State Electoral Votes in 2004

The map of the United States shown here is distorted to show the relative [weight of the states]
in terms of the electoral votes in 2004, following the changes required b[y]
A candidate must win 270 electoral vores to be elected pres[ident.]

2004 Presidential Election Results

George W. Bush won 286 electoral votes

John F. Kerry won 252 electoral votes

www.wadsworth.com

wadsworth.com is the World Wide Web site for Wadsworth and is your direct source to dozens of online resources.

At *wadsworth.com* you can find out about supplements, demonstration software, and student resources. You can also send e-mail to many of our authors and preview new publications and exciting new technologies.

wadsworth.com
Changing the way the world learns®

American Government and Politics Today

2005-2006 EDITION

STEFFEN W.   MACK C.   BARBARA A.
SCHMIDT SHELLEY BARDES

THOMSON
——— ™
WADSWORTH

Australia • Canada • Mexico • Singapore • Spain
United Kingdom • United States

THOMSON

WADSWORTH

Publisher: Clark Baxter
Executive Editor: David Tatom
Development: Catherine Wein
Assistant Editor: Julie Yardley
Marketing Manager: Janise Fry
Project Editor: Katy German and Ann Borman
Print Buyer: Barbara Britton
Permissions Editor: Joohee Lee
Production and Design: Bill Stryker

Photo Researcher: Anne Sheroff
Copy Editor: Pat Lewis
Illustrator: Bill Stryker
Cover Designer: Bill Stryker
Cover Images: PhotoDisc
Text and Cover Printer: Transcontinental
Compositor: Parkwood Composition Service

Printed in Canada
1 2 3 4 5 6 7 8 07 06 05 04

For more information about our products, contact us at:
Thomson Learning Academic Resource Center
1-800-423-0563
For permission to use material from this text, contact us by:
Phone: 1-800-730-2214
Fax: 1-800-730-2215
Web: http://www.thomsonrights.com

Library of Congress ISSN: 1079–0071
ISBN: 0–534–63162–2

Thomson Higher Education
10 Davis Drive
Belmont, CA 94002-3098
USA

ASIA (including India)
Thomson Learning
5 Shenton Way
#01-01 UIC Building
Singapore 068808

AUSTRALIA/NEW ZEALAND
Thomson Learning Australia
102 Dodds Street
Southbank, Victoria 3006
Australia

LATIN AMERICA
Thomson Learning
Seneca, 53
Colonia Polanco
11560 Mexico
D.F.Mexico

CANADA
Thomson Nelson
1120 Birchmount Road
Toronto, Ontario
Canada M1K 5G4

UK/EUROPE/MIDDLE
EAST/AFRICA
Thomson Learning
High Holborn House
50-51 Bedford Road
London WC1R 4LR
United Kingdom

SPAIN (includes Portugal)
Thomson Paraninfo
Calle Magallanes, 25
28015 Madrid, Spain

Part One
The American System

Part Two
Civil Rights and Liberties

Part Three
People and Politics

v

CONTENTS

Part One

★★★★★★★★★★★★★★★★★★★★★★★★★★★★

The American System

Chapter 1

The Democratic Republic   1

Chapter 2
The Constitution   29

Chapter 3
Federalism 79

Part Two

★★★★★★★★★★★★★★★★★★★★★★★★★★★★★★★

Civil Rights and Liberties

Chapter 4
Civil Liberties 111

CHAPTER 4 FEATURES

WHICH SIDE ARE YOU ON?
Should We Be One Nation "under God"? 117

GLOBAL VIEW
The Head Scarves Issue 123

AMERICA'S SECURITY
Military Tribunals for Suspected Terrorists 139

Chapter 5
Civil Rights   149

CHAPTER 5 FEATURES

GLOBAL VIEW
The Struggle for Women's Rights around the World   165

WHICH SIDE ARE YOU ON?
Zero-Tolerance Policies   182

Part Three

★★★★★★★★★★★★★★★★★★★★★★★★★★★★★★★★★★★★

People and Politics

Chapter 6
Public Opinion and Political Socialization   189

CHAPTER 6 FEATURES

GLOBAL VIEW
Polling in Baghdad   206

POLITICS AND POLLS
The Issue of Push Polls   208

Chapter 7
Interest Groups   219

Chapter 8
Political Parties   249

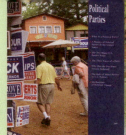

CHAPTER 8 FEATURES

POLITICS AND ELECTIONS
The 2004 Democratic Primary Elections   263

WHICH SIDE ARE YOU ON?
Should Voters Ignore Third-Party Candidates?   277

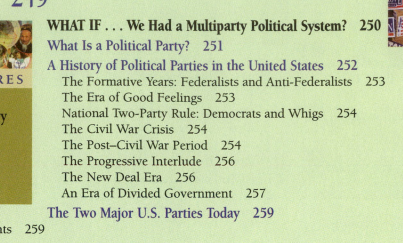

Chapter 9
Campaigns, Nominations, and Elections 287

Chapter 10
The Media and Cyberpolitics   325

CHAPTER 10 FEATURES

AMERICA'S SECURITY
Press Censorship in Times
of Crisis   331

WHICH SIDE ARE YOU ON?
Are Internet Campaigns
the Wave of the Future?   341

POLITICS AND DIVERSITY
Racial Profiling
in the Media   349

xvi

Part Four

★★★★★★★★★★★★★★★★★★★★★★★★★★★★★

Political Institutions

Chapter 11

The Congress   353

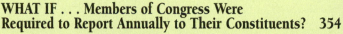

Chapter 12
The President   389

CHAPTER 12 FEATURES

Chapter 13
The Bureaucracy   423

Chapter 14
The Courts 453

CHAPTER 14 FEATURES

AMERICA'S SECURITY
Holding U.S. Citizens as "Enemy Combatants" 462

WHICH SIDE ARE YOU ON?
Is the Process of Confirming Judicial Nominees Too Political? 470

GLOBAL VIEW
When the Supreme Court Looks to Other Nations' Laws 474

Part Five

Public Policy

Chapter 15
Domestic Policy   483

CHAPTER 15 FEATURES

POLITICS AND HEALTH CARE
Health Care for Members
of Congress   491

WHICH SIDE ARE YOU ON?
Should Welfare Mothers Work
outside the Home?   497

GLOBAL VIEW
Day Care in
Western Europe   498

AMERICA'S SECURITY
Those Colored Alert Levels   508

Chapter 16
Economic Policy   521

CHAPTER 16 FEATURES

POLITICS AND TRADE
The High Cost of Saving
U.S. Jobs   535

POLITICS AND ECONOMICS
Outsourcing: A Political Hot-
Button Issue   538

WHICH SIDE ARE YOU ON?
Should Social Security Be
Partially Privatized?   543

xxii

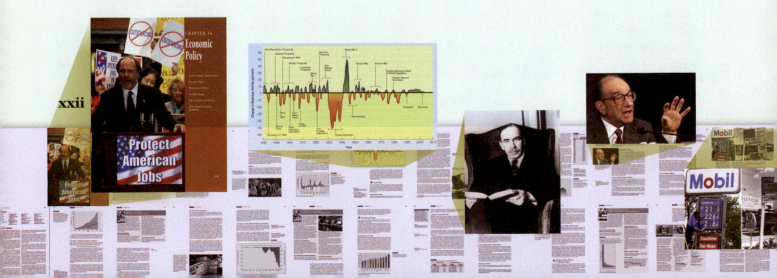

Chapter 17
Foreign Policy   547

CHAPTER 17 FEATURES

Part Six

★★★★★★★★★★★★★★★★★★★★★★★★★★★★★★★★★★★★

State and Local Politics

Chapter 18

State and Local Government   579

The 2005–2006 edition of *American Government and Politics Today* contains some of the most thoroughgoing revisions we have ever made to this text. Many of these changes were made necessary by the dramatic developments in the war on terrorism since September 11, 2001, and the turmoil and unrest that marked the occupation of Iraq following the invasion of that country in 2003.

During the presidential election campaign of 2004, Republican incumbent George W. Bush and Democratic challenger John Kerry both had to address a series of questions: How should the American exit from Iraq be managed? What balance should be struck between the need for protection against terrorist attacks and the civil liberties that Americans have traditionally enjoyed? How should the nation handle the growing budget deficits predicted for future years? The reelection of Bush and the Republican sweep of the Senate and the House of Representatives ensured that Republicans would take the lead in looking for answers.

The changes we have made to this edition, however, are not limited to bringing the text up to date. We have also made major revisions based on the latest research. Finally, pedagogy in the profession has evolved over time, and this edition represents our latest and best approach to introducing American government and politics to today's students.

2004 Election Results Included and Analyzed

Our experience has been that students respond to up-to-date information about political events. Consequently, we have included results of the November 2004 elections. We also analyze how these results will affect our political processes at the national, state, and local levels. While we have updated all of the text to be consistent with these results, in particular we have added numerous special *Elections 2004* features that are distributed throughout the text.

The Interactive Focus of This Text

Whether it be voter participation, terrorism, or the problems that face the president, we constantly strive to involve the student reader in the analysis. We make sure that the reader comes to understand that politics is not an abstract process but a very human enterprise. We emphasize how different outcomes can affect students' civil rights and liberties, employment opportunities, and economic welfare.

Throughout the text, we encourage the reader to think critically. Almost all of the features end with questions designed to pique the student's interest. A feature titled *Which Side Are You On?* challenges the reader to find a connection between controversial issues facing the nation and the reader's personal positions on these issues. We further encourage interaction with the political system by ending each chapter with a feature titled *Making a Difference*, which shows students not only what they can do to become politically involved but why they should care enough to do so. Online exercises (to be discussed shortly) that conclude each chapter show students how to access and analyze political information.

The Most Complete Web Connection

We continue to make sure that our text leads the industry in its integration with the Web. For this edition, you will find the following Web-based resources:

■ **The Wadsworth American Government Resource Center**—at http://politicalscience.wadsworth.com/amgov. The American Government Resource Center provides a rich array of tools that help students understand the American political process. These materials are organized around nineteen core topics, each of which features a set of student activities designed to inspire and motivate active citizenship.

■ **A text-specific site for this book**—accessible through the Wadsworth American Government Resource Center's site or directly at http://politicalscience.wadsworth.com/schmidt12, where students will find a free Study Guide to this book. For each chapter, there are two online quizzes to help students master the material—the PolyPrep Self-Study Assessment and the Tutorial Quiz.

■ **The PoliPrep Self-Study Assessment**—this system provides a pre-test for each major section of the chapter. PoliPrep then generates a customized study plan. After the student completes the study plan, a post-test evaluates the student's progress.

■ **The Tutorial Quiz**—for each chapter, this test provides questions on the chapter contents, including the features. The questions are organized to match the major sections of the chapter.

■ **InfoTrac® College Edition**—an online search engine that will take the student exactly where he or she needs to go to find relevant information, including full-text articles in important political science journals and other sources. A sample exercise at the end of each chapter introduces the student to this resource.

■ **American Government Internet Activities**—a free booklet that takes the student on a grand tour of numerous Web sites, each related to a specific major topic in American government.

■ **Online testing**—which allows instructors to provide and grade examinations online using *ExamView*.

■ **WebTutor on WebCT or Blackboard**—a content-rich, easy-to-use, Web-based study aid for students that includes presentations of concepts, flashcards with audio clips, Web links, tutorials, discussion questions, and more.

Special Pedagogy and Features

The 2005–2006 Edition of *American Government and Politics Today* contains many pedagogical aids and high-interest features to assist both students and instructors. The following list summarizes the special elements that can be found in each chapter:

- *What If . . .* —a discussion of a hypothetical situation.

- *Margin Definitions*—for all important terms.

- *Did You Know . . . ?*—margin features presenting various facts and figures that add interest to the learning process.

- *Which Side Are You On?*—a feature designed to elicit student responses to controversial issues.

- *America's Security*—a case-study feature that examines how today's security-conscious America is dealing with terrorist threats.

- *Global View*—a feature that compares the American experience with developments, events, or government structures in other nations.

- *Politics and . . .* —a feature that examines the influence of politics on a variety of issues. Several of these features focus on the theme of *Politics and Diversity.* Others address topics such as *Politics and Elections* or *Politics and the Presidency.*

- *Why Is It Important Today?*—a concluding section in each chapter that discusses how the challenges in American government affect every citizen today.

- *Making a Difference*—a chapter-ending feature that gives the student some specific reasons why he or she should care about the topics covered in the chapter and provides ways in which she or he can become actively involved in American politics.

- *Key Terms*—a chapter-ending list, with page numbers, of all terms in the chapter that were boldfaced and defined in the margins.

- *Chapter Summary*—a point-by-point summary of the chapter text.

- *Selected Print and Media Resources*—offers suggested scholarly readings as well as popular books and films relevant to chapter topics.

- *E-mocracy*—a feature that discusses politics and the Internet and suggests Web sites and Internet activities related to the chapter's topics.

Appendices

Because we know that this book serves as a reference, we have included important documents for the student of American government to have close at hand. A fully annotated copy of the U.S. Constitution appears at the end of Chapter 2, as an appendix to that chapter. In addition, we have included the following appendices:

- The Declaration of Independence.

- How to Read Case Citations and Find Court Decisions.

- *Federalist Papers* No. 10, No. 51, and No. 78.

- Justices of the U.S. Supreme Court since 1900.

- Party Control of Congress since 1900.

- Spanish Equivalents for Important Terms in American Government.

Useful material is also located immediately inside the front and back covers of this text. Inside the front cover, you will find a simple reference map of the United States plus a cartogram that distorts the size of the various states to indicate their relative weight in the Electoral College. Inside the back cover you will find a list of the presidents of the United States.

A Comprehensive Supplements Package

We are proud to be the authors of a text that has the most comprehensive, accessible, and fully integrated supplements package on the market. Together, the text and the supplements listed below constitute a total learning/teaching package for you and your students. For further information on any of these supplements, contact your Wadsworth/Thomson Learning sales representative.

Supplements for Instructors

- *Instructor's Resource CD-ROM*—Includes the Instructor's Manual, Test Bank, Exam View, PowerPoint slides containing the figures from the text, and the Video Case Study Instructor's Manual.

- *Instructor's Manual.*

- *Online Instructor's Manual* (password protected).

- *Multimedia Manager for Political Science: A Microsoft PowerPoint Link Tool.*

- *My Course 2.0.*

- *Test Bank.*

- *ExamView*, including questions on the features.

- *American Government Transparency Acetates Package*, 2003 Edition.

- *Political Science Video Library.*

- *CNN Today: American Government*, Volumes I, II, III, and IV (VHS videos).

- *Video Case Studies in American Government.* A collection of twelve videos on topics such as the impeachment of Bill Clinton, the contested 2000 election, presidential leadership styles, how the federal government forced the states to raise the drinking age, gun control, and affirmative action. The videos feature interviews with prominent individuals on all sides of the issues.

- *Video Case Studies Instructor's Manual.*

Supplements for Students

- *Study Guide.*

- *WebTutor on WebCT or Blackboard.*

- *American Government: An Introduction Using MicroCase ExplorIT*, Seventh Edition.

- *America at Odds* CD-ROM.

- *American Government Internet Activities*, Third Edition.

- *Readings in American Government*, Fourth Edition.

- *Supplemental government texts for California and Texas.*

- *An Introduction to Critical Thinking and Writing in American Politics.*

- *Handbook of Selected Court Cases* (third edition).

- *Thinking Globally, Acting Locally.*

- *Handbook of Selected Legislation and Other Documents* (third edition).

■ *College Survival Guide: Hints and References to Aid College Students*, Fourth Edition.

■ *InfoTrac® College Edition.*

■ *InfoTrac® College Edition Student Guide for Political Science.*

For Users of the Previous Edition

As usual, we thank you for your past support of our work. We have made numerous changes to this text for the 2005–2006 edition, many of which we list below. We have rewritten much of the text, added numerous new features, and updated the book to reflect the results of the 2004 elections.

New *What If . . .* Features

■ "What If . . . National Laws Were Put to a Popular Vote?" (Chapter 1).

■ "What If . . . An Immigrant Could Become President?" (Chapter 2).

■ "What If . . . Education Were a National Responsibility?" (Chapter 3).

■ "What If . . . One State's Same-Sex Marriages Had to Be Recognized Nationwide?" (Chapter 5).

■ "What If . . . Exit Polls Were Regulated?" (Chapter 6).

■ "What If . . . Retired Government Employees Could Not Work for Interest Groups?" (Chapter 7).

■ "What If . . . We Had a Multiparty Political System?" (Chapter 8).

■ "What If . . . We Had Public Financing for All Political Campaigns?" (Chapter 9).

■ "What If . . . The Media Were Truly Independent?" (Chapter 10).

■ "What If . . . Members of Congress Were Required to Report Annually to Their Constituents?" (Chapter 11).

■ "What If . . . The Public Graded Federal Bureaucracies?" (Chapter 13).

■ "What If . . . The National Parks Were Privatized?" (Chapter 15).

■ "What If . . . Every Adult Were Guaranteed a Job?" (Chapter 16).

■ "What If . . . North Korea Exploded a Nuclear Bomb?" (Chapter 17).

Significant Changes within Chapters

Each chapter contains new features, updated facts and tabular data, and, whenever feasible, the most current information available on the problems facing the nation. In addition, significant changes have been made to the chapters listed below:

■ Chapter 1 (The Democratic Republic)—This chapter has been retitled and completely rewritten. The section on ideology has been greatly expanded.

■ Chapter 3 (Federalism)—The coverage of dual federalism and cooperative federalism has been expanded, and a new section examines Democratic and Republican approaches to federalism from the 1960s to the present.

■ Chapter 5 (Civil Rights)—Added topics include the violence accompanying segregation and the urban disturbances of the 1960s and 1970s. The section on women's rights has been extensively updated to reflect the most recent research.

■ Chapter 6 (Public Opinion and Political Socialization)—All material relating to political socialization and voting behavior is now concentrated in this chapter. We have also added new analyses of the impact of religion and economic class on political socialization.

■ Chapter 8 (Political Parties)—The chapter has been completely rewritten. The history of U.S. political parties now more fully describes the impact of cultural and economic factors on the evolving two-party system. We explain how, in recent years, cultural politics has altered the parties' appeals to their traditional constituents. A new section discusses "realignment," "dealignment," and "tipping."

■ Chapter 9 (Campaigns, Nominations, and Elections)—All material on campaign finance is now included in this chapter. The chapter also contains new material on campaign finance law and nonparty "shadow organizations" and new research on voter turnout.

■ Chapter 14 (The Courts)—The chapter now includes a new discussion of strict versus broad construction of the Constitution.

■ Chapter 15 (Domestic Policy)—This chapter has been largely rewritten. It examines the Medicare prescription drug benefit, health-care costs, Medicare, the uninsured, and various policy alternatives. The sections on poverty and welfare, as well as the section on crime, have been revised and new material has been added on prisons. The material on the environment has been expanded.

■ Chapter 16 (Economic Policy)—New to this edition, this chapter first covers unemployment, inflation, and the business cycle, and then explains the tools that the government uses to manage economic policy. Sections on world trade and taxes are included.

■ Chapter 17 (Foreign Policy)—This chapter has been revised to reflect recent developments, especially those in postwar Iraq.

Acknowledgments

Since we started this project a number of years ago, a sizable cadre of individuals has helped us in various phases of the undertaking. The following academic reviewers offered numerous constructive criticisms, comments, and suggestions during the preparation of all previous editions:

Danny M. Adkison
Oklahoma State University, Stillwater

Sharon Z. Alter
William Rainey Harper College, Illinois

Hugh M. Arnold
Clayton College and State University, Georgia

William Arp III
Louisiana State University

Kevin Bailey
North Harris Community College, Texas

Orlando N. Bama
McLennan Community College, Texas

Dr. Charles T. Barber
University of Southern Indiana, Evansville

Clyde W. Barrow
Texas A&M University

Shari Garber Bax
Central Missouri State University, Warrensburg

David S. Bell
Eastern Washington University, Cheney

David C. Benford, Jr.
Tarrant County Junior College, Texas

John A. Braithwaite
Coastline College, California

Lynn R. Brink
North Lake College, Irving, Texas

Barbara L. Brown
Southern Illinois University at Carbondale

Richard G. Buckner
Santa Fe Community College

Kenyon D. Bunch
Fort Lewis College, Durango, Colorado

Ralph Bunch
Portland State University, Oregon

Carol Cassell
University of Alabama

Frank T. Colon
Lehigh University, Bethlehem, Pennsylvania

Frank J. Coppa
Union County College, Cranford, New Jersey

Robert E. Craig
University of New Hampshire

Doris Daniels
Nassau Community College, New York

Carolyn Grafton Davis
North Harris County College, Texas

Paul B. Davis
Truckee Meadows Community College, Nevada

Richard D. Davis
Brigham Young University

Ron Deaton
Prince George's Community College, Maryland

Marshall L. DeRosa
Louisiana State University, Baton Rouge

Michael Dinneen
Tulsa Junior College, Oklahoma

Gavan Duffy
University of Texas at Austin

Gregory Edwards
Amarillo College, Texas

George C. Edwards III
Texas A&M University

Mark C. Ellickson
Southwestern Missouri State University,
Springfield

Larry Elowitz
Georgia College, Milledgeville

John W. Epperson
Simpson College, Indianola, Indiana

Victoria A. Farrar-Myers
University of Texas at Arlington

Daniel W. Fleitas
University of North Carolina at Charlotte

Elizabeth N. Flores
Del Mar College, Texas

Joel L. Franke
Blinn College, Brenham, Texas

Barry D. Friedman
North Georgia College, Dahlonega

Robert S. Getz
SUNY–Brockport, New York

Kristina Gilbert
Riverside Community College, California

William A. Giles
Mississippi State University

Donald Gregory
Stephen F. Austin State University, Texas

Forest Grieves
University of Montana

Dale Grimnitz
Normandale Community College,
Bloomington, Minnesota

Stefan D. Haag
Austin Community College, Texas

Justin Halpern
Northeastern State University, Oklahoma

Willie Hamilton
Mount San Jacinto College, California

Jean Wahl Harris
University of Scranton, Pennsylvania

David N. Hartman
Rancho Santiago College,
Santa Ana, California

Robert M. Herman
Moorpark College, California

Richard J. Herzog
Stephen F. Austin State University,
Nacogdoches, Texas

Paul Holder
McClennan Community College, Waco, Texas

Michael Hoover
Seminole Community College,
Sanford, Florida

J. C. Horton
San Antonio College, Texas

Robert Jackson
Washington State University, Pullman

Willoughby Jarrell
Kennesaw State University, Georgia

Loch K. Johnson
University of Georgia

Donald L. Jordan
United States Air Force Academy, Colorado

John D. Kay
Santa Barbara City College, California

Charles W. Kegley
University of South Carolina

Bruce L. Kessler
Shippensburg University, Pennsylvania

Jason F. Kirksey
Oklahoma State University, Stillwater

Nancy B. Kral
Tomball College, Texas

Dale Krane
Mississippi State University

Samuel Krislov
University of Minnesota

William W. Lamkin
Glendale Community College

Harry D. Lawrence
Southwest Texas Junior College, Uvaide, Texas

Ray Leal
Southwest Texas State University, San Marcos

Sue Lee
Center for Telecommunications, Dallas
County Community College District

Carl Lieberman
University of Akron, Ohio

Orma Linford
Kansas State University, Manhattan

James J. Lopach
University of Montana

Eileen Lynch
Brookhaven College, Texas

James D. McElyea
Tulsa Junior College, Oklahoma

Thomas J. McGaghie
Kellogg Community College, Michigan

William P. McLauchlan
Purdue University, Indiana

William W. Maddox
University of Florida

S. J. Makielski, Jr.
Loyola University, New Orleans

Jarol B. Manheim
George Washington University,
District of Colombia

J. David Martin
Midwestern State University,
Wichita Falls, Texas

Bruce B. Mason
Arizona State University

Thomas Louis Masterson
Butte College, California

Steve J. Mazurana
University of Northern Colorado, Greeley

Stanley Melnick
Valencia Community College, Florida

Robert Mittrick
Luzurne County Community College,
Pennsylvania

Helen Molanphy
Richland College, Texas

James Morrow
Tulsa Community College

Keith Nicholls
University of Alabama

Stephen Osofsky
Nassau Community College, New York

John P. Pelissero
Loyola University of Chicago

Neil A. Pinney
Western Michigan University, Kalamazoo

George E. Pippin
Jones County Community College,
Mississippi

Walter V. Powell
Slippery Rock University, Pennsylvania

Michael A. Preda
Midwestern State University,
Wichita Falls, Texas

Mark E. Priewe
University of Texas at San Antonio

Charles Prysby
University of North Carolina

Donald R. Ranish
Antelope Valley College, California

John D. Rausch
Fairmont State University, West Virginia

Renford Reese
California State Polytechnic University—
Pomona

Curt Reichel
University of Wisconsin

Russell D. Renka
Southeast Missouri State University,
Cape Girardeau

Paul Rozycki
Charles Stewart Mott Community College,
Flint, Michigan

Bhim Sandhu
West Chester University, Pennsylvania

Pauline Schloesser
Texas Southern University, Houston

Eleanor A. Schwab
South Dakota State University, Brookings

Len Shipman
Mount San Antonio College, California

Scott Shrewsbury
Mankato State University, Minnesota

Alton J. Slane
Muhlenberg College, Pennsylvania

Joseph L. Smith
Grand Valley State University, Michigan

Michael W. Sonnlietner
Portland Community College, Oregon

Gilbert K. St. Clair
University of New Mexico

Carol Stix
Pace University, Pleasantville, New York

Gerald S. Strom
University of Illinois at Chicago

Regina Swopes
Northeastern Illinois University, Chicago

John R. Todd
North Texas State University

Ron Velton
Grayson County College, Texas

Albert C. Waite
Central Texas College

Benjamin Walter
Vanderbilt University, Tennessee

B. Oliver Walter
University of Wyoming, Laramie

Mark J. Wattier
Murray State University, Kentucky

Thomas L. Wells
Old Dominion University, Virginia

Jean B. White
Weber State College, Utah

Lance Widman
El Camino College, California

Allan Wiese
Mankato State University, Minnesota

J. David Woodard
Clemson University, South Carolina

Robert D. Wrinkle
Pan American University, Texas

The 2005–2006 Edition of this text is the result of our working closely with reviewers who each offered us penetrating criticisms, comments, and suggestions. Although we have not been able to take account of all requests, each of the reviewers listed below will see many of his or her suggestions taken to heart.

Evelyn Ballard
Houston Community College, Texas

Dewey Clayton
University of Louisville, Kentucky

Don Thomas Dugi
Transylvania University, Louisville, Kentucky

Jeffrey L. Prewitt
Brewton-Parker College, Mt. Vernon, Georgia

Gregory Schaller
Villanova University, Villanova, Pennsylvania, and St. Joseph's University, Philadelphia

Charles R. Shedlak
Ivy Tech State College, South Bend, Indiana

Dr. Robert E. Sterken, Jr.
University of Texas, Tyler

In preparing this edition of *American Politics and Government Today*, we were the beneficiaries of the expert guidance of a skilled and dedicated team of publishers and editors. We would like, first of all, to thank Susan Badger, the CEO of Thomson Learning Higher Education Group, for the support she has shown for this project. We have benefited greatly from the supervision and encouragement given by David Tatom, executive editor, and Clark Baxter, editorial director. Catherine Wein, our developmental editor, also deserves our thanks for her efforts in coordinating reviews and in many other aspects of project development. We are also indebted to editorial assistants Reena Thomas and Cheryl Lee for their contributions to this project.

We are grateful to Bill Stryker, our production manager, for a remarkable design and for making it possible to get the text out on time. We also thank Anne Sheroff, who worked on graphics issues. In addition, our gratitude goes to all of those who worked on the various supplements offered with this text, especially supplements coordinator Rebecca F. Green, and to Michelle Vardeman, who coordinates the Web site. We would also like to thank Janise Fry, marketing manager, for her tremendous efforts in marketing the text.

Many other people helped during the research and editorial stages of this edition. Gregory Scott skillfully coordinated the authors' efforts and provided editorial and research assistance from the outset of the project to the end. Suzie Franklin DeFazio's copyediting and the proofreading of Mary Berry, Pat Lewis, and Beverly Peavler contributed greatly to the book. We are grateful to Joy Westberg for her work on the visual preface. We also thank Roxie Lee for her proofreading and other assistance, which helped us to meet our ambitious schedule, and Sue Jasin of K&M Consulting for her contributions to the smooth running of the project.

Any errors remain our own. We welcome comments from instructors and students alike. Suggestions that we have received in the past have helped us to improve this text and to adapt it to the changing needs of instructors and students.

Steffen Schmidt   Mack Shelley   Barbara Bardes

About the Authors

Steffen W. Schmidt

Steffen W. Schmidt is a professor of political science at Iowa State University. He grew up in Colombia, South America, and studied in Colombia, Switzerland, and France. He obtained his Ph.D. from Columbia University, New York, in public law and government.

Schmidt has published six books and over 150 journal articles. He is also the recipient of numerous prestigious teaching prizes, including the Amoco Award for Lifetime Career Achievement in Teaching and the Teacher of the Year award. He is a pioneer in the use of Web-based and real-time video courses and is a member of the American Political Science Association's section on computers and multimedia. He is on the editorial board of the *Political Science Educator* and is the technology and teaching editor of the *Journal of Political Science Education.*

Schmidt has a political talk show on WOI radio, where he is known as Dr. Politics, streaming live once a week at http://www.wol.org. The show has been broadcast live from various U.S. and international venues. He is a frequent political commentator for *CNN en Español* and the British Broadcasting Corporation.

Schmidt likes to snow ski, ride hunter jumper horses, race sailboats, and scuba dive.

Mack C. Shelley II

Mack C. Shelley II is professor of political science, professor of statistics, and director of the Research Institute for Studies in Education at Iowa State University. After receiving his bachelor's degree from American University in Washington, D.C., he completed graduate studies at the University of Wisconsin at Madison, where he received a master's degree in economics and a Ph.D. in political science. He taught for two years at Mississippi State University before arriving at Iowa State in 1979.

Shelley has published numerous articles, books, and monographs on public policy. From 1993 to 2002, he served as elected coeditor of the *Policy Studies Journal.* His published books include *The Permanent Majority: The Conservative Coalition in the United States Congress; Biotechnology and the Research Enterprise* (with William F. Woodman and Brian J. Reichel); *American Public Policy: The Contemporary Agenda* (with Steven G. Koven and Bert E. Swanson); and *Redefining Family Policy: Implications for the 21st Century* (with Joyce M. Mercier and Steven Garasky). Other recent work has focused on electronic government and the "digital divide," learning communities, how to improve student life (especially in residence halls), and public health.

His leisure time includes travel, working with students, and playing with the family dog and three cats.

Barbara A. Bardes

Barbara A. Bardes is a professor of political science at the University of Cincinnati. She received her bachelor of arts degree and master of arts degree from Kent State University. After completing her Ph.D. at the University of Cincinnati, she held faculty positions at Mississippi State University and Loyola University in Chicago. She returned to the University of Cincinnati as dean of one of its colleges. She has also worked as a political consultant and directed polling for a research center.

Bardes has written articles on public opinion and foreign policy, and on women and politics. She has authored *Thinking about Public Policy; Declarations of Independence: Women and Political Power in Nineteenth-Century American Fiction;* and *Public Opinion: Measuring the American Mind* (with Robert W. Oldendick). Her current research interests include public opinion on terrorism and homeland security and media effects in elections.

Bardes's home is located in a very small hamlet in Kentucky called Rabbit Hash, famous for its 150-year-old general store. Her hobbies include travel, gardening, needlework, and antique collecting.

The Democratic Republic

WHAT IF . . .
National Laws Were Put to a Popular Vote?

BACKGROUND

The United States is a democratic republic, or a *representative democracy.* In a representative democracy, the people elect representatives who make the laws. Governors and presidents are elected to carry out these laws. Representative democracy is not the only possible democratic system. An alternative is *direct democracy,* in which the people, rather than their representatives, make decisions. In ancient Greece, in the city of Athens, the citizens of the entire city gathered together in an assembly to make laws, to declare war, and to decide important issues.

Such an assembly is clearly not possible in a large country. But what if citizens could cast votes in elections on issues of national policy? After all, such votes are common at the state level. Depending on state law, citizens can vote for new laws in a number of ways. In a *referendum,* the legislature submits an issue to the voters. In an *initiative,* the voters themselves put an issue on the ballot by collecting a specified number of signatures. Some states, in addition, allow *recall elections,* in which the voters can remove elected officials before their terms of office expire.

WHAT IF NATIONAL LAWS WERE PUT TO A POPULAR VOTE?

If national laws were put to a popular vote, citizens would have a much more direct voice in government. Today, for example, public opinion polls indicate that a sizeable number of Americans support the use of marijuana for medical purposes. If voters approved such use in a national referendum, medical marijuana would be legal in all states.

A LACK OF DELIBERATION

Giving voters more say on legislation might lead to some serious problems. For one thing, voters might not be able to explore fully the consequences of their decisions. Before passing legislation, Congress normally looks at the possible ramifications of its decisions. For example, Congress often consults with federal agencies that have expertise in an area. In contrast, few voters could take the time or would have the resources to thoroughly assess the trade-offs involved in a particular issue.

If a spending proposal were put to a referendum, the voters would not be able to evaluate the impact of the proposal on the overall federal budget. California can serve as an example of this problem. By some estimates, the voters in that state have earmarked almost 80 percent of the state's revenues for particular purposes. As a result, when preparing a budget, elected officials face an almost impossible task if a recession reduces tax revenues.

Furthermore, the federal government does not have to balance its budget as some state governments do. Voters in a national referendum could thus authorize new spending without raising taxes (or cut taxes without reducing spending), pushing the federal government further into debt.

CONSTITUTIONAL DIFFICULTIES

As a practical matter, the U.S. Constitution makes no provision for referenda, initiatives, or recalls. It also does not ban such procedures. The United States Supreme Court, however, has strongly opposed any delegation of the congressional power to draft legislation. Some years ago, for example, Congress passed a "line-item veto" law that allowed the president to block part of a spending bill without rejecting the entire package. The Supreme Court found this law to be an unconstitutional delegation of congressional power. The membership and opinions of the Court can change, but the existing Court would surely never permit a binding national referendum.

Of course, Congress could always sponsor a purely advisory referendum. It is unlikely that the Court would block such a procedure, as long as Congress retained the right to accept or to ignore the results of the vote.

FOR CRITICAL ANALYSIS

1. *If Congress could refer issues to a vote of the people, what kinds of issues do you think it might put to a vote?*
2. *If the people instead of Congress decided an issue, how might the people vote differently than Congress?*

Politics, for many people, is the "great game"—better than soccer, better than chess. Scores may only be tallied every two years, at elections, but the play continues at all times. The game, furthermore, is played for high stakes. Politics can affect what you have in your purse or wallet. It can determine what you can legally do in your spare time. In worst-case circumstances, it can even threaten your life. Few topics are so entertaining—and so important.

Given the importance of political decisions, should the people be able to vote on major issues directly at the national level? We examined this question in the *What If . . .* feature that opened this chapter.

★ Politics and Government

What is politics? **Politics** can be understood as the process of resolving conflicts and deciding, as political scientist Harold Lasswell put it, "who gets what, when, and how."[1] More specifically, politics is the struggle over power or influence within organizations or informal groups that can grant benefits or privileges.

We can identify many such groups and organizations. In families, all members may meet together to decide on values, priorities, and actions. Wherever there is a community that makes decisions through formal or informal rules, politics exists. For example, when a church decides to construct a new building or hire a new minister, the decision may be made politically. Politics can be found in schools, social groups, and any other organized collection of people. Of all of the organizations that are controlled by political activity, however, the most important is the government.

What is the government? Certainly, it is an **institution**—that is, an ongoing organization with a life separate from the lives of the individuals who are part of it at any given moment in time. The **government** can be defined as an institution within which decisions are made that resolve conflicts or allocate benefits and privileges. The government is also the *preeminent* institution within society. It is unique because it has the ultimate authority for making decisions and allocating values.

Politics
The struggle over power or influence within organizations or informal groups that can grant or withhold benefits or privileges.

Institution
An ongoing organization that performs certain functions for society.

Government
The institution in which decisions are made that resolve conflicts or allocate benefits and privileges. It is unique because it has the ultimate authority within society.

★ Why Is Government Necessary?

Perhaps the best way to assess the need for government is to examine circumstances in which government, as we normally understand it, does not exist. What happens when multiple groups compete with each other for power within a society? There are places around the world where such circumstances exist. A current example is the African nation of Somalia. Since 1991, Somalia has not had a central government. Mogadishu, the capital, is divided among several warlords, each of whom controls a bloc of neighborhoods. When Somali warlords compete for the control of a particular locality, the result is war, generalized devastation, and famine. In general, multiple armed forces compete by fighting, and the absence of a unified government is equivalent to civil war.

The Need for Security

As the example of Somalia shows, one of the original purposes of government is the maintenance of security, or **order.** By keeping the peace, the government protects the people from violence at the hands of private or foreign armies. It dispenses justice and protects the people against the violence of criminals. If order is not present, it is not possible to provide any of the other benefits that people expect from government.

Order
A state of peace and security. Maintaining order by protecting members of society from violence and criminal activity is the oldest purpose of government.

---

[1]Harold Lasswell, *Politics: Who Gets What, When, and How* (New York: McGraw-Hill, 1936).

Consider the situation in Iraq. In March and April 2003, U.S. and British coalition forces entered that nation, which was governed by the dictator Saddam Hussein. The relatively small number of coalition troops had little trouble in defeating their military opponents, but they experienced serious difficulties in establishing order within Iraq when the war was over.

Once it became clear that Saddam Hussein was no longer in control of the country, widespread looting broke out. Ordinary citizens entered government buildings and made off with the furniture. Looters stole crucial supplies from hospitals, making it difficult to treat Iraqis injured during the war. Thieves stripped the copper from electrical power lines, which made it impossible to quickly restore electrical power. In various localities, demonstrators confronted coalition troops, often with fatal results. Only when security and order were restored was it possible to begin the reconstructing of Iraqi society. Order is a political value that we will return to later in this chapter.

Limiting Government Power

Order cannot be the only important political value. Under Saddam Hussein, Iraq certainly experienced a kind of order. For many unfortunate Iraqi citizens, that order took the form of the "peace of the grave"—large numbers of people were killed by Saddam Hussein's security forces, sometimes for trivial reasons. Protection from the violence of domestic criminals or foreign armies is not enough. Citizens also need protection from abuses of power by the government.

U.S. President George W. Bush and British Prime Minister Tony Blair believed—probably mistakenly, as it turned out—that Saddam Hussein possessed weapons of mass destruction. Eliminating those weapons was a principal goal of the war. A second major goal, however, was to promote stability in the greater Middle East by freeing the Iraqi people from a despotic regime. Eliminating Saddam Hussein would not be enough to guarantee the freedom of the Iraqi people. Iraqis are divided among themselves by religion and language. How could each of the various groups that make up Iraq be prevented from oppressing the others? To protect the liberties of the Iraqi people, it would be necessary to limit the powers of the new Iraqi government.

Sallama al-Khafaji, an Iraqi Shiite member of the Iraqi Governing Council, signs the new constitution in Baghdad, Iraq, on March 8, 2004. The signing was delayed once by terror attacks in Karbala and Baghdad, and then by last-minute Shiite reservations. The constitution was signed nine days after the proposed deadline. (EPA/NABIL MOUNZER)

Liberty—the greatest freedom of the individual consistent with the freedom of other individuals—is a second major political value, along with order. Liberty is a value that may be promoted by government but can also be invoked *against* government. We will discuss this value further later in this chapter.

Authority and Legitimacy

Every government must have **authority**—that is, the right and power to enforce its decisions. Ultimately, the government's authority rests on its control of the armed forces and the police. Virtually no one in the United States, however, bases his or her day-to-day activities on fear of the government's enforcement powers. Most people, most of the time, obey the law because this is what they have always done. Also, if they did not obey the law they would face the disapproval of friends and family. Consider an example: Do you avoid injuring your friends or stealing their possessions because you are afraid of the police—or because if you did these things, you would no longer have friends?

Under normal circumstances, the government's authority has broad popular support. People accept the government's right to establish rules and laws. When authority is broadly accepted, we say that it has **legitimacy.** Authority without legitimacy is a recipe for trouble. Iraq can again serve as an example. While many Iraqis were happy to see the end of Saddam Hussein's regime, they were also not pleased that their nation was occupied by foreign troops. Many Iraqis, especially in districts inhabited by Sunni Arabs (the former politically dominant group in Iraq) did not accept the legitimacy of the U.S.–led Coalition Provisional Authority (CPA). Terrorists and other groups hostile to the CPA could organize attacks on coalition troops or the new Iraqi police, knowing that their neighbors would not report their activities. The country would not be fully at peace until the CPA yielded authority to a government chosen by the Iraqis themselves—a government with substantial legitimacy, rather than one imposed by outside forces.

Democracy and Other Forms of Government

There are a variety of different types of government, which can be classified according to which person or group of people controls society through the government.

Types of Government

At one extreme is a society governed by a **totalitarian regime.** In such a political system, a small group of leaders or a single individual—a dictator—makes all political decisions for the society. Every aspect of political, social, and economic life is controlled by the government. The power of the ruler is total (thus, the term *totalitarianism*).

A second type of system is authoritarian government. **Authoritarianism** differs from totalitarianism in that only the government itself is fully controlled by the ruler. Social and economic institutions exist that are not under the government's control.

Many of our terms for describing the distribution of political power are derived from the ancient Greeks, who were the first Western people to study politics systematically. One form of rule by the few was known as **aristocracy,** literally meaning "rule by the best." In practice, this meant rule by wealthy members of ancient families.

The Greek term for rule by the people was **democracy.** Within the limits of their culture, some of the Greek city-states operated as democracies. Today, in much of the world, the people will not grant legitimacy to a government unless it is based on democracy.

Liberty
The greatest freedom of individuals that is consistent with the freedom of other individuals in the society.

Authority
The right and power of a government or other entity to enforce its decisions and compel obedience.

Legitimacy
Popular acceptance of the right and power of a government or other entity to exercise authority.

Totalitarian Regime
A form of government that controls all aspects of the political and social life of a nation.

Authoritarianism
A type of regime in which only the government itself is fully controlled by the ruler. Social and economic institutions exist that are not under the government's control.

Aristocracy
Rule by the "best"; in reality, rule by an upper class.

Democracy
A system of government in which political authority is vested in the people. Derived from the Greek words *demos* ("the people") and *kratos* ("authority").

The 2004 Elections and American Values

The reelection of Republican George W. Bush as president of the United States was based on an appeal to several basic American values that are described in this chapter. Above all, Bush was able to appeal to the value of order or security, which we have just discussed. Bush presented himself—successfully—as a wartime commander in chief who should be allowed to finish the job he had started. Democratic challenger John Kerry also presented himself as a commander in chief, but he was not able to match Bush in this regard. On the economy, Kerry appealed to the value of equality, or fairness, which we discuss later in this chapter. He gained little traction with this appeal, however.

Direct Democracy as a Model

The Athenian system of government in ancient Greece is usually considered the purest model for **direct democracy** because the citizens of that community debated and voted directly on all laws, even those put forward by the ruling council of the city. Is direct democracy possible today? We looked at one aspect of that question in the *What If . . .* feature at the beginning of this chapter.

The most important feature of Athenian democracy was that the **legislature** was composed of all of the citizens. Women, foreigners, and slaves, however, were excluded because they were not citizens. This form of government required a high level of participation from every citizen; that participation was seen as benefiting the individual and the city-state. The Athenians believed that although a high level of participation might lead to instability in government, citizens, if informed about the issues, could be trusted to make wise decisions.

Direct Democracy Today.   Direct democracy also has been practiced in Switzerland and, in the United States, in New England town meetings. At New England town meetings, which can include all of the voters who live in the town, impor-

Direct Democracy
A system of government in which political decisions are made by the people directly, rather than by their elected representatives; probably attained most easily in small political communities.

Legislature
A governmental body primarily responsible for the making of laws.

This town meeting in Vermont allows every citizen of the town to vote directly and in person for elected officials, for proposed policies, and, in some cases, for the town budget. To be effective, such a form of direct democracy requires that the citizens stay informed about local politics, attend town meetings, and devote time to discussion and decision making. (AP Photo/Toby Talbot)

tant decisions—such as levying taxes, hiring city officials, and deciding local ordinances—are made by majority vote. Some states provide a modern adaptation of direct democracy for their citizens; representative democracy is supplemented by the **initiative** or the **referendum**—a process by which the people may vote directly on laws or constitutional amendments. The **recall** process, which is available in many states, allows the people to vote to remove an official from state office.

Teledemocracy.   Because of the Internet, Americans have more access to political information than ever before. Voters can now go online to examine the record of any candidate for any office. Constituents can badger their congressional representatives and state legislators by sending them e-mail. Individuals can easily and relatively inexpensively form political interest groups using the Internet. They can even contribute to a particular politician's campaign through the Internet. Therefore, to some extent, we are gradually progressing toward a type of teledemocracy in which citizens and their political representatives communicate with each other easily and frequently online. In 2000, Colorado offered its citizens the opportunity of voting online.[2]

The Dangers of Direct Democracy

Although they were aware of the Athenian model, the framers of the U.S. Constitution were opposed to such a system. Democracy was considered to be dangerous and to lead to instability. But in the 1700s and 1800s, the idea of government based on the **consent of the people** gained increasing popularity. Such a government was the main aspiration of the American Revolution, the French Revolution in 1789, and many subsequent revolutions. At the time of the American Revolution, however, the masses were still considered to be too uneducated to govern themselves, too prone to the influence of demagogues (political leaders who manipulate popular prejudices), and too likely to subordinate minority rights to the tyranny of the majority.

James Madison defended the new scheme of government set forth in the U.S. Constitution, while warning of the problems inherent in a "pure democracy":

A common passion or interest will, in almost every case, be felt by a majority of the whole . . . and there is nothing to check the inducements to sacrifice the weaker party or an obnoxious individual. Hence it is that such democracies have ever been spectacles of turbulence and contention, and have ever been found incompatible with personal security or the rights of property; and have in general been as short in their lives as they have been violent in their deaths.[3]

Like other politicians of his time, Madison feared that pure, or direct, democracy would deteriorate into mob rule. What would keep the majority of the people, if given direct decision-making power, from abusing the rights of minority groups?

A Democratic Republic

The framers of the U.S. Constitution chose to craft a **republic,** meaning a government in which sovereign power rests with the people, rather than with a king or monarch. A republic is based on **popular sovereignty.** To Americans of the 1700s, the idea of a republic also meant a government based on common beliefs and virtues that would be fostered within small communities. The rulers were to be amateurs—good citizens who would take turns representing their fellow citizens.

Initiative
A procedure by which voters can propose a law or a constitutional amendment.

Referendum
An electoral device whereby legislative or constitutional measures are referred by the legislature to the voters for approval or disapproval.

Recall
A procedure allowing the people to vote to dismiss an elected official from state office before his or her term has expired.

Consent of the People
The idea that governments and laws derive their legitimacy from the consent of the governed.

Republic
A form of government in which sovereignty rests with the people, as opposed to a king or monarch.

Popular Sovereignty
The concept that ultimate political authority is based on the will of the people.

---

[2]Dave Brady, "Netting Voters," *The Industry Standard,* June 26, 2000, p. 119.
[3]James Madison, in Alexander Hamilton, James Madison, and John Jay, *The Federalist Papers,* No. 10 (New York: Mentor Books, 1964), p. 81. See Appendix C of this textbook.

Volunteers register voters in the Spanish Harlem section of New York City. By setting up a table in the neighborhood, the election officials make registration more convenient for voters, as well as less threatening. Supporters of both political parties often conduct voter-registration drives in the months before general elections. Does the voter-registration process make it harder for some kinds of people to exercise their right to vote? (Lisa Quinones, Stock Photo)

Democratic Republic
A republic in which representatives elected by the people make and enforce laws and policies.

Representative Democracy
A form of government in which representatives elected by the people make and enforce laws and policies; may retain the monarchy in a ceremonial role.

Universal Suffrage
The right of all adults to vote for their representatives.

Majority
More than 50 percent.

Majority Rule
A basic principle of democracy asserting that the greatest number of citizens in any political unit should select officials and determine policies.

The U.S. Constitution created a form of republican government that we now call a **democratic republic.** The people hold the ultimate power over the government through the election process, but all policy decisions are made by elected officials. For the founders, even this distance between the people and the government was not sufficient. The Constitution made sure that the Senate and the president would be selected by political elites rather than by the people, although later changes to the Constitution allowed the voters to elect members of the Senate directly.

Despite these limits, the new American system was unique in the amount of power it granted to the ordinary citizen. Over the course of the following two centuries, democratic values became more and more popular, at first in the West and then throughout the rest of the world. The spread of democratic principles gave rise to another name for our system of government—**representative democracy.** The term *representative democracy* has almost the same meaning as *democratic republic,* with one exception. Recall that in a republic, not only are the people sovereign, but there is no king. What if a nation develops into a democracy, but preserves the monarchy as a largely ceremonial institution? This is exactly what happened in Britain. Not surprisingly, the British found the term *democratic republic* to be unacceptable, and they described their system as a representative democracy instead.

Principles of Democratic Government. All representative democracies rest on the rule of the people as expressed through the election of government officials. In the 1790s in the United States, only free white males were able to vote, and in some states they had to be property owners as well. Women did not receive the right to vote in national elections in the United States until 1920, and the right to vote was not secured in all states by African Americans until the 1960s. Today, **universal suffrage** is the rule.

Because everyone's vote counts equally, the only way to make fair decisions is by some form of **majority** will. But to ensure that **majority rule** does not become oppressive, modern democracies also provide guarantees of minority rights. If political minorities were not protected, the majority might violate the fundamental rights of members of certain groups, especially groups that are unpopular or dissimilar to the majority population, such as racial minorities.

To guarantee the continued existence of a representative democracy, there must be free, competitive elections. Thus, the opposition always has the opportunity to win elective office. For such elections to be totally open, freedom of the press and speech must be preserved so that opposition candidates may present their criticisms of the government.

Constitutional Democracy. Another key feature of Western representative democracy is that it is based on the principle of **limited government.** Not only is the government dependent on popular sovereignty, but the powers of the government are also clearly limited, either through a written document or through widely shared beliefs. The U.S. Constitution sets down the fundamental structure of the government and the limits to its activities. Such limits are intended to prevent political decisions based on the whims or ambitions of individuals in government rather than on constitutional principles.

★★★★★★★★★★★★★★
DID YOU KNOW . . .
That the phrase "In God We Trust" was made the national motto on July 30, 1956, but had appeared on U.S. coins as early as 1864**?**

Limited Government
The principle that the powers of government should be limited, usually by institutional checks.

★ What Kind of Democracy Do We Have?

Political scientists have developed a number of theories about American democracy, including *majoritarian* theory, *elite* theory, and theories of *pluralism*. Advocates of these theories use them to describe American democracy either as it actually is or as they believe it should be.

Democracy for Everyone

Many people believe that in a democracy, the government ought to do what the majority of the people want. This simple proposition is the heart of majoritarian theory. As a theory of what democracy should be like, **majoritarianism** is popular among both political scientists and ordinary citizens. Many scholars, however, consider majoritarianism to be a surprisingly poor description of how U.S. democracy actually works. They point to the low level of turnout for elections. Polling data have shown that many Americans are neither particularly interested in politics nor well informed. Few are able to name the persons running for Congress in their districts, and even fewer can discuss the candidates' positions.

Majoritarianism
A political theory holding that in a democracy, the government ought to do what the majority of the people want.

Democracy for the Few

If ordinary citizens are not really making policy decisions with their votes, who is? One answer suggests that elites really govern the United States. American democracy, in other words, is a sham democracy. **Elite theory** is usually used simply to describe the American system. Few people today believe it is a good idea for the country to be run by a privileged minority. In the past, however, many people believed that it was appropriate for the country to be run by an elite. Consider the words of Alexander Hamilton, one of the framers of the Constitution:

Elite Theory
A perspective holding that society is ruled by a small number of people who exercise power to further their self-interest.

> All communities divide themselves into the few and the many. The first are the rich and the wellborn, the other the mass of the people. . . . The people are turbulent and changing; they seldom judge or determine right. Give therefore to the first class a distinct, permanent share in the government. They will check the unsteadiness of the second, and as they cannot receive any advantage by a change, they therefore will ever maintain good government.[4]

---

[4]Alexander Hamilton, "Speech in the Constitutional Convention on a Plan of Government," in *Writings,* ed. Joanne B. Freeman (New York: Library of America, 2001).

Some versions of elite theory posit a small, cohesive, elite class that makes almost all the important decisions for the nation,[5] whereas others suggest that voters choose among competing elites. New members of the elite are recruited through the educational system so that the brightest children of the masses allegedly have the opportunity to join the elite stratum.

Democracy for Groups

A different school of thought holds that our form of democracy is based on group interests. Even if the average citizen cannot keep up with political issues or cast a deciding vote in any election, the individual's interests will be protected by groups that represent her or him.

Theorists who subscribe to **pluralism** see politics as a struggle among groups to gain benefits for their members. Given the structures of the American political system, group conflicts tend to be settled by compromise and accommodation. Because there are a multitude of interests, no one group can dominate the political process. Furthermore, because most individuals have more than one interest, conflict among groups need not divide the nation into hostile camps.

Many political scientists believe that pluralism works very well as a descriptive theory. As a theory of how democracy *should* function, however, pluralism has problems. Poor citizens are rarely represented by interest groups. At the same time, rich citizens are often overrepresented. As political scientist E. E. Schattschneider observed, "The flaw in the pluralist heaven is that the heavenly chorus sings with a strong upper-class accent."[6] There are also serious doubts as to whether group decision making always reflects the best interests of the nation.

Indeed, critics see a danger that groups may become so powerful that all policies become compromises crafted to satisfy the interests of the largest groups. The interests of the public as a whole, then, are not considered. Critics of pluralism have suggested that a democratic system can be virtually paralyzed by the struggle among interest groups. We will discuss interest groups at greater length in Chapter 7.

Some scholars argue that none of these three theories—majoritarianism, elite theory, or pluralism—fully describes the workings of American democracy. These experts say that each theory captures a part of the true reality but that we need all three theories to gain a full understanding of American politics.

Pluralism
A theory that views politics as a conflict among interest groups. Political decision making is characterized by bargaining and compromise.

 # Fundamental Values

The writers of the American Constitution believed that the structures they had created would provide for both democracy and a stable political system. They also believed that the nation would be sustained by its **political culture**—a concept defined as a patterned set of ideas, values, and ways of thinking about government and politics.

Political Socialization

There is considerable consensus among American citizens about certain concepts basic to the U.S. political system. Given that the vast majority of Americans are descendants of immigrants having diverse cultural and political backgrounds, how can we account for this consensus? Primarily, it is the result of **political socialization**—the process by which beliefs and values are transmitted to new

Political Culture
The collection of beliefs and attitudes toward government and the political process held by a community or nation.

Political Socialization
The process through which individuals learn a set of political attitudes and form opinions about social issues. The family and the educational system are two of the most important forces in the political socialization process.

---

[5]Michael Parenti, *Democracy for the Few,* 7th ed. (Belmont, Calif.: Wadsworth Publishing, 2001).
[6]E. E. Schattschneider, *The Semi-Sovereign People* (Hinsdale, Ill.: The Dryden Press, 1975; originally published 1960).

immigrants and to our children. The nation depends on several different agents to transmit the precepts of our national culture.

The most obvious source of political socialization is the family. Parents teach their children about the value of participating in the political system through their example and through their approval. One of the primary functions of the public education system in the United States is to teach the values of the political culture to students through history courses, discussions of political issues, and the rituals of pledging allegiance to the flag and celebrating national holidays.

The most fundamental concepts of the American political culture are those of the **dominant culture.** The dominant culture in the United States has its roots in Western European civilization. From that civilization, American politics has inherited a bias toward individualism, private property, and Judeo-Christian ethics. Other cultural heritages honor community or family over individualism and sometimes place far less emphasis on materialism. Additionally, changes in our own society have brought about the breakdown of some values, such as the sanctity of the family structure, and the acceptance of others, such as women's pursuit of careers in the workplace. How do American values differ from those of other nations? We look at that question in this chapter's *Global View* feature on the next page.

Dominant Culture
The values, customs, and language established by the group or groups that traditionally have controlled politics and government in a society.

Liberty versus Order

In the United States, our civil liberties include religious freedom—both the right to practice whatever religion one chooses and freedom from any state-imposed religion. Our civil liberties also include freedom of speech—the right to express our opinions freely on all matters, including government actions. Freedom of speech is perhaps one of our most prized liberties, because a democracy could not endure without it. These and many other basic guarantees of liberty are found in the Bill of Rights, the first ten amendments to the Constitution.

Liberty, however, is not the only value widely held by Americans. A substantial portion of the American electorate believes that certain kinds of liberty threaten the traditional social order. The right to privacy is a particularly controversial liberty. The United States Supreme Court has held that the right to privacy can be derived from other rights that are explicitly stated in the Bill of Rights. The Supreme Court has also held that under the right to privacy, the government

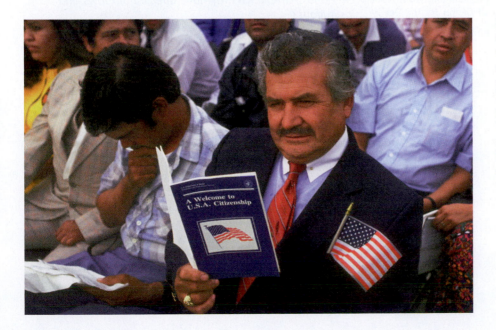

Each year thousands of immigrants are sworn in as new U.S. citizens. The U.S. Constitution, in Article I, Section 8, declares that Congress shall have the power to "establish a uniform Rule of Naturalization." Naturalization is the process by which individuals become U.S. citizens. Are the values that immigrants bring with them from their homelands likely to influence the values of their new country? (Chris Smith, Getty Images-Archive)

GLOBAL VIEW
America: The Exceptional Country?

Citizens of the United States have always believed that there was something exceptional about their country, and a belief in "American exceptionalism" has not been limited to Americans. Throughout the 1800s, European observers were unanimous in describing the United States as unlike other countries. Two characteristics made the United States stand out. One was the nation's uniquely democratic political system. The other was its unrivaled prosperity.

Since then, democratic values and economic prosperity have spread to other countries, and the United States is no longer unique in its wealth and democracy. Are the nations of the world, then, converging on a single model, or does the United States continue to be the exception in various ways?

This question has been raised more frequently in recent years. The Western nations were divided over the appropriateness of the war with Iraq in 2003. Differences between the United States and Europe, downplayed in the past, now often seem more important. Many have claimed that Americans and Europeans hold fundamentally different values. Worldwide public opinion surveys can help us determine whether this is true.

A COMMITMENT TO RELIGION

Among citizens of economically advanced nations, Americans stand out in their religious commitment. In a recent survey by the Pew Research Center,* 58 percent of those surveyed in the United States believe that "it is necessary to believe in God to be a moral person." This statement is actually more popular in most of the economically undeveloped countries of Africa, Latin America, and the Islamic world than in the United States. In Europe and Japan, however, strong majorities disagree with the statement. Only 13 percent of French respondents agree with it.

A COMMITMENT TO SELF-RELIANCE

Americans have a remarkably strong commitment to a philosophy of self-reliance. While a majority of Americans believe that "the government has a responsibility to help the poor," that majority is much smaller than in Europe. The most marked single difference between the United States and other countries, however, was in response to the statement that "success is determined by forces outside our control." Americans strongly disagree with this statement—much more so than the citizens of any other nation. Only Canadians even come close to disagreeing with the statement as often as Americans.

SHARED VALUES

Americans do share a number of basic values with most of the rest of the world. The Pew survey reported that democracy and a free market economy enjoy nearly universal approval. A degree of skepticism toward government is also almost universal, and not a peculiarly American trait.

FOR CRITICAL ANALYSIS

In what ways do you think that U.S. attitudes toward religion and self-reliance may have affected our laws and institutions?

*The Pew Global Attitudes Project, *Views of a Changing World: June 2003* (Washington, D.C.: The Pew Research Center for the People and the Press).

cannot ban either abortion[7] or private homosexual behavior by consenting adults.[8] Cultural conservatives believe that such rights threaten the sanctity of the family and the general cultural commitment to moral behavior. Of course, other Americans disagree with this point of view.

Security is another issue. When Americans feel particularly fearful or vulnerable, the government has emphasized national security over civil liberties. Such was the case after the Japanese attack on Pearl Harbor in 1941, which led to the U.S. entry into World War II. Thousands of Japanese Americans were held in internment camps, based on the assumption that their loyalty to this country was in question. More recently, the terrorist attacks on the Pentagon and the World Trade Center on September 11, 2001, renewed calls for greater security at the expense of some civil liberties. (See this chapter's feature entitled *America's Security: Loss of Liberty in Wartime* on page 14.)

---

[7]*Roe v. Wade*, 410 U.S. 113 (1973).
[8]*Lawrence v. Texas*, 123 S.Ct. 2472 (2003).

Equality versus Liberty

The Declaration of Independence states, "All men are created equal." The proper meaning of equality, however, has been disputed by Americans since the Revolution.[9] Much of American history—and indeed, world history—is the story of how the value of **equality** has been extended and elaborated.

First, the right to vote was granted to all adult white males regardless of whether they owned property. The Civil War resulted in the end of slavery and established that, in principle at least, all citizens were equal before the law. The civil rights movement of the 1950s and 1960s sought to make that promise of equality a reality for African Americans. Other movements have sought equality for other racial and ethnic groups, for women, for persons with disabilities, and for gay men and lesbians. We discuss these movements in Chapter 5.

To promote equality, it is often necessary to place limits on the right to treat people unequally. In this sense, equality and liberty are conflicting values. Today, the right to refuse equal treatment to the members of a particular race has very few defenders. Yet as recently as fifty years ago, this right was a cultural norm.

Economic Equality. Equal treatment regardless of race, religion, gender, and other characteristics is a popular value today. Equal opportunity for individuals to develop their talents and skills is also a value with substantial support. Equality of economic status, however, is a controversial value.

For much of history, the idea that the government could do anything about the division of society between rich and poor was not something about which people even thought. Most people assumed that such an effort was either impossible or undesirable. This assumption began to lose its force in the 1800s. As a result of the growing wealth of the Western world, and a visible increase in the ability of government to take on large projects, some people began to advocate the value of universal equality, or *egalitarianism*. Some radicals dreamed of a revolutionary transformation of society that would establish an egalitarian system—that is, a system in which wealth and power were redistributed on a more equal basis.

Many others rejected this vision but still came to endorse the values of eliminating poverty and at least reducing the degree of economic inequality in society. Antipoverty advocates believed then and believe now that such a program could prevent much suffering. In addition, they believed that reducing economic inequality would promote fairness and enhance the moral tone of society generally.

Property Rights and Capitalism. The value of reducing economic inequality is in conflict with the right to **property**. This is because reducing economic inequality typically involves the transfer of property (usually in the form of money) from some people to others. For many people, liberty and property are closely entwined. Our capitalist system is based on private property rights. Under **capitalism**, property consists not only of personal possessions but also of wealth-creating assets such as farms and factories. The investor-owned corporation is in many ways the preeminent capitalist institution. The funds invested by the owners of a corporation are known as *capital*—hence the very name of the system. Capitalism is also typically characterized by considerable freedom to make binding contracts and by relatively unconstrained markets for goods, services, and investments.

Property—especially wealth-creating property—can be seen as giving its owner political power and the liberty to do whatever he or she wants. At the same

Equality
As a political value, the idea that all people are of equal worth.

Property
Anything that is or may be subject to ownership. As conceived by the political philosopher John Locke, the right to property is a natural right superior to human law (laws made by government).

Capitalism
An economic system characterized by the private ownership of wealth-creating assets and also by free markets and freedom of contract.

August 8, 1963, civil rights march on Washington, D.C. (Library of Congress)

[9]Richard J. Ellis, "Rival Visions of Equality in American Political Culture," *Review of Politics,* Vol. 54 (Spring 1992), p. 254.

AMERICA'S SECURITY
Loss of Liberty in Wartime

Iraqi men rest in the shade of a wall, painted with graffiti concerning the Abu Ghraib prison mistreatment scandal, in the Sadr City district of Baghdad, Iraq. (AP Photo/Karim Kadim)

What happens to liberty in times of war? On April 28, 2004, the CBS news program *Sixty Minutes II* aired photographs taken at Abu Ghraib prison in Baghdad, Iraq. The pictures showed what appeared to be sexual and physical abuse of Iraqi prisoners. In some photographs, inmates were hooded, piled naked on top of each other, and made to crawl on leashes. Other photos, which were released to members of Congress, showed even greater abuses. In the months before the photographs came to light, the U.S Army had already arrested several U.S. soldiers in connection with the case. The photos, however, turned what had been a minor story into a major scandal.

Reporters learned that the abuse was part of an intimidation process designed to elicit information from prisoners. U.S. prison guards believed that the inmates subjected to the abuse were among the "worst of the worst" and that interrogation of these persons could yield intelligence that could save the lives of other American soldiers. The guards who were charged with crimes as a result of the abuse claimed that military intelligence personnel had encouraged them to "soften up" the prisoners. These claims raised the question of whether higher levels in the chain of command bore any responsibility for the scandal.

INTELLIGENCE GATHERING VERSUS HUMAN RIGHTS

Whether in Iraq or in the United States, developing intelligence that can be used to prevent terrorist attacks is of major importance. The actions used to obtain such intelligence, however, can come into conflict with other valued principles, such as the right of detainees to receive humane treatment and a fair trial and the right of the people to know what their government is doing.

After the terrorist attacks of September 11, 2001, for example, the federal government arrested approximately 1,200 noncitizens in the United States, largely for visa violations. These persons were interned in secret, and the government did not release even the names of those detained. None of these individuals was ever charged with a terrorism-related offense. Also, in November 2001 President George W. Bush issued an executive order authorizing military tribunals for noncitizens, in which "it is not practicable to apply . . . the principles of law and the rules of evidence generally recognized in the trial of criminal cases in the United States district courts."

THE GENEVA CONVENTIONS

Measures designed to obtain information from prisoners are strictly limited by the Geneva Conventions, a set of treaties ratified by the United States after World War II (1939–1945). After 9/11, however, the Bush administration limited American adherence to the conventions. White House Counsel Alberto Gonzales wrote to the president in January 2002: "As you have said, the war against terrorism is a new kind of war. The nature of the new war places a high premium on other factors, such as the ability to quickly obtain information from captured terrorists and their sponsors. . . . In my judgment, this . . . renders obsolete Geneva's strict limitations on questioning of enemy prisoners and renders quaint some of its provisions." Officially, rejection of the Geneva Conventions was limited to the war in Afghanistan and was not extended to Iraq.

Abandoning the conventions, even for Afghanistan, raises some serious questions. If U.S. troops become prisoners of war, can we expect that they will be treated in accordance with the conventions if we refuse to adhere to them? A further question is whether forceful interrogation methods (or even torture) can yield good intelligence. Many experts in this field believe that prisoners subjected to such methods will say anything that they believe their interrogators wish to hear, regardless of whether it is true.

FOR CRITICAL ANALYSIS

To what extent might the news of abuses such as those that took place at Abu Ghraib prison cause greater security problems in Iraq?

Members of the Florida National Guard armed with M-16 assault rifles march past Starbucks at Jacksonville International Airport in Florida, soon after the September 11 terrorist attack. The Florida National Guard was deployed to augment security. How much liberty should we be prepared to give up in exchange for enhanced security? (AP photo/Oscar Sosa)

time, the ownership of property immediately creates inequality in society. The desire to own property, however, is so widespread among all classes of Americans that radical egalitarian movements have had a difficult time securing a wide following here.

Can the values of property and order come into conflict? We look at a circumstance in which they do in this chapter's *Which Side Are You On?* feature on the following page.

 ## Political Ideologies

A political **ideology** is a closely linked set of beliefs about politics. Political ideologies offer their adherents well-organized theories that propose goals for the society and the means by which those goals can be achieved. At the core of every political ideology is a set of guiding values. The two ideologies most commonly referred to in discussions of American politics are *liberalism* and *conservatism*.

Liberalism versus Conservatism

The set of beliefs called **conservatism** includes a limited role for the government in helping individuals. Conservatism also includes support for traditional values. These values usually include a strong sense of patriotism. Conservatives believe that the private sector probably can outperform the government in almost any activity. Believing that the individual is primarily responsible for his or her own well-being, conservatives typically oppose government programs to redistribute income or change the status of individuals. Conservatives play a dominant role in the Republican Party.

The set of beliefs called **liberalism** includes advocacy of government action to improve the welfare of individuals, support for civil rights, and tolerance for social change. American liberals believe that government should take positive action to reduce poverty, to redistribute income from wealthier classes to poorer ones, and to regulate the economy. Liberals are an influential force within the Democratic Party but do not dominate the party to the same extent that conservatives dominate the Republican Party.

Ideology
A comprehensive set of beliefs about the nature of people and about the role of an institution or government.

Conservatism
A set of beliefs that includes a limited role for the national government in helping individuals, support for traditional values and lifestyles, and a cautious response to change.

Liberalism
A set of beliefs that includes the advocacy of positive government action to improve the welfare of individuals, support for civil rights, and tolerance for political and social change.

WHICH SIDE ARE YOU ON?
Forfeiture and the War on Drugs

At the heart of most political controversies lies a conflict between two values held by the American people. *Forfeiture* (the loss of property without compensation) counterpoises the values of order and property.

Under the forfeiture provisions of the drug laws, the government can seize houses, cars, and other assets if it suspects that they were used in illegal drug sales or were bought with money from such sales.

These seizures are conducted under the *civil* law, rather than the *criminal* law. In a criminal case, a person is presumed innocent until proved guilty beyond a reasonable doubt. In civil forfeiture cases, however, the government only needs to show that there is a "preponderance of evidence" that the property was used in a drug-law violation, or that the asset may have been bought with money from a drug crime. To get the property back, the *owner* has to prove that the government has no right to seize the property. Proving that you are innocent of a crime is not enough. For example, if you lend your car to someone who uses it while selling drugs, you can lose ownership of the vehicle even if you are unaware of the sale.

FORFEITURE IS A VITAL TOOL IN THE WAR ON DRUGS

Some maintain that forfeitures are essential to the war on drugs. The United States Supreme Court has argued that the laws force people to exercise greater care in loaning their property. Forfeiture can also encourage property owners to undertake vigorous steps to prevent drug violations. According to the courts, *consent* to the use of illegal drugs includes the failure by the building owner to take all reasonable steps to stop the use of illegal drugs once the owner has been notified that drugs are being used.

FORFEITURE DESTROYS OUR CONSTITUTIONAL RIGHTS

Opponents point out that forfeiture laws can threaten us with the loss of our homes and other property if we do not take drastic measures to ensure that no one we do business with has been involved with drugs. Forcing citizens to spy on each other is the hallmark of a totalitarian society.

Consider the experience of Joseph Haji, who owns the Sunshine Market in Detroit. The Detroit police brought drug-sniffing dogs into Haji's market. The dogs found three one-dollar bills in the cash register that smelled of cocaine. The police confiscated the $3, plus the additional $4,381 in the cash register. To no avail, Haji objected, noting that his store is in a drug-plagued neighborhood: "I'm supposed to inspect the money?" A recent study has determined that over 90 percent of U.S. paper money is contaminated with traces of cocaine.

WHAT'S YOUR POSITION?

Forfeiture provisions have also been introduced into antiterrorism laws. Are the threats of terrorism and drugs so great that we must give up certain protections to let the government fight these evils more effectively? Or do forfeiture provisions go too far?

GOING ONLINE

You can find links to a variety of articles on civil forfeiture at **http://dmoz.org/Society/Issues/Property_Rights/Forfeiture**.

The Traditional Political Spectrum

A traditional method of comparing political ideologies is to array them on a continuum from left to right, based primarily on how much power the government should exercise to promote economic equality. Table 1–1 shows how ideologies can be arrayed in a traditional political spectrum. In addition to liberalism and conservatism, this example includes the ideologies of socialism and libertarianism.

Socialism falls on the left side of the spectrum. Socialists play a minor role in the American political arena, although socialist parties and movements have been important in other countries around the world. In the past, socialists typically advocated replacing investor ownership of major businesses with either government ownership or ownership by employee cooperatives. Socialists believed that such steps would break the power of the very rich and lead to an egalitarian society. In more recent times, socialists in Western Europe have advocated more limited programs that redistribute income.

Socialism
A political ideology based on strong support for economic and social equality. Socialists traditionally envisioned a society in which major businesses were taken over by the government or by employee cooperatives.

TABLE 1–1

The Traditional Political Spectrum

	SOCIALISM	LIBERALISM	CONSERVATISM	LIBERTARIANISM
How much power should the government have over the economy?	Active government control of major economic sectors.	Positive government action in the economy.	Positive government action to support capitalism.	Almost no regulation of the economy.
What should the government promote?	Economic equality, community.	Economic security, equal opportunity, social liberty.	Economic liberty, morality, social order.	Total economic and social liberty.

On the right side of the spectrum is **libertarianism**, a philosophy of skepticism toward most government activities. Libertarians strongly support property rights and typically oppose regulation of the economy and redistribution of income. Libertarians support *laissez-faire* capitalism. (*Laissez faire* is French for "let it be.") Libertarians also tend to oppose government attempts to regulate personal behavior and promote moral values.

Libertarianism
A political ideology based on skepticism or opposition toward almost all government activities.

"Classical" Liberalism

The word *liberal* has an odd history. It comes from the same root as *liberty,* and originally it simply meant "free." In that broad sense, the United States as a whole is a liberal country, and all popular American ideologies are variants of liberalism. In a more restricted definition, a *liberal* was a person who believed in limited government and who opposed religion in politics. A hundred years ago, liberalism referred to a philosophy that in some ways resembled modern-day libertarianism. For that reason, many libertarians today refer to themselves as *classical liberals.*

How did the meaning of the word *liberal* change? In the 1800s, the Democratic Party was seen as the more liberal of the two parties. The Democrats of that time stood for limited government and opposition to moralism in politics. Democrats opposed Republican projects such as building roads, freeing the slaves, and prohibiting the sale of alcoholic beverages. Beginning with Democratic president Woodrow Wilson (1913–1921), however, the party's economic policies began to change. By the time of President Franklin Delano Roosevelt (1933–1945), the Democrats stood for positive government action to help the economy. Although Roosevelt stood for new policies, he kept the old language—as Democrats had long done, he called himself a liberal. We will discuss the history of the two parties in greater detail in Chapter 8.

Outside the United States and Canada, the meaning of the word *liberal* never changed. For this reason, you might hear a left-of-center European denounce U.S. president Ronald Reagan (1981–1989) or British prime minister Margaret Thatcher (1979–1990) for their "liberalism." What is meant, of course, is that these two leaders were enthusiastic advocates of *laissez-faire* capitalism.

Problems with the Traditional Political Spectrum

Many political scientists believe that the traditional left-to-right spectrum is not sufficiently complete. Take the example of libertarians. In Table 1–1, libertarians are placed to the right of conservatives. If the only question is how much power the government should have over the economy, this is where they belong. Libertarians, however, advocate the most complete possible freedom in social matters. They oppose government action to promote traditional moral values, although such action is often favored by other groups on the political right. Their strong

"You'll be happy to know, Father, he's not a Liberal, Moderate or Conservative. Jason's a nothing."

support for civil liberties seems to align them more closely with modern liberals than with conservatives.

Liberalism is often described as an ideology that supports "big government." If the objective is to promote equality, the description has some validity. In the moral sphere, however, conservatives tend to support more government regulation of social values and moral decisions than do liberals. Thus, conservatives tend to oppose gay rights legislation and propose stronger curbs on pornography. Liberals usually show greater tolerance for alternative life choices and oppose government attempts to regulate personal behavior and morals.

A Four-Cornered Ideological Grid

For a more sophisticated breakdown of American popular ideologies, many scholars use a four-cornered grid, as shown in Figure 1–1. The grid provides four possible ideologies. Each quadrant contains a substantial portion of the American electorate. Individual voters may fall anywhere on the grid, depending on the strength of their beliefs about economic and cultural issues.

Note that there is no generally accepted term for persons in the lower-left position, which we have labeled "economic liberals, cultural conservatives." Some scholars have used terms such as *populist* to describe this point of view, but these words can be misleading.

Individuals who are economic liberals and cultural conservatives tend to support government action both to promote the values of economic equality and fairness and to defend traditional values such as the family and marriage. These individuals may describe themselves as conservative or moderate. They are more likely to be Democrats than Republicans but often do not identify strongly with any party.

Libertarian, as a position on our two-way grid, does not refer to the small Libertarian Party, which has only a minor role in the American political arena. Rather, libertarians more typically support the Republican Party. They are more likely than conservatives to vote for a compatible Democrat, however.

Classifying the Voters.   If the traditional political spectrum held, most voters would fall into the liberal or conservative quarters of our ideological grid. Actually, there are a substantial number of voters in each quadrant. Asking whether the government should guarantee everyone a job, for example, divides the electorate roughly in half on the economic dimension. Certain questions about abortion also divide the electorate in half on the social dimension. Knowing how a voter answered one of these questions, however, does not tell us how he or she answered the other one. There are many people who would give a "liberal" answer to the jobs question but a "conservative" answer to the abortion question; also, many people would give a "conservative" answer to the jobs question and a "liberal" answer on abortion.

Conservative Popularity.   Even though all four ideologies are popular, it does not follow that the various labels we have used in the four-cornered grid are equally favored. Voters are much more likely to describe themselves as conservative than as liberal. There are a variety of reasons for this, but one is that *liberal* has come to imply "radical" to many people, while *conservative* often implies "moderate." Because most Americans value moderation, the conservative label has an advantage, and few politicians today willingly describe themselves as liberal. The designation *libertarian* has an even more radical flavor than *liberal,* and the number of voters with obvious libertarian tendencies far exceeds the number who are willing to adopt the label. We will look further at popular ideologies in Chapter 6.

FIGURE 1–1

A Four-Cornered Ideological Grid

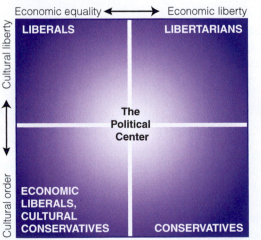

Totalitarian Ideologies

Two other important ideologies fit poorly into the traditional political spectrum. These are **communism** and **fascism**. Neither ideology ever had a significant following in the United States. Their impact on Europe and Asia, however, determined the course of twentieth-century history.

The first communists were a radical breakaway from the socialist movement. Traditionally, socialists had always considered themselves to be democrats. The communists, however, believed that they could abolish capitalism and institute socialism through a severe partisan dictatorship. The Soviet Union, founded by Russian communists after World War I (1914–1918), succeeded in establishing government control of farms, factories, and businesses of all kinds and in replacing the market system with central planning. Under Joseph Stalin (1924–1953), the Soviet Union also developed into a brutal totalitarian regime.

The most famous example of fascism was Nazi Germany (1933–1945). As with communism, the success of fascism depended on a large body of disciplined followers and a populist appeal. Fascism, however, championed elitism rather than egalitarianism. It was strongly influenced by Charles Darwin's concept of "the survival of the fittest." It valued action over rational deliberation and explicitly rejected liberal individualism—it exalted the national collective, united behind an absolute ruler. Fascism appealed to patriotism or nationalism, but it shaped these common sentiments into virulent racism.

Totalitarianism in the Islamic World

The terrorists who attacked the World Trade Center and the Pentagon on September 11, 2001, were ideologically motivated. These terrorists were members of the al Qaeda[10] network led by Osama bin Laden. Al Qaeda's ideology is based on a radical and fundamentalist interpretation of Islam, an interpretation sometimes called *Islamism*. Al Qaeda rejects all Western democratic values and calls for the

Communism
A revolutionary variant of socialism that favors a partisan (and often totalitarian) dictatorship, government control of all enterprises, and the replacement of free markets by central planning.

Fascism
A twentieth-century ideology—often totalitarian—that exalts the national collective united behind an absolute ruler. Fascism rejects liberal individualism, values action over rational deliberation, and glorifies war.

---

[10]*Al Qaeda,* sometimes transliterated as *al Qaida* or *al-Qa'idah,* is Arabic for "the base."

Osama Bin Laden is pictured here in one of his numerous televised broadcasts. While bin Laden's al Qaeda terrorist network was significantly disrupted by the U.S. intervention in Afghanistan, other radical groups in the Middle East and elsewhere have adopted al Qaeda's ideology and techniques. What effect may these developments have on the fight against terrorism? (AP Photo/ Al Jazeera)

establishment of a worldwide Islamic political order (the *caliphate*). Al Qaeda's
Islamist allies in Afghanistan—the Taliban—were, in fact, able to impose a totalitarian government until they were brought down by U.S. intervention.

Saddam Hussein's Baath Party in Iraq can also be called a totalitarian movement. One of the many surprises faced by the U.S.–led coalition after it took control of Iraq was the durability of the Baath Party.[11] Unlike the Iraqi army, the Baath
Party did not dissolve on Hussein's defeat but continued to try to hold power until
it could be dislodged by coalition forces. Baathists played a prominent role in the
subsequent terrorist attacks on coalition troops. The Baath Party gained strength
from the fact that it is ideologically based and was not created for the sole purpose
of supporting Hussein.

The Baath Party was founded by Syrian ideologue Michel Aflaq. While Baathists
are often referred to as Arab nationalists, Baath ideology goes beyond pan-Arab
nationalism and actually views the Arabs as a kind of master race. Baathism glorifies constant struggle and is relatively nonreligious. The ideological similarity
between Baathism and fascism is quite striking. Hussein also borrowed organizational techniques from Stalin's Communist Party and openly cited the Soviet
leader as a role model.

Even before the Second Gulf War in 2003, Baathism had limited appeal in the
Arab world. Radical Islamism is a more attractive and dangerous ideology. The
United States may be responding to Islamist movements for many years to come.

★ The Changing Face of America

The face of America is changing as its citizens age, become more diverse, and generate new needs for laws and policies. Long a nation of growth, the United States
has also become a middle-aged nation with a low birthrate and an increasing
number of older citizens who want services from the government. Both the aging
of the population and its changing ethnic composition will have significant political consequences.

The Aging of America

Like other economically advanced countries, the United States has in recent
decades experienced falling birthrates and an increase in the number of older citizens. The "aging of America" is a weaker phenomenon than in many other
wealthy countries, however. Currently, the median age of the population is 35.5
in the United States and 37.7 in Europe. By 2050, the median age in the United
States is expected to rise slightly to 36.2. In Europe, it is expected to reach 52.7.

The United States, while it is aging, is not aging quickly enough to halt the
growth of its population. One reason for this is immigration. Of course, new immigrants directly add to the population of the country. In addition, however, a great
many new immigrants are of exactly the right age to become mothers and fathers.

Figure 1–2 shows the predicted change in the proportion of the retirement-age
population in the United States over the next half-century. By 2025, that proportion is expected to be about one and a half times what it is today. As a result, the
government will be under pressure to revise the Social Security system. A larger
portion of each worker's wages will have to go toward taxes to support benefits
for the retired population—or else the benefits may be reduced.

The larger number of older persons will also strain health-care budgets. Not only
do older persons require more medical care, but we can expect that advances in
medical science will cause the demand for medical services to rise in future years.

---

[11]*Baath* is Arabic for "renaissance."

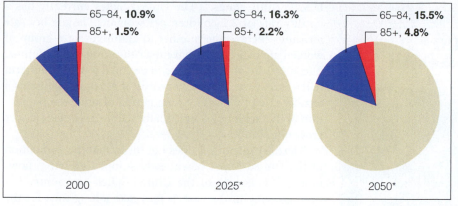

65–84, **10.9%**
85+, **1.5%**

2000

65–84, **16.3%**
85+, **2.2%**

2025*

65–84, **15.5%**
85+, **4.8%**

2050*

*Data for 2025 and 2050 are projections.
Source: U.S. Bureau of the Census.

FIGURE 1–2

The Aging of America
The figures show that the portion of the population over age sixty-five will increase during the next half-century. Growth in the proportion of the elderly will slow by 2050 due to the effects of immigration.

Our Growing Population

The United States differs from most economically advanced nations in the growth of its population. In 2050, there are expected to be about 420 million Americans, up from 295 million today.

The End of the Population Explosion.   In recent decades, population growth rates have been falling throughout the world. The great population explosion of the late twentieth century is reaching its end—the world's population, currently just over 6 billion, is expected to stabilize at perhaps 9 billion by 2050. While growth rates remain high in many African and Muslim nations, most economically advanced nations will have smaller populations in 2050 than they do today.[12] The United States will continue to grow during these years, however. For that reason, by 2050 the portion of the world's population living in the United States will be close to what it is today.

[12]Exceptions include countries with large immigrant populations, such as Canada and Australia; also, Britain and France are expected to post modest population gains.

An elementary school teacher confers with a multiethnic family on their daughter's progress in school. The increasing number of multiethnic families is a relatively new development in the United States. (Copyright ©Robin Sachs/Photo Edit—All rights reserved)

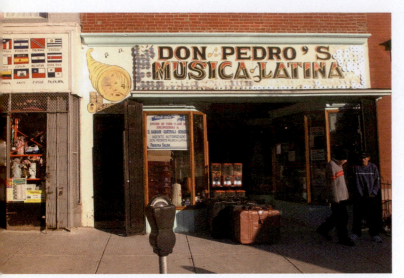

Don Pedro's Musica Latina shop in "Spanish Town" on Broadway Street in the Fells Point section of Baltimore. Hispanics are the fastest growing minority in the country. (AP Photo/*The Daily Record*, Eric Stocklin)

U.S. Fertility Rates. The United States currently has a fertility rate of 2.1 children per woman. The *fertility rate* measures the average number of children that a group of women are expected to have over the course of a lifetime. A fertility rate of 2.1 happens to be equal to the "long-term replacement rate." In other words, if a nation maintains a fertility rate of 2.1 over a long period of time, the population of that nation will eventually stabilize—it will neither grow nor shrink.

A fertility rate of 2.1 does not mean that the population of the United States has already stopped growing, however. If—as is true of the United States—a country has been growing in the past, it may take a long time for the population to stabilize. Because of past growth, the median age of the population is younger than it would otherwise be. This means that there are more potential mothers and fathers. Only after its residents age will the population of a country stabilize.

Ethnic Change

The ethnic character of the United States is also changing. Non-Hispanic white Americans have a fertility rate of just over 1.8. African Americans have a fertility rate of 2.1. Hispanic Americans, however, have a current fertility rate of almost 3.0. (The fertility rate in Mexico is only 2.5.) Figure 1-3 shows the projected changes in the U.S. ethnic distribution in future years.

A large share of all new immigrants are Hispanic, which also serves to increase the Hispanic proportion of the U.S. population. A **Hispanic** is someone who can claim a heritage from a Spanish-speaking country. Table 1-2 shows the places of origin for immigrants entering the United States in 2002. In part because of the growth in the Hispanic American population, non-Hispanic white Americans no longer make up a majority of the population in California. By 2015, they will no longer be the majority in Texas. The number of persons who identify themselves as "multiracial" is also growing. What might be the consequences of a large multiracial population? We look at that question in this chapter's *Politics and Diversity* feature on page 24.

Hispanic
Someone who can claim a heritage from a Spanish-speaking country. The term is used only in the United States or other countries that receive immigrants—Spanish-speaking persons living in Spanish-speaking countries do not normally apply the term to themselves.

FIGURE 1–3

Distribution of the U.S. Population by Race and Hispanic Origin, 1980 to 2075

By about 2060, minorities will constitute a majority of the U.S. population.

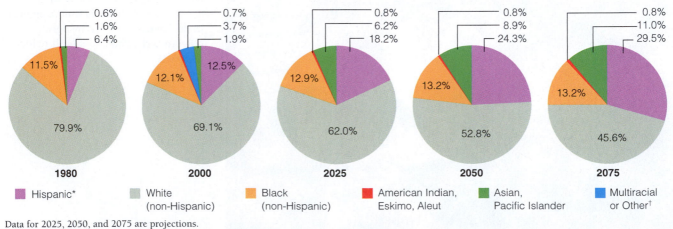

Data for 2025, 2050, and 2075 are projections.
*Persons of Hispanic origin can be of any race.
†The "multiracial or other" category in 2000 is not an official census category but represents all non-Hispanics who chose either "some other race" or two or more races in the 2000 census.
SOURCE: U.S. Bureau of the Census.

TABLE 1–2

Places of Origin of Immigrants into the United States, 2002

REGION OR COUNTRY	NUMBER	PERCENT
Mexico	219,380	20.6
El Salvador	31,168	2.9
Cuba	28,272	2.7
Dominican Republic	22,604	2.1
Haiti	20,268	1.9
Canada	19,519	1.8
Guatemala	16,229	1.5
Jamaica	14,898	1.4
Other North America	32,099	3.0
Colombia	18,845	1.8
Other South America	55,661	5.2
India	71,105	6.7
China	61,282	5.8
Philippines	51,308	4.8
Vietnam	33,627	3.2
Korea	21,021	2.0
Pakistan	13,743	1.3
Iran	13,029	1.2
Other Asia	76,984	7.2
Bosnia	25,373	2.4
Ukraine	21,217	2.0
Russia	20,833	2.0
Britain	16,181	1.5
Other Europe	90,605	8.5
Africa	60,269	5.7
Oceania	5,557	0.5
Unknown	2,655	0.2
TOTAL	1,063,732	100.0

SOURCE: Bureau of Citizenship and Immigration Services.

Who Are the Hispanics?

To the U.S. Census Bureau, *Hispanics* are those who identify themselves by that term. Hispanics can be of any race. Hispanics can be new immigrants or the descendants of families that have lived in the United States for centuries.

Hispanics may come from any of about twenty Spanish-speaking countries,[13] and they differ among themselves in many ways. Hispanic Americans, as a result, are a highly diverse population. The three largest Hispanic groups are Mexican Americans at 58.5 percent of all Hispanics; Puerto Ricans (all of whom are U.S. citizens) at 9.6 percent of the total; and Cuban Americans at 3.5 percent.

The term *Hispanic* itself, although used by the government, is not entirely popular among Hispanic Americans. Some prefer the term *Latino*. Most prefer a name that identifies their heritage more specifically—many Mexican Americans would rather be called that than Hispanic.

---

[13]According to the census definition, "Hispanic" includes the relatively small number of Americans whose ancestors came directly from Spain itself. Few of these people are likely to check the "Hispanic" box on a census form, however.

POLITICS AND DIVERSITY
The Problem of Racial Classifications

Today, the lines separating racial groups are becoming increasingly blurred, in part because of marriage between men and women of different races. Illegal in sixteen states until a 1967 ruling by the United States Supreme Court,* interracial marriage has become more common in recent decades. When Oprah Winfrey asked golfer Tiger Woods about his ethnicity, Woods said he was not a black but a "Cablinasian"—a combination of Caucasian, black, Indian, and Asian.

WHAT ARE THE NUMBERS?

Interracial marriage is especially common among races with relatively small populations. For example, about 43 percent of married non-Hispanic American Indian women have spouses of a different category. "Out-marriage" by African Americans is less common—only 4 percent of African American women are married to men of a different race. In contrast, 22 percent of Asian American women are married outside the Asian American category, and 18 percent of Hispanic women are married to non-Hispanic men.

These figures are for all marriages, and they include older married persons who found their mates at a time when interracial marriage was often unacceptable. Younger people are more likely to intermarry. New immigrants, however, are less likely to intermarry than native-born citizens, and so our growing immigrant population also holds down the total number of interracial marriages.

A POLITICAL ISSUE

The U.S. government uses racial classifications to determine who is eligible for certain benefits, notably protections against discrimination. Yet how can these classifications be applied to the millions of Americans with mixed backgrounds? Before the 2000 census, the U.S. Congress debated which questions should appear on the census forms. A group of multiracial activists campaigned for a "multiracial" option on the census and received support from the Republican leadership.

This proposal was opposed, however, by established civil rights organizations. The problem was not just that a multiracial option might reduce the official number of African Americans and therefore reduce black political influence. Some opponents of the classification argued that multiracialism did not really exist. Traditionally, a person with any identifiable African ancestry has been considered black in the United States. In effect, the multiracial activists and the African American leadership were at odds over deeply held but conflicting definitions of identity.

In the end, the multiracial option was not created. Census respondents were allowed to check more than one racial box, however, and 2.4 percent of all respondents did so. Some activists have since argued that the government should not collect information on racial identity at all. An initiative to prevent the state of California from collecting such data was placed on the ballot in 2003 but was voted down by large margins.

FOR CRITICAL ANALYSIS

Some people have suggested that, partly due to intermarriage, Americans will eventually begin to see groups such as Japanese Americans and Chinese Americans as essentially "white." What impact would this have on African Americans?

* *Loving v. Virginia,* 388 U.S. 1 (1967).

The diversity among Hispanic Americans results in differing political behavior. The majority of Hispanic Americans vote Democratic. In 2000, they backed Democratic presidential candidate Al Gore over Republican George W. Bush by 67 to 31 percent. Cuban Americans, however, are usually Republican. Most Cuban Americans left Cuba because of Fidel Castro's communist regime, and their strong anticommunism translates into conservative politics.

Other Trends

Various other social trends reveal changes that are under way in American society. Among the most important shifts has been the increasing number of women participating in the labor force. In 1960, only 36 percent of women over the age of sixteen were working outside the home or actively seeking work. By the time of the 2000 census, it was 58 percent.[14] An interesting point is that during the

---

[14]Though it is now several years old, the 2000 census is still the most accurate source for many kinds of data and will remain valuable until the next census is taken in 2010.

same years, labor force participation by men actually dropped. In 1960, the participation rate was 80 percent. By 2000, it was 71 percent. Likely causes of this decline include more years spent in higher education and earlier retirement.

Americans today are better educated than in the past. In 1960, only two-fifths of the population over the age of twenty-five had graduated from high school. By 2000, about four-fifths of all adults were high school graduates. In 1960, only 8 percent of Americans had a college degree. Today, one-fourth have a degree.

Abortion is a major political and social issue. Abortion rates rose sharply after abortion was legalized in 1973 but have declined since. The rate of divorce, another social indicator, rose from 2.5 divorces a year for every 1,000 people in 1965 to 4.8 in 1975. Over the last ten years the rate has begun to drop, and by 2002 it was at 4.0 divorces for every 1,000 people. The abortion and divorce rates parallel a large number of other indicators of social trouble, such as the murder rate—years of increases were followed by significant declines over the last decade.

 ## American Politics: Why Is It Important Today?

A presidential election year reminds us of the importance of American politics. A presidential election can be enormously fascinating. The two candidates were closely matched for most of the year and were very close in the public opinion polls right up to the end, when Bush finally emerged victorious. Beyond the entertainment value of the campaign lay important issues, even issues of life or death. Which candidate could do a better job of protecting us against terrorism? Which candidate had the better approach to war and peace? Which candidate could do best on the economy? Which candidate could best promote moral values?

Even as we chose a president, we also elected the entire House of Representatives, large numbers of senators and governors, and thousands of other officials from state legislators on down. The combined decisions of all of these political leaders will have an enormous impact on your economic well-being. Jobs, taxes—these are important issues. But other matters may affect you even more directly. Do you attend a state school? The level of support that your state can provide to your school may determine how much tuition you must pay. When you graduate, you will probably look for a job. Government policy may affect whether your employer is able to offer you health insurance. When you retire, how much will Social Security be able to help—and how much will you have to set aside out of your earnings?

> **DID YOU KNOW . . .**
> That about 14 percent of all legal immigrants to the United States plan to live in the Los Angeles/Long Beach, California, area ?

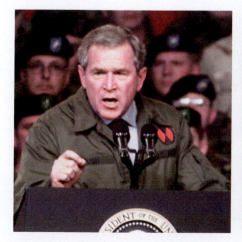

The presidential candidates in the 2004 elections. On the left, President George W. Bush, the Republican candidate, addresses soldiers at Fort Carson, Colorado. On the right, Senator John F. Kerry, the Democratic candidate, speaks in Toledo, Ohio. (Kerry/Photo by Sharon Farmer) (Bush/Photo by Spc. Aimee Felix)

MAKING A DIFFERENCE   ★ Seeing Democracy in Action

One way to begin to understand the American political system is to observe a legislative body in action. There are thousands of elected legislatures in the United States at all levels of government. You might choose to visit a city council, a school board, a township board of trustees, a state legislature, or the U.S. Congress.

Why Should You Care?

State and local legislative bodies can have a direct impact on your life. For example, local councils or commissions typically oversee the police, and the behavior of the police is a matter of interest even if you live on-campus. If you live off-campus, local authorities are responsible for an even greater number of issues that affect you directly. Are there items that the Sanitation Department refuses to pick up? You might be able to change its policies by lobbying your councilperson.

Even if there are no local issues that concern you, there are still benefits to be gained from observing a local legislative session. You may discover that local government works rather differ-

ently than you expected. You might learn, for example, that the representatives of your political party do not serve your interests as well as you thought—or that the other party is much more sensible than you had presumed.

What Can You Do?

To find out when and where local legislative bodies meet, look up the number of the city hall or county building in the telephone directory, and call the clerk of the council. In many communities, city council meetings and county board meetings can be seen on public access TV channels. Many cities and almost all state governments have Internet Web sites.

Before attending a business session of the legislature, try to find out how the members are elected. Are the members chosen by the "at-large" method of election so that each member represents the whole community, or are they chosen by specific geographic districts or wards? Is there a chairperson or official leader who controls the meetings? What are the responsibilities of this legislature?

When you visit the legislature, keep in mind the theory of representative democracy. The legislators or council members are elected to represent their constituents (those who voted them into office). Observe how often the members refer to their constituents or to the special needs of their community or electoral district. Listen for sources of conflict within a community. If there is a debate, for example, over a zoning proposal that involves the issue of land use, try to figure out why some members oppose the proposal.

If you want to follow up on your visit, try to get a brief interview with one of the members of the council or board. In general, legislators are very willing to talk to students, particularly students who also are voters. Ask the member how he or she sees the job of representative. How can the wishes of the constituents be identified? How does the representative balance the needs of the ward or district with the good of the entire community? You can write to many legislators via e-mail. You might ask how much e-mail they receive and who actually answers it.

 **Key Terms**

aristocracy 5	elite theory 9	libertarianism 17	popular sovereignty 7
authoritarianism 5	equality 13	liberty 5	property 13
authority 5	fascism 19	limited government 9	recall 7
capitalism 13	government 3	majoritarianism 9	referendum 7
communism 19	Hispanic 22	majority 8	representative democracy 8
consent of the people 7	ideology 15	majority rule 8	republic 7
conservatism 15	initiative 7	order 3	socialism 16
democracy 5	institution 3	pluralism 10	totalitarian regime 5
democratic republic 8	legislature 6	political culture 10	universal suffrage 8
direct democracy 6	legitimacy 5	political socialization 10	
dominant culture 11	liberalism 15	politics 3	

Chapter Summary

1 Politics is the process by which people decide which members of society get certain benefits or privileges and which members do not. It is the struggle over power or influence within institutions and organizations that can grant benefits or privileges. Government is the institution within which decisions are made that resolve conflicts or allocate benefits and privileges. It is unique because it has the ultimate authority within society.

2 Two fundamental political values are order, which includes security against violence, and liberty, the greatest freedom of the individual consistent with the freedom of other individuals. Liberty can be both promoted by government and invoked against government. To be effective, government authority must be backed up by legitimacy.

3 In a direct democracy, such as ancient Athens, the people themselves make the important political decisions. The United States is a representative democracy, where the people elect representatives to make the decisions.

4 Theories of American democracy include majoritarianism, in which the government does what the majority wants; elite theory, in which the real power lies with one or more elites; and pluralist theories, in which organized interest groups contest for power.

5 Fundamental American values include liberty, order, equality, and property. Not all of these values are fully compatible. The value of order often competes with civil liberties, and economic equality competes with property rights.

6 Popular political ideologies can be arrayed from left (liberal) to right (conservative). We can also analyze economic liberalism and conservatism separately from cultural liberalism and conservatism.

7 The face of America is changing as the population ages and becomes more ethnically diverse. Other changes—including the growing number of women in the work force and higher levels of education—are also altering the face of the nation.

Selected Print and Media Resources

SUGGESTED READINGS

Harrison, Lawrence E., and Samuel P. Huntington, eds. *Culture Matters: How Values Shape Human Progress.* New York: Basic Books, 2001. Each of the essays included in this book gives insight into an important question: How and why do some cultures do a better job of creating freedom, prosperity, and justice than others?

Lasswell, Harold. *Politics: Who Gets What, When and How.* New York: McGraw-Hill, 1936. This classic work defines the nature of politics.

Tocqueville, Alexis de. *Democracy in America.* Edited by Phillips Bradley. New York: Vintage Books, 1945. Life in the United States is described by a French writer who traveled through the nation in the 1820s.

White, John Kenneth. *The Values Divide: American Politics and Culture in Transition.* Chatham, N.J.: Chatham House, 2003. In this insightful book, a noted political science professor concludes that America is less a place than a "dream." He notes that the American dream is alive and well and that a vast majority of Americans believe that it is possible to achieve it—and that many Americans feel that they have achieved it.

Zakaria, Fareed. *The Future of Freedom: Illiberal Democracy at Home and Abroad.* New York: W. W. Norton & Co., 2003. The author argues that democratic elections are likely to lead to negative results unless liberal values have been established first. Liberal values, in this sense, include provisions for limited government, civil liberties, and minority rights.

MEDIA RESOURCES

All Things Considered—A daily broadcast of National Public Radio that provides extensive coverage of political, economic, and social news stories.

The Conservatives—A program that shows the rise of the conservative movement in America from the 1940s, through the presidential candidacy of Barry Goldwater, to the presidency of Ronald Reagan. In addition to Goldwater and Reagan, leaders interviewed include William F. Buckley, Jr., Norman Podhoretz, and Milton Friedman.

Liberalism vs. Conservatism—A 2001 film from Teacher's Video that focuses on two contrasting views of the role of government in society.

Mr. Smith Goes to Washington—A classic movie, produced in 1939, starring Jimmy Stewart as the honest citizen who goes to Congress trying to represent his fellow citizens. The movie dramatizes the clash between representing principles and representing corrupt interests.

The Values Issue and American Politics: Values Matter Most—Ben Wattenberg travels around the country in this 1995 program speaking to a broad range of ordinary Americans. He examines what he calls the "value issue"—the issues of crime, welfare, race, discipline, drugs, and prayer in the schools. Wattenberg believes that candidates who can best address these issues will win elections.

e-mocracy ★ Connecting to American Government and Politics

The Web has become a virtual library, a telephone directory, a contact source, and a vehicle to improve your understanding of American government and politics today. To help you become familiar with Web resources, we conclude each chapter in this book with an *E-mocracy* feature. The *Logging On* section in each of these features includes Internet addresses, or uniform resource locators (URLs), that will take you to Web sites focusing on topics or issues discussed in the chapter. Realize that Web sites come and go continually, so some of the Web sites that we include in the *Logging On* section may not exist by the time you read this book.

Each *E-mocracy* feature also includes an InfoTrac Internet activity. These activities are designed to lead you to Web sites that you can explore to learn more about an important political issue.

A word of caution about Internet use: Many students surf the Web for political resources. When doing so, you need to remember to approach these sources with care. For one thing, you should be very careful when giving out information about yourself. You also need to use good judgment because the reliability or intent of any given Web site is often unknown. Some sites are more concerned with accuracy than others, and some sites are updated to include current information while others are not.

Logging On

We have a powerful and interesting Web site for the textbook, which you can access through the Wadsworth American Government Resource Center. Go to

http://politicalscience.wadsworth.com/ amgov

You may also want to visit the home page of Dr. Politics—offered by Steffen

Schmidt, one of the authors of this book—for some interesting ideas and activities relating to American government and politics. Go to

http://www.public.iastate.edu/~sws/ homepage.html

Information about the rules and requirements for immigration and citizenship can be found at the Web site of the U.S. Bureau of Citizenship and Immigration Services:

http://www.immigration.gov/graphics/ index.htm.

For a basic "front door" to almost all U.S. government Web sites, click onto the very useful site maintained by the University of Michigan:

http://www.lib.umich.edu/govdocs/ govweb.html

For access to federal government offices and agencies, go to the U.S. government's official Web site at

http://www.firstgov.gov

To learn about the activities of one of the nation's oldest liberal political organizations, go to the Web site of the Americans for Democratic Action (ADA) at the following URL:

http://adaction.org

You can find a wealth of information about the changing face of America at the Web site of the Bureau of the Census:

http://www.census.gov

Using InfoTrac for Political Research

You can research a large number of topics by using the InfoTrac online library. Access to InfoTrac is provided with this textbook.

As noted in this chapter, the ideology of Islamism (which is not the same thing as the religion of Islam) will probably pose major problems for the United States in years to come. To use InfoTrac to research Islamism, go to

http://www.infotrac-college.com

Log on and go to InfoTrac College Edition, then go to the Keyword guide. Type "islamism" in the search field. InfoTrac will present you with a list of relevant articles, with the most recent articles shown first. Read several of the articles and use the information they provide to draw your own conclusions.

ONLINE REVIEW

At **http://politicalscience.wadsworth. com/schmidt12**, you will find a free Study Guide to this book. For each chapter, there are two online quizzes to help you master the material.

• The **PoliPrep Self Study Assessment** provides a pre-test for each major section of the chapter. PoliPrep then generates a customized study plan. After you complete the study plan, a post-test evaluates your progress.

• The **Tutorial Quiz** for each chapter provides questions on the chapter contents, including the features. The questions are organized to match the major sections of the chapter.

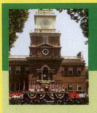

WHAT IF . . .
An Immigrant Could Become President?

BACKGROUND

The U.S. Constitution sets few rules on who can be elected president. An eligible candidate must be at least thirty-five years old, must have lived in the United States for the last fourteen years, and must be a "natural born Citizen." Presumably, this last provision means that a presidential candidate must be a citizen by birth, rather than through naturalization.

Naturalization is the procedure by which immigrants into the United States become citizens. Some persons, such as adopted children, can be naturalized simply by application. Normal requirements for persons over eighteen include five years as a legal permanent resident and the ability to read and write English. (There are exemptions to the English requirement for long-term elderly residents.) Applicants must be of "good moral character" and must pass a test on U.S. history and government.

WHAT IF AN IMMIGRANT COULD BECOME PRESIDENT?

When the Constitution was adopted, the population of the United States was small, and the founders were concerned that the new country might fall under the influence of one of the great European powers. Ensuring that the president would be natural born was one small safeguard against foreign domination.

The safeguard was probably unnecessary. For most of our history, American suspicion of any foreign connection has been a powerful force. Today, however, the U.S. electorate possesses great self-confidence. Diversity of origin is not an issue. Many of us can now imagine electing an immigrant to the highest office.

Certainly, Austrian-born Arnold Schwarzenegger, governor of California, can imagine such a possibility. "There are so many people . . . that are immigrants, that are doing such a terrific job with their work, bringing businesses here, that there's no reason why not," said Schwarzenegger. "Look at the kind of contribution that people like Henry Kissinger have made, Madeleine Albright." Kissinger and Albright are both former secretaries of state who immigrated from Europe.

WOULD ELECTING AN IMMIGRANT MAKE A DIFFERENCE?

Electing an immigrant would certainly showcase the virtue of diversity. Yet even if the voters could draw from a larger pool of talent than they do today, they would surely apply the same standards to potential presidents. The voters expect that, in foreign policy, any president will be a strong champion of American national interests. This suggests that electing an immigrant as president would not change much.

The ability to elect an immigrant, however, might provide a tactical advantage to particular politicians or viewpoints. What if Schwarzenegger were a Republican contender?

Schwarzenegger's particular variety of Republicanism (he is more liberal than most Republicans on cultural issues) has attracted independents and some Democrats in California and might do so nationally. Also, a presidential candidate who is a naturalized citizen might appeal across party boundaries to other naturalized citizens and members of ethnic minorities who are first-generation Americans. Such a candidate might even encourage resident aliens to seek citizenship.

AMENDING THE CONSTITUTION

The requirement that the president be natural born has, over the years, prevented a number of popular figures from contemplating a run for the presidency. In addition to Schwarzenegger, Kissinger, and Albright, we can include Michigan Democratic governor Jennifer Granholm, born in Canada.

The idea of amending the Constitution to permit immigrants to run for president was first raised in the 1970s by Republicans who were impressed by Kissinger's performance as secretary of state. The proposal did not go far, however. Constitutional amendments require overwhelming national support both in the Congress and in state legislatures.

FOR CRITICAL ANALYSIS

1. *Do you think that today's citizens would be reluctant to vote for a foreign-born presidential candidate?*
2. *Why might a naturalized leader be more nationalistic than a natural-born one?*

We the People of the United States, in Order to form a more perfect Union, establish Justice, insure domestic Tranquility, provide for the common defence, promote the general Welfare, and secure the Blessings of Liberty to ourselves and our Posterity, do ordain and establish this Constitution for the United States of America.

Every schoolchild in America has at one time or another been exposed to these famous words from the Preamble to the U.S. Constitution. The document itself is remarkable. The U.S. Constitution, compared with others in the fifty states and in the world, is relatively short. Because amending it is difficult (as we point out in this chapter's *What If . . .* feature), it also has relatively few amendments. The Constitution has remained largely intact for over two hundred years. To a great extent, this is because the principles set forth in the Constitution are sufficiently broad that they can be adapted to meet the needs of a changing society.

How and why the U.S. Constitution was created is a story that has been told and retold. It is worth repeating, because knowing the historical and political context in which this country's governmental machinery was formed is essential to understanding American government and politics today. The Constitution did not result just from creative thinking. Many of its provisions were grounded in the political philosophy of the time. The delegates to the Constitutional Convention in 1787 brought with them two important sets of influences: their political culture and their political experience. In the years between the first settlements in the New World and the writing of the Constitution, Americans had developed a political philosophy about how people should be governed and had tried out several forms of government. These experiences gave the founders the tools with which they constructed the Constitution.

 ## The Colonial Background

In 1607, the English government sent a group of farmers to establish a trading post, Jamestown, in what is now Virginia. The Virginia Company of London was the first to establish a permanent English colony in the Americas. The king of England gave the backers of this colony a charter granting them "full power and authority" to make laws "for the good and welfare" of the settlement. The colonists at Jamestown instituted a **representative assembly,** setting a precedent in government that was to be observed in later colonial adventures.

Jamestown was not a commercial success. Of the 105 men who landed, 67 died within the first year. But 800 new arrivals in 1609 added to their numbers. By the spring of the next year, frontier hazards had cut their numbers to 60. Of the 6,000 people who left England for Virginia between 1607 and 1623, 4,800 perished. This period is sometimes referred to as the "starving time for Virginia." Climatological researchers suggest that this "starving time" may have been brought about by a severe drought in the Jamestown area, which lasted from 1607 to 1612.

Separatists, the *Mayflower,* and the Compact

The first New England colony was established in 1620. A group of mostly extreme Separatists, who wished to break with the Church of England, came over on the ship *Mayflower* to the New World, landing at Plymouth (Massachusetts). Before going onshore, the adult males—women were not considered to have any political status—drew up the Mayflower Compact, which was signed by forty-one of the forty-four men aboard the ship on November 21, 1620. The reason for the compact was obvious. This group was outside the jurisdiction of the Virginia Company of London, which had chartered its settlement in Virginia, not Massachusetts. The Separatist leaders feared that some of the *Mayflower* passengers might conclude that they were no longer under any obligations of civil obedience.

Representative Assembly
A legislature composed of individuals who represent the population.

The signing of the compact aboard the *Mayflower*. In 1620, the Mayflower Compact was signed by almost all of the men aboard the ship *Mayflower,* just before disembarking at Plymouth, Massachusetts. It stated, "We . . . covenant and combine ourselves togeather into a civil body politick . . . ; and by vertue hearof to enacte, constitute, and frame such just and equal laws . . . as shall be thought [necessary] for the generall good of the Colonie." (The Granger Collection)

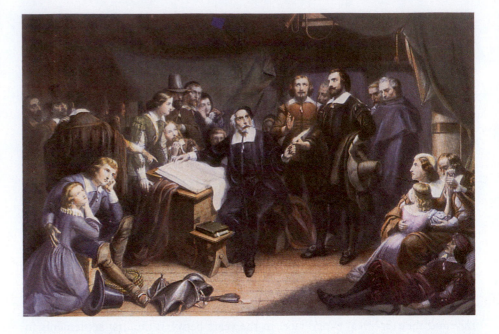

MILESTONES IN EARLY U.S. POLITICAL HISTORY

1607 Jamestown established; Virginia Company lands settlers.
1620 Mayflower Compact signed.
1630 Massachusetts Bay Colony set up.
1639 Fundamental Orders of Connecticut adopted.
1641 Massachusetts Body of Liberties adopted.
1682 Pennsylvania Frame of Government passed.
1701 Pennsylvania Charter of Privileges written.
1732 Last of the thirteen colonies (Georgia) established.
1756 French and Indian War declared.
1765 Stamp Act; Stamp Act Congress meets.
1774 First Continental Congress.
1775 Second Continental Congress; Revolutionary War begins.
1776 Declaration of Independence signed.
1777 Articles of Confederation drafted.
1781 Last state (Maryland) signs Articles of Confederation.
1783 "Critical period" in U.S. history begins; weak national government until 1789.
1786 Shays' Rebellion.
1787 Constitutional Convention.
1788 Ratification of Constitution.
1791 Ratification of Bill of Rights.

Therefore, some form of public authority was imperative. As William Bradford (one of the Separatist leaders) recalled in his accounts, there were "discontented and mutinous speeches that some of the strangers amongst them had let fall from them in the ship; That when they came a shore they would use their owne libertie; for none had power to command them."[1]

The compact was not a constitution. It was a political statement in which the signers agreed to create and submit to the authority of a government, pending the receipt of a royal charter. The Mayflower Compact's historical and political significance is twofold: it depended on the consent of the affected individuals, and it served as a prototype for similar compacts in American history. According to Samuel Eliot Morison, the compact proved the determination of the English immigrants to live under the rule of law, based on the *consent of the people.*[2]

More Colonies, More Government

Another outpost in New England was set up by the Massachusetts Bay Colony in 1630. Then followed Rhode Island, Connecticut, New Hampshire, and others. By 1732, the last of the thirteen colonies, Georgia, was established. During the colonial period, Americans developed a concept of limited government, which followed from the establishment of the first colonies under Crown charters. Theoretically, London governed the colonies. In practice, owing partly to the colonies' distance from London, the colonists exercised a large measure of self-government. The colonists were able to make their own laws, as in the Fundamental Orders of Connecticut in 1639. The Massachusetts Body of Liberties in 1641 supported the protection of individual rights and was made a part of colonial law. In 1682, the Pennsylvania Frame of Government was passed. Along with the Pennsylvania Charter of Privileges of 1701, it foreshadowed our modern Constitution and Bill of Rights. All of this legislation enabled the colonists to acquire crucial political experience. After independence was declared in 1776, the states quickly set up their own new constitutions.

---

[1]John Camp, *Out of the Wilderness: The Emergence of an American Identity in Colonial New England* (Middleton, Conn.: Wesleyan University Press, 1990).
[2]See Morison's "The Mayflower Compact" in Daniel J. Boorstin, ed., *An American Primer* (Chicago: University of Chicago Press, 1966), p. 18.

British Restrictions and Colonial Grievances

The conflict between Britain and the American colonies, which ultimately led to the Revolutionary War, began in the 1760s when the British government decided to raise revenues by imposing taxes on the American colonies. Policy advisers to Britain's young King George III, who ascended the throne in 1760, decided that it was only logical to require the American colonists to help pay the costs of Britain's defending them during the French and Indian War (1756–1763). The colonists, who had grown accustomed to a large degree of self-government and independence from the British Crown, viewed the matter differently.

In 1764, the British Parliament passed the Sugar Act. Many colonists were unwilling to pay the tax imposed by the act. Further regulatory legislation was to come. In 1765, Parliament passed the Stamp Act, providing for internal taxation—or, as the colonists' Stamp Act Congress, assembled in 1765, called it, "taxation without representation." The colonists boycotted the purchase of English commodities in return. The success of the boycott (the Stamp Act was repealed a year later) generated a feeling of unity within the colonies. The British, however, continued to try to raise revenues in the colonies. When Parliament passed duties on glass, lead, paint, and other items in 1767, the colonists again boycotted British goods. The colonists' fury over taxation climaxed in the Boston Tea Party: colonists dressed as Mohawk Indians dumped almost 350 chests of British tea into Boston Harbor as a gesture of tax protest. In retaliation, Parliament passed the Coercive Acts (the "Intolerable Acts") in 1774, which closed Boston Harbor and placed the government of Massachusetts under direct British control. The colonists were outraged—and they responded.

The Colonial Response: The Continental Congresses

New York, Pennsylvania, and Rhode Island proposed the convening of a colonial congress. The Massachusetts House of Representatives requested that all colonies hold conventions to select delegates to be sent to Philadelphia for such a congress.

The First Continental Congress

The First Continental Congress was held at Carpenter's Hall on September 5, 1774. It was a gathering of delegates from twelve of the thirteen colonies (delegates from Georgia did not attend until 1775). At that meeting, there was little talk of independence. The Congress passed a resolution requesting that the colonies send a petition to King George III expressing their grievances. Resolutions were also passed requiring that the colonies raise their own troops and boycott British trade. The British government condemned the Congress's actions, treating them as open acts of rebellion.

The delegates to the First Continental Congress declared that in every county and city, a committee was to be formed whose mission was to spy on the conduct of friends and neighbors and to report to the press any violators of the trade ban. The formation of these committees was an act of cooperation among the colonies, which represented a step toward the creation of a national government.

The Second Continental Congress

By the time the Second Continental Congress met in May 1775 (this time all of the colonies were represented), fighting already had broken out between the British and the colonists. One of the main actions of the Second Congress was to establish an army. It did this by declaring the militia that had gathered around

King George III (1738–1820) was king of Great Britain and Ireland from 1760 until his death on January 29, 1820. Under George III, the British Parliament attempted to tax the American colonies. Ultimately, the colonies, exasperated at repeated attempts at taxation, proclaimed their independence on July 4, 1776. (National Portrait Gallery)

Boston an army and naming George Washington as commander in chief. The participants in that Congress still attempted to reach a peaceful settlement with the British Parliament. One declaration of the Congress stated explicitly that "we have not raised armies with ambitious designs of separating from Great Britain, and establishing independent states." But by the beginning of 1776, military encounters had become increasingly frequent.

Public debate was acrimonious. Then Thomas Paine's *Common Sense* appeared in Philadelphia bookstores. The pamphlet was a colonial best seller. (To do relatively as well today, a book would have to sell between eight and ten million copies in its first year of publication.) Many agreed that Paine did make common sense when he argued that

> a government of our own is our natural right: and when a man seriously reflects on the precariousness [instability, unpredictability] of human affairs, he will become convinced, that it is infinitely wiser and safer, to form a constitution of our own in a cool and deliberate manner, while we have it in our power, than to trust such an interesting event to time and chance.[3]

Students of Paine's pamphlet point out that his arguments were not new—they were common in tavern debates throughout the land. Rather, it was the near poetry of his words—which were at the same time as plain as the alphabet—that struck his readers.

★ Declaring Independence

On April 6, 1776, the Second Continental Congress voted for free trade at all American ports with all countries except Britain. This act could be interpreted as an implicit declaration of independence. The next month, the Congress suggested that each of the colonies establish state governments unconnected to Britain. Finally, in July, the colonists declared their independence from Britain.

The Resolution of Independence

On July 2, the Resolution of Independence was adopted by the Second Continental Congress:

> RESOLVED, That these United Colonies are, and of right ought to be free and independent States, that they are absolved from allegiance to the British Crown, and that all political connection between them and the state of Great Britain is, and ought to be, totally dissolved.

The actual Resolution of Independence was not legally significant. On the one hand, it was not judicially enforceable, for it established no legal rights or duties. On the other hand, the colonies were already, in their own judgment, self-governing and independent of Britain. Rather, the Resolution of Independence and the subsequent Declaration of Independence were necessary to establish the legitimacy of the new nation in the eyes of foreign governments, as well as in the eyes of the colonists themselves. What the new nation needed most were supplies for its armies and a commitment of foreign military aid. Unless it appeared to the world as a political entity separate and independent from Britain, no foreign government would enter into a contract with its leaders.

July 4, 1776—The Declaration of Independence

By June 1776, Thomas Jefferson already was writing drafts of the Declaration of Independence in the second-floor parlor of a bricklayer's house in Philadelphia. On adoption of the Resolution of Independence, Jefferson argued that a declara-

"You know, the idea of taxation with representation doesn't appeal to me very much either."

Drawing by Handelsman; © 1970 The New Yorker Magazine, Inc.

---

[3] *The Political Writings of Thomas Paine,* Vol. 1 (Boston: J. P. Mendum Investigator Office, 1870), p. 46.

tion clearly putting forth the causes that compelled the colonies to separate from Britain was necessary. The Second Congress assigned the task to him, and he completed his work on the declaration, which enumerated the colonists' major grievances against Britain. Some of his work was amended to gain unanimous acceptance (for example, his condemnation of the slave trade was eliminated to satisfy Georgia and North Carolina), but the bulk of it was passed intact on July 4, 1776. On July 19, the modified draft became "the unanimous declaration of the thirteen United States of America." On August 2, it was signed by the members of the Second Continental Congress.

Famous Worldwide. The Declaration of Independence has become one of the world's most famous and significant documents. The words opening the second paragraph of the Declaration are known everywhere:

> We hold these Truths to be self-evident, that all Men are created equal, that they are endowed by their Creator with certain unalienable Rights, that among these are Life, Liberty, and the Pursuit of Happiness—That to secure these Rights, Governments are instituted among Men, deriving their just Powers from the Consent of the Governed, that whenever any Form of Government becomes destructive of these Ends, it is the Right of the People to alter or abolish it, and to institute new Government.

Natural Rights and a Social Contract. The assumption that people have **natural rights** ("unalienable Rights"), including the rights to "Life, Liberty, and the Pursuit of Happiness," was a revolutionary concept at that time. Its use by Jefferson reveals the influence of the English philosopher John Locke (1632–1704), whose writings were familiar to educated American colonists, including Jefferson.[4] In his *Two Treatises on Government,* published in 1690, Locke had argued that all people possess certain natural rights, including the rights to life, liberty, and property, and that the primary purpose of government was to protect these rights. Furthermore,

Natural Rights
Rights held to be inherent in natural law, not dependent on governments. John Locke stated that natural law, being superior to human law, specifies certain rights of "life, liberty, and property." These rights, altered to become "life, liberty, and the pursuit of happiness," are asserted in the Declaration of Independence.

---

[4]Not all scholars believe that Jefferson was truly influenced by Locke. For example, Jay Fliegelman states that "Jefferson's fascination with Homer, Ossian, Patrick Henry, and the violin is of greater significance than his indebtedness to Locke." Jay Fliegelman, *Declaring Independence: Jefferson, Natural Language, and the Culture of Performance* (Stanford, Calif.: Stanford University Press, 1993).

Members of the Second Continental Congress adopted the Declaration of Independence on July 4, 1776. Minor changes were made in the document in the following two weeks. On July 19, the modified draft became the "unanimous declaration of the thirteen United States of America." On August 2, the members of the Second Continental Congress signed it. The first official printed version carried only the signatures of the Congress's president, John Hancock, and its secretary, Charles Thompson. (Painting by John Trumbull, 1819. Library of Congress)

Social Contract

A voluntary agreement among individuals to secure their rights and welfare by creating a government and abiding by its rules.

government was established by the people through a **social contract**—an agreement among the people to form a government and abide by its rules. As you read earlier, such contracts, or compacts, were not new to Americans. The Mayflower Compact was the first of several documents that established governments or governing rules based on the consent of the governed. In citing the "pursuit of happiness" instead of "property" as a right, Jefferson clearly meant to go beyond Locke's thinking.

After setting forth these basic principles of government, the Declaration of Independence goes on to justify the colonists' revolt against Britain. Much of the remainder of the document is a list of what "He" (King George III) had done to deprive the colonists of their rights. (See Appendix A at the end of this book for the complete text of the Declaration of Independence.)

Once it had fulfilled its purpose of legitimating the American Revolution, the Declaration of Independence was all but forgotten for many years. According to scholar Pauline Maier, the Declaration did not become enshrined as what she calls "American Scripture" until the 1800s.[5]

★ The Rise of Republicanism

Although the colonists had formally declared independence from Britain, the fight to gain actual independence continued for five more years—until the British general Cornwallis surrendered at Yorktown in 1781. In 1783, after Britain formally recognized the independent status of the United States in the Treaty of Paris, Washington disbanded the army. During these years of military struggles, the states faced the additional challenge of creating a system of self-government for an independent United States.

Some colonists in the middle and lower southern colonies had demanded that independence be preceded by the formation of a strong central government. But the anti-Royalists in New England and Virginia, who called themselves Republicans, were against a strong central government. They opposed monarchy, executive authority, and virtually any form of restraint on the power of local groups. These Republicans were a major political force from 1776 to 1780. Indeed, they almost prevented victory over the British by their unwillingness to cooperate with any central authority.

During this time, all of the states adopted written constitutions. Eleven of the constitutions were completely new. Two of them—those of Connecticut and Rhode Island—were old royal charters with minor modifications. Republican sentiment led to increased power for the legislatures. In Pennsylvania and Georgia, **unicameral** (one-body) **legislatures** were unchecked by executive or judicial authority. Basically, the Republicans attempted to maintain the politics of 1776. In almost all states, the legislature was predominant.

Unicameral Legislature

A legislature with only one legislative chamber, as opposed to a bicameral (two-chamber) legislature, such as the U.S. Congress. Today, Nebraska is the only state in the Union with a unicameral legislature.

Confederation

A political system in which states or regional governments retain ultimate authority except for those powers they expressly delegate to a central government. A voluntary association of independent states, in which the member states agree to limited restraints on their freedom of action.

State

A group of people occupying a specific area and organized under one government; may be either a nation or a subunit of a nation.

★ The Articles of Confederation: Our First Form of Government

The fear of a powerful central government led to the passage of the Articles of Confederation, which created a weak central government. The term **confederation** is important; it means a voluntary association of *independent* **states,** in which the member states agree to only limited restraints on their freedom of action. As a result, confederations seldom have an effective executive authority.

In June 1776, the Second Continental Congress began the process of drafting what would become the Articles of Confederation. The final form of the Articles

---

[5]See Pauline Maier, *American Scripture: Making the Declaration of Independence* (New York: Knopf, 1997).

was achieved by November 15, 1777. It was not until March 1, 1781, however, that the last state, Maryland, agreed to ratify what was called the Articles of Confederation and Perpetual Union. Well before the final ratification of the Articles, however, many of them were implemented: the Continental Congress and the thirteen states conducted American military, economic, and political affairs according to the standards and the form specified by the Articles.[6]

Under the Articles, the thirteen original colonies, now states, established on March 1, 1781, a government of the states—the Congress of the Confederation. The Congress was a unicameral assembly of so-called ambassadors from each state, with each state possessing a single vote. Each year, the Congress would choose one of its members as its president, but the Articles did not provide for a president of the United States.

The Congress was authorized in Article X to appoint an executive committee of the states "to execute in the recess of Congress, such of the powers of Congress as the United States, in Congress assembled, by the consent of nine [of the thirteen] states, shall from time to time think expedient to vest with them." The Congress was also allowed to appoint other committees and civil officers necessary for managing the general affairs of the United States. In addition, the Congress could regulate foreign affairs and establish coinage and weights and measures. But it lacked an independent source of revenue and the necessary executive machinery to enforce its decisions throughout the land. Article II of the Articles of Confederation guaranteed that each state would retain its sovereignty. Figure 2–1 illustrates the structure of the government under the Articles of Confederation; Table 2–1 summarizes the powers—and the lack of powers—of Congress under the Articles of Confederation.

Accomplishments under the Articles

The new government had some accomplishments during its eight years of existence under the Articles of Confederation. Certain states' claims to western lands were settled. Maryland had objected to the claims of the Carolinas, Connecticut, Georgia, Massachusetts, New York, and Virginia. It was only after these states

---

[6]Robert W. Hoffert, *A Politics of Tensions: The Articles of Confederation and American Political Ideas* (Niwot, Colo.: University Press of Colorado, 1992).

FIGURE 2–1

The Confederal Government Structure under the Articles of Confederation

Congress
Congress had one chamber. Each state had two to seven members, but only one vote. The exercise of most powers required approval of at least nine states. Amendments to the Articles required the consent of all of the states.

Committee of the States
A committee of representatives from all of the states was empowered to act in the name of Congress between sessions.

Officers
Congress appointed officers to do some of the executive work.

The States

TABLE 2–1

Powers of the Congress of the Confederation

CONGRESS HAD POWER TO	CONGRESS LACKED POWER TO
▪ Declare war and make peace. ▪ Enter into treaties and alliances. ▪ Establish and control armed forces. ▪ Requisition men and money from states. ▪ Regulate coinage. ▪ Borrow money and issue bills of credit. ▪ Fix uniform standards of weight and measurement. ▪ Create admiralty courts. ▪ Create a postal system. ▪ Regulate Indian affairs. ▪ Guarantee citizens of each state the rights and privileges of citizens in the several states when in another state. ▪ Adjudicate disputes between states on state petition.	▪ Provide for effective treaty-making power and control foreign relations; it could not compel states to respect treaties. ▪ Compel states to meet military quotas; it could not draft soldiers. ▪ Regulate interstate and foreign commerce; it left each state free to set up its own tariff system. ▪ Collect taxes directly from the people; it had to rely on states to collect and forward taxes. ▪ Compel states to pay their share of government costs. ▪ Provide and maintain a sound monetary system or issue paper money; this was left up to the states, and monies in circulation differed tremendously in value.

consented to give up their land claims to the United States as a whole that Maryland signed the Articles of Confederation. Another accomplishment under the Articles was the passage of the Northwest Ordinance of 1787, which established a basic pattern of government for new territories north of the Ohio River. All in all, the Articles represented the first real pooling of resources by the American states.

Weaknesses of the Articles

In spite of these accomplishments, the Articles of Confederation had many defects. Although Congress had the legal right to declare war and to conduct foreign policy, it did not have the right to demand revenues from the states. It could only ask for them. Additionally, the actions of Congress required the consent of nine states. Any amendments to the Articles required the unanimous consent of the Congress and confirmation by every state legislature. Furthermore, the Articles did not create a national system of courts.

Basically, the functioning of the government under the Articles depended on the goodwill of the states. Article III of the Articles simply established a "league of friendship" among the states—no national government was intended.

Probably the most fundamental weakness of the Articles, and the most basic cause of their eventual replacement by the Constitution, was the lack of power to raise money for the militia. The Articles contained no language giving Congress coercive power to raise money (by levying taxes) to provide adequate support for the military forces controlled by Congress. When states refused to send money to support the government (not one state met the financial requests made by Congress under the Articles), Congress resorted to selling off western lands to speculators or issuing bonds that sold for less than their face value. Due to a lack of resources, the Continental Congress was forced to disband the army, even in the face of serious Spanish and British military threats.

Shays' Rebellion and the Need for Revision of the Articles

Because of the weaknesses of the Articles of Confederation, the central government could do little to maintain peace and order in the new nation. The states bickered among themselves and increasingly taxed each other's goods. At times they prevented trade altogether. By 1784, the country faced a serious economic depression. Banks were calling in old loans and refusing to give new ones. People who could not pay their debts were often thrown into prison.

By 1786, in Concord, Massachusetts, the scene of one of the first battles of the Revolution, there were three times as many people in prison for debt as there were for all other crimes combined. In Worcester County, Massachusetts, the ratio was even higher—twenty to one. Most of the prisoners were small farmers who could not pay their debts because of the disorganized state of the economy.

In August 1786, mobs of musket-bearing farmers led by former revolutionary captain Daniel Shays seized county courthouses and disrupted the trials of debtors in Springfield, Massachusetts. Shays and his men then launched an attack on the federal arsenal at Springfield, but they were repulsed. Shays' Rebellion demonstrated that the central government could not protect the citizenry from armed rebellion or provide adequately for the public welfare. The rebellion spurred the nation's political leaders to action. As John Jay wrote to Thomas Jefferson,

> Changes are Necessary, but what they ought to be, what they will be, and how and when to be produced, are arduous Questions. I feel for the Cause of Liberty. . . . If it should not take Root in this Soil[,] Little Pains will be taken to cultivate it in any other.[7]

---

[7]Excerpt from a letter from John Jay to Thomas Jefferson written in October 1786, as reproduced in Winthrop D. Jordan *et al., The United States,* combined ed., 6th ed. (Englewood Cliffs, N.J.: Prentice Hall, 1987), p. 135.

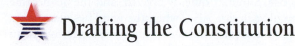 Drafting the Constitution

The Virginia legislature called for a meeting of all the states to be held at Annapolis, Maryland, on September 11, 1786—ostensibly to discuss commercial problems only. It was evident to those in attendance (including Alexander Hamilton and James Madison) that the national government had serious weaknesses that had to be addressed if it were to survive. Among the important problems to be solved were the relationship between the states and the central government, the powers of the national legislature, the need for executive leadership, and the establishment of policies for economic stability.

The result of this meeting was a petition to the Continental Congress for a general convention to meet in Philadelphia in May 1787 "to consider the exigencies of the union." Congress approved the convention in February 1787. When those who favored a weak central government realized that the Philadelphia meeting would in fact take place, they endorsed the convention. They made sure, however, that the convention would be summoned "for the sole and express purpose of revising the Articles of Confederation." Those in favor of a stronger national government had different ideas.

The designated date for the opening of the convention at Philadelphia, now known as the Constitutional Convention, was May 14, 1787. Because few of the delegates had actually arrived in Philadelphia by that time, however, the convention was not formally opened in the East Room of the Pennsylvania State House until May 25.[8] Fifty-five of the seventy-four delegates chosen for the convention actually attended. (Of those fifty-five, only about forty played active roles at the convention.) Rhode Island was the only state that refused to send delegates.

Who Were the Delegates?

Who were the fifty-five delegates to the Constitutional Convention? They certainly did not represent a cross-section of American society in the 1700s. Indeed, most were members of the upper class. Consider the following facts:

1. Thirty-three were members of the legal profession.
2. Three were physicians.
3. Almost 50 percent were college graduates.
4. Seven were former chief executives of their respective states.
5. Six were owners of large plantations.
6. Eight were important businesspersons.

They were also relatively young by today's standards: James Madison was thirty-six, Alexander Hamilton was only thirty-two, and Jonathan Dyton of New Jersey was twenty-six. The venerable Benjamin Franklin, however, was eighty-one and had to be carried in on a portable chair borne by four prisoners from a local jail. Not counting Franklin, the average age was just over forty-two.

The Working Environment

The conditions under which the delegates worked for 115 days were far from ideal and were made even worse by the necessity of maintaining total secrecy. The framers of the Constitution believed that if public debate took place on particular positions, delegates would have a more difficult time compromising or backing down to reach agreement. Consequently, the windows were usually shut in

---

[8]The State House was later named Independence Hall. This was the same room in which the Declaration of Independence had been signed eleven years earlier.

the East Room of the State House. Summer quickly arrived, and the air became heavy, humid, and hot by noon of each day. Also, when the windows were open, flies swarmed into the room. The delegates did, however, have a nearby tavern and inn to which they retired each evening. The Indian Queen became the informal headquarters of the delegates.

Factions among the Delegates

We know much about the proceedings at the convention because James Madison kept a daily, detailed personal journal. A majority of the delegates were strong nationalists—they wanted a central government with real power, unlike the central government under the Articles of Confederation. George Washington and Benjamin Franklin preferred limited national authority based on a separation of powers. They were apparently willing to accept any type of national government, however, as long as the other delegates approved it. A few advocates of a strong central government, led by Gouverneur Morris of Pennsylvania and John Rutledge of South Carolina, distrusted the ability of the common people to engage in self-government.

Among the nationalists, several went so far as to support monarchy. This group included Alexander Hamilton, who was chiefly responsible for the Annapolis Convention's call for the Constitutional Convention. In a long speech on June 18, he presented his views: "I have no scruple in declaring . . . that the British government is the best in the world and that I doubt much whether anything short of it will do in America."

Another important group of nationalists were of a more democratic stripe. Led by James Madison of Virginia and James Wilson of Pennsylvania, these democratic nationalists wanted a central government founded on popular support.

Still another faction consisted of nationalists who were less democratic in nature and who would support a central government only if it were founded on very narrowly defined republican principles. This group was made up of a relatively small number of delegates, including Edmund Randolph and George Mason of Virginia, Elbridge Gerry of Massachusetts, and Luther Martin and John Francis Mercer of Maryland.

Many of the other delegates from Connecticut, Delaware, Maryland, New Hampshire, and New Jersey were concerned about only one thing—claims to western lands. As long as those lands became the common property of all of the states, they were willing to support a central government.

Finally, there was a group of delegates who were totally against a national authority. Two of the three delegates from New York quit the convention when they saw the nationalist direction of its proceedings.

Politicking and Compromises

The debates at the convention started on the first day. James Madison had spent months reviewing European political theory. When his Virginia delegation arrived ahead of most of the others, it got to work immediately. By the time George Washington opened the convention, Governor Edmund Randolph of Virginia was prepared to present fifteen resolutions. In retrospect, this was a masterful stroke on the part of the Virginia delegation. It set the agenda for the remainder of the convention—even though, in principle, the delegates had been sent to Philadelphia for the sole purpose of amending the Articles of Confederation. They had not been sent to write a new constitution.

The Virginia Plan.   Randolph's fifteen resolutions proposed an entirely new national government under a constitution. It was, however, a plan that favored the large states, including Virginia. Basically, it called for the following:

Elbridge Gerry (1744–1814), from Massachusetts, was a patriot during the Revolution. He was a signatory of the Declaration of Independence and later became governor of Massachusetts (1810–1812). He became James Madison's new vice president when Madison was reelected in December 1812. (The Library of Congress)

1. A **bicameral** (two-chamber) **legislature,** with the lower chamber chosen by the people and the smaller upper chamber chosen by the lower chamber from nominees selected by state legislatures. The number of representatives would be proportional to a state's population, thus favoring the large states. The legislature could void any state laws.
2. The creation of an unspecified national executive, elected by the legislature.
3. The creation of a national judiciary appointed by the legislature.

It did not take long for the smaller states to realize they would fare poorly under the Virginia plan, which would enable Virginia, Massachusetts, and Pennsylvania to form a majority in the national legislature. The debate on the plan dragged on for a number of weeks. It was time for the small states to come up with their own plan.

The New Jersey Plan. On June 15, lawyer William Paterson of New Jersey offered an alternative plan. After all, argued Paterson, under the Articles of Confederation all states had equality; therefore, the convention had no power to change this arrangement. He proposed the following:

1. The fundamental principle of the Articles of Confederation—one state, one vote—would be retained.
2. Congress would be able to regulate trade and impose taxes.
3. All acts of Congress would be the supreme law of the land.
4. Several people would be elected by Congress to form an executive office.
5. The executive office would appoint a Supreme Court.

Basically, the New Jersey plan was simply an amendment of the Articles of Confederation. Its only notable feature was its reference to the **supremacy doctrine**, which was later included in the Constitution.

The "Great Compromise." The delegates were at an impasse. Most wanted a strong national government and were unwilling even to consider the New Jersey plan. But when the Virginia plan was brought up again, the small states threatened to leave. It was not until July 16 that the **Great Compromise** was achieved. Roger Sherman of Connecticut proposed the following:

1. A bicameral legislature in which the lower chamber, the House of Representatives, would be apportioned according to the number of free inhabitants in each state, plus three-fifths of the slaves.

Bicameral Legislature
A legislature made up of two parts, called chambers. The U.S. Congress, composed of the House of Representatives and the Senate, is a bicameral legislature.

Supremacy Doctrine
A doctrine that asserts the priority of national law over state laws. This principle is rooted in Article VI of the Constitution, which provides that the Constitution, the laws passed by the national government under its constitutional powers, and all treaties constitute the supreme law of the land.

Great Compromise
The compromise between the New Jersey and Virginia plans that created one chamber of the Congress based on population and one chamber representing each state equally; also called the Connecticut Compromise.

George Washington presided over the Constitutional Convention of 1787. Although the convention was supposed to have started on May 14, 1787, few of the delegates had actually arrived in Philadelphia by that date. It formally opened in the East Room of the Pennsylvania State House (later named Independence Hall) on May 25. Only Rhode Island did not send any delegates. (The Granger Collection)

2. An upper chamber, the Senate, which would have two members from each state elected by the state legislatures.

This plan, also called the Connecticut Compromise because of the role of the Connecticut delegates in the proposal, broke the deadlock. It did exact a political price, however, because it permitted each state to have equal representation in the Senate. Having two senators represent each state in effect diluted the voting power of citizens living in more heavily populated states and gave the smaller states disproportionate political powers. But the Connecticut Compromise resolved the large-state/small-state controversy. In addition, the Senate acted as part of a checks-and-balances system against the House, which many feared would be dominated by, and responsive to, the masses.

The Three-Fifths Compromise. The Great Compromise also settled another major issue—how to deal with slaves in the representational scheme. Slavery was still legal in many northern states, but it was concentrated in the South. Many delegates were opposed to slavery and wanted it banned entirely in the United States. Charles Pinckney of South Carolina led strong southern opposition to a ban on slavery. Furthermore, the South wanted slaves to be counted along with free persons in determining representation in Congress. Delegates from the northern states objected. Sherman's three-fifths proposal was a compromise between northerners who did not want the slaves counted at all and southerners who wanted them counted in the same way as free whites. Actually, Sherman's Connecticut plan spoke of three-fifths of "all other persons" (and that is the language of the Constitution itself). It is not hard to figure out, though, who those other persons were.

The three-fifths compromise illustrates the power of the southern states at the convention.[9] The three-fifths rule meant that the House of Representatives and the electoral college would be apportioned in part on the basis of *property*—specifically, property in slaves. Modern commentators have referred to the three-fifths rule as valuing African Americans only three-fifths as much as whites. Actually, the additional southern representatives elected because of the three-fifths rule did not represent the slaves at all. Rather, these extra representatives were a gift to the slave owners—the additional representatives enhanced the power of the South in Congress.

The three-fifths compromise did not completely settle the slavery issue. There was also the question of the slave trade. Eventually, the delegates agreed that Congress could not ban the importation of slaves until after 1808. The compromise meant that the matter of slavery itself was never addressed directly. The South won twenty years of unrestricted slave trade and a requirement that escaped slaves in free states be returned to their owners in slave states. Could the authors of the Constitution have done more to address the issue of slavery? See this chapter's *Politics and Diversity* feature for a further discussion of this question.

Other Issues. The South also worried that the northern majority in Congress would pass legislation unfavorable to its economic interests. Because the South depended on agricultural exports, it feared the imposition of export taxes. In return for acceding to the northern demand that Congress be able to regulate commerce among the states and with other nations, the South obtained a promise that export taxes would not be imposed. As a result, the United States is among the few countries that do not tax their exports.

There were other disagreements. The delegates could not decide whether to establish only a Supreme Court or to create lower courts as well. They deferred the issue by mandating a Supreme Court and allowing Congress to establish

---

[9]See Garry Wills, *"Negro President": Jefferson and the Slave Power* (New York: Houghton Mifflin, 2003).

POLITICS AND DIVERSITY
Could the Founders Have Banned Slavery Outright?

One of the most hotly debated issues at the Constitutional Convention concerned slavery. As we discussed elsewhere, the three-fifths compromise was the result of that debate. There was also another compromise: the importation of slaves would not be banned until after 1808. The debate over slavery—or, more specifically, over how the founders dealt with it—continues to this day. Some contend that those delegates who opposed slavery should have made greater efforts to ban it completely.*

DID THE FOUNDERS HAVE NO OTHER CHOICE?

Some historians argue that the founders had no choice. The South was an important part of the economy, and the southern states had over 600,000 slaves. Major leaders from Virginia, such as George Washington, had serious doubts about slavery. It appears, however, that the delegates from North Carolina, South Carolina, and Georgia would never have agreed to the Constitution if slavery had been threatened—meaning that these states would not have remained part of the Union. The founders believed, as James Madison said, "Great as the evil is, a dismemberment of the Union would be worse. . . . If those states should disunite from the other states, . . . they might solicit and obtain aid from foreign powers."† Benjamin Franklin, then president of the Pennsylvania Society for the Abolition of Slavery, also feared that without a slavery compromise, delegates from the South would abandon the convention.

CRITICS STATE THAT ETHICS SHOULD HAVE PREVAILED

Critics of the founders' actions nonetheless believe that any compromise on slavery implicitly acknowledged the validity of the institution. According to these critics, the delegates who opposed slavery had a moral obligation to make greater efforts to ban it. Many of the delegates' contemporaries considered the compromise to be a "betrayal" of the Declaration of Independence's principle of equality among all men.

An American slave market in Philadelphia as depicted in an 1863 drawing. The writers of the Constitution did not ban slavery in the United States but did agree to limit the importation of new slaves after 1808. Nowhere are the words *slavery* or *slaves* used in the Constitution. Instead, the Constitution uses such language as "no person held in service" and "all other persons." (Library of Congress Prints and Photographs Division)

FOR CRITICAL ANALYSIS

Do you think that antislavery delegates to the convention could have obtained a better result if they had taken a stronger stand? If Georgia and the Carolinas had stayed out of the Union, what would subsequent American history have been like? Would the eventual freedom of the slaves have been advanced—or delayed?

GOING ONLINE

To learn more about the founders' discussion of the slavery issue, go to the following Web sites: **http://www.yale.edu/lawweb/avalon/debates/debcont.htm** (click on "August 8" for James Madison's notes on the discussion of whether slaves should count as part of a state's population for purposes of representation, as well as about banning the slave trade) and **http://www.yale.edu/lawweb/avalon/federal/fed.htm** (click on "No. 42" to access *Federalist Paper* No. 42, which indicates how difficult it was for the founders simply to ban the slave trade in 1808).

*See Paul Finkelman's criticism of the founders' actions on the slavery issue in *Slavery and the Founders: Race and Liberty in the Age of Jefferson,* 2d ed. (Armonk, N.Y.: M. E. Sharpe, 2000).
†Speech before the Virginia ratifying convention on June 17, 1788, as cited in Bruno Leone, ed., *The Creation of the Constitution* (San Diego: Greenhaven Press, 1995), p. 159.

lower courts. They also disagreed over whether the president or the Senate would choose the Supreme Court justices. A compromise was reached with the agreement that the president would nominate the justices and the Senate would confirm the nominations.

These compromises, as well as others, resulted from the recognition that if one group of states refused to ratify the Constitution, it was doomed.

Working toward Final Agreement

The Connecticut Compromise was reached by mid-July. The make-up of the executive branch and the judiciary, however, was left unsettled. The remaining work of the convention was turned over to a five-man Committee of Detail, which presented a rough draft of the Constitution on August 6. It made the executive and judicial branches subordinate to the legislative branch.

The Madisonian Model—Separation of Powers. The major issue of **separation of powers** had not yet been resolved. The delegates were concerned with structuring the government to prevent the imposition of tyranny—either by the majority or by a minority. It was Madison who proposed a governmental scheme—sometimes called the **Madisonian model**—to achieve this: the executive, legislative, and judicial powers of government were to be separated so that no one branch had enough power to dominate the others. The separation of powers was by function, as well as by personnel, with Congress passing laws, the president enforcing and administering laws, and the courts interpreting laws in individual circumstances.

Each of the three branches of government would be independent of the others, but they would have to cooperate to govern. According to Madison, in *Federalist Paper* No. 51 (see Appendix C), "the great security against a gradual concentration of the several powers in the same department consists in giving to those who administer each department the necessary constitutional means and personal motives to resist encroachments of the others."

The Madisonian Model—Checks and Balances. The "constitutional means" Madison referred to is a system of **checks and balances** through which each branch of the government can check the actions of the others. For example, Congress can enact laws, but the president has veto power over congressional acts. The Supreme Court has the power to declare acts of Congress and of the executive unconstitutional, but the president appoints the justices of the Supreme Court, with the advice and consent of the Senate. (The Supreme Court's power to declare acts unconstitutional was not mentioned in the Constitution, although arguably the framers assumed that the Court would have this power—see the discussion of judicial review later in this chapter.) Figure 2–2 outlines these checks and balances.

Madison's ideas of separation of powers and checks and balances were not new. Indeed, the influential French political thinker Baron de Montesquieu (1689–1755) had explored these concepts in his book *The Spirit of the Laws,* published in 1748. Montesquieu not only discussed the "three sorts of powers" (executive, legislative, and judicial) that were necessarily exercised by any government but also gave examples of how, in some nations, certain checks on these powers had arisen and had been effective in preventing tyranny.

In the years since the Constitution was ratified, the checks and balances built into it have evolved into a sometimes complex give-and-take among the branches of government. Generally, for nearly every check that one branch has over another, the branch that has been checked has found a way of getting around it.

Separation of Powers
The principle of dividing governmental powers among different branches of government.

Madisonian Model
A structure of government proposed by James Madison in which the powers of the government are separated into three branches: executive, legislative, and judicial.

Checks and Balances
A major principle of the American system of government whereby each branch of the government can check the actions of the others.

James Madison (1751–1836) earned the title "master builder of the Constitution" because of his persuasive logic during the Constitutional Convention. His contributions to the *Federalist Papers* showed him to be a brilliant political thinker and writer. (National Archives)

For example, suppose that the president checks Congress by vetoing a bill. Congress can override the presidential veto by a two-thirds vote. Additionally, Congress holds the "power of the purse." If it disagrees with a program endorsed by the executive branch, it can simply refuse to appropriate the funds necessary to operate that program. Similarly, the president can impose a countercheck on Congress if the Senate refuses to confirm a presidential appointment, such as a judicial appointment. The president can simply wait until Congress is in recess and then make what is called a "recess appointment," which does not require the Senate's approval.

The Executive. Some delegates favored a plural executive made up of representatives from the various regions. This was abandoned in favor of a single chief executive. Some argued that Congress should choose the executive. To make the presidency completely independent of the proposed Congress, however, an **electoral college** was adopted. To be sure, the electoral college created a cumbersome presidential election process (see Chapter 9). The process even made it possible for a candidate who came in second in the popular vote to become president by being the top vote getter in the electoral college, which happened in 2000. The electoral college insulated the president, however, from direct popular control. The seven-year single term that some of the delegates had proposed was replaced by a four-year term and the possibility of reelection.

Electoral College
A group of persons called electors selected by the voters in each state and the District of Columbia (D.C.); this group officially elects the president and vice president of the United States. The number of electors in each state is equal to the number of each state's representatives in both chambers of Congress. The Twenty-third Amendment to the Constitution grants D.C. as many electors as the state with the smallest population.

FIGURE 2–2

Checks and Balances

The major checks and balances among the three branches are illustrated here. The Constitution does not mention some of these checks, such as judicial review—the power of the courts to declare federal or state acts unconstitutional—and the president's ability to refuse to enforce judicial decisions or congressional legislation. Checks and balances can be thought of as a confrontation of powers or responsibilities. Each branch checks the action of another; two branches in conflict have powers that can result in balances or stalemates, requiring one branch to give in or both to reach a compromise.

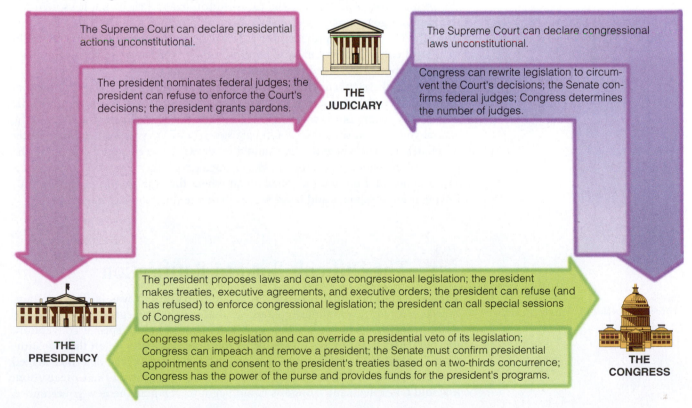

The Supreme Court can declare presidential actions unconstitutional.

The Supreme Court can declare congressional laws unconstitutional.

The president nominates federal judges; the president can refuse to enforce the Court's decisions; the president grants pardons.

THE JUDICIARY

Congress can rewrite legislation to circumvent the Court's decisions; the Senate confirms federal judges; Congress determines the number of judges.

The president proposes laws and can veto congressional legislation; the president makes treaties, executive agreements, and executive orders; the president can refuse (and has refused) to enforce congressional legislation; the president can call special sessions of Congress.

THE PRESIDENCY

Congress makes legislation and can override a presidential veto of its legislation; Congress can impeach and remove a president; the Senate must confirm presidential appointments and consent to the president's treaties based on a two-thirds concurrence; Congress has the power of the purse and provides funds for the president's programs.

THE CONGRESS

Federal System
A system of government in which power is divided between a central government and regional, or subdivisional, governments. Each level must have some domain in which its policies are dominant and some genuine political or constitutional guarantee of its authority.

★ The Final Document

On September 17, 1787, the Constitution was approved by thirty-nine delegates. Of the fifty-five who had attended originally, only forty-two remained. Three delegates refused to sign the Constitution. Others disapproved of at least parts of it but signed anyway to begin the ratification debate.

The Constitution that was to be ratified established the following fundamental principles:

1. Popular sovereignty, or control by the people.
2. A republican government in which the people choose representatives to make decisions for them.
3. Limited government with written laws, in contrast to the powerful British government against which the colonists had rebelled.
4. Separation of powers, with checks and balances among branches to prevent any one branch from gaining too much power.
5. A federal system that allows for states' rights, because the states feared too much centralized control.

You will read about federalism in detail in Chapter 3. Suffice it to say here that in the **federal system** established by the founders, sovereign powers—ruling powers—are divided between the states and the national government. The Constitution expressly granted certain powers to the national government. For example, the national government was given the power to regulate commerce among the states. The Constitution also declared that the president is the nation's chief executive and the commander in chief of the armed forces. Additionally, the Constitution made it clear that laws made by the national government take priority over conflicting state laws. At the same time, the Constitution provided for extensive states' rights, including the right to control commerce within state borders and to exercise those governing powers that were not delegated to the national government.

The federal system created by the founders was a novel form of government at that time—no other country in the world had such a system. It was invented by the founders as a compromise solution to the controversy over whether the states or the central government should have ultimate sovereignty. As you will read in Chapter 3, the debate over where the line should be drawn between states' rights and the powers of the national government has characterized American politics ever since. The founders did not go into detail about where this line should be drawn, thus leaving it up to scholars and court judges to divine the founders' intentions.

★ The Difficult Road to Ratification

Ratification
Formal approval.

The founders knew that **ratification** of the Constitution was far from certain. Indeed, because it was almost guaranteed that many state legislatures would not ratify it, the delegates agreed that each state should hold a special convention. Elected delegates to these conventions would discuss and vote on the Constitution. Further departing from the Articles of Confederation, the delegates agreed that as soon as nine states (rather than all thirteen) approved the Constitution, it would take effect, and Congress could begin to organize the new government.

The Federalists Push for Ratification

The two opposing forces in the battle over ratification were the Federalists and the Anti-Federalists. The **Federalists**—those in favor of a strong central government and the new Constitution—had an advantage over their opponents, called the **Anti-Federalists,** who wanted to prevent the Constitution as drafted from being ratified. In the first place, the Federalists had assumed a positive name, leaving their opposition the negative label of *Anti*-Federalist.[10] More important, the Federalists had attended the Constitutional Convention and knew of all the deliberations that had taken place. Their opponents had no such knowledge, because those deliberations had not been open to the public. Thus, the Anti-Federalists were at a disadvantage in terms of information about the document. The Federalists also had time, power, and money on their side. Communications were slow. Those who had access to the best communications were Federalists— mostly wealthy bankers, lawyers, plantation owners, and merchants living in urban areas, where communications were better. The Federalist campaign was organized relatively quickly and effectively to elect Federalists as delegates to the state ratifying conventions.

The Anti-Federalists, however, had at least one strong point in their favor: they stood for the status quo. In general, the greater burden is always placed on those advocating change.

The *Federalist Papers.* In New York, opponents of the Constitution were quick to attack it. Alexander Hamilton answered their attacks in newspaper columns over the signature "Caesar." When the Caesar letters had little effect, Hamilton switched to the pseudonym Publius and secured two collaborators—John Jay and James Madison. In a very short time, those three political figures wrote a series of eighty-five essays in defense of the Constitution and of a republican form of government.

These widely read essays, called the *Federalist Papers,* appeared in New York newspapers from October 1787 to August 1788 and were reprinted in the newspapers of other states. Although we do not know for certain who wrote every one, it is apparent that Hamilton was responsible for about two-thirds of the essays. These included the most important ones interpreting the Constitution, explaining the various powers of the three branches, and presenting a theory of *judicial review*—to be discussed later in this chapter. Madison's *Federalist Paper* No. 10 (see Appendix C), however, is considered a classic in political theory; it deals with the nature of groups—or factions, as he called them. In spite of the rapidity with which the *Federalist Papers* were written, they are considered by many to be perhaps the best example of political theorizing ever produced in the United States.[11]

The Anti-Federalist Response. The Anti-Federalists used such pseudonyms as Montezuma and Philadelphiensis in their replies. Many of their attacks on the Constitution were also brilliant. The Anti-Federalists claimed that the Constitution was written by aristocrats and would lead to aristocratic tyranny. More important, the Anti-Federalists believed that the Constitution would create an overbearing and overburdening central government hostile to personal liberty. (The Constitution said nothing about freedom of the press, freedom of religion,

Federalist
The name given to one who was in favor of the adoption of the U.S. Constitution and the creation of a federal union with a strong central government.

Anti-Federalist
An individual who opposed the ratification of the new Constitution in 1787. The Anti-Federalists were opposed to a strong central government.

---

[10]There is some irony here. At the Constitutional Convention, those opposed to a strong central government pushed for a federal system because such a system would allow the states to retain some of their sovereign rights (see Chapter 3). The label *Anti-Federalists* thus contradicted their essential views.
[11]Some scholars believe that the *Federalist Papers* played only a minor role in securing ratification of the Constitution. Even if this is true, they still have lasting value as an authoritative explanation of the Constitution.

or any other individual liberty.) They wanted to include a list of guaranteed liberties, or a bill of rights. Finally, the Anti-Federalists decried the weakened power of the states.

The Anti-Federalists cannot be dismissed as unpatriotic extremists. They included such patriots as Patrick Henry and Samuel Adams. They were arguing what had been the most prevalent view of the time. This view derived from the French political philosopher Montesquieu, who, as mentioned earlier, was an influential political theorist at that time. Montesquieu believed that liberty was safe only in relatively small societies governed by direct democracy or by a large legislature with small districts. The Madisonian view favoring a large republic, particularly expressed in *Federalist Papers* No. 10 and No. 51 (see Appendix C), was actually the more *un*popular view at the time. Madison was probably convincing because citizens were already persuaded that a strong national government was necessary to combat foreign enemies and to prevent domestic insurrections. Still, some researchers believe it was mainly the bitter experiences with the Articles of Confederation, rather than Madison's arguments, that persuaded the state conventions to ratify the Constitution.[12]

The March to the Finish

The struggle for ratification continued. Strong majorities were procured in Delaware, Pennsylvania, New Jersey, Georgia, and Connecticut. After a bitter struggle in Massachusetts, that state ratified the Constitution by a narrow margin on February 6, 1788. By the spring, Maryland and South Carolina had ratified by sizable majorities. Then on June 21 of that year, New Hampshire became the ninth state to ratify the Constitution. Although the Constitution was formally in effect, this meant little without Virginia and New York—the latter did not ratify for another month (see Table 2–2).

---

[12]Of particular interest is the view of the Anti-Federalist position contained in Herbert J. Storing, *What the Anti-Federalists Were For* (Chicago: University of Chicago Press, 1981). Storing also edited seven volumes of the Anti-Federalist writings, *The Complete Anti-Federalist* (Chicago: University of Chicago Press, 1981). See also Josephine F. Pacheco, *Antifederalism: The Legacy of George Mason* (Fairfax, Va.: George Mason University Press, 1992).

TABLE 2–2

Ratification of the Constitution

State	Date	Vote For–Against
Delaware	Dec. 7, 1787	30–0
Pennsylvania	Dec. 12, 1787	43–23
New Jersey	Dec. 18, 1787	38–0
Georgia	Jan. 2, 1788	26–0
Connecticut	Jan. 9, 1788	128–40
Massachusetts	Feb. 6, 1788	187–168
Maryland	Apr. 28, 1788	63–11
South Carolina	May 23, 1788	149–73
New Hampshire	June 21, 1788	57–46
Virginia	June 25, 1788	89–79
New York	July 26, 1788	30–27
North Carolina	Nov. 21, 1789*	194–77
Rhode Island	May 29, 1790	34–32

*Ratification was originally defeated on August 4, 1788, by a vote of 84–184.

Did the Majority of Americans Support the Constitution?

In 1913, historian Charles Beard published *An Economic Interpretation of the Constitution of the United States*.[13] This book launched a debate that has continued ever since—the debate over whether the Constitution was supported by a majority of Americans.

Beard's Thesis.   Beard's central thesis was that the Constitution had been produced primarily by wealthy property owners who desired a stronger government able to protect their property rights. Beard also claimed that the Constitution had been imposed by undemocratic methods to prevent democratic majorities from exercising real power. He pointed out that there was never any popular vote on whether to hold a constitutional convention in the first place.

Furthermore, even if such a vote had been taken, state laws generally restricted voting rights to property-owning white males, meaning that most people in the country (white males without property, women, American Indians, and slaves) were not eligible to vote. Finally, Beard pointed out that even the word *democracy* was distasteful to the founders. The term was often used by conservatives to smear their opponents.

State Ratifying Conventions.   As for the various state ratifying conventions, the delegates had been selected by only 150,000 of the approximately four million citizens. That does not seem very democratic—at least not by today's standards. Some historians have suggested that if a Gallup poll could have been taken at that time, the Anti-Federalists would probably have outnumbered the Federalists.[14]

Certainly, some of the delegates to state ratifying conventions from poor, agrarian areas feared that an elite group of Federalists would run the country just as oppressively as the British had governed the colonies. Amos Singletary, a delegate to the Massachusetts ratifying convention, contended that those who urged the adoption of the Constitution "expect to get all the power and all the money into their own hands, and then they will swallow up all us little folks . . . just as the whale swallowed Jonah."[15] Others who were similarly situated, though, felt differently. Jonathan Smith, who was also a delegate to the Massachusetts ratifying convention, regarded a strong national government as a "cure for disorder"—referring to the disorder caused by the rebellion of Daniel Shays and his followers.[16]

Support Was Probably Widespread.   Much has also been made of the various machinations used by the Federalists to ensure the Constitution's ratification (and they did resort to a variety of devious tactics, including purchasing at least one printing press to prevent the publication of Anti-Federalist sentiments). Yet the perception that a strong central government was necessary to keep order and protect the public welfare appears to have been fairly pervasive among all classes—rich and poor alike.

Further, although the need for strong government was a major argument in favor of adopting the Constitution, even the Federalists sought to craft a limited government. Compared with constitutions adopted by other nations in later years, the U.S. Constitution, through its checks and balances, favors limited government over "energetic" government to a marked degree.

★ ★ ★ ★ ★ ★ ★ ★ ★ ★ ★ ★ ★ ★ ★ ★

DID YOU KNOW . . .
That 64 percent of Americans believe that the Constitution declared English to be the national language of the United States**?**

---

[13]Charles A. Beard, *An Economic Interpretation of the Constitution of the United States* (New York: Macmillan, 1913; New York: Free Press, 1986).
[14]Jim Powell, "James Madison—Checks and Balances to Limit Government Power," *The Freeman*, March 1996, p. 178.
[15]As quoted in Bruno Leone, ed., *The Creation of the Constitution* (San Diego: Greenhaven Press, 1995), p. 215.
[16]*Ibid.*, p. 217.

★ The Bill of Rights

The U.S. Constitution would not have been ratified in several important states if the Federalists had not assured the states that amendments to the Constitution would be passed to protect individual liberties against incursions by the national government. Many of the recommendations of the state ratifying conventions included specific rights that were considered later by James Madison as he labored to draft what became the Bill of Rights.

A "Bill of Limits"

Although called the Bill of Rights, essentially the first ten amendments to the Constitution were a "bill of limits," because the amendments limited the powers of the national government over the rights and liberties of individuals. (Do non-citizens have liberties that are protected by the Bill of Rights and other parts of the Constitution? We address that question in this chapter's *America's Security* feature.)

Ironically, a year earlier Madison had told Jefferson, "I have never thought the omission [of the Bill of Rights] a material defect" of the Constitution. But Jefferson's enthusiasm for a bill of rights apparently influenced Madison, as did his desire to gain popular support for his election to Congress. Madison promised in his campaign letter to voters that, once elected, he would force Congress to "prepare and recommend to the states for ratification, the most satisfactory provisions for all essential rights."

Madison had to cull through more than two hundred state recommendations.[17] It was no small task, and in retrospect he chose remarkably well. One of the rights appropriate for constitutional protection that he left out was equal protection under the laws—but that was not commonly regarded as a basic right at that time. Not until 1868 did the states ratify an amendment guaranteeing that no state shall deny equal protection to any person. (The Supreme Court has since applied this guarantee to certain actions of the federal government as well.)

The final number of amendments that Madison and a specially appointed committee came up with was seventeen. Congress tightened the language somewhat and eliminated five of the amendments. Of the remaining twelve, two—dealing with the apportionment of representatives and the compensation of the members of Congress—were not ratified immediately by the states. Eventually, Supreme Court decisions led to reform of the apportionment process. The amendment on the compensation of members of Congress was ratified 203 years later—in 1992!

No Explicit Limits on State Government Powers

On December 15, 1791, the national Bill of Rights was adopted when Virginia agreed to ratify the ten amendments. On ratification, the Bill of Rights became part of the U.S. Constitution. The basic structure of American government had already been established. Now the fundamental rights and liberties of individuals were protected, at least in theory, at the national level. The proposed amendment that Madison characterized as "the most valuable amendment in the whole lot"— which would have prohibited the states from infringing on the freedoms of conscience, press, and jury trial—had been eliminated by the Senate. Thus, the Bill of Rights as adopted did not limit state power, and individual citizens had to rely on the guarantees contained in a particular state constitution or state bill of rights. The country had to wait until the violence of the Civil War before signifi-

---

[17]For details on these recommendations, including their sources, see Leonard W. Levy, *Origins of the Bill of Rights* (New Haven, Conn.: Yale University Press, 1999).

AMERICA'S SECURITY
The Constitutional Rights of Foreign Citizens

Among the most obvious characteristics of the terrorists who attacked the United States on September 11, 2001, is that they were all foreign citizens. After the attack, the government tightened the procedures for admitting foreign nationals into the country. In 2003, the Bureau of Immigration and Customs Enforcement was organized under the new Department of Homeland Security and given responsibility for immigration-related law enforcement. This includes deportation cases.

Deportation law raises a question: Do noncitizens have constitutional rights? The Bill of Rights contains no language that limits its protections to citizens. The Fourteenth Amendment specifies that all *persons* shall enjoy "due process of law." In practice, however, the courts have often deferred to government assertions that noncitizens have no right to make constitutional claims. The events of 9/11 have reinforced that judicial deference.

PUBLIC TRIALS

Immediately after 9/11, the government arrested over 1,200 foreign citizens on suspicion of terrorism. These persons were cleared of terrorism, but most were deported for violating immigration rules. The deportation hearings were secret, a reversal of past procedure. Even the names of the persons held were not released. In June 2003, a federal appellate court ruled that the government was within its rights to maintain such secrecy.* The United States Supreme Court refused to review the issue. As a result, the public will never know how these cases were handled or whether any of the deportations were unjust.

FREEDOM OF SPEECH

A case in February 1999 involved a group of noncitizens associated with the Popular Front for the Liberation of

Palestine (PFLP). The PFLP has carried out terrorist acts in Israel, but there was no evidence of criminal conduct by the group arrested in the United States. In *Reno v. American-Arab Anti-Discrimination Committee,*† the Supreme Court ruled that aliens have no First Amendment rights to object to deportation even if the deportation is based on their political associations. This ruling also covers permanent residents—noncitizens with "green cards" that allow them to live and work in the United States on a long-term basis.

EX POST FACTO LAWS

Article I, Section 9, of the Constitution prohibits *ex post facto* laws—laws that inflict punishments for acts that were not illegal when they were committed. This provision may not apply to immigrants, however. The 1996 Illegal Immigrant Reform and Immigration Responsibility Act provides mandatory deportation for noncitizens convicted of an aggravated felony, even if the crime took place before 1996.

The term *aggravated felony* sounds serious, but under immigration law it can include misdemeanors. Possession of marijuana is usually an aggravated felony. Under the 1996 law, many permanent residents have been deported to nations that they left when they were small children. In some cases, deported persons do not even speak the language of the country to which they are deported.

FOR CRITICAL ANALYSIS

The Supreme Court has stated, "In exercise of its broad power over naturalization and immigration, Congress may make rules as to aliens that would be unacceptable if applied to citizens."‡ Is this guideline necessary to protect America's security, or does it go too far? Why?

*Center for National Security Studies v. U.S. Dept. of Justice, 331 F.3d 918 (D.C. Cir. 2003).

†525 U.S. 471 (1999).
‡See, for example, *Demore v. Hyung Joon Kim,* 538 U.S. 510 (2003).

cant limitations on state power in the form of the Fourteenth Amendment became part of the national Constitution.

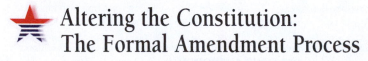

Altering the Constitution: The Formal Amendment Process

The U.S. Constitution consists of 7,000 words. It is shorter than any state constitution except that of Vermont, which has 6,880 words. One of the reasons the federal Constitution is short is that the founders intended it to be only a framework for the new government, to be interpreted by succeeding generations. One of the reasons it has remained short is that the formal amending procedure does not allow for changes to be made easily. Article V of the Constitution outlines the ways in which amendments may be proposed and ratified (see Figure 2–3).

Two formal methods of proposing an amendment to the Constitution are available: (1) a two-thirds vote in each chamber of Congress or (2) a national convention that is called by Congress at the request of two-thirds of the state legislatures (the second method has never been used).

Ratification can occur by one of two methods: (1) by a positive vote in three-fourths of the legislatures of the various states or (2) by special conventions called in the states and a positive vote in three-fourths of them. The second method has been used only once, to repeal Prohibition (the ban on the production and sale of alcoholic beverages). That situation was exceptional because it involved an amendment (the Twenty-first) to repeal an amendment (the Eighteenth, which had created Prohibition). State conventions were necessary for repeal of the Eighteenth Amendment because the "pro-dry" legislatures in the most conservative states would never have passed the repeal. (Note that Congress determines the method of ratification to be used by all states for each proposed constitutional amendment.)

Many Amendments Proposed, Few Accepted

Congress has considered more than eleven thousand amendments to the Constitution. Many proposed amendments have been advanced to address highly specific problems. An argument against such "narrow" amendments has been that amendments ought to embody broad principles, in the way that the existing Constitution does. For that reason, many people have opposed such narrow amendments as one to protect the American flag.

Only thirty-three amendments have been submitted to the states after having been approved by the required two-thirds vote in each chamber of Congress, and only twenty-seven have been ratified—see Table 2–3. (The full, annotated text of the U.S. Constitution, including its amendments, is presented in a special appendix at the end of this chapter.) It should be clear that the amendment process is much more difficult than a graphic depiction such as Figure 2–3 can indicate. Because of competing social and economic interests, the requirement that two-thirds of both the House and Senate approve the amendments is difficult to achieve. Thirty-four senators, representing only seventeen sparsely populated states, could block any amendment. For example, the Republican-controlled

FIGURE 2–3

The Formal Constitutional Amending Procedure

There are two ways of proposing amendments to the U.S. Constitution and two ways of ratifying proposed amendments. Among the four possibilities, the usual route has been proposal by Congress and ratification by state legislatures.

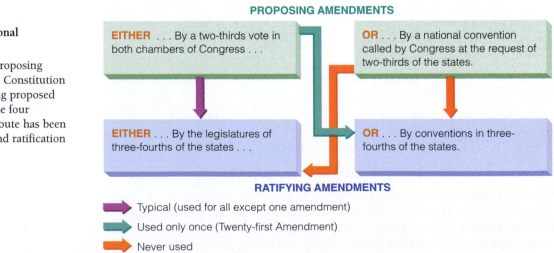

PROPOSING AMENDMENTS

EITHER . . . By a two-thirds vote in both chambers of Congress . . .

OR . . . By a national convention called by Congress at the request of two-thirds of the states.

EITHER . . . By the legislatures of three-fourths of the states . . .

OR . . . By conventions in three-fourths of the states.

RATIFYING AMENDMENTS

➡ Typical (used for all except one amendment)

➡ Used only once (Twenty-first Amendment)

➡ Never used

TABLE 2–3

Amendments to the Constitution

AMENDMENT	SUBJECT	YEAR ADOPTED	TIME REQUIRED FOR RATIFICATION
1st–10th	The Bill of Rights	1791	2 years, 2 months, 20 days
11th	Immunity of states from certain suits	1795	11 months, 3 days
12th	Changes in electoral college procedure	1804	6 months, 3 days
13th	Prohibition of slavery	1865	10 months, 3 days
14th	Citizenship, due process, and equal protection	1868	2 years, 26 days
15th	No denial of vote because of race, color, or previous condition of servitude	1870	11 months, 8 days
16th	Power of Congress to tax income	1913	3 years, 6 months, 22 days
17th	Direct election of U.S. senators	1913	10 months, 26 days
18th	National (liquor) prohibition	1919	1 year, 29 days
19th	Women's right to vote	1920	1 year, 2 months, 14 days
20th	Change of dates for congressional and presidential terms	1933	10 months, 21 days
21st	Repeal of the Eighteenth Amendment	1933	9 months, 15 days
22d	Limit on presidential tenure	1951	3 years, 11 months, 3 days
23d	District of Columbia electoral vote	1961	9 months, 13 days
24th	Prohibition of tax payment as a qualification to vote in federal elections	1964	1 year, 4 months, 9 days
25th	Procedures for determining presidential disability and presidential succession and for filling a vice presidential vacancy	1967	1 year, 7 months, 4 days
26th	Prohibition of setting minimum voting age above eighteen in any election	1971	3 months, 7 days
27th	Prohibition of Congress's voting itself a raise that takes effect before the next election	1992	203 years

House approved the Balanced Budget Amendment within the first one hundred days of the 104th Congress in 1995, but it was defeated in the Senate by one vote.

After approval by Congress, the process becomes even more arduous. Three-fourths of the state legislatures must approve the amendment. Only those amendments that have wide popular support across parties and in all regions of the country are likely to be approved.

Why was the amendment process made so difficult? The framers feared that a simple amendment process could lead to a tyranny of the majority, which could pass amendments to oppress disfavored individuals and groups. The cumbersome amendment process does not seem to stem the number of amendments that are proposed each year in Congress, however, particularly in recent years.

Limits on Ratification

A reading of Article V of the Constitution reveals that the framers of the Constitution specified no time limit on the ratification process. The Supreme Court has held that Congress can specify a time for ratification as long as it is "reasonable." Since 1919, most proposed amendments have included a requirement that ratification be obtained within seven years. This was the case with the proposed Equal Rights Amendment, which sought to guarantee equal rights for women. When three-fourths of the states had not ratified in the allotted seven years, however, Congress extended the limit by an additional three years and three months. That extension expired on June 30, 1982, and the amendment still had not been ratified. Another proposed amendment, which would have guaranteed congressional representation to the District of Columbia, fell far short of the thirty-eight state ratifications needed before its August 22, 1985, deadline.

Supporters of marriage rights for gay and lesbian couples rally in front of the Massachusetts Statehouse in Boston. The signs held by the demonstrators indicate opposition to an amendment to the Massachusetts constitution that would ban same-sex marriages. It takes at least two years to get a constitutional amendment on the ballot in Massachusetts. What problems might result if such mandatory delays existed on the national level? (REUTERS/Jim Bourg/Landov)

On May 7, 1992, Michigan became the thirty-eighth state to ratify the Twenty-seventh Amendment (on congressional compensation)—one of the two "lost" amendments of the twelve that originally were sent to the states in 1789. Because most of the amendments proposed in recent years have been given a time limit of only seven years by Congress, it was questionable for a time whether the amendment would take effect even if the necessary number of states ratified it. Is 203 years too long a lapse of time between the proposal and the final ratification of an amendment? It apparently was not, because the amendment was certified as legitimate by archivist Don Wilson of the National Archives on May 18, 1992.

The National Convention Provision

The Constitution provides that a national convention requested by the legislatures of two-thirds of the states can propose a constitutional amendment. Congress has received approximately 400 convention applications since the Constitution was ratified; every state has applied at least once. Fewer than 20 applications were submitted during the Constitution's first 100 years, but more than 150 have been filed in the last two decades. No national convention has been held since 1787, and many national political and judicial leaders are uneasy about the prospect of convening a body that conceivably could do as the Constitutional Convention did—create a new form of government. The state legislative bodies that originate national convention applications, however, do not appear to be uncomfortable with such a constitutional modification process; more than 230 state constitutional conventions have been held.

★ Informal Methods of Constitutional Change

Formal amendments are one way of changing our Constitution, and, as is obvious from their small number, they have been resorted to infrequently. If we discount the first ten amendments (the Bill of Rights), which were adopted soon after the ratification of the Constitution, there have been only seventeen formal alterations of the Constitution in the more than two hundred years of its existence.

But looking at the sparse number of formal constitutional amendments gives us an incomplete view of constitutional change. The brevity and ambiguity of the original document have permitted great alterations in the Constitution by way of varying interpretations over time. As the United States grew, both in population and territory, new social and political realities emerged. Congress, presidents, and the courts found it necessary to interpret the Constitution's provisions in light of these new realities. The Constitution has proved to be a remarkably flexible document, adapting itself time and again to new events and concerns.

Congressional Legislation

The Constitution gives Congress broad powers to carry out its duties as the nation's legislative body. For example, Article I, Section 8, of the Constitution gives Congress the power to regulate foreign and interstate commerce. Although there is no clear definition of foreign commerce or interstate commerce in the Constitution, Congress has cited the *commerce clause* as the basis for passing thousands of laws that have defined the meaning of foreign and interstate commerce. Similarly, Article III, Section 1, states that the national judiciary shall consist of one supreme court and "such inferior courts, as Congress may from time to time ordain and establish." Through a series of acts, Congress has used this broad provision to establish the federal court system of today.

Presidential Actions

Even though the Constitution does not expressly authorize the president to propose bills or even budgets to Congress,[18] presidents since the time of Woodrow Wilson (who served as president from 1913 to 1921) have proposed hundreds of bills to Congress each year. Presidents have also relied on their Article II authority as commander in chief of the nation's armed forces to send American troops abroad into combat, although the Constitution provides that Congress has the power to declare war. Presidents have also conducted foreign affairs by the use of **executive agreements,** which are legally binding documents made between the president and a foreign head of state. The Constitution does not mention such agreements.

Executive Agreement
An international agreement between chiefs of state that does not require legislative approval.

Judicial Review

Another way of changing the Constitution—or of making it more flexible—is through the power of judicial review. **Judicial review** refers to the power of U.S. courts to examine the constitutionality of actions undertaken by the legislative and executive branches of government. A state court, for example, may rule that a statute enacted by the state legislature is unconstitutional. Federal courts (and ultimately, the United States Supreme Court) may rule unconstitutional not only acts of Congress and decisions of the national executive branch but also state statutes, state executive actions, and even provisions of state constitutions.

Judicial Review
The power of the Supreme Court or any court to declare unconstitutional federal or state laws and other acts of government.

Not a Novel Concept. The Constitution does not specifically mention the power of judicial review. Those in attendance at the Constitutional Convention, however,

---

[18]Note, though, that the Constitution, in Article II, Section 3, does state that the president "shall from time to time . . . recommend to [Congress's] consideration such measures as he shall judge necessary and expedient." Some scholars interpret this phrase to mean that the president has the constitutional authority to propose bills and budgets to Congress for consideration.

DID YOU KNOW . . .
That the states have still not ratified an amendment (introduced by Congress in 1810) barring U.S. citizens from accepting titles of nobility from foreign governments **?**

The members of the United States Supreme Court. From left to right, the justices are William Rehnquist (chief justice), John Paul Stevens, Sandra Day O'Connor, Antonin Scalia, Anthony Kennedy, David Souter, Clarence Thomas, Ruth Bader Ginsberg, and Stephen Breyer. (Paul Hosefros/The New York Times)

probably expected that the courts would have some authority to review the legality of acts by the executive and legislative branches, because, under the common law tradition inherited from England, courts exercised this authority. Indeed, Alexander Hamilton, in *Federalist Paper* No. 78 (see Appendix C), explicitly outlined the concept of judicial review. Whether the power of judicial review can be justified constitutionally is a question that has been subject to some debate, particularly in recent years. For now, suffice it to say that in 1803, the Supreme Court claimed this power for itself in *Marbury v. Madison*,[19] in which the Court ruled that a particular provision of an act of Congress was unconstitutional.

Allows Court to Adapt the Constitution.   Through the process of judicial review, the Supreme Court adapts the Constitution to modern situations. Electronic technology, for example, did not exist when the Constitution was ratified. Nonetheless, the Supreme Court has used the Fourth Amendment guarantees against unreasonable searches and seizures to place limits on the use of wiretapping and other electronic eavesdropping methods by government officials. At some point, the Court may need to decide whether certain new antiterrorism laws passed by Congress or state legislatures violate the Fourth Amendment or other constitutional provisions. Additionally, the Supreme Court has changed its interpretation of the Constitution in accordance with changing values. It ruled in 1896 that "separate-but-equal" public facilities for African Americans were constitutional; but by 1954 the times had changed, and the Supreme Court reversed that decision.[20] Woodrow Wilson summarized the Supreme Court's work when he described it as "a constitutional convention in continuous session." Basically, the law is what the Supreme Court says it is at any point in time.

---

[19]5 U.S. 137 (1803). See Chapter 14 for a further discussion of the *Marbury v. Madison* case.
[20]*Brown v. Board of Education of Topeka,* 347 U.S. 483 (1954).

Interpretation, Custom, and Usage

The Constitution has also been changed through interpretation by both Congress and the president. Originally, the president had a staff consisting of personal secretaries and a few others. Today, because Congress delegates specific tasks to the president and the chief executive assumes political leadership, the executive office staff alone has increased to several thousand persons. The executive branch provides legislative leadership far beyond the expectations of the founders.

Changes in the ways of doing political business have also altered the Constitution. The Constitution does not mention political parties, yet these informal, "extraconstitutional" organizations make the nominations for offices, run the campaigns, organize the members of Congress, and in fact change the election system from time to time. The emergence and evolution of the party system, for example, have changed the way the president is elected. The Constitution calls for the electoral college to choose the president. Today, the people vote for electors who are pledged to the candidate of their party, effectively choosing the president themselves. Perhaps most striking, the Constitution has been adapted from serving the needs of a small, rural republic to providing a framework of government for an industrial giant with vast geographic, natural, and human resources.

The Constitution: Why Is It Important Today?

Our Constitution is a flexible one. If it were not, it would not have lasted for over two hundred years. It is now the longest-lived written constitution in the world. It is also the most imitated constitution in the world. There is a good reason why our Constitution has lasted so long and been imitated so much—it promised such a large number of rights and liberties.

Nevertheless, just because our Constitution has endured for over two hundred years does not mean that we can take it for granted. In other words, citizens nationwide have to be ever vigilant to make sure that our government does not chip away at our rights and liberties. The individual protections afforded by the Constitution do not and should not vanish even though we face an increased threat of terrorism. What is the trade-off involved here? How much privacy and personal freedom should we give up in order to obtain more security? This question is one that you and every other American must consider.

Benjamin Franklin is said to have answered a question from a curious citizen about what kind of government the Constitutional Convention had given the United States by saying, "A republic, if you can keep it." Many countries have a constitution that includes the rights of free speech, religion, and assembly. There is, however, a big difference between what is written and what is reality. The U.S. Constitution is not just a group of words conveying beautiful concepts. It is a true governing document—but to remain effective it must be supported by the American people *and* enforced by the government.

Ultimately, we, the people, decide how many of our liberties will endure. Indeed, as the noted American jurist Judge Learned Hand once stated, "Liberty lies in the hearts of men and women; when it dies there, no constitution . . . can ever do much to help it."

MAKING A DIFFERENCE

★ How Can You Affect the U.S. Constitution?

The Constitution is an enduring document that has survived more than two hundred years of turbulent history. It is also a changing document, however. Twenty-seven amendments have been added to the original Constitution. How can you, as an individual, actively help to rewrite the Constitution?

Why Should You Care?

The laws of the nation have a direct impact on your life, and none more so than the Constitution—the supreme law of the land. The most important issues in society are often settled by the Constitution. For example, for the first seventy-five years of the republic, the Constitution implicitly protected the institution of slavery. If the Constitution had never been changed through the amendment process, slavery might still be legal today.

Since the passage of the Fourteenth Amendment in 1868, the Constitution has defined who is a citizen and who is entitled to the protections the Constitution provides. Constitutional provisions define our liberties. The First Amendment protects our freedom of speech more thoroughly than do the laws of many other nations. Few other countries have constitutional provisions governing the right to own firearms (the Second

Amendment). All of these are among the most fundamental issues we face.

What Can You Do?

Consider how one person decided to affect the Constitution. Shirley Breeze, head of the Missouri Women's Network, decided to bring the Equal Rights Amendment (ERA) back to life after its "death" in 1982. She spearheaded a movement that has gained significant support. Today, bills to ratify the ERA have been introduced not only in Missouri but also in other states that did not ratify it earlier, including Illinois, Oklahoma, and Virginia.

At the time of this writing, national coalitions of interest groups are supporting or opposing a number of proposed amendments. One hotly debated proposed amendment concerns abortion. If you are interested in this issue and would like to make a difference, you can contact one of several groups.

An organization whose primary goal is to secure the passage of the Human Life Amendment is

American Life League
P.O. Box 1350
Stafford, VA 22555
540-659-4171

http://www.all.org

The Human Life Amendment would recognize in law the "personhood" of the unborn, secure human rights protections for an unborn child from the time of fertilization, and prohibit abortion under any circumstances.

A political action and information organization working on behalf of "pro-choice" issues—that is, the right of women to have control over reproduction—is

NARAL Pro-Choice America (formerly the National Abortion and Reproductive Rights Action League)
1156 15th St., Suite 700
Washington, DC 20005
202-973-3000

http://www.naral.org

There is also another way that you can affect the Constitution—by protecting your existing rights and liberties under it. In the wake of the 9/11 attacks, a number of new laws have been enacted that many believe go too far in curbing our constitutional rights. If you agree and want to join with others who are concerned about this issue, a good starting point is the Web site of the American Civil Liberties Union (ACLU) at

http://www.aclu.org

Key Terms

Anti-Federalist 47	executive agreement 55	Madisonian model 44	social contract 36
bicameral legislature 41	federal system 46	natural rights 35	state 36
checks and balances 44	Federalist 47	ratification 46	supremacy doctrine 41
confederation 36	Great Compromise 41	representative assembly 31	unicameral legislature 36
electoral college 45	judicial review 55	separation of powers 44	

★ Chapter Summary

1 The first permanent English colonies were established at Jamestown in 1607 and Plymouth in 1620. The Mayflower Compact created the first formal government for the British colonists. By the mid-1700s, other British colonies had been established along the Atlantic seaboard from Georgia to Maine.

2 In 1763, the British tried to impose on their increasingly independent-minded colonies a series of taxes and legislative acts. The colonists responded with boycotts of British products and protests. Representatives of the colonies formed the First Continental Congress in 1774. The delegates sent a petition to the British king expressing their grievances. The Second Continental Congress established an army in 1775 to defend colonists against attacks by British soldiers.

3 On July 4, 1776, the Second Continental Congress approved the Declaration of Independence. Perhaps the most revolutionary aspects of the Declaration were its assumptions that people have natural rights to life, liberty, and the pursuit of happiness; that governments derive their power from the consent of the governed; and that people have a right to overthrow oppressive governments. During the Revolutionary War, the colonies adopted written constitutions that severely curtailed the power of executives, thus giving their legislatures predominant powers. By the end of the Revolutionary War, the states had signed the Articles of Confederation, creating a weak central government with few powers. The Articles proved to be unworkable because the national government had no way to ensure compliance by the states with such measures as securing tax revenues.

4 General dissatisfaction with the Articles of Confederation prompted the call for a convention at Philadelphia in 1787. Although the delegates ostensibly convened to amend the Articles, the discussions soon focused on creating a constitution for a new form of government. The Virginia plan and the New Jersey plan did not garner widespread support. A compromise offered by Connecticut helped to break the large-state/small-state disputes dividing the delegates. The final version of the Constitution provided for the separation of powers, checks and balances, and a federal form of government.

5 Fears of a strong central government prompted the addition of the Bill of Rights to the Constitution. The Bill of Rights secured for Americans a wide variety of freedoms, including the freedoms of religion, speech, and assembly. It was initially applied only to the federal government, but amendments to the Constitution following the Civil War made it clear that the Bill of Rights would apply to the states as well.

6 An amendment to the Constitution may be proposed either by a two-thirds vote in each house of Congress or by a national convention called by Congress at the request of two-thirds of the state legislatures. Ratification can occur either by a positive vote in three-fourths of the legislatures of the various states or by special conventions called in the states for the specific purpose of ratifying the proposed amendment and a positive vote in three-fourths of these state conventions. Informal methods of constitutional change include congressional legislation, presidential actions, judicial review, and changing interpretations of the Constitution.

★ Selected Print and Media Resources

SUGGESTED READINGS

Bailyn, Bernard. *To Begin the World Anew: The Genius and Ambiguities of the American Founders.* New York: Knopf, 2003. In a series of essays, a two-time Pulitzer Prize–winning historian discusses the themes of order and liberty in the *Federalist Papers* and the advantages of the founders' provincialism.

Dahl, Robert A. *How Democratic Is the American Constitution?* New Haven, Conn.: Yale University Press, 2002. This book compares the U.S. Constitution with the constitutions of other democratic countries in the world.

Hamilton, Alexander, *et al. The Federalist: The Famous Papers on the Principles of American Government.* Benjamin F. Wright, ed. New York: Friedman/Fairfax Publishing, 2002. This is an updated version of the famous papers written by Alexander Hamilton, James Madison, and John Jay, and published in the *New York Packet,* in support of the ratification of the Constitution.

Wills, Garry. *"Negro President": Jefferson and the Slave Power.* New York: Houghton Mifflin, 2003. Wills is usually an admirer of Jefferson, but here he argues that many of Jefferson's actions defended the interests of southern slave owners. Wills notes that Jefferson would not have been elected president in 1800 were it not for the three-fifths rule. The volume also profiles Timothy Pickering, a long-time Federalist opponent of Jefferson and an advocate of the abolition of slavery.

MEDIA RESOURCES

In the Beginning—A 1987 Bill Moyers program that features discussions with three prominent historians about the roots of the Constitution and its impact on our society.

John Locke—A 1994 video exploring the character and principal views of John Locke.

Thomas Jefferson—A 1996 documentary by acclaimed director Ken Burns. The film covers Jefferson's entire life, including his writing of the Declaration of Independence, his presidency, and his later years in Virginia. Historians and writers interviewed include Daniel Boorstin, Garry Wills, Gore Vidal, and John Hope Franklin.

e-mocracy ★ The Internet and Our Constitution

Today, you can find online many important documents from the founding period, including descriptions of events leading up to the American Revolution, the Articles of Confederation, notes on the Constitutional Convention, the Federalists' writings, and the Anti-Federalists' responses.

You are able to access the Internet and explore a variety of opinions on every topic imaginable because you enjoy the freedoms—including freedom of speech—guaranteed by our Constitution. Even today, more than two hundred years after the U.S. Bill of Rights was ratified, citizens in some countries do not enjoy the right to free speech. Nor can they surf the Web freely, as U.S. citizens do.

For example, the Chinese government employs a number of methods to control Internet use. One method is to use filtering software to block electronic pathways to objectionable sites, including the sites of Western news organizations. Another technique is to prohibit Internet users from sending or discussing information that has not been publicly released by the government. Still another practice is to monitor the online activities of Internet users. None of these methods is foolproof, however. Indeed, some observers claim that the Internet, by exposing citizens in politically oppressive nations to a variety of views on politics and culture, will eventually transform those nations.

We should note that such restrictions also can exist in the United States. For example, there have been persistent efforts by Congress and many courts to limit access to Web sites deemed porno-graphic. Free speech advocates have attacked these restrictions as unconstitutional, as you will read in Chapter 4.

Logging On

For U.S. founding documents, including the Declaration of Independence, scanned originals of the U.S. Constitution, and the *Federalist Papers,* go to Emory University School of Law's Web site at

http://www.law.emory.edu/erd/docs/federalist

The University of Oklahoma Law Center has a number of U.S. historical documents online, including many of those discussed in this chapter. Go to

http://www.law.ou.edu/hist

The National Constitution Center provides information on the Constitution—including its history, current debates over constitutional provisions, and news articles—at the following site:

http://www.constitutioncenter.org

To look at state constitutions, go to

http://www.findlaw.com/casecode/state.html

Using InfoTrac for Political Research

You can find a large number of articles on the Constitution in InfoTrac. The main problem may be limiting your search so that you can obtain a useful selection of material. To access InfoTrac, go to

http://www.infotrac-college.com

Log on, go to InfoTrac College Edition, and then go to the Keyword search page. Type "united states constitution" into the text box and then add other words to limit your search. To find information on a First Amendment topic, add either "religion" or "free speech." Then click on "Search." InfoTrac will provide you with a list of articles sorted by date. Choose a selection of recent articles on the same topic and use them to prepare a report.

ONLINE REVIEW

At **http://politicalscience.wadsworth.com/schmidt12**, you will find a free Study Guide to this book. For each chapter, there are two online quizzes to help you master the material.

• The **PoliPrep Self Study Assessment** provides a pre-test for each major section of the chapter. PoliPrep then generates a customized study plan. After you complete the study plan, a post-test evaluates your progress.

• The **Tutorial Quiz** for each chapter provides questions on the chapter contents, including the features. The questions are organized to match the major sections of the chapter.

The Constitution of the United States*

The Preamble

We the People of the United States, in Order to form a more perfect Union, establish Justice, insure domestic Tranquility, provide for the common defence, promote the general Welfare, and secure the Blessings of Liberty to ourselves and our Posterity, do ordain and establish this Constitution for the United States of America.

The Preamble declares that "We the People" are the authority for the Constitution (unlike the Articles of Confederation, which derived their authority from the states). The Preamble also sets out the purposes of the Constitution.

Article I. (Legislative Branch)

The first part of the Constitution, Article 1, deals with the organization and powers of the lawmaking branch of the national government, the Congress.

Section 1. Legislative Powers

All legislative Powers herein granted shall be vested in a Congress of the United States, which shall consist of a Senate and House of Representatives.

Section 2. House of Representatives

Clause 1: Composition and Election of Members. The House of Representatives shall be composed of Members chosen every second Year by the People of the several States, and the Electors in each State shall have the Qualifications requisite for Electors of the most numerous Branch of the State Legislature.

Each state has the power to decide who may vote for members of Congress. Within each state, those who may vote for state legislators may also vote for members of the House of Representatives (and, under the Seventeenth Amendment, for U.S. senators). When the Constitution was written, nearly all states limited voting rights to white male property owners or taxpayers at least twenty-one years old. Subsequent amendments granted voting power to African American men, all women, and eighteen-year-olds.

Clause 2: Qualifications. No Person shall be a Representative who shall not have attained to the Age of twenty five Years, and been seven Years a Citizen of the United States, and who shall not, when elected, be an Inhabitant of that State in which he shall be chosen.

Each member of the House must be at least twenty-five years old, a citizen of the United States for at least seven years, and a resident of the state in which she or he is elected.

Clause 3: Apportionment of Representatives and Direct Taxes. Representatives [and direct Taxes][1] shall be apportioned among the several States which may be included within this Union, according to their respective Numbers [which shall be determined by adding to the whole Number of free Persons, including those bound to Service for a Term of Years, and excluding Indians not taxed, three fifths of all other Persons].[2] The actual Enumeration shall be made within three Years after the first Meeting of the Congress of the United States, and within every subsequent Term of ten Years, in such Manner as they shall by Law direct. The Number of Representatives shall not exceed one for every thirty Thousand, but each State shall have at Least one Representative; and until such enumeration shall be made, the State of New Hampshire shall be entitled to chuse three, Massachusetts eight, Rhode Island and Providence Plantations one, Connecticut five, New York six, New Jersey four, Pennsylvania eight, Delaware one, Maryland six, Virginia ten, North Carolina five, South Carolina five, and Georgia three.

A state's representation in the House is based on the size of its population. Population is counted in each decade's census, after which Congress reapportions House seats. Since early in the twentieth century, the number of seats has been limited to 435.

Clause 4: Vacancies. When vacancies happen in the Representation from any State, the Executive Authority thereof shall issue Writs of Election to fill such Vacancies.

The "Executive Authority" is the state's governor. When a vacancy occurs in the House, the governor calls a special election to fill it.

Clause 5: Officers and Impeachment. The House of Representatives shall chuse their Speaker and other Officers; and shall have the sole Power of Impeachment.

---

*The spelling, capitalization, and punctuation of the original have been retained here. Brackets indicate passages that have been altered by amendments to the Constitution. We have added article titles (in parentheses), section titles, and clause designations. We have also inserted annotations in blue italic type.

---

[1]Modified by the Sixteenth Amendment.
[2]Modified by the Fourteenth Amendment.

The power to impeach is the power to accuse. In this case, it is the power to accuse members of the executive or judicial branch of wrongdoing or abuse of power. Once a bill of impeachment is issued, the Senate holds the trial.

Section 3. The Senate

Clause 1: Term and Number of Members.   The Senate of the United States shall be composed of two Senators from each State [chosen by the Legislature thereof],[3] for six Years; and each Senator shall have one Vote.

Every state has two senators, each of whom serves for six years and has one vote in the upper chamber. Since the Seventeenth Amendment in 1913, all senators have been elected directly by voters of the state during the regular election.

Clause 2: Classification of Senators.   Immediately after they shall be assembled in Consequence of the first Election, they shall be divided as equally as may be into three Classes. The Seats of the Senators of the first Class shall be vacated at the Expiration of the second Year, of the second Class at the Expiration of the fourth Year, and of the third Class at the Expiration of the sixth Year, so that one third may be chosen every second Year; [and if Vacancies happen by Resignation, or otherwise, during the Recess of the Legislature of any State, the Executive thereof may make temporary Appointments until the next Meeting of the Legislature, which shall then fill such Vacancies].[4]

One-third of the Senate's seats are open to election every two years (in contrast, all members of the House are elected simultaneously).

Clause 3: Qualifications.   No Person shall be a Senator who shall not have attained to the Age of thirty Years, and been nine Years a Citizen of the United States, and who shall not, when elected, be an Inhabitant of that State for which he shall be chosen.

Every senator must be at least thirty years old, a citizen of the United States for a minimum of nine years, and a resident of the state in which he or she is elected.

Clause 4: The Role of the Vice President.   The Vice President of the United States shall be President of the Senate, but shall have no Vote, unless they be equally divided.

The vice president presides over meetings of the Senate but cannot vote unless there is a tie. The Constitution gives no other official duties to the vice president.

Clause 5: Other Officers.   The Senate shall chuse their other Officers, and also a President pro tempore, in the Absence of the Vice President, or when he shall exercise the Office of President of the United States.

The Senate votes for one of its members to preside when the vice president is absent. This person is usually called the president pro tempore because of the temporary nature of the position.

Clause 6: Impeachment Trials.   The Senate shall have the sole Power to try all Impeachments. When sitting for that Purpose, they shall be on Oath or Affirmation. When the President of the United States is tried, the Chief Justice shall preside: And no Person shall be convicted without the Concurrence of two thirds of the Members present.

The Senate conducts trials of officials that the House impeaches. The Senate sits as a jury, with the vice president presiding if the president is not on trial.

Clause 7: Penalties for Conviction.   Judgment in Cases of Impeachment shall not extend further than to removal from Office, and disqualification to hold and enjoy any Office of honor, Trust, or Profit under the United States: but the Party convicted shall nevertheless be liable and subject to Indictment, Trial, Judgment, and Punishment, according to Law.

On conviction of impeachment charges, the Senate can only force an official to leave office and prevent him or her from holding another office in the federal government. The individual, however, can still be tried in a regular court.

Section 4. Congressional Elections: Times, Manner, and Places

Clause 1: Elections.   The Times, Places and Manner of holding Elections for Senators and Representatives, shall be prescribed in each State by the Legislature thereof; but the Congress may at any time by Law make or alter such Regulations, except as to the Places of chusing Senators.

Congress set the Tuesday after the first Monday in November in even-numbered years as the date for congressional elections. In states with more than one seat in the House, Congress requires that representatives be elected from districts within each state. Under the Seventeenth Amendment, senators are elected at the same places as other officials.

Clause 2: Sessions of Congress.   [The Congress shall assemble at least once in every Year, and such Meeting shall be on the first Monday in December, unless they shall by Law appoint a different Day.][5]

---

[3]Repealed by the Seventeenth Amendment.
[4]Modified by the Seventeenth Amendment.

[5]Changed by the Twentieth Amendment.

Congress has to meet every year at least once. The regular session now begins at noon on January 3 of each year, subsequent to the Twentieth Amendment, unless Congress passes a law to fix a different date. Congress stays in session until its members vote to adjourn. Additionally, the president may call a special session.

Section 5. Powers and Duties of the Houses

Clause 1: Admitting Members and Quorum. Each House shall be the Judge of the Elections, Returns, and Qualifications of its own Members, and a Majority of each shall constitute a Quorum to do Business; but a smaller Number may adjourn from day to day, and may be authorized to compel the Attendance of absent Members, in such Manner, and under such Penalties as each House may provide.

Each chamber may exclude or refuse to seat a member-elect.

The quorum rule requires that 218 members of the House and 51 members of the Senate be present to conduct business. This rule normally is not enforced in the handling of routine matters.

Clause 2: Rules and Discipline of Members. Each House may determine the Rules of its Proceedings, punish its Members for disorderly Behaviour, and, with the Concurrence of two thirds, expel a Member.

The House and the Senate may adopt their own rules to guide their proceedings. Each may also discipline its members for conduct that is deemed unacceptable. No member may be expelled without a two-thirds majority vote in favor of expulsion.

Clause 3: Keeping a Record. Each House shall keep a Journal of its Proceedings, and from time to time publish the same, excepting such Parts as may in their Judgment require Secrecy; and the Yeas and Nays of the Members of either House on any question shall, at the Desire of one fifth of those Present, be entered on the Journal.

The journals of the two chambers are published at the end of each session of Congress.

Clause 4: Adjournment. Neither House, during the Session of Congress, shall, without the Consent of the other, adjourn for more than three days, nor to any other Place than that in which the two Houses shall be sitting.

Congress has the power to determine when and where to meet, provided, however, that both chambers meet in the same city. Neither chamber may recess for more than three days without the consent of the other.

Section 6. Rights of Members

Clause 1: Compensation and Privileges. The Senators and Representatives shall receive a Compensation for their services, to be ascertained by Law, and paid out of the Treasury of the United States. They shall in all Cases, except Treason, Felony and Breach of the Peace, be privileged from Arrest during their Attendance at the Session of their respective Houses, and in going to and returning from the same; and for any Speech or Debate in either House, they shall not be questioned in any other Place.

Congressional salaries are to be paid by the U.S. Treasury rather than by the members' respective states. The original salaries were $6 per day; in 1857 they were $3,000 per year. Both representatives and senators were paid $157,000 in 2004.

Treason is defined in Article III, Section 3. A felony is any serious crime. A breach of the peace is any indictable offense less than treason or a felony. Members cannot be arrested for things they say during speeches and debates in Congress. This immunity applies to the Capitol Building itself and not to their private lives.

Clause 2: Restrictions. No Senator or Representative shall, during the Time for which he was elected, be appointed to any civil Office under the Authority of the United States, which shall have been created, or the Emoluments whereof shall have been encreased during such time; and no Person holding any Office under the United States, shall be a Member of either House during his Continuance in Office.

During the term for which a member was elected, he or she cannot concurrently accept another federal government position.

Section 7. Legislative Powers: Bills and Resolutions

Clause 1: Revenue Bills. All Bills for raising Revenue shall originate in the House of Representatives; but the Senate may propose or concur with Amendments as on other Bills.

All tax and appropriation bills for raising money have to originate in the House of Representatives. The Senate, though, often amends such bills and may even substitute an entirely different bill.

Clause 2: The Presidential Veto. Every Bill which shall have passed the House of Representatives and the Senate, shall, before it becomes a Law, be presented to the President of the United States; If he approve he shall sign it, but if not he shall return it, with his Objections to the House in which it shall have originated, who shall enter the Objections at large on their Journal, and proceed to reconsider it. If after such Reconsideration two thirds of that House shall agree to pass the Bill, it shall be sent together with the Objections, to the other House, by which it shall likewise be reconsidered, and if approved by two thirds of that House, it shall become a Law. But in all such Cases the Votes of both Houses shall be determined by Yeas and Nays, and the Names of the Persons voting for and against the Bill shall be entered on the Journal of each House respectively. If any Bill shall not be returned by the President within ten Days (Sundays excepted) after it shall have been presented to him, the Same shall be a Law, in like Manner as if he had signed it, unless the Congress by their Adjournment prevent its Return in which Case it shall not be a Law.

When Congress sends the president a bill, he or she can sign it (in which case it becomes law) or send it back to the chamber in which it originated. If it is sent back, a two-thirds majority of each chamber must pass it again for it to become law. If the president neither signs it nor sends it back within ten days, it becomes law anyway, unless Congress adjourns in the meantime.

Clause 3: Actions on Other Matters. Every Order, Resolution, or Vote to which the Concurrence of the Senate and House of Representatives may be necessary (except on a question of Adjournment) shall be presented to the President of the United States; and before the Same shall take Effect, shall be approved by him, or being disapproved by him, shall be repassed by two thirds of the Senate and House of Representatives, according to the Rules and Limitations prescribed in the Case of a Bill.

The president must have the opportunity to either sign or veto everything that Congress passes, except votes to adjourn and resolutions not having the force of law.

Section 8. The Powers of Congress
Clause 1: Taxing. The Congress shall have Power To lay and collect Taxes, Duties, Imposts and Excises, to pay the Debts and provide for the common Defence and general Welfare of the United States; but all Duties, Imposts and Excises shall be uniform throughout the United States;

Duties are taxes on imports and exports. Impost is a generic term for tax. Excises are taxes on the manufacture, sale, or use of goods.

Clause 2: Borrowing. To borrow Money on the credit of the United States;

Congress has the power to borrow money, which is normally carried out through the sale of U.S. treasury bonds on which interest is paid. Note that the Constitution places no limit on the amount of government borrowing.

Clause 3: Regulation of Commerce. To regulate Commerce with foreign Nations, and among the several States, and with the Indian Tribes;

This is the commerce clause, which gives to Congress the power to regulate interstate and foreign trade. Much of the activity of Congress is based on this clause.

Clause 4: Naturalization and Bankruptcy. To establish an uniform Rule of Naturalization, and uniform Laws on the subject of Bankruptcies throughout the United States;

Only Congress may determine how aliens can become citizens of the United States. Congress may make laws with respect to bankruptcy.

Clause 5: Money and Standards. To coin Money, regulate the Value thereof, and of foreign Coin, and fix the Standard of Weights and Measures;

Congress mints coins and prints and circulates paper money. Congress can establish uniform measures of time, distance, weight, and so on. In 1838, Congress adopted the English system of weights and measurements as our national standard.

Clause 6: Punishing Counterfeiters. To provide for the Punishment of counterfeiting the Securities and current Coin of the United States;

Congress has the power to punish those who copy American money and pass it off as real. Currently, the fine is up to $5,000 and/or imprisonment for up to fifteen years.

Clause 7: Roads and Post Offices. To establish Post Offices and post Roads;

Post roads include all routes over which mail is carried—highways, railways, waterways, and airways.

Clause 8: Patents and Copyrights. To promote the Progress of Science and useful Arts, by securing for limited Times to Authors and Inventors the exclusive Right to their respective Writings and Discoveries;

Authors' and composers' works are protected by copyrights established by copyright law, which currently is the Copyright Act of 1976, as amended. Copyrights are valid for the life of the author or composer plus seventy years. Inventors' works are protected by patents, which vary in length of protection from fourteen to twenty years. A patent gives a person the exclusive right to control the manufacture or sale of her or his invention.

Clause 9: Lower Courts. To constitute Tribunals inferior to the supreme Court;

Congress has the authority to set up all federal courts, except the Supreme Court, and to decide what cases those courts will hear.

Clause 10: Punishment for Piracy. To define and punish Piracies and Felonies committed on the high Seas, and Offences against the Law of Nations;

Congress has the authority to prohibit the commission of certain acts outside U.S. territory and to punish certain violations of international law.

Clause 11: *Declaration of War.* To declare War, grant Letters of Marque and Reprisal, and make Rules concerning Captures on Land and Water;

Only Congress can declare war, although the president, as commander in chief, can make war without Congress's formal declaration. Letters of marque and reprisal authorized private parties to capture and destroy enemy ships in wartime. Since the middle of the nineteenth century, international law has prohibited letters of marque and reprisal, and the United States has honored the ban.

Clause 12: *The Army.* To raise and support Armies, but no Appropriation of Money to that Use shall be for a longer Term than two Years;

Congress has the power to create an army; the money used to pay for it must be appropriated for no more than two-year intervals. This latter restriction gives ultimate control of the army to civilians.

Clause 13: *Creation of a Navy.* To provide and maintain a Navy;

This clause allows for the maintenance of a navy. In 1947, Congress created the U.S. Air Force.

Clause 14: *Regulation of the Armed Forces.* To make Rules for the Government and Regulation of the land and naval Forces;

Congress sets the rules for the military mainly by way of the Uniform Code of Military Justice, which was enacted in 1950 by Congress.

Clause 15: *The Militia.* To provide for calling forth the Militia to execute the Laws of the Union, suppress Insurrections and repel Invasions;

The militia is known today as the National Guard. Both Congress and the president have the authority to call the National Guard into federal service.

Clause 16: *How the Militia Is Organized.* To provide for organizing, arming, and disciplining the Militia, and for governing such Part of them as may be employed in the Service of the United States, reserving to the States respectively, the Appointment of the Officers, and the Authority of training the Militia according to the discipline prescribed by Congress;

This clause gives Congress the power to "federalize" state militia (National Guard). When called into such service, the

National Guard is subject to the same rules that Congress has set forth for the regular armed services.

Clause 17: *Creation of the District of Columbia.* To exercise exclusive Legislation in all Cases whatsoever, over such District (not exceeding ten Miles square) as may, by Cession of particular States, and the Acceptance of Congress, become the Seat of the Government of the United States, and to exercise like Authority over all Places purchased by the Consent of the Legislature of the State in which the Same shall be, for the Erection of Forts, Magazines, Arsenals, dock-Yards, and other needful Buildings;—And

Congress established the District of Columbia as the national capital in 1791. Virginia and Maryland had granted land for the District, but Virginia's grant was returned because it was believed it would not be needed. Today, the District covers sixty-nine square miles.

Clause 18: *The Elastic Clause.* To make all Laws which shall be necessary and proper for carrying into Execution the foregoing Powers, and all other Powers vested by this Constitution in the Government of the United States, or in any Department or Officer thereof.

This clause—the necessary and proper clause, or the elastic clause—grants no specific powers, and thus it can be stretched to fit different circumstances. It has allowed Congress to adapt the government to changing needs and times.

Section 9. The Powers Denied to Congress

Clause 1: *Question of Slavery.* The Migration or Importation of such Persons as any of the States now existing shall think proper to admit, shall not be prohibited by the Congress prior to the Year one thousand eight hundred and eight, but a Tax or duty may be imposed on such Importation, not exceeding ten dollars for each Person.

"Persons" referred to slaves. Congress outlawed the slave trade in 1808.

Clause 2: *Habeas Corpus.* The privilege of the Writ of Habeas Corpus shall not be suspended, unless when in Cases of Rebellion or Invasion the public Safety may require it.

A writ of habeas corpus is a court order directing a sheriff or other public officer who is detaining another person to "produce the body" of the detainee so the court can assess the legality of the detention.

Clause 3: *Special Bills.* No Bill of Attainder or ex post facto Law shall be passed.

A bill of attainder is a law that inflicts punishment without a trial. An ex post facto law is a law that inflicts punishment for an act that was not illegal when it was committed.

Clause 4: Direct Taxes. [No Capitation, or other direct, Tax shall be laid, unless in Proportion to the Census or Enumeration herein before directed to be taken.][6]

A capitation is a tax on a person. A direct tax is a tax paid directly to the government, such as a property tax. This clause was intended to prevent Congress from levying a tax on slaves per person and thereby taxing slavery out of existence.

Clause 5: Export Taxes. No Tax or Duty shall be laid on Articles exported from any State.

Congress may not tax any goods sold from one state to another or from one state to a foreign country. (Congress does have the power to tax goods that are bought from other countries, however.)

Clause 6: Interstate Commerce. No Preference shall be given by any Regulation of Commerce or Revenue to the Ports of one State over those of another: nor shall Vessels bound to, or from, one State, be obliged to enter, clear, or pay Duties in another.

Congress may not treat different ports within the United States differently in terms of taxing and commerce powers. Congress may not give one state's port a legal advantage over the ports of another state.

Clause 7: Treasury Withdrawals. No Money shall be drawn from the Treasury, but in Consequence of Appropriations made by Law; and a regular Statement and Account of the Receipts and Expenditures of all public Money shall be published from time to time.

Federal funds can be spent only as Congress authorizes. This is a significant check on the president's power.

Clause 8: Titles of Nobility. No Title of Nobility shall be granted by the United States: And no Person holding any Office of Profit or Trust under them, shall, without the Consent of the Congress, accept of any present, Emolument, Office, or Title, of any kind whatever, from any King, Prince, or foreign State.

No person in the United States may hold a title of nobility, such as duke or duchess. This clause also discourages bribery of American officials by foreign governments.

Section 10. Those Powers Denied to the States

Clause 1: Treaties and Coinage. No State shall enter into any Treaty, Alliance, or Confederation; grant Letters of Marque and Reprisal; coin Money; emit Bills of Credit; make any Thing but gold and silver Coin a Tender in Payment of Debts; pass any Bill of Attainder, ex post facto Law, or Law

---

[6]Modified by the Sixteenth Amendment.

impairing the Obligation of Contracts, or grant any Title of Nobility.

Prohibiting state laws "impairing the Obligation of Contracts" was intended to protect creditors. (Shays' Rebellion—an attempt to prevent courts from giving effect to creditors' legal actions against debtors—occurred only one year before the Constitution was written.)

Clause 2: Duties and Imposts. No State shall, without the Consent of the Congress, lay any Imports or Duties on Imports or Exports, except what may be absolutely necessary for executing its inspection Laws; and the net Produce of all Duties and Imposts, laid by any State on Imports or Exports, shall be for the Use of the Treasury of the United States; and all such Laws shall be subject to the Revision and Controul of the Congress.

Only Congress can tax imports. Further, the states cannot tax exports.

Clause 3: War. No State shall, without the Consent of Congress, lay any Duty of Tonnage, keep Troops, or Ships of War in time of Peace, enter into any Agreement or Compact with another State, or with a foreign Power or engage in War, unless actually invaded, or in such imminent Danger as will not admit of delay.

A duty of tonnage is a tax on ships according to their cargo capacity. No states may tax ships according to their cargo unless Congress agrees. Additionally, this clause forbids any state to keep troops or warships during peacetime or to make a compact with another state or foreign nation unless Congress so agrees. A state, in contrast, can maintain a militia, but its use has to be limited to disorders that occur within the state—unless, of course, the militia is called into federal service.

Article II. (Executive Branch)

Section 1. The Nature and Scope of Presidential Power

Clause 1: Four-Year Term. The executive Power shall be vested in a President of the United States of America. He shall hold his Office during the Term of four Years, and, together with the Vice President, chosen for the same Term, be elected, as follows.

The president has the power to carry out laws made by Congress, called the executive power. He or she serves in office for a four-year term after election. The Twenty-second Amendment limits the number of times a person may be elected president.

Clause 2: Choosing Electors from Each State. Each State shall appoint, in such Manner as the Legislature thereof may direct, a Number of Electors, equal to the whole Number of Senators and Representatives to which the State may be entitled in the Congress; but no Senator or Representative, or Person holding an Office of Trust or Profit under the United States, shall be appointed an Elector.

The "Electors" are known more commonly as the "electoral college." The president is elected by electors—that is, representatives chosen by the people—rather than by the people directly.

Clause 3: The Former System of Elections. [The Electors shall meet in their respective States, and vote by Ballot for two Persons, of whom one at least shall not be an Inhabitant of the same State with themselves. And they shall make a List of all the Persons voted for, and of the Number of Votes for each; which List they shall sign and certify, and transmit sealed to the Seat of the Government of the United States, directed to the President of the Senate. The President of the Senate shall, in the Presence of the Senate and House of Representatives, open all the Certificates, and the Votes shall then be counted. The Person having the greatest Number of Votes shall be the President, if such Number be a Majority of the whole Number of Electors appointed; and if there be more than one who have such Majority, and have an equal Number of Votes, then the House of Representatives shall immediately chuse by Ballot one of them for President; and if no Person have a Majority, then from the five highest on the List the said House shall in like Manner chuse the President. But in chusing the President, the Votes shall be taken by States, the Representation from each State having one Vote; A quorum for this Purpose shall consist of a Member or Members from two thirds of the States, and a Majority of all the States shall be necessary to a Choice. In every Case, after the Choice of the President, the Person having the greater Number of Votes of the Electors shall be the Vice President. But if there should remain two or more who have equal Votes, the Senate shall chuse from them by Ballot the Vice President.][7]

The original method of selecting the president and vice president was replaced by the Twelfth Amendment. Apparently, the framers did not anticipate the rise of political parties and the development of primaries and conventions.

Clause 4: The Time of Elections. The Congress may determine the Time of chusing the Electors, and the Day on which they shall give their Votes; which Day shall be the same throughout the United States.

Congress set the Tuesday after the first Monday in November every fourth year as the date for choosing electors. The electors cast their votes on the Monday after the second Wednesday in December of that year.

Clause 5: Qualifications for President. No person except a natural born Citizen, or a Citizen of the United States, at the time of the Adoption of this Constitution, shall be eligible to the Office of President; neither shall any Person be eligible to that Office who shall not have attained to the Age of thirty five Years, and been fourteen Years a Resident within the United States.

The president must be a natural-born citizen, be at least thirty-five years of age when taking office, and have been a resident within the United States for at least fourteen years.

Clause 6: Succession of the Vice President. [In Case of the Removal of the President from Office, or of his Death, Resignation or Inability to discharge the Powers and Duties of the said Office, the same shall devolve on the Vice President, and the Congress may by Law provide for the Case of Removal, Death, Resignation or Inability, both of the President and Vice President, declaring what Officer shall then act as President, and such Officer shall act accordingly, until the Disability be removed, or a President shall be elected.][8]

This section provided for the method by which the vice president was to succeed to the presidency, but its wording is ambiguous. It was replaced by the Twenty-fifth Amendment.

Clause 7: The President's Salary. The President shall, at stated Times, receive for his Services, a Compensation, which shall neither be encreased nor diminished during the Period for which he shall have been elected, and he shall not receive within that Period any other Emolument from the United States, or any of them.

The president maintains the same salary during each four-year term. Moreover, she or he may not receive additional cash payments from the government. Originally set at $25,000 per year, the salary is currently $400,000 a year plus a $50,000 non-taxable expense account.

Clause 8: The Oath of Office. Before he enter on the Execution of his Office, he shall take the following Oath or Affirmation: "I do solemnly swear (or affirm) that I will faithfully execute the Office of President of the United States, and will to the best of my Ability, preserve, protect and defend the Constitution of the United States."

The president is "sworn in" prior to beginning the duties of the office. Currently, the taking of the oath of office occurs on January 20, following the November election. The ceremony is called the inauguration. *The oath of office is administered by the chief justice of the United States Supreme Court.*

---

[7]Changed by the Twelfth Amendment.

[8]Modified by the Twenty-fifth Amendment.

Section 2. Powers of the President

Clause 1: Commander in Chief. The President shall be Commander in Chief of the Army and Navy of the United States, and of the Militia of the several States, when called into the actual Service of the United States; he may require the Opinion, in writing, of the principal Officer in each of the executive Departments, upon any Subject relating to the Duties of their respective Offices, and he shall have Power to grant Reprieves and Pardons for Offences against the United States, except in Cases of Impeachment.

The armed forces are placed under civilian control because the president is a civilian but still commander in chief of the military. The president may ask for the help of the head of each of the executive departments (thereby creating the cabinet). The cabinet members are chosen by the president with the consent of the Senate, but they can be removed without Senate approval.

The president's clemency powers extend only to federal cases. In those cases, he or she may grant a full or conditional pardon, or reduce a prison term or fine.

Clause 2: Treaties and Appointment. He shall have Power, by and with the Advice and Consent of the Senate, to make Treaties, provided two thirds of the Senators present concur; and he shall nominate, and by and with the Advice and Consent of the Senate, shall appoint Ambassadors, other public Ministers and Consuls, Judges of the supreme Court, and all other Officers of the United States, whose Appointments are not herein otherwise provided for, and which shall be established by Law; but the Congress may by Law vest the Appointment of such inferior Officers, as they think proper, in the President alone, in the Courts of Law, or in the Heads of Departments.

Many of the major powers of the president are identified in this clause, including the power to make treaties with foreign governments (with the approval of the Senate by a two-thirds vote) and the power to appoint ambassadors, Supreme Court justices, and other government officials. Most such appointments require Senate approval.

Clause 3: Vacancies. The President shall have Power to fill up all Vacancies that may happen during the Recess of the Senate, by granting Commissions which shall expire at the end of their next Session.

The president has the power to appoint temporary officials to fill vacant federal offices without Senate approval if the Congress is not in session. Such appointments expire automatically at the end of Congress's next term.

Section 3. Duties of the President

He shall from time to time give to the Congress Information of the State of the Union, and recommend to their Consid-eration such Measures as he shall judge necessary and expedient; he may, on extraordinary Occasions, convene both Houses, or either of them, and in Case of Disagreement between them, with Respect to the Time of Adjournment, he may adjourn them to such Time as he shall think proper; he shall receive Ambassadors and other public Ministers; he shall take Care that the Laws be faithfully executed, and shall Commission all the Officers of the United States.

Annually, the president reports on the state of the union to Congress, recommends legislative measures, and proposes a federal budget. The State of the Union speech is a statement not only to Congress but also to the American people. After it is given, the president proposes a federal budget and presents an economic report. At any time, the president may send special messages to Congress while it is in session. The president has the power to call special sessions, to adjourn Congress when its two chambers do not agree on when to adjourn, to receive diplomatic representatives of other governments, and to ensure the proper execution of all federal laws. The president further has the ability to empower federal officers to hold their positions and to perform their duties.

Section 4. Impeachment

The President, Vice President and all civil Officers of the United States, shall be removed from Office on Impeachment for, and Conviction of, Treason, Bribery, or other high Crimes and Misdemeanors.

Treason denotes giving aid to the nation's enemies. The definition of high crimes and misdemeanors is usually given as serious abuses of political power. In either case, the president or vice president may be accused by the House (called an impeachment) and then removed from office if convicted by the Senate. (Note that impeachment does not mean removal but rather refers to an accusation of treason or high crimes and misdemeanors.)

Article III. (Judicial Branch)

Section 1. Judicial Powers, Courts, and Judges

The judicial Power of the United States, shall be vested in one supreme Court, and in such inferior Courts as the Congress may from time to time ordain and establish. The Judges, both of the supreme and inferior Courts, shall hold their Offices during good Behaviour, and shall, at stated Times, receive for their Services a Compensation, which shall not be diminished during their Continuance in Office.

The Supreme Court is vested with judicial power, as are the lower federal courts that Congress creates. Federal judges serve in their offices for life unless they are impeached and convicted by Congress. The payment of federal judges may not be reduced during their time in office.

Section 2. *Jurisdiction*

Clause 1: Cases under Federal Jurisdiction. The judicial Power shall extend to all Cases, in Law and Equity, arising under this Constitution, the Laws of the United States, and Treaties made, or which shall be made, under their Authority;—to all Cases affecting Ambassadors, other public Ministers and Consuls;—to all Cases of admiralty and maritime Jurisdiction;—to Controversies to which the United States shall be a Party;—to Controversies between two or more States; [—between a State and Citizens of another State;—][9] between Citizens of different States;—between Citizens of the same State claiming Lands under Grants of different States, [and between a State, or the Citizens thereof, and foreign States, Citizens or Subjects.][10]

The federal courts take on cases that concern the meaning of the U.S. Constitution, all federal laws, and treaties. They also can take on cases involving citizens of different states and citizens of foreign nations.

Clause 2: Cases for the Supreme Court. In all Cases affecting Ambassadors, other public Ministers and Consuls, and those in which a State shall be a Party, the supreme Court shall have original Jurisdiction. In all the other Cases before mentioned, the supreme Court shall have appellate Jurisdiction, both as to Law and Fact, with such Exceptions, and under such Regulations as the Congress shall make.

In a limited number of situations, the Supreme Court acts as a trial court and has original jurisdiction. These cases involve a representative from another country or involve a state. In all other situations, the cases must first be tried in the lower courts and then can be appealed to the Supreme Court. Congress may, however, make exceptions. Today, the Supreme Court acts as a trial court of first instance on rare occasions.

Clause 3: The Conduct of Trials. The Trial of all Crimes, except in Cases of Impeachment, shall be by Jury; and such Trial shall be held in the State where the said Crimes shall have been committed; but when not committed within any State, the Trial shall be at such Place or Places as the Congress may by Law have directed.

Any person accused of a federal crime is granted the right to a trial by jury in a federal court in that state in which the crime was committed. Trials of impeachment are an exception.

Section 3. *Treason*

Clause 1: The Definition of Treason. Treason against the United States, shall consist only in levying War against them, or, in adhering to their Enemies, giving them Aid and Comfort. No Person shall be convicted of Treason unless on the Testimony of two Witnesses to the same overt Act, or on Confession in open Court.

Treason is the making of war against the United States or giving aid to its enemies.

Clause 2: Punishment. The Congress shall have Power to declare the Punishment of Treason, but no Attainder of Treason shall work Corruption of Blood, or Forfeiture except during the Life of the Person attainted.

Congress has provided that the punishment for treason ranges from a minimum of five years in prison and/or a $10,000 fine to a maximum of death. "No Attainder of Treason shall work Corruption of Blood" prohibits punishment of the traitor's heirs.

Article IV. (Relations among the States)

Section 1. *Full Faith and Credit*

Full Faith and Credit shall be given in each State to the public Acts, Records, and judicial Proceedings of every other State. And the Congress may by general Laws prescribe the Manner in which such Acts, Records and Proceedings shall be proved, and the Effect thereof.

All states are required to respect one another's laws, records, and lawful decisions. There are exceptions, however. A state does not have to enforce another state's criminal code. Nor does it have to recognize another state's grant of a divorce if the person obtaining the divorce did not establish legal residence in the state in which it was given.

Section 2. *Treatment of Citizens*

Clause 1: Privileges and Immunities. The Citizens of each State shall be entitled to all Privileges and Immunities of Citizens in the several States.

A citizen of a state has the same rights and privileges as the citizens of another state in which he or she happens to be.

Clause 2: Extradition. A Person charged in any State with Treason, Felony, or other Crime, who shall flee from Justice, and be found in another State, shall on Demand of the executive Authority of the State from which he fled, be delivered up, to be removed to the State having Jurisdiction of the Crime.

Any person accused of a crime who flees to another state must be returned to the state in which the crime occurred.

Clause 3: Fugitive Slaves. [No Person held to Service or Labour in one State, under the Laws thereof, escaping into another, shall, in Consequence of any Law or Regulation

---

[9]Modified by the Eleventh Amendment.
[10]Modified by the Eleventh Amendment.

therein, be discharged from such Service or Labour, but shall be delivered up on Claim of the Party to whom such Service or Labour may be due.][11]

This clause was struck down by the Thirteenth Amendment, which abolished slavery in 1865.

Section 3. Admission of States
Clause 1: The Process.   New States may be admitted by the Congress into this Union; but no new State shall be formed or erected within the Jurisdiction of any other State; nor any State be formed by the Junction of two or more States, or Parts of States, without the Consent of the Legislatures of the States concerned as well as of the Congress.

Only Congress has the power to admit new states to the union. No state may be created by taking territory from an existing state unless the state's legislature so consents.

Clause 2: Public Land.   The Congress shall have Power to dispose of and make all needful Rules and Regulations respecting the Territory or other Property belonging to the United States; and nothing in this Constitution shall be so construed as to Prejudice any Claims of the United States, or of any particular State.

The federal government has the exclusive right to administer federal government public lands.

Section 4. Republican Form of Government
The United States shall guarantee to every State in this Union a Republican Form of Government, and shall protect each of them against Invasion; and on Application of the Legislature, or of the Executive (when the Legislature cannot be convened) against domestic Violence.

Each state is promised a republican form of government—that is, one in which the people elect their representatives. The federal government is bound to protect states against any attack by foreigners or during times of trouble within a state.

Article V. (Methods of Amendment)

The Congress, whenever two thirds of both Houses shall deem it necessary, shall propose Amendments to this Constitution, or on the Application of the Legislatures of two thirds of the several States, shall call a Convention for proposing Amendments, which, in either Case, shall be valid to all Intents and Purposes, as Part of this Constitution, when ratified by the Legislatures of three fourths of the several States, or by Conventions in three fourths thereof, as the

one or the other Mode of Ratification may be proposed by the Congress; Provided that no Amendment which may be made prior to the Year One thousand eight hundred and eight shall in any Manner affect the first and fourth Clauses in the Ninth Section of the First Article; and that no State, without its Consent, shall be deprived of its equal Suffrage in the Senate.

Amendments may be proposed in either of two ways: a two-thirds vote of each chamber (Congress) or at the request of two-thirds of the states. Ratification of amendments may be carried out in two ways: by the legislatures of three-fourths of the states or by the voters in three-fourths of the states. No state may be denied equal representation in the Senate.

Article VI. (National Supremacy)

Clause 1: Existing Obligations.   All Debts contracted and Engagements entered into, before the Adoption of this Constitution shall be as valid against the United States under this Constitution, as under the Confederation.

During the Revolutionary War and the years of the Confederation, Congress borrowed large sums. This clause pledged that the new federal government would assume those financial obligations.

Clause 2: Supreme Law of the Land.   This Constitution, and the Laws of the United States which shall be made in Pursuance thereof; and all Treaties made, or which shall be made, under the Authority of the United States, shall be the supreme Law of the Land; and the Judges in every State shall be bound thereby, any Thing in the Constitution or Laws of any State to the Contrary notwithstanding.

This is typically called the supremacy clause; it declares that federal law takes precedence over all forms of state law. No government at the local or state level may make or enforce any law that conflicts with any provision of the Constitution, acts of Congress, treaties, or other rules and regulations issued by the president and his or her subordinates in the executive branch of the federal government.

Clause 3: Oath of Office.   The Senators and Representatives before mentioned, and the Members of the several State Legislatures, and all executive and judicial Officers, both of the United States and of the several States, shall be bound by Oath or Affirmation, to support this Constitution; but no religious Test shall ever be required as a Qualification to any Office or public Trust under the United States.

Every federal and state official must take an oath of office promising to support the U.S. Constitution. Religion may not be used as a qualification to serve in any federal office.

---

[11]Repealed by the Thirteenth Amendment.

Article VII. (Ratification)

The Ratification of the Conventions of nine States shall be sufficient for the Establishment of this Constitution between the States so ratifying the Same.

Nine states were required to ratify the Constitution. Delaware was the first and New Hampshire the ninth.

Done in Convention by the Unanimous Consent of the States present the Seventeenth Day of September in the Year of our Lord one thousand seven hundred and Eighty seven and of the Independence of the United States of America the Twelfth. In witness whereof we have hereunto subscribed our Names,

Attest William Jackson Secretary

Go. WASHINGTON
Presid't.
and deputy from Virginia

DELAWARE
{
Geo. Read
Gunning Bedford jun
John Dickinson
Richard Bassett
Jaco. Broom
}

MARYLAND
{
James McHenry
Dan of St. Thos. Jenifer
Danl. Carroll
}

VIRGINIA
{
John Blair
James Madison Jr.
}

NORTH CAROLINA
{
Wm. Blount
Richd. Dobbs Spaight
Hu. Williamson
}

SOUTH CAROLINA
{
J. Rutledge
Charles Cotesworth Pinckney
Charles Pinckney
Pierce Butler
}

GEORGIA
{
William Few
Abr. Baldwin
}

NEW HAMPSHIRE
{
John Langdon
Nicholas Gilman
}

MASSACHUSETTS
{
Nathaniel Gorham
Rufus King
}

CONNECTICUT
{
Wm. Saml. Johnson
Roger Sherman
}

NEW YORK
{
Alexander Hamilton
}

NEW JERSEY
{
Wh. Livingston
David Brearley
Wm. Paterson
Jona. Dayton
}

PENNSYLVANIA
{
B. Franklin
Thomas Mifflin
Robt. Morris
Geo. Clymer
Thos. FitzSimons
Jared Ingersoll
James Wilson
Gouv. Morris
}

Articles in addition to, and amendment of, the Constitution of the United States of America, proposed by Congress and ratified by the Legislatures of the several states, pursuant to the Fifth Article of the original Constitution.

Amendments to the Constitution of the United States

(The Bill of Rights)[12]

Amendment I.
(Religion, Speech, Assembly, and Petition)

Congress shall make no law respecting an establishment of religion, or prohibiting the free exercise thereof; or abridging the freedom of speech, or of the press; or the right of the people peaceably to assemble, and to petition the Government for a redress of grievances.

Congress may not create an official church or enact laws limiting the freedom of religion, speech, the press, assembly, and petition. These guarantees, like the others in the Bill of Rights (the first ten amendments), are not absolute—each may be exercised only with regard to the rights of other persons.

Amendment II.
(Militia and the Right to Bear Arms)

A well regulated Militia, being necessary to the security of a free State, the right of the people to keep and bear Arms, shall not be infringed.

To protect itself, each state has the right to maintain a volunteer armed force. States and the federal government regulate the possession and use of firearms by individuals.

Amendment III.
(The Quartering of Soldiers)

No Soldier shall, in time of peace be quartered in any house, without the consent of the Owner, nor in time of war, but in a manner to be prescribed by law.

Before the Revolutionary War, it had been common British practice to quarter soldiers in colonists' homes. Military troops do not have the power to take over private houses during peacetime.

---

[12]On September 25, 1789, Congress transmitted to the state legislatures twelve proposed amendments, two of which, having to do with congressional representation and congressional pay, were not adopted. The remaining ten amendments became the Bill of Rights. In 1992, the amendment concerning congressional pay was adopted as the Twenty-seventh Amendment.

Amendment IV.
(Searches and Seizures)

The right of the people to be secure in their persons, houses, papers, and effects, against unreasonable searches and seizures, shall not be violated, and no Warrants shall issue, but upon probable cause, supported by Oath or affirmation, and particularly describing the place to be searched, and the persons or things to be seized.

Here the word warrant means "justification" and refers to a document issued by a magistrate or judge indicating the name, address, and possible offense committed. Anyone asking for the warrant, such as a police officer, must be able to convince the magistrate or judge that an offense probably has been committed.

Amendment V.
(Grand Juries, Self-Incrimination, Double Jeopardy, Due Process, and Eminent Domain)

No person shall be held to answer for a capital, or otherwise infamous crime, unless on a presentment or indictment of a Grand Jury, except in cases arising in the land or naval forces, or in the Militia, when in actual service in time of War or public danger; nor shall any person be subject for the same offence to be twice put in jeopardy of life or limb; nor shall be compelled in any criminal case to be a witness against himself, nor be deprived of life, liberty, or property, without due process of law; nor shall private property be taken for public use, without just compensation.

There are two types of juries. A grand jury considers physical evidence and the testimony of witnesses and decides whether there is sufficient reason to bring a case to trial. A petit jury hears the case at trial and decides it. "For the same offence to be twice put in jeopardy of life or limb" means to be tried twice for the same crime. A person may not be tried for the same crime twice or forced to give evidence against herself or himself. No person's right to life, liberty, or property may be taken away except by lawful means, called the due process of law. Private property taken for use in public purposes must be paid for by the government.

Amendment VI.
(Criminal Court Procedures)

In all criminal prosecutions, the accused shall enjoy the right to a speedy and public trial, by an impartial jury of the State and district wherein the crime shall have been committed, which district shall have been previously ascertained by law, and to be informed of the nature and cause of the accusation; to be confronted with the witnesses against him; to have compulsory process for obtaining witnesses in his favor, and to have the Assistance of Counsel for his defence.

Any person accused of a crime has the right to a fair and public trial by a jury in the state in which the crime took place. The charges against that person must be indicated. Any accused person has the right to a lawyer to defend him or her and to question those who testify against him or her, as well as the right to call people to speak in his or her favor at trial.

Amendment VII.
(Trial by Jury in Civil Cases)

In Suits at common law, where the value in controversy shall exceed twenty dollars, the right of trial by jury shall be preserved, and no fact tried by jury, shall be otherwise re-examined in any Court of the United States, than according to the rules of the common law.

A jury trial may be requested by either party in a dispute in any case involving more than $20. If both parties agree to a trial by a judge without a jury, the right to a jury trial may be put aside.

Amendment VIII.
(Bail, Cruel and Unusual Punishment)

Excessive bail shall not be required, nor excessive fines imposed, nor cruel and unusual punishments inflicted.

Bail is that amount of money that a person accused of a crime may be required to deposit with the court as a guarantee that she or he will appear in court when requested. The amount of bail required or the fine imposed as punishment for a crime must be reasonable compared with the seriousness of the crime involved. Any punishment judged to be too harsh or too severe for a crime shall be prohibited.

Amendment IX.
(The Rights Retained by the People)

The enumeration in the Constitution, of certain rights, shall not be construed to deny or disparage others retained by the people.

Many civil rights that are not explicitly enumerated in the Constitution are still held by the people.

Amendment X.
(Reserved Powers of the States)

The powers not delegated to the United States by the Constitution, nor prohibited by it to the States, are reserved to the States respectively, or to the people.

Those powers not delegated by the Constitution to the federal government or expressly denied to the states belong to the states and to the people. This amendment in essence allows the states to pass laws under their "police powers."

Amendment XI.
(Ratified on February 7, 1795—
Suits against States)

The Judicial power of the United States shall not be construed to extend to any suit in law or equity, commenced or prosecuted against one of the United States by Citizens of another State, or by Citizens or Subjects of any Foreign State.

This amendment has been interpreted to mean that a state cannot be sued in federal court by one of its own citizens, by a citizen of another state, or by a foreign country.

Amendment XII.
(Ratified on June 15, 1804—
Election of the President)

The Electors shall meet in their respective states, and vote by ballot for President and Vice-President, one of whom, at least, shall not be an inhabitant of the same State with themselves; they shall name in their ballots the person voted for as President, and in distinct ballots the person voted for as Vice-President, and they shall make distinct lists of all persons voted for as President, and of all persons voted for as Vice-President, and of the number of votes for each, which lists they shall sign and certify, and transmit sealed to the seat of the government of the United States, directed to the President of the Senate;—The President of the Senate shall, in the presence of the Senate and House of Representatives, open all the certificates and the votes shall then be counted;—The person having the greatest number of votes for President, shall be the President, if such number be a majority of the whole number of Electors appointed; and if no person have such majority, then from the persons having the highest numbers not exceeding three on the list of those voted for as President, the House of Representatives shall choose immediately, by ballot, the President. But in choosing the President, the votes shall be taken by States, the representation from each State having one vote; a quorum for this purpose shall consist of a member or members from two-thirds of the States, and a majority of all States shall be necessary to a choice. [And if the House of Representatives shall not choose a President whenever the right of choice shall devolve upon them, before the fourth day of March next following, then the Vice-President shall act as President, as in the case of the death or other constitutional disability of the President.][13]—The person having the greatest number of votes as Vice-President, shall be the Vice-President, if such number be a majority of the whole number of Electors appointed, and if no person have a majority, then from the two highest numbers on the list, the Senate shall choose the Vice-President; a quorum for the purpose

---

[13]Changed by the Twentieth Amendment.

shall consist of two-thirds of the whole number of Senators, and a majority of the whole number shall be necessary to a choice. But no person constitutionally ineligible to the office of President shall be eligible to that of Vice-President of the United States.

The original procedure set out for the election of president and vice president in Article II, Section 1, resulted in a tie in 1800 between Thomas Jefferson and Aaron Burr. It was not until the next year that the House of Representatives chose Jefferson to be president. This amendment changed the procedure by providing for separate ballots for president and vice president.

Amendment XIII.
(Ratified on December 6, 1865—
Prohibition of Slavery)

Section 1.
Neither slavery nor involuntary servitude, except as a punishment for crime whereof the party shall have been duly convicted, shall exist within the United States, or any place subject to their jurisdiction.

Some slaves had been freed during the Civil War. This amendment freed the others and abolished slavery.

Section 2.
Congress shall have power to enforce this article by appropriate legislation.

Amendment XIV.
(Ratified on July 9, 1868—
Citizenship, Due Process, and
Equal Protection of the Laws)

Section 1.
All persons born or naturalized in the United States, and subject to the jurisdiction thereof, are citizens of the United States and of the State wherein they reside. No State shall make or enforce any law which shall abridge the privileges or immunities of citizens of the United States; nor shall any State deprive any person of life, liberty, or property, without due process of law; nor deny to any person within its jurisdiction the equal protection of the laws.

Under this provision, states cannot make or enforce laws that take away rights given to all citizens by the federal government. States cannot act unfairly or arbitrarily toward, or discriminate against, any person.

Section 2.
Representatives shall be apportioned among the several States according to their respective numbers, counting the whole number of persons in each State, excluding Indians not taxed. But when the right to vote at any election for the choice of electors for President and Vice President of the United States, Representatives in Congress, the Executive

and Judicial officers of a State, or the members of the Legislature thereof, is denied to any of the male inhabitants of such State, being [twenty-one][14] years of age, and citizens of the United States, or in any way abridged, except for participation in rebellion, or other crime, the basis of representation therein shall be reduced in the proportion which the number of such male citizens shall bear to the whole number of male citizens twenty-one years of age in such State.

Section 3.
No person shall be a Senator or Representative in Congress, or elector of President and Vice President, or hold any office, civil or military, under the United States, or under any State, who having previously taken an oath, as a member of Congress, or as an officer of the United States, or as a member of any State legislature, or as an executive or judicial officer of any State, to support the Constitution of the United States, shall have engaged in insurrection or rebellion against the same, or given aid or comfort to the enemies thereof. But Congress may by a vote of two-thirds of each House, remove such disability.

This provision forbade former state or federal government officials who had acted in support of the Confederacy during the Civil War to hold office again. It limited the president's power to pardon those persons. Congress removed this "disability" in 1898.

Section 4.
The validity of the public debt of the United States, authorized by law, including debts incurred for payment of pensions and bounties for services in suppressing insurrection or rebellion, shall not be questioned. But neither the United States nor any State shall assume or pay any debt or obligation incurred in aid of insurrection or rebellion against the United States, or any claim for the loss or emancipation of any slave, but all such debts, obligations and claims shall be held illegal and void.

Section 5.
The Congress shall have power to enforce, by appropriate legislation, the provisions of this article.

Amendment XV.
(Ratified on February 3, 1870—
The Right to Vote)

Section 1.
The right of citizens of the United States to vote shall not be denied or abridged by the United States or by any State on account of race, color, or previous condition of servitude.

No citizen can be refused the right to vote simply because of race or color or because that person was once a slave.

---

[14]Changed by the Twenty-sixth Amendment.

Section 2.

The Congress shall have power to enforce this article by appropriate legislation.

Amendment XVI.
(Ratified on February 3, 1913— Income Taxes)

The Congress shall have power to lay and collect taxes on incomes, from whatever source derived, without apportionment among the several States, and without regard to any census or enumeration.

This amendment allows Congress to tax income without sharing the revenue so obtained with the states according to their population.

Amendment XVII.
(Ratified on April 8, 1913— The Popular Election of Senators)

Section 1.

The Senate of the United States shall be composed of two Senators from each State, elected by the people thereof, for six years; and each Senator shall have one vote. The electors in each State shall have the qualifications requisite for electors of the most numerous branch of the State legislatures.

Section 2.

When vacancies happen in the representation of any State in the Senate, the executive authority of such State shall issue writs of election to fill such vacancies: *Provided,* That the legislature of any State may empower the executive thereof to make temporary appointments until the people fill the vacancies by election as the legislature may direct.

Section 3.

This amendment shall not be so construed as to affect the election or term of any Senator chosen before it becomes valid as part of the Constitution.

This amendment modified portions of Article I, Section 3, that related to election of senators. Senators are now elected by the voters in each state directly. When a vacancy occurs, either the state may fill the vacancy by a special election, or the governor of the state involved may appoint someone to fill the seat until the next election.

Amendment XVIII.
(Ratified on January 16, 1919— Prohibition)

Section 1.

After one year from the ratification of this article the manufacture, sale, or transportation of intoxicating liquors within, the importation thereof into, or the exportation thereof from the United States and all territory subject to the jurisdiction thereof for beverage purposes is hereby prohibited.

Section 2.

The Congress and the several States shall have concurrent power to enforce this article by appropriate legislation.

Section 3.

This article shall be inoperative unless it shall have been ratified as an amendment to the Constitution by the legislatures of the several States, as provided in the Constitution, within seven years from the date of the submission hereof to the States by the Congress.[15]

This amendment made it illegal to manufacture, sell, and transport alcoholic beverages in the United States. It was repealed by the Twenty-first Amendment.

Amendment XIX.
(Ratified on August 18, 1920— Women's Right to Vote)

Section 1.

The right of citizens of the United States to vote shall not be denied or abridged by the United States or by any State on account of sex.

Section 2.

Congress shall have power to enforce this article by appropriate legislation.

Women were given the right to vote by this amendment, and Congress was given the power to enforce this right.

Amendment XX.
(Ratified on January 23, 1933— The Lame Duck Amendment)

Section 1.

The terms of the President and Vice President shall end at noon on the 20th day of January, and the terms of Senators and Representatives at noon on the 3d day of January, of the years in which such terms would have ended if this article had not been ratified; and the terms of their successors shall then begin.

This amendment modified Article I, Section 4, Clause 2, and other provisions relating to the president in the Twelfth Amendment. The taking of the oath of office was moved from March 4 to January 20.

Section 2.

The Congress shall assemble at least once in every year, and such meeting shall begin at noon on the 3d day of January, unless they shall by law appoint a different day.

Congress changed the beginning of its term to January 3. The reason the Twentieth Amendment is called the Lame Duck

---

[15]The Eighteenth Amendment was repealed by the Twenty-first Amendment.

Amendment is because it shortens the time between when a member of Congress is defeated for reelection and when he or she leaves office.

Section 3.

If, at the time fixed for the beginning of the term of the President, the President elect shall have died, the Vice President elect shall become President. If a President shall not have been chosen before the time fixed for the beginning of his term, or if the President elect shall have failed to qualify, then the Vice President elect shall act as President until a President shall have qualified; and the Congress may by law provide for the case wherein neither a President elect nor a Vice President elect shall have qualified, declaring who shall then act as President, or the manner in which one who is to act shall be selected, and such person shall act accordingly until a President or Vice President shall have qualified.

This part of the amendment deals with problem areas left ambiguous by Article II and the Twelfth Amendment. If the president dies before January 20 or fails to qualify for office, the presidency is to be filled as described in this section.

Section 4.

The Congress may by law provide for the case of the death of any of the persons from whom the House of Representatives may choose a President whenever the rights of choice shall have devolved upon them, and for the case of the death of any of the persons from whom the Senate may choose a Vice President whenever the right of choice shall have devolved upon them.

Congress has never created legislation pursuant to this section.

Section 5.

Sections 1 and 2 shall take effect on the 15th day of October following the ratification of this article.

Section 6.

This article shall be inoperative unless it shall have been ratified as an amendment to the Constitution by the legislatures of three-fourths of the several States within seven years from the date of its submission.

Amendment XXI.
(Ratified on December 5, 1933— The Repeal of Prohibition)

Section 1.

The eighteenth article of amendment to the Constitution of the United States is hereby repealed.

Section 2.

The transportation or importation into any State, Territory, or possession of the United States for delivery or use therein of intoxicating liquors, in violation of the laws thereof, is hereby prohibited.

Section 3.

This article shall be inoperative unless it shall have been ratified as an amendment to the Constitution by conventions in the several States, as provided in the Constitution, within seven years from the date of the submission hereof to the States by the Congress.

The amendment repealed the Eighteenth Amendment but did not make alcoholic beverages legal everywhere. Rather, they remained illegal in any state that so designated them. Many such "dry" states existed for a number of years after 1933. Today, there are still "dry" counties within the United States, in which the sale of alcoholic beverages is illegal.

Amendment XXII.
(Ratified on February 27, 1951— Limitation of Presidential Terms)

Section 1.

No person shall be elected to the office of the President more than twice, and no person who has held the office of President, or acted as President, for more than two years of a term to which some other person was elected President shall be elected to the office of President more than once. But this Article shall not apply to any person holding the office of President when this Article was proposed by the Congress, and shall not prevent any person who may be holding the office of President, or acting as President, during the term within which this Article becomes operative from holding the office of President or acting as President during the remainder of such term.

Section 2.

This article shall be inoperative unless it shall have been ratified as an amendment to the Constitution by the legislatures of three-fourths of the several States within seven years from the date of its submission to the States by the Congress.

No president may serve more than two elected terms. If, however, a president has succeeded to the office after the halfway point of a term in which another president was originally elected, then that president may serve for more than eight years, but not to exceed ten years.

Amendment XXIII.
(Ratified on March 29, 1961— Presidential Electors for the District of Columbia)

Section 1.

The District constituting the seat of Government of the United States shall appoint in such manner as the Congress may direct:

A number of electors of President and Vice President equal to the whole number of Senators and Representatives in Congress to which the District would be entitled if it were a State, but in no event more than the least populous State; they shall be in addition to those appointed by the States, but they shall be considered, for the purposes of the election of President and Vice President, to be electors appointed by a State; and they shall meet in the District and perform such duties as provided by the twelfth article of amendment.

Section 2.

The Congress shall have power to enforce this article by appropriate legislation.

Citizens living in the District of Columbia have the right to vote in elections for president and vice president. The District of Columbia has three presidential electors, whereas before this amendment it had none.

Amendment XXIV.
(Ratified on January 23, 1964—
The Anti–Poll Tax Amendment)

Section 1.

The right of citizens of the United States to vote in any primary or other election for President or Vice President, for electors for President or Vice President, or for Senator or Representative in Congress, shall not be denied or abridged by the United States, or any State by reason of failure to pay any poll tax or other tax.

Section 2.

The Congress shall have power to enforce this article by appropriate legislation.

No government shall require a person to pay a poll tax to vote in any federal election.

Amendment XXV.
(Ratified on February 10, 1967—
Presidential Disability and
Vice Presidential Vacancies)

Section 1.

In case of the removal of the President from office or of his death or resignation, the Vice President shall become President.

Whenever a president dies or resigns from office, the vice president becomes president.

Section 2.

Whenever there is a vacancy in the office of the Vice President, the President shall nominate a Vice President who shall take office upon confirmation by a majority vote of both Houses of Congress.

Whenever the office of the vice presidency becomes vacant, the president may appoint someone to fill this office, provided Congress consents.

Section 3.

Whenever the President transmits to the President pro tempore of the Senate and the Speaker of the House of Representatives his written declaration that he is unable to discharge the powers and duties of his office, and until he transmits to them a written declaration to the contrary, such powers and duties shall be discharged by the Vice President as Acting President.

Whenever the president believes she or he is unable to carry out the duties of the office, she or he shall so indicate to Congress in writing. The vice president then acts as president until the president declares that she or he is again able to carry out the duties of the office.

Section 4.

Whenever the Vice President and a majority of either the principal officers of the executive departments or of such other body as Congress may by law provide, transmit to the President pro tempore of the Senate and the Speaker of the House of Representatives their written declaration that the President is unable to discharge the powers and duties of his office, the Vice President shall immediately assume the powers and duties of the office as Acting President.

Thereafter, when the President transmits to the President pro tempore of the Senate and the Speaker of the House of Representatives his written declaration that no inability exists, he shall resume the powers and duties of his office unless the Vice President and a majority of either the principal officers of the executive department or of such other body as Congress may by law provide, transmit within four days to the President pro tempore of the Senate and the Speaker of the House of Representatives their written declaration that the President is unable to discharge the powers and duties of his office. Thereupon Congress shall decide the issue, assembling within forty-eight hours for that purpose if not in session. If the Congress, within twenty-one days after receipt of the latter written declaration, or, if Congress is not in session, within twenty-one days after Congress is required to assemble, determines by two-thirds vote of both Houses that the President is unable to discharge the powers and duties of his office, the Vice President shall continue to discharge the same as Acting President; otherwise, the President shall resume the powers and duties of his office.

Whenever the vice president and a majority of the members of the cabinet believe that the president cannot carry out her or his duties, they shall so indicate in writing to Congress. The vice president shall then act as president. When the president believes that she or he is able to carry out her or his duties again, she or he shall so indicate to the Congress. However, if the vice president and a majority of the cabinet do not agree, Congress must decide by a two-thirds vote within three weeks who shall act as president.

Amendment XXVI.
(Ratified on July 1, 1971— The Eighteen-Year-Old Vote)

Section 1.
The right of citizens of the United States, who are eighteen years of age or older, to vote shall not be denied or abridged by the United States or by any State on account of age.

No one over eighteen years of age can be denied the right to vote in federal or state elections by virtue of age.

Section 2.
The Congress shall have power to enforce this article by appropriate legislation.

Amendment XXVII.
(Ratified on May 7, 1992— Congressional Pay)

No law, varying the compensation for the services of the Senators and Representatives, shall take effect, until an election of representatives shall have intervened.

This amendment allows the voters to have some control over increases in salaries for congressional members. Originally submitted to the states for ratification in 1789, it was not ratified until 203 years later, in 1992.

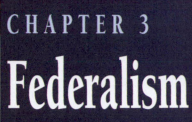

CHAPTER 3
Federalism

- Three Systems of Government

- Why Federalism?

- The Constitutional Basis for American Federalism

- Defining Constitutional Powers—The Early Years

- States' Rights and the Resort to Civil War

- The Continuing Dispute over the Division of Power

- The Politics of Federalism

- Federalism and the Supreme Court Today

WHAT IF . . .
Education Were a National Responsibility?

BACKGROUND

The U.S. Constitution provides us with a federal form of government, in which powers are *shared* by the national and state governments. The Constitution expressly grants certain powers to the national government and reserves the rest to the states. Still, the limits of national and state authority have been debated throughout our history.

Education traditionally has been a state responsibility, but in recent years, the national government has become more involved, notably through federal grants. These grants typically come with "strings attached" that require state governments to meet various standards as a condition for receiving funds. One example is the No Child Left Behind Act of 2002 (the NCLB), which requires regular testing of schoolchildren. What would it be like if the national government, instead of relying on conditional grants, had complete responsibility for the public schools?

WHAT IF EDUCATION WERE A NATIONAL RESPONSIBILITY?

If education were a national responsibility, there would certainly be more uniformity in education. Currently, educational procedures and curriculum requirements vary from state to state—and from locality to locality. If the national government were in control of education, this would change. Educational establishments might be run like other national government institutions. The army and the post office are examples: staff members of the post office or the army must adhere to an enormous body of rules. The rules are created in part to provide equal treatment for everyone by setting up uniform ways of doing things.

NATIONAL STANDARDS

No set of rules can cover every possible circumstance. Furthermore, a centralized system lacks flexibility. It was once said in France that the top education official in Paris could find out what every student in the country was doing just by looking at his watch. A national school system in the United States would have national standards that might cover everything from teacher training requirements to student dress codes. Schools in some small towns might have to stop offering certain foreign languages because they cannot find instructors with the certifications mandated by the national

government. Students in South Dakota might discover that they could not wear certain items of clothing because the items signify gang membership in Los Angeles.

The No Child Left Behind Act (NCLB) of 2002 is a step in the direction of national standards. The act can also serve as an example of some of the problems that elaborate national standards can create. Some of the standards imposed by the NCLB may, in the long run, be impossible to meet. By 2014, all students in all schools are expected to pass state tests. If a *single student* fails a test, the student's school will be "in need of improvement." Any school that remains in need of improvement for over five years must be "restructured," which may involve replacing staff or turning school operations over to a private firm or the state education agency. These provisions inspired one school principal to liken the 1,100-page NCLB to a Russian novel. "That's because it's long, it's complicated, and in the end, everybody gets killed."*

WHO WOULD PAY?

In a truly national system, the national government would pay for the schools. Probably, the schools would be funded

out of income taxes, rather than local property taxes. In our federal system, however, it is more likely that the national government would pay only a part of the costs. The national government would try to "bribe" the states into adopting a uniform system by making acceptance of national rules a condition for receiving national funds. A common complaint is that the existing NCLB is an "underfunded mandate," meaning that the national government does not provide sufficient funds to cover the costs of the program. For example, New Hampshire has estimated that its net cost of implementing the NCLB is $498 per student per year.[†]

FOR CRITICAL ANALYSIS

1. *How might the national government approach designing an education system if it were to assume complete control over education, rather than sharing authority in this area with the states?*

2. *What problems might result from imposing a uniform educational system on a large country that has great cultural and economic diversity?*

---

*Sherry Posnick-Goodwin, "Sizing Up the EISA," *California Educator,* February 2003. Available online at http://www.cta.org/CaliforniaEducator/v7i5/Feature_1.htm.

[†]William Mathis, "No Child Left Behind: Costs and Benefits," *Phi Delta Kappan,* May 2003. Available online at http://www.pdkintl.org/kappan/k0305mat.htm.

In the United States, rights and powers are reserved to the states by the Tenth Amendment. It may appear that since September 11, 2001, the federal government, sometimes called the national or central government, predominates. Nevertheless, that might be a temporary exaggeration, for there are 87,900 separate governmental units in this nation, as you can see in Table 3–1.

Visitors from France or Spain are often awestruck by the complexity of our system of government. Consider that a criminal action can be defined by state law, by national law, or by both. Thus, a criminal suspect can be prosecuted in the state court system or in the federal court system (or both). Often, economic regulation over exactly the same matter exists at the local level, the state level, and the national level—generating multiple forms to be completed, multiple procedures to be followed, and multiple laws to be obeyed. Many programs are funded by the national government but administered by state and local governments.

Relations between central governments and local units are structured in various ways. *Federalism* is one of these ways. Understanding federalism and how it differs from other forms of government is important in understanding the American political system. Indeed, many political issues today, including the education issue discussed in this chapter's opening *What If . . .* feature, would not arise if we did not have a federal form of government in which governmental authority is divided between the central government and various subunits.

 ## Three Systems of Government

There are almost two hundred independent nations in the world today. Each of these nations has its own system of government. Generally, though, we can describe how nations structure relations between central governments and local units in terms of three models: (1) the unitary system, (2) the confederal system, and (3) the federal system. The most popular, both historically and today, is the unitary system.

TABLE 3–1

Governmental Units in the United States

With almost 88,000 separate governmental units in the United States today, it is no wonder that intergovernmental relations in the United States are so complicated. Actually, the number of school districts has decreased over time, but the number of special districts created for single purposes, such as flood control, has increased from only about 8,000 during World War II to over 35,000 today.

Federal government		1
State governments		50
Local governments		87,849
Counties	3,034	
Municipalities	19,431	
(mainly cities or towns)		
Townships	16,506	
(less extensive powers)		
Special districts	35,356	
(water, sewer, and so on)		
School districts	13,522	
TOTAL		87,900

SOURCE: U.S. Census Bureau.

A third grader raises her reading test in the air to indicate to her teacher that she is finished. The test took place at the W. L. Smith Elementary School in Petal, Mississippi. Across Mississippi, test scores for public school students showed improvement in almost every subject and grade level, but state education officials said that hundreds of schools might not make the grade under the new No Child Left Behind law. How might teachers respond to the pressure to pass nationally sponsored tests? (AP Photo/*Hattiesburg American*, Gavin Averill)

Unitary System
A centralized governmental system in which local or subdivisional governments exercise only those powers given to them by the central government.

Confederal System
A system consisting of a league of independent states, each having essentially sovereign powers. The central government created by such a league has only limited powers over the states.

A Unitary System

A **unitary system** of government is the easiest to define. Unitary systems allow ultimate governmental authority to rest in the hands of the national, or central, government. Consider a typical unitary system—France. There are regions, departments, and municipalities (communes) in France. The regions, departments, and communes have elected and appointed officials. So far, the French system appears to be very similar to the U.S. system, but the similarity is only superficial. Under the unitary French system, the decisions of the lower levels of government can be overruled by the national government. The national government also can cut off the funding of many local government activities. Moreover, in a unitary system such as that in France, all questions of education, police, the use of land, and welfare are handled by the national government. Britain, Egypt, Ghana, Israel, Japan, the Philippines, and Sweden—in fact, most countries today—have unitary systems of government.[1]

A Confederal System

You were introduced to the elements of a **confederal system** of government in Chapter 2, when we examined the Articles of Confederation. A confederation is the opposite of a unitary governing system. It is a league of independent states in which a central government or administration handles only those matters of common concern expressly delegated to it by the member states. The central government has no ability to make laws directly applicable to member states unless the members explicitly support such laws. The United States under the Articles of Confederation was a confederal system.

Few, if any, confederations of this kind exist. One possible exception is the European Union, a league of countries that is developing unifying institutions, such as a common currency. Nations have also formed organizations with one another for limited purposes, such as military or peacekeeping cooperation. Examples are the North Atlantic Treaty Organization and the United Nations. These organizations, however, are not true confederations.

A Federal System

The federal system lies between the unitary and confederal forms of government. As mentioned in Chapter 2, in a *federal system,* authority is divided, usually by a written constitution, between a central government and regional, or subdivisional, governments (often called *constituent governments*). The central government and the constituent governments both act directly on the people through laws and through the actions of elected and appointed governmental officials. Within each government's sphere of authority, each is supreme, in theory. Thus, a federal system differs sharply from a unitary one in which the central government is supreme and the constituent governments derive their authority from it. Australia, Brazil, Canada, Germany, India, and Mexico are other examples of nations with federal systems. See Figure 3–1 for a comparison of the three systems.

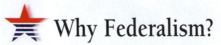 **Why Federalism?**

Why did the United States develop in a federal direction? We look here at that question, as well as at some of the arguments for and against a federal form of government.

---

[1]Recent legislation has altered somewhat the unitary character of the French political system. In Britain, the unitary nature of the government has been modified by the creation of the Scottish Parliament.

A Practical Solution

As you saw in Chapter 2, the historical basis of our federal system was laid down in Philadelphia at the Constitutional Convention, where advocates of a strong national government opposed states' rights advocates. This dichotomy continued through to the ratifying conventions in the several states. The resulting federal system was a compromise. The supporters of the new Constitution were political pragmatists—they realized that without a federal arrangement, there would be no ratification of the new Constitution. The appeal of federalism was that it retained state traditions and local power while establishing a strong national government capable of handling common problems.

Even if the colonial leaders had agreed on the desirability of a unitary system, size and regional isolation would have made such a system difficult operationally. At the time of the Constitutional Convention, the thirteen colonies taken together were much larger geographically than England or France. Slow travel and communication, combined with geographic spread, contributed to the isolation of many regions within the colonies. It could take several weeks for all of the colonies to be informed about a particular political decision.

Other Arguments for Federalism

The arguments for federalism in the United States and elsewhere involve a complex set of factors, some of which we already have noted. First, for big countries, such as the United States, India, and Canada, federalism allows many functions to be "farmed out" by the central government to the states or provinces. The lower levels of government that accept these responsibilities thereby can become the focus of political dissatisfaction rather than the national authorities. Second, even with modern transportation and communications systems, the large area or population of some nations makes it impractical to locate all political authority in one place. Finally, federalism brings government closer to the people. It allows more direct access to, and influence on, government agencies and policies, rather than leaving the population restive and dissatisfied with a remote, faceless, all-powerful central authority.

DID YOU KNOW . . .
That under Article I, Section 10, of the Constitution, no state is allowed to enter into any treaty, alliance, or confederation?

FIGURE 3–1

The Flow of Power in Three Systems of Government

In a unitary system, power flows from the central government to the local and state governments. In a confederal system, power flows in the opposite direction—from the state governments to the central government. In a federal system, the flow of power, in principle, goes both ways.

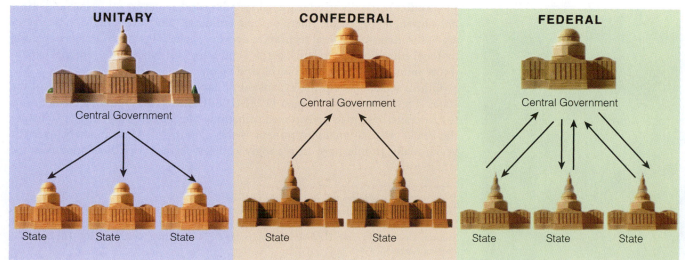

Air pollution in Los Angeles, California. In our federal system of government, states have often been the testing grounds for programs later adopted by the federal government for nationwide implementation. Air-pollution control, for example, was initiated in California to cope with the threatening conditions produced by a large population in a relatively enclosed valley. (Ron Watts, Stock Photo)

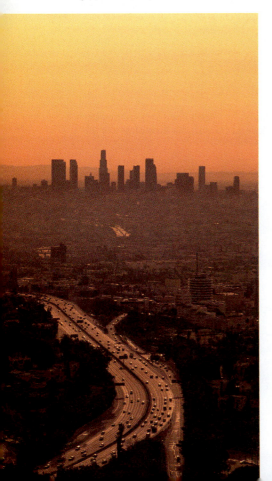

Benefits for the United States.   In the United States, federalism historically has yielded many benefits. State governments long have been a training ground for future national leaders. Many presidents made their political mark as state governors. The states themselves have been testing grounds for new government initiatives. As United States Supreme Court justice Louis Brandeis once observed:

> It is one of the happy incidents of the federal system that a single courageous state may, if its citizens choose, serve as a laboratory and try novel social and economic experiments without risk to the rest of the country.[2]

Examples of programs pioneered at the state level include unemployment compensation, which began in Wisconsin, and air-pollution control, which was initiated in California. Currently, states are experimenting with policies ranging from educational reforms to the medical use of marijuana to homeland security defense strategies. Since the passage of the 1996 welfare reform legislation—which gave more control over welfare programs to state governments—states have also been experimenting with different methods of delivering welfare assistance.

Federalism Allows for Many Political Subcultures.   The American way of life always has been characterized by a number of political subcultures, which divide along the lines of race and ethnic origin, region, wealth, education, and, more recently, degree of religious fundamentalism and sexual preference. The existence of diverse political subcultures would appear to be incompatible with a political authority concentrated solely in a central government. Had the United States developed into a unitary system, various political subcultures certainly would have been less able to influence government behavior than they have been, and continue to be, in our federal system.

Arguments against Federalism

Not everyone thinks federalism is such a good idea. Some see it as a way for powerful state and local interests to block progress and impede national plans. Smaller political units are more likely to be dominated by a single political group, and the dominant groups in some cities and states have resisted implementing equal rights for minority groups. (This was essentially the argument that James Madison put forth in *Federalist Paper* No. 10, which you can read in Appendix C of this text.) Some argue, however, that the dominant factions in other states have been more progressive than the national government in many areas, such as the environment.

Critics of federalism also argue that too many Americans suffer as a result of the inequalities across the states. As you will read later in this chapter, individual states differ markedly in educational spending and achievement, crime and crime prevention, and even the safety of their buildings. Not surprisingly, these critics argue for increased federal legislation and oversight. This might involve creating national educational standards, national building code standards, national expenditure minimums for crime control, and so on.

Others see dangers in the expansion of national powers at the expense of the states. President Ronald Reagan (1981–1989) said, "The Founding Fathers saw the federalist system as constructed something like a masonry wall. The States are the bricks, the national government is the mortar. . . . Unfortunately, over the years, many people have increasingly come to believe that Washington is the whole wall."[3]

---

[2]*New State Ice Co. v. Liebmann,* 285 U.S. 262 (1932).

[3]Text of the address by the president to the National Conference of State Legislatures, Atlanta, Georgia (Washington, D.C.: The White House, Office of the Press Secretary, July 30, 1981), as quoted in Edward Millican, *One United People: The Federalist Papers and the National Idea* (Lexington, Ky.: The University Press of Kentucky, 1990).

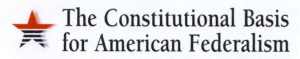

The Constitutional Basis for American Federalism

The term "federal system" cannot be found in the U.S. Constitution. Nor is it possible to find a systematic division of governmental authority between the national and state governments in that document. Rather, the Constitution sets out different types of powers. These powers can be classified as (1) the powers of the national government, (2) the powers of the states, and (3) prohibited powers. The Constitution also makes it clear that if a state or local law conflicts with a national law, the national law will prevail.

Powers of the National Government

The powers delegated to the national government include both expressed and implied powers, as well as the special category of inherent powers. Most of the powers expressly delegated to the national government are found in Article I, Section 8, of the Constitution. These **enumerated powers** include coining money, setting standards for weights and measures, making uniform naturalization laws, admitting new states, establishing post offices, and declaring war. Another important enumerated power is the power to regulate commerce among the states—a topic we deal with later in this chapter.

Enumerated Powers
Powers specifically granted to the national government by the Constitution. The first seventeen clauses of Article I, Section 8, specify most of the enumerated powers of the national government.

The Necessary and Proper Clause. The implied powers of the national government are also based on Article I, Section 8, which states that the Congress shall have the power

> [t]o make all Laws which shall be necessary and proper for carrying into Execution the foregoing Powers, and all other Powers vested by this Constitution in the Government of the United States, or in any Department or Officer thereof.

This clause is sometimes called the **elastic clause,** or the **necessary and proper clause,** because it provides flexibility to our constitutional system. It gives Congress all of those powers that can be reasonably inferred but that are not expressly stated in the brief wording of the Constitution. The clause was first used in the Supreme Court decision of *McCulloch v. Maryland*[4] (discussed later in this chapter) to develop the concept of implied powers. Through this concept, the national government has succeeded in strengthening the scope of its authority to meet the numerous problems that the framers of the Constitution did not, and could not, anticipate.

Elastic Clause, or Necessary and Proper Clause
The clause in Article I, Section 8, that grants Congress the power to do whatever is necessary to execute its specifically delegated powers.

Inherent Powers. A special category of national powers that is not implied by the necessary and proper clause consists of what have been labeled the inherent powers of the national government. These powers derive from the fact that the United States is a sovereign power among nations, and so its national government must be the only government that deals with other nations. Under international law, it is assumed that all nation-states, regardless of their size or power, have an *inherent* right to ensure their own survival. To do this, each nation must have the ability to act in its own interest among and with the community of nations—by, for instance, making treaties, waging war, seeking trade, and acquiring territory. Note that no specific clause in the Constitution says anything about the acquisition of additional land. Nonetheless, through the federal government's inherent powers, we made the Louisiana Purchase in 1803 and then went on to acquire Florida, Texas, Oregon, Alaska, Hawaii, and other lands. The United States grew from a mere thirteen states to fifty states, plus several "territories."

---

[4]4 Wheaton 316 (1819).

The national government has these inherent powers whether or not they have been enumerated in the Constitution. Some constitutional scholars categorize inherent powers as a third type of power, completely distinct from the delegated powers (both expressed and implied) of the national government.

Powers of the State Governments

The Tenth Amendment states that the powers not delegated to the United States by the Constitution, nor prohibited by it to the states, are reserved to the states, or to the people. These are the reserved powers that the national government cannot deny to the states. Because these powers are not expressly listed—and because they are not limited to powers that are expressly listed—there is sometimes a question as to whether a certain power is delegated to the national government or reserved to the states. State powers have been held to include each state's right to regulate commerce within its borders and to provide for a state militia. States also have the reserved power to make laws on all matters not prohibited to the states by the U.S. Constitution or state constitutions and not expressly, or by implication, delegated to the national government. Furthermore, the states have **police power**—the authority to legislate for the protection of the health, morals, safety, and welfare of the people. Their police power enables states to pass laws governing such activities as crimes, marriage, contracts, education, intrastate transportation, and land use.

The ambiguity of the Tenth Amendment has allowed the reserved powers of the states to be defined differently at different times in our history. When there is widespread support for increased regulation by the national government, the Tenth Amendment tends to recede into the background. When the tide turns the other way (in favor of states' rights), the Tenth Amendment is resurrected to justify arguments supporting increased states' rights.

Concurrent Powers

In certain areas, the states share **concurrent powers** with the national government. Most concurrent powers are not specifically listed in the Constitution; they are only implied. An example of a concurrent power is the power to tax. The types of taxation are divided between the levels of government. For example, states may not levy a tariff (a set of taxes on imported goods); only the national government may do this. Neither government may tax the facilities of the other. If the state governments did not have the power to tax, they would not be able to function other than on a ceremonial basis. Other concurrent powers include the power to borrow funds, to establish courts, and to charter banks and corporations. To a limited extent, the national government exercises police power, and to the extent that it does, police power is also a concurrent power. Concurrent powers exercised by the states are normally limited to the geographic area of each state and to those functions *not* granted by the Constitution exclusively to the national government (such as the coinage of money and the negotiation of treaties).

Prohibited Powers

The Constitution prohibits or denies a number of powers to the national government. For example, the national government has expressly been denied the power to impose taxes on goods sold to other countries (exports). Moreover, any power not granted expressly or implicitly to the federal government by the Constitution is prohibited to it. For example, the national government cannot create a national divorce law system. The states are also denied certain powers. For example, no state is allowed to enter into a treaty on its own with another country.

Police Power
The authority to legislate for the protection of the health, morals, safety, and welfare of the people. In the United States, most police power is reserved to the states.

Concurrent Powers
Powers held jointly by the national and state governments.

The Supremacy Clause

The supremacy of the national constitution over subnational laws and actions is established in the **supremacy clause** of the Constitution. The supremacy clause (Article VI, Clause 2) states the following:

> This Constitution, and the Laws of the United States which shall be made in Pursuance thereof; and all Treaties made . . . under the Authority of the United States, shall be the supreme Law of the Land; and the Judges in every State shall be bound thereby, any Thing in the Constitution or Laws of any State to the Contrary notwithstanding.

In other words, states cannot use their reserved or concurrent powers to thwart national policies. All national and state officers, including judges, must be bound by oath to support the Constitution. Hence, any legitimate exercise of national governmental power supersedes any conflicting state action.[5] Of course, deciding whether a conflict actually exists is a judicial matter, as you will soon read when we discuss the case of *McCulloch v. Maryland.*

National government legislation in a concurrent area is said to *preempt* (take precedence over) conflicting state or local laws or regulations in that area. One of the ways in which the national government has extended its powers, particularly during the twentieth century, is through the preemption of state and local laws by national legislation. In the first decade of the twentieth century, fewer than 20 national laws preempted laws and regulations issued by state and local governments. By the beginning of the twenty-first century, the number had risen to nearly 120.

Some political scientists believe that national supremacy is critical for the longevity and smooth functioning of a federal system. Nonetheless, the application of this principle has been a continuous source of conflict. Indeed, as you will see, the most extreme example of this conflict was the Civil War.

Vertical Checks and Balances

Recall from Chapter 2 that one of the concerns of the founders was to prevent the national government from becoming too powerful. For that reason, they divided the government into three branches—legislative, executive, and judicial. They also created a system of checks and balances that allowed each branch to check the actions of the others. The federal form of government created by the founders also involves checks and balances. These are sometimes called *vertical checks and balances* because they involve relationships between the states and the national government. They can be contrasted with *horizontal checks and balances,* in which the branches of government that are on the same level—either state or national—can check one other.

For example, the reserved powers of the states act as a check on the national government. Additionally, the states' interests are represented in the national legislature (Congress), and the citizens of the various states determine who will head the executive branch (the presidency). The founders also made it impossible for the central government to change the Constitution without the states' consent, as you read in Chapter 2. Finally, national programs and policies are administered by the states, which gives the states considerable control over the ultimate shape of those programs and policies.

Supremacy Clause
The constitutional provision that makes the Constitution and federal laws superior to all conflicting state and local laws.

---

[5]An example of this is President Dwight Eisenhower's disciplining of Arkansas governor Orval Faubus in 1957 by federalizing the National Guard to enforce the court-ordered desegregation of Little Rock High School.

Interstate compacts have long been used as a way to address issues that affect more than one state. An interstate compact between New York and New Jersey in 1921 created the Port Authority of New York and New Jersey to develop and maintain harbor facilities in that area, including the Port Authority Bus Terminal shown here. Today, there are over two hundred interstate compacts. (Robert Brenner, PhotoEdit)

Interstate Compact

An agreement between two or more states. Agreements on minor matters are made without congressional consent, but any compact that tends to increase the power of the contracting states relative to other states or relative to the national government generally requires the consent of Congress. Such compacts serve as a means by which states can solve regional problems.

The national government, in turn, can check state policies by exercising its constitutional powers under the clauses just discussed, as well as under the commerce clause (to be examined later). Furthermore, the national government can influence state policies indirectly through federal grants, as you will learn later in this chapter.

Interstate Relations

So far we have examined only the relationship between central and state governmental units. The states, however, have constant commercial, social, and other dealings among themselves. The national Constitution imposes certain "rules of the road" on interstate relations. These rules have had the effect of preventing any one state from setting itself apart from the other states. The three most important clauses governing interstate relations in the Constitution, all taken from the Articles of Confederation, require each state to do the following:

1. Give full faith and credit to every other state's public acts, records, and judicial proceedings (Article IV, Section 1).
2. Extend to every other state's citizens the privileges and immunities of its own citizens (Article IV, Section 2).
3. Agree to return persons who are fleeing from justice in another state back to their home state when requested to do so (Article IV, Section 2).

Following these constitutional mandates is not always easy for the states. For example, one question that has arisen in recent years is whether states will be constitutionally obligated to recognize same-sex marriages performed in other states. Another issue is the following: How can the states collect taxes on goods sold on Indian reservations? For a discussion of tribal rights under federalism, see the *Politics and Diversity* feature on the next page.

Additionally, states may enter into agreements called **interstate compacts**—if consented to by Congress. In reality, congressional consent is necessary only if such a compact increases the power of the contracting states relative to other states (or to the national government). Typical examples of interstate compacts are the establishment of the Port Authority of New York and New Jersey by an interstate compact between those two states in 1921 and the regulation of the production of crude oil and natural gas by the Interstate Oil and Gas Compact of 1935.

Defining Constitutional Powers—The Early Years

Recall from Chapter 2 that constitutional language, to be effective and to endure, must have some degree of ambiguity. Certainly, the powers delegated to the national government and the powers reserved to the states contain elements of ambiguity, thus leaving the door open for different interpretations of federalism. Disputes over the boundaries of national versus state powers have characterized this nation from the beginning. In the early 1800s, the most significant disputes arose over differing interpretations of the implied powers of the national government under the necessary and proper clause and over the respective powers of the national government and the states to regulate commerce.

Although political bodies at all levels of government play important roles in the process of settling such disputes, ultimately it is the Supreme Court that casts the final vote. As might be expected, the character of the referee will have an impact on the ultimate outcome of any dispute. From 1801 to 1835, the Supreme Court was headed by Chief Justice John Marshall, a Federalist who advocated a

POLITICS AND DIVERSITY
Tribal Governments and Federalism

One feature of American federalism is the existence of American Indian tribal governments. Under interpretations of the Constitution that date back to the founding of our nation, Indian affairs are a national, not a state, responsibility. Indian tribes are "domestic dependent nations" under the protection of the national government. The tribes exercise inherent sovereign powers over their members and territories. State governments have powers over reservation lands only when Congress has explicitly granted such powers to the states.

INDIAN GAMBLING CASINOS

American Indians have always been the most poverty-stricken ethnic group in the nation, and Indian leaders have long sought to promote economic development. In the 1980s, several tribes devised a solution that depended on their exemption from state laws. The plan was to organize bingo gambling on reservation lands. In the United States, the regulation of gambling has always been a state responsibility. As an example, for decades Nevada was the only state in the union to permit gambling casinos. Our federal system meant that neither the national government nor any other state could interfere in Nevada's gambling operations.

Indian leaders reasoned that because reservations were exclusively subject to national law, and because there was no national law against reservation gambling, they could establish bingo gambling enterprises. The United States Supreme Court agreed. In 1987, the Court ruled that when a state allowed other forms of gambling, it could not forbid Indian tribes from pursuing the same businesses. Only if a state banned all gambling (as is done in Utah and Hawaii) could it ban gambling on reservations.*

In reaction, Congress passed the Indian Gaming Regulatory Act of 1988. Under the act, to sponsor horse races, casinos, slot machines, or video poker, reservations had to negotiate compacts with state governments. (Bingo is exempt from this requirement.) Today, there are more than 310 tribal gambling operations, about 220 of which are Nevada-style casinos. A relatively limited number of people receive the benefits, not all of them Indians. Of the 558 federally recognized tribes, 22 collect 56 percent of the revenues. Indian poverty remains widespread. Still, gambling has become the most successful economic development scheme in Indian history.

A blackjack dealer deals cards for a player at her table in the Casino Sandia on the Sandia Pueblo, a reservation twelve miles north of Albuquerque, New Mexico. What problems could result when Indian tribes rely on gambling as a source of revenue? © Miguel Gandert/CORBIS

"A RIGHT WITHOUT A REMEDY"

A more heated controversy in relations between tribal and state governments is over the taxation of goods sold by tribally owned stores. In 1994, the Supreme Court ruled that states have the right to collect taxes on sales to non-Indian customers.[†] Because the tribes are sovereign entities, however, the states cannot sue the tribes if they fail to pay taxes. In legal language, the states have "a right without a remedy." This standoff has led to a number of unfortunate incidents. For example, in July 2003, the Rhode Island State Police raided a tobacco shop run by the Narragansett tribe. In the resulting scuffle, eight people were injured and eight Indians were arrested, including the tribe's leader.

FOR CRITICAL ANALYSIS

How might Congress resolve the issue of tax-free sales on reservations?

---

*California v. Cabazon Band of Mission Indians, 480 U.S. 202 (1987).

[†]Department of Taxation and Finance of New York v. Milhelm Attea & Bros, Inc., 512 U.S. 61 (1994).

strong central government. We look here at two cases decided by the Marshall Court: *McCulloch v. Maryland*[6] and *Gibbons v. Ogden*.[7] Both cases are considered milestones in the movement toward national government supremacy.

McCulloch v. Maryland (1819)

The U.S. Constitution says nothing about establishing a national bank. Nonetheless, at different times Congress chartered two banks—the First and Second Banks of the United States—and provided part of their initial capital; thus they were national banks. The government of Maryland imposed a tax on the Second Bank's Baltimore branch in an attempt to put that branch out of business. The branch's cashier, James William McCulloch, refused to pay the Maryland tax. When Maryland took McCulloch to its state court, the state of Maryland won. The national government appealed the case to the Supreme Court.

One of the issues before the Court was whether the national government had the implied power, under the necessary and proper clause, to charter a bank and contribute capital to it. The other important question before the Court was the following: If the bank was constitutional, could a state tax it? In other words, was a state action that conflicted with a national government action invalid under the supremacy clause?

Chief Justice Marshall held that if establishing such a national bank aided the national government in the exercise of its designated powers, then the authority to set up such a bank could be implied. Having established this doctrine of implied powers, Marshall then answered the other important question before the Court and established the doctrine of national supremacy. Marshall ruled that no state could use its taxing power to tax an arm of the national government. If it could, "the declaration that the Constitution . . . shall be the supreme law of the land, is [an] empty and unmeaning [statement]."

Marshall's decision enabled the national government to grow and to meet problems that the Constitution's framers were unable to foresee. Today, practically every expressed power of the national government has been expanded in one way or another by use of the necessary and proper clause.

---

[6]4 Wheaton 316 (1819).
[7]9 Wheaton 1 (1824).

John Marshall (1755–1835) was the fourth chief justice of the Supreme Court. When Marshall took over, the Court had little power and almost no influence over the other two branches of government. Some scholars have declared that Marshall is the true architect of the American constitutional system, because he single-handedly gave new power to the Constitution. What consequences might have followed if Marshall had taken a more restrictive view of the national government's powers? (The Library of Congress)

Gibbons v. Ogden (1824)

One of the most important parts of the Constitution included in Article I, Section 8, is the so-called **commerce clause,** in which Congress is given the power "[t]o regulate Commerce with foreign Nations, and among the several States, and with the Indian Tribes." The meaning of this clause was at issue in *Gibbons v. Ogden*.

Commerce Clause
The section of the Constitution in which Congress is given the power to regulate trade among the states and with foreign countries.

The Background of the Case. Robert Fulton and Robert Livingston secured a monopoly on steam navigation on the waters in New York State from the New York legislature in 1803. They licensed Aaron Ogden to operate steam-powered ferryboats between New York and New Jersey. Thomas Gibbons, who had obtained a license from the U.S. government to operate boats in interstate waters, decided to compete with Ogden, but he did so without New York's permission. Ogden sued Gibbons. The New York state courts prohibited Gibbons from operating in New York waters. Gibbons appealed to the Supreme Court.

There were actually several issues before the Court in this case. The first issue was how the term *commerce* should be defined. New York's highest court had defined the term narrowly to mean only the shipment of goods, or the interchange of commodities, *not* navigation or the transport of people. The second issue was whether the national government's power to regulate interstate commerce extended to commerce within a state (*intra*state commerce) or was limited strictly to commerce among the states (*inter*state commerce). The third issue was whether the power to regulate interstate commerce was a concurrent power (as the New York court had concluded) or an exclusive national power.

Marshall's Ruling. Marshall defined *commerce* as *all* commercial intercourse—all business dealings—including navigation and the transport of people. Marshall also held that the commerce power of the national government could be exercised in state jurisdictions, even though it cannot reach *solely* intrastate commerce. Finally, Marshall emphasized that the power to regulate interstate commerce was an *exclusive* national power. Marshall held that because Gibbons was duly authorized by the national government to navigate in interstate waters, he could not be prohibited from doing so by a state court.

Marshall's expansive interpretation of the commerce clause in *Gibbons v. Ogden* allowed the national government to exercise increasing authority over all areas of economic affairs throughout the land. Congress did not immediately exploit this broad grant of power. In the 1930s and subsequent decades, however, the commerce clause became the primary constitutional basis for national government regulation—as you will read later in this chapter.

★ States' Rights and the Resort to Civil War

The controversy over slavery that led to the Civil War took the form of a dispute over national government supremacy versus the rights of the separate states. Essentially, the Civil War brought to an ultimate and violent climax the ideological debate that had been outlined by the Federalist and Anti-Federalist parties even before the Constitution was ratified.

The Shift Back to States' Rights

As we have seen, while John Marshall was chief justice of the Supreme Court, he did much to increase the power of the national government and to reduce that of the states. During the Jacksonian era (1829–1837), however, a shift back to states' rights began. The question of the regulation of commerce became one of the major issues in federal-state relations. When Congress passed a tariff in 1828, the state of South Carolina unsuccessfully attempted to nullify the tariff (render it void), claiming that in cases of conflict between a state and the national government, the state should have the ultimate authority over its citizens.

Over the next three decades, the North and South became even more sharply divided—over tariffs that mostly benefited northern industries and over the slavery issue. On December 20, 1860, South Carolina formally repealed its ratification of the Constitution and withdrew from the Union. On February 4, 1861, representatives from six southern states met at Montgomery, Alabama, to form a new government called the Confederate States of America.

War and the Growth of the National Government

The ultimate defeat of the South in 1865 permanently ended any idea that a state could successfully claim the right to secede, or withdraw, from the Union. Ironically, the Civil War—brought about in large part because of the South's desire for increased states' rights—resulted in the opposite: an increase in the political power of the national government.

The War Effort.   Thousands of new employees were hired to run the Union war effort and to deal with the social and economic problems that had to be handled in the aftermath of war. A billion-dollar ($1.3 billion, which is over $11.5 billion in today's dollars) national government budget was passed for the first time in 1865 to cover the increased government expenditures. The first (temporary) income tax was imposed on citizens to help pay for the war. This tax and the increased national government spending were precursors to the expanded future role of the national government in the American federal system. Civil liberties were curtailed in the Union and in the Confederacy in the name of the wartime emergency. The distribution of pensions and widows' benefits also boosted the national government's social role. Many scholars contend that the North's victory set the nation on the path to a modern industrial economy and society.

A painting of a Civil War battle by H. Charles McBarron, Jr., shows the First U.S. Infantry Battalion fighting up-slope at Vicksburg, Mississippi, in 1863. How did the Civil War change attitudes toward the government in the South and in the North? (The Granger Collection, New York)

The Civil War Amendments. The expansion of the national government's authority during the Civil War was reflected in the passage of the Civil War amendments to the Constitution. Before the war, it was a bedrock constitutional principle that the national government should not interfere with slavery in the states. The Thirteenth Amendment, ratified in 1865, did more than interfere with slavery—it abolished the institution altogether. By abolishing slavery, the amendment also in effect abolished the rule by which three-fifths of the slaves were counted when apportioning seats in the House of Representatives. (See Chapter 2.) African Americans were now counted in full.

The Fourteenth Amendment (1868) defined who was a citizen of each state. It sought to guarantee equal rights under state law, stating that

> [no] State [shall] deprive any person of life, liberty, or property, without due process of law; nor deny to any person within its jurisdiction the equal protection of the laws.

In time, the courts interpreted these words to mean that the national Bill of Rights applied to state governments, a development that we will examine in Chapter 4. The Fourteenth Amendment also confirmed the abolition of the three-fifths rule. Finally, the Fifteenth Amendment (1870) gave African Americans the right to vote in all elections, including state elections—although a century would pass before that right was enforced.

★ The Continuing Dispute over the Division of Power

Although the outcome of the Civil War firmly established the supremacy of the national government and put to rest the idea that a state could secede from the Union, the war by no means ended the debate over the division of powers between the national government and the states. In fact, many current political issues raise questions about states' rights and federalism. For example, should the states have the right to legalize medical marijuana? We look at that question in this chapter's *Which Side Are You On?* feature on the following page.

The debate over the division of powers in our federal system can be viewed as progressing through at least two general stages since the Civil War: dual federalism and cooperative federalism.

Dual Federalism and the Retreat of National Authority

During the decades following the Civil War, the prevailing model was what political scientists have called **dual federalism**—a doctrine that emphasizes a distinction between federal and state spheres of government authority. Various images have been used to describe different configurations of federalism over time. Dual federalism is commonly depicted as a layer cake, because the state governments and the national government are viewed as separate entities, like separate layers in a cake. The national government is the top layer of the cake; the state government is the bottom layer. Nevertheless, the two layers are physically separate. They do not mix. For the most part, advocates of dual federalism did not believe that the state and national governments should exercise authority in the same areas.

A Return to Normal Conditions. The doctrine of dual federalism represented a revival of states' rights following the expansion of national authority during the Civil War. Dual federalism, after all, was a fairly accurate model of the prewar

Dual Federalism
A system in which the states and the national government each remain supreme within their own spheres. The doctrine looks on nation and state as co-equal sovereign powers. Neither the state government nor the national government should interfere in the other's sphere.

WHICH SIDE ARE YOU ON?
The Debate over Marijuana

In the last decade, nine states—Alaska, Arizona, California, Colorado, Maine, Nevada, Oregon, Vermont, and Washington—and Washington, D.C., have adopted laws legalizing marijuana, or cannabis, for medical use. Typically, laws legalizing marijuana use for medical reasons allow physicians to prescribe marijuana only for patients who are suffering from a terminal illness, such as cancer or AIDS.

The adoption of "medical marijuana" laws has triggered further debate over whether marijuana should be legalized for certain purposes. Because federal drug policy prohibits the use of marijuana for any purpose, the debate is whether drug policy should be dictated by the national government or left to the states.

Doug McVay and Charles Thomas handcuff themselves to the White House fence. The pair were protesting against the arrest of patients who use marijuana for medical reasons. (REUTERS/ Hyungwon Kang/Landov)

NATIONAL DRUG POLICY PREVAILS

State laws legalizing marijuana for medical purposes directly conflict with the federal Controlled Substances Act of 1970. This act defines marijuana as a substance subject to national control, and those who possess marijuana are subject to federal criminal penalties. The Constitution states, in the supremacy clause, that the Constitution and national laws and treaties are the supreme law of the land. Thus, if a state law conflicts with a national law, the national law takes priority. This means that state laws authorizing the use of marijuana for medical purposes, when challenged, may be invalidated by the courts. In one case involving an Oakland, California, cooperative that distributed cannabis to those who wanted it for medical purposes, the United States Supreme Court held that the national law prevailed.* (In December 2003, however, a federal appeals court ruled that the national government may have no authority when medical marijuana is not sold or transported across state lines.[†] This case will likely go to the Supreme Court.)

Many Americans believe that drug policy should be left in the hands of the national government. They argue that if each state could create its own laws on drugs, citizens would not have uniform protection against the problems stemming from drug use and abuse. After all, the use and sale of illegal drugs are nationwide problems.

LET THE STATES DECIDE

Proponents of medical marijuana argue that the national government should respect the wishes of the majority of the voters in the states that have legalized marijuana use for medical purposes. If this means revising federal drug policy, then that should be done. They also point out that several other nations, including England and Canada, have

legalized medical marijuana. Why shouldn't the United States do so as well?

Some supporters of medical marijuana go even further and contend that the mere possession of small amounts of marijuana for any purpose should be decriminalized. These advocates contend that marijuana is more like alcohol than like heroin or cocaine and therefore should not be treated like heroin or cocaine by the law.

Clearly, however, the national government has no interest in letting the states determine their own policies on marijuana. In 2002 and 2003, John P. Walters, director of the White House Office of National Drug Control Policy, undertook a nationwide tour to campaign against state ballot proposals that sought to reduce state penalties for marijuana possession. Nevada complained that Walters was, in effect, using federal funds to influence the outcome of a state election and accused Walters of refusing to file a Nevada campaign spending report.

WHAT'S YOUR POSITION?

If an initiative to legalize the use of marijuana for medical purposes were placed on your state's ballot, how would you vote? Why?

GOING ONLINE

The Marijuana Policy Project seeks to minimize the harm associated with marijuana (the greatest harm being, in its opinion, imprisonment) by promoting the legalization of marijuana for certain purposes, including medical uses. Visit its Web site at **http://www.mpp.org** for its views, as well as for information on recent developments in this area. The National Institute on Drug Abuse believes that more studies need to be undertaken before allowing marijuana to be prescribed for medical purposes. It offers information on marijuana and its effects at **http://www. nida.nih.gov/MarijBroch/Marijintro.html**.

*United States v. Oakland Cannabis Buyers' Cooperative, 532 U.S. 483 (2001).
[†]Raich v. Ashcroft, 352 F.3d 1222 (9th Cir. 2003).

consensus on state-national relations. For many people, it therefore represented a return to normal. The national income tax, used to fund the war effort and the reconstruction of the South, was ended in 1872. The most significant step to reverse the wartime expansion of national power took place in 1877, when President Rutherford B. Hayes withdrew the last federal troops from the South. This meant that the national government was no longer in a position to regulate state actions that affected African Americans. While the black population was now free, it was again subject to the authority of southern whites.

The Role of the Supreme Court.   The Civil War crisis drastically reduced the influence of the United States Supreme Court. In the prewar *Dred Scott* decision,[8] the Court had attempted to abolish the power of the national government to restrict slavery in the territories. In so doing, the Court placed itself on the losing side of the impending conflict. After the war, Congress took the unprecedented step of exempting the entire process of southern reconstruction from judicial review. The Court had little choice but to acquiesce.

In time, the Supreme Court reestablished itself as the legitimate constitutional umpire. Its decisions tended to support dual federalism, defend states' rights, and limit the powers of the national government. In 1895, for example, the Court ruled that a national income tax was unconstitutional.[9] In subsequent years, the Court gradually backed away from this decision and might eventually have overturned it. In 1913, however, the Sixteenth Amendment explicitly authorized a national income tax.

For the Court, dual federalism meant that the national government could intervene in state activities through grants and subsidies, but in most cases it was barred from regulating matters that the Court considered to be purely local. The Court generally limited the exercise of police power to the states. For example, in 1918, the Court ruled that a 1916 national law banning child labor was unconstitutional because it attempted to regulate a local problem.[10] In effect, the Court placed severe limits on the ability of Congress to legislate under the commerce clause of the Constitution.

---

[8]*Dred Scott v. Sanford,* 19 Howard 393 (1857).

[9]*Pollock v. Farmers' Loan & Trust Co.,* 157 U.S. 429 (1895); *Pollock v. Farmers' Loan & Trust Co.,* 158 U.S. 601 (1895).

[10]*Hammer v. Dagenhart,* 247 U.S. 251 (1918). This decision was overruled in *United States v. Darby,* 312 U.S. 100 (1940).

This photograph shows teenagers and young boys leaving a coal mine near Fairmont, West Virginia. In the 1800s, even very young children worked in coal mines. Today, national child-labor laws prohibit employers from hiring young workers for dangerous occupations. Why do you think the parents of these youths and children allowed them to work at such dangerous jobs? If no child-labor laws existed today, would a large percentage of children still be working in dangerous occupations? Why or why not? (Lewis Hine, The Library of Congress)

The New Deal and Cooperative Federalism

The doctrine of dual federalism receded into the background in the 1930s as the nation attempted to deal with the Great Depression. Franklin D. Roosevelt was inaugurated on March 4, 1933, as the thirty-second president of the United States. In the previous year, nearly 1,500 banks had failed (and 4,000 more would fail in 1933). Thirty-two thousand businesses had closed down, and almost one-fourth of the labor force was unemployed. The public expected the national government to do something about the disastrous state of the economy. But for the first three years of the Great Depression (1930–1932), the national government did very little.

The "New Deal."   President Herbert Hoover (1929–1933) clung to the doctrine of dual federalism and insisted that unemployment and poverty were local issues. The states, not the national government, had the sole responsibility for combating the effects of unemployment and providing relief to the poor. Roosevelt, however, did not feel bound by this doctrine, and his new Democratic administration energetically intervened in the economy. Roosevelt's "New Deal" included large-scale emergency antipoverty programs. In addition, the New Deal introduced major new laws regulating economic activity, such as the National Industrial Recovery Act of 1933, which established the National Recovery Administration (NRA). The NRA, initially the centerpiece of the New Deal, provided codes for every industry to restrict competition and regulate labor relations.

The End of Dual Federalism.   Roosevelt's expansion of national authority was challenged by the Supreme Court, which continued to adhere to the doctrine of dual federalism. In 1935, the Court ruled that the NRA program was unconstitutional.[11] The NRA had turned out to be largely unworkable and was unpopular. The Court, however, rejected the program on the ground that it regulated intrastate, not interstate, commerce. This position appeared to rule out any alternative recovery plans that might be better designed. Subsequently, the Court struck down the Agricultural Adjustment Act, the Bituminous Coal Act, a railroad retirement plan, legislation to protect farm mortgages, and a municipal bankruptcy act.

---

[11]*Schechter Poultry Corp. v. United States,* 295 U.S. 495 (1935).

President Franklin Delano Roosevelt (1933–1944). Roosevelt's national approach to addressing the effects of the Great Depression was overwhelmingly popular, although many of his specific initiatives were controversial. How did the Great Depression change the political beliefs of many ordinary Americans? (UPI)

In 1937, Roosevelt proposed legislation that would allow him to add up to six new justices to the Supreme Court. Presumably, the new justices would be more friendly to the exercise of national power than the existing members were. Roosevelt's move was widely seen as an assault on the Constitution. Congressional Democrats refused to support the measure, and it failed. Nevertheless, the "court-packing scheme" had its intended effect. Although the membership of the Court did not change, after 1937 the Court ceased its attempts to limit the national government's powers under the commerce clause. For the next half-century, the commerce clause would provide Congress with an unlimited justification for regulating the economic life of the country.

Cooperative Federalism.   Some political scientists have described the era since 1937 as characterized by **cooperative federalism,** in which the states and the national government cooperate in solving complex common problems. Roosevelt's New Deal programs, for example, often involved joint action between the national government and the states. The pattern of national-state relationships during these years gave rise to a new metaphor for federalism—that of a marble cake. Unlike a layer cake, in a marble cake the two types of cake are intermingled, and any bite contains cake of both flavors.

As an example of how national and state governments work together under the cooperative federalism model, consider Aid to Families with Dependent Children (AFDC), a welfare program that was initially established during the New Deal. (AFDC was replaced by Temporary Assistance to Needy Families—TANF—in 1996.) Under the AFDC program, the national government provided most of the funding, but state governments established benefit levels and eligibility requirements for recipients. Local welfare offices were staffed by state, not national, employees. In return for national funding, the states had to conform to a series of regulations on how the program was to be carried out. These regulations tended to become more elaborate over time.

The 1960s and 1970s were a time of even greater expansion of the national government's role in domestic policy. The evolving pattern of national-state-local government relationships during the 1960s and 1970s gave rise to yet another metaphor—**picket-fence federalism,** a concept devised by political scientist Terry Sanford. The horizontal boards in the fence represent the different levels of government (national, state, and local), while the vertical pickets represent the various programs and policies in which each level of government is involved. Officials at each level of government work together to promote and develop the policy represented by each picket.

Methods of Implementing Cooperative Federalism

Even before the Constitution was adopted, the national government gave grants to the states in the form of land to finance education. The national government also provided land grants for canals, railroads, and roads. In the twentieth century, federal grants increased significantly, especially during Roosevelt's administration during the Great Depression and again during the 1960s, when the dollar amount of grants quadrupled. These funds were used for improvements in education, pollution control, recreation, and highways. With this increase in grants, however, came a bewildering number of restrictions and regulations.

Categorical Grants.   By 1985, **categorical grants** amounted to more than $100 billion a year. They were spread out across four hundred separate programs, but the largest five accounted for over 50 percent of the revenues spent. These five programs involved Medicaid (health care for the poor), highway construction, unemployment benefits, housing assistance, and welfare programs to assist mothers

Cooperative Federalism
The theory that the states and the national government should cooperate in solving problems.

Picket-Fence Federalism
A model of federalism in which specific programs and policies (depicted as vertical pickets in a picket fence) involve all levels of government—national, state, and local (depicted by the horizontal boards in a picket fence).

Categorical Grants
Federal grants to states or local governments that are for specific programs or projects.

with dependent children and people with disabilities. For fiscal year 2005, the national government gave an estimated $225 billion to the states through federal grants. The shift toward a greater role for the central government in the United States can be clearly seen in Figure 3–2, which shows the increase in central government spending as a percentage of total government spending.

Before the 1960s, most categorical grants by the national government were *formula grants*. These grants take their name from the method used to allocate funds. They fund state programs using a formula based on such variables as the state's needs, population, or willingness to come up with matching funds. Beginning in the 1960s, the national government began increasingly to offer *program grants*. These grants require states to apply for grants for specific programs. The applications are evaluated by the national government, and the applications may compete with one another. Program grants give the national government a much greater degree of control over state activities than formula grants.

Why have federal grants to the states increased so much? One reason is that Congress has decided to offload some programs to the states and provide a major part of the funding for them. Also, Congress continues to use grants to persuade states and cities to operate programs devised by the federal government. Finally, states often are happy to apply for grants because they are relatively "free," requiring only that the state match a small portion of each grant. States can still face criticism for accepting the grants because their matching funds may be diverted from other state projects.

Feeling the Pressure—The Strings Attached to Federal Grants.   No dollars sent to the states are completely free of "strings," however; all funds come with requirements that must be met by the states. Often, through the use of grants, the national government has been able to exercise substantial control over matters that traditionally have been under the purview of state governments. When the federal government gives federal funds for highway improvements, for example, it may condition the funds on the state's cooperation with a federal policy. This is exactly what the federal government did in the 1980s and 1990s to force the states to raise their minimum drinking age to twenty-one.

Block Grants.   **Block grants** lessen the restrictions on federal grants given to state and local governments by grouping a number of categorical grants under

Block Grants
Federal programs that provide funds to state and local governments for general functional areas, such as criminal justice or mental-health programs.

FIGURE 3–2

The Shift toward Central Government Spending

Before the Great Depression, local governments accounted for 60 percent of all government spending, with the federal government accounting for only 17 percent. By 2005, federal government spending was almost two-thirds of the total.

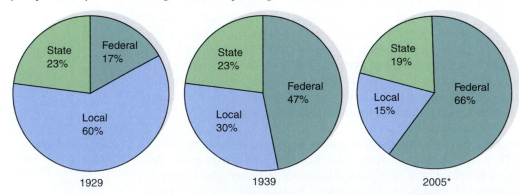

*Estimated.
SOURCE: U.S. Department of Commerce, Bureau of the Census and Bureau of Economic Analysis; Congressional Budget Office.

one broad heading. Governors and mayors generally prefer block grants because such grants give the states more flexibility in how the money is spent.

One major set of block grants provides aid to state welfare programs. The Personal Responsibility and Work Opportunity Reconciliation Act of 1996 ended the AFDC program. The TANF program that replaced AFDC provided a welfare block grant to each state. Each grant has an annual cap. According to some, this is one of the most successful block grant programs. Although state governments prefer block grants, Congress generally favors categorical grants because the expenditures can be targeted according to congressional priorities.

Federal Mandates.   For years, the federal government has passed legislation requiring that states improve environmental conditions and the civil rights of certain groups. Since the 1970s, the national government has enacted literally hundreds of **federal mandates** requiring the states to take some action in areas ranging from the way voters are registered, to ocean-dumping restrictions, to the education of persons with disabilities. The Unfunded Mandates Reform Act of 1995 requires the Congressional Budget Office to identify mandates that cost state and local governments more than $50 million to implement. Nonetheless, the federal government routinely continues to pass mandates for state and local governments that cost more than that to implement. Consider a recent federal mandate involving the expansion of eligibility for Medicaid, the federally subsidized but state-operated health-care program for low-income Americans. Some researchers predict that this mandate alone will have cost the states $70 *billion* a year during the first few years of the twenty-first century.

One way in which the national government has moderated the burden of federal mandates is by granting *waivers,* which allow individual states to try out innovative approaches to carrying out the mandates. For example, Oregon received a waiver to experiment with a new method of rationing health-care services under the federally mandated Medicaid program. Does Oregon's method show promise for improving the health of the poor? We look at that program in the *Politics and Diversity* feature on the next page.

Federal Mandate
A requirement in federal legislation that forces states and municipalities to comply with certain rules.

Under the No Child Left Behind Act (discussed in the *What If . . .* feature at the beginning of this chapter), a school that is rated "in need of improvement" over a period of five years must be "restructured." Presumably, this could mean closing the school, as suggested by the cartoonist. The No Child Left Behind Act imposes serious federal mandates on the states in return for funding by the national government.

POLITICS AND DIVERSITY
The Oregon Plan for Medicaid

Federalism is based on the recognition that the United States is geographically diverse. Waivers, which permit state experiments in managing national programs, are one expression of federalism. Medicaid, the national health-care system for the poor, has issued major program waivers to fifteen states. Medicaid is jointly funded by the national and state governments.

A DIFFERENT WAY TO RATION MEDICAL CARE

The Medicaid waiver that has drawn the most attention is the "Oregon Plan." Ordinarily, when states have difficulty paying for their share of Medicaid, they limit the number of people eligible for the program. In contrast, Oregon sought to reduce the cost of the Medicaid benefit package without seriously affecting the health of the participants. The savings would be used to extend coverage to members of the "working poor" who lacked health insurance. This concept became known as the Oregon Plan.

Under the plan, a state commission of physicians created a list of 745 medical diagnoses and treatments and ranked them by effectiveness. At the bottom of the list were those treatments that were least likely to help the patient. The plan would not pay for treatments falling below an arbitrary line on the list. In previous years, when states had achieved savings by removing people from

Medicaid altogether, there had been little public outcry. Explicitly rationing care by treatment was unusual, however, and there were widespread objections (though not in Oregon itself). In 1993, however, the Clinton administration accepted a modified version of the plan.

RESULTS OF THE OREGON PLAN

As a result of the plan, Oregon increased the number of Medicaid participants by 39 percent. The percentage of Oregonians without health insurance dropped from 14 percent to 12 percent during a time when the national figure rose from 14 percent to 15 percent. Unfortunately, Oregon was hard-hit by the 2001 recession. For several years, the state had the highest unemployment rate in the nation, and state finances were severely squeezed. In February 2004, through an initiative, Oregon voters repealed an emergency income tax increase, forcing major spending cuts. The working poor who had been added to the Medicaid program were removed. While the prioritized list of services remains, the savings are no longer allocated to increasing the number of persons covered but to reducing the overall cost of the program.

FOR CRITICAL ANALYSIS

What problems may arise as a result of rationing health care by a prioritized list of services?

The Politics of Federalism

As we have observed, the allocation of powers between the national and state governments continues to be a major issue. Traditionally, conservatives have been seen as advocates for the states, and liberals as supporters of the national government. For conservatives, support for states' rights is often a matter of principle. In addition, conservatives believe that leaving issues to the states often favors conservative policies. Liberals generally do not have the same level of ideological commitment to national power that conservatives have to states' rights. Liberal support for national authority is usually based solely on the belief that the national government is more likely than state governments to promote liberal goals such as alleviating poverty.

What Has National Authority Accomplished?

Why is it that conservatives have favored the states and liberals have favored the national government? One answer is that throughout American history, the expansion of national authority has typically been an engine of social change. Far more than the states, the national government has been willing to alter the status quo. The expansion of national authority during the Civil War freed the slaves—a major social revolution. During the New Deal, the expansion of national authority meant unprecedented levels of government intervention in the economy. In both the Civil War and New Deal eras, support for states' rights was a method of opposing these changes and supporting the status quo.

Some scholars believe that this equation was also a subtext in the Supreme Court's defense of states' rights between the Civil War and 1937. These scholars argue that the Supreme Court, in those years, came increasingly under the influence of *laissez-faire* economics—a belief that any government intervention in the economy was improper. When the Court struck down national legislation against child labor, for example, it was acting not only in defense of the states; an underlying motivation was the Court's belief that laws banning child labor were wrong no matter which level of government implemented them.

Civil Rights and the War on Poverty. A final example of the use of national power to change society was the presidency of Lyndon B. Johnson (1963–1969). Johnson oversaw the greatest expansion of national authority since the New Deal. Under Johnson, a series of civil rights acts forced the states to grant African Americans equal treatment under the law. Crucially, these acts included the abolition of all measures designed to prevent African Americans from voting. Johnson's Great Society and War on Poverty programs resulted in major increases in spending by the national government. As before, states' rights were invoked to support the status quo—states' rights meant no action on civil rights and no increase in antipoverty spending.

Why Should the States Favor the Status Quo? When state governments have authority in a particular field, there may be great variations from state to state in how the issues are handled. Inevitably, some states will be more conservative than others. Therefore, bringing national authority to bear on a particular issue may have the effect of imposing national standards on states that, for whatever reason, have not adopted such standards. One example is the voting rights legislation passed under President Johnson. By the 1960s, there was a national consensus that all citizens, regardless of race, should have the right to vote. A majority of the white electorate in certain states, however, did not share this view. National legislation was necessary to impose the national consensus on the recalcitrant states.

Another factor that may make the states more receptive to limited government, especially on economic issues, is competition among the states. It is widely believed that major corporations are more likely to establish new operations in states with a "favorable business climate." Such a climate may mean low taxes and therefore relatively more limited social services. If states compete with one another to offer the best business climate, the competition may force down taxes all around. Competition of this type may also dissuade states from implementing environmental regulations that restrict certain business activities. Those who deplore the effect of such competition often refer to it as a "race to the bottom." National legislation, in contrast, is not constrained by interstate competition.

A final factor that may encourage the states to favor the status quo is the relative power of local economic interests. A large corporation in a small state, for example, may have a substantial amount of political influence. Such a corporation, which has experienced success within the existing economic framework, may be opposed to any changes to that framework. These local economic interests may have less influence at the national level. This observation echoes James Madison's point in *Federalist Paper* No. 10 (see Appendix C of this text). Madison argued that a large federal republic would be less subject to the danger of "factions" than a small state.

Devolution
The transfer of powers from a national or central government to a state or local government.

Federalism Becomes a Republican Issue

In the years after 1968, the **devolution** of power from the national government to the states became a major ideological theme for the Republican Party. This devolution of power is commonly referred to as "federalism." This is a relatively new meaning for the word *federalism*, which was traditionally used to describe the American system generally, regardless of where the line between national and state power was to be drawn. Advocates of federalism today, however, have in mind a much stronger role for the states.

The "New Federalism."   The architects of Lyndon Johnson's War on Poverty were reluctant to let state governments have a role in the new programs. This reluctance was a response to the resistance of many southern states to African American civil rights. The Johnson administration did not trust the states to administer antipoverty programs in an impartial and efficient manner.

Republican president Richard Nixon (1969–1974), who succeeded Johnson in office, saw political opportunity in the Democrats' suspicion of state governments. Nixon advocated what he called a "New Federalism" that would devolve authority from the national government to the states. In part, the New Federalism involved the conversion of categorical grants into block grants, thereby giving state governments greater flexibility in spending. A second part of Nixon's New Federalism was *revenue sharing*. Under the revenue-sharing plan, the national government provided direct, unconditional financial support to state and local governments.

Nixon was able to obtain only a limited number of block grants from Congress. The block grants he did obtain, plus revenue sharing, substantially increased financial support to state governments. Republican president Ronald Reagan (1981–1989) was also a strong advocate of federalism, but some of his policies withdrew certain financial support from the states. Reagan was more successful than Nixon in obtaining block grants, but Reagan's block grants, unlike Nixon's, were less generous to the states than the categorical grants they replaced. Under Reagan, revenue sharing was eliminated.

President George W. Bush signs the No Child Left Behind Act into law in 2002 at Hamilton High School in Hamilton, Ohio. Why would the national government want to intervene in a traditionally local activity, such as evaluating the performance of the public schools?

Federalism in the Twenty-First Century. Today, federalism (in the sense of limited national authority) continues to be an important element in conservative ideology. At this point, however, it is not clear whether competing theories of federalism truly divide the Republicans from the Democrats in practice. Consider that under Democratic president Bill Clinton (1993–2001), Congress replaced the AFDC, a categorical welfare program, with the TANF block grants. This replacement was part of the Welfare Reform Act of 1996, which was perhaps the most significant domestic policy initiative of Clinton's administration. In contrast, a major domestic initiative of Republican president George W. Bush was increased federal funding and control of education—long a preserve of state and local governments. (We examined this issue in the chapter-opening *What If . . .* feature.)

Also, in some circumstances, liberals today may benefit from states' rights. One example is the issue of same-sex marriages, which we will examine more closely in Chapter 5. A minority of the states are much more receptive than the rest of the nation to same-sex marriages or to "civil unions" for gay male or lesbian partners. Liberals who favor such marriages or civil unions therefore have an incentive to oppose national legislation or an amendment to the national Constitution on this topic.

★ Federalism and the Supreme Court Today

The United States Supreme Court, which normally has the final say on constitutional issues, necessarily plays a significant role in determining the line between federal and state powers. Consider the decisions rendered by Chief Justice John Marshall in the cases discussed earlier in this chapter. Since the 1930s, Marshall's broad interpretation of the commerce clause has made it possible for the national government to justify its regulation of virtually any activity, even when an activity would appear to be purely local in character.

Since the 1990s, however, the Supreme Court has been reining in somewhat the national government's powers under the commerce clause. The Court also has given increased emphasis to state powers under the Tenth and Eleventh Amendments to the Constitution.

Reining in the Commerce Power

In a widely publicized 1995 case, *United States v. Lopez,*[12] the Supreme Court held that Congress had exceeded its constitutional authority under the commerce clause when it passed the Gun-Free School Zones Act in 1990. The Court stated that the act, which banned the possession of guns within one thousand feet of any school, was unconstitutional because it attempted to regulate an area that had "nothing to do with commerce, or any sort of economic enterprise." This marked the first time in sixty years that the Supreme Court had placed a limit on the national government's authority under the commerce clause.

In 2000, in *United States v. Morrison,*[13] the Court held that Congress had overreached its authority under the commerce clause when it passed the Violence against Women Act in 1994. The Court invalidated a key section of the act that provided a federal remedy for gender-motivated violence, such as rape. The Court noted that in enacting this law, Congress had extensively documented that violence against women had an adverse "aggregate" effect on interstate commerce: it deterred potential victims from traveling, from engaging in employment, and

---

[12]514 U.S. 549 (1995).
[13]529 U.S. 598 (2000).

from transacting business in interstate commerce. It also diminished national productivity and increased medical and other costs. Nonetheless, the Court held that evidence of an aggregate effect on commerce was not enough to justify national regulation of noneconomic, violent criminal conduct.

State Sovereignty and the Eleventh Amendment

In recent years, the Supreme Court has issued a series of decisions that bolstered the authority of state governments under the Eleventh Amendment to the Constitution. As interpreted by the Court, that amendment in most circumstances precludes lawsuits against state governments for violations of rights established by federal laws unless the states consent to be sued. For example, in a 1999 case, *Alden v. Maine,*[14] the Court held that Maine state employees could not sue the state for violating the overtime pay requirements of a federal act. According to the Court, state immunity from such lawsuits "is a fundamental aspect of the sovereignty which [the states] enjoyed before the ratification of the Constitution, and which they retain today."

In 2000, in *Kimel v. Florida Board of Regents,*[15] the Court held that the Eleventh Amendment precluded employees of a state university from suing the state to enforce a federal statute prohibiting age-based discrimination. In 2003, however, in *Nevada v. Hibbs,* the Court ruled that state employers must abide by the federal Family and Medical Leave Act (FMLA). The reasoning was that the FMLA seeks to outlaw gender bias, and government actions that may discriminate on the basis of gender must receive a "heightened review status" compared with actions that may discriminate on the basis of age or disability.[16] Also, in 2004 the Court ruled that the Eleventh Amendment could not shield states from suits by handicapped individuals who had been denied access to courtrooms located on the upper floors of buildings.[17]

Tenth Amendment Issues

The Tenth Amendment states: "The powers not delegated to the United States by the Constitution, nor prohibited by it to the States, are reserved to the States respectively, or to the people." In 1992, the Court held that requirements imposed on the state of New York under a federal act regulating low-level radioactive waste were inconsistent with the Tenth Amendment and thus unconstitutional. According to the Court, the act's "take title" provision, which required states to accept ownership of waste or regulate waste according to Congress's instructions, exceeded the enumerated powers of Congress. Although Congress can regulate the handling of such waste, "it may not conscript state governments as its agents" in an attempt to enforce a program of federal regulation.[18]

In 1997, the Court revisited this Tenth Amendment issue. In *Printz v. United States,*[19] the Court struck down the provisions of the federal Brady Handgun Violence Prevention Act of 1993 that required state employees to check the backgrounds of prospective handgun purchasers. Said the Court:

> [T]he federal government may neither issue directives requiring the States to address particular problems, nor command the States' officers, or those of their political subdivisions, to administer or enforce a federal regulatory program.

---

[14]527 U.S. 706 (1999).
[15]528 U.S. 62 (2000).
[16]538 U.S. 721 (2003).
[17]*Tennessee v. Lane,* 124 S.Ct. 1978 (2004).
[18]*New York v. United States,* 505 U.S. 144 (1992).
[19]521 U.S. 898 (1997).

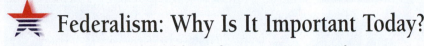

Federalism: Why Is It Important Today?

The fact that we have a federal form of government can touch your personal life in significant ways. For example, consider the federal-state conflict over the right to die. If you or one of your loved ones ends up suffering from a terminal illness, a pressing issue for you may be whether the state in which you live has a law allowing physician-assisted suicide and whether the federal government has allowed that law to stand.

Our federal form of government also means diversity—because different state and local governments have different laws, policies, and the like. For example, there is no one uniform body of national laws that set criminal penalties for persons found guilty by state courts. (There are, of course, national standards for federal courts.) For wrongdoers, the amount of time spent in prison often depends as much on where the crime was committed as on the crime itself—the sentences received for various crimes differ significantly from one region of the country to another (see Table 3–2). Even at the county level, there are great differences in criminal sentencing—just another reason why federalism is important. Consider the state of Georgia. Cocaine dealers sentenced in Henry and Butts Counties receive, on average, a sentence of nearly eighteen years in prison, while their counterparts in Fulton, Dekalb, Douglas, and Clayton Counties usually get six years or less.

Where you live will also determine your monthly welfare payment if you ever find yourself in need. The average welfare payment in Alaska is $827 per month, whereas the average payment in Texas is $127 per month. The chances that an application for welfare assistance will be granted vary greatly as well. In one recent period, North Carolina accepted 100 percent of 25,118 new applications for assistance, while Ohio denied 99.5 percent of 94,278 applications. Where you live also determines how much is spent per year for your child's education in the public schools. This amount ranges from over $11,000 per child in New York, Connecticut, and New Jersey to under $5,000 per child in Utah and North Dakota. In contrast, in a unitary system of government, government spending per year per pupil is effectively the same throughout the country. Generally, the diversity offered by a federal system means that you can "vote with your feet"—you can move to a state where more money is spent on education, welfare payments are higher, or politicians are "tougher on crime."

TABLE 3–2

Regional Sentencing Differences

As this table shows, punishment for crimes can vary significantly, depending on the region of the country in which the crime is prosecuted.

CRIME	MEAN PRISON SENTENCE IN SOUTH (IN MONTHS)	MEAN PRISON SENTENCE OUTSIDE SOUTH (IN MONTHS)
Rape	183	142
Robbery	130	96
Burglary	84	53

SOURCE: Bureau of Justice Statistics, *State Court Sentencing of Convicted Felons,* 1996 (Washington, D.C.: U.S. Department of Justice, 2000), 56–57, Tables 5.2 and 5.3.

MAKING A DIFFERENCE

★ Writing Letters to the Editor

Our federal system encourages debate over whether a particular issue should be a national, state, or local question. Also, because many questions are, in fact, state or local ones, it is easier for you to make a significant contribution to the discussion on these issues. Even in the largest states, there are many fewer people to persuade than in the nation as a whole. Attempts to influence your fellow citizens, by letters to the editor or other methods, can therefore be more effective.

Why Should You Care?

In this chapter, we have described a variety of issues arising from our federal system that may concern you directly. While the national government provides aid to educational programs, education is still primarily a state and local responsibility. The total amount of money spent on education is determined by state and local governments. Therefore, you can address this issue at the state or local level. As we have noted, welfare payments and sentences for crimes are also set at the state level. Gambling laws are another state responsibility. Do you enjoy gambling—or do you believe that the effects of gambling make it a social disaster? State law—or state negotiations with Indian tribes—determines the availability of gambling.

The question of which level of government should handle an issue may also affect you directly. Are you concerned that you might need medical marijuana someday, or do you believe that access to medical marijuana will subvert the drug laws and lead to greater problems from drug use? Either way, in any state that seeks to permit medical marijuana, the question of national versus state authority will determine the outcome of the debate.

What Can You Do?

One of the best ways to make your point on these or other issues is by writing an effective letter to the editor of your local newspaper (or even to a national newspaper such as the *New York Times*). First, you should familiarize yourself with the kinds of letters that are accepted by the newspapers to which you want to write. Then follow these rules for writing an effective letter:

1. Use a computer, and double-space the lines. If possible, use a spelling checker and grammar checker.

2. Your lead topic sentence should be short, to the point, and powerful.
3. Keep your thoughts on target—choose only one topic to discuss in your letter. Make sure it is newsworthy and timely.
4. Make sure your letter is concise; never let your letter exceed a page and a half in length (double-spaced).
5. If you know that facts were misstated or left out in current news stories about your topic, supply the facts. The public wants to know.
6. Don't be afraid to express moral judgments. You can go a long way by appealing to the readers' sense of justice.
7. Personalize the letter by bringing in your own experiences, if possible.
8. Sign your letter, and give your address (including your e-mail address, if you have one) and your telephone number.
9. Send your letter to the editorial office of the newspaper or magazine of your choice. Virtually all publications now have e-mail addresses and home pages on the Web. The Web sites usually give information on where you can send mail.

Key Terms

block grants 98	cooperative federalism 97	enumerated powers 85	police power 86
categorical grants 97	devolution 102	federal mandate 99	supremacy clause 87
commerce clause 91	dual federalism 93	interstate compact 88	unitary system 82
concurrent powers 86	elastic clause, or necessary and proper clause 85	picket-fence federalism 97	
confederal system 82			

Chapter Summary

1 There are three basic models for ordering relations between central governments and local units: (a) a unitary system (in which ultimate power is held by the national government), (b) a confederal system (in which ultimate power is retained by the states), and (c) a federal system (in which governmental powers are divided between the national government and the states). A major reason for the creation of a federal system in the United States is that it reflected a compromise between the views of the Federalists (who wanted a strong national government) and those of the Anti-Federalists (who wanted the states to retain their sovereignty).

2 The Constitution expressly delegated certain powers to the national government in Article I, Section 8. In addition to these expressed powers, the national government has implied and inherent powers. Implied powers are those that are reasonably necessary to carry out the powers expressly delegated to the national government. Inherent powers are those held by the national government by virtue of its being a sovereign state with the right to preserve itself.

3 The Tenth Amendment to the Constitution states that powers not delegated to the United States by the Constitution, nor prohibited by it to the states, are reserved to the states, or to the people. In certain areas, the Constitution provides for concurrent powers, such as the power to tax, which are powers that are held jointly by the national and state governments. The Constitution also denies certain powers to both the national government and the states.

4 The supremacy clause of the Constitution states that the Constitution, congressional laws, and national treaties are the supreme law of the land. States cannot use their reserved or concurrent powers to override national policies. "Vertical" checks and balances allow the states to influence the national government and vice versa.

5 The three most important clauses in the Constitution on interstate relations require that (a) each state give full faith and credit to every other state's public acts, records, and judicial proceedings; (b) each state extend to every other state's citizens the privileges and immunities of its own citizens; and (c) each state agree to return persons who are fleeing from justice back to their home state when requested to do so.

6 Two landmark Supreme Court cases expanded the constitutional powers of the national government. Chief Justice John Marshall's expansive interpretation of the necessary and proper clause of the Constitution in *McCulloch v. Maryland* (1819) enhanced the implied power of the national government. Marshall's broad interpretation of the commerce clause in *Gibbons v. Ogden* (1824) further extended the constitutional regulatory powers of the national government.

7 The controversy over slavery that led to the Civil War took the form of a fight over national government supremacy versus the rights of the separate states. Ultimately, the effect of the South's desire for increased states' rights and the subsequent Civil War was an increase in the political power of the national government.

8 Since the Civil War, federalism has evolved through at least two general phases: dual federalism and cooperative federalism. In dual federalism, each of the states and the federal government remain supreme within their own spheres. The era since the Great Depression has sometimes been labeled one of cooperative federalism, in which states and the national government cooperate in solving complex common problems.

9 Categorical grants from the federal government to state governments help finance many projects, such as Medicaid, highway construction, unemployment benefits, and welfare programs. By attaching special conditions to the receipt of federal grants, the national government can effect policy changes in areas typically governed by the states. Block grants, which group a number of categorical grants together, usually have fewer strings attached, thus giving state and local governments more flexibility in using funds. Federal mandates—laws requiring states to implement certain policies, such as policies to protect the environment—have generated controversy because of their cost.

10 Traditionally, conservatives have favored states' rights, and liberals have favored national authority. In part, this is because the national government has historically been an engine of change, while state governments have been more content with the status quo. States also have been reluctant to increase social spending because of a fear that the resulting taxes could interfere with a "favorable business climate" and cause new business enterprises to avoid the state.

11 Resistance to African American civil rights by the southern states prejudiced many people against states' rights in the 1960s. Renamed "federalism," the states' rights cause received Republican support in the 1970s and 1980s. Republican presidents Richard Nixon and Ronald Reagan sought to return power to the states through block grants and other programs. Under Republican president George W. Bush, however, the national government has gained power relative to the states.

12 The United States Supreme Court plays a significant role in determining the line between state and federal powers. Since the 1990s, the Court has been reining in somewhat the national government's powers under the commerce clause and has given increased emphasis to state powers under the Tenth and Eleventh Amendments to the Constitution.

 Selected Print and Media Resources

SUGGESTED READINGS

Farber, Daniel A. *Lincoln's Constitution.* Chicago: University of Chicago Press, 2003. The author discusses the Constitution as Lincoln found it on taking office. He then looks at the unprecedented constitutional issues that Lincoln faced during the Civil War.

Hamilton, Alexander, *et al. The Federalist: The Famous Papers on the Principles of American Government.* Benjamin F. Wright, ed. New York: Friedman/Fairfax Publishing, 2002. These essays remain an authoritative exposition of the founders' views on federalism.

Nagel, Robert F. *The Implosion of American Federalism.* New York: Oxford University Press, 2002. The author contends that despite the states' rights trend of recent years, which has been given force by the Supreme Court in several of its decisions, the nation faces the danger of increasingly centralized power.

Warren, Robert Penn. *All the King's Men,* rev. ed. Chicago: Harcourt Brace, 2001. This book is a fictionalized account of Governor Huey Long of Louisiana, one of the nation's "most astounding politicians."

MEDIA RESOURCES

Can the States Do It Better?—A 1996 film in which various experts discuss how much power the national government should have. The film uses documentary footage and other resources to illustrate this debate.

City of Hope—A 1991 movie by John Sayles. The film is a story of life, work, race, and politics in a modern New Jersey city. An African American alderman is one of the several major characters.

The Civil War—The PBS documentary series that made director Ken Burns famous. *The Civil War,* first shown in 1990, marked a revolution in documentary technique. Photographs, letters, eyewitness memoirs, and music are used to bring the war to life. The DVD version was released in 2002.

McCulloch v. Maryland and *Gibbons v. Ogden*—These programs are part of the series *Equal Justice under Law: Landmark Cases in Supreme Court History.* They provide more details on cases that defined our federal system.

e-mocracy ★ Your Federal, State, and Local Governments Are Available at a Click of Your Mouse

Although online voting remains rare, your access to federal, state, and local government offices has improved dramatically since the Internet entered just about everybody's life. The number of government services available online is growing rapidly. Some bureaucrats now talk about *e-government*. Instead of waiting in line to renew car registrations, residents of Scottsdale, Arizona, can renew online. In Colorado, heating and air-conditioning contractors can obtain permits from a Web site run by Net-Clerk, Inc. In many jurisdictions, all parking tickets can be handled with a credit card and a computer connected to the Internet.

At most colleges, it is now possible to apply online for financial aid. The federal government allows online applications for Social Security benefits and strongly encourages taxpayers to file their income tax returns electronically. Many citizens have found that e-government programs such as these make interactions with the government much simpler. It is no longer necessary to wait in line or to put up with the "bureaucratic shuffle."

Logging On

You can learn how some communities have benefited from implementing online government through EzGov, Inc., by reading some of the comments at EzGov's Web site. Go to

http://www.ezgov.com/customers

Federalism is an important aspect of our democracy. To learn more about the establishment of our federal form of government and about some of today's

issues relating to federalism, visit the Web sites listed in the remainder of this *Logging On* section.

To learn the founders' views on federalism, you can access the *Federalist Papers* online at

http://www.law.emory.edu/ erd/docs/federalist

The following site has links to U.S. state constitutions, the *Federalist Papers,* and international federations, such as the European Union:

http://www.constitution.org/cs_feder.htm

The Web site of the Council of State Governments is a good source for information on state responses to federalism issues:

http://www.csg.org

Another good source of information on issues facing state governments and federal-state relations is the National Governors Association's Web site at

http://www.nga.org

You can find a directory of numerous federalism links at

http://www.gmu.edu

The Brookings Institution's policy analyses and recommendations on a variety of issues, including federalism, can be accessed at

http://www.brook.edu

For a libertarian approach to issues relating to federalism, go to the Cato Institute's Web page at

http://www.cato.org

Using InfoTrac for Political Research

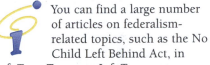

You can find a large number of articles on federalism-related topics, such as the No Child Left Behind Act, in InfoTrac. To access InfoTrac, go to

http://www.infotrac-college.com

Log on, go to InfoTrac College Edition, and then go to the Keyword search page. Type "no child left behind" into the text box, then click on "Search." InfoTrac will provide you with a list of articles sorted by date. Choose a selection of recent articles that address one of these questions: Is the act adequately funded? Do the tests mandated by the act make sense?

ONLINE REVIEW

At **http://politicalscience.wadsworth. com/schmidt12**, you will find a free Study Guide to this book. For each chapter, there are two online quizzes to help you master the material.

• The **PoliPrep Self Study Assessment** provides a pre-test for each major section of the chapter. PoliPrep then generates a customized study plan. After you complete the study plan, a post-test evaluates your progress.

• The **Tutorial Quiz** for each chapter provides questions on the chapter contents, including the features. The questions are organized to match the major sections of the chapter.

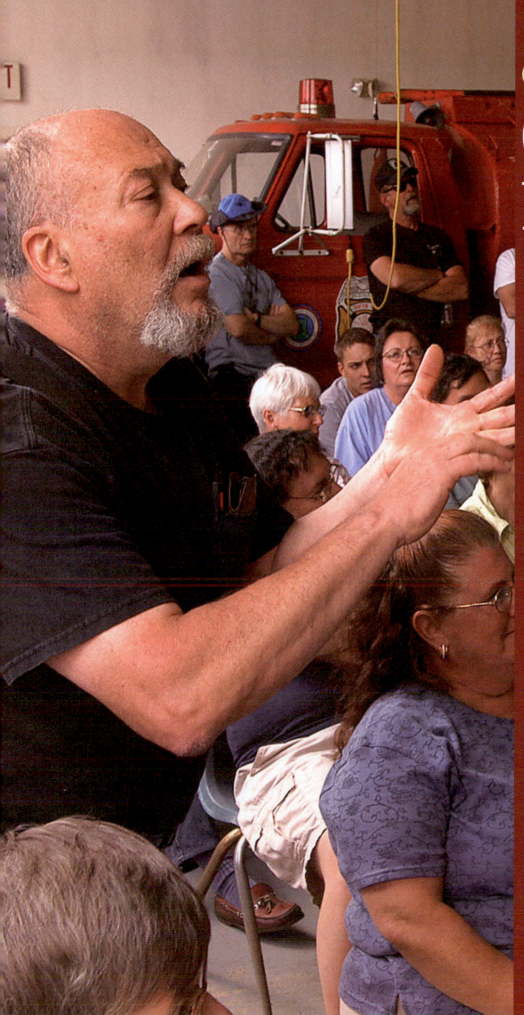

Civil Liberties

WHAT IF . . .
You Had to Carry a National Identification Card?

BACKGROUND

Many countries require their citizens to carry national identification cards. For example, in Spain this document is compulsory for anyone over fourteen years of age. Spaniards carry their national ID cards the same way we carry our driver's licenses. Most other countries in the European Union have mandatory state-issued identity card systems as well. Clearly, the precedent exists if the United States wishes to proceed with a national identification system. Traditionally, Americans have been opposed to a national ID card, but that changed after the terrorist attacks of September 11, 2001, when, at least for a short time, a majority of Americans were in favor of a national ID system.

WHAT IF YOU HAD TO CARRY A NATIONAL ID CARD?

We could have a system that would require every resident of the United States to obtain a national ID card at a certain age. On what basis would a card be issued? According to Joseph Atick, head of a New Jersey biometric information system manufacturer, "ID documents in the United States aren't worth the plastic they are printed on." Birth certificates are easily forged today, and fake driver's licenses are readily available on the Internet.

PERHAPS BIOMETRIC IDENTIFICATION SHOULD BE REQUIRED

An effective, but not 100 percent foolproof, national ID system might use some form of biometric identification involving facial or fingerprint scans. The ID card then could include retinal scans, palm prints, or standard thumbprints. Banks and other check-cashing facilities are already using thumbprints.

One problem with incorporating biometric information into cards is that they would be expensive. Such a system could take up to five years to implement and would cost billions of dollars.

USING SMART CARDS

A typical ID system uses "dumb" cards that can provide only the information actually printed on the cards. So-called smart cards, in contrast, contain a magnetic stripe, a computer chip, or some other technology that links each card to a central database. Such cards are used as debit cards in Europe already. U.S. passports are, in effect, smart cards because they contain a magnetic stripe. When you reenter the United States, your U.S. passport is swiped through a card-reading machine. The information is then linked to a central database. The same could be done with any national ID card system.

If we had a national ID system using smart cards, border-crossing guards, gun dealers, and airline employees could use card readers to monitor the persons with whom they are dealing. Required background checks for the purchase of firearms would be relatively inexpensive for the individual gun dealer instituting a check. (This ignores, of course, the multibillion-dollar cost of initiating and implementing such a system.)

We could also institute, along with a national ID system, background checks before an ID card is issued. All such information would be kept in a central database.

IS A NATIONAL ID SYSTEM IN OUR FUTURE?

A national ID system remains politically controversial. President George W. Bush has not overtly favored it. In contrast, Senator Dick Durbin (D., Ill.) has proposed federal funding for developing such a system. He wants to give state motor vehicle authorities access to computer databases maintained by the Social Security Administration, law enforcement agencies, and especially the U.S. Bureau of Citizenship and Immigration Services.

Durbin's concept mirrors that of many other supporters of such a system. Nonetheless, others simply want to improve current driver's licenses by making them harder to forge and allowing background checks.

Opponents of a national ID system have stood firm: they oppose it because of privacy problems. A national database could be used for inappropriate purposes—for example, an insurance company might use it to deny coverage to someone with a poor medical history. Opponents believe that the long-term erosion of privacy rights will far outweigh any benefits that a national ID card might offer in our fight against terrorism.

FOR CRITICAL ANALYSIS

1. *If you were convinced that a national ID system would help prevent future terrorism, would you support such a system despite its possible abuse?*
2. *How might a potential terrorist thwart any national ID system?*

"The land of the free." When asked what makes the United States distinctive, Americans will commonly say that it is a free country. Americans have long believed that limits on the power of government are an essential part of what makes this country free. The first ten amendments to the U.S. Constitution—the Bill of Rights—place such limits on the national government. Of these amendments, none is more famous than the First Amendment, which guarantees freedom of religion, speech, the press, and other rights.

Most other democratic nations have laws to protect these and other **civil liberties,** but none of the laws is quite like the First Amendment. Take the issue of "hate speech." What if someone makes statements that stir up hatred toward a particular race or other group of people? In Germany, where memories of Nazi anti-Semitism remain alive, such speech is unquestionably illegal. In the United States, the issue is not so clear. The courts have often extended constitutional protection to this kind of speech.

In this chapter, we describe the civil liberties provided by the Bill of Rights and some of the controversies that surround them. In addition to First Amendment liberties, we look at the right to privacy, which we touched on in the *What If . . .* feature that opened this chapter. We also examine the rights of defendants in criminal cases.

> **DID YOU KNOW . . .**
> That one of the proposed initial constitutional amendments,—"No State shall infringe the equal rights of conscience, nor the freedom of speech, nor of the press, nor of the right of trial by jury in criminal cases"—was never sent to the states for approval because the states' rights advocates in the First Congress defeated this proposal**?**

Civil Liberties
Those personal freedoms that are protected for all individuals. Civil liberties typically involve restraining the government's actions against individuals.

★ The Bill of Rights

As you read through this chapter, bear in mind that the Bill of Rights, like the rest of the Constitution, is relatively brief. The framers set forth broad guidelines, leaving it up to the courts to interpret these constitutional mandates and apply them to specific situations. Thus, judicial interpretations shape the true nature of the civil liberties and rights that we possess. Because judicial interpretations change over time, so do our liberties and rights. As you will read in the following pages, there have been many conflicts over the meaning of such simple phrases as *freedom of religion* and *freedom of the press*. To understand what freedoms we actually have, we need to examine how the courts—and particularly the United States Supreme Court—have resolved some of those conflicts. One important conflict was over the issue of whether the Bill of Rights in the federal Constitution limited state governments as well as the national government.

Extending the Bill of Rights to State Governments

Many citizens do not realize that, as originally intended, the Bill of Rights limited only the powers of the national government. At the time the Bill of Rights was ratified, there was little concern over the potential of state governments to curb civil liberties. For one thing, state governments were closer to home and easier to control. For another, most state constitutions already had bills of rights. Rather, the fear was of the potential tyranny of the national government. The Bill of Rights begins with the words, "Congress shall make no law . . . ." It says nothing about *states* making laws that might abridge citizens' civil liberties. In 1833, in *Barron v. Baltimore,*[1] the United States Supreme Court held that the Bill of Rights did not apply to state laws.

We mentioned that most states had bills of rights. These bills of rights were similar to the national one, but there were some differences. Furthermore, each state's judicial system interpreted the rights differently. Citizens in different states, therefore, effectively had different sets of civil rights. It was not until after the Fourteenth Amendment was ratified in 1868 that civil liberties guaranteed by the

---

[1]7 Peters 243 (1833).

Incorporation Theory
The view that most of the protections of the Bill of Rights apply to state governments through the Fourteenth Amendment's due process clause.

national Constitution began to be applied to the states. Section 1 of that amendment provides, in part, as follows:

> No State shall . . . deprive any person of life, liberty, or property, without due process of law.

Incorporation of the Fourteenth Amendment

There was no question that the Fourteenth Amendment applied to state governments. For decades, however, the courts were reluctant to define the liberties spelled out in the national Bill of Rights as constituting "due process of law," which was protected under the Fourteenth Amendment. Not until 1925, in *Gitlow v. New York*,[2] did the United States Supreme Court hold that the Fourteenth Amendment protected the freedom of speech guaranteed by the First Amendment to the Constitution.

Only gradually, and never completely, did the Supreme Court accept the **incorporation theory**—the view that most of the protections of the Bill of Rights are incorporated into the Fourteenth Amendment's protection against state government actions. Table 4–1 shows the rights that the Court has incorporated into the Fourteenth Amendment and the case in which it first applied each protection. As you can see in that table, in the fifteen years following the *Gitlow* decision, the Supreme Court incorporated into the Fourteenth Amendment the other basic freedoms (of the press, assembly, the right to petition, and religion) guaranteed by the First Amendment. These and the later Supreme Court decisions listed in Table 4–1 have bound the fifty states to accept for their citizens most of the rights and freedoms that are set forth in the U.S. Bill of Rights. We now look at some of those rights and freedoms, beginning with the freedom of religion.

★ Freedom of Religion

In the United States, freedom of religion consists of two principal precepts as they are presented in the First Amendment. The first precept guarantees the separation of church and state, and the second guarantees the free exercise of religion.

---

[2]268 U.S. 652 (1925).

TABLE 4–1

Incorporating the Bill of Rights into the Fourteenth Amendment

Year	Issue	Amendment Involved	Court Case
1925	Freedom of speech	I	*Gitlow v. New York*, 268 U.S. 652.
1931	Freedom of the press	I	*Near v. Minnesota*, 283 U.S. 697.
1932	Right to a lawyer in capital punishment cases	VI	*Powell v. Alabama*, 287 U.S. 45.
1937	Freedom of assembly and right to petition	I	*De Jonge v. Oregon*, 299 U.S. 353.
1940	Freedom of religion	I	*Cantwell v. Connecticut*, 310 U.S. 296.
1947	Separation of church and state	I	*Everson v. Board of Education*, 330 U.S. 1.
1948	Right to a public trial	VI	*In re Oliver*, 333 U.S. 257.
1949	No unreasonable searches and seizures	IV	*Wolf v. Colorado*, 338 U.S. 25.
1961	Exclusionary rule	IV	*Mapp v. Ohio*, 367 U.S. 643.
1962	No cruel and unusual punishment	VIII	*Robinson v. California*, 370 U.S. 660.
1963	Right to a lawyer in all criminal felony cases	VI	*Gideon v. Wainwright*, 372 U.S. 335.
1964	No compulsory self-incrimination	V	*Malloy v. Hogan*, 378 U.S. 1.
1965	Right to privacy	I, III, IV, V, IX	*Griswold v. Connecticut*, 381 U.S. 479.
1966	Right to an impartial jury	VI	*Parker v. Gladden*, 385 U.S. 363.
1967	Right to a speedy trial	VI	*Klopfer v. North Carolina*, 386 U.S. 213.
1969	No double jeopardy	V	*Benton v. Maryland*, 395 U.S. 784.

The Separation of Church and State—The Establishment Clause

The First Amendment to the Constitution states, in part, that "Congress shall make no law respecting an establishment of religion." In the words of Thomas Jefferson, the **establishment clause** was designed to create a "wall of separation of Church and State." Perhaps Jefferson was thinking about the religious intolerance that characterized the first colonies. Many of the American colonies were founded by groups that were in pursuit of religious freedom. Nonetheless, the early colonists were quite intolerant of religious beliefs that did not conform to those held by the majority of citizens within their own communities. Jefferson undoubtedly was also aware that state churches (denominations) were the rule; among the original thirteen American colonies, nine had *official* churches.

As interpreted by the Supreme Court, the establishment clause in the First Amendment means at least the following:

> Neither a state nor the federal government can set up a church. Neither can pass laws which aid one religion, aid all religions, or prefer one religion over another. Neither can force nor influence a person to go to or to remain away from church against his will or force him to profess a belief or disbelief in any religion. No person can be punished for entertaining or professing religious beliefs or disbeliefs, for church attendance or nonattendance. No tax in any amount, large or small, can be levied to support any religious activities or institutions, whatever they may be called, or whatever form they may adopt to teach or practice religion. Neither a state nor the federal government can, openly or secretly, participate in the affairs of any religious organizations or groups and vice versa.[3]

The establishment clause covers all conflicts about such matters as the legality of state and local government aid to religious organizations and schools, allowing or requiring school prayers, the teaching of evolution versus fundamentalist theories of creation, the posting of the Ten Commandments in schools or public places, and discrimination against religious groups in publicly operated institutions. The

---

[3]*Everson v. Board of Education,* 330 U.S. 1 (1947).

Establishment Clause
The part of the First Amendment prohibiting the establishment of a church officially supported by the national government. It is applied to questions of state and local government aid to religious organizations and schools, questions of the legality of allowing or requiring school prayers, and questions of the teaching of evolution versus fundamentalist theories of creation.

John Ashcroft, attorney general in the George W. Bush administration, defends the USA Patriot Act of 2001 at a meeting in Washington. Critics of the act argued that it threatens the civil liberties of American citizens. How can we simultaneously protect the country from terrorism and guard against the abuse of power by the government? (Reuters/ Larry Downing © Reuters/Corbis)

establishment clause's mandate that government can neither promote nor discriminate against religious beliefs raises particularly knotty questions at times. Should the courts hold that reciting the Pledge of Allegiance in public schools violates the establishment clause—because the pledge contains the words "under God"? (See this chapter's *Which Side Are You On?* feature for a discussion of this issue.)

Aid to Church-Related Schools.   Throughout the United States, all property owners except religious, educational, fraternal, literary, scientific, and similar nonprofit institutions must pay property taxes. A large part of the proceeds of such taxes goes to support public schools. But not all children attend public schools. Fully 12 percent of school-age children attend private schools, of which 85 percent have religious affiliations. Many cases have reached the Supreme Court in which the Court has tried to draw a fine line between permissible public aid to students in church-related schools and impermissible public aid to religion. These issues have arisen most often at the elementary and secondary levels.

In 1971, in *Lemon v. Kurtzman,*[4] the Court ruled that direct state aid could not be used to subsidize religious instruction. The Court in the *Lemon* case gave its most general statement on the constitutionality of government aid to religious schools, stating that the aid had to be secular (nonreligious) in aim, that it could not have the primary effect of advancing or inhibiting religion, and that the government must avoid "an excessive government entanglement with religion." All laws under the establishment clause are now subject to the three-part *Lemon* test. How the test is applied, however, has varied over the years.

In a number of cases, the Supreme Court has held that state programs helping church-related schools are unconstitutional. The Court also has denied state reimbursements to religious schools for field trips and for developing achievement tests. In a series of other cases, however, the Supreme Court has allowed states to use tax funds for lunches, textbooks, diagnostic services for speech and hearing problems, standardized tests, and transportation for students attending church-operated elementary and secondary schools. In 2000, in *Mitchell v. Helms,*[5] the Court held that the use of public funds to provide all schools, including parochial schools, with computers and Internet links did not violate the Constitution.

A Change in the Court's Position.   Generally, today's Supreme Court has shown a greater willingness to allow the use of public funds for programs in religious schools than was true at times in the past. Consider that in 1985, in *Aguilar v. Felton,*[6] the Supreme Court ruled that state programs providing special educational services for disadvantaged students attending religious schools violated the establishment clause. In 1997, however, when the Supreme Court revisited this decision, the Court reversed its position. In *Agostini v. Felton,*[7] the Court held that *Aguilar* was "no longer good law." What had happened between 1985 and 1997 to cause the Court to change its mind? Justice Sandra Day O'Connor answered this question in the *Agostini* opinion: what had changed since *Aguilar,* she stated, was "our understanding" of the establishment clause. Between 1985 and 1997, the Court's make-up had changed significantly. In fact, six of the nine justices who participated in the 1997 decision were appointed after the 1985 *Aguilar* decision.

School Vouchers.   Questions about the use of public funds for church-related schools are likely to continue as state legislators search for new ways to improve the

---

[4]403 U.S. 602 (1971).
[5]530 U.S. 793 (2000).
[6]473 U.S. 402 (1985).
[7]521 U.S. 203 (1997).

WHICH SIDE ARE YOU ON?
Should We Be One Nation "under God"?

The Pledge of Allegiance was first published in a children's magazine in 1892. It was endorsed by the U.S. Congress in 1942, during World War II. Since that time, the ritual of reciting the Pledge of Allegiance has been repeated time and again in the public schools. The wording of the pledge has changed slightly over the years. In 1954, Congress replaced the words "one nation" with "one nation under God" as part of a campaign against "godless communism." Now, this question has been raised: Should a pledge containing the words "under God" be recited at all in the public schools, or should the pre-1954 version of the pledge, which did not include these words, be reinstated?

INCLUDING "UNDER GOD" IN THE PLEDGE IS UNCONSTITUTIONAL

According to the U.S. Court of Appeals for the Ninth Circuit, a public school may not invite students to recite a pledge to "one nation under God." The court was reviewing a case brought by Michael Newdow, an atheist whose eight-year-old daughter attended a public school. In 1943, the Supreme Court made it clear that no child could be required to recite the pledge. Nonetheless, Newdow claimed that his daughter's constitutional rights were violated by having to "watch and listen" as her teacher led her classmates "in a ritual proclaiming that there is a God."

The federal appellate court agreed with Newdow's argument and held that the words "under God" in the Pledge of Allegiance violated the establishment clause. The court concluded that the words "under God" did not constitute a religiously neutral expression. Rather, it was equivalent to saying we are one nation "under Jesus" or some other deity. Reciting the pledge, said the court, is the same as swearing allegiance not only to the values for which the flag has traditionally stood but also to monotheism."*

Newdow later told news reporters that it "makes our country stronger when everyone's views are given equality, especially when it comes to religion." Newdow is not alone in taking this position, nor is he alone in being an atheist. Some 30 million Americans proclaim themselves to be nonreligious, atheistic, or agnostic. Another million, including Buddhists and Hindus, are not monotheistic and might find it hard to swear an oath of allegiance to a monotheistic deity.

LEAVE THE PLEDGE ALONE

Needless to say, the Ninth Circuit's ruling provoked a nationwide outcry. President George W. Bush harshly criticized the opinion and promised that the Justice Department would fight to overturn it. Polls revealed that a strong majority (84 percent) of Americans shared the president's sentiments.

Some of those who believe that the pledge should be left alone feel that acknowledging God in the pledge strengthens the nation. Indeed, in 1954, when President Dwight D. Eisenhower authorized the addition of the words "under God" to the pledge, he emphasized that we were strengthening "those spiritual weapons which forever will be our country's most powerful resource in peace and war."

Others believe that the words "under God" do not refer to any specific religion or deity but simply acknowledge the nation's religious heritage. They point out that references to God have been part and parcel of our national identity since its beginning. Today, many of our institutions of government, including the Supreme Court and both chambers of Congress, invoke God's blessing before sessions. Supporters contend that reciting the pledge is largely a ceremonial activity; it should not be regarded as an oath to a religious deity.

In June 2004, the United States Supreme Court ruled against Newdow on a technicality. The Court found that Newdow (who was divorced) did not have sufficient custody rights over his daughter to bring a suit on her behalf.† The Court therefore avoided ruling on the constitutionality of the Pledge, and the fundamental issue in this case remains unresolved.

WHAT'S YOUR POSITION?

Do you believe that public schools should invite students to recite a pledge that contains the words "under God" in it? Why or why not?

GOING ONLINE

Michael Newdow has set up a Web site on which he has posted information about his case. To access the site, go to **http://www.restorethepledge.com**. You can find an argument in favor of retaining the words "under God" in the pledge by reading the dissenting opinion in the Ninth Circuit's 2002 case. To find the case, key in the words "Newdow v. U.S. Congress" in any major search engine, such as Yahoo.

*Newdow v. U.S. Congress, 292 F.3d 597 (2002).

†Elk Grove Unified School District v. Newdow, 124 S.Ct. 2301 (2004).

educational system in this country. An issue that has come to the forefront in recent years is school vouchers. In a voucher system, educational vouchers (state-issued credits) can be used to "purchase" education at any school, public or private.

School districts in Florida, Ohio, and Wisconsin have all been experimenting with voucher systems. In 2000, the courts reviewed a case involving Ohio's voucher program. Under that program, some $10 million in public funds is spent annually to send 4,300 Cleveland students to fifty-one private schools, all but five of which are Catholic schools. The case presented a straightforward constitutional question: Is it a violation of the principle of separation of church and state for public tax money to be used to pay for religious education?

In 2002, the Supreme Court held that the Cleveland voucher program was constitutional.[8] The Court concluded, by a five-to-four vote, that Cleveland's use of taxpayer-paid school vouchers to send children to private schools was constitutional even though more than 95 percent of the students use the vouchers to attend Catholic or other religious schools. The Court's majority reasoned that the program did not unconstitutionally entangle church and state, because families theoretically could use the vouchers for their children to attend religious schools, secular private academies, suburban public schools, or charter schools, even though few public schools had agreed to accept vouchers. The Court's decision raised a further question that will need to be decided—whether religious and private schools that accept government vouchers must comply with disability and civil rights laws, as public schools currently are required to do.

The Issue of School Prayer—*Engel v. Vitale*.   Do the states have the right to promote religion in general, without making any attempt to establish a particular religion? That is the question in the matter of school prayer and was the precise issue presented in 1962 in *Engel v. Vitale*,[9] the so-called Regents' Prayer case in New York. The State Board of Regents of New York had suggested that a prayer be spoken aloud in the public schools at the beginning of each day. The recommended prayer was as follows:

> Almighty God, we acknowledge our dependence upon Thee,
> And we beg Thy blessings upon us, our parents, our teachers, and our Country.

Such a prayer was implemented in many New York public schools.

The parents of a number of students challenged the action of the regents, maintaining that it violated the establishment clause of the First Amendment. At trial, the parents lost. The Supreme Court, however, ruled that the regents' action was unconstitutional because "the constitutional prohibition against laws respecting an establishment of a religion must mean at least that in this country it is no part of the business of government to compose official prayers for any group of the American people to recite as part of a religious program carried on by any government." The Court's conclusion was based in part on the "historical fact that governmentally established religions and religious persecutions go hand in hand." In *Abington School District v. Schempp*[10] (1963), the Supreme Court outlawed officially sponsored daily readings of the Bible and recitation of the Lord's Prayer in public schools.

The Debate over School Prayer Continues.   Although the Supreme Court has ruled repeatedly against officially sponsored prayer and Bible-reading sessions in public schools, other means for bringing some form of religious expression into public education have been attempted. In 1983, the Tennessee legislature passed a bill requiring public school classes to begin each day with a minute of silence.

Children pray outside a Texas school. Officially organized prayer in public schools is in violation of Supreme Court rulings based on the First Amendment. If the Court were to hold that officially sponsored prayer in the schools did not violate the Constitution, what consequences might follow? (AP Photo/ *The Lufkin News,* Joel Andrews)

---

[8]*Zelman v. Simmons-Harris,* 536 U.S. 639 (2002).
[9]370 U.S. 421 (1962).
[10]374 U.S. 203 (1963).

Alabama had a similar law. In *Wallace v. Jaffree*[11] (1985), the Supreme Court struck down as unconstitutional the Alabama law authorizing one minute of silence for prayer or meditation in all public schools. Applying the three-part *Lemon* test, the Court concluded that the law violated the establishment clause because it was "an endorsement of religion lacking any clearly secular purpose."

Since then, the lower courts have interpreted the Supreme Court's decision to mean that states can require a moment of silence in the schools as long as they make it clear that the purpose of the law is secular, not religious. For example, in 2001 a federal appellate court upheld a Virginia law requiring public schools to observe a moment of silence at the beginning of the day. The Virginia law states that schools must pause for a minute of silence so that students may meditate, pray, or sit quietly.[12]

Prayer outside the Classroom.   The courts have also dealt with cases involving prayer in public schools outside the classroom, particularly prayer during graduation ceremonies. In 1992, in *Lee v. Weisman*,[13] the United States Supreme Court held that it was unconstitutional for a school to invite a rabbi to deliver a non-sectarian prayer at graduation. The Court said nothing about *students* organizing and leading prayers at graduation ceremonies and other school events, however, and these issues continue to come before the courts. A particularly contentious question in the last few years involves student-initiated prayers before sporting events, such as football games. In 2000, the Supreme Court held that while school prayer at graduation did not violate the establishment clause, students could not use a school's public-address system to lead prayers at sporting events.[14]

In spite of the Court's ruling, students in a number of schools in Texas continue to pray over public-address systems at sporting events. In other areas, the Court's ruling is skirted by avoiding the use of the public-address system. For example, in a school in North Carolina, a pregame prayer was broadcast over a local radio station and heard by fans who took radios to the game for that purpose.

The Ten Commandments.   A related church-state issue is whether the Ten Commandments may be displayed in public schools—or on any public property. In recent years, a number of states have considered legislation that would allow or even require schools to post the Ten Commandments in school buildings. Supporters of the "Hang Ten" movement claim that schoolchildren are not being taught the fundamental religious and family values that frame the American way of life. They argue further that the Ten Commandments are more than just religious documents. The commandments are also secular in nature because they constitute a part of the official and permanent history of American government.

Opponents of such laws claim that they are an unconstitutional government entanglement with the religious life of citizens. They point out that the Supreme Court, in its 1980 decision in *Stone v. Graham*,[15] held that a Kentucky law requiring that the Ten Commandments be posted in every public school classroom in the state violated the establishment clause. Still, various Ten Commandments installations have been found to be constitutional. For example, a U.S. court of appeals ruled in 2003 that a granite monument on the grounds of the Texas state capitol that contained the commandments was constitutional because of the secular nature of the monument as a whole.[16]

> ★★★★★★★★★★★★★★★★★
> **DID YOU KNOW . . .**
> That according to Gallup polls, only 10 percent of Americans say they hold a secular evolutionist view of the world, while 44 percent believe in strict biblical creationism**?**

---

[11]472 U.S. 38 (1985).
[12]*Brown v. Gilmore*, 258 F.3d 265 (4th Cir. 2001).
[13]505 U.S. 577 (1992).
[14]*Santa Fe Independent School District v. Doe*, 530 U.S. 290 (2000).
[15]449 U.S. 39 (1980).
[16]*Van Orden v. Perry*, 351 F.3d 173 (5th Cir. 2003).

Workers prepare to remove a monument of the Ten Commandments from the rotunda of the Alabama Supreme Court building in Montgomery, Alabama, in August 2003. Alabama Supreme Court chief justice Roy S. Moore had refused to remove the monument and, as a result, was expelled from the judiciary. The incident drew protests from a variety of Christian groups. In what circumstances might a religious symbol in a public building *not* violate the establishment clause? (Reuters/Tami Chappell © Reuters/Corbis)

The Ten Commandments controversy took an odd twist in 2003 when, in the middle of the night, Alabama chief justice Roy Moore installed a two-and-a-half-ton granite monument featuring the commandments in the rotunda of the state courthouse. When Moore refused to obey a federal judge's order to remove the monument, the Alabama Court of the Judiciary was forced to expel him from the judicial bench. The monument was wheeled away to a storage room.

Forbidding the Teaching of Evolution.   For many decades, certain religious groups, particularly in southern states, have opposed the teaching of evolution in the schools. To these groups, evolutionary theory directly counters their religious belief that human beings did not evolve but were created fully formed, as described in the biblical story of the creation. State and local attempts to forbid the teaching of evolution, however, have not passed constitutional muster in the eyes of the United States Supreme Court. For example, in 1968 the Supreme Court held, in *Epperson v. Arkansas,*[17] that an Arkansas law prohibiting the teaching of evolution violated the establishment clause, because it imposed religious beliefs on students. The Louisiana legislature passed a law requiring the teaching of the biblical story of the creation alongside the teaching of evolution. In 1987, in *Edwards v. Aguillard,*[18] the Supreme Court declared that this law was unconstitutional, in part because it had as its primary purpose the promotion of a particular religious belief.

Subsequently, a Louisiana school board required teachers in its district to recite disclaimers that evolution lessons are "not intended to influence or dissuade the Biblical version of Creation or any other concept." In 2000, a federal appellate court held that the disclaimer violated the establishment clause because it was aimed at the "protection and maintenance of a particular religious viewpoint."[19]

Nonetheless, state and local groups around the country, particularly in the so-called Bible Belt, continue their efforts against the teaching of evolution. The

[17]393 U.S. 97 (1968).
[18]482 U.S. 578 (1987).
[19]*Freiler v. Tangipahoa Parish Board of Education,* 201 F.3d 602 (5th Cir. 2000).

Tennessee legislature recently considered a bill that would allow a school to fire any teacher who presents evolution as fact. Alabama has approved a disclaimer to be inserted in biology textbooks, indicating that evolution is "a controversial theory some scientists present as a scientific explanation for the origin of living things." No doubt, these laws and policies will be challenged on constitutional grounds.

Religious Speech. Another controversy in the area of church-state relations concerns religious speech in public schools or universities. For example, in *Rosenberger v. University of Virginia*,[20] the issue was whether the University of Virginia violated the establishment clause when it refused to fund a Christian group's newsletter but granted funds to more than one hundred other student organizations. The Supreme Court ruled that the university's policy unconstitutionally discriminated against religious speech. The Court pointed out that the money came from student fees, not general taxes, and was used for the "neutral" payment of bills for student groups.

Later, the Supreme Court reviewed a case involving a similar claim of discrimination against a religious group, the Good News Club. The club offers religious instruction to young schoolchildren. The club sued the school board of a public school in Milford, New York, when the board refused to allow the club to meet on school property after the school day ended. The club argued that the school board's refusal to allow the club to meet on school property, when other groups, such as the Girl Scouts and the 4-H Club, were permitted to do so, amounted to discrimination on the basis of religion. Ultimately, the Supreme Court agreed, ruling in *Good News Club v. Milford Central School*[21] that the Milford school board's decision violated the establishment clause.

The Free Exercise Clause

The First Amendment constrains Congress from prohibiting the free exercise of religion. Does this **free exercise clause** mean that no type of religious practice can be prohibited or restricted by government? Certainly, a person can hold any religious belief that he or she wants, or a person can have no religious belief. When, however, religious *practices* work against public policy and the public welfare, the government can act. For example, regardless of a child's or parent's religious beliefs, the government can require certain types of vaccinations. Additionally, public school students can be required to study from textbooks chosen by school authorities.

The extent to which government can regulate religious practices has always been a subject of controversy. For example, in 1990, in *Oregon v. Smith*,[22] the United States Supreme Court ruled that the state of Oregon could deny unemployment benefits to two drug counselors who had been fired for using peyote, an illegal drug, in their religious services. The counselors had argued that using peyote was part of the practice of a Native American religion. Many criticized the decision as going too far in the direction of regulating religious practices.

The Religious Freedom Restoration Act. In 1993, Congress responded to the public's criticism by passing the Religious Freedom Restoration Act (RFRA). One of the specific purposes of the act was to overturn the Supreme Court's decision in *Oregon v. Smith*. The act required national, state, and local governments to "accommodate religious conduct" unless the government could show that there

Free Exercise Clause
The provision of the First Amendment guaranteeing the free exercise of religion.

[20]515 U.S. 819 (1995).
[21]533 U.S. 98 (2001).
[22]494 U.S. 872 (1990).

was a *compelling* reason not to do so. Moreover, if the government did regulate a religious practice, it had to use the least restrictive means possible.

Some people believed that the RFRA went too far in the other direction—it accommodated practices that were contrary to the public policies of state governments. Proponents of states' rights complained that the act intruded into an area traditionally governed by state laws, not by the national government. In 1997, in *City of Boerne v. Flores*,[23] the Supreme Court agreed and held that Congress had exceeded its constitutional authority when it passed the RFRA. According to the Court, the act's "sweeping coverage ensures its intrusion at every level of government, displacing laws and prohibiting official actions of almost every description and regardless of subject matter."

Free Exercise in the Public Schools.   The courts have repeatedly held that U.S. governments at all levels must remain neutral on issues of religion. In the *Good News Club* decision mentioned above, the Supreme Court ruled that "state power is no more to be used to handicap religions than it is to favor them." Nevertheless, by overturning the RFRA, the Court cleared the way for public schools to set regulations that, while ostensibly neutral, effectively limited religious expression by students. An example is a rule banning hats, which has been created by many schools as a way of discouraging the display of gang insignia. This rule has also been interpreted as barring yarmulkes, the small caps worn by strictly observant Jewish boys and men. Can there be good reasons for preventing public school students from displaying religious symbols? We examine that issue in this chapter's *Global View* feature.

Recently, the national government has found a new way to ensure that public schools do not excessively restrict religion. This method employs the No Child Left Behind Act of 2002, which we described in the *What If . . .* feature in Chapter 3. To receive funds under the act, schools must certify in writing that they do not ban prayer or other expressions of religion as long as they are made in a constitutionally appropriate manner.

★ Freedom of Expression

Perhaps the most frequently invoked freedom that Americans have is the right to free speech and a free press without government interference. Each of us has the right to have our say, and all of us have the right to hear what others say. For the most part, Americans can criticize public officials and their actions without fear of reprisal by any branch of our government.

No Prior Restraint

Prior Restraint
Restraining an action before the activity has actually occurred. When expression is involved, this means censorship.

Restraining an activity before that activity has actually occurred is called **prior restraint.** When expression is involved, prior restraint means censorship, as opposed to subsequent punishment. Prior restraint of expression would require, for example, that a permit be obtained before a speech could be made, a newspaper published, or a movie or TV show exhibited. Most, if not all, Supreme Court justices have been very critical of any governmental action that imposes prior restraint on expression. The Court clearly displayed this attitude in *Nebraska Press Association v. Stuart*,[24] a case decided in 1976:

> A prior restraint on expression comes to this Court with a "heavy presumption" against its constitutionality. . . . The government thus carries a heavy burden of showing justification for the enforcement of such a restraint.

---

[23]521 U.S. 507 (1997).
[24]427 U.S. 539 (1976). See also *Near v. Minnesota*, 283 U.S. 697 (1931).

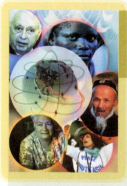

GLOBAL VIEW
The Head Scarves Issue

Under our federal system, it is up to state and local authorities to decide whether students are allowed to display religious insignia in the public schools. Given the strong religious beliefs of many Americans, however, few schools ban Christian crosses, the Jewish Star of David, or other religious symbols. Head coverings receive less protection, even though several religions endorse such coverings either for men or for women.

FRANCE BANS THE HEAD SCARF

In February 2004, the French National Assembly overwhelmingly approved a ban on religious apparel and symbols in the public schools. The law, which took effect in September 2004, was clearly aimed at the head scarves worn by many Muslim schoolgirls. The law was denounced fiercely in much of the Islamic world. It was also criticized by the Roman Catholic Church and by observers in other countries. Polls indicated, however, that Muslim women in France were split, with about half supporting and half opposing the ban. Many Muslim women welcome the law because it allows them to resist pressure from family members to wear a head scarf. For these women, the head scarf does not represent religious devotion but the second-class status of women in traditional Islamic societies.

A seventeen-year-old girl attends class in an all-girls Muslim school in Chicago. Students at this school typically wear head scarves. If this student attended a U.S. public school, could the school prohibit her from wearing such a scarf? Why or why not? (AP Photo/Aynsley Floyd)

THE BACKGROUND OF THE BAN

France has the largest Muslim minority in Western Europe. In recent years, the ideology of radical Islamism (see Chapter 1) has taken root in the Muslim districts of urban areas. Head scarves—previously rarely worn by Muslim schoolgirls in France—are widely seen as a symbol not just of Islamic piety but also of radical Islamism.

For the French authorities, one of the most dangerous characteristics of Islamism is its association with anti-Semitism. In 2002, France experienced a wave of anti-Semitic vandalism and attacks attributed to Islamists.

In January 2004, a march against the head scarf ban, which drew seven thousand participants, was organized by a leading Muslim anti-Semite. The march was boycotted by every mainstream Muslim organization in France. American

critics of the ban have often expressed concern that it also encompasses Jewish yarmulkes. This criticism is probably moot, however. By the early 2000s, observant Jewish schoolboys in much of France had already ceased to wear yarmulkes because of anti-Semitic harassment.

FOR CRITICAL ANALYSIS

Some say that the ban on head scarves in France is similar to the ban on gang insignia in a number of U.S. schools. Is this comparison reasonable? What difference does it make if head scarves are an expression of religious belief?

One of the most famous cases concerning prior restraint was *New York Times v. United States*[25] (1971), the so-called Pentagon Papers case. The *Times* and the *Washington Post* were about to publish the Pentagon Papers, an elaborate secret history of the U.S. government's involvement in the Vietnam War (1964–1975). The secret documents had been obtained illegally by a disillusioned former Pentagon official. The government wanted a court order to bar publication of the documents, arguing that national security was threatened and that the documents

---

[25]403 U.S. 713 (1971).

These protesters are burning an American flag as a symbolic expression of their opposition to government policy. Would a constitutional amendment to prohibit such actions place unacceptable limitations on symbolic speech? (Les Stone/Corbis Sygma)

Symbolic Speech
Nonverbal expression of beliefs, which is given substantial protection by the courts.

Commercial Speech
Advertising statements, which increasingly have been given First Amendment protection.

had been stolen. The newspapers argued that the public had a right to know the information contained in the papers and that the press had the right to inform the public. The Supreme Court ruled six to three in favor of the newspapers' right to publish the information. This case affirmed the no-prior-restraint doctrine.

Typically, prior restraints have been associated with the press. In 1999, though, the California Supreme Court issued a ruling that, according to some commentators, amounts to prior restraint in the workplace. The case involved several Hispanic employees who claimed that their supervisor's insults and racist comments had created a hostile work environment. The lower court agreed and awarded damages to the employees. In upholding the ruling, the California Supreme Court took the bold step of issuing a list of offensive words that can no longer be used in any workplace in the state, even among Hispanic Americans themselves. Three justices harshly dissented from the majority opinion, referring to it as "the exception that swallowed the First Amendment."[26]

The Protection of Symbolic Speech

Not all expression is in words or in writing. Articles of clothing, gestures, movements, and other forms of expressive conduct are considered **symbolic speech.** Such speech is given substantial protection today by our courts. For example, in a landmark decision issued in 1969, *Tinker v. Des Moines School District,*[27] the United States Supreme Court held that the wearing of black armbands by students in protest against the Vietnam War was a form of speech protected by the First Amendment. The case arose after a school administrator in Des Moines, Iowa, issued a regulation prohibiting students in the Des Moines School District from wearing the armbands. The Supreme Court reasoned that the school district was unable to show that the wearing of the armbands had disrupted normal school activities. Furthermore, the school district's policy was discriminatory, as it banned only certain forms of symbolic speech (the black armbands) and not others (such as lapel crosses and fraternity rings).

In 1989, in *Texas v. Johnson,*[28] the Supreme Court ruled that state laws that prohibited the burning of the American flag as part of a peaceful protest also violated the freedom of expression protected by the First Amendment. Congress responded by passing the Flag Protection Act of 1989, which was ruled unconstitutional by the Supreme Court in June 1990.[29] Congress and President George H. W. Bush immediately pledged to work for a constitutional amendment to "protect our flag"—an effort that has yet to be successful. Freedom of speech can also apply to group-sponsored events. In 1995, the Supreme Court held that forcing the organizers of Boston's St. Patrick's Day parade to include gays and lesbians violated the organizers' freedom of speech.[30]

In 2003, however, the Supreme Court held that a Virginia statute prohibiting the burning of a cross with "an intent to intimidate" did not violate the First Amendment. The Court concluded that a burning cross is an instrument of racial terror so threatening that it overshadows free speech concerns.[31]

The Protection of Commercial Speech

Commercial speech usually is defined as advertising statements. Can advertisers use their First Amendment rights to prevent restrictions on the content of com-

---

[26]*Aguilar v. Avis Rent A Car System,* 21 Cal.4th 121 (1999).
[27]393 U.S. 503 (1969).
[28]488 U.S. 884 (1989).
[29]*United States v. Eichman,* 496 U.S. 310 (1990).
[30]*Hurley v. Irish-American Gay, Lesbian and Bisexual Group of Boston,* 515 U.S. 557 (1995).
[31]*Virginia v. Black,* 538 U.S. 343 (2003).

mercial advertising? Until the 1970s, the Supreme Court held that such speech was not protected at all by the First Amendment. By the mid-1970s, however, more and more commercial speech had been brought under First Amendment protection. According to Justice Harry A. Blackmun, "Advertising, however tasteless and excessive it sometimes may seem, is nonetheless dissemination of information as to who is producing and selling what product for what reason and at what price."[32] Nevertheless, the Supreme Court will consider a restriction on commercial speech valid as long as it (1) seeks to implement a substantial government interest, (2) directly advances that interest, and (3) goes no further than necessary to accomplish its objective. In particular, a business engaging in commercial speech can be subject to liability for factual inaccuracies in ways that do not apply to noncommercial speech.

An interesting question is whether speech by a corporation is commercial when it does not take the form of an obvious advertisement. In 2003, in a surprise decision, the United States Supreme Court reversed itself and refused to hear *Nike v. Kasky,*[33] a case in which the California Supreme Court had held that almost any statement by a corporation constituted commercial speech. (The Court had earlier accepted the case for decision.) The case was settled out of court later in 2003.

Permitted Restrictions on Expression

At various times, restrictions on expression have been permitted. A description of several such restrictions follows.

Clear and Present Danger. When a person's remarks present a clear and present danger to the peace or public order, they can be curtailed constitutionally. Justice Oliver Wendell Holmes used this reasoning in 1919 when examining the case of a socialist who had been convicted for violating the Espionage Act by distributing a leaflet that opposed the military draft. Holmes stated:

> The question in every case is whether the words are used in such circumstances and are of such a nature as to create a *clear and present danger* that they will bring about the substantive evils that Congress has a right to prevent. It is a question of proximity and degree. [Emphasis added.][34]

According to the **clear and present danger test,** then, expression may be restricted if evidence exists that such expression would cause a condition, actual or imminent, that Congress has the power to prevent. Commenting on this test, Justice Louis D. Brandeis in 1920 said, "Correctly applied, it will reserve the right of free speech . . . from suppression by tyrannists, well-meaning majorities, and from abuse by irresponsible, fanatical minorities."[35]

Modifications to the Clear and Present Danger Rule. Since the clear and present danger rule was first enunciated, the United States Supreme Court has modified it. In *Gitlow v. New York,*[36] the Court introduced the *bad-tendency rule*. According to this rule, speech or other First Amendment freedoms may be curtailed if there is a possibility that such expression might lead to some "evil." In the *Gitlow* case, a member of a left-wing group was convicted of violating New York State's criminal anarchy statute when he published and distributed a pamphlet urging the violent overthrow of the U.S. government. In its majority opinion, the Supreme Court held that although the First Amendment afforded

★★★★★★★★★★★★★★★★★★

DID YOU KNOW . . .
That a local newspaper in Winchester, Indiana, refused to print a proposed antipornography ordinance because the newspaper considered the language of the ordinance too "obscene" to print?

Clear and Present Danger Test
The test proposed by Justice Oliver Wendell Holmes for determining when government may restrict free speech. Restrictions are permissible, he argued, only when speech presents a "clear and present danger" to the public order.

---

[32]*Virginia State Board of Pharmacy v. Virginia Citizens Consumer Council, Inc.,* 425 U.S. 748 (1976).
[33]119 Cal.Rptr.2d 296 (2002).
[34]*Schenck v. United States,* 249 U.S. 47 (1919).
[35]*Schaefer v. United States,* 251 U.S. 466 (1920).
[36]268 U.S. 652 (1925).

protection against state incursions on freedom of expression, Gitlow could be punished legally in this particular instance because his expression would tend to bring about evils that the state had a right to prevent.

The Supreme Court again modified the clear and present danger test in a 1951 case, *Dennis v. United States.*[37] At the time, there was considerable tension between the United States and the Soviet Union, a communist-ruled country that included Russia and several other modern-day nations. Twelve members of the American Communist Party were convicted of violating a statute that made it a crime to conspire to teach, advocate, or organize the violent overthrow of any government in the United States. The Supreme Court affirmed the convictions, significantly modifying the clear and present danger test in the process. The Court applied a *grave and probable danger rule.* Under this rule, "the gravity of the 'evil' discounted by its improbability justifies such invasion of free speech as is necessary to avoid the danger." This rule gave much less protection to free speech than did the clear and present danger test.

Some claim that the United States did not achieve true freedom of political speech until 1969. In that year, in *Brandenburg v. Ohio,*[38] the Supreme Court overturned the conviction of a Ku Klux Klan leader for violating a state statute. The statute prohibited anyone from advocating "the duty, necessity, or propriety of sabotage, violence, or unlawful methods of terrorism as a means of accomplishing industrial or political reform." The Court held that the guarantee of free speech does not permit a state "to forbid or proscribe advocacy of the use of force or of law violation except where such advocacy is directed to inciting or producing imminent lawless actions and is likely to incite or produce such action." The *incitement test* enunciated by the Court in this case is a difficult one for prosecutors to meet. As a result, the Court's decision significantly broadened the protection given to advocacy speech.

Unprotected Speech: Obscenity

A large number of state and federal statutes make it a crime to disseminate obscene materials. Generally, the courts have not been willing to extend constitutional protections of free speech to what they consider obscene materials. But what is obscenity? Justice Potter Stewart once stated, in *Jacobellis v. Ohio,*[39] a 1964 case, that even though he could not define *obscenity,* "I know it when I see it." The problem, of course, is that even if it were agreed on, the definition of *obscenity* changes with the times. Victorians deeply disapproved of the "loose" morals of the Elizabethan Age. The works of Mark Twain and Edgar Rice Burroughs at times have been considered obscene (after all, Tarzan and Jane were not legally wedded).

Definitional Problems.　The Supreme Court has grappled from time to time with the difficulty of specifying an operationally effective definition of *obscenity.* In 1973, in *Miller v. California,*[40] Chief Justice Warren Burger created a formal list of requirements that currently must be met for material to be legally obscene. Material is obscene if (1) the average person finds that it violates contemporary community standards; (2) the work taken as a whole appeals to a prurient interest in sex; (3) the work shows patently offensive sexual conduct; and (4) the work lacks serious redeeming literary, artistic, political, or scientific merit. The problem, of course, is that one person's prurient interest is another person's medical interest or artistic pleasure. The Court went on to state that the definition of *prurient interest* would be determined by the community's standards. The Court

---

[37]341 U.S. 494 (1951).
[38]395 U.S. 444 (1969).
[39]378 U.S. 184 (1964).
[40]413 U.S. 5 (1973).

avoided presenting a definition of *obscenity,* leaving this determination to local and state authorities. Consequently, the *Miller* case has been applied in a widely inconsistent manner.

Protecting Children.   The Supreme Court has upheld state laws making it illegal to sell materials showing sexual performances by minors. In 1990, in *Osborne v. Ohio,*[41] the Court ruled that states can outlaw the possession of child pornography in the home. The Court reasoned that the ban on private possession is justified because owning the material perpetuates commercial demand for it and for the exploitation of the children involved. At the federal level, the Child Protection Act of 1984 made it a crime to receive knowingly through the mails sexually explicit depictions of children.

Pornography on the Internet.   A significant problem facing Americans and their lawmakers today is how to control obscenity and child pornography that are disseminated by way of the Internet. In 1996, Congress first attempted to protect minors from pornographic materials on the Internet by passing the Communications Decency Act (CDA). The act made it a crime to make available to minors online any "obscene or indecent" message that "depicts or describes, in terms patently offensive as measured by contemporary community standards, sexual or excretory activities or organs." The act was immediately challenged in court as an unconstitutional infringement on free speech. The Supreme Court held that the act imposed unconstitutional restraints on free speech and was therefore invalid.[42] In the eyes of the Court, the terms *indecent* and *patently offensive* covered large amounts of nonpornographic material with serious educational or other value.

Later attempts by Congress to curb pornography on the Internet also encountered stumbling blocks. For example, the Child Online Protection Act (COPA) of 1998 banned the distribution of material "harmful to minors" without an age-verification system to separate adult and minor users. In 2002, the Supreme Court upheld a lower court injunction suspending COPA, and in 2004 the Court again upheld the suspension of the law on the ground that it was probably unconstitutional.[43] In

---

[41]495 U.S. 103 (1990).
[42]*Reno v. American Civil Liberties Union,* 521 U.S. 844 (1997).
[43]*Ashcroft v. American Civil Liberties Union,* 124 S.Ct. 2783 (2004).

Children use computers at a public library in Boston in June 2003, on the day after the United States Supreme Court upheld the Children's Internet Protection Act (CIPA). Under the act, public schools and libraries must install filtering software on their computers to prevent children from viewing pornographic material. What problems might the CIPA pose for adult library patrons? (AP Photo/Chitose Suzuki)

2000, Congress enacted the Children's Internet Protection Act (CIPA), which requires public schools and libraries to install filtering software to prevent children from viewing Web sites with "adult" content. In 2002, a U.S. district court found the CIPA unconstitutional when applied to public libraries. In 2003, however, the Supreme Court reversed the district court and upheld the act.[44]

Should "Virtual" Pornography Be Deemed a Crime? In 2001, the Supreme Court agreed to review a case challenging the constitutionality of another federal act attempting to protect minors in the online environment—the Child Pornography Prevention Act (CPPA) of 1996. This act made it illegal to distribute or possess computer-generated images that appear to depict minors engaging in lewd and lascivious behavior. At issue was whether digital child pornography should be considered a crime when no actual children are involved, only digitally rendered images.

The Supreme Court, noting that virtual child pornography is not the same as child pornography, held that the CPPA's ban on virtual child pornography restrained a substantial amount of lawful speech.[45] The Court stated, "The statute proscribes the visual depiction of an idea—that of teenagers engaging in sexual activity—that is a fact of modern society and has been a theme in art and literature throughout the ages." The Court concluded that the act was overbroad and thus unconstitutional.

Unprotected Speech: Slander

Can you say anything you want about someone else? Not really. Individuals are protected from **defamation of character,** which is defined as wrongfully hurting a person's good reputation. The law imposes a general duty on all persons to refrain from making false, defamatory statements about others. Breaching this duty orally is the wrongdoing called **slander.** Breaching it in writing is the wrongdoing called *libel,* which we discuss later. The government itself does not bring charges of slander or libel. Rather, the defamed person may bring a civil suit for damages.

Legally, slander is the public uttering of a false statement that harms the good reputation of another. Slanderous public uttering means that the defamatory statements are made to, or within the hearing of, persons other than the defamed party. If one person calls another dishonest, manipulative, and incompetent to his or her face when no one else is around, that does not constitute slander. The message is not communicated to a third party. If, however, a third party accidentally overhears defamatory statements, the courts have generally held that this constitutes a public uttering and therefore slander, which is prohibited.

Campus Speech

In recent years, students have been facing free speech challenges on campuses. One issue has to do with whether a student should have to subsidize, through student activity fees, organizations that promote causes that the student finds objectionable.

Student Activity Fees. In 2000, this question came before the United States Supreme Court in a case brought by several University of Wisconsin students. The students argued that their mandatory student activity fees—which helped to fund liberal causes with which they disagreed, including gay rights—violated their First Amendment rights of free speech, free association, and free exercise of religion. They contended that they should have the right to choose whether to

---

Defamation of Character
Wrongfully hurting a person's good reputation. The law imposes a general duty on all persons to refrain from making false, defamatory statements about others.

Slander
The public uttering of a false statement that harms the good reputation of another. The statement must be made to, or within the hearing of, persons other than the defamed party.

---

[44]*U.S. v. American Library Association, Inc.,* 539 U.S. 194 (2003).
[45]*Ashcroft v. Free Speech Coalition,* 535 U.S. 234 (2002).

fund organizations that promoted political and ideological views that were offensive to their personal beliefs. To the surprise of many, the Supreme Court rejected the students' claim and ruled in favor of the university. The Court stated that "the university may determine that its mission is well served if students have the means to engage in dynamic discussions of philosophical, religious, scientific, social and political subjects in their extracurricular life. If the university reaches this conclusion, it is entitled to impose a mandatory fee to sustain an open dialogue to these ends."[46]

Campus Speech and Behavior Codes.   Another free speech issue is the legitimacy of campus speech and behavior codes. Some state universities have established codes that challenge the boundaries of the protection of free speech provided by the First Amendment. These codes are designed to prohibit so-called hate speech—abusive speech attacking persons on the basis of their ethnicity, race, or other criteria. For example, a University of Michigan code banned "any behavior, verbal or physical, that stigmatizes or victimizes an individual on the basis of race, ethnicity, religion, sex, sexual orientation, creed, national origin, ancestry, age, marital status, handicap" or Vietnam-veteran status. A federal court found that the code violated students' First Amendment rights.[47]

Although the courts generally have held, as in the University of Michigan case, that campus speech codes are unconstitutional restrictions on the right to free speech, such codes continue to exist. Whether hostile speech should be banned on high school campuses has also become an issue. In view of school shootings and other violent behavior in the schools, school officials have become concerned about speech that consists of veiled threats or that could lead to violence. Some schools have even prohibited students from wearing clothing, such as T-shirts, bearing verbal messages (such as sexist or racist comments) or symbolic messages (such as the Confederate flag) that might generate "ill will or hatred."[48]

Defenders of campus speech codes argue that they are necessary not only to prevent violence but also to promote equality among different cultural, ethnic, and racial groups on campus and greater sensitivity to the needs and feelings of others. Most educators acknowledge that a certain degree of civility is required for productive campus discourse. Moreover, some hostile speech can rise to the level of illegal threats or illegal forms of harassment. A number of students also support restraints on campus hate speech. In 2002, for example, the student assembly at Wesleyan University passed a resolution declaring that the "right to speech comes with implicit responsibilities to respect community standards."

Hate Speech on the Internet

Extreme hate speech appears on the Internet, including racist materials and denials of the Holocaust (the murder of millions of Jews by the Nazis during World War II). Can the federal government restrict this type of speech? Should it? Content restrictions can be difficult to enforce. Even if Congress succeeded in passing a law prohibiting particular speech on the Internet, an army of "Internet watchers" would be needed to enforce it. Also, what if other countries attempt to impose their laws that restrict speech on U.S. Web sites? This is not a theoretical issue. In 2000, a French court found Yahoo in violation of French laws banning the display of Nazi memorabilia. In 2001, however, a U.S. district court held that this ruling could not be enforced against Yahoo in the United States.[49]

---

[46]*Board of Regents of the University of Wisconsin System v. Southworth,* 529 U.S. 217 (2000).
[47]*Doe v. University of Michigan,* 721 F.Supp. 852 (1989).
[48]Shannon P. Duffy, "Right to a 'Redneck' T-Shirt," *The National Law Journal,* October 14, 2002, p. A4.
[49]*Yahoo! Inc. v. La Ligue Contre le Racisme et l'Antisemitisme,* 169 F.Supp.2d 1181 (N.D.Cal. 2001).

★ Freedom of the Press

Freedom of the press can be regarded as a special instance of freedom of speech. Of course, at the time of the framing of the Constitution, the press meant only newspapers, magazines, and books. As technology has modified the ways in which we disseminate information, the laws touching on freedom of the press have been modified. What can and cannot be printed still occupies an important place in constitutional law, however.

Defamation in Writing

Libel
A written defamation of a person's character, reputation, business, or property rights.

Libel is defamation in writing (or in pictures, signs, films, or any other communication that has the potentially harmful qualities of written or printed words). As with slander, libel occurs only if the defamatory statements are observed by a third party. If one person writes to another a private letter wrongfully accusing him or her of embezzling funds, that does not constitute libel. It is interesting that the courts have generally held that dictating a letter to a secretary constitutes communication of the letter's contents to a third party, and therefore, if defamation has occurred, the wrongdoer can be sued.

New York Times Co. v. Sullivan[50] (1964) explored an important question regarding libelous statements made about public officials. The Supreme Court held that only when a statement was made with **actual malice**—that is, with either knowledge of its falsity or a reckless disregard of the truth—against a public official could damages be obtained.

Actual Malice
Either knowledge of a defamatory statement's falsity or a reckless disregard for the truth.

Public Figures
Public officials, movie stars, and other persons known to the public because of their positions or activities.

The standard set by the Court in the *New York Times* case has since been applied to **public figures** generally. Public figures include not only public officials but also public employees who exercise substantial governmental power and any persons who are generally in the public limelight. Statements made about public figures, especially when they are made through a public medium, usually are related to matters of general public interest; they are made about people who substantially affect all of us. Furthermore, public figures generally have some access to a public medium for answering disparaging falsehoods about themselves, whereas private individuals do not. For these reasons, public figures have a greater burden of proof (they must prove that the statements were made with actual malice) in defamation cases than do private individuals.

A Free Press versus a Fair Trial: Gag Orders

Another major issue relating to freedom of the press concerns media coverage of criminal trials. The Sixth Amendment to the Constitution guarantees the right of criminal suspects to a fair trial. In other words, the accused have rights. The First Amendment guarantees freedom of the press. What if the two rights appear to be in conflict? Which one prevails?

Gag Order
An order issued by a judge restricting the publication of news about a trial or a pretrial hearing to protect the accused's right to a fair trial.

Jurors certainly may be influenced by reading news stories about the trial in which they are participating. In the 1970s, judges increasingly issued **gag orders**, which restricted the publication of news about a trial in progress or even a pretrial hearing. In a landmark 1976 case, *Nebraska Press Association v. Stuart*,[51] the Supreme Court unanimously ruled that a Nebraska judge's gag order had violated the First Amendment's guarantee of freedom of the press. Chief Justice Warren Burger indicated that even pervasive adverse pretrial publicity did not necessarily

[50]376 U.S. 254 (1964).
[51]427 U.S. 539 (1976).

lead to an unfair trial and that prior restraints on publication were not justified. Some justices even went so far as to suggest that gag orders are never justified.

In spite of the *Nebraska Press Association* ruling, the Court has upheld certain types of gag orders. In *Gannett Co. v. De Pasquale*[52] (1979), for example, the highest court held that if a judge found a reasonable probability that news publicity would harm a defendant's right to a fair trial, the court could impose a gag rule: "Members of the public have no constitutional right under the Sixth and Fourteenth Amendments to *attend* criminal trials."

The *Nebraska* and *Gannett* cases, however, involved pretrial hearings. Could a judge impose a gag order on an entire trial, including pretrial hearings? In *Richmond Newspapers, Inc. v. Virginia*[53] (1980), the Court ruled that actual trials must be open to the public except under unusual circumstances.

Films, Radio, and TV

As we have noted, only in a few cases has the Supreme Court upheld prior restraint of published materials. The Court's reluctance to accept prior restraint is less evident with respect to motion pictures. In the first half of the twentieth century, films were routinely submitted to local censorship boards. In 1968, the Supreme Court ruled that a film can be banned only under a law that provides for a prompt hearing at which the film is shown to be obscene. Today, few local censorship boards exist. Instead, the film industry regulates itself primarily through the industry's rating system.

Radio and television broadcasting has the least First Amendment protection. Broadcasting initially received less protection than the printed media because, at that time, the number of airwave frequencies was limited. In 1934, the national government established the Federal Communications Commission (FCC) to regulate electromagnetic wave frequencies. No one has a right to use the airwaves without a license granted by the FCC. The FCC grants licenses for limited periods and imposes a variety of regulations on broadcasting. For example, the FCC can impose sanctions on radio or TV stations that broadcast "filthy words," even if the words are not legally obscene.

---

[52]443 U.S. 368 (1979).
[53]448 U.S. 555 (1980).

Radio "shock jock" Howard Stern offended the sensibilities of the Federal Communications Commission (FCC). That regulatory body fined Stern's radio station owner hundreds of thousands of dollars for Stern's purportedly obscene outbursts on radio in 1992 and again in 2004. The extent to which the FCC can regulate speech over the air involves the First Amendment. Why is it that what is permissible and acceptable on radio and TV today probably would have been considered "obscene" three decades ago? (Bill Swersey/Getty Images)

★ The Right to Assemble and to Petition the Government

The First Amendment prohibits Congress from making any law that abridges "the right of the people peaceably to assemble, and to petition the Government for a redress of grievances." Inherent in such a right is the ability of private citizens to communicate their ideas on public issues to government officials, as well as to other individuals. The Supreme Court has often put this freedom on a par with the freedom of speech and the freedom of the press. Nonetheless, it has allowed municipalities to require permits for parades, sound trucks, and demonstrations, so that public officials can control traffic or prevent demonstrations from turning into riots.

This became a major issue in 1977 when the American Nazi Party wanted to march through the largely Jewish suburb of Skokie, Illinois. The American Civil Liberties Union defended the Nazis' right to march (in spite of its opposition to the Nazi philosophy). The Supreme Court let stand a lower court's ruling that the city of Skokie had violated the Nazis' First Amendment guarantees by denying them a permit to march.[54]

Street Gangs

An issue that has surfaced in recent years is whether communities can prevent gang members from gathering together on the streets without violating their right of assembly or associated rights. Although some actions taken by cities to prevent gang members from gathering together or "loitering" in public places have passed constitutional muster, others have not. For example, in a 1997 case, the California Supreme Court upheld a lower court's order preventing gang members from appearing in public together.[55] In 1999, however, the United States Supreme Court held that Chicago's "antiloitering" ordinance violated the constitutional right to due process of law because, among other things, it left too much power to the police to determine what constituted "loitering."[56]

Online Assembly

A question for Americans today is whether individuals should have the right to "assemble" online for the purpose of advocating violence against certain groups (such as physicians who perform abortions) or advocating values that are opposed to our democracy (such as terrorism). While some online advocacy groups promote interests consistent with American political values, other groups have as their goal the destruction of those values. Whether First Amendment freedoms should be sacrificed (by the government's monitoring of Internet communications, for example) in the interests of national security is a question that will no doubt be debated for some time to come.

★ More Liberties under Scrutiny: Matters of Privacy

No explicit reference is made anywhere in the Constitution to a person's right to privacy. Until relatively recently, the courts did not take a very positive approach toward the right to privacy. For example, during Prohibition, suspected bootleg-

About 1,000 union workers and other protesters gather across from a Fifth Avenue outlet of the Gap in New York's largest protest in connection with the World Economic Forum. A ring of police officers, part of a 4,000-member contingent assigned to handle demonstrators, enclosed the exterior of the store as demonstrators protesting the globalization of industry listened to speakers, including AFL-CIO president John Sweeney. (AP Photo/Steve Chernin)

[54]*Smith v. Collin,* 439 U.S. 916 (1978).
[55]*Gallo v. Acuna,* 14 Cal.4th 1090 (1997).
[56]*City of Chicago v. Morales,* 527 U.S. 41 (1999).

gers' telephones were tapped routinely, and the information obtained was used as a legal basis for prosecution. In *Olmstead v. United States*[57] (1928), the Supreme Court upheld such an invasion of privacy. Justice Louis Brandeis, a champion of personal freedoms, strongly dissented from the majority decision in this case. He argued that the framers of the Constitution gave every citizen the right to be left alone. He called such a right "the most comprehensive of rights and the right most valued by civilized men."

In the 1960s, the highest court began to modify the majority view. In 1965, in *Griswold v. Connecticut*,[58] the Supreme Court overthrew a Connecticut law that effectively prohibited the use of contraceptives, holding that the law violated the right to privacy. Justice William O. Douglas formulated a unique way of reading this right into the Bill of Rights. He claimed that the First, Third, Fourth, Fifth, and Ninth Amendments created "penumbras [shadows], formed by emanations from those guarantees that help give them life and substance," and he went on to describe zones of privacy that are guaranteed by these rights. When we read the Ninth Amendment, we can see the foundation for his reasoning: "The enumeration in the Constitution, of certain rights, shall not be construed to deny or disparage others retained by the people." In other words, just because the Constitution, including its amendments, does not specifically talk about the right to privacy does not mean that this right is denied to the people.

Some of today's most controversial issues relate to privacy rights. One issue involves the erosion of privacy rights in an information age, as computers make it easier to compile and distribute personal information. Other issues concern abortion and the "right to die." Since the terrorist attacks of September 11, 2001, Americans have faced another crucial question regarding privacy rights: To what extent should Americans sacrifice privacy rights in the interests of national security?

Privacy Rights in an Information Age

An important privacy issue, created in part by new technology, is the amassing of information on individuals by government agencies and private businesses, such as marketing firms. Personal information on the average American citizen is filed away in dozens of agencies—such as the Social Security Administration and the Internal Revenue Service. Because of the threat of indiscriminate use of private information by unauthorized individuals, Congress passed the Privacy Act in 1974. This was the first law regulating the use of federal government information about private individuals. Under the Privacy Act, every citizen has the right to obtain copies of personal records collected by federal agencies and to correct inaccuracies in such records.

The ease with which personal information can be obtained by using the Internet for marketing and other purposes has led to unique privacy issues. Some fear that privacy rights in personal information soon may be a thing of the past. Whether privacy rights can survive in an information age is a question that Americans and their leaders continue to confront.

Privacy Rights and Abortion

Historically, abortion was not a criminal offense before the "quickening" of the fetus (the first movement of the fetus in the uterus, usually between the sixteenth and eighteenth weeks of pregnancy). During the last half of the nineteenth century, however, state laws became more severe. By 1973, performing an abortion at any time during pregnancy was a criminal offense in a majority of the states.

---

[57]277 U.S. 438 (1928). This decision was overruled later in *Katz v. United States,* 389 U.S. 347 (1967).
[58]381 U.S. 479 (1965).

Roe v. Wade.   In *Roe v. Wade*[59] (1973), the United States Supreme Court accepted the argument that the laws against abortion violated "Jane Roe's" right to privacy under the Constitution. The Court held that during the first trimester (three months) of pregnancy, abortion was an issue solely between a woman and her physician. The state could not limit abortions except to require that they be performed by licensed physicians. During the second trimester, to protect the health of the mother, the state was allowed to specify the conditions under which an abortion could be performed. During the final trimester, the state could regulate or even outlaw abortions except when necessary to preserve the life or health of the mother.

After *Roe,* the Supreme Court issued decisions in a number of cases defining and redefining the boundaries of state regulation of abortion. During the 1980s, the Court twice struck down laws that required a woman who wished to have an abortion to undergo counseling designed to discourage abortions. In the late 1980s and early 1990s, however, the Court took a more conservative approach. For example, in *Webster v. Reproductive Health Services*[60] (1989), the Court upheld a Missouri statute that, among other things, banned the use of public hospitals or other taxpayer-supported facilities for performing abortions. And, in *Planned Parenthood v. Casey*[61] (1992), the Court upheld a Pennsylvania law that required preabortion counseling, a waiting period of twenty-four hours, and, for girls under the age of eighteen, parental or judicial permission. As a result, abortions are now more difficult to obtain in some states than others.

The Controversy Continues.   Abortion continues to be a divisive issue. Right-to-life forces continue to push for laws banning abortion, to endorse political candidates who support their views, and to organize protests. Because of several

---

[59]410 U.S. 113 (1973). Jane Roe was not the real name of the woman in this case. It is a common legal pseudonym used to protect a person's privacy.
[60]492 U.S. 490 (1989).
[61]505 U.S. 833 (1992).

Right-to-life groups increased their demonstrations against abortion facilities in the 1990s and early 2000s. The clash between right-to-life and freedom-of-choice forces has resulted in restrictions on demonstrations around abortion clinics. (Christopher Brown/ Stock Boston)

episodes of violence attending protests at abortion clinics, in 1994 Congress passed the Freedom of Access to Clinic Entrances Act. The act prohibits protesters from blocking entrances to such clinics. The Supreme Court ruled in 1993 that such protesters can be prosecuted under laws governing racketeering,[62] and in 1998 a federal court in Illinois convicted right-to-life protesters under these laws. In 1997, the Supreme Court upheld the constitutionality of prohibiting protesters from entering a fifteen-foot "buffer zone" around abortion clinics and from giving unwanted counseling to those entering the clinics.[63]

In another decision in 2000, the Court upheld a Colorado law requiring demonstrators to stay at least eight feet away from people entering and leaving clinics unless people consented to be approached. The Court concluded that the law's restrictions on speech-related conduct did not violate the free speech rights of abortion protesters.[64]

In the same year, the Supreme Court again addressed the abortion issue directly when it reviewed a Nebraska law banning "partial-birth" abortions. Similar laws have been passed by at least twenty-seven states. A partial-birth abortion, which physicians call intact dilation and extraction, is a procedure that can be used during the second trimester of pregnancy. Abortion rights advocates claim that in limited circumstances the procedure is the safest way to perform an abortion, and that the government should never outlaw specific medical procedures. Opponents argue that the procedure has no medical merit and that it ends the life of a fetus that might be able to live outside the womb. The Supreme Court invalidated the Nebraska law on the ground that, as written, the law could be used to ban other abortion procedures and because it contained no provisions for protecting the health of the pregnant woman.[65] In 2003, legislation similar to the Nebraska statute was passed by the U.S. Congress and signed into law by president George W. Bush. It was immediately challenged in court.

ELECTIONS 2004
Civil Liberties and the 2004 Elections

The reelection of George W. Bush by a 3.5 million popular vote margin probably signaled a path of little change on the civil liberties front. Polls indicated that because of the terrorism threat, a majority of Americans favored the USA Patriot Act—despite challenges it poses to civil liberties. During their nominating convention the Democrats did claim that the act infringed on our civil liberties, but the issue never arose again during the campaign. There now appears to be little likelihood that the USA Patriot Act will be strengthened—or repealed.

Privacy Rights and the "Right to Die"

A 1976 case involving Karen Ann Quinlan was one of the first publicized right-to-die cases.[66] The parents of Quinlan, a young woman who had been in a coma for nearly a year and who had been kept alive during that time by a respirator, wanted her respirator removed. In 1976, the New Jersey Supreme Court ruled

---

[62]*National Organization of Women v. Joseph Scheidler,* 509 U.S. 951 (1993).
[63]*Schenck v. ProChoice Network,* 519 U.S. 357 (1997).
[64]*Hill v. Colorado,* 530 U.S. 703 (2000).
[65]*Stenberg v. Carhart,* 530 U.S. 914 (2000).
[66]*In re Quinlan,* 70 N.J. 10 (1976).

that the right to privacy includes the right of a patient to refuse treatment and that patients unable to speak can exercise that right through a family member or guardian. In 1990, the Supreme Court took up the issue. In *Cruzan v. Director, Missouri Department of Health,*[67] the Court stated that a patient's life-sustaining treatment can be withdrawn at the request of a family member only if there is "clear and convincing evidence" that the patient did not want such treatment.

What If There Is No Living Will?   Since the 1976 *Quinlan* decision, most states have enacted laws permitting people to designate their wishes concerning life-sustaining procedures in "living wills" or durable health-care powers of attorney. These laws and the Supreme Court's *Cruzan* decision have resolved the right-to-die controversy for cases in which a living will has been drafted. Disputes are still possible if there is no living will. An example is the case of Terri Schiavo, a Florida woman who has been in a persistent vegetative state for over a decade. Schiavo's husband sought to have her feeding tube removed on the basis of oral statements that she would not want her life prolonged in such circumstances. Schiavo's parents fought this move in court but lost on the ground that a spouse, not a parent, is the appropriate legal guardian for a married person. In October 2003, however, the Florida state legislature took the unprecedented step of passing a special law that in effect applied only to Schiavo, which allowed Governor Jeb Bush to overrule the courts. In September 2004, the Florida Supreme Court ruled that "Terri's Law" violated the state constitution.[68]

Physician-Assisted Suicide.   In the 1990s, another issue surfaced: Do privacy rights include the right of terminally ill people to end their lives through physician-assisted suicide? Until 1996, the courts consistently upheld state laws that prohibited this practice, either through specific statutes or under their general homicide statutes. In 1996, after two federal appellate courts ruled that state laws banning assisted suicide (in Washington and New York) were unconstitutional, the issue reached the United States Supreme Court. In 1997, in *Washington v. Glucksberg,*[69] the Court stated, clearly and categorically, that the liberty interest protected by the Constitution does not include a right to commit suicide, with or without assistance. To hold otherwise, said the Court, would be "to reverse centuries of legal doctrine and practice, and strike down the considered policy choice of almost every state."

In effect, the Supreme Court left the decision in the hands of the states. Since then, assisted suicide has been allowed in only one state—Oregon. Even in that state, however, it is uncertain whether physicians will continue to be able to prescribe lethal drugs for terminal patients. This is a point of controversy between the federal government (which controls prescription drugs) and the state.

Privacy Rights versus Security Issues

As former Supreme Court justice Thurgood Marshall once said, "Grave threats to liberty often come in times of urgency, when constitutional rights seem too extravagant to endure." Not surprisingly, antiterrorist legislation since the attacks on September 11, 2001, has eroded certain basic rights, in particular the Fourth Amendment protections against unreasonable searches and seizures. Current legislation allows the government to conduct "roving" wiretaps.

Previously, only specific telephone numbers, cell phone numbers, or computer terminals could be tapped. Now a particular person under suspicion can be monitored electronically no matter what form of electronic communication he or she

---

[67]497 U.S. 261 (1990).
[68]___ So.2d ___ (Florida Supreme Court, 1990).
[69]521 U.S. 702 (1997).

uses. Such roving wiretaps contravene the Supreme Court's interpretation of the Fourth Amendment, which requires a judicial warrant to describe the *place* to be searched, not just the person. One of the goals of the framers was to avoid *general* searches. Further, once a judge approves an application for a roving wiretap, when, how, and where the monitoring occurs will be left to the FBI's discretion. As an unavoidable result, a third party will have access to the conversations and e-mails of hundreds of people who falsely believe them to be private.

★ The Great Balancing Act: The Rights of the Accused versus the Rights of Society

The United States has one of the highest murder rates in the industrialized world. It is not surprising, therefore, that many citizens have extremely strong opinions about the rights of those accused of violent crimes. When an accused person, especially one who has confessed to some criminal act, is set free because of an apparent legal "technicality," many people believe that the rights of the accused are being given more weight than the rights of society and of potential or actual victims. Why, then, give criminal suspects rights? The answer is partly to avoid convicting innocent people, but mostly because all criminal suspects have the right to due process of law and fair treatment.

The courts and the police must constantly engage in a balancing act of competing rights. At the basis of all discussions about the appropriate balance is, of course, the U.S. Bill of Rights. The Fourth, Fifth, Sixth, and Eighth Amendments deal specifically with the rights of criminal defendants. (You will learn about some of your rights under the Fourth Amendment in the *Making a Difference* feature at the end of this chapter.)

Rights of the Accused

The basic rights of criminal defendants are outlined below. When appropriate, the specific constitutional provision or amendment on which a right is based also is given.

Limits on the Conduct of Police Officers and Prosecutors
- No unreasonable or unwarranted searches and seizures (Amend. IV).
- No arrest except on probable cause (Amend. IV).
- No coerced confessions or illegal interrogation (Amend. V).
- No entrapment.
- On questioning, a suspect must be informed of her or his rights.

Defendant's Pretrial Rights
- **Writ of *habeas corpus*** (Article I, Section 9).
- Prompt **arraignment** (Amend. VI).
- Legal counsel (Amend. VI).
- Reasonable bail (Amend. VIII).
- To be informed of charges (Amend. VI).
- To remain silent (Amend. V).

Trial Rights
- Speedy and public trial before a jury (Amend. VI).
- Impartial jury selected from a cross-section of the community (Amend. VI).
- Trial atmosphere free of prejudice, fear, and outside interference.
- No compulsory self-incrimination (Amend. V).

Writ of *Habeas Corpus*
Habeas corpus means, literally, "you have the body." A writ of *habeas corpus* is an order that requires jailers to bring a prisoner before a court or judge and explain why the person is being held.

Arraignment
The first act in a criminal proceeding, in which the defendant is brought before a court to hear the charges against him or her and enter a plea of guilty or not guilty.

- Adequate counsel (Amend. VI).
- No cruel and unusual punishment (Amend. VIII).
- Appeal of convictions.
- No double jeopardy (Amend. V).

Some worry that the Bush administration's prosecution of suspected terrorists in military tribunals instead of regular criminal courts represents a threat to the constitutional rights of accused persons. For a discussion of this issue, see this chapter's *America's Security* feature.

Extending the Rights of the Accused

During the 1960s, the Supreme Court, under Chief Justice Earl Warren, significantly expanded the rights of accused persons. In a case decided in 1963, *Gideon v. Wainwright,*[70] the Court held that if a person is accused of a felony and cannot afford an attorney, an attorney must be made available to the accused person at the government's expense. Although the Sixth Amendment to the Constitution provides for the right to counsel, the Supreme Court had established a precedent twenty-one years earlier in *Betts v. Brady,*[71] when it held that only criminal defendants in capital cases automatically had a right to legal counsel.

Miranda v. Arizona.   In 1966, the Court issued its decision in *Miranda v. Arizona.*[72] The case involved Ernesto Miranda, who was arrested and charged with the kidnapping and rape of a young woman. After two hours of questioning, Miranda confessed and was later convicted. Miranda's lawyer appealed his conviction, arguing that the police had never informed Miranda that he had a right to remain silent and a right to be represented by counsel. The Court, in ruling in Miranda's favor, enunciated the *Miranda* rights that are now familiar to virtually all Americans:

> Prior to any questioning, the person must be warned that he has a right to remain silent, that any statement he does make may be used against him, and that he has a right to the presence of an attorney, either retained or appointed.

---

[70]372 U.S. 335 (1963).
[71]316 U.S. 455 (1942).
[72]384 U.S. 436 (1966).

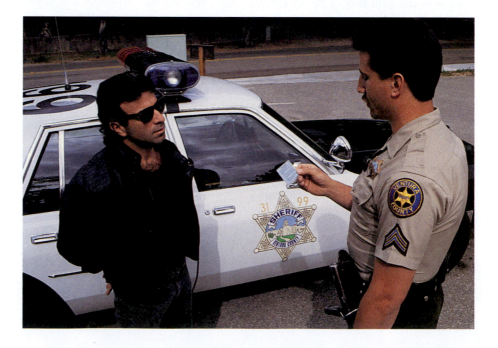

This man is being read his *Miranda* rights by the arresting officer. Suspects often waive, or forgo, their *Miranda* rights. Why might arrested persons choose not to exercise these rights? (Elana Rooraid, PhotoEdit)

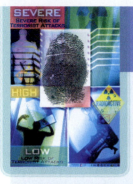

AMERICA'S SECURITY
Military Tribunals for Suspected Terrorists

About two months after the terrorist attacks on September 11, 2001, Attorney General John Ashcroft and Vice President Dick Cheney announced that suspected terrorists who were noncitizens would be prosecuted in American military tribunals. There was an immediate outcry against this violation of constitutional safeguards. Nonetheless, President George W. Bush called military trials "absolutely the right thing to do."

In times of crisis, particularly war, the United States has used military tribunals routinely. During the Civil War, for example, the Union Army conducted over four thousand trials by military tribunals. In the last days of the war, several nonmilitary personnel were hanged after being convicted by military tribunals of spying for the South. In 1942, during World War II, German agents who had traveled by submarine to Florida, Long Island, and New York were convicted and sentenced to death by military tribunals.

REDUCED RIGHTS OF THE ACCUSED

In November 2001, President Bush promulgated an executive order setting up military tribunals for noncitizens. The defendant was to have far fewer rights than any military defendant facing a court-martial.

In March 2002, in response to public criticism of the proposed tribunals, the Pentagon made public a revised set of rules that allow suspected terrorists to have the presumption of innocence and the right to remain silent. The prosecution must prove that the defendant is guilty beyond a reasonable doubt. The military judges can convict a defendant by a two-thirds majority vote. For the death penalty to be imposed, the judges' decision must be unanimous. Defendants in such trials, however, do not have the right to a jury trial. Hearsay can be accepted as evidence. Finally, there can be no civilian review of the judges' decisions.

In June 2004, the United States Supreme Court ruled that federal courts may consider challenges to the custody of noncitizens held as prisoners at the U.S. naval base at Guantanamo Bay, Cuba. These prisoners had been confined for years without facing any courts. The Supreme Court's decision does not rule out the use of military tribunals for the Guantanamo prisoners but does allow the federal courts to review the detention of persons held indefinitely without recourse to any tribunal, military or otherwise.* In response, the Bush administration set up military panels to review the grounds for detaining each prisoner.

THE REASONING BEHIND MILITARY TRIBUNALS

The Bush administration argued that, in view of these "extraordinary times," secret military tribunals were necessary to safeguard evidence that could be used to prevent future terrorist attacks on Americans and their country. Moreover, the government does not want to give terrorist leaders and supporters a forum for expressing their anti-American views.

Consider also that in a normal criminal trial, evidence can be thrown out based on the exclusionary rule—which is used to keep evidence that is gathered illegally from being admitted in court. The administration does not think that people bent on destroying this country should have such constitutional rights.

In 2004, the government finally began the process of bringing Guantanamo prisoners before military tribunals. By July 2004, fifteen prisoners had been scheduled for trial.

FOR CRITICAL ANALYSIS

The military tribunal issue is an example of how the values of liberty and security can collide. Under what circumstances should terrorist suspects have the same constitutional rights that criminal suspects have in our normal criminal justice system?

*Rasul v. Bush, 124 S.Ct. 2686 (2004).

Two years after the Supreme Court's *Miranda* decision, Congress passed the Omnibus Crime Control and Safe Streets Act of 1968. Section 3501 of the act reinstated a rule that had been in effect for 180 years before *Miranda*—that statements by defendants can be used against them if the statements were voluntarily made. The Justice Department immediately disavowed Section 3501 as unconstitutional and has continued to hold this position. As a result, Section 3501, although it was never repealed, has never been enforced. In 2000, after a surprise move by a federal appellate court held that the all-but-forgotten provision was enforceable, the Supreme Court held that the *Miranda* warnings were constitutionally based and could not be overruled by a legislative act.[73]

---

[73]*Dickerson v. United States,* 530 U.S. 428 (2000).

Exceptions to the *Miranda* Rule.   As part of a continuing attempt to balance the rights of accused persons against the rights of society, the Supreme Court has made a number of exceptions to the *Miranda* rule. In 1984, for example, the Court recognized a "public safety" exception to the rule. The need to protect the public warranted the admissibility of statements made by the defendant (in this case, indicating where he had placed a gun) as evidence in a trial, even though the defendant had not been informed of his *Miranda* rights.[74]

In 1985, the Court further held that a confession need not be excluded even though the police failed to inform a suspect in custody that his attorney had tried to reach him by telephone.[75] In an important 1991 decision, the Court stated that a suspect's conviction will not be automatically overturned if the suspect was coerced into making a confession. If the other evidence admitted at trial is strong enough to justify the conviction without the confession, then the fact that the confession was obtained illegally in effect can be ignored.[76] In yet another case, in 1994, the Supreme Court ruled that suspects must unequivocally and assertively state their right to counsel in order to stop police questioning. Saying, "Maybe I should talk to a lawyer" during an interrogation after being taken into custody is not enough. The Court held that police officers are not required to decipher the suspect's intentions in such situations.[77]

Video Recording of Interrogations.   In view of the numerous exceptions, there are no guarantees that the *Miranda* rule will survive indefinitely. Increasingly, though, law enforcement personnel are using digital cameras to record interrogations. According to some scholars, the recording of *all* custodial interrogations would satisfy the Fifth Amendment's prohibition against coercion and in the process render the *Miranda* warnings unnecessary. Others argue, however, that recorded interrogations can be misleading.

The Exclusionary Rule

At least since 1914, judicial policy has prohibited the admission of illegally seized evidence at trials in federal courts. This is the so-called **exclusionary rule.** Improperly obtained evidence, no matter how telling, cannot be used by prosecutors. This includes evidence obtained by police in violation of a suspect's *Miranda* rights or of the Fourth Amendment. The Fourth Amendment protects against unreasonable searches and seizures and provides that a judge may issue a search warrant to a police officer only on probable cause (a demonstration of facts that permit a reasonable belief that a crime has been committed). The question that must be determined by the courts is what constitutes an "unreasonable" search and seizure.

The reasoning behind the exclusionary rule is that it forces police officers to gather evidence properly, in which case their due diligence will be rewarded by a conviction. Nevertheless, the exclusionary rule has always had critics who argue that it permits guilty persons to be freed because of innocent errors.

This rule was first extended to state court proceedings in a 1961 United States Supreme Court decision, *Mapp v. Ohio.*[78] In this case, the Court overturned the conviction of Dollree Mapp for the possession of obscene materials. Police found pornographic books in her apartment after searching it without a search warrant and despite her refusal to let them in.

Exclusionary Rule
A policy forbidding the admission at trial of illegally seized evidence.

---

[74]*New York v. Quarles,* 467 U.S. 649 (1984).
[75]*Moran v. Burbine,* 475 U.S. 412 (1985).
[76]*Arizona v. Fulminante,* 499 U.S. 279 (1991).
[77]*Davis v. United States,* 512 U.S. 452 (1994).
[78]367 U.S. 643 (1961).

Over the last several decades, the Supreme Court has diminished the scope of the exclusionary rule by creating some exceptions to its applicability. For example, in 1984 the Court held that illegally obtained evidence could be admitted at trial if law enforcement personnel could prove that they would have obtained the evidence legally anyway.[79] In another case decided in the same year, the Court held that a police officer who used a technically incorrect search warrant form to obtain evidence had acted in good faith and therefore the evidence was admissible at trial. The Court thus created the "good faith" exception to the exclusionary rule.[80]

 **The Death Penalty**

Capital punishment remains one of the most debated aspects of our criminal justice system. Those in favor of the death penalty maintain that it serves as a deterrent to serious crime and satisfies society's need for justice and fair play. Those opposed to the death penalty do not believe it has any deterrent value and hold that it constitutes a barbaric act in an otherwise civilized society.

Cruel and Unusual Punishment?

The Eighth Amendment prohibits cruel and unusual punishment. Throughout history, "cruel and unusual" referred to punishments that were more serious than the crimes—the phrase referred to torture and to executions that prolonged the agony of dying. The Supreme Court never interpreted "cruel and unusual" to prohibit all forms of capital punishment in all circumstances. Indeed, a number of states had imposed the death penalty for a variety of crimes and allowed juries to decide when the condemned could be sentenced to death. Many believed, however, and in 1972 the Supreme Court agreed, in *Furman v. Georgia*,[81] that the imposition of the death penalty was random and arbitrary.

---

[79]*Nix v. Williams,* 467 U.S. 431 (1984).
[80]*Massachusetts v. Sheppard,* 468 U.S. 981 (1984).
[81]408 U.S. 238 (1972).

A death penalty opponent at a rally in California. The rally took place at the capitol building in Sacramento. A major death penalty issue is whether the penalty has a deterrent effect. Why might the death penalty have such an effect—and why might it not? (AP Photo/Rich Pedroncelli)

★ ★ ★ ★ ★ ★ ★ ★ ★ ★ ★ ★ ★ ★ ★

DID YOU KNOW ...
That in eighteenth-century England, pocket picking and similar crimes were punishable by the death penalty?

The Supreme Court's 1972 decision stated that the death penalty, as then applied, violated the Eighth and Fourteenth Amendments. The Court ruled that capital punishment is not necessarily cruel and unusual if the criminal has killed or attempted to kill someone. In its opinion, the Court invited the states to enact more precise laws so that the death penalty would be applied more consistently. By 1976, twenty-five states had adopted a two-stage, or *bifurcated*, procedure for capital cases. In the first stage, a jury determines the guilt or innocence of the defendant for a crime that has been determined by statute to be punishable by death. If the defendant is found guilty, the jury reconvenes in the second stage and considers all relevant evidence to decide whether the death sentence is, in fact, warranted.

In *Gregg v. Georgia,*[82] the Supreme Court ruled in favor of Georgia's bifurcated process, holding that the state's legislative guidelines had removed the ability of a jury to "wantonly and freakishly impose the death penalty." The Court upheld similar procedures in Texas and Florida, establishing a "road map" for all states to follow that would assure them protection from lawsuits based on Eighth Amendment grounds. On January 17, 1977, Gary Mark Gilmore became the first American to be executed (by Utah) under the new laws.

The Death Penalty Today

Today, thirty-seven states (see Figure 4–1) and the federal government have capital punishment laws based on the guidelines established by the *Gregg* case. State governments are responsible for almost all executions in this country. The executions of Timothy McVeigh and Juan Raul Garza in 2001 marked the first death sentences carried out by the federal government since 1963. Currently, there are about 3,700 prisoners on death row across the nation.

The number of executions per year reached a high in 1998 at ninety-eight and then began to fall. Some believe that the declining number of executions reflects the waning support among Americans for the imposition of the death penalty. In 1994, polls indicated that 80 percent of Americans supported the death penalty. Recent polls, however, suggest that this number has dropped to between 50 and 60 percent, depending on the poll.

The number of executions may decline even further due to the Supreme Court's 2002 ruling in *Ring v. Arizona.*[83] The Court held that only juries, not judges, could

[82]428 U.S. 153 (1976).
[83]536 U.S. 548 (2002).

FIGURE 4–1

States That Allow the Death Penalty

Today, as shown in this figure, thirty-seven states have laws permitting capital punishment. On June 24, 2004, the New York Court of Appeals (that state's highest court) ruled that New York's death penalty law violated the state constitution. Also, New Hampshire has a death penalty statute, but that state has not sentenced any defendants to death since 1972. Connecticut, Kansas, New Jersey, and South Dakota have inmates on "death row," but none of these states has actually executed anyone since 1972.

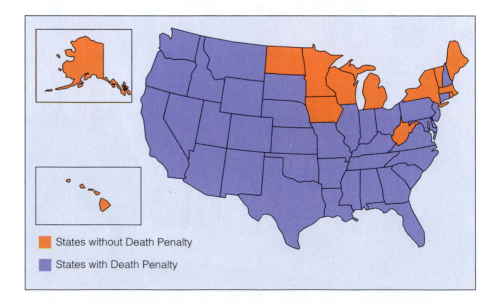

■ States without Death Penalty

■ States with Death Penalty

impose the death penalty, thus invalidating the laws of five states that allow judges to make this decision. The ruling meant that the death sentences of 168 death row inmates would have to be reconsidered by the relevant courts. The sentences of many of these inmates will likely be commuted to life in prison.

Time Limits for Death Row Appeals

In 1996, Congress passed the Anti-Terrorism and Effective Death Penalty Act. The law sharply limits federal court access for all defendants convicted in state courts. It also imposes a severe time limit on death row appeals. The law requires federal judges to hear these appeals and issue their opinions within a specified time period. Many are concerned that the shortened appeals process increases the possibility that innocent persons may be put to death. Recently, DNA testing has shown that a large number of innocent people may have been convicted unjustly of murder. Since 1973, ninety-eight prisoners have been freed from death row after new evidence suggested that they were convicted wrongfully. On average, it takes about seven years to exonerate someone on death row. In recent years, however, the time between conviction and execution has been shortened from an average of ten to twelve years to an average of six to eight years.

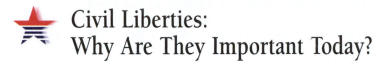

Civil Liberties: Why Are They Important Today?

In the past, every time there was a crisis, civil liberties were jeopardized because of fears of disloyalty among some part of the populace. During World War II, we removed more than 110,000 Americans of Japanese descent from their homes on the West Coast and sent them to special "internment camps" because we were afraid that they would not remain loyal to the United States. The fear was that they would be potential spies for Japan, our enemy. In the 1950s, when we worried that the Soviet Union's communist doctrine would spread to our shores, the "red scare" ensued.[84] Various "witch hunts" attempted to expose communists and their sympathizers within the American movie industry, the universities, and elsewhere.

Today, we are in another time of crisis, and our civil liberties are indeed being threatened. You may think that you could never be affected by a reduction in this nation's civil liberties, but consider this: You could be identified mistakenly as a member or a supporter of a subversive group. If you are in the United States on a visa, even if you have permanent residency, you could be picked up and held, sometimes without the possibility of communicating with others, if you are suspected of being involved in terrorism.

On a broader basis, most Americans take their civil liberties for granted. Americans traveling to other countries often are surprised by the visible presence of armed military in the streets. Citizens in some other countries often must be careful of what they say and to whom they say it, because there may be serious repercussions for openly criticizing their government or for being too friendly with foreign visitors, such as Americans. When you go abroad, you need to be careful too about being active politically. You can be jailed, or worse, in other countries for allegedly or actually engaging in antigovernment activities. An example is Lori Berenson, an American traveler in Peru who in 1995 was sentenced to jail until 2016 for allegedly supporting terrorist acts against the Peruvian government.

★★★★★★★★★★★★★★★★★

DID YOU KNOW . . .
That more people were executed in the United States during the Great Depression than during any other decade for which reliable records are available?

---

[84]Communists were called "reds" because of their choice of red as the color for their flag. When the Soviet Union was formed after the Russian Revolution in 1917, that nation also adopted a red flag.

MAKING A DIFFERENCE

★ Your Civil Liberties: Searches and Seizures

Our civil liberties include numerous provisions, many of them listed in the Bill of Rights, that protect persons who are suspected of criminal activity. Among these are limits on how the police—as agents of the government—can conduct searches and seizures.

Why Should You Care?

You may be the most law-abiding person in the world, but that will not guarantee that you will never be stopped, arrested, or searched by the police. Sooner or later, the great majority of all citizens will have some kind of interaction with the police. People who do not understand their rights or how to behave toward law enforcement officers can find themselves in serious trouble. The words of advice in this feature actually provide you with key survival skills for life in the modern world.

What Can You Do?

How should you behave if you are stopped by police officers? Your civil liberties protect you from having to provide information other than your name and address. Normally, even if you have not been placed under arrest, the officers have the right to frisk you for weapons, and you must let them proceed. The officers cannot, however, check your person or your clothing further if, in their judgment, no weaponlike object is produced.

The officers may search you only if they have a search warrant or probable cause to believe that a search will likely produce incriminating evidence.

What if the officers do not have probable cause or a warrant? Physically resisting their attempt to search you can lead to disastrous results. It is best simply to refuse orally to give permission for the search, preferably in the presence of a witness. Being polite is better than acting out of anger and making the officers irritable. It is usually advisable to limit what you say to the officers. If you are arrested, it is best to keep quiet until you can speak with a lawyer.

If you are in your car and are stopped by the police, the same fundamental rules apply. Always be ready to show your driver's license and car registration. You may be asked to get out of the car. The officers may use a flashlight to peer inside if it is too dark to see otherwise. None of this constitutes a search. A true search requires either a warrant or probable cause. No officer has the legal right to search your car simply to find out if you may have committed a crime. Police officers can conduct searches that are incident to lawful arrests, however.

If you are in your home and a police officer with a search warrant appears, you can ask to examine the warrant before granting entry. A warrant that is correctly made out will state the place or persons to be searched, the object sought, the date of the warrant (which should be no more than ten days old), and it will bear the signature of a judge or magistrate. If the warrant is in order, you need not make any statement. If you believe the warrant to be invalid, or if no warrant is produced, you should make it clear orally that you have not consented to the search, preferably in

the presence of a witness. If the search later is proved to be unlawful, normally any evidence obtained cannot be used in court.

Officers who attempt to enter your home without a search warrant can do so only if they are pursuing a suspected felon into the house. Rarely is it advisable to give permission for a warrantless search. You, as the resident, must be the one to give permission if any evidence obtained is to be considered legal. The landlord, manager, or head of a college dormitory cannot give legal permission. A roommate, however, can give permission for a search of his or her room, which may allow the police to search areas where you have belongings.

If you are a guest in a place that is being legally searched, you may be legally searched as well. But unless you have been placed under arrest, you cannot be compelled to go to the police station or get into a squad car.

If you would like to find out more about your rights and obligations under the laws of searches and seizures, you might wish to contact the following organization:

The American Civil Liberties
    Union
125 Broad St., 18th Floor
New York, NY 10004
212-549-2500
    http://www.aclu.org

 **Key Terms**

actual malice 130	commercial speech 124	gag order 130	slander 128
arraignment 137	defamation of character 128	incorporation theory 114	symbolic speech 124
civil liberties 113	establishment clause 115	libel 130	writ of *habeas corpus* 137
clear and present danger	exclusionary rule 140	prior restraint 122	
test 125	free exercise clause 121	public figures 130	

 **Chapter Summary**

1 Originally, the Bill of Rights limited only the power of the national government, not that of the states. Gradually and selectively, however, the Supreme Court accepted the incorporation theory, under which no state can violate most provisions of the Bill of Rights.

2 The First Amendment protects against government interference with freedom of religion by requiring a separation of church and state (under the establishment clause) and by guaranteeing the free exercise of religion. Controversial issues that arise under the establishment clause include aid to church-related schools, school prayer, the teaching of evolution versus creationism, school vouchers, the posting of the Ten Commandments in public places, and discrimination against religious speech. The government can interfere with the free exercise of religion only when religious practices work against public policy or the public welfare.

3 The First Amendment protects against government interference with freedom of speech, which includes symbolic speech (expressive conduct). The Supreme Court has been especially critical of government actions that impose prior restraint on expression. Commercial speech (advertising) by businesses has received limited First Amendment protection. Restrictions on expression are permitted when the expression presents a clear and present danger to the peace or public order. Speech that has not received First Amendment protection includes expression judged to be obscene or slanderous.

4 The First Amendment protects against government interference with the freedom of the press, which can be regarded as a special instance of freedom of speech. Speech by the press that does not receive protection includes libelous statements. Publication of news about a criminal trial may be restricted by a gag order in some circumstances.

5 The First Amendment protects the right to assemble peaceably and to petition the government. Permits may be required for parades, sound trucks, and demonstrations to maintain the public order, and a permit may be denied to protect the public safety.

6 Under the Ninth Amendment, rights not specifically mentioned in the Constitution are not necessarily denied to the people. Among these unspecified rights protected by the courts is a right to privacy, which has been inferred from the First, Third, Fourth, Fifth, and Ninth Amendments. A major privacy issue today is how best to protect privacy rights in cyberspace. Whether an individual's privacy rights include a right to an abortion or a "right to die" continues to provoke controversy. Another major challenge concerns the extent to which Americans must forfeit privacy rights to control terrorism.

7 The Constitution includes protections for the rights of persons accused of crimes. Under the Fourth Amendment, no one may be subject to an unreasonable search or seizure or be arrested except on probable cause. Under the Fifth Amendment, an accused person has the right to remain silent. Under the Sixth Amendment, an accused person must be informed of the reason for his or her arrest. The accused also has the right to adequate counsel, even if he or she cannot afford an attorney, and the right to a prompt arraignment and a speedy and public trial before an impartial jury selected from a cross-section of the community.

8 In *Miranda v. Arizona* (1966), the Supreme Court held that criminal suspects, before interrogation by law enforcement personnel, must be informed of certain constitutional rights, including the right to remain silent and the right to counsel.

9 The exclusionary rule forbids the admission in court of illegally seized evidence. There is a "good faith exception" to the exclusionary rule: illegally seized evidence need not be thrown out owing to, for example, a technical defect in a search warrant. Under the Eighth Amendment, cruel and unusual punishment is prohibited. Whether the death penalty is cruel and unusual punishment continues to be debated.

★ Selected Print and Media Resources

SUGGESTED READINGS

Epps, Garrett. *To an Unknown God: Religious Freedom on Trial.* New York: St. Martin's Press, 2001. The author chronicles the journey through the courts of *Oregon v. Smith* (discussed earlier in this chapter), a case concerning religious practices decided by the Supreme Court in 1990. The author regards this case as one of the Supreme Court's most momentous decisions on religious freedom in the last fifty years.

Gottlieb, Roger S. *Joining Hands: Politics and Religion Together for Social Change.* Boulder, Colo.: Westview Press, 2002. In this exploration of the political role of religion and the spiritual component of politics, the author argues that religious belief and spiritual practice are integral to the politics of social change in the United States.

Leone, Richard C., and Anrig Greg, Jr., eds. *The War on Our Freedoms: Civil Liberties in an Age of Terrorism.* New York: PublicAffairs, 2003. In this book, experts from various fields argue that measures taken since the attacks of September 11, 2001, threaten our liberties.

Lewis, Anthony. *Gideon's Trumpet.* New York: Vintage, 1964. This classic work discusses the background and facts of *Gideon v. Wainwright,* the 1963 Supreme Court case in which the Court held that the state must make an attorney available for any person accused of a felony who cannot afford a lawyer.

MEDIA RESOURCES

The Abortion War: Thirty Years after Roe v. Wade—An ABC News program released in 2003 that examines the current state of the abortion issue.

The Chamber—A movie, based on John Grisham's novel by the same name, about a young lawyer who defends a man (his grandfather) who has been sentenced to death and faces imminent execution.

Execution at Midnight—A video presenting the arguments and evidence on both sides of the controversial death penalty issue.

Gideon's Trumpet—An excellent 1980 movie about the *Gideon v. Wainwright* case. Henry Fonda plays the role of the convicted petty thief Clarence Earl Gideon.

May It Please the Court: The First Amendment—A set of audiocassette recordings and written transcripts of the oral arguments made before the Supreme Court in sixteen key First Amendment cases. Participants in the recording include nationally known attorneys and several Supreme Court justices.

The People versus Larry Flynt—An R-rated 1996 film that clearly articulates the conflict between freedom of the press and how a community defines pornography.

Skokie: Rights or Wrong?—A documentary by Sheila Chamovitz. The film documents the legal and moral crisis created when American Nazis attempted to demonstrate in Skokie, Illinois, a predominantly Jewish suburb that was home to many concentration camp survivors.

e-mocracy ★ Understanding Your Civil Liberties

Today, the online world offers opportunities for Americans to easily access information concerning the nature of their civil liberties, how they originated, and how they may be threatened by various government actions. Several of the Web sites in the *Logging On* section of Chapter 2 present documents that set forth and explain the civil liberties guaranteed by the Constitution. In the *Logging On* section that follows, we list other Web sites you can visit to gain insights into the nature of these liberties.

Logging On

The American Civil Liberties Union (ACLU), the nation's leading civil liberties organization, provides an extensive array of information and links concerning civil rights issues at

http://www.aclu.org

The Liberty Counsel describes itself as "a nonprofit religious civil liberties education and legal defense organization established to preserve religious freedom." The URL for its Web site is

http://www.lc.org

Summaries and the full text of Supreme Court decisions concerning consitutional law, plus a virtual tour of the Supreme Court, are available at

http://www.oyez.org/oyez/frontpage

If you want to read historic Supreme Court decisions, you can search for them at

http://supct.law.cornell.edu/ supct/search/index.html

The Center for Democracy and Technology (CDT) focuses on how developments in communications technology are affecting the constitutional liberties of Americans. You can access the CDT's site at

http://www.cdt.org

The American Library Association's Web site provides information on free speech issues, especially issues of free speech on the Internet. Go to

http://www.ala.org

You can find current information on Internet privacy issues at the Electronic Privacy Information Center's Web site. Go to

http://www.epic.org/privacy

For the history of flag protection and the First Amendment, as well as the status of the proposed flag amendment in Congress, go to

http://www.freedomforum.org/ packages/first/Flag/timeline.htm

Using InfoTrac for Political Research

 As you read in this chapter, governments, including the federal, state, and local governments, are restrained from interfering with certain individual freedoms. The Bill of Rights contained in the U.S. Constitution and the bills of rights contained in the various state constitutions all protect the individual from particular government actions. Nonetheless, governments frequently take action against individual liberties. Various groups monitor these government infringements on civil liberties. One of the most well-known groups is the American Civil Liberties Union (ACLU).

To use InfoTrac to research the ACLU, go to

http://www.infotrac-college.com

Log in and go to InfoTrac College Edition. If you want to obtain a broad view of the kinds of activities in which the ACLU is involved, you can simply type "aclu" in the search box on the Keyword search page. InfoTrac will present you with a long list of articles on the ACLU, starting with the most recent one. If you would like to narrow your search somewhat, you could type a key word into the search box along with "aclu." For example, you might search on "aclu religion" or "aclu speech." You can also

look for material on the ACLU using the Subject search page.

After you have generated a list of articles, read a few that address a particular issue. Do you think this is an important civil liberty to defend? Do you agree with the ACLU's position on the issue? Is there anything concerning the issue that surprised you, or did you learn about a government law or action that you have never heard about before?

At **http://politicalscience.wadsworth. com/schmidt12**, you will find a free Study Guide to this book. For each chapter, there are two online quizzes to help you master the material.

• The **PoliPrep Self Study Assessment** provides a pre-test for each major section of the chapter. PoliPrep then generates a customized study plan. After you complete the study plan, a post-test evaluates your progress.

• The **Tutorial Quiz** for each chapter provides questions on the chapter contents, including the features. The questions are organized to match the major sections of the chapter.

Civil Rights

WHAT IF . . .
One State's Same-Sex Marriages
Had to Be Recognized Nationwide?

BACKGROUND

As you learned in Chapter 3, the Constitution requires that each state give full faith and credit to every other state's public acts. If a man and woman are married under the laws of Nevada, the other forty-nine states must recognize that marriage. But what if one state recognizes same-sex marriages? Does that mean that all other states must recognize such marriages and give each partner the benefits accorded to partners in opposite-sex marriages?

In 1996, Congress attempted to prevent such a result through the Defense of Marriage Act, which allows state governments to ignore same-sex marriages performed in other states. But what would happen if the United States Supreme Court ruled that the Defense of Marriage Act is unconstitutional? If this happened, then all of the state laws that refuse to recognize same-sex marriages performed in another state would be unconstitutional as well, because the U.S. Constitution is the supreme law of the land.

WHAT IF ONE STATE'S SAME-SEX MARRIAGES HAD TO BE RECOGNIZED NATIONWIDE?

If same-sex marriages were allowed, then same-sex relationships would be much more conspicuous. There are many contexts in which marriage is an issue—everything from registering at a hotel to applying for a line of credit. Hotel clerks or bankers who would prefer not to deal with same-sex couples would be forced to confront the reality of these relationships.

What about federal benefits? The national government has traditionally left marriage to the states. In the past, the Internal Revenue Service, the Social Security Administration, and other federal agencies recognized marriages when, and only when, the states recognized them. The Defense of Marriage Act is the first occasion on which the national government has established its own definition of marriage. Under the act, no matter what the states do, federal agencies cannot recognize same-sex marriages. If the Defense of Marriage Act were declared unconstitutional, however, the federal government might again have to accept all state-defined marriages, and a same-sex marriage in a state that allowed such unions would entitle the couple to federal benefits.

ENFORCING THE LAW

A majority of the American electorate is opposed to marriages that unite two lesbians or two gay men. In some parts of the country, such opposition may be overwhelming. If same-sex marriages were legal nationwide, officials in conservative states might refuse to recognize such marriages, regardless of the law. It could take a long campaign of lawsuits to enforce widespread compliance.

Currently, it is advocates of same-sex marriage who have challenged the legal process. In February 2004, San Francisco began issuing marriage licenses to same-sex couples even though the marriages were against California law. By March, officials in other jurisdictions had begun to copy San Francisco. In effect, these officials—and the people they married—were engaging in acts of civil disobedience on behalf of same-sex marriage. (We discuss civil disobedience in the African American civil rights movement later in this chapter.)

HOW IT COULD HAPPEN

There are two requirements for nationwide recognition of same-sex marriages. One is that the Defense of Marriage Act be ruled unconstitutional. It is open to question whether the Supreme Court would actually issue such a ruling. The other requirement, however—legalization of same-sex marriage by one or more states—may be in place already. In November 2003, the Massachusetts Supreme Judicial Court ruled that same-sex couples have a right to civil marriage under the Massachusetts state constitution.* The court also ruled that civil unions would not suffice. *Civil unions* are legally recognized partnerships that provide some or all of the state benefits provided to married couples. As of 2004, Vermont is the only state with a law that recognizes civil unions for same-sex couples.

FOR CRITICAL ANALYSIS

1. President George W. Bush has endorsed an amendment to the U.S. Constitution to ban same-sex marriage. What difficulties do the advocates of this amendment face in getting it adopted?
2. What impact would widespread same-sex marriage have on American culture generally?

*Goodridge v. Department of Public Health, 798 N.E.2d 941 (Mass. 2003).

The topic of this chapter's opening *What If . . .* feature—the right to same-sex marriage—certainly was not an issue in the early years of this nation. In spite of the words set forth in the Declaration of Independence that "all Men are created equal," the concept of equal treatment under the law was a distant dream in those years. In fact, the majority of the population had few rights. As you learned in Chapter 2, the framers of the Constitution permitted slavery to continue. Slaves thus were excluded from the political process. Women also were excluded for the most part, as were Native Americans, African Americans who were not slaves, and even white men who did not own property. Indeed, it has taken this nation more than two hundred years to approach even a semblance of equality among all Americans. Today, in contrast, we have numerous civil rights. Indeed, some people claim that we have too many rights and that the expansion of civil rights has circumvented reasonable approaches to handling social problems.

Equality is at the heart of the concept of civil rights. Generally, the term **civil rights** refers to the rights of all Americans to equal treatment under the law, as provided for by the Fourteenth Amendment to the Constitution. Although the terms *civil rights* and *civil liberties* are sometimes used interchangeably, scholars make a distinction between the two. As you learned in Chapter 4, civil liberties are basically *limitations* on government; they specify what the government *cannot* do. Civil rights, in contrast, specify what the government *must* do—to ensure equal protection and freedom from discrimination.

Essentially, the history of civil rights in America is the story of the struggle of various groups to be free from discriminatory treatment. In this chapter, we first look at two movements that had significant consequences for the history of civil rights in America: the civil rights movement of the 1950s and 1960s and the women's movement, which began in the mid-1800s and continues today. Each of these movements resulted in legislation that secured important basic rights for all Americans—the right to vote and the right to equal protection under the laws. We then explore a question with serious implications for today's voters and policymakers: What should the government's responsibility be when equal protection under the law is not enough to ensure truly equal opportunities for Americans?

Note that most minorities in this nation have suffered—and some continue to suffer—from discrimination. Hispanics, Native Americans, Asian Americans, Arab Americans from Middle Eastern countries, and persons from India all have had to struggle for equal treatment, as have people from various island nations and other countries. The fact that these groups are not singled out for special attention in the following pages should not be construed to mean that their struggle for equality is any less significant than the struggles of those groups that we do discuss.

★ African Americans and the Consequences of Slavery in the United States

Before 1863, the Constitution protected slavery and made equality impossible in the sense in which we use the word today. African American leader Frederick Douglass pointed out that "Liberty and Slavery—opposite as Heaven and Hell— are both in the Constitution." As Abraham Lincoln stated sarcastically, "All men are created equal, except Negroes."

The constitutionality of slavery was confirmed just a few years before the outbreak of the Civil War in the famous *Dred Scott v. Sanford*[1] case of 1857. The Supreme Court held that slaves were not citizens of the United States, nor were

[1] 19 Howard 393 (1857).

Civil Rights
Generally, all rights rooted in the Fourteenth Amendment's guarantee of equal protection under the law.

This is a portrait of Dred Scott (1795–1858), an American slave who was born in Virginia and who later moved with his owner to Illinois, where slavery was illegal. He was the nominal plaintiff in a test case that sought to obtain his freedom on the ground that he lived in the free state of Illinois. Although the Supreme Court ruled against him, he was soon emancipated and became a hotel porter in St. Louis. (Missouri Historical Society)

they entitled to the rights and privileges of citizenship. The Court also ruled that the Missouri Compromise, which banned slavery in the territories north of 36°30' latitude (the southern border of Missouri), was unconstitutional. The *Dred Scott* decision had grave consequences. Most observers contend that the ruling contributed to making the Civil War inevitable.

Ending Servitude

With the emancipation of the slaves by President Lincoln's Emancipation Proclamation in 1863 and the passage of the Thirteenth, Fourteenth, and Fifteenth Amendments during the Reconstruction period following the Civil War, constitutional inequality was ended.

The Thirteenth Amendment (1865) states that neither slavery nor involuntary servitude shall exist within the United States. The Fourteenth Amendment (1868) tells us that *all* persons born or naturalized in the United States are citizens of the United States. It states, furthermore, that "[n]o State shall make or enforce any law which shall abridge the privileges or immunities of citizens of the United States; nor shall any State deprive any person of life, liberty, or property, without due process of law; nor deny to any person within its jurisdiction the equal protection of the laws." Note the use of the terms *citizen* and *person* in this amendment. *Citizens* have political rights, such as the right to vote and run for political office. Citizens also have certain privileges or immunities (see Chapter 3). All *persons,* however, including noncitizen immigrants, have a right to due process of law and equal protection under the law.

The Fifteenth Amendment (1870) reads as follows: "The right of citizens of the United States to vote shall not be denied or abridged by the United States or by any State on account of race, color, or previous condition of servitude."

The Civil Rights Acts of 1865 to 1875

From 1865 to 1875, Congress passed a series of civil rights acts that were aimed at enforcing these amendments. The Civil Rights Act of 1866 extended citizen-

Abraham Lincoln reads the Emancipation Proclamation on July 22, 1862. The Emancipation Proclamation did not abolish slavery (that was done by the Thirteenth Amendment, in 1865), but it ensured that slavery would be abolished if and when the North won the Civil War. After the Battle of Antietam on September 17, 1862, Lincoln publicly announced the Emancipation Proclamation and declared that all slaves residing in states that were still in rebellion against the United States on January 1, 1863, would be freed once those states came under the military control of the Union Army. (The Granger Collection)

ship to anyone born in the United States and gave African Americans full equality before the law. The act further authorized the president to enforce the law with national armed forces. The Enforcement Act of 1870 set out specific criminal sanctions for interfering with the right to vote as protected by the Fifteenth Amendment and by the Civil Rights Act of 1866. Equally important was the Civil Rights Act of 1872, known as the Anti–Ku Klux Klan Act. This act made it a federal crime for anyone to use law or custom to deprive an individual of rights, privileges, and immunities secured by the Constitution or by any federal law. The Second Civil Rights Act, passed in 1875, declared that everyone is entitled to full and equal enjoyment of public accommodations, theaters, and other places of public amusement, and it imposed penalties for violators.

DID YOU KNOW . . .
That by the end of the Civil War, 180,000 African American troops were in arms for the North, providing services that included occupying conquered territory, and that Lincoln said the war could never have been concluded without these forces**?**

The Ineffectiveness of the Civil Rights Laws

The Reconstruction statutes, or civil rights acts, ultimately did little to secure equality for African Americans. Both the *Civil Rights Cases* and the case of *Plessy v. Ferguson* effectively nullified these acts. Additionally, various barriers were erected that prevented African Americans from exercising their right to vote.

The *Civil Rights Cases*. The Supreme Court invalidated the 1875 Civil Rights Act when it held, in the *Civil Rights Cases*[2] of 1883, that the enforcement clause of the Fourteenth Amendment (which states that "[n]o State shall make or enforce any law which shall abridge the privileges or immunities of citizens") was limited to correcting actions by states in their *official* acts; thus, the discriminatory acts of *private* citizens were not illegal. ("Individual invasion of individual rights is not the subject matter of the Amendment.") The 1883 Supreme Court decision met with widespread approval throughout most of the United States.

Twenty years after the Civil War, the white majority was all too willing to forget about the Civil War amendments and the civil rights legislation of the 1860s and 1870s. The other civil rights laws that the Court did not specifically invalidate became dead letters in the statute books, although they were never repealed by Congress. At the same time, many former proslavery secessionists had regained political power in the southern states.

Plessy v. Ferguson: Separate but Equal. A key decision during this period concerned Homer Plessy, a Louisiana resident who was one-eighth African American. In 1892, he boarded a train in New Orleans. The conductor made him leave the car, which was restricted to whites, and directed him to a car for nonwhites. At that time, Louisiana had a statute providing for separate railway cars for whites and African Americans.

Plessy went to court, claiming that such a statute was contrary to the Fourteenth Amendment's equal protection clause. In 1896, the United States Supreme Court rejected Plessy's contention. The Court concluded that the Fourteenth Amendment "could not have been intended to abolish distinctions based upon color, or to enforce social . . . equality." The Court stated that segregation alone did not violate the Constitution: "Laws permitting, and even requiring, their separation in places where they are liable to be brought into contact do not necessarily imply the inferiority of either race to the other."[3] So was born the **separate-but-equal doctrine.**

Plessy v. Ferguson became the judicial cornerstone of racial discrimination throughout the United States. Even though *Plessy* upheld segregated facilities in railway cars only, it was assumed that the Supreme Court was upholding

Separate-but-Equal Doctrine
The doctrine holding that separate-but-equal facilities do not violate the equal protection clause.

---

[2]109 U.S. 3 (1883).
[3]*Plessy v. Ferguson*, 163 U.S. 537 (1896).

segregation everywhere as long as the separate facilities were equal. The result was a system of racial segregation, particularly in the South—supported by laws collectively known as Jim Crow laws—that required separate drinking fountains; separate seats in theaters, restaurants, and hotels; separate public toilets; and separate waiting rooms for the two races. "Separate" was indeed the rule, but "equal" was never enforced, nor was it a reality.

Voting Barriers.   The brief enfranchisement of African Americans ended after 1877, when the federal troops that occupied the South during the Reconstruction era were withdrawn. Southern politicians regained control of state governments and, using everything except race as a formal criterion, passed laws that effectively deprived African Americans of the right to vote. By using the ruse that political parties were private bodies, the Democratic Party was allowed to keep black voters from its primaries. The **white primary** was upheld by the Supreme Court until 1944 when, in *Smith v. Allwright*,[4] the Court ruled it a violation of the Fifteenth Amendment.

Another barrier to African American voting was the **grandfather clause**, which restricted voting to those who could prove that their grandfathers had voted before 1867. **Poll taxes** required the payment of a fee to vote; thus, poor African Americans—as well as poor whites—who could not afford to pay the tax were excluded from voting. Not until the Twenty-fourth Amendment to the Constitution was ratified in 1964 was the poll tax eliminated as a precondition to voting. **Literacy tests** were also used to deny the vote to African Americans. Such tests asked potential voters to read, recite, or interpret complicated texts, such as a section of the state constitution, to the satisfaction of local registrars—who were, of course, never satisfied with the responses of African Americans.

Extralegal Methods of Enforcing White Supremacy.   The second-class status of African Americans was also a matter of social custom, especially in the South. In their interactions with southern whites, African Americans were expected to observe an informal but detailed code of behavior that confirmed their inferiority. The most serious violation of the informal code was "familiarity" toward a white woman by an African American man or boy. The code was backed up by

---

[4]321 U.S. 649 (1944).

White Primary
A state primary election that restricts voting to whites only; outlawed by the Supreme Court in 1944.

Grandfather Clause
A device used by southern states to disenfranchise African Americans. It restricted voting to those whose grandfathers had voted before 1867.

Poll Tax
A special tax that must be paid as a qualification for voting. The Twenty-fourth Amendment to the Constitution outlawed the poll tax in national elections, and in 1966 the Supreme Court declared it unconstitutional in all elections.

Literacy Test
A test administered as a precondition for voting, often used to prevent African Americans from exercising their right to vote.

Jim Crow laws required the segregation of the races, particularly in public facilities such as this theater. The name "Jim Crow," which came from a vaudeville character of the 1800s, was applied to laws and practices that enforced segregation. Facilities provided to African Americans under segregation were almost always inferior to the ones provided to whites. What factors may have led to this kind of discrimination? (Library of Congress)

the common practice of *lynching*—mob action to murder an accused individual, usually by hanging and sometimes accompanied by torture. Lynching was a common response to an accusation of "familiarity." Of course, lynching was illegal, but southern authorities rarely prosecuted these cases, and white juries would not convict.

African Americans outside the South were subject to a second kind of violence—race riots. In the early twentieth century, race riots were typically initiated by whites. Frequently, the riots were caused by competition for employment. For example, there were a number of serious riots during World War II (1939–1945), when labor shortages forced northern employers to hire more black workers.

The End of the Separate-but-Equal Doctrine

A successful attack on the separate-but-equal doctrine began with a series of lawsuits in the 1930s that sought to admit African Americans to state professional schools. By 1950, the Supreme Court had ruled that African Americans who were admitted to a state university could not be assigned to separate sections of classrooms, libraries, and cafeterias.

In 1951, Oliver Brown decided that his eight-year-old daughter, Linda Carol Brown, should not have to go to an all-nonwhite elementary school twenty-one blocks from her home, when there was a white school only seven blocks away. The National Association for the Advancement of Colored People (NAACP), formed in 1909, decided to support Oliver Brown. The outcome would have a monumental impact on American society.

Brown v. Board of Education of Topeka.   The 1954 unanimous decision of the United States Supreme Court in *Brown v. Board of Education of Topeka*[5] established that segregation of races in the public schools violates the equal protection clause of the Fourteenth Amendment. Chief Justice Earl Warren said that separation implied inferiority, whereas the majority opinion in *Plessy v. Ferguson* had said the opposite.

"With All Deliberate Speed."   The following year, in *Brown v. Board of Education*[6] (sometimes called the second *Brown* decision), the Court declared that the lower courts needed to ensure that African Americans would be admitted to schools on a nondiscriminatory basis "with all deliberate speed." The district courts were to consider devices in their desegregation orders that might include "the school transportation system, personnel, [and] revision of school districts and attendance areas into compact units to achieve a system of determining admission to the public schools on a nonracial basis."

Reactions to School Integration

The white South did not let the Supreme Court ruling go unchallenged. Governor Orval Faubus of Arkansas used the state's National Guard to block the integration of Central High School in Little Rock in September 1957. The federal court demanded that the troops be withdrawn. Finally, President Dwight Eisenhower had to federalize the Arkansas National Guard and send in the Army's 101st Airborne Division to quell the violence. Central High became integrated.

The universities in the South, however, remained segregated. When James Meredith, an African American student, attempted to enroll at the University of Mississippi in Oxford in 1962, violence flared there, as it had in Little Rock. The

[5]347 U.S. 483 (1954).
[6]349 U.S. 294 (1955).

De Facto Segregation
Racial segregation that occurs because of past social and economic conditions and residential racial patterns.

De Jure Segregation
Racial segregation that occurs because of laws or administrative decisions by public agencies.

Busing
In the context of civil rights, the transportation of public school students from areas where they live to schools in other areas to eliminate school segregation based on residential patterns.

white riot at Oxford was so intense that President John Kennedy was forced to send in 30,000 U.S. combat troops, a larger force than the one then stationed in Korea. There were 375 military and civilian injuries, many from gunfire, and two bystanders were killed. Ultimately, peace was restored, and Meredith began attending classes.[7]

An Integrationist Attempt at a Cure: Busing

In most parts of the United States, residential concentrations by race have made it difficult to achieve racial balance in schools. Although it is true that a number of school boards in northern districts created segregated schools by drawing school district lines arbitrarily, the residential concentration of African Americans and other minorities in well-defined geographic locations has contributed to the difficulty of achieving racial balance. This concentration results in ***de facto* segregation,** as distinct from ***de jure* segregation,** which results from laws or administrative decisions.

Court-Ordered Busing.   The obvious solution to both *de facto* and *de jure* segregation seemed to be transporting some African American schoolchildren to white schools and some white schoolchildren to African American schools. Increasingly, the courts ordered school districts to engage in such **busing** across neighborhoods. Busing led to violence in some northern cities, such as in south Boston, where African American students were bused into blue-collar Irish Catholic neighborhoods. Indeed, busing was unpopular with many groups. In the mid-1970s, almost 50 percent of African Americans interviewed were opposed to busing, and approximately three-fourths of the whites interviewed held the same opinion. Nonetheless, through the next decade, the Supreme Court fairly consistently upheld busing plans in the cases it decided.

The End of Integration?   During the 1980s and the early 1990s, the Supreme Court tended to back away from its earlier commitment to busing and other methods of desegregation. By the late 1990s and early 2000s, the federal courts

[7]William Doyle, *An American Insurrection: James Meredith and the Battle of Oxford, Mississippi, 1962* (New York: Anchor, 2003).

For a number of years after the *Brown* decision, whites reacted aggressively to attempts at desegregation. In Little Rock, Arkansas, Governor Orval Faubus sent in the state's National Guard to prevent African American students from entering Little Rock Central High School on September 2, 1957. On September 24, President Dwight Eisenhower sent in five hundred soldiers to enforce integration. Many of them remained there for the rest of the school year. (Burt Glinn/Magnum)

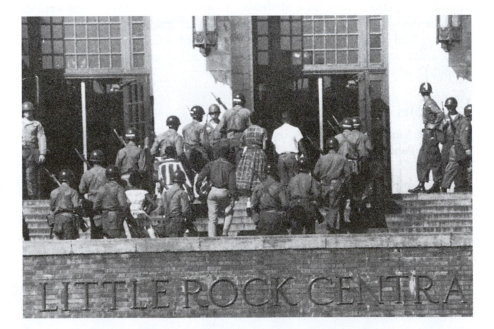

were increasingly unwilling to uphold race-conscious policies designed to further school integration and diversity—outcomes that are not mandated by the Constitution. For example, in 2001, a federal appellate court held that the Charlotte-Mecklenburg school district in North Carolina had achieved the goal of integration,[8] meaning that race-based admission quotas could no longer be imposed constitutionally.

The Resurgence of Minority Schools.   Today, schools around the country are becoming segregated again, in large part because of *de facto* segregation. The rapid decline in the relative proportion of whites who live in large cities and high minority birthrates have increased the minority presence in those urban areas. Today, one out of every three African American and Hispanic students goes to a school with more than 90 percent minority enrollment. In the largest U.S. cities, fifteen out of sixteen African American and Hispanic students go to schools with almost no non-Hispanic whites.

Generally, Americans are now taking another look at what desegregation means. The attempt to integrate the schools, particularly through busing, has largely failed to improve educational resources and achievement for African American children. The goal of racially balanced schools envisioned in the 1954 *Brown v. Board of Education of Topeka* decision is giving way to the goal of better education for children, even if that means educating them in schools in which students are of the same race or in which race is not considered.

The Civil Rights Movement

The *Brown* decision applied only to public schools. Not much else in the structure of existing segregation was affected. In December 1955, a forty-three-year-old African American woman, Rosa Parks, boarded a public bus in Montgomery, Alabama. When the bus became crowded and several white people stepped

---

[8]*Belk v. Charlotte-Mecklenburg Board of Education,* 269 F.3d 305 (4th Cir. 2001).

Born in Alabama, Rosa Parks was active in the Montgomery Voters' League and the NAACP (National Association for the Advancement of Colored People) League Council. After the successful boycott of the Montgomery bus system, which was sparked by her actions, she was fired from her job and subsequently moved to Detroit. Can actions by an ordinary person change history? Why or why not? (AP Photo/Paul Warner)

aboard, Parks was asked to move to the rear of the bus, the "colored" section. She refused, was arrested, and was fined $10; but that was not the end of the matter. For an entire year, African Americans boycotted the Montgomery bus line. The protest was headed by a twenty-seven-year-old Baptist minister, Dr. Martin Luther King, Jr. During the protest period, he went to jail, and his house was bombed. In the face of overwhelming odds, King won. In 1956, a federal district court issued an injunction prohibiting the segregation of buses in Montgomery. The era of civil rights protests had begun.

King's Philosophy of Nonviolence

Civil Disobedience
A nonviolent, public refusal to obey allegedly unjust laws.

The following year, in 1957, King formed the Southern Christian Leadership Conference (SCLC). King advocated nonviolent **civil disobedience** as a means to achieve racial justice. King's philosophy of civil disobedience was influenced, in part, by the life and teachings of Mahatma Gandhi (1869–1948). Gandhi had led resistance to the British colonial system in India from 1919 to 1947. He used tactics such as demonstrations and marches, as well as nonviolent, public disobedience to unjust laws. King's followers successfully used these methods to gain wider public acceptance of their cause.

Dr. Martin Luther King, Jr., acknowledges the crowd at the August 1963 March on Washington for Jobs and Freedom. Nearly a quarter-million African Americans and sympathetic whites participated in the march. The march is best remembered for King's eloquent "I have a dream" speech and the assembled multitude singing "We Shall Overcome," the anthem of the civil rights movement. (AP Photo)

Nonviolent Demonstrations.   For the next decade, African Americans and sympathetic whites engaged in sit-ins, freedom rides, and freedom marches. In the beginning, such demonstrations were often met with violence, and the contrasting image of nonviolent African Americans and violent, hostile whites created strong public support for the civil rights movement. When African Americans in Greensboro, North Carolina, were refused service at a Woolworth's lunch counter, they organized a sit-in that was aided day after day by sympathetic whites and other African Americans. Enraged customers threw ketchup on the protesters. Some spat in their faces. The sit-in movement continued to grow, however. Within six months of the first sit-in at the Greensboro Woolworth's, hundreds of lunch counters throughout the South were serving African Americans.

The sit-in technique also was successfully used to integrate interstate buses and their terminals, as well as railroads engaged in interstate transportation. Although buses and railroads engaged in interstate transportation were prohibited by law from segregating African Americans from whites, they stopped doing so only after the sit-in protests.

Marches and Demonstrations.   One of the most famous of the violence-plagued protests occurred in Birmingham, Alabama, in 1963, when Police Commissioner Eugene "Bull" Connor unleashed police dogs and used electric cattle prods against the protesters. People throughout the country viewed the event on television with indignation and horror. King himself was thrown in jail. The media coverage of the Birmingham protest and the violent response by the city government played a key role in the process of ending Jim Crow in the United States. The ultimate result was the most important civil rights act in the nation's history, the Civil Rights Act of 1964 (to be discussed shortly).

In August 1963, African American leaders A. Philip Randolph and Bayard Rustin organized a massive March on Washington for Jobs and Freedom. Before nearly a quarter-million white and African American spectators and millions watching on television, King told the world his dream: "I have a dream that my four little children will one day live in a nation where they will not be judged by the color of their skin but by the content of their character."

Malcolm X opposed the philosophy of nonviolence espoused by Martin Luther King, Jr., and he urged African Americans to "fight back" against white supremacy. Some people have argued that such a militant approach is almost always counterproductive. Others believe that a militant alternative may have made King's peaceful appeal more attractive. Are either of these arguments persuasive? Why or why not? (AP Photo)

Another Approach—Black Power

Not all African Americans agreed with King's philosophy of nonviolence or with the idea that King's strong Christian background should represent the core spirituality of African Americans. Black Muslims and other African American separatists advocated a more militant stance and argued that desegregation should not result in cultural assimilation. During the 1950s and 1960s, when King was spearheading nonviolent protests and demonstrations to achieve civil rights for African Americans, black power leaders insisted that African Americans should "fight back" instead of turning the other cheek. Indeed, some would argue that without the fear generated by black militants, a "moderate" such as King would not have garnered such widespread support from white America.

Malcolm Little (who became Malcolm X when he joined the Black Muslims in 1952) and other leaders in the black power movement believed that African Americans fell into two groups: the "Uncle Toms," who peaceably accommodated the white establishment, and the "New Negroes," who took pride in their color and culture and who preferred and demanded racial separation as well as power. Malcolm X was assassinated in 1965, but he became an important reference point for a new generation of African Americans and a symbol of African American identity.

 ## The Climax of the Civil Rights Movement

Police-dog attacks, cattle prods, high-pressure water hoses, beatings, bombings, the March on Washington, and black militancy—all of these events and developments led to an environment in which Congress felt compelled to act on behalf of African Americans. The second era of civil rights acts, sometimes referred to as the second Reconstruction period, was under way.

Civil Rights Legislation

As the civil rights movement mounted in intensity, equality before the law came to be "an idea whose time has come," in the words of Republican Senate Minority Leader Everett Dirksen.

The Civil Rights Act of 1964. The Civil Rights Act of 1964, the most far-reaching bill on civil rights in modern times, forbade discrimination on the basis of race, color, religion, gender, and national origin. The major provisions of the act were as follows:

1. It outlawed arbitrary discrimination in voter registration.
2. It barred discrimination in public accommodations, such as hotels and restaurants, whose operations affect interstate commerce.
3. It authorized the federal government to sue to desegregate public schools and facilities.
4. It expanded the power of the Civil Rights Commission and extended its life.
5. It provided for the withholding of federal funds from programs administered in a discriminatory manner.
6. It established the right to equality of opportunity in employment.

Title VII of the Civil Rights Act of 1964 is the cornerstone of employment-discrimination law. It prohibits discrimination in employment based on race, color, religion, gender, or national origin. Under Title VII, executive orders were issued that banned employment discrimination by firms that received any federal funding. The 1964 Civil Rights Act created a five-member commission, the Equal Employment Opportunity Commission (EEOC), to administer Title VII.

The EEOC can issue interpretive guidelines and regulations, but these do not have the force of law. Rather, they give notice of the commission's enforcement policy. The EEOC also has investigatory powers. It has broad authority to require the production of documentary evidence, to hold hearings, and to **subpoena** and examine witnesses under oath.

Subpoena
A legal writ requiring a person's appearance in court to give testimony.

The Voting Rights Act of 1965. As late as 1960, only 29.1 percent of African Americans of voting age were registered in the southern states, in stark contrast to 61.1 percent of whites. The Voting Rights Act of 1965 addressed this issue. The act had two major provisions. The first one outlawed discriminatory voter-registration

President Lyndon Johnson shakes hands with civil rights leader Martin Luther King, Jr., during the signing of the Civil Rights Act of 1964. Some of the objectives of the act, such as equal voting rights, proved to be easier to obtain than others (for example, desegregated schools). Why would some goals of the act be more difficult to reach? (© Bettmann/CORBIS)

tests. The second authorized federal registration of voters and federally administered voting procedures in any political subdivision or state that discriminated electorally against a particular group. In part, the act provided that certain political subdivisions could not change their voting procedures and election laws without federal approval. The act targeted counties, mostly in the South, in which less than 50 percent of the eligible population was registered to vote. Federal voter registrars were sent to these areas to register African Americans who had been kept from voting by local registrars. Within one week after the act was passed, forty-five federal examiners were sent to the South. A massive voter-registration drive covered the country.

Urban Riots.   Even as the civil rights movement was experiencing its greatest victories, a series of riots swept through African American inner-city neighborhoods. These urban riots were different in character from the race riots described earlier in this chapter. The riots in the first half of the twentieth century were street battles between whites and blacks. The urban riots of the late 1960s and early 1970s, however, were not directed against individual whites—in some cases whites actually participated in small numbers. The riots were primarily civil insurrections, although these disorders were accompanied by large-scale looting of stores. Inhabitants of the affected neighborhoods attributed the riots to racial discrimination.[9] The riots dissipated much of the goodwill toward the civil rights movement that had been built up earlier in the decade among northern whites. Together with widespread student demonstrations against the Vietnam War (1964–1975), the riots pushed many Americans toward conservatism.

The Civil Rights Act of 1968 and Other Housing Reform Legislation.   Martin Luther King, Jr., was assassinated on April 4, 1968. Despite King's message of peace, his death was followed by the most widespread rioting to date. Nine days after King's death, President Johnson signed the Civil Rights Act of 1968, which forbade discrimination in most housing and provided penalties for those attempting to interfere with individual civil rights (giving protection to civil rights workers, among others). Subsequent legislation added enforcement provisions to the federal government's rules against discriminatory mortgage-lending practices. Today, all lenders must report to the federal government the race, gender, and income of all mortgage-loan seekers, along with the final decision on their loan applications.

Consequences of Civil Rights Legislation

As a result of the Voting Rights Act of 1965 and its amendments, and the large-scale voter-registration drives in the South, the number of African Americans registered to vote climbed dramatically. By 1980, 55.8 percent of African Americans of voting age in the South were registered. In recent elections, the percentage of voting-age African Americans who have registered to vote has been just slightly less than the percentage of voting-age whites who have done so.

Political Participation by African Americans.   Today, there are more than 8,500 African American elected officials in the United States. The movement of African American citizens into high elected office has been sure, if exceedingly slow.

---

[9]Angus Campbell and Howard Schuman, *ICPSR 3500: Racial Attitudes in Fifteen American Cities, 1968* (Ann Arbor: Inter-university Consortium for Political and Social Research, 1997). Campbell and Schuman's survey documents both white participation and the attitudes of the inhabitants of affected neighborhoods. This survey is available online at **http://www.grinnell.edu/academic/data/sociology/minorityresearch/raceatt1968**.

DID YOU KNOW . . .
That after the assassination of Martin Luther King, Jr., riots took place in over 100 cities, 75,000 troops and members of the National Guard were mobilized, 27,000 African Americans were jailed, and 39 African Americans were killed**?**

In recent years, African American candidates for president have been taken more seriously than in the past. Here, several Democratic presidential candidates gather after a debate in 2003. They include, from left to right, former Illinois senator Carol Moseley Braun, Massachusetts senator John Kerry, the Reverend Al Sharpton of New York, Missouri representative Dick Gephardt, and North Carolina senator John Edwards. If an African American were to become president in the future, what kind of background and experience might that person have? (AP Photo/Matt York)

Notably, recent polling data show that most Americans do not consider race a significant factor in choosing a president. In 1958, when the Gallup poll first asked whether respondents would be willing to vote for an African American as president, only 38 percent of the public said yes. By 2004, this number had reached 95 percent. This high figure may have been attained, at least in part, because of the emergence of an African American who is widely considered to be of presidential caliber—Colin Powell, formerly chair of the Joint Chiefs of Staff and later secretary of state under President George W. Bush.

Political Participation by Other Minorities.   As mentioned earlier, the civil rights movement focused primarily on the rights of African Americans. Yet the legislation resulting from the movement has ultimately benefited virtually all minority groups. The Civil Rights Act of 1964, for example, prohibits discrimination against any person because of race, color, or national origin. Subsequent amendments to the Voting Rights Act of 1965 extended its protections to other minorities, including Hispanic Americans, Asian Americans, Native Americans, and Native Alaskans. To further protect the voting rights of minorities, the law now provides that states must make bilingual ballots available in counties where 5 percent or more of the population speaks a language other than English.

The political participation of other minority groups in the United States has also been increasing. For example, Hispanics are gaining political power in several states. Even though political participation by minorities has increased dramatically since the 1960s, the number of political offices held by members of minority groups remains disproportionately low compared with their numbers in the overall population. This will likely change in the future due to the continued influx of immigrants, particularly from Mexico. Collectively, Hispanics, African Americans, Native Americans, and Asian Americans are now a majority of the populations in California, Hawaii, and New Mexico. It is estimated that by 2015 minority populations will collectively outnumber whites in Texas as well.

Lingering Social and Economic Disparities.   According to Joyce Ladner of the Brookings Institution, one of the difficulties with the race-based civil rights agenda of the 1950s and 1960s is that it did not envision remedies for cross-racial problems. How, for example, should the nation address problems, such as poverty and urban violence, that affect underclasses in all racial groups? In 1967, when Martin Luther King, Jr., proposed a Poor People's Campaign, he recognized that a civil rights coalition based entirely on race would not be sufficient to address the problem of poverty among whites as well as blacks. During his 1984 and 1988 presidential campaigns, African American leader Jesse Jackson also acknowledged the inadequacy of a race-based model of civil rights when he attempted to form a "Rainbow Coalition" of minorities, women, and other underrepresented groups, including the poor.[10]

Some, including many liberals, contend that government intervention is necessary to eliminate the social and economic disparities that persist within the American population. Others, including a number of conservatives, believe that the most effective means of addressing these issues is through coalitions of government groups, private businesses, community-based groups, and individuals. Indeed, a number of civil rights activists today are pursuing the latter strategy.

Finally, even today, race consciousness continues to divide African Americans and white Americans. Whether we are talking about college attendance, media stereotyping, racial profiling, or academic achievement, the black experience is different from the white one. As a result, African Americans view the nation and many specific issues differently than their white counterparts do.[11] In survey after survey, when blacks are asked whether they have achieved racial equality, few believe that they have. In contrast, whites are five times more likely than blacks to believe that racial equality has been achieved.[12] In spite of the civil rights movement and civil rights legislation, African Americans continue to feel a sense of injustice in matters of race, and this feeling is often not apparent to, or appreciated by, the majority of white America.

★ Women's Struggle for Equal Rights

Like African Americans and other minorities, women also have had to struggle for equality. During the first phase of this struggle, the primary goal of women was to obtain the right to vote. Some women had hoped that the founders would provide such a right in the Constitution. The Constitution did not include a provision guaranteeing women the right to vote, but neither did it deny to women—or to any others—this right. Rather, the founders left it up to the states to decide such issues, and, as mentioned earlier, by and large, the states limited the franchise to adult white males who owned property.

Early Women's Political Movements

The first political cause in which women became actively engaged was the movement to abolish slavery. Yet even male abolitionists felt that women should not take an active role on the subject in public. When the World Antislavery Convention was held in London in 1840, women delegates were barred from active participation. Partly in response to this rebuff, two American delegates, Lucretia Mott and Elizabeth Cady Stanton, returned from that meeting with plans to work for women's rights in the United States.

In 1848, Mott and Stanton organized the first women's rights convention in Seneca Falls, New York. The three hundred people who attended approved a

Elizabeth Cady Stanton (1815–1902) was a social reformer and a women's suffrage leader. At her wedding to Henry B. Stanton in 1840, she insisted on dropping the word *obey* from the marriage vows. She wrote *The History of Women's Suffrage*, which was published in 1886. (Corbis/Bettmann)

---

[10]Joyce A. Ladner, "A New Civil Rights Agenda," *The Brookings Review*, Vol. 18, No. 2 (Spring 2000), pp. 26–28.
[11]Lawerence D. Bobo et al., "Through the Eyes of Black America," *Public Perspective*, May/June 2001, p. 13.
[12]*Ibid.*, p. 15, Figure 2.

Declaration of Sentiments: "We hold these truths to be self-evident: that all men *and women* are created equal." In the following twelve years, groups that supported women's rights held seven conventions in different cities in the Midwest and East. With the outbreak of the Civil War, however, advocates of women's rights were urged to put their support behind the war effort, and most agreed.

Women's Suffrage Associations

Susan B. Anthony and Elizabeth Cady Stanton formed the National Woman Suffrage Association in 1869. In their view, women's **suffrage** was a means to achieve major improvements in the economic and social situation of women in the United States. In other words, the vote was to be used to seek broader goals. Nowadays, we commonly see the women's rights movement as a liberal cause, but many of the broader goals of the suffrage advocates would not be regarded as liberal today. An example was the prohibition of alcoholic beverages, which received widespread support among women in general and women's rights activists in particular. It should be noted that many women considered prohibition to be a method of combating domestic violence.

Unlike Anthony and Stanton, Lucy Stone, a key founder of the rival American Woman Suffrage Association, believed that the vote was the only major issue. Members of the American Woman Suffrage Association traveled to each state; addressed state legislatures; and wrote, published, and argued their convictions. They achieved only limited success. In 1880, the two organizations joined forces. The resulting National American Woman Suffrage Association had only one goal—the enfranchisement of women—but it made little progress.

The Congressional Union, founded in the early 1900s by Alice Paul, rejected the state-by-state approach. Instead, the Union adopted a national strategy of obtaining an amendment to the U.S. Constitution. The Union also employed militant tactics. It sponsored large-scale marches and civil disobedience—which resulted in hunger strikes, arrests, and jailings. Finally, in 1920, the Nineteenth Amendment was passed: "The right of citizens of the United States to vote shall not be denied or abridged by the United States or by any State on account of sex." (Today, the word *gender* is typically used instead of *sex*.) Although it may seem that the United States was slow to give women the vote, it was really not too far behind the rest of the world (see Table 5–1). For more on women's rights around the world, see the *Global View* feature on the next page.

The Modern Women's Movement

Historian Nancy Cott contends that the word *feminism* first began to be used around 1910. At that time, **feminism** meant, as it does today, political, social, and economic equality for women—a radical notion that gained little support among members of the suffrage movement.

After gaining the right to vote in 1920, women engaged in little independent political activity until the 1960s. The civil rights movement of that decade resulted in a growing awareness of rights for all groups, including women. Increased partic-

Susan B. Anthony (1820–1906), a leader of the women's suffrage movement, was also active in the antialcohol and antislavery movements. In 1869, with Elizabeth Cady Stanton, she founded the National Woman Suffrage Association. In 1888, she organized the International Council of Women and, in 1904, the International Women's Suffrage Alliance, in Berlin. (Corbis/Bettmann)

Suffrage
The right to vote; the franchise.

Feminism
The movement that supports political, economic, and social equality for women.

TABLE 5–1

Years, by Country, in Which Women Gained the Right to Vote

1893: New Zealand	1919: Germany	1945: Italy	1953: Mexico
1902: Australia	1920: United States	1945: Japan	1956: Egypt
1913: Norway	1930: South Africa	1947: Argentina	1963: Kenya
1918: Britain	1932: Brazil	1950: India	1971: Switzerland
1918: Canada	1944: France	1952: Greece	1984: Yemen

SOURCE: Center for the American Woman and Politics.

GLOBAL VIEW
The Struggle for Women's Rights around the World

Although in the last several decades women's rights have emerged as a global issue, progress has been slow. The struggle for women's rights in countries where cultural or legal practices perpetuate the inequality of women is especially difficult.

THE PROBLEM OF VIOLENCE

Most people consider the right to be free from violence as one of the most basic human rights. Women's rights advocates point out that this right is threatened in societies that do not accept the premise that men and women are equal. Some parts of India, for example, implicitly tolerate the practice of dowry killing. (A dowry is a sum of money given to a husband by the bride's family.) In a number of cases, husbands, dissatisfied with the size of dowries, have killed their wives in order to remarry for a "better deal"—a crime that is rarely prosecuted.

THE SITUATION IN AFGHANISTAN

In 2001, a startling documentary, "Behind the Veil," was aired repeatedly on CNN. A courageous female reporter had secretly filmed Afghan women being beaten in the streets, killed in public for trivial offenses, and generally subjugated in extreme ways. For the first time ever, women's rights became a major issue in our foreign policy. Americans learned that Afghan girls were barred from schools, and by law women were not allowed to work. Women who had lost their husbands during Afghanistan's civil wars were forced into begging and prostitution. Women had no access to medical care. Any woman found with an unrelated man could be executed by stoning, and many were.

NATION BUILDING AND WOMEN'S RIGHTS

After the collapse of the Taliban regime, the United States and its allies were able to influence the status of Afghan women. The draft constitution of Afghanistan, adopted in January 2004, gave women equality before the law and 20 percent of the seats in the National Assembly. Much of the country remained outside the control of the national government, however. Women continued to face daunting

Iraqi girls wait for the start of class at the Eastern Secondary School in Baghdad. The role of women in the new Iraq remains uncertain. What negative consequences could result if discriminatory laws forced Iraqi women—among the region's most educated—to retreat to their homes? (AP Photo/Alexander Zemlianichenko)

abuse, including arson attacks on girls' schools, forced marriages, and imposition of the all-covering burka garment.

Women in Iraq have enjoyed greater equality than in most Arab nations. In line with the secular ideology of the Baath Party (see Chapter 1), Saddam Hussein tended to tyrannize over men and women alike. A problem for the U.S.–led Coalition Provisional Authority (CPA) that governed Iraq until June 2004 was ensuring that women did not lose ground under the new regime. Some members of the Iraqi Governing Council, for example, advocated traditional Islamic laws that would have deprived women of equal rights. Women's organizations campaigned against these provisions, and they were vetoed by the CPA. The interim Iraqi constitution, adopted in March 2004, allotted 25 percent of the seats in the parliament to women.

FOR CRITICAL ANALYSIS

Is it fair or appropriate for one country to judge the cultural practices of another? Why or why not?

ipation in the work force gave many women greater self-confidence. Additionally, the publication of Betty Friedan's *The Feminine Mystique* in 1963 focused national attention on the unequal status of women in American life.

In 1966, Friedan and others who were dissatisfied with existing women's organizations, and especially with the failure of the Equal Employment Opportunity Commission to address discrimination against women, formed the National Organization for Women (NOW). Many observers consider the founding of NOW to be the beginning of the modern women's movement—the feminist movement.

NOW immediately adopted a blanket resolution designed "to bring women into full participation in the mainstream of American society *now*, exercising all the privileges and responsibilities thereof in truly equal partnership with men."

Feminism gained additional impetus from young women who entered politics to support the civil rights movement or to oppose the Vietnam War. Many of them found that despite the egalitarian principles of these movements, women remained in second-class positions. These young women sought their own movement. In the late 1960s, "women's liberation" organizations began to spring up on college campuses. Women also began organizing independent "consciousness-raising groups" in which they discussed how gender issues affected their lives. The new women's movement experienced explosive growth, and by 1970 it had emerged as a major social force.

Who are the feminists today? It is difficult to measure the support for feminism at present because the word means different things to different people. When the dictionary definition of *feminist*—"someone who supports political, economic, and social equality for women"—was read to respondents in a survey, 67 percent labeled themselves as feminists.[13] In the absence of such prompting, however, the term *feminist* (like the term *liberal*) implies radicalism to many people, who therefore shy away from it.

The Equal Rights Amendment.   The initial focus of the modern women's movement was not on expanding the political rights of women. Rather, leaders of NOW and other liberal women's rights advocates sought to eradicate gender inequality through a constitutional amendment. The proposed Equal Rights Amendment (ERA), which was first introduced in Congress in 1923 by leaders of the National Women's Party (a successor to the Congressional Union), states as follows: "Equality of rights under the law shall not be denied or abridged by the United States or by any state on account of sex." For years the amendment was not even given a hearing in Congress, but finally it was approved by both chambers and sent to the state legislatures for ratification in 1972.

As was noted in Chapter 2, any constitutional amendment must be ratified by the legislatures (or conventions) in three-fourths of the states before it can become law. Since the early 1900s, most proposed amendments have required that ratification occur within seven years of Congress's adoption of the amendment. The necessary thirty-eight states failed to ratify the ERA within the seven-year period specified by Congress, even though it was supported by numerous national party platforms, six presidents, and both chambers of Congress. To date, efforts to reintroduce the amendment have not succeeded.

During the national debate over the ratification of the ERA, a women's countermovement emerged. Many women perceived the goals pursued by NOW and other liberal women's organizations as a threat to their way of life. At the head of the countermovement was Republican Phyllis Schlafly and her conservative organization, Eagle Forum. Eagle Forum's "Stop-ERA" campaign found significant support among fundamentalist religious groups and various other conservative organizations. The campaign was effective in blocking the ratification of the ERA.

Additional Women's Issues.   While NOW concentrated on the ERA, a large number of other women's groups, many of them entirely local, addressed a spectrum of added issues. One of these was the issue of *domestic violence*—that is, assaults within the family. Typically, this meant husbands or boyfriends assaulting their wives or girlfriends. During the 1970s, feminists across the country began opening *battered women's shelters* to house victims of abuse.

---

[13]Nancy E. McGlen and Karen O'Connor, *Women, Politics, and American Society,* 2d ed. (Upper Saddle River, N.J.: Prentice Hall, 1998), p. 11.

Abortion soon emerged as a key concern. Virtually the entire organized women's movement united behind the "freedom-of-choice" position, at the cost of alienating potential women's rights supporters who favored the "right-to-life" position instead. Because abortion was a national issue, the campaign was led by national organizations such as NARAL Pro-Choice America, formerly the National Abortion Rights Action League. (For information about organizations on both sides of this debate, see the *Making a Difference* feature in Chapter 2.)

Another issue—pornography—tended to divide the women's movement rather than unite it. While a majority of feminists found pornography demeaning to women, many were also strong supporters of free speech. Others, notably activists Andrea Dworkin and Catharine Mackinnon, believed that pornography was so central to the subjugation of women that First Amendment protections should not apply. In some ways, the campaign against pornography was reminiscent of the "social control" tendencies of the suffrage movement that had been expressed in such issues as prohibition.

Challenging Gender Discrimination in the Courts. When ratification of the ERA did not take place, women's rights organizations began a campaign to win more limited national and state laws that would guarantee the equality of women. This more limited campaign met with much success. Women's rights organizations also challenged discriminatory statutes and policies in the federal courts, contending that **gender discrimination** violated the Fourteenth Amendment's equal protection clause. Since the 1970s, the Supreme Court has tended to scrutinize gender classifications closely and has invalidated a number of such statutes and policies. For example, in 1977 the Court held that police and firefighting units cannot establish arbitrary rules, such as height and weight requirements, that tend to keep women from joining those occupations.[14] In 1983, the Court ruled that life insurance companies cannot charge different rates for women and men.[15]

A question that the Court has not ruled on is whether women should be allowed to participate in military combat. Generally, the Supreme Court has left this decision up to Congress and the Department of Defense. Recently, women have been allowed to serve as combat pilots and on naval warships. To date, however, they have not been allowed to join infantry direct-combat units, although they are now permitted to serve in combat-support units. In 1996, the Supreme Court held that the state-financed Virginia Military Institute's policy of accepting only males violated the equal protection clause.[16]

Expanding Women's Political Opportunities. Following the failure of the ERA, in addition to fighting discrimination in the courts, the women's movement began to work for increased representation in government. Several women's political organizations that are active today concentrate their efforts on getting women elected to political offices. These organizations include the National Women's Political Caucus, the Coalition for Women's Appointments, the Feminist Majority Foundation, and the National Education for Women's Leadership (the NEW Leadership).

Women in Politics Today

The efforts of women's rights advocates have helped to increase the number of women holding political offices at all levels of government.

DID YOU KNOW . . .
That in 2003–2004, women had to work nearly sixteen months—from January 1, 2003, to April 15, 2004 ("Equal Pay Day")—to match the salary earned by men in the twelve months of 2003 **?**

Gender Discrimination
Any practice, policy, or procedure that denies equality of treatment to an individual or to a group because of gender.

---

[14]*Dothard v. Rawlinson*, 433 U.S. 321 (1977).
[15]*Arizona v. Norris*, 463 U.S. 1073 (1983).
[16]*United States v. Virginia*, 518 U.S. 515 (1996).

Women in Congress.   Although a men's club atmosphere still prevails in Congress, the number of women holding congressional seats has increased significantly in recent years. Elections during the 1990s brought more women to Congress than either the Senate or the House had seen before. In 2001, for the first time, a woman was elected to a leadership post in Congress. Nancy Pelosi of California was elected as the Democrats' minority whip in the U.S. House of Representatives. In 2002, she became minority leader.

ELECTIONS 2004 Political Leadership by Women

Women increased their presence in the House of Representatives to a total of sixty-eight members. Eight new female representatives were elected for a net gain of five members. All of the incumbent women senators were elected with little difficulty, although two female candidates for open seats were defeated. In both cases, the wave of Republican victories on Bush's coattails may have contributed to their defeat. Women continued to capture leadership positions at the state level.

Nancy Pelosi of California is the Democratic leader in the House of Representatives. Here, she holds a whip that she received on becoming House minority whip in 2001. Pelosi was the first woman to be elected to a leadership post in Congress. Why might some voters actually prefer female candidates? (AP Photo/Joe Marquette)

Women in the Executive and Judicial Branches.   Although no woman has yet been nominated for president by a major political party, in 1984 a woman, Geraldine Ferraro, became the Democratic nominee for vice president. Another woman, Elizabeth Dole, made a serious run for the Republican presidential nomination in the 2000 campaigns. A recent Gallup poll found that 92 percent of Americans said that they would vote for a qualified woman for president if she were nominated by their party.

Increasing numbers of women are also being appointed to cabinet posts. President Bill Clinton (1993–2001) appointed four women to his cabinet, more than any previous president. Madeleine Albright was appointed to the important post of secretary of state. President George W. Bush appointed three women to cabinet positions and two women to other significant federal offices.

Increasing numbers of women are sitting on federal judicial benches as well. President Ronald Reagan (1981–1989) was credited with a historic first when he appointed Sandra Day O'Connor to the Supreme Court in 1981. President Clinton appointed a second woman, Ruth Bader Ginsburg, to the Court.

Continuing Disproportionate Leadership.   For all their achievements in the political arena, the number of women holding political offices remains disproportionately low compared with their participation as voters. In recent elections, the turnout of female voters nationally has been slightly higher than that of male voters.

★ Gender-Based Discrimination in the Workplace

Traditional cultural beliefs concerning the proper role of women in society continue to be evident not only in the political arena but also in the workplace. Since the 1960s, however, women have gained substantial protection against discrimination through laws mandating equal employment opportunities and equal pay.

Title VII of the Civil Rights Act of 1964

Title VII of the Civil Rights Act of 1964 prohibits gender discrimination in employment and has been used to strike down employment policies that discriminate against employees on the basis of gender. Even so-called protective policies have been held to violate Title VII if they have a discriminatory effect. In 1991, for example, the Supreme Court held that a fetal protection policy established by Johnson Controls, Inc., the country's largest producer of automobile batteries, violated Title VII. The policy required all women of childbearing age working in jobs that entailed periodic exposure to lead or other hazardous materials to prove that they were infertile or to transfer to other positions. Women who agreed to transfer often had to accept cuts in pay and reduced job responsibilities. The Court concluded that women who are "as capable of doing their jobs as their male counterparts may not be forced to choose between having a child and having a job."[17]

In 1978, Congress amended Title VII to expand the definition of gender discrimination to include discrimination based on pregnancy. Women affected by pregnancy, childbirth, or related medical conditions must be treated—for all employment-related purposes, including the receipt of benefits under employee benefit programs—the same as other persons not so affected but similar in ability to work.

Sexual Harassment

The Supreme Court has also held that Title VII's prohibition of gender-based discrimination extends to **sexual harassment** in the workplace. Sexual harassment occurs when job opportunities, promotions, salary increases, and so on are given in return for sexual favors. A special form of sexual harassment, called hostile-environment harassment, occurs when an employee is subjected to sexual conduct or comments that interfere with the employee's job performance or are so pervasive or severe as to create an intimidating, hostile, or offensive environment.

In two 1998 cases, the Supreme Court clarified the responsibilities of employers in preventing sexual harassment. In *Faragher v. City of Boca Raton,* the question was the following: Should an employer be held liable for a supervisor's sexual harassment of an employee even though the employer was unaware of the harassment? The Court ruled that the employer in this case was liable but stated that the employer might have avoided such liability if it had taken reasonable care to prevent harassing behavior—which the employer had not done. In the second case, *Burlington Industries v. Ellerth,* the Court similarly held that an employer was liable for sexual harassment caused by a supervisor's actions even though the employee had suffered no tangible job consequences as a result of those actions. Again, the Court emphasized that a key factor in holding the employer liable was whether the employer had exercised reasonable care to prevent and promptly correct any sexually harassing behavior.[18]

In another 1998 case, *Oncale v. Sundowner Offshore Services, Inc.,*[19] the Supreme Court addressed a further issue: Should Title VII protection be extended to cover situations in which individuals are harassed by members of the same sex? The Court answered this question in the affirmative.

Wage Discrimination

By 2010, women will constitute a majority of U.S. workers. Although Title VII and other legislation since the 1960s have mandated equal employment opportunities for men and women, women continue to earn less, on average, than men do.

Sexual Harassment
Unwanted physical or verbal conduct or abuse of a sexual nature that interferes with a recipient's job performance, creates a hostile work environment, or carries with it an implicit or explicit threat of adverse employment consequences.

---

[17]*United Automobile Workers v. Johnson Controls, Inc.,* 499 U.S. 187 (1991).
[18]524 U.S. 725 (1998) and 524 U.S. 742 (1998).
[19]523 U.S. 75 (1998).

Female members of the U.S. Marine Corps pass weapons and gear down the chain to the rear of the landing craft utility vessel as their unit goes ashore in Iraq. What impact might the presence of female soldiers have in a country where women have traditionally been barred from such activities? (U.S. Navy photo by Photographer's Mate 1st Class Bart A. Bauer.)

The Equal Pay Act of 1963. The issue of wage discrimination was first addressed during World War II (1939–1945), when the War Labor Board issued an "equal pay for women" policy. In implementing the policy, the board often evaluated jobs for their comparability and required equal pay for comparable jobs. The board's authority ended with the war. Although it was supported by the next three presidential administrations, the Equal Pay Act was not enacted until 1963 as an amendment to the Fair Labor Standards Act of 1938.

Basically, the Equal Pay Act requires employers to provide equal pay for substantially equal work. In other words, males cannot legally be paid more than females who perform essentially the same job. The Equal Pay Act did not address the fact that certain types of jobs traditionally held by women pay lower wages than the jobs usually held by men. For example, more women than men are salesclerks and nurses, whereas more men than women are construction workers and truck drivers. Even if all clerks performing substantially similar jobs for a company earned the same salaries, they typically would still be earning less than the company's truck drivers.

When Congress passed the Equal Pay Act in 1963, a woman, on average, made 59 cents for every dollar earned by a man. Figures recently released by the U.S. Department of Labor suggest that women now earn 76 cents for every dollar that men earn. In some areas, the wage gap is widening. According to the results of a General Accounting Office survey reported in 2002, female managers in ten industries made less money relative to male managers in 2000 than they did in 1995. In the entertainment industry, for example, in 2000 female managers earned 62 cents for every dollar earned by male managers—down from 83 cents in 1995.[20]

The Glass Ceiling. Although greater numbers of women are holding jobs in professions or business enterprises that were once dominated by men, few women hold top positions in their firms. Less than 12 percent of the Fortune 500 companies in America—America's leading corporations—have a woman as one of their five highest-paid executives. In all, according to Census Bureau statistics, men still hold 93 percent of the top corporate management positions in this country. Because the barriers faced by women in the corporate world are subtle and not easily pinpointed, they have been referred to as the "glass ceiling."

Over the last decade, women have been breaking through the glass ceiling in far greater numbers than before. Alternatively, some corporations have offered a "mommy track" to high-achieving women. The mommy track allows a woman more time to pursue a family life but usually rules out promotion to top jobs. The mommy track therefore tends to reinforce the glass ceiling.

★ Civil Rights: Extending Equal Protection

As noted earlier in this chapter, the Civil Rights Act of 1964 prohibited discrimination against any person on the basis of race, color, national origin, religion, or gender. The act also established the right to equal opportunity in employment. A basic problem remained, however: minority groups and women, because of past discrimination, often lacked the education and skills to compete effectively in the marketplace. In 1965, the federal government attempted to remedy this problem by implementing the concept of affirmative action. **Affirmative action** policies attempt to "level the playing field" by giving special preferences in educational admissions and employment decisions to groups that have been discriminated

Affirmative Action
A policy in educational admissions or job hiring that gives special attention or compensatory treatment to traditionally disadvantaged groups in an effort to overcome present effects of past discrimination.

---

[20]The results of this survey are online at **http://www.gao.gov/audit.htm**. To view a copy of the results, enter "GAO-02-156" in the search box. In 2004, the name of this agency was changed to the "Government Accountability Office."

against in the past. These policies go beyond a strict interpretation of the equal protection clause of the Fourteenth Amendment. So do a number of other laws and programs established by the government during and since the 1960s.

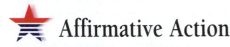 Affirmative Action

In 1965, President Lyndon Johnson ordered that affirmative action policies be undertaken to remedy the effects of past discrimination. All government agencies, including those of state and local governments, were required to implement such policies. Additionally, affirmative action requirements were imposed on companies that sell goods or services to the federal government and on institutions that receive federal funds. Affirmative action policies were also required whenever an employer had been ordered to develop such a plan by a court or by the Equal Employment Opportunity Commission because of evidence of past discrimination. Finally, labor unions that had been found to discriminate against women or minorities in the past were required to establish and follow affirmative action plans.

Affirmative action programs have been controversial because they allegedly result in discrimination against majority groups, such as white males (or discrimination against other minority groups that may not be given preferential treatment under a particular affirmative action program). At issue in the current debate over affirmative action programs is whether such programs, because of their discriminatory nature, violate the equal protection clause of the Fourteenth Amendment to the Constitution.

The *Bakke* Case

The first Supreme Court case addressing the constitutionality of affirmative action plans examined a program implemented by the University of California at Davis. Allan Bakke, a white student who had been turned down for medical school at the Davis campus, discovered that his academic record was better than those of some of the minority applicants who had been admitted to the program. He sued the University of California regents, alleging **reverse discrimination.** The UC–Davis Medical School had held sixteen places out of one hundred for educationally "disadvantaged students" each year, and the administrators at that campus admitted to using race as a criterion for admission for these particular minority slots. At trial in 1974, Bakke said that his exclusion from medical school violated his rights under the Fourteenth Amendment's provision for equal protection of the laws. The trial court agreed. On appeal, the California Supreme Court agreed also. Finally, the regents of the university appealed to the United States Supreme Court.

In 1978, the Supreme Court handed down its decision in *Regents of the University of California v. Bakke.*[21] The Court did not rule against affirmative action programs. Rather, it held that Bakke must be admitted to the UC–Davis Medical School because its admissions policy had used race as the sole criterion for the sixteen "minority" positions. Justice Lewis Powell, speaking for the Court, indicated that while race can be considered "as a factor" among others in admissions (and presumably hiring) decisions, race cannot be the sole factor. So affirmative action programs, but not specific quota systems, were upheld as constitutional.

Further Limits on Affirmative Action

A number of cases decided during the 1980s and 1990s placed further limits on affirmative action programs. In a landmark decision in 1995, *Adarand Constructors,*

Reverse Discrimination
The charge that an affirmative action program discriminates against those who do not have minority status.

---

[21]438 U.S. 265 (1978).

Inc. v. Peña,[22] the Supreme Court held that any federal, state, or local affirmative action program that uses racial or ethnic classifications as the basis for making decisions is subject to "strict scrutiny" by the courts. Under a strict-scrutiny analysis, to be constitutional, a discriminatory law or action must be narrowly tailored to meet a *compelling* government interest. In effect, the Court's opinion in *Adarand* means that an affirmative action program cannot make use of quotas or preferences for unqualified persons, and once the program has succeeded in achieving that compelling government interest, the program must be changed or dropped.

In 1996, a federal appellate court went even further. In *Hopwood v. State of Texas,*[23] two white law school applicants sued the University of Texas School of Law in Austin, alleging that they had been denied admission because of the school's affirmative action program. The program allowed admissions officials to take race and other factors into consideration. The federal appellate court held that the program violated the equal protection clause because it discriminated in favor of minority applicants. Significantly, the court directly challenged the *Bakke* decision by stating that the use of race even as a means of achieving diversity on college campuses "undercuts the Fourteenth Amendment."

In 2003, however, in two cases involving the University of Michigan, the Supreme Court indicated that limited affirmative action programs continued to be acceptable and that diversity was a legitimate goal. The Court struck down the affirmative action plan used for undergraduate admissions at the university, which automatically awarded a substantial number of points to applicants based on minority status.[24] At the same time, it approved the admissions plan used by the law school, which took race into consideration as part of a complete examination of each applicant's background.[25]

State Ballot Initiatives

A ballot initiative passed by California voters in 1996 amended that state's constitution to end all state-sponsored affirmative action programs. The law was challenged immediately in court by civil rights groups and others. These groups claimed that the law violated the Fourteenth Amendment by denying racial minorities and women the equal protection of the laws. In 1997, however, a federal appellate court upheld the constitutionality of the amendment. Thus, affirmative action is now illegal in California in all state-sponsored institutions, including state agencies and educational institutions. In 1998, Washington voters also approved a law banning affirmative action in that state.

★ Special Protection for Older Americans

Americans are getting older. In colonial times, about half the population was under the age of sixteen. In 2000, fewer than one in four Americans was under the age of sixteen. Today, about 38 million Americans (nearly 13 percent of the population) are aged sixty-five or older. By the year 2025, this figure is projected to reach about 70 million. By 2050, the portion of the population over age sixty-five will have almost doubled from the current figure.

Older citizens face a variety of difficulties unique to their group. One problem that seems to endure, despite government legislation designed to prevent it, is age discrimination in employment.

On the University of Michigan campus, students react to a federal appeals court decision in 2002 to uphold the use of race in admissions to the university's law school. The two students in the back are supporting affirmative action. The student in the front is opposing it. (AP Photo/Danny Moloshok)

---

[22]515 U.S. 200 (1995).
[23]84 F.3d 720 (5th Cir. 1996).
[24]*Gratz v. Bollinger,* 539 U.S. 244 (2003).
[25]*Grutter v. Bollinger,* 539 U.S. 306 (2003).

Age Discrimination in Employment

Age discrimination is potentially the most widespread form of discrimination, because anyone—regardless of race, color, national origin, or gender—could be a victim at some point in life. The unstated policies of some companies not to hire or to demote or dismiss people they feel are "too old" have made it difficult for some older workers to succeed in their jobs or continue with their careers. Additionally, older workers have fallen victim at times to cost-cutting efforts by employers. To reduce operational costs, companies may replace older, higher-salaried workers with younger, lower-salaried workers.

The Age Discrimination in Employment Act of 1967

In an attempt to protect older employees from such discriminatory practices, Congress passed the Age Discrimination in Employment Act (ADEA) in 1967. The act, which applies to employers, employment agencies, and labor organizations and covers individuals over the age of forty, prohibits discrimination against individuals on the basis of age unless age is shown to be a bona fide occupational qualification reasonably necessary to the normal operation of the particular business.

To succeed in a suit for age discrimination, an employee must prove that the employer's action, such as a decision to fire the employee, was motivated, at least in part, by age bias. Even if an older worker is replaced by a younger worker falling under the protection of the ADEA—that is, by a younger worker who is also over the age of forty—the older worker is entitled to bring a suit under the ADEA.[26] As discussed in Chapter 3 in the context of federalism, in 2000 the Supreme Court limited the applicability of the ADEA in its decision in *Kimel v. Florida Board of Regents*.[27] The Court held that the sovereign immunity granted the states by the Eleventh Amendment to the Constitution precluded suits against a state by private parties alleging violations of the ADEA. Victims of age discrimination can bring actions under state statutes, however, and most states have laws protecting their citizens from age discrimination.

The ADEA, as initially passed, did not address one of the major problems facing older workers—**mandatory retirement** rules, which require employees to retire when they reach a certain age. Mandatory retirement rules often mean that competent, well-trained employees who want to continue working are unable to do so. In 1978, in an amendment to the ADEA, Congress prohibited mandatory retirement rules for most employees under the age of seventy. In 1986, Congress outlawed mandatory retirement rules entirely for all but a few selected occupations, such as firefighting.

Mandatory Retirement
Forced retirement when a person reaches a certain age.

★ Securing Rights for Persons with Disabilities

Like older Americans, persons with disabilities did not fall under the protective umbrella of the Civil Rights Act of 1964. In 1973, however, Congress passed the Rehabilitation Act, which prohibited discrimination against persons with disabilities in programs receiving federal aid. A 1978 amendment to the act established the Architectural and Transportation Barriers Compliance Board. Regulations for ramps, elevators, and the like in all federal buildings were implemented. Congress passed the Education for All Handicapped Children Act in 1975. It guarantees that all children with disabilities will receive an "appropriate" education. The most

---

[26]*O'Connor v. Consolidated Coil Caterers Corp.*, 517 U.S. 308 (1996).
[27]528 U.S. 62 (2000).

significant federal legislation to protect the rights of persons with disabilities, however, is the Americans with Disabilities Act (ADA), which Congress passed in 1990.

The Americans with Disabilities Act of 1990

The ADA requires that all public buildings and public services be accessible to persons with disabilities. The act also mandates that employers must reasonably accommodate the needs of workers or potential workers with disabilities. Physical access means ramps; handrails; wheelchair-accessible restrooms, counters, drinking fountains, telephones, and doorways; and easily accessible mass transit. In addition, other steps must be taken to comply with the act. Car rental companies must provide cars with hand controls for disabled drivers. Telephone companies are required to have operators to pass on messages from speech-impaired persons who use telephones with keyboards.

The ADA requires employers to "reasonably accommodate" the needs of persons with disabilities unless to do so would cause the employer to suffer an "undue hardship." The ADA defines persons with disabilities as persons who have physical or mental impairments that "substantially limit" their everyday activities. Health conditions that have been considered disabilities under federal law include blindness, alcoholism, heart disease, cancer, muscular dystrophy, cerebral palsy, paraplegia, diabetes, acquired immune deficiency syndrome (AIDS), and infection with the human immunodeficiency virus (HIV) that causes AIDS.

The ADA does not require that *unqualified* applicants with disabilities be hired or retained. If a job applicant or an employee with a disability, with reasonable accommodation, can perform essential job functions, however, then the employer must make the accommodation. Required accommodations may include installing ramps for a wheelchair, establishing more flexible working hours, creating or modifying job assignments, and creating or improving training materials and procedures.

Limiting the Scope and Applicability of the ADA

Beginning in 1999, the Supreme Court has issued a series of decisions that effectively limit the scope of the ADA. In 1999, for example, the Court held in *Sutton v. United Airlines, Inc.*[28] that a condition (in this case, severe nearsightedness) that can be corrected with medication or a corrective device (in this case, eyeglasses) is not considered a disability under the ADA. In other words, the determination of whether a person is substantially limited in a major life activity is based on how the person functions when taking medication or using corrective devices, not on how the person functions without these measures. Since then, the courts have held that plaintiffs with bipolar disorder, epilepsy, diabetes, and other conditions do not fall under the ADA's protections if the conditions can be corrected with medication or corrective devices—even though the plaintiffs contended that they were discriminated against because of their conditions.

In a 2002 decision, the Court held that carpal tunnel syndrome did not constitute a disability under the ADA. The Court stated that although an employee with carpal tunnel syndrome could not perform the manual tasks associated with her job, the injury did not constitute a disability under the ADA because it did not "substantially limit" the major life activity of performing manual tasks.[29]

The Supreme Court has also limited the applicability of the ADA by holding that lawsuits under the ADA cannot be brought against state government employers.[30] In a 2001 case, the Court concluded—as it did with the ADEA, as mentioned earlier—that states, as sovereigns, are immune from lawsuits brought against them by private parties under the federal ADA.

A man and a woman communicating in sign language at work. Sign language is not a method of representing English but is an entirely unique language system. Despite the fact that it is not English, could sign language be exempted from the effects of "English-only" laws that have been adopted in some jurisdictions? Why or why not? (Copyright ©Michael Newman/Photo Edit—All rights reserved)

---

[28]527 U.S. 471 (1999).
[29]*Toyota Manufacturing, Kentucky, Inc. v. Williams,* 534 U.S. 184 (2002).
[30]*Board of Trustees of the University of Alabama v. Garret,* 531 U.S. 356 (2001).

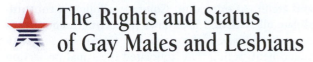

The Rights and Status of Gay Males and Lesbians

On June 27, 1969, patrons of the Stonewall Inn, a New York City bar popular with gay men and lesbians, responded to a police raid by throwing beer cans and bottles because they were angry at what they felt was unrelenting police harassment. In the ensuing riot, which lasted two nights, hundreds of gay men and lesbians fought with police. Before Stonewall, the stigma attached to homosexuality and the resulting fear of exposure had tended to keep most gay men and lesbians quiescent. In the months immediately after Stonewall, however, "gay power" graffiti began to appear in New York City. The Gay Liberation Front and the Gay Activist Alliance were formed, and similar groups sprang up in other parts of the country. Thus, Stonewall has been called "the shot heard round the homosexual world."

Growth in the Gay Male and Lesbian Rights Movement

The Stonewall incident marked the beginning of the movement for gay and lesbian rights. Since then, gay men and lesbians have formed thousands of organizations to exert pressure on legislatures, the media, schools, churches, and other organizations to recognize their right to equal treatment.

To a great extent, lesbian and gay groups have succeeded in changing public opinion—and state and local laws—relating to their status and rights. Nevertheless, they continue to struggle against age-old biases against homosexuality, often rooted in deeply held religious beliefs, and the rights of gay men and lesbians remain an extremely divisive issue in American society. These attitudes were clearly illustrated in a widely publicized case involving the Boy Scouts of America. The case arose after a Boy Scout troop in New Jersey refused to allow gay activist James Dale to be a Scout leader. In 2000, the case came before the Supreme Court, which held that, as a private organization, the Boy Scouts had the right to determine the requirements for becoming a Scout leader.[31]

State and Local Laws Targeting Gay Men and Lesbians

Before the Stonewall incident, forty-nine states had sodomy laws that made various kinds of sexual acts, including homosexual acts, illegal (Illinois, which had repealed its sodomy law in 1962, was the only exception). During the 1970s and 1980s, more than half of these laws were either repealed or struck down by the courts.

The trend toward repealing state antigay laws was suspended in 1986 with the Supreme Court's decision in *Bowers v. Hardwick*.[32] In that case, the Court upheld, by a five-to-four vote, a Georgia law that made homosexual conduct between two adults a crime. In 2003, the Court reversed its earlier position on sodomy with its decision in *Lawrence v. Texas*.[33] In this case, the Court held that laws against sodomy violate the due process clause of the Fourteenth Amendment. The Court stated: "The liberty protected by the Constitution allows homosexual persons the right to choose to enter upon relationships in the confines of their homes and their own private lives and still retain their dignity as free persons." The result of *Lawrence v. Texas* was to invalidate all remaining sodomy laws throughout the country.

Today, twelve states[34] and more than 230 cities and counties have special laws protecting lesbians and gay men against discrimination in employment, housing,

James Dale was not allowed to be a Boy Scout leader because he is gay. Although a New Jersey state appeals court ruled that the Boy Scouts of America's ban on admitting gay individuals violated New Jersey's laws against discrimination, the United States Supreme Court held that the Boy Scouts, as a private organization, had the right to bar gay men from becoming Scout leaders. (AP Photo/Stuart Ramson)

---

[31]*Boy Scouts of America v. Dale,* 530 U.S. 640 (2000).
[32]478 U.S. 186 (1986).
[33]539 U.S. 558 (2003).
[34]California, Connecticut, Hawaii, Maryland, Massachusetts, Minnesota, Nevada, New Hampshire, New Jersey, Rhode Island, Vermont, and Wisconsin. Maine also had a law protecting gay and lesbian rights until February 1998, when the law was repealed in a referendum.

public accommodations, and credit. At one point, Colorado adopted a constitutional amendment to invalidate all state and local laws protecting homosexuals from discrimination. Ultimately, however, the Supreme Court, in *Romer v. Evans*,[35] invalidated the amendment, ruling that it violated the equal protection clause of the U.S. Constitution because it denied to homosexuals in Colorado—but to no other Colorado residents—"the right to seek specific protection of the law." Several laws at the national level have also been changed over the past two decades. Among other things, the government has lifted a ban on hiring gay men and lesbians and voided a 1952 law prohibiting gay men and lesbians from immigrating to the United States.

The Gay Community and Politics

Politicians at the national level have not overlooked the potential significance of homosexual issues in American politics. While conservative politicians generally have been critical of efforts to secure gay and lesbian rights, liberals, by and large, have been speaking out for gay rights in the last twenty-five years. In 1980, the Democratic platform included a gay plank for the first time.

President Bill Clinton long embraced much of the gay rights agenda and became the first sitting president to address a gay rights organization. In 1997, in a speech intentionally reminiscent of Harry Truman's 1947 speech to an African American civil rights group, Clinton pledged his support for equal rights for gay and lesbian Americans at a fund-raiser sponsored by the Human Rights Campaign Fund. In 2000, George W. Bush became the first Republican presidential candidate to meet with a large group of openly gay leaders to discuss their issues. Although Bush asserted that he would continue to oppose gay marriage and adoption, he also said that being openly gay would not disqualify a person from serving in a prominent position in his administration.

While to date, eleven openly gay men and lesbians have been elected to the House of Representatives, none has succeeded yet in gaining a seat in the Senate. Gay rights groups continue to work for increased political representation in Congress, however.

Former Navy lieutenant Paul Thomasson speaks to reporters outside the U.S. Court of Appeals in Richmond, Virginia. Thomasson was discharged from the Navy after giving a letter to his commander stating, "I am gay." The first federal appeals court to rule on the Clinton administration's "don't ask, don't tell" policy upheld the measure in 1996, ruling that openly gay service members can be banned from the military. (AP Photo/*Richmond Times-Dispatch*/Masaaki Okada)

Gay Men and Lesbians in the Military

The U.S. Department of Defense traditionally has viewed homosexuality as incompatible with military service. Supporters of gay and lesbian rights have attacked this policy in recent years, and in 1993 the policy was modified. In that year, President Clinton announced that a new policy, generally characterized as "don't ask, don't tell," would be in effect. Enlistees would not be asked about their sexual orientation, and gay men and lesbians would be allowed to serve in the military so long as they did not declare that they were gay or lesbian or commit homosexual acts. Military officials endorsed the new policy, after opposing it initially, but supporters of gay rights were not enthusiastic. Clinton had promised during his presidential campaign to repeal outright the long-standing ban.

Several gay men and lesbians who have been discharged from military service have protested their discharges by bringing suit against the Defense Department. Often at issue in these cases are the constitutional rights to free speech, privacy, and the equal protection of the laws. A widely publicized 1998 case involved the Navy's dismissal of a naval officer, Timothy McVeigh,[36] on the ground that he had entered "gay" on a profile page for his account with America Online (AOL). Naval

---

[35]517 U.S. 620 (1996).
[36]This is not the Timothy McVeigh who was convicted for the 1995 bombing of the Alfred P. Murrah Federal Building in Oklahoma City.

officers claimed that this amounted to a public declaration of McVeigh's gay status and thus justified his discharge. McVeigh argued that it was not a public declaration. Furthermore, contended McVeigh, the Navy had violated a 1986 federal privacy law governing electronic communications by obtaining information from AOL without a warrant or a court order. In 1998, a federal court judge agreed and ordered the Navy to reinstate McVeigh.[37]

Same-Sex Marriages

Perhaps one of the most sensitive political issues with respect to the rights of gay and lesbian couples is whether they should be allowed to marry, just as heterosexual couples are. The controversy over this issue was fueled in 1993 when the Hawaii Supreme Court ruled that denying marriage licenses to gay couples might violate the equal protection clause of the Hawaii constitution.[38] In the wake of this event, other states began to worry about whether they might have to treat gay men or lesbians who were legally married in another state as married couples in their state as well. Opponents of gay rights pushed for state laws banning same-sex marriages, and a number of states enacted such laws. At the federal level, Congress passed the Defense of Marriage Act of 1996 (discussed in this chapter's opening *What If . . .* feature), which bans federal recognition of lesbian and gay couples and allows state governments to ignore same-sex marriages performed in other states. Ironically, the Hawaii court decisions that gave rise to these concerns have largely come to naught. In 1998, residents in that state voted for a state constitutional amendment that allows the Hawaii legislature to ban same-sex marriages.

The controversy over gay marriages was fueled again by developments in the state of Vermont. In 1999, the Vermont Supreme Court ruled that gay couples are entitled to the same benefits of marriage as opposite-sex couples.[39] Subsequently, in April 2000, the Vermont legislature passed a law permitting gay and lesbian

---

[37]*McVeigh v. Cohen*, 983 F.Supp. 215 (D.C. 1998).
[38]*Baehr v. Lewin*, 852 P.2d 44 (Hawaii 1993).
[39]*Baker v. Vermont*, 744 A.2d 864 (Vermont 1999).

Gay men and lesbians demonstrate in New York City's Bryant Park in favor of same-sex marriages. They want the state of New York to legalize such marriages. Why might many gay men and lesbians find civil unions to be an inadequate alternative to marriage? (Ilkka Uimonen)

couples to form "civil unions." The law entitled partners forming civil unions to receive some three hundred state benefits available to married couples, including the rights to inherit a partner's property and to decide on medical treatment for an incapacitated partner. It did not, however, entitle those partners to receive any benefits allowed to married couples under federal law, such as spousal Social Security benefits. Some felt that the Vermont legislature did not go far enough—it should have allowed full legal marriage rights to same-sex couples.

Child Custody and Adoption

Gay men and lesbians also have faced difficulties in obtaining child-custody and adoption rights. Courts around the country, when deciding which of two parents should have custody, have wrestled with how much weight, if any, should be given to a parent's sexual orientation. For some time, the courts were split fairly evenly on this issue. In about half the states, courts held that a parent's sexual orientation should not be a significant factor in determining child custody. Courts in other states, however, tended to give more weight to sexual orientation. In one case, a court even went so far as to award custody to a father because the child's mother was a lesbian, even though the father had served eight years in prison for killing his first wife. Today, however, courts in the majority of states no longer deny custody or visitation rights to persons solely on the basis of their sexual orientation.

The last decade has also seen a sharp climb in the number of gay men and lesbians who are adopting children. To date, twenty-two states have allowed lesbians and gay men to adopt children through state-operated or private adoption agencies.

★ The Rights and Status of Juveniles

Approximately 76 million Americans—almost 30 percent of the total population—are under twenty-one years of age. The definition of *children* ranges from persons under age sixteen to persons under age twenty-one. However defined, children in the United States have fewer rights and protections than any other major group in society.

The reason for this lack of rights is the common presumption of society and its lawmakers that children basically are protected by their parents. This is not to say that children are the exclusive property of the parents. Rather, an overwhelming case in favor of *not* allowing parents to control the actions of their children must be presented before children can be given authorization to act without parental consent (or before the state can be given authorization to act on children's behalf without regard to their parents' wishes).

Supreme Court decisions affecting children's rights began a process of slow evolution with *Brown v. Board of Education of Topeka*, the landmark civil rights case of 1954 discussed earlier in this chapter. In *Brown*, the Court granted children the status of rights-bearing persons. In 1967, in *In re Gault*,[40] the Court expressly held that children have a constitutional right to be represented by counsel at the government's expense in a criminal action. Five years later, the Court acknowledged that "children are 'persons' within the meaning of the Bill of Rights. We have held so over and over again."[41] In 1976, the Court recognized a girl's right to have an abortion without consulting her parents.[42] (More recently, however, the Court has allowed state laws to dictate whether the child must obtain consent.)

---

[40]387 U.S. 1 (1967).
[41]*Wisconsin v. Yoder*, 406 U.S. 205 (1972).
[42]*Planned Parenthood of Central Missouri v. Danforth*, 428 U.S. 52 (1976).

A teacher gathers voter registration forms from graduating seniors in Verona, Wisconsin, in 2004. In a matter of minutes, nearly half of the school's 310 seniors registered. Why did the latest generation of young voters not follow their predecessor's tendency to stay away from the polls? (AP Photo/Andy Manis)

Voting Rights and the Young

The Twenty-sixth Amendment to the Constitution, ratified on July 1, 1971, reads as follows:

> The right of citizens of the United States, who are eighteen years of age or older, to vote shall not be denied or abridged by the United States or by any State on account of age.

Before this amendment was ratified, the age at which citizens could vote was twenty-one in most states. Why did the Twenty-sixth Amendment specify age eighteen? Why not seventeen or sixteen? And why did it take until 1971 to allow those between the ages of eighteen and twenty-one to vote? One of the arguments used for granting suffrage to eighteen-year-olds was that, because they could be drafted to fight in the country's wars, they had a stake in public policy. At the time, the example of the Vietnam War (1964–1975) was paramount.

Have eighteen- to twenty-year-olds used their right to vote? Yes and no. In 1972, immediately after the passage of the Twenty-sixth Amendment, 58 percent of eighteen- to twenty-year-olds were registered to vote, and 48.4 percent reported that they had voted. But by the 2000 presidential elections, of the 11.8 million American residents in the eighteen-to-twenty age bracket, 40.5 percent were registered, and 28.4 percent reported that they had voted. Subsequent elections have shown similar results. In contrast, voter turnout among Americans aged sixty-five or older is very high, usually between 60 and 70 percent.

The Rights of Children in Civil and Criminal Proceedings

Children today have limited rights in civil and criminal proceedings in our judicial system. Different procedural rules and judicial safeguards apply in civil and criminal laws. **Civil law** relates in part to contracts among private individuals or companies. **Criminal law** relates to crimes against society that are defined by society acting through its legislatures.

Civil Law
The law regulating conduct between private persons over noncriminal matters. Under civil law, the government provides the forum for the settlement of disputes between private parties in such matters as contracts, domestic relations, and business interactions.

Criminal Law
The law that defines crimes and provides punishment for violations. In criminal cases, the government is the prosecutor because crimes are violations of the public order.

Majority
Full age; the age at which a person is entitled by law to the right to manage her or his own affairs and to the full enjoyment of civil rights.

Necessaries
In contract law, necessaries include whatever is reasonably necessary for suitable subsistence as measured by age, state, condition in life, and so on.

Civil Rights of Juveniles.   The civil rights of children are defined exclusively by state law with respect to private contract negotiations, rights, and remedies. The legal definition of **majority** varies from eighteen to twenty-one years of age, depending on the state. As a rule, an individual who is legally a minor cannot be held responsible for contracts that he or she forms with others. In most states, only contracts entered into for so-called **necessaries** (things necessary for sub-sistence, as determined by the courts) can be enforced against minors. Also, when minors engage in negligent behavior, typically their parents are liable. If, for example, a minor destroys a neighbor's fence, the neighbor may bring suit against the child's parent but not against the child.

Civil law also encompasses the area of child custody. Child-custody rulings traditionally have given little weight to the wishes of the child. Courts have main-tained the right to act on behalf of the child's "best interests" but have sometimes been constrained from doing so by the "greater" rights possessed by adults. For instance, a widely publicized Michigan Supreme Court ruling awarded legal cus-tody of a two-and-a-half-year-old Michigan resident to an Iowa couple, the child's biological parents. A Michigan couple, who had cared for the child since shortly after its birth and who had petitioned to adopt the child, lost out in the custody battle. The court said that the law had allowed it to consider only the parents' rights and not the child's best interests.

Children's rights and their ability to articulate their rights for themselves in custody matters were strengthened, however, by several well-publicized rulings involving older children. In one case, for example, an eleven-year-old Florida boy filed suit in his own name, assisted by his own privately retained legal counsel, to terminate his relationship with his biological parents and to have the court affirm his right to be adopted by foster parents. The court granted his request, although it did not agree procedurally with the method by which the boy initiated the

This juvenile is being arrested in the same way that an adult would be, but he does not have the full rights of an adult under criminal law. Juveniles normally receive less severe punishment than adults do for similar crimes, however. (Bart Bartholomew/Stock Photo)

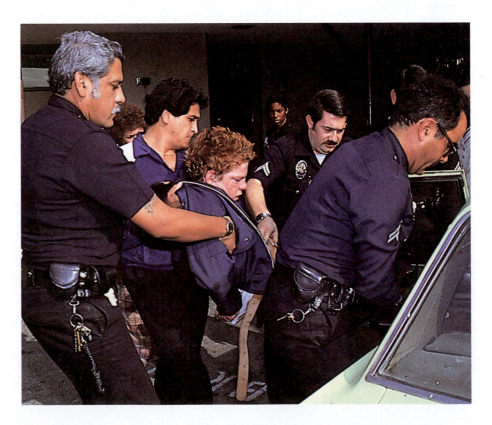

suit.[43] The news media characterized the case as the first instance in which a minor child had "divorced" himself from his parents.

Criminal Rights of Juveniles. One of the main requirements for an act to be criminal is intent. The law has given children certain defenses against criminal prosecution because of their presumed inability to have criminal intent. Under the **common law,** children up to seven years of age were considered incapable of committing a crime because they did not have the moral sense to understand that they were doing wrong. Children between the ages of seven and fourteen were also presumed to be incapable of committing a crime, but this presumption could be challenged by showing that the child understood the wrongful nature of the act. Today, states vary in their approaches. Most states retain the common law approach, although age limits vary from state to state. Other states have simply set a minimum age for criminal responsibility.

All states have juvenile court systems that handle children below the age of criminal responsibility who commit delinquent acts. The aim of juvenile courts is allegedly to reform rather than to punish. In states that retain the common law approach, children who are above the minimum age but are still juveniles can be turned over to the criminal courts if the juvenile court determines that they should be treated as adults. Children still do not have the right to trial by jury or to post bail. Also, in most states parents can commit their minor children to state mental institutions without allowing the child a hearing.

Although minors do not usually have the full rights of adults in criminal proceedings, they have certain advantages. In felony, manslaughter, murder, armed robbery, and assault cases, traditionally juveniles were not tried as adults. They were often sentenced to probation or "reform" school for a relatively short term regardless of the seriousness of their crimes. Today, however, most states allow juveniles to be tried as adults (often at the discretion of the judge) for certain crimes, such as murder. When they are tried as adults, they are given due process

[43]*Kingsley v. Kingsley,* 623 So.2d 780 (Fla.App. 1993).

Common Law
Judge-made law that originated in England from decisions shaped according to prevailing customs. Decisions were applied to similar situations and thus gradually became common to the nation.

Michael Humphreys is led out of a courthouse in Washington state following a court appearance. Humphreys, a thirteen-year-old boy accused of fatally shooting a neighbor and wounding the man's wife, was convicted and received a sentence of fifty-eight years. What are the best ways of handling very young persons who commit violent felonies? (AP Photo/*The Columbian*/Jeremiah Coughlan)

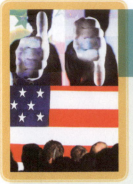

WHICH SIDE ARE YOU ON?
Zero-Tolerance Policies

Because of fears of violence among America's youth, both in and out of school, a large number of school districts have implemented zero-tolerance rules.

Under zero-tolerance rules, students have faced mandatory expulsion for threats of violence, disobedience, defiance of authority, disruptive behavior, profanity, and possession of drugs or alcohol. Obviously, enforcement varies from school district to school district.

The federal government estimates that almost 100,000 students each year are expelled under zero-tolerance rules. In the Chicago public schools alone, about 2,500 students are expelled each year and another 13,000 are suspended.

ZERO-TOLERANCE POLICIES SEND A CLEAR MESSAGE

Supporters of zero-tolerance policies say that they send a clear message that certain behavior will not be tolerated in school. These people argue that the impartiality of these policies is their greatest strength. Zero tolerance can eliminate discrimination, because school administrators cannot be more lenient toward a white student from a middle-class background than a poor, minority student who breaks the same rule.

Former American Federation of Teachers president Sandra Feldman recalls a tough high school in the Bronx. The discipline code was not consistently enforced, and students wandered into class whenever they felt like it. A new principal worked out a plan. When the bell rang, teachers would shut their doors, and students who were in the hall would be sent to detention. On the first day, despite warnings, dozens of students were shut out of class. In a few weeks, however, lateness was no longer a problem, and the whole atmosphere of the school was changing.

ZERO-TOLERANCE POLICIES SOMETIMES LEAD TO THE ABSURD

Opponents of zero tolerance point out that many students have been suspended for trivial actions. A Massachusetts girl was expelled for bringing a plastic knife with her lunch. A Pennsylvania boy was suspended for having a soft plastic toy axe as part of his Halloween firefighter costume. Two Chicago eighth graders were arrested for bringing bags of colored powder to school. The bags contained Kool-Aid. Only after the children's attorneys forced the authorities to test the substance were the charges dropped.

Benjamin Ratner, an eighth grader at a middle school in Virginia, took a knife away from a schoolmate who said she was considering suicide. He was suspended for four

Taylor Hess, a sixteen-year-old honors student at L.D. Bell High School in Texas, poses with some of the awards he has received. Because of the school district's zero-tolerance policy toward weapons, Hess was expelled from school after a butter knife was found in the bed of his pickup truck. (AP Photo/ Dawn Dietrich)

months because he was caught holding the knife. The school has a zero-tolerance policy.

Given these examples, why do zero-tolerance policies remain popular among school administrators? "I think it has more to do with the fear of lawsuits than anything else," says Rutgers University psychology professor Maurice Elias. "On a deeper level, I think it bespeaks adults trying to stake their moral authority when there are really many shades of gray."

WHAT'S YOUR POSITION?

School-ground killings make the news, but they constitute less than 0.6 percent of all youth homicides. Do these statistics justify the loosening of zero-tolerance policies? Why or why not?

GOING ONLINE

To learn about the problems that can occur if schools do not have strong discipline policies, see the Web site of the American Federation of Teachers. Articles on discipline are at **http://www.aft.org/topics/discipline/index.htm**. For a more critical approach to the topic, see the Web site of the New York University Child Study Center at **http://www.aboutourkids.org/aboutour/articles/zerotolerance.html**. For a look at the effect of zero-tolerance policies on special education students, see **http://www.wrightslaw.com/info/discipl.index.htm**.

of law and tried for the crime, rather than being given the paternalistic treatment reserved for the juvenile delinquent. Juveniles who are tried as adults may also face adult penalties, including the death penalty. Currently, about seventy people are on the nation's death rows for crimes that they committed when they were sixteen or seventeen years old.

Approaches to Dealing with Crime by Juveniles. What to do about crime committed by juveniles is a pressing problem for today's political leaders. One approach to the problem is to treat juveniles as adults, which more and more judges seem to be doing. There appears to be widespread public support for this approach, as well as for lowering the age at which juveniles should receive adult treatment in criminal proceedings. Polling data show that two-thirds of U.S. adults think that juveniles under the age of thirteen who commit murder should be tried as adults. Another method is to hold parents responsible for the crimes of their minor children (a minority of the states do so under so-called parental-responsibility laws). These are contradictory approaches, to be sure. Yet they perhaps reflect the divided opinion in our society concerning the rights of children versus the rights of parents.

In the wake of crimes committed in the schools, many districts have implemented what are called zero-tolerance policies. These policies have become controversial in recent years because, according to some, they are enforced without regard to the particular circumstances surrounding an incident. Should they be modified or revoked? See this chapter's *Which Side Are You On?* feature on the facing page for a discussion of this issue.

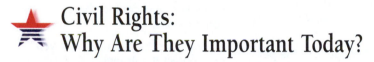

Civil Rights: Why Are They Important Today?

Fifty years ago, the laws protecting most of the groups discussed in this chapter were largely nonexistent. The reason we now have laws protecting minorities, women, older Americans, persons with disabilities, and gay males and lesbians is that these and other groups pressured the government to enact such laws. If no one had taken action on these issues, you can be sure that these groups would still have few, if any, legal protections. Certainly, they would not enjoy the degree of equal protection under the laws that they enjoy today.

That said, it is clear that the struggle for equality is far from over. Civil rights continue to be very important in our society, particularly for those who continue to face discrimination because of their race, color, national origin, religion, disability, age, gender, or sexual preferences. How equality can best be attained continues to generate controversy. The debate over affirmative action is illustrative. Is it time to go beyond affirmative action plans based on race, ethnicity, and gender to programs based on other criteria, such as economic disadvantage? Should affirmative action be banned entirely?

Some contend that what we need today is a new civil rights agenda that puts less emphasis on race, ethnic origin, and gender and more on social and economic needs. Already, a new generation of civil rights activists is focusing simply on the challenge of improving the plight of the poor, without regard to race, ethnic origin, or gender. However these issues are decided, you can be sure that the outcome will have a significant effect on American society.

MAKING A DIFFERENCE

★ Dealing with Discrimination

Anyone applying for a job may be subjected to a variety of possibly discriminatory practices based on race, color, gender, religion, age, sexual preference, or disability. There may be tests, some of which could have a discriminatory effect. At both the state and federal levels, the government continues to examine the fairness and validity of criteria used in job-applicant screening, and as a result, there are ways of addressing the problem of discrimination.

Why Should You Care?

Some people may think that discrimination is only a problem for members of racial or ethnic minorities. Actually, almost everyone can be affected. Consider that in some instances, white men have actually experienced "reverse discrimination"—and have obtained redress for it. Also, discrimination against women is common, and women constitute half the population. Even if you are male, you probably have female friends whose well-being is of interest to you. Therefore, the knowledge of how to proceed when you suspect discrimination is another useful tool to have when living in the modern world.

What Can You Do?

If you believe that you have been discriminated against by a potential employer, consider the following steps:

1. Evaluate your own capabilities, and determine if you are truly qualified for the position.
2. Analyze the reasons why you were turned down. Would others agree with you that you have been the object of discrimination, or would they uphold the employer's claim?
3. If you still believe that you have been treated unfairly, you have recourse to several agencies and services.

You should first speak to the personnel director of the company and explain politely that you believe you have not been evaluated adequately. If asked, explain your concerns clearly. If necessary, go into explicit detail, and indicate that you may have been discriminated against.

If a second evaluation is not forthcoming, contact your local state employment agency. If you still do not obtain adequate help, contact one or more of the following state agencies, usually listed in your telephone directory under "State Government."

1. If a government entity is involved, a state ombudsperson or citizen aide may be available to mediate.
2. You can contact the state civil rights commission, which at least will give you advice even if it does not wish to take up your case.
3. The state attorney general's office normally has a division dealing with discrimination and civil rights.
4. There may be a special commission or department specifically set up to help you, such as a women's status commission or a commission on Hispanics or Asian Americans. If you are a woman or a member of such a minority group, contact these commissions.

Finally, at the national level, you can contact the American Civil Liberties Union, 125 Broad St., New York, N.Y. 10004-2400, 212-549-2500, or check

http://www.aclu.org

You can also contact the most appropriate federal agency: the Equal Employment Opportunity Commission, 1801 L St. N.W., Washington, DC 20507, 202-663-4900, or go to

http://www.eeoc.gov

 **Key Terms**

affirmative action 170

busing 156

civil law 179

civil disobedience 158

civil rights 151

common law 181

criminal law 179

de facto segregation 156

de jure segregation 156

feminism 164

gender discrimination 166

grandfather clause 154

literacy test 154

majority 180

mandatory retirement 173

necessaries 180

poll tax 154

reverse discrimination 171

separate-but-equal doctrine 153

sexual harassment 169

subpoena 160

suffrage 164

white primary 154

Chapter Summary

1 The civil rights movement started with the struggle by African Americans for equality. Before the Civil War, most African Americans were slaves, and slavery was protected by the Constitution and the Supreme Court. Constitutional amendments after the Civil War legally ended slavery, and African Americans gained citizenship, the right to vote, and other rights through legislation. This legal protection was largely a dead letter by the 1880s, however, and politically and socially African American inequality continued.

2 Legal segregation was declared unconstitutional by the Supreme Court in *Brown v. Board of Education of Topeka* (1954), in which the Court stated that separation implied inferiority. In *Brown v. Board of Education* (1955), the Supreme Court ordered federal courts to ensure that public schools were desegregated "with all deliberate speed." Also in 1955, the modern civil rights movement began with a boycott of segregated public transportation in Montgomery, Alabama. Of particular impact was the Civil Rights Act of 1964. The act bans discrimination on the basis of race, color, religion, gender, or national origin in employment and public accommodations. The act created the Equal Employment Opportunity Commission to administer the legislation's provisions.

3 The Voting Rights Act of 1965 outlawed discriminatory voter-registration tests and authorized federal registration of persons and federally administered procedures in any state or political subdivision evidencing electoral discrimination or low registration rates. The Voting Rights Act and other protective legislation passed during and since the 1960s apply not only to African Americans but to other ethnic groups as well. Minorities have been increasingly represented in national and state politics, although they have yet to gain representation proportionate to their numbers in the U.S. population. Lingering social and economic disparities have led to a new civil rights agenda—one focusing less on racial differences and more on economic differences.

4 In the early history of the United States, women were considered citizens, but by and large they had no political rights. After the first women's rights convention in 1848, the women's movement gained momentum. Not until 1920, when the Nineteenth Amendment was ratified, did women finally obtain the right to vote. The modern women's movement began in the 1960s in the wake of the civil rights and anti–Vietnam War movements. The National Organization for Women (NOW) was formed in 1966 to bring about complete equality for women in all walks of life. Efforts to secure the ratification of the Equal Rights Amendment failed, but the women's movement was successful in obtaining new laws, changes in social customs, and increased political representation of women.

5 Although women have found it difficult to gain positions of political leadership, their numbers in Congress and in other government bodies increased significantly in the 1990s and early 2000s. Women continue to struggle against gender discrimination in employment. Federal government efforts to eliminate gender discrimination in the workplace include Title VII of the Civil Rights Act of 1964, which prohibits, among other things, gender-based discrimination, including sexual harassment on the job. Wage discrimination also continues to be a problem for women, as does the "glass ceiling" that prevents them from rising to the top of business or professional firms.

6 Affirmative action programs have been controversial because they can lead to reverse discrimination against majority groups or even other minority groups. Supreme Court decisions have limited affirmative action programs, and voters in California and Washington passed initiatives banning state-sponsored affirmative action in those states. Two Supreme Court decisions in cases brought against the University of Michigan have confirmed the principle that limited affirmative action programs are constitutional.

7 Problems associated with aging and retirement are becoming increasingly important as the number of older persons in the United States increases. The Age Discrimination in Employment Act of 1967 prohibited job-related discrimination against individuals who are over forty years old on the basis of age, unless age is shown to be a bona fide occupational qualification reasonably necessary to the normal operation of the business. Amendments to the act prohibit mandatory retirement except in a few selected professions.

8 The Rehabilitation Act of 1973 prohibited discrimination against persons with disabilities in programs receiving federal aid. Regulations implementing the act provide for ramps, elevators, and the like in federal buildings. The Education for All Handicapped Children Act (1975) provides that children with disabilities should receive an "appropriate" education. The Americans with Disabilities Act of 1990 prohibits job discrimination against persons with physical and mental disabilities, requiring that positive steps be taken to comply with the act. The act also requires expanded access to public facilities, including transportation, and to services offered by such private concerns as car rental and telephone companies.

9 Gay and lesbian rights groups, which first began to form in 1969, now number in the thousands. These groups work to promote laws protecting gay men and lesbians from discrimination and to repeal antigay laws. After 1969, sodomy laws that criminalized specific sexual practices were repealed or struck down by the courts in all but eighteen states, and in 2003 a Supreme Court decision effectively invalidated all remaining sodomy laws nationwide. Twelve states and more than 230 cities and counties now have laws prohibiting discrimination based on sexual orientation. Gay men and lesbians are no longer barred from federal employment or from immigrating to this country. Since 1980, liberal Democrats at the national level have supported gay and lesbian rights and sought electoral support from these groups. The military's "don't ask, don't tell" policy has fueled extensive controversy, as have same-sex marriages and child-custody issues.

10 Although children form a large group of Americans, they have the fewest rights and protections, in part because it is commonly presumed that parents protect their children. The Twenty-sixth Amendment grants the right to vote to those aged eighteen or older. In most states, only contracts entered into for necessaries can be enforced against minors. When minors engage in negligent acts, their parents may be held liable. Minors have some defense against criminal prosecution because of their presumed inability to have criminal intent below certain ages. For those under the age of criminal responsibility, there are state juvenile courts. When minors are tried as adults, they are entitled to the procedural protections afforded to adults and are subject to adult penalties, including the death penalty.

★ Selected Print and Media Resources

SUGGESTED READINGS

Anderson, Terry H. *The Pursuit of Fairness: A History of Affirmative Action.* New York: Oxford University Press, 2004. Anderson offers an evenhanded history of affirmative action. His account extends from the administrations of Franklin D. Roosevelt and Harry Truman in the 1940s to the 2003 University of Michigan cases that have established the current constitutional parameters of affirmative action policies.

Chappell, David L. *A Stone of Hope: Prophetic Religion and the Death of Jim Crow.* Chapel Hill: University of North Carolina Press, 2003. In a controversial reinterpretation, Chappell argues that the religious dimension of the African American civil rights movement has been underestimated. Chappell, in fact, calls the movement a religious revival with political and social dimensions.

Friedan, Betty. *The Feminine Mystique.* New York: W. W. Norton & Co., 2001. Friedan's work is the feminist classic that helped launch the modern women's movement in the United States. This edition contains an up-to-date introduction by columnist Anna Quindlen.

Moats, David. *Civil Wars: A Battle for Gay Marriage.* New York: Harcourt, 2004. Moats, a Pulitzer Prize–winning Vermont journalist, chronicles the battle over same-sex marriage in Vermont. The result was a law legalizing civil unions.

Walker, Alice. *The Color Purple.* Chicago: Harcourt Brace, 1992. This Pulitzer Prize–winning novel, which was originally published in 1982, is about a black woman's struggle for justice, dignity, and empowerment. The book is rich in themes that concern women's issues.

Woodward, C. Vann. *The Strange Career of Jim Crow.* New York: Oxford University Press, 1957. This is the classic study of how segregation was created in the southern states.

MEDIA RESOURCES

Beyond the Glass Ceiling—A CNN–produced program showing the difficulties women face in trying to rise to the top in corporate America.

G.I. Jane—A 1997 film about a woman who is out to prove that she can survive Navy SEAL training that is so rigorous that many (60 percent) of the men do not make it.

I Have a Dream—A film on Martin Luther King, Jr., focusing on the 1963 march on Washington and King's "I have a dream" speech, which some consider to be one of the greatest speeches of all time.

Malcolm X—A 1992 film, directed by Spike Lee and starring Denzel Washington, that depicts the life of the controversial "black power" leader Malcolm X. Malcolm X, who was assassinated on February 21, 1965, clearly had a different vision from that of Martin Luther King, Jr., regarding how to achieve civil rights, respect, and equality for black Americans.

Separate but Equal—A video focusing on Thurgood Marshall, the lawyer (and later Supreme Court justice) who took the struggle for equal rights to the Supreme Court, and on the rise and demise of segregation in America.

Shot by a Kid—A film documenting the relationship among children, guns, and violence in four major cities of the United States.

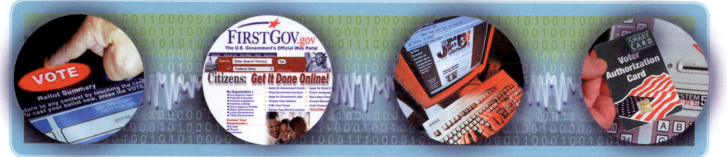

e-mocracy ★ Civil Rights Information Online

Today, thanks to the Internet, information on civil rights issues is literally at your fingertips. By simply accessing the American Civil Liberties Union's Web site (the URL for this organization is given below, in the *Logging On* section), you can learn about the major civil rights issues facing Americans today. A host of other Web sites offer data on the extent to which groups discussed in this chapter are protected under state and federal laws. You can also find numerous advocacy sites that indicate what you can do to help promote the rights of a certain group.

Logging On

For information on, and arguments in support of, affirmative action and the rights of the groups discussed in this chapter, a good source is the American Civil Liberties Union's Web site. Go to

http://www.aclu.org

The National Organization for Women (NOW) offers online information and updates on the status of women's rights, including affirmative action cases involving women. Go to

http://www.now.org

An excellent source of information on issues facing African Americans is the Web site of the National Association for the Advancement of Colored People at

http://www.naacp.org

You can find information on the Americans with Disabilities Act (ADA) of 1990, including the act's text, at

http://www.jan.wvu.edu/links/ adalinks.htm

You can access the Web site of the Human Rights Campaign Fund, the nation's largest gay and lesbian political organization, at

http://www.hrc.org

If you are interested in children's rights and welfare, a good starting place is the Web site of the Child Welfare Institute. Go to

http://www.gocwi.org

Using InfoTrac for Political Research

Imagine that you are the owner of a new franchise business and are hiring your first employees. You expect that your employees will be both male and female. You will not always be on-site to monitor the behavior of your employees; you will be hiring shift managers as supervisors. You therefore want to develop an employment manual that contains, among other things, explicit rules against sexual harassment.

Use the InfoTrac Web site to find materials that will help you develop the sexual-harassment section of your manual. Go to

http://www.infotrac-college.com

Log on, go to InfoTrac College Edition, and then go to the Subject search page. Type "sexual harassment" into the search box. InfoTrac will offer you a large number of articles that you can use in your research. Consider the information that you find using Info-Trac. To what extent would you rely on this information when you write an employment manual? What other resources might you also check?

ONLINE REVIEW

At **http://politicalscience.wadsworth. com/schmidt12**, you will find a free Study Guide to this book. For each chapter, there are two online quizzes to help you master the material.

• The **PoliPrep Self Study Assessment** provides a pre-test for each major section of the chapter. PoliPrep then generates a customized study plan. After you complete the study plan, a post-test evaluates your progress.

• The **Tutorial Quiz** for each chapter provides questions on the chapter contents, including the features. The questions are organized to match the major sections of the chapter.

CHAPTER 6

Public Opinion and Political Socialization

- Defining Public Opinion

- How Public Opinion Is Formed: Political Socialization

- Political Preferences and Voting Behavior

- Measuring Public Opinion

- Technology and Opinion Polls

- Public Opinion and the Political Process

WHAT IF . . .
Exit Polls Were Regulated?

BACKGROUND

The media compete fiercely to be the first source to project winners on election day. To project winners, they use the results of exit polls. These polls are conducted at selected precincts in each state. Trained interviewers visit each of the selected precincts and take a systematic sample of voters at different times during the day. Sampled voters are asked to fill out a written questionnaire indicating their age, ethnic group, income, gender, political party, and how they voted. The media can make projections based on exit polls within one hour after the voting booths close. Because of inaccurate projections during the 2000 presidential elections, however, many politicians and citizens alike have suggested that exit polls be regulated or even banned.

WHAT IF EXIT POLLS WERE REGULATED?

Frequently, television networks have declared the winning presidential candidate before all the polling places across the country were closed. Remarkably, the networks did this even in 2000, which by some measures was the closest presidential election in American history. The networks announced that the next president would be . . . Al Gore. (Over a month later, George W. Bush became the actual winner.)

Not surprisingly, the networks were criticized strongly. More significantly, the networks' premature declarations may have caused some potential voters to stay home. Some have proposed that the networks should be prevented from predicting election outcomes based on exit polling in any state where the polls are still open. Such a restriction might increase voter participation, especially in western states, where the polls close late because of time zone differences.

THE CANADIAN EXAMPLE

In Canada, there actually is a law that bans anyone from broadcasting election results while the polls are open. As a result, the Canadian Broadcasting Corporation (CBC) begins its election-night coverage in each province only when the polls in that province are closed. The CBC's coverage begins in the Maritime Provinces on the Atlantic coast. At one-hour intervals, the broadcast becomes available in Ontario and Quebec, then in the Prairie Provinces, and finally in British Columbia.

THE PRESS AND THE FIRST AMENDMENT

Congress could pass a law that banned the broadcast of election predictions based on exit polling in states where the polls have not closed. The constitutionality of such a law would be questionable, however. In general, the First Amendment does not allow the government to restrict what the news media can do.

There are ways, though, in which such a law might be found constitutional. One point is that the law would not ban reports altogether but would merely postpone them for a few hours. A second point follows from the fact that the national government in effect owns the broadcast frequencies and leases them out to television and radio companies. The courts have long held that in return for allowing broadcasters to use the airwaves, the government can impose various requirements on them. In some cases, these requirements have affected broadcasters' free speech rights.

Cable networks, however, do not rely on government-owned frequencies and cannot be kept from reporting projected election results. Also, Internet Web sites cannot as yet be restrained by federal requirements.

One possible alternative would be an agreement among the major broadcast and cable networks not to release the results of exit polls in states where the polls are still open. Almost certainly, however, some information sources would refuse to adhere to such an agreement, and any West Coast resident who seriously wanted to find out what was happening elsewhere in the country would still be able to do so.

FOR CRITICAL ANALYSIS

1. *In what ways might reduced voter turnout in the West affect a national election?*
2. *Political scientists and politicians glean much valuable information from exit polls. What could be done to allow the collection of such data without influencing the outcome of the elections?*

In a democracy, the ability of the people to freely express their opinions is fundamental. Americans can express their opinions in many ways. They can write letters to newspapers. They can organize politically. They can vote. They can respond to opinion polls, including the exit polls discussed in the chapter-opening *What If . . .* feature. Public opinion clearly plays an important role in our political system, just as it does in any democracy.

President George W. Bush found out how important public opinion was when he announced that the administration was going to try terrorist suspects in military tribunals where the defendants would have few rights. Public opinion was so negative that Bush felt forced to announce new rules for the tribunals that gave defendants more rights. (See the *America's Security* feature in Chapter 4 for a further discussion of the rights of defendants in the military tribunals.)

In contrast, Bush's war on terrorism received widespread support from Americans. This support bolstered the Bush administration's authority during a time of crisis. Indeed, Bush's approval ratings of slightly over 90 percent were the highest ever recorded in the history of the Gallup poll, which is conducted by one of the major polling organizations. By 2004, however, Bush's approval ratings were around 50 percent, and he was locked in an extremely close contest for the presidency with Senator John F. Kerry of Massachusetts.

There is no doubt that public opinion can be powerful. Political scientists often point to two presidential decisions to illustrate this power. In 1968, President Lyndon Johnson decided not to run for reelection because of the intense and negative public reaction to the war in Vietnam. In 1974, President Richard Nixon resigned in the wake of a scandal when it was obvious that public opinion no longer supported him. The extent to which public opinion affects policymaking is not always so clear, however. For example, suppose that public opinion strongly supports a certain policy. If political leaders adopt that position, is it because they are responding to public opinion or to their own views on the issue? In addition, to some extent, political leaders themselves can shape public opinion. For these and other reasons, scholars must deal with many uncertainties when analyzing the impact of public opinion on policymaking.

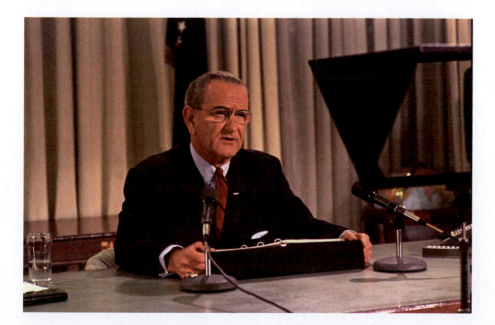

President Lyndon B. Johnson addresses the nation from the Oval Office in 1968, announcing a halt to the bombing in Vietnam and his intention not to run for reelection. (Photo by Yoichi R. Okamoto, LBJ Presidential Library)

★ Defining Public Opinion

There is no single public opinion, because there are many different "publics." In a nation of about 295 million people, there may be innumerable gradations of opinion on an issue. What we do is describe the distribution of opinions among the members of the public about a particular question. Thus, we define **public opinion** as the aggregate of individual attitudes or beliefs shared by some portion of the adult population.

Typically, public opinion is distributed among several different positions, and the distribution of opinion can tell us how divided the public is on an issue and whether compromise is possible. When a large proportion of the American public appears to express the same view on an issue, we say that a **consensus** exists, at least at the moment the poll was taken. Figure 6–1 shows a pattern of opinion that might be called consensual. Issues on which the public holds widely differing attitudes result in **divisive opinion** (see Figure 6–2). Sometimes, a poll shows a distribution of opinion indicating that most Americans either have no information about the issue or are not interested enough in the issue to formulate a position. Politicians may believe that the lack of public knowledge of an issue gives them more room to maneuver, or they may be wary of taking any action for fear that opinion will crystallize after a crisis.

An interesting question arises as to when *private* opinion becomes *public* opinion. Everyone probably has a private opinion about the competence of the president, as well as private opinions about more personal concerns, such as the state of a neighbor's lawn. We say that private opinion becomes public opinion when the opinion is publicly expressed and concerns public issues. When someone's private opinion becomes so strong that the individual is willing to go to the polls to vote for or against a candidate or an issue—or is willing to participate in a demonstration, discuss the issue at work, speak out on television or radio, or participate in the political process in any one of a dozen other ways—then the opinion becomes public opinion.

Public Opinion
The aggregate of individual attitudes or beliefs shared by some portion of the adult population.

Consensus
General agreement among the citizenry on an issue.

Divisive Opinion
Public opinion that is polarized between two quite different positions.

FIGURE 6–1

Consensus Opinion

Question: Do you approve or disapprove of the way George W. Bush handled his job as president in the first few weeks after the September 11 terrorist attacks?

Approve—88%
Disapprove—10%
No Opinion—2%

SOURCE: The Gallup Poll, January 23–25, 2003.

FIGURE 6–2

Divisive Opinion

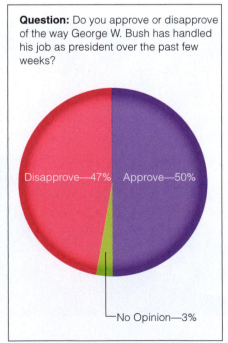

Question: Do you approve or disapprove of the way George W. Bush has handled his job as president over the past few weeks?

Disapprove—47%   Approve—50%

No Opinion—3%

SOURCE: The Gallup Poll, March 8–11, 2004.

How Public Opinion Is Formed: Political Socialization

Most Americans are willing to express opinions on political issues when asked. How do people acquire these opinions and attitudes? Typically, views that are expressed as political opinions are acquired through the process of **political socialization.** By this we mean that people acquire their political attitudes, often including their party identification, through relationships with their families, friends, and co-workers.

Political Socialization
The process by which people acquire political beliefs and attitudes.

Models of Political Socialization

Although family and teachers were once seen as the primary agents of political socialization, many scholars believe that the media are beginning to displace these traditional agents. Compared with the amount of time that young people spend in face-to-face contact with parents and teachers, time spent with television and the Internet has increased substantially over the years.

Additionally, scholars question how accurately we can predict political behavior today based on old notions of political socialization. It is less likely now than in the past, for example, that the children of conservatives will grow up to be conservatives and the children of liberals will grow up to be liberals. Even though the influence of the family on political socialization may be changing, however, it is still an obvious place to start our examination.

The Family and the Social Environment

Not only do our parents' political attitudes and actions affect our opinions, but the family also links us to other factors that affect opinion, such as race, social class, educational environment, and religious beliefs. How do parents transmit their political attitudes to their offspring?

Studies suggest that the influence of parents is due to two factors: communication and receptivity. Parents communicate their feelings and preferences to children constantly. Because children have such a strong need for parental approval, they are very receptive to their parents' views. Children are less likely to influence their parents, because parents expect deference from their children.[1]

Nevertheless, other studies show that if children are exposed to political ideas at school and in the media, they will share these ideas with their parents, giving the parents what some scholars call a "second chance" at political socialization. Children also can expose their parents to new media, such as the Internet.[2]

Education as a Source of Political Socialization. From the early days of the republic, schools were perceived to be important transmitters of political information and attitudes. Children in the primary grades learn about their country mostly in patriotic ways. They learn about the Pilgrims, the flag, and some of the nation's presidents. They also learn to celebrate national holidays. Later, in the

---

[1]Barbara A. Bardes and Robert W. Oldendick, *Public Opinion: Measuring the American Mind,* 2d ed. (Belmont, Calif.: Wadsworth Publishing Co., 2003), p. 73.
[2]For a pioneering study in this area, see Michael McDevitt and Steven H. Chaffee, "Second Chance Political Socialization: 'Trickle-up' Effects of Children on Parents," in Thomas J. Johnson *et al.,* eds., *Engaging the Public: How Government and the Media Can Reinvigorate American Democracy* (Lanham, Md.: Rowman & Littlefield Publishers, 1998), pp. 57–66.

An eight-year-old boy looks at a map of Europe under the gaze of his mother. Parents constantly communicate with their children on a variety of matters that influence their views on the world. How might parents pass on political beliefs without even realizing that they are doing so? (Tannen Maury/Landov)

middle grades, children learn more historical facts and come to understand the structure of government and the functions of the president, judges, and Congress. By high school, students have a more complex understanding of the political system, may identify with a political party, and may take positions on issues.

Generally, education is closely linked to political participation. The more education a person receives, the more likely it is that the person will be interested in politics, be confident in his or her ability to understand political issues, and be an active participant in the political process. Public opinion polls, however, suggest that even well-educated younger Americans are not strongly interested in politics.[3]

Peers and Peer Group Influence.   Once a child enters school, the child's friends become an important influence on behavior and attitudes. For children and for adults, friendships and associations in **peer groups** affect political attitudes. We must, however, separate the effects of peer group pressure on opinions and attitudes in general from the effects of peer group pressure on political opinions. For the most part, associations among peers are nonpolitical. Political attitudes are more likely to be shaped by peer groups when the peer groups are involved directly in political activities.

Individuals who join interest groups based on ethnic identity may find, for example, a common political bond through working for the group's civil liberties and rights. African American activist groups may consist of individuals who join together to support government programs that will aid the African American population. Members of a labor union may be strongly influenced to support certain pro-labor candidates.

Peer Group
A group consisting of members sharing common social characteristics. These groups play an important part in the socialization process, helping to shape attitudes and beliefs.

---

[3]Adam Clymer, "College Students Not Drawn to Voting or Politics," *The New York Times,* January 12, 2000, p. A14.

Opinion Leaders' Influence. We are all influenced by those with whom we are closely associated or whom we hold in high regard—friends at school, family members and other relatives, and teachers. In a sense, these people are **opinion leaders,** but on an *informal* level; that is, their influence on our political views is not necessarily intentional or deliberate. We are also influenced by *formal* opinion leaders, such as presidents, lobbyists, congresspersons, news commentators, and religious leaders, who have as part of their jobs the task of swaying people's views. Their interest lies in defining the political agenda in such a way that discussions about policy options will take place on their terms.

Opinion Leader
One who is able to influence the opinions of others because of position, expertise, or personality.

The Impact of the Media

Clearly, the **media**—newspapers, television, radio, and Internet sources— strongly influence public opinion. This is because the media inform the public about the issues and events of our times and thus have an **agenda-setting** effect. In other words, to borrow from Bernard Cohen's classic statement about the media and public opinion, the media may not be successful in telling people what to think, but they are "stunningly successful in telling their audience what to think about."[4]

Media
The channels of mass communication.

Agenda-Setting
Determining which public-policy questions will be debated or considered.

Today, many contend that the media's influence on public opinion has grown to equal that of the family. For example, in her analysis of the role played by the media in American politics,[5] media scholar Doris A. Graber points out that high school students, when asked where they obtain the information on which they base their attitudes, mention the mass media far more than they mention their families, friends, and teachers. This trend, combined with the increasing popularity of such information sources as talk shows and the Internet, may alter significantly the nature of the media's influence on public debate in the future. The media's influence will be discussed in more detail in Chapter 10.

[4]*The Press and Foreign Policy* (Princeton, N.J.: Princeton University Press, 1963), p. 81.
[5]See Doris A. Graber, *Mass Media and American Politics,* 6th ed. (Chicago: University of Chicago Press, 2001).

A young mother in Vermilion, Ohio, tries to watch President George W. Bush's televised State of the Union address while her children play nearby. People are no longer limited to viewing news produced by the three major networks, as they were years ago. Could the multiplicity of news outlets today limit the ability of the media to affect people's politics? Why or why not? (AP Photo/*The Plain Dealer*/John Kuntz)

The Influence of Political Events

It is somewhat surprising that a person's chronological age has little consistent effect on political beliefs. In some years, young people have tended to favor the Republicans, and in other years they have tended to favor the Democrats. It is true that young adults are somewhat more liberal than older people on such issues as same-sex marriage, civil disobedience, and racial and gender equality. Nevertheless, a more important factor than a person's age is the impact of important political events that shape the political attitudes of an entire generation. When events produce such a long-lasting result, we refer to it as a **generational effect** (also called the *cohort effect*).

Voters who grew up in the 1930s during the Great Depression were likely to form lifelong attachments to the Democratic Party, the party of Franklin D. Roosevelt. In the 1960s and 1970s, the war in Vietnam and the **Watergate break-in** and the subsequent presidential cover-up fostered widespread cynicism toward government. There is evidence that the years of economic prosperity under President Ronald Reagan during the 1980s led many young people to identify with the Republican Party. It is less clear whether more recent presidents—including Democrat Bill Clinton (1993–2001) and Republican George W. Bush—have been able to affect the party identification of young voters.

★ Political Preferences and Voting Behavior

Various socioeconomic and demographic factors appear to influence political preferences. These factors include education, income and **socioeconomic status,** religion, race, gender, geographic region, and similar traits. People who share the same religion, occupation, or any other demographic trait are likely to influence each other and may also have common political concerns that follow from the common characteristic. Other factors, such as party identification, perception of the candidates, and issue preferences, are closely connected to the electoral process itself. Table 6–1 illustrates the impact of some of these variables on voting behavior.

Demographic Influences

Demographic influences reflect the individual's personal background and place in society. Some factors have to do with the family into which a person was born: race and (for most people) religion. Others may be the result of choices made throughout an individual's life: place of residence, educational achievement, and profession.

It is also clear that many of these factors are interrelated. People who have more education are likely to have higher incomes and to hold professional jobs. Similarly, children born into wealthier families are far more likely to complete college than children from poor families. Many other interrelationships are not so immediately obvious; for example, many people might not guess that 88 percent of African Americans report that religion is very important in their lives, compared with only 57 percent of whites.[6]

Education. In the past, having a college education tended to be associated with voting for Republicans. In recent years, however, this correlation has become weaker. In particular, individuals with a postgraduate education—more than a bachelor's degree—have become increasingly Democratic. Also, a higher percent-

---

Generational Effect
A long-lasting effect of the events of a particular time on the political opinions of those who came of political age at that time.

Watergate Break-in
The 1972 illegal entry into the Democratic National Committee offices by participants in President Richard Nixon's reelection campaign.

Socioeconomic Status
The value assigned to a person due to occupation or income. An upper-class person, for example, has high socioeconomic status.

---

[6]The Gallup Poll, "A Look at Americans and Religion Today," March 23, 2004.

TABLE 6–1

Votes by Groups in Presidential Elections, 1988–2000 (in Percentages)

	1988		1992			1996		2000		2004	
	DUKAKIS (DEM.)	BUSH (REP.)	CLINTON (DEM.)	BUSH (REP.)	PEROT (REF.)	CLINTON (DEM.)	DOLE (REP.)	GORE (DEM.)	BUSH (REP.)	KERRY (DEM.)	BUSH (REP.)
Total vote	45	53	43	38	19	49	41	48	48	48	51
Sex											
Men	41	57	41	38	21	43	44	42	53	44	55
Women	49	50	46	37	17	54	38	54	43	51	48
Race											
White	40	59	39	41	20	43	46	42	54	41	58
Black	86	12	82	11	7	84	12	90	8	88	11
Hispanic	69	30	62	25	14	72	21	67	31	54	44
Educational Attainment											
Not a high school graduate	56	43	55	28	17	59	28	59	39	50	50
High school graduate	49	50	43	36	20	51	35	48	49	47	52
College graduate	37	62	40	41	19	44	46	45	51	46	52
Postgraduate education	48	50	49	36	15	52	40	52	44	54	45
Religion											
White Protestant	33	66	33	46	21	36	53	34	63	32	68
Catholic	47	52	44	36	20	53	37	49	47	47	52
Jewish	64	35	78	12	10	78	16	79	19	75	24
White Fundamentalist	18	81	23	61	15	na	na	na	na	21	79
Union Status											
Union household	57	42	55	24	21	59	30	59	37	59	40
Family Income											
Under $15,000	62	37	59	23	18	59	28	57	37	63	37
$15,000–29,000	50	49	45	35	20	53	36	54	41	57	41
$30,000–49,000	44	56	41	38	21	48	40	49	48	50	49
Over $50,000	42	56	40	42	18	44	48	45	52	43	56
Size of Place											
Population over 500,000	62	37	58	28	13	68	25	71	26	60	40
Population 50,000 to 500,000	52	47	50	33	16	50	39	57	40	50	50
Population 10,000 to 50,000	38	61	39	42	20	48	41	38	59	48	51
Rural	44	55	39	40	20	44	46	37	59	39	60

NA = not asked.

SOURCES: *The New York Times;* Voter News Service; CBS News.

age of voters with only a high school education voted Republican in 2000, compared with the pattern in previous elections, in which that group of voters tended to favor Democrats.

Many people with postgraduate degrees are professionals, such as physicians, attorneys, and college instructors. Typically, a postgraduate degree is an occupational requirement for professionals. Despite the recent popularity of the master of business administration (MBA) degree, businesspersons are more likely to have only a bachelor's diploma. They are also much more likely to vote Republican.

The Influence of Economic Status. Family income is a strong predictor of economic liberalism or conservatism. Those with low incomes tend to favor government action to benefit the poor or to promote economic equality. Those with high incomes tend to oppose government intervention in the economy or to support it only when it benefits business. On economic issues, therefore, the traditional economic spectrum described in Chapter 1 on page 17 is a useful tool. The rich tend toward the right; the poor tend toward the left.

If we examine cultural as well as economic issues, however, the four-cornered ideological grid discussed in Chapter 1 on page 18 becomes important. It happens

A Jewish grandmother and granddaughter light the menorah candles during the Hanukkah holiday in December. Despite their modern-day prosperity, a majority of American Jews continue to support liberal politics. Why might Jewish voters continue to be more interested in traditionally liberal values than in "voting their pocketbooks"? (© Ariel Skelley/CORBIS)

that upper-class voters are more likely to endorse cultural liberalism, and lower-class individuals are more likely to favor cultural conservatism. Support for the right to have an abortion, for example, rises with income. It follows that libertarians—those who oppose government action on both economic and social issues—are concentrated among the wealthier members of the population. (Libertarians constitute the upper-right-hand corner of the grid in Figure 1–1 in Chapter 1.) Those who favor government action both to promote traditional moral values and to promote economic equality—economic liberals, cultural conservatives—are concentrated among groups that are less well off. (This group fills up the lower-left-hand corner of the grid.)

Economic Status and Voting Behavior. Normally, the higher a person's income, the more likely the person will be to vote Republican. Manual laborers, factory workers, and especially union members are more likely to vote Democratic (see Table 6–2). If socioeconomic status is measured by profession, then traditionally those of higher socioeconomic status—professionals and businesspersons, as well as white-collar workers—have tended to vote Republican.

There are no hard-and-fast rules, however. Some very poor individuals are devoted Republicans, just as some extremely wealthy people support the Democratic Party. Indeed, recent research indicates that a realignment is occurring among those of higher economic status: as just mentioned, professionals now tend to vote Democratic, while small-business owners, managers, and corporate executives tend to vote Republican.[7]

Religious Influence: Denomination. Traditionally, scholars have examined the impact of religion on political attitudes by dividing the population into such categories as Protestant, Catholic, and Jewish. In recent decades, however, such a breakdown has become less valuable as a means of predicting someone's political

[7]Thomas B. Edsall, "Voters Thinking Less with Their Wallets," *International Herald Tribune,* March 27, 2001, p. 3.

TABLE 6–2

Percentage of Union Households Voting Republican

Although union members are more likely to identify themselves as Democrats than Republicans and labor organizations are far more likely to support Democratic candidates, the data below show that in seven of thirteen presidential elections, Republicans have captured at least 40 percent of the votes from union households.

Year	Union Households Voting Republican for President Candidates	Percentage
1952	Eisenhower vs. Stevenson	44
1956	Eisenhower vs. Stevenson	57
1960	Kennedy vs. Nixon	36
1964	Johnson vs. Goldwater	17
1968	Nixon vs. Humphrey	44
1972	Nixon vs. McGovern	57
1976	Carter vs. Ford	36
1980	Reagan vs. Carter	45
1984	Reagan vs. Mondale	43
1988	Bush vs. Dukakis	42
1992	Clinton vs. Bush	24
1996	Clinton vs. Dole	30
2000	Gore vs. Bush	37
2004	Kerry vs. Bush	40

SOURCES: *CQ Researcher,* June 28, 1996, p. 560; *The New York Times,* November 10, 1996, p. 16; and authors' updates.

preferences. It is true that in the past, Jewish voters were notably more liberal than members of other groups, on both economic and cultural issues, and they continue to be more liberal today. Persons reporting no religion are very liberal on social issues but have mixed economic views. Northern Protestants and Catholics, however, do not differ that greatly from each other, and neither do southern Protestants and Catholics. This represents something of a change—in the late 1800s and early 1900s, northern Protestants were distinctly more likely to vote Republican, and northern Catholics were more likely to vote Democratic.

Religious Influence: Commitment.   Nevertheless, two factors do turn out to be major predictors of political attitudes among members of the various Christian denominations. One is the degree of religious commitment, as measured by such actions as regular churchgoing. The other is the degree to which the voter adheres to religious beliefs that (depending on the denomination) can be called conservative, evangelical, or fundamentalist. High scores on either factor are associated with cultural conservatism on political issues—that is, with beliefs that place a high value on social order. (See Chapter 1 for a discussion of the contrasting values of order and liberty.) These religious factors have much less influence on economic views.

As a result, voters who are more devout, regardless of their church affiliation, are tending to vote Republican, while voters who are less devout are more often Democrats. In 2000, for example, Protestants who regularly attended church gave 84 percent of their votes to Republican candidate George W. Bush, compared with 55 percent of those who attended church less often. Among Catholics, there was a similar pattern: a majority of Catholics who attended church regularly voted Republican, while a majority of Catholics who were not regular churchgoers voted for Democratic candidate Al Gore.[8] There is an exception to this trend: African Americans of all religions have been strongly supportive of Democrats.

The Influence of Race and Ethnicity.   Although African Americans are, on average, somewhat conservative on certain cultural issues such as same-sex marriage and abortion, they tend to be more liberal than whites on social-welfare matters, civil liberties, and even foreign policy. African Americans voted principally for

[8]Ronald Brownstein, "Attendance, Not Affiliation, Key to Religious Voters," *The Los Angeles Times,* July 16, 2001, p. A10.

Appealing to African American churchgoers as part of their campaigns for the presidency, Senator John Kerry and President George W. Bush speak during Sunday services. Kerry is at the Greater Bethlehem Temple Apostolic Faith Church in Jackson, Mississippi. Bush is visiting the Union Bethel African Methodist Episcopal Church in New Orleans. How might Bush have attempted to win the support of these voters? How might Kerry have crafted his appeal? (REUTERS/Jim Bourg/Landov)

An Asian American family standing outside their new home. The median family income of Asian Americans is about $10,000 more than the median income for all households. As a result, Asian Americans, especially those from Japan, China, and India, are sometimes seen as "model minorities" who are succeeding through education and hard work. Despite the "model minority" designation, some Asian Americans continue to live in poverty or experience discrimination. Asian Americans are more likely to vote Republican than members of most other minority groups.

Republicans until Democrat Franklin Roosevelt's New Deal in the 1930s. Since then, they have largely identified with the Democratic Party. Indeed, Democratic presidential candidates have received, on average, more than 80 percent of the African American vote since 1956. As you learned in Chapter 1, Hispanics also favor the Democrats by a margin of about two to one. Hispanics of Cuban ancestry, however, are predominantly Republican. Most Asian American groups lean toward the Democrats, although often by narrow margins. Muslim American immigrants and their descendants are an interesting category.[9] In 2000, a majority of Muslim Americans of Middle Eastern ancestry voted for Republican George W. Bush because they shared his cultural conservatism and believed that he would do a better job of defending their civil liberties than Democrat Al Gore. In the 2004 election campaign, however, the civil liberties issue propelled many of these voters toward the Democrats.[10]

The Gender Gap. Until the 1980s, there was little evidence that men's and women's political attitudes were very different. Following the election of Ronald Reagan in 1980, however, scholars began to detect a **gender gap.** A May 1983 Gallup poll revealed that men were more likely than women to approve of Reagan's job performance. The gender gap has reappeared in subsequent presidential elections, with women being more likely than men to support the Democratic candidate. In the 2000 elections, 54 percent of women voted for Democrat Al Gore, compared with 42 percent of men. A similar gender gap was evident in the 2002 midterm elections: 55 percent of women favored Democratic candidates, compared with 43 percent of men.

Women also appear to hold different attitudes from their male counterparts on a range of issues other than presidential preferences. They are much more likely

Gender Gap
The difference between the percentage of women who vote for a particular candidate and the percentage of men who vote for the candidate.

---

[9]At least a third of U.S. Muslims actually are African Americans whose ancestors have been in this country for a long time. In terms of political preferences, African American Muslims are more likely to resemble other African Americans than Muslim immigrants from the Middle East.

[10]For up-to-date information on Muslim American issues, see the Web site of the Council on American-Islamic Relations at http://www.cair-net.org.

than men to oppose capital punishment and the use of force abroad. Studies also have shown that women are more concerned about risks to the environment, more supportive of social welfare, and more in agreement with extending civil rights to gay men and lesbians than are men. In contrast, women are also more concerned than men about the security issues raised by the events of 9/11. This last fact may have pushed women in a more conservative direction, at least for a time.

Reasons for the Gender Gap.   What is the cause of the gender gap? A number of explanations have been offered, including the increase in the number of working women, feminism, and women's concerns over abortion rights and other social issues. Researchers Lena Edlund and Rohini Pande of Columbia University, however, found that the major factor leading to the gender gap has been the disparate economic impact on men and women of not being married. In the last three decades, men and women have tended to marry later in life or stay single even after having children. The divorce rate has also risen dramatically. Edlund and Pande argue that this decline in marriage has tended to make men richer and women relatively poorer. Consequently, support for Democrats is high among single women, particularly single mothers.[11]

Researchers have also found that the gender gap grows wider as men and women become better educated. This result seems to contradict Edlund and Pande's theory, at least in part—it does not seem likely that well-educated women would be suffering economically, and there is some evidence that the gender gap persists even among well-educated married women.[12]

Geographic Region.   Finally, where you live can influence your political attitudes. In one way, regional differences are less important today than just a few decades ago. The former solid (Democratic) South has crumbled in national elections. Only 43 percent of the votes from the southern states went to Democrat Al Gore in 2000, while 55 percent went to Republican George W. Bush.

There is a tendency today, at least in national elections, for the South, the Great Plains, and the Rocky Mountain states to favor the Republicans and for the West Coast and the Northeast to favor the Democrats. Perhaps more important than region is residence—urban, suburban, or rural. People in large cities tend to be liberal and Democratic. Those who live in smaller communities tend to be conservative and Republican.

Election-Specific Factors

Factors such as party identification, perception of the candidates, and issue preferences may have an effect on how people vote in particular elections. While most people do not change their party identification from year to year, candidates and issues can change greatly, and voting behavior can therefore change as well.

Party Identification.   With the possible exception of race, party identification has been the most important determinant of voting behavior in national elections. Party affiliation is influenced by family and peer groups, by generational effects, by the media, and by the voter's assessment of candidates and issues.

In the middle to late 1960s, party attachment began to weaken. Whereas independent voters were a little more than 20 percent of the eligible electorate during

DID YOU KNOW . . .
That Britain had a major gender gap for much of the twentieth century—because women were much more likely than men to support the Conservative Party rather than the more left-wing Labor Party?

---

[11]For an online video presentation of Edlund and Pande's research, go to http://www.Columbia.edu/cu/news/media/02/edlund_pande/index.html.

[12]Susan Page, "'Til Politics Do Us Part: Gender Gap Widens," *USA Today*, December 18, 2003, p. 1A–2A.

the 1950s, they constituted over 30 percent of all voters by the mid-1990s. Independent voting seems to be more common among new young voters. While party identification may have little effect on the voting behavior of independents, it remains a crucial determinant for the majority of the voters, who have established party identifications.

Perception of the Candidates.   The image of the candidate also seems to be important in a voter's choice, especially of a president. To some extent, voter attitudes toward candidates are based on emotions (such as trust) rather than on any judgment about experience or policy. In some years, voters have been attracted to a candidate who appeared to share their concerns and worries. (President Bill Clinton was one example.) In other years, voters have sought a candidate who appeared to have high integrity and honesty. Voters have been especially attracted to these candidates in elections that follow a major scandal, such as Richard Nixon's Watergate scandal (1972–1974) or Clinton's sex scandal (1998–1999).

Issue Preferences.   Issues make a difference in presidential and congressional elections. Although personality or image factors may be very persuasive, most voters have some notion of how the candidates differ on basic issues or at least know which candidates want a change in the direction of government policy.

Historically, economic concerns have been among the most powerful influences on public opinion. When the economy is doing well, it is very difficult for a challenger, especially at the presidential level, to defeat the incumbent. In contrast, inflation, unemployment, or high interest rates are likely to work to the disadvantage of the incumbent. Some studies seem to show that people vote on the basis of their personal economic well-being, while other research suggests that people vote on the basis of the nation's overall economic health.[13]

★ Measuring Public Opinion

In a democracy, people express their opinions in a variety of ways, as mentioned in this chapter's introduction. One of the most common means of gathering and measuring public opinion on specific issues is, of course, through the use of **opinion polls.**

The History of Opinion Polls

During the 1800s, certain American newspapers and magazines spiced up their political coverage by doing face-to-face straw polls (unofficial polls indicating the trend of political opinion) or mail surveys of their readers' opinions. In the early twentieth century, the magazine *Literary Digest* further developed the technique of opinion polling by mailing large numbers of questionnaires to individuals, many of whom were its own subscribers, to determine their political opinions. From 1916 to 1936, more than 70 percent of the magazine's election predictions were accurate.

Literary Digest's polling activities suffered a setback in 1936, however, when the magazine predicted, based on more than two million returned questionnaires, that Republican candidate Alfred Landon would win over Democratic candidate Franklin D. Roosevelt. Landon won in only two states. A major problem with the

Opinion Poll
A method of systematically questioning a small, selected sample of respondents who are deemed representative of the total population.

---

[13]Warren E. Miller and J. Merrill Shanks, *The New American Voter* (Cambridge, Mass.: Harvard University Press, 1996). See page 270 for voting on the basis of personal income and page 196 for voting on the basis of the state of the economy.

Digest's polling technique was its use of nonrepresentative respondents. In 1936, at the bottom of the Great Depression, the magazine's subscribers were, for one thing, considerably more affluent than the average American. In other words, they did not accurately represent all of the voters in the U.S. population.

Several newcomers to the public opinion poll industry accurately predicted Roosevelt's landslide victory. These newcomers are still active in the poll-taking industry today: the Gallup poll of George Gallup and the Roper poll founded by Elmo Roper. Gallup and Roper, along with Archibald Crossley, developed the modern polling techniques of market research. Using personal interviews with small samples of selected voters (less than two thousand), they showed that they could predict with accuracy the behavior of the total voting population.

By the 1950s, improved methods of sampling and a whole new science of survey research had been developed. Survey research centers sprang up throughout the United States, particularly at universities. Some of these survey groups are the American Institute of Public Opinion at Princeton, New Jersey; the National Opinion Research Center at the University of Chicago; and the Survey Research Center at the University of Michigan.

Sampling Techniques

How can interviewing fewer than two thousand voters tell us what tens of millions of voters will do? Clearly, it is necessary that the sample of individuals be representative of all voters in the population. Consider an analogy. Let's say we have a large jar containing ten thousand pennies of various dates, and we want to know how many pennies were minted within certain decades (1950–1959, 1960–1969, and so on).

Representative Sampling.   One way to estimate the distribution of the dates on the pennies—without examining all ten thousand—is to take a representative sample. This sample would be obtained by mixing the pennies up well and then removing a handful of them—perhaps one hundred pennies. The distribution of dates might be as follows:

- *1950–1959: 5 percent.*
- *1960–1969: 5 percent.*
- *1970–1979: 20 percent.*
- *1980–1989: 30 percent.*
- *1990–present: 40 percent.*

If the pennies are very well mixed within the jar, and if you take a large enough sample, the resulting distribution will probably approach the actual distribution of the dates of all ten thousand coins.

The Principle of Randomness.   The most important principle in sampling, or poll taking, is randomness. Every penny or every person should have a known chance, and especially an *equal chance,* of being sampled. If this happens, then a small sample should be representative of the whole group, both in demographic characteristics (age, religion, race, region, and the like) and in opinions. The ideal way to sample the voting population of the United States would be to put all voter names into a jar—or a computer—and randomly sample, say, two thousand of them. Because this is too costly and inefficient, pollsters have developed other ways to obtain good samples. One technique is simply to choose a random selection of telephone numbers and interview the respective households. This technique produces a relatively accurate sample at a low cost.

To ensure that the random samples include respondents from relevant segments of the population—rural, urban, northeastern, southern, and so on—most survey organizations randomly choose, say, urban areas that they will consider as representative of all urban areas. Then they randomly select their respondents within those areas. A generally less accurate technique is known as *quota sampling*. Here, survey researchers decide how many persons of certain types they need in the survey—such as minorities, women, or farmers—and then send out interviewers to find the necessary number of these types. Not only is this method often less accurate, but it also may be biased if, say, the interviewer refuses to go into certain neighborhoods or will not interview after dark.

Generally, the national survey organizations take great care to select their samples randomly, because their reputations rest on the accuracy of their results. The Gallup and Roper polls usually interview about 1,500 individuals, and their results have a very high probability of being correct—within a margin of 3 percentage points. The accuracy with which the Gallup poll has predicted presidential election results is shown in Table 6–3.

Problems with Polls

Public opinion polls are snapshots of the opinions and preferences of the people at a specific moment in time and as expressed in response to a specific question. Given that definition, it is fairly easy to understand situations in which the polls are wrong. For example, opinion polls leading up to the 1980 presidential election showed President Jimmy Carter defeating challenger Ronald Reagan. Only a few analysts noted the large number of "undecided" respondents a week before the election. Those voters shifted massively to Reagan at the last minute, and Reagan won the election.

The famous photo of Harry Truman showing the front page that declared his defeat in the 1948 presidential elections is another tribute to the weakness of polling. Again, the poll that predicted his defeat was taken more than a week before election day.

President Harry Truman holds up the front page of the *Chicago Daily Tribune* issue that predicted his defeat on the basis of a Gallup poll. The poll had indicated that Truman would lose the 1948 contest for his reelection by a margin of 55.5 to 44.5 percent. The Gallup poll was completed more than a week before the election, so it missed a shift by undecided voters to Truman. Truman won the election with 49.9 percent of the vote. (Corbis/UPI/Bettmann)
.

TABLE 6–3

Gallup Poll Accuracy Record

YEAR	GALLUP FINAL SURVEY, PERCENTAGE		ELECTION RESULTS, PERCENTAGE		DEVIATION
2004	49.0	Bush	51.0	Bush	−2.0
2000	50.0	Bush	48.0	Bush	+2.0
1996	52.0	Clinton	49.0	Clinton	+3.0
1992	49.0	Clinton	43.2	Clinton	+5.8
1988	56.0	Bush	53.9	Bush	+2.1
1984	59.0	Reagan	59.1	Reagan	−0.1
1980	47.0	Reagan	50.8	Reagan	−3.8
1976	48.0	Carter	50.0	Carter	−2.0
1972	62.0	Nixon	61.8	Nixon	+0.2
1968	43.0	Nixon	43.5	Nixon	−0.5
1964	64.0	Johnson	61.3	Johnson	+2.7
1960	51.0	Kennedy	50.1	Kennedy	+0.9
1956	59.5	Eisenhower	57.8	Eisenhower	+1.7
1952	51.0	Eisenhower	55.4	Eisenhower	−4.4
1948	44.5	Truman	49.9	Truman	−5.4
1944	51.5	Roosevelt	53.3	Roosevelt	−1.8
1940	52.0	Roosevelt	55.0	Roosevelt	−3.0
1936	55.7	Roosevelt	62.5	Roosevelt	−6.8

SOURCES: *The Gallup Poll Monthly,* November 1992; *Time,* November 21, 1994; *The Wall Street Journal,* November 6, 1996; and authors' updates.

Sampling Errors. Polls may also report erroneous results because the pool of respondents was not chosen in a scientific manner; that is, the form of sampling and the number of people sampled may be too small to overcome **sampling error,** which is the difference between the sample result and the true result if the entire population had been interviewed. The sample would be biased, for example, if the poll interviewed people by telephone and did not correct for the fact that more women than men answer the telephone and that some populations (college students and very poor individuals, for example) cannot be found so easily by telephone. Unscientific mail-in polls, telephone call-in polls, and polls completed by the workers in a campaign office are usually biased and do not give an accurate picture of the public's views. Because of these and other problems with polls, some have suggested that polling be regulated by the government (see the chapter-opening *What If . . .* feature).

As poll takers get close to election day, they become even more concerned about their sample of respondents. Some pollsters continue to interview eligible voters, meaning those over eighteen and registered to vote. Many others use a series of questions in the poll and other weighting methods to try to identify "likely voters" so that they can be more accurate in their election-eve predictions. When a poll changes its method from reporting the views of eligible voters to reporting those of likely voters, the results tend to change dramatically.

Poll Questions. It makes sense to expect that the results of a poll will depend on the questions that are asked. Depending on what question is asked, voters could be said either to support a particular proposal or to oppose it. One of the problems with many polls is the yes/no answer format. For example, suppose that a poll question asks, "Are you in favor of abortion?" A respondent who is in favor of abortion in some circumstances but not in others has no way of indicating this view because "yes" and "no" are the only possible answers. Furthermore, respondents' answers are also influenced by the order in which questions are asked, by

Sampling Error

The difference between a sample's results and the true result if the entire population had been interviewed.

"One final question: Do you now own or have you ever owned a fur coat?"
Drawing by Mick Stevens, *The New Yorker.*

the possible answers from which they are allowed to choose, and, in some cases, by their interaction with the interviewer. To a certain extent, people try to please the interviewer. They answer questions about which they have no information and avoid some answers to try to measure up to the interviewer's expectations. Is it possible that in some foreign countries, the problem of developing appropriate questions would be even greater than in the United States? We look at one recent example of foreign polling in this chapter's *Global View* feature.

Push Polls. Some campaigns have begun using "push polls," in which the respondents are given misleading information in the questions asked to persuade them to vote against a candidate. Obviously, the answers given are likely to be influenced by such techniques. Are push pools unfair, and if they are, what can be

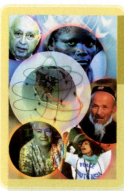

GLOBAL VIEW
Polling in Baghdad

While Americans take polling for granted, it is relatively uncommon in the Islamic world. Many Muslim-majority countries are dictatorships or absolute monarchies, and poll respondents might therefore believe that it is unsafe to speak freely with interviewers. The U.S.–led occupation of Iraq, however, opened up possibilities for poll takers.

The Gallup organization took advantage of the opportunity. Initially, its polling was limited to Baghdad. Baghdad residents were "incredibly responsive"—Gallup achieved a 97 percent cooperation rate, which is unprecedented by Western standards. Later, polling was extended to the rest of the country.

OPINIONS ON THE OCCUPATION

In the initial polls, most Baghdad residents believed that ousting Saddam Hussein was worth the hardships endured since the invasion. In October 2003, 85 percent of the respondents believed that immediate withdrawal of the coalition forces would result in anarchy. Still, 20 percent believed that attacks on U.S. forces could be justified in whole or in part.

By April 2004, however (when polling had gone nationwide), Iraqi opinions about the occupation were much more negative. Thirty percent of respondents believed that attacks on U.S. forces could be justified in whole or in part—and in the "Sunni triangle" west of Baghdad, 62 percent believed that the attacks could be justified completely. On the conduct of U.S. forces, 58 percent of Iraqis described it as "bad." In Baghdad, 81 percent of the respondents described the conduct as "bad," up from 29 percent in 2003. Still, there was no change in the number of persons who believed that getting rid of Saddam Hussein had been "worth it."

POLITICAL OPINIONS

In Baghdad, freedom of speech was endorsed by an impressive 98 percent of the respondents, and freedom of religious practice was supported by 86 percent. Separation of "mosque and state," however, was opposed, 52 percent to 40 percent. When asked what forms of government would be acceptable for the country, about half endorsed a multiparty parliamentary democracy. An equal number of respondents favored a system based on the Islamic concept of *shura,* whereby leaders work through a process of consultation and consensus. A *shura* system was especially favored by the less well educated. An Iranian-style theocracy, in which religious leaders hold most of the power, was acceptable to only 23 percent.

CULTURAL ATTITUDES

Gallup asked Baghdad respondents to describe what, if anything, they most resented about the West. About 36 percent responded that Western culture undermined morality by spreading sexually indecent influences and corruption. Nationally, 53 percent believed that women should follow more traditional roles than they did before the invasion. Only 26 percent wanted more freedom for women than before. Responses by women did not differ greatly from those by men. Responses by the Kurdish minority, however, were dramatically different—only 10 percent of Kurds favored traditional roles for women, while 82 percent favored more freedom. Stark differences between Kurds and Arabs on this and many other questions may pose a problem for the new Iraqi government.

FOR CRITICAL ANALYSIS

Baghdad residents were eager to participate in the polling. What reasons might they have had for this attitude?

done about them? We take a closer look at push polls in this chapter's *Politics and Polls* feature on the following page.

Because of these problems with polls, you need to be especially careful when evaluating poll results. For some suggestions on how to be a critical consumer of public opinion polls, see the *Making a Difference* feature at the end of this chapter. Some have suggested that during times of crisis, it is particularly important for pollsters to avoid these kinds of problems and try to obtain accurate results.

The Accuracy of the 2004 Polls

All of the major news outlets, plus a variety of research groups, took polls every week from Labor Day until November. After the Democratic convention, Kerry moved up smartly in the polls, as did Bush after the Republican convention. Bush kept his lead until the presidential debates, when the race became "too close to call." Gallup and other polls, however, had difficulties in determining the impact of the anticipated high voter turnout. On Election Day, news leaked that network exit polls had Kerry as the winner. The network anchors were cautious, however, and made no mention of these predictions on the air.

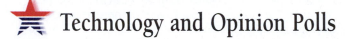 Technology and Opinion Polls

Public opinion polling is based on scientific principles, particularly with respect to randomness. Today, technological advances allow polls to be taken over the Internet, but serious questions have been raised about the ability of pollsters to obtain truly random samples using this medium. The same was said not long ago when another technological breakthrough changed public opinion polling—the telephone.

The Advent of Telephone Polling

During the 1970s, telephone polling began to predominate over in-person polling. Obviously, telephone polling is less expensive than sending interviewers to poll respondents in their homes. Additionally, telephone interviewers do not have to worry about safety problems, particularly in high-crime areas. Finally, telephone interviews can be conducted relatively quickly. They allow politicians or the media to poll one evening and report the results the next day.

Telephone Polling Problems. Somewhat ironically, the success of telephone polling has created major problems for the technique. The telemarketing industry in general has become so pervasive that people increasingly refuse to respond to telephone polls. More and more households either use caller ID systems to screen calls or have their calls picked up by an answering machine. Most people can determine within the first thirty seconds of a call whether the call is legitimate or of interest to them, and they hang up if it is not.

Nonresponse Rates Have Skyrocketed. Nonresponses in telephone polling include unreachable numbers, refusals, answering machines, and call-screening devices. The nonresponse rate has increased to as high as 80 percent for most telephone polls. Such a high nonresponse rate undercuts confidence in the survey

POLITICS AND POLLS
The Issue of Push Polls

The notion that candidates can use polls to "push" the respondents into voting for the candidate sponsoring the poll is relatively new to politics. Nonetheless, this type of polling is increasingly being used in political campaigns.

WHAT IS A PUSH POLL?

The National Council on Public Polls defines a *push poll* as

a technique in which telephone calls are used to canvass vast numbers of potential voters, feeding them false and damaging "information" about a candidate under the guise of taking a poll to see how this "information" affects voter preferences. In fact, the intent is to "push" the voters away from one candidate and towards the opposing candidate.

Push polls are typically used in an effort to reach a high percentage of voters just before the close of an election campaign. Whereas a normal polling interview lasts from a few minutes to over thirty minutes, a push poll typically lasts no longer than sixty seconds, and sometimes only twenty seconds.

THE INCREASING USE OF PUSH POLLS

Designing polling questions so as to influence the respondents' votes has become common. Indeed, the practice has spread throughout all levels of U.S. politics—local, state, and federal. In 1996, in a random survey of forty-five candidates, researchers found that thirty-five of them claimed to have been victimized by negative push-polling techniques used by their opponents.* Now even advocacy groups, as well as candidates for political offices, are using push polls.

During the 2000 presidential primaries, Republican presidential hopeful John McCain accused the Bush camp of making more than 200,000 "advocacy" calls, asking voters about their likely choices in the elections. The calls used long questions containing information about McCain's record. The Bush camp said that the information was accurate. In contrast, McCain saw this as negative "push polling."

Push polling continued during the 2002 congressional campaigns and the campaigns in 2004. Its use was widespread in campaigns for governorships and other state offices.

FOR CRITICAL ANALYSIS

Is it possible to tell whether a survey question is worded "neutrally" or is worded in a biased manner in an effort to elicit a particular response?

*Karl T. Feld, "When Push Comes to Shove: A Polling Industry Call to Arms," *Public Perspective,* September/October 2001, p. 38.

---

results. In most cases, polling only 20 percent of those on the list cannot lead to a random sample. Even more important for politicians is the fact that polling organizations are not required to report their response rates.

Enter Internet Polling

Obviously, Internet polling is not done on a one-on-one basis, since there is no voice communication. In spite of the potential problems, the Harris Poll, a widely respected national polling organization, conducted online polls during the 1998 elections. Its election predictions were accurate in many states. Nonetheless, it made a serious error in one southern gubernatorial election. The Harris group subsequently refined its techniques and continues to conduct online polls. This organization believes that proper weighting of the results will achieve the equivalent of a random-sampled poll.

Public opinion experts argue that the Harris Poll procedure violates the mathematical basis of random sampling. Nonetheless, the Internet population is looking more like the rest of America: almost as many women go online as men, 43 percent of African American adults are online, and so are 59 percent of Hispanics (compared with 67 percent of non-Hispanic whites).[14]

---

[14]Pew Internet and American Life Project, *May–June 2004 Tracking Survey.* The Pew Internet surveys are online at http://www.pewinternet.org.

"Nonpolls" on the Internet.   Even if organizations such as the Harris Poll succeed in obtaining the equivalent of a random sample when polling on the Internet, another problem will remain: the proliferation of "nonpolls" on the Internet. Every media outlet that maintains a Web site allows anyone to submit her or his opinion. Numerous organizations and for-profit companies send polls to individuals via e-mail. Mister Poll (http://www.mrpoll.com) bills itself as the Internet's largest online polling database. Mister Poll allows you to create your own polls just for fun or to include them on your home page. In general, Mister Poll, like many other polling sites, asks a number of questions on various issues and seeks answers from those who log on to its site. Although the Mister Poll Web site states, "None of these polls is scientific," sites such as this one undercut the efforts of legitimate pollsters to use the Internet scientifically.

Will Internet Polling Go the Way of Telephone Polling?   Perhaps the greatest threat to the science of polling, whether polls are conducted via the Internet or otherwise, is simply that Americans are overwhelmed with polling data. They are tired of pollsters' attempts to poll them, and they are overwhelmed by the deluge of poll results. Although some results may be legitimate and derive from truly scientific work, many are obtained from cheap, quick, and poorly executed polls. How can any American determine which data are legitimate?

If all polls appear equal, will the American public believe any of them? If polls and polling come to be regarded as inaccurate, then the practice of scientific polling could disappear.

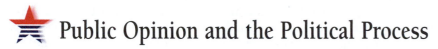

Public Opinion and the Political Process

Public opinion affects the political process in many ways. Politicians, whether in office or in the midst of a campaign, see public opinion as important to their careers. The president, members of Congress, governors, and other elected officials realize that strong support by the public as expressed in opinion polls is a source of power in dealing with other politicians. It is far more difficult for a senator to say no to the president if the president is immensely popular and if polls show approval of the president's policies. Public opinion also helps political candidates identify the most important concerns among the people and may help them shape their campaigns successfully.

Nevertheless, surveys of public opinion are not equivalent to elections in the United States. Although opinion polls may influence political candidates or government officials, elections are the major vehicle through which Americans can bring about changes in their government.

Political Culture and Public Opinion

Americans are divided into a multitude of ethnic, religious, regional, and political subgroups. Given the diversity of American society and the wide range of opinions contained within it, how is it that the political process continues to function without being stalemated by conflict and dissension? One explanation is rooted in the concept of the American political culture, which can be described as a set of attitudes and ideas about the nation and the government. As discussed in Chapter 1, our political culture is widely shared by Americans of many different backgrounds. To some extent, it consists of symbols, such as the American flag, the Liberty Bell, and the Statue of Liberty. The elements of our political culture also include certain shared beliefs about the most important values in the American political system, including (1) liberty, equality, and property; (2) support for religion; and

Political Trust
The degree to which individuals express trust in the government and political institutions, usually measured through a specific series of survey questions.

(3) community service and personal achievement. The structure of the government—particularly federalism, the political parties, the powers of Congress, and popular rule—is also an important value.

Political Culture and Support for Our Political System.   The political culture provides a general environment of support for the political system. If the people share certain beliefs about the system and a reservoir of good feeling exists toward the institutions of government, the nation will be better able to weather periods of crisis. Such was the case after the 2000 presidential elections when, for several weeks, it was not certain who the next president would be and how that determination would be made. At the time, some contended that the nation was facing a true constitutional crisis. Certainly, in many nations of today's world this would be the case. In fact, however, the broad majority of Americans did not believe that the uncertain outcome of the elections had created a constitutional crisis. Polls taken during this time found that, on the contrary, most Americans were confident in our political system's ability to decide the issue peaceably and in a lawful manner.[15]

Political Trust.   The political culture also helps Americans evaluate their government's performance. At times in our history, **political trust** in government has reached relatively high levels. As you can see in Table 6–4, a poll taken two weeks after the 9/11 attacks found that trust in government was higher than it had been for more than three decades. At other times, political trust in government has fallen to low levels. For example, during the 1960s and 1970s, during the Vietnam War and the Watergate scandals, surveys showed that the overall level of political trust in government had declined steeply. A considerable proportion of Americans seemed to feel that they could not trust government officials and that they could not count on officials to care about the ordinary person. This index of political trust reached an all-time low in the early 1990s but then climbed steadily until 2001 (see Table 6–4).

Public Opinion about Government

A vital component of public opinion in the United States is the considerable ambivalence with which the public regards many major national institutions. Table 6–5 shows trends from 1977 to 2003 in opinion polls asking respondents, at regularly spaced intervals, how much confidence they had in the institutions listed. Over the years, military and religious organizations have ranked highest.

---

[15]As reported in *Public Perspective,* March/April 2002, p. 11, summarizing the results of Gallup/CNN/ *USA Today* polls conducted between November 11 and December 10, 2000.

TABLE 6–4

Trends in Political Trust

QUESTION: HOW MUCH OF THE TIME DO YOU THINK YOU CAN TRUST THE GOVERNMENT IN WASHINGTON TO DO WHAT IS RIGHT—JUST ABOUT ALWAYS, MOST OF THE TIME, OR ONLY SOME OF THE TIME?

	1968	1972	1974	1976	1978	1980	1982	1984	1986	1988	1990	1992	1994	1996	1998	2000	2001	2002	2003
Percentage saying: Always/Most of the time	61	53	36	33	29	25	32	46	42	44	27	23	20	25	34	40	64	46	33
Some of the time	36	45	61	63	67	73	64	51	55	54	73	75	79	71	66	59	35	52	58

SOURCES: *New York Times*/CBS News Surveys; University of Michigan Survey Research Center, National Election Studies; Pew Research Center for the People and the Press; Council for Excellence in Government; *Washington Post* poll, September 25–27, 2001; and Gallup polls, September 2–4, 2002, and October 24–26, 2003.

A command sergeant major delivers copies of the *Stars and Stripes* newspaper to American marines in Iraq. When Americans express high levels of confidence in the military, which events or which people are they likely to be thinking about?

Note, however, the decline in confidence in churches in 2002 following a substantial number of sex-abuse allegations against Catholic priests. Note also the somewhat heightened regard for the military after the first Gulf War in 1991. Since that time, the public has consistently had more confidence in the military than in any of the other institutions shown in Table 6–5. In 2002 and 2003, confidence in the military soared even higher, most likely because Americans recognized the central role to be played by the military in the war on terrorism.

The United States Supreme Court and the banking industry have scored well over time. Less confidence is expressed in newspapers, television, big business,

TABLE 6–5

Confidence in Institutions Trend

QUESTION: I AM GOING TO READ A LIST OF INSTITUTIONS IN AMERICAN SOCIETY. WOULD YOU PLEASE TELL ME HOW MUCH CONFIDENCE YOU, YOURSELF, HAVE IN EACH ONE—A GREAT DEAL, QUITE A LOT, SOME, OR VERY LITTLE?

	PERCENTAGE SAYING "A GREAT DEAL" OR "QUITE A LOT"														
	1979	1981	1983	1985	1987	1989	1991	1993	1995	1997	1999	2001	2002	2003	2004
Military	54	50	53	61	61	63	69	67	64	60	68	66	79	82	75
Church or organized religion	65	64	62	66	61	52	56	53	57	56	58	60	45	50	53
Banks and banking	60	46	51	51	51	42	30	38	43	41	43	44	47	50	53
U.S. Supreme Court	45	46	42	56	52	46	39	43	44	50	49	50	50	47	46
Public schools	53	42	39	48	50	43	35	39	40	40	36	38	38	40	41
Television	38	25	25	29	28	NA	24	21	33	34	34	34	35	35	30
Newspapers	51	35	38	35	31	NA	32	31	30	35	33	36	35	33	30
Congress	34	29	28	39	NA	32	18	19	21	22	26	26	29	29	30
Organized labor	36	28	26	28	26	NA	22	26	26	23	28	26	26	28	31
Big business	32	20	28	31	NA	NA	22	23	21	28	30	28	20	22	24

NA = Not asked.
SOURCE: Gallup poll, May 21–23, 2004.

and organized labor. In 1991, following a scandal involving congressional banking practices, confidence in Congress fell to a record low of 18 percent. Confidence in Congress has yet to return to the levels reported in the 1970s and 1980s.

At times, popular confidence in all institutions may rise or fall, reflecting optimism or pessimism about the general state of the nation. For example, between 1979 and 1981 there was a collapse of confidence affecting most institutions. This reflected public dissatisfaction with the handling of the hostage crisis in Iran and with some of the highest levels of inflation in U.S. history. Some of this confidence was restored by 1985, however, when conditions had improved.

Although people may not have much confidence in government institutions, they nonetheless turn to government to solve what they perceive to be the major problems facing the country. Table 6–6, which is based on Gallup polls conducted from the years 1975 to 2003, shows that the leading problems have changed over time. The public tends to emphasize problems that are immediate. It is not at all unusual to see fairly sudden, and even apparently contradictory, shifts in public perceptions of what government should do. In recent years, education, the economy, and terrorism have reached the top of the problems list.

Public Opinion and Policymaking

If public opinion is important for democracy, are policymakers really responsive to public opinion? A study by political scientists Benjamin I. Page and Robert Y. Shapiro suggests that in fact the national government is very responsive to the public's demands for action.[16] In looking at changes in public opinion poll results over time, Page and Shapiro show that when the public supports a policy change, the following occurs: policy changes in a direction consistent with the change in public opinion 43 percent of the time, policy changes in a direction opposite to the change in opinion 22 percent of the time, and policy does not change at all 33 percent of the time. Page and Shapiro also show, as should be no surprise, that when public opinion changes dramatically—say, by 20 percentage points rather than by just 6 or 7 percentage points—government policy is much more likely to follow changing public attitudes.

Setting Limits on Government Action. Although opinion polls cannot give exact guidance on what the government should do in a specific instance, the

---

[16]See the extensive work of Page and Shapiro in Benjamin I. Page and Robert Y. Shapiro, *The Rational Public: Fifty Years of Trends in Americans' Policy Preferences* (Chicago: University of Chicago Press, 1992).

TABLE 6–6

Most Important Problem Trend, 1975 to Present

Year	Problem	Year	Problem
1975	High cost of living, unemployment	1990	War in Middle East
1976	High cost of living, unemployment	1991	Economy
1977	High cost of living, unemployment	1992	Unemployment, budget deficit
1978	High cost of living, energy problems	1993	Health care, budget deficit
1979	High cost of living, energy problems	1994	Crime, violence, health care
1980	High cost of living, unemployment	1995	Crime, violence
1981	High cost of living, unemployment	1996	Budget deficit
1982	Unemployment, high cost of living	1997	Crime, violence
1983	Unemployment, high cost of living	1998	Crime, violence
1984	Unemployment, fear of war	1999	Crime, violence
1985	Fear of war, unemployment	2000	Morals, family decline
1986	Unemployment, budget deficit	2001	Economy, education
1987	Unemployment, economy	2002	Terrorism, economy
1988	Economy, budget deficit	2003	Terrorism, economy
1989	War on drugs	2004	War in Iraq, economy

SOURCES: *New York Times*/CBS News poll, January 1996; Gallup polls, 2000, 2002, 2003, and 2004.

opinions measured in polls do set an informal limit on government action. For example, consider the highly controversial issue of abortion. Most Americans are moderates on this issue; they do not approve of abortion as a means of birth control, but they do feel that it should be available under certain circumstances. Yet sizable groups of people express very intense feelings both for and against legalized abortion. Given this distribution of opinion, most elected officials would rather not try to change policy to favor either of the extreme positions. To do so would clearly violate the opinion of the majority of Americans. In this case, as in many others, *public opinion does not make public policy; rather, it restrains officials from taking truly unpopular actions.* If officials do act in the face of public opposition, the consequences will be determined at the ballot box.

To what degree should public opinion influence policymaking? It would appear that members of the public view this issue differently than policy leaders do. The results of a recent poll about polls showed that whereas 68 percent of the public feel that public opinion should have a great deal of influence on policy, only 43 percent of policy leaders hold this opinion.[17] Why would a majority of policy leaders *not* want to be strongly influenced by public opinion? One answer to this question is that public opinion polls can provide only a limited amount of guidance to policymakers.

The Limits of Polling. Policymakers cannot always be guided by opinion polls. In the end, politicians must make their own choices. When they do so, their choices necessarily involve trade-offs. If politicians vote for increased spending to improve education, for example, by necessity there must be fewer resources available for other worthy projects.

Individuals who are polled do not have to make such trade-offs when they respond to questions. Indeed, survey respondents usually are not even given a choice of trade-offs in their policy opinions. Pollsters typically ask respondents whether they want more or less spending in a particular area, such as education. Rarely, though, is a dollar amount assigned. Additionally, broad poll questions often provide little guidance for policymakers. What does it mean if a majority of those polled want "free" medical treatment for everyone in need? Obviously, medical care is never free. Certain individuals may receive medical care free of charge, but society as a whole has to pay for it. In short, polling questions usually do not reflect the cost of any particular policy choice. Moreover, to make an informed policy choice requires an understanding not only of the policy area but also of the consequences of any given choice. Virtually no public opinion polls make sure that those polled have such information.

Finally, government decisions cannot be made simply by adding up individual desires. Politicians engage in a type of "horse trading." All politicians know that they cannot satisfy every desire of every constituent. Therefore, each politician attempts to maximize the *net* benefits to his or her constituents, while keeping within whatever the politician believes the government can afford.

★ Public Opinion: Why Is It Important Today?

Public opinion is important today because it can lead to changes in policy. Earlier in this chapter, we described how public opinion put pressure on President George W. Bush to change his policy on military tribunals. We also pointed out that positive public opinion can give a politician greater leeway when making

> **DID YOU KNOW . . .**
> That the number of radio and television stations with a dominant talk-show format grew from 308 in 1989 to over 1,000 in 2003?

---

[17]Mollyann Brodie *et al.*, "Polling and Democracy: The Will of the People," *Public Perspective,* July/August 2001, pp. 10–14.

policy, as evidenced by the public's strong support for the war in Afghanistan in 2001 and 2002 and the fairly consistent support of a majority of Americans for the war against Iraq in the early months of 2003.

Remember, though, that the relationship between changes in public opinion and changes in public policy is more indirect than direct: the public's preferences provide broad guidelines within which policymakers can operate. In essence, the importance of public opinion lies more in its ability to prevent totally objectionable policies than in its ability to specify particular policy mandates. The result is that any publicly considered policy will at least be tolerable for most people.

Public opinion is only as effective as the polls that measure it, however. No one in America can avoid public opinion polls. One can scarcely glance at the nightly news without seeing the results of the latest poll about some important (or superfluous) issue. Certainly, public opinion polls are important to the political process today. Otherwise, it would be hard to explain why politicians spend so many millions of dollars each year for such information. Both policymakers and the public need to be critical consumers of opinion polls, as discussed in this chapter's *Making a Difference* feature.

MAKING A DIFFERENCE ★ Be a Critical Consumer of Opinion Polls

Americans are inundated with the results of public opinion polls. The polls purport to tell us a variety of things: whether the president's popularity is up or down, whether gun control is more in favor now than previously, or who is leading the pack for the next presidential nomination. What must be kept in mind with this blizzard of information is that all poll results are not equally good or equally believable.

Why Should You Care?

As a critical consumer, you need to be aware of what makes one set of public opinion poll results valid and other results useless or even dangerously misleading. Knowing what makes a poll accurate is especially important if you plan to participate actively in politics. Successful participation depends on accurate information, and that includes knowing what your fellow citizens are thinking. If large numbers of other people really agree with you that a particular policy needs to be changed, there may be a good chance that the policy can actually be altered. If almost no one agrees with you on a particular issue, there may be no point in trying to change policy immediately; the best you can do is to try to sway the opin-

ions of others, in the hope that someday enough people will agree with you to make policy changes possible.

What Can You Do?

Pay attention only to opinion polls that are based on scientific, or random, samples. In these so-called *probability samples,* a known probability is used to select each person interviewed. Do not give credence to the results of opinion polls that consist of shopping-mall interviews or the like. The main problem with this kind of opinion taking is that not everyone has an equal chance of being in the mall when the interview takes place. Also, it is almost certain that the people in the mall are not a reasonable cross-section of a community's entire population.

Probability samples are useful because you can calculate the range within which the results would have fallen if everybody had been interviewed. Well-designed probability samples will allow the pollster to say, for example, that he or she is 95 percent sure that 61 percent of the public, plus or minus 4 percentage points, supports national health insurance. It turns out that if you want to be twice as precise about a poll result, you need to

collect a sample four times as large. This tends to make accurate polls expensive and difficult to conduct.

Pay attention as well to how people were contacted for the poll—by mail, by telephone, in person in their homes, or in some other way (such as via the Internet). Because of its lower cost, polling firms have turned more and more to telephone interviewing. This method can produce highly accurate results. Its disadvantage is that telephone interviews typically need to be short and to deal with questions that are fairly easy to answer. Interviews in person are better for getting useful information about why a particular response was given. They take much longer to complete, however. Results from mailed questionnaires should be taken with a grain of salt. Usually, only a small percentage of people send them back.

When viewers or listeners of television or radio shows are encouraged to call in their opinions to an 800 telephone number, the polling results are meaningless. Users of the Internet also have an easy way to make their views known. Only people who own computers and are interested in the topic will take the trouble to respond, however, and that group is not representative of the general public.

★ Key Terms

★ Chapter Summary

1 Public opinion is the aggregate of individual attitudes or beliefs shared by some portion of the adult population. A consensus exists when a large proportion of the public appears to express the same view on an issue. Divisive opinion exists when the public holds widely different attitudes on an issue. Sometimes, a poll shows a distribution of opinion indicating that most people either have no information about an issue or are not interested enough in the issue to form a position on it.

2 People's opinions are formed through the political socialization process. Important factors in this process are the family, educational experiences, peer groups, opinion leaders, the media, and political events. The influence of the media as a socialization factor may be growing relative to the family. Voting behavior is influenced by demographic factors such as education, economic status, religion, race and ethnicity, gender, and region. It is also influenced by election-specific factors such as party identification, perception of the candidates, and issue preferences.

3 Most descriptions of public opinion are based on the results of opinion polls. The accuracy of polls depends on sampling techniques that include a representative sample of the population being polled and that ensure randomness in the selection of respondents.

4 Problems with polls include sampling errors (which may occur when the pool of respondents is not chosen in a scientific manner), the difficulty of knowing the degree to which responses are influenced by the type and order of questions asked, the use of a yes/no format for answers to the questions, and the interviewer's techniques. Many are concerned about the use of "push polls" (in which the questions "push" the respondent toward a particular candidate).

5 Advances in technology have changed polling techniques over the years. During the 1970s, telephone polling came to be widely used. Today, largely because of extensive telemarketing, people often refuse to answer calls, and nonresponse rates in telephone polling have skyrocketed. Due to the difficulty of obtaining a random sample in the online environment, Internet polls are often "nonpolls." Whether Internet polls can overcome this problem remains to be seen.

6 Public opinion affects the political process in many ways. The political culture provides a general environment of support for the political system, allowing the nation to weather periods of crisis. The political culture also helps Americans to evaluate their government's performance. At times, the level of trust in government has been relatively high; at other times, the level of trust has declined steeply. Similarly, Americans' confidence in government institutions varies over time, depending on a number of circumstances. Generally, though, Americans turn to government to solve what they perceive to be the major problems facing the country. In 2004, Americans ranked the War in Iraq and the economy as the two most significant problems facing the nation.

7 Public opinion also plays an important role in policymaking. Although polling data show that a majority of Americans would like policy leaders to be influenced to a great extent by public opinion, politicians cannot always be guided by opinion polls. This is because the respondents often do not understand the costs and consequences of policy decisions or the trade-offs involved in making such decisions. An important function of public opinion is to set limits on government action through public pressure.

★ Selected Print and Media Resources

SUGGESTED READINGS

Asher, Herbert. *Polling and the Public: What Every Citizen Should Know.* Washington, D.C.: CQ Press, 2004. This clearly written and often entertaining book explains what polls are, how they are conducted and interpreted, and how the wording and ordering of survey questions, as well as the interviewer's techniques, can significantly affect the respondents' answers.

Bardes, Barbara A., and Robert W. Oldendick. *Public Opinion: Measuring the American Mind,* 2d ed. Belmont, Calif.: Wadsworth Publishing Co., 2003. This examination of public opinion polling looks at the uses of public opinion data and recent technological issues in polling in addition to providing excellent coverage of public opinion on important issues over a period of decades.

Berinsky, Adam J. *Silent Voices: Public Opinion and Political Participation in America.* Princeton, N.J.: Princeton University Press, 2004. Berinsky argues that people who do not respond to survey questions may differ significantly from those who do.

Jacobsen, Clay. *Circle of Seven.* Nashville, Tenn.: Broadman & Holman, 2000. A gripping novel pitting one man, a television reporter, against a media group that manipulates opinion polls and the media to further its own ends.

Newport, Frank. *Polling Matters: Why Leaders Must Listen to the Wisdom of the People.* New York: Warner Books, 2004. Newport, the editor-in-chief of the Gallup Poll, offers a spirited defense of the polling process. Newport believes that polls reflect the country's collective wisdom, and he disputes the argument that citizens are too uninformed to offer useful opinions.

MEDIA RESOURCES

Faith and Politics: The Christian Right—This 1995 documentary was hosted by Dan Rather and produced by CBS News. It focuses on the efforts of the Christian conservative movement to affect educational curriculums and public policy. Members of the Christian right who are interviewed include Ralph Reed and Gary Bauer. Critics of the Christian right who are interviewed include Senator Arlen Specter.

Vox Populi: Democracy in Crisis—A PBS special focusing on why public confidence in government, which has plummeted during recent decades, still has not recovered.

Wag the Dog—A 1997 film that provides a very cynical look at the importance of public opinion. The film, which features Dustin Hoffman and Robert De Niro, follows the efforts of a presidential political consultant who stages a foreign policy crisis to divert public opinion from a sex scandal in the White House.

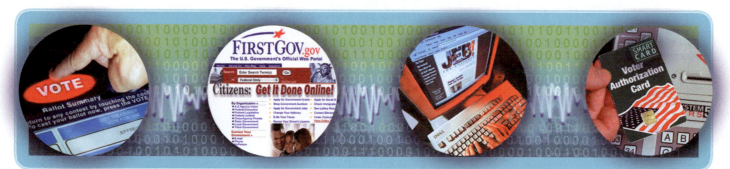

e-mocracy ★ Online Polling and Poll Data

News organizations, interest groups, not-for-profit groups, and online e-zines are now using online polling to gather the opinions of their readers and viewers. All the user has to do is log on to the Web site and click on the box indicating the preferred response. People can respond to online polls more easily than to call-in polls, and in most cases, they are free to the user. Realize, though, that online polls are totally nonscientific because the respondents are all self-selected. Essentially, Internet polls are pseudopolls because only those who choose to do so respond, making the polls much more likely to be biased and based on an unrepresentative sample.

At the same time, the Internet is an excellent source for finding reliable polling reports and data. All of the major polling organizations have Web sites that include news releases about polls they have conducted. Some sites make the polling data available for free to users; others require that a user pay a subscription fee before accessing the polling archives on the site.

Logging On

Yale University Library, one of the world's great research institutions, offers access to social science libraries and information services. If you want to browse through library sources of public opinion data, this is an interesting site to visit. Go to

http://www.library.yale.edu/socsci/opinion

According to its home page, the mission of National Election Studies (NES) "is to produce high quality data on voting, public opinion, and political participation that serves the research needs of social scientists, teachers, students, and policymakers concerned with understanding the theoretical and empirical foundations of mass politics in a democratic society." This is a good place to obtain information on public opinion. Find it at

http://www.umich.edu/~nes

The Polling Report Web site offers polls and their results organized by topic. It is up to date and easy to use:

http://www.pollingreport.com

The Gallup organization's Web site offers not only polling data (although a user must pay a subscription fee to obtain access to many polling reports) but also information on how polls are constructed, conducted, and interpreted. Go to

http://www.gallup.com

Another site that features articles and polling data on public opinion is the Web site of the Zogby poll at

http://www.zogby.com

Using InfoTrac for Political Research

Use the InfoTrac Web site to sharpen your skills in using public opinion data. Go to

http://www.infotrac-college.com

Log on, go to InfoTrac College Edition, and then go to the Subject search page. Type "public opinion polls" into the search box. InfoTrac will offer you a large number of articles that report poll results.

Pick one or more articles that contain detailed information about a poll. Then conduct an analysis. First, ask how large was the sample, and how big is the "confidence" interval cited in the study? Do you know who commissioned the poll and to whom the results were given? Second, examine at least three questions and responses, and answer the following: How might the wording of the question have influenced the responses? How can you tell if the survey respondents had any information about the question asked? Was the number of respondents who could not answer the question substantial? Can you tell if respondents could answer the question without much information? Finally, consider how much a political leader could learn from this poll.

ONLINE REVIEW

At **http://politicalscience.wadsworth. com/schmidt12**, you will find a free Study Guide to this book. For each chapter, there are two online quizzes to help you master the material.

• The **PoliPrep Self Study Assessment** provides a pre-test for each major section of the chapter. PoliPrep then generates a customized study plan. After you complete the study plan, a post-test evaluates your progress.

• The **Tutorial Quiz** for each chapter provides questions on the chapter contents, including the features. The questions are organized to match the major sections of the chapter.

Interest Groups

BACKGROUND

Many interest groups employ *lobbyists* to influence legislation and the administrative decisions of government. About half of the paid lobbyists in Washington are former government employees or former members of Congress. Interest groups place a high value on lobbyists who "know their way around Washington," and former government employees and elected officials qualify in this regard. Often, retired government employees or congresspersons retain personal friendships with their former colleagues. There are rules in place to prevent former government employees from lobbying their former colleagues for a limited period of time after retirement. Congresspersons and their staff members also face such limits. Still, retirees can immediately engage in activities that do not *technically* qualify as lobbying, and they can begin full-scale lobbying as soon as the time limits expire. Some critics believe that interest groups that hire former government employees gain an improper influence on government.

WHAT IF RETIRED GOVERNMENT EMPLOYEES COULD NOT WORK FOR INTEREST GROUPS?

Some people have argued that because interest groups gain improper influence by hiring former government employees, such hiring should not merely be restricted but should be banned altogether. If this were to happen, interest groups that frequently hire former government employees would be less effective. Which groups are these, and what do they seek to accomplish?

A large number of interest groups represent particular industries. Typically, such groups are concerned with legislation and administrative rules that are specific to their industry and that are of little interest to the general public. Therefore, the press pays little attention to these laws and regulations. Industry lobbying can "fly under the radar."

A retired government employee with expert knowledge of the specific subject matter and of the processes and people involved in making administrative rules can be a formidable lobbyist. Likewise, a former member of Congress can offer invaluable assistance when an interest group seeks to affect lawmaking. If these knowledgeable retirees were not available to interest groups, those groups would have less influence on administrative rulemaking and on legislation. Of course, campaign contributions by interest groups are also part of the process of influencing Congress. (You will learn more about campaign finance in Chapter 9.)

CORPORATE WELFARE

As an example of an interest group, consider the pharmaceutical industry. This industry spends about $88 million a year on lobbying, and over half of its 623 registered lobbyists are former members of Congress or former government employees. The pharmaceutical industry has a history of inserting beneficial provisions into pending legislation. In 2001, for example, an amendment was added to the Homeland Security Act to protect the makers of vaccine preservatives from lawsuits charging that their drugs cause autism in children.

Industry-specific legislation can include tariffs on imports, tax breaks, and direct subsidies. The cost of this legislation adds up. The Cato Institute, a libertarian research group, has estimated the cost of what it calls "corporate welfare" to be about $93 billion a year. Barring former government employees from working for interest groups might reduce these kinds of unnecessary subsidies.

Interest groups that address issues of broader concern generally do not need to hire experts with government experience to be effective. There can be little doubt, for example, that the influence of the National Rifle Association does not depend on its ability to hire retired government employees.

THE IMPACT ON FORMER EMPLOYEES

Some government employees—and many congresspersons—look forward to lobbying as a final stage of their careers. A government career may be more attractive if it ends with a few years of highly paid, comfortable employment. Banning such employment might make government service less appealing to some.

FOR CRITICAL ANALYSIS

1. *Why would interest groups argue that a ban on hiring retired government employees would be an unfair (or even an unconstitutional) restriction on their activities?*

2. *In what ways might a ban on the hiring of retired government employees be unfair to the former employees themselves?*

The structure of American government invites the participation of **interest groups** at various stages of the policymaking process. For example, interest groups played a role in the legislation passed by Congress after the terrorist attacks of September 11, 2001. In a show of national unity, the House of Representatives and the Senate voted overwhelmingly to give President George W. Bush authority to use military force in response to the attacks and passed a $40 billion emergency spending bill to pay for the response.

Two weeks after the attacks, life on Capitol Hill returned to the more normal process of dissension and debate. The president's requests for further antiterrorism legislation spurred furious action by interest groups, which quickly sent their **lobbyists** to persuade Congress to adopt their positions on these bills. The airlines, which constitute a powerful interest group, expressed their need for congressional help. They were gratified by an airline bailout bill to make up for the sizable losses they suffered as a result of the closure of U.S. airspace after the attacks and the drop in the number of passengers in the weeks that followed. After the bill passed, however, lobbyists for the many other industries—including car rental firms, the hotel industry, and travel and tourism companies—that were hurt by the attacks began asking for their own assistance packages. Perhaps the oddest lobbying efforts were seen during the debate over the aviation security bill. We look at these efforts in this chapter's *America's Security* feature on the next page.

Interest Group
An organized group of individuals sharing common objectives who actively attempt to influence policymakers.

Lobbyist
An organization or individual who attempts to influence legislation and the administrative decisions of government.

Interest Groups: A Natural Phenomenon

Alexis de Tocqueville observed in 1834 that "in no country of the world has the principle of association been more successfully used or applied to a greater multitude of objectives than in America."[1] The French traveler was amazed at the degree to which Americans formed groups to solve civic problems, establish

[1]Alexis de Tocqueville, *Democracy in America,* Vol. 1, edited by Phillips Bradley (New York: Knopf, 1980), p. 191.

Lobbying activity becomes most intense the day a vote is being taken on an important issue. Not surprisingly, lobbyists are often found in the lobbies of Congress. (Dennis Brack/Black Star)

AMERICA'S SECURITY
Interest Groups and Aviation Security

In November 2001, President George W. Bush signed into law an aviation security bill. Before this bill passed, baggage and passenger screening at airports had been the responsibility of the airlines and local airport authorities. Generally, an airport would contract with one of a handful of international corporations for security screeners. The job required little education or experience, and workers typically received very low pay. Background checks for airport security personnel were extremely limited.

THE DEMAND FOR IMPROVED SECURITY

After 9/11, the president, Congress, and the public demanded that airport security be improved. The Senate favored making airport security a federal responsibility and making all screeners federal employees. The Republican majority in the House favored letting the private security firms continue, but under federal oversight. A little-known interest group, the Airline Security Association, launched a lobbying effort to keep private security corporations in business. Its lobbyists cited the excellent work of many security agencies and named the "airport screener of the year."

As the debate continued, it became clear that the price of requiring airport screening personnel to be employees of the federal government would be high, both for the gov-

Surrounded by members of Congress and representatives of the airline industry, President George W. Bush signs the aviation security bill. (AP Photo/J. Scott Applewhite)

ernment and for existing employees who wanted to continue in their jobs. To be eligible for these new federal jobs, current employees would need to pass background checks and have high school diplomas. One proposal would have required that all screeners have been U.S. citizens for at least five years. About one-third of those who were then working as screeners, however, were not high school graduates, and a significant number were not U.S. citizens. Groups that represent immigrants and the Hispanic Congressional Caucus opposed these requirements.*

Unions were also unhappy with the proposed bill because it would not have given these new federal employees normal civil service protections. Other groups that tried to influence the bill included the airline pilots, the flight attendants, the airlines' trade group, and the makers of screening equipment.

THE END RESULT—A COMPROMISE

The end result was a compromise. Aviation security became a federal responsibility, and all passenger and baggage screeners were required to become federal employees within one year. After two years under this system, an airport could go back to private contractors, but only under federal supervision. To gain business support for this version of the bill, Republicans slipped in some provisions to protect enterprises hurt by the terrorist attacks.†

While this debate was going on, Americans continued to cut down on air travel, and airline companies suffered further losses. It was clear that the American public wanted assurance that air travel would again be safe, but the interested parties continued to lobby and jockey over this important legislation. Although this lobbying may have seemed out of place in a national emergency, interest groups representing individuals, businesses, and other kinds of associations have roots deep in American history and culture.

FOR CRITICAL ANALYSIS

Do you think it is appropriate for interest groups to lobby for their positions in times of national emergency? Can you imagine circumstances in which people can be hurt by delays in passing legislation due to intense lobbying?

*James C. Benton and Peter Cohn, "White House, Aviation Safety Conferees Grope Their Way toward Compromise," *Congressional Quarterly Weekly,* November 10, 2001, p. 2676.

†"Aviation Security," *Congressional Quarterly Weekly,* December 22, 2001, p. 3055.

social relationships, and speak for their economic or political interests. Perhaps James Madison, when he wrote *Federalist Paper* No. 10 (see Appendix C), had already judged the character of his country's citizens similarly. He supported the creation of a large republic with many states to encourage the formation of multiple interests. The multitude of interests, in Madison's view, would work to discourage the formation of an oppressive majority interest.

Surely, neither Madison nor de Tocqueville foresaw the formation of more than a hundred thousand associations in the United States. Poll data show that more than two-thirds of all Americans belong to at least one group or association. While the majority of these affiliations could not be classified as "interest groups" in the political sense, Americans do understand the principles of working in groups.

Today, interest groups range from the elementary school parent-teacher association and the local "Stop the Sewer Plant Association" to the statewide association of insurance agents. They include small groups such as local environmental organizations and national groups such as the Boy Scouts of America, the American Civil Liberties Union, the National Education Association, and the American League of Lobbyists.

Alexis de Tocqueville (1805–1859), a French social historian and traveler, commented on Americans' predilection for joining groups. (Corbis/Bettmann)

Interest Groups and Social Movements

Interest groups are often spawned by mass **social movements.** Such movements represent demands by a large segment of the population for change in the political, economic, or social system. Social movements are often the first expression of latent discontent with the existing system. They may be the authentic voice of weaker or oppressed groups in society that do not have the means or standing to organize as interest groups. For example, the women's movement of the 1800s suffered disapproval from most mainstream political and social leaders. Because women were unable to vote or take an active part in the political system, it was difficult for women who desired greater freedoms to organize formal groups. After the Civil War, when more women became active in professional life, the first real women's rights group, the National Woman Suffrage Association, came into being.

African Americans found themselves in an even more disadvantaged situation after the end of the Reconstruction period. They were unable to exercise political rights in many southern and border states, and their participation in any form of organization could lead to economic ruin, physical harassment, or even death. The civil rights movement of the 1950s and 1960s was clearly a social movement. Although several formal organizations worked to support the movement—including the Southern Christian Leadership Conference, the National Association for the Advancement of Colored People, and the Urban League—only a social movement could generate the kinds of civil disobedience that took place in hundreds of towns and cities across the country.

Social movements are often precursors of interest groups. They may generate interest groups with specific goals that successfully recruit members through the incentives the group offers. In the case of the women's movement of the 1960s, the National Organization for Women was formed in part out of a demand to end gender-segregated job advertising in newspapers.

Why So Many?

Whether based in a social movement or created to meet an immediate crisis, interest groups continue to form and act in American society. One reason for the multitude of interest groups is that the right to join a group is protected by the First Amendment to the U.S. Constitution (see Chapter 4). Not only are all

Social Movement
A movement that represents the demands of a large segment of the public for political, economic, or social change.

people guaranteed the right "peaceably to assemble," but they are also guaranteed the right "to petition the Government for a redress of grievances." This constitutional provision encourages Americans to form groups and to express their opinions to the government or to their elected representatives as members of a group. Group membership makes the individual's opinions appear more powerful and strongly conveys the group's ability to vote for or against a representative.

In addition, our federal system of government provides thousands of "pressure points" for interest group activity. Americans can form groups in their neighborhoods or cities and lobby the city council and their state government. They can join statewide groups or national groups and try to influence government policy through the Congress or through one of the executive agencies or cabinet departments. Representatives of giant corporations may seek to influence the president personally at social events or fund-raisers. When attempts to influence government through the executive and legislative branches fail, interest groups turn to the courts, filing suit in state or federal court to achieve their political objectives. Pluralist theorists, as discussed in Chapter 1, point to the openness of the American political structure as a major factor in the power of groups in American politics.

★ Why Do Americans Join Interest Groups?

One puzzle that has fascinated political scientists is why some people join interest groups, whereas many others do not. Everyone has some interest that could benefit from government action. For many individuals, however, those concerns remain unorganized interests, or **latent interests.**

Latent Interests
Public-policy interests that are not recognized or addressed by a group at a particular time.

According to political theorist Mancur Olson,[2] it simply may not be rational for individuals to join most groups. In his classic work on this topic, Olson introduced the idea of the "collective good." This concept refers to any public benefit that, if available to any member of the community, cannot be denied to any other member, whether or not he or she participated in the effort to gain the good.

Although collective benefits are usually thought of as coming from such public goods as clean air or national defense, benefits are also bestowed by the government on subsets of the public. Price subsidies to dairy farmers and loans to college students are examples. Olson used economic theory to propose that it is not rational for interested individuals to join groups that work for group benefits. In fact, it is often more rational for the individual to wait for others to procure the benefits and then share them. How many college students, for example, join the American Association of Community Colleges, an organization that lobbies the government for increased financial aid to students? The difficulty interest groups face in recruiting members when the benefits can be obtained without joining is referred to as the **free rider problem.**

Free Rider Problem
The difficulty interest groups face in recruiting members when the benefits they achieve can be gained without joining the group.

If so little incentive exists for individuals to join together, why are there thousands of interest groups lobbying in Washington? According to the logic of collective action, if the contribution of an individual *will* make a difference to the effort, then it is worth it to the individual to join. Thus, smaller groups, which seek benefits for only a small proportion of the population, are more likely to enroll members who will give time and funds to the cause. Larger groups, which represent general public interests (the women's movement or the American Civil Liberties Union, for example), will find it relatively more difficult to get individuals to join. People need an incentive—material or otherwise—to participate.

[2]Mancur Olson, *The Logic of Collective Action* (Cambridge, Mass.: Harvard University Press, 1965).

Solidary Incentives

Interest groups offer **solidary incentives** for their members. Solidary incentives include companionship, a sense of belonging, and the pleasure of associating with others. Although the National Audubon Society was originally founded to save the snowy egret from extinction, today most members join to learn more about birds and to meet and share their pleasure with other individuals who enjoy bird-watching as a hobby. Even though the incentive might be solidary for many members, this organization nonetheless also pursues an active political agenda, working to preserve the environment and to protect endangered species. Most members may not play any part in working toward larger, more national goals unless the organization can convince them to take political action or unless some local environmental issue arises.

Solidary Incentive
A reason or motive having to do with the desire to associate with others and to share with others a particular interest or hobby.

Material Incentives

For other individuals, interest groups offer direct **material incentives.** A case in point is the AARP (formerly the American Association of Retired Persons), which provides discounts, insurance plans, and organized travel opportunities for its members. Because of its exceptionally low dues ($12.50 annually) and the benefits gained through membership, the AARP has become the largest—and a very powerful—interest group in the United States. The AARP can claim to represent the interests of millions of senior citizens and can show that they actually have joined the group. For most seniors, the material incentives outweigh the membership costs.

Many other interest groups offer indirect material incentives for their members. Such groups as the American Dairy Association and the National Association of Automobile Dealers do not give discounts or freebies to their members, but they do offer indirect benefits and rewards by, for example, protecting the material

Material Incentive
A reason or motive having to do with economic benefits or opportunities.

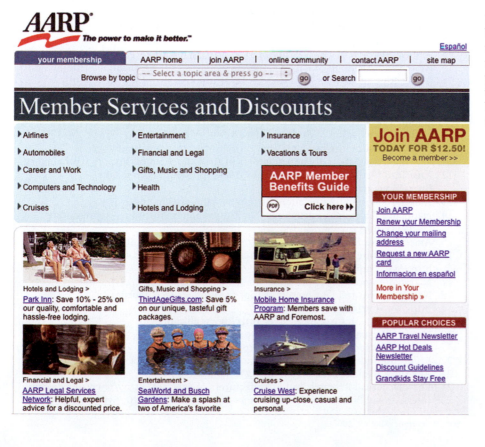

The AARP's Web site lists the many benefits and discounts available to members for an annual fee of $12.50. If many members of an organization join purely for the membership benefits, is it appropriate for the organization to lobby aggressively for specific policies that not all members may endorse?

Purposive Incentive

A reason for supporting or participating in the activities of a group that is based on agreement with the goals of the group. For example, someone with a strong interest in human rights might have a purposive incentive to join Amnesty International.

interests of their members from government policymaking that is injurious to their industry or business.

Purposive Incentives

Interest groups also offer the opportunity for individuals to pursue political, economic, or social goals through joint action. **Purposive incentives** offer individuals the satisfaction of taking action when the goals of a group correspond to their beliefs or principles. The individuals who belong to a group focusing on the abortion issue or gun control, for example, do so because they feel strongly enough about the issues to support the group's work with money and time.

Some scholars have argued that many people join interest groups simply for the discounts, magazine subscriptions, and other tangible benefits and are not really interested in the political positions taken by the groups. According to William P. Browne, however, research shows that people really do care about the policy stance of an interest group. Members of a group seek people who share the group's views and then ask them to join. As one group leader put it, "Getting members is about scaring the hell out of people."[3] People join the group and then feel that they are doing something about a cause that is important to them.

---

[3]William P. Browne, *Groups, Interests, and U.S. Public Policy* (Washington, D.C.: Georgetown University Press, 1998), p. 23.

TABLE 7–1

Fortune's "Power 25"—The Twenty-Five Most Effective Interest Groups

1. National Rifle Association of America (the NRA—opposed to gun control): http://www.nra.org
2. AARP (formerly the American Association of Retired Persons): http://www.aarp.org
3. National Federation of Independent Business: http://www.nfibonline.com
4. American Israel Public Affairs Committee (AIPAC—a pro-Israel group): http://www.aipac.org
5. Association of Trial Lawyers of America: http://www.atla.org
6. American Federation of Labor–Congress of Industrial Organizations (the AFL–CIO—a federation of most U.S. labor unions): http://www.aflcio.org
7. Chamber of Commerce of the United States of America (an association of businesses): http://www.uschamber.org
8. National Beer Wholesalers Association: http://www.nbwa.org
9. National Association of Realtors: http://www.realtor.com
10. National Association of Manufacturers (NAM): http://www.nam.org
11. National Association of Home Builders of the United States: http://www.nahb.org
12. American Medical Association (the AMA—representing physicians): http://www.ama-assn.org
13. American Hospital Association: http://www.aha.org/aha/index.jsp
14. National Education Association of the United States (the NEA—representing teachers): http://www.nea.org
15. American Farm Bureau Federation (representing farmers): http://www.fb.org
16. Motion Picture Association of America (representing movie studios): http://www.mpaa.org/home.htm
17. National Association of Broadcasters: http://www.nab.org
18. National Right to Life Committee (opposed to legalized abortion): http://www.nrlc.org
19. America's Health Insurance Plans: http://www.ahip.org
20. National Restaurant Association: http://www.restaurant.org
21. National Governors' Association: http://www.nga.org
22. Recording Industry Association of America: http://www.riaa.com
23. American Bankers Association: http://www.aba.com
24. Pharmaceutical Research and Manufacturers of America: http://www.phrma.org
25. International Brotherhood of Teamsters (a labor union): http://www.teamster.org

SOURCE: *Fortune*, May 28, 2001.

Types of Interest Groups

Thousands of groups exist to influence government. Among the major types of interest groups are those that represent the main sectors of the economy. In addition, a number of "public-interest" organizations have been formed to represent the needs of the general citizenry, including some "single-issue" groups. The interests of foreign governments and foreign businesses are also represented in the American political arena. The names and Web addresses of some major interest groups are shown in Tables 7–1 and 7–2.

Economic Interest Groups

More interest groups are formed to represent economic interests than any other set of interests. The variety of economic interest groups mirrors the complexity of the American economy. The major sectors that seek influence in Washington, D.C., include business, agriculture, labor unions and their members, government workers, and professionals.

Business Interest Groups. Thousands of business groups and trade associations work to influence government policies that affect their respective industries. "Umbrella groups" represent certain types of businesses or companies that deal in a particular type of product. The U.S. Chamber of Commerce, for example, is an umbrella group that represents businesses, and the National Association of Manufacturers is an umbrella group that represents only manufacturing concerns. The American Pet Products Manufacturers Association works for the good of manufacturers of pet food, pet toys, and other pet products, as well as for pet shops. This group strongly opposes increased regulation of stores that sell animals and restrictions on importing pets. Other major organizations that represent

---

TABLE 7–2

Some Other Important Interest Groups (Not on *Fortune*'s "Power 25" List)

American Civil Liberties Union (the ACLU): http://www.aclu.org
American Legion (a veterans' group): http://www.legion.org
American Library Association: http://www.ala.org
The American Society for the Prevention of Cruelty to Animals (the ASPCA): http://www.aspca.org
Amnesty International USA (promotes human rights): http://www.amnesty.org
Handgun Control, Inc. (favors gun control): http://www.bradycampaign.org
League of United Latin American Citizens (LULAC): http://www.lulac.org
Mothers Against Drunk Driving (MADD): http://www.madd.org
NARAL Pro-Choice America (formerly the National Abortion and Reproductive Rights Action League—favors legalized abortion): http://www.naral.org
National Association for the Advancement of Colored People (the NAACP—represents African Americans): http://www.naacp.org
National Audubon Society (an environmentalist group): http://www.audubon.org
National Gay and Lesbian Task Force: http://www.ngltf.org
National Organization for Women (NOW—a feminist group): http://www.now.org
National Urban League (a civil rights organization): http://www.nul.org
National Wildlife Federation: http://www.thetaskforce.org
The Nature Conservancy: http://nature.org
Sierra Club (an environmentalist group): http://www.sierraclub.org
Veterans of Foreign Wars of the United States: http://www.vfw.org
World Wildlife Fund: http://www.wwf.org

business interests, such as the Better Business Bureaus, take positions on policies but do not actually lobby in Washington, D.C.[4]

Some business groups are decidedly more powerful than others. The U.S. Chamber of Commerce, which has more than 200,000 member companies, can bring constituent influence to bear on every member of Congress. Another powerful lobbying organization is the National Association of Manufacturers. With a staff of more than sixty people in Washington, D.C., the organization can mobilize dozens of well-educated, articulate lobbyists to work the corridors of Congress on issues of concern to its members.

Although business interest groups are likely to agree on anything that reduces government regulation or taxation, they often do not concur on the specifics of policy, and the sector has been troubled by disagreement and fragmentation within its ranks. For example, should states be able to collect sales tax on purchases made using the Internet? Businesses have come down on both sides of this issue, which we discuss in this chapter's *Which Side Are You On?* feature.

Business groups and trade associations used to lobby at cross-purposes because they had no way to coordinate their messages. Faced with increasing efforts by organized labor to support Democratic candidates for Congress, business interests agreed in 1996 to form "the Coalition," an informal organization that raises funds specifically to help Republican candidates for Congress.[5]

Agricultural Interest Groups.   American farmers and their employees represent less than 2 percent of the U.S. population. In spite of this, farmers' influence on legislation beneficial to their interests has been significant. Farmers have succeeded in their aims because they have very strong interest groups. They are geographically dispersed and therefore have many representatives and senators to speak for them.

The American Farm Bureau Federation, established in 1919, has several million members (many of whom are not actually farmers) and is usually seen as conservative. It was instrumental in getting government guarantees of "fair" prices during the Great Depression in the 1930s.[6] Another important agricultural interest organization is the National Farmers' Union (NFU), which is considered more liberal. As farms have become larger and "agribusiness" has become a way of life, single-issue farm groups have emerged. The American Dairy Association, the Peanut Growers Group, and the National Soybean Association, for example, work to support their respective farmers and associated businesses. In recent years, agricultural interest groups have become active on many new issues. Among other things, they have opposed immigration restrictions and are very involved in international trade matters as they seek new markets. One of the newest agricultural groups is the American Farmland Trust, which supports policies to conserve farmland and protect natural resources.

As proof of how powerful the agricultural lobby still is in the United States, in May 2002 President George W. Bush signed the Farm Security and Rural Investment Act, which authorized the largest agricultural subsidy in U.S. history.

Labor Movement
Generally, the economic and political expression of working-class interests; politically, the organization of working-class interests.

Labor Interest Groups.   Interest groups representing the **labor movement** date back to at least 1886, when the American Federation of Labor (AFL) was formed. In 1955, the AFL joined forces with the Congress of Industrial Organizations

---

[4]Charles S. Mack, *Business, Politics, and the Practice of Government Relations* (Westport, Conn.: Quorum Books, 1997), p. 14.
[5]H. R. Mahood, *Interest Groups in American National Politics: An Overview* (New York: Prentice Hall, 2000), p. 34.
[6]The Agricultural Adjustment Act of 1933 (declared unconstitutional) was replaced by the 1937 Agricultural Adjustment Act and later changed and amended several times.

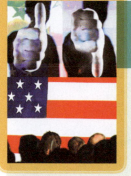

WHICH SIDE ARE YOU ON?
Should the Internet Be Taxed?

Sales taxes are one of the most important ways in which state governments can raise revenue. But what happens when consumers in one state buy goods and services in another, using the mail, the telephone, or the Internet? Many states impose a *use tax* on such transactions that is identical to their sales tax. If you buy something through the Internet or a mail-order catalogue, however, the vendor you are dealing with might not collect a tax for your state. The United States Supreme Court ruled in *Quill Corp. v. North Dakota* (1992) that no state can compel a business located outside the state to collect use taxes from the state's residents.* The only way a state can collect these taxes is to go after customers directly, but the states usually have no idea who the customers are or what they bought.

States could tax Internet access instead. In 1998, however, Congress banned such taxes. Congress has not prohibited use taxes, but as noted, they are hard to collect. The Supreme Court, however, explicitly stated in the *Quill* decision that under its power to regulate interstate commerce, Congress could establish a nationwide system for collecting state use taxes. Should Congress take such a step?

TAXATION IS NOT FAIR UNLESS EVERYONE PAYS

Most state governments favor such a step. State governments constitute an important lobby in Washington, and they are currently under severe financial pressure. Businesses that must collect sales taxes because they operate "brick-and-mortar" stores also support this viewpoint. These businesses argue that competitors who are not required to collect taxes have an unfair advantage.

*504 U.S. 298 (1992). Under the ruling in the *Quill* case, a state can require a business to collect sales or use taxes only if the business has a "substantial physical presence" in the state.

Many state government officials believe they are losing billions of dollars in revenues because they cannot collect use taxes on e-commerce. If that revenue could be collected, some of the current pressure on state government finances might be relieved.

THE INTERNET IS SPECIAL

Opponents of any plan to make use taxes collectible include almost every interest group involved with the Internet—online and mail-order vendors, the computer and telecommunications industries, and e-commerce shoppers. Opponents argue that taxing the Internet might impede the growth of e-commerce. Also, mail-order and Internet vendors must charge shipping fees, which in some cases exceed the sales taxes collected by brick-and-mortar stores. The large number of different tax rates would complicate any use-tax collection system. Further, stores such as Wal-Mart receive benefits that include police and fire protection, garbage collection, and road construction, all of which are paid for by sales taxes. Online vendors do not enjoy these benefits. Finally, those who want to limit taxes in general argue that e-commerce may force states to keep sales taxes low so that local merchants can compete.

WHAT'S YOUR POSITION?

Should Congress make it possible for states to collect use taxes? Why do the antitax forces currently have the upper hand?

GOING ONLINE

Annette Nellen of San Jose State University sponsors a Web site that provides a substantial amount of material on e-commerce taxation. To view this site, go to **http://www.cob.sjsu.edu/facstaff/nellen_a/e-links.html**.

(CIO). Today, the combined AFL–CIO is a large union with a membership exceeding 13 million workers and an active political arm called the Committee on Political Education. In a sense, the AFL–CIO is a union of unions.

The role of unions in American society has weakened in recent years, as witnessed by a decline in union membership (see Figure 7–1 on the following page). In the age of automation and with the rise of the **service sector**, blue-collar workers in basic industries (autos, steel, and the like) represent a smaller and smaller percentage of the total working population. Because of this decline in the industrial sector of the economy, national unions are looking to nontraditional areas for their membership, including migrant farm workers, service workers, and, most

Service Sector
The sector of the economy that provides services—such as health care, banking, and education—in contrast to the sector that produces goods.

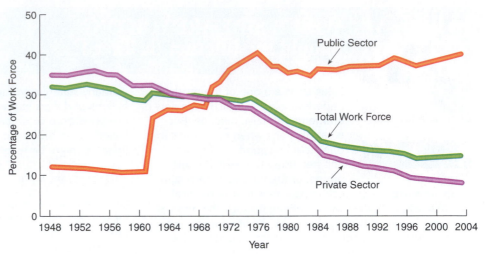

FIGURE 7–1

Decline in Union Membership, 1948 to Present

As shown in this figure, the percentage of the total work force that is represented by labor unions has declined precipitously over the last two decades. Note, however, that in contrast to the decline in union representation in the private sector, the percentage of government workers who are unionized has increased significantly.

SOURCE: Bureau of Labor Statistics, 2004.

recently, public employees—such as police officers, firefighting personnel, and teachers, including college professors and graduate assistants. Indeed, public-sector unions are the fastest-growing labor organizations.

Although the proportion of the work force that belongs to a union has declined over the years, American labor unions have not given up their efforts to support sympathetic candidates for Congress or for state office. Currently, the AFL–CIO, under the leadership of John J. Sweeney, has a political budget that exceeds $30 million for each two-year political cycle, which it uses to help Democratic candidates nationwide. Although interest groups that favor Republicans continue to

Members of the Operating Engineers, Laborers, and Carpenters unions protest the policies of a construction company, claiming that this company's actions are undermining union wages and benefits. Labor unions have wielded considerable political power since the early 1900s. Why has that power declined somewhat in recent years? (AP Photo/*The Capital Times*/David Sandell)

assist their candidates, the efforts of labor are more sustained and more targeted. Labor offers a candidate (such as Democratic presidential candidate John Kerry in 2004) a corps of volunteers in addition to campaign contributions. A massive turnout by labor union members in critical elections can significantly increase the final vote totals for Democratic candidates.

Public Employee Unions.   The degree of unionization in the private sector has declined since 1965, but this has been partially offset by growth in the unionization of public employees. Figure 7–1 displays the growth in public-sector unionization. With a total membership of more than 7.1 million, public-sector unions are likely to continue expanding.

Both the American Federation of State, County, and Municipal Employees and the American Federation of Teachers are members of the AFL–CIO's Public Employee Department. Over the years, public employee unions have become quite militant and are often involved in strikes. Most of these strikes are illegal, because almost no public employees have the right to strike.

A powerful interest group lobbying on behalf of public employees is the National Education Association (NEA), a nationwide organization of about 2.5 million teachers and others connected with education. Many NEA locals function as labor unions. The NEA lobbies intensively for increased public funding of education.

Interest Groups of Professionals.   Numerous professional organizations exist, including the American Bar Association, the Association of General Contractors of America, the Institute of Electrical and Electronic Engineers, and others. Some professional groups, such as lawyers and doctors, are more influential than others because of their social status. Lawyers have a unique advantage—a large number of members of Congress share their profession. In terms of money spent on lobbying, however, one professional organization stands head and shoulders above the rest—the American Medical Association (AMA). Founded in 1847, it is now affiliated with more than 2,000 local and state medical societies and has a total membership of 300,000.

Members of the American Bar Association (ABA) gather at the organization's national convention. The delegates are discussing a proposed overhaul of the code of ethics for lawyers. Many members of Congress are lawyers. Would it benefit the country if more legislators were drawn from other occupations? Why or why not? (AP Photo/Charles Bennett)

At the Haitian community center in Miami in 2004, leaders of the Florida Immigrant Advocacy Center opposed plans to return Haitian refugees to that country. "Given the current political crisis in Haiti," the speaker said, "we could be returning people to their death." How can an interest group representing nonvoters gain political leverage? (AP Photo/J.Pat Carter)

Sierra Club president Adam Werbach holds a press conference in San Francisco to announce that the Sierra Club will not call for major curbs on immigration. Why might an environmental organization take a position on immigration? (AP Photo/Paul Sakuma)

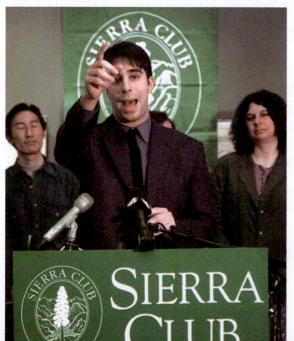

The Unorganized Poor.   Some have argued that the system of interest group politics leaves out poor Americans or U.S. residents who are not citizens and cannot vote. Americans who are disadvantaged economically cannot afford to join interest groups; if they are members of the working poor, they may hold two or more jobs just to survive, leaving them no time to participate in interest groups. Other groups in the population—including non-English-speaking groups, resident aliens, single parents, disabled Americans, and younger voters—probably do not have the time or expertise even to find out what group might represent them. Consequently, some scholars suggest that interest groups and lobbyists are the privilege of upper-middle-class Americans and those who belong to unions or other special groups.

R. Allen Hays examines the plight of poor Americans in his book *Who Speaks for the Poor?*[7] Hays studied groups and individuals who have lobbied for public housing and other issues related to the poor and concluded that the poor depend largely on indirect representation. Most efforts on behalf of the poor come from a policy network of groups—including public housing officials, welfare workers and officials, religious groups, public-interest groups, and some liberal general interest groups—that speak loudly and persistently for the poor. Poor Americans themselves remain outside the interest group network and have little direct voice of their own.

Environmental Groups

Environmental interest groups are not new. We have already mentioned the National Audubon Society, which was founded in 1905 to protect the snowy egret from the commercial demand for hat decorations. The patron of the Sierra Club, John Muir, worked for the

---

[7]R. Allen Hays, *Who Speaks for the Poor?* (New York: Routledge, 2001).

The Coast Guard keeps a Greenpeace boat from getting too close to a tanker near the harbor of Long Beach, California. The environmentalist group was protesting the impact of oil use on the world's climate. How effective are such tactics by environmentalist groups in influencing government policy? (AP Photo/Reed Saxon)

creation of national parks more than a century ago. But the blossoming of national environmental groups with mass memberships did not occur until the 1970s. Since the first Earth Day, organized in 1972, many interest groups have sprung up to protect the environment in general or unique ecological niches. The groups range from the National Wildlife Federation, with a membership of more than 4.5 million and an emphasis on education, to the more elite Environmental Defense Fund, with a membership of 300,000 and a focus on influencing federal policy. Other groups include the Nature Conservancy, which uses members' contributions to buy up threatened natural areas and either give them to state or local governments or manage them itself, and the more radical Greenpeace Society and Earth First.

Public-Interest Groups

Public interest is a difficult term to define because, as we noted in Chapter 6, there are many publics in our nation of about 295 million. It is almost impossible for one particular public policy to benefit everybody, which makes it practically impossible to define the public interest. Nonetheless, over the past few decades, a variety of lobbying organizations have been formed "in the public interest."

Public Interest
The best interests of the overall community; the national good, rather than the narrow interests of a particular group.

Nader Organizations. The best-known and perhaps the most effective public-interest groups are those organized under the leadership of consumer activist Ralph Nader. Nader's rise to the top began after the publication, in 1965, of his book *Unsafe at Any Speed,* a lambasting critique of the purported attempt by General Motors (GM) to keep from the public detrimental information about its rear-engine Corvair. Partly as a result of Nader's book, Congress began to consider an automobile safety bill. GM made a clumsy attempt to discredit Nader's background. Nader sued, the media exploited the story, and when GM settled out of court for $425,000,

Ralph Nader, testifying on automobile safety before a Senate Government Operations subcommittee in 1966. Nader, an attorney, was the author of the book *Unsafe at Any Speed*. Nader campaigned for president in 2000 and 2004 but received only a small share of the votes. How might his political ambitions have affected the public-interest organizations that he helped found? (AP Photo)

Nader became a recognized champion of consumer interests. Since then, Nader has turned over much of his income to the more than sixty public-interest groups that he has formed or sponsored. Nader ran for president in 2000 on the Green Party ticket and again in 2004 as an independent.

Other Public-Interest Groups.   Partly in response to the Nader organizations, numerous conservative public-interest law firms have sprung up that are often pitted against the consumer groups in court. Some of these are the Mountain States Legal Defense Foundation, the Pacific Legal Foundation, the National Right-to-Work Legal Defense Foundation, the Washington Legal Foundation, the Institute for Justice, and the Mid-Atlantic Legal Foundation.

One of the largest public-interest groups is Common Cause, founded in 1968. Its goal is to reorder national priorities toward "the public" and to make governmental institutions more responsive to the needs of the public. Anyone willing to pay dues of $20 a year can become a member. Members are polled regularly to obtain information about local and national issues requiring reassessment. Some of the activities of Common Cause have been (1) helping to ensure the passage of the Twenty-sixth Amendment (giving eighteen-year-olds the right to vote), (2) achieving greater voter registration in all states, (3) supporting the complete withdrawal of all U.S. forces from South Vietnam in the 1970s, and (4) promoting legislation that would limit campaign spending.

Other public-interest groups include the League of Women Voters, founded in 1920. Although nominally nonpartisan, it has lobbied for the Equal Rights Amendment and for government reform. The Consumer Federation of America is an alliance of about two hundred local and national organizations interested in consumer protection. The American Civil Liberties Union dates back to World War I (1914–1918), when, under a different name, it defended draft resisters. It generally enters into legal disputes related to Bill of Rights issues.

Other Interest Groups

Single-interest groups, being narrowly focused, may be able to call attention to their causes because they have simple and straightforward goals and because their members tend to care intensely about the issues. Thus, such groups can easily motivate their members to contact legislators or to organize demonstrations in support of their policy goals.

A number of interest groups focus on just one issue. The abortion debate has created various groups opposed to abortion (such as the Right to Life organization) and groups in favor of abortion rights (such as NARAL Pro-Choice America). Other single-issue groups are the National Rifle Association, the Right to Work Committee (an antiunion group), and the American Israel Public Affairs Committee (a pro-Israel group).

Still other groups represent Americans who share a common characteristic, such as age or ethnicity. Such interest groups may lobby for legislation that benefits their members in terms of rights or just represent a viewpoint.

The AARP, as mentioned earlier, is one of the most powerful interest groups in Washington, D.C., and, according to some, the strongest lobbying group in the United States. It is certainly the nation's largest interest group, with a membership of over 35 million. The AARP has accomplished much for its members over the years. It played a significant role in the creation of Medicare and Medicaid, as well as in obtaining cost-of-living increases in Social Security payments. In 2003, the AARP supported the Republican bill to add prescription drug coverage to Medicare. (The plan also made other changes to the system.) Some observers believe that the AARP's support tipped the balance and allowed Congress to pass the measure on a closely divided vote.

Foreign Governments

Homegrown interests are not the only players in the game. Washington, D.C., is also the center for lobbying by foreign governments as well as private foreign interests. The governments of the largest U.S. trading partners, such as Japan, South Korea, Canada, and the European Union (EU) countries, maintain substantial research and lobbying staffs. Even smaller nations, such as those in the Caribbean, engage lobbyists when vital legislation affecting their trade interests is considered. Frequently, these foreign interests hire former representatives or former senators to promote their positions on Capitol Hill.

★ What Makes an Interest Group Powerful?

At any time, thousands of interest groups are attempting to influence state legislatures, governors, Congress, and members of the executive branch of the U.S. government. What characteristics make some of those groups more powerful than others and more likely to have influence over government policy? Generally, interest groups attain a reputation for being powerful through their membership size, leadership, financial resources, and cohesiveness.

Size and Resources

No legislator can deny the power of an interest group that includes thousands of his or her own constituents among its members. Labor unions and organizations such as the AARP and the American Automobile Association are able to claim voters in every congressional district. Having a large membership—more than 13 million in the case of the AFL–CIO—carries a great deal of weight with government

The job of lobbyists never stops. These Washington lobbyists are scrutinizing news reports to ascertain the positions of members of Congress on policy issues relevant to the interests that the lobbyists represent. While many critics of lobbyists and interest groups argue that they distort the actions of government, the First Amendment prohibits the government from regulating their speech. (Tom McCarthy/PhotoEdit)

A senior citizen poses a question to her congressional representative at a town hall meeting in Laurel, Maryland. The discussion centered on the new Medicare legislation and on the Maryland state health plan. The high turnout of elderly voters gives additional clout to the interest groups that represent them. (AP Photo/Gerald Herbert)

officials. The AARP now has more than 35 million members and a budget of $435 million for its operations. In addition, the AARP claims to represent all older Americans, close to 20 percent of the population, whether they join the organization or not.

Having a large number of members, even if the individual membership dues are relatively small, provides an organization with a strong financial base. Those funds pay for lobbyists, television advertisements, mailings to members, a Web site, and many other resources that help an interest group make its point to politicians. The business organization with the largest membership is probably the U.S. Chamber of Commerce, which has more than 200,000 members. The Chamber uses its members' dues to pay for staff and lobbyists, as well as a sophisticated communications network so that it can contact members in a timely way. All of the members can receive e-mail and check the Web site to get updates on the latest legislative proposals.

Other organizations may have fewer members but nonetheless can muster significant financial resources. The pharmaceutical lobby, which represents many of the major drug manufacturers, is one of the most powerful interest groups in Washington due to its financial resources. This lobby has over six hundred registered lobbyists and spent close to $200 million in the last presidential election cycle for lobbying and campaign expenditures.

Leadership

Money is not the only resource that interest groups need to have. Strong leaders who can develop effective strategies are also important. For example, the election of John Sweeney as the president of the AFL–CIO in 1995 brought a new vision to the American labor movement. Under his leadership, the labor movement became a revitalized force in American politics. Beginning with the 2000 election

Celebrated actor and NRA president Charlton Heston holds up a musket as he tells an NRA convention that "they [the government] can have my gun when they pry it from my cold dead hands." Heston, who received a standing ovation, was forced to step down in 2003 due to ill health. The NRA is one of the most powerful interest groups in the country. Why is it so effective? (AP Photo/Ric Feld)

campaign, American labor leaders adopted another effective strategy when they attempted to attract immigrants as new members of their organizations.

Other interest groups, including some with few financial resources, succeed in part because they are led by individuals with charisma and access to power, such as Jesse Jackson of the Rainbow Coalition. Sometimes, choosing a leader with a particular image can be an effective strategy for an organization. The National Rifle Association (NRA) had more than organizational skills in mind when it elected actor Charlton Heston as its president. The strategy of using an actor identified with powerful roles as the spokesperson for the organization worked to improve its national image.

Cohesiveness

Regardless of an interest group's size or the amount of money in its coffers, the motivation of an interest group's members is a key factor in determining how powerful it is. If the members of a group hold their beliefs strongly enough to send letters to their representatives, join a march on Washington, or work together to defeat a candidate, that group is considered powerful. As described earlier, the American labor movement's success in electing Democratic candidates made the labor movement a more powerful lobby.

In contrast, although groups that oppose abortion rights have had little success in influencing policy, they are considered powerful because their members are vocal and highly motivated. Other measures of cohesion include the ability of a group to get its members to contact Washington quickly or to give extra money when needed. The U.S. Chamber of Commerce excels at both of these strategies. In comparison, the AARP cannot claim that it can get its 35 million members to contact their congressional representatives, but it does seem to influence the opinions of older Americans and their views of political candidates.

 Interest Group Strategies

Interest groups employ a wide range of techniques and strategies to promote their policy goals. Although few groups are successful at persuading Congress and the president to completely endorse their programs, many are able to block—or at least weaken—legislation injurious to their members. The key to success for

Direct Technique
An interest group activity that involves interaction with government officials to further the group's goals.

Indirect Technique
A strategy employed by interest groups that uses third parties to influence government officials.

interest groups is access to government officials. To gain such access, interest groups and their representatives try to cultivate long-term relationships with legislators and government officials. The best of these relationships are based on mutual respect and cooperation. The interest group provides the official with excellent sources of information and assistance, and the official in turn gives the group opportunities to express its views.

The techniques used by interest groups can be divided into direct and indirect techniques. With **direct techniques,** the interest group and its lobbyists approach the officials personally to present their case. With **indirect techniques,** in contrast, the interest group uses the general public or individual constituents to influence the government on behalf of the interest group.

Direct Techniques

Lobbying, publicizing ratings of legislative behavior, building coalitions, and providing campaign assistance are the four main direct techniques used by interest groups.

Lobbying Techniques.   As might be guessed, the term *lobbying* comes from the activities of private citizens regularly congregating in the lobbies of legislative chambers before a session to petition legislators. In the latter part of the 1800s, railroad and industrial groups openly bribed state legislators to pass legislation beneficial to their interests, giving lobbying a well-deserved bad name. Most lobbyists today are professionals. They are either consultants to a company or interest group or members of one of the Washington, D.C., law firms that specialize in providing such services. Such firms employ hundreds of former members of Congress and former government officials—for example, former presidential candidates Bob Dole and Walter Mondale. Lobbyists are valued for their network of contacts in Washington. As Ed Rollins, a former White House aide, put it, "I've got many friends who are all through the agencies and equally important, I don't have many enemies. . . . I tell my clients I can get your case moved to the top of the pile."[8]

Lobbyists engage in an array of activities to influence legislation and government policy. These include the following:

1. Engaging in private meetings with public officials, including the president's advisers, to make known the interests of the lobbyists' clients. Although acting on behalf of their clients, lobbyists often furnish needed information to senators and representatives (and government agency appointees) that these officials could not easily obtain on their own. It is to the lobbyists' advantage to provide accurate information so that policymakers will rely on this source in the future.
2. Testifying before congressional committees for or against proposed legislation.
3. Testifying before executive rulemaking agencies—such as the Federal Trade Commission or the Consumer Product Safety Commission—for or against proposed rules.
4. Assisting legislators or bureaucrats in drafting legislation or prospective regulations. Often, lobbyists furnish advice on the specific details of legislation.
5. Inviting legislators to social occasions, such as cocktail parties, boating expeditions, and other events, including conferences at exotic locations. Most lobbyists believe that meeting legislators in a relaxed social setting is effective.
6. Providing political information to legislators and other government officials. Often, the lobbyists have better information than the party leadership about how other legislators are going to vote. In this case, the political information they furnish may be a key to legislative success.
7. Supplying nominations for federal appointments to the executive branch.

---

[8]As quoted in Mahood, *Interest Groups in American National Politics,* p. 51.

The Ratings Game. Many interest groups attempt to influence the overall behavior of legislators through their rating systems. Each year, the interest group selects legislation that it believes is most important to the organization's goals and then monitors how legislators vote on it. Each legislator is given a score based on the percentage of times that he or she voted in favor of the group's position. The usual scheme ranges from 0 to 100 percent. In the ratings scheme of the liberal Americans for Democratic Action, for example, a rating of 100 means that a member of Congress voted with the group on every issue and is, by that measure, very liberal.

Ratings are a shorthand way of describing members' voting records for interested citizens. They can also be used to embarrass members. For example, an environmental group identifies the twelve representatives who the group believes have the worst voting records on environmental issues and labels them "the Dirty Dozen," and a watchdog group describes those representatives who took home the most "pork" for their districts or states as the biggest "pigs."

Building Alliances. Another direct technique used by interest groups is to form a coalition with other groups concerned about the same legislation. Often, these groups will set up a paper organization with an innocuous name to represent their joint concerns. In the early 1990s, for example, environmental, labor, and consumer groups formed an alliance called the Citizens Trade Campaign to oppose the passage of the North American Free Trade Agreement.

Members of such a coalition share expenses and multiply the influence of their individual groups by combining their efforts. Other advantages of forming a coalition are that it blurs the specific interests of the individual groups involved and makes it appear that larger public interests are at stake. These alliances also are efficient devices for keeping like-minded groups from duplicating one another's lobbying efforts.

Campaign Assistance. Interest groups have additional strategies to use in their attempts to influence government policies. Groups recognize that the greatest concern of legislators is to be reelected, so they focus on the legislators' campaign needs. Associations with large memberships, such as labor unions, are able to provide workers for political campaigns, including precinct workers to get out the vote, volunteers to put up posters and pass out literature, and people to staff telephone banks for campaign headquarters.

In many states where certain interest groups have large memberships, candidates vie for the groups' endorsements in the campaign. Gaining those endorsements may be automatic, or it may require that the candidates participate in debates or interviews with the interest groups. Endorsements are important because an interest group usually publicizes its choices in its membership publication and because the candidate can use the endorsement in her or his campaign literature. Traditionally, labor unions have endorsed Democratic Party candidates. Republican candidates, however, often try to persuade union locals at least to refrain from any endorsement. Making no endorsement can then be perceived as disapproval of the Democratic Party candidate.

Senator John Kerry received labor union endorsements in Milwaukee on the day of the Wisconsin primary election in 2004. Kerry appeared with Missouri representative Dick Gephardt, who earlier had been the unions' favorite candidate. Shortly before the Wisconsin vote, however, Gephardt dropped out of the presidential race and endorsed Kerry. (AP Photo/Charles Krupa)

ELECTIONS 2004

Interest Groups: The Candidates of Choice

Despite attempts at campaign-finance reform, the 2004 election boasted record campaign spending. The usual array of interest groups—labor unions, professional groups, and business associations—gathered contributions to their PACs and distributed them to the candidates. Most labor contributions went to Democratic candidates, while a majority of business contributions went to Republicans. Some groups, such as realtors, gave evenly to both parties. At the same time, the new campaign groups, the so-called 527 organizations—tax-exempt associations focused on influencing political elections—raised more than $400 million dollars in unregulated contributions and used them for campaign activities and advertising. Some national interest groups, such as the Laborer's Union, the National Association of Realtors, and the Sierra Club, created their own 527 organizations to spend funds for advertising and other political activities. The flood of unregulated funds supported massive advertising campaigns in the last months of the campaign.

Indirect Techniques

Interest groups can also try to influence government policy by working through others, who may be constituents or the general public. Indirect techniques mask the interest group's own activities and make the effort appear to be spontaneous. Furthermore, legislators and government officials are often more impressed by contacts from constituents than from an interest group's lobbyist.

Generating Public Pressure.   In some instances, interest groups try to produce a "groundswell" of public pressure to influence the government. Such efforts may include advertisements in national magazines and newspapers, mass mailings, television publicity, and demonstrations. The Internet and satellite links make communication efforts even more effective. Interest groups may commission polls to find out what the public's sentiments are and then publicize the results. The intent of this activity is to convince policymakers that public opinion overwhelmingly supports the group's position.

Some corporations and interest groups also engage in a practice that might be called **climate control.** With this strategy, public relations efforts are aimed at improving the public image of the industry or group and are not necessarily related to any specific political issue. Contributions by corporations and groups in support of public television programs, sponsorship of special events, and commercials extolling the virtues of corporate research are some ways of achieving climate control. For example, to improve its image in the wake of litigation against tobacco companies, Philip Morris began advertising its assistance to community agencies, including halfway houses for teen offenders and shelters for battered women. By building a reservoir of favorable public opinion, groups believe that their legislative goals will be less likely to encounter opposition by the public.

Using Constituents as Lobbyists.   Interest groups also use constituents to lobby for the group's goals. In the "shotgun" approach, the interest group tries to mobilize large numbers of constituents to write, phone, or send e-mails to their legislators or the president. Often, the group provides postcards or form letters for constituents to fill out and mail. These efforts are effective on Capitol Hill only

Climate Control
The use of public relations techniques to create favorable public opinion toward an interest group, industry, or corporation.

when there is a very large number of responses, however, because legislators know that the voters did not initiate the communications on their own. Artificially manufactured grassroots activity has been aptly labeled *Astroturf lobbying.*

A more powerful variation of this technique uses only important constituents. With this approach, known as the "rifle" technique or the "Utah plant manager theory," the interest group might, for example, ask the manager of a local plant in Utah to contact the senator from Utah.[9] Because the constituent is seen as responsible for many jobs or other resources, the legislator is more likely to listen carefully to the constituent's concerns about legislation than to a paid lobbyist.

Unconventional Forms of Pressure. Sometimes, interest groups may employ forms of pressure that are outside the ordinary political process. These can include marches, rallies, or demonstrations. Such assemblies, as long as they are peaceful, are protected by the First Amendment. In Chapter 5, we described the civil disobedience techniques of the African American civil rights movement in the 1950s and 1960s. The 1963 March on Washington in support of civil rights was one of the most effective demonstrations ever organized. The women's suffrage movement of the early 1900s also employed marches and demonstrations to great effect.

Demonstrations, however, are not always peaceable. Violent demonstrations have a long history in America, dating back to the antitax Boston Tea Party described in Chapter 2. The Vietnam War (1964–1975) provoked a large number of demonstrations, some of which were violent. In 1999, at a meeting of the World Trade Organization in Seattle, demonstrations against "globalization" turned violent. These demonstrations were repeated in the early 2000s at various sites around the world. Still, violent demonstrations can be counterproductive—instead of putting pressure on the authorities, they may simply alienate the public. For example, historians continue to debate whether the demonstrations against the Vietnam War were effective or counterproductive.

Another unconventional form of pressure is the **boycott**—a refusal to buy a particular product or deal with a particular business. To be effective, boycotts must

Boycott
A form of pressure or protest—an organized refusal to purchase a particular product or deal with a particular business.

---

[9]Kay Lehman Schlozman and John T. Tierney, *Organized Interests and American Democracy* (New York: Harper & Row, 1986), p. 293.

In Virginia, members of the Sierra Club, Public Citizen, and Common Cause protest the Bush administration's environmental policies while Bush speaks at a campaign fund-raiser. How effective are demonstrations as a method of influencing policy? (AP Photo/Adele Starr)

command widespread support. One example was the African American boycott of buses in Montgomery, Alabama, during 1955, described in Chapter 5. Another was the boycott of California grapes that were picked by nonunion workers, as part of a campaign to organize Mexican American farmworkers. The first grape boycott lasted from 1965 to 1970; a series of later boycotts was less effective.

 # Regulating Lobbyists

Congress made its first attempt to control lobbyists and lobbying activities through Title III of the Legislative Reorganization Act of 1946, otherwise known as the Federal Regulation of Lobbying Act. The act actually provided for public disclosure more than for regulation, and it neglected to specify which agency would enforce its provisions. The 1946 legislation defined a lobbyist as any person or organization that received money to be used principally to influence legislation before Congress. Such persons and individuals were supposed to "register" their clients and the purposes of their efforts and report quarterly on their activities.

The legislation was tested in a 1954 Supreme Court case, *United States v. Harriss,*[10] and was found to be constitutional. The Court agreed that the lobbying law did not violate due process, freedom of speech or of the press, or the freedom to petition. The Court narrowly construed the act, however, holding that it applied only to lobbyists who were influencing federal legislation *directly.*

The Results of the 1946 Act

The immediate result of the act was that a minimal number of individuals registered as lobbyists. National interest groups, such as the National Rifle Association and the American Petroleum Institute, could employ hundreds of staff members who were, of course, working on legislation but only register one or two lobbyists who were engaged *principally* in influencing Congress. There were no reporting requirements for lobbying the executive branch, federal agencies, the courts, or congressional staff.

Approximately seven thousand individuals and organizations registered annually as lobbyists, although most experts estimated that ten times that number were actually employed in Washington to exert influence on the government.

The Reforms of 1995

The reform-minded Congress of 1995–1996 overhauled the lobbying legislation, fundamentally changing the ground rules for those who seek to influence the federal government. Lobbying legislation passed in 1995 included the following provisions:

1. A lobbyist is defined as anyone who spends at least 20 percent of his or her time lobbying members of Congress, their staffs, or executive-branch officials.
2. Lobbyists must register with the clerk of the House and the secretary of the Senate within forty-five days of being hired or of making their first contacts. The registration requirement applies to organizations that spend more than $20,000 in one year or to individuals who are paid more than $5,000 annually for lobbying work.
3. Semiannual reports must disclose the general nature of the lobbying effort, specific issues and bill numbers, the estimated cost of the campaign, and a list of the branches of government contacted. The names of the individuals contacted need not be reported.

---

[10]347 U.S. 612 (1954).

4. Representatives of U.S.–owned subsidiaries of foreign-owned firms and lawyers who represent foreign entities also are required to register.

5. The requirements exempt "grassroots" lobbying efforts and those of tax-exempt organizations, such as religious groups.

As they debated the 1995 law, both the House and the Senate adopted new rules on gifts and travel expenses: the House adopted a flat ban on gifts, and the Senate limited gifts to $50 in value and to no more than $100 in gifts from a single source in a year. There are exceptions for gifts from family members and for home-state products and souvenirs, such as T-shirts and coffee mugs. Both chambers banned all-expenses-paid trips, golf outings, and other such junkets. An exception applies for "widely attended" events, however, or if the member is a primary speaker at an event. These gift rules stopped the broad practice of taking members of Congress to lunch or dinner, but the various exemptions and exceptions have caused much controversy as the Senate and House Ethics Committees have considered individual cases.

★ Interest Groups and Representative Democracy

The role played by interest groups in shaping national policy has caused many to question whether we really have a democracy at all. Most interest groups have a middle-class or upper-class bias. Members of interest groups can afford to pay the membership fees, are generally fairly well educated, and normally participate in the political process to a greater extent than the "average" American.

Furthermore, leaders of interest groups tend to constitute an "elite within an elite" in the sense that they usually are from a higher social class than their members. The most powerful interest groups—those with the most resources and political influence—are primarily business, trade, or professional groups. In contrast, public-interest groups or civil rights groups make up only a small percentage of the interest groups lobbying Congress.

Interest Groups: Elitist or Pluralist?

Remember from Chapter 1 that the elite theory of politics presumes that most Americans are uninterested in politics and are willing to let a small, elite group of citizens make decisions for them. Pluralist theory, in contrast, views politics as a struggle among various interest groups to gain benefits for their members. The pluralist approach views compromise among various competing interests as the essence of political decision making. In reality, neither theory fully describes American politics.

If interest groups led by elite, upper-class individuals are the dominant voices in Congress, then what we see is a conflict among elite groups—which would lend as much support to the elitist theory as to the pluralist approach.

Interest Group Influence

The results of lobbying efforts—congressional legislation—do not always favor the interests of the most powerful groups, however. In part, this is because not all interest groups have an equal influence on government. Each group has a different combination of resources to use in the policymaking process. While some groups are composed of members who have high social status and significant economic resources, such as the National Association of Manufacturers, other groups derive influence from their large memberships. The AARP, for example, has more members than any other interest group. Its large membership allows it to wield significant power over legislators. Still other groups, such as environmentalists, have causes that can claim strong public support even from people who have no direct stake in the issue. Groups such as the National Rifle Association are well organized and have highly motivated members. This enables them to channel a stream of mail or electronic messages toward Congress with a few days' effort.

Even the most powerful interest groups do not always succeed in their demands. Whereas the U.S. Chamber of Commerce may be accepted as having a justified interest in the question of business taxes, many legislators might feel that the group should not engage in the debate over the future of Social Security. In other words, groups are seen as having a legitimate concern in the issues closest to their interests but not necessarily in broader issues. This may explain why some of the most successful groups are those that focus on very specific issues—such as tobacco farming, funding of abortions, or handgun control—and do not get involved in larger conflicts.

Complicating the question of interest group influence is the fact that many groups' lobbyists are former colleagues, friends, or family members of current members of Congress.

★ Interest Groups: Why Are They Important Today?

The role of interest groups in American politics has been in question since the writing of the Constitution. James Madison, among many others, worried about how to control the "mischiefs of faction" while recognizing that the very business of a democracy is to resolve the conflicts between interests. Today, the power of interest groups is probably greater than ever before. Interest groups are able to raise and spend large sums to support candidates and parties. Politicians admit that such support buys access, if not influence. Groups use modern technology, and increasingly the Internet, to rally their members.

The existence of interest groups, nonetheless, has advantages for a democracy. By participating in such groups, individual citizens are empowered to influence government in ways far beyond the ballot. Groups do increase the interest and participation of voters in the system. And, without a doubt, these groups can protect the rights of minorities through their access to all branches of the government. Thus, the future could see a continued expansion of interest groups. No doubt, numerous groups, particularly among segments of society that have been left out of the debate, will take advantage of the Internet to promote their interests at lower cost. In any event, it is unlikely that these political associations will disappear soon.

MAKING A DIFFERENCE

★ The Gun Control Issue

Some interest groups focus on issues that concern only a limited number of people. Others are involved in causes in which almost everyone has a stake. Gun control is one of the issues that concerns a large number of people. The question of whether the possession of handguns should be regulated or even banned is at the heart of a long-term and heated battle among organized interest groups. The fight is fueled by the one million gun incidents occurring in the United States each year—murders, suicides, assaults, accidents, and robberies in which guns are involved.

Why Should You Care?

The passionate feelings that are brought to bear on both sides of the gun control issue are evidence of its importance. The problem of crime is central to the gun control issue. Public opinion poll respondents cited crime as one the nation's most important problems throughout the 1990s, and it continues to be a major concern in the 2000s.

Does the easy availability of handguns promote crime? Do people have a right to possess firearms to defend home and hearth? In other words, are guns part of the problem of crime—or part of the solution? Either way, the question is important to you personally. Even if you are fortunate enough not to be victimized by crime, you will

probably find yourself limiting your activities from time to time out of a fear of crime.

What Can You Do?

Almost every year, Congress and the various state legislatures debate measures that would alter gun laws for the nation or for the individual states. As a result, there are plenty of opportunities to get involved.

Issues in the debate include child-safety features on guns and the regulation of gun dealers who sell firearms at gun shows. Proponents of gun control seek safety locks and more restrictions on gun purchases—if not to ban hand guns entirely. Proponents of firearms claim that firearms are a constitutional right and meet a vital defense need for individuals. They contend that the problem lies not in the sale and ownership of weapons but in their use by criminals.

The National Coalition to Ban Handguns favors a total ban, taking the position that handguns "serve no valid purpose, except to kill people." Such a ban is opposed by the National Rifle Association of America (NRA). The NRA, founded in 1871, is currently one of the most powerful single-issue groups in the United States. The NRA believes that gun laws will not reduce the number of crimes. It is illogical to assume, according to the NRA, that persons

who refuse to obey laws prohibiting rape, murder, and other crimes will obey a gun law.

Many proponents of gun control insist that controlling the purchase of weapons would reduce the availability of guns to children. In response, some states have passed laws that hold adults liable for not locking away their firearms. In addition, a number of cities have sued gun manufacturers for not controlling the flow of their products to dealers who sell guns to criminals and gang members.

To find out more about the NRA's position, contact that organization at the following address:

The National Rifle Association
11250 Waples Mill Rd.
Fairfax, VA 22030
703-267-1000
http://www.nra.org

To learn about the positions of gun control advocates, contact:

The Coalition to Stop Gun Violence
1023 15th St. N.W., Suite 600
Washington, DC 20036
202-408-0061
http://www.csgv.org

Brady Center to Prevent Gun Violence
1225 Eye St. N.W., Suite 1100
Washington, DC 20005
202-289-7319
http://www.bradycampaign.org

★ Key Terms

boycott 241

climate control 240

direct technique 238

free rider problem 224

indirect technique 238

interest group 221

labor movement 228

latent interests 224

lobbyist 221

material incentive 225

public interest 233

purposive incentive 226

service sector 229

social movement 223

solidary incentive 225

★ Chapter Summary

1 An interest group is an organization whose members share common objectives and who actively attempt to influence government policy. Interest groups proliferate in the United States because they can influence government at many points in the political structure and because they offer solidary, material, and purposive incentives to their members. Interest groups are often created out of social movements.

2 Major types of interest groups include business, agricultural, labor, public employee, professional, and environmental groups. Other important groups may be considered public-interest groups. In addition, special interest groups and foreign governments lobby the government.

3 Interest groups use direct and indirect techniques to influence government. Direct techniques include testifying before committees and rulemaking agencies, providing information to legislators, rating legislators' voting records, aiding political campaigns, and building alliances. Indirect techniques to influence government include campaigns to

rally public sentiment, letter-writing campaigns, efforts to influence the climate of opinion, and the use of constituents to lobby for the group's interest. Unconventional methods of applying pressure include demonstrations and boycotts.

4 The 1946 Legislative Reorganization Act was the first attempt to control lobbyists and their activities through registration requirements. The Supreme Court narrowly construed the act as applying only to lobbyists who directly seek to influence federal legislation.

5 In 1995, Congress approved new legislation requiring anyone who spends 20 percent of his or her time influencing legislation to register. Also, any organization spending $20,000 or more and any individual who is paid more than $5,000 annually for his or her work must register. Semi-annual reports must include the names of clients, the bills in which they are interested, and the branches of government contacted. Grassroots lobbying and the lobbying efforts of tax-exempt organizations are exempt from the rules.

★ Selected Print and Media Resources

SUGGESTED READINGS

Ainsworth, Scott H. *Analyzing Interest Groups: Group Influence on People and Policies.* New York: W. W. Norton, 2002. The author provides an insightful analysis of the role of interest groups in American government and specific examples of how interest groups influence both the public and the policymaking process.

Cigler, Allan J., and Burdett A. Loomis, eds. *Interest Group Politics,* 6th ed. Washington, D.C.: CQ Press, 2002. This collection of essays examines the politics of a range of different interest groups at work in the American political arena.

Goldstein, Kenneth M. *Interest Groups, Lobbying, and Participation in America.* New York: Cambridge University Press, 2003. What kind of people join interest groups, and how do such people seek to influence legislation? The author looks for answers using survey data and interviews with activists.

Patrick, Brian Anse. *The National Rifle Association and the Media: The Motivating Force of Negative Coverage.* Vol. 1 of *Frontiers in Political Communications.* New York: Peter Lang Publishing, 2004. Patrick argues that the NRA (the National Rifle Association) actually benefits from negative media coverage, which has served to mobilize participants in the "gun culture."

Sifry, Micah, and Nancy Watzman. *Is That a Politician in Your Pocket? Washington on $2 Million a Day.* New York: John Wiley & Sons, 2004. The authors, who are staff members at Public Campaign, provide a clearly written and detailed exposé of how financial

contributions by interest groups drive politics. Chapters cover pharmaceuticals, gun control, agribusiness, oil and chemical corporations, and cable TV.

MEDIA RESOURCES

Bowling for Columbine—Michael Moore's documentary won an Academy Award in 2003. Moore seeks to understand why the United States leads the industrialized world in firearms deaths. While the film is hilarious, it takes a strong position in favor of gun control and is critical of the National Rifle Association.

Norma Rae—A 1979 Hollywood movie about an attempt by a northern union organizer to unionize workers in the southern textile industry; stars Sally Field, who won an Academy Award for her performance.

Organizing America: The History of Trade Unions—A 1994 documentary that incorporates interviews, personal accounts, and archival footage to tell the story of the American labor movement. The film is a Cambridge Educational Production.

The West Wing—A popular television series that is widely regarded as being an accurate portrayal of the issues and political pressures faced by a liberal president and his White House staff.

e-mocracy ★ Interest Groups and the Internet

The Internet may have a strong equalizing effect in the world of lobbying and government influence. The first organizations to use electronic means to reach their constituents and drum up support for action were the large economic coalitions, including the Chamber of Commerce and the National Association of Manufacturers. Groups such as these, as well as groups representing a single product such as tobacco, quickly realized that they could set up Web sites and mailing lists to provide information more rapidly to their members. Members could check the Web every day to see how legislation was developing in Congress or anywhere in the world. National associations could send e-mail to all of their members with one keystroke, mobilizing them to contact their representatives in Congress.

Logging On

Almost every interest group or association has its own Web site. To find one, use your favorite search engine (Lycos, Google, or another search engine) and search for the association by name. For a sense of the breadth of the kinds of interest groups that have Web sites, take a look at one or two of those listed here.

Those interested in the gun control issue may want to visit the National Rifle Association's site at

http://www.nra.org

You can learn more about the labor movement by visiting the AFL–CIO's site at

http://www.aflcio.org

The AARP (formerly the American Association of Retired Persons) has a site at

http://www.aarp.org

Information on environmental issues is available at a number of sites. The Environmental Defense Fund's site is

http://www.environmentaldefense. org/home.cfm

You can also go to the National Resource Defense Council's site for information on environmental issues. Its URL is

http://www.nrdc.org

Using InfoTrac for Political Research

You can find much information on the interest groups mentioned in this chapter by visiting InfoTrac. To access InfoTrac, go to

http://www.infotrac-college.com

Log on, go to InfoTrac College Edition, and then go to the Keyword search page. Type the name of an interest group into the text box and click on "Search."

Tables 7–1 and 7–2 in this chapter provide you with lists of important interest groups that you can research. Examine a group such as the National Beer Wholesalers Association. It may surprise you that the beer wholesalers are considered one of the nation's most influential lobbying groups. If you enter the name of the group into Keyword search, you will also discover that InfoTrac contains a very large number of articles on the beer wholesalers. As you research this group, consider these questions: What are the goals of the beer wholesalers? What strategies do the wholesalers employ to reach these goals? Why have they been so effective?

ONLINE REVIEW

At **http://politicalscience.wadsworth. com/schmidt12**, you will find a free Study Guide to this book. For each chapter, there are two online quizzes to help you master the material.

• The **PoliPrep Self Study Assessment** provides a pre-test for each major section of the chapter. PoliPrep then generates a customized study plan. After you complete the study plan, a post-test evaluates your progress.

• The **Tutorial Quiz** for each chapter provides questions on the chapter contents, including the features. The questions are organized to match the major sections of the chapter.

WHAT IF . . .
We Had a Multiparty Political System?

BACKGROUND

The two-party system is an enduring feature of American government. In most elections, the contest is between two candidates, one from each of the major parties. In modern times, most members of Congress and state legislatures and all of the presidents have been either Democrats or Republicans.

Minor, or "third," parties have entered the arena, but historically elections have been mostly two-party affairs. With few exceptions, the two major parties have accounted for over 90 percent of the total popular vote since the 1800s.

But what if we had a multiparty system instead? In fact, through public opinion polls, a large number of Americans have expressed a desire for a party other than the Republicans and the Democrats. Could this desire be satisfied?

WHAT IF WE HAD A MULTIPARTY POLITICAL SYSTEM?

Actually, systems with multiple competing political parties are much more common in Western democracies than the two-party system. As a modern, complex society with a wide variety of interests and opinions, the United States might be a likely candidate for a multiparty system.

To implement such a system, we would probably need proportional representation. Legislative seats would be allocated to parties in proportion to the percentage of votes they won in the nation or a state. If a party or its candidates received 20 percent of the total vote, the party would have 20 percent of the seats in the legislature. One party would be unlikely to have exclusive control of the government. In a proportional representation scheme, for example, if the vote for the House of Representatives were similar to the vote for president in the 2000 elections, the Democrats might win 215 seats, the Republicans might receive 212, and the Green Party might have 8. No party would enjoy a majority of the 435 seats in the House.

HOW A MULTIPARTY SYSTEM MIGHT FUNCTION

If there were many parties, each one might be similar to a large interest group. Although still acting like a party, each one would carry out functions that in a two-party system only an interest group can perform. Parties representing interests would bargain with each other much as interest groups today negotiate with each other within a party. A party would not have to win support from a large and heterogeneous group as our parties now do but would achieve success by appealing to special groups.

How many parties would we require to represent the diversity of American society? We could have parties representing many different groups: a farmers' party, a Hispanic party, a western party, a labor party, and perhaps others. To gain support for his or her program, a president would have to build a coalition of several parties by persuading each party that its members would benefit from the coalition. The major difficulty in a multiparty political system is, of course, that parties will withdraw from the coalition when they fail to benefit from it. Holding a coalition together for more than one issue is sometimes impossible.

IS PROPORTIONAL REPRESENTATION CONSTITUTIONAL?

Would proportional representation for the House of Representatives violate the Constitution? The short answer is "no." The Constitution mandates only that House members be chosen state by state by a vote of the people. Congress has the constitutional right to establish rules for national elections. Provided that Congress did not alter the relative number of representatives coming from each state, it could establish proportional representation for House elections simply by passing a law. Note, however, that because of the specific constitutional procedures for electing senators, proportional representation in the Senate is impossible under the Constitution.

FOR CRITICAL ANALYSIS

1. *What groups might be better served by a multiparty system?*
2. *Why might members of the existing Congress be hostile to a plan for proportional representation?*

Every two years, usually starting in early fall, the media concentrate on the state of the political parties. For example, near the end of the 2004 campaigns, the media offered continuous commentaries on how Democratic candidate John F. Kerry and Republican incumbent George W. Bush were faring. As the elections drew near, the polls also concentrated on discovering to which political party each potential voter believed he or she "belongs." Prior to an election, a typical poll usually asks the following question: "Do you consider yourself to be a Republican, a Democrat, or an independent?" Generally, the responses indicate that Americans divide fairly evenly among these three choices, with about one-third describing themselves as **independents.** Of course, independents as such are not represented in Congress. This circumstance could change if we had *proportional representation,* a concept discussed in this chapter's opening *What If . . .* feature.

After the elections are over, the media publish the election results. Among other things, Americans learn which party controls the presidency and how many Democrats and Republicans will be sitting in the House of Representatives and the Senate when the new Congress convenes.

Notice that in the first paragraph, when discussing party membership, we put the word *belongs* in quotation marks. We did this because hardly anyone actually "belongs" to a political party in the sense of being a card-carrying member. To become a member of a political party, you do not have to pay dues, pass an examination, or swear an oath of allegiance. Therefore, at this point we can ask an obvious question: If it takes nothing to be a member of a political party, what, then, is a political party?

 ## What Is a Political Party?

A **political party** might be formally defined as a group of political activists who organize to win elections, operate the government, and determine public policy. This definition explains the difference between an interest group and a political party. Interest groups do not want to operate the government, and they do not put forth political candidates—even though they support candidates who will promote their interests if elected or reelected. Another important distinction is that interest groups tend to sharpen issues, whereas American political parties tend to blur their issue positions to attract voters.

Political parties differ from **factions,** which are smaller groups that are trying to obtain power or benefits.[1] Factions generally preceded the formation of political parties in American history, and the term is still used to refer to groups within parties that follow a particular leader or share a regional identification or an ideological viewpoint. For example, the Republican Party sometimes is seen as having a northeastern faction that holds more moderate positions than the dominant conservative majority of the party. Factions are subgroups within parties that may try to capture a nomination or get a position adopted by the party. A key difference between factions and parties is that factions do not have a permanent organization, whereas political parties do.

Political parties in the United States engage in a wide variety of activities, many of which are discussed in this chapter. Through these activities, parties perform a number of functions for the political system. These functions include the following:

1. *Recruiting candidates for public office.* Because it is the goal of parties to gain control of government, they must work to recruit candidates for all elective offices. Often, this means recruiting candidates to run against powerful incumbents. If parties did not search out and encourage political hopefuls, far more offices would be uncontested, and voters would have limited choices.

Independent
A voter or candidate who does not identify with a political party.

Political Party
A group of political activists who organize to win elections, operate the government, and determine public policy.

Faction
A group or bloc in a legislature or political party acting in pursuit of some special interest or position.

---

[1]See James Madison's comments on factions in Chapter 2.

One function of a political party is to serve as the "loyal opposition" when the party is not in power. For some time after September 11, 2001, however, the Democrats found it hard to formulate a foreign-policy alternative to the Bush administration's policies. Here, in March 2003, Senate Democratic leader Tom Daschle accuses Bush of having failed "miserably" at diplomacy before launching the attack on Iraq. Few other Democrats were willing to criticize the president's actions at such an early date. The Democrats, though, were not so reserved during the 2004 presidential campaign season. In an upset, Daschle failed to gain reelection in 2004. (Chris Kleponis/Bloomberg News/Landov)

Two-Party System
A political system in which only two parties have a reasonable chance of winning.

2. *Organizing and running elections.* Although elections are a government activity, political parties actually organize the voter-registration drives, recruit the volunteers to work at the polls, provide most of the campaign activity to stimulate interest in the election, and work to increase voter participation.

3. *Presenting alternative policies to the electorate.* In contrast to factions, which are often centered on individual politicians, parties are focused on a set of political positions. The Democrats or Republicans in Congress who vote together do so because they represent constituencies that have similar expectations and demands.

4. *Accepting responsibility for operating the government.* When a party elects the president or governor and members of the legislature, it accepts the responsibility for running the government. This includes staffing the executive branch with loyal party supporters and developing linkages among the elected officials to gain support for policies and their implementation.

5. *Acting as the organized opposition to the party in power.* The "out" party, or the one that does not control the government, is expected to articulate its own policies and oppose the winning party when appropriate. By organizing the opposition to the "in" party, the opposition party forces debate on the policy alternatives.

The major functions of American political parties are carried out by a small, relatively loose-knit nucleus of party activists. This arrangement is quite different from the more highly structured, mass-membership party organization typical of many European parties. American parties concentrate on winning elections rather than on signing up large numbers of deeply committed, dues-paying members who believe passionately in the party's program.

★ A History of Political Parties in the United States

Although it is difficult to imagine a political system in the United States with four, five, six, or seven major political parties, other democratic systems have three-party, four-party, or even ten-party systems. In some European nations, parties are clearly tied to ideological positions; parties that represent Marxist, socialist, liberal, conservative, and ultraconservative positions appear on the political continuum. Some nations have political parties representing regions of the nation that have separate cultural identities, such as the French-speaking and Flemish-speaking regions of Belgium. Some parties are rooted in religious differences. Parties also exist that represent specific economic interests—agricultural, maritime, or industrial—and some, such as monarchist parties, speak for alternative political systems.

The United States has a **two-party system,** and that system has been around since about 1800. The function and character of the political parties, as well as the emergence of the two-party system itself, have much to do with the unique historical forces operating from this country's beginning as an independent nation. Indeed, James Madison (1751–1836) linked the emergence of political parties to the form of government created by our Constitution.

Generally, we can divide the evolution of our nation's political parties into seven periods:

1. The creation of parties, from 1789 to 1816.
2. The era of one-party rule, or personal politics, from 1816 to 1828.

3. The period from Andrew Jackson's presidency to just before the Civil War, from 1828 to 1860.
4. The Civil War and post–Civil War period, from 1860 to 1896.
5. The Republican ascendancy and the progressive period, from 1896 to 1932.
6. The New Deal period, from 1932 to about 1968.
7. The modern period, from approximately 1968 to the present.

The Formative Years: Federalists and Anti-Federalists

The first partisan political division in the United States occurred before the adoption of the Constitution. As you will recall from Chapter 2, the Federalists were those who pushed for the adoption of the Constitution, whereas the Anti-Federalists were against ratification.

In September 1796, George Washington, who had served as president for almost two full terms, decided not to run again. In his farewell address, he made a somber assessment of the nation's future. Washington felt that the country might be destroyed by the "baneful [harmful] effects of the spirit of party." He viewed parties as a threat to both national unity and the concept of popular government. Early in his career, Thomas Jefferson did not like political parties either. In 1789, he stated, "If I could not go to heaven but with a party, I would not go there at all."[2]

Nevertheless, in the years after the ratification of the Constitution, Americans came to realize that something more permanent than a faction would be necessary to identify candidates for office and represent political differences among the people. The result was two political parties.

One party was the Federalists, which included John Adams, the second president (1797–1801). The Federalists represented commercial interests such as merchants and large planters. They supported a strong national government.

Thomas Jefferson led the other party, which came to be called the Republicans. (These Republicans should not be confused with the later Republican Party of Abraham Lincoln. To avoid confusion, some scholars refer to Jefferson's party as the Democratic-Republicans, but this name was never used during the time that the party existed.) Jefferson's Republicans represented artisans and farmers. They strongly supported states' rights. In 1800, when Jefferson defeated Adams in the presidential contest, one of the world's first peaceful transfers of power from one party to another was achieved.

The Era of Good Feelings

From 1800 to 1820, a majority of U.S. voters regularly elected Republicans to the presidency and to Congress. By 1816, the Federalist Party had virtually collapsed, and two-party competition did not really exist. Although during elections the Republicans opposed the Federalists' call for a stronger, more active central government, they undertook such active government policies as acquiring the Louisiana Territory and Florida and establishing a national bank. Because there was no real political opposition to the Republicans and thus little political debate, the

Thomas Jefferson, founder of the first Republican Party. His election to the presidency in 1800 was one of the world's first transfers of power through a free election. (Library of Congress)

---

[2]Letter to Francis Hopkinson written from Paris while Jefferson was minister to France. In John P. Foley, ed., *The Jeffersonian Cyclopedia* (New York: Russell & Russell, 1967), p. 677.

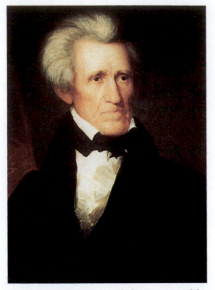

Andrew Jackson earned the name "Old Hickory" for exploits during the War of 1812. In 1828, Jackson was elected president as the candidate of the new Democratic Party. (Corbis/Bettmann)

Era of Good Feelings
The years from 1817 to 1825, when James Monroe was president and there was, in effect, no political opposition.

Democratic Party
One of the two major American political parties evolving out of the Republican Party of Thomas Jefferson.

Whig Party
A major party in the United States during the first half of the nineteenth century, formally established in 1836. The Whig Party was anti-Jackson and represented a variety of regional interests.

Republican Party
One of the two major American political parties. It emerged in the 1850s as an antislavery party and consisted of former northern Whigs and antislavery Democrats.

administration of James Monroe (1817–1825) came to be known as the **era of good feelings.** Since political competition now took place among individual Republican aspirants, this period can also be called the *era of personal politics*.

National Two-Party Rule: Democrats and Whigs

Organized two-party politics returned in 1824. With the election of John Quincy Adams as president, the Republican Party split in two. The followers of Adams called themselves National Republicans. The followers of Andrew Jackson, who defeated Adams in 1828, formed the **Democratic Party.** Later, the National Republicans took the name **Whig Party,** which had been a traditional name for British liberals. The Whigs stood, among other things, for federal spending on "internal improvements," such as roads. The Democrats opposed this policy. The Democrats, who were the stronger of the two parties, favored personal liberty and opportunity for the "common man." It was understood implicitly that the "common man" was a white man—hostility toward African Americans was an important force holding the disparate Democratic groups together.[3]

The Civil War Crisis

In the 1850s, hostility between the North and South over the issue of slavery divided both parties. The Whigs were the first to split in two. The Whigs had been the party of an active federal government, but southerners had come to believe that "a government strong enough to build roads is a government strong enough to free your slaves." The southern Whigs therefore ceased to exist as an organized party. The northern Whigs united with antislavery Democrats and members of the radical antislavery Free Soil Party to form the modern **Republican Party.**

The Post–Civil War Period

After the Civil War, the Democratic Party was able to heal its divisions. Southern resentment of the Republicans' role in defeating the South and fears that the federal government would intervene on behalf of African Americans ensured that the Democrats would dominate the white South for the next century.

"Rum, Romanism, and Rebellion." Northern Democrats feared a strong government for other reasons. The Republicans thought that the government should promote business and economic growth, but many Republicans also wanted to use the power of government to impose evangelical Protestant moral values on society. Democrats opposed what they saw as culturally coercive measures. Many Republicans wanted to limit or even prohibit the sale of alcohol. They favored the establishment of public schools—with a Protestant curriculum. As a result, Catholics were strongly Democratic. In 1884, Protestant minister Samuel Burchard described the Democrats as the party of "rum, Romanism, and rebellion." This remark was offensive to Catholics, and Republican presidential candidate James Blaine later claimed that it cost him the White House. Offensive as it may have been, Burchard's characterization of the Democrats contained an element of truth.

The Triumph of the Republicans. In this period, the parties were very evenly matched in strength. The abolition of the three-fifths rule, described in Chapter 2, meant that African Americans would be counted fully when allocating House seats and electoral votes to the South. The Republicans therefore had to carry

---

[3]Edward Pessen, *Jacksonian America: Society, Personality, and Politics* (Homewood, Ill.: Dorsey Press, 1969). See especially pages 246–247. The small number of free blacks who could vote were overwhelmingly Whig.

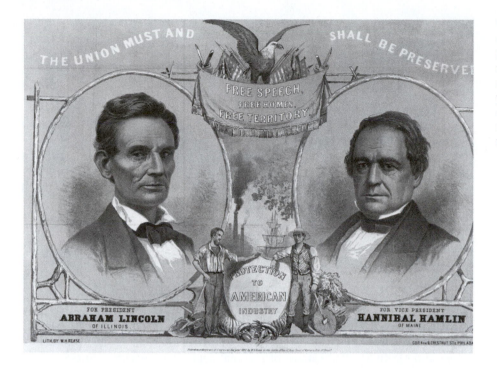

This handbill was used in the election campaign of 1860. It shows Abraham Lincoln with his first vice-presidential running mate, Senator Hannibal Hamlin of Maine. Handbills served the same purpose as today's direct-mail and e-mail advertisements, appealing directly to the voters with the candidate's message. (Corbis/Bettmann)

almost every northern state to win, and this was not always possible. In the 1890s, however, the Republicans gained a decisive edge. In that decade, the populist movement emerged in the West and South to champion the interests of small farmers, who were often greatly in debt. Populists supported inflation, which benefited debtors by reducing the value of outstanding debts. In 1896, when William Jennings Bryan became the Democratic candidate for president, the Democrats embraced populism.

As it turned out, the few western farmers who were drawn to the Democrats by this step were greatly outnumbered by urban working-class voters who believed that inflation would reduce the value of their paychecks and who therefore became Republicans. William McKinley, the Republican candidate, was

Republican presidential candidate William McKinley campaigned in 1896 on a platform draped with the American flag. A century later, candidates still use the same type of decorations. What sort of messages are modern-day candidates attempting to send by frequent displays of the flag? (The Smithsonian)

FIGURE 8–1

The 1896 Presidential Election

In 1896, the agrarian, populist appeal of Democrat William Jennings Bryan (blue states) won western states for the Democrats at the cost of losing more populous eastern states to Republican William McKinley (red states). This pattern held in subsequent presidential elections.

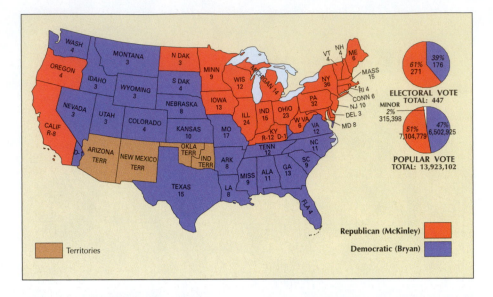

elected with a solid majority of the votes. Figure 8–1 shows the states taken by Bryan and McKinley. The pattern of regional support shown in Figure 8–1 persisted for many years. From 1896 until 1932, the Republicans were able successfully to present themselves as the party that knew how to manage the economy.

The Progressive Interlude

In the early 1900s, a spirit of political reform arose in both major parties. Called *progressivism,* this spirit was compounded of a fear of the growing power of great corporations and a belief that honest, impartial government could regulate the economy effectively. In 1912, the Republican Party temporarily split as former Republican president Theodore Roosevelt campaigned for the presidency on a third-party Progressive ticket. The Republican split permitted the election of Woodrow Wilson, the Democratic candidate, along with a Democratic Congress.

Like Roosevelt, Wilson considered himself a progressive, although he and Roosevelt did not agree on how progressivism ought to be implemented. Wilson's progressivism marked the beginning of a radical change in Democratic policies. Dating back to its very foundation, the Democratic Party had been the party of limited government. Under Wilson, the Democrats became for the first time at least as receptive as the Republicans to government action in the economy. (Wilson's progressivism did not extend to race relations—for African Americans, the Wilson administration was something of a disaster.)

The New Deal Era

The Republican ascendancy resumed after Wilson left office. It ended with the election of 1932, in the depths of the Great Depression. Republican Herbert Hoover was president when the depression began in 1929. While Hoover took some measures to fight the depression, they fell far short of what the public demanded. Significantly, Hoover opposed federal relief for the unemployed and the destitute. In 1932, Democrat Franklin D. Roosevelt was elected president by overwhelming margins.

The Great Depression shattered the working-class belief in Republican economic competence. Under Roosevelt, the Democrats began to make major interventions in the economy in an attempt to combat the depression and to relieve the suffering of the unemployed. Roosevelt's New Deal relief programs were open to all citizens, both black and white. As a result, African Americans began to support the Democratic Party in large numbers—a development that would have stunned any American politician of the 1800s.

Roosevelt's political coalition was broad enough to establish the Democrats as the new majority party, in place of the Republicans. In the 1950s, Republican Dwight D. Eisenhower, the leading U.S. general during World War II, won two terms as president. Otherwise, with minor interruptions, the Democratic ascendancy lasted until 1968.

An Era of Divided Government

The New Deal coalition managed the unlikely feat of including both African Americans and whites who were hostile to African American advancement. This balancing act came to an end in the 1960s, a decade that was marked by the civil rights movement, by several years of "race riots" in major cities, and by increasingly heated protests against the Vietnam War. For many economically liberal, socially conservative voters, especially in the South, social issues had become more important than economic ones, and these voters left the Democrats. These voters outnumbered the new voters who joined the Democrats—newly enfranchised African Americans and former liberal Republicans in New England and the upper Midwest.

Unemployed workers filing benefit claims in the 1930s. Unemployment insurance was first introduced during the "New Deal" of Democratic president Franklin D. Roosevelt. The Great Depression did not end until 1941 (on the eve of World War II), but Roosevelt's attempts to alleviate suffering caused by the Depression made him very popular. (Franklin D. Roosevelt Presidential Library and Museum)

The Parties in Balance. The result, since 1968, has been a nation almost evenly divided in politics. In presidential elections, the Republicans have had more success than the Democrats. Until recently, Congress remained Democratic, but official party labels can be misleading. Some of the Democrats were southern conservatives who normally voted with the Republicans on issues. As these conservative Democrats retired, they were largely replaced by Republicans.

In the thirty-six years between the elections of 1968 and 2004, there were only eight years when one of the two major parties controlled the presidency, the House of Representatives, and the Senate. The Democrats controlled all three institutions during the presidency of Jimmy Carter (1977–1981) and during the first two years of the presidency of Bill Clinton (1993–2001). The Republicans controlled all three institutions during the third and fourth years of George W. Bush's presidency.[4] Before the election of 1992, the electorate seemed to prefer, in most circumstances, to match a Republican president with a Democratic Congress. Under Bill Clinton, that state of affairs was reversed, with a Democratic president facing a Republican Congress.

Red State, Blue State. The pattern of a Republican Congress and a Democratic president would have continued after the election of 2000 if Democratic presidential candidate Al Gore had received 538 more popular votes in Florida. George W. Bush actually lost the popular vote count by over half a million votes and carried the electoral college (which coincidentally has 538 members) by five votes. The extreme closeness of the vote in the electoral college led the press to repeatedly publish the state map of the results, shown in Figure 8–2 on the next page. Commentators have discussed at length the supposed differences between the Republican "red states"

---

[4]The Republicans also were in control of all three institutions for the first four months after Bush's inauguration. This initial period of control came to an end when Senator James Jeffords of Vermont left the Republican Party, giving the Democrats control of the Senate.

FIGURE 8–2

The Presidential Election of 2000

In 2000, Republican George W. Bush (red states) defeated Democrat Al Gore (blue states) in one of the closest presidential elections ever. Note the almost complete reversal of the geographic pattern of 1896. This reversal parallels the transformation of the Democrats from an anti–civil rights to a pro–civil rights party and from a party that supports limited government to a party that favors positive government action.

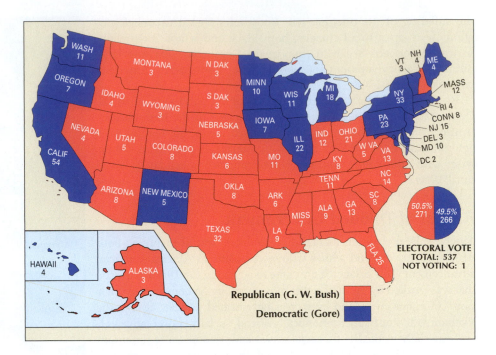

ELECTORAL VOTE
TOTAL: 537
NOT VOTING: 1

Republican (G. W. Bush)
Democratic (Gore)

and the Democratic "blue states." The pattern revealed in 2000 was, in fact, a representative outcome. The states carried by Bush were identical to the states that voted Republican at least twice between 1988 and 2000, plus Ohio and West Virginia.

An interesting characteristic of the 2000 map is that it is an almost complete reversal of the geographic pattern of 1896, shown in Figure 8–1. This reversal parallels the transformation of the Democratic Party from a party that stood for limited government, states' rights, and racial segregation to a party of active government, national authority, and civil rights for African Americans.

Partisan Trends in the 2004 Elections

Despite the presidential victory of Republican George W. Bush and the improved Republican margins of control in the House and Senate, the 2004 elections revealed a nation that continued to be closely divided between the two parties. As you can see in Figure 8–3, only three states with sixteen electoral votes changed hands between 2000 and 2004. Cultural politics may have played a more important role than was expected by most observers before the election. In exit polls, more voters cited "moral values" as the most important election issue than mentioned the war in Iraq or the economy—a result not seen in opinion polls conducted earlier in the year. The emphasis on moral issues caused some commentators to wonder whether same-sex marriage, which became a major issue in 2004, may have persuaded many culturally conservative voters to turn out and vote Republican. Democratic senator John F. Kerry, with his New England reserve, could not easily appeal to these voters, although clearly he tried. In the wake of the election, some Democrats called for a candidate in 2008 who, like presidents Bill Clinton and Jimmy Carter, could make a stronger appeal to religious voters.

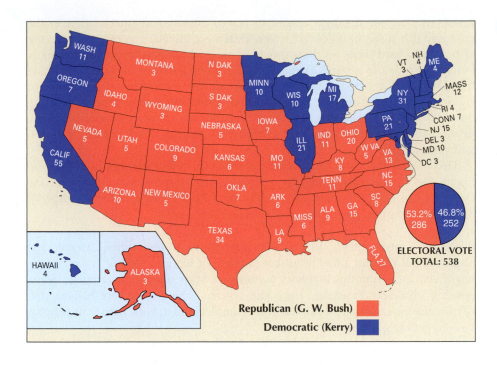

FIGURE 8–3

The Presidential Election of 2004

Between the presidential elections of 2000 and 2004, only three states changed hands. Winning candidate George W. Bush picked up New Mexico and Iowa, but lost New Hampshire. Bush also won the popular vote by well over three million votes in 2004. He lost the popular vote by about half a million in 2000.

 The Two Major U.S. Parties Today

It is sometimes said that the major American political parties are like Tweedledee and Tweedledum, the twins in Lewis Carroll's *Through the Looking Glass*. Labels such as "Repubocrats" are especially popular among supporters of third parties, such as the Green Party and the Libertarian Party. Third-party advocates, of course, have an interest in claiming that there is no difference between the two major parties—their chances of gaining support are much greater if the major parties are seen as indistinguishable. Despite such allegations, the major parties do have substantial differences, both in their policies and in their constituents.

The Parties' Core Constituents

You learned in Chapter 6 how demographic factors affect support for the two parties. Democrats receive disproportionate support not only from the least well educated voters but also from individuals with advanced degrees. Upper-income voters are more Republican than lower-income voters; businesspersons are much more likely to vote Republican than labor union members. The Jewish electorate is heavily Democratic; white evangelical Christians who are regular churchgoers tend to be Republicans. Hispanics are strongly Democratic; African Americans are overwhelmingly so. Women are somewhat more Democratic than men. City dwellers tend to be Democrats; rural people tend to be Republicans. In presidential elections, the South, the Rocky Mountain states, and the Great Plains states typically vote Republican; the West Coast and the Northeast are more likely to favor the Democrats. These tendencies represent the influences of economic interests and cultural values, which are often in conflict with each other.

Economic Beliefs

A coalition of the labor movement and various racial and ethnic minorities has been the core of Democratic Party support since the presidency of Franklin D.

Roosevelt. The social programs and increased government intervention in the economy that made up Roosevelt's New Deal were intended to ease the pressure of economic hard times on these groups. This goal remains important for many Democrats today. In general, Democratic identifiers are more likely to approve of social-welfare spending, to support government regulation of business, to endorse measures to improve the situation of minorities, and to support assisting the elderly with their medical expenses. Republicans are more supportive of the private marketplace and believe more strongly in an ethic of self-reliance and limited government.

These traditional party beliefs are reflected in the public opinion poll results in Figure 8–4. On economic and health-care issues, respondents considered the Democrats in Congress more trustworthy than Republican president George W. Bush. President Bush showed strength on security issues.

Economic Convergence?   In his 1996 State of the Union address, Democratic president Bill Clinton announced that "the era of big government is over." One might conclude from this that both parties now favor limited government. Some political observers, however, argue the reverse. These observers believe that despite the tax cuts that Republicans have implemented, both parties in practice now favor "big government."

Harvard University professor Jeffrey Frankel goes even further. "When it comes to White House economic policy," Frankel writes, "the Republican and Democratic parties have switched places since the 1960s." Frankel points out that budget deficits rose during the administrations of Republicans Ronald Reagan (1981–1989) and George W. Bush but fell under Bill Clinton. Federal employment grew under Reagan and George W. Bush but fell under Clinton. Reagan and Bush both introduced "protectionist" measures to restrict imports, such as Bush's tariffs on imported steel and timber. Clinton, despite the protectionist beliefs of

FIGURE 8–4

Republican Issues and Democratic Issues

A public opinion poll conducted immediately before President Bush's State of the Union address in 2004 asked respondents whether they trusted President Bush or the Democrats in Congress to handle certain issues facing the nation.

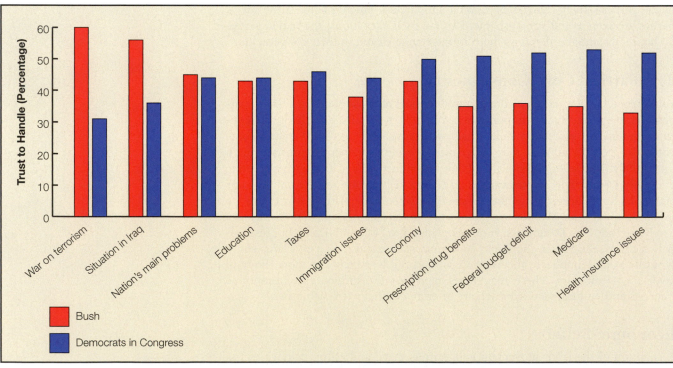

SOURCE: ABC News/*Washington Post* poll conducted January 15–18, 2004.

many Democrats in Congress, was in practice more supportive of free trade.[5] Despite these facts, Clinton was not really a supporter of limited government. If his 1993 plan for universal health insurance had been accepted by Congress, the size and cost of the federal government would have increased considerably.

Republican and Democratic Budgets. Other observers have noted a contrast in budgets. Reagan faced a Congress controlled by the Democrats. Clinton in turn faced a Republican Congress for most of his administration. Reagan regularly submitted budgets larger than the ones that the Democratic Congress eventually passed, however, while Clinton's budgets were typically smaller than those approved by the Republican Congress. During the first three years of George W. Bush's presidency, discretionary federal spending rose by 27 percent, compared with 10 percent under Clinton's two full terms in office. Finally, it was a Republican majority in Congress that passed a new Medicare prescription drug benefit in 2003.

Despite these paradoxes, the perception is that the Democrats still tend to favor the less well off, while the Republicans tend to favor the prosperous. Democrats have argued, for example, that President Bush's tax cuts were weighted heavily toward the upper end of the economic spectrum. In addition, there is another class of issues on which the differences between the parties have become greater than ever—cultural issues.

Cultural Politics

In recent years, cultural values may have become more important than they previously were in defining the beliefs of the two major parties. For example, in 1987, Democrats were almost as likely to favor stricter abortion laws (40 percent) as Republicans were (48 percent). Today, Republicans are twice as likely to favor stricter abortion laws (50 percent to 25 percent).[6]

Cultural Politics and Socioeconomic Status. Thomas Frank, writing in *Harper's Magazine,* reported the following bumper sticker at a gun show in Kansas City: "A working person voting for the Democrats is like a chicken voting for Colonel Sanders." (Colonel Sanders is the mascot of KFC, the chain of fried chicken restaurants.) In light of the economic traditions of the two parties, this seems to be an odd statement. In fact, the sticker is an exact reversal of an earlier one directed against the Republicans.

You can make sense of such a sentiment by remembering what you learned in Chapter 6—although economic conservatism is associated with higher incomes, social conservatism is relatively more common among lower-income groups. The individual who displayed the bumper sticker, therefore, was in effect claiming that cultural concerns—in this example, presumably the right to own handguns—are far more important than economic ones. Frank argues that despite Republican control of the national government during the George W. Bush administration, cultural conservatives continued to view themselves as embattled "ordinary Americans" under threat from a liberal, cosmopolitan elite.[7]

The Regional Factor in Cultural Politics. Conventionally, some parts of the country are viewed as culturally liberal, and others as culturally conservative. On a regional basis, cultural liberalism (as opposed to economic liberalism) may be

[5]Jeffrey Frankel, "Republican and Democratic Presidents Have Switched Economic Policies," *Milken Institute Review,* Vol. 5, No. 1 (First Quarter 2003), pp. 18–25.
[6]The Pew Research Center for the People and the Press, *The 2004 Political Landscape: Evenly Divided and Increasingly Polarized,* November 5, 2003. This survey is online at http:// people-press.org/reports.
[7]Thomas Frank, "Lie Down for America," *Harper's Magazine,* April 2004, p. 33.

★★★★★★★★★★★★★★★★★

DID YOU KNOW . . .
That it took 103 ballots for John W. Davis to be nominated at the Democratic National Convention in 1924 **?**

Reverse-Income Effect
A tendency for wealthier states or regions to favor the Democrats and for less wealthy states or regions to favor the Republicans. The effect appears paradoxical because it reverses traditional patterns of support.

associated with economic dynamism. The San Francisco Bay Area can serve as an example. The greater Bay Area contains Silicon Valley, the heart of the micro-computer industry; it has the highest per capita personal income of any metro-politan area in America. It also is one of the most liberal regions of the country. San Francisco liberalism is largely cultural—one sign of this liberalism is that the city has a claim to be the "capital" of gay America. There is not much evidence, however, that the region's wealthy citizens are in favor of higher taxes.

To further illustrate this point, we can compare the political preferences of rel-atively wealthy states with relatively poor ones. Of the ten states with the highest per capita personal incomes in 2000, eight voted for Democrat Al Gore in the presidential election of that year. Of the twenty-five states with the lowest per capita incomes in 2000, twenty voted for Republican George W. Bush.

Given these data, it seems hard to believe that upper-income voters really are more Republican than lower-income ones. Within any given state or region, how-ever, upscale voters are more likely to be Republican regardless of whether the area as a whole leans Democratic or Republican. States that vote Democratic are often northern states that contain large cities. At least part of this **reverse-income effect** may simply be that urban areas are more prosperous, culturally liberal, and Democratic than the countryside, and that the North is more prosperous, cultur-ally liberal, and Democratic than the South.

The 2004 Election: Economics and National Security

Despite the importance of cultural beliefs in determining party allegiance, Republican incumbent George W. Bush and Democratic challenger John F. Kerry avoided cultural issues in the 2004 elections whenever possible. Both candidates believed that national security and economic concerns would be the most important issues for undecided voters. How did Kerry become the Democratic presidential can-didate? We examine this question in this chapter's *Politics and Elections* feature.

Kerry at first stressed economics. He claimed that the economic recovery of 2003 and 2004 had not created significant numbers of new jobs. Bush cam-paigned as the national security candidate—a leader who merited reelection on the basis of his actions in the years following the terrorist attacks of September 11, 2001. These contrasting campaigns were based on the traditional beliefs of the two parties. Kerry's appeal to economic fairness was an expression of the value of equality; Bush's emphasis on security was an expression of the value of order, a key value for cultural conservatives. (These values were defined and described in Chapter 1 of this text.)

During the Democratic National Convention, however, Kerry sought to por-tray himself as a better choice for commander-in-chief by playing up his Vietnam War record and by using patriotic symbolism. Kerry claimed that Bush had need-lessly antagonized our traditional allies. Meanwhile, Bush continued to attack Kerry's credibility as a potential president by branding him as a "flip-flopper."

★ The Three Faces of a Party

Although American parties are known by a single name and, in the public mind, have a common historical identity, each party really has three major components. The first component is the **party-in-the-electorate.** This phrase refers to all those individuals who claim an attachment to the political party. They need not partic-ipate in election campaigns. Rather, the party-in-the-electorate is the large num-ber of Americans who feel some loyalty to the party or who use partisanship as a cue to decide who will earn their vote. Party membership is not really a rational choice; rather, it is an emotional tie somewhat analogous to identifying with a

Party-in-the-Electorate
Those members of the general public who identify with a political party or who express a preference for one party over another.

POLITICS AND ELECTIONS
The 2004 Democratic Primary Elections

In early 2003, John F. Kerry appeared to be the strongest Democratic presidential candidate. By March 2004, he had decisively won the Democratic presidential nomination. The Democratic Party had designed its nominating process to produce such a result. The primary and caucus schedule was heavily "front-loaded," with many delegates chosen in the opening weeks. Such a system should favor a front-runner endorsed by the party establishment. An insurgent would not have the funds needed to maintain a national campaign after the very first events—the Iowa caucuses and the New Hampshire primary.

The great shock of the primary season was that the system actually produced the intended result. As late as December 2003, hardly anyone thought that would happen.

THE CONTENDERS

Three candidates other than Kerry showed promise. Howard Dean had been governor of Vermont, and governors have had great success in presidential elections. Claiming to represent the "democratic wing of the Democratic Party," Dean strongly opposed the war in Iraq. Wesley Clark, a retired general, also opposed the war. His background was unusual for a Democratic candidate, but many Democrats considered it advantageous. Finally, John Edwards of North Carolina enjoyed some support, although he was only in his first term in the Senate.

THE RISE AND FALL OF HOWARD DEAN

Rank-and-file Democrats loved Dean's sharp criticisms of the Bush administration. Dean also made strikingly effective use of the Internet to raise funds and organize his campaign. On the eve of the Iowa caucuses in January, he had become the front-runner. His unguarded speech damaged him, however. For example, in a radio interview four years earlier, Dean had lambasted the Iowa caucus process and its participants. On losing the caucuses to Kerry, Dean tried to cheer his followers with a speech so intense that many television viewers thought that he had "lost control." In the following weeks, Kerry's support skyrocketed. Democrats across the country told poll-takers that they would vote for Kerry because he was the candidate most likely to defeat Bush. A sign in Iowa seemed to say it all: "Dated Dean, Married Kerry."

Edwards finished second in Iowa and gave Kerry his strongest competition in the subsequent primaries. Although his résumé was thin, Edwards turned out to be a

Democratic presidential candidate Howard Dean gives a yell while addressing his supporters on the night of the Iowa caucuses in January 2004. Dean's performance was ridiculed on the Web as the "Dean goes nuts" speech. As a result of this and other missteps, many Democrats began to view Dean as unelectable, and he quickly lost support in the primaries. (AP Photo/Paul Sancya)

strikingly effective orator. He had developed his skills by appealing to jurors as one of North Carolina's most successful trial lawyers. Many Democrats believed that Edwards ought to be the party's vice-presidential nominee, and in July 2004 Kerry asked Edwards to join the ticket.

FOR CRITICAL ANALYSIS

Why might an antiwar candidate not have been the strongest opponent for Bush?

Party Organization
The formal structure and leadership of a political party, including election committees; local, state, and national executives; and paid professional staff.

Party-in-Government
All of the elected and appointed officials who identify with a political party.

region or a baseball team. Although individuals may hold a deep loyalty to or identification with a political party, there is no need for members of the party-in-the-electorate to speak out publicly, to contribute to campaigns, or to vote all Republican or all Democratic. Needless to say, the party leaders pay close attention to the affiliation of their members in the electorate.

The second component, the **party organization,** provides the structural framework for the political party by recruiting volunteers to become party leaders; identifying potential candidates; and organizing caucuses, conventions, and election campaigns for its candidates, as will be discussed in more detail shortly. It is the party organization and its active workers that keep the party functioning between elections, as well as make sure that the party puts forth electable candidates and clear positions in the elections. If the party-in-the-electorate declines in numbers and loyalty, the party organization must try to find a strategy to rebuild the grassroots following.

The **party-in-government** is the third component of American political parties. The party-in-government consists of those elected and appointed officials who identify with a political party. Generally, elected officials do not also hold official party positions within the formal organization, although they often have the informal power to appoint party executives.

Party Organization

Each of the American political parties is often seen as having a pyramid-shaped organization, with the national chairperson and committee at the top and the local precinct chairperson on the bottom. This structure, however, does not accurately reflect the relative power of the individual components of the party organization. If it did, the national chairperson of the Democratic Party or the Republican Party, along with the national committee, could simply dictate how the organization was to be run, just as if it were ExxonMobil Corporation or Ford Motor Company. In reality, the political parties have a confederal structure, in which each unit has significant autonomy and is linked only loosely to the other units.

The National Party Organization

National Convention
The meeting held every four years by each major party to select presidential and vice presidential candidates, to write a platform, to choose a national committee, and to conduct party business.

Party Platform
A document drawn up at each national convention, outlining the policies, positions, and principles of the party.

Each party has a national organization, the most clearly institutional part of which is the **national convention,** held every four years. The convention is used to nominate the presidential and vice presidential candidates. In addition, the **party platform** is developed at the national convention. The platform sets forth the party's position on the issues and makes promises to initiate certain policies if the party wins the presidency.

After the convention, the platform frequently is neglected or ignored by party candidates who disagree with it. Because candidates are trying to win votes from a wide spectrum of voters, it is counterproductive to emphasize the fairly narrow and sometimes controversial goals set forth in the platform. Political scientist Gerald M. Pomper discovered decades ago, however, that once elected, the parties do try to carry out platform promises and that roughly three-fourths of the promises eventually become law.[8] Of course, some general goals, such as economic prosperity, are included in the platforms of both parties.

Convention Delegates.   The party convention provides the most striking illustration of the difference between the ordinary members of a party, or party iden-

---

[8]Gerald M. Pomper and Susan S. Lederman, *Elections in America: Control and Influence in Democratic Politics,* 2d ed. (New York: Longman, 1980).

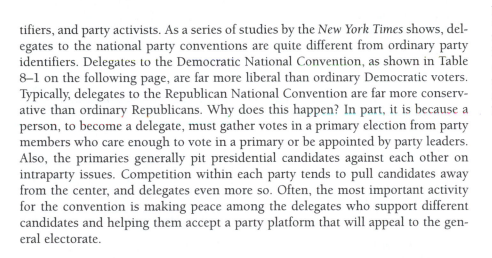

Delegates at the 2004 Republican National Convention in New York (left photos) and at the Democratic National Convention in Boston (right photos). Do national party conventions still have a function in an era in which presidential candidates are actually chosen by primary elections and caucuses open to all party members? (Dennis Brack/Bloomberg News/Landov)

tifiers, and party activists. As a series of studies by the *New York Times* shows, delegates to the national party conventions are quite different from ordinary party identifiers. Delegates to the Democratic National Convention, as shown in Table 8–1 on the following page, are far more liberal than ordinary Democratic voters. Typically, delegates to the Republican National Convention are far more conservative than ordinary Republicans. Why does this happen? In part, it is because a person, to become a delegate, must gather votes in a primary election from party members who care enough to vote in a primary or be appointed by party leaders. Also, the primaries generally pit presidential candidates against each other on intraparty issues. Competition within each party tends to pull candidates away from the center, and delegates even more so. Often, the most important activity for the convention is making peace among the delegates who support different candidates and helping them accept a party platform that will appeal to the general electorate.

The National Committee.   At the national convention, each of the parties formally chooses a national standing committee, elected by the individual state parties. This **national committee** directs and coordinates party activities during the following four years. The Democrats include at least two members, a man and a woman, from each state, from the District of Columbia, and from the several territories. Governors, members of Congress, mayors, and other officials may be included as at-large members of the national committee. The Republicans, in addition, add state chairpersons from every state carried by the Republican Party in the preceding presidential, gubernatorial, or congressional elections. The selections of national committee members are ratified by the delegations to the national convention.

   One of the jobs of the national committee is to ratify the presidential nominee's choice of a national chairperson, who in principle acts as the spokesperson for the party. The national chairperson and the national committee plan the next

National Committee
A standing committee of a national political party established to direct and coordinate party activities between national party conventions.

TABLE 8–1

Convention Delegates and Voters: How Did They Compare on the Issues in 2004?

PERCENTAGE OF . . .	DEMOCRATIC DELEGATES	DEMOCRATIC VOTERS	ALL VOTERS	REPUBLICAN VOTERS	REPUBLICAN DELEGATES
SCOPE OF GOVERNMENT					
Government should do more to . . .					
solve the nation's problems	79	48	42	35	7
promote traditional values	15	26	40	61	55
ECONOMIC POLICY					
The budget deficit is a very serious problem for the country	86	68	51	28	13
All or most of the tax cuts Congress has passed since 2000 should be made permanent	7	33	49	68	95
FOREIGN POLICY					
The United States did the right thing in taking military action against Iraq	7	21	46	78	96
It is extremely important for the Unites States to work through the United Nations to solve international problems	79	66	49	31	7
DOMESTIC POLICY					
New anti-terrorism laws excessively restrict the average person's civil liberties	77	53	43	25	15
Gay couples should be allowed to legally marry	44	36	26	11	3
Abortion should be generally available to those who want it	75	49	34	17	13
The penalty for murder should be death, rather than life in prison without chance of parole	19	39	50	65	57
IDEOLOGY					
Your political ideology is . . .					
liberal	41	34	20	8	1
moderate	52	45	42	30	33
conservative	3	19	36	61	63

SOURCE: *The New York Times,* July 25, 2004 and August 29, 2004.

campaign and the next convention, obtain financial contributions, and publicize the national party.

Picking a National Chairperson.   In general, the party's presidential candidate chooses the national chairperson. (If that candidate loses, however, the chairperson is often changed.) The national chairperson performs such jobs as establish-

Ed Gillespie (left), the national chairman of the Republican National Committee, and Terry McAuliffe (right), the national chairman of the Democratic National Committee. Is the function of a national party chairperson similar to the function of a chairperson of a corporate board of directors? (Left: Alex Wong/ Getty Images; right: © LEFRANC DAVID/GAMMA)

ing a national party headquarters, raising campaign funds and distributing them to state parties and to candidates, and appearing in the media as a party spokesperson. The national chairperson, along with the national committee, attempts to maintain some sort of liaison among the different levels of the party organization. The fact, though, is that the real strength and power of a national party are at the state level.

The State Party Organization

There are fifty states in the Union, plus the District of Columbia and the territories, and an equal number of party organizations for each major party. Therefore, there are more than a hundred state parties (and even more, if we include local parties and minor parties). Because every state party is unique, it is impossible to describe what an "average" state political party is like. Nonetheless, state parties have several organizational features in common.

Each state party has a chairperson, a committee, and a number of local organizations. In theory, the role of the **state central committee**—the principal organized structure of each political party within each state—is similar in the various states. The committee, usually composed of members who represent congressional districts, state legislative districts, or counties, has responsibility for carrying out the policy decisions of the party's state convention. In some states the state committee can issue directives to the state chairperson.

Also, like the national committee, the state central committee has control over the use of party campaign funds during political campaigns. Usually, the state central committee has little, if any, influence on party candidates once they are elected. In fact, state parties are fundamentally loose alliances of local interests and coalitions of often bitterly opposed factions.

State parties are also important in national politics because of the **unit rule,** which awards electoral votes in presidential elections as an indivisible bloc (except in Maine and Nebraska). Presidential candidates concentrate their efforts in states in which voter preferences seem to be evenly divided or in which large numbers of electoral votes are at stake.

State Central Committee
The principal organized structure of each political party within each state. This committee is responsible for carrying out policy decisions of the party's state convention.

Unit Rule
A rule by which all of a state's electoral votes are cast for the presidential candidate receiving a plurality of the popular vote in that state.

Local Party Machinery: The Grassroots

The lowest layer of party machinery is the local organization, supported by district leaders, precinct or ward captains, and party workers. Much of the work is coordinated by county committees and their chairpersons.

Patronage
Rewarding faithful party workers and followers with government employment and contracts.

Patronage and City Machines.   In the 1800s, the institution of **patronage**—rewarding the party faithful with government jobs or contracts—held the local organization together. For immigrants and the poor, the political machine often furnished important services and protections. The big-city machine was the archetypal example. Tammany Hall, or the Tammany Society, which dominated New York City government for nearly two centuries, was perhaps the most famous instance of this political form.

The last big-city local political machine to exercise substantial power was run by Chicago's Mayor Richard J. Daley, who was also an important figure in national Democratic politics. Daley, as mayor, ran the Chicago Democratic machine from 1955 until his death in 1976. The current mayor of Chicago, Richard M. Daley, son of the former mayor, does not have the kind of machine that his father had.

City machines are now dead, mostly because their function of providing social services (and reaping the reward of votes) has been taken over by state and national agencies. This trend began in the 1930s, when the social legislation of the New Deal established Social Security and unemployment insurance. The local party machine has little, if anything, to do with deciding who is eligible to receive these benefits.

Local Party Organizations Today.   Local political organizations, whether located in cities, in townships, or at the county level, still can contribute a great deal to local election campaigns. These organizations are able to provide the foot soldiers of politics—individuals who pass out literature and get out the vote on election day, which can be crucial in local elections. In many regions, local Democratic and Republican organizations still exercise some patronage, such as awarding courthouse jobs, contracts for street repair, and other lucrative construction contracts. The constitutionality of awarding—or not awarding—contracts on the basis of

Florida Democratic Party chairperson Scott Maddox holds a voter registration form during a campaign to enroll university students. In past elections, younger citizens have not voted as often as older ones. What might have been the reasons? (AP Photo/Steve Cannon)

political affiliation has been subject to challenge, however. The Supreme Court has ruled that failing to hire or firing individuals because of their political affiliation is an infringement of the employees' First Amendment rights to free expression.[9] Local party organizations are also the most important vehicles for recruiting young adults into political work, because political involvement at the local level offers activists many opportunities to gain experience.

The Party-in-Government

After the election is over and the winners are announced, the focus of party activity shifts from getting out the vote to organizing and controlling the government. As you will see in Chapter 11, party membership plays an important role in the day-to-day operations of Congress, with partisanship determining everything from office space to committee assignments and power on Capitol Hill. For the president, the political party furnishes the pool of qualified applicants for political appointments to run the government. (Although it is uncommon to do so, presidents can and occasionally do appoint executive personnel, such as cabinet members, from the opposition party.) As we will note in Chapter 12, there are not as many of these appointed positions as presidents might like, and presidential power is limited by the permanent bureaucracy. Judicial appointments also offer a great opportunity to the winning party. For the most part, presidents are likely to appoint federal judges from their own party.

Republican National Committee chairman Ed Gillespie unveils a fifty-six-foot eighteen-wheeler that the Republicans used to register voters across the country. The Republicans hoped to register one million voters with the vehicle, named "Reggie the Registration Rig." (AP Photo/Evan Vucci)

Divided Government.   All of these party appointments suggest that the winning political party, whether at the national, state, or local level, has a great deal of control in the American system. Because of the checks and balances and the relative lack of cohesion in American parties, however, such control is an illusion. One reason is that for some time many Americans have seemed to prefer a **divided government**, with the executive and legislative branches controlled by different parties. The trend toward **ticket splitting**—splitting votes between the president and members of Congress—has increased sharply since 1952. This practice may indicate a lack of trust in government or the relative weakness of party identification among many voters. Voters have often seemed comfortable with having a president affiliated with one party and a Congress controlled by the other.

The Limits of Party Unity.   There are other ways in which the power of the parties is limited. Consider how major laws are passed in Congress. Traditionally, legislation has rarely been passed by a vote strictly along party lines. Although most Democrats may oppose a bill, for example, some Democrats may vote for it. Their votes, combined with the votes of Republicans, may be enough to pass the bill. Similarly, support from some Republicans may enable a bill sponsored by the Democrats to pass. This is not to say that Congress *never* votes along strict party lines. A notable example of such partisan voting occurred in the House of Representatives in 1998. The

Divided Government

A situation in which one major political party controls the presidency and the other controls the chambers of Congress, or in which one party controls a state governorship and the other controls the state legislature.

Ticket Splitting

Voting for candidates of two or more parties for different offices. For example, a voter splits her ticket if she votes for a Republican presidential candidate and for a Democratic congressional candidate.

---

[9]*Rutan v. Republican Party of Illinois*, 497 U.S. 62 (1990).

Safe Seat
A district that returns the legislator with 55 percent of the vote or more.

issue at hand was whether to impeach President Bill Clinton. Almost all votes were strictly along party lines—Democrats against, and Republicans for.

One reason that the political parties find it so hard to rally all of their members in Congress to vote along party lines is that parties in this country do not have a "boss system." In other words, the head of a political party in most instances cannot handpick candidates who share his or her views and who will be beholden to that boss and to that party. In America, the candidates who win most elections largely do so on their own, without significant help from a political party. An individual generally gains a nomination through her or his own hard work and personal political organization. This means, though, that the parties have very little control over the candidates who run under the party labels. In fact, a candidate could run as a Republican, for example, and advocate beliefs repugnant to the national party, such as racism. No one in the Republican Party organization could stop this person from being nominated or even elected.

Party Polarization.   Despite the forces that act against party-line voting, there have been times when the two parties in Congress have been polarized, and defections from the party line have been rare. One such period was the mid-1990s, after the Republicans gained control of both the House and the Senate. Under House Speaker Newt Gingrich, the Republicans maintained strict discipline in an attempt to use their new majority to sponsor a specific legislative agenda. In 2003, polarization peaked again. "People genuinely hate each other," lamented Louisiana senator John Breaux, a moderate Democrat.[10]

One cause of polarization is the use of sophisticated computer programs to create House districts that are "safe" for each party. A safe Republican district, for example, would contain such a large share of Republican voters that no Democratic candidate would have a chance of winning. (You will learn more about congressional redistricting in Chapter 11.) With **safe seats,** Republicans and Democrats alike find it advantageous to appeal to their party's most committed supporters, rather than to independents. The close party division in Congress also enhances the spirit of political competition.

Writers and advocates in the media, who find that stridency sells, also tend to encourage an atmosphere of polarization. Some commentators, however, do not believe that this spirit of polarization extends very far into the general electorate. They contend that a majority of Americans are strongly committed to tolerance of opposing political views.[11]

★ Why Has the Two-Party System Endured?

There are several reasons why two major parties have dominated the political landscape in the United States for almost two centuries. These reasons have to do with (1) the historical foundations of the system, (2) political socialization and practical considerations, (3) the winner-take-all electoral system, and (4) state and federal laws favoring the two-party system.

The Historical Foundations of the Two-Party System

As we have seen, at many times in American history there has been one preeminent issue or dispute that divided the nation politically. In the beginning, Americans were at odds over ratifying the Constitution. After the Constitution went into effect, the power of the federal government became the major national issue.

---

[10]Jackie Calmes, "Set This House on Fire," *The Wall Street Journal Europe,* December 1, 2003, p. A7.
[11]Robert J. Samuelson, "Polarization Myths," *The Washington Post,* December 3, 2003, p. A29.

Thereafter, the dispute over slavery divided the nation by section, North versus South. At times—for example, in the North after the Civil War—cultural differences have been important, with advocates of government-sponsored morality (such as banning alcoholic beverages) pitted against advocates of personal liberty.

During much of the 1900s, economic differences were preeminent. In the New Deal period, the Democrats became known as the party of the working class, while the Republicans became known as the party of the middle and upper classes and commercial interests.

When politics is based on an argument between two opposing points of view, advocates of each viewpoint can mobilize most effectively by forming a single, unified party. Also, when a two-party system has been in existence for almost two centuries, it becomes difficult to imagine an alternative.

Political Socialization and Practical Considerations

Given that the majority of Americans identify with one of the two major political parties, it is not surprising that most children learn at a fairly young age to think of themselves as either Democrats or Republicans. This generates a built-in mechanism to perpetuate a two-party system. Also, many politically oriented people who aspire to work for social change consider that the only realistic way to capture political power in this country is to be either a Republican or a Democrat.

The Winner-Take-All Electoral System

At virtually every level of government in the United States, the outcome of elections is based on the **plurality**, winner-take-all principle. In a plurality system, the winner is the person who obtains the most votes, even if that person does not receive a majority (over 50 percent) of the votes. Whoever gets the most votes gets everything. Most legislators in the United States are elected from single-member districts in which only one person represents the constituency, and the candidate who finishes second in such an election receives nothing for the effort.

Plurality
A number of votes cast for a candidate that is greater than the number of votes for any other candidate but not necessarily a majority.

Presidential Voting. The winner-take-all system also operates in the election of the U.S president. Recall that the voters in each state do not vote for a president directly but vote for **electoral college** delegates who are committed to the various presidential candidates. These delegates are called *electors*.

In all but two states (Maine and Nebraska), if a presidential candidate wins a plurality in the state, then *all* of the state's votes go to that candidate. For example, let us say that the electors pledged to a particular presidential candidate receive a plurality of 40 percent of the votes in a state. That presidential candidate will receive all of the state's votes in the electoral college. Minor parties have a difficult time competing under such a system. Because voters know that minor parties cannot win any electoral votes, they often will not vote for minor-party candidates, even if the candidates are in tune with them ideologically.

Electoral College
A group of persons, called electors, who are selected by the voters in each state. This group officially elects the president and the vice president of the United States.

Popular Election of the Governors and the President. In most of Europe, the chief executive (usually called the prime minister) is elected by the legislature, or parliament. If the parliament contains three or more parties, as is usually the case, two or more of the parties can join together in a coalition to choose the prime minister and the other leaders of the government. In the United States, however, the people elect the president and the governors of all fifty states. There is no opportunity for two or more parties to negotiate a coalition. Here, too, the winner-take-all principle discriminates powerfully against any third party.

Proportional Representation.   Many other nations use a system of proportional representation with multimember districts. If, during the national election, party X obtains 12 percent of the vote, party Y gets 43 percent of the vote, and party Z gets the remaining 45 percent of the vote, then party X gets 12 percent of the seats in the legislature, party Y gets 43 percent of the seats, and party Z gets 45 percent of the seats. Because even a minor party may still obtain at least a few seats in the legislature, the smaller parties have a greater incentive to organize under such electoral systems than they do in the United States.

The relative effects of proportional representation versus our system of single-member districts are so strong that many scholars have made them one of the few "laws" of political science. "Duverger's Law," named after French political scientist Maurice Duverger, states that electoral systems based on single-member districts tend to produce two parties, while systems of proportional representation produce multiple parties.[12] Still, many countries with single-member districts have more than two political parties—Britain and Canada are examples. (The question of what American elections would be like if the United States had a multiparty system was addressed in the *What If . . .* feature that opened this chapter.)

State and Federal Laws Favoring the Two Parties

Many state and federal election laws offer a clear advantage to the two major parties. In some states, the established major parties need to gather fewer signatures to place their candidates on the ballot than minor parties or independent candidates do. The criterion for determining how many signatures will be required is often based on the total party vote in the last general election, thus penalizing a new political party that did not compete in that election.

At the national level, minor parties face different obstacles. All of the rules and procedures of both houses of Congress divide committee seats, staff members, and other privileges on the basis of party membership. A legislator who is elected on a minor-party ticket, such as the Conservative Party of New York, must choose to be counted with one of the major parties to obtain a committee assignment. The Federal Election Commission (FEC) rules for campaign financing also place restrictions on minor-party candidates. Such candidates are not eligible for federal matching funds in either the primary or the general election. In the 1980 election, John Anderson, running for president as an independent, sued the FEC for campaign funds. The commission finally agreed to repay part of his campaign costs after the election in proportion to the votes he received. Giving funds to a candidate when the campaign is over is, of course, much less helpful than providing funds while the campaign is still under way.

 The Role of Minor Parties in U.S. Politics

For the reasons just discussed, minor parties have a difficult, if not impossible, time competing within the American two-party political system. Nonetheless, minor parties have played an important role in our political life. Parties other than the Republicans or Democrats are usually called **third parties.** (Technically, of course, there could be fourth, fifth, or sixth parties as well, but we use the term *third party* because it has endured.) Third parties can come into existence in a number of ways. They may be founded from scratch by individuals or groups who are committed to a particular interest, issue, or ideology. They can split off from one of the major parties when a group becomes dissatisfied with the major party's

Third Party
A political party other than the two major political parties (Republican and Democratic).

---

[12]As cited in Todd Landman, *Issues and Methods in Comparative Politics* (New York: Routledge, 2003), page 14.

Jill Stein, the Green Party candidate for governor of Massachusetts, meets supporters outside the first debate between gubernatorial candidates in 2002. Stein was not allowed to participate in the debate with the Democratic and Republican candidates. What criteria should be used to determine whether third-party candidates can participate in debates? (AP Photo/Steven Senne)

policies. Finally, they can be organized around a particular charismatic leader and serve as that person's vehicle for contesting elections.

Frequently, third parties have acted as barometers of changes in the political mood. Such barometric indicators have forced the major parties to recognize new issues or trends in the thinking of Americans. Political scientists also believe that third parties have acted as safety valves for dissident groups, perhaps preventing major confrontations and political unrest. In some instances, third parties have functioned as way stations for voters en route from one of the major parties to the other. Table 8–2 lists significant third-party presidential campaigns in American history; Table 8–3 (page 274) provides a brief description of third-party beliefs.

Ideological Third Parties

The longest-lived third parties have been those with strong ideological foundations that are typically at odds with the majority mind-set. The Socialist Party is

TABLE 8–2

The Most Successful Third-Party Presidential Campaigns since 1864

The following list includes all third-party candidates winning over 5 percent of the popular vote or any electoral votes since 1864. (We ignore isolated "unfaithful electors" in the electoral college who fail to vote for the candidate to which they are pledged.)

Year	Major Third Party	Third-Party Presidential Candidate	Percent of of the Popular Vote	Electoral Votes	Winning Presidential Candidate and Party
1892	Populist	James Weaver	8.5	22	Grover Cleveland (D)
1912	Progressive	Theodore Roosevelt	27.4	88	Woodrow Wilson (D)
	Socialist	Eugene Debs	6.0	—	
1924	Progressive	Robert LaFollette	16.6	13	Calvin Coolidge (R)
1948	States' Rights	Strom Thurmond	2.4	39	Harry Truman (D)
1960	Independent Democrat	Harry Byrd	0.4	15*	John Kennedy (D)
1968	American Independent	George Wallace	13.5	46	Richard Nixon (R)
1980	National Union	John Anderson	6.6	—	Ronald Reagan (R)
1992	Independent	Ross Perot	18.9	—	Bill Clinton (D)
1996	Reform	Ross Perot	8.4	—	Bill Clinton (D)

*Byrd received fifteen electoral votes from unpledged electors in Alabama and Mississippi.
SOURCE: *Dave Leip's Atlas of U.S. Presidential Elections*, at http://www.uselectionatlas.org.

TABLE 8–3

Policies of Selected American Third Parties since 1864

Populist: This pro-farmer party of the 1890s advocated progressive reforms. It also advocated replacing gold with silver as the basis of the currency in hopes of creating a mild inflation in prices. (It was believed by many that inflation would help debtors and stimulate the economy.)

Socialist: This party advocated a "cooperative commonwealth" based on government ownership of industry. It was pro-labor, often antiwar, and in later years, anticommunist. It was dissolved in 1972 and replaced by nonparty advocacy groups (Democratic Socialists of America and Social Democrats USA).

Communist: This left-wing breakaway from the Socialists was the U.S. branch of the worldwide communist movement. The party was pro-labor and advocated full equality for African Americans. It was also slavishly devoted to the communist-led Soviet Union, which provoked great hostility among most Americans.

Progressive: This name was given to several successive splinter parties built around individual political leaders. Theodore Roosevelt, who ran in 1912, advocated federal regulation of industry to protect consumers, workers, and small businesses. Robert LaFollette, who ran in 1924, held similar viewpoints.

American Independent: Built around George Wallace, this party opposed any further promotion of civil rights and advocated a militant foreign policy. Wallace's supporters were mostly former Democrats who were soon to be Republicans.

Libertarian: This party opposes most government activity.

Reform: The Reform Party was built initially around businessman Ross Perot but later was taken over by others. Under Perot, the party was a middle-of-the-road group opposed to federal budget deficits. Under Patrick Buchanan, it came to represent right-wing nationalism and opposition to free trade.

Green: The Greens are a left-of-center pro-environmental party; they are also generally hostile to globalization.

an example. The party was founded in 1901 and lasted until 1972, when it was finally dissolved. (A smaller party later took up the name.)

Ideology has at least two functions. First, the members of the minor party regard themselves as outsiders and look to one another for support; ideology provides great psychological cohesiveness. Second, because the rewards of ideological commitment are partly psychological, these minor parties do not think in terms of immediate electoral success. A poor showing at the polls therefore does not dissuade either the leadership or the grassroots participants from continuing their quest for change in American government (and, ultimately, American society).

Currently active ideological parties include the Libertarian Party and the Green Party. As you learned in Chapter 1, the Libertarian Party supports a *laissez-faire* ("let it be") capitalist economic program, together with a hands-off policy on regulating matters of moral conduct. The Green Party began as a grassroots environmentalist organization with affiliated political parties across North America and Western Europe. It was established in the United States as a national party in 1996 and nominated Ralph Nader to run for president in 2000. Nader campaigned against what he called "corporate greed," advocated universal health insurance, and promoted environmental concerns.[13] He ran again for president as an independent in 2004.

---

[13]Ralph Nader offers his own entertaining account of his run for the presidency in 2000 in *Crashing the Party: How to Tell the Truth and Still Run for President* (New York: St. Martin's Press, 2002).

Independent presidential candidate Ralph Nader (shown here) and former candidate Howard Dean debated the legitimacy of third-party campaigns in July 2004. After Dean's own bid for the presidency failed, the former Vermont governor became the Democratic Party's leading critic of Nader's campaign. What might have happened if Dean himself had mounted a third-party effort, as some of his supporters wished? (REUTERS/Molly Riley/Landov)

Splinter Parties

Some of the most successful minor parties have been those that split from major parties. The impetus for these **splinter parties**, or factions, has usually been a situation in which a particular personality was at odds with the major party. The most successful of these splinter parties was the Bull Moose Progressive Party, formed in 1912 to support Theodore Roosevelt for president. The Republican national convention of that year denied Roosevelt the nomination, despite the fact that he had won most of the primaries. He therefore left the Republicans and ran against Republican "regular" William Howard Taft in the general election. Although Roosevelt did not win the election, he did split the Republican vote so that Democrat Woodrow Wilson became president.

Third parties have also been formed to back individual candidates who were not rebelling against a particular party. Ross Perot, for example, who challenged Republican George H. W. Bush and Democrat Bill Clinton in 1992, had not previously been active in a major party. Perot's supporters, likewise, probably would have split their votes between Bush and Clinton had Perot not been in the race. In theory, Perot ran in 1992 as a nonparty independent; in practice, he had to create a campaign organization. By 1996, Perot's organization was formalized as the Reform Party.

Splinter Party
A new party formed by a dissident faction within a major political party. Often, splinter parties have emerged when a particular personality was at odds with the major party.

The Impact of Minor Parties

Third parties have rarely been able to affect American politics by actually winning elections. (One exception is that third-party and independent candidates have occasionally won races for state governorships—for example, Jesse Ventura was elected governor of Minnesota on the Reform Party ticket in 1998.) Instead, the impact of third parties has taken two forms. First, third parties can influence one of the major parties to take up one or more issues. Second, third parties can determine the outcome of a particular election by pulling votes from one of the major-party candidates in what is called the "spoiler effect."

Influencing the Major Parties. One of the most clear-cut examples of a major party adopting the issues of a minor party took place in 1896, when the Democratic

Theodore Roosevelt, president of the United States from 1901 to 1909, became president after William McKinley was assassinated. Roosevelt was reelected in 1904. In 1912, unable to gain the nomination of the Republican Party, Roosevelt formed a splinter group named the Bull Moose Progressive Party but was unsuccessful in his effort to regain the presidency. (The National Archives)

Party took over the Populist demand for "free silver"—that is, a policy of coining enough new money to create an inflation. As you learned on pages 255 and 256, however, absorbing the Populists cost the Democrats votes overall.

Affecting the Outcome of an Election. The presidential election of 2000 was one instance in which a minor party may have altered the outcome. Green candidate Ralph Nader received almost one hundred thousand votes in Florida, a majority of which would probably have gone to Democrat Al Gore if Nader had not been in the race. The real question, however, is not whether Nader's vote had an effect—clearly, it did—but whether the effect was important.

The problem is that in an election as close as the presidential election of 2000, *any* factor with an impact on the outcome can be said to have determined the results of the election. Discussing his landslide loss to Democrat Lyndon Johnson in 1964, Republican Barry Goldwater wrote, "When you've lost an election by that much, it isn't the case of whether you made the wrong speech or wore the wrong necktie. It was just the wrong time."[14] With the opposite situation, a humorist might speculate that Gore would have won the election had he worn a better tie! Nevertheless, given that Nader garnered almost three million votes nationwide, many people believe that the Nader campaign was an important reason for Gore's loss. Should voters ignore third parties to avoid spoiling the chances of a preferred major-party candidate? We discuss this question in this chapter's *Which Side Are You On?* feature.

---

[14] Barry Goldwater, *With No Apologies* (New York: William Morrow, 1979).

WHICH SIDE ARE YOU ON?
Should Voters Ignore Third-Party Candidates?

Many people argue that if Green Party presidential candidate Ralph Nader had not run in 2000, a majority of his votes would have gone to Democrat Al Gore. In turn, Gore would have defeated Republican George W. Bush. But did Green voters "shoot themselves in the foot" by not supporting Gore, who was arguably the "greenest" major-party presidential candidate in U.S. history?

VOTERS SHOULD VOTE THEIR CONSCIENCES, REGARDLESS

Third-party advocates claim that a vote for their candidate is the only way to bring new issues into the national debate. The major-party candidates, fearful of offending any large constituency, will always blur the issues and avoid controversy. Furthermore, why should anyone assume that third-party voters would support a particular major-party candidate if the third party were not in the race? It is just as likely that these voters would stay home if no candidate represented their beliefs.

Voters should consider how close either of the two major candidates is to the positions they prefer. Gore may have been a rather green Democrat, but what if the Libertarian Party truly represents your beliefs? Bush, Gore, and 2004 Democratic candidate John Kerry were all a long way from having a libertarian philosophy.

A final point is that not all elections are close. In 2004, third-party voters in Massachusetts knew that Kerry was sure to carry his home state, and everyone knew that nothing could keep Texas from going for Bush. In these states, third-party supporters could vote for their preferred candidate secure in the knowledge that their votes would not affect the election outcome.

ACTIONS SHOULD BE JUDGED BY THEIR CONSEQUENCES

Third-party opponents argue that pure intentions may get you into heaven, but elections are a part of this world. Nader supporters cannot escape the simple truth that they helped elect Bush in 2000. Furthermore, backing the Green Party was not necessary to get environmental concerns onto the table. Gore's 1992 book, *Earth in the Balance: Ecology and the Human Spirit,** was so controversial that it may have done his campaign as much damage as Nader was able to inflict. Instead of getting Gore, the Greens got

In February 2004, a Nader supporter had harsh words with a demonstrator who wanted Nader to stay out of the 2004 presidential race. Later that year, Nader failed to win the nomination of the Green Party but continued to run as an independent. What effect, if any, could Nader's failure to win the nomination have had on those who where considering whether to support him? (REUTERS/Jonathan Ernst/Landov)

Bush, who wanted to open new federally owned lands for logging and oil drilling, who opposed many steps to address global warming, and who sought to roll back some pollution-control standards for the benefit of industry.

WHAT'S YOUR POSITION?

Should voters support a third-party candidate even if they prefer one of the major-party candidates to the other? What considerations should such a voter take into account?

GOING ONLINE

Anyone who is contemplating a vote for a third party should first learn what that party believes. Visiting the party's Web site is a good place to begin. You can find the Green Party at **http://www.gp.org** and the Libertarian Party at **http://www.lp.org**. You can find a comprehensive list of parties and partylike organizations at **http://www. politics1.com/parties.htm**.

*Albert Gore, Jr., *Earth in the Balance: Ecology and the Human Spirit* (1992; repr., New York: Houghton Mifflin Co., 2000).

⬟ Mechanisms of Political Change

What does the twenty-first century hold for the Democrats and the Republicans? Support for the two major parties is roughly balanced today. In the future, could one of the two parties decisively overtake the other and become the "natural party of government"? The Republicans held this status from 1896 until 1932, and the Democrats enjoyed it for many years after the election of Franklin D. Roosevelt in 1932. Not surprisingly, political advisers in both parties dream of circumstances that could grant them lasting political hegemony, or dominance.

Realignment

Realignment
A process in which a substantial group of voters switches party allegiance, producing a long-term change in the political landscape.

One mechanism by which a party might gain dominance is called **realignment.** In this process, major constituencies shift their allegiance from one party to another, creating a long-term alteration in the political environment. Realignment has often been associated with particular elections, called *realigning elections.* The election of 1896, which established a Republican ascendancy, was clearly a realigning election. So was the election of 1932, which made the Democrats the leading party.

Realignment: The Myth of Dominance. A number of myths have grown up around the concept of realignment. One is that in realignment, a newly dominant party must replace the previously dominant party. Actually, realignment could easily strengthen an already dominant party. Alternatively, realignment could result in a tie. This has happened—twice. One example was the realignment of the 1850s, which resulted in Abraham Lincoln's election as president in 1860. After the Civil War, the Republicans and the Democrats were almost evenly matched nationally.

The most recent realignment—which also resulted in two closely matched parties—has sometimes been linked to the election of 1968. Actually, the realignment was a gradual process that took place over many years. In 1968, Democrat Hubert Humphrey, Republican Richard Nixon, and third-party candidate George Wallace of Alabama all vied for the presidency. Following the Republican victory in that election, Nixon adopted a "southern strategy" aimed at drawing dissatisfied southern Democrats into the Republican Party.[15] At the presidential level, the strategy was an immediate success, although years would pass before the Republicans could gain dominance in the South's delegation to Congress or in state legislatures. Nixon's southern strategy helped create the political environment in which we live today. Another milestone in the progress of the Republicans was Ronald Reagan's sweeping victory in the presidential election of 1980.

Realignment: The Myth of Predictability. A second myth concerning realignments is that they take place, like clockwork, every thirty-six years. Supposedly, there were realigning elections in 1860, 1896, 1932, and 1968, and therefore 2004 must have been a year for realignment. No such event appears to have taken place. In fact, there is no force that could cause political realignments at precise thirty-six-year intervals. Further, as we observed earlier in this section, realignments are not always tied to particular elections. The most recent realignment, in which conservative southern Democrats became conservative southern Republicans, was not closely linked to a particular election. The realignment of the 1850s, following the creation of the modern Republican Party, also took place over a number of years.

---

[15]The classic work on Nixon's southern strategy is Kirkpatrick Sales, *The Emerging Republican Majority* (New Rochelle, N.Y.: Arlington House, 1969).

Is Realignment Still Possible?   The nature of American political parties created the pattern of realignment in American history. The sheer size of the country, combined with the inexorable pressure toward a two-party system, resulted in parties made up of voters with conflicting interests or values. The pre–Civil War party system involved two parties—Whigs and Democrats—with support in both the North and the South. This system could survive only by burying, as deeply as possible, the issue of slavery. We should not be surprised that the structure eventually collapsed. The Republican ascendancy of 1896–1932 united capitalists and industrial workers under the Republican banner, despite serious economic conflicts between the two. The New Deal Democratic coalition after 1932 brought African Americans and ardent segregationists into the same party.

For realignment to occur, a substantial body of citizens must come to believe that their party can no longer represent their interests or values. The problem must be fundamental and not attributable to the behavior of an individual politician. It is not easy to identify groups of Republicans or Democrats today who might reach such a conclusion. Despite the confusion that the major parties sometimes display on policy matters, the values that unite each party are relatively coherent, and their constituents are reasonably compatible. Therefore, the current party system should be more stable than in the past, and a major realignment is not likely to take place in the foreseeable future.

Dealignment

Among political scientists, one common argument has been that realignment is no longer likely because voters are not as committed to the two major parties as they were in the 1800s and early 1900s. In this view, called **dealignment** theory, large numbers of independent voters may result in political volatility, but the absence of strong partisan attachments means that it is no longer easy to "lock in" political preferences for decades.

Independent Voters.   Figure 8–5 shows trends in **party identification,** as measured by standard polling techniques from 1937 to the present. The chart displays a rise in the number of independent voters throughout the period combined with a

Dealignment
A decline in party loyalties that reduces long-term party commitment.

Party Identification
Linking oneself to a particular political party.

FIGURE 8–5

Party Identification from 1937 to the Present

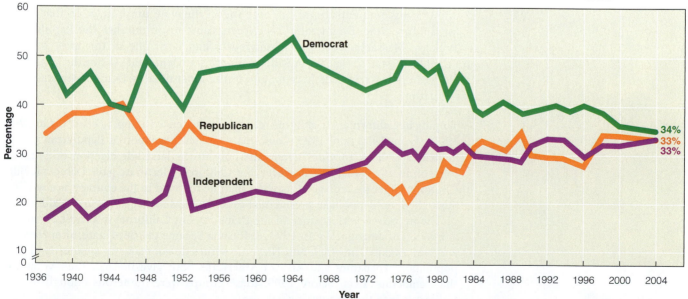

SOURCES: *Gallup Report,* August 1995; *New York Times*/CBS poll, June 1996; *Gallup Report,* February 1998; The Pew Research Center for the People and the Press, November 2003; and authors' update.

fall in support for the Democrats from the mid-1960s on. The decline in Democratic identification may be due to the consolidation of Republican support in the South since 1968, a process that by now may be substantially complete. In any event, the traditional Democratic advantage in party identification has vanished.

Not only has the number of independents grown over the last half-century, but voters are also less willing to vote a straight ticket—that is, to vote for all the candidates of one party. In the early 1900s, **straight-ticket voting** was nearly universal. By midcentury, 12 percent of voters engaged in ticket splitting. In recent presidential elections, between 20 and 40 percent of the voters engaged in split-ticket voting. This trend, along with the increase in the number of voters who call themselves independents, suggests that parties have lost much of their hold on the loyalty of the voters.

Not-So-Independent Voters.   A problem with dealignment theory is that many "independent" voters are not all that independent. Polling organizations estimate that of the 33 percent of voters who identify themselves as independents, 11 percent vote as if they were Democrats in almost all elections, and 12 percent vote as if they were Republicans. If these "leaners" are deducted from the independent category, only 10 percent of the voters remain. These true independents are **swing voters**—they can swing back and forth between the parties. These voters are important in deciding elections. Some analysts believe, however, that swing voters are far less numerous today than they were two or three decades ago.

Tipping

Realignment is not the only mechanism that can alter the political landscape. Political transformation can also result from changes in the composition of the electorate. Even when groups of voters never change their party preferences, if one group becomes more numerous over time, it can become dominant for that reason alone. We call this kind of demographically based change **tipping**. Immigration is one cause of this phenomenon.

Tipping in Massachusetts.   Consider Massachusetts, where for generations Irish Catholics confronted Protestant Yankees in the political arena. Most of the Yankees were Republican; most of the Irish were Democrats. The Yankees were numerically dominant from the founding of the state until 1928. In that year, for the first time, Democratic Irish voters came to outnumber the Republican Yankees. Massachusetts, which previously had been one of the most solidly Republican states, cast its presidential vote for Democrat Al Smith. Within a few years, Massachusetts became one of the most reliably Democratic states in the nation.

Tipping in California?   California may have experienced a tipping effect during the 1990s. From 1952 until 1992, California consistently supported Republican presidential candidates, turning Democratic only in the landslide election of Lyndon Johnson in 1964. In 1992, however, the California electorate gave Democrat Bill Clinton a larger percentage of its votes than he received in the country as a whole. Since then, no Republican presidential candidate has managed to carry California.

The improved performance of the Democrats in California is almost certainly a function of demography. In 1999, California became the third state, after Hawaii and New Mexico, in which non-Hispanic whites do *not* make up a majority of the population. Hispanics and African Americans both give most of their votes to the Democrats. Even before 1999, these groups were numerous enough to tip California into the Democratic column.

Straight-Ticket Voting
Voting exclusively for the candidates of one party.

Swing Voters
Voters who frequently swing their support from one party to another.

Tipping
A phenomenon that occurs when a group that is becoming more numerous over time grows large enough to change the political balance in a district, state, or country.

On to the Future

Some speculation about the future is reasonable, as long as we remember that unexpected events can make any prediction obsolete. We can anticipate that party advocates will continue to hope that events will propel their party into a dominant position. Either party could lose substantial support if it were identified with a major economic disaster. Noneconomic events could have an impact as well.

Republican strategists will seek to encourage substantial numbers of voters to abandon the Democrats, perhaps on the basis of cultural issues. Some of these strategists believe that the relative conservatism of Hispanic Americans on cultural matters may provide an opening for the Republicans. (The 2004 elections were encouraging—44 percent of Hispanic voters picked Bush.) Others point to the increasing numbers of Americans with investments in the stock market as a possible indicator of growing economic conservatism. Finally, Republicans look at the decline in Democratic Party identification since the 1960s (see Figure 8–5 on page 279) and project that trend into the future.

Democratic strategists hope that the tolerant spirit of many younger voters (in attitudes toward gay rights, for example) may work to their advantage. Hispanic voters are of interest to the Democrats as well. Demographic changes have turned once reliably Republican states such as Florida into swing states that can decide national elections. As noted in Chapter 1, some time after 2015, Texas—now among the most Republican states—will no longer have a non-Hispanic white majority. If the Republicans do not succeed in detaching Hispanics from the Democratic Party, Texas could eventually tip into the Democratic column and possibly tip the country as a whole to the Democrats as well.

★ Political Parties: Why Are They Important Today?

Although party machines no longer dominate local politics in our major cities, political parties remain important to you today. The party in power ends up with most of the important leadership positions in Congress. Therefore, a political party's electoral success may lead to new laws and regulations that affect your daily life. You may pay higher or lower taxes, face greater or fewer employment opportunities, or experience changes in the social environment around you—all depending on which political party prevailed in the last election.

With our two-party system, the political parties are also important because they impart stability to our government, a stability that is unknown in many parts of the world. While one party (the "in" party) governs, the other party (the "out" party) continues to present alternatives. The out party acts as the "loyal opposition," making sure that the party in power is unable to do something wildly out of line with what Americans want. Even though the Republicans controlled both chambers of Congress and the presidency after the 2004 elections, their margin of control in Congress was not large. This meant that they had somewhat limited room in which to maneuver.

Congress and most state legislatures organize themselves by party. Therefore, a newly elected legislator, even one who claims to be independent, must ally herself or himself with one of the two major parties to obtain seats on committees and even office space. If, at some future date, a political movement were to arise that could challenge the dominance of the two major parties, that movement would have to organize as a party if it wished to participate in running the government. Therefore, political parties remain essential to the political system today.

★★★★★★★★★★★★★★★★★★

DID YOU KNOW . . .

That 72 percent of Americans between the ages of eighteen and twenty-nine favor the formation of a third political party❓

MAKING A DIFFERENCE

★ Electing Convention Delegates

The most exciting political party event, staged every four years, is the national convention. State conventions also take place on a regular basis. Surprising as it might seem, there are opportunities for the individual voter to become involved in nominating delegates to a state or national convention or to become a delegate.

Why Should You Care?

How would you like to exercise a small amount of real political power yourself—power that goes beyond simply voting in an election? You might be able to become a delegate to a county, district, or even state party convention. Many of these conventions nominate candidates for various offices. For example, in Michigan, the state party conventions nominate the candidates for the Board of Regents of the state's three top public universities. The regents set university policies, so these are nominations in which students have an obvious interest. In Michigan, if you are elected as a party precinct delegate, you can attend your party's state convention.

In much of the country, there are more openings for party precinct delegates than there are people willing to serve. In such circumstances, almost anyone can become a delegate by collecting a handful of signatures on a nominating petition or by mounting a small-scale write-in campaign. You are then eligible to take part in one of the most educational political experiences available to an ordinary citizen. You will get a firsthand look at how political persuasion takes place, how resolutions are written and passed, and how candidates seek out support

among their fellow party members. In some states, party caucuses bring debate even closer to the grassroots level.

What Can You Do?

When the parties choose delegates for the national convention, the process begins at the local level—either the congressional district or the state legislative district. Delegates may be elected in party primary elections or chosen in neighborhood or precinct caucuses.

If the delegates are elected in a primary, persons who want to run for these positions must first file petitions with the board of elections. If you are interested in committing yourself to a particular presidential candidate and running for the delegate position, check with the local county committee or with the party's national committee about the rules you must follow.

It is even easier to get involved in the grassroots politics of presidential caucuses. In some states—Iowa being the earliest and most famous example—delegates are first nominated at the local precinct caucus. According to the rules of the Iowa caucuses, anyone can participate in a caucus if he or she is eighteen years old, a resident of the precinct, and registered as a party member. These caucuses, in addition to being the focus of national media attention in January or February, select delegates to the county conventions who are pledged to specific presidential candidates. This is the first step toward the national convention.

At both the county caucus and the convention levels, both parties try to find younger members to fill some of the seats. Contact the state or county political party to find out when the caucuses or primaries will be held. Then gather local supporters and friends, and prepare to join in an occasion during which political debate is at its best.

For further information about these opportunities (some states hold caucuses and state conventions in every election year), contact the state party office or your local state legislator for specific dates and regulations. You can also write to the national committee for information on how to become a delegate.

Republican National Committee
Republican National Headquarters
310 First St. S.E.
Washington, DC 20003
202-863-8500
http://www.rnc.org

Democratic National Committee
Democratic National Headquarters
430 Capital St. S.E.
Washington, DC 20003
202-863-8000
**http://www.democrats.org/
index.html**

Key Terms

dealignment 279	national convention 264	political party 251	swing voters 280
Democratic Party 254	party identification 279	realignment 278	third party 272
divided government 269	party-in-government 264	Republican Party 254	ticket splitting 269
electoral college 271	party-in-the-electorate 262	reverse-income effect 262	tipping 280
era of good feelings 254	party organization 264	safe seat 270	two-party system 252
faction 251	party platform 264	splinter party 275	unit rule 267
independent 251	patronage 268	state central committee 267	Whig Party 254
national committee 265	plurality 271	straight-ticket voting 280	

Chapter Summary

1 A political party is a group of political activists who organize to win elections, operate the government, and determine public policy. Political parties recruit candidates for public office, organize and run elections, present alternative policies to the voters, assume responsibility for operating the government, and act as the opposition to the party in power.

2 The evolution of our nation's political parties can be divided into seven periods: (a) the creation and formation of political parties from 1789 to 1816; (b) the era of one-party rule, or personal politics, from 1816 to 1828; (c) the period from Andrew Jackson's presidency to the Civil War, from 1828 to 1860; (d) the Civil War and post–Civil War period, from 1860 to 1896; (e) the Republican ascendency and progressive period, from 1896 to 1932; (f) the New Deal period, from 1932 to about 1968; and (g) the modern period, from approximately 1968 to the present.

3 A political party consists of three components: the party-in-the-electorate, the party organization, and the party-in-government. Each party component maintains linkages to the others to keep the party strong. Each level of the party—local, state, and national—has considerable autonomy. The national party organization is responsible for holding the national convention in presidential election years, writing the party platform, choosing the national committee, and conducting party business.

4 The party-in-government comprises all of the elected and appointed officeholders of a party. The linkage of party members is crucial to building support for programs among the branches and levels of government.

5 Many of the differences between the two parties date from the time of Franklin D. Roosevelt's New Deal. The Democrats have advocated government action to help labor and minorities, and the Republicans have championed self-reliance and limited government. The constituents of the two parties continue to differ. A close look at policies actually enacted in recent years, however, suggests that despite rhetoric to the contrary, both parties are committed to a large and active government. Today, cultural differences are at least as important as economic issues in determining party allegiance.

6 Two major parties have dominated the political landscape in the United States for almost two centuries. The reasons for this include (a) the historical foundations of the system, (b) political socialization and practical considerations, (c) the winner-take-all electoral system, and (d) state and federal laws favoring the two-party system. For these reasons, minor parties have found it extremely difficult to win elections.

7 Minor, or third, parties have emerged from time to time, sometimes as dissatisfied splinter groups from within major parties, and have acted as barometers of changes in the political mood. Splinter parties have emerged when a particular personality was at odds with the major party, as when Teddy Roosevelt's differences with the Republican Party resulted in the formation of the Bull Moose Progressive Party. Other minor parties, such as the Socialist Party, have formed around specific issues or ideologies. Third parties can affect the political process (even if they do not win) if major parties adopt their issues or if they determine which major party wins an election.

8 One mechanism of political change is realignment, in which major blocs of voters switch allegiance from one party to another. Realignments were manifested in the elections of 1896 and 1932. Realignment need not leave one party dominant—it can result in two parties of roughly equal strength. Some scholars speak of dealignment—that is, the loss of strong party attachments. In fact, the share of the voters who describe themselves as independents has grown since the 1930s, and the share of self-identified Democrats has shrunk since the 1960s. Many independents actually vote as if they were Democrats or Republicans, however. Demographic change can also "tip" a district or state from one party to another.

★ Selected Print and Media Resources

SUGGESTED READINGS

Black, Earl, and Merle Black. *The Rise of Southern Republicans.* Cambridge, Mass.: Belkmap Press, 2003. This book analyzes the shift in politics in the southern states over the last four decades.

Dubose, Lou, Jan Reid, and Carl M. Cannon. *Boy Genius: Karl Rove, the Brains behind the Remarkable Political Triumph of George W. Bush.* New York: PublicAffairs, 2003. Presidential advisor Karl Rove was George W. Bush's chief political strategist dating from Bush's first run for governor of Texas. In addition to describing Rove's relationship with Bush, this account details Rove's role in the political realignment that turned Texas into a reliably Republican state.

Gould, Lewis. *Grand Old Party: A History of the Republicans.* New York: Random House, 2003. A companion volume to the history of the Democrats by Jules Witcover, listed below. Gould provides a sweeping history of the Republican Party from its origins as an antislavery coalition to the present. A major theme of the work is the evolution of the Republicans from a party of active government to the more conservative party that it is today.

Green, John C., and Paul S. Hernson, eds. *Responsible Partisanship: The Evolution of American Political Parties since 1950.* Lawrence: University Press of Kansas, 2003. This collection of scholarly essays explores the roles and functions of political parties, both as parties-in-the-electorate and parties-in-government.

Judis, John B., and Ruy Teixeira. *The Emerging Democratic Majority.* New York: Scribner, 2004. The authors make the controversial argument that the Democrats will again become the largest party because they appeal to ethnic groups and professions that make up a growing share of the population.

Nader, Ralph. *Crashing the Party: How to Tell the Truth and Still Run for President.* New York: St. Martin's Press, 2002. This is Nader's own entertaining and detailed account of his run for the presidency as a Green in 2000.

Sifry, Micah L. *Spoiling for a Fight: Third-Party Politics in America.* Florence, Ky.: Routledge, 2002. The author looks closely at Ralph Nader's run for the presidency in 2000 and at the importance and potential of alternative parties in American politics and government.

Witcover, Jules. *Party of the People: A History of the Democrats.* New York: Random House, 2003. A companion volume to the history of the Republicans by Lewis Gould, listed above. Witcover describes the transformation of the Democrats from a party of limited government to a party of national authority, but he also finds a common thread that connects modern Democrats to the past—a belief in social and economic justice.

MEDIA RESOURCES

The American President—A 1995 film starring Michael Douglas as a president who must balance partisanship and friendship (Republicans in Congress promise to approve the president's crime bill only if he modifies an environmental plan sponsored by his liberal girlfriend).

The Best Man—A 1964 drama based on Gore Vidal's play of the same name. The film, which deals with political smear campaigns by presidential party nominees, focuses on political party power and ethics.

The Last Hurrah—A classic 1958 political film starring Spencer Tracy as a corrupt politician who seeks his fifth nomination for mayor of a city in New England.

A Third Choice—A film that examines America's experience with third parties and independent candidates throughout the nation's political history.

e-mocracy ★ Political Parties and the Internet

Today's political parties use the Internet to attract voters, organize campaigns, obtain campaign contributions, and the like. Voters, in turn, can go online to learn more about specific parties and their programs. Those who use the Internet for information on the parties, though, need to exercise some caution. Besides the parties' official sites, there are satirical sites mimicking the parties, sites distributing misleading information about the parties, and sites that are raising money for their own causes rather than for political parties.

Logging On

The political parties all have Web sites. The Democratic Party is online at

http://www.democrats.org

The Republican National Committee is at

http://www.rnc.org

The Libertarian Party has a Web site located at

http://www.lp.org

The Green Party of the United States can be found at

http://www.gp.org

Politics1.com offers extensive information on U.S. political parties, including the major parties and fifty minor parties. Go to

http://www.politics1.com/parties.htm

The Pew Research Center for the People and the Press offers survey data online on how the parties fared during the most recent elections, voter typology, and numerous other issues. To access this site, go to

http://people-press.org

Using InfoTrac for Political Research

A large amount of information has been published that seeks to explain the outcome of the 2004 presidential and congressional elections. As an exercise, try to determine what impact partisan and ideological preferences had on the outcome of the election. You can find relevant information by visiting InfoTrac. To access InfoTrac, go to

http://www.infotrac-college.com

Log on, go to InfoTrac College Edition, and then go to the Keyword search page. Type "party identification" into the text box and click on "Search." Read a dozen or so short articles that seem, from their titles, to be helpful in understanding the 2004 election.

ONLINE REVIEW

At **http://politicalscience.wadsworth.com/schmidt12**, you will find a free Study Guide to this book. For each chapter, there are two online quizzes to help you master the material.

• The **PoliPrep Self Study Assessment** provides a pre-test for each major section of the chapter. PoliPrep then generates a customized study plan. After you complete the study plan, a post-test evaluates your progress.

• The **Tutorial Quiz** for each chapter provides questions on the chapter contents, including the features. The questions are organized to match the major sections of the chapter.

Campaigns, Nominations, and Elections

WHAT IF . . .
We Had Public Financing for All Political Campaigns?

BACKGROUND

To run for office, most American politicians must fund their own campaigns. As campaigns become more expensive, many candidates find themselves spending more time raising donations than campaigning. In 1974, Congress created a system to fund a share of the presidential primary and general election campaigns publicly. By 2004, however, some candidates were turning down public financing because they believed they needed even more funds to win than the government could provide. (Politicians accepting public funds are not allowed to accept private support as well.)

WHAT IF WE HAD PUBLIC FINANCING FOR ALL POLITICAL CAMPAIGNS?

Recent campaign-finance reforms took aim at unregulated contributions by special interests and the political parties but did nothing to reduce the need for fund-raising by candidates themselves. Campaigns, especially those that rely on television advertising, continue to become more expensive. In addition, the entrance of millionaire contenders into the political scene means that candidates who are not as wealthy cannot raise enough funds to compete effectively. How would the character of American elections change if the government provided public funds for all campaigns for federal office—or, as is done in several European countries, if the government simply provided free television time for advertising for all candidates of major parties?

THE ISSUE OF FAIRNESS

Over the years, a number of public interest groups have advocated public financing of campaigns. Public financing would make it easier for newcomers to challenge the power of incumbent members of Congress. If challengers received as much funding as incumbents, there might be more new faces in Congress. Also, there probably would be less advertising overall in the campaign season, something many viewers would prefer. Less advertising might make it more difficult for voters to learn about candidates and issues, however.

The public financing of campaigns, though, would not be enough to stop special interest groups from buying advertising time. While the United States Supreme Court has approved a new sixty-day limit on advertisements purchased by independent groups that mention a candidate before an election, the general right to take a position on television or in the newspaper is protected by the First Amendment for all groups.

WHO WOULD PAY?

Public financing of campaigns, of course, would be paid for by the taxpayer. It is unlikely that the funding would be anywhere close to the current levels for two reasons. First, Congress would find it difficult to justify an expenditure of several billion dollars in the face of other national priorities. Second, incumbents likely would set the amount low, believing that special interests would also raise funds for them outside the system. As a result, candidates might rely on less expensive means of reaching voters, such as telemarketing and the Internet.

An alternative plan is common in Europe. Because governments everywhere own the broadcast spectrum, they can require the networks to provide free airtime to the political parties in exchange for their broadcast licenses. Many European governments impose this requirement. Naturally, American networks are strongly against this idea.

FOR CRITICAL ANALYSIS

1. *What are the potential benefits of changing the electoral system through public financing?*
2. *Even if campaigns were financed publicly, what would prevent interest groups from raising funds for campaigns on an independent basis?*

Free elections are the cornerstone of the American political system. Voters choose one candidate over another to hold political office by casting ballots in local, state, and federal elections. In 2004, the voters chose George W. Bush and Dick Cheney to be president and vice president of the United States for the next four years. In addition, voters elected all of the members of the House of Representatives and one-third of the members of the Senate. The campaigns were bitter, long, and extremely expensive. The total cost for all federal elections in the 2003–2004 cycle was well into the billions of dollars.

Voters and candidates frequently criticize the American electoral process. It is said to favor wealthier candidates, to further the aims of special interest groups, and to be dominated by older voters and those with better education and higher income. Recent reforms of the campaign-finance laws were tested for the first time in 2004. Although the new laws had some effect on campaign strategy, fund-raising outside the system and extensive use of television advertising dominated the election season. One question that is often raised is whether we should have public financing of all federal campaigns. We discussed this question in the *What If . . .* feature that opened this chapter.

★ Who Wants to Be a Candidate?

For an election to be competitive, there must be more than one strong candidate seeking office. If there is only one candidate for any office, the election may be regarded as undemocratic. Who, then, are the people who seek to run for office?

There are thousands of elective offices in the United States. The political parties strive to provide a slate of candidates for every election. Recruiting candidates is easier for some offices than for others. Political parties may have difficulty finding candidates for the board of the local water control district, but they generally find a sufficient number of candidates for county commissioner or sheriff. The higher the office and the more prestige attached to it, the more candidates are likely to want to run. In many areas of the country, however, one political party may be considerably stronger than another. In those situations, the minority party may have more difficulty finding nominees for elections in which victory is unlikely.

The presidential campaign provides the most colorful and exciting look at candidates and how they prepare to compete for office—in this instance, the highest office in the land. The men and women who wanted to be candidates in the 2004 presidential campaign faced a long and obstacle-filled path. First, they needed to raise enough money to tour the nation, particularly the states with early **presidential primaries,** to see if they had enough local supporters. They needed funds to create an organization, to devise a plan to win primary votes, and to win the party's nomination at the national convention. Finally, they needed funds to finance a successful campaign for president. Always, at every turn, there was the question of whether they would have enough funds to wage a campaign.

Presidential Primary
A statewide primary election of delegates to a political party's national convention, held to determine a party's presidential nominee.

Why They Run

People who choose to run for office can be divided into two groups—the "self-starters" and those who are recruited. The volunteers, or self-starters, get involved in political activities to further their careers, to carry out specific political programs, or in response to certain issues or events. The campaign of Senator Eugene McCarthy in 1968 to deny Lyndon Johnson's renomination grew out of McCarthy's opposition to the Vietnam War. Ralph Nader's campaigns for the presidency in 2000 and 2004 were rooted in his belief that the two major parties were ignoring vital issues, such as environmental protection and the influence of corporate wealth on American politics. Howard Dean's primary campaign in 2004

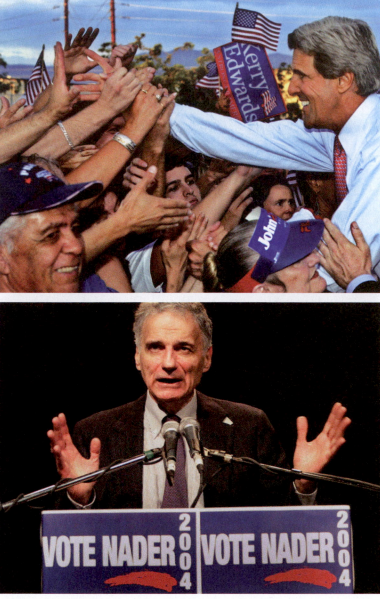

The 2004 candidates. President George W. Bush (left) speaks at a campaign rally in Kalamazoo, Michigan; Massachusetts Senator John F. Kerry (top right) shakes hands after a rally in Albuquerque, New Mexico; Ralph Nader (lower right) speaks with supporters at a gathering in Portland, Oregon. (AP Photo/Gerald Herbert; Sharon Farmer; AP Photo/Rick Bowmer)

stemmed from his desire to get Americans, especially younger voters, engaged in politics.

Issues are important, but self-interest and personal goals—status, career objectives, prestige, and income—are central in motivating some candidates to enter political life. Political office is often seen as the stepping-stone to achieving certain career goals. A lawyer or an insurance agent may run for office only once or twice and then return to private life with enhanced status. Other politicians may aspire to long-term political office—for example, county offices such as commissioner or sheriff sometimes offer attractive opportunities for power, status, and income and are in themselves career goals. Finally, we think of ambition as the desire for ever more important offices and higher status. Politicians who run for lower offices and then set their sights on Congress or a governorship may be said to have "progressive" ambitions.[1]

[1]See the discussion of this topic in Linda Fowler, *Candidates, Congress, and the American Democracy* (Ann Arbor: University of Michigan Press, 1993), pp. 56–59.

The Nomination Process

Individuals become official candidates through the process of nomination. Generally, nominating processes for all offices are controlled by state laws and usually favor the two major political parties. For most minor offices, individuals become candidates by submitting petitions to the local election board. Political parties may help individuals obtain the petitions, pay whatever filing fee is required, and gather signatures. In most states, a candidate from one of the two major parties faces far fewer requirements to get on the ballot than a candidate who is an independent or who represents a minor or new party.

In some states, candidates are placed on the party ballot by a party **caucus** or by a local or state party convention. A caucus is a small, local meeting typically of party regulars who agree on a nominee, while the convention is a countywide or statewide gathering of party members who agree on a slate of nominees. Frequently, the results of petitions, caucuses, or conventions are then voted on by a broader set of party members in a primary election. If there are no opponents to the party's chosen candidates, however, a primary election may be unnecessary. Contested primary elections sometimes signal division within a political party at the local or state level. Alternatively, there may simply be more than one ambitious individual who wishes to run for a particular office, making a primary election necessary.

The American system of nominations, caucuses, and primary elections is one of the most complex in the world. In a majority of European nations, the political party's choice of candidates is final, and no primary elections are ever held.

Who Is Eligible?

There are few constitutional restrictions on who can become a candidate in the United States. As detailed in the Constitution, the formal requirements for national office are as follows:

1. *President.* Must be a natural-born citizen, have attained the age of thirty-five years, and be a resident of the country for fourteen years by the time of inauguration.
2. *Vice president.* Must be a natural-born citizen, have attained the age of thirty-five years, and not be a resident of the same state as the candidate for president.[2]

---

[2]Technically, a presidential and vice presidential candidate can be from the same state, but if they are, one of the two must forfeit the electoral votes of their home state.

★★★★★★★★★★★★★★★★★★★

DID YOU KNOW . . .

That five women received votes for vice president at the Democratic convention in 1924, the first held after women received the right to vote in 1920**?**

Caucus
A meeting of party members designed to select candidates and propose policies.

Voters choose candidates during a Washington state presidential caucus in Seattle February 2004. A state party spokesperson estimated that the turnout would top the 100,000 mark for the first time. Caucusing is a more participatory process than voting in a primary, but normally fewer people turn out. Does enhanced participation by those who attend caucuses make up for the fact that fewer people participate in caucuses than in primaries? Why or why not? (AP Photo/Elaine Thompson)

One of the many "firsts" of the 2000 elections was the campaign of a former first lady for national office. Hillary Rodham Clinton succeeded in winning one of New York's seats in the U.S. Senate. Why might New York be willing to elect candidates who lack long-standing ties to the state? (Peter Kramer/ Getty Images)

3. *Senator.* Must be a citizen for at least nine years, have attained the age of thirty by the time of taking office, and be a resident of the state from which elected.
4. *Representative.* Must be a citizen for at least seven years, have attained the age of twenty-five by the time of taking office, and be a resident of the state from which elected.

The qualifications for state legislators are set by the state constitutions and likewise include age, place of residence, and citizenship. (Usually, the requirements for the upper chamber of a legislature are somewhat higher than those for the lower chamber.) The legal qualifications for running for governor or other state office are similar.

Who Runs?

In spite of these minimal legal qualifications for office at both the national and state levels, a quick look at the slate of candidates in any election—or at the current members of the U.S. House of Representatives—will reveal that not all segments of the population take advantage of these opportunities. Holders of political office in the United States are overwhelmingly white and male. Until the twentieth century, presidential candidates were of northern European origin and of Protestant heritage.[3] Laws that effectively denied voting rights made it impossible to elect African American public officials in many areas in which African Americans constituted a significant portion of the population. As a result of the passage of major civil rights legislation in the 1960s, however, the number of African American public officials has increased throughout the United States.

Women as Candidates.   Until recently, women generally were considered to be appropriate candidates only for lower-level offices, such as state legislator or school board member. The last twenty years have seen a tremendous increase in the number of women who run for office, not only at the state level but for the U.S. Congress as well. Figure 9–1 shows the increase in female candidates. In 2004, 138 women ran for Congress, and 68 were elected. Women were not recruited in the past because they had not worked their way up through the party organization or because they were thought to have no chance of winning. Women also had a more difficult time raising campaign funds. Today, it is clear that women are just as likely as men to participate in many political activities, and a majority of Americans say they would vote for a qualified woman for president of the United States.

Lawyers as Candidates.   Candidates are likely to be professionals, particularly lawyers. Political campaigning and officeholding are simply easier for some occupational groups than for others, and political involvement can make a valuable contribution to certain careers. Lawyers, for example, have more flexible schedules than do many other professionals, can take time off for campaigning, and can leave their jobs to hold public office full-time. Furthermore, holding political office is good publicity for their professional practice, and they usually have partners or associates to keep the firm going while they are in office. Perhaps most important, many jobs that lawyers aspire to—federal or state judgeships, state attorney offices, or work in a federal agency—can be attained by political appointment. Such appointments often go to loyal partisans who have served their party by running for and holding office. Personal ambitions, then, are well served for certain groups by participation in the political arena, whereas it could be a sacrifice for others whose careers demand full-time attention for many years.

---

[3]A number of early presidents were Unitarian. The Unitarian Church is not Protestant, but it is historically rooted in the Protestant tradition.

FIGURE 9–1

Women Running for Congress (and Winning)

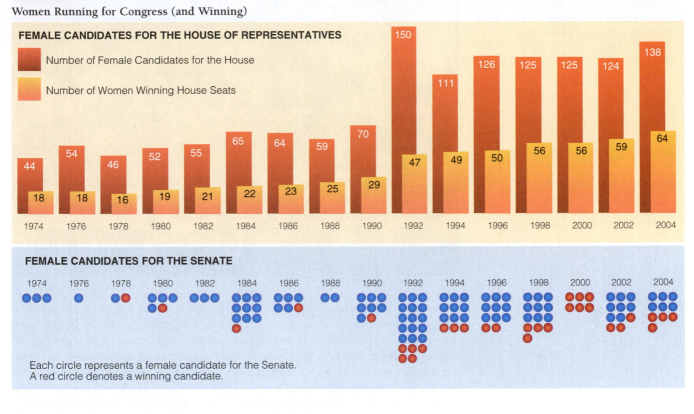

FEMALE CANDIDATES FOR THE HOUSE OF REPRESENTATIVES

■ Number of Female Candidates for the House

■ Number of Women Winning House Seats

FEMALE CANDIDATES FOR THE SENATE

Each circle represents a female candidate for the Senate.
A red circle denotes a winning candidate.

★ The Twenty-First-Century Campaign

After the candidates have been nominated, the most exhausting and expensive part of the election process begins—the general election campaign. The contemporary political campaign is becoming more complex and more sophisticated with every election. Even with the most appealing of candidates, today's campaigns require a strong organization; expertise in political polling and marketing; professional assistance in fund-raising, accounting, and financial management; and technological capabilities in every aspect of the campaign.

The Changing Campaign

The goal is the same for all campaigns—to convince voters to choose a candidate or a slate of candidates for office. Part of the reason for the increased intensity of campaigns in the last decade is that they are no longer centered on the party but are centered on the candidate. The candidate-centered campaign emerged in response to several developments: changes in the electoral system, the increased importance of television in campaigns, technological innovations such as computers, and the increased cost of campaigning.

To run a successful and persuasive campaign, the candidate's organization must be able to raise funds for the effort, obtain coverage from the media, produce and pay for political commercials and advertising, schedule the candidate's time effectively, convey the candidate's position on the issues to the voters, conduct research on the opposing candidate, and get the voters to go to the polls. When party identification was stronger among voters and before the advent of television campaigning, a strong party organization at the local, state, or national

Dwight D. Eisenhower campaigns for president in 1952. Why do few presidential candidates take the time to ride in parades today? (Minnesota Historical Society)

level could furnish most of the services and expertise that the candidate needed. Political parties provided the funds for campaigning until the 1970s. Parties used their precinct organizations to distribute literature, register voters, and get out the vote on election day. Less effort was spent on advertising each candidate's positions and character, because the party label presumably communicated that information to many voters.

One of the reasons that campaigns no longer depend on parties is that fewer people identify with them (see Chapter 8), as is evident from the increased number of political independents. In 1952, about one-fifth of adults identified themselves as independents, whereas in 2004, about one-third considered themselves independents. Political independents include not only adults who are well educated and issue oriented but also many individuals who are not very interested in politics or well informed about candidates or issues.

The Professional Campaign

Whether the candidate is running for the state legislature, for the governor's office, for the U.S. Congress, or for the presidency, every campaign has some fundamental tasks to accomplish. Today, in national elections, most of these tasks are handled by paid professionals rather than volunteers or amateur politicians.

Political Consultant
A paid professional hired to devise a campaign strategy and manage a campaign.

The most sought-after and possibly the most criticized campaign expert is the **political consultant,** who, for a large fee, devises a campaign strategy, thinks up a campaign theme, oversees the advertising, and possibly chooses the campaign colors and the candidate's official portrait. Political consultants began to displace volunteer campaign managers in the 1960s, about the same time that television became a force in campaigns. The paid consultant monitors the campaign's progress, plans all media appearances, and coaches the candidate for debates. The consultants and the firms they represent are not politically neutral; most will work only for candidates from one party.

 ## The Strategy of Winning

In the United States, unlike some European countries, there are no rewards for a candidate who comes in second; the winner takes all. The campaign organization must plan a strategy that maximizes the candidate's chances of winning. In American politics, candidates seek to capture all the votes of their party's supporters, to convince a majority of the independent voters to vote for them, and to gain a few votes from supporters of the other party. To accomplish these goals, candidates must consider their visibility, their message, and their campaign strategy.

Candidate Visibility and Appeal

One of the most important concerns is how well known the candidate is. If she or he is a highly visible incumbent, there may be little need for campaigning except to remind the voters of the office-holder's good deeds. If, however, the candidate is an unknown challenger or a largely unfamiliar character attacking a well-known public figure, the campaign must devise a strategy to get the candidate before the public.

In the case of the independent candidate or the candidate representing a minor party, the problem of name recognition is serious. Such candidates must present an overwhelming case for the voter to reject the major-party candidate. Both Democratic and Republican candidates use the strategic ploy of labeling third-party candidates as "not serious" and therefore not worth the voter's time.

The Use of Opinion Polls

One of the major sources of information for both the media and the candidates is opinion polls. Poll taking is widespread during the primaries. Presidential hopefuls have private polls taken to make sure that there is at least some chance they could be nominated and, if nominated, elected. During the presidential campaign itself, polling is even more frequent. Polls are taken not only by the regular pollsters—Roper, Harris, Gallup, and others—but also privately by each candidate's campaign organization. These private polls are for the exclusive and secret use of the candidate and his or her campaign organization. As the election approaches, many candidates use **tracking polls,** which are polls taken almost every day, to find out how well they are competing for votes. Tracking polls enable consultants to fine-tune the advertising and the candidate's speeches in the last days of the campaign.

Focus Groups

Another tactic is to use a **focus group** to gain insights into public perceptions of the candidate. Professional consultants organize a discussion of the candidate or of certain political issues among ten to fifteen ordinary citizens. The citizens are selected from specific target groups in the population—for example, working men, blue-collar men, senior citizens, or young voters. Recent campaigns have tried to reach groups such as "soccer moms" or "NASCAR dads."[4] The group discusses personality traits of the candidate, political advertising, and other candidate-related issues. The conversation is videotaped (and often observed from behind a mirrored wall). Focus groups are expected to reveal more emotional responses to candidates or the deeper anxieties of voters—feelings that consultants believe often are not tapped by more impersonal telephone surveys. The campaign then can shape its messages to respond to these feelings and perceptions.

A volunteer campaign worker uses the telephone to collect polling information from potential voters. (Bob Dammerich/ Stock Boston)

Tracking Poll
A poll taken for the candidate on a nearly daily basis as election day approaches.

Focus Group
A small group of individuals who are led in discussion by a professional consultant to gather opinions on and responses to candidates and issues.

---

[4]NASCAR stands for the "National Association of Stock Car Auto Racing."

★ Financing the Campaign

In a book published in 1932 entitled *Money in Elections,* Louise Overacker had the following to say about campaign financing:

> The financing of elections in a democracy is a problem which is arousing increasing concern. Many are beginning to wonder if present-day methods of raising and spending campaign funds do not clog the wheels of our elaborately constructed mechanism of popular control, and if democracies do not inevitably become [governments ruled by small groups].[5]

Although writing more than seventy years ago, Overacker touched on a sensitive issue in American political campaigns—the connection between money and elections. It is estimated that over $3 billion was spent at all levels of campaigning in the 1999–2000 election cycle. At the federal level alone, a total of more than $500 million is estimated to have been spent in races for the House of Representatives, $300 million in senatorial races, and $800 million in the presidential campaign. The 2004 campaigns certainly cost even more. Except for the presidential campaigns, all of this money has to be provided by the candidates and their families, borrowed, or raised by contributions from individuals or *political action committees,* described later in this chapter. For the presidential campaigns, some of the funds come from the federal government.

Regulating Campaign Financing

The way campaigns are financed has changed dramatically in the last two and a half decades. Today, candidates and political parties must operate within the constraints imposed by complicated laws regulating campaign financing.

A variety of federal **corrupt practices acts** have been designed to regulate campaign financing. The first, passed in 1925, limited primary and general elec-

Corrupt Practices Acts
A series of acts passed by Congress in an attempt to limit and regulate the size and sources of contributions and expenditures in political campaigns.

[5]Louise Overacker, *Money in Elections* (New York: Macmillan, 1932), p. vii.

George W. Bush, left, is applauded by supporters at a Bush/Cheney 2004 fund-raising dinner in Los Angeles. Bush's recipe for very successful fund-raising had been honed to precision since his first campaign for Texas governor in 1994. John Kerry, the Democratic challenger, also raised impressive sums in 2004. In what ways could the need to raise funds distort the political process? (AP Photo/Charles Dharapak)

tion expenses for congressional candidates. In addition, it required disclosure of election expenses and, in principle, put controls on contributions by corporations. There were many loopholes in the restrictions, and the acts proved to be ineffective.

The **Hatch Act** (Political Activities Act) of 1939 is best known for restricting the political activities of civil servants. The act also, however, made it unlawful for a political group to spend more than $3 million in any campaign and limited individual contributions to a political group to $5,000. Of course, such restrictions were easily circumvented by creating additional political groups.

In the 1970s, Congress passed additional legislation to reshape the nature of campaign financing. In 1971, it passed the Federal Election Campaign Act to reform the process. Then in 1974, in the wake of the Watergate scandal (see Chapter 6), Congress enacted further reforms.

Hatch Act
An act passed in 1939 that restricted the political activities of government employees. It also prohibited a political group from spending more than $3 million in any campaign and limited individual contributions to a campaign committee to $5,000.

The Federal Election Campaign Act

The Federal Election Campaign Act (FECA) of 1971, which became effective in 1972, essentially replaced all past laws. The act placed no limit on overall spending but restricted the amount that could be spent on mass media advertising, including television. It limited the amount that candidates could contribute to their own campaigns (a limit later ruled unconstitutional) and required disclosure of all contributions and expenditures over $100. In principle, the FECA limited the role of labor unions and corporations in political campaigns. It also provided for a voluntary $1 check-off on federal income tax returns for general campaign funds to be used by major-party presidential candidates.

Further Reforms in 1974. For many, the 1971 act did not go far enough. Amendments to the FECA passed in 1974 did the following:

1. *Created the Federal Election Commission.* This commission consists of six nonpartisan administrators whose duties are to enforce compliance with the requirements of the act.
2. *Provided public financing for presidential primaries and general elections.* Any candidate running for president who is able to obtain sufficient contributions in at least twenty states can obtain a subsidy from the U.S. Treasury to help pay for primary campaigns. In 2004, however, neither George W. Bush nor John Kerry accepted public financing for the primaries. This allowed both of them to spend much more on advertising and other expenses than they could have if they had accepted public funding. Each of the two did accept $74.62 million for the general election campaign.
3. *Limited presidential campaign spending.* Any candidate accepting federal support must agree to limit campaign expenditures to the amount prescribed by federal law.
4. *Limited contributions.* Under the 1974 amendments, citizens could contribute up to $1,000 to each candidate in each federal election or primary; the total limit on all contributions from an individual to all candidates was $25,000 per year. Groups could contribute up to a maximum of $5,000 to a candidate in any election. (As you will read shortly, some of these limits were changed by the 2002 campaign-reform legislation.)
5. *Required disclosure.* Each candidate must file periodic reports with the Federal Election Commission, listing who contributed, how much was spent, and for what the money was spent.

Buckley v. Valeo. The 1971 act had limited the amount that each individual could spend on his or her own behalf. The Supreme Court declared the provision unconstitutional in 1976, in *Buckley v. Valeo*,[6] stating that it was unconstitutional to restrict in any way the amount congressional candidates could spend on their own behalf: "The candidate, no less than any other person, has a First Amendment right to engage in the discussion of public issues and vigorously and tirelessly to advocate his own election."

The *Buckley v. Valeo* decision, which has often been criticized, was directly countered by a 1997 Vermont law. The law, known as Act 64, imposed spending limits ranging from $2,000 to $300,000 (depending on the office sought) by candidates for state offices in Vermont. A number of groups, including the American Civil Liberties Union and the Republican Party, challenged the act, claiming that it violated the First Amendment's guarantee of free speech. In a landmark decision in August 2002, a federal appellate court disagreed and upheld the law. The court stated that Vermont had shown that, without spending limits, "the fundraising practices in Vermont will continue to impair the accessibility which is essential to any democratic political system. The race for campaign funds has compelled public officials to give preferred access to contributors, selling their time in order to raise campaign funds."[7]

The court's decision opened the door to further controversy over the Supreme Court's ruling in *Buckley v. Valeo*. Ultimately, the Supreme Court may have to revisit that ruling and reevaluate the issue of whether such spending limits violate the First Amendment.

★ Interest Groups and Campaign Money

In the last two decades, interest groups and individual companies have found new, very direct ways to support elected officials through campaign donations. Elected officials, in turn, have become dependent on these donations to run increasingly expensive campaigns. Interest groups and corporations funnel money to political candidates through several devices: **political action committees (PACs), soft money** contributions, and **issue advocacy advertising.** These devices developed as a means of circumventing the campaign-financing reforms of the early 1970s, which limited contributions by individuals and unions to set amounts.

PACs and Political Campaigns

The 1974 and 1976 amendments to the Federal Election Campaign Act of 1971 allow corporations, labor unions, and other interest groups to set up PACs to raise money for candidates. For a federal PAC to be legitimate, the money must be raised from at least fifty volunteer donors and must be given to at least five candidates in the federal election. PACs can contribute up to $5,000 to each candidate in each election. Each corporation or each union is limited to one PAC. As you might imagine, corporate PACs obtain funds from executives and managers in their firms, and unions obtain PAC funds from their members.

The number of PACs has grown significantly since 1976, as has the amount they spend on elections. There were about 1,000 PACs in 1976; today, there are more than 4,500. Total spending by PACs grew from $19 million in 1973 to almost $900 million in 1999–2000. About 42 percent of all campaign money raised by House candidates in 2002 came from PACs.[8]

Interest groups funnel PAC money to the candidates they think can do the most good for them. Frequently, they make the maximum contribution of $5,000 per election to candidates who face little or no opposition. The summary of PAC con-

Political Action Committee (PAC)
A committee set up by and representing a corporation, labor union, or special interest group. PACs raise and give campaign donations.

Soft Money
Campaign contributions unregulated by federal or state law, usually given to parties and party committees to help fund general party activities.

Issue Advocacy Advertising
Advertising paid for by interest groups that support or oppose a candidate or a candidate's position on an issue without mentioning voting or elections.

---

[6]424 U.S. 1 (1976).
[7]*Landell v. Vermont Public Interest Research Group,* 300 F.3d 129 (2d Cir. 2002).
[8]Center for Responsive Politics, 2004, at http://www.opensecrets.org.

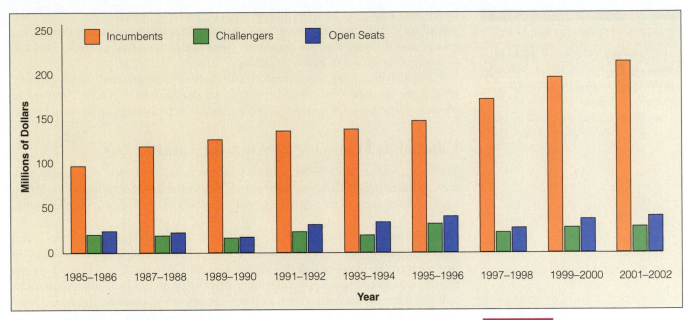

SOURCE: Federal Election Commission, 2004.

FIGURE 9–2

PAC Contributions to Congressional Candidates, 1986 to 2002

tributions given in Figure 9–2 shows that the great bulk of campaign contributions goes to incumbent candidates rather than to challengers. Table 9–1 shows the amounts contributed by the top twenty PACs during the 2001–2002 election cycle.

As Table 9–1 also shows, many PACs give most of their contributions to candidates of one party. Other PACs, particularly corporate PACs, tend to give money to Democrats in Congress as well as to Republicans, because, with both chambers of Congress so closely divided, predicting which party will be in control after an election is almost impossible. Why, you might ask, would business leaders give to

TABLE 9–1

The Top Twenty Contributors to Federal Candidates, 2001–2002 Election Cycle*

RANK	PAC NAME	TOTAL	DEM. %	REP. %
1	National Association of Realtors	$3,269,426	48%	52%
2	Laborers Union	2,537,000	88	12
3	Machinists/Aerospace Workers Union	2,249,850	99	1
4	Association of Trial Lawyers of America	2,235,753	87	12
5	National Automobile Dealers Association	2,221,250	35	65
6	American Medical Association	2,104,319	43	57
7	Teamsters Union	1,967,971	84	16
8	American Federation of State, County and Municipal Employees	1,899,000	96	3
9	International Brotherhood of Electrical Workers	1,878,800	95	4
10	Carpenters and Joiners Union	1,789,000	73	27
11	Credit Union National Association	1,699,773	45	55
12	United Food and Commercial Workers Union	1,603,044	99	1
13	United Auto Workers	1,578,250	98	1
14	National Association of Home Builders	1,534,100	39	61
15	Service Employees International Union	1,485,309	89	9
16	National Beer Wholesalers Association	1,435,750	24	76
17	SBC Communications	1,398,749	40	60
18	American Federation of Teachers	1,364,315	99	1
19	Ironworkers Union	1,363,500	88	12
20	AFL–CIO	1,329,074	94	6

*Includes subsidiaries and affiliated PACs, if any.
SOURCE: Center for Responsive Politics, 2003.

Democrats who may be more liberal than themselves? Interest groups see PAC contributions as a way to ensure *access* to powerful legislators, even though the groups may disagree with the legislators some of the time. PAC contributions are, in a way, an investment in a relationship.

Campaign-financing regulations clearly limit the amount that a PAC can give to any one candidate, but there is no limit on the amount that a PAC can spend on issue advocacy, either on behalf of a candidate or party or in opposition to one.

Campaign Financing beyond the Limits

Within a few years after the establishment of the tight limits on contributions, new ways to finance campaigns were developed that skirted the reforms and made it possible for huge sums of money to be raised, especially by the major political parties.

Contributions to Political Parties.   Candidates, PACs, and political parties found ways to generate *soft money*—that is, campaign contributions to political parties that escaped the limits of federal election law. Although the FECA limited contributions that would be spent on elections, there were no limits on contributions to political parties for activities such as voter education and voter-registration drives. This loophole enabled the parties to raise millions of dollars from corporations and individuals. It was not unusual for some corporations to give more than a million dollars to the Democratic National Committee or to the Republican Party.[9] As shown in Table 9–2, nearly twice as much soft money was raised in the 1999–2000 presidential election cycle as in the previous (1995–1996) presidential election cycle. The parties spent this money for their conventions, for registering voters, and for advertising to promote the general party position. The parties also sent a great deal of the money to state and local party organizations, which used it to support their own tickets.

 **2004 Campaigns and Elections**

Predictions of Election Day foul-ups similar to those experienced in 2000 did not come true. Voter turnout increased and there were long lines in many states, but the election proceeded smoothly. In Ohio, however, a potential problem surfaced: 150,000 provisional ballots were cast by individuals who claimed that they had registered but whose registration could not be immediately verified. These ballots could have taken weeks to process and led to disputes in the courts. Kerry, however, concluded that there were not enough outstanding provisional ballots to change the results in Ohio, and he conceded the next morning.

Although soft money contributions to the national parties were outlawed after election day 2002 (as you will read shortly), political parties saw no contradiction in raising and spending as much soft money as possible during this election cycle. By October 2002, the parties together had raised more than $400 million in soft money, four times as much as they had raised eight years before. President George W. Bush raised even more money for his party than Bill Clinton had raised for the Democrats in previous election cycles.

Independent Expenditures.   Business corporations, labor unions, and other interest groups discovered that it was legal to make **independent expenditures** in an election campaign so long as the expenditures were not coordinated with

Independent Expenditures
Nonregulated contributions from PACs, organizations, and individuals. The funds may be spent on advertising or other campaign activities so long as those expenditures are not coordinated with those of a candidate.

[9]Paul Allen Beck, *Party Politics in America,* 8th ed. (New York: Longman Publishers, 1997), pp. 293–294.

TABLE 9–2

Soft Money Raised by Political Parties, 1993 to 2002

	1993–1994	1995–1996	1997–1998	1999–2000	2001–2002
Democratic Party	$ 45.6 million	$122.3 million	$ 92.8 million	$243.0 million	$199.6 million
Republican Party	59.5 million	141.2 million	131.6 million	244.4 million	221.7 million
Total	105.1 million	263.5 million	224.4 million	487.4 million	421.3 million

SOURCES: *Congressional Quarterly Weekly Report,* September 6, 1997, p. 2065; and authors' update.

those of the candidate or political party. Hundreds of unique committees and organizations blossomed to take advantage of this campaign tactic. Although a 1990 United States Supreme Court decision, *Austin v. Michigan State Chamber of Commerce,*[10] upheld the right of the states and the federal government to limit independent, direct corporate expenditures (such as for advertisements) on behalf of *candidates,* the decision did not stop business and other types of groups from making independent expenditures on *issues.*

Issue Advocacy. Indeed, issue advocacy—spending unregulated money on advertising that promotes positions on issues rather than candidates—has become a common tactic in recent years. Interest groups routinely wage their own issue campaigns. For example, the Christian Coalition, which is incorporated, annually raises millions of dollars to produce and distribute voter guidelines and other direct-mail literature to describe candidates' positions on various issues and to promote its agenda. In 2004, the interest group "MoveOn.org" began running issue ads attacking the Bush record shortly after Senator John Kerry had clinched the Democratic nomination. The Bush campaign responded by beginning its own advertising campaign. Are voters aware of who sponsors the ads? This question is discussed in this chapter's *Politics and Campaigns* feature on the next page.

Although promoting issue positions is very close to promoting candidates who support those positions, the courts repeatedly have held, in accordance with the *Buckley v. Valeo* decision mentioned earlier, that interest groups have a First Amendment right to advocate their positions. The Supreme Court clarified, in a 1996 decision,[11] that political parties may also make independent expenditures on

---

[10]494 U.S. 652 (1990).
[11]*Colorado Republican Federal Campaign Committee v. Federal Election Commission,* 518 U.S. 604 (1996).

Former Democratic representative Tom Andrews speaks on behalf of MoveOn.org and Win Without War in 2004. The two organizations called on Congress to censure President Bush for misleading the public prior to the war in Iraq. Such a demand goes well beyond anything advocated by the Democratic candidate, Senator Kerry. How can independent expenditures on political advertisements create problems for a candidate who is the apparent beneficiary of the ads? (Mark Wilson/Getty Images)

POLITICS AND CAMPAIGNS
Who Is Paying for Those Television Commercials?

Beginning with the primary elections in 2004, television viewers began to see candidates at the end of campaign commercials saying, "I'm George Bush (or John Kerry), and I approved this message." Why were these "tag lines" being aired? Other political commercials did not contain tag lines—why did these other commercials not include them?

CAMPAIGN COMMERCIALS AND INDEPENDENT COMMERCIALS

The commercials that contained a candidate approval statement were paid for by the candidates' campaign committees. Campaign advertising that is sponsored by, or coordinated with, the candidate's own committee must contain the tag line. This requirement was established by the Bipartisan Campaign Reform Act of 2002, better known as the McCain-Feingold Act.

Political advertisers who were independent of the campaigns were not required to display a tag line. These advertisers include new groups such as America Coming Together, the Media Fund, and Americans for a Better Country. Why were the new groups organized, and why were they running so many advertisements?

SOFT MONEY

To understand why the new groups exist, you must understand the history of *soft money*. Soft money, which was given to the parties in the past, consisted of contributions by organizations and individual contributions that exceeded statutory limits. Soft money could not be used for advertisements that named the candidates, but it could be used for more general advertisements and for activities such as get-out-the-vote drives. Of the two major parties, the Republicans have always had a much larger base of supporters willing to make donations directly to campaigns. The Democrats made up for this disadvantage by raising soft money from organizations such as labor unions and from a limited number of wealthy liber-

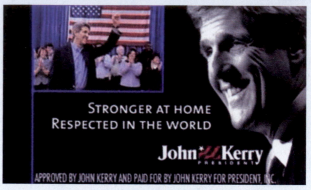

In the voice-over accompanying this image, Democratic candidate John Kerry states that "I approved this message." This is an example of the tag line required on commercials paid for by the candidate's own committee. (Courtesy of JohnKerry.com)

als. The McCain-Feingold Act, however, banned soft money contributions to the national parties.

THE SHADOW PARTIES

Interest groups that previously gave soft money to the Democratic Party responded to the McCain-Feingold Act by setting up new organizations outside of the party, often called "527" organizations after the provision of the tax code that covers them. These groups sought to perform tasks that the Democratic Party could no longer afford, such as voter registration. Because of their role, these groups have been called a "shadow Democratic Party." By 2004, Republican supporters were also organizing shadow groups. These new bodies were responsible for much of the independent advertising during the 2003–2004 election cycle.

FOR CRITICAL ANALYSIS

Some observers claim that diverting large campaign contributions to groups that are organizationally separate from the candidates' campaigns reduces the possibility of corrupt influence. How likely is this?

behalf of candidates—as long as the parties do so *independently* of the candidates. In other words, the parties must not coordinate such expenditures with the candidates' campaigns.

The Bipartisan Campaign Reform Act of 2002

Campaign reform had been in the air for so long that it was almost anticlimactic when President George W. Bush signed the Bipartisan Campaign Reform Act on March 27, 2002. This act, which amended the 1971 FECA, took effect on the day after the congressional elections were held on November 5, 2002.

Key Elements of the New Law. The 2002 law bans the large, unlimited contributions to national political parties that are known as soft money. It places curbs on, but does not entirely eliminate, the use of campaign ads by outside special interest groups advocating the election or defeat of specific candidates. Such ads are allowed up to sixty days before a general election and up to thirty days before a primary election.

In 1974, contributions by individuals to federal candidates were limited to $1,000 per individual. The 2002 act increased this limit to $2,000. In addition, the maximum amount that an individual can give to all federal candidates was raised from $25,000 per year to $95,000 over a two-year election cycle.

The act did not ban soft money contributions to state and local parties. These parties can accept such contributions as long as they are limited to $10,000 per year per individual.

Consequences of the 2002 Act. One of the consequences of the 2002 act was a set of constitutional challenges by groups negatively affected. In December 2003, however, the Supreme Court upheld almost all of the clauses of the act.[12]

The regulation prohibiting the national parties from raising unregulated "soft dollars" may have some unintended consequences. The two national parties have contributed to the stability of our political system by, in essence, usurping most minor parties and bringing almost everyone inside a "big tent." The strength of the Democratic and Republican parties has rested in part on their ability to raise large sums of money. Therefore, one unintended consequence of the 2002 campaign-financing reform law may be to undermine the stabilizing role of the two major parties. Without large amounts of soft money, the two major parties will no longer have the power they previously had to finance get-out-the-vote drives and phone banks. This task will fall to the state parties or nonparty organizations, which may not do such a good job.

---

[12]*McConnell v. Federal Election Commission,* 124 S.Ct. 619 (2003).

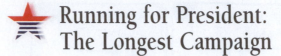

★ Running for President: The Longest Campaign

The American presidential election is the culmination of two different campaigns linked by the parties' national conventions. The presidential primary campaign lasts from January until June of the election year. Traditionally, the final campaign heats up around Labor Day, although in 2004 it began much earlier.

Primary elections were first mandated in 1903 in Wisconsin. The purpose of the primary was to open the nomination process to ordinary party members and to weaken the influence of party bosses in the nomination procedure. Until 1968, however, there were fewer than twenty primary elections for the presidency. They were often **"beauty contests"** in which the candidates competed for popular votes, but the results had little or no impact on the selection of delegates to the national convention. National conventions were meetings of the party elite—legislators, mayors, county chairpersons, and loyal party workers—who were mostly appointed to their delegations. National conventions saw numerous trades and bargains among competing candidates, and the leaders of large blocs of delegates could direct their delegates to support a favorite candidate.

Reforming the Primaries

In recent decades, the character of the primary process and the make-up of the national convention have changed dramatically. The public, rather than party elites, now generally controls the nomination process. After the disruptive riots outside the doors of the 1968 Democratic convention in Chicago, many party leaders pushed for serious reforms of the convention process. They saw the general dissatisfaction with the convention, and the riots in particular, as being caused by the inability of the average party member to influence the nomination system.

The Democratic National Committee appointed a special commission to study the problems of the primary system. Called the McGovern-Fraser Commission, the group over the next several years formulated new rules for delegate selection that had to be followed by state Democratic Parties.

"Beauty Contest"
A presidential primary in which contending candidates compete for popular votes but the results do not control the selection of delegates to the national convention.

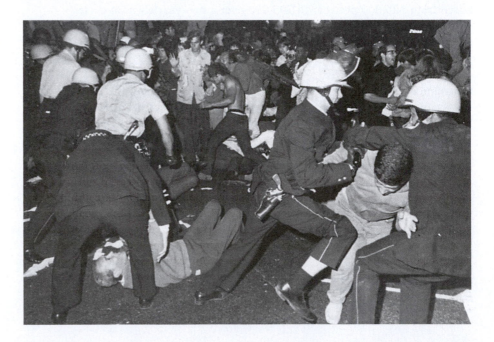

Demonstrations outside the 1968 Democratic convention in Chicago were shown on national TV. Dissatisfaction with the convention influenced the party to reform its delegate selection rules. (Paul Conklin/PhotoEdit)

The reforms instituted by the Democratic Party, which were imitated in most states by the Republicans, revolutionized the nomination process for the presidency. The most important changes require that a majority of the convention delegates not be nominated by party elites; they must be elected by the voters in primary elections, in caucuses held by local parties, or at state conventions. Delegates are normally pledged to a particular candidate, although the pledge is not always formally binding at the convention. The delegation from each state must also include a proportion of women, younger party members, and representatives of the minority groups within the party. At first, virtually no special privileges were given to elected party officials, such as senators and governors. In 1984, however, many of these officials returned to the Democratic convention as **superdelegates.**

Types of Primaries

Primary elections differ from state to state. Among the most common types are those discussed here.

Closed Primary. In a **closed primary,** only avowed or declared members of a party can vote in that party's primary. In other words, voters must declare their party affiliation, either when they register to vote or at the primary election. A closed-primary system tries to make sure that registered voters cannot cross over into the other party's primary in order to nominate the weakest candidate of the opposing party or to affect the ideological direction of that party.

Open Primary. An **open primary** is a primary in which voters can vote in either party primary without disclosing their party affiliation. Basically, the voter makes the choice in the privacy of the voting booth. The voter must, however, choose one party's list from which to select candidates. Open primaries place no restrictions on independent voters.

Blanket Primary. A *blanket primary* is one in which the voter can vote for candidates of more than one party. Alaska, Louisiana, and Washington have blanket primaries. Blanket-primary campaigns may be much more costly because each candidate for every office is trying to influence all the voters, not just those in his or her party.

In 2000, the United States Supreme Court issued a decision that will alter significantly the use of the blanket primary. The case arose when political parties in California challenged the constitutionality of a 1996 ballot initiative authorizing the use of the blanket primary in that state. The parties contended that the blanket primary violated their First Amendment right of association. Because the nominees represent the party, they argued, party members—not the general electorate—should have the right to choose the party's nominee. The Supreme Court ruled in favor of the parties, holding that the blanket primary violated parties' First Amendment associational rights.[13]

The Court's ruling called into question the constitutional validity of blanket primaries in other states as well. The question before these states is how to devise a primary election system that will comply with the Supreme Court's ruling yet offer independent voters a chance to participate in the primary elections.

Run-Off Primary. Some states have a two-primary system. If no candidate receives a majority of the votes in the first primary, the top two candidates must compete in another primary, called a *run-off primary.*

---

[13]*California Democratic Party v. Jones,* 530 U.S. 567 (2000).

★ ★ ★ ★ ★ ★ ★ ★ ★ ★ ★ ★ ★ ★ ★ ★

DID YOU KNOW . . .
That you can be listed on the New Hampshire primary ballot merely by paying a $1,000 filing fee **?**

Superdelegate
A party leader or elected official who is given the right to vote at the party's national convention. Superdelegates are not elected at the state level.

Closed Primary
A type of primary in which the voter is limited to choosing candidates of the party of which he or she is a member.

Open Primary
A primary in which any registered voter can vote (but must vote for candidates of only one party).

Front-Loading the Primaries

As soon as politicians and potential presidential candidates realized that winning as many primary elections as possible guaranteed them the party's nomination for president, their tactics changed dramatically. For example, candidates running in the 2004 primaries, such as Howard Dean, concentrated on building organizations in states that held early, important primary elections. Candidates realized that winning early contests, such as the Iowa caucuses or the New Hampshire primary election (both in January), meant that the media instantly would label the winner as the **front-runner,** thus increasing the candidate's media exposure and escalating the pace of contributions to his or her campaign fund.

The Rush to Be First.   The states and state political parties began to see that early primaries had a much greater effect on the outcome of the presidential election and, accordingly, began to hold their primaries earlier in the season to secure that advantage. While New Hampshire held on to its claim to be the first primary, other states moved theirs to the following week. A group of mostly southern states decided to hold their primaries on the same date, known as Super Tuesday, in the hope of nominating a moderate southerner at the Democratic convention. When California, which had held the last primary (in June), moved its primary to March, the primary season was curtailed drastically. Due to this process of **front-loading** the primaries, in 2000 the presidential nominating process was over in March, with both George W. Bush and Al Gore having enough convention delegate votes to win their nominations. This meant that the campaign was essentially without news until the conventions in August, a gap that did not appeal to the politicians or the media. Both parties discussed whether more changes in the primary process were necessary.

Consequences of Early Primaries.   Despite the apparent problems with the front-loaded primary season in 2000, the Democratic Party decided to hold some of its primaries even earlier in the 2003–2004 presidential election cycle. For example, the Democratic Iowa caucus was advanced to January 19, to be followed eight days later by the New Hampshire primary. The Democrats' goal in moving up their primaries was obvious: settle on a candidate early so that she or he would have a long time during which to raise funds to unseat the incumbent president, George W. Bush.

Critics of this strategy suggested that the shortened primary period might not allow the voters time to evaluate the candidates' character, ideology, and issue positions. In addition, the earliest tests of the candidates would take place in Iowa and New Hampshire, states that are overwhelmingly non-Hispanic white and that do not reflect the national demographics of the Democratic Party. Several southern primaries, however, were also moved to an early position in the calendar, and the population in those states does include more minority voters. Finally, critics expressed concern that the candidates with the most campaign funds by January 1, 2004, would have a great advantage over the rest of the field.

The 2004 Primary Contest.   The contest for the Democratic nomination drew a large and diverse field of candidates in 2004. Former Vermont governor Howard Dean got off to the strongest start, in part due to his effective use of the Internet to recruit supporters and raise funds. Senators John Kerry of Massachusetts and John Edwards of North Carolina were also strong contenders. A late entry to the race was General Wesley Clark, who claimed expertise in national security and defense. Two African American candidates made a run for the nomination—former Illinois senator Carol Moseley Braun and the Reverend Al Sharpton. Other candidates included Connecticut senator Joe Lieberman, a former vice presiden-

Front-Runner
The presidential candidate who appears to be ahead at a given time in the primary season.

Front-Loading
The practice of moving presidential primary elections to the early part of the campaign to maximize the impact of these primaries on the nomination.

tial candidate; Ohio representative Dennis Kucinich; and representative Dick Gephardt of Missouri.

The Dean campaign had great momentum before the primaries actually began, but by January all of the other Democratic candidates were attacking Dean on his positions and experience. Senator John Kerry, who won the Iowa caucuses, was catapulted into the lead, while Howard Dean destroyed his own campaign by seeming to lose control during a speech to his followers. It was an amazing example of how one moment in a campaign, shown over and over on television, can affect an election. In the primaries that followed, Edwards was Kerry's only real competition. By March 2, Kerry had clinched the nomination.

On to the National Convention

Presidential candidates have been nominated by the convention method in every election since 1832. The delegates are sent from each state and are apportioned on the basis of state representation. Extra delegates are allowed to attend from states that had voting majorities for the party in the preceding elections. Parties also accept delegates from the District of Columbia, the territories, and certain overseas groups.

Seating the Delegates. At the convention, each political party uses a **credentials committee** to determine which delegates may participate. The credentials committee usually prepares a roll of all delegates entitled to be seated. Controversy may arise when rival groups claim to be the official party organization for a county, district, or state. The Mississippi Democratic Party split along racial lines in 1964 at the height of the civil rights movement in the Deep South. Separate all-white and mixed white and African American sets of delegates were selected, and both factions showed up at the national convention. After much debate on party rules, the committee decided to seat the pro–civil rights delegates and exclude those who represented the traditional "white" party.

Convention Activities. The typical convention lasts only a few days. The first day consists of speech making, usually against the opposing party. During the

Credentials Committee
A committee used by political parties at their national conventions to determine which delegates may participate. The committee inspects the claim of each prospective delegate to be seated as a legitimate representative of his or her state.

The first 2004 Democratic presidential candidate debate was held in Albuquerque, New Mexico, in September 2003. The Democratic presidential candidates (from the left) were Senator Bob Graham, Representative Dick Gephardt, former senator Carol Moseley Braun, Senator John Kerry, Representative Dennis Kucinich, Senator John Edwards, Senator Joe Lieberman, and former governor Howard Dean. (EPA/POOL/Landov)

second day, there are committee reports, and during the third day, there is presidential balloting. Because delegates generally arrive at the convention committed to presidential candidates, no convention since 1952 has required more than one ballot to choose a nominee, and since 1972, candidates have usually come into the convention with enough committed delegates to win. On the fourth day, a vice presidential candidate is usually nominated, and the presidential nominee gives the acceptance speech.

In 2004, the outcome of the two conventions was so predictable that the national networks devoted only three hours of prime-time coverage to each convention—barely enough time to include speeches by the candidates. However, gavel-to-gavel coverage was available on several cable networks and Internet sites.

★ The Electoral College

Elector
A member of the electoral college, which selects the president and vice president. Each state's electors are chosen in each presidential election year according to state laws.

Many people who vote for the president and vice president think that they are voting directly for a candidate. In actuality, they are voting for **electors** who will cast their ballots in the electoral college. Article II, Section 1, of the Constitution outlines in detail the method of choosing electors for president and vice president. The framers of the Constitution wanted to avoid the selection of president and vice president by the "excitable masses." Rather, they wished the choice to be made by a few supposedly dispassionate, reasonable men (but not women).

The Choice of Electors

Each state's electors are selected during each presidential election year. The selection is governed by state laws. After the national party convention, the electors are pledged to the candidates chosen. The total number of electors today is 538, equal to 100 senators, 435 members of the House, and 3 electors for the District of Columbia (the Twenty-third Amendment, ratified in 1961, added electors for the District of Columbia). Each state's number of electors equals that state's number of senators (two) plus its number of representatives. A graphic inside the front cover of this book shows how the electoral votes are apportioned by state.

The Electors' Commitment

When a plurality of voters in a state chooses a slate of electors, those electors are pledged to cast their ballots on the first Monday after the second Wednesday in December in the state capital for the presidential and vice presidential candidates of their party.[14] The Constitution does not, however, *require* the electors to cast their ballots for the candidates of their party.

The ballots are counted and certified before a joint session of Congress early in January. The candidates who receive a majority of the electoral votes (270) are certified as president-elect and vice president–elect. According to the Constitution, if no candidate receives a majority of the electoral votes, the election of the president is decided in the House from among the candidates with the three highest numbers of votes, with each state having one vote (decided by a plurality of each state delegation). The selection of the vice president is determined by the Senate in a choice between the two candidates with the most votes, each senator having one vote. Congress was required to choose the president and vice president in

[14]In Maine and Nebraska, electoral votes are based on congressional districts. Each district chooses one elector. The remaining two electors are chosen statewide.

1801 (Thomas Jefferson and Aaron Burr), and the House chose the president in 1825 (John Quincy Adams).[15]

It is possible for a candidate to become president without obtaining a majority of the popular vote. There have been many minority presidents in our history, including Abraham Lincoln, Woodrow Wilson, Harry Truman, John F. Kennedy, Richard Nixon (in 1968), and Bill Clinton. Such an event becomes more likely when there are important third-party candidates.

Perhaps more distressing is the possibility of a candidate's being elected when an opposing candidate receives a plurality of the popular vote. This has occurred on four occasions—in the elections of John Quincy Adams in 1824, Rutherford B. Hayes in 1876, Benjamin Harrison in 1888, and George W. Bush in 2000, all of whom won elections in which an opponent received a plurality of the popular vote.

Criticisms of the Electoral College

Besides the possibility of a candidate's becoming president even though an opponent obtains more popular votes, there are other complaints about the electoral college. The idea of the Constitution's framers was to have electors use their own discretion to decide who would make the best president. But electors no longer perform the selecting function envisioned by the founders, because they are committed to the candidate who has a plurality of popular votes in their state in the general election.[16]

One can also argue that the current system, which in most states gives all of the electoral votes to the candidate who has a statewide plurality, is unfair to other candidates and their supporters. The current system of voting also means that presidential campaigning will be concentrated in those states that have the largest number of electoral votes and in those states in which the outcome is likely to be

---

[15]For a detailed account of the process, see Michael J. Glennon, *When No Majority Rules: The Electoral College and Presidential Succession* (Washington, D.C.: Congressional Quarterly Press, 1993), p. 20.
[16]Note, however, that there have been revolts by so-called *faithless electors*—in 1796, 1820, 1948, 1956, 1960, 1968, 1972, 1976, 1988, and 2000.

close. The other states may receive second-class treatment during the presidential campaign. It can also be argued that there is something of a bias favoring states with smaller populations, because including Senate seats in the electoral vote total partly offsets the edge of the more populous states in the House. Wyoming (with two senators and one representative) gets an electoral vote for roughly each 164,594 people (based on the 2000 census), for example, whereas Iowa gets one vote for each 418,046 people, and California has one vote for every 615,848 inhabitants. Note that many of the smallest states have Republican majorities.

Many proposals for reform of the electoral college system have been advanced, particularly after the turmoil resulting from the 2000 elections. The most obvious is to get rid of it completely and simply allow candidates to be elected on a popular-vote basis; in other words, have a direct election, by the people, of the president and vice president. Because abolishing the electoral college would require a constitutional amendment, however, the chances of electing the president by a direct vote are remote.

The major parties are not in favor of eliminating the electoral college, fearing that it would give minor parties a more influential role. Also, less populous states are not in favor of direct election of the president because they believe they would be overwhelmed by the large-state vote.

★ How Are Elections Conducted?

The United States uses the **Australian ballot**—a secret ballot that is prepared, distributed, and counted by government officials at public expense. Since 1888, all states have used the Australian ballot. Before that, many states used the alternatives of oral voting and differently colored ballots prepared by the parties. Obviously, knowing which way a person was voting made it easy to apply pressure on the person to change his or her vote, and vote buying was common.

Office-Block and Party-Column Ballots

Two types of Australian ballots are used in the United States in general elections. The first, called an **office-block ballot,** or sometimes a **Massachusetts ballot,** groups all the candidates for a particular elective office under the title of that office. Parties dislike the office-block ballot because it places more emphasis on the office than on the party; it discourages straight-ticket voting and encourages split-ticket voting.

A **party-column ballot** is a form of general election ballot in which all of a party's candidates are arranged in one column under the party's label and symbol. It is also called the **Indiana ballot.** In some states, it allows voters to vote for all of a party's candidates for local, state, and national offices by simply marking a single "X" or by pulling a single lever. Most states use this type of ballot. As it encourages straight-ticket voting, the two major parties favor this form. When a party has an exceptionally strong presidential or gubernatorial candidate to head the ticket, the use of the party-column ballot increases the **coattail effect** (the influence of a popular candidate on the success of other candidates on the same party ticket).

Voting by Mail

Although voting by mail has been accepted for absentee ballots for many decades (for example, for those who are doing business away from home or for members of the armed forces), only recently have several states offered mail ballots to all of their voters. The rationale for using the mail ballot is to make voting easier for

Australian Ballot
A secret ballot prepared, distributed, and tabulated by government officials at public expense. Since 1888, all states have used the Australian ballot rather than an open, public ballot.

Office-Block, or Massachusetts, Ballot
A form of general election ballot in which candidates for elective office are grouped together under the title of each office. It emphasizes voting for the office and the individual candidate, rather than for the party.

Party-Column, or Indiana, Ballot
A form of general election ballot in which all of a party's candidates for elective office are arranged in one column under the party's label and symbol. It emphasizes voting for the party, rather than for the office or individual.

Coattail Effect
The influence of a popular candidate on the electoral success of other candidates on the same party ticket. The effect is increased by the party-column ballot, which encourages straight-ticket voting.

On the day before the 2003 California gubernatorial election, a clerk at the Registrar-Recorder/County Clerk office in Los Angeles scans absentee ballots so that the validity of the signatures can be confirmed. What problems might result when large numbers of citizens vote without ever visiting a polling place? (AP Photo/Ric Francis)

the voters. A startling result came in a special election in Oregon in spring 1996: with the mail ballot, turnout was 66 percent, and the state saved more than $1 million. In the 2000 presidential elections, in which Oregon voters were allowed to mail in their ballots, voter participation was over 80 percent. Although voters in a number of states now have the option of voting by mail, Oregon is the only state to have abandoned precinct polling places completely.

Problems with Mail Voting. Norman Ornstein, an early critic of mail-in voting, has suggested that mail balloting subverts the whole election process. In part, this is because the voter casts her or his ballot at any time, perhaps before any debates or other dialogues are held between candidates. Thus, the voter may be casting an uninformed ballot.[17] When voting methods came under scrutiny after the 2000 elections, the authors of three prominent national reports[18] also criticized mail-in voting for this reason. The reports also concluded that mail-in voting deprives voters of the secrecy guaranteed by polling-place voting, provides more opportunities for fraud, and represents the abandonment of an important civic rite of going to the polls on election day.

Benefits of Mail Voting. Others, however, see the mail ballot as the best way to increase voter participation when many are too busy to vote or have little interest in the process. The next step in making voting easier may be Internet voting. In 2004, the federal government conducted a pilot study of Internet voting for members of the military. The study was aimed at making sure that absentee ballots can be received and counted without delay. In the end, however, the government decided not to implement the plan due to security concerns.[19]

---

[17]Norman Ornstein, "Vote-by-Mail: Is It Good for Democracy?" *Campaigns and Elections,* May 1996, page 47.
[18]These reports were based on studies conducted by a commission led by former presidents Gerald Ford and Jimmy Carter, by the Constitution Project at Georgetown University, and by a consortium of the Massachusetts Institute of Technology and the California Institute of Technology.
[19]CBSNEWS.com, "Americans Abroad to Vote Online," July 12, 2003, at http://www.cbsnews.com/stories/2003/07/12/politics/main562983.shtml.

Vote Fraud

Vote fraud is something regularly suspected but seldom proved. Voting in the 1800s, when secret ballots were rare and people had a cavalier attitude toward the open buying of votes, was probably much more conducive to fraud than modern elections are. Larry J. Sabato and Glenn R. Simpson, however, claim that the potential for vote fraud is high in many states, particularly through the use of phony voter registrations and absentee ballots.[20]

The Danger of Fraud. In California, for example, it is very difficult to remove a name from the polling list even if the person has not cast a ballot in the last two years. Thus, many persons are still on the rolls even though they no longer live in California. Enterprising political activists could use these names for absentee ballots. Other states have registration laws that are meant to encourage easy registration and voting. Such laws can be taken advantage of by those who seek to vote more than once.

After the 2000 elections, Larry Sabato again emphasized the problem of voting fraud. "It's a silent scandal," said Sabato, "and the problem is getting worse with increases in absentee voting, which is the easiest way to commit fraud." He noted that in 2000, one-third of Florida's counties found that more than 1,200 votes were cast illegally by felons, and in one county alone nearly 500 votes were cast by unregistered voters. In two precincts, the number of ballots cast was greater than the number of people who voted.[21]

Mistakes by Voting Officials. Some observers claim, however, that errors leading to fraud are trivial in number and that a few mistakes are inevitable in a system involving millions of voters. These people argue that an excessive concern with vote fraud makes it harder for minorities and poor people to vote.

For example, in 2000, Kathleen Harris, Florida's top election official, oversaw a purge of the voter rolls while simultaneously serving as co-chair of the Florida Bush campaign. According to the *New York Times,* when attempting to remove the names of convicted felons from the list of voters:

> Ms. Harris's office overruled the advice of the private firm that compiled the felon list and called for removing not just names that were an exact match, but ones that were highly inexact. Thousands of Florida voters wound up being wrongly purged . . . . In Missouri, elected officials charged for years that large numbers of St. Louis residents were casting votes from vacant lots. A study conducted by The [St. Louis] *Post Dispatch* in 2001 found that in the vast majority of cases, the voters lived in homes that had been wrongly classified by the city."[22]

In both the Florida and Missouri examples, a majority of the affected voters were African American.

As a result of the confusion generated by the 2000 elections, many states are now in the process of improving their voting systems and procedures. Some claim that certain reforms, such as requiring voters to show a voter-registration card or photo identification when they go to the polls, will help to curb voting fraud. Would a standardized national voting system help? We examine this question in this chapter's *Which Side Are You On?* feature.

An ex-felon (front) joins other demonstrators outside a courthouse in Miami. Inside the courthouse, judges were hearing arguments on whether the state was doing enough to help ex-felons regain their voting rights. This individual finished his sentence ten years ago. Should ex-felons be allowed to vote? Why or why not? (AP Photo/ J. Pat Carter)

---

[20]Larry J. Sabato and Glenn R. Simpson, *Dirty Little Secrets: The Persistence of Corruption in American Politics* (New York: Random House, 1996).
[21]As cited in "Blind to Voter Fraud," *The Wall Street Journal,* March 2, 2001, p. A10.
[22]"How America Doesn't Vote," *The New York Times: The News of the Week in Review,* February 15, 2004, p. 10.

WHICH SIDE ARE YOU ON?
Should There Be One Voting System for All States?

After the 2000 presidential elections, the entire country watched as Florida state officials, representatives of both candidates, and state and federal courts struggled with deciding which candidate would receive the state's electoral votes. Election officials in Florida taught American voters a new vocabulary of election terms. We came to understand that a "hanging chad" is the little piece of cardboard that dangles from a punch card if it is not fully punched out. We learned how and why votes are recounted at the county level.

In the 2004 election, 32 percent of American voters used some sort of optical scanning system (pencil-in-the-blocks, for example), 29 percent used touch screens, 19 percent used punch cards, 13 percent used voting machines with levers, and less than 1 percent used paper ballots. With so many different systems still in place, major issues in counting ballots remain.

Critics claim that touch-screen voting systems, such as this one, are vulnerable to tampering and do not provide a "paper trail" for auditing voting results.

SHOULD THE BEST SYSTEM BE ADOPTED NATIONALLY?

After 2000, members of Congress vowed that voters in all states should use systems that would prevent the kinds of mistakes seen in some Florida jurisdictions. Suggestions ranged from letting voters see printouts of their ballots to providing every precinct with touch-screen machines that register votes on a computer.

Should there be one voting system for the whole nation? Congress might pass a law requiring that all states adopt touch screens or computerized optical scanning devices. Although Congress probably could not compel states to follow this law, funding could be available to purchase such systems as an incentive for state cooperation.

WE DO NOT EVEN KNOW WHAT THE BEST SYSTEM IS YET

A number of issues would be raised by a requirement for a national voting system. Who would decide which system to use, and which companies might manufacture the

machines? Would a national system necessarily be more secure? Critics of touch-screen machines, for example, say that the computer program that counts the votes could be tampered with and the votes changed. Imagine the confusion that would occur if fraud were suspected in every state in a national election.

Also, replacing old systems in all of the states that use them would be very expensive. After a year of study, Congress authorized over $3 billion to assist states in the replacement process. As of 2004, however, only $650 million has actually gone to the states.

WHAT'S YOUR POSITION?

How could voting systems be improved to raise the public's confidence in the election process and make citizens more willing to vote?

GOING ONLINE

Several major studies are being conducted on voting technology. One is the Caltech–MIT/Voting Technology Project, which you can find at **http://www.vote.caltech.edu**. The Center for the Study of Technology and Society also provides extensive resources on its Web site: **http://www.tecsoc.org/govpol/focusnetvote.htm**.

 # Turning Out to Vote

In 2004, the voting-age population was about 221 million people. Of that number, 120 million, or 54.2 percent of the voting-age population, actually went to the polls. When only half of the voting-age population participates in elections, it means, among other things, that the winner of a close presidential election may be voted in by only about one-fourth of the voting-age population (see Table 9–3 on the following page).

Voter Turnout
The percentage of citizens taking part in the election process; the number of eligible voters that actually "turn out" on election day to cast their ballots.

Figure 9–3 shows **voter turnout** for presidential and congressional elections from 1900 to 2004. According to these statistics, the last good year for voter turnout was 1960, when almost 65 percent of the voting-age population actually voted. Each of the peaks in the figure represents voter turnout in a presidential election. Thus, we can also see that turnout for congressional elections is influenced greatly by whether there is a presidential election in the same year.

The same is true at the state level. When there is a race for governor, more voters participate both in the general election for governor and in the election for state representatives. Voter participation rates in gubernatorial elections are also greater in presidential election years. The average turnout in state elections is about 14 percentage points higher when a presidential election is held.

Now consider local elections. In races for mayor, city council, county auditor, and the like, it is fairly common for only 25 percent or less of the electorate to vote. Is something amiss here? It would seem that people should be more likely to vote in elections that directly affect them. At the local level, each person's vote counts more (because there are fewer voters). Furthermore, the issues—crime control, school bonds, sewer bonds, and so on—touch the immediate interests of the voters. The facts, however, do not fit the theory. Potential voters are most interested in national elections, when a presidential choice is involved. Otherwise, voter participation in our representative government is very low (and, as we have seen, it is not overwhelmingly great even at the presidential level).

The Effect of Low Voter Turnout

There are two schools of thought concerning low voter turnout. Some view low voter participation as a threat to our representative democratic government. Too few individuals are deciding who wields political power in our society. In addi-

TABLE 9–3

Elected by a Majority?

Most presidents have won a majority of the votes cast in the election. We generally judge the extent of their victory by whether they have won more than 51 percent of the votes. Some presidential elections have been proclaimed *landslides,* meaning that the candidates won by an extraordinary majority of votes cast. As indicated below, however, no modern president has been elected by more than 38 percent of the total voting-age population.

YEAR—WINNER (PARTY)	PERCENTAGE OF TOTAL POPULAR VOTE	PERCENTAGE OF VOTING-AGE POPULATION
1932—Roosevelt (D)	57.4	30.1
1936—Roosevelt (D)	60.8	34.6
1940—Roosevelt (D)	54.7	32.2
1944—Roosevelt (D)	53.4	29.9
1948—Truman (D)	49.6	25.3
1952—Eisenhower (R)	55.1	34.0
1956—Eisenhower (R)	57.4	34.1
1960—Kennedy (D)	49.7	31.2
1964—Johnson (D)	61.1	37.8
1968—Nixon (R)	43.4	26.4
1972—Nixon (R)	60.7	33.5
1976—Carter (D)	50.1	26.8
1980—Reagan (R)	50.7	26.7
1984—Reagan (R)	58.8	31.2
1988—Bush (R)	53.4	26.8
1992—Clinton (D)	43.3	23.1
1996—Clinton (D)	49.2	23.2
2000—Bush (R)	47.8	24.5
2004—Bush (R)	51.0	27.6

SOURCES: *Congressional Quarterly Weekly Report,* January 31, 1989, p. 137; *The New York Times,* November 5, 1992; *The New York Times,* November 7, 1996; and *The New York Times,* November 12, 2000.

FIGURE 9–3

Voter Turnout for Presidential and Congressional Elections, 1900 to 2004

The peaks represent turnout in presidential election years; the troughs represent turnout in off-presidential-election years.

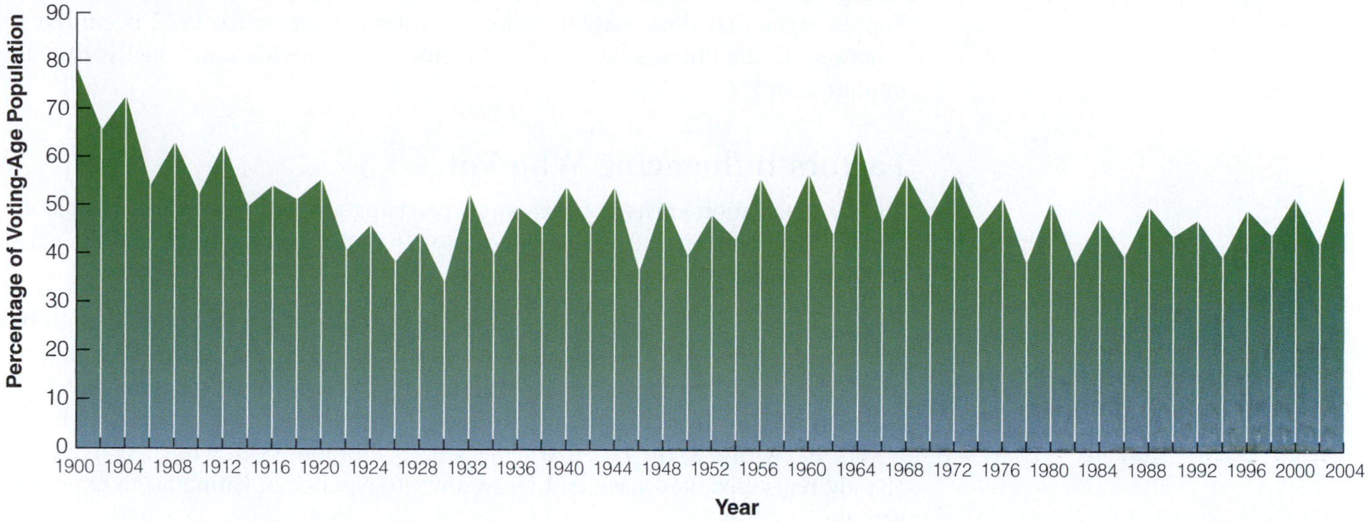

SOURCES: Historical Data Archive, Inter-university Consortium for Political and Social Research; U.S. Department of Commerce, *Statistical Abstract of the United States: 1980,* 101st ed. (Washington, D.C.: U.S. Government Printing Office, 1980), p. 515; William H. Flanigan and Nancy H. Zingale, *Political Behavior of the American Electorate,* 5th ed. (Boston: Allyn and Bacon, 1983), p. 20; *Congressional Quarterly,* various issues; and authors' updates.

tion, low voter participation presumably signals apathy about our political system in general. It also may signal that potential voters simply do not want to take the time to learn about the issues. When only a handful of people take the time to research the issues, it will be easier, say the alarmists, for an authoritarian figure to take over our government.

Others are less concerned about low voter participation. They believe that low voter participation simply indicates more satisfaction with the status quo. Also, they believe that representative democracy is a reality even if a very small percentage of eligible voters vote. If everyone who does not vote believes that the outcome of the election will accord with his or her own desires, then representative democracy is working. The nonvoters are obtaining the type of government—with the type of people running it—that they want to have anyway.

Is Voter Turnout Declining?

During many recent elections, the media have voiced the concern that voter turnout is declining. Indeed, Figure 9–3 appears to show lower voter turnout than the 1960s. Pundits have blamed the low turnout on negative campaigning and broad public cynicism about the political process. But is voter turnout actually as low as it seems?

One problem with widely used measurements of voter turnout—as exemplified by Figure 9–3—is that they compare the number of people who actually vote with the voting-age population, not the population of *eligible voters*. These figures are not the same. The figure for the voting-age population includes felons and ex-felons who have lost the right to vote. Above all, it includes new immigrants who are not yet citizens. Finally, it does not include Americans living abroad, who can cast absentee ballots.

In 2004, the voting-age population included 3.2 million ineligible felons and ex-felons and an estimated 17.5 million noncitizens. It did not include 3.3 million Americans abroad. As stated earlier in this chapter, the voting-age population in 2004 was 221 million people. The number of eligible voters, however, was only

204 million. That means that voter turnout in 2000 was not 54.2 percent, as is often reported, but 58.9 percent.

As you learned in Chapter 1, the United States has experienced high rates of immigration in recent decades. Political scientists Michael McDonald and Samuel Popkin argue that the apparent decline in voter turnout since 1972 is entirely a function of the increasing size of the ineligible population, chiefly due to immigration.[23]

Factors Influencing Who Votes

A clear association exists between voter participation and the following characteristics: age, educational attainment, minority status, income level, and the existence of two-party competition.

1. *Age.* Look at Table 9–4, which shows the breakdown of voter participation by age group for the 2000 presidential election. It would appear from these figures that age is a strong factor in determining voter turnout on election day. The reported turnout increases with older age groups. Greater participation with age is very likely due to the fact that older voters are more settled in their lives, are already registered, and have had more time to experience voting as an expected activity.

2. *Educational attainment.* Education also influences voter turnout. In general, the more education you have, the more likely you are to vote. This pattern is clearly evident in the 2000 election results, as you can see in Table 9–5. Reported turnout was over 30 percentage points higher for those who had some college education than it was for people who had never been to high school.

3. *Minority status.* Race and ethnicity are important, too, in determining the level of voter turnout. Non-Hispanic whites in 2000 voted at a 60.4 percent rate, whereas the non-Hispanic African American turnout rate was 54.1 percent. For Hispanics, the turnout rate was 27.5 percent, and for Asian Americans the rate was slightly lower, at 25.4 percent. These low rates are largely due to the fact that many Hispanic and Asian American immigrants are not yet citizens.

4. *Income level.* As you can see in Table 9–6, differences in income also correlate with differences in voter turnout. Wealthier people tend to be overrepresented

---

[23]Michael P. McDonald and Samuel L. Popkin, "The Myth of the Vanishing Voter," *American Political Science Review,* Vol. 95, No. 4 (December 2001), p. 963.

TABLE 9–4

Voting in the 2000 Presidential Elections by Age Group

Turnout is given as a percentage of the voting-age population.

AGE	REPORTED TURNOUT
18–24	32.3
25–34	43.7
35–44	55.0
45–54	62.3
55–64	66.8
65–74	69.9
75 years and over	64.9

SOURCE: U.S. Bureau of the Census, February 27, 2002.

TABLE 9–5

Voting in the 2000 Presidential Elections by Education Level

Turnout is given as a percentage of the voting-age population.

YEARS OF SCHOOL COMPLETED	REPORTED TURNOUT
Less than 9th grade	26.8
9th to 12th grade, no diploma	33.6
High school graduate	49.4
Some college or associate degree	60.3
Bachelor's degree	70.3
Advanced degree	75.5

SOURCE: U.S. Bureau of the Census, February 27, 2002.

TABLE 9–6

Voting in the 2000 Presidential Elections by Income

Turnout is given as a percentage of the voting-age population.

INCOME	REPORTED TURNOUT
Under $5,000	28.2
$5,000 to $9,999	34.7
$10,000 to $14,999	37.7
$15,000 to $24,999	43.4
$25,000 to $34,999	51.0
$35,000 to $49,999	57.5
$50,000 to $74,999	65.2
$75,000 and over	71.5

SOURCE: U.S. Bureau of the Census, February 27, 2002.

among voters who turn out on election day. In 2000, turnout varied from 28.2 percent for those with annual family incomes under $5,000 to about 71.5 percent for people with annual family incomes of $75,000 or more.

5. *Two-party competition.* Another factor in voter turnout is the extent to which elections are competitive within a state. More competitive states generally have higher turnout rates, and turnout increases considerably in states where there is an extremely competitive race in a particular year. In addition, turnout can be increased through targeted get-out-the-vote drives among minority voters.

These statistics reinforce one another. White voters are likely to be wealthier than African American voters, who are also less likely to have obtained a college education.

Why People Do Not Vote

For many years, political scientists believed that one reason voter turnout in the United States was so much lower than in other Western nations was that it was very difficult to register to vote. In most states, registration required a special trip to a public office far in advance of elections. Many experts are now proposing other explanations for low U.S. voter turnout.

Uninformative Media Coverage and Negative Campaigning. Some scholars contend that one of the reasons why some people do not vote has to do with media coverage of campaigns. Many researchers have shown that the news media tend to provide much more news about "the horse race," or which candidates are ahead in the polls, than about the actual policy positions of the candidates. Thus, voters are not given the kind of information that would provide an incentive to go to the polls on election day. Additionally, negative campaigning is thought to have an adverse effect on voter turnout. By the time citizens are ready to cast their ballots, most of the information they have heard about the candidates has been so negative that no candidate is appealing.

According to a year-long study conducted in 2000 by Harvard University's Center on the Press, Politics, and Public Policy, nonvoters and voters alike shared the same criticisms of the way the media cover campaigns: most thought the media treated campaigns like theater or entertainment. Nonvoters, however, were much more cynical about government and politicians than were voters. As the director of the study put it, "All the polls, the spin, the attack ads, the money and the negative news have soured Americans on the way we choose our president."[24]

The Rational Ignorance Effect. Another explanation of low voter turnout suggests that citizens are making a logical choice in not voting. If citizens believe that their votes will not affect the outcome of an election, then they have little incentive to seek the information they need to cast intelligent votes. The lack of incentive to obtain costly (in terms of time, attention, and so on) information about politicians and political issues has been called the **rational ignorance effect.** That term may seem contradictory, but it is not. Rational ignorance is a condition in which people purposely and rationally decide not to obtain information—to remain ignorant.

Why, then, do even one-third to one-half of U.S. citizens bother to show up at the polls? One explanation is that most citizens receive personal satisfaction from

Democratic presidential candidate Kerry, as seen in a Bush campaign advertisement entitled "Differences." The ad accused Kerry of making overly expensive campaign promises that threatened the U.S. economy. How might negative advertisements such as this one affect voter turnout? (AP Photo/Bush-Cheney 2004)

Rational Ignorance Effect
An effect produced when people purposely and rationally decide not to become informed on an issue because they believe that their vote on the issue is not likely to be a deciding one; a lack of incentive to seek the necessary information to cast an intelligent vote.

[24]Thomas E. Patterson, *The Vanishing Voter: Public Involvement in an Age of Uncertainty* (New York: Alfred A. Knopf Publishers, 2002). You can continue to track the Vanishing Voter Project at the study's Web site, http://www.vanishingvoter.org.

the act of voting. It makes them feel that they are good citizens and that they are doing something patriotic. Even among voters who are registered and who plan to vote, if the cost of voting goes up (in terms of time and inconvenience), the number of registered voters who actually vote will fall. In particular, bad weather on election day means that, on average, a smaller percentage of registered voters will go to the polls.

Plans for Improving Voter Turnout.   Mail-in voting, Internet voting, registering to vote when you apply for a driver's license—these are all ideas that have been either suggested or implemented in the hope of improving voter turnout. Nonetheless, voter turnout remains low.

Two other ideas seemed promising. The first was to allow voters to visit the polls up to three weeks before election day. The second was to allow voters to vote by absentee ballot without having to give any particular reason for doing so. The Committee for the Study of the American Electorate discovered, however, that in areas that had implemented these plans, neither plan increased voter turnout. Indeed, voter turnout actually fell in those jurisdictions. In other words, states that did *not* permit early voting or unrestricted absentee voting had *better* turnout rates than states that did. Apparently, these two innovations appeal mostly to people who already intended to vote.

What is left? One possibility is to declare election day a national holiday. In this way, more eligible voters will find it easier to go to the polls.

★ Legal Restrictions on Voting

Legal restrictions on voter registration have existed since the founding of our nation. Most groups in the United States have been concerned with the suffrage issue at one time or another.

Historical Restrictions

In colonial times, only white males who owned property with a certain minimum value were eligible to vote, leaving a greater number of Americans ineligible than eligible to take part in the democratic process.

Property Requirements.   Many government functions concern property rights and the distribution of income and wealth, and some of the founders of our nation believed it was appropriate that only people who had an interest in property should vote on these issues. The idea of extending the vote to all citizens was, according to Charles Pinckney, a South Carolina delegate to the Constitutional Convention, merely "theoretical nonsense."

The logic behind the restriction of voting rights to property owners was questioned seriously by Thomas Paine in his pamphlet *Common Sense:*

> Here is a man who today owns a jackass, and the jackass is worth $60. Today the man is a voter and goes to the polls and deposits his vote. Tomorrow the jackass dies. The next day the man comes to vote without his jackass and cannot vote at all. Now tell me, which was the voter, the man or the jackass?[25]

The writers of the Constitution allowed the states to decide who should vote. Thus, women were allowed to vote in Wyoming in 1870 but not in the entire nation until the Nineteenth Amendment was ratified in 1920. By about 1850, most white adult males in virtually all the states could vote without any property

African American voters in New York circa 1945. Until the 1965 Voting Rights Act, African Americans faced obstacles when trying to exercise their right to vote, especially in the South. If part of the population cannot vote, what impact is that likely to have on the types of legislation passed by Congress or state legislatures? (Library of Congress, NAACP Collection)

[25]Thomas Paine, *Common Sense* (London: H. D. Symonds, 1792), p. 28.

qualification. North Carolina was the last state to eliminate its property test for voting—in 1856.

Further Extensions of the Franchise. Extension of the franchise to black males occurred with the passage of the Fifteenth Amendment in 1870. This enfranchisement was short lived, however, as the "redemption" of the South by white racists had rolled back these gains by the end of the century. As discussed in Chapter 5, it was not until the 1960s that African Americans, both male and female, were able to participate in the electoral process in all states. Women received full national voting rights with the Nineteenth Amendment in 1920. The most recent extension of the franchise occurred when the voting age was reduced to eighteen by the Twenty-sixth Amendment in 1971. In the years since the amendment was passed, however, young people have traditionally had a low turnout.

Is the Franchise Still Too Restrictive? There continue to be certain classes of people who do not have the right to vote. These include noncitizens and, in most states, convicted felons who have been released from prison. They also include current prison inmates, election law violators, and people who are mentally incompetent. Also, no one under the age of eighteen can vote. Some political activists have argued that some of these groups should be allowed to vote. Most other democracies do not prevent persons convicted of a crime from voting after they have completed their sentences. In the 1800s, many states let noncitizen immigrants vote. In Nicaragua, the minimum voting age is sixteen.

One discussion concerns the voting rights of convicted felons who are no longer in prison or on parole. Some contend that voting should be a privilege, not a right, and we should not want the types of people who commit felonies participating in decision making. Others believe that it is wrong to further penalize those who have paid their debt to society. These people argue that barring felons from the polls injures minority groups because minorities make up a disproportionately large share of former prison inmates.

A Republican campaign worker registers a citizen to vote during the 2004 campaign in New York's Times Square. How do voter registration drives affect election outcomes? (AP Photo/Jennifer Szymaszek)

Registration
The entry of a person's name onto the list of registered voters for elections. To register, a person must meet certain legal requirements of age, citizenship, and residency.

Current Eligibility and Registration Requirements

Voting generally requires **registration,** and to register, a person must satisfy the following voter qualifications, or legal requirements: (1) citizenship, (2) age (eighteen or older), and (3) residency—the duration varies widely from state to state and with types of elections. Since 1972, states cannot impose residency requirements of more than thirty days.

Each state has different qualifications for voting and registration. In 1993, Congress passed the "motor voter" bill, which requires that states provide voter-registration materials when people receive or renew driver's licenses, that all states allow voters to register by mail, and that voter-registration forms be made available at a wider variety of public places and agencies. In general, a person must register well in advance of an election, although voters in Idaho, Maine, Minnesota, Oregon, Wisconsin, and Wyoming are allowed to register up to, and on, election day. North Dakota has no voter registration at all.

Some argue that registration requirements are responsible for much of the non-participation in our political process. Certainly, since their introduction in the late 1800s, registration laws have had the effect of reducing the voting participation of African Americans and immigrants. There also is a partisan dimension to the debate over registration and nonvoting. Republicans generally fear that an expanded electorate would help to elect more Democrats.

The question arises as to whether registration is really necessary. If it decreases participation in the political process, perhaps it should be dropped altogether. Still, as those in favor of registration requirements argue, such requirements may prevent fraudulent voting practices, such as multiple voting or voting by noncitizens.

★ Campaigns, Nominations, and Elections: Why Are They Important Today?

Campaigns and elections are not just for show. They perform a valuable function in a democracy. Without political campaigns, how would you learn about the candidates? How would you learn about the issues at stake in an upcoming election and which positions the candidates have taken on those issues? The culmination of all that campaigning, the election itself, is equally important. Who wins an election may determine how much you pay in taxes, whether more funds will be made available for education in your state, how much government aid you will receive if you become ill or lose your job, and the size of the Social Security check you will receive during your retirement years.

Because campaigns and elections are so important in our political system, it is critical to ensure that voting procedures and methods yield fair and accurate results. The importance of voting systems throughout the states became clear after the 2000 presidential elections. One of the biggest problems with campaigns is, of course, the high cost of running for a national or even a state political office. This problem is important because as long as the campaign process remains so expensive, numerous Americans who would like to run for office will not do so simply because they cannot raise the funds necessary to compete in the race.

MAKING A DIFFERENCE   ★ Registering and Voting

In nearly every state, before you are allowed to cast a vote in an election, you must first register. Registration laws vary considerably from state to state. Depending in part on how difficult a state's laws make it to register, some states have much lower rates of registration and voting participation than do others.

Why Should You Care?

To vote, you must register. But why bother to vote? After all, the electorate is large, many elections are not close, and often your vote will not have an important effect on the election outcome. If you do vote, however, you increase the amount of attention that politicians pay to people like you. When Congress, state legislatures, or city councils consider new laws and regulations, these bodies typically give more weight to the interests of groups that are more likely to vote. So even if your single vote does not determine the outcome of an election, it does add, to a small degree, to the voter turnout for your constituency. Your vote therefore increases the chances of legislation that benefits you or that meets with your approval.

What Can You Do?

What do you have to do to register and cast a vote? In general, you must be a citizen of the United States, at least eighteen years old on or before election day, and a resident of the state in which you intend to register. Most states require that you meet minimum-residency requirements. In other words, you must have lived in the state in which you plan to be registered for a specified period of time. If you have not lived in the state long enough to register before an upcoming election, you may retain your previous registration in another state and cast an absentee vote, if that state permits it. Minimum residency requirements vary among the states. By a ruling of the United States Supreme Court, no state can require more than thirty days of residency. Some states require a much shorter period—for example, ten days in New Hampshire and Wisconsin and one day in Alabama. Twenty states do not have a minimum-residency requirement at all.

Nearly every state also specifies a closing date by which you must be registered before an election. In other words, even if you have met a residency requirement, you still may not be able to vote if you register too close to the day of the election. The closing date is different in certain states (Connecticut, Delaware, and Louisiana) for primary elections than for other elections. The closing date for registration varies from election day itself (Idaho, Maine, Minnesota, Oregon, Wisconsin, and Wyoming) to thirty days before the election (Arizona). In North Dakota, no registration is necessary.

In most states, your registration can be revoked if you do not vote within a certain number of years. This process of automatically "purging" the voter-registration lists of nonactive voters happens every two years in about a dozen states, every three years in Georgia, every four years in more than twenty other states, every five years in Maryland and Rhode Island, every eight years in North Carolina, and every ten years in Michigan. Ten states do not require this purging at all.

Let us look at Iowa as an example. Iowa voters normally register through the local county auditor or when they obtain a driver's license (under the "motor voter" law of 1993). A voter who moves to a new address within the state must change his or her registration by contacting the auditor. Postcard registrations must be postmarked or delivered to the county auditor no later than the twenty-fifth day before an election. Voters can declare or change their party affiliation when they register or reregister, or they can change or declare a party when they go to the polls on election day. Postcard registration forms in Iowa are available at many public buildings, from labor unions, at political party headquarters, at the county auditors' offices, or from campus groups. Registrars who will accept registrations at other locations may be located by calling a party headquarters or a county auditor.

For more information on voting registration, contact your county or state officials, party headquarters, labor union, or local chapter of the League of Women Voters. The Web site for the League of Women Voters is

http://www.lwv.org.

Key Terms

Australian ballot 310

"beauty contest" 304

caucus 291

closed primary 305

coattail effect 310

corrupt practices acts 296

credentials committee 307

elector 308

focus group 295

front-loading 306

front-runner 306

Hatch Act 297

independent expenditures 300

issue advocacy advertising 298

office-block, or Massachusetts, ballot 310

open primary 305

party-column, or Indiana, ballot 310

political action committee (PAC) 298

political consultant 294

presidential primary 289

rational ignorance effect 317

registration 320

soft money 298

superdelegate 305

tracking poll 295

voter turnout 314

Chapter Summary

1 People may choose to run for political office to further their careers, to carry out specific political programs, or in response to certain issues or events. The legal qualifications for holding political office are minimal at both the state and local levels, but holders of political office still are predominantly white and male and are likely to be from the professional class.

2 American political campaigns are lengthy and extremely expensive. In the last decade, they have become more candidate centered rather than party centered in response to technological innovations and decreasing party identification. Candidates have begun to rely less on the party and more on paid professional consultants to perform the various tasks necessary to wage a political campaign. The crucial task of professional political consultants is image building. The campaign organization devises a campaign strategy to maximize the candidate's chances of winning. Candidates use public opinion polls and focus groups to gauge their popularity and to test the mood of the country.

3 The amount of money spent in financing campaigns is increasing steadily. A variety of corrupt practices acts have been passed to regulate campaign finance. The Federal Election Campaign Act of 1971 and its amendments in 1974 and 1976 instituted major reforms by limiting spending and contributions; the acts allowed corporations, labor unions, and interest groups to set up political action committees (PACs) to raise money for candidates. New techniques, including "soft money" contributions to the parties and independent expenditures, were later developed. The Bipartisan Campaign Reform Act of 2002 banned soft money contributions to the national parties, limited advertising by interest groups, and increased the limits on individual contributions.

4 After the Democratic convention of 1968, the McGovern-Fraser Commission formulated new rules for primaries, which were adopted by all Democrats and by Republicans in many states. These reforms opened up the nomination process for the presidency to all voters.

5 A presidential primary is a statewide election to help a political party determine its presidential nominee at the national convention. Some states use the caucus method of choosing convention delegates. The primary campaign recently has been shortened to the first few months of the election year.

6 The voter technically does not vote directly for president but chooses between slates of presidential electors. In most states, the slate that wins the most popular votes throughout the state gets to cast all the electoral votes for the state. The candidate receiving a majority (270) of the electoral votes wins. Both the mechanics and the politics of the electoral college have been criticized sharply. There have been many proposed reforms, including a proposal that the president be elected on a popular-vote basis in a direct election.

7 The United States uses the Australian ballot, a secret ballot that is prepared, distributed, and counted by government officials. The office-block ballot groups candidates according to office. The party-column ballot groups candidates according to their party labels and symbols.

8 Voter participation in the United States is low compared with that of other countries. Some view low voter turnout as a threat to representative democracy, whereas others believe it simply indicates greater satisfaction with the status quo. There is an association between voting and a person's age, education, minority status, and income level. Another factor affecting voter turnout is the extent to which elections are competitive within a state. It is also true that the number of eligible voters is smaller than the number of people of voting age because of ineligible felons and immigrants who are not yet citizens.

9 In colonial times, only white males with a certain minimum amount of property were eligible to vote. The suffrage issue has concerned, at one time or another, most groups in the United States. Currently, to be eligible to vote, a person must satisfy registration, citizenship, and age and residency requirements. Each state has different qualifications. Some claim that these requirements are responsible for much of the nonparticipation in the political process in the United States.

★ Selected Print and Media Resources

SUGGESTED READINGS

Crouse, Timothy. *The Boys on the Bus.* New York: Random House, 1973. This classic book, which reads like a novel, is about political spin-doctoring in the 1972 Nixon/McGovern presidential campaigns, as seen by the press corps.

Faucheux, Ronald A. *Running for Office: The Strategies, Techniques, and Messages Modern Political Candidates Need to Win Elections.* New York: M. Evans & Co., 2002. A variety of guides on how to run a campaign are available. Typically, these guides are oriented toward first-time candidates for state or local office. Faucheux's well-regarded manual is among the most recent.

Green, Donald P., and Alan S. Gerber. *Get Out the Vote: How to Increase Voter Turnout.* Washington, D.C.: Brookings Institution Press, 2004. This volume is a practical guide for activists seeking to mount get-out-the-vote (GOTV) campaigns. It differs from other guides in that it is based on research and experiments in actual electoral settings—Green and Gerber are political science professors at Yale University. The authors discover that many widely used GOTV tactics are less effective than is often believed.

MoveOn. *MoveOn's 50 Ways to Love Your Country: How to Find Your Political Voice and Become a Catalyst for Change.* Makawao, Maui, Hawaii: Inner Ocean Publishing, 2004. This book contains fifty short chapters in which individuals describe how they sought to make a difference by getting involved in the political process. As we explained earlier in this chapter, MoveOn is a "shadow party" to the Democrats. Nevertheless, the techniques described here could be used just as easily by Republicans. The volume is also available on audiotape.

Sabato, Larry J., ed. *Overtime! The Election 2000 Thriller.* Reading, Mass.: Addison Wesley Longman, 2001. This collection of essays offers firsthand accounts (including some by members of the presidential candidates' legal teams) of the political and legal drama that unfolded after the 2000 elections.

Wayne, Stephen J. *The Road to the White House, 2004: The Politics of Presidential Elections.* Belmont, Calif.: Wadsworth Publishing, 2003. Stephen Wayne examines the changes in the election process since 1996 and provides an excellent analysis of the presidential selection process.

MEDIA RESOURCES

Bulworth—A 1998 satirical film starring Warren Beatty and Halle Berry. Jay Bulworth, a senator who is fed up with politics and life in general, hires a hit man to carry out his own assassination. He then throws political caution to the wind in campaign appearances by telling the truth and behaving the way he really wants to behave.

The Candidate—A 1972 film, starring the young Robert Redford, that effectively investigates and satirizes the decisions that a candidate for the U.S. Senate must make. A political classic.

If You Can't Say Anything Nice—Negative campaigning seems to have become the norm in recent years. This 1999 program looks at the resulting decline in popularity of politics among the electorate and suggests approaches to restoring faith in the process.

Money Talks: The Influence of Money on American Politics—Bill Moyers reports on the influence of money on our political system. Produced in 1994.

Primary Colors—A 1998 film starring John Travolta as a southern governor who is plagued by a sex scandal during his run for the presidency.

e-mocracy ★ Elections and the Web

Today's voters have a significant advantage over those in past decades. It is now possible to obtain extensive information about candidates and issues simply by going online. Some sites present point-counterpoint articles about the candidates or issues in an upcoming election. Other sites support some candidates and positions and oppose others. The candidates themselves all now have Web sites that you can visit if you want to learn more about them and their positions. You can also obtain information online about election results by going to sites such as those listed in the *Logging On* section. While the Internet has proved to be a valuable vehicle for communicating information about elections, it is not clear whether it will be used for actual voting in national elections at some future time. Although Internet voting seems like a great idea, it also raises many concerns, particularly about security.

Logging On

For detailed information about current campaign-financing laws and for the latest filings of finance reports, see the site maintained by the Federal Election Commission at

http://www.fec.gov

To find excellent reports on where campaign money comes from and how it is spent, be sure to view the site maintained by the Center for Responsive Politics at

http://www.opensecrets.org

You can learn about the impact of different voting systems on election strategies and outcomes at the Center for Voting and Democracy, which maintains the following Web site:

http://www.fairvote.org

Another excellent site for investigating voting records and campaign-financing information is that of Project Vote Smart. Go to

http://www.vote-smart.org

Using InfoTrac for Political Research

How was the presidential election of 2004 different from previous presidential elections? In what ways was it the same? You can find answers to these questions by using InfoTrac. To use InfoTrac to research the 2004 election, go to

http://www.infotrac-college.com

Log in and go to InfoTrac College Edition, then go to the Subject guide. Type "elections" in the search box. InfoTrac will present you with a list of election topics. Click on the button labeled "Narrow by subdivision." InfoTrac will then present a series of election topics, including articles for each recent election year. If you click on 2004, you will find a listing of relevant articles on the most recent presidential election, sorted by date. Clicking on 2000 provides you with articles on the 2000 presidential election. Use a selection of articles on each election year to address the topic of what changed in 2004 and what remained the same.

ONLINE REVIEW

At **http://politicalscience.wadsworth. com/schmidt12**, you will find a free Study Guide to this book. For each chapter, there are two online quizzes to help you master the material.

• The **PoliPrep Self Study Assessment** provides a pre-test for each major section of the chapter. PoliPrep then generates a customized study plan. After you complete the study plan, a post-test evaluates your progress.

• The **Tutorial Quiz** for each chapter provides questions on the chapter contents, including the features. The questions are organized to match the major sections of the chapter.

The Media and Cyberpolitics

WHAT IF
The Media Were Truly Independent?

BACKGROUND

Americans often assume that our country has the freest press in the world. After all, the First Amendment prevents the government from regulating the media in ways that are common in other nations. The government, however, is not the only force that can compromise the independence of the media.

The media in the United States have always relied primarily on advertisers for support. Such reliance leaves the media exposed to pressure from advertisers, who can threaten to withdraw their ads. Reporters usually can resist the demands of individual advertisers. They may find it harder to ignore concerns that most advertisers have in common, such as a desire that reporters have a positive attitude toward business in general. After all, most advertisers are profit-making businesses, and most media companies are also motivated by profits. What if the media were free from these commercial concerns?

WHAT IF THE MEDIA WERE TRULY INDEPENDENT?

If the media were truly independent, no one outside the journalistic community would be able to set standards for journalists. Presumably, reporters would set professional standards for themselves. If journalists were to set their own standards, however, a remaining source of bias might be the personal prejudices of highly educated professionals. Modern reporters are well educated and generally upper middle class. As a result, they are likely to share the biases and preconceptions of other well-educated, well-paid professionals. Furthermore, those journalists who are most likely to influence their colleagues are also usually the best paid. Such persons may be liberal on cultural issues but may also be conservative on economic ones. It would take a strong commitment to objectivity to overcome these tendencies.

HOW WOULD AN INDEPENDENT MEDIA BE FUNDED?

If the media were truly independent, where would the funding come from? One possible model is public television, such as the Public Broadcasting System (PBS) in the United States. PBS relies on contributions from its viewers as well as grants from governments and corporations. These funding sources are more uncertain than commercial advertising, however. PBS is constantly teetering on the brink of financial disaster. Therefore, threats by sponsors to withdraw their support may have an even greater impact on PBS than on commercial networks. Indeed, legislators often advocate withdrawing governmental support from PBS.

True independence would mean that the media enjoyed a funding source that could not be taken away easily. One agency that enjoys such a funding source is the British Broadcasting Corporation (BBC). The BBC is funded primarily by a tax on televisions, currently set at over $200 per household. In principle, the British government could reduce or eliminate this tax, but threatening to do so would be politically dangerous for any British leader.

Could such a system be established in the United States? It would be highly unlikely. Americans and their representatives surely would never approve a tax on television sets. Also, such a levy would probably be subject to massive tax evasion. The government simply has no idea who owns television sets, or how many.

INDEPENDENCE MAY NOT ELIMINATE MEDIA BIAS

Given the personal prejudices of many journalists, some observers believe that bias would still be a problem even for independent media. Consider that even though the BBC prides itself on its independence and is seen as independent by much of the British public, some believe that its news coverage is still biased. Critics claim that the BBC is left of center, antiwar, and too critical of Israel. Defenders of the network point out, however, that on many of these issues, the BBC's apparent bias corresponds to British popular opinion. These people contend that the BBC's reporting is cautious, and that the most powerful influence on the BBC's reporting may, in fact, be its spirit of professionalism.

FOR CRITICAL ANALYSIS

1. *What kinds of reporting are advertisers likely to prefer? What kinds of reporting would they dislike?*
2. *How might the personal biases of reporters affect how they cover specific news stories?*

The study of people and politics—of how people gain the information that they need to be able to choose among political candidates, to organize for their own interests, and to formulate opinions on the policies and decisions of the government—must take into account the role played by the media. Historically, the print media played the most important role in informing public debate. The print media developed, for the most part, our understanding of how news is to be reported. Today, however, more than 90 percent of Americans use television news as their primary source of information. In addition, the Internet has become a source for political communication and fund-raising. As Internet use grows, the system of gathering and sharing news and information is changing from one in which the media have a primary role to one in which the individual citizen may play a greater part. With that in mind, it is important to analyze the current relationship between the media and politics. The question of who owns the media has an impact on this relationship, as we pointed out in the chapter-opening *What If . . .* feature.

The Media's Functions

The mass media perform a number of different functions in any country. In the United States, we can list at least six. Almost all of them can have political implications, and some are essential to the democratic process. These functions are as follows: (1) entertainment, (2) reporting the news, (3) identifying public problems, (4) socializing new generations, (5) providing a political forum, and (6) making profits.

Entertainment

By far the greatest number of radio and television hours are dedicated to entertaining the public. The battle for prime-time ratings indicates how important successful entertainment is to the survival of networks and individual stations.

Although there is no direct linkage between entertainment and politics, network dramas often introduce material that may be politically controversial and that may stimulate public discussion. An example is *The West Wing,* a TV series that many people believe promotes liberal political values. Made-for-TV movies have focused on a number of controversial topics, including AIDS, incest, and wife battering.

Reporting the News

A primary function of the mass media in all their forms—newspapers and magazines, radio, television, cable, and online news services—is the reporting of news. The media provide words and pictures about events, facts, personalities, and ideas. The protections of the First Amendment are intended to keep the flow of news as free as possible, because it is an essential part of the democratic process. If citizens cannot obtain unbiased information about the state of their communities and their leaders' actions, how can they make voting decisions? One of the most incisive comments about the importance of the media was made by James Madison, who said, "A people who mean to be their own governors must arm themselves with the power

Democratic vice presidential hopeful Senator John Edwards of North Carolina, photographed here surrounded by the media after attending an event at Allen Temple Church in Greenville, South Carolina. (EPA/TANNEN MAURY/Landov)

knowledge gives. A popular government without popular information or the means of acquiring it, is but a prologue to a farce or a tragedy or perhaps both."[1]

Identifying Public Problems

Public Agenda
Issues that are perceived by the political community as meriting public attention and governmental action.

The power of the media is important not only in revealing what the government is doing but also in determining what the government ought to do—in other words, in setting the **public agenda.** The mass media identify public issues, such as the placement of convicted sex offenders in residential neighborhoods on release from prison. The media then influence the passage of legislation, such as "Megan's Law," which requires police to notify neighbors about the release and/or resettlement of certain offenders. American journalists also work in a long tradition of uncovering public wrongdoing, corruption, and bribery and of bringing such wrongdoing to the public's attention. Closely related to this investigative function is that of presenting policy alternatives. Public policy is often complex and difficult to make entertaining, but programs devoted to public policy increasingly are being scheduled for prime-time television. Most networks produce shows with a "news magazine" format that sometimes include segments on foreign policy and other issues.

Socializing New Generations

As mentioned in Chapter 6, the media, and particularly television, strongly influence the beliefs and opinions of Americans. Because of this influence, the media play a significant role in the political socialization of the younger generation, as well as immigrants to this country. Through the transmission of historical information (sometimes fictionalized), the presentation of American culture, and the portrayal of the diverse regions and groups in the United States, the media teach young people and immigrants about what it means to be an American. TV talk shows, such as the *Oprah Winfrey Show,* sometimes focus on controversial issues (such as abortion or assisted suicide) that relate to basic American values (such as liberty). Many children's shows are designed not only to entertain young viewers but also to instruct them in the traditional moral values of American society. In recent years, the public has become increasingly concerned about the level of violence depicted on children's programs and on other shows during prime time.

Republican presidential candidate George W. Bush chats with talk show host Oprah Winfrey. What types of voters would Bush appeal to by appearing on this show? (AP Photo/Wilfredo Lee)

Providing a Political Forum

As part of their news function, the media also provide a political forum for leaders and the public. Candidates for office use news reporting to sustain interest in their campaigns, while officeholders use the media to gain support for their policies or to present an image of leadership. Presidential trips abroad are an outstanding way for the chief executive to get colorful, positive, and exciting news coverage that makes the president look "presidential." The media also offer ways for citizens to participate in public debate, through letters to the editor, televised editorials, or electronic mail. The question of whether more public access should be provided will be discussed later in this chapter.

[1]James Madison, "Letter to W. T. Barry" (August 4, 1822), in Gaillard P. Hunt, ed., IX *The Writings of James Madison* 103 (1910).

Making Profits

Most of the news media in the United States are private, for-profit corporate enterprises. One of their goals is to make profits for expansion and for dividends to the stockholders who own the companies. In general, profits are made as a result of charging for advertising. Advertising revenues usually are related directly to circulation or to listener/viewer ratings.

For the most part, the media depend on advertisers to obtain revenues to make profits. Media outlets that do not succeed in generating sufficient revenues from advertising either go bankrupt or are sold. Consequently, reporters may feel pressure from media owners and from advertisers. Media owners may take their cues from what advertisers want. If an important advertiser does not like the political bent of a particular reporter, the reporter could be asked to alter his or her "style" of writing. The Project for Excellence in Journalism in 2001 discovered that 53 percent of local news directors said that advertisers try to tell them what to air and what not to air.[2]

Advertisers have been known to pull ads from newspapers and TV stations whenever they read or view negative publicity about their own companies or products. For example, CBS ran a *60 Minutes* show about Dillard's and other department stores that claimed store security guards used excessive force and racial profiling. In response, Dillard's pulled its ads from CBS. This example can be multiplied many times over.

Several well-known media outlets, in contrast, are publicly owned—public television stations in many communities and National Public Radio. These operate without extensive commercials, are locally supported, and are often subsidized by the government and corporations. A complex relationship exists among the for-profit and nonprofit media, the government, and the public. Throughout the rest of this chapter, we examine some of the many facets of this relationship.

★ A History of the Media in the United States

Many years ago Thomas Jefferson wrote, "Were it left to me to decide whether we should have a government without newspapers, or newspapers without a government, I should not hesitate a moment to prefer the latter."[3] Although the media have played a significant role in politics since the founding of this nation, they were not as overwhelmingly important in the past as they are today. For one thing, politics was controlled by a small elite who communicated personally. For another, during the early 1800s and before, news traveled slowly. If an important political event occurred in New York, it was not known until five days later in Philadelphia; ten days later in the capital cities of Connecticut, Maryland, and Virginia; and fifteen days later in Boston.

Roughly three thousand newspapers were being published by 1860. Some of these, such as the *New York Tribune,* were mainly sensation mongers that concentrated on crimes, scandals, and the like. The *New York Herald* specialized in self-improvement and what today would be called practical news. Although sensational and biased reporting often created political divisiveness (this was true particularly during the Civil War), many historians believe that the growth of the print media also played an important role in unifying the country.

---

[2]Project for Excellence in Journalism, "Gambling with the Future," *Columbia Journalism Review,* November/December 2001.

[3]Thomas Jefferson, "Letter to Edward Carrington" (1787), in Lipscomb and Bergh, eds., *The Writings of Thomas Jefferson,* Memorial Edition 6:57, Washington, D.C., 1903–04.

The Rise of the Political Press

Americans may cherish the idea of an unbiased press, but in the early years of the nation's history, the number of politically sponsored newspapers was significant. The sole reason for the existence of such periodicals was to further the interests of the politicians who paid for their publication. As chief executive of our government during this period, George Washington has been called a "firm believer" in **managed news.** Although acknowledging that the public had a right to be informed, he believed that some matters should be kept secret and that news that might damage the image of the United States should be censored (not published). Washington, however, made no attempt to control the press. (In times of crisis, should the government be allowed to censor news articles in the interests of protecting the nation's security? For a discussion of this issue, see this chapter's *America's Security* feature.)

Managed News
Information generated and distributed by the government in such a way as to give government interests priority over candor.

The Development of Mass-Readership Newspapers

Two inventions in the nineteenth century led to the development of mass-readership newspapers. The first was the high-speed rotary press; the second was the telegraph. Faster presses meant lower per-unit costs and lower subscription prices. By 1848, the Associated Press had developed the telegraph into a nationwide apparatus for the dissemination of all types of information on a systematic basis.

Along with these technological changes came a growing population and increasing urbanization. A larger, more urban population could support daily newspapers, even if the price per paper was only a penny. Finally, the burgeoning, diversified economy encouraged the growth of advertising, which meant that newspapers could obtain additional revenues from merchants who seized the opportunity to promote their wares to a larger public.

The Popular Press and Yellow Journalism

Students of the history of journalism have ascertained a change in the last half of the 1800s, not in the level of biased news reporting but in its origin. Whereas politically sponsored newspapers had expounded a particular political party's point of view, the post–Civil War mass-based newspapers expounded whatever political philosophy the owner of the newspaper happened to have.

" INTERESTING.....IT'S LIKE A PORTABLE 500K FILE and YOU DON'T HAVE TO WAIT FOR IT TO DOWNLOAD.... AND YOU SAY IT'S CALLED A NEWSPAPER ?"

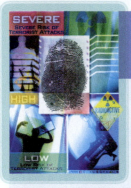

AMERICA'S SECURITY
Press Censorship in Times of Crisis

During periods of crisis, Americans have tended to rally around the president and other political leaders. The war on terrorism has been no different. But this war has presented new kinds of challenges for Americans and for their government. How do we defend ourselves against this new kind of enemy—one that is stateless, unpredictable, and at times intractable? To enable our security forces—including the Federal Bureau of Investigation, the Central Intelligence Agency, the police, and the armed forces—to do the best job possible, should the government prevent the media from publishing information that could harm those efforts? This would constitute a form of censorship, even if self-imposed by the media.

A DIVISIVE ISSUE

Americans are quite divided in their opinions about restricting the freedom of the press in the present crisis. A Pew Research Center poll taken after the terrorist attacks in September 2001 found that 53 percent of the respondents wanted the government to censor news that might threaten national security. A significant minority (almost 40 percent of the respondents), however, thought that the media should always report news that is in the national interest.

A similar split in opinion was reflected in another poll taken after 9/11 that asked the following question: Should Americans publicly criticize presidential decisions on military issues? According to the poll's results, 54 percent of the respondents thought that Americans should not criticize presidential decisions on these issues; 41 percent of the respondents, though, believed that it was all right to engage in such criticism. One year after 9/11, however,

the proportion of respondents who considered such criticism acceptable had already risen to 60 percent.*

A related issue concerns the degree to which the press should support the administration's position. The Pew Research Center poll mentioned above also asked that particular question. Almost three-fourths of those polled wanted news coverage that reflects all points of view. The American public wants a press that thinks independently and does not serve as a propaganda machine, even in times of crisis.

THE THORNY ISSUE OF NO PRIOR RESTRAINT

Since the ratification of the Bill of Rights, America has prided itself on its free press. Whenever the government has tried to prevent the publication of information that the media believed to be in the public interest, the courts have struck down such prior restraints. A key Supreme Court case on this issue was decided in 1971. The *New York Times* and the *Washington Post* were planning to publish a secret history of the U.S. government's involvement in the war in Vietnam (1964–1975). The government attempted to prevent the publication of those documents, arguing that national security was threatened. The Supreme Court ruled in favor of the newspapers' right to publish.

FOR CRITICAL ANALYSIS

In times of severe crisis, should the government be allowed to interfere with the media's attempts to publish information on America's security?

*CBS News poll, November 2001, as reported in *Public Perspective*, January/February 2002, p. 47; and CBS News poll, September 24, 2002, as reported at **http://www.cbsnews.com/stories/2002/09/24/opinion/polls/main523130.shtml**.

Even if newspaper owners did not have a particular political axe to grind, they often allowed their editors to engage in sensationalism and what is known as **yellow journalism.** The questionable or simply personal activities of a prominent businessperson, politician, or socialite were front-page material. Newspapers, then as now, made their economic way by maximizing readership. As the *National Enquirer* demonstrates with its current circulation of almost two million, sensationalism is still rewarded by high levels of readership.

Yellow Journalism
A term for sensationalistic, irresponsible journalism. Reputedly, the term is an allusion to the cartoon "The Yellow Kid" in the old *New York World,* a newspaper especially noted for its sensationalism.

The Age of the Electromagnetic Signal

The first scheduled radio program in the United States featured politicians. On the night of November 2, 1920, KDKA–Pittsburgh transmitted the returns of the presidential-election race between Warren G. Harding and James M. Cox. The listeners were a few thousand people tuning in on very primitive, homemade sets.

By 1924, there were nearly 1,400 radio stations. But it was not until 8 P.M. on November 15, 1926, that the electronic media came into their own in the United States. On that night, the National Broadcasting Company (NBC) made its debut with a four-hour program broadcast by twenty-five stations in twenty-one cities. Network broadcasting had become a reality.

Even with the advent of national radio in the 1920s and television in the late 1940s, many politicians were slow to understand the significance of the **electronic media.** The 1952 presidential campaign was the first to involve a real role for television. Television coverage of the Republican convention helped Dwight Eisenhower win over delegates and secure the nomination. His vice presidential running mate, Richard Nixon, put TV to good use. Accused of hiding a secret slush fund, Nixon replied to his critics with his famous "Checkers" speech. He denied the attacks, cried real tears, and said that the only thing he ever received from a contributor for his personal use was his dog, Checkers, and a "Republican cloth coat" for his wife, Pat. It was a highly effective performance.

Today, television dominates the campaign strategy of every would-be national politician, as well as that of every elected official. Politicians think of ways to continue to be newsworthy, thereby gaining access to the electronic media. Attacking the president's programs is one way of becoming newsworthy; other ways include holding highly visible hearings on controversial subjects, going on "fact-finding" trips, and employing gimmicks (such as taking a walking tour of a state).

The Revolution in the Electronic Media

Just as technological change was responsible for the end of politically sponsored periodicals, technology is increasing the number of alternative news sources today. The advent of pay TV, cable TV, subscription TV, satellite TV, and the Internet has completely changed the electronic media landscape. With hundreds, if not thousands, of potential outlets for specialized programs, the electronic media are becoming more and more like the print media in catering to specialized tastes. This is sometimes referred to as **narrowcasting.** Both cable television and the Internet offer the public unparalleled access to specialized information on everything from gardening and home repair to sports and religion. Most viewers are able to choose among several sources for their favorite type of programming.

Electronic Media
Communication channels that involve electronic transmissions, such as radio, television, and, to an increasing extent, the Internet.

Narrowcasting
Broadcasting that is targeted to one small sector of the population.

The Web site of the Fox News cable network. All of the major TV news providers now have Web sites at which viewers can find up-to-the-minute breaking stories. Fox News has been widely accused of bias in favor of conservative causes and the Republican Party. The network claims, however, that it is impartial. How might you judge the political bias of a network?

In recent years, narrowcasting has become increasingly prevalent. The broadcast networks' audiences are declining. Between 1982 and 2005, their share of the audience fell from 72 percent to 55 percent. At the same time, the percentage of households having access to the Internet grew from zero to more than 65 percent.

Talk-Show Politics and Internet Broadcasting

Multiple news outlets have given rise to literally thousands of talk shows on television, radio, and the Internet. By 2005, there were more than two dozen national television talk shows; their hosts ranged from Jerry Springer, who is regarded as a sensationalist, to Larry King, whose show has become a political necessity for candidates. In 2003, Arnold Schwarzenegger actually announced his candidacy for governor of California on Jay Leno's *Tonight Show.*

The real blossoming of "talk" has occurred on the radio. The number of radio stations that program only talk shows has increased from about 300 in 1989 to more than 1,200 today. The topics of talk shows range from business and investment, to psychology, to politics. There has been considerable criticism of the political talk shows, especially those hosted by Rush Limbaugh, G. Gordon Liddy, and other conservatives, on the ground that these shows focus on personal attacks rather than policy issues. Critics contend that such shows increase the level of intolerance and irrationality in American politics. The listeners to those shows are self-selected and tend to share the viewpoint of the host.

Responding to conservative dominance of "talk radio," in 2003 and 2004 a number of liberal groups began considering the possibilities of left-of-center talk shows. In 2004, liberal comedian Al Franken went live with his highly partisan take on the news. Although Franken is willing to match rhetoric with conservative talk-show hosts such as Rush Limbaugh, Franken's broadcast was initially carried by only 5 stations, as opposed to the 650 stations that carry Limbaugh.

The Internet makes it possible for a Web site to be highly ideological or partisan and to encourage online chat with others of the same persuasion. One of the

Radio talk show host Rush Limbaugh has a very large number of enthusiastic listeners across the country. Limbaugh, who is strongly conservative, is famous for harsh language he aims at liberals and liberal ideas. What are the political implications of the conservative dominance of talk radio? Does it unbalance the national discourse—or does it balance liberal voices in other branches of the media? (AP Photo/ Lennox McLendon)

potential hazards of narrowcasting of this kind is that people will be less open to dialogue with those whose opinions differ from their own, resulting in increased political extremism.

★ The Primacy of Television

Television is the most influential medium. It is also big business. National news TV personalities such as Peter Jennings may earn millions of dollars per year from their TV contracts alone. They are paid so much because they command large audiences, and large audiences command high prices for advertising on national news shows. Indeed, news *per se* has become a major factor in the profitability of TV stations.

The Increase in News-Type Programming

In 1963, the major networks—ABC, CBS, and NBC—devoted only eleven minutes daily to national news. A twenty-four-hour-a-day news cable channel—CNN—started operating in 1980. With the addition of CNN–Headline News, CNBC, MSNBC, Fox News, and other news-format cable channels since the 1980s, the amount of news-type programming has continued to increase. By 2005, the amount of time on the networks devoted to news-type programming had increased to about three hours. In recent years, all of the major networks have also added Internet sites to try to capture that market, but they face hundreds of competitors on the Web.

Television's Influence on the Political Process

Television's influence on the political process today is recognized by all who engage in the process. Television news is often criticized for being superficial, particularly compared with the detailed coverage available in the print media, such as the *New York Times*. In fact, television news is constrained by its technical characteristics, the most important being the limitations of time—stories must be reported in only a few minutes.

Jon Stewart of *The Daily Show*, an award-winning production of the Comedy Central channel. Stewart was highly critical of the Bush administration during 2004. The program regularly features political guests—Democratic senator John Edwards formally announced his candidacy for president on the show. Many voters report that they get most of their political news from programming that is primarily slanted toward entertainment. How would such information differ from that which is available on the evening news? (Courtesy of *The Daily Show*)

The most interesting aspect of television is, of course, the fact that it relies on pictures rather than words to attract the viewer's attention. Therefore, the video-tapes or slides that are chosen for a particular political story have exaggerated importance. Viewers do not know what other photos may have been taken or what other events may have been recorded—they see only those appearing on their screens. Television news can also be exploited for its drama by well-constructed stories. Some critics suggest that there is pressure to produce television news that has a "story line," like a novel or movie. The story should be short, with exciting pictures and a clear plot. In the extreme case, the news media are satisfied with a **sound bite,** a several-second comment selected or crafted for its immediate impact on the viewer.

It has been suggested that these formatting characteristics—or necessities—of television increase its influence on political events. (Newspapers and news magazines are also limited by their formats, but to a lesser extent.) As you are aware, real life is usually not dramatic, nor do all events have a neat or an easily understood plot. Political campaigns are continuing events, lasting perhaps as long as two years. The significance of their daily turns and twists is only apparent later. The "drama" of Congress, with its 535 players and dozens of important committees and meetings, is also difficult for the media to present. What television requires is dozens of daily three-minute stories.

Sound Bite
A brief, memorable comment that can easily be fit into news broadcasts.

★ The Media and Political Campaigns

All forms of the media—television, newspapers, radio, magazines, and online services—have a significant political impact on American society. Media influence is most obvious during political campaigns. News coverage of a single event, such as the results of the Iowa caucuses or the New Hampshire primary, may be the most important factor in having a candidate be referred to in the media as the front-runner in a presidential campaign. It is not too much of an exaggeration to say that almost all national political figures, starting with the president, plan every public appearance and statement to attract media coverage.

Vice President Dick Cheney unclips his microphone after a live TV interview at the Bush Cheney 2004 national campaign headquarters in Arlington, Virginia. How much of an impact do vice presidential candidates have on a presidential race? (AP Photo/Gerald Herbert)

Because television is the primary news source for the majority of Americans, candidates and their consultants spend much of their time devising strategies that use television to their benefit. Three types of TV coverage are generally employed in campaigns for the presidency and other offices: advertising, management of news coverage, and campaign debates.

Advertising

Perhaps one of the most effective political ads of all time was a thirty-second spot created by President Lyndon Johnson's media adviser in 1964. In this ad, a little girl stood in a field of daisies. As she held a daisy, she pulled the petals off and quietly counted to herself. Suddenly, when she reached number ten, a deep bass voice cut in and began a countdown: "10, 9, 8, 7, 6 . . . ." When the voice intoned "zero," the unmistakable mushroom cloud of an atomic bomb began to fill the screen. Then President Johnson's voice was heard: "These are the stakes. To make a world in which all of God's children can live, or to go into the dark. We must either love each other or we must die." At the end of the commercial, the message read, "Vote for President Johnson on November 3."

To understand how effective this "daisy girl" commercial was, you must know that Johnson's opponent was Barry Goldwater, a Republican conservative candidate known for his expansive views on the role of the U.S. military. The ad's impli-

President Lyndon Johnson's "daisy girl" ad contrasted the innocence of childhood with the horror of an atomic attack.

A pair of TV attack ads. The anti-Bush ad (left) was produced by MoveOn.org and paid for by the Media Fund, both of which are liberal organizations. The anti-Kerry ad (right) was produced and paid for by a conservative group called the Club for Growth. All of these organizations are "shadow groups," also known as "527 organizations" after the section of the tax code that applies to them. These groups are not allowed to coordinate their efforts with those of the presidential campaigns or the major parties. In what ways might attack ads backfire?

cation was that Goldwater would lead the United States into nuclear war. Although the ad was withdrawn within a few days, it has a place in political campaign history as the classic negative campaign advertisement. The ad's producer, Tony Schwartz, describes the effect in this way: "It was comparable to a person going to a psychiatrist and seeing dirty pictures in a Rorschach pattern. The daisy commercial evoked Goldwater's pro-bomb statements. They were like dirty pictures in the audience's mind."[4]

Since the daisy girl advertisement, negative advertising has come into its own. Candidates vie with one another to produce "attack" ads and then to counterattack when the opponent responds. The public claims not to like negative advertising, but as one consultant put it, "Negative advertising works." The most important effect of negative advertisements may not be to transfer votes from the candidate who is under attack to the candidate running the ads. Rather, the negative ads can demoralize the supporters of the candidate who is under attack. Some supporters, as a result, may not bother to vote. The widespread use of negative ads, therefore, can lead to reduced political participation and a general cynicism about politics.

As noted in Chapter 9, "advocacy ads," which argue for or against a policy or an issue (and, indirectly, for or against candidates who support that policy or issue), are another form of political advertising. These ads are very effective at conveying political messages to voters.

Management of News Coverage

Using political advertising to get a message across to the public is a very expensive tactic. Coverage by the news media, however, is free; it simply demands that the campaign ensure that coverage takes place. In recent years, campaign managers have shown increasing sophistication in creating newsworthy events for journalists to cover. As Doris Graber points out, "To keep a favorable image of their candidates in front of the public, campaign managers arrange newsworthy events to familiarize potential voters with their candidates' best aspects."[5]

[4]As quoted in Kathleen Hall Jamieson, *Packaging the Presidency: A History and Criticism of Presidential Campaign Advertising,* 3d ed. (New York: Oxford University Press, 1996), p. 200.
[5]Doris Graber, *Mass Media and American Politics,* 5th ed. (Washington, D.C.: Congressional Quarterly Press, 1997), p. 59.

Spin
An interpretation of campaign events or election results that is favorable to the candidate's campaign strategy.

Spin Doctor
A political campaign adviser who tries to convince journalists of the truth of a particular interpretation of events.

The campaign staff uses several methods to try to influence the quantity and type of coverage the campaign receives. First, the campaign staff understands the technical aspects of media coverage—camera angles, necessary equipment, timing, and deadlines—and plans political events to accommodate the press. Second, the campaign organization is aware that political reporters and their sponsors—networks or newspapers—are in competition for the best stories and can be manipulated through the granting of favors, such as a personal interview with the candidate. Third, the scheduler in the campaign has the important task of planning events that will be photogenic and interesting enough for the evening news. A related goal, although one that is more difficult to attain, is to convince reporters that a particular interpretation of an event is correct.

Today, the art of putting the appropriate **spin** on a story or event is highly developed. Each presidential candidate's press advisers, often referred to as **spin doctors,** try to convince the journalists that their interpretations of the political events are correct. For example, in 2004, George W. Bush's camp tried to persuade the media that criticisms of the administration by former administration officials were motivated by self-interest. These critics included former treasury secretary Paul O'Neill and former counterterrorism official Richard Clarke. Journalists have begun to report on the different spins and on how the candidates are trying to manipulate campaign news coverage.

Going for the Knockout Punch—Presidential Debates

In presidential elections, perhaps just as important as political advertisements is the performance of the candidate in televised presidential debates. After the first such debate in 1960, in which John Kennedy, the young senator from Massachusetts, took on the vice president of the United States, Richard Nixon, candidates became aware of the great potential of television for changing the momentum of a campaign. In general, challengers have much more to gain from

A family watches the 1960 Kennedy-Nixon debates on television. After the debate, TV viewers thought Kennedy had won, whereas radio listeners thought Nixon had won. (The Library of Congress)

Senator John Kerry (left) speaks as President George W. Bush (right) listens during the first 2004 presidential candidates' debate. The debate was held at the University of Miami in Florida on September 30, 2004. Coming into the debates, Kerry was trailing in the Gallup Poll and in other polls. After the first debate, however, Gallup reported that Kerry and Bush were tied. The race was again too close to call, as it had been for much of 2004. (Dennis Brack/Bloomberg News/Landov)

debating than do incumbents. Challengers hope that the incumbent will make a mistake in the debate and undermine the "presidential" image. Incumbent presidents are loath to debate their challengers, because it puts their opponents on an equal footing with them, but the debates have become so widely anticipated that it is difficult for an incumbent to refuse.

Debates can affect the outcome of a race. Some people believe that Democrat Al Gore hurt himself during the 2000 debates by appearing arrogant. In 2004, John F. Kerry came close to saving his campaign with a strong debate performance, though in the end George W. Bush won the election. During the debates, Kerry appeared calm and forceful—in a word, presidential. Kerry badly needed to project this image to counter repeated Republican accusations that he lacked the character to serve as commander in chief. In contrast, Bush seemed somewhat rattled by Kerry's criticisms, especially during the first debate.

Although debates are justified publicly as an opportunity for the voters to find out how candidates differ on the issues, what the candidates want is to capitalize on the power of television to project an image. They view the debate as a strategic opportunity to improve their own images or to point out the failures of their opponents. Candidates also know that the morning-after interpretation of the debate by the news media may play a crucial role in what the public thinks. Regardless of the risks of debating, the potential for gaining votes is so great that candidates undoubtedly will continue to seek televised debates.

Political Campaigns and the Internet

Without a doubt, the Internet has become an important vehicle for campaign advertising and news coverage, as well as for soliciting campaign contributions. This was made clear during the 2004 presidential elections. A Pew Research Study poll conducted in December 2003 and January 2004 revealed that even at that early stage of the election process, 22 percent of all Internet users had gone online to obtain news or information about the campaigns. This figure equals the number who had done this by the end of the 2002 elections, so use of the Internet was clearly rising. Of all Internet users, 7 percent had participated in online campaign activities. (Internet users included about two-thirds of all American adults.)

Democratic presidential candidate Senator John Kerry of Massachusetts waves after making his arrival onstage on a Harley-Davidson motorcycle during the *Tonight Show* as host Jay Leno applauds. Television and radio talk shows have become important forums for political candidates. Is there any downside to a candidate appearing on a popular TV or radio talk show? (AP Photo/Reed Saxon)

Today, the campaign staff of virtually every candidate running for a significant political office includes an Internet campaign strategist—a professional hired to create and maintain the campaign Web site. The work of this strategist includes designing a user-friendly and attractive Web site for the candidate, managing the candidate's e-mail communications, and tracking campaign contributions made through the site. Additionally, virtually all major interest groups in the United States now use the Internet to promote their causes. Prior to elections, various groups engage in issue advocacy from their Web sites. At little or no cost, they can promote positions taken by favored candidates and solicit contributions.

Only a few years ago, some speculated that the Internet would soon dominate political campaign advertising and news coverage. The traditional media—television, radio, and printed newspapers and magazines—would play a far less significant role than in the past. Will this, in fact, happen? We examine this question in this chapter's *Which Side Are You On?* feature.

The Media's Impact on the Voters

The question of how much influence the media have on voting behavior is difficult to answer. Generally, individuals watch television, read newspapers, or log on to a Web site with certain preconceived ideas about political issues and candidates. These attitudes and opinions act as a kind of perceptual screen that filters out information that makes people feel uncomfortable or that does not fit with their own ideas.

Voters watch campaign commercials and news about political campaigns with "selective attentiveness"—that is, they tend to watch those commercials that support the candidates they favor and tend to pay attention to news stories about their own candidates. This selectivity also affects their perceptions of the content of a news story or commercial and whether it is remembered. Apparently, the media have the most influence on those persons who have not formed an opinion about political candidates or issues. Studies have shown that the flurry of television commercials and debates immediately before election day has the greatest impact on those voters who are truly undecided. Few voters who have already formed their opinions change their minds under the influence of the media.

In 2004, as in earlier years, the media focused on the "horse race" aspects of the presidential campaigns. While some media outlets did present careful analyses of the issues and critiques of the candidates' advertising spots, most of the television coverage focused on the ever-present polls. Both presidential candidates, John Kerry and George W. Bush, took advantage of every opportunity to be on prime-time television: they visited with Oprah, David Letterman, and Larry King, among others. In fact, a national poll has indicated that some 20 percent of the voters said that they learned about politics from late-night talk shows.

One possible way in which the media might have affected the race was the continuous news from Iraq, which mostly reported murderous attacks on American soldiers and Iraqi policemen. This drumbeat of grim news, however, did not appear to shake the belief of a majority of the American people that it was necessary to see the situation in Iraq through to the end.

WHICH SIDE ARE YOU ON?
Are Internet Campaigns the Wave of the Future?

In December 2002, Vermont governor Howard Dean did not look like a candidate who could win the Democratic presidential nomination, although his fiery speeches were popular among the faithful. By December 2003, Dean was propelled to the head of the Democratic pack by a campaign that took unique advantage of the Internet. In January 2004, however, Dean's support collapsed. While Dean was on the rise, many observers claimed that Internet-based campaigns were indeed the wave of the future. But after January, some pundits compared Dean's campaign to the tech boom of the 1990s—"an overinflated bubble that left its naïve believers drenched in soap scum."*

THE INTERNET WILL DEMOCRATIZE POLITICAL CAMPAIGNS

Internet advocates say that new technology can bring more people into the democratic process. Activists can sign up online for face-to-face meetings through Web sites such as Meetup.com. Supporters can create independent Web logs, or *blogs,* that give them a stake in the campaign. Above all, the Web is a very effective way of mobilizing campaign contributions. Finally, the Web can be used to distribute advertisements at almost no cost. Web ads can be more hard hitting than TV ads because the Internet is not subject to government regulation.

Web advocates argue that Dean's political collapse was due to his deficiencies as a candidate, not the technology he employed. As technology expert Esther Dyson observed, "The best way to kill a bad product is good advertising."†

THE INTERNET IS SERIOUSLY OVERSOLD

Web critics question whether the Web is truly transformative. After all, Dean failed. Many of the young campaign workers he recruited through the Web, through their inexperience, may have turned off more voters than they were able to mobilize. A "flash mob" psychology can lead Web users to rally behind candidates who have not been tested by the pressure of a national campaign. The Web also promotes extreme political positions. This can pull campaigns away from the political center, where most of the votes are located. Finally, the Internet cannot be used to persuade marginal voters to get out and vote, and get-out-the-vote drives have been key to the success of most recent campaigns.

WHAT'S YOUR POSITION?

Do you think that Internet campaigns are essential or that they are overhyped? Might the Web be more useful for lobbying than for organizing campaigns?

GOING ONLINE

You can find the Meetup service at **http://www.meetup.com**. Meetup participants can set the location and agenda of a meeting online. You can obtain information on registering to vote at **http://www.declareyourself.org**. Web site technologies for candidates are for sale at **http://www.electionmall.com**, an entertaining site.

* Steven Levy, "Dean's Net Effect Is Just the Start," *Newsweek,* March 29, 2004, p. 73.

†Ibid.

★ The Media and the Government

The mass media not only wield considerable power when it comes to political campaigns, but they also, in one way or another, can wield power over the affairs of government and over government officials. For example, in April 2004 President George W. Bush tried to keep National Security Adviser Condoleezza Rice from testifying before the bipartisan 9/11 investigation commission by citing the doctrine of executive privilege. After several weeks during which this decision was widely criticized in the print and electronic media, Bush reversed himself and allowed Rice to testify.

The Role of the Media in the 2004 Elections

The media campaigns of all candidates included the usual mind-numbing cascade of TV commercials and radio spots, many of which were "attack" ads. As usual, the networks paid scant attention to the two conventions. Nonetheless, the poll numbers for Kerry jumped after the public got to see him for an entire hour. In the months that followed, Kerry's frequent TV ads did not seem to help him, whereas the Bush ads were effective in raising questions about Kerry's leadership abilities. What was new to the 2004 campaign was the way in which the Internet supplemented standard media coverage. Thousands of so-called Web-based "blogs" were set up to pitch views for and against various candidates.

President Ronald Reagan (1981–1989) in a speech from the White House. Reagan was called "the great communicator" for his effective use of the media. He was an actor before entering politics, and that experience helped him develop his skills. Reagan accumulated decades of political experience before becoming president. Still, some people held his acting career against him. Why might that be so? (AP Photo/Barry Thumma)

The Media and the Presidency

The relationship between the media and the president usually is reciprocal: each needs the other to thrive. Because of this codependency, both the media and the president work hard to exploit one another. The media need news to report, and the president needs coverage.

In the United States, the prominence of the president is accentuated by a **White House press corps** that is assigned full-time to cover the presidency. These reporters even have a lounge in the White House where they spend their days, waiting for a story to break. Most of the time, they simply wait for the daily or twice-daily briefing by the president's **press secretary.** Because of the press corps' physical proximity to the president, the chief executive cannot even take a brief stroll around the presidential swimming pool without its becoming news. Perhaps no other nation allows the press such access to its highest government official. Consequently, no other democratic nation has its airwaves and print media so filled with absolute trivia regarding the personal lives of the chief executive and his family.

One of the first presidents to make truly effective use of the media was President Franklin D. Roosevelt (1933–1945), who brought new spirit to a demoralized country and led it through the Great Depression with his radio broadcasts. His "fireside chats" brought hope to millions. Through his speeches, Roosevelt was able to forge a common emotional bond among his listeners. His decisive announcement in 1933 on the reorganization of the banks, for example, calmed a jittery nation and prevented the collapse of the banking industry. (Nervous depositors were withdrawing their assets, which threatened to create a "run" on the banks.) His famous Pearl Harbor speech, following the Japanese attack on the U.S. Pacific fleet on December 7, 1941 ("a day that will live in infamy"), mobilized the nation for World War II.

Setting the Public Agenda

According to a number of studies, the media play an important part in setting the public agenda. Evidence is strong that whatever public problems receive the greatest media treatment will be cited by the public in contemporary surveys as the most important problems. Although the media do not make policy decisions, they do influence to a significant extent the policy issues that will be decided—and this is an important part of the political process. Because those who control the media are not elected representatives of the people, the agenda-setting role of the media necessarily is a controversial one. The relationship of the media to

White House Press Corps
The reporters assigned full-time to cover the presidency.

Press Secretary
The presidential staff member responsible for handling White House media relations and communications.

President Franklin D. Roosevelt, the first president to fully exploit the airwaves for his benefit, reported to the nation through radio "fireside chats." How did such capabilities change the nature of the presidency? (Photo Researchers)

agenda setting remains complex, though, because politicians are able to manipulate media coverage to control some of its effects, as well as to exploit the media to further their agendas with the public.

Government Regulation of the Media

The United States has one of the freest presses in the world. Nonetheless, regulation of the media does exist, particularly of the electronic media. Many aspects of this regulation were discussed in Chapter 4, when we examined First Amendment rights and the press.

The First Amendment does not mention electronic media, which did not exist when the Bill of Rights was written. For many reasons, the government has much greater control over the electronic media than it does over printed media. Through the Federal Communications Commission (FCC), which regulates communications by radio, television, wire, and cable, the number of radio stations has been controlled for many years, even though technologically we could have many more radio stations than now exist. Also, the FCC created a situation in which the three major TV networks dominated the airwaves.

Controlling Ownership of the Media

Many FCC rules have dealt with ownership of news media, such as how many stations a network can own. Recently, the FCC has decided to auction off hundreds of radio frequencies, allowing the expansion of cellular telephone applications.

In 1996, Congress passed legislation that has far-reaching implications for the communications industry—the Telecommunications Act. The act ended the rule that kept telephone companies from entering the cable business and other communications markets. What this means is that a single corporation—whether AOL/Time-Warner or Disney—can offer long-distance and local telephone services, cable television, satellite television, Internet services, and, of course, libraries of films and entertainment. The act opened the door to competition and led to more options for consumers, who now can choose among multiple competitors for all of these services delivered to the home. At the same time, it launched a race among competing companies to control media ownership.

Media Conglomerates.   Many media outlets are now owned by corporate conglomerates. A single entity may own a television network; the studios that produce shows, news, and movies; and the means to deliver that content to the home via cable, satellite, or the Internet. The question to be faced in the future is how to ensure competition in the delivery of news so that citizens have access to multiple points of view from the media.

Within the past decade, all of the prime-time television networks have been purchased by major American corporations and have become part of corporate conglomerates. The Turner Broadcasting/CNN network was also purchased by a major corporation, Time Warner. Later, Time Warner was acquired by America Online (AOL), a merger that combined the world's then-largest media company with the world's then-largest online company. Fox Television has always been a part of Rupert Murdoch's publishing and media empire. In addition to taking part in mergers and acquisitions, many of these companies have formed partnerships with computer software makers, such as Microsoft, for joint electronic publishing ventures.

Reevaluating the Rules.   In 2002, in response to a series of decisions by the U.S. Court of Appeals for the District of Columbia, the FCC began to reevaluate its

The Reverend Jesse Jackson leads a protest outside the headquarters of the Federal Communications Commission (the FCC) in Washington, D.C. In 2003, the FCC voted to relax its media-ownership rules, opening the door for media conglomerates to buy more local television stations and newspapers. Why might someone believe that the media coverage would be less balanced under conglomerate ownership? (Chris Kleponis/Bloomberg News/Landov)

rules that limited the concentration of media ownership. In June 2003, the FCC announced new proposed rules that would have allowed large media corporations to own a significantly greater number of television stations in any given media market. In addition, the new rules would, for the first time, have permitted a company to own both a TV station and the local newspaper in any of the larger markets. A wide variety of interest groups, on learning of the proposed new rules, opposed them strongly. Congress reacted with unusual speed and barred the FCC from implementing the proposed rules.

Government Control of Content

On the face of it, the First Amendment would seem to apply to all media. In fact, the United States Supreme Court has often been slow to extend free speech and free press guarantees to new media. For example, in 1915, the Court held that "as a matter of common sense," free speech protections did not apply to cinema. Only in 1952 did the Court find that motion pictures were covered by the First Amendment.[6] In contrast, the Court extended full protection to the Internet almost immediately by striking down provisions of the 1996 Telecommunications Act.[7] Cable TV also received broad protection in 2000.[8]

Control of Broadcasting. While the Court has held that the First Amendment is relevant to radio and television, it has never extended full protection to these media. The Court has used a number of arguments to justify this stand—initially, the scarcity of broadcast frequencies. The Court later held that the government could restrict "indecent" programming based on the "pervasive" presence of

---

[6]*Joseph Burstyn, Inc. v. Wilson*, 343 U.S. 495 (1952).
[7]*Reno v. American Civil Liberties Union*, 521 U.S. 844 (1997).
[8]*United States v. Playboy Entertainment Group*, 529 U.S. 803 (2000).

During the Second Gulf War, the U.S. military allowed journalists to join military units for the duration of their presence in the Middle East. This program was called "embedding." Here, journalists from around the world gather at the Kuwait Hilton Hotel and wait to join their assigned units. How might such close contact between reporters and soldiers affect what the reporters write?

broadcasting in the home.[9] On this basis, the FCC has the authority to fine broadcasters for indecency or profanity.

Indecency in broadcasting became a major issue in 2004. In the first three months of that year, the FCC levied fines that exceeded those imposed in the previous nine years combined. Including older fines, radio personality Howard Stern has cost his employers almost $2 million. Another triggering episode was singer Janet Jackson's "wardrobe malfunction" during a 2004 Super Bowl halftime performance. Legislation was introduced in Congress to increase the maximum fine that the FCC can impose to $500,000 per incident.

Government Control of the Media during the Second Gulf War.   During the First Gulf War in 1991, the U.S. government was strongly criticized for not providing accurate information to the media. Stung by this criticism, the Bush administration tried a two-pronged strategy during the Second Gulf War in 2003. Every day, reporters at the central command post in Qatar were able to hear briefings from top commanders. (Reporters complained, however, that they did not hear enough about the true progress of the war.) The administration also allowed more than five hundred journalists to travel with the combat forces as "embedded" journalists. Reports from the field were very favorable to the military. This was understandable, given that the journalists quickly identified with the troops and their difficulties. The Bush administration, however, was unable to control reports from foreign and Arab media.

The Public's Right to Media Access

Media Access
The public's right of access to the media. The Federal Communications Commission and the courts gradually have taken the stance that citizens do have a right to media access.

Does the public have a right to **media access?** Both the FCC and the courts gradually have taken the stance that citizens do have a right of access to the media, particularly the electronic media. The argument is that because the airwaves are public, the government has the right to dictate how they are used. The government could, for example, require the broadcast networks to provide free airtime to candidates. Republican senator John McCain of Arizona, a major proponent of

---

[9]*FCC v. Pacifica Foundation,* 438 U.S. 230 (1978). In this case, the Court banned seven swear words (famously used by comedian George Carlin) during hours when children could hear them.

campaign-finance reform, has proposed—so far without success—legislation that would provide such free airtime.

Technology is giving more citizens access to the electronic media and, in particular, to television. As more cable operators have more airtime to sell, some of it will remain unused and will be available for public access. At the same time, the Internet makes media access by the public very easy, although not everyone has the resources to take advantage of it.

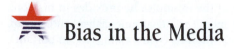

Bias in the Media

Many studies have been undertaken to try to identify the sources and direction of **bias** in the media, and these studies have reached different conclusions. Some claim that the press has a liberal bias. Others conclude that the press shows a conservative bias. Still others do not see any notable partisan bias.

Bias
An inclination or a preference that interferes with impartial judgment.

Do the Media Have a Partisan Bias?

In a classic study conducted in the 1980s, researchers found that media producers, editors, and reporters (the "media elite") exhibited a notably liberal and "left-leaning" bias in their news coverage.[10] Since then, the contention that the media have a liberal bias has been repeated time and again. Joining the ranks of those who assert that the media has a liberal bias is Bernard Goldberg, a veteran CBS broadcaster. Goldberg argues that liberal bias is responsible for the declining number of viewers who watch network news. He claims that this liberal bias, which "comes naturally to most reporters," has given viewers less reason to trust the big news networks.[11] Conservative journalist William McGowan also claims that the press exhibits a liberal bias. He maintains that most news reporters have liberal views on the issues they cover (he cites a survey of journalists in which over 80 percent of the respondents said that they were in favor of abortion rights) and that this bias prevents them from investigating and reporting on opposing viewpoints.[12]

In contrast to Goldberg and McGowan, journalist Eric Alterman argues that the media have, on the whole, a conservative bias. Alterman claims that the unwarranted perception of a liberal bias has intimidated the media into presenting more conservative opinions. Alterman finds conservative bias to be strongest in the media's coverage of economic issues. He also observes that the almost complete dominance of talk radio by conservatives has given the political right an outlet that the political left cannot counter. Alterman does find a degree of cultural liberalism among journalists, however, as demonstrated by the resolutely nonreligious nature of mainstream reporting.[13]

A poll by the Pew Research Center for the People and the Press in January 2004 confirmed that Americans were divided over the issue of whether news organizations favor one political party or the other. While 42 percent of self-identified Republicans saw positive bias toward the Democrats, 29 percent of the Democrats saw positive bias toward the Republicans.

[10]S. Robert Lichter, Stanley Rothman, and Linda S. Lichter, *The Media Elite* (New York: Adler and Adler, 1986).
[11]Bernard Goldberg, *Bias: A CBS Insider Exposes How the Media Distort the News* (Washington, D.C.: Regnery Publishing, 2001).
[12]William McGowan, *Coloring the News: How Crusading for Diversity Has Corrupted American Journalism* (San Francisco: Encounter Books, 2001).
[13]Eric Alterman, *What Liberal Media? The Truth about Bias and the News* (New York: Basic Books, 2003).

A Commercial Bias?

According to Andrew Kohut, director of the Pew Research Center in Washington, D.C., however, the majority of those responding to Pew Research Center polls see no ideological or partisan pattern in media bias. Rather, what people mean when they say the press is biased in its political reporting is that it is biased toward its own self-interest—the need to gain higher ratings and thus more advertising revenues.

Interestingly, even though Bernard Goldberg, as just mentioned, argues that there is a liberal bias in the media, some of the examples he provides in his book would indicate that the bias in the press is more toward commercialism and elitism. For example, he states that during "sweeps" months (when ratings are important), the networks deliberately avoid featuring blacks, Hispanics, and poor or unattractive people on their prime-time news magazine shows. This, asserts Goldberg, is because such coverage might "turn off" the white, middle-class viewers that the networks want to attract so that they can build the ratings that advertisers want. When the media do cover minority groups, are the images they use misleading? We examine this question in this chapter's *Politics and Diversity* feature.

Other Theories of Media Bias

Others see the media as biased toward the "status quo," meaning that the media are biased toward supporting corporate America and its aims. This group believes that the press tends to downplay the complaints made by people who are seen as being on the fringes of the political spectrum, especially on the left.

Still others contend that the media are biased against "losers." For example, Kathleen Hall Jamieson, director of the Annenberg Public Policy Center at the University of Pennsylvania, concludes that if there is a bias in the press, it is not a partisan bias but a bias against losers. A candidate who falls behind in a race is immediately labeled a "loser," making it even more difficult for that candidate to regain favor in the voters' eyes.[14]

Calvin F. Exoo has offered yet another theory. In his study of politics in the media,[15] he concluded that journalists are constrained by both the pro-America bias of the media's owners and the journalists' own code of objectivity. Most are more interested in improving their career prospects by covering the winning candidate and pleasing their editors to get better assignments than they are in discussing public policies. Thus, the bias in the media is toward not criticizing the American system and on producing "news" that will attract viewers and readers without threatening the American way of life. This analysis would support Thomas E. Patterson's view that the bias of the news media is to emphasize bad news and cynicism rather than any partisan position.[16]

The Media: Why Are They Important Today?

The media, particularly during elections, can influence your everyday life in many ways. The media are always present with political stories, issues, and debates. In the print media, you cannot avoid political discussions because they are regular features. When you watch the news on TV, you see political stories every day. If you listen to commercial radio, you hear political news at least once

---

[14]Kathleen Hall Jamieson, *Everything You Think You Know about Politics . . . and Why You're Wrong* (New York: Basic Books, 2000).
[15]Calvin F. Exoo, *The Politics of the Mass Media* (St. Paul: West, 1994).
[16]Thomas E. Patterson, *Out of Order* (New York: Knopf, 1993).

POLITICS AND DIVERSITY
Racial Profiling in the Media

Racial profiling is the act of routinely making negative assumptions about individuals based on race. The term was first used to describe the behavior of certain police officers who habitually stopped African American motorists more frequently than white ones, often on minor pretexts. African Americans have described these incidents as stops for "driving while black." Some observers have charged that the media—television in particular—engage in racial profiling in their reporting on minority group members.

IMAGES ON TV

Those who believe that the media engage in racial profiling point to common stereotypes that journalists often use when illustrating news stories. For example, a study found that while African Americans constituted 29 percent of the nation's poor, they made up 65 percent of the images of the poor shown on leading network news programs. In addition to being disproportionately portrayed as black, the poor were also largely represented by the persons least likely to command sympathy—unemployed adults. The elderly and the working poor were underrepresented.*

*Martin Gilens, "Race and Poverty in America: Public Misperceptions and the American News Media," *Public Opinion Quarterly,* vol. 6 (1996).

Critics of racial profiling also argue that African Americans are regularly used to illustrate drug abusers or dealers, even though a majority of users are white, and that images of criminals in general are disproportionately black.

Americans of Middle Eastern ancestry have also complained about profiling. In this instance, the stereotype is of the Arab terrorist. Of course, such people exist, but like African American criminals, they make up a small part of the group's population.

DIVERSITY IN THE NEWSROOM

Today's newsrooms are increasingly diverse. One survey revealed that minority group members made up 18 percent of the employees in television journalism, and African Americans made up 10 percent. Such a substantial minority presence may serve to prevent egregious examples of racial profiling. Some even argue that racial and ethnic diversity in the work force leads television journalists to "pull their punches" when reporting on minority group members.

FOR CRITICAL ANALYSIS

Although part of the newsroom work force is made up of minority group members, network executives and news directors are predominantly white and male. In what ways could this reduce minority influence?

---

an hour. During campaigns, you encounter paid political announcements on a regular basis in all media.

You may find the media annoying when they cover something you think is silly or insignificant. Nevertheless, the media remain important simply because they are the vehicles through which you obtain information about the current state of affairs both within and outside the United States. Certainly, in a world where security concerns have become paramount, you must be aware of what steps your government is taking to improve national security. If you do not, you may find that radical changes have been made—changes that may affect some of the basic freedoms that you take for granted.

Today, in addition to traditional news media, the Internet provides easy access to an expanded set of viewpoints. Not only can you access the Web sites of TV news shows, domestic newspapers and magazines, and a variety of sources of political commentary, but in addition you can access foreign newspapers. Foreign views of the United States are often very different from the views expressed in the U.S. media, particularly on issues relating to U.S. foreign policy. The Internet also provides access to the "alternative press," such as the *Nation*, the *Progressive*, and the *Washington Monthly*. Of course, the consumer of news publicized via the Internet must always be vigilant, must know what sources the news reporter used, and must be able to analyze news stories. We treat this topic further in this chapter's *Making a Difference* feature.

MAKING A DIFFERENCE   ★ Being a Critical Consumer of the News

Television and newspapers provide a wide range of choices for Americans who want to stay informed. Still, critics of the media argue that a substantial amount of programming and print is colored either by the subjectivity of editors and producers or by the demands of profit making. Few Americans take the time to become critical consumers of the news.

Why Should You Care?

Even if you do not plan to engage in political activism, you have a stake in ensuring that your beliefs are truly your own and that they represent your values and interests. To guarantee this result, you need to obtain accurate information from the media and avoid being swayed by subliminal appeals, loaded terms, or outright bias. If you do not take care, you could find yourself voting for a candidate who is opposed to what you believe in or voting against measures that are in your interest.

Even when journalists themselves are relatively successful in an attempt to remain objective, they will of necessity give airtime to politicians and interest group representatives who are far from impartial. You need the ability to determine what motivates the players in the political game and to what extent they are "shading"

the news or even propagating outright lies. You also need to determine which news outlets are reliable.

What Can You Do?

To become a critical news consumer, you must practice reading a newspaper with a critical eye toward editorial decisions. For example, ask yourself what stories are given prominence on the front page of the paper and which ones merit a photograph. What is the editorial stance of the newspaper? Which columnists are given space on the "op-ed" page opposite the paper's own editorial page? For a contrast to most daily papers, occasionally pick up an outright political publication such as the *National Review* or the *New Republic* and take note of the editorial positions.

Watching the evening news can be far more rewarding if you look at how much the news depends on video effects. You will note that stories on the evening news tend to be no more than three minutes long, that stories with excellent videotape get more attention, and that considerable time is taken up with "happy talk" or human interest stories.

Another way to critically evaluate news coverage is to compare how the news is covered in different media. For example, you might compare the

evening news with the daily paper. You will see that the paper is perhaps half a day behind television in reporting the news but that the printed story contains far more information.

If you wish to obtain more information on the media, you can contact one of the following organizations:

National Association of Broadcasters
1771 N St. N.W.
Washington, DC 20036
202-429-5300
http://www.nab.org

National Newspaper Association
129 Neff Annex
Columbia, MO 65211
1-800-829-4NNA
http://www.nna.org

Accuracy in Media
(a conservative group)
4455 Connecticut Ave. N.W.,
Suite 330
Washington, DC 20008
202-364-4401
http://www.aim.org

People for the American Way
(a liberal group)
2000 M St. N.W., Suite 400
Washington, DC 20036
202-467-4999
http://www.pfaw.org

 ## Key Terms

bias 347	media access 346	public agenda 328	spin doctor 338
electronic media 332	narrowcasting 332	sound bite 335	White House press corps 343
managed news 330	press secretary 343	spin 338	yellow journalism 331

★ Chapter Summary

1 The media are enormously important in American politics today. They perform a number of functions, including (a) entertainment, (b) news reporting, (c) identifying public problems, (d) socializing new generations, (e) providing a political forum, and (f) making profits.

2 The media have always played a significant role in American politics. In the 1800s and earlier, however, news traveled slowly, and politics was controlled by small groups whose members communicated personally. The high-speed rotary press and the telegraph led to self-supported newspapers and mass readership.

3 Broadcast media (television and radio) have been important means of communication since the early twentieth century. New technologies, such as cable television and the Internet, are giving broadcasters the opportunity to air a greater number of specialized programs.

4 The media wield great power during political campaigns and over the affairs of government and government officials by focusing attention on their actions. Today's political campaigns use political advertising and expert management of news coverage. For presidential candidates, how they appear in presidential debates is of major importance.

5 The relationship between the media and the president is close; each uses the other—sometimes positively, sometimes negatively. The media play an important role in investigating the government, in getting government officials to understand better the needs and desires of American society, and in setting the public agenda.

6 The electronic media are subject to government regulation. Many Federal Communications Commission rules have dealt with ownership of TV and radio stations. Legislation has removed many rules about co-ownership of several forms of media, although the most recent steps taken by Congress have been to halt any further deregulation.

7 Studies of bias in the media have reached different conclusions. Some claim that the media have a liberal bias; others contend that the press shows a conservative bias. Still others conclude that the press is biased toward its own self-interest—the need to gain higher ratings and thus more advertising revenues. Other studies have found other types of biases, such as a bias in favor of the status quo or a bias against losers.

★ Selected Print and Media Resources

SUGGESTED READINGS

Alterman, Eric. *What Liberal Media? The Truth about Bias and the News.* New York: Basic Books, 2003. Based on extensive research, Alterman's book argues that the media have a conservative bias overall, especially on economic issues.

Gillmor, Dan. *We the Media: Grassroots Journalism by the People, for the People.* Sebastopol, Calif.: O'Reilly, 2004. Web logs, or "blogs," have become an increasingly important part of the media. In 2004, for the first time, bloggers were awarded press credentials to cover the national political conventions. Newspaper journalist Dan Gillmor, a blogger himself, covers the new movement.

Goldberg, Bernard. *Arrogance: Rescuing America from the Media Elite.* New York: Warner, 2003. This is Goldberg's second book in which he argues that the media have a liberal bias and is a follow-up to *Bias: A CBS Insider Exposes How the Media Distort the News.* Goldberg argues that the media elite constitute an inbred, insular group.

NBC, Marc Robinson, Tom Brokaw, *et al. Brought to You in Living Color: Seventy-five Years of Great Moments in Television and Radio from NBC.* Somerset, N.J.: Wiley, 2002. Although this book focuses on the history of NBC, it also provides an entertaining and informative history of network programming and entertainment over the past seventy-five years.

MEDIA RESOURCES

All the President's Men—A film, produced by Warner Brothers in 1976, starring Dustin Hoffman and Robert Redford as the two *Washington Post* reporters, Bob Woodward and Carl Bernstein, who broke the story on the Watergate scandal. The film is an excellent portrayal of the *Washington Post* newsroom and the decisions that editors make in such situations.

Citizen Kane—A 1941 film, based on the life of William Randolph Hearst and directed by Orson Welles, that has been acclaimed as one of the best movies ever made. Welles himself stars as the newspaper tycoon. The film also stars Joseph Cotten and Alan Ladd.

Disconnected: Politics, the Press, and the Public—This 2000 seminar, introduced by Peter Jennings of ABC News and moderated by Arthur Miller of Harvard Law School, examines how the media affect the national agenda and the standards of political debate. Panelists include Dan Rather of CBS News, Jeff Greenfield of CNN, Democratic congressman Barney Frank, Republican political consultant Ed Rollins, and others.

The Insider—A 1999 film, starring Russell Crowe and Al Pacino, about the real-life drama that took place behind the scenes of the CBS news magazine *60 Minutes* when CBS corporate executives tried to pull the plug on a news story about a tobacco-industry whistleblower.

e-mocracy ★ The Media and the Internet

Today, the Internet offers a great opportunity to those who want to access the news. All of the major news organizations, including radio and television stations and newspapers, are online. Most local newspapers include at least some of their news coverage and features on their Web sites, and all national newspapers are online. Even foreign newspapers can now be accessed online within a few seconds. Also available are purely Web-based news publications, including e-zines (online news magazines) such as *Slate, Salon,* and *Hotwired.* Because it is relatively simple for anyone or any organization to put up a home page or Web site, a wide variety of sites have appeared that critique the news media or give alternative interpretations of the news and the way it is presented.

Logging On

The Web site of the *American Journalism Review* includes features from the magazine and original content created specifically for online reading. Go to

http://www.ajr.org

The *Drudge Report* home page, posted by Matt Drudge, provides a handy guide to the Web's best spots for news and opinions. Its mission is one-click access to breaking news and recent columns. It provides links to specific columnists and opinion pages for magazines and major daily newspapers. Go to

http://www.drudgereport.com

The American Review Web page critiques the media, promotes media activism, and calls for media reform. Its URL is

http://www.AmericanReview.us

To view *Slate,* the e-zine of politics and culture published by Microsoft, go to

http://Slate.msn.com

"Blogs," or Web logs, have become a major feature of the Internet. A large number of blogs deal with political topics. For a listing of several hundred political blogs, go to the Blog Search Engine at:

http://www.blogsearchengine.com/ political_blogs.html

For an Internet site that provides links to news media around the world, including alternative media, go to

http://www.mediachannel.org

Using InfoTrac for Political Research

The question of to what extent—and in which direction—the media are biased is key to anyone who is concerned about truth. You can research this by using InfoTrac. To use InfoTrac to research media bias, go to

http://www.infotrac-college.com

Log in and go to InfoTrac College Edition, then go to the Keyword guide. Type "media bias" in the search field. InfoTrac will present you with a list of articles, with the most recent ones listed first. When choosing articles for your analysis, be sure to pick ones that represent multiple points of view. You will quickly discover that commentators who discuss bias are often strongly opinionated. It may take some work to extract real evidence of biased reporting from these opinion pieces.

ONLINE REVIEW

At **http://politicalscience.wadsworth. com/schmidt12**, you will find a free Study Guide to this book. For each chapter, there are two online quizzes to help you master the material.

• The **PoliPrep Self Study Assessment** provides a pre-test for each major section of the chapter. PoliPrep then generates a customized study plan. After you complete the study plan, a post-test evaluates your progress.

• The **Tutorial Quiz** for each chapter provides questions on the chapter contents, including the features. The questions are organized to match the major sections of the chapter.

CHAPTER 11

The Congress

353

WHAT IF . . .
Members of Congress Were Required to Report Annually to Their Constituents?

BACKGROUND

Each year, members of Congress vote on hundreds of bills and hold thousands of conversations with colleagues, lobbyists, and constituents. But how do constituents find out what their representative or senator is actually doing? There are sources that record the formal votes and actions of members of Congress, but there is no requirement for members to report to the voters, although they are entitled to free postage for such mailings. Many members of Congress do communicate with their constituents using newsletters, Web sites, and newspaper columns. These communications are generally self-serving, however, and report only those activities that the members want to highlight.

WHAT IF MEMBERS OF CONGRESS WERE REQUIRED TO REPORT ANNUALLY TO THEIR CONSTITUENTS?

Requiring all members of Congress to issue a report to their constituents would certainly provide citizens with more information about their legislators than ever before. Each member of the House of Representatives could mail a document to every district resident reporting votes on every bill presented to the House and listing every meeting with a lobbyist, constituent, or colleague. The report could also include official trips, the number of days spent at home in the district, and the budget for that member's office. Constituents might be surprised at the number of individual constituent requests serviced by the member's office staff.

STRENGTHENING PUBLIC SUPPORT FOR CONGRESS

One of the issues facing Congress is a lack of public support for its work. Because it is difficult for the media to capture the tasks of Congress, voters tend to hear only about scandals, junkets to foreign lands, and projects that appear to be wasteful. By providing an annual report to the citizens, members would make public the amount of

work they do. Simply publishing the schedule of committee meetings and Senate or House sessions attended would show the voters that members work hard at their jobs.

Voters would also be surprised by the range of issues that members must vote on in a given session. Many of the votes have little relevance for their own districts, yet such votes require attention by Congress as a whole. Members often must vote on tax or spending bills that can run up to hundreds of pages.

Finally, voters could see the list of people who actually meet with members of the House and Senate. In addition to lobbyists, representatives of the administration, staff members, and colleagues, members meet with and respond to hundreds of individual constituents each year. Reporting these meetings might encourage more constituents to contact their representatives in Washington.

THE USEFULNESS OF THIS INFORMATION

Requiring such a report would help voters appreciate the work done by their members of Congress. The annual report, however, could also raise new considerations for the relationship between constituent and representative.

Some voters would comb through the report and come away with hard questions about how their representatives spend their time in office. Are the members really paying attention to the issues that face their constituents, or are they taking care of special interests? Do they spend enough time at home to know the concerns of their constituents? Why is it necessary for a member to travel to a NATO meeting in Rome, for example?

Members of the opposition party would find information in the report to use against the legislator in the next election. Many meetings, trips, and votes are difficult to explain to the general public, and some may truly be suspect. Members of the media would also search the report for newsworthy items.

Finally, the size and complexity of the report could overwhelm many voters and perhaps reduce their interest in government even further.

354

Most Americans view Congress in a less than flattering light. In recent years, Congress has appeared to be deeply split, highly partisan in its conduct, and not very responsive to public needs. Polls show that only about 40 percent of the public have favorable opinions about Congress as a whole. Yet individual members of Congress often receive much higher approval ratings from the voters in their districts. This is one of the paradoxes of the relationship between the people and Congress. Members of the public hold the institution in relatively low regard compared with the satisfaction they express with their individual representatives.

Part of the explanation for these seemingly contradictory appraisals is that members of Congress spend considerable time and effort serving their **constituents.** If the federal bureaucracy makes a mistake, the senator's or representative's office tries to resolve the issue. What most Americans see of Congress, therefore, is the work of their own representatives in their home states. As suggested in this chapter's opening *What If . . .* feature, the tie between members of Congress and the voters might be even stronger if members had to report to their constituents annually.

Constituent
One of the persons represented by a legislator or other elected or appointed official.

Congress, however, was created to work not just for local constituents but also for the nation as a whole. Understanding the nature of the institution and the process of lawmaking is an important part of understanding how the policies that shape our lives are made. In this chapter, we describe the functions of Congress, including constituent service, representation, lawmaking, and oversight of the government. We review how the members of Congress are elected and how Congress organizes itself when it meets. We also examine how bills pass through the legislative process.

Why Was Congress Created?

The founders of the American republic believed that the bulk of the power that would be exercised by a national government should be in the hands of the legislature. The leading role envisioned for Congress in the new government is apparent from its primacy in the Constitution. Article I deals with the structure, the powers, and the operation of Congress, beginning in Section 1 with an application of the basic principle of separation of powers: "All legislative Powers herein granted shall be vested in a Congress of the United States, which shall consist of a Senate and House of Representatives." These legislative powers are spelled out in detail in Article I and elsewhere.

The **bicameralism** of Congress—its division into two legislative houses—was in part the result of the Connecticut Compromise, which tried to balance the large-state population advantage, reflected in the House, and the small-state demand for equality in policymaking, which was satisfied in the Senate. Beyond that, the two chambers of Congress also reflected the social class biases of the founders. They wished to balance the interests and the numerical superiority of the common citizens with the property interests of the less numerous landowners, bankers, and merchants. They achieved this goal by providing in Sections 2 and 3 of Article I that members of the House of Representatives should be elected directly by "the People," whereas members of the Senate were to be chosen by the elected representatives sitting in state legislatures, who were more likely to be members of the elite. (The latter provision was changed in 1913 by the passage of the Seventeenth Amendment, which provides that senators also are to be elected directly by the people.)

Bicameralism
The division of a legislature into two separate assemblies.

The logic of separate constituencies and separate interests underlying the bicameral Congress was reinforced by differences in length of tenure. Members of the House are required to face the electorate every two years, whereas senators can serve for a much more secure term of six years—even longer than the four-year term provided for the president. Furthermore, the senators' terms are staggered so that only one-third of the senators face the electorate every two years, along with all of the House members.

★ The Functions of Congress

The bicameral structure of Congress was designed to enable the legislative body and its members to perform certain functions for the political system. These functions include the following: lawmaking, representation, oversight, public education, and conflict resolution. Of these, the two most important and the ones that are most often in conflict are lawmaking and representation.

The Lawmaking Function

The principal and most obvious function of any legislature is **lawmaking**. Congress is the highest elected body in the country charged with making binding rules for all Americans. Lawmaking requires decisions about the size of the federal budget, about health-care reform and gun control, and about the long-term prospects for war or peace. This does not mean, however, that Congress initiates most of the ideas for legislation that it eventually considers. A majority of the bills that Congress acts on originate in the executive branch, and many other bills are traceable to interest groups and political party organizations. Through the processes of compromise and **logrolling** (offering to support a fellow member's bill in exchange for that member's promise to support your bill in the future), as well as debate and discussion, backers of legislation attempt to fashion a winning majority coalition to create policies for the nation.

The Representation Function

Representation includes both representing the desires and demands of the constituents in the member's home district or state and representing larger national interests such as farmers or the environment. Because the interests of constituents in a specific district may be at odds with the demands of national policy, the representation function is often in conflict with the lawmaking function for individ-

Lawmaking
The process of establishing the legal rules that govern society.

Logrolling
An arrangement in which two or more members of Congress agree in advance to support each other's bills.

Representation
The function of members of Congress as elected officials representing the views of their constituents.

Representative William Jefferson, a Democrat from Louisiana, shakes hands with a constituent during a visit to his home district. Jefferson represents the Second District in Louisiana, which includes most of the city of New Orleans. After a tough fight to win his seat in 1990, Jefferson has been reelected with ease. (Philip Gould/ Corbis)

ual lawmakers and sometimes for Congress as a whole. For example, although it may be in the interest of the nation to reduce defense spending by closing military bases, such closures are not in the interest of the states and districts that will lose jobs and local spending. Every legislator faces votes that set representational issues against lawmaking realities.

How should the legislators fulfill the representation function? There are several views on how this should be accomplished.

The Trustee View of Representation. The first approach to the question of how representation should be achieved is that legislators should act as **trustees** of the broad interests of the entire society. They should vote against the narrow interests of their constituents if their conscience and their perception of national needs so dictate. For example, in 1999 a number of Republican legislators supported strong laws regulating the tobacco industry in spite of the views of some of their constituents.

The Instructed-Delegate View of Representation. Directly opposed to the trustee view of representation is the notion that the members of Congress should behave as **instructed delegates;** that is, they should mirror the views of the majority of the constituents who elected them to power in the first place. On the surface, this approach is plausible and rewarding. For it to work, however, we must assume that constituents actually have well-formed views on the issues that are decided in Congress and, further, that they have clear-cut preferences about these issues. Neither condition is likely to be satisfied very often.

Generally, most legislators hold neither a pure trustee view nor a pure instructed-delegate view. Typically, they combine both perspectives in a pragmatic mix that is often called the "politico" style.

Service to Constituents

Individual members of Congress are expected by their constituents to act as brokers between private citizens and the imposing, often faceless federal government. This function of providing service to constituents usually takes the form of

Trustee
A legislator who acts according to her or his conscience and the broad interests of the entire society.

Instructed Delegate
A legislator who is an agent of the voters who elected him or her and who votes according to the views of constituents regardless of personal beliefs.

Republican Joseph R. Pitts, House member from Pennsylvania, discusses tax issues with constituents. Pitts' newsletter simultaneously champions tax cuts and celebrates federal spending in his district. This is common in congressional newsletters. How might a representative justify the apparent contradiction? (Photo courtesy of Congressman Pitts)

Casework
Personal work for constituents by members of Congress.

Ombudsperson
A person who hears and investigates complaints by private individuals against public officials or agencies.

casework. The legislator and her or his staff spend a considerable portion of their time in casework activities, such as tracking down a missing Social Security check, explaining the meaning of particular bills to people who may be affected by them, promoting a local business interest, or interceding with a regulatory agency on behalf of constituents who disagree with proposed agency regulations.

Legislators and many analysts of congressional behavior regard this **ombudsperson** role as an activity that strongly benefits the members of Congress. A government characterized by a large, confusing bureaucracy and complex public programs offers innumerable opportunities for legislators to come to the assistance of (usually) grateful constituents. Morris P. Fiorina once suggested, somewhat mischievously, that senators and representatives prefer to maintain bureaucratic confusion to maximize their opportunities for performing good deeds on behalf of their constituents:

> Some poor, aggrieved constituent becomes enmeshed in the tentacles of an evil bureaucracy and calls upon Congressman St. George to do battle with the dragon. . . . In dealing with the bureaucracy, the congressman is not merely one vote of 435. Rather, he is a nonpartisan power, someone whose phone call snaps an office to attention. He is not kept on hold. The constituent who receives aid believes that his congressman and his congressman alone got results.[1]

The Oversight Function

Oversight
The process by which Congress follows up on laws it has enacted to ensure that they are being enforced and administered in the way Congress intended.

Oversight of the bureaucracy is essential if the decisions made by Congress are to have any force. **Oversight** is the process by which Congress follows up on the laws it has enacted to ensure that they are being enforced and administered in the way Congress intended. This is done by holding committee hearings and investigations, changing the size of an agency's budget, and cross-examining high-level presidential nominees to head major agencies.

Senators and representatives increasingly see their oversight function as a critically important part of their legislative activities. In part, oversight is related to the concept of constituency service, particularly when Congress investigates alleged arbitrariness or wrongdoing by bureaucratic agencies.

The Public-Education Function

Educating the public is a function that is performed whenever Congress holds public hearings, exercises oversight over the bureaucracy, or engages in committee and floor debate on such major issues and topics as political assassinations, aging, illegal drugs, and the concerns of small businesses. In so doing, Congress presents a range of viewpoints on pressing national questions. Congress also decides what issues will come up for discussion and decision; this **agenda setting** is a major facet of its public-education function.

Agenda Setting
Determining which public-policy questions will be debated or considered.

The Conflict-Resolution Function

Congress is commonly seen as an institution for resolving conflicts within American society. Organized interest groups and representatives of different racial, religious, economic, and ideological interests look on Congress as an access point for airing their grievances and seeking help. This puts Congress in the position of trying to resolve the differences among competing points of view by passing laws to accommodate as many interested parties as possible. To the extent that Congress meets pluralist expectations in accommodating competing interests, it tends to build support for the entire political process.

---

[1]Morris P. Fiorina, *Congress: Keystone of the Washington Establishment,* 2d ed. (New Haven, Conn.: Yale University Press, 1989), pp. 44, 47.

 The Powers of Congress

The Constitution is both highly specific and extremely vague about the powers that Congress may exercise. The first seventeen clauses of Article I, Section 8, specify most of the **enumerated powers** of Congress—that is, powers expressly given to that body.

Enumerated Powers

The enumerated, or expressed, powers of Congress include the right to impose taxes and import tariffs; borrow money; regulate interstate commerce and international trade; establish procedures for naturalizing citizens; make laws regulating bankruptcies; coin (and print) money and regulate its value; establish standards of weights and measures; punish counterfeiters; establish post offices and postal routes; regulate copyrights and patents; establish the federal court system; punish illegal acts on the high seas; declare war; raise and regulate an army and a navy; call up and regulate the state militias to enforce laws, to suppress insurrections, and to repel invasions; and govern the District of Columbia.

The most important of the domestic powers of Congress, listed in Article I, Section 8, are the rights to collect taxes, to spend, and to regulate commerce. The most important foreign policy power is the power to declare war. Other sections of the Constitution allow Congress to establish rules for its own members, to regulate the electoral college, and to override a presidential veto. Congress may also regulate the extent of the Supreme Court's authority to review cases decided by the lower courts, regulate relations among states, and propose amendments to the Constitution.

Powers of the Senate. Some functions are restricted to one chamber. The Senate must advise on, and consent to, the ratification of treaties and must accept or reject presidential nominations of ambassadors, Supreme Court justices, and "all other

Enumerated Power
A power specifically granted to the national government by the Constitution. The first seventeen clauses of Article I, Section 8, specify most of the enumerated powers of Congress.

A U.S. Postal Service employee collects tax returns from last-minute filers outside a Massachusetts post office on the night of April 15. The most important of the domestic powers of Congress is the right to impose taxes, including taxes on income. Is it appropriate for persons with higher incomes to pay a greater percentage of their income in taxes? Why or why not? (AP Photo/*The Republican/*Christopher Evans)

Officers of the United States." But the Senate may delegate to the president or lesser officials the power to make lower-level appointments.

Consitutional Amendments.   Amendments to the Constitution provide for other congressional powers. Congress must certify the election of a president and a vice president or itself choose these officers if no candidate has a majority of the electoral vote (Twelfth Amendment). It may levy an income tax (Sixteenth Amendment) and determine who will be acting president in case of the death or incapacity of the president or vice president (Twentieth Amendment and Twenty-fifth Amendment). In addition, Congress explicitly is given the power to enforce, by appropriate legislation, the provisions of several other amendments.

The Necessary and Proper Clause

Beyond these numerous specific powers, Congress enjoys the right under Article I, Section 8 (the "elastic," or "necessary and proper," clause), "[t]o make all Laws which shall be necessary and proper for carrying into Execution the foregoing Powers [of Article I], and all other Powers vested by this Constitution in the Government of the United States, or in any Department or Officer thereof." As discussed in Chapter 3, this vague statement of congressional responsibilities provided, over time, the basis for a greatly expanded national government. It also constituted, at least in theory, a check on the expansion of presidential powers.

★ House-Senate Differences

Congress is composed of two markedly different—but co-equal—chambers. Although the Senate and the House of Representatives exist within the same legislative institution, each has developed certain distinctive features that clearly distinguish one from the other. A summary of these differences is given in Table 11–1 below.

TABLE 11–1

Differences between the House and the Senate

HOUSE*	SENATE*
Members chosen from local districts	Members chosen from an entire state
Two-year term	Six-year term
Originally elected by voters	Originally (until 1913) elected by state legislatures
May impeach (indict) federal officials	May convict federal officials of impeachable offenses
Larger (435 voting members)	Smaller (100 members)
More formal rules	Fewer rules and restrictions
Debate limited	Debate extended
Less prestige and less individual notice	More prestige and more media attention
Originates bills for raising revenues	Has power to advise the president on, and to consent to, presidential appointments and treaties
Local or narrow leadership	National leadership
More partisan	Less party loyalty

*Some of these differences, such as the term of office, are provided for in the Constitution. Others, such as debate rules, are not.

Size and Rules

The central difference between the House and the Senate is simply that the House is much larger than the Senate. The House has 435 representatives, plus delegates from the District of Columbia, Puerto Rico, Guam, American Samoa, and the Virgin Islands, compared with just 100 senators. This size difference means that a greater number of formal rules are needed to govern activity in the House, whereas correspondingly looser procedures can be followed in the less crowded Senate. This difference is most obvious in the rules governing debate on the floors of the two chambers.

The Senate normally permits extended debate on all issues that arise before it. In contrast, the House operates with an elaborate system in which its **Rules Committee** normally proposes time limitations on debate for any bill, and a majority of the entire body accepts or modifies those suggested time limits. As a consequence of its stricter time limits on debate, the House, despite its greater size, often is able to act on legislation more quickly than the Senate.

Rules Committee
A standing committee of the House of Representatives that provides special rules under which specific bills can be debated, amended, and considered by the House.

Debate and Filibustering

The Senate tradition of the **filibuster,** or the use of unlimited debate as a blocking tactic, dates back to 1790. In that year, a proposal to move the U.S. capital from New York to Philadelphia was stalled by such time-wasting maneuvers. This unlimited-debate tradition—which also existed in the House until 1811—is not absolute, however.

Under Senate Rule 22, debate may be ended by invoking *cloture.* Cloture shuts off discussion on a bill. Amended in 1975 and 1979, Rule 22 states that debate may be closed off on a bill if sixteen senators sign a petition requesting it and if, after two days have elapsed, three-fifths of the entire membership (sixty votes, assuming no vacancies) vote for cloture. After cloture is invoked, each senator may speak on a bill for a maximum of one hour before a vote is taken.

In 1979, the Senate refined Rule 22 to ensure that a final vote must take place within one hundred hours of debate after cloture has been imposed. It further limited the use of multiple amendments to stall postcloture final action on a bill.

Filibuster
The use of the Senate's tradition of unlimited debate as a delaying tactic to block a bill.

Orrin Hatch, Republican of Utah, speaks in the Senate chamber. Hatch chairs the Senate Judiciary Committee. Hatch spoke during the thirty-ninth hour of a marathon session organized by Republicans to protest Democratic filibusters. The Democrats were blocking Bush nominees for federal court judgeships. Why might senators seek to block a president's judicial candidates? (AP Photo/APTN)

Prestige

As a consequence of the greater size of the House, representatives generally cannot achieve as much individual recognition and public prestige as can members of the Senate. Senators are better able to gain media exposure and to establish careers as spokespersons for large national constituencies. To obtain recognition for his or her activities, a member of the House generally must do one of two things. He or she might survive in office long enough to join the ranks of the leadership on committees or within the party. Alternatively, the representative could become an expert on some specialized aspect of legislative policy—such as tax laws, the environment, or education.

★ Congresspersons and the Citizenry: A Comparison

Members of the U.S. Senate and the U.S. House of Representatives are not typical American citizens. Members of Congress are older than most Americans, partly because of constitutional age requirements and partly because a good deal of political experience normally is an advantage in running for national office. Members of Congress are also disproportionately white, male, and trained in high-status occupations. Lawyers are by far the largest occupational group among congresspersons, although the proportion of lawyers in the House is lower now than it was in the past. Compared with the average American citizen, members of Congress are well paid. In 2004, annual congressional salaries were $157,000. Increasingly, members of Congress are also much wealthier than the average citizen. Whereas fewer than 1 percent of Americans have assets exceeding $1 million, about one-third of the members of Congress are millionaires. Table 11–2 summarizes selected characteristics of the members of Congress.

TABLE 11–2

Characteristics of the 109th Congress, 2005–2007

CHARACTERISTIC	U.S. POPULATION (2000)*	HOUSE	SENATE
Age (median)	35.3	55.1	60.3
Percentage minority	24.9	15.6	5
Religion			
Percentage church members	61.0	97.9	100
Percentage Roman Catholic	39.0	29.4	24
Percentage Protestant	56.0	57.7	57
Percentage Jewish	4.0	6.0	11
Percentage female	50.9	15.6	14
Percentage with advanced degrees	5.0	64.4	78
Occupation			
Percentage lawyers	0.4	36.8	58
Percentage blue-collar workers	20.1	1.8	3
Family income			
Percentage of families earning over $50,000 annually	22.0	100.0	100
Personal wealth			
Percentage with assets over $1 million†	0.7	16.0	33

SOURCE: Congressional Quarterly.
*Estimates based on 2000 census.
†107th Congress.

Compared with the composition of Congress over the past two hundred years, however, the House and Senate today are significantly more diverse in gender and ethnicity than ever before. There are almost sixty women in the House of Representatives (about 14 percent) and fourteen women in the Senate (also 14 percent). Minority group members fill over 15 percent of the seats in the House. The 108th Congress has significant numbers of members born in 1946 or later, the so-called Baby Boomers. A majority of House members (54 percent) and a large minority of the Senate (41 percent) belong to this postwar generation. This shift in the character of Congress may prompt consideration of the issues that will affect the Boomers, such as Social Security and Medicare.

Congress after the 2004 Elections

The 2004 congressional election results were good news for Republicans and the Bush administration. Republicans increased their majorities in both the House and the Senate. They looked forward to reforming Social Security and the tax code, while continuing their support of business interests. The Democrats were dismayed by the defeat of Senate minority leader Tom Daschle of South Dakota (the first time this has happened in fifty years) but elated by the election of Barack Obama of Illinois, who became the only African American member of the Senate. In the House, incumbents of both parties continued to display an almost insurmountable ability to win reelection. Outside of Texas, where a new gerrymander ousted four senior Democrats, only three incumbents actually lost reelection to challengers.

Congressional Elections

The process of electing members of Congress is decentralized. Congressional elections are conducted by the individual state governments. The states, however, must conform to the rules established by the U.S. Constitution and by national statutes. The Constitution states that representatives are to be elected every second year by popular ballot, and the number of seats awarded to each state is to be determined every ten years by the results of the census. Each state has at least one representative, with most congressional districts having about half a million residents. Senators are elected by popular vote (since the passage of the Seventeenth Amendment) every six years; approximately one-third of the seats are chosen every two years. Each state has two senators. Under Article I, Section 4, of the Constitution, state legislatures are given control over "[t]he Times, Places and Manner of holding Elections for Senators and Representatives"; however, "the Congress may at any time by Law make or alter such Regulations."

Only states can elect members of Congress. Therefore, territories such as Puerto Rico and Guam are not represented, though they do elect nonvoting delegates that sit in the House. The District of Columbia is also represented only by a nonvoting delegate. Should D.C. be allowed to elect representatives who can vote? We examine this question in the *Politics and Diversity* feature on page 364.

POLITICS AND DIVERSITY
Representation for the District of Columbia

Washington, D.C., casts three electoral votes in presidential elections, the same number as the state with the smallest population. The citizens of the capital also elect a delegate who sits in the House of Representatives, but that delegate cannot vote. The District is not represented in the Senate at all. There have been a number of proposals to give D.C. voting representation in Congress. In 1978, Congress approved a constitutional amendment to give the District the representation it would have if it were a state, including two senators. The amendment was not ratified, however. More recently, District citizens have campaigned to make D.C. a state. New states can be admitted to the union without amending the Constitution.

POLITICAL CONSEQUENCES

About 60 percent of Washington's population is African American, and District voters are heavily Democratic. If D.C. were a state, its congressional delegation would probably always be Democratic. Clearly, the Republican Party has no interest in such a result. Also, statehood for D.C. would make the Senate even more unrepresentative than it is now. The only state with a smaller population than the District is Wyoming.

ALTERNATIVE SOLUTIONS

In 2003, Representative Tom Davis, a Republican from Virginia, proposed a plan to give the District a voting representative. His plan would also give an additional representative to the strongly Republican state of Utah. Historian John Steele Gordon has another proposal. He notes that until 1801, Washington's inhabitants voted as if they were residents of Maryland. (The District was created from land ceded by Maryland.) Gordon suggests that District citizens again vote as if they lived in Maryland. In 2004, he drafted

Dressed as George Washington, a demonstrator protests the District of Columbia's lack of congressional representation at a rally for the D.C. delegates to the Democratic National Convention. The delegates are gathered at Union Station in Washington before a train trip to Boston. Why do you think the two major parties grant the District representation at their national conventions? (AP Photo/Lauren Burke)

a constitutional amendment that would allow this. Actually, an amendment might not be necessary, although the legislature of Maryland would probably have to agree to any proposal. Many District residents oppose both of these plans because neither would give D.C. two senators.

FOR CRITICAL ANALYSIS

Which solution to the D.C. representation issue would be the most just? Why?

Candidates for Congressional Elections

Candidates for congressional seats may be self-selected. In districts where one party is very strong, however, there may be a shortage of candidates willing to represent the weaker party. In such circumstances, leaders of the weaker party must often actively recruit candidates. Candidates may resemble the voters of the district in ethnicity or religion, but they are also likely to be very successful individuals who have been active in politics before. House candidates are especially likely to have local ties to their districts. Candidates usually choose to run because they believe they would enjoy the job and its accompanying status. They also may be thinking of a House seat as a stepping-stone to future political office as a senator, governor, or president.

Congressional Campaigns and Elections. Congressional campaigns have changed considerably in the past two decades. Like all other campaigns, they are much more expensive, with the average cost of a winning Senate campaign now $5 million and a winning House campaign averaging more than $890,000. Campaign funds include direct contributions by individuals, contributions by political action committees (PACs), and "soft money" funneled through state party committees. As you read in Chapter 9, all of these contributions are regulated by laws, including the Federal Election Campaign Act of 1971, as amended, and most recently the Bipartisan Campaign Reform Act of 2002. Once in office, legislators spend time almost every day raising funds for their next campaign.

Most candidates for Congress must win the nomination through a **direct primary**, in which **party identifiers** vote for the candidate who will be on the party ticket in the general election. To win the primary, candidates may take more liberal or more conservative positions to get the votes of party identifiers. In the general election, they may moderate their views to attract the votes of independents and voters from the other party.

Presidential Effects. Congressional candidates are always hopeful that a strong presidential candidate on the ticket will have "coattails" that will sweep in senators and representatives of the same party. In fact, coattail effects have been quite limited and in recent presidential elections have not materialized at all. One way to measure the coattail effect is to look at the subsequent midterm elections, held in the even-numbered years following the presidential contests. In these years, voter turnout falls sharply. In the past, the party controlling the White House normally lost seats in Congress in the midterm elections, in part because the coattail effect ceased to apply. Members of Congress who were from contested districts or who were in their first term were more likely not to be reelected. In recent years, however, this "midterm effect" has often failed to materialize. Table 11–3 shows the pattern for midterm elections since 1942.

The Power of Incumbency

The power of incumbency in the outcome of congressional elections cannot be overemphasized. Table 11–4 shows that a sizable majority of representatives and

TABLE 11–3

Midterm Gains and Losses by the Party of the President, 1942 to 2002

SEATS GAINED OR LOST BY THE PARTY OF THE PRESIDENT IN THE HOUSE OF REPRESENTATIVES	
1942	−45 (D.)
1946	−55 (D.)
1950	−29 (D.)
1954	−18 (R.)
1958	−47 (R.)
1962	−4 (D.)
1966	−47 (D.)
1970	−12 (R.)
1974	−48 (R.)
1978	−15 (D.)
1982	−26 (R.)
1986	−5 (R.)
1990	−8 (R.)
1994	−52 (D.)
1998	+5 (D.)
2002	+5 (R.)

Direct Primary
An intraparty election in which the voters select the candidates who will run on a party's ticket in the subsequent general election.

Party Identifier
A person who identifies with a political party.

TABLE 11–4

The Power of Incumbency

	ELECTION YEAR													
	1978	**1980**	**1982**	**1984**	**1986**	**1988**	**1990**	**1992**	**1994**	**1996**	**1998**	**2000**	**2002**	**2004**
House														
Number of incumbent candidates	382	398	393	411	394	409	406	368	387	384	402	403	393	404
Reelected	358	361	354	392	385	402	390	325	349	361	395	394	383	397
Percentage of total	93.7	90.7	90.1	95.4	97.7	98.3	96.0	88.3	90.2	94.0	98.3	97.8	97.5	98.3
Defeated	24	37	39	19	9	7	16	43	38	23	7	9	10	7
In primary	5	6	10	3	3	1	1	19	4	2	1	3	3	1
In general election	19	31	29	16	6	6	15	24	34	21	6	6	7	6
Senate														
Number of incumbent candidates	25	29	30	29	28	27	32	28	26	21	29	29	28	26
Reelected	15	16	28	26	21	23	31	23	24	19	26	23	24	25
Percentage of total	60.0	55.2	93.3	89.6	75.0	85.2	96.9	82.1	92.3	90.5	89.7	79.3	85.7	96.2
Defeated	10	13	2	3	7	4	1	5	2	2	3	6	4	1
In primary	3	4	0	0	0	0	0	1	0	1	0	0	1	0
In general election	7	9	2	3	7	4	1	4	2	1	3	6	3	1

SOURCES: Norman Ornstein, Thomas E. Mann, and Michael J. Malbin, *Vital Statistics on Congress, 2001–2002* (Washington, D.C.: The AEI Press, 2002); and authors' update.

a slightly smaller proportion of senators who decide to run for reelection are successful. This conclusion holds for both presidential-year and midterm elections. A number of scholars contend that the pursuit of reelection is the strongest motivation behind the activities of members of Congress. The reelection goal is pursued in several ways. Incumbents can use the mass media, make personal appearances with constituents, and send newsletters—all to produce a favorable image and to make the incumbent's name a household word. Members of Congress generally try to present themselves as informed, experienced, and responsive to people's needs. Legislators also can point to things that they have done to benefit their constituents—by fulfilling the congressional casework function or bringing money for mass transit to the district, for example. Finally, incumbents can demonstrate the positions that they have taken on key issues by referring to their voting records in Congress.

Party Control of Congress after the 2004 Elections

The Republican majorities in both the House and the Senate were increased after the 2004 elections. Republicans now have fifty-five seats in the Senate and face forty-four Democrats (and one independent— James Jeffords of Vermont—who caucuses with the Democrats). This margin may make it easier for the Republicans to pass legislation. The Republicans need sixty votes, however, to stop Democratic filibusters over judicial nominations and other controversial legislation. Several retiring southern Democrats were replaced by Republicans, enhancing the Republican position in the South. In the House of Representatives, the Republicans hold a twenty-seven-seat majority. While this will give them control of the agenda and all committee chairmanships, the diverse constituencies represented in both parties will make cohesive voting difficult on many issues. Members of both parties, but especially the Republicans, will have to grapple with how to balance spending on Iraq, homeland security, and pork-barrel projects for their districts against the growing budget deficit.

★ Congressional Apportionment

Reapportionment
The allocation of seats in the House of Representatives to each state after each census.

Redistricting
The redrawing of the boundaries of the congressional districts within each state.

Justiciable Question
A question that may be raised and reviewed in court.

Two of the most complicated aspects of congressional elections are apportionment issues—**reapportionment** (the allocation of seats in the House to each state after each census) and **redistricting** (the redrawing of the boundaries of the districts within each state). In a landmark six-to-two vote in 1962, the United States Supreme Court made the apportionment of state legislative districts a **justiciable** (that is, a reviewable) **question**.[2] The Court did so by invoking the Fourteenth Amendment principle that no state can deny to any person "the equal protection of the laws." In 1964, the Court held that *both* chambers of a state legislature must be apportioned so that all districts are equal in population.[3] Later that year, the Court applied this "one person, one vote" principle to U.S. congressional districts on the basis of Article I, Section 2, of the Constitution, which requires that members of the House be chosen "by the People of the several States."[4]

[2]*Baker v. Carr*, 369 U.S. 186 (1962). The term *justiciable* is pronounced juhs-*tish*-a-buhl.
[3]*Reynolds v. Sims*, 377 U.S. 533 (1964).
[4]*Wesberry v. Sanders*, 376 U.S. 1 (1964).

Severe malapportionment of congressional districts before 1964 resulted in some districts containing two or three times the populations of other districts in the same state, thereby diluting the effect of a vote cast in the more populous districts. This system generally benefited the conservative populations of rural areas and small towns and harmed the interests of the more heavily populated and liberal cities. In fact, suburban areas have benefited the most from the Court's rulings, as suburbs account for an increasingly larger proportion of the nation's population, while cities include a correspondingly smaller segment of the population.

Gerrymandering

Although the general issue of apportionment has been dealt with fairly successfully by the one person, one vote principle, the **gerrymandering** issue has not yet been resolved. This term refers to the legislative boundary-drawing tactics that were used under Elbridge Gerry, the governor of Massachusetts, in the 1812 elections (see Figure 11–1). A district is said to have been gerrymandered when its shape is altered substantially by the dominant party in a state legislature to maximize its electoral strength at the expense of the minority party.

In 1986, the Supreme Court heard a case that challenged gerrymandered congressional districts in Indiana. The Court ruled for the first time that redistricting for the political benefit of one group could be challenged on constitutional grounds. In this specific case, *Davis v. Bandemer*,[5] however, the Court did not agree that the districts were drawn unfairly, because it could not be proved that a group of voters would consistently be deprived of influence at the polls as a result of the new districts.

Redistricting after the 2000 Census

In the meantime, political gerrymandering continues. Redistricting decisions are often made by a small group of political leaders within a state legislature.

---

[5]478 U.S. 109 (1986).

Gerrymandering

The drawing of legislative district boundary lines for the purpose of obtaining partisan or factional advantage. A district is said to be gerrymandered when its shape is manipulated by the dominant party in the state legislature to maximize electoral strength at the expense of the minority party.

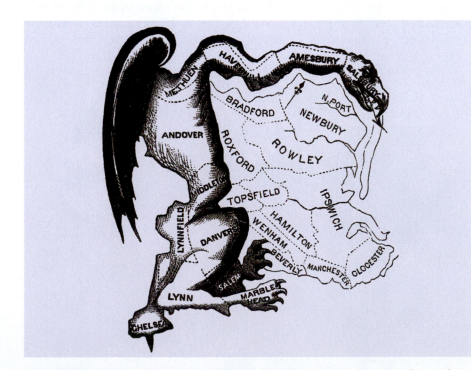

SOURCE: *Congressional Quarterly's Guide to Congress*, 3d ed. (Washington, D.C.: Congressional Quarterly Press, 1982), p. 695.

FIGURE 11–1

The Original Gerrymander

The practice of "gerrymandering"—the excessive manipulation of the shape of a legislative district to benefit a certain incumbent or party—is probably as old as the republic, but the name originated in 1812. In that year, the Massachusetts legislature carved out of Essex County a district that historian John Fiske said had a "dragonlike contour." When the painter Gilbert Stuart saw the misshapen district, he penciled in a head, wings, and claws and exclaimed, "That will do for a salamander!" Editor Benjamin Russell replied, "Better say a Gerrymander" (after Elbridge Gerry, then governor of Massachusetts).

Typically, their goal is to shape voting districts in such a way as to maximize their party's chances of winning state legislative seats as well as seats in Congress. Two of the techniques they use are called "packing" and "cracking." With the use of powerful computers and software, they *pack* voters supporting the opposing party into as few districts as possible or *crack* the opposing party's supporters into different districts. Consider that in Michigan, the Republicans who dominated redistricting efforts succeeded in packing six Democratic incumbents into only three congressional seats.

Clearly, partisan redistricting aids incumbents. The party that dominates a state's legislature will be making redistricting decisions. Through gerrymandering tactics such as packing and cracking, districts can be redrawn in such a way as to ensure that party's continued strength in the state legislature or Congress. Some have estimated that only between 30 and 50 of the 435 seats in the House of Representatives were open for any real competition in the 2002 congressional elections. Perhaps, though, there is an alternative to partisan redistricting, a possibility that we examine in this chapter's *Which Side Are You On?* feature.

"Minority-Majority" Districts

In the early 1990s, the federal government encouraged a type of gerrymandering that made possible the election of a minority representative from a "minority-majority" area. Under the mandate of the Voting Rights Act of 1965, the Justice Department issued directives to states after the 1990 census instructing them to create congressional districts that would maximize the voting power of minority groups—that is, create districts in which minority voters were the majority. The result was a number of creatively drawn congressional districts—see, for example, the depiction of Illinois's Fourth Congressional District in Figure 11–2 below, which is commonly described as "a pair of earmuffs."

Constitutional Challenges

Many of these "minority-majority" districts were challenged in court by citizens who claimed that creating districts based on race or ethnicity alone violates the equal protection clause of the Constitution. In 1995, the Supreme Court agreed

FIGURE 11–2

The Fourth Congressional District of Illinois

This district, which is mostly within Chicago's city limits, was drawn to connect two Hispanic neighborhoods separated by an African American majority district.

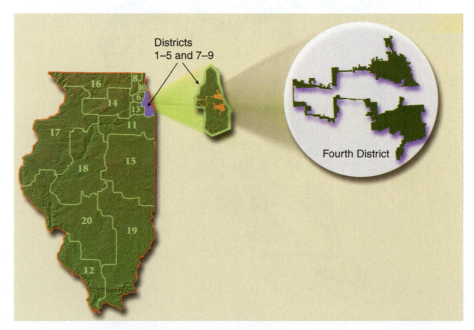

SOURCE: *The New York Times,* July 15, 2001, p. 16.

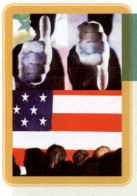

WHICH SIDE ARE YOU ON?
Should Nonpartisan Commissions Take Charge of Redistricting?

As you have learned, incumbents are routinely reelected to office. One of the reasons this is so is the partisan nature of the redistricting process each decade. Those in Congress enlist the help of party leaders in their states, who redistrict in such a way as to make congressional members' seats safe for reelection if they choose to run. According to one critic, "Those who draw the lines have become some of the most powerful people in America. They can reward legislators for good behavior and punish them for disloyalty."*

REDISTRICTING SHOULD NO LONGER BE PARTISAN

It used to be that on election day, Americans chose their representatives. Today, however, the opposite seems to be occurring—the representatives are choosing the voters through the political redistricting process. As mentioned, this gives incumbents an advantage—in addition to the many other advantages they enjoy. Simply as part of their job, for example, members of Congress appear in the news and enjoy free publicity on such networks as C-SPAN.

Some have suggested that the way redistricting is currently undertaken is shamefully biased. To ensure neutrality in redistricting, they propose that nonpartisan state commissions should be established to make redistricting decisions. Iowa and Arizona already use nonpartisan boards to redistrict. Canada and Britain use this process, too, with great success. The boundaries are universally respected, and the legislative seats are more competitive.

*Stephen E. Gottlieb, "Incumbents Rule," *The National Law Journal*, February 25, 2002, p. A21.

"IF IT AIN'T BROKE, DON'T FIX IT"

Others contend that there is no truly neutral way to engage in this complicated activity every ten years. Indeed, while the United States Supreme Court has held that partisan gerrymandering can be challenged on constitutional grounds, it has also made the task of proving that a partisan gerrymander is unconstitutional very difficult.[†] As a result, no redistricting plan has ever been thrown out on these grounds. The courts have held that minimizing contests between incumbents and pairing minority party incumbents in the same district are not sufficient grounds to reject a plan.

One of the reasons the American democratic system has remained so stable is that we respect political tradition. The so-called faults of partisan redistricting have been part of that system for over two hundred years. Why should we change it if the end result has been a strong republic?

WHAT'S YOUR POSITION?

If you were on a nonpartisan redistricting board, how might you go about redrawing congressional district boundaries after each census?

GOING ONLINE

The Center for Voting and Democracy has a page on its Web site devoted to the topic of redistricting, including the use of nonpartisan boards. Visit **http://www.fairvote.org/redistricting**. The National Conference of State Legislatures also maintains a site on the process of redistricting, including the latest news on the topic. Go to **http://www.ncsl.org/public/issues.htm** and select "redistricting" from the pop-up menu.

[†]*Davis v. Bandemer*, 478 U.S. 109 (1986).

with this argument when it declared that Georgia's new Eleventh District was unconstitutional. The district stretched from Atlanta to the Atlantic, splitting eight counties and five municipalities along the way. The Court referred to the district as a "monstrosity" linking "widely spaced urban centers that have absolutely nothing to do with each other." The Court went on to say that when a state assigns voters on the basis of race, "it engages in the offensive and demeaning assumption that voters of a particular race, because of their race, think alike, share the same political interests, and will prefer the same candidates at the polls." The Court also chastised the Justice Department for concluding that race-based districting was mandated under the Voting Rights Act of 1965: "When the Justice Department's interpretation of the Act compels race-based districting, it by definition raises a serious constitutional question."[6] In subsequent rulings, the

[6]*Miller v. Johnson*, 515 U.S. 900 (1995).

Court affirmed its position that when race is the dominant factor in the drawing of congressional district lines, the districts are unconstitutional.

Changing Directions

In the early 2000s, the Supreme Court seemed to take a new direction on racial redistricting challenges. In a 2000 case, the Court limited the federal government's authority to invalidate changes in state and local elections on the basis that the changes were discriminatory. The case involved a proposed school redistricting plan in Louisiana. The Court held that federal approval for the plan could not be withheld simply because the plan was discriminatory. Rather, the test was whether the plan left racial and ethnic minorities worse off than they were before.[7]

In 2001, the Supreme Court reviewed, for a second time, a case involving North Carolina's Twelfth District. The district was 165 miles long, following Interstate 85 for the most part. According to a local joke, the district was so narrow that a car traveling down the interstate highway with both doors open would kill most of the voters in the district. In 1996, the Supreme Court had held that the district was unconstitutional because race had been the dominant factor in drawing the district's boundaries. Shortly thereafter, the boundaries were redrawn, but the district was again challenged as a racial gerrymander. A federal district court agreed and invalidated the new boundaries as unconstitutional. In 2001, however, the Supreme Court held that there was insufficient evidence for the lower court's conclusion that race had been the dominant factor when the boundaries were redrawn.[8] The Twelfth District's boundaries remained as drawn.

★ Perks and Privileges

Legislators have many benefits that are not available to most workers. For example, members of Congress are granted generous **franking** privileges that permit them to mail newsletters, surveys, and other correspondence to their constituents. The annual cost of congressional mail has risen from $11 million in 1971 to over $60 million today. Typically, the costs for these mailings rise substantially during election years.

Permanent Professional Staffs

More than 30,000 people are employed in the Capitol Hill bureaucracy. About half of them are personal and committee staff members. The personal staff includes office clerks and secretaries; professionals who deal with media relations, draft legislation, and satisfy constituency requests for service; and staffers who maintain local offices in the member's home district or state.

The average Senate office on Capitol Hill employs about thirty staff members, and twice that number work on the personal staffs of senators from the most populous states. House office staffs typically are about half as large as those of the Senate. The number of staff members has increased dramatically since 1960. With the bulk of those increases coming in assistants to individual members, some scholars question whether staff members are really advising on legislation or are primarily aiding constituents and gaining votes in the next election.

Congress also benefits from the expertise of the professional staffs of agencies that were created to produce information for members of the House and Senate.

Franking
A policy that enables members of Congress to send material through the mail by substituting their facsimile signature (frank) for postage.

---

[7]*Reno v. Bossier Parish School Board*, 120 S.Ct. 886 (2000).
[8]*Easley v. Cromartie*, 532 U.S. 234 (2001).

For example, the Congressional Research Service, the Government Accountability Office, and the Congressional Budget Office all provide reports, audits, and policy recommendations for review by members of Congress.

Privileges and Immunities under the Law

Members of Congress also benefit from a number of special constitutional protections. Under Article I, Section 6, of the Constitution, they "shall in all Cases, except Treason, Felony and Breach of the Peace, be privileged from Arrest during their Attendance at the Session of their respective Houses, and in going to and returning from the same; and for any Speech or Debate in either House, they shall not be questioned in any other Place." The arrest immunity clause is not really an important provision today. The "speech or debate" clause, however, means that a member may make any allegations or other statements he or she wishes in connection with official duties and normally not be sued for libel or slander or otherwise be subject to legal action.

Congressional Caucuses: Another Source of Support

All members of Congress are members of one or more caucuses. The most important caucuses are those established by the parties in each chamber. These Democratic and Republican meetings provide information to the members and devise legislative strategy for the party. Other caucuses have been founded, such as the Democratic Study Group and the Congressional Black Caucus, to support subgroups of members. In 1995, concerned with the growth of caucuses supported by public funds, the Republican majority in the House passed a rule that prohibited using free space for caucuses or using public funds to finance them.

The number of caucuses has not declined, however. Instead, the number has increased. There are now more than two hundred caucuses, including small ones (the Albanian Issues Caucus, the Potato Caucus) and large ones (the Sportsmen's Caucus). These organizations, which are now funded by businesses and special interests, provide staff assistance and information for members of Congress and help them build support among specific groups of voters.

The congressional Hispanic Caucus gathers in Albuquerque, New Mexico, the site of the first debate among the 2004 Democratic presidential hopefuls. From the left are Hispanic Caucus chair Ciro Rodriguez, Democrat of Texas; Democratic National Committee chair Terry McAuliffe; and New Mexico governor Bill Richardson (who is Hispanic despite his Anglo-sounding name). (AP Photo/*The Albuquerque Journal*/Pat Vasquez-Cunningham)

★ The Committee Structure

Most of the actual work of legislating is performed by the committees and sub-committees within Congress. Thousands of bills are introduced in every session of Congress, and no single member can possibly be adequately informed on all the issues that arise. The committee system is a way to provide for specialization, or a division of the legislative labor. Members of a committee can concentrate on just one area or topic—such as taxation or energy—and develop sufficient exper-tise to draft appropriate legislation when needed. The flow of legislation through both the House and the Senate is determined largely by the speed with which the members of these committees act on bills and resolutions.

The Power of Committees

Sometimes called "little legislatures," committees usually have the final say on pieces of legislation.[9] Committee actions may be overturned on the floor by the House or Senate, but this rarely happens. Legislators normally defer to the exper-tise of the chairperson and other members of the committee who speak on the floor in defense of a committee decision. Chairpersons of committees exercise control over the scheduling of hearings and formal action on a bill. They also decide which subcommittee will act on legislation falling within their committee's jurisdiction.

Committees only very rarely are deprived of control over a bill—although this kind of action is provided for in the rules of each chamber. In the House, if a bill has been considered by a standing committee for thirty days, the signatures of a majority (218) of the House membership on a **discharge petition** can pry a bill out of an uncooperative committee's hands. From 1909 to 2005, however, although over nine hundred such petitions were initiated, only slightly more than two dozen resulted in successful discharge efforts. Of those, twenty resulted in bills that passed the House.[10]

Discharge Petition
A procedure by which a bill in the House of Representatives may be forced (discharged) out of a committee that has refused to report it for consideration by the House. The petition must be signed by an absolute majority (218) of representatives and is used only on rare occasions.

---

[9]The term *little legislatures* is from Woodrow Wilson, *Congressional Government* (New York: Meridian Books, 1956 [first published in 1885]).

[10]Congressional Quarterly, Inc., *Guide to Congress,* 5th ed. (Washington, D.C.: CQ Press, 2000); and authors' update.

Representative Pat Roberts, Republican from Kansas, speaks with General John P. Abizaid, head of the U.S. Army Central Command, before Abizaid's testimony to the Senate Armed Services Committee in May 2004. Congress continues to investigate the abuse and humiliation of Iraqi prisoners at the Abu Ghraib prison outside Baghdad by U.S. personnel. (EPA/Mike Theiler/ Landov)

Types of Congressional Committees

Over the past two centuries, Congress has created several different types of committees, each of which serves particular needs of the institution.

Standing Committees. By far the most important committees in Congress are the **standing committees**—permanent bodies that are established by the rules of each chamber of Congress and that continue from session to session. A list of the standing committees of the 109th Congress is presented in Table 11–5. In addition, most of the standing committees have created subcommittees to carry out their work. For example, in the 108th Congress, there were sixty-eight subcommittees in the Senate and eighty-eight in the House.[11] Each standing committee is given a specific area of legislative policy jurisdiction, and almost all legislative measures are considered by the appropriate standing committees.

Because of the importance of their work and the traditional influence of their members in Congress, certain committees are considered to be more prestigious than others. Seats on standing committees that handle spending issues are especially sought after because members can use these positions to benefit their constituents. Committees that control spending include the Appropriations Committee in either chamber and the Ways and Means Committee in the House. Members also normally seek seats on committees that handle matters of special interest to their constituents. A member of the House from an agricultural district, for example, will have an interest in joining the House Agriculture Committee.

Select Committees. In principle, a **select committee** is created for a limited time and for a specific legislative purpose. For example, a select committee may be

---

[11]*Congressional Directory* (Washington, D.C.: U.S. Government Printing Office, various editions).

Standing Committee
A permanent committee in the House or Senate that considers bills within a certain subject area.

Select Committee
A temporary legislative committee established for a limited time period and for a special purpose.

TABLE 11–5

Standing Committees of the 109th Congress, 2005–2007

HOUSE COMMITTEES	SENATE COMMITTEES
Agriculture	Agriculture, Nutrition, and Forestry
Appropriations	Appropriations
Armed Services	Armed Services
Budget	Banking, Housing, and Urban Affairs
Education and the Workforce	Budget
Energy and Commerce	Commerce, Science, and Transportation
Financial Services	Energy and Natural Resources
Government Reform	Environment and Public Works
House Administration	Finance
International Relations	Foreign Relations
Judiciary	Governmental Affairs
Resources	Health, Education, Labor, and Pensions
Rules	Judiciary
Science	Rules and Administration
Small Business	Small Business and Entrepreneurship
Standards of Official Conduct	Veterans Affairs
Transportation and Infrastructure	
Veterans Affairs	
Ways and Means	

In 2002, the House and Senate select committees on intelligence held joint closed hearings to examine the events of September 11, 2001. From left to right, the committee leaders are House ranking Democrat Nancy Pelosi of California, Senate ranking Republican Richard C. Shelby of Alabama, Senate Democratic chair Bob Graham of Florida, and House Republican chair Porter J. Goss of Florida. (REUTERS/ Hyungwon Kang/Landov)

formed to investigate a public problem, such as child nutrition or aging. In practice a select committee, such as the Select Committee on Intelligence in each chamber, may continue indefinitely. Select committees rarely create original legislation.

Joint Committee
A legislative committee composed of members from both chambers of Congress.

Joint Committees. A **joint committee** is formed by the concurrent action of both chambers of Congress and consists of members from each chamber. Joint committees, which may be permanent or temporary, have dealt with the economy, taxation, and the Library of Congress.

Conference Committee
A special joint committee appointed to reconcile differences when bills pass the two chambers of Congress in different forms.

Conference Committees. Special joint committees—**conference committees**— are formed for the purpose of achieving agreement between the House and the Senate on the exact wording of legislative acts when the two chambers pass legislative proposals in different forms. No bill can be sent to the White House to be signed into law unless it first passes both chambers in identical form. Sometimes called the "third house" of Congress, conference committees are in a position to make significant alterations to legislation and frequently become the focal point of policy debates.

The House Rules Committee. Because of its special "gatekeeping" power over the terms on which legislation will reach the floor of the House of Representatives, the House Rules Committee holds a uniquely powerful position. A special committee rule sets the time limit on debate and determines whether and how a bill may be amended. This practice dates back to 1883. The Rules Committee has the unusual power to meet while the House is in session, to have its resolutions considered immediately on the floor, and to initiate legislation on its own.

The Selection of Committee Members

Seniority System
A custom followed in both chambers of Congress specifying that the member of the majority party with the longest term of continuous service will be given preference when a committee chairperson (or a holder of some other significant post) is selected.

In both chambers, members are appointed to standing committees by the Steering Committee of their party. The majority-party member with the longest term of continuous service on a standing committee is given preference when the committee selects its chairperson. This is not a law but an informal, traditional process, and it applies to other significant posts in Congress as well. The **seniority system,** although it deliberately treats members unequally, provides a predictable means of assigning positions of power within Congress. The most senior member of the minority party is called the *ranking* committee member for that party.

The general pattern until the 1970s was that members of the House or Senate who represented **safe seats** would be reelected continually and eventually would accumulate enough years of continuous committee service to enable them to become the chairpersons of their committees. In the 1970s, a number of reforms in the chairperson selection process somewhat modified the seniority system. The reforms introduced the use of a secret ballot in electing House committee chairpersons and allowed for the possibility of choosing a chairperson on a basis other than seniority. The Democrats immediately replaced three senior chairpersons who were out of step with the rest of their party. In 1995, under Speaker Newt Gingrich, the Republicans chose relatively junior House members as chairpersons of several key committees, thus ensuring conservative control of the committees. The Republicans also passed a rule limiting the term of a chairperson to six years.

Safe Seat
A district that returns a legislator with 55 percent of the vote or more.

★ The Formal Leadership

The limited amount of centralized power that exists in Congress is exercised through party-based mechanisms. Congress is organized by party. When the Democratic Party, for example, wins a majority of seats in either the House or the Senate, Democrats control the official positions of power in that chamber, and every important committee has a Democratic chairperson and a majority of Democratic members. The same process holds when Republicans are in the majority.

We consider the formal leadership positions in the House and Senate separately, but you will note some broad similarities in the way leaders are selected and in the ways they exercise power in the two chambers.

Leadership in the House

The House leadership is made up of the Speaker, the majority and minority leaders, and the party whips.

The Speaker. The foremost power holder in the House of Representatives is the **Speaker of the House.** The Speaker's position is technically a nonpartisan one, but in fact, for the better part of two centuries, the Speaker has been the official leader of the majority party in the House. When a new Congress convenes in January of odd-numbered years, each party nominates a candidate for Speaker. All Democratic members of the House are expected to vote for their party's nominee, and all Republicans are expected to support their candidate. The vote to organize the House is the one vote in which representatives must vote with their party. In a sense, this vote defines a member's partisan status.

The influence of modern-day Speakers is based primarily on their personal prestige, persuasive ability, and knowledge of the legislative process—plus the acquiescence or active support of other representatives. The major formal powers of the Speaker include the following:

Speaker of the House
The presiding officer in the House of Representatives. The Speaker is always a member of the majority party and is the most powerful and influential member of the House.

1. Presiding over meetings of the House.
2. Appointing members of joint committees and conference committees.
3. Scheduling legislation for floor action.
4. Deciding points of order and interpreting the rules with the advice of the House parliamentarian.
5. Referring bills and resolutions to the appropriate standing committees of the House.

Dennis Hastert, a Republican member of Congress from Illinois, became Speaker of the House in 1999. What benefits could a state receive when one of its senators or representatives wins a leadership post? (AP Photo/Ron Edmonds)

A Speaker may take part in floor debate and vote, as can any other member of Congress, but recent Speakers usually have voted only to break a tie. Since 1975, the Speaker, when a Democrat, has also had the power to appoint the Democratic Steering Committee, which determines new committee assignments for House party members.

In general, the powers of the Speaker are related to his or her control over information and communications channels in the House. This is a significant power in a large, decentralized institution in which information is a very important resource. With this control, the Speaker attempts to ensure the smooth operation of the chamber and to integrate presidential and congressional policies.

Majority Leader of the House
A legislative position held by an important party member in the House of Representatives. The majority leader is selected by the majority party in caucus or conference to foster cohesion among party members and to act as spokesperson for the majority party in the House.

The Majority Leader.   The **majority leader of the House** is elected by a caucus of the majority party to foster cohesion among party members and to act as a spokesperson for the party. The majority leader influences the scheduling of debate and acts as the chief supporter of the Speaker. The majority leader cooperates with the Speaker and other party leaders, both inside and outside Congress, to formulate the party's legislative program and to guide that program through the legislative process in the House. The Democrats often recruit future Speakers from those who hold that position.

Minority Leader of the House
The party leader elected by the minority party in the House.

The Minority Leader.   The **minority leader of the House** is the candidate nominated for Speaker by a caucus of the minority party. Like the majority leader, the leader of the minority party has as her or his primary responsibility the maintaining of cohesion within the party's ranks. The minority leader works for cohesion among the party's members and speaks on behalf of the president if the minority party controls the White House. In relations with the majority party, the minority leader consults with both the Speaker and the majority leader on recognizing members who wish to speak on the floor, on House rules and procedures, and on the scheduling of legislation. Minority leaders have no actual power in these areas, however.

Whips. The leadership of each party includes assistants to the majority and minority leaders, known as **whips.** The whips are members of Congress who assist the party leaders by passing information down from the leadership to party members and by ensuring that members show up for floor debate and cast their votes on important issues. Whips conduct polls among party members about the members' views on legislation, inform the leaders about whose vote is doubtful and whose is certain, and may exert pressure on members to support the leaders' positions. In the House, serving as a whip is the first step toward positions of higher leadership.

Leadership in the Senate

The Senate is less than one-fourth the size of the House. This fact alone probably explains why a formal, complex, and centralized leadership structure is not as necessary in the Senate as it is in the House.

The two highest-ranking formal leadership positions in the Senate are essentially ceremonial in nature. Under the Constitution, the vice president of the United States is the president (that is, the presiding officer) of the Senate and may vote to break a tie. The vice president, however, is only rarely present for a meeting of the Senate. The Senate elects instead a **president pro tempore** ("pro tem") to preside over the Senate in the vice president's absence. Ordinarily, the president pro tem is the member of the majority party with the longest continuous term of service in the Senate. The president pro tem is mostly a ceremonial position. Junior senators take turns actually presiding over the sessions of the Senate.

The real leadership power in the Senate rests in the hands of the **Senate majority leader,** the **Senate minority leader,** and their respective whips. The Senate

Whip
A member of Congress who aids the majority or minority leader of the House or the Senate.

President Pro Tempore
The temporary presiding officer of the Senate in the absence of the vice president.

Senate Majority Leader
The chief spokesperson of the majority party in the Senate, who directs the legislative program and party strategy.

Senate Minority Leader
The party officer in the Senate who commands the minority party's opposition to the policies of the majority party and directs the legislative program and strategy of his or her party.

Republican senator William Frist of Tennessee, left, was elected Senate majority leader in 2002. Democratic representative Nancy Pelosi of California, right, is the first woman to hold a leadership position in Congress. She was elected House minority leader in 2002. It is very rare for a congressional leader to become president. How might a leadership position interfere with presidential aspirations? (Left: UPI Photo/Michael Kleinfeld/Landov; right: Chris Kleponis/Bloomberg News/Landov)

majority and minority leaders have the right to be recognized first in debate on the floor and generally exercise the same powers available to the House majority and minority leaders. They control the scheduling of debate on the floor in conjunction with the majority party's Policy Committee, influence the allocation of committee assignments for new members or for senators attempting to transfer to a new committee, influence the selection of other party officials, and participate in selecting members of conference committees. The leaders are expected to mobilize support for partisan legislative initiatives or for the proposals of a president who belongs to their party. The leaders act as liaisons with the White House when the president is of their party, try to obtain the cooperation of committee chairpersons, and seek to facilitate the smooth functioning of the Senate through the senators' unanimous consent. The majority and minority leaders are elected by their respective party caucuses.

Senate party whips, like their House counterparts, maintain communication within the party on platform positions and try to ensure that party colleagues are present for floor debate and important votes. The Senate whip system is far less elaborate than its counterpart in the House, simply because there are fewer members to track.

A list of the formal party leaders of the 108th Congress is presented in Table 11–6. Party leaders are a major source of influence over the decisions about public issues that senators and representatives must make every day.

★ How Members of Congress Decide

Each member of Congress casts hundreds of votes in each session. Each member compiles a record of votes during the years that he or she spends in the national legislature. There are usually a number of different reasons why any particular vote is cast. Research shows that the best predictor of a member's vote is party

TABLE 11–6

Party Leaders in the 109th Congress, 2005–2007
Senate minority leader Tom Daschle of South Dakota failed to gain reelection in 2004. Senator Harry Reid is expected to replace Daschle as minority leader.

POSITION	INCUMBENT	PARTY/ STATE	LEADER SINCE
House			
Speaker	J. Dennis Hastert	R., Ill.	Jan. 1999
Majority leader	Tom DeLay	R., Tex.	Jan. 2003
Majority whip	Roy Blunt	R., Mo.	Jan. 2003
Chair of the Republican Conference	Deborah Pryce	R., Ohio	Jan. 2003
Minority leader	Nancy Pelosi	D., Calif.	Jan. 2003
Minority whip	Steny Hoyer	D., Md.	Jan. 2003
Chair of the Democratic Caucus	Robert Menendez	D., N.J.	Jan. 2003
Senate			
President pro tempore	Ted Stevens	R., Alaska	Jan. 2003
Majority leader	William Frist	R., Tenn.	Jan. 2003
Majority whip	Mitch McConnell	R., Ky.	Jan. 2003
Chair of the Republican Conference	Rick Santorum	R., Pa.	Jan. 2001
Minority leader	to be determined		
Minority whip	Harry Reid	D., Nev.	Jan. 1999
Chair of the Democratic Conference	to be determined		

affiliation. Obviously, party members do have common opinions on some, if not all, issues facing the nation. In addition, the party leadership in each house works hard to build cohesion and agreement among the members through the activities of the party caucuses and conferences. In recent years, the increase in partisanship in both the House and the Senate has meant that most Republicans are voting in opposition to most Democrats.

The Conservative Coalition

Political parties are not always unified. In the 1950s and 1960s, the Democrats in Congress were often split between northern liberals and southern conservatives. This division gave rise to the **conservative coalition,** a voting bloc made up of conservative Democrats and conservative (which is to say, most) Republicans. This coalition was able to win many votes over the years. Today, however, most southern conservatives are Republicans, so the coalition has almost disappeared.

Conservative Coalition
An alliance of Republicans and southern Democrats that can form in the House or the Senate to oppose liberal legislation and support conservative legislation.

"Crossing Over"

On some votes, individual representatives and senators will vote against their party, "crossing over to the other side," because the interests of their states or districts differ from the interests that prevail within the rest of their party. In some cases, members vote a certain way because of the influence of regional or national interests. Other voting decisions are based on the members' religious or ideological beliefs. Votes on issues such as abortion or gay rights may be motivated by a member's religious views.

There are, however, far too many voting decisions for every member to be fully informed on each issue. Research suggests that many voting decisions are based on cues provide by trusted colleagues or the party leadership. A member who sits on the committee that wrote a law may become a reliable source of information about that law. Alternatively, a member may turn to a colleague who represents a district in the same state or one who represents a similar district for cues on voting. Cues may also come from fellow committee members, from leaders, and from the administration.

★ How a Bill Becomes Law

Each year, Congress and the president propose and approve many laws. Some are budget and appropriation laws that require extensive bargaining but must be passed for the government to continue to function. Other laws are relatively free of controversy and are passed with little dissension. Still other proposed legislation is extremely controversial and reaches to the roots of differences between Democrats and Republicans and between the executive and legislative branches.

As detailed in Figure 11–3 on the following page, each law begins as a bill, which must be introduced in either the House or the Senate. Often, similar bills are introduced in both chambers. A "money bill," however, must start in the House. In each chamber, the bill follows similar steps. It is referred to a committee and its subcommittees for study, discussion, hearings, and rewriting ("mark up"). When the bill is reported out to the full chamber, it must be scheduled for debate (by the Rules Committee in the House and by the leadership in the Senate). After the bill has been passed in each chamber, if it contains different provisions, a conference committee is formed to write a compromise bill, which must be approved by both chambers before it is sent to the president to sign or veto.

Another form of congressional action, the *joint resolution,* differs little from a bill in how it is proposed or debated. Once it is approved by both chambers and

FIGURE 11–3

How a Bill Becomes Law

This illustration shows the most typical way in which proposed legislation is enacted into law. Most legislation begins as similar bills introduced into the House and the Senate. The process is illustrated here with two hypothetical bills, House bill No. 100 (HR 100) and Senate bill No. 200 (S 200). The path of HR 100 is shown on the left, and that of S 200, on the right.

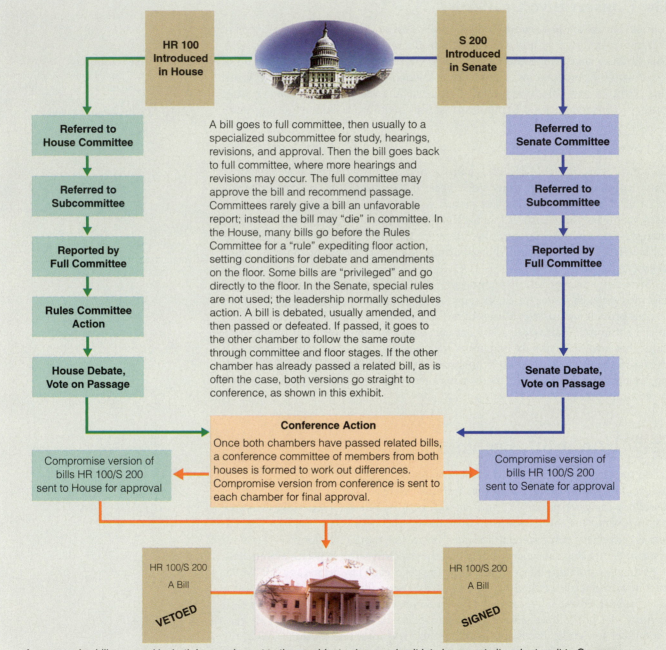

HR 100 Introduced in House

Referred to House Committee

Referred to Subcommittee

Reported by Full Committee

Rules Committee Action

House Debate, Vote on Passage

A bill goes to full committee, then usually to a specialized subcommittee for study, hearings, revisions, and approval. Then the bill goes back to full committee, where more hearings and revisions may occur. The full committee may approve the bill and recommend passage. Committees rarely give a bill an unfavorable report; instead the bill may "die" in committee. In the House, many bills go before the Rules Committee for a "rule" expediting floor action, setting conditions for debate and amendments on the floor. Some bills are "privileged" and go directly to the floor. In the Senate, special rules are not used; the leadership normally schedules action. A bill is debated, usually amended, and then passed or defeated. If passed, it goes to the other chamber to follow the same route through committee and floor stages. If the other chamber has already passed a related bill, as is often the case, both versions go straight to conference, as shown in this exhibit.

S 200 Introduced in Senate

Referred to Senate Committee

Referred to Subcommittee

Reported by Full Committee

Senate Debate, Vote on Passage

Conference Action

Once both chambers have passed related bills, a conference committee of members from both houses is formed to work out differences. Compromise version from conference is sent to each chamber for final approval.

Compromise version of bills HR 100/S 200 sent to House for approval

Compromise version of bills HR 100/S 200 sent to Senate for approval

HR 100/S 200 A Bill

VETOED

HR 100/S 200 A Bill

SIGNED

A compromise bill approved by both houses is sent to the president, who can sign it into law or veto it and return it to Congress.

Congress may override a veto by a two-thirds majority vote in both houses; the bill then becomes law without the president's signature.

signed by the president, it has the force of law.[12] A joint resolution to amend the Constitution, however, after it is approved by two-thirds of both chambers, is sent not to the president but to the states for ratification.

DID YOU KNOW . . .
That retiring members of Congress can start collecting a pension at age fifty after twenty years of work or at age sixty after ten years of service?

How Much Will the Government Spend?

The Constitution is very clear about where the power of the purse lies in the national government: all taxing or spending bills must originate in the House of Representatives. Today, much of the business of Congress is concerned with approving government expenditures through the budget process and with raising the revenues to pay for government programs.

From 1922, when Congress required the president to prepare and present to the legislature an **executive budget,** until 1974, the congressional budget process was so disjointed that it was difficult to visualize the total picture of government finances. The president presented the executive budget to Congress in January. It was broken down into thirteen or more appropriations bills. Some time later, after all of the bills had been debated, amended, and passed, it was more or less possible to estimate total government spending for the next year.

Executive Budget
The budget prepared and submitted by the president to Congress.

Frustrated by the president's ability to impound, or withhold, funds and dissatisfied with the entire budget process, Congress passed the Budget and Impoundment Control Act of 1974 to regain some control over the nation's spending. The act required the president to spend the funds that Congress had appropriated, ending the president's ability to kill programs by withholding funds. The other major accomplishment of the act was to force Congress to examine total national taxing and spending at least twice in each budget cycle.

The budget cycle of the federal government is described in the rest of this section. (See Figure 11–4 for a graphic illustration of the budget cycle.)

[12]In contrast, *simple resolutions* and *concurrent resolutions* do not carry the force of law but rather are used by one or both chambers of Congress, respectively, to express facts, principles, or opinions. For example, a concurrent resolution is used to set the time when Congress will adjourn.

FIGURE 11–4
The Budget Cycle

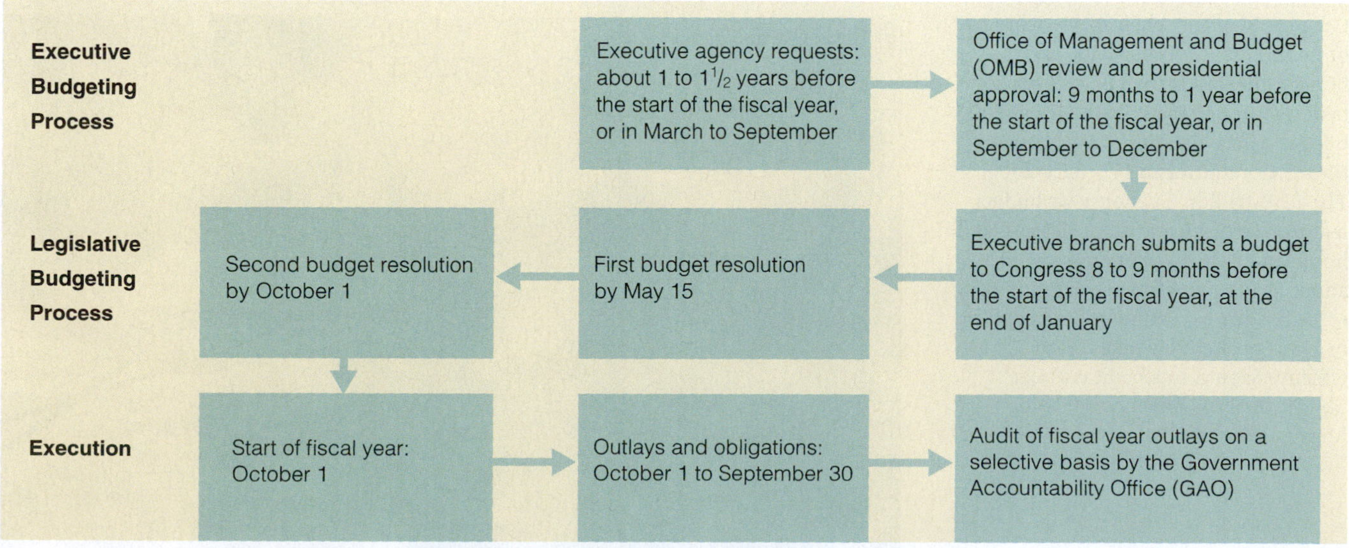
Executive Budgeting Process
Executive agency requests: about 1 to 1½ years before the start of the fiscal year, or in March to September
Office of Management and Budget (OMB) review and presidential approval: 9 months to 1 year before the start of the fiscal year, or in September to December
Legislative Budgeting Process
Executive branch submits a budget to Congress 8 to 9 months before the start of the fiscal year, at the end of January
First budget resolution by May 15
Second budget resolution by October 1
Execution
Start of fiscal year: October 1
Outlays and obligations: October 1 to September 30
Audit of fiscal year outlays on a selective basis by the Government Accountability Office (GAO)

Fiscal Year (FY)
A twelve-month period that is used for bookkeeping, or accounting, purposes. Usually, the fiscal year does not coincide with the calendar year. For example, the federal government's fiscal year runs from October 1 through September 30.

Spring Review
The annual process in which the Office of Management and Budget requires federal agencies to review their programs, activities, and goals and submit their requests for funding for the next fiscal year.

Fall Review
The annual process in which the Office of Management and Budget, after receiving formal federal agency requests for funding for the next fiscal year, reviews the requests, makes changes, and submits its recommendations to the president.

Authorization
A formal declaration by a legislative committee that a certain amount of funding may be available to an agency. Some authorizations terminate in a year; others are renewable automatically without further congressional action.

Preparing the Budget

The federal government operates on a **fiscal year (FY)** cycle. The fiscal year runs from October through September, so that fiscal 2006, or FY06, runs from October 1, 2005, through September 30, 2006. Eighteen months before a fiscal year starts, the executive branch begins preparing the budget. The Office of Management and Budget (OMB) receives advice from the Council of Economic Advisers and the Treasury Department. The OMB outlines the budget and then sends it to the various departments and agencies. Bargaining follows, in which—to use only two of many examples—the Department of Health and Human Services argues for more welfare spending, and the armed forces argue for more defense spending.

Even though the OMB has only six hundred employees, it is one of the most powerful agencies in Washington. It assembles the budget documents and monitors federal agencies throughout each year. Every year, it begins the budget process with a **spring review,** in which it requires all of the agencies to review their programs, activities, and goals. At the beginning of each summer, the OMB sends out a letter instructing agencies to submit their requests for funding for the next fiscal year. By the end of the summer, each agency must submit a formal request to the OMB.

In actuality, the "budget season" begins with the **fall review.** At this time, the OMB looks at budget requests and, in almost all cases, routinely cuts them back. Although the OMB works within guidelines established by the president, specific decisions often are left to the OMB director and the director's associates. By the beginning of November, the director's review begins. The director meets with cabinet secretaries and budget officers. Time becomes crucial. The budget must be completed by January so that it can be included in the *Economic Report of the President.*

Congress Faces the Budget

In January, nine months before the fiscal year starts, the president takes the OMB's proposed budget, approves it, and submits it to Congress. Then the congressional budgeting process takes over. The budgeting process involves two steps. First, Congress must authorize funds to be spent. The **authorization** is a formal declaration by the appropriate congressional committee that a certain amount of fund-

Gregory Mankow, chair of the Council of Economic Advisers (left), and budget director Joshua Bolten (right) testified on President Bush's fiscal 2005 budget before the House Ways and Means Committee in February 2004. The $2.4 trillion election-year budget featured large increases for defense and homeland security. Congress could adopt a rule that all new spending has to be funded by cutting other spending or by imposing new taxes. How effective would this be in curbing budget deficits? (AP Photo/Pablo Martinez Monsivais)

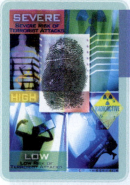

AMERICA'S SECURITY
The Spoils of War

To pay for the costs of the war in Iraq, President George W. Bush requested two supplementary appropriations in 2003. The first, submitted in March, was for $75 billion; the second, submitted in September, was for $87 billion. These two requests together amounted to about $550 for every person in the United States. The second of these requests was politically controversial, in part because it was unexpected. The first appropriation, because it received less publicity, became an ideal vehicle for special interest add-ons by Congress and the White House. When Congress passed the bill, the cost was $4 billion more than the president had initially requested.

SOME ITEMS IN THE FIRST BILL

Some rather large items in the first bill appeared to have little direct connection to the war in Iraq. For example, the airline industry received a $2.3 billion tax rebate. The bill increased Israel's foreign aid budget by $1 billion and provided Israel with $9 billion in loan guarantees. Other items included the following:

- $110 million for the National Animal Disease Center in Ames, Iowa.
- $3.3 million in payments to the European Community resulting from a music licensing dispute.

- $2 million for the U.S. Fish and Wildlife Service.
- $231,000 for abstinence education and related services for a Lutheran ministry in Allentown, Pennsylvania.

WHAT ARE WE VOTING ON?

One reason that bills can contain large amounts of questionable spending is that members of Congress do not always know what a bill contains when they vote on it. In the example of the first bill, only a single copy of the conference report—the final compromise between the House and Senate versions of the bill—was available to the members before the final vote. Members of the conference committee could insert anything they wanted into the final bill without any scrutiny at all. This bill had to be rushed through because it was an emergency measure. Conference committees, however, often slip questionable last-minute changes into ordinary spending bills.

FOR CRITICAL ANALYSIS

What institutional reforms could help legislators understand what is in each bill before they vote on it?

---

ing may be available to an agency. Congressional committees and subcommittees look at the proposals from the executive branch and the Congressional Budget Office in making the decision to authorize funds. After the funds are authorized, they must be appropriated by Congress. The appropriations committees of both the House and the Senate forward spending bills to their respective bodies. The **appropriation** of funds occurs when the final bill is passed.

The budget process involves large sums. For example, President George W. Bush's proposed budget for fiscal year 2005 called for expenditures of $2.4 trillion, or $2,400,000,000,000. When forming the budget for a given year, Congress and the president must take into account revenues, primarily in the form of taxes, as well as expenditures to balance the budget. If spending exceeds the amount brought in by taxes, the government runs a budget deficit (and increases the public debt). For example, although President Bush's proposed budget for fiscal year 2005 called for expenditures of approximately $2.4 trillion, projected revenues from taxes amounted to only about $2.0 trillion—leaving a deficit of $364 billion.

With these large sums in play, representatives and senators who chair key committees find it relatively easy to slip spending proposals into a variety of bills. These proposals may have nothing to do with the ostensible purpose of the bill. Are such earmarked appropriations good policy? We look at one example of such spending in this chapter's *America's Security* feature.

Appropriation
The passage, by Congress, of a spending bill specifying the amount of authorized funds that actually will be allocated for an agency's use.

First Budget Resolution

A resolution passed by Congress in May that sets overall revenue and spending goals for the following fiscal year.

Second Budget Resolution

A resolution passed by Congress in September that sets "binding" limits on taxes and spending for the following fiscal year.

Continuing Resolution

A temporary funding law that Congress passes when an appropriations bill has not been decided by the beginning of the new fiscal year on October 1.

Budget Resolutions

The **first budget resolution** by Congress is scheduled to be passed in May. It sets overall revenue goals and spending targets. During the summer, bargaining among all the concerned parties takes place. Spending and tax laws that are drawn up during this period are supposed to be guided by the May congressional budget resolution.

By September, Congress is scheduled to pass its **second budget resolution,** one that will set "binding" limits on taxes and spending for the fiscal year beginning October 1. Bills passed before that date that do not fit within the limits of the budget resolution are supposed to be changed.

In actuality, between 1978 and 1996, Congress did not pass a complete budget by October 1. In other words, generally, Congress does not follow its own rules. Budget resolutions are passed late, and when they are passed, they are not treated as binding. In each fiscal year that starts without a budget, every agency operates on the basis of a **continuing resolution,** which enables the agency to keep on doing whatever it was doing the previous year with the same amount of funding. Even continuing resolutions have not always been passed on time.

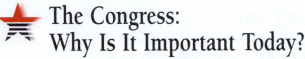

The Congress: Why Is It Important Today?

Despite the public's sometimes cynical attitude toward the institution, Congress affects our lives in immediate and profound ways. One of the most important decisions Congress makes that affects our lives every day is how much the government spends. How much will the government spend to regulate job safety, the environment, or airline security? How much will be spent on intelligence gathering and military actions in the war on terrorism? How many guards will be paid to patrol our borders, protect our national infrastructure, or ride airplanes as air marshals?

Congress makes these important decisions, and in turn, Congress decides how much we pay in taxes, which fund the government. Tax rates, deductions, and credits are all legislated by Congress. Although polls show that Americans give the president more credit than Congress for legislation that is enacted, members of Congress are more aware of the local needs of their states and districts than is the president, whose constituency is nationwide.

Members of Congress frequently go home to their districts and, in most cases, build trusting relationships with their constituents. Voters have opportunities to meet their representatives, argue for or against legislation, and express their needs and concerns. Congress was created for just this purpose. Local and state interests are fully represented in our federal system of government through Congress. Just one representative from one district in one state has the power to influence how or whether a bill becomes a law.

MAKING A DIFFERENCE

★ Learning about Your Representatives

Do you know the names of your senators and your representative in Congress? A surprising number of Americans do not. Even if you know the names and parties of your elected delegates, there is still much more you could learn about them that would be useful.

Why Should You Care?

The legislation that Congress passes can directly affect your life. Consider, for example, the Medicare prescription drug benefit passed in November 2003. Some might think that such a benefit, which only helps persons over the age of sixty-five, would be of no interest to college students. Actually, legislation such as this could affect you long before you reach retirement age. Funding the new benefit may mean that you will have to pay higher taxes when you join the work force. Also, some students may be affected even sooner than that. Most students are part of a family, and family finances are often important in determining whether a family will help pay for the student's tuition. There are families in which the cost of medicine for the oldest members is a substantial burden.

You can make a difference in our democracy simply by going to the polls on election day and voting for the candidates you would like to rep-

resent you in Congress. It goes without saying, though, that to cast an informed vote, you need to know how your congressional representatives stand on the issues and, if they are incumbents, how they have voted on bills that are important to you.

What Can You Do?

To contact a member of Congress, start by going to the Web sites of the U.S. House of Representatives (at **http://www.house.gov**) and the U.S. Senate (at **http://www.senate.gov**).

Although you can communicate easily with your representatives by e-mail, using e-mail has some drawbacks. Representatives and senators are now receiving large volumes of e-mail from constituents, and they rarely read it themselves. They have staff members who read and respond to e-mail instead. Many interest groups argue that U.S. mail, or even express mail or a phone call, is more likely to capture the attention of the representative than e-mail. You can contact your representatives using one of the following addresses or phone numbers:

United States House of
Representatives
Washington, DC 20515
202-224-3121

United States Senate
Washington, DC 20510
202-224-3121

Performance Evaluations

Interest groups also track the voting records of members of Congress and rate the members on the issues. Project Vote Smart tracks the performance of over 13,000 political leaders, including their campaign finances, issue positions, and voting records. You can contact Project Vote Smart at:

Project Vote Smart
One Common Ground
Philipsburg, MT 59858
Voter Hotline toll free 1-888-VOTE-
SMART (1-888-868-3762)
http://www.vote-smart.org

Finally, if you want to know how your representatives funded their campaigns, contact the Center for Responsive Politics (CRP), a research group that tracks money in politics, campaign fund-raising, and similar issues. You can contact the CRP at:

The Center for Responsive Politics
1101 14th St. N.W., Suite 1030
Washington, DC 20005
202-857-0044
http://www.opensecrets.org

Key Terms

agenda setting 358	executive budget 381	majority leader of the House 376	safe seat 375
appropriation 383	fall review 382	minority leader of the House 376	second budget resolution 384
authorization 382	filibuster 361		select committee 373
bicameralism 355	first budget resolution 384	ombudsperson 358	Senate majority leader 377
casework 358	fiscal year (FY) 382	oversight 358	Senate minority leader 377
conference committee 374	franking 370	party identifier 365	seniority system 374
conservative coalition 379	gerrymandering 367	president pro tempore 377	Speaker of the House 375
constituent 355	instructed delegate 357	reapportionment 366	spring review 382
continuing resolution 384	joint committee 374	redistricting 366	standing committee 373
direct primary 365	justiciable question 366	representation 356	trustee 357
discharge petition 372	lawmaking 356	Rules Committee 361	whip 377
enumerated power 359	logrolling 356		

Chapter Summary

1 The authors of the Constitution believed that the bulk of national power should be in the legislature. The Constitution states that Congress will consist of two chambers. A result of the Connecticut Compromise, this bicameral structure established a balanced legislature, with the membership in the House of Representatives based on population and the membership in the Senate based on the equality of states.

2 The functions of Congress include (a) lawmaking, (b) service to constituents, (c) representation, (d) oversight, (e) public education, and (f) conflict resolution.

3 The first seventeen clauses of Article I, Section 8, of the Constitution specify most of the enumerated, or expressed, powers of Congress, including the right to impose taxes, to borrow money, to regulate commerce, and to declare war. Besides its enumerated powers, Congress enjoys the right to "make all Laws which shall be necessary and proper for carrying into Execution the foregoing Powers, and all other Powers vested by this Constitution in the Government of the United States, or in any Department or Officer thereof." This is called the elastic, or necessary and proper, clause.

4 There are 435 members in the House of Representatives and 100 members in the Senate. Owing to its larger size, the House has a greater number of formal rules. The Senate tradition of unlimited debate dates back to 1790 and has been used over the years to frustrate the passage of bills. Under Senate Rule 22, cloture can be used to shut off debate on a bill.

5 Members of Congress are not typical American citizens. They are older and wealthier than most Americans, disproportionately white and male, and more likely to be trained in professional occupations.

6 Congressional elections are operated by the individual state governments, which must abide by rules established by the Constitution and national statutes. Most candidates for Congress must win nomination through a direct primary. The overwhelming majority of incumbent representatives and a smaller proportion of senators who run for reelection are successful. A complicated aspect of congressional elections is apportionment—the allocation of legislative seats to constituencies. The Supreme Court's "one person, one vote" rule has been applied to equalize the populations of congressional and state legislative districts.

7 Members of Congress are well paid and enjoy benefits such as franking privileges. Members of Congress have personal and committee staff members available to them and also enjoy a number of legal privileges and immunities.

8 Most of the actual work of legislating is performed by committees and subcommittees within Congress. Legislation introduced into the House or Senate is assigned to the appropriate standing committees for review. Select committees are created for a limited time for a specific purpose. Joint committees are formed by the concurrent action of both chambers and consist of members from each chamber. Conference committees are special joint committees set up to achieve agreement between the House and the Senate on the exact wording of legislative acts passed by both chambers in different forms. The seniority rule, which is usually followed, specifies that the longest-serving member of the majority party will be the chairperson of a committee.

9 The foremost power holder in the House of Representatives is the Speaker of the House. Other leaders are the House majority leader, the House minority leader, and the majority and minority whips. Formally, the vice president is the presiding officer of the Senate, with the most senior member of the majority party serving as the president pro tempore to preside when the vice president is absent. Actual leadership in the Senate rests with the majority leader, the minority leader, and their whips.

10 A bill becomes law by progressing through both chambers of Congress and their appropriate standing and joint committees to the president.

11 The budget process for a fiscal year begins with the preparation of an executive budget by the president. This is reviewed by the Office of Management and Budget and then sent to Congress, which is supposed to pass a final budget by the end of September. Since 1978, Congress has not generally followed its own time rules.

★ Selected Print and Media Resources

SUGGESTED READINGS

Barone, Michael, and Grant Ujifusa. *The Almanac of American Politics, 2004.* Washington, D.C.: National Journal, 2003. This book, which is published biannually, is a comprehensive summary of current political information on each member of Congress, his or her state or congressional district, recent congressional election results, key votes, ratings by various organizations, sources of campaign contributions, and records of campaign expenditures.

Brown, Sherrod. *Congress from the Inside: Observations from the Majority and the Minority.* Kent, Ohio: Kent State University Press, 2004. A congressional member's view of what Congress actually does. Brown, a four-term representative from Ohio, looks at election campaigns, committee service, working with constituents, and the Democratic Party's struggle to deal with its loss of a House majority. Brown avoids self-puffery, but his liberal stance is evident.

Davidson, Roger H., and Walter J. Oleszek. *Congress and Its Members,* 9th ed. Washington, D.C.: CQ Press, 2003. This classic looks carefully at the "two Congresses," the one in Washington and the role played by congresspersons at home.

Just, Ward S. *The Congressman Who Loved Flaubert.* New York: Carrol and Graf Publishers, 1990. This fictional account of a career politician was first published in 1973 and is still a favorite with students of political science. Ward Just is renowned for his political fiction, and particularly for his examination of character and motivation.

Rosenthal, Cindy Simon, ed. *Women Transforming Congress (Congressional Studies Series,* Vol. 4). Norman: University of Oklahoma Press, 2003. This collection of essays written by women in the political arena focuses on how the political activities of women have transformed the predominantly male institution of Congress.

Silverberg, David. *Congress for Dummies.* Hoboken, N.J.: For Dummies, 2002. This introduction to how Congress works has forewords by Speaker of the House Dennis Hastert and Senate Minority Leader Tom Daschle. Silverberg is the editor of *The Hill,* a weekly that covers Congress. He has covered Congress as a reporter for over twenty years.

MEDIA SOURCES

The Congress—In one of his earlier efforts (1988), filmmaker Ken Burns profiles the history of Congress. Narration is by David McCullough, and those interviewed include David Broker, Alistair Cooke, and Cokie Roberts. PBS Home Video re-released this film on DVD in 2003.

Congress: A Day in the Life of a Representative—From political meetings to social functions to campaigning, this 1995 program examines what politicians really do. Featured representatives are Tim Roemer (a Democrat from Indiana) and Sue Myrick (a Republican from North Carolina).

Mr. Smith Goes to Washington—A 1939 film in which Jimmy Stewart plays the naïve congressman who is quickly educated in Washington. A true American political classic.

The Seduction of Joe Tynan—A 1979 film in which Alan Alda plays a young senator who must face serious decisions about his political role and his private life.

e-mocracy ★ Elections and the Web

Virtually all senators and representatives now have Web sites that you can find simply by keying in their names in a search engine. As you read in this chapter's *Making a Difference* feature, you can easily learn the names of your congressional representatives by going to the Web site of the House or Senate (see the following *Logging On* section for the URLs for these sites). Once you know the names of your representatives, you can go to their Web sites to learn more about them and their positions on specific issues. You can also check the Web sites of the groups listed in the *Making a Difference* feature to track your representatives' voting records and discover the names of their campaign contributors.

Note that some members of Congress also provide important services to their constituents via their Web sites. Some sites, for example, allow constituents to apply for internships in Washington, D.C., apply for appointments to military academies, order flags, order tours of the Capitol, and register complaints electronically. Other sites may provide forms from certain government agencies, such as the Social Security Administration, that constituents can use to request assistance from those agencies or register complaints.

Logging On

To find out about the schedule of activities taking place in Congress, use the following Web sites:

http://www.senate.gov

http://www.house.gov

The Congressional Budget Office is online at

http://www.cbo.gov

The URL for the Government Printing Office is

http://www.gpoaccess.gov

For the real inside facts on what's going on in Washington, D.C., you can look at the following resources:

RollCall, the newspaper of the Capitol:

http://www.rollcall.com

Congressional Quarterly, a publication that reports on Congress:

http://www.cq.com

The Hill, which investigates various activities of Congress:

http://www.hillnews.com

Using InfoTrac for Political Research

You can examine a particular piece of legislation to learn how various influences act on Congress. A useful example is energy policy. Many different forces have shaped energy legislation—and in 2003, at least, ensured that a major bill proposed by the president would fail. Special interests, the president, and the ideological orientation of members of Congress have all played a role. You can research energy legislation using InfoTrac. To use

InfoTrac to research such legislation, go to

http://www.infotrac-college.com

Log in and go to InfoTrac College Edition, then go to the Subject guide. Type "united states congress" in the search field. InfoTrac will present you with a list of subjects. Select "United States. Congress" and click on "Narrow by subdivision." You will see a more detailed list of topics. Scroll down to "energy policy" and click on "View." You will now see a long list of articles, sorted by date. Choose a number of the most recent articles and try to discover the current state of legislation on energy policy. Which interests or forces seem to be especially influential?

ONLINE REVIEW

At **http://politicalscience.wadsworth. com/schmidt12**, you will find a free Study Guide to this book. For each chapter, there are two online quizzes to help you master the material.

• The **PoliPrep Self Study Assessment** provides a pre-test for each major section of the chapter. PoliPrep then generates a customized study plan. After you complete the study plan, a post-test evaluates your progress.

• The **Tutorial Quiz** for each chapter provides questions on the chapter contents, including the features. The questions are organized to match the major sections of the chapter.

The President

WHAT IF . . .
There Were No Executive Privilege?

BACKGROUND

When a U.S. president wishes to keep information secret, he or she can invoke *executive privilege*. Typically, administrations use executive privilege to safeguard national security secrets. Although there is no mention of executive privilege in the Constitution, presidents from George Washington to George W. Bush have invoked this privilege in response to perceived encroachments on the executive branch by Congress and by the judiciary.

Nonetheless, Congress could pass a law prohibiting the executive branch from using executive privilege as a defense to requests for information. Alternatively, the Supreme Court could hold that executive privilege is an unconstitutional exercise of executive power.

WHAT IF THERE WERE NO EXECUTIVE PRIVILEGE?

If there were no executive privilege, a president would have to be aware that all of his or her words, documents, and actions could be made public. We know from twentieth-century history that when a president does not have full executive privilege to protect information, the results can be devastating. President Richard Nixon (1969–1974) had tape-recorded hundreds of hours of conversations in the Oval Office. During a scandal involving a cover-up (the Watergate scandal, as you will read later in this chapter), Congress requested those tapes. Nixon invoked executive privilege and refused to turn them over. Ultimately, the Supreme Court ordered him to do so, however, and the tapes provided damning information about Nixon's role in the purported cover-up of illegal activities. Rather than face impeachment, Nixon resigned the presidency.

Clearly, if executive privilege were eliminated, it is unlikely that conversations between the president and other members of the executive branch would be recorded or otherwise documented. As a result, we would have fewer records of an administration's activities than we do today.

EXECUTIVE PRIVILEGE IN A WORLD FILLED WITH TERRORISM

Following the terrorist attacks on September 11, 2001, Attorney General John Ashcroft advised federal agencies "to lean toward withholding information whenever possible." In some instances, the Bush administration attempted to withhold information from Congress and the courts, not just the public. One troubling example was the threat to fire a top civil servant if he told Congress the true projected cost of the administration's Medicare prescription drug bill.

Of course, without executive privilege, the president might experience problems in waging a war on terrorism. While Congress and the courts have procedures that can be used to guard sensitive information, both branches of government are unaccustomed to keeping secrets, and often find it hard to do so.

PAST, PRESENT, AND FUTURE PRESIDENTIAL PAPERS

The White House is allowed to decide what is classified as top secret. Even if Congress requests top secret material, the White House does not have to release it. In general, not all transcripts of private conversations between past presidents and foreign heads of state are made available to congressional committees, for example.

If executive privilege were eliminated, the White House would have a difficult time regulating the flow of past presidential records into the public forum. Future presidents, of course, would know that virtually every word and act could be released to the public. The behavior of presidents and their administrations would certainly change. They might simply insist that there be no record of sensitive conversations. If so, future Americans would lose much of the historical background for America's domestic and international actions.

FOR CRITICAL ANALYSIS

1. The history of executive privilege dates back to 1796, when President George Washington refused a request by the House for certain documents. Given the changes that have taken place since that time, should executive privilege be eliminated? Or should it be retained as even more necessary today than it was at that time?

2. What would be the costs to the nation if executive privilege were eliminated?

The writers of the Constitution created the presidency of the United States without any models to follow. Nowhere else in the world was there a democratically selected chief executive. What the founders did not want was a king. In fact, given their previous experience with royal governors in the colonies, many of the delegates to the Constitutional Convention wanted to create a very weak executive who could not veto legislation. Other delegates, especially those who had witnessed the need for a strong leader in the Revolutionary Army, believed a strong executive would be necessary for the new republic. The delegates, after much debate, created a chief executive who had enough powers granted in the Constitution to balance those of Congress.[1]

The power exercised by each president who has held the office has been scrutinized and judged by historians, political scientists, the media, and the public. The executive privilege enjoyed by presidents has also been subject to scrutiny and debate, as you learned in the chapter-opening *What If . . .* feature. Indeed, it would seem that Americans are fascinated by presidential power and by the persons who hold the office. In this chapter, after looking at who can become president and at the process involved, we examine closely the nature and extent of the constitutional powers held by the president.

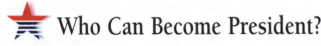

★ Who Can Become President?

The requirements for becoming president, as outlined in Article II, Section 1, of the Constitution, are not overwhelmingly stringent:

> No person except a natural born Citizen, or a Citizen of the United States, at the time of the Adoption of this Constitution, shall be eligible to the Office of President; neither shall any Person be eligible to that Office who shall not have attained to the Age of thirty-five Years, and been fourteen Years a Resident within the United States.

The only question that arises about these qualifications relates to the term *natural born Citizen*. Does that mean only citizens born in the United States and its

---

[1]Forrest McDonald, *The American Presidency: An Intellectual History* (Lawrence, Kans.: University Press of Kansas, 1994), p. 179.

Harry Truman, left, when he was the proprietor of a Kansas City, Missouri, men's clothing store, about 1920. Ronald Reagan, right, is shown as a frontier marshal in the movie *Law and Order*, released in 1953. Compared to members of Congress, presidents have had a more varied background. How would varied life experiences benefit a president? (Both photos © CORBIS)

territories? What about a child born to a U.S. citizen (or to a couple who are U.S. citizens) visiting or living in another country? Although the question has not been dealt with directly by the Supreme Court, it is reasonable to expect that someone would be eligible if her or his parents were Americans. The first presidents, after all, were not even American citizens at birth, and others were born in areas that did not become part of the United States until later. These questions were debated when George Romney, who was born in Chihuahua, Mexico, made a serious bid for the Republican presidential nomination in the 1960s.[2]

The American dream is symbolized by the statement that "anybody can become president of this country." It is true that in modern times, presidents have included a haberdasher (Harry Truman—for a short period of time), a peanut farmer (Jimmy Carter), and an actor (Ronald Reagan). But if you examine the list of presidents inside the back cover of this book, you will see that the most common previous occupation of presidents in this country has been the law. Out of forty-three presidents, twenty-six have been lawyers, and many have been wealthy. (There have been fewer lawyers in the last century, however.)

Although the Constitution states that the minimum-age requirement for the presidency is thirty-five years, most presidents have been much older than that when they assumed office. John F. Kennedy, at the age of forty-three, was the youngest elected president, and the oldest was Ronald Reagan, at age sixty-nine. The average age at inauguration has been fifty-four. There has clearly been a demographic bias in the selection of presidents. All have been male, white, and from the Protestant tradition, except for John F. Kennedy, a Roman Catholic. Presidents have been men of great stature—such as George Washington—and men in whom leadership qualities were not so pronounced—such as Warren Harding (1921–1923). A presidential candidate usually has experience as a vice president, senator, or state governor. Former governors have been especially successful at winning the presidency. Does service in the Senate actually handicap potential presidential candidates? We look at that question in the *Politics and the Presidency* feature.

★ The Process of Becoming President

Major and minor political parties nominate candidates for president and vice president at national conventions every four years. As discussed in Chapter 9, the nation's voters do not elect a president and vice president directly but rather cast ballots for presidential electors, who then vote for president and vice president in the electoral college.

Because the election is governed by a majority in the electoral college, it is conceivable that someone could be elected to the office of the presidency without having a plurality of the popular vote cast. Indeed, in four cases, candidates won elections even though their major opponents received more popular votes. One of those cases occurred in 2000, when George W. Bush won the electoral college vote and became president even though his opponent, Al Gore, won the popular vote. In elections when more than two candidates were running for office, many presidential candidates have won with less than 50 percent of the total popular votes cast for all candidates—including Abraham Lincoln, Woodrow Wilson, Harry Truman, John F. Kennedy, Richard Nixon, and in 1992, Bill Clinton. Independent candidate Ross Perot garnered a surprising 19 percent of the vote in 1992. Remember from Chapter 9 that no president has won a majority of votes from the entire voting-age population.

---

[2]George Romney was governor of Michigan from 1963 to 1969. Romney was not nominated, and the issue remains unresolved.

POLITICS AND THE PRESIDENCY
Senators as Presidential Candidates

Senators often aspire to become president. In the contest to become the 2004 Democratic presidential candidate, four of the top eight contenders were senators or former senators. John F. Kerry, the winner, was a senator from Massachusetts. Over the years, however, few senators have actually made it to the presidency. Of the nineteen presidents elected between 1900 and 2000, only two came directly from the Senate. The most recent one was Democrat John F. Kennedy (1961–1963). In contrast, nine presidents were former governors, and five were former vice presidents. Why have senators had such a hard time winning, when so many of them run?

THE VOTING RECORD PROBLEM

To succeed, senators must learn the art of compromise. A senator who votes against a bill may not be completely opposed to it. Instead, he or she may hope that if a particular bill is defeated, the Senate will draft a better one. A senator may vote to report an important bill out of committee simply to let the entire Senate vote on it. Then, on the floor of the Senate, he or she may vote against it. These kinds of votes may be hard to explain. For example, Kerry cast hundreds of votes in his Senate career. It was easy for the Bush campaign to criticize selected votes, such as votes against defense or intelligence funding. But without determining the context of each vote, it is impossible to know why Kerry cast the vote he did. Was it an amendment or a final vote? Was it a key vote—or a noncontroversial bipartisan measure? Governors do not usually have as much trouble as legislators in explaining their past decisions.

THE SENATE MAY PROMOTE POOR SPEAKING HABITS

As you learned in Chapter 11, unlike the House, the Senate imposes no limits on debate. Senators do not have to be succinct. Therefore, they may lose (or never learn) the kind of speaking skills needed in a presidential campaign. Columnist George F. Will made the following observation: "It takes years of . . . seasoning in the Senate's habits of unlimited debate and its belief that self-congratulatory sonorousness is eloquence, to produce a person as inarticulate as [1996 Republican presidential candidate] Bob Dole."* Some believe that, at least intially, Kerry suffered from this problem as well.

FOR CRITICAL ANALYSIS

How important is eloquence in a presidential candidate? Can an inarticulate candidate win if he or she stands for popular policies?

*George F. Will, "Handicapped on the Hill," *Newsweek,* October 27, 2003.

Two "JFK" senators from Massachusetts campaign for the presidency. On the left, Senator John F. Kennedy, the 1960 Democratic presidential nominee, thanks supporters for selecting him. On the right, Senator John F. Kerry shakes hands with supporters following a rally in Grand Rapids, Michigan in 2004. (Left photo © Corbis/Bettmann; right photo courtesy of Kerry-Edwards 2004, Inc., photographer Sharon Farmer)

Twelfth Amendment
An amendment to the Constitution, adopted in 1804, that specifies the separate election of the president and vice president by the electoral college.

Head of State
The role of the president as ceremonial head of the government.

From left to right, the first cabinet—Henry Knox, Thomas Jefferson, Edmund Randolph, Alexander Hamilton—and the first president, George Washington. (The Granger Collection)

On occasion, the electoral college has failed to give any candidate a majority. At this point, the election is thrown into the House of Representatives. The president is then chosen from among the three candidates having the most electoral college votes, as noted in Chapter 9. Only two times in our past has the House had to decide on a president. Thomas Jefferson and Aaron Burr tied in the electoral college in 1800. This happened because the Constitution had not been explicit in indicating which of the two electoral votes was for president and which was for vice president. In 1804, the **Twelfth Amendment** clarified the matter by requiring that the president and vice president be chosen separately. In 1824, the House again had to make a choice, this time among William H. Crawford, Andrew Jackson, and John Quincy Adams. It chose Adams, even though Jackson had more electoral and popular votes.

★ The Many Roles of the President

The Constitution speaks briefly about the duties and obligations of the president. Based on this brief list of powers and on the precedents of history, the presidency has grown into a very complicated job that requires balancing at least five constitutional roles. These are (1) head of state, (2) chief executive, (3) commander in chief of the armed forces, (4) chief diplomat, and (5) chief legislator of the United States. Here we examine each of these significant presidential functions, or roles. It is worth noting that one person plays all these roles simultaneously and that the needs of these roles may at times come into conflict.

Head of State

Every nation has at least one person who is the ceremonial head of state. In most democratic governments, the role of **head of state** is given to someone other than the chief executive, who leads the executive branch of government. In Britain, for example, the head of state is the queen. In much of Europe, the prime minister is the chief executive, and the head of state is the president. But in the United States, the president is both chief executive and head of state. According to William Howard Taft, as head of state the president symbolizes the "dignity and majesty" of the American people.

As head of state, the president engages in a number of activities that are largely symbolic or ceremonial, such as the following:

- Decorating war heroes.
- Throwing out the first ball to open the baseball season.
- Dedicating parks and post offices.
- Receiving visiting heads of state at the White House.
- Going on official state visits to other countries.
- Making personal telephone calls to astronauts.
- Representing the nation at times of national mourning, such as after the terrorist attacks of September 11, 2001, and after the loss of the space shuttle *Columbia* in 2003.

Some students of the American political system believe that having the president serve as both the chief executive and the head of state drastically limits the time available to do "real" work. Not all presidents have agreed with this conclusion, however—particularly those presidents who have skillfully blended these two roles with their role as politician. Being head of state gives the president tremendous public exposure, which can be an important asset in a campaign for reelection. When that exposure is positive, it helps the president deal with Congress over proposed legislation and increases the chances of being reelected—or getting the candidates of the president's party elected.

Chief Executive

According to the Constitution, "The executive Power shall be vested in a President of the United States of America. . . . [H]e may require the Opinion, in writing, of the principal Officer in each of the executive Departments, upon any Subject relating to the Duties of their respective Offices . . . and he shall nominate, and by and with the Advice and Consent of the Senate, shall appoint . . . Officers of the United States. . . . [H]e shall take Care that the Laws be faithfully executed."

As **chief executive,** the president is constitutionally bound to enforce the acts of Congress, the judgments of federal courts, and treaties signed by the United States. The duty to "faithfully execute" the laws has been a source of constitutional power for presidents. To assist in the various tasks of the chief executive, the president has a federal bureaucracy (see Chapter 13), which currently consists of over 2.7 million federal civilian employees.

The Powers of Appointment and Removal.   You might think that the president, as head of the largest bureaucracy in the United States, wields enormous power. The president, however, only nominally runs the executive bureaucracy. Most government positions are filled by **civil service** employees, who generally gain government employment through a merit system rather than presidential appointment.[3] Therefore, even though the president has important **appointment power,** it is limited to cabinet and subcabinet jobs, federal judgeships, agency

---

[3]See Chapter 13 for a discussion of the Civil Service Reform Act.

Chief Executive
The role of the president as head of the executive branch of the government.

Civil Service
A collective term for the body of employees working for the government. Generally, civil service is understood to apply to all those who gain government employment through a merit system.

Appointment Power
The authority vested in the president to fill a government office or position. Positions filled by presidential appointment include those in the executive branch and the federal judiciary, commissioned officers in the armed forces, and members of the independent regulatory commissions.

President George W. Bush is shown here working in the Oval Office. This oval-shaped office in the White House is often used to represent the power of the presidency and of the United States. (AP Photo/Doug Mills)

heads, and about two thousand lesser jobs. This means that most of the 2.7 million federal employees owe no political allegiance to the president. They are more likely to owe loyalty to congressional committees or to interest groups representing the sector of the society that they serve. Table 12–1 shows what percentage of the total employment in each executive department is available for political appointment by the president.

The president's power to remove from office those officials who are not doing a good job or who do not agree with the president is not explicitly granted by the Constitution and has been limited. In 1926, however, a Supreme Court decision prevented Congress from interfering with the president's ability to fire those executive-branch officials whom the president had appointed with Senate approval.[4] There are ten agencies whose directors the president can remove at any time. These agencies include the Arms Control and Disarmament Agency, the Commission on Civil Rights, the Environmental Protection Agency, the General Services Administration, and the Small Business Administration. In addition, the president can remove all heads of cabinet departments, all individuals in the Executive Office of the President, and all of the 5,332 political appointees listed in Table 12–1.

Harry Truman spoke candidly of the difficulties a president faces in trying to control the executive bureaucracy. On leaving office, he referred to the problems that Dwight Eisenhower, as a former general of the army, was going to have: "He'll sit here and he'll say do this! do that! and nothing will happen. Poor Ike—it won't be a bit like the Army. He'll find it very frustrating."[5]

---

[4]*Meyers v. United States,* 272 U.S. 52 (1926).
[5]Quoted in Richard E. Neustadt, *Presidential Power: The Politics of Leadership* (New York: Wiley, 1960), p. 9. Truman may not have considered the amount of politics involved in decision making in the upper reaches of the army.

TABLE 12–1

Total Civilian Employment in Cabinet Departments Available for Political Appointment by the President

EXECUTIVE DEPARTMENT	TOTAL NUMBER OF EMPLOYEES	POLITICAL APPOINTMENTS AVAILABLE	PERCENTAGE
Agriculture	100,084	439	0.43
Commerce	39,151	446	1.13
Defense	670,568	466	0.06
Education	4,581	186	4.06
Energy	15,689	433	2.75
Health and Human Services	63,323	391	0.61
Homeland Security	(not yet created)	N/A	N/A
Housing and Urban Development	10,154	156	1.53
Interior	72,982	240	0.32
Justice	126,711	501	0.39
Labor	16,016	188	1.17
State	28,054	1,066	3.79
Transportation	64,131	274	0.42
Treasury	159,274	231	0.14
Veterans Affairs	223,137	315	0.14
TOTAL	1,593,855	5,332	0.33

SOURCES: *Policy and Supporting Positions* (Washington, D.C.: Government Printing Office, 2000); U.S. Office of Personnel Management, 2004.

The Power to Grant Reprieves and Pardons. Section 2 of Article II of the Constitution gives the president the power to grant **reprieves** and **pardons** for offenses against the United States except in cases of impeachment. All pardons are administered by the Office of the Pardon Attorney in the Department of Justice. In principle, a pardon is granted to remedy a mistake made in a conviction.

The Supreme Court upheld the president's power to grant reprieves and pardons in a 1925 case concerning a pardon granted by the president to an individual convicted of contempt of court. The judiciary had contended that only judges had the authority to convict individuals for contempt of court when court orders were violated and that the courts should be free from interference by the executive branch. The Supreme Court simply stated that the president could grant reprieves or pardons for all offenses "either before trial, during trial, or after trial, by individuals, or by classes, conditionally or absolutely, and this without modification or regulation by Congress."[6]

In a controversial decision, President Gerald Ford pardoned former president Richard Nixon for his role in the Watergate affair before any charges were brought in court. Just before George W. Bush's inauguration in 2001, President Bill Clinton announced pardons for more than one hundred persons. Some of these pardons were controversial.

Commander in Chief

The president, according to the Constitution, "shall be Commander in Chief of the Army and Navy of the United States, and of the Militia of the several States, when called into the actual Service of the United States." In other words, the armed forces are under civilian, rather than military, control.

Wartime Powers. Certainly, those who wrote the Constitution had George Washington in mind when they made the president the **commander in chief.** Although we do not expect our president to lead the troops into battle, presidents as commanders in chief have wielded dramatic power. Harry Truman made the awesome decision to drop atomic bombs on Hiroshima and Nagasaki in 1945 to force Japan to surrender and thus bring World War II to an end. Lyndon Johnson ordered bombing missions against North Vietnam in the 1960s, and he personally

---

[6]*Ex parte Grossman,* 267 U.S. 87 (1925).

★★★★★★★★★★★★★★★★★
DID YOU KNOW . . .
That President Richard Nixon served 56 days without a vice president, and that President Gerald Ford served 132 days without a vice president**?**

Reprieve
A formal postponement of the execution of a sentence imposed by a court of law.

Pardon
A release from the punishment for or legal consequences of a crime; a pardon can be granted by the president before or after a conviction.

Commander in Chief
The role of the president as supreme commander of the military forces of the United States and of the state National Guard units when they are called into federal service.

ELECTIONS 2004 · The 2004 Presidential Elections

Leading up to the 2004 elections, current events appeared to pose a problem for incumbent George W. Bush. American solders were getting killed every day in Iraq. Job growth was historically slow. In addition, opinion polls revealed that Bush was seriously unpopular in Europe and throughout most of the world. But Bush's domestic favorable ratings stabilized above 50 percent by Election Day, and Bush succeeded in convincing enough undecided voters that he should remain commander in chief during this war on terrorism. More than that, his 3.5 million-vote margin over Kerry—the largest in any presidential election in thirty years—and the increased Republican majorities in both chambers of Congress gave Bush a chance at meeting his second-term goals. These included reform of the tax system and Social Security, as well as improved standards in our schools.

War Powers Resolution
A law passed in 1973 spelling out the conditions under which the president can commit troops without congressional approval.

selected some of the targets. Richard Nixon decided to invade Cambodia in 1970. Ronald Reagan sent troops to Lebanon and Grenada in 1983 and ordered U.S. fighter planes to attack Libya in 1986. George H. W. Bush sent troops to Panama in 1989 and to the Middle East in 1990. Bill Clinton sent troops to Haiti in 1994 and to Bosnia in 1995, ordered missile attacks on alleged terrorist bases in 1998, and sent American planes to bomb Serbia in 1999. Most recently, George W. Bush invaded Iraq in 2003. Can the use of military power to establish democracy in other countries enhance our security? We examine that question in this chapter's *America's Security* feature.

The president is the ultimate decision maker in military matters. Everywhere the president goes, so too goes the "football"—a briefcase filled with all the codes necessary to order a nuclear attack. Only the president has the power to order the use of nuclear force.

As commander in chief, the president has probably exercised more authority than in any other role. Constitutionally, Congress has the sole power to declare war, but the president can send the armed forces into a country in situations that are certainly the equivalent of war. Harry Truman dispatched troops to Korea in 1950. Kennedy, Johnson, and Nixon waged an undeclared war in Southeast Asia, where more than 58,000 Americans were killed and 300,000 were wounded. In neither of these situations had Congress declared war.

The War Powers Resolution.　In an attempt to gain more control over such military activities, in 1973 Congress passed the **War Powers Resolution**—over President Nixon's veto—requiring that the president consult with Congress when sending American forces into action. Once they are sent, the president must report to Congress within forty-eight hours. Unless Congress approves the use of troops within sixty days or extends the sixty-day time limit, the forces must be withdrawn. The War Powers Resolution was tested in the fall of 1983, when Reagan requested that troops be left in Lebanon. The resulting compromise was a congressional resolution allowing troops to remain there for eighteen months. Shortly

President George W. Bush carries a platter of turkey and fixings as he visits U.S. troops on Thanksgiving Day in 2003. Bush secretly traveled to Baghdad to pay the surprise visit. What other steps could a president take to boost the morale of the armed forces? (REUTERS/ Anja Niedringhaus, Pool/Landov)

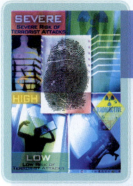

AMERICA'S SECURITY
Do We Need a Democratic World to Be Safe?

A fundamental reason that President George W. Bush went to war in Iraq was the belief that a democratic Iraq could be a source of peace and progress for the entire Middle East. Will a democratic Iraq have such an effect? More broadly, is a democratic world a way to ensure America's security? Bush appeared to believe this. "[T]here's an historic opportunity here to change the world," he said about Iraq. "I feel strongly that the course this administration has taken will make America more secure and the world more free, and, therefore the world more peaceful."*

DEMOCRACY AND PEACE

Some political scientists have claimed that the statement, "Democracies do not go to war with each other" is so true that it can be called a "law" of political science.[†] It follows that a democratic world would be a world without war. Some observers, however, do not believe that nations have to be democratic to remain at peace with one another. Since they became independent, the nations of both South America and Africa have experienced constant dictatorships

*George W. Bush, press conference on April 13, 2004.
[†]As cited in Todd Landman, *Issues and Methods in Comparative Politics* (New York: Routledge, 2003), p. 14.

and civil upheaval. Yet wars *between* nations on these continents have been rare. Some argue that while dictatorship is a necessary requirement to produce a belligerent nation, it is far from the only requirement. There must also be a belligerent dictator—such as Saddam Hussein, who invaded Kuwait in 1990.

DEMOCRACY AND WAR

Democracy may also not be a perfect protection against war. The U.S. Civil War (1860–1865) is one example. Despite the existence of slavery in the South, both parties to the conflict had constitutions that were fundamentally democratic—at least from the viewpoint of whites in both sections.

Of more relevance to the Middle East is the argument, advanced by many, that the greatest source of animosity toward the United States in the region is America's role in the Israeli-Palestinian conflict. These people contend that even a fully democratic Middle East will not guarantee America's security if the Israeli-Palestinian dispute is not settled.

FOR CRITICAL ANALYSIS

Why might a democratic Middle East be inhospitable territory for Islamist radicals such as Osama bin Laden?

---

after the resolution was passed, however, more than 240 sailors and Marines were killed in a suicide bombing of a U.S. military housing compound in Beirut. That event provoked a furious congressional debate over the role American troops were playing in the Middle East, and all troops were withdrawn shortly thereafter.

In spite of the War Powers Resolution, the powers of the president as commander in chief are more extensive today than they were in the past. These powers are linked closely to the president's powers as chief diplomat, or chief crafter of foreign policy.

Chief Diplomat

The Constitution gives the president the power to recognize foreign governments; to make treaties, with the **advice and consent** of the Senate; and to make special agreements with other heads of state that do not require congressional approval. In addition, the president nominates ambassadors. As **chief diplomat,** the president dominates American foreign policy, a role that has been supported many times by the Supreme Court.

Diplomatic Recognition.   An important power of the president as chief diplomat is that of **diplomatic recognition,** or the power to recognize—or refuse to recognize—foreign governments. In the role of ceremonial head of state, the president

Advice and Consent
Terms in the Constitution describing the U.S. Senate's power to review and approve treaties and presidential appointments.

Chief Diplomat
The role of the president in recognizing foreign governments, making treaties, and effecting executive agreements.

Diplomatic Recognition
The formal acknowledgment of a foreign government as legitimate.

President George H. W. Bush
(1989–1993) meets with Prince Saud
Al-Faisal, foreign minister of Saudi
Arabia, in 1990. George H. W. Bush is
the father of George W. Bush, making
the Bush family a true political dynasty.
It is not uncommon for the children of
elected officials to go into politics. (AP
Photo/Barry Thumma)

has always received foreign diplomats. In modern times, the simple act of receiving a foreign diplomat has been equivalent to accrediting the diplomat and officially recognizing his or her government. Such recognition of the legitimacy of another country's government is a prerequisite to diplomatic relations or treaties between that country and the United States.

Deciding when to recognize a foreign power is not always simple. The United States, for example, did not recognize the Soviet Union until 1933—sixteen years after the Russian Revolution of 1917. It was only after all attempts to reverse the effects of that revolution—including military invasion of Russia and diplomatic isolation—had proved futile that Franklin Roosevelt extended recognition to the Soviet government. U.S. presidents faced a similar problem with the Chinese communist revolution. In December 1978, long after the communist victory in China in 1949, Jimmy Carter granted official recognition to the People's Republic of China.[7]

A diplomatic recognition issue that faced the Clinton administration involved recognizing a former enemy—the Republic of Vietnam. Many Americans, particularly those who believed that Vietnam had not been forthcoming in the efforts to find the remains of missing American soldiers or to find out about former prisoners of war, opposed any formal relationship with that nation. After the U.S. government had negotiated with the Vietnamese government for many years over the missing-in-action issue and engaged in limited diplomatic contacts for several years, President Clinton announced on July 11, 1995, that the United States would recognize the government of Vietnam and move to establish normal diplomatic relations.

Proposal and Ratification of Treaties.   The president has the sole power to negotiate treaties with other nations. These treaties must be presented to the Senate, where they may be modified and must be approved by a two-thirds vote. After ratification, the president can approve the senatorial version of the treaty. Approval poses a problem when the Senate has tacked on substantive amendments or reservations to a treaty, particularly when such changes may require reopening negotiations with the other signatory governments. Sometimes a president may decide to withdraw a treaty if the senatorial changes are too extensive—as Woodrow Wilson did with the Versailles Treaty in 1919. Wilson believed that the senatorial reservations would weaken the treaty so much that it would be ineffective. His refusal to accept the senatorial version of the treaty led to the eventual refusal of the United States to join the League of Nations.

President Carter was successful in lobbying for the treaties that provided for the return of the Panama Canal to Panama by the year 2000 and neutralizing the canal. President Bill Clinton won a major political and legislative victory in 1993 by persuading Congress to ratify the North American Free Trade Agreement (NAFTA). In so doing, he had to overcome opposition from Democrats and most of organized labor. In 1998, he worked closely with Senate Republicans to ensure Senate approval of a treaty governing the use of chemical weapons. In 2000, President Clinton won another major legislative victory when Congress voted to permanently normalize trade relations with China.

Before September 11, 2001, President George W. Bush indicated his intention to steer the United States in a unilateral direction on foreign policy. He rejected the Kyoto Agreement on global warming and proposed ending the 1972 Anti-Ballistic Missile (ABM) Treaty that was part of the first Strategic Arms Limitation

[7]The Nixon administration first encouraged new relations with the People's Republic of China by allowing a cultural exchange of ping-pong teams.

Allied leaders attend the Versailles peace conference in 1919 after World War I. U.S. President Woodrow Wilson is second from the left. Wilson failed to get the resulting peace treaty approved by the U.S. Senate. To what extent should Congress defer to the president in making foreign policy? (National Archives)

Treaty (SALT I). After the terrorist attacks of 9/11, however, President Bush sought cooperation from U.S. allies in the war on terrorism. Bush's return to multilateralism was exemplified in the signing of a nuclear weapons reduction treaty with Russia in 2002. Nonetheless, his attempts to gain international support for a war against Iraq to overthrow that country's government were not as successful as he had hoped.

Executive Agreements.   Presidential power in foreign affairs is enhanced greatly by the use of **executive agreements** made between the president and other heads of state. Such agreements do not require Senate approval, although the House and Senate may refuse to appropriate the funds necessary to implement them. Whereas treaties are binding on all succeeding administrations, executive agreements require each new president's consent to remain in effect.

Among the advantages of executive agreements are speed and secrecy. The former is essential during a crisis; the latter is important when the administration fears that open senatorial debate may be detrimental to the best interests of the United States or to the interests of the president.[8] There have been far more executive agreements (about 9,000) than treaties (about 1,300). Many executive agreements contain secret provisions calling for American military assistance or other support. For example, Franklin Roosevelt (1933–1945) used executive agreements to bypass congressional isolationists when he traded American destroyers for British Caribbean naval bases and when he arranged diplomatic and military affairs with Canada and Latin American nations.

Executive Agreement
An international agreement made by the president, without senatorial ratification, with the head of a foreign state.

Chief Legislator

Constitutionally, presidents must recommend to Congress legislation that they judge necessary and expedient. Not all presidents have wielded their powers as **chief legislator** in the same manner. Some presidents have been almost completely unsuccessful in getting their legislative programs implemented by Congress. Presidents Franklin Roosevelt and Lyndon Johnson, however, saw much of their proposed legislation put into effect.

Chief Legislator
The role of the president in influencing the making of laws.

---

[8]The Case Act of 1972 requires that all executive agreements be transmitted to Congress within sixty days after the agreement takes effect. Secret agreements are transmitted to the foreign relations committees as classified information.

Each year the president presents the State of the Union message, which is required by Article II, Section 3, of the Constitution and is usually given in late January. Attendees include all members of Congress, and usually also include the justices of the U.S. Supreme Court and the heads of most of the executive departments. Vice President Dick Cheney (left) and House Speaker Dennis Hastert (right) listen behind the president. (Kevin Lamarque/POOL via Bloomberg News/Landov)

State of the Union Message

An annual message to Congress in which the president proposes a legislative program. The message is addressed not only to Congress but also to the American people and to the world.

In modern times, the president has played a dominant role in creating the congressional agenda. In the president's annual **State of the Union message,** which is required by the Constitution (Article II, Section 3) and is usually given in late January shortly after Congress reconvenes, the president as chief legislator presents a program. The message gives a broad, comprehensive view of what the president wishes the legislature to accomplish during its session. It is as much a message to the American people and to the world as it is to Congress. Its impact on public opinion can determine the way in which Congress responds to the president's agenda.

Getting Legislation Passed.   The president can propose legislation. Congress, however, is not required to pass—or even introduce—any of the administration's bills. How, then, does the president get those proposals made into law? One way is by exercising the power of persuasion. The president writes to, telephones, and meets with various congressional leaders; makes public announcements to influence public opinion; and, as head of the party, exercises legislative leadership through the congresspersons of that party.

A president whose party holds a majority in both chambers of Congress may have an easier time getting legislation passed than does a president who faces a hostile Congress. But one of the ways in which a president who faces a hostile Congress still can wield power is through the ability to veto legislation.

Veto Message

The president's formal explanation of a veto when legislation is returned to Congress.

Saying No to Legislation.   The president has the power to say no to legislation through use of the veto, by which the White House returns a bill unsigned to Congress with a **veto message** attached.[9] Because the Constitution requires that every bill passed by the House and the Senate be sent to the president before it becomes law, the president must act on each bill.

1. If the bill is signed, it becomes law.
2. If the bill is not sent back to Congress after ten congressional working days, it becomes law without the president's signature.
3. The president can reject the bill and send it back to Congress with a veto message setting forth objections. Congress then can change the bill, hoping to secure presidential approval and repass it. Or Congress can simply reject the president's

---

[9]*Veto* in Latin means "I forbid."

objections by overriding the veto with a two-thirds roll-call vote of the members present in both the House and the Senate.

4. If the president refuses to sign the bill and Congress adjourns within ten working days after the bill has been submitted to the president, the bill is killed for that session of Congress. This is called a **pocket veto.** If Congress wishes the bill to be reconsidered, the bill must be reintroduced during the following session.

Presidents employed the veto power infrequently until after the Civil War, but it has been used with increasing vigor since then (see Table 12–2). The total

Pocket Veto
A special veto exercised by the chief executive after a legislative body has adjourned. Bills not signed by the chief executive die after a specified period of time. If Congress wishes to reconsider such a bill, it must be reintroduced in the following session of Congress.

TABLE 12–2
Presidential Vetoes, 1789 to Present

Years	President	Regular Vetoes	Vetoes Overridden	Pocket Vetoes	Total Vetoes
1789–1797	Washington	2	0	0	2
1797–1801	J. Adams	0	0	0	0
1801–1809	Jefferson	0	0	0	0
1809–1817	Madison	5	0	2	7
1817–1825	Monroe	1	0	0	1
1825–1829	J. Q. Adams	0	0	0	0
1829–1837	Jackson	5	0	7	12
1837–1841	Van Buren	0	0	1	1
1841–1841	Harrison	0	0	0	0
1841–1845	Tyler	6	1	4	10
1845–1849	Polk	2	0	1	3
1849–1850	Taylor	0	0	0	0
1850–1853	Fillmore	0	0	0	0
1853–1857	Pierce	9	5	0	9
1857–1861	Buchanan	4	0	3	7
1861–1865	Lincoln	2	0	5	7
1865–1869	A. Johnson	21	15	8	29
1869–1877	Grant	45	4	48	93
1877–1881	Hayes	12	1	1	13
1881–1881	Garfield	0	0	0	0
1881–1885	Arthur	4	1	8	12
1885–1889	Cleveland	304	2	110	414
1889–1893	Harrison	19	1	25	44
1893–1897	Cleveland	42	5	128	170
1897–1901	McKinley	6	0	36	42
1901–1909	T. Roosevelt	42	1	40	82
1909–1913	Taft	30	1	9	39
1913–1921	Wilson	33	6	11	44
1921–1923	Harding	5	0	1	6
1923–1929	Coolidge	20	4	30	50
1929–1933	Hoover	21	3	16	37
1933–1945	F. Roosevelt	372	9	263	635
1945–1953	Truman	180	12	70	250
1953–1961	Eisenhower	73	2	108	181
1961–1963	Kennedy	12	0	9	21
1963–1969	L. Johnson	16	0	14	30
1969–1974	Nixon	26*	7	17	43
1974–1977	Ford	48	12	18	66
1977–1981	Carter	13	2	18	31
1981–1989	Reagan	39	9	39	78
1989–1993	G. H. W. Bush	29	1	15	44
1993–2001	Clinton	37†	2	1	38
2001–	G. W. Bush	0	0	0	0
TOTAL		1,485	106	1,066	2,551

*Two pocket vetoes by President Nixon, overruled in the courts, are counted here as regular vetoes.
†President Clinton's line-item vetoes are not included.

SOURCE: Office of the Clerk.

Line-Item Veto
The power of an executive to veto
individual lines or items within a piece of
legislation without vetoing the entire bill.

Constitutional Power
A power vested in the president by Article
II of the Constitution.

Statutory Power
A power created for the president through
laws enacted by Congress.

Expressed Power
A power of the president that is expressly
written into the Constitution or into
statutory law.

number of vetoes from George Washington through George W. Bush's term in office was 2,551, with about two-thirds of those vetoes being exercised by Grover Cleveland, Franklin Roosevelt, Harry Truman, and Dwight Eisenhower.

Somewhat surprisingly, George W. Bush issued no vetoes at all from the time he took office through 2004. Not since Martin Van Buren (1837–1841) has a president served a full term in office without exercising the veto power. Bush had the benefit of a Republican Congress that passed legislation he was willing to sign. He occasionally threatened to use the veto and certainly used it when he was governor of Texas. Still, Bush's acceptance of all legislation passed by Congress is evidence of a unique style of management.

The Line-Item Veto. Ronald Reagan lobbied strenuously for Congress to give another tool to the president—the **line-item veto,** which would allow the president to veto *specific* spending provisions of legislation that was passed by Congress. Reagan saw the line-item veto as the only way that he could control overall congressional spending. In 1996, Congress passed the Line Item Veto Act, which provided for the line-item veto. Signed by President Clinton, the law granted the president the power to rescind any item in an appropriations bill unless Congress passed a resolution of disapproval. Of course, the congressional resolution could be, in turn, vetoed by the president. The law did not take effect until after the 1996 election.

President Clinton used the line-item veto on several occasions, beginning on August 11, 1997. While his early vetoes were of little consequence to the members of Congress, the next set of vetoes—of thirty-eight military construction projects—caused an uproar, and Congress passed a disapproval bill to rescind the vetoes. The act also was challenged in court as an unconstitutional delegation of legislative powers to the executive branch. In 1998, by a six-to-three vote, the United States Supreme Court agreed and overturned the act. The Court stated that "there is no provision in the Constitution that authorizes the president to enact, to amend or to repeal statutes."[10]

Congress's Power to Override Presidential Vetoes. A veto is a clear-cut indication of the president's dissatisfaction with congressional legislation. Congress, however, can override a presidential veto, although it rarely exercises this power. Consider that two-thirds of the members of each chamber who are present must vote to override the president's veto in a roll-call vote. This means that if only one-third plus one of the members voting in one of the chambers of Congress do not agree to override the veto, the veto holds. It was not until the administration of John Tyler (1841–1845) that Congress overrode a presidential veto. In the first sixty-five years of American federal government history, out of thirty-three regular vetoes, Congress overrode only one, or about 3 percent. Overall, only about 7 percent of all vetoes have been overridden.

Other Presidential Powers

The powers of the president just discussed are called **constitutional powers**, because their basis lies in the Constitution. In addition, Congress has established by law, or statute, numerous other presidential powers—such as the ability to declare national emergencies. These are called **statutory powers.** Both constitutional and statutory powers have been labeled the **expressed powers** of the president, because they are expressly written into the Constitution or into law.

---

[10]*Clinton v. City of New York,* 524 U.S. 417 (1998).

Presidents also have what have come to be known as **inherent powers.** These depend on the statements in the Constitution that "the executive Power shall be vested in a President" and that the president should "take Care that the Laws be faithfully executed." The most common example of inherent powers are those emergency powers invoked by the president during wartime. Franklin Roosevelt, for example, used his inherent powers to move the Japanese and Japanese Americans living in the United States into internment camps for the duration of World War II.

Clearly, modern U.S. presidents have many powers at their disposal. According to some critics, among the powers exercised by modern presidents are certain powers that rightfully belong to Congress but that Congress has yielded to the executive branch.

Inherent Power
A power of the president derived from the statements in the Constitution that "the executive Power shall be vested in a President" and that the president should "take Care that the Laws be faithfully executed"; defined through practice rather than through law.

Patronage
The practice of rewarding faithful party workers and followers with government employment and contracts.

★ The President as Party Chief and Superpolitician

Presidents are by no means above political partisanship, and one of their many roles is that of chief of party. Although the Constitution says nothing about the function of the president within a political party (the mere concept of political parties was abhorrent to most of the authors of the Constitution), today presidents are the actual leaders of their parties.

The President as Chief of Party

As party leader, the president chooses the national committee chairperson and can try to discipline party members who fail to support presidential policies. One way of exerting political power within the party is through **patronage**—appointing individuals to government or public jobs. This power was more extensive in the past, before the establishment of the civil service in 1883 (see Chapter 13), but the president still retains important patronage power. As we noted earlier, the president can appoint several thousand individuals to jobs in the cabinet, the White House, and the federal regulatory agencies.

Perhaps the most important partisan role that the president played in the late 1900s and early 2000s was that of fund-raiser. The president is able to raise large amounts for the party through appearances at dinners, speaking engagements, and other social occasions. President Clinton may have raised more than half a billion dollars for the Democratic Party during his two terms. President Bush was even more successful than Clinton.

Presidents have a number of other ways of exerting influence as party chief. The president may make it known that a particular congressperson's choice for federal judge will not be appointed unless that member of Congress is more supportive of the president's legislative program.[11] The president may agree to campaign for a particular program or for a particular candidate. Presidents also reward loyal members of Congress with support for the funding of local projects, tax breaks for regional industries, and other forms of "pork."

Constituencies and Public Approval

All politicians worry about their constituencies, and presidents are no exception. Presidents are also concerned with public approval ratings.

The flag-draped casket of Ronald Reagan, the fortieth president of the United States, during his funeral at the National Cathedral in Washington in June 2004. Reagan, the first president to receive a state funeral in over thirty years, was a formidable politician. What measures are appropriate to honor past presidents? (EPA/Shawn Thew /Landov)

---

[11]"Senatorial courtesy" (see Chapter 14) often puts the judicial appointment in the hands of the Senate, however.

Washington Community
Individuals regularly involved with politics in Washington, D.C.

Presidential Constituencies.   Presidents have many constituencies. In principle, they are beholden to the entire electorate—the public of the United States—even those who did not vote. They are certainly beholden to their party, because its members helped to put them in office. The president's constituencies also include members of the opposing party whose cooperation the president needs. Finally, the president must take into consideration a constituency that has come to be called the **Washington community.** This community consists of individuals who—whether in or out of political office—are intimately familiar with the workings of government, thrive on gossip, and measure on a daily basis the political power of the president.

Public Approval.   All of these constituencies are impressed by presidents who maintain a high level of public approval, partly because this is very difficult to accomplish. Presidential popularity, as measured by national polls, gives the president an extra political resource to use in persuading legislators or bureaucrats to pass legislation. After all, refusing to do so might be going against public sentiment. President Bill Clinton showed significant strength in the public opinion polls for a second-term chief executive, as Figure 12–1 indicates.

George W. Bush and the Public Opinion Polls.   The impact of popular approval on a president's prospects was placed in sharp relief by the experiences of President Bush. Immediately after 9/11, Bush had the highest approval ratings ever recorded. His popularity then entered a steep decline that was interrupted only briefly by high ratings during the Second Gulf War. Such a decline appeared to threaten his reelection, and in many periods during the campaign, Kerry's supporters were certain that Bush would be rejected by the voters. In the end, however, Bush's popularity stabilized at just over 50 percent, reflecting the continued support of his political "base." Bush's support may have come from a narrow majority of the voters, but their support was firm.

"Going Public."   Since the early 1900s, presidents have spoken more to the public and less to Congress. In the 1800s, only 7 percent of presidential speeches were addressed to the public; since 1900, 50 percent have been addressed to the

FIGURE 12–1

Public Popularity of Modern Presidents

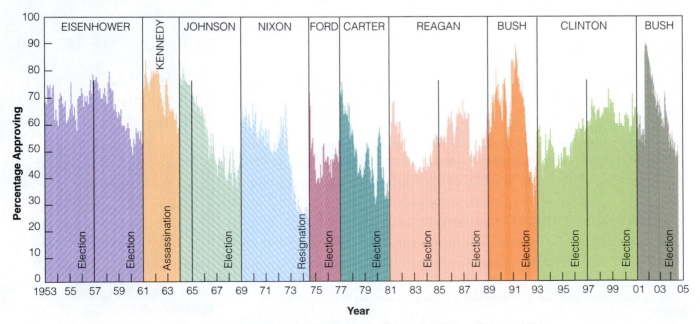

SOURCES: The Roper Center for Public Opinion Research; Gallup and *USA Today*/CNN Polls, March 1992 through August 2004.

"I don't think you can distance yourself from the White House on this one. After all, you <u>are</u> the President."

public. One scholar, Samuel Kernell, has proposed that the style of presidential leadership has changed since World War II, owing partly to the influence of television, with a resulting change in the balance of national politics.[12] Presidents frequently go over the heads of Congress and the political elites, taking their cases directly to the people. For example, in early 2001 President George W. Bush appealed directly to the public to support his proposed tax cut and budget. In a prime-time television speech, Bush urged Americans to send a message in favor of tax relief to their congressional representatives and senators. "After all," he said, "the surplus is your money."

This strategy, which Kernell dubbed "going public," gives the president additional power through the ability to persuade and manipulate public opinion. By identifying their own positions so clearly, presidents make compromises with Congress much more difficult and weaken the legislators' positions. Given the increasing importance of the media as the major source of political information for citizens and elites, presidents will continue to use public opinion as part of their arsenal of weapons to gain support from Congress and to achieve their policy goals. Can admitting to a mistake ever help a president gain public support? We examine this question in the *Which Side Are You On?* feature on the next page.

★ Special Uses of Presidential Power

Presidents have at their disposal a variety of special powers and privileges not available in the other branches of the U.S. government. These include (1) emergency powers, (2) executive orders, and (3) executive privilege.

---

[12]Samuel Kernell, *Going Public: New Strategies of Presidential Leadership,* 3d ed. (Washington, D.C.: Congressional Quarterly Press, 1997).

WHICH SIDE ARE YOU ON?
Should a President Ever Admit to Making a Mistake?

"The best defense is a good offense." This often-used saying is applied to football teams and embattled politicians. But should the president of the United States employ this philosophy as well? Some political analysts argue that President Bush and his administration made mistakes in responding to terrorism by first assuming that all of Bill Clinton's actions to counter terrorism were wrong. Next, Bush and his team may have been overly obsessed with Iraq, and therefore did not pay enough attention to Osama bin Laden. Whatever the truth may be, assume for the sake of argument that the president did make mistakes. Should he admit to them?

IT'S OKAY TO MAKE A MISTAKE AND 'FESS UP

Many believe that a president who admits to making a mistake will obtain positive public reaction. Moreover, the issues at hand—in this instance, whether Bush did enough to prevent 9/11—might be put to rest. In 1961, President John F. Kennedy admitted that he was responsible for a disastrous failed invasion at the Bay of Pigs in Cuba. In the days that followed, his public approval ratings increased by 11 percentage points. In 1980, President Carter admitted that his administration had failed to rescue hundreds of U.S. citizens taken hostage in Iran, although this admission did not help him win reelection.

Also consider that there is something else at stake today. How can you fix a system that is obviously broken if you are not willing to say that something is wrong? If the president of the United States does not admit that mistakes were made before the terrorist attacks in 2001, how can we be assured that such attacks will not happen again?

President Jimmy Carter took full responsibility for the failed rescue mission of U.S. hostages in Iran in 1980. Carter lost his reelection bid later that year. During much of the hostage crisis—which lasted over 380 days—Carter benefited from a "rally 'round the flag" effect. Why might this effect have eventually worn off? (Wally McNamee, © Corbis)

IF PRESIDENTS ADMIT TO MISTAKES, THEY WILL LOSE POWER AND RESPECT

In contrast, many political commentators believe that a president should never admit to a mistake. Even if the Bush administration made mistakes in the period before 9/11, how would it benefit for the nation to hear an admission of errors? And, who should admit the errors? The CIA, the FBI, former Clinton administration officials, or only Bush? Such admission actually could weaken the effort to root out terrorists by discouraging Americans and other nations from assisting in the effort. People elect presidents to lead this country, not to engage in contriteness. Moreover, presidents who admit to a mistake give their domestic political enemies a campaign issue that can be used to attack them.

WHAT'S YOUR POSITION?

Do you think that it is better for a president to admit to a mistake or to carry on regardless?

GOING ONLINE

Newspaper columnists devote considerable attention to presidential behavior. You can find links to the Web sites of more than seven hundred commentators by visiting **http://www.blueagle.com**.

Political books played an unusually important role in the 2004 campaign. One way to obtain a summary of what is in a book—for example, *Plan of Attack* by Bob Woodward—is to visit **http://www.amazon.com**, locate the book using Amazon's search engine, and read the reviews.

Emergency Powers

If you were to read the Constitution, you would find no mention of the additional powers that the executive office may exercise during national emergencies. Indeed, the Supreme Court has indicated that an "emergency does not create power."[13] But it is clear that presidents have used their inherent powers during times of emergency, particularly in the realm of foreign affairs. The **emergency powers** of the president were first enunciated in the Supreme Court's decision in *United States v. Curtiss-Wright Export Corp.*[14] In that case, President Franklin Roosevelt, without authorization by Congress, ordered an embargo on the shipment of weapons to two warring South American countries. The Court recognized that the president may exercise inherent powers in foreign affairs and that the national government has primacy in these affairs.

Examples of emergency powers are abundant, coinciding with crises in domestic and foreign affairs. Abraham Lincoln suspended civil liberties at the beginning of the Civil War (1861–1865) and called the state militias into national service. These actions and his subsequent governance of conquered areas and even of areas of northern states were justified by claims that they were essential to preserve the Union. Franklin Roosevelt declared an "unlimited national emergency" following the fall of France in World War II (1939–1945) and mobilized the federal budget and the economy for war.

President Harry Truman authorized the federal seizure of steel plants and their operation by the national government in 1952 during the Korean War. Truman claimed that he was using his inherent emergency power as chief executive and commander in chief to safeguard the nation's security, as an ongoing steel mill strike threatened the supply of weapons to the armed forces. The Supreme Court did not agree, holding that the president had no authority under the Constitution to seize private property or to legislate such action.[15] According to legal scholars, this was the first time a limit was placed on the exercise of the president's emergency powers.

> **Emergency Power**
> An inherent power exercised by the president during a period of national crisis.

Executive Orders

Congress allows the president (as well as administrative agencies) to issue **executive orders** that have the force of law. These executive orders can do the following: (1) enforce legislative statutes, (2) enforce the Constitution or treaties with foreign nations, and (3) establish or modify rules and practices of executive administrative agencies.

An executive order, then, represents the president's legislative power. The only apparent requirement is that under the Administrative Procedure Act of 1946, all executive orders must be published in the *Federal Register,* a daily publication of the U.S. government. Executive orders have been used to establish procedures to appoint noncareer administrators, to implement national affirmative action regulations, to restructure the White House bureaucracy, to ration consumer goods and to administer wage and price controls under emergency conditions, to classify government information as secret, to regulate the export of restricted items, and to establish military tribunals for suspected terrorists.

> **Executive Order**
> A rule or regulation issued by the president that has the effect of law. Executive orders can implement and give administrative effect to provisions in the Constitution, to treaties, and to statutes.

> **Federal Register**
> A publication of the U.S. government that prints executive orders, rules, and regulations.

Executive Privilege

Another inherent executive power that has been claimed by presidents concerns the ability of the president and the president's executive officials to withhold

---

[13]*Home Building and Loan Association v. Blaisdell,* 290 U.S. 398 (1934).
[14]299 U.S. 304 (1936).
[15]*Youngstown Sheet and Tube Co. v. Sawyer,* 343 U.S. 579 (1952).

Executive Privilege
The right of executive officials to withhold information from or to refuse to appear before a legislative committee.

information from or refuse to appear before Congress or the courts. This is called **executive privilege,** and it relies on the constitutional separation of powers for its basis.

As discussed in this chapter's opening *What If . . .* feature, presidents have frequently invoked executive privilege to avoid having to disclose information to Congress on actions of the executive branch. For example, President George W. Bush claimed executive privilege to keep the head of the newly established Office of Homeland Security, Tom Ridge, from testifying before Congress. The Bush administration also resisted attempts by the congressional Government Accountability Office to obtain information about meetings and documents related to Vice President Dick Cheney's actions as chair of the administration's energy policy task force. Bush, like presidents before him, claimed that a certain degree of secrecy is essential to national security. Critics of executive privilege believe that it can be used to shield from public scrutiny actions of the executive branch that should be open to Congress and to the American citizenry.

Limiting Executive Privilege.   Limits to executive privilege went untested until the Watergate affair in the early 1970s. Five men had broken into the headquarters of the Democratic National Committee and were caught searching for documents that would damage the candidacy of the Democratic nominee, George McGovern. Later investigation showed that the break-in was planned by members of Richard Nixon's campaign committee and that Nixon and his closest advisers had devised a strategy for impeding the investigation of the crime. After it became known that all of the conversations held in the Oval Office had been tape-recorded on a secret system, Nixon was ordered to turn over the tapes to the special prosecutor.

As you read in this chapter's opening *What If . . .* feature, Nixon refused to do so, claiming executive privilege. He argued that "no president could function if the private papers of his office, prepared by his personal staff, were open to public scrutiny." In 1974, in one of the Supreme Court's most famous cases, *United States v. Nixon,*[16] the justices unanimously ruled that Nixon had to hand over the tapes. The Court held that executive privilege could not be used to prevent evidence from being heard in criminal proceedings.

Clinton's Attempted Use of Executive Privilege.   The claim of executive privilege was also raised by the Clinton administration as a defense against the aggressive investigation of Clinton's relationship with Monica Lewinsky by Independent Counsel Kenneth Starr. The Clinton administration claimed executive privilege for several presidential aides who might have discussed the situation with the president. In addition, President Clinton asserted that his White House counsel did not have to testify before the Starr grand jury due to attorney-client privilege. Finally, the Department of Justice claimed that members of the Secret Service who guard the president could not testify about his activities due to a "protective function privilege" inherent in their duties. The federal judge overseeing the case denied the claims of privilege, however, and the decision was upheld on appeal.

Richard Nixon (right) leaves the White House after his resignation on August 9, 1974. Next to him are his wife, Pat, Betty Ford, and Gerald Ford, the new president. (Don Carl Steffan/Photo Researchers)

★ Abuses of Executive Power and Impeachment

Presidents normally leave office either because their first term has expired and they have not sought (or won) reelection or because, having served two full terms, they are not allowed to be elected for a third term (owing to the Twenty-second Amendment, passed in 1951). Eight presidents have died in office. But

---

[16]318 U.S. 683 (1974).

there is still another way for a president to leave office—by **impeachment** and conviction. Articles I and II of the Constitution authorize the House and Senate to remove the president, the vice president, or other civil officers of the United States for committing "Treason, Bribery, or other high Crimes and Misdemeanors." According to the Constitution, the impeachment process begins in the House, which impeaches (accuses) the federal officer involved. If the House votes to impeach the officer, it draws up articles of impeachment and submits them to the Senate, which conducts the actual trial.

In the history of the United States, no president has ever actually been impeached and also convicted—and thus removed from office—by means of this process. President Andrew Johnson (1865–1869), who succeeded to the office after the assassination of Abraham Lincoln, was impeached by the House but acquitted by the Senate. More than a century later, the House Judiciary Committee approved articles of impeachment against President Richard Nixon for his involvement in the cover-up of the Watergate break-in of 1972. Informed by members of his own party that he had no hope of surviving the trial in the Senate, Nixon resigned on August 9, 1974, before the full House voted on the articles. Nixon is the only president to have resigned from office.

The second president to be impeached by the House but not convicted by the Senate was President Bill Clinton. In September 1998, Independent Counsel Kenneth Starr sent to Congress the findings of his investigation of the president on the charges of perjury and obstruction of justice. The House approved two charges against Clinton: lying to the grand jury about his affair with Monica Lewinsky and obstruction of justice. The articles of impeachment were then sent to the Senate, which acquitted Clinton.

Impeachment
An action by the House of Representatives to accuse the president, vice president, or other civil officers of the United States of committing "Treason, Bribery, or other high Crimes and Misdemeanors."

On December 19, 1998, the House of Representatives voted to impeach President Bill Clinton for perjury and obstruction of justice. That same day, Clinton addressed lawmakers and staff outside the Oval Office, surrounded by supporters. President Clinton was later acquitted by the Senate, but the events raised important issues about presidential privacy and ethics. To what extent should the president's personal life be the subject of public scrutiny while he or she is in office? (AP Photo/Doug Mills)

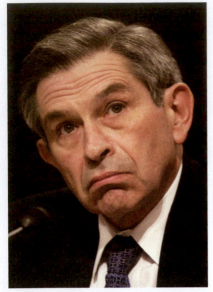

Deputy Secretary of Defense Paul Wolfowitz was a prime architect of the Bush administration's Iraq policy in the years following the 9/11 attack. Wolfowitz received much criticism for his optimistic forecasts of how easy it would be to administer Iraq after the war. (Chris Kleponis/Bloomberg News/Landov)

Cabinet
An advisory group selected by the president to aid in making decisions. The cabinet includes the heads of fifteen executive departments and others named by the president.

Kitchen Cabinet
The informal advisers to the president.

The Executive Organization

Gone are the days when presidents answered their own mail, as George Washington did. It was not until 1857 that Congress authorized a private secretary for the president, to be paid by the federal government. Woodrow Wilson typed most of his correspondence, even though he did have several secretaries. At the beginning of Franklin Roosevelt's long tenure in the White House, the entire staff consisted of thirty-seven employees. With the New Deal and World War II, however, the presidential staff became a sizable organization.

Today, the executive organization includes a White House Office staff of about 600, including some workers who are part-time employees and others who are borrowed from their departments by the White House. Not all of these employees have equal access to the president, nor are all of them likely to be equally concerned about the administration's political success. The more than 360 employees who work in the White House Office itself are closest to the president. They often include many individuals who worked on the president's campaign. These assistants are most concerned with preserving the president's reputation. Also included in the president's staff are a number of councils and advisory organizations, such as the National Security Council. Although the individuals who hold staff positions in these offices are appointed by the president, they are really more concerned with their own areas than with the president's overall success. The group of appointees who perhaps are least helpful to the president is the cabinet, each member of which is the principal officer of a government department.

The Cabinet

Although the Constitution does not include the word *cabinet,* it does state that the president "may require the Opinion, in writing, of the principal Officer in each of the executive Departments." Since the time of George Washington, there has been an advisory group, or **cabinet,** to which the president turns for counsel.

Members of the Cabinet. Originally, the cabinet consisted of only four officials—the secretaries of state, treasury, and war, and the attorney general. Today, the cabinet numbers fourteen department secretaries and the attorney general. (See Table 12–1 on page 396 for the names of the cabinet departments and Chapter 13 for a detailed discussion of these units.)

The cabinet may include others as well. The president at his or her discretion can, for example, ascribe cabinet rank to the vice president, the head of the Office of Management and Budget, the national security adviser, the ambassador to the United Nations, or others.

Often, a president will use a **kitchen cabinet** to replace the formal cabinet as a major source of advice. The term *kitchen cabinet* originated during the presidency of Andrew Jackson, who relied on the counsel of close friends who often met with him in the kitchen of the White House. A kitchen cabinet is a very informal group of advisers; usually, they are friends with whom the president worked before being elected.

Presidential Use of Cabinets. Because neither the Constitution nor statutory law requires the president to consult with the cabinet, its use is purely discretionary. Some presidents have relied on the counsel of their cabinets more than others. Dwight Eisenhower was used to the team approach to solving problems from his experience as supreme allied commander during World War II, and therefore he frequently turned to his cabinet for advice on a wide range of issues.

The National Security Council meets at the White House on September 12, 2001, the day after the 9/11 attacks. From left to right, those shown are CIA Director George Tenet, Attorney General John Ashcroft, Secretary of Defense Donald Rumsfeld, Secretary of State Colin Powell, President George W. Bush, Vice President Dick Cheney, Chairman of the Joint Chiefs of Staff General Henry Shelton, and National Security Adviser Condoleezza Rice. (AP Photo/Doug Mills)

More often, presidents have solicited the opinions of their cabinets and then did what they wanted to do anyway. Lincoln supposedly said—after a cabinet meeting in which a vote was seven nays against his one aye—"Seven nays and one aye, the ayes have it." In general, few presidents have relied heavily on the advice of their cabinet members.

It is not surprising that presidents tend not to rely on their cabinet members' advice. Often, the departmental heads are more responsive to the wishes of their own staffs or to their own political ambitions than they are to the president. They may be more concerned with obtaining resources for their departments than with achieving the goals of the president. So there is often a strong conflict of interest between presidents and their cabinet members.

The Executive Office of the President

When President Franklin Roosevelt appointed a special committee on administrative management, he knew that the committee would conclude that the president needed help. Indeed, the committee proposed a major reorganization of the executive branch. Congress did not approve the entire reorganization, but it did create the **Executive Office of the President (EOP)** to provide staff assistance for the chief executive and to help coordinate the executive bureaucracy. Since that time, a number of agencies have been created within the EOP to supply the president with advice and staff help. These agencies include the following:

Executive Office of the President (EOP)
An organization established by President Franklin D. Roosevelt to assist the president in carrying out major duties.

- White House Office.
- White House Military Office.
- Office of the Vice President.
- Council of Economic Advisers.
- Council on Environmental Quality.
- National Security Council.
- Office of Management and Budget.
- Office of National AIDS Policy.
- Office of National Drug Control Policy.
- Office of Science and Technology Policy.
- Office of the United States Trade Representative.
- President's Critical Infrastructure Protection Board.
- President's Foreign Intelligence Advisory Board.

Several of the offices within the EOP are especially important, including the White House Office, the Office of Management and Budget, and the National Security Council.

The White House Office.   The **White House Office** includes most of the key personal and political advisers to the president. Among the jobs held by these aides are those of legal counsel to the president, secretary, press secretary, and appointments secretary. Often, the individuals who hold these positions are recruited from the president's campaign staff. Their duties—mainly protecting the president's political interests—are similar to campaign functions. In all recent administrations, one member of the White House Office has been named **chief of staff.** This person, who is responsible for coordinating the office, is also one of the president's chief advisers.

The president may establish special advisory units within the White House to address topics the president finds especially important. Such units include the long-established Domestic Policy Council and the National Economic Council. Under George W. Bush, these units also include the Office of Faith-Based and Community Initiatives and the USA Freedom Corps. The White House Office also includes the staff members who support the first lady.

In addition to civilian advisers, the president is supported by a large number of military personnel, who are organized under the White House Military Office. These members of the military provide communications, transportation, medical care, and food services to the president and the White House staff.

Employees of the White House Office have been both envied and criticized. The White House Office, according to most former staffers, grants its employees access and power. They are able to use the resources of the White House to contact virtually anyone in the world by telephone, cable, fax, or electronic mail as well as to use the influence of the White House to persuade legislators and citizens. Because of this influence, staffers are often criticized for overstepping the bounds of the office. It is the appointments secretary who is able to grant or deny senators, representatives, and cabinet secretaries access to the president. It is the press secretary who grants to the press and television journalists access to any information about the president.

White House staff members are closest to the president and may have considerable influence over the administration's decisions. Often, when presidents are under fire for their decisions, the staff is accused of keeping the chief executive too isolated from criticism or help. Presidents insist that they will not allow the staff to become too powerful, but given the difficulty of the office, each president eventually turns to staff members for loyal assistance and protection.

The Office of Management and Budget.   The **Office of Management and Budget (OMB)** was originally the Bureau of the Budget, which was created in 1921 within the Department of the Treasury. Recognizing the importance of this agency, Franklin Roosevelt moved it into the White House Office in 1939. Richard Nixon reorganized the Bureau of the Budget in 1970 and changed its name to reflect its new managerial function. It is headed by a director, who must make up the annual federal budget that the president presents to Congress each January for approval. In principle, the director of the OMB has broad fiscal powers in planning and estimating various parts of the federal budget, because all agencies must submit their proposed budget to the OMB for approval. In reality, it is not so clear that the OMB truly can affect the greater scope of the federal budget. The OMB may be more important as a clearinghouse for legislative proposals initiated in the executive agencies.

The National Security Council.   The **National Security Council (NSC)** is a link between the president's key foreign and military advisers and the president.

White House Office
The personal office of the president, which tends to presidential political needs and manages the media.

Chief of Staff
The person who is named to direct the White House Office and advise the president.

Office of Management and Budget (OMB)
A division of the Executive Office of the President. The OMB assists the president in preparing the annual budget, clearing and coordinating departmental agency budgets, and supervising the administration of the federal budget.

National Security Council (NSC)
An agency in the Executive Office of the President that advises the president on national security.

National security adviser Condoleezza Rice testifies before the 9/11 Commission in 2004. What problems could result when a top adviser to the president is required to give public testimony? (Greg E. Mathieson/MAI/ Landov)

Its members consist of the president, the vice president, and the secretaries of state and defense, plus other informal members. Included in the NSC is the president's special assistant for national security affairs. In 2001, Condoleezza Rice became the first woman to serve as a president's national security adviser.

★ The Vice Presidency

The Constitution does not give much power to the vice president. The only formal duty is to preside over the Senate—which is rarely necessary. This obligation is fulfilled when the Senate organizes and adopts its rules and when the vice president is needed to decide a tie vote. In all other cases, the president pro tem manages parliamentary procedures in the Senate. The vice president is expected to participate only informally in senatorial deliberations, if at all.

The Vice President's Job

Vice presidents have traditionally been chosen by presidential nominees to balance the ticket to attract groups of voters or appease party factions. If a presidential nominee is from the North, it is not a bad idea to have a vice presidential nominee who is from the South. If the presidential nominee is from a rural state, perhaps someone with an urban background would be most suitable as a running mate. Presidential nominees who are strongly conservative or strongly liberal would do well to have vice presidential nominees who are more in the middle of the political road.

Strengthening the Ticket. In recent presidential elections, vice presidents have often been selected for other reasons. Bill Clinton picked Al Gore to be his running mate in 1992 even though both were southern and moderates. The ticket appealed to southerners and moderates, both of whom were crucial to the election. In 2000, both vice presidential selections were intended to shore up the respective presidential candidates' perceived weaknesses. Republican George W. Bush, who was subject to criticism for his lack of government experience and his "lightweight" personality, chose Dick Cheney, a former member of Congress who had also served as secretary of defense. Democrat Al Gore chose Senator Joe Lieberman of Connecticut, whose reputation for moral integrity (as an Orthodox

Vice President Dick Cheney assembled a task force in 2001 to advise the president on his energy policy. The task force recommended the disbursement of millions of federal dollars to energy companies. The Government Accountability Office, the investigative arm of Congress, sued Cheney for the release of documents prepared for the task force. Cheney claimed that release of the information would affect the president's ability to obtain candid opinions from people outside government. Should all government meetings become public information? (AP Photo/John Todd)

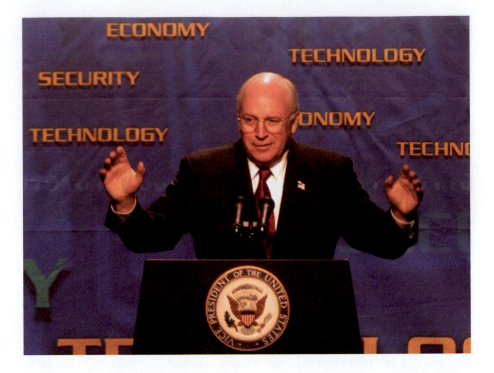

Jew) could help counteract the effects of Bill Clinton's sex scandals. In 2004, Democratic presidential candidate John Kerry made a more traditional choice in Senator John Edwards of North Carolina. Edwards provided regional balance and also a degree of socioeconomic balance because unlike Kerry, he had been born in relatively humble circumstances.

Supporting the President.   The job of vice president is not extremely demanding, even when the president gives some specific task to the vice president. Typically, vice presidents spend their time supporting the president's activities. During the Clinton administration (1993–2001), however, Vice President Al Gore did much to strengthen the position of vice president by his aggressive support for environmental protection policies on a global basis. He also took a special interest in areas of emerging technology and was instrumental in providing subsidies to public schools for Internet use. Vice President Dick Cheney, as one of President George W. Bush's key advisers, clearly was an influential figure in the Bush administration. Of course, the vice presidency takes on more significance if the president becomes disabled or dies in office—and the vice president becomes president.

Vice presidents sometimes have become elected presidents in their own right. John Adams and Thomas Jefferson were the first to do so. Richard Nixon was elected president in 1968 after he had served as Dwight D. Eisenhower's vice president during 1953–1961. In 1988, George H. W. Bush was elected to the presidency after eight years as Ronald Reagan's vice president.

Presidential Succession

Eight vice presidents have become president because of the death of the president. John Tyler, the first to do so, took over William Henry Harrison's position after only one month. No one knew whether Tyler should simply be a caretaker until a new president could be elected three and a half years later or whether he actually should be president. Tyler assumed that he was supposed to be the chief executive and he acted as such—although he was commonly referred to as "His

An attempted assassination of Ronald Reagan occurred on March 31, 1981. In the foreground, two men bend over Press Secretary James Brady, who lies seriously wounded. In the background, President Reagan is watched over by a U.S. Secret Service agent with an automatic weapon. A Washington, D.C., police officer, Thomas Delahanty, lies to the left after also being shot. (AP Photo/Ron Edmonds)

Accidency." Since then, vice presidents taking over the position of the presidency because of the incumbent's death have assumed the presidential powers.

But what should a vice president do if a president becomes incapable of carrying out necessary duties while in office? When James Garfield was shot in 1881, he remained alive for two and a half months. What was Vice President Chester Arthur's role?

This question was not addressed in the original Constitution. Article II, Section 1, says only that "[i]n Case of the Removal of the President from Office, or of his Death, Resignation, or Inability to discharge the Powers and Duties of the said Office, the same shall devolve on [the same powers shall be exercised by] the Vice President." There have been many instances of presidential disability. When Dwight Eisenhower became ill a second time in 1958, he entered into a pact with Richard Nixon specifying that the vice president could determine whether the president was incapable of carrying out his duties if the president could not communicate. John Kennedy and Lyndon Johnson entered into similar agreements with their vice presidents. Finally, in 1967, the **Twenty-fifth Amendment** was passed, establishing procedures in case of presidential incapacity.

The Twenty-Fifth Amendment

According to the Twenty-fifth Amendment, when a president believes that he or she is incapable of performing the duties of office, the president must inform Congress in writing. Then the vice president serves as acting president until the president can resume normal duties. When the president is unable to communicate, a majority of the cabinet, including the vice president, can declare that fact to Congress. Then the vice president serves as acting president until the president resumes normal duties. If a dispute arises over the return of the president's ability, a two-thirds vote of Congress is required to decide whether the vice president shall remain acting president or whether the president shall resume normal duties.

In 2002, President George W. Bush formally invoked the Twenty-fifth Amendment for the first time by officially transferring presidential power to Vice President Dick Cheney while the president underwent a colonoscopy, a twenty-minute procedure. He commented that he undertook this transfer of power "because we're at war," referring to the war on terrorism. The only other time the

Twenty-fifth Amendment
A 1967 amendment to the Constitution that establishes procedures for filling presidential and vice presidential vacancies and makes provisions for presidential disability.

TABLE 12–3

Line of Succession to the Presidency of the United States

1. Vice president
2. Speaker of the House of Representatives
3. Senate president pro tempore
4. Secretary of state
5. Secretary of the treasury
6. Secretary of defense
7. Attorney general (head of the Justice Department)
8. Secretary of the interior
9. Secretary of agriculture
10. Secretary of commerce
11. Secretary of labor
12. Secretary of health and human services
13. Secretary of housing and urban development
14. Secretary of transportation
15. Secretary of energy
16. Secretary of education
17. Secretary of veterans affairs
18. Secretary of homeland security

provisions of the Twenty-fifth Amendment have been used was during President Reagan's colon surgery in 1985, although Reagan did not formally invoke the amendment.

When the Vice Presidency Becomes Vacant

The Twenty-fifth Amendment also addresses the issue of how the president should fill a vacant vice presidency. Section 2 of the amendment simply states, "Whenever there is a vacancy in the office of the Vice President, the President shall nominate a Vice President who shall take office upon confirmation by a majority vote of both Houses of Congress." This is exactly what occurred when Richard Nixon's vice president, Spiro Agnew, resigned in 1973 because of his alleged receipt of construction contract kickbacks during his tenure as governor of Maryland. Nixon turned to Gerald Ford as his choice for vice president. After extensive hearings, both chambers of Congress confirmed the appointment. Then, when Nixon resigned on August 9, 1974, Ford automatically became president and nominated as his vice president Nelson Rockefeller. Congress confirmed Ford's choice. For the first time in the history of the country, neither the president nor the vice president had been elected to their positions.

The question of who shall be president if both the president and vice president die is answered by the Succession Act of 1947. If the president and vice president die, resign, or are disabled, the Speaker of the House will become president, after resigning from Congress. Next in line is the president pro tem of the Senate, followed by the cabinet officers in the order of the creation of their departments (see Table 12–3).

★ The Presidency: Why Is It Important Today?

Some suggest that the presidency is virtually "in your face" day in and day out in this country. Certainly, the media inundate us, often on a daily basis, with every single activity in which the president is involved. To be sure, most of the media coverage of the president provides entertainment value only. Yet it can generally be said that no other country puts its head of state under such a microscope.

Today, the powers of the U.S. president are more extensive than perhaps ever before, and these powers may significantly affect you, your family, or your friends. The president acts as chief legislator by submitting proposed legislation to Congress. The president can veto legislation. As commander in chief, the president can deploy troops without the approval of Congress. The president also has the ability to act while Congress is not in session. For example, Lincoln suspended certain constitutional liberties, blockaded southern ports, and banned "treasonable correspondence" from the U.S. mails during a congressional recess.

President George W. Bush certainly continued in the tradition of expanding presidential powers. He used an executive order—just one of 13,600 that have been issued in this nation's history—to create military tribunals to try foreigners accused of terrorism. (See Chapter 4 for a further discussion of this important issue.) President Bush, as did many of his predecessors, sent American men and women into combat—in this instance, in Afghanistan and Iraq. Clearly, the president, while constrained by the Constitution, has a range of powers that impact every citizen and resident of this nation.

MAKING A DIFFERENCE

★ Communicating with the White House

Writing the president is a traditional way for citizens to express their opinions. Every day, the White House receives several thousand letters and other communications.

Why Should You Care?

Should you consider sending a message to the president? There are reasons why you might want to engage in this form of political participation. Presidents typically claim that they do not set their policies by looking at the public opinion polls. Yet any president must pay attention to public opinion, and few presidents have been able to avoid changing policy when the public is pressing them to do so. President Bush has been no exception.

In 2003 and 2004, in response to the situation in Iraq, a number of Democratic and Republican legislators began raising the idea of reinstating a military draft of young people. Such a measure would probably need the support of the president to succeed. A military draft might affect you or your friends directly. If you have opinions on a topic such as this, you may well want to "cast your vote" by adding your letter to the many others that the president receives on this issue.

What Can You Do?

The most traditional form of communication with the White House is, of course, by letter. Letters to the president should be addressed to

> The President
>   of the United States
> The White House
> 1600 Pennsylvania Avenue N.W.
> Washington, DC 20500

Letters may be sent to the first lady at the same address. Will you get an answer? Almost certainly. The White House mail room is staffed by volunteers and paid employees who sort the mail for the president and tally the public's concerns. You may receive a standard response to your comments or a more personal, detailed response.

You can also call the White House on the telephone and leave a message for the president or first lady. To call the switchboard, call 202-456-1414, a number publicized by former Secretary of State James Baker when he told the Israelis through the media, "When you're serious about peace, call us at . . . ." The switchboard received more than eight thousand calls in the next twenty-four hours.

The White House also has a round-the-clock comment line, which you can reach at 202-456-1111. When you call that number, an operator will take down your comments and forward them to the president's office.

The home page for the White House is

www.whitehouse.gov

It is designed to be entertaining and to convey information about the president. You can also send your comments and ideas to the White House using e-mail. Send comments to the president at

President@whitehouse.gov

Address e-mail to the first lady at

First.Lady@whitehouse.gov

In 2003, the White House deployed a new and somewhat complicated system for sending messages to President Bush. It involves navigating successive Web pages and filling out a form. You must choose one of a limited number of topics selected by the White House. Once the message is sent, the writer must wait for an automated e-mail response that asks for a confirmation.

Key Terms

advice and consent 399	emergency power 409	kitchen cabinet 412	State of the Union message 402
appointment power 395	executive agreement 401	line-item veto 404	statutory power 404
cabinet 412	Executive Office of the President (EOP) 413	National Security Council (NSC) 414	Twelfth Amendment 394
chief diplomat 399	executive order 409	Office of Management and Budget (OMB) 414	Twenty-fifth Amendment 417
chief executive 395	executive privilege 410	pardon 397	veto message 402
chief legislator 401	expressed power 404	patronage 405	War Powers Resolution 398
chief of staff 414	*Federal Register* 409	pocket veto 403	Washington community 406
civil service 395	head of state 394	reprieve 397	White House Office 414
commander in chief 397	impeachment 411		
constitutional power 404	inherent power 405		
diplomatic recognition 399			

Chapter Summary

1 The office of the presidency in the United States, combining as it does the functions of chief of state and chief executive, was, when created, unique. The framers of the Constitution were divided over whether the president should be a weak or a strong executive.

2 The requirements for the office of the presidency are outlined in Article II, Section 1, of the Constitution. The president's roles include both formal and informal duties. The roles of the president include chief of state, chief executive, commander in chief, chief diplomat, chief legislator, and party chief.

3 As head of state, the president is ceremonial leader of the government. As chief executive, the president is bound to enforce the acts of Congress, the judgments of the federal courts, and treaties. The chief executive has the power of appointment and the power to grant reprieves and pardons.

4 As commander in chief, the president is the ultimate decision maker in military matters. As chief diplomat, the president recognizes foreign governments, negotiates treaties, signs agreements, and nominates and receives ambassadors.

5 The role of chief legislator includes recommending legislation to Congress, lobbying for the legislation, approving laws, and exercising the veto power. In addition to constitu-

tional and inherent powers, the president has statutory powers written into law by Congress. Presidents are also leaders of their political parties. Presidents use their power to persuade and their access to the media to fulfill this function.

6 Presidents have a variety of special powers not available to other branches of the government. These include emergency power and the power to issue executive orders and invoke executive privilege.

7 Abuses of executive power are dealt with by Articles I and II of the Constitution, which authorize the House and Senate to impeach and remove the president, vice president, or other officers of the federal government for committing "Treason, Bribery, or other high Crimes and Misdemeanors."

8 The president receives assistance from the cabinet and from the Executive Office of the President (including the White House Office).

9 The vice president is the constitutional officer assigned to preside over the Senate and to assume the presidency in case of the death, resignation, removal, or disability of the president. The Twenty-fifth Amendment, passed in 1967, established procedures to be followed in case of presidential incapacity and when filling a vacant vice presidency.

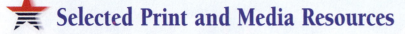

Selected Print and Media Resources

SUGGESTED READINGS

Clinton, Bill. *My Life*. New York: Knopf, 2004. President Clinton's autobiography devotes ample space to illuminating stories from his childhood. In contrast, some may find the account of his presidential years excessively detailed. Still, the book is essential source material on one of the most important and controversial political figures of our time.

Frum, David. *The Right Man: The Surprise Presidency of George Bush*. New York: Random House, 2003. The author, who was a speechwriter for George W. Bush during his first year as president, provides an inside look at this period of the Bush presidency.

Greenfield, Meg. *Washington*. New York: Public Affairs, 2001. The author, a longtime *Washington Post* reporter, takes a candid look at Washington, D.C., politics and political players.

Greenstein, Fred I. *The Presidential Difference: Leadership Style from Roosevelt to Clinton*. Old Tappan, N.J.: Free Press, 2000. In this book, an eminent presidential scholar examines and discusses the leadership styles of eleven chief executives. Greenstein assesses each president in several categories including organization, skill, vision, and emotional intelligence.

Kranish, Michael, Brian C. Mooney, and Nina J. Easton. *John F. Kerry: The Complete Biography by the Boston Globe Reporters Who Know Him Best*. New York: PublicAffairs, 2004. Unlike other books on Kerry, this comprehensive account reports on Kerry's political career all the way through his years in the Senate. Though the authors strive for objectivity, Kerry's supporters may find the tone a bit harsh.

Mann, James. *Rise of the Vulcans: The History of Bush's War Cabinet*. New York: Viking Books, 2004. This is a collective biography of George W. Bush's foreign policy team (not all of whom are actually in the cabinet). The self-described Vulcans include Donald Rumsfeld, secretary of defense; Vice President Dick Cheney; Colin Powell, secretary of state; Paul Wolfowitz, deputy secretary of defense; Richard Armitage, deputy secretary of state; and Condoleezza Rice, national security adviser. While these individuals have never been in perfect agreement, they share basic values.

Woodward, Bob. *Bush at War*. New York: Simon & Schuster, 2002. Noted investigative journalist Woodward takes a close look at presidential decision making in the months following the terrorist attacks of September 11, 2001. His account of the Bush White House and his analysis of President Bush's leadership style are especially notable.

MEDIA RESOURCES

CNN—Election 2000—A politically balanced look at the extraordinarily close presidential election of 2000, which pitted Republican George W. Bush against Democrat Al Gore. The race was eventually settled by the United States Supreme Court. CNN's Bill Hemmer narrates this 2001 production.

Fahrenheit 9/11—Michael Moore's scathing 2004 critique of the Bush administration has been called "one long political attack ad." It is also the highest-grossing documentary ever made. While the film may be unfair, it is—like all of Moore's productions—entertaining.

LBJ: A Biography—An acclaimed biography of Lyndon Johnson that covers his rise to power, his presidency, and the events of the Vietnam War, which ended his presidency; produced in 1991 as part of PBS's *The American Experience* series.

Nixon—An excellent 1995 film exposing the events of Richard Nixon's troubled presidency. Anthony Hopkins plays the embattled but brilliant chief executive.

Sunrise at Campobello—An excellent portrait of one of the greatest presidents, Franklin Delano Roosevelt; produced in 1960 and starring Ralph Bellamy.

e-mocracy ★ The Presidency and the Internet

Today, the Internet has become such a normal part of most Americans' lives that it is almost hard to imagine what life was like without it. Certainly, accessing the latest press releases from the White House was much more difficult ten years ago than it is today. It was not until the Clinton administration (1993–2001) that access to the White House via the Internet became possible. President Bill Clinton supported making many White House documents available on the White House Web site. Correspondence with the president and the first lady quickly moved from ordinary handwritten letters to e-mail. During the Clinton presidency, most agencies of the government, as well as congressional offices, also began to provide access and information on the Internet. Today, you can access the White House Web site (see the *Logging On* section) to find White House press releases, presidential State of the Union messages and other speeches, historical data on the presidency, and much more.

Logging On

This site offers extensive information on the White House and the presidency:

http://www.whitehouse.gov

Inaugural addresses of American presidents from George Washington to George W. Bush can be found at

http://www.bartleby.com/124

You can find an excellent collection of data and maps describing all U.S. presidential elections at Dave Leip's Atlas of U.S. Presidential Elections. Go to

http://uselectionatlas.org

Using InfoTrac for Political Research

You can use InfoTrac to research the 2004 presidential campaign and learn more about the way in which the candidates' stands on particular issues may have helped determine the result. To use InfoTrac to research issues in the 2004 campaign, go to

http://www.infotrac-college.com

Log in and go to InfoTrac College Edition, then go to the Keyword guide. Type the names of the two candidates into the search field and also type in a keyword for a particular type of issue. For example, you could enter "bush kerry environment" or "kerry bush terrorism." InfoTrac will present you with a list of articles, sorted by date. If the list is long, choose a number of the most recent ones to use when making your evaluation.

ONLINE REVIEW

At **http://politicalscience.wadsworth.com/schmidt12**, you will find a free Study Guide to this book. For each chapter, there are two online quizzes to help you master the material.

• The **PoliPrep Self Study Assessment** provides a pre-test for each major section of the chapter. PoliPrep then generates a customized study plan. After you complete the study plan, a post-test evaluates your progress.

• The **Tutorial Quiz** for each chapter provides questions on the chapter contents, including the features. The questions are organized to match the major sections of the chapter.

CHAPTER 13

The Bureaucracy

- The Nature of Bureaucracy

- The Size
  of the Bureaucracy

- The Organization of the
  Federal Bureaucracy

- Staffing the Bureaucracy

- Modern Attempts
  at Bureaucratic Reform

- Bureaucrats as Politicians
  and Policymakers

- Congressional Control
  of the Bureaucracy

WHAT IF . . .
The Public Graded Federal Bureaucracies?

BACKGROUND

Congress has repeatedly reformed the civil service since 1883. In addition, each modern administration has claimed that it would make bureaucrats more accountable. In spite of all efforts, however, bureaucrats are far from accountable to their bosses in the executive branch, to Congress, and, least of all, to the public—the taxpayers who fund their salaries. Would bureaucrats be more accountable if report cards graded their efforts?

WHAT IF THE PUBLIC GRADED FEDERAL BUREAUCRACIES?

On taking office, President George W. Bush created a plan known as performance-based budgeting to increase bureaucratic accountability. As part of this plan, the Office of Management and Budget (OMB) was to examine how well each agency met specific performance criteria and create a report card for each agency.

The government could also prepare report cards that summarize public input. Many commercial businesses actively solicit feedback from their customers on whether staff members were polite, whether problems were resolved quickly, and whether the customer was satisfied with the transaction overall. Similarly, the government could print evaluation forms to be distributed to citizens every time they interacted with the government. Taxpayers could even insert their evaluations of the Internal Revenue Service into the same envelope as their tax returns.

MAKING SENSE OF THE EVALUATIONS

The number of federal agencies is very large, and the average citizen usually deals with only a few of them. Therefore, if report cards were based on responses from a federal agency's "customers," they might not represent the opinions of the general public. For some agencies, this probably would

not matter. If customers rated the performance of the Department of Veterans Affairs, their responses would probably not be much different from what the public would have thought.

But what about the Federal Bureau of Investigation (FBI)? Criminals arrested by the FBI will never be happy with that experience. Less dramatically, businesses that deal with regulatory agencies may never be satisfied with the regulations imposed on them, even if most people believe that these regulations are essential to the public's health or safety. To make sense, any report card must indicate which groups of people are assigning the grades.

MAKING USE OF THE EVALUATIONS

Under the Bush administration's plan for performance-based budgeting, budgetary payouts were to be linked to specific performance criteria for each program. Unfortunately, it is not always possible to cut the funding of a program that is performing poorly. The program may be so essential that it cannot be cut. It may be performing badly because it is underfunded—and cutting back will only make matters worse.

Bad publicity might be a better tool for making bureaucrats more responsive. Already, numerous private groups bring ridicule to the federal government by discovering laughable programs and

actions by federal bureaucrats that virtually no one could justify. If agencies were compared with other agencies and had to fear criticism if their performance fell below average, they might have an incentive to improve the quality of their work.

A BASIS FOR DISCIPLINE

Many observers believe that the greatest obstacle to making the federal bureaucracy responsive is that it is very hard to fire federal bureaucrats. If bureaucrats in private businesses do not perform, their bosses simply fire them. The federal bureaucracy, in contrast, is so extensively governed by rules and regulations about firing that virtually no one is ever dismissed.

Congress could make it easier for bureaucrats to be fired. If it did so, perhaps poor performance on a public report card could lead to discipline and, in due course, discharge. Threats against individual bureaucrats might be more effective than a threat to cut a program's budget—a threat that the government might not be able to carry out.

FOR CRITICAL ANALYSIS

1. *What specific items ought to be listed on a report card that is used to evaluate a federal bureaucracy?*
2. *If Congress tried to make civil servants easier to fire, what political forces might stand in the way?*

Faceless bureaucrats—this image provokes a negative reaction from many, if not most, Americans. Polls consistently report that the majority of Americans support "less government." The same polls, however, report that the majority of Americans support almost every specific program that the government undertakes. The conflict between the desire for small government and the benefits that only a large government can provide has been a constant feature of American politics. For example, the goal of preserving endangered species has widespread support. At the same time, many people believe that restrictions imposed under the Endangered Species Act violate the rights of landowners. Helping the elderly pay their medical bills is a popular objective, but hardly anyone enjoys paying the Medicare tax that supports this effort.

In this chapter, we describe the size, organization, and staffing of the federal bureaucracy. We review modern attempts at bureaucratic reform and the process by which Congress exerts ultimate control over the bureaucracy. We also discuss the bureaucracy's role in making rules and setting policy.

★ The Nature of Bureaucracy

Every modern president, at one time or another, has proclaimed that his administration was going to "fix government." All modern presidents also have put forth plans to end government waste and inefficiency (see Table 13–1). Their success has been, in a word, underwhelming. Presidents generally have been powerless to affect the structure and operation of the federal bureaucracy significantly.

A **bureaucracy** is the name given to a large organization that is structured hierarchically to carry out specific functions. Generally, most bureaucracies are characterized by an organization chart. The units of the organization are divided according to the specialization and expertise of the employees.

Bureaucracy
A large organization that is structured hierarchically to carry out specific functions.

Public and Private Bureaucracies

We should not think of bureaucracy as unique to government. Any large corporation or university can be considered a bureaucratic organization. The fact is that the handling of complex problems requires a division of labor. Individuals must concentrate their skills on specific, well-defined aspects of a problem and depend on others to solve the rest of it.

Public or government bureaucracies differ from private organizations in some important ways, however. A private corporation, such as Microsoft, has a single set of leaders—its board of directors. Public bureaucracies, in contrast, do not have a single set of leaders. Although the president is the chief administrator of the federal system, all bureaucratic agencies are subject to Congress for their

TABLE 13–1

Selected Presidential Plans to End Government Inefficiency

PRESIDENT	NAME OF PLAN
Lyndon Johnson (1963–1969)	Programming, Planning, and Budgeting Systems
Richard Nixon (1969–1974)	Management by Objectives
Jimmy Carter (1977–1981)	Zero-Based Budgeting
Ronald Reagan (1981–1989)	President's Private Sector Survey on Cost Control (the Grace Commission)
George H. W. Bush (1989–1993)	Right-Sizing Government
Bill Clinton (1993–2001)	Reinventing Government
George W. Bush (2001–)	Performance-Based Budgeting

German sociologist Max Weber,
(1864–1920)

Weberian Model
A model of bureaucracy developed by the German sociologist Max Weber, who viewed bureaucracies as rational, hierarchical organizations in which decisions are based on logical reasoning.

Acquisitive Model
A model of bureaucracy that views top level bureaucrats as seeking to expand the size of their budgets and staffs to gain greater power.

Monopolistic Model
A model of bureaucracy that compares bureaucracies to monopolistic business firms. Lack of competition in either circumstance leads to inefficient and costly operations.

funding, staffing, and, indeed, their continued existence. Furthermore, public bureaucracies supposedly serve the citizenry.

One other important difference between private corporations and government bureaucracies is that government bureaucracies are not organized to make a profit. Rather, they are supposed to perform their functions as efficiently as possible to conserve the taxpayers' dollars. Perhaps it is this ideal that makes citizens hostile toward government bureaucracy when they experience inefficiency and red tape.

Models of Bureaucracy

Several theories have been offered to help us understand better the ways in which bureaucracies function. Each of these theories focuses on specific features of bureaucracies.

Weberian Model.   The classic model, or **Weberian model,** of the modern bureaucracy was proposed by the German sociologist Max Weber.[1] He argued that the increasingly complex nature of modern life, coupled with the steadily growing demands placed on governments by their citizens, made the formation of bureaucracies inevitable. According to Weber, most bureaucracies—whether in the public or private sector—are organized hierarchically and governed by formal procedures. The power in a bureaucracy flows from the top downward. Decision-making processes in bureaucracies are shaped by detailed technical rules that promote similar decisions in similar situations. Bureaucrats are specialists who attempt to resolve problems through logical reasoning and data analysis instead of "gut feelings" and guesswork. Individual advancement in bureaucracies is supposed to be based on merit rather than political connections. Indeed, the modern bureaucracy, according to Weber, should be an apolitical organization.

Acquisitive Model.   Other theorists do not view bureaucracies in terms as benign as Weber's. Some believe that bureaucracies are acquisitive in nature. Proponents of the **acquisitive model** argue that top-level bureaucrats will always try to expand, or at least to avoid any reductions in, the size of their budgets. Although government bureaucracies are not-for-profit enterprises, bureaucrats want to maximize the size of their budgets and staffs, because these things are the most visible trappings of power in the public sector. These efforts are also prompted by the desire of bureaucrats to "sell" their products—national defense, public housing, agricultural subsidies, and so on—to both Congress and the public.

Monopolistic Model.   Because government bureaucracies seldom have competitors, some theorists have suggested that these bureaucratic organizations may be explained best by a **monopolistic model.** The analysis is similar to that used by economists to examine the behavior of monopolistic firms. Monopolistic bureaucracies—like monopolistic firms—essentially have no competitors and act accordingly. Because monopolistic bureaucracies usually are not penalized for chronic inefficiency, they have little reason to adopt cost-saving measures or to make more productive use of their resources. Some economists have argued that such problems can be cured only by privatizing certain bureaucratic functions.

Bureaucracies Compared

The federal bureaucracy in the United States enjoys a greater degree of autonomy than do federal or national bureaucracies in many other nations. Much of the insularity that is commonly supposed to characterize the bureaucracy in this

---

[1]Max Weber, *Theory of Social and Economic Organization,* edited by Talcott Parsons (New York: Oxford University Press, 1974).

Ear tags were used to trace the path of a cow that died of mad cow disease in Washington state in 2003. Canadian officials conducted DNA tests on the dead cow to see if it came from Canada. Protection against communicable diseases in animals (and in humans) often requires cooperation among agencies from many countries. (EPA/Barry Sweet/Landov)

country may stem from the sheer size of the government organizations needed to implement a budget that exceeds $2 trillion. Because the lines of authority often are not well defined, some bureaucracies may be able to operate with a significant degree of autonomy.

The federal nature of the American government also means that national bureaucracies regularly provide financial assistance to their state counterparts. Both the Department of Education and the Department of Housing and Urban Development, for example, distribute funds to their counterparts at the state level. In contrast, most bureaucracies in European countries have a top-down command structure so that national programs may be implemented directly at the lower level. This is due not only to the smaller size of most European countries but also to the fact that public ownership of such businesses as telephone companies, airlines, railroads, and utilities is far more common in Europe than in the United States.

The fact that the U.S. government owns relatively few enterprises does not mean, however, that its bureaucracies are comparatively powerless. Indeed, there are many **administrative agencies** in the federal bureaucracy—such as the Environmental Protection Agency, the Nuclear Regulatory Commission, and the Securities and Exchange Commission—that regulate private companies.

Administrative Agency
A federal, state, or local government unit established to perform a specific function. Administrative agencies are created and authorized by legislative bodies to administer and enforce specific laws.

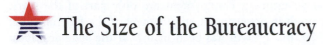 ## The Size of the Bureaucracy

In 1789, the new government's bureaucracy was minuscule. There were three departments—State (with nine employees), War (with two employees), and Treasury (with thirty-nine employees)—and the Office of the Attorney General (which later became the Department of Justice). The bureaucracy was still small in 1798. At that time, the secretary of state had seven clerks and spent a total of $500 (about $8,145 in 2005 dollars) on stationery and printing. In that same year, the Appropriations Act allocated $1.4 million to the War Department (or $22.8 million in 2005 dollars).[2]

---

[2]Leonard D. White, *The Federalists: A Study in Administrative History, 1789–1801* (New York: Free Press, 1948).

FIGURE 13–1

Federal Agencies and Their Respective Numbers of Civilian Employees

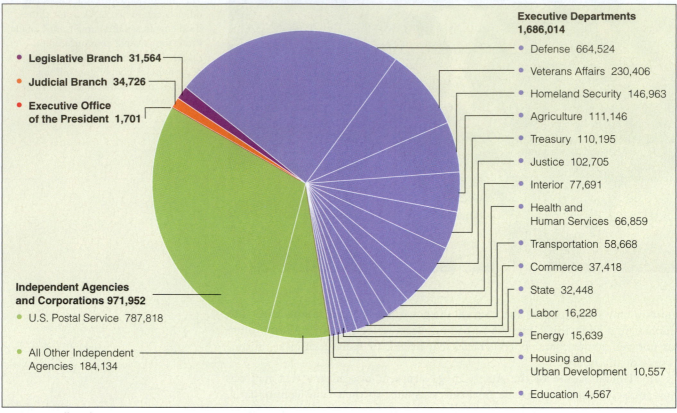

SOURCE: U.S. Office of Personnel Management, September 2004.

FIGURE 13–2

Government Employment at the Federal, State, and Local Levels

There are more local government employees than federal or state employees combined.

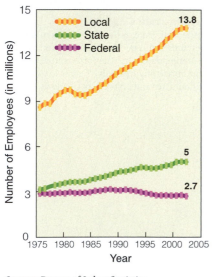

SOURCE: Bureau of Labor Statistics.

Times have changed, as we can see in Figure 13–1, which lists the various federal agencies and the number of civilian employees in each. Excluding the military, the federal bureaucracy includes approximately 2.7 million government employees. That number has remained relatively stable for the last several decades. It is somewhat deceiving, however, because many other individuals work directly or indirectly for the federal government as subcontractors or consultants and in other capacities. In fact, according to some studies, the federal work force vastly exceeds the number of official federal workers.[3]

The figures for federal government employment are only part of the story. Figure 13–2 shows the growth in government employment at the federal, state, and local levels. Since 1970, this growth has been mainly at the state and local levels. If all government employees are included, more than 15 percent of all civilian employment is accounted for by government.

The costs of the bureaucracy are commensurately high. The share of the gross domestic product accounted for by all government spending was only 8.5 percent in 1929. Today, it exceeds 30 percent. Could we reduce the cost of government by eliminating unnecessary spending? We look at one example of questionable spending in the *Politics and Subsidies* feature.

---

[3]See, for example, Paul C. Light, *The True Size of Government* (Washington, D.C.: Brookings Institution Press, 1999).

POLITICS AND SUBSIDIES
Amtrak—A Public Railroad, No Matter What the Cost

Thirty-five years ago, after several private rail companies went bankrupt, Congress created a public railway system called Amtrak. Today, Amtrak links 500 American towns and cities in 46 states with over 22,000 miles of rail. Amtrak runs 41 long-distance routes such as the "Sunset Limited" between Orlando and Los Angeles, but its most popular routes are along the Northeast corridor. While Amtrak appears impressive, it has many critics both in and outside Congress.

THE RED INK KEEPS FLOWING

During Amtrak's existence, American taxpayers have subsidized it to the tune of over $25 billion. Current subsidies typically exceed $1 billion a year—$2 billion was requested in 2004. As Republican representative Harold Rogers of Kentucky has pointed out, "Every time a passenger boards a train, Uncle Sam writes a check for $138.71, on average." For example, the aforementioned Sunset Limited route costs the taxpayers $347 for each passenger served. The subsidy on a round-trip Amtrak ride between Los Angeles and New York is $1,270. You can buy a cross-country airline ticket from a discounter for around $400 to $500.

THE RATIONALE FOR KEEPING SUBSIDIES

Those in favor of the Amtrak subsidies argue that Amtrak provides essential transportation for the poor. Actually, the percentage of users with incomes above $40,000 is higher for Amtrak than for any other intercity transportation option. Upper-middle-income suburbanites in the Northeast are its main users.

Amtrak supporters believe that it relieves congestion on the highways and at airports. Because so few people use Amtrak, though, if the system disappeared, the airlines could easily accommodate its customers in presently unsold seats on existing flights. On the majority of Amtrak routes, if customers used their automobiles instead, only one or two vehicles per lane per hour would be added.

An Amtrak train rolls through a station near Wilmington, Delaware. Publicly owned passenger railroad systems run at a loss in most countries, but few are as unprofitable per mile traveled as Amtrak. Why might a passenger rail system in the United States be especially unprofitable? (Reuters/Tim Shaffer/Landov)

PRIVATIZATION EFFORTS

Some members of Congress have suggested that Amtrak be sold off to the highest bidder. The U.S. Department of Transportation has also considered allowing states or groups of states to bid on portions of Amtrak. Under either proposal, Amtrak's responsibilities as a federal corporation would be phased out. Not surprisingly, Amtrak President David Gun has voiced skepticism over privatization efforts.

FOR CRITICAL ANALYSIS

Who might gain and who might lose if Amtrak were privatized?

The Organization of the Federal Bureaucracy

Within the federal bureaucracy are a number of different types of government agencies and organizations. Figure 13–3 on the following page outlines the several bodies within the executive branch, as well as the separate organizations that provide services to Congress, to the courts, and directly to the president. In Chapter 12, we

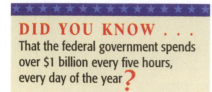

DID YOU KNOW . . .
That the federal government spends over $1 billion every five hours, every day of the year ?

discussed those agencies that are considered to be part of the Executive Office of the President.

The executive branch, which employs most of the government's staff, has four major types of structures. They are (1) cabinet departments, (2) independent executive agencies, (3) independent regulatory agencies, and (4) government corporations. Each has a distinctive relationship to the president, and some have unusual internal structures, overall goals, and grants of power.

FIGURE 13–3

Organization Chart of the Federal Government

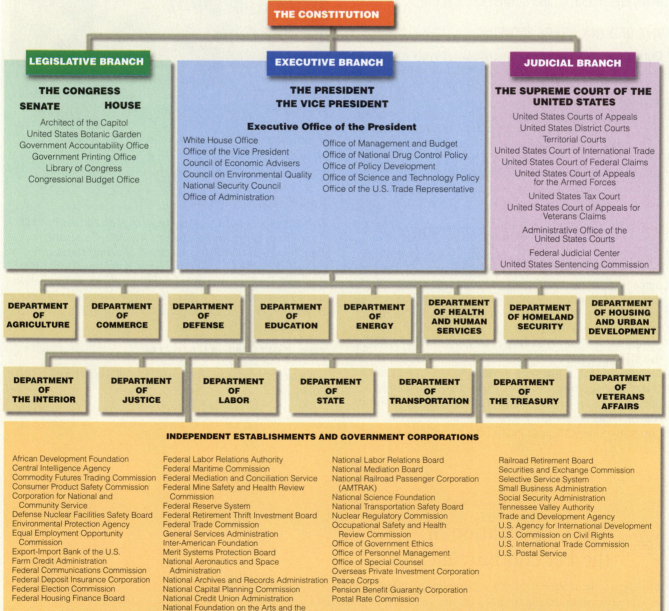

SOURCE: *United States Government Manual, 2003–2004* (Washington, D.C.: U.S. Government Printing Office, 2003).

Cabinet Departments

The fifteen **cabinet departments** are the major service organizations of the federal government. They can also be described in management terms as **line organizations.** This means that they are directly accountable to the president and are responsible for performing government functions, such as printing money and training troops. These departments were created by Congress when the need for each department arose. The first department to be created was State, and the most recent one was Homeland Security, established in 2003. A president might ask that a new department be created or an old one abolished, but the president has no power to do so without legislative approval from Congress.

Each department is headed by a secretary (except for the Justice Department, which is headed by the attorney general). Each also has several levels of undersecretaries, assistant secretaries, and so on.

Presidents theoretically have considerable control over the cabinet departments, because presidents are able to appoint or fire all of the top officials. Even cabinet departments do not always respond to the president's wishes, though. One reason that presidents are frequently unhappy with their departments is that the entire bureaucratic structure below the top political levels is staffed by permanent employees, many of whom are committed to established programs or procedures and who resist change. As we can see from Table 13–2 on the following page, each cabinet department employs thousands of individuals, only a handful of whom are under the control of the president. The table also describes some of the functions of each of the departments. The most recently created cabinet department is the Department of Homeland Security. How effective is the new department at fighting terrorism? We examine this question in the *America's Security* feature on page 433.

Cabinet Department
One of the fifteen departments of the executive branch (State, Treasury, Defense, Justice, Interior, Agriculture, Commerce, Labor, Health and Human Services, Homeland Security, Housing and Urban Development, Education, Energy, Transportation, and Veterans Affairs).

Line Organization
In the federal government, an administrative unit that is directly accountable to the president.

Gwen Gunn, a manager for the Federal Emergency Management Agency (FEMA) in San Diego, explains the work of the local center to Homeland Security Secretary Tom Ridge. Why might it be reasonable for the Department of Homeland Security to oversee recovery from natural disasters? What might a natural disaster and a terrorist attack have in common? (Kevin Galvin/FEMA News Photo)

TABLE 13–2
Executive Departments

DEPARTMENT AND YEAR ESTABLISHED	PRINCIPAL FUNCTIONS	SELECTED SUBAGENCIES
State (1789) (32,448 employees)	Negotiates treaties; develops foreign policy; protects citizens abroad.	Passport Agency; Bureau of Diplomatic Security; Foreign Service; Bureau of Human Rights and Humanitarian Affairs; Bureau of Consular Affairs.
Treasury (1789) (110,195 employees)	Pays all federal bills; borrows money; collects federal taxes; mints coins and prints paper currency; supervises national banks.	Internal Revenue Service; U.S. Mint.
Interior (1849) (77,691 employees)	Supervises federally owned lands and parks; supervises Native American affairs.	U.S. Fish and Wildlife Service; National Park Service; Bureau of Indian Affairs; Bureau of Land Management.
Justice (1870)* (102,705 employees)	Furnishes legal advice to the president; enforces federal criminal laws; supervises federal prisons.	Federal Bureau of Investigation; Drug Enforcement Administration; Bureau of Prisons.
Agriculture (1889) (111,146 employees)	Provides assistance to farmers and ranchers; conducts agricultural research; works to protect forests.	Soil Conservation Service; Agricultural Research Service; Food Safety and Inspection Service; Federal Crop Insurance Corporation; Commodity Credit Corporation; Forest Service.
Commerce (1913)† (37,418 employees)	Grants patents and trademarks; conducts a national census; monitors the weather; protects the interests of businesses.	Bureau of the Census; Bureau of Economic Analysis; Patent and Trademark Office; National Oceanic and Atmospheric Administration.
Labor (1913)† (16,228 employees)	Administers federal labor laws; promotes the interests of workers.	Occupational Safety and Health Administration; Bureau of Labor Statistics; Employment Standards Administration; Employment and Training Administration.
Defense (1947)‡ (664,524 employees)	Manages the armed forces (army, navy, air force, and marines); operates military bases; is responsible for civil defense.	National Security Agency; Joint Chiefs of Staff; Departments of the Air Force, Navy, Army; Defense Advanced Research Projects Agency; Defense Intelligence Agency; the service academies.
Housing and Urban Development (1965) (10,557 employees)	Deals with the nation's housing needs; develops and rehabilitates urban communities; oversees resale of mortgages.	Government National Mortgage Association; Office of Community Planning and Development; Office of Fair Housing and Equal Opportunity.
Transportation (1967) (58,668 employees)	Finances improvements in mass transit; develops and administers programs for highways, railroads, and aviation.	Federal Aviation Administration; Federal Highway Administration; National Highway Traffic Safety Administration; Federal Transit Administration.
Energy (1977) (15,630 employees)	Promotes the conservation of energy and resources; analyzes energy data; conducts research and development.	Federal Energy Regulatory Commission; National Nuclear Security Administration.
Health and Human Services (1979)§ (66,859 employees)	Promotes public health; enforces pure food and drug laws; conducts and sponsors health-related research.	Food and Drug Administration; Public Health Service; Centers for Disease Control; National Institutes of Health; Centers for Medicare and Medicaid Services.
Education (1979)§ (4,567 employees)	Coordinates federal programs and policies for education; administers aid to education; promotes educational research.	Office of Special Education and Rehabilitation Service; Office of Elementary and Secondary Education; Office of Postsecondary Education; Office of Vocational and Adult Education; Office of Federal Student Aid.
Veterans Affairs (1988) (230,406 employees)	Promotes the welfare of veterans of the U.S. armed forces.	Veterans Health Administration; Veterans Benefits Administration; National Cemetery Systems.
Homeland Security (2003) (146,963 employees)	Attempts to prevent terrorist attacks within the United States, control America's borders, and minimize the damage from natural disasters.	U.S. Customs Service; U.S. Coast Guard; Secret Service; Federal Emergency Management Agency; Bureau of Citizenship and Immigration Services.

*Formed from the Office of the Attorney General (created in 1789).
†Formed from the Department of Commerce and Labor (created in 1903).
‡Formed from the Department of War (created in 1789) and the Department of the Navy (created in 1798).
§Formed from the Department of Health, Education, and Welfare (created in 1953).
Employment figures as of September 2003.

AMERICA'S SECURITY
Unifying the Antiterrorism Effort

The creation of the Department of Homeland Security (DHS) in 2003 was the largest reorganization of the U.S. government since 1947. President George W. Bush claimed that consolidating twenty-two agencies with responsibilities for preventing terrorism into a single department would promote efficiency and improve coordination.

SAFER AIR TRAVEL

Homeland Security officials point to a number of successes. The department introduced several new security programs on schedule and without serious problems. These include the deployment of 50,000 trained airport screeners and a high-tech baggage-screening program. Thomas Winkowski, head of Customs and Border Protection for South Florida, claims that arrests of Cuban, Haitian, and Dominican migrants have skyrocketed because of greater coordination between Immigration and Customs Enforcement officers and the Coast Guard. (Both units are part of the DHS.)

BUT HUGE IMMIGRATION BACKLOGS

Unfortunately, consolidation of the department has diverted a substantial amount of management energy that could have been devoted to the war on terrorism. Even though the DHS brought together agencies with budgets totaling $37 billion, Bush's 2004 budget request for the DHS was $36 billion, so some functions actually had to be trimmed. The 2005 budget request was $40 billion, which helped. Still, fewer than one hundred inspectors are assigned to overseas ports to inspect millions of cargo containers bound for the United States. In late 2003, the department had a backlog of almost seven million immigration applications.

THE DHS, THE FBI, AND THE CIA

A fundamental reality is that for all its 147,000 employees, the DHS does not actually unify the antiterrorist effort. The most important antiterrorist agencies are the Federal Bureau of Investigation (FBI) and the Central Intelligence Agency (CIA). Neither agency is part of the DHS. Both have reputations for defending their turfs. Many people believe that the number-one problem in addressing terrorism has been the failure of the FBI and the CIA to exchange information with each other. Indeed, some have observed that officers of these agencies have been reluctant to share information with others in their own agency, let alone outsiders. For that reason, some members of Congress have

John Brennan (left), director of the Terrorist Threat Integration Center, testifies before the Senate Government Affairs Committee. Also present are John Pistole, assistant director of the FBI's counterterrorism division; Lieutenant General Patrick Hughes of the Department of Homeland Security; and Philip Mudd, deputy director of the CIA's counterterrorist center. (AP Photo/Dennis Cook)

called for the creation of a completely new domestic security service. Already in 2003, Bush created a Terrorist Threat Integration Center in *addition* to the DHS, the FBI, and the CIA. The danger exists that a multiplication of new entities will only increase the coordination problem. In July 2004, the bipartisan 9/11 Commission recommended the creation of a new national intelligence director to centralize efforts now spread over six cabinet departments plus the CIA. The panel also called for a national counterterrorism center that would be stronger than the existing Terrorist Threat Integration Center.

FOR CRITICAL ANALYSIS

How could the government encourage officers of different agencies to communicate with each other more freely?

Independent Executive Agencies

Independent Executive Agency
A federal agency that is not part of a cabinet department but reports directly to the president.

Independent executive agencies are bureaucratic organizations that are not located within a department but report directly to the president, who appoints their chief officials. When a new federal agency is created—the Environmental Protection Agency, for example—Congress decides where it will be located in the bureaucracy. In recent decades, presidents often have asked that a new organization be kept separate or independent rather than added to an existing department, particularly if a department may be hostile to the agency's creation. Table 13–3 describes the functions of several selected independent executive agencies.

Independent Regulatory Agencies

Independent Regulatory Agency
An agency outside the major executive departments charged with making and implementing rules and regulations.

The **independent regulatory agencies** are typically responsible for a specific type of public policy. Their function is to make and implement rules and regulations in a particular sphere of action to protect the public interest. The earliest such agency was the Interstate Commerce Commission (ICC), which was established in 1887 when Americans began to seek some form of government control over the rapidly growing business and industrial sector. This new form of organization, the independent regulatory agency, was supposed to make technical, nonpolitical decisions about rates, profits, and rules that would be for the benefit of all and that did not require congressional legislation. In the years that followed the creation of the ICC, other agencies were formed to regulate communication (the Federal Communications Commission), nuclear power (the Nuclear Regulatory Commission), and so on. (The ICC was abolished on December 30, 1995.)

The Purpose and Nature of Regulatory Agencies.   In practice, the regulatory agencies are administered independently of all three branches of government. They were set up because Congress felt it was unable to handle the complexities and technicalities required to carry out specific laws in the public interest. The

TABLE 13–3

Selected Independent Executive Agencies

NAME	DATE FORMED	PRINCIPAL FUNCTIONS
The Smithsonian Institution (5,245 employees)	1846	Runs the government's museums and the National Zoo.
Central Intelligence Agency (CIA) (number of employees not released)	1947	Gathers and analyzes political and military information about foreign countries; conducts covert operations outside the United States.
General Services Administration (GSA) (12,757 employees)	1949	Purchases and manages property of the federal government; acts as the business arm of the federal government in overseeing federal government spending projects; discovers overcharges in government programs.
National Science Foundation (NSF) (1,315 employees)	1950	Promotes scientific research; provides grants to all levels of schools for instructional programs in the sciences.
Small Business Administration (SBA) (3,630 employees)	1953	Protects the interests of small businesses; provides low-cost loans and management information to small businesses.
National Aeronautics and Space Administration (NASA) (18,954 employees)	1958	Is responsible for the U.S. space program, including the building, testing, and operating of space vehicles.
Environmental Protection Agency (EPA) (18,217 employees)	1970	Undertakes programs aimed at reducing air and water pollution; works with state and local agencies to help fight environmental hazards.

regulatory commissions in fact combine some functions of all three branches of government—executive, legislative, and judicial. They are legislative in that they make rules that have the force of law. They are executive in that they provide for the enforcement of those rules. They are judicial in that they decide disputes involving the rules they have made.

Members of regulatory agency boards or commissions are appointed by the president with the consent of the Senate, although they do not report to the president. By law, the members of regulatory agencies cannot all be from the same political party. Presidents can influence regulatory agency behavior by appointing people of their own parties or individuals who share their political views when vacancies occur, in particular when the chair is vacant. Members may be removed by the president only for causes specified in the law creating the agency. Table 13–4 describes the functions of selected independent regulatory agencies.

Agency Capture.   Over the last several decades, some observers have concluded that these agencies, although nominally independent, may in fact not always be so. They contend that many independent regulatory agencies have been **captured** by the very industries and firms that they were supposed to regulate. The results have been less competition rather than more competition, higher prices rather than lower prices, and less choice rather than more choice for consumers.

Deregulation and Reregulation.   During the presidency of Ronald Reagan (1981–1989), some significant deregulation (the removal of regulatory restraints—the opposite of regulation) occurred, much of which had started under President Jimmy Carter (1977–1981). For example, President Carter appointed a chairperson of the Civil Aeronautics Board (CAB) who gradually eliminated regulation of airline fares and routes. Then, under Reagan, the CAB was eliminated on January 1, 1985.

★★★★★★★★★★★★★★★★

DID YOU KNOW . . .
That the Commerce Department's U.S. Travel and Tourism Administration gave away $440,000 in disaster relief to western ski resort operators because there hadn't been enough snow**?**

Capture
The act by which an industry being regulated by a government agency gains direct or indirect control over agency personnel and decision makers.

TABLE 13–4

Selected Independent Regulatory Agencies

NAME	DATE FORMED	PRINCIPAL FUNCTIONS
Federal Reserve System Board of Governors (Fed) (1,068 employees)	1913	Determines policy with respect to interest rates, credit availability, and the money supply.
Federal Trade Commission (FTC) (1,068 employees)	1914	Prevents businesses from engaging in unfair trade practices; stops the formation of monopolies in the business sector; protects consumer rights.
Securities and Exchange Commission (SEC) (3,261 employees)	1934	Regulates the nation's stock exchanges, in which shares of stocks are bought and sold; requires full disclosure of the financial profiles of companies that wish to sell stocks and bonds to the public.
Federal Communications Commission (FCC) (2,051 employees)	1934	Regulates all communications by telegraph, cable, telephone, radio, and television.
National Labor Relations Board (NLRB) (1,931 employees)	1935	Protects employees' rights to join unions and bargain collectively with employers; attempts to prevent unfair labor practices by both employers and unions.
Equal Employment Opportunity Commission (EEOC) (2,589 employees)	1964	Works to eliminate discrimination based on religion, gender, race, color, national origin, age, or disability; examines claims of discrimination.
Nuclear Regulatory Commission (NRC) (3,083 employees)	1974	Ensures that electricity-generating nuclear reactors in the United States are built and operated safely; regularly inspects the operations of such reactors.

Government Corporation
An agency of government that administers
a quasi-business enterprise. These
corporations are used when activities are
primarily commercial.

During the administration of George H. W. Bush (1989–1993), calls for reregulation of many businesses increased. Indeed, during that administration, the Americans with Disabilities Act of 1990, the Civil Rights Act of 1991, and the Clean Air Act Amendments of 1991, all of which increased or changed the regulation of many businesses, were passed. Additionally, the Cable Reregulation Act of 1992 was passed.

Under President Bill Clinton (1993–2001), the Interstate Commerce Commission was eliminated, and the banking and telecommunications industries, along with many other sectors of the economy, were deregulated. At the same time, there was extensive regulation to protect the environment.

Government Corporations

Another form of bureaucratic organization in the United States is the **government corporation.** Although the concept is borrowed from the world of business, distinct differences exist between public and private corporations.

A private corporation has shareholders (stockholders) who elect a board of directors, who in turn choose the corporate officers, such as president and vice president. When a private corporation makes a profit, it must pay taxes (unless it avoids them through various legal loopholes). It either distributes part or all of the after-tax profits to shareholders as dividends or plows the profits back into the corporation to make new investments.

A government corporation has a board of directors and managers, but it does not have any stockholders. We cannot buy shares of stock in a government corporation. If the government corporation makes a profit, it does not distribute the profit as dividends. Also, if it makes a profit, it does not have to pay taxes; the profits remain in the corporation. Table 13–5 describes the functions of selected government corporations.

A mail clerk unloads mail from a "sweeper" at the Main Post Office in St. Louis during the Christmas rush. The U.S. Postal Service is a government corporation. The United States enjoys one of the lowest rates for domestic letter postage in the industrialized world—$0.37. In U.S. dollars, the rate is $0.51 in Britain, $0.62 in France, and $0.73 in Japan. (UPI Photo/Bill Greenblatt/Landov)

TABLE 13-5

Selected Government Corporations

Name	Date Formed	Principal Functions
Tennessee Valley Authority (TVA) (13,379 employees)	1933	Operates a Tennessee River control system and generates power for a seven-state region and for the U.S. aeronautics and space programs; promotes the economic development of the Tennessee Valley region; controls floods and promotes the navigability of the Tennessee River.
Federal Deposit Insurance Corporation (FDIC) (5,473 employees)	1933	Insures individuals' bank deposits up to $100,000; oversees the business activities of banks.
Export-Import Bank of the United States (Ex-Im Bank) (394 employees)	1933	Promotes the sale of American-made goods abroad; grants loans to foreign purchasers of American products.
National Railroad Passenger Corporation (AMTRAK) (22,000 employees)	1970	Provides a national and intercity rail passenger service; controls 22,000 miles of track and serves 500 communities.
U.S. Postal Service* (787,818 employees)	1970	Delivers mail throughout the United States and its territories; is the largest government corporation.

*Formed from the Post Office Department (an executive department) in 1970.

★ Staffing the Bureaucracy

There are two categories of bureaucrats: political appointees and civil servants. As noted earlier, the president is able to make political appointments to most of the top jobs in the federal bureaucracy. The president also can appoint ambassadors to foreign posts. All of the jobs that are considered "political plums" and that usually go to the politically well connected are listed in *Policy and Supporting Positions,* a book published by the Government Printing Office after each presidential election. Informally (and appropriately), this has been called "The Plum Book." The rest of the national government's employees belong to the civil service and obtain their jobs through a much more formal process.

Political Appointees

To fill the positions listed in "The Plum Book," the president and the president's advisers solicit suggestions from politicians, businesspersons, and other prominent individuals. Appointments to these positions offer the president a way to pay off outstanding political debts. But the president must also take into consideration such things as the candidate's work experience, intelligence, political affiliations, and personal characteristics. Presidents have differed in the importance they attach to appointing women and minorities to plum positions. Presidents often use ambassadorships, however, to reward individuals for their campaign contributions.

The Aristocracy of the Federal Government. Political appointees are in some sense the aristocracy of the federal government. But their powers, although appearing formidable on paper, are often exaggerated. Like the president, a political appointee will occupy her or his position for a comparatively brief time. Political appointees often leave office before the president's term actually ends. In fact, the average term of service for political appointees is less than two years. As a result, most appointees have little background for their positions and may be mere figureheads. Often, they only respond to the paperwork that flows up from below. Additionally, the professional civil servants who make up the permanent civil service may not feel compelled to carry out their current boss' directives quickly, because they know that he or she will not be around for very long.

The Difficulty in Firing Civil Servants.   This inertia is compounded by the fact that it is very difficult to discharge civil servants. In recent years, fewer than one-tenth of 1 percent of federal employees have been fired for incompetence. Because discharged employees may appeal their dismissals, many months or even years can pass before the issue is resolved conclusively. This occupational rigidity helps to ensure that most political appointees, no matter how competent or driven, will not be able to exert much meaningful influence over their subordinates, let alone implement dramatic changes in the bureaucracy itself.

History of the Federal Civil Service

When the federal government was formed in 1789, it had no career public servants but rather consisted of amateurs who were almost all Federalists. When Thomas Jefferson took over as president, few in his party were holding federal administrative jobs, so he fired more than one hundred officials and replaced them with his own supporters. Then, for the next twenty-five years, a growing body of federal administrators gained experience and expertise, becoming in the process professional public servants. These administrators stayed in office regardless of who was elected president. The bureaucracy had become a self-maintaining, long-term element within government.

To the Victor Belong the Spoils.   When Andrew Jackson took over the White House in 1828, he could not believe how many appointed officials (appointed before he became president, that is) were overtly hostile toward him and his Democratic Party. As the bureaucracy was reluctant to carry out his programs, Jackson did the obvious: he fired federal officials—more than had all his predecessors combined. The **spoils system**—an application of the principle that to the victor belong the spoils—became the standard method of filling federal positions. Whenever a new president was elected from a party different from the party of the

Spoils System
The awarding of government jobs to political supporters and friends.

On September 19, 1881, President James A. Garfield was assassinated by a disappointed office seeker, Charles J. Guiteau. The long-term effect of this event was to replace the spoils system with a permanent career civil service. This process began with the passage of the Pendleton Act in 1883, which established the Civil Service Commission. (Library of Congress)

WASHINGTON, D. C.—THE ATTACK ON THE PRESIDENT'S LIFE—SCENE IN THE LADIES' ROOM OF THE BALTIMORE AND OHIO RAILROAD DEPOT—THE ARREST OF THE ASSASSIN.

previous president, there would be an almost complete turnover in the staffing of the federal government.

The Civil Service Reform Act of 1883. Jackson's spoils system survived for a number of years, but it became increasingly corrupt. Also, as the size of the bureaucracy increased by 300 percent between 1851 and 1881, the cry for civil service reform became louder. Reformers began to look to the example of several European countries, in particular, Germany, which had established a professional civil service that operated under a **merit system** in which job appointments were based on competitive examinations.

In 1883, the **Pendleton Act**—or **Civil Service Reform Act**—was passed, placing the first limits on the spoils system. The act established the principle of employment on the basis of open, competitive examinations and created the **Civil Service Commission** to administer the personnel service. Only 10 percent of federal employees were covered by the merit system initially. Later laws, amendments, and executive orders, however, increased the coverage to more than 90 percent of federal employees. The effects of these reforms were felt at all levels of government.

The Supreme Court strengthened the civil service system in *Elrod v. Burns*[4] in 1976 and *Branti v. Finkel*[5] in 1980. In those two cases, the Court used the First Amendment to forbid government officials from discharging or threatening to discharge public employees solely for *not* being supporters of the political party in power unless party affiliation is an appropriate requirement for the position. Additional enhancements to the civil service system were added in *Rutan v. Republican Party of Illinois*[6] in 1990. The Court's ruling effectively prevented the use of partisan political considerations as the basis for hiring, promoting, or transferring most public employees. An exception was permitted, however, for senior policymaking positions, which usually go to officials who will support the programs of the elected leaders.

The Civil Service Reform Act of 1978. In 1978, the Civil Service Reform Act abolished the Civil Service Commission and created two new federal agencies to perform its duties. To administer the civil service laws, rules, and regulations, the act created the Office of Personnel Management (OPM). The OPM is empowered to recruit, interview, and test potential government workers and determine who should be hired. The OPM makes recommendations to the individual agencies as to which persons meet the standards (typically, the top three applicants for a position), and the agencies then decide whom to hire. To oversee promotions, employees' rights, and other employment matters, the act created the Merit Systems Protection Board (MSPB). The MSPB evaluates charges of wrongdoing, hears employee appeals from agency decisions, and can order corrective action against agencies and employees.

Federal Employees and Political Campaigns. In 1933, when President Franklin D. Roosevelt set up his New Deal, a virtual army of civil servants was hired to staff the numerous new agencies that were created. Because the individuals who worked in these agencies owed their jobs to the Democratic Party, it seemed natural for them to campaign for Democratic candidates. The Democrats controlling Congress in the mid-1930s did not object. But in 1938, a coalition of conservative Democrats and Republicans took control of Congress and forced

Merit System
The selection, retention, and promotion of government employees on the basis of competitive examinations.

Pendleton Act (Civil Service Reform Act)
An act that established the principle of employment on the basis of merit and created the Civil Service Commission to administer the personnel service.

Civil Service Commission
The initial central personnel agency of the national government; created in 1883.

---

[4]427 U.S. 347 (1976).
[5]445 U.S. 507 (1980).
[6]497 U.S. 62 (1990).

DID YOU KNOW . . .
That federal officials spent $333,000 building a deluxe, earthquake-proof outhouse for hikers in Pennsylvania's remote Delaware Water Gap recreation area**?**

through the Hatch Act—or Political Activities Act—of 1939. The act prohibited federal employees from actively participating in the political management of campaigns. It also forbade the use of federal authority to influence nominations and elections and outlawed the use of bureaucratic rank to pressure federal employees to make political contributions.

The Hatch Act created a controversy that lasted for decades. Many contended that the act deprived federal employees of their First Amendment freedoms of speech and association. In 1972, a federal district court declared the act unconstitutional. The United States Supreme Court, however, reaffirmed the challenged portion of the act in 1973, stating that the government's interest in preserving a nonpartisan civil service was so great that the prohibitions should remain.[7] Twenty years later, Congress addressed the criticisms of the Hatch Act by passing the Federal Employees Political Activities Act of 1993. This act, which amended the Hatch Act, lessened the harshness of the 1939 act in several ways. Among other things, the 1993 act allowed federal employees to run for office in nonpartisan elections, participate in voter-registration drives, make campaign contributions to political organizations, and campaign for candidates in partisan elections.

★ Modern Attempts at Bureaucratic Reform

As long as the federal bureaucracy exists, there will continue to be attempts to make it more open, efficient, and responsive to the needs of U.S. citizens. The most important actual and proposed reforms in the last several decades include sunshine and sunset laws, privatization, incentives for efficiency, and more protection for so-called whistleblowers.

Sunshine Laws before and after 9/11

Government in the Sunshine Act
A law that requires all committee-directed federal agencies to conduct their business regularly in public session.

In 1976, Congress enacted the **Government in the Sunshine Act.** It required for the first time that all multiheaded federal agencies—agencies headed by a committee instead of an individual—hold their meetings regularly in public session.

---

[7]*United States Civil Service Commission v. National Association of Letter Carriers,* 413 U.S. 548 (1973).

"Who do I see to get big government off my back?"

The bill defined *meetings* as almost any gathering, formal or informal, of agency members, including a conference telephone call. The only exceptions to this rule of openness are discussions of matters such as court proceedings or personnel problems, and these exceptions are specifically listed in the bill. Sunshine laws now exist at all levels of government.

Information Disclosure.   Sunshine laws are consistent with the policy of information disclosure that has been supported by the government for decades. For example, beginning in the 1960s, a number of consumer protection laws have required that certain information be disclosed to consumers—when purchasing homes, borrowing funds, and so on. In 1966, the federal government passed the Freedom of Information Act, which required federal government agencies, with certain exceptions, to disclose to individuals, on their request, any information about them contained in government files. (You will learn more about this act in the *Making a Difference* feature at the end of this chapter.)

Curbs on Information Disclosure.   Since September 11, 2001, the trend toward government in the sunshine and information disclosure has been reversed at both the federal and state levels. Within weeks after September 11, 2001, numerous federal agencies removed hundreds, if not thousands, of documents from Internet sites, public libraries, and reading rooms found in various federal government departments. Information contained in some of the documents included diagrams of power plants and pipelines, structural details on dams, and safety plans for chemical plants. The military also immediately started restricting information about its current and planned activities, as did the Federal Bureau of Investigation. These agencies were concerned that terrorists could make use of this information to plan attacks.

State and local governments control and supervise police forces, dams, electricity sources, and water supplies. Consequently, it is not surprising that many state and local governments followed in the footsteps of the federal government in curbing access to certain public records and information.

Such actions constitute a broad attempt by state and local governments to keep terrorists from learning about local emergency preparedness plans. It is possible, however, that as soon as the public starts to believe that the threat has lessened, some groups will take state and local governments to court in an effort to increase public access to state and local records by reimposing the sunshine laws that were in effect before 9/11.

Sunset Laws

Potentially, the size and scope of the federal bureaucracy can be controlled through **sunset legislation,** which places government programs on a definite schedule for congressional consideration. Unless Congress specifically reauthorizes a particular federally operated program at the end of a designated period, it would be terminated automatically; that is, its sun would set.

The idea of sunset legislation was initially suggested by Franklin D. Roosevelt when he created the plethora of New Deal agencies in the 1930s. His assistant, William O. Douglas, recommended that each agency's charter should include a provision allowing for its termination in ten years. Only an act of Congress could revitalize it. The proposal was never adopted. It was not until 1976 that a state

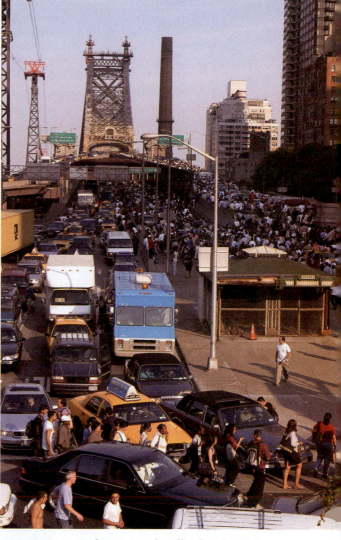

Pedestrians and traffic clog the 59th Street Bridge in New York City during the power outage of August 14, 2003. Parts of the Northeast, the Midwest, and Canada struggled to resume normal operations after the biggest electrical blackout in North American history. What steps can the federal government take to address the causes of this type of disaster? (James Patrick Cooper/Bloomberg News/Landov)

Sunset Legislation
Laws requiring that existing programs be reviewed regularly for their effectiveness and be terminated unless specifically extended as a result of these reviews.

legislature—Colorado's—adopted sunset legislation for state regulatory commissions, giving them a life of six years before their suns set. Today, most states have some type of sunset law.

Privatization

Privatization
The replacement of government services with services provided by private firms.

Another approach to bureaucratic reform is **privatization,** which occurs when government services are replaced by services from the private sector. For example, the government might contract with private firms to operate prisons. Supporters of privatization argue that some services could be provided more efficiently by the private sector. Another scheme is to furnish vouchers to "clients" in lieu of services. For example, instead of supplying housing, the government could offer vouchers that recipients could use to "pay" for housing in privately owned buildings.

The privatization, or contracting out, strategy has been most successful on the local level. Municipalities, for example, can form contracts with private companies for such things as trash collection. This approach is not a cure-all, however, as there are many functions, particularly on the national level, that cannot be contracted out in any meaningful way. For example, the federal government could not contract out most of the Defense Department's functions to private firms. Whether Social Security should be partially privatized is a topic currently being debated.

Incentives for Efficiency and Productivity

An increasing number of state governments are beginning to experiment with a variety of schemes to run their operations more efficiently and capably. They focus on maximizing the efficiency and productivity of government workers by providing incentives for improved performance.[8] For example, many governors, mayors, and city administrators are considering ways in which government can be made more entrepreneurial. Some of the most promising measures have included such tactics as permitting agencies that do not spend their entire budgets to keep some of the difference and rewarding employees with performance-based bonuses.

Government Performance and Results Act.   At the federal level, the Government Performance and Results Act of 1997 was designed to improve efficiency in the federal work force. The act required that all government agencies (except the Central Intelligence Agency) describe their new goals and establish methods for determining whether those goals are met. Goals may be broadly crafted (for example, reducing the time it takes to test a new drug before allowing it to be marketed) or narrowly crafted (for example, reducing the number of times a telephone rings before it is answered).

The "performance-based budgeting" implemented by President George W. Bush took this results-oriented approach a step further. Performance-based budgeting links agency funding to actual agency performance. Agencies are given specific performance criteria to meet, and the Office of Management and Budget rates each agency to determine how well it has performed. In theory, the amount of funds that each agency will receive in the next annual budget should be determined by the extent to which it has met the performance criteria.

Bureaucracy Changed Little, Though.   Efforts to improve bureaucratic efficiency are supported by the assertion that although society and industry have

[8]See, for example, David Osborne and Ted Gaebler, *Reinventing Government: How the Entrepreneurial Spirit Is Transforming the Public Sector* (Reading, Mass.: Addison-Wesley, 1992); and David Osborne and Peter Plastrik, *Banishing Bureaucracy: The Five Strategies for Reinventing Government* (Reading, Mass.: Addison-Wesley, 1997).

changed enormously in the past century, the form of government used in Washington, D.C., and in most states has remained the same. Some observers believe that the nation's diverse economic base cannot be administered competently by traditional bureaucratic organizations. Consequently, government must become more responsive to cope with the increasing number of demands placed on it. Political scientists Joel Aberbach and Bert Rockman take issue with this contention. They argue that the bureaucracy has changed significantly over time in response to changes desired by various presidential administrations. In their opinion, many of the problems attributed to the bureaucracy are, in fact, a result of the political decision-making process. Therefore, attempts to "reinvent" government by reforming the bureaucracy are misguided.[9]

Other analysts have suggested that the problem lies not so much with traditional bureaucratic organizations as with the people who run them. According to policy specialist Taegan Goddard and journalist Christopher Riback, what needs to be "reinvented" is not the machinery of government but public officials. After each election, new appointees to bureaucratic positions may find themselves managing complex, multimillion-dollar enterprises, yet they often are untrained for their jobs. According to these authors, if we want to reform the bureaucracy, we should focus on preparing newcomers for the task of "doing" government.[10]

Saving Costs through E-Government.   Many contend that the communications revolution brought about by the Internet has not only improved the efficiency with which government agencies deliver services to the public but also helped to reduce the cost of government. Agencies can now communicate with members of the public, as well as other agencies, via e-mail. Additionally, every federal agency now has a Web site to which citizens can go to find information about agency services instead of calling or appearing in person at a regional agency office. Since 2003, federal agencies have also been required by the Government Paperwork Elimination Act of 1998 to use electronic commerce whenever it is practical to do so and will save on costs.

Helping Out the Whistleblowers

The term **whistleblower** as applied to the federal bureaucracy has a special meaning: it is someone who blows the whistle on a gross governmental inefficiency or illegal action. Whistleblowers may be clerical workers, managers, or even specialists, such as scientists. The 1978 Civil Service Reform Act prohibits reprisals against whistleblowers by their superiors, and it set up the Merit Systems Protection Board as part of this protection. Many federal agencies also have toll-free hot lines that employees can use anonymously to report bureaucratic waste and inappropriate behavior. About 35 percent of all calls result in agency action or follow-up.

Further protection for whistleblowers was provided in 1989, when Congress passed the Whistle-Blower Protection Act. That act established an independent agency, the Office of Special Counsel (OSC), to investigate complaints brought by government employees who have been demoted, fired, or otherwise sanctioned for reporting government fraud or waste. There is little evidence, though, that potential whistleblowers truly have received more protection as a result of these endeavors. More than 40 percent of the employees who turned to the OSC for assistance in a recent three-year period stated that they were no longer employees of the government agencies on which they blew the whistle.

DID YOU KNOW . . .
That each year, federal administrative agencies produce rules that fill 7,500 pages in the *Code of Federal Regulations*?

Whistleblower
Someone who brings to public attention gross governmental inefficiency or an illegal action.

---

[9]Joel D. Aberbach and Bert A. Rockman, *In the Web of Politics: Three Decades of the U.S. Federal Executive* (Washington, D.C.: Brookings Institution Press, 2000).
[10]Taegan D. Goddard and Christopher Riback, *You Won—Now What? How Americans Can Make Democracy Work from City Hall to the White House* (New York: Scribner, 1998).

Some state and federal laws encourage employees to blow the whistle on their employers' wrongful actions by providing monetary incentives to the whistleblowers. At the federal level, the False Claims Act of 1986 allows a whistleblower who has disclosed information about a fraud against the U.S. government to receive a monetary award. If the government chooses to prosecute the case and wins, the whistleblower receives between 15 and 25 percent of the proceeds. If the government declines to intervene, the whistleblower can bring suit on behalf of the government, and if the suit is successful, will receive between 25 and 30 percent of the proceeds.

★ Bureaucrats as Politicians and Policymakers

Because Congress is unable to oversee the day-to-day administration of its programs, it must delegate certain powers to administrative agencies. Congress delegates the power to implement legislation to agencies through what is called **enabling legislation.** For example, the Federal Trade Commission was created by the Federal Trade Commission Act of 1914, the Equal Employment Opportunity Commission was created by the Civil Rights Act of 1964, and the Occupational Safety and Health Administration was created by the Occupational Safety and Health Act of 1970. The enabling legislation generally specifies the name, purpose, composition, functions, and powers of the agency.

In theory, the agencies should put into effect laws passed by Congress. Laws are often drafted in such vague and general terms, however, that they provide relatively little guidance to agency administrators as to how the laws should be implemented. This means that the agencies themselves must decide how best to carry out the wishes of Congress.

The discretion given to administrative agencies is not accidental. Congress has long realized that it lacks the technical expertise and the resources to monitor the implementation of its laws. Hence, the administrative agency is created to fill the gaps. This gap-filling role requires the agency to formulate administrative rules (regulations) to put flesh on the bones of the law. But it also forces the agency itself to become an unelected policymaker.

The Rulemaking Environment

Rulemaking does not occur in a vacuum. Suppose that Congress passes a new air-pollution law. The Environmental Protection Agency (EPA) might decide to implement the new law through a technical regulation on factory emissions. This proposed regulation would be published in the *Federal Register,* a daily government publication, so that interested parties would have an opportunity to comment on it. Individuals and companies that opposed parts or all of the rule might then try to convince the EPA to revise or redraft the regulation. Some parties might try to persuade the agency to withdraw the proposed regulation altogether. In any event, the EPA would consider these comments in drafting the final version of the regulation following the expiration of the comment period.

Waiting Periods and Court Challenges.   Once the final regulation has been published in the *Federal Register,* there is a sixty-day waiting period before the rule can be enforced. During that period, businesses, individuals, and state and local governments can ask Congress to overturn the regulation. After that sixty-day period has lapsed, the regulation can still be challenged in court by a party having a direct interest in the rule, such as a company that expects to incur significant costs in complying with it. The company could argue that the rule misinterprets the applic-

Enabling Legislation
A statute enacted by Congress that authorizes the creation of an administrative agency and specifies the name, purpose, composition, functions, and powers of the agency being created.

able law or goes beyond the agency's statutory purview. An allegation by the company that the EPA made a mistake in judgment probably would not be enough to convince the court to throw out the rule. The company instead would have to demonstrate that the rule itself was "arbitrary and capricious." To meet this standard, the company would have to show that the rule reflected a serious flaw in the EPA's judgment.

Controversies.   How agencies implement, administer, and enforce legislation has resulted in controversy. Decisions made by agencies charged with administering the Endangered Species Act have led to protests from farmers, ranchers, and others whose economic interests have been harmed. For example, the government decided to cut off the flow of irrigation water from Klamath Lake in Oregon in the summer of 2001. That action, which affected irrigation water for more than one thousand farmers in southern Oregon and northern California, was undertaken to save endangered suckerfish and salmon. It was believed that the lake's water level was so low that further use of the water for irrigation would harm these fish. The results of this decision were devastating for many farmers.

Negotiated Rulemaking

Since the end of World War II (1939–1945), companies, environmentalists, and other special interest groups have challenged government regulations in court. In the 1980s, however, the sheer wastefulness of attempting to regulate through litigation became more and more apparent. Today, a growing number of federal agencies encourage businesses and public-interest groups to become directly involved in drafting regulations. Agencies hope that such participation may help to prevent later courtroom battles over the meaning, applicability, and legal effect of the regulations.

Congress formally approved such a process, which is called *negotiated rulemaking,* in the Negotiated Rulemaking Act of 1990. The act authorizes agencies to allow those who will be affected by a new rule to participate in the rule-drafting process. If an agency chooses to engage in negotiated rulemaking, it must publish in the *Federal Register* the subject and scope of the rule to be developed, the parties affected significantly by the rule, and other information. Representatives of the affected groups and other interested parties then may apply to be members of the negotiating committee. The agency is represented on the committee, but a neutral third party (not the agency) presides over the proceedings. Once the committee members have reached agreement on the terms of the proposed rule, a notice is published in the *Federal Register,* followed by a period for comments by any person or organization interested in the proposed rule. Negotiated rulemaking often is conducted under the condition that the participants promise not to challenge in court the outcome of any agreement to which they were a party.

Bureaucrats Are Policymakers

Theories of public administration once assumed that bureaucrats do not make policy decisions but only implement the laws and policies promulgated by the president and legislative bodies. Many people continue to make this assumption. A more realistic view, which is now held by most bureaucrats and elected officials, is that the agencies and departments of government play important roles in policymaking. As we have seen, many government rules, regulations, and programs are in fact initiated by the bureaucracy, based on its expertise and scientific studies. How a law passed by Congress eventually is translated into concrete

A northern spotted owl sits on a tree in a national forest in Oregon. Environmentalists filed a lawsuit in 2003 seeking to stop logging on federal lands in southwestern Oregon, claiming the U.S. Fish and Wildlife Service had ignored the need to protect critical habitat for the owl, a threatened species. How should we balance the desire to protect rare species with our need for natural resources? (AP Photo/File)

action—from the forms to be filled out to decisions about who gets the benefits—usually is determined within each agency or department. Even the evaluation of whether a policy has achieved its purpose usually is based on studies that are commissioned and interpreted by the agency administering the program.

The bureaucracy's policymaking role often has been depicted by what traditionally has been called the "iron triangle." Recently, the concept of an "issue network" has been viewed as a more accurate description of the policymaking process.

Iron Triangles. In the past, scholars often described the bureaucracy's role in the policymaking process by using the concept of an **iron triangle**—a three-way alliance among legislators in Congress, bureaucrats, and interest groups. Consider as an example the development of agricultural policy. Congress, as one component of the triangle, includes two major committees concerned with agricultural policy, the House Committee on Agriculture and the Senate Committee on Agriculture, Nutrition, and Forestry. The Department of Agriculture, the second component of the triangle, has over 100,000 employees, plus thousands of contractors and consultants. Agricultural interest groups, the third component of the iron triangle in agricultural policymaking, include many large and powerful associations, such as the American Farm Bureau Federation, the National Cattleman's Association, and the Corn Growers Association. These three components of the iron triangle work together, formally or informally, to create policy.

For example, the various agricultural interest groups lobby Congress to develop policies that benefit their groups' interests. Members of Congress cannot afford to ignore the wishes of interest groups because those groups are potential sources of voter support and campaign contributions. The legislators in Congress also work closely with the Department of Agriculture, which, in implementing a policy, can develop rules that benefit—or at least do not hurt—certain industries or groups. The Department of Agriculture, in turn, supports policies that enhance the department's budget and powers. In this way, according to theory, agricultural policy is created that benefits all three components of the iron triangle. In 2002, the result was the Farm Security and Rural Investment Act, the largest agricultural subsidy act in U.S. history. What kind of bureaucracy does it take to administer subsidies on this scale? We look at this question in the *Politics and the Bureaucracy* feature.

Issue Networks. To be sure, the preceding discussion presents a much simplified picture of how the iron triangle works. With the growth in the complexity of government, policymaking also has become more complicated. The bureaucracy is larger, Congress has more committees and subcommittees, and interest groups are more powerful than ever. Although iron triangles still exist, often they are inadequate as descriptions of how policy is actually made. Frequently, different interest groups concerned about a certain area of policy have conflicting demands, which makes agency decision making difficult. Additionally, divided government in recent years has meant that departments are pressured by the president to take one approach and by Congress to take another.

Many scholars now use the term *issue network* to describe the policymaking process. An **issue network** consists of individuals or organizations that support a particular policy position on the environment, taxation, consumer safety, or some other issue. Typically, an issue network includes legislators and/or their staff members, interest groups, bureaucrats, scholars and other experts, and representatives from the media. Members of a particular issue network work together to influence the president, members of Congress, administrative agencies, and the

Iron Triangle
The three-way alliance among legislators, bureaucrats, and interest groups to make or preserve policies that benefit their respective interests.

Issue Network
A group of individuals or organizations—which may consist of legislators and legislative staff members, interest group leaders, bureaucrats, the media, scholars, and other experts—that supports a particular policy position on a given issue.

POLITICS AND THE BUREAUCRACY
Administering Farm Subsidies

In 1996, President Bill Clinton signed the Freedom to Farm Act. The goal of the new bill was to reduce the dependence of farmers on federal handouts. By 2000, however, subsidies were again high, providing 49 percent of net farm income. The Farm Security Act, signed by President Bush in 2002, increased the cost of the farm program by 77 percent. The bill even added new subsidies on several crops, including lentils and chickpeas.

OPPOSITION TO THE BILL

Naturally, the farm bill of 2002 was very popular in farm states, several of which were closely contested in the 2004 presidential election. Nevertheless, some conservatives who were opposed to increased government spending believed that the Republicans who drafted the bill had betrayed their principles.

Others worried about the implications for U.S. foreign policy. Mexican peasants, for example, find it difficult to grow corn as cheaply as subsidized American farmers. Putting rural Mexicans out of business may result in greater levels of illegal immigration into the United States. U.S. farm subsidies were an important cause of the collapse of the world trade talks held in September 2003 at Cancun, Mexico. Many economists have argued that opening markets for farmers in poor countries would do more to fight world poverty than any amount of foreign aid.

ADMINISTERING THE SUBSIDIES

The U.S. farm program is very complex, and therefore a substantial bureaucracy is needed to administer it. Had the philosophy behind the Freedom to Farm Act been allowed to continue, the size of the U.S. Department of Agriculture (USDA) bureaucracy would have shrunk. As it is, there are over 5,600 USDA offices spread throughout the United States. In many midwestern county seats, the post office and the "ag office" are the only two representatives of the federal government in town.

There is some justification for the large number of offices. The farm program is difficult for many farmers to understand. In addition to crop subsidies, there are conservation programs and set-aside programs (which pay farmers to take land out of production). To participate, farmers need detailed information on their land, including crop-yield histories. Farmers can ask for help from local USDA office personnel, but they often must visit the USDA office many times in a season to get the paperwork right.

FOR CRITICAL ANALYSIS

Much of the legislation Congress enacts is quite complicated. These complications lead to an extensive bureaucratic regime. Why do you think Congress creates complicated laws?

courts to affect public policy on a specific issue. Each policy issue may involve conflicting positions taken by two or more issue networks.

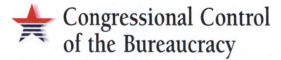

Congressional Control of the Bureaucracy

Many political pundits doubt whether Congress can meaningfully control the federal bureaucracy. These commentators forget that Congress specifies in an agency's "enabling legislation" the powers of the agency and the parameters within which it can operate. Additionally, Congress has the power of the purse and theoretically could refuse to authorize or appropriate funds for a particular agency (see the discussion of the budgeting process in Chapter 11). Whether Congress would actually take such a drastic measure would depend on the circumstances. It is clear, however, that Congress does have the legal authority to decide whether to fund or not to fund administrative agencies. Congress also can exercise oversight over agencies through investigations and hearings.

Congressional committees conduct investigations and hold hearings to oversee an agency's actions, reviewing them to ensure compliance with congressional intentions. The agency's officers and employees can be ordered to testify before a committee about the details of an action. Through these oversight activities, especially in the questions and comments of members of the House or Senate during the hearings, Congress indicates its positions on specific programs and issues.

Congress can ask the Government Accountability Office (GAO) to investigate particular agency actions as well. The Congressional Budget Office (CBO) also conducts oversight studies. The results of a GAO or CBO study may encourage Congress to hold further hearings or make changes in the law. Even if a law is not changed explicitly by Congress, however, the views expressed in any investigations and hearings are taken seriously by agency officials, who often act on those views.

In 1996, Congress passed the Congressional Review Act. The act created special procedures that can be employed to express congressional disapproval of particular agency actions. These procedures have rarely been used, however. Since the act's passage, the executive branch has issued over 15,000 regulations. Yet only eight resolutions of disapproval have been introduced, and none of these was passed by either chamber.

★ The Bureaucracy: Why Is It Important Today?

Federal bureaucrats have taken over an often-misunderstood policymaking function. They write rules and regulations that affect virtually every aspect of your life, including the car that you drive, the food that you eat, the education benefits that you receive, the way that you build your house, the places that you can go hiking, and the chemicals that are allowed in what you drink.

While everyone believes that Congress makes the laws, these laws are usually so vaguely worded that the federal bureaucracy must interpret them. Through their rulemaking functions, regulatory agencies staffed by bureaucrats create much of the "law" in the United States. Most of the body of environmental law, for example, consists of regulations issued by the Environmental Protection Agency. Some federal agencies have even levied taxes—a power that presumably only Congress can exercise. The federal bureaucracy has become so powerful and so pervasive in our everyday lives that some political scientists have called it the fourth branch of government.

MAKING A DIFFERENCE

★ What the Government Knows about You

The federal government collects billions of pieces of information on tens of millions of Americans each year. These data are stored in files and sometimes are exchanged among agencies. You are probably the subject of several federal records (for example, in the Social Security Administration; the Internal Revenue Service; and, if you are a male, the Selective Service).

Why Should You Care?

Verifying the information that the government has on you can be important. On several occasions, the records of two people with similar names have become confused. Sometimes innocent persons have had the criminal records of other persons erroneously inserted in their files. Such disasters are not always caused by bureaucratic error. One of the most common crimes in today's world is "identity theft," in which one person makes use of another person's personal identifiers (such as a Social Security number) to commit fraud. In some instances, identity thieves have been arrested or even jailed under someone else's name.

What Can You Do?

The 1966 Freedom of Information Act (FOIA) requires that the federal government release, at your request, any identifiable information it has about you or about any other subject. Ten categories of material are exempted, however (classified material, confidential material on trade secrets, internal personnel rules, personal medical files, and the like). To request material, write directly to the Freedom of Information Act officer at the agency in question (say, the Department of Education). You must have a relatively specific idea about the document or information you want to obtain.

A second law, the Privacy Act of 1974, gives you access specifically to information the government may have collected about you. This law allows you to review records on file with federal agencies and to check those records for possible inaccuracies.

If you want to look at any records or find out if an agency has a record on you, write to the agency head or Privacy Act officer, and address your letter to the specific agency. State that "under the provisions of the Privacy Act of 1974, 5 U.S.C. 522a, I hereby request a copy of (or access to) _____." Then describe the record that you wish to investigate.

The American Civil Liberties Union (ACLU) has published a manual, called *Your Right to Government Information,* that guides you through the steps of obtaining information from the federal government. You can order it online at the following Web site:

http://www.aclu.org

In the search box at the bottom of the page, enter "Marwick" (the name of the author). Alternatively, you can order the manual from the ACLU at the following address:

ACLU Publications
P.O. Box 4713
Trenton, NJ 08650-4713
1-800-775-ACLU

Key Terms

★ Chapter Summary

1 Bureaucracies are hierarchical organizations characterized by division of labor and extensive procedural rules. Bureaucracy is the primary form of organization of most major corporations and universities as well as governments.

2 Several theories have been offered to explain bureaucracies. The Weberian model posits that bureaucracies are rational, hierarchical organizations in which decisions are based on logical reasoning. The acquisitive model views top level bureaucrats as pressing for ever-larger budgets and staffs to augment their own sense of power and security. The monopolistic model focuses on the environment in which most government bureaucracies operate, stating that bureaucracies are inefficient and excessively costly to operate because they have no competitors.

3 Since the founding of the United States, the federal bureaucracy has grown from 50 to about 2.7 million employees (excluding the military). Federal, state, and local employees together make up over 15 percent of the nation's civilian labor force. The federal bureaucracy consists of fifteen cabinet departments, as well as a large number of independent executive agencies, independent regulatory agencies, and government corporations. These entities enjoy varying degrees of autonomy, visibility, and political support.

4 A federal bureaucracy of career civil servants was formed during Thomas Jefferson's presidency. Andrew Jackson implemented a spoils system through which he appointed his own political supporters. A civil service based on professionalism and merit was the goal of the Civil Service Reform Act of 1883. Concerns that the civil service be freed from the pressures of politics prompted the passage of the Hatch Act in 1939. Significant changes in the administration of the civil service were made by the Civil Service Reform Act of 1978.

5 There have been many attempts to make the federal bureaucracy more open, efficient, and responsive to the needs of U.S. citizens. The most important reforms have included sunshine and sunset laws, privatization, strategies to provide incentives for increased productivity and efficiency, and protection for whistleblowers.

6 Congress delegates much of its authority to federal agencies when it creates new laws. The bureaucrats who run these agencies may become important policymakers, because Congress has neither the time nor the technical expertise to oversee the administration of its laws. In the agency rulemaking process, a proposed regulation is published. A comment period follows, during which interested parties may offer suggestions for changes. Because companies and other organizations have challenged many regulations in court, federal agencies now are authorized to allow parties that will be affected by new regulations to participate in the rule-drafting process.

7 Congress exerts ultimate control over all federal agencies, because it controls the federal government's purse strings. It also establishes the general guidelines by which regulatory agencies must abide. The appropriations process may provide a way to send messages of approval or disapproval to particular agencies, as do congressional hearings and investigations of agency actions.

★ Selected Print and Media Resources

SUGGESTED READINGS

Burrough, Bryan. *Public Enemies: America's Greatest Crime Wave and the Birth of the F.B.I., 1933–1934.* New York: Penguin Press, 2004. Burroughs strips the myths from such romanticized criminals as John Dillinger while simultaneously showing how incompetent the F.B.I. often was in its initial years.

Gronlund, Ake, ed. *Electronic Government: Design, Applications, and Management.* Hershey, Pa.: Idea Group Publishing, 2002. This collection of essays focuses on how electronic government might improve government services as well as increase citizen participation in democratic processes.

Hilts, Philip J. *Protecting America's Health: The FDA, Business, and One Hundred Years of Regulation.* New York: Knopf, 2003. This history of the Food and Drug Administration (FDA) explains the origin and nature of the drug-approval process and the importance of clinical trials. The book provides a thorough examination of an important regulatory agency. Hilts is sympathetic to the agency and relatively critical of the pharmaceutical industry.

Light, Paul C. *Government's Greatest Achievements: From Civil Rights to Homeland Security.* Washington, D.C.: The Brookings Institution, 2002. The author stresses that for all of the criticisms made of bureaucracy, the government does work—as witnessed by its many achievements over the past half-century.

Wilson, James Q. *Bureaucracy: What Government Agencies Do and Why They Do It.* New York: Basic Books, 2000. Wilson provides a thorough description of the federal bureaucracy, with examples. He argues that bureaucracy behaves in consistent—and therefore predictable—ways and that institutional culture is a major determinant of an agency's behavior.

MEDIA RESOURCES

The Bureaucracy of Government: John Lukacs—A 1988 Bill Moyers special. Historian John Lukacs discusses the common political lament over the giant but invisible mechanism called bureaucracy.

Yes, Minister—A new member of the British cabinet bumps up against the machinations of a top civil servant in a comedy of manners. This popular 1980 BBC comedy is now available on DVD.

e-mocracy ★ E-Government

All federal government agencies (and virtually all state agencies) now have Web pages. Citizens can access these Web sites to find information and forms that, in the past, could normally be obtained only by going to a regional or local branch of the agency. For example, if you or a member of your family wants to learn about Social Security benefits available on retirement, you can simply access the Social Security Administration's Web site to find that information. A number of federal government agencies have also been active in discovering and prosecuting fraud perpetrated on citizens via the Internet.

Logging On

Numerous links to federal agencies and information on the federal government can be found at the U.S. government's official Web site. Go to

http://www.firstgov.gov

The Federal Web Locator is an excellent site to access if you want to find information on the bureaucracy. Its URL is

http://www.infoctr.edu/fwl

You may want to examine two publications available from the federal government to learn more about the federal bureaucracy. The first is the *Federal Register,* which is the official publication for executive-branch documents. You can find it at

http://www.gpoaccess.gov/fr/ browse.html

The second is the *United States Government Manual,* which describes the origins, purposes, and administrators of every federal department and agency. It is available at

http://www.gpoaccess.gov/gmanual/ browse.html

"The Plum Book," which lists the bureaucratic positions that can be filled by presidential appointment, is online at

http://www.gpoaccess.gov/plumbook/ index.html

To find telephone numbers for government agencies and personnel, you can go to

http://www.firstgov.gov/Agencies.shtml

Using InfoTrac for Political Research

You can use InfoTrac to research how the bureaucracy addresses a particular issue. A good example is the Endangered Species Act. Significant controversy exists around the implementation of this act. To use InfoTrac to research the Endangered Species Act, go to

http://www.infotrac-college.com

Log in and go to InfoTrac College Edition, then go to the Keyword guide. Type "endangered species act" in the search field. InfoTrac will present you with a list of articles, sorted by date. Choose a number of the most recent ones to use when making your analysis. Be sure to read articles that defend the act, as well as articles that criticize it.

ONLINE REVIEW

At **http://politicalscience.wadsworth. com/schmidt12**, you will find a free Study Guide to this book. For each chapter, there are two online quizzes to help you master the material.

• The **PoliPrep Self Study Assessment** provides a pre-test for each major section of the chapter. PoliPrep then generates a customized study plan. After you complete the study plan, a post-test evaluates your progress.

• The **Tutorial Quiz** for each chapter provides questions on the chapter contents, including the features. The questions are organized to match the major sections of the chapter.

CHAPTER 14

The Courts

BACKGROUND

The nine justices who sit on the bench of the Supreme Court are not elected to their posts. Rather, they are appointed by the president (and confirmed by the Senate). They also hold their offices for life, barring gross misconduct. Nevertheless, these justices are among the most important policymakers of this nation because they have the final say on how the U.S. Constitution—the "supreme law of the land"—should be interpreted.

In recent years, the Supreme Court has been strongly criticized by some for being too remote from the real world of politics and for making policy decisions on issues without regard for the practical consequences of those decisions. Would the justices act differently if they were elected and therefore had to campaign for their positions on the Court?

WHAT IF SUPREME COURT JUSTICES HAD TO CAMPAIGN?

Under the existing system, once approved by the Senate and seated on the high court's bench, a justice is free to decide cases as he or she wishes. Because they hold their offices for life, Supreme Court justices do not need to worry about job security. If, however, the justices were voted for and had to campaign for election and reelection, the situation could change dramatically.

For one thing, very likely the justices would have to devote a substantial amount of their time to their campaigns, just as members of Congress do. This would take time away from their judicial work, and decisions might receive significantly less deliberation than under the current system. Additionally, if the justices had to run for reelection to maintain their seats on the high court, it is only natural that public opinion and particularly the wishes of major campaign contributors would come into play.

INTEREST GROUPS AND CAMPAIGN COSTS

If state judicial campaigns and elections can serve as a guide, it is likely that interest groups that made sizable contributions to the justices' campaigns would wield at least some influence over the justices' decisions. In the thirty-nine states where members of the judiciary are elected, judges increasingly are using their discretion in deciding cases to satisfy public opinion and campaign contributors. Typically, the largest donors to state judicial campaigns are attorneys, political parties, and interest groups involved in civil litigation before the judges they are helping to elect.

In a survey of Texas judges sponsored by that state's supreme court, 48 percent of the judges responded that campaign contributions were "fairly influential" or "very influential" in guiding their decisions. In fact, the degree to which elected state judges are influenced by their political and financial supporters has caused some to claim that justice is increasingly "for sale."

POLITICAL IDEOLOGY

Humorist Finley Peter Dunne once said that "th' Supreme Court follows th' iliction returns." In other words, Democratic presidents tend to appoint liberal judges and justices to federal benches, and Republican presidents tend to appoint conservative judges and justices. Ultimately, then, the federal judiciary, including the Supreme Court, does change in response to election returns, but this process takes time.

Justices on the nation's highest court, because they are at the top of the judicial career ladder, sometimes end up sitting on the Supreme Court for decades. If these justices were elected, the ideological complexion of the Court probably would change much more quickly. A voting bloc of liberal or conservative justices might be short lived, with new alliances being formed after the next election. As a result, the decisions made by the Court, as the final interpreter of the Constitution, might not be very "final."

If the next election brought in justices with different ideological views, the Court could overturn the precedents set by the Court during the previous term. Of course, staggered terms could be used, as in the Senate, to ensure more continuity in judicial decision making.

FOR CRITICAL ANALYSIS

1. *Should Supreme Court justices be influenced by public opinion when making their decisions? Why or why not?*
2. *If Supreme Court justices were elected, would their decisions be less authoritative? Explain.*

As indicated in this chapter's opening *What If . . .* feature, the justices of the Supreme Court are not elected but rather are appointed by the president and confirmed by the Senate. The same is true for all other federal court judges. This fact does not mean that the federal judiciary is apolitical, however. Indeed, our courts play a larger role in making public policy than courts in most other countries in the world today.

As Alexis de Tocqueville, a French commentator on American society in the 1800s, noted, "scarcely any political question arises in the United States that is not resolved, sooner or later, into a judicial question."[1] Our judiciary forms part of our political process. The instant that judges interpret the law, they become actors in the political arena—policymakers working within a political institution. The most important political force within our judiciary is the United States Supreme Court.

How do courts make policy? Why do the federal courts play such an important role in American government? The answers to these questions lie, in part, in our colonial heritage. Most of American law is based on the English system, particularly the English *common law tradition*. In that tradition, the decisions made by judges constitute an important source of law. We open this chapter with an examination of this tradition and of the various sources of American law. We then look at the federal court system—its organization, how its judges are selected, how these judges affect policy, and how they are restrained by our system of checks and balances.

★ The Common Law Tradition

In 1066, the Normans conquered England, and William the Conqueror and his successors began the process of unifying the country under their rule. One of the ways they did this was to establish king's courts. Before the conquest, disputes had been settled according to local custom. The king's courts sought to establish a common or uniform set of rules for the whole country. As the number of courts and cases increased, portions of the most important decisions of each year were gathered together and recorded in *Year Books*. Judges settling disputes similar to ones that had been decided before used the *Year Books* as the basis for their decisions. If a case was unique, judges had to create new laws, but they based their decisions on the general principles suggested by earlier cases. The body of judge-made law that developed under this system is still used today and is known as the **common law.**

The practice of deciding new cases with reference to former decisions—that is, according to **precedent**—became a cornerstone of the English and American judicial systems and is embodied in the doctrine of ***stare decisis*** (pronounced *ster*-ay dih-si-ses), a Latin phrase that means "to stand on decided cases." The doctrine of *stare decisis* obligates judges to follow the precedents set previously by their own courts or by higher courts that have authority over them.

For example, a lower state court in California would be obligated to follow a precedent set by the California Supreme Court. That lower court, however, would not be obligated to follow a precedent set by the supreme court of another state, because each state court system is independent. Of course, when the United States Supreme Court decides an issue, all of the nation's other courts are obligated to abide by the Court's decision—because the Supreme Court is the highest court in the land.

The doctrine of *stare decisis* provides a basis for judicial decision making in all countries that have common law systems. Today, the United States, Britain,

Common Law
Judge-made law that originated in England from decisions shaped according to prevailing custom. Decisions were applied to similar situations and gradually became common to the nation.

Precedent
A court rule bearing on subsequent legal decisions in similar cases. Judges rely on precedents in deciding cases.

Stare Decisis
To stand on decided cases; the judicial policy of following precedents established by past decisions.

---

[1]Alexis de Tocqueville, *Democracy in America* (New York: Harper & Row, 1966), p. 248.

and several dozen other countries have common law systems. Generally, those
countries that were once colonies of Britain, including Australia, Canada, India,
and New Zealand, have retained their English common law heritage.

★ Sources of American Law

The body of American law includes the federal and state constitutions, statutes
passed by legislative bodies, administrative law, and case law—the legal principles
expressed in court decisions.

Constitutions

The constitutions of the federal government and the states set forth the general
organization, powers, and limits of government. The U.S. Constitution is the
supreme law of the land. A law in violation of the Constitution, no matter what
its source, may be declared unconstitutional and thereafter cannot be enforced.
Similarly, the state constitutions are supreme within their respective borders
(unless they conflict with the U.S. Constitution or federal laws and treaties made
in accordance with it). The Constitution thus defines the political playing field on
which state and federal powers are reconciled. The idea that the Constitution
should be supreme in certain matters stemmed from widespread dissatisfaction
with the weak federal government that had existed previously under the Articles
of Confederation adopted in 1781.

Statutes and Administrative Regulations

Although the English common law provides the basis for both our civil and criminal legal systems, statutes (laws enacted by legislatures) increasingly have
become important in defining the rights and obligations of individuals. Federal
statutes may relate to any subject that is a concern of the federal government and
may apply to areas ranging from hazardous waste to federal taxation. State
statutes include criminal codes, commercial laws, and laws covering a variety of

The courts are sometimes asked to
make decisions that have an impact on
our federal system. Here, New York
attorney general Elliot Spitzer points to
images of the polar ice caps at a press
conference. Eight states and New York
City have sued the federal government
to compel the Environmental Protection
Agency (EPA) to revise national
regulations governing power plant
emissions. Carbon dioxide emissions
from these plants are blamed in part for
global warming that is melting the polar
ice. If states employ the federal courts
in an attempt to change national
regulations, the courts may find
themselves in controversial territory.
(EPA/Jason Szenes/Landov)

other matters. Cities, counties, and other local political bodies also pass statutes, which are called ordinances. These ordinances may deal with such issues as zoning proposals and public safety. Rules and regulations issued by administrative agencies are another source of law. Today, much of the work of the courts consists of interpreting these laws and regulations and applying them to circumstances in cases before the courts.

Case Law

Because we have a common law tradition, in which the doctrine of *stare decisis* (described under "The Common Law Tradition" above) plays an important role, the decisions rendered by the courts also form an important body of law, collectively referred to as **case law.** Case law includes judicial interpretations of common law principles and doctrines as well as interpretations of the types of law just mentioned—constitutional provisions, statutes, and administrative agency regulations. As you learned in previous chapters, it is up to the courts, and particularly the Supreme Court, to decide what a constitutional provision or a statutory phrase means. In doing so, the courts, in effect, establish law. (We will discuss this policymaking function of the courts in more detail later in the chapter.)

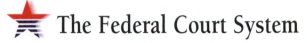

The Federal Court System

The United States has a dual court system. There are state courts and federal courts. Each of the fifty states, as well as the District of Columbia, has its own independent system of courts. This means that there are fifty-two court systems in total. Here we focus on the federal courts.

Basic Judicial Requirements

In any court system, state or federal, before a case can be brought before a court, certain requirements must be met. Two important requirements are jurisdiction and standing to sue.

Jurisdiction. A state court can exercise **jurisdiction** (the authority of the court to hear and decide a case) over the residents of a particular geographic area, such as a county or district. A state's highest court, or supreme court, has jurisdictional authority over all residents within the state. Because the Constitution established a federal government with limited powers, federal jurisdiction is also limited.

Article III, Section 1, of the U.S. Constitution limits the jurisdiction of the federal courts to cases that involve either a federal question or diversity of citizenship. A **federal question** arises when a case is based, at least in part, on the U.S. Constitution, a treaty, or a federal law. A person who claims that her or his rights under the Constitution, such as the right to free speech, have been violated could bring a case in a federal court. **Diversity of citizenship** exists when the parties to a lawsuit are from different states or (more rarely) when the suit involves a U.S. citizen and a government or citizen of a foreign country. The amount in controversy must be at least $75,000 before a federal court can take jurisdiction in a diversity case, however.

Standing to Sue. Another basic judicial requirement is standing to sue, or a sufficient "stake" in a matter to justify bringing suit. The party bringing a lawsuit must have suffered a harm, or have been threatened by a harm, as a result of the action that led to the dispute in question. Standing to sue also requires that the controversy at issue be a justiciable controversy. A *justiciable controversy* is a

Case Law
Judicial interpretations of common law principles and doctrines, as well as interpretations of constitutional law, statutory law, and administrative law.

Jurisdiction
The authority of a court to decide certain cases. Not all courts have the authority to decide all cases. Where a case arises and what its subject matter is are two jurisdictional issues.

Federal Question
A question that has to do with the U.S. Constitution, acts of Congress, or treaties. A federal question provides a basis for federal jurisdiction.

Diversity of Citizenship
The condition that exists when the parties to a lawsuit are citizens of different states, or when the parties are citizens of a U.S. state and citizens or the government of a foreign country. Diversity of citizenship can provide a basis for federal jurisdiction.

controversy that is real and substantial, as opposed to hypothetical or academic. In other words, a court will not give advisory opinions on hypothetical questions.

Types of Federal Courts

As you can see in Figure 14–1, the federal court system is basically a three-tiered model consisting of (1) U.S. district courts and various specialized courts of limited jurisdiction (not all of the latter are shown in the figure), (2) intermediate U.S. courts of appeals, and (3) the United States Supreme Court.

U.S. District Courts. The U.S. district courts are trial courts. **Trial courts** are what their name implies—courts in which trials are held and testimony is taken. The U.S. district courts are courts of **general jurisdiction,** meaning that they can hear cases involving a broad array of issues. Federal cases involving most matters typically are heard in district courts. The other courts on the lower tier of the model shown in Figure 14–1 are courts of **limited jurisdiction,** meaning that they can try cases involving only certain types of claims, such as tax claims or bankruptcy petitions.

There is at least one federal district court in every state. The number of judicial districts can vary over time owing to population changes and corresponding caseloads. Currently, there are ninety-four federal judicial districts. A party who is dissatisfied with the decision of a district court can appeal the case to the appropriate U.S. court of appeals, or federal **appellate court.** Figure 14–2 shows the jurisdictional boundaries of the district courts (which are state boundaries, unless otherwise indicated by dotted lines within a state) and of the U.S. courts of appeals.

U.S. Courts of Appeals. There are thirteen U.S. courts of appeals—also referred to as U.S. circuit courts of appeals. Twelve of these courts, including the U.S. Court of Appeals for the District of Columbia, hear appeals from the federal district courts located within their respective judicial circuits (geographic areas over which they exercise jurisdiction). The Court of Appeals for the Thirteenth Circuit, called the Federal Circuit, has national appellate jurisdiction over certain

Trial Court
The court in which most cases begin.

General Jurisdiction
Exists when a court's authority to hear cases is not significantly restricted. A court of general jurisdiction normally can hear a broad range of cases.

Limited Jurisdiction
Exists when a court's authority to hear cases is restricted to certain types of claims, such as tax claims or bankruptcy petitions.

Appellate Court
A court having jurisdiction to review cases and issues that were originally tried in lower courts.

FIGURE 14–1

The Federal Court System

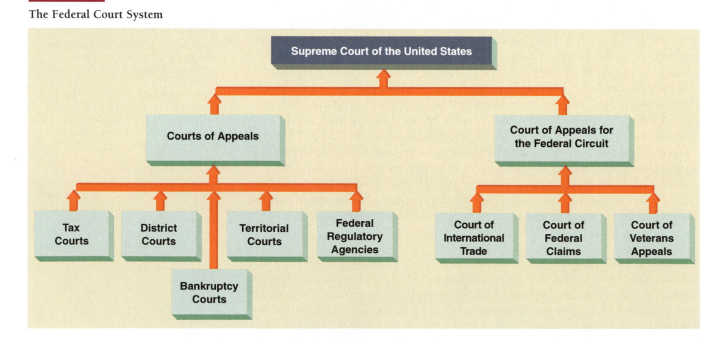

types of cases, such as cases involving patent law and those in which the U.S. government is a defendant.

Note that when an appellate court reviews a case decided in a district court, the appellate court does not conduct another trial. Rather, a panel of three or more judges reviews the record of the case on appeal, which includes a transcript of the trial proceedings, and determines whether the trial court committed an error. Usually, appellate courts do not look at questions of *fact* (such as whether a party did, in fact, commit a certain action, such as burning a flag) but at questions of *law* (such as whether the act of flag burning is a form of speech protected by the First Amendment to the Constitution). An appellate court will challenge a trial court's finding of fact only when the finding is clearly contrary to the evidence presented at trial or when there is no evidence to support the finding.

A party can petition the United States Supreme Court to review an appellate court's decision. The likelihood that the Supreme Court will grant the petition is slim, however, because the Court reviews only a very few of the cases decided by the appellate courts. This means that decisions made by appellate judges usually are final.

The United States Supreme Court. The highest level of the three-tiered model of the federal court system is the United States Supreme Court. When the Supreme Court came into existence in 1789, it had five justices. In the following years, more justices were added. Since 1869 there have been nine justices on the Court.

According to the language of Article III of the U.S. Constitution, there is only one national Supreme Court. All other courts in the federal system are considered

FIGURE 14–2

Geographic Boundaries of Federal District Courts and Circuit Courts of Appeals

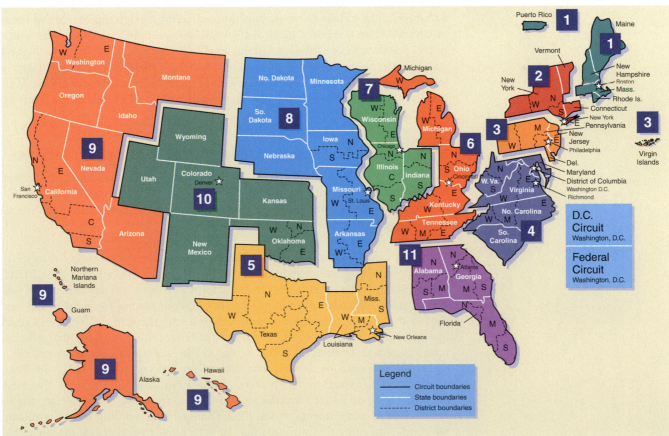

SOURCE: Administrative Office of The United States Courts.

"Do you ever have one of those days when everything seems un-Constitutional?"

"inferior." Congress is empowered to create other inferior courts as it deems necessary. The inferior courts that Congress has created include the district courts, the federal courts of appeals, and the federal courts of limited jurisdiction.

Although the Supreme Court can exercise original jurisdiction (that is, act as a trial court) in certain cases, such as those affecting foreign diplomats and those in which a state is a party, most of its work is as an appellate court. The Court hears appeals not only from the federal appellate courts but also from the highest state courts. Note, though, that the United States Supreme Court can review a state supreme court decision only if a federal question is involved. Because of its importance in the federal court system, we will look more closely at the Supreme Court starting on page 463.

Specialized Federal Courts and the War on Terrorism

As noted, the federal court system includes a variety of trial courts of limited jurisdiction, dealing with matters such as tax claims or international trade. The government's attempts to combat terrorism have drawn attention to certain specialized courts that meet in secret.

The FISA Court. The federal government created the first secret court in 1978. In that year, Congress passed the Foreign Intelligence Surveillance Act (FISA), which established a court to hear requests for warrants for the surveillance of suspected spies. Officials can request warrants without having to reveal to the suspect or to the public the information used to justify the warrant. The FISA court has approved almost all of the thousands of requests for warrants that officials have submitted. There is no public access to the court's proceedings or records.

In the aftermath of the terrorist attacks on September 11, 2001, the Bush administration expanded the powers of the FISA court. Previously, the FISA allowed secret domestic surveillance only if the "purpose" was foreign intelligence. Recent amendments to the FISA changed this wording to "a significant purpose"—meaning that warrants may now be requested to obtain evidence that can be used in criminal trials. Additionally, the court has the authority to approve physical as well as electronic searches, which means that officials may search a suspect's property without obtaining a warrant in open court and without notifying the subject.

Alien "Removal Courts." The FISA court is not the only court in which suspects' rights have been reduced. In response to the Oklahoma City bombing in 1995, Congress passed the Anti-Terrorism and Effective Death Penalty Act of 1996. The act included a provision creating an alien "removal court" to hear evidence against suspected "alien terrorists." The judges rule on whether there is probable cause for deportation. If so, a public deportation proceeding is held in a U.S. district court. The prosecution does not need to follow procedures that normally apply in criminal cases. In addition, the defendant cannot see the evidence that the prosecution used to secure the hearing.

Secret courts are not the only way in which terrorism has affected our legal system. In 2004, the United States Supreme Court decided two cases of historic importance. Both cases raised a significant issue: Should the government have the right to hold a U.S. citizen in indefinite custody without his being able to challenge his designation as an "enemy combatant"? We examine this issue in the *America's Security* feature on the following page.

Parties to Lawsuits

In most lawsuits, the parties are the plaintiff (the person or organization that initiates the lawsuit) and the defendant (the person or organization against whom the lawsuit is brought). There may be a number of plaintiffs and defendants in a single lawsuit. In the last several decades, many lawsuits have been brought by interest groups (see Chapter 7). Interest groups play an important role in our judicial system, because they **litigate**—bring to trial—or assist in litigating most cases of racial or gender-based discrimination, virtually all civil liberties cases,

Litigate
To engage in a legal proceeding or seek relief in a court of law; to carry on a lawsuit.

Counsel questions a witness as the judge and jury look on. Most jury trials have between six and twelve jurors. Some trials are held without juries. (John Neubauer/PhotoEdit)

AMERICA'S SECURITY
Holding U.S. Citizens as "Enemy Combatants"

In May 2002, at O'Hare International Airport in Chicago, agents of the Federal Bureau of Investigation arrested José Padilla, a U.S. citizen, as he entered the United States. U.S. attorney general John Ashcroft stated that the arrest disrupted "an unfolding terrorist plot to attack the United States by exploding a radioactive dirty bomb." Born in Brooklyn, Padilla was raised in Chicago, where he was convicted of numerous street crimes. He converted to Islam while in prison and later traveled to the Middle East, where, according to federal authorities, he joined the al Qaeda terrorist network.[*]

On the left is José Padilla, as shown in an undated driver's license photo. On the right is Yaser Esam Hamdi. (REUTERS/Florida DMV/Handout/Landov)

THE PRESIDENT MAKES A STATEMENT

Soon after Padilla's arrest, President George W. Bush declared him an "enemy combatant." The government argued that it could detain an enemy combatant indefinitely without bringing criminal charges and without permitting a court to rule on whether the "enemy combatant" designation was appropriate. Padilla was not permitted to see a lawyer for the next two years. In April 2004, however, his case came before the United States Supreme Court. The Court also heard the case of Yaser Esam Hamdi, a U.S. citizen who, unlike Padilla, was arrested in Afghanistan where he was allegedly fighting on behalf of the Taliban. Born in Louisiana, Hamdi enjoyed joint U.S.–Saudi Arabian citizenship at the time of his arrest.

HABEAS CORPUS

Article 1, Section 9, of the Constitution states the following: "The privilege of the Writ of Habeas Corpus shall not be suspended, unless when in Cases of Rebellion or Invasion the Public Safety may require it." A writ of *habeas corpus* is a court order directing the government to "produce the body" of a detainee so that the court can assess the legality of the detention. If *habeas corpus* applied to Padilla, he could ask a court to rule on his detention. A court might find no evidence that Padilla was an enemy combatant. It might also find that the detention violated the Constitution.

During the Civil War (1861–1865), Abraham Lincoln assumed that the president (as opposed to Congress) has the power to suspend *habeas corpus* in a national crisis. The Civil War, however, clearly qualified as a "Rebellion or Invasion," in the language of the Constitution. The question before the Supreme Court in the *Padilla* and *Hamdi* cases was this: Is the war on terrorism enough of an emergency to justify the suspension of *habeas corpus*?

THE VERDICT

The Court ruled on the *Padilla* and *Hamdi* cases in June 2004. In the end, Padilla's suit, which initially had seemed the strongest because he had been arrested in the United States, was dismissed on a technicality. The Court ruled that Padilla's lawyers had filed the case in the wrong court and against the wrong federal official.[†]

The Court chose the *Hamdi* case to affirm the rights of designated enemy combatants. Justice Sandra Day O'Connor wrote that "due process demands that a citizen held in the United States as an enemy combatant be given a meaningful opportunity to contest the factual basis for that detention before a neutral decisionmaker. . . . a state of war is not a blank check for the president when it comes to the rights of the nation's citizens."[‡]

On the same day that it ruled on *Padilla* and *Hamdi,* the Court also found that the noncitizen detainees held at Guantanamo Bay in Cuba were entitled to challenge the grounds for their confinement. (We presented this ruling in Chapter 4.)

In July 2004, Padilla's lawyers renewed his suit in accordance with the Court's guidelines and, in October, Hamdi was released following a settlement with the government under which he agreed to renounce his U.S. citizenship and return to Saudi Arabia.

FOR CRITICAL ANALYSIS

Under the Constitution, the government had the right to charge either of these individuals with the crime of treason. Why did the government not do this?

[*]Deborah Sontag, "Terror Suspect's Path from Streets to Brig," *The New York Times,* April 25, 2004, p. 1.

[†]*Rumsfeld v. Padilla,* 124 S.Ct. 2711 (2004).
[‡]*Hamdi v. Rumsfeld,* 124 S.Ct. 2633 (2004).

and more than one-third of the cases involving business matters. Interest groups also file *amicus curiae* (pronounced ah-*mee*-kous *kur*-ee-eye) **briefs,** or "friend of the court" briefs, in more than 50 percent of these kinds of cases.

Sometimes interest groups or other plaintiffs will bring a **class-action suit,** in which whatever the court decides will affect all members of a class similarly situated (such as users of a particular product manufactured by the defendant in the lawsuit). The strategy of class-action lawsuits was pioneered by such groups as the National Association for the Advancement of Colored People (NAACP), the Legal Defense Fund, and the Sierra Club, whose leaders believed that the courts would offer a more sympathetic forum for their views than would Congress.

Procedural Rules

Both the federal and the state courts have established procedural rules that shape the litigation process. These rules are designed to protect the rights and interests of the parties, to ensure that the litigation proceeds in a fair and orderly manner, and to identify the issues that must be decided by the court—thus saving court time and costs. Court decisions may also apply to trial procedures. For example, the Supreme Court has held that the parties' attorneys cannot discriminate against prospective jurors on the basis of race or gender. Some lower courts have also held that people cannot be excluded from juries because of their sexual orientation or religion.

The parties must comply with procedural rules and with any orders given by the judge during the course of the litigation. When a party does not follow a court's order, the court can cite him or her for contempt. A party who commits *civil* contempt (failing to comply with a court's order for the benefit of another party to the proceeding) can be taken into custody, fined, or both, until the party complies with the court's order. A party who commits *criminal* contempt (obstructing the administration of justice or bringing the court into disrespect) also can be taken into custody and fined but cannot avoid punishment by complying with a previous order.

Throughout this text, you have read about how technology is affecting all areas of government. The judiciary is no exception. Today's courts continue to place opinions and other information online. Increasingly, lawyers are expected to file court documents electronically. There is little doubt that in the future we will see more court proceedings being conducted through use of the Internet.

The Supreme Court at Work

The Supreme Court begins its regular annual term on the first Monday in October and usually adjourns in late June or early July of the next year. Special sessions may be held after the regular term ends, but only a few cases are decided in this way. More commonly, cases are carried over until the next regular session.

Of the total number of cases that are decided each year, those reviewed by the Supreme Court represent less than one-half of 1 percent. Included in these, however, are decisions that profoundly affect our lives. In recent years, the United States Supreme Court has decided issues involving capital punishment, affirmative action programs, religious freedom, assisted suicide, abortion, busing, term limits for congresspersons, sexual harassment, pornography, states' rights, limits on federal jurisdiction, and many other matters with significant consequences for the nation. Because the Supreme Court exercises a great deal of discretion over the types of cases it hears, it can influence the nation's policies by issuing decisions in some types of cases and refusing to hear appeals in others, thereby allowing lower court decisions to stand.

Amicus Curiae **Brief**
A brief (a document containing a legal argument supporting a desired outcome in a particular case) filed by a third party, or *amicus curiae* (Latin for "friend of the court"), who is not directly involved in the litigation but who has an interest in the outcome of the case.

Class-Action Suit
A lawsuit filed by an individual seeking damages for "all persons similarly situated."

Which Cases Reach the Supreme Court?

Many people are surprised to learn that in a typical case, there is no absolute right of appeal to the United States Supreme Court. The Court's appellate jurisdiction is almost entirely discretionary—the Court can choose which cases it will decide. The justices never explain their reasons for hearing certain cases and not others, so it is difficult to predict which case or type of case the Court might select. Chief Justice William Rehnquist, in his description of the selection process in *The Supreme Court: How It Was, How It Is*,[2] said that the decision of whether to accept a case "strikes me as a rather subjective decision, made up in part of intuition and in part of legal judgment."

Factors That Bear on the Decision.   Factors that bear on the decision include whether a legal question has been decided differently by various lower courts and needs resolution by the highest court, whether a lower court's decision conflicts with an existing Supreme Court ruling, and whether the issue could have significance beyond the parties to the dispute. In its 2004–2005 term, the Court agreed to review a variety of cases of great importance. Questions before the Court

[2]William H. Rehnquist, *The Supreme Court: How It Was, How It Is* (New York: Morrow, 1987).

In her chambers, Justice Ruth Bader Ginsburg works on her caseload with one of her law clerks. Each justice has four law clerks, who typically are culled from the "best and the brightest" graduates from U.S. law schools. Some critics of the Supreme Court's practices argue that the clerks have too much power and influence over the Court's decision making. (Paul Conklin/PhotoEdit)

included the following: In a criminal jury trial, must sentences be based exclusively on facts proven before the jury? Can states decriminalize medical marijuana in circumstances where the commerce clause of the Constitution does not apply? Do consumers have a right to purchase wine that is shipped directly from out-of-state wineries? Can the government seize property under its powers of eminent domain and then turn the property over to a private developer?

Another factor is whether the solicitor general is pressuring the Court to take a case. The solicitor general, a high-ranking presidential appointee within the Justice Department, represents the national government before the Supreme Court and promotes presidential policies in the federal courts. He or she decides what cases the government should ask the Supreme Court to review and what position the government should take in cases before the Court.

Granting Petitions for Review. If the Court decides to grant a petition for review, it will issue a **writ of *certiorari*** (pronounced sur-shee-uh-*rah*-ree). The writ orders a lower court to send the Supreme Court a record of the case for review. More than 90 percent of the petitions for review are denied. A denial is not a decision on the merits of a case, nor does it indicate agreement with the lower court's opinion. (The judgment of the lower court remains in force, however.) Therefore, denial of the writ has no value as a precedent. The Court will not issue a writ unless at least four justices approve of it. This is called the **rule of four.**[3]

Writ of *Certiorari*
An order issued by a higher court to a lower court to send up the record of a case for review.

Rule of Four
A United States Supreme Court procedure by which four justices must vote to grant a petition for review if a case is to come before the full court.

Deciding Cases

Once the Supreme Court grants *certiorari* in a particular case, the justices do extensive research on the legal issues and facts involved in the case. (Of course, some preliminary research is necessary before deciding to grant the petition for review.) Each justice is entitled to four law clerks, who undertake much of the research and preliminary drafting necessary for the justice to form an opinion.[4]

The Court normally does not hear any evidence, as is true with all appeals courts. The Court's consideration of a case is based on the abstracts, the record, and the briefs. The attorneys are permitted to present **oral arguments.** All statements and the justices' questions are tape-recorded during these sessions. Unlike the practice in most courts, lawyers addressing the Supreme Court can be (and often are) questioned by the justices at any time during oral argument.

The justices meet to discuss and vote on cases in conferences held throughout the term. In these conferences, in addition to deciding cases currently before the Court, the justices determine which new petitions for *certiorari* to grant. These conferences take place in the oak-paneled chamber and are strictly private—no stenographers, tape recorders, or video cameras are allowed. Two pages used to be in attendance to wait on the justices while they were in conference, but fear of information leaks caused the Court to stop this practice.[5]

Oral Arguments
The verbal arguments presented in person by attorneys to an appellate court. Each attorney presents reasons to the court why the court should rule in her or his client's favor.

Decisions and Opinions

When the Court has reached a decision, its opinion is written. The **opinion** contains the Court's ruling on the issue or issues presented, the reasons for its decision, the rules of law that apply, and other information. In many cases, the decision of

Opinion
The statement by a judge or a court of the decision reached in a case. The opinion sets forth the applicable law and details the reasoning on which the ruling was based.

---

[3]The "rule of four" is modified when seven or fewer justices participate, which occurs from time to time. When that happens, as few as three justices can grant *certiorari*.

[4]For a former Supreme Court law clerk's account of the role these clerks play in the high court's decision-making process, see Edward Lazarus, *Closed Chambers: The First Eyewitness Account of the Epic Struggles inside the Supreme Court* (New York: Times Books, 1998).

[5]It turned out that one supposed information leak came from lawyers making educated guesses.

Affirm
To declare that a court ruling is valid and must stand.

Reverse
To annul or make void a court ruling on account of some error or irregularity.

Remand
To send a case back to the court that originally heard it.

Unanimous Opinion
A court opinion or determination on which all judges agree.

Majority Opinion
A court opinion reflecting the views of the majority of the judges.

Concurring Opinion
A separate opinion prepared by a judge who supports the decision of the majority of the court but who wants to make or clarify a particular point or to voice disapproval of the grounds on which the decision was made.

Dissenting Opinion
A separate opinion in which a judge dissents from (disagrees with) the conclusion reached by the majority on the court and expounds his or her own views about the case.

the lower court is **affirmed,** resulting in the enforcement of that court's judgment or decree. If the Supreme Court believes that a reversible error was committed during the trial or that the jury was instructed improperly, however, the decision will be **reversed.** Sometimes the case will be **remanded** (sent back to the court that originally heard the case) for a new trial or other proceeding. For example, a lower court might have held that a party was not entitled to bring a lawsuit under a particular law. If the Supreme Court holds to the contrary, it will remand (send back) the case to the trial court with instructions that the trial go forward.

The Court's written opinion sometimes is unsigned; this is called an opinion *per curiam* ("by the court"). Typically, the Court's opinion is signed by all the justices who agree with it. When in the majority, the chief justice assigns the opinion and often writes it personally. When the chief justice is in the minority, the senior justice on the majority side decides who writes the opinion.

When all justices unanimously agree on an opinion, the opinion is written for the entire Court (all the justices) and can be deemed a **unanimous opinion.** When there is not a unanimous opinion, a **majority opinion** is written, outlining the views of the majority of the justices involved in the case. Often, one or more justices who feel strongly about making or emphasizing a particular point that is not made or emphasized in the unanimous or majority written opinion will write a **concurring opinion.** That means the justice writing the concurring opinion agrees (concurs) with the conclusion given in the majority written opinion, but for different reasons. Finally, in other than unanimous opinions, one or more dissenting opinions are usually written by those justices who do not agree with the majority. The **dissenting opinion** is important because it often forms the basis of the arguments used years later if the Court reverses the previous decision and establishes a new precedent.

Shortly after the opinion is written, the Supreme Court announces its decision from the bench. At that time, the opinion is made available to the public at the office of the clerk of the Court. The clerk also releases the opinion for online publication. Ultimately, the opinion is published in the *United States Reports,* which is the official printed record of the Court's decisions.

★ The Selection of Federal Judges

All federal judges are appointed. The Constitution, in Article II, Section 2, states that the president appoints the justices of the Supreme Court with the advice and consent of the Senate. Congress has provided the same procedure for staffing other federal courts. This means that the Senate and the president jointly decide who shall fill every vacant judicial position, no matter what the level.

There are over 850 federal judgeships in the United States. Once appointed to such a judgeship, a person holds that job for life. Judges serve until they resign, retire voluntarily, or die. Federal judges who engage in blatantly illegal conduct may be removed through impeachment, although such action is rare.

Judicial Appointments

Judicial candidates for federal judgeships are suggested to the president by the Department of Justice, senators, other judges, the candidates themselves, and lawyers' associations and other interest groups. In selecting a candidate to nominate for a judgeship, the president considers not only the person's competence but also other factors, including the person's political philosophy (as will be discussed shortly), ethnicity, and gender.

The nomination process—no matter how the nominees are obtained—always works the same way. The president makes the actual nomination, transmitting the name to the Senate. The Senate then either confirms or rejects the nomination. To reach a conclusion, the Senate Judiciary Committee (operating through subcommittees) invites testimony, both written and oral, at its various hearings. A practice used in the Senate, called **senatorial courtesy,** is a constraint on the president's freedom to appoint federal district judges. Senatorial courtesy allows a senator of the president's political party to veto a judicial appointment in her or his state. During much of American history, senators from the "opposition" party (the party to which the president did not belong) also enjoyed the right of senatorial courtesy, although their veto power varied over time.

Federal District Court Judgeship Nominations. Although the president officially nominates federal judges, in the past the nomination of federal district court judges actually originated with a senator or senators of the president's party from the state in which there was a vacancy. In effect, judicial appointments were a form of political patronage. President Jimmy Carter (1977–1981) ended this tradition by establishing independent commissions to oversee the initial nomination process. President Ronald Reagan (1981–1989) abolished Carter's nominating commissions and established complete presidential control of nominations.

In 2000, Orrin Hatch, Republican chair of the Senate Judiciary Committee, announced that the opposition party (at that point, the Democrats) would no longer be allowed to invoke senatorial courtesy. The implementation of the new policy was delayed when Republican senator James Jeffords of Vermont left the Republican Party. Jeffords' departure turned control of the Senate over to the Democrats. After the 2002 elections, however, when the Republicans regained control of the Senate, they put the new policy into effect.[6]

Federal Courts of Appeals Appointments. There are many fewer federal courts of appeals appointments than federal district court appointments, but they are more important. This is because federal appellate judges handle more important matters, at least from the point of view of the president, and therefore presidents take a keener interest in the nomination process for such judgeships. Also, the U.S. courts of appeals have become "stepping-stones" to the Supreme Court.

---

[6]John Anthony Maltese, "Anatomy of a Confirmation Mess: Recent Trends in the Federal Judicial Selection Process," April 15, 2004. This article is available as part of a *Jurist* online symposium. Go to http://jurist.law.pitt.edu/forum/symposium-jc/index.php.

Senatorial Courtesy
In federal district court judgeship nominations, a tradition allowing a senator to veto a judicial appointment in his or her state.

Republican senators call for an end to a Democratic filibuster. From left to right are senators Kay Bailey Hutchinson of Texas, Rick Santorum of Pennsylvania, and Orrin Hatch of Utah. The filibuster blocked a vote on federal appeals court nominee Miguel Estrada, a conservative Hispanic attorney. Should minority group members support a nominee from their own group even when the nominee's political philosophy might not be shared by most group members? Why or why not? (REUTERS/Brendan McDermid/Landov)

Supreme Court Appointments.   As we have described, the president nominates Supreme Court justices.[7] As you can see in Table 14–1, which summarizes the background of all Supreme Court justices to 2005, the most common occupational background of the justices at the time of their appointment has been private legal practice or state or federal judgeship. Those nine justices who were in federal executive posts at the time of their appointment held the high offices of secretary of state, comptroller of the treasury, secretary of the navy, postmaster general, secretary of the interior, chairman of the Securities and Exchange

[7]For a discussion of the factors that may come into play during the process of nominating Supreme Court justices, see David A. Yalof, *Pursuit of Justices: Presidential Politics and the Selection of Supreme Court Nominees* (Chicago: University of Chicago Press, 1999).

TABLE 14–1

Background of Supreme Court Justices to 2005

	NUMBER OF JUSTICES (108 = TOTAL)
Occupational Position before Appointment	
Private legal practice	25
State judgeship	21
Federal judgeship	28
U.S. attorney general	7
Deputy or assistant U.S. attorney general	2
U.S. solicitor general	2
U.S. senator	6
U.S. representative	2
State governor	3
Federal executive post	9
Other	3
Religious Background	
Protestant	83
Roman Catholic	11
Jewish	6
Unitarian	7
No religious affiliation	1
Age on Appointment	
Under 40	5
41–50	31
51–60	58
61–70	14
Political Party Affiliation	
Federalist (to 1835)	13
Jeffersonian Republican (to 1828)	7
Whig (to 1861)	1
Democrat	44
Republican	42
Independent	1
Educational Background	
College graduate	92
Not a college graduate	16
Gender	
Male	106
Female	2
Race	
White	106
African American	2

SOURCES: Congressional Quarterly, *Congressional Quarterly's Guide to the U.S. Supreme Court* (Washington, D.C.: Congressional Quarterly Press, 1996); and authors' update.

Commission, and secretary of labor. In the "Other" category under "Occupational Position before Appointment" in Table 14–1 are two justices who were professors of law (including William H. Taft, a former president) and one justice who was a North Carolina state employee with responsibility for organizing and revising the state's statutes.

Partisanship and Judicial Appointments

Ideology plays an important role in the president's choices for judicial appointments. In most circumstances, the president appoints judges or justices who belong to the president's own political party. Presidents see their federal judiciary appointments as the one sure way to institutionalize their political views long after they have left office. By 1993, for example, Presidents Ronald Reagan and George H. W. Bush together had appointed nearly three-quarters of all federal court judges. This preponderance of Republican-appointed federal judges strengthened the legal moorings of the conservative social agenda on a variety of issues, ranging from abortion to civil rights. Nevertheless, President Bill Clinton had the opportunity to appoint about two hundred federal judges, thereby shifting the ideological make-up of the federal judiciary.

By the time you read this book, one or more of the Supreme Court justices may have retired. Should this happen, the president will be in a position to exercise considerable influence over the future ideological make-up of the Supreme Court. As many presidents have learned, however, there is no guarantee that once a justice is appointed to the bench, that justice's decisions will please the president.

The Senate's Role

Ideology also plays a large role in the Senate's confirmation hearings, and presidential nominees to the Supreme Court have not always been confirmed. In fact, almost 20 percent of presidential nominations to the Supreme Court have been either rejected or not acted on by the Senate. There have been many acrimonious battles over Supreme Court appointments when the Senate and the president have not seen eye to eye about political matters.

The U.S. Senate had a long record of refusing to confirm the president's judicial nominations from the beginning of Andrew Jackson's presidency in 1829 to the end of Ulysses Grant's presidency in 1877. From 1894 until 1968, however, only three nominees were not confirmed. Then, from 1968 through 1987, four presidential nominees to the highest court were rejected. One of the most controversial Supreme Court nominations was that of Clarence Thomas, who underwent an extremely volatile confirmation hearing in 1991, replete with charges against him of sexual harassment. He was ultimately confirmed by the Senate, however.

President Bill Clinton had little trouble gaining approval for both of his nominees to the Supreme Court: Ruth Bader Ginsburg and Stephen Breyer. Clinton found it more difficult, however, to secure Senate approval for his judicial nominations to the lower courts, as did President George W. Bush. In fact, during the late 1990s and early 2000s the duel between the Senate and the president aroused considerable concern about the consequences of the increasingly partisan and ideological tension over federal judicial appointments. As a result of Senate delays in confirming nominations, the number of judicial vacancies mounted, as did the backlog of cases pending in the federal courts. Especially given the backlog of judicial appointments, is it appropriate for senators to consider purely political questions when voting on a judicial nominee? We look at this question in the *Which Side Are You On?* feature on the next page.

★ ★ ★ ★ ★ ★ ★ ★ ★ ★ ★ ★ ★ ★

DID YOU KNOW . . .
That Justice Clarence Thomas is often called the "silent justice" because he asks so few questions during oral arguments **?**

WHICH SIDE ARE YOU ON?
Is the Process of Confirming Judicial Nominees Too Political?

In January 2004, President George W. Bush appointed Charles Pickering as a federal appellate court judge using a temporary "recess appointment." In so doing, he abandoned his attempt to push Pickering's appointment through the Senate. Pickering was far from being the only one of Bush's judicial nominees to be blocked by a politicized confirmation process. President Bill Clinton also had a great deal of trouble in getting his nominees confirmed. Has the politicization of the confirmation process gone too far?

JUDICIAL CONFIRMATIONS HAVE BECOME TOO POLITICAL

Since 1987, when the Senate refused to confirm the appointment of Robert Bork to the Supreme Court, serious battles over judicial nominees have become commonplace. Those who believe that the confirmation process has become too political claim that these attempts to block nominees are based on a doctrine of "payback"—making trouble for one party's nominees because that party made trouble for your nominees in the past. Instead, nominees should be assessed on the basis of their qualifications alone. The ideology of a judge should not matter, because judges should base their rulings on the law, not their personal preferences.

POLITICS CANNOT BE AVOIDED

Others say that the system is working as it should. Politics have played a role in selecting judges since the administration of George Washington. Most nominees are confirmed without dispute. As of 2004, the vacancy rate on the federal bench was at its lowest point in thirteen years. Those nominees who run into trouble are usually the most conservative Republican nominees or the most liberal Democratic ones. It is legitimate to evaluate a candidate's judicial ideology when that ideology is strongly held and likely to influence the judge's rulings.

Senator Barbara Boxer, Democrat of California, speaks during a thirty-hour filibuster on President Bush's judicial nominees. Next to Boxer is a chart claiming that the Democrats were blocking fewer Bush nominees than the Republicans had blocked when Bill Clinton was president. (AP Photo/APTN)

WHAT'S YOUR POSITION?

If it is impossible to eliminate politics completely from the confirmation process, in what ways can the effects of politics be minimized?

GOING ONLINE

You can find an online symposium on the judicial confirmation process at the Jurist Web site. Go to **http://jurist.law.pitt.edu/forum/symposium-jc/index.php**. *Jurist* is a gateway to legal instruction, information, and scholarship. It is edited by a team of professors from law schools across the United States and around the world. *Jurist* is hosted by the University of Pittsburgh.

 Policymaking and the Courts

The partisan battles over judicial appointments reflect an important reality in today's American government: the importance of the judiciary in national politics. Because appointments to the federal bench are for life, the ideology of judicial appointees can affect national policy for years to come. Although the primary function of judges in our system of government is to interpret and apply the laws, inevitably judges make policy when carrying out this task. One of the major policymaking tools of the federal courts is their power of judicial review.

Judicial Review

Remember from Chapter 2 that the power of the courts to determine whether a law or action by the other branches of government is constitutional is known as the power of *judicial review*. This power enables the judicial branch to act as a check on the other two branches of government, in line with the system of checks and balances established by the U.S. Constitution.

The power of judicial review is not mentioned in the Constitution, however. Rather, it was established by the United States Supreme Court's decision in *Marbury v. Madison*.[8] In that case, in which the Court declared that a law passed by Congress violated the Constitution, the Court claimed such a power for the judiciary:

> It is emphatically the province and duty of the Judicial Department to say what the law is. Those who apply the rule to a particular case must of necessity expound and interpret that rule. If two laws conflict with each other, the courts must decide on the operation of each.

If a federal court declares that a federal or state law or policy is unconstitutional, the court's decision affects the application of the law or policy only within that court's jurisdiction. For this reason, the higher the level of the court, the greater the impact of the decision on society. Because of the Supreme Court's national jurisdiction, its decisions have the greatest impact. For example, when the Supreme Court held that an Arkansas state constitutional amendment limiting the terms of congresspersons was unconstitutional, laws establishing term limits in twenty-three other states also were invalidated.[9]

Some claim that the power of judicial review gives unelected judges and justices on federal court benches too much influence over national policy. Others argue that the powers exercised by the federal courts, particularly the power of judicial review, are necessary to protect our constitutional rights and liberties. Built into our federal form of government is a system of checks and balances. If the federal courts did not have the power of judicial review, there would be no governmental body to check Congress's lawmaking authority.

Judicial Activism and Judicial Restraint

Judicial scholars like to characterize different judges and justices as being either "activist" or "restraintist." The doctrine of **judicial activism** rests on the conviction that the federal judiciary should take an active role by using its powers to check the activities of Congress, state legislatures, and administrative agencies when those governmental bodies exceed their authority. One of the Supreme Court's most activist eras was the period from 1953 to 1969, when the Court was headed by Chief Justice Earl Warren. The Warren Court propelled the civil rights movement forward by holding, among other things, that laws permitting racial segregation violated the equal protection clause.

In contrast, the doctrine of **judicial restraint** rests on the assumption that the courts should defer to the decisions made by the legislative and executive branches, because members of Congress and the president are elected by the people whereas members of the federal judiciary are not. Because administrative agency personnel normally have more expertise than the courts do in the areas regulated by the agencies, the courts likewise should defer to agency rules and decisions. In other words, under the doctrine of judicial restraint, the courts should not thwart the implementation of legislative acts and agency rules unless they are clearly unconstitutional.

Judicial Activism
A doctrine holding that the Supreme Court should take an active role by using its powers to check the activities of governmental bodies when those bodies exceed their authority.

Judicial Restraint
A doctrine holding that the Supreme Court should defer to the decisions made by the elected representatives of the people in the legislative and executive branches.

---

[8]5 U.S. 137 (1803).
[9]*U.S. Term Limits v. Thornton*, 514 U.S. 779 (1995).

Judicial activism sometimes is linked with liberalism, and judicial restraint with conservatism. In fact, though, a conservative judge can be activist, just as a liberal judge can be restraintist. In the 1950s and 1960s, the Supreme Court was activist and liberal. Some observers believe that the Rehnquist Court, with its conservative majority, has become increasingly activist since the 1990s. Some go even further and claim that the federal courts, including the Supreme Court, wield too much power in our democracy.

Strict versus Broad Construction

Strict Construction
A judicial philosophy that looks to the "letter of the law" when interpreting the Constitution or a particular statute.

Broad Construction
A judicial philosophy that looks to the context and purpose of a law when making an interpretation.

Other terms that are often used to describe a justice's philosophy are *strict construction* and *broad construction*. Justices who believe in **strict construction** look to the "letter of the law" when they attempt to interpret the Constitution or a particular statute. Those who favor **broad construction** try to determine the context and purpose of the law.

As with the doctrines of judicial restraint and judicial activism, strict construction is often associated with conservative political views, and broad construction is often linked with liberalism. These traditional political associations sometimes appear to be reversed, however. Consider the Eleventh Amendment to the Constitution, which rules out lawsuits in federal courts "against one of the United States by Citizens of another State, or by Citizens or Subjects of any Foreign State." Nothing is said about citizens suing their *own* states, and strict construction would therefore find such suits to be constitutional. Conservative justices, however, have construed this amendment broadly to deny citizens the constitutional right to sue their own states in most circumstances. John T. Noonan, Jr., a federal appellate court judge who was appointed by a Republican president, has described these rulings as "adventurous."[10]

Ideology and the Rehnquist Court

William H. Rehnquist became the sixteenth chief justice of the Supreme Court in 1986, after fifteen years as an associate justice. He was known as a strong anchor of the Court's conservative wing. With Rehnquist's appointment as chief justice, it seemed to observers that the Court necessarily would become more conservative.

This, in fact, has happened. The Court began to take a rightward shift shortly after Rehnquist became chief justice, and the Court's rightward movement continued as other conservative appointments to the bench were made during the Reagan and George H. W. Bush administrations. Today, three of the justices (William Rehnquist, Antonin Scalia, and Clarence Thomas) are notably conservative in their views. Four of the justices (John Paul Stevens, David Souter, Ruth Bader Ginsburg, and Stephen Breyer) hold liberal-to-moderate views. The middle of the Court is now occupied by two moderate-to-conservative justices, Sandra Day O'Connor and Anthony Kennedy. O'Connor and Kennedy usually provide the "swing votes" on the Court in controversial cases. The ideological alignments on the Court vary, however, depending on the issues involved in particular cases.

Certainly, today's Supreme Court has moved far from the liberal positions taken by the Court under Earl Warren (1953–1969) and under Warren Burger (1969–1986). Since the mid-1990s, the Court has issued many conservative rulings, some of which you have already read about in this text. Another judicial controversy with ideological overtones is the following: Should the Supreme Court ever consider rulings by foreign judges when drafting its opinions? We examine this question in the *Global View* feature on page 474.

---

[10]John T. Noonan, Jr., *Narrowing the Nation's Power: The Supreme Court Sides with the States* (Berkeley: University of California Press, 2002).

CONSERVATIVE

William Rehnquist   Antonin Scalia   Clarence Thomas

SWING VOTES

Sandra Day O'Connor   Anthony Kennedy

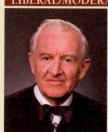

LIBERAL/MODERATE

John Paul Stevens   David Souter   Ruth Bader Ginsburg   Stephen Breyer

FIGURE 14–3

The Rehnquist Court

The members of the United States Supreme Court as of 2005, grouped by their philosophical positions.

Federalism. Several of these rulings reflect a conservative approach to constitutional law that emphasizes states' rights. For example, in 1995 the Court curbed—for the first time in sixty years—the national government's constitutional power under the commerce clause to regulate intrastate activities. The Court held that a federal law regulating the possession of guns in school zones had nothing to do with interstate commerce, and therefore Congress had overreached its powers by attempting to regulate this activity.[11] In 2000, the Court held that Congress had overreached its authority under the commerce clause when it included a federal remedy for gender-motivated violence, such as rape or stalking, in the Federal Violence against Women Act of 1994. The Court concluded that the effect of such violence on interstate commerce was not sufficient to justify national regulation of noneconomic, violent criminal conduct.[12]

As discussed in Chapter 5 (and on the previous page), the Court has also bolstered states' rights by holding that states have sovereign immunity, under the Eleventh Amendment, from lawsuits brought by state employees under federal laws prohibiting certain types of discrimination. Some observers fear that the Court's decisions on states' rights are threatening the federal structure of the nation.[13]

[11]*United States v. Lopez,* 514 U.S. 549 (1995).
[12]*United States v. Morrison,* 529 U.S. 598 (2000).
[13]See, for example, Simon Lazarus, "The Most Dangerous Branch," *The Atlantic Monthly,* June 2002.

GLOBAL VIEW
When the Supreme Court Looks to Other Nations' Laws

Over the last several years, a number of justices on the United States Supreme Court have referred to foreign law when deciding important issues. For example, in 2003 the Court cited foreign law in a controversial case in which it struck down sodomy laws.* (As you learned in Chapter 5, these laws made various kinds of sexual acts, including homosexual ones, illegal.)

In the majority opinion, Justice Anthony Kennedy noted that the European Court of Human Rights and other foreign courts have, in recent years, stated that homosexuals have a right "to engage in intimate, consensual conduct." This comment sparked debate over whether the Supreme Court, or other U.S. courts, should ever consider world opinion or cite foreign law as a persuasive authority.

IS FOREIGN LAW IRRELEVANT?

The practice of citing foreign law has many opponents, including Justice Antonin Scalia, who believes that foreign opinions are irrelevant. There is considerable historical and popular weight behind this view. Many Americans are highly distrustful of foreign practices and attitudes. Judges who have cited foreign law typically look to other democratic countries, such as Canada, Australia, and the nations of

Western Europe. These countries are the most likely to provide useful precedents. The political consensus in almost all of these countries, however, is several degrees to the left of the consensus in America. It follows that conservatives have some reason to be skeptical of foreign examples.

AN INTERNATIONAL PERSPECTIVE

Other Supreme Court justices, including Justices Ruth Bader Ginsburg, Stephen Breyer, and Sandra Day O'Connor, believe that in our increasingly global community we should not ignore the opinions of courts in the rest of the world. Certainly, no one on the Court is suggesting that foreign law should set precedents—it should be only one source among many. U.S. courts habitually cite a wide variety of sources when explaining their reasoning. These may include articles by law professors, sociological studies, or even the works of Shakespeare.

FOR CRITICAL ANALYSIS

Some people have argued that U.S. participation in a system of international law is a "win-win" situation—it promises stability to the world, while at the same time providing the United States with the benefits of international cooperation. What might America gain from such international participation? What might it lose?

*Lawrence v. Texas, 539 U.S. 558 (2003).

In view of the Court's support for states' rights, many scholars were surprised when the Court involved itself in the dispute over the manual recounting of the Florida votes after the 2000 elections. Nonetheless, in a historic decision, the Court reversed the Florida Supreme Court's order to manually recount the votes in selected Florida counties—a decision that effectively handed the presidency to George W. Bush.[14]

Civil Rights.　In civil rights cases, the Rehnquist Court's generally conservative (strict) interpretation of the Constitution has had mixed results. In one decision, the Court refused to extend the constitutional right to privacy to include the right of terminally ill persons to end their lives through physician-assisted suicide. Therefore, a state law banning this practice did not violate the Constitution.[15] (Essentially, the Court left it up to the states to decide whether to ban—or to permit—assisted suicide; to date, only one state, Oregon, has passed a law permitting the practice.) In another decision, the Court held that a federal statute expanding religious liberties was an unconstitutional attempt by Congress to rewrite the Constitution.[16]

[14]*Bush v. Gore,* 531 U.S. 98 (2000).
[15]*Washington v. Glucksberg,* 521 U.S. 702 (1997).
[16]*City of Boerne v. Flores,* 521 U.S. 507 (1997).

University of Michigan law students attend a rally outside the U.S. Supreme Court to defend the university's affirmative action programs. In 2003, the Court ruled that the affirmative action plan used to select law students was constitutional, but the plan used to choose undergraduates was not. What might happen if all affirmative action programs were ruled unconstitutional? (Photo by Alex Wong/Getty Images)

A series of cases decided by the Court in 2003 had a major impact on civil rights issues. In two cases involving the University of Michigan, the Court held that limited affirmative action plans in pursuit of diversity were constitutional.[17] In a Texas case, the Court ruled that laws against homosexual conduct violate the due process clause of the Fourteenth Amendment.[18]

 What Checks Our Courts?

Our judicial system is one of the most independent in the world. But the courts do not have absolute independence, for they are part of the political process. Political checks limit the extent to which courts can exercise judicial review and engage in an activist policy. These checks are exercised by the executive branch, the legislature, the public, and, finally, the judiciary itself.

Executive Checks

President Andrew Jackson was once supposed to have said, after Chief Justice John Marshall made an unpopular decision, "John Marshall has made his decision; now let him enforce it."[19] This purported remark goes to the heart of **judicial implementation**—the enforcement of judicial decisions in such a way that those decisions are translated into policy. The Supreme Court simply does not have any enforcement powers, and whether a decision will be implemented depends on the cooperation of the other two branches of government. Rarely, though, will a president refuse to enforce a Supreme Court decision, as President Jackson did. To take such an action could mean a significant loss of public support because of the Supreme Court's stature in the eyes of the nation.

More commonly, presidents exercise influence over the judiciary by appointing new judges and justices as federal judicial seats become vacant. Additionally, as mentioned earlier, the U.S. solicitor general plays a significant role in the federal court system, and the person holding this office is a presidential appointee.

Judicial Implementation
The way in which court decisions are translated into action.

---

[17]*Gratz v. Bollinger,* 539 U.S. 244 (2003); and *Grutter v. Bollinger,* 539 U.S. 306 (2003).
[18]*Lawrence v. Texas,* 539 U.S. 558 (2003).
[19]The decision referred to was *Cherokee Nation v. Georgia,* 30 U.S. 1 (1831).

Executives at the state level also may refuse to implement court decisions with which they disagree. A notable example of such a refusal occurred in Arkansas after the Supreme Court ordered schools to desegregate "with all deliberate speed" in 1955.[20] Arkansas governor Orval Faubus refused to cooperate with the decision and used the state's National Guard to block the integration of Central High School in Little Rock. Ultimately, President Dwight Eisenhower had to federalize the Arkansas National Guard and send federal troops to Little Rock to quell the violence that had erupted.

Legislative Checks

Courts may make rulings, but often the legislatures at local, state, and federal levels are required to appropriate funds to carry out the courts' rulings. A court, for example, may decide that prison conditions must be improved, but it is up to the legislature to authorize the funds necessary to carry out the ruling. When such funds are not appropriated, the court that made the ruling, in effect, has been checked.

Constitutional Amendments.   Courts' rulings can be overturned by constitutional amendments at both the federal and state levels. Many of the amendments to the U.S. Constitution (such as the Fourteenth, Fifteenth, and Twenty-sixth Amendments) check the state courts' ability to allow discrimination, for example. Proposed constitutional amendments that were created in an effort to reverse courts' decisions on school prayer and abortion have failed.

Rewriting Laws.   Finally, Congress or a state legislature can rewrite (amend) old laws or enact new ones to overturn a court's rulings if the legislature concludes that the court is interpreting laws or legislative intentions erroneously. For example, Congress passed the Civil Rights Act of 1991 in part to overturn a series of conservative rulings in employment-discrimination cases. In 1993, Congress enacted the Religious Freedom Restoration Act (RFRA), which broadened religious liberties, after Congress concluded that a 1990 Supreme Court ruling restricted religious freedom to an unacceptable extent.[21]

According to political scientist Walter Murphy, "A permanent feature of our constitutional landscape is the ongoing tug and pull between elected government and the courts."[22] Certainly, today's Supreme Court and the other two branches of government have been at odds on several occasions in the last decade. Consider the battle over religious rights and the RFRA. On signing the RFRA, President Clinton stated that the act was necessary to reverse the Court's erroneous interpretation of the Constitution in its 1990 decision. According to the president, the elected government's view of religious liberty was "far more consistent with the intent of the founders than [was] the Supreme Court." The Supreme Court responded in kind. In 1997, it invalidated the RFRA, declaring that the act represented an unconstitutional attempt by Congress to add new rights to the Constitution.[23] The Court proclaimed horror at the prospect that "[s]hifting legislative majorities could change the Constitution."

Public Opinion

Public opinion plays a significant role in shaping government policy, and certainly the judiciary is not excepted from this rule. For one thing, persons affected

---

[20]*Brown v. Board of Education,* 349 U.S. 294 (1955)—the second *Brown* decision.
[21]*Employment Division, Department of Human Resources of Oregon v. Smith,* 494 U.S. 872 (1990).
[22]As quoted in Neal Devins, "The Last Word Debate: How Social and Political Forces Shape Constitutional Values," *American Bar Association Journal,* October 1997, p. 48.
[23]*City of Boerne v. Flores,* 521 U.S. 507 (1997).

by a Supreme Court decision that is noticeably at odds with their views may simply ignore it. Officially sponsored prayers were banned in public schools in 1962, yet it was widely known that the ban was (and still is) ignored in many southern districts. What can the courts do in this situation? Unless someone complains about the prayers and initiates a lawsuit, the courts can do nothing.

The public also can pressure state and local government officials to refuse to enforce a certain decision. As already mentioned, judicial implementation requires the cooperation of government officials at all levels, and public opinion in various regions of the country will influence whether such cooperation is forthcoming.

Additionally, the courts themselves necessarily are influenced by public opinion to some extent. After all, judges are not "islands" in our society; their attitudes are influenced by social trends, just as the attitudes and beliefs of all persons are. Courts generally tend to avoid issuing decisions that they know will be noticeably at odds with public opinion. In part, this is because the judiciary, as a branch of the government, prefers to avoid creating divisiveness among the public. Also, a court—particularly the Supreme Court—may lose stature if it decides a case in a way that markedly diverges from public opinion. For example, in 2002 the Supreme Court ruled that the execution of mentally retarded criminals violates the Eighth Amendment's ban on cruel and unusual punishment. In its ruling, the Court indicated that the standards of what constitutes cruel and unusual punishment are influenced by public opinion and that there is "powerful evidence that today our society views mentally retarded offenders as categorically less culpable than the average criminal."[24]

Judicial Traditions and Doctrines

Supreme Court justices (and other federal judges) typically exercise self-restraint in fashioning their decisions. In part, this restraint stems from their knowledge that the other two branches of government and the public can exercise checks on the judiciary, as previously discussed. To a large extent, however, this restraint is mandated by various judicially established traditions and doctrines. For example, in exercising its discretion to hear appeals, the Supreme Court will not hear a meritless appeal just so it can rule on the issue. Also, when reviewing a case, the Supreme Court typically narrows its focus to just one issue or one aspect of an issue involved in the case. The Court rarely makes broad, sweeping decisions on issues. Furthermore, the doctrine of *stare decisis* acts as a restraint because it obligates the courts, including the Supreme Court, to follow established precedents when deciding cases. Only rarely will courts overrule a precedent.

Hypothetical and Political Questions. Other judicial doctrines and practices also act as restraints. As already mentioned, the courts will hear only what are called justiciable disputes—disputes that arise out of actual cases. In other words, a court will not hear a case that involves a merely hypothetical issue. Additionally, if a political question is involved, the Supreme Court often will exercise judicial restraint and refuse to rule on the matter. A **political question** is one that the Supreme Court declares should be decided by the elected branches of government—the executive branch, the legislative branch, or those two branches acting together. For example, the Supreme Court has refused to rule on the controversy regarding the rights of gay men and lesbians in the military, preferring instead to defer to the executive branch's decisions on the matter. Generally, fewer questions are deemed political questions by the Supreme Court today than in the past.

★★★★★★★★★★★★★★★★★

DID YOU KNOW . . .
That in 1930, Justice Oliver Wendell Holmes, Jr., dissenting from the Supreme Court's majority opinion striking down economic legislation as violative of due process, wrote, "I see hardly any limit but the sky" to the Court's invalidation of statutes**?**

Political Question
An issue that a court believes should be decided by the executive or legislative branch.

---

[24]*Atkins v. Virginia*, 536 U.S. 304 (2002).

The Impact of the Lower Courts. Higher courts can reverse the decisions of lower courts. Lower courts can act as a check on higher courts, too. Lower courts can ignore—and have ignored—Supreme Court decisions. Usually, this is done indirectly. A lower court might conclude, for example, that the precedent set by the Supreme Court does not apply to the exact circumstances in the case before the court; or the lower court may decide that the Supreme Court's decision was ambiguous with respect to the issue before the lower court. The fact that the Supreme Court rarely makes broad and clear-cut statements on any issue makes it easier for the lower courts to interpret the Supreme Court's decisions in a different way.

★ The Judiciary: Why Is It Important Today?

John Marshall, chief justice of the United States Supreme Court from 1801 to 1835, stated, "The Judicial Department comes home in its effects to every man's fireside: it passes on his property, his reputation, his life, his all." Whether it is a Supreme Court decision on prayer in the schools or a local court decision against a neighbor, what the courts say and do strongly influences American life and politics.

The federal judiciary is one of the most important institutions in American political life. Indeed, it would be hard to imagine what life in this country would be like if the judiciary were not an independent branch of government but were under the control, say, of Congress. As you learned in this chapter, there is an ongoing interplay among the judiciary, Congress, and the executive branch. Time and again, through the process of judicial review, the federal courts have checked attempts by Congress to pass laws that are not consistent with the U.S. Constitution. In turn, Congress at times has enacted legislation specifically to overturn Supreme Court decisions. On some occasions, the courts have also checked actions of the executive branch.

Because the United States Supreme Court is the highest court in the nation, its decisions must be followed by all other courts in the United States. Thus, Supreme Court decisions can directly affect the everyday lives of millions of Americans. Consider just one example—the Supreme Court's decision in *Brown v. Board of Education of Topeka* (1954). This decision, which outlawed segregation in public schools, dramatically changed the course of race relations throughout America. Furthermore, the Supreme Court has played a significant role in determining the nature and scope of our constitutional rights and liberties. For example, privacy rights were not specifically mentioned in the Constitution. The Supreme Court, however, has held that such rights can be inferred from other constitutional provisions.

MAKING A DIFFERENCE ★ Changing the Legal System

The U.S. legal system may seem too complex to be influenced by one individual, but its power nonetheless depends on the support of individuals. The public has many ways of resisting, modifying, or overturning statutes and rulings of the courts.

Why Should You Care?

Legislative bodies may make laws and ordinances, but legislation is given its practical form by court rulings. Therefore, if you care about the effects of a particular law, you may have to pay attention to how the courts are interpreting it. For example, do you believe that sentences handed down for certain crimes are too lenient—or too strict? Legislative bodies can attempt to establish sentences for various offenses, but the courts inevitably retain considerable flexibility in determining what happens in any particular case.

What Can You Do?

Public opinion can have an effect on judicial policies. One example of the

kind of pressure that can be exerted on the legal system began with a tragedy. In 1980, thirteen-year-old Cari Lightner was hit from behind and killed by a drunk driver while she was walking in a bicycle lane. The driver was a forty-seven-year-old man with two prior drunk-driving convictions. He was at that time out on bail after a third arrest. Cari's mother, Candy, quit her job as a real estate agent to form Mothers Against Drunk Driving (MADD) and launched a campaign to stiffen penalties for drunk-driving convictions.

The organization now has three million members and supporters. Outraged by the thousands of lives lost every year because of drunk driving, the group seeks stiff penalties against drunk drivers. MADD, by becoming involved, has gotten results. Owing to its efforts and the efforts of other citizen-activist groups, many states have responded with stiffer penalties and deterrents. If you feel strongly about this issue and want to get involved, contact:

MADD
P.O. Box 541688
Dallas, TX 75354-1688
1-800-GET-MADD
http://www.madd.org

If you want information about the Supreme Court, contact the following by telephone or letter:

Clerk of the Court
The Supreme Court of the
　United States
1 First St. N.E.
Washington, DC 20543
202-479-3000

You can access online information about the Supreme Court at the following site:

http://www.oyez.org/oyez/ frontpage

Key Terms

affirm 466	dissenting opinion 466	limited jurisdiction 458	reverse 466
amicus curiae brief 463	diversity of citizenship 457	litigate 461	rule of four 465
appellate court 458	federal question 457	majority opinion 466	senatorial courtesy 467
broad construction 472	general jurisdiction 458	opinion 465	*stare decisis* 455
case law 457	judicial activism 471	oral arguments 465	strict construction 472
class-action suit 463	judicial implementation 475	political question 477	trial court 458
common law 455	judicial restraint 471	precedent 455	unanimous opinion 466
concurring opinion 466	jurisdiction 457	remand 466	writ of *certiorari* 465

★ Chapter Summary

1 American law is rooted in the common law tradition, which is part of our heritage from England. The common law doctrine of *stare decisis* (which means "to stand on decided cases") obligates judges to follow precedents established previously by their own courts or by higher courts that have authority over them. Precedents established by the United States Supreme Court, the highest court in the land, are binding on all lower courts. Fundamental sources of American law include the U.S. Constitution and state constitutions, statutes enacted by legislative bodies, regulations issued by administrative agencies, and case law.

2 Article III, Section 1, of the U.S. Constitution limits the jurisdiction of the federal courts to cases involving (a) a federal question—which is a question based, at least in part, on the U.S. Constitution, a treaty, or a federal law; or (b) diversity of citizenship—which arises when parties to a lawsuit are from different states or when the lawsuit involves a foreign citizen or government. The federal court system is a three-tiered model consisting of (a) U.S. district (trial) courts and various lower courts of limited jurisdiction; (b) U.S. courts of appeals; and (c) the United States Supreme Court. Cases may be appealed from the district courts to the appellate courts. In most cases, the decisions of the federal appellate courts are final because the Supreme Court hears relatively few cases.

3 The Supreme Court's decision to review a case is influenced by many factors, including the significance of the issues involved and whether the solicitor general is pressing the Court to take the case. After a case is accepted, the justices undertake research (with the help of their law clerks) on the issues involved in the case, hear oral arguments from the parties, meet in conference to discuss and vote on the issue, and announce the opinion, which is then released for publication.

4 Federal judges are nominated by the president and confirmed by the Senate. Once appointed, they hold office for life, barring gross misconduct. The nomination and confirmation process, particularly for Supreme Court justices, is often extremely politicized. Democrats and Republicans alike realize that justices may occupy seats on the Court for decades and naturally want to have persons appointed who share their basic views. Nearly 20 percent of all Supreme Court appointments have been either rejected or not acted on by the Senate.

5 In interpreting and applying the law, judges inevitably become policymakers. The most important policymaking tool of the federal courts is the power of judicial review. This power was not mentioned specifically in the Constitution, but John Marshall claimed the power for the Court in his 1803 decision in *Marbury v. Madison.*

6 Judges who take an active role in checking the activities of the other branches of government sometimes are characterized as "activist" judges, and judges who defer to the other branches' decisions sometimes are regarded as "restraintist" judges. The Warren Court of the 1950s and 1960s was activist in a liberal direction, whereas today's Rehnquist Court seems to be increasingly activist in a conservative direction. Several politicians and scholars argue that judicial activism has gotten out of hand.

7 Checks on the powers of the federal courts include executive checks, legislative checks, public opinion, and judicial traditions and doctrines.

★ Selected Print and Media Resources

SUGGESTED READINGS

Finkelman, Paul, and Melvin I. Urofsky. *Landmark Decisions of the United States Supreme Court.* Washington, D.C.: CQ Press, 2002. The authors look at numerous Supreme Court decisions in U.S. history and analyze their impact on American society.

Foskett, Ken. *Judging Thomas: The Life and Times of Clarence Thomas.* New York: William Morrow, 2004. Foskett, an Atlanta journalist, delves into the intellectual development of Justice Thomas, one of the nation's most prominent African American conservatives.

Klarman, Michael J. *From Jim Crow to Civil Rights: The Supreme Court and the Struggle for Racial Equality.* New York: Oxford University Press, 2004. Klarman, a professor of constitutional law, provides a detailed history of the Supreme Court's changing attitudes toward equality. Klarman argues that the Civil Rights movement would have revolutionized the status of African Americans even if the Court had not outlawed segregation.

Meador, Daniel John. *American Courts,* second edition. Eagan, Minn.: West Publishing, 2000. Professor Meador describes our state and national court system in this short, clearly written volume. Meador gives special attention to judges and also describes the role of lawyers.

Murphy, Bruce Allen. *Wild Bill: The Legend and Life of William O. Douglas.* New York: Random House, 2003. As a member of the Supreme Court from 1939 to 1975, William O. Douglas played a leading role in championing individual liberties. Murphy's biography provides much detail not only on the Court but also on American politics in general. (Murphy also reveals that the private Douglas was much less admirable than the public figure.)

O'Connor, Sandra Day. *The Majesty of the Law: Reflections of a Supreme Court Justice.* New York: Random House, 2003. As the Supreme Court's most prominent swing vote, Justice O'Connor may be the most powerful member of that body. O'Connor gives a basic introduction to the Court, reflects on past discrimination against women in the law, tells amusing stories about fellow justices, and calls for improving the treatment of jury members.

Raskin, Jamin B. *We the Students: Supreme Court Cases for and about Students,* 2d ed. Washington, D.C.: CQ Press, 2003. This book explores, in an interactive format, a number of cases reviewed by the Supreme Court on issues of high interest to students.

MEDIA RESOURCES

Amistad—A 1997 movie, starring Anthony Hopkins, about a slave ship mutiny in 1839. Much of the story revolves around the prosecution, ending at the Supreme Court, of the slave who led the revolt.

Court TV—This TV channel covers high-profile trials, including those of O. J. Simpson, the Unabomber, British nanny Louise Woodward, and Timothy McVeigh. (You can learn how to access Court TV from your area at its Web site—see the *Logging On* section on the next page for its URL.)

Gideon's Trumpet—A 1980 film, starring Henry Fonda as the small-time criminal James Earl Gideon, which makes clear the path a case takes to the Supreme Court and the importance of cases decided there.

Justice Sandra Day O'Connor—In a 1994 program, Bill Moyers conducts Justice O'Connor's first television interview. Topics include women's rights, O'Connor's role as the Supreme Court's first woman justice, and her difficulties breaking into the male-dominated legal profession. O'Connor defends her positions on affirmative action and abortion.

The Magnificent Yankee—A 1950 movie, starring Louis Calhern and Ann Harding, that traces the life and philosophy of Oliver Wendell Holmes, Jr., one of the Supreme Court's most brilliant justices.

Marbury v. Madison—A 1987 video on the famous 1803 case that established the principle of judicial review.

e-mocracy ★ Courts on the Web

Most courts in the United States now have sites on the Web. These sites vary in what they include. Some courts simply display contact information for court personnel. Others include recent judicial decisions along with court rules and forms. Many federal courts permit attorneys to file documents electronically. The information available on these sites continues to grow as courts try to avoid being left behind in the information age. One day, courts may decide to implement *virtual courtrooms,* in which judicial proceedings take place totally via the Internet. The Internet may ultimately provide at least a partial solution to the twin problems of overloaded dockets and the high time and money costs of litigation.

Logging On

The home page of the federal courts is a good starting point for learning about the federal court system in general. At this site, you can even follow the "path" of a case as it moves through the federal court system. Go to

http://www.uscourts.gov

To access the Supreme Court's official Web site, on which Supreme Court decisions are made available within hours of their release, go to

http://supremecourtus.gov

Several Web sites offer searchable databases of Supreme Court decisions. You can access Supreme Court cases since 1970 at FindLaw's site:

http://www.findlaw.com

The following Web site also offers an easily searchable index to Supreme Court opinions, including some important historic decisions:

http://supct.law.cornell.edu/supct

You can find information on the justices of the Supreme Court, as well as their decisions, at

http://www.oyez.org/oyez/frontpage

Court TV's Web site offers information ranging from its program schedule and how you can find Court TV in your area to famous cases and the wills of celebrities. For each case included on the site, you can read a complete history as well as selected documents filed with the court and court transcripts. You can access this site at

http://www.courttv.com

Using InfoTrac for Political Research

You can use InfoTrac to research how the United States Supreme Court has responded to controversial issues. To use InfoTrac to research Supreme Court rulings, go to

http://www.infotrac-college.com

Log in and go to InfoTrac College Edition, then go to the Keyword guide. Type "united states supreme court" in the search field. In addition, type in one or more words that will narrow the search to a particular issue or group of issues. Words that you might choose include "affirmative action," "first amendment," "gay marriage," "abortion," or "pollution." (Note that the key word "environment" will turn up many sexual-harassment cases because of the "hostile-environment" doctrine. Also, if you do not type in the words "United States," you will receive many articles on state and foreign supreme courts.) InfoTrac will present you with a list of articles, sorted by date. Choose a number of recent ones that all appear to address the same topic, and use them to make your analysis.

ONLINE REVIEW

At **http://politicalscience.wadsworth.com/schmidt12**, you will find a free Study Guide to this book. For each chapter, there are two online quizzes to help you master the material.

• The **PoliPrep Self Study Assessment** provides a pre-test for each major section of the chapter. PoliPrep then generates a customized study plan. After you complete the study plan, a post-test evaluates your progress.

• The **Tutorial Quiz** for each chapter provides questions on the chapter contents, including the features. The questions are organized to match the major sections of the chapter.

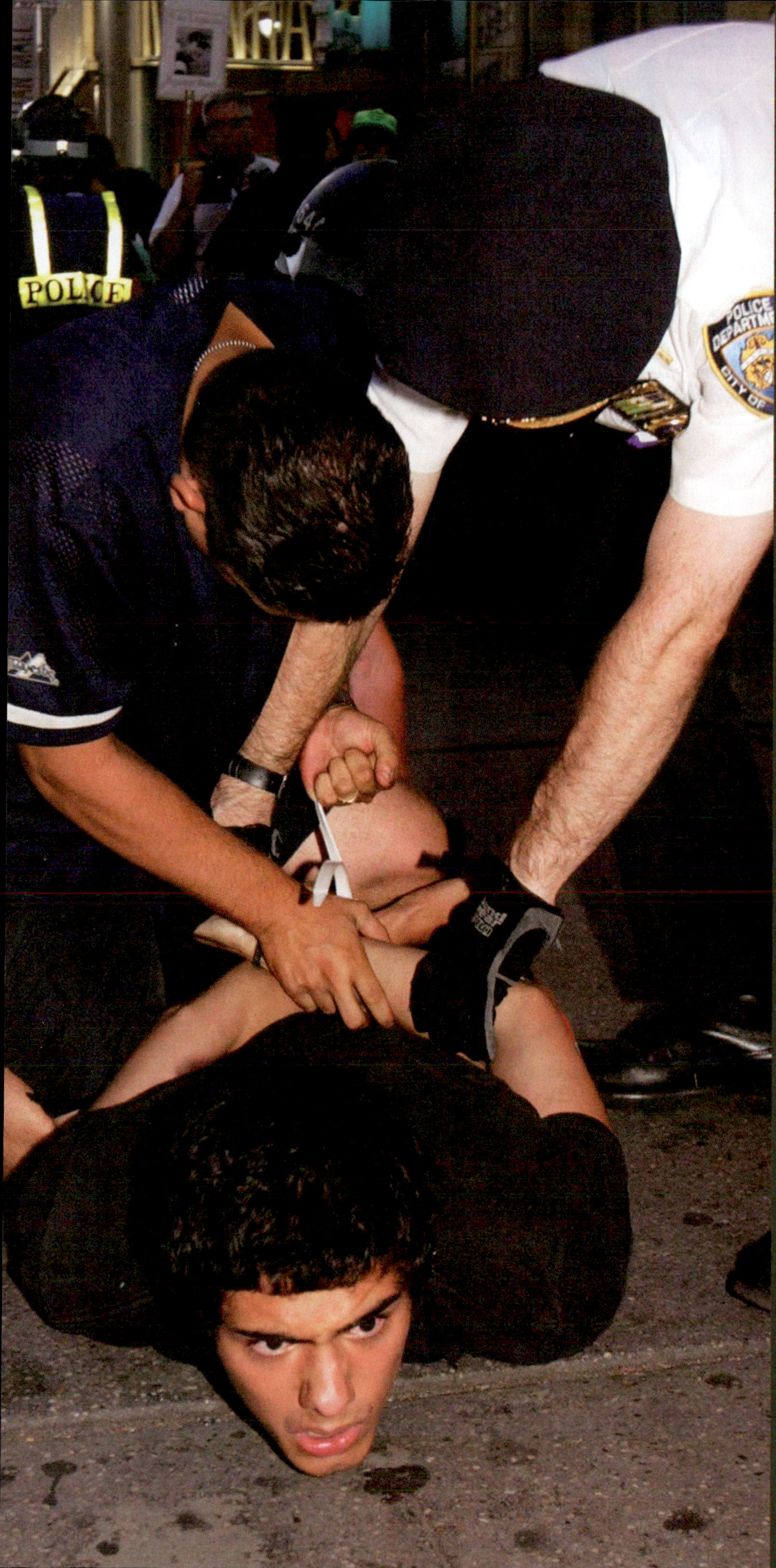

CHAPTER 15

Domestic Policy

- The Policymaking Process

- Health Care

- Poverty and Welfare

- Immigration

- Crime in the Twenty-First Century

- Environmental Policy

WHAT IF . . .
The National Parks Were Privatized?

BACKGROUND

Large federal budget deficits have generated pressure to restrain federal spending. One agency that has felt the effects of funding cuts is the National Park Service, an agency within the Department of the Interior. While the Park Service's budget increased during the Clinton and Bush administrations, the Park Service had to absorb $200 million in hurricane and forest-fire repair costs in 2003 alone. Furthermore, some western law enforcement rangers have been transferred to eastern parts of the country to guard monuments and memorials against potential terrorist attacks.

As a result of these developments, visitors to the parks will find that some parks are not open on Sundays and holidays, bathrooms are serviced less frequently or even closed, and certain parks have eliminated guided ranger tours and lifeguards at beaches. One solution to the financial squeeze proposed by the Bush administration was contracting out more park services to the private sector. (The government already contracts out some park services, including food services and other concessions.) Suppose, though, that the government went even further and privatized all park administration and services. What might result?

WHAT IF THE NATIONAL PARKS WERE PRIVATIZED?

If the national parks were completely privatized, they would probably be better maintained. Private companies contracting with the government to run the parks would want to make profits from the ventures and would therefore wish to make the parks more accommodating to visitors. Facilities would be improved, visitors would be able to access more areas within the parks, and there would be better lodging facilities and more restaurants. Private companies would probably provide more tours, historical displays, museums, theaters, and other enticements to draw visitors.

At the same time, to pay for the new attractions and facilities, the price of admission to the parks might increase dramatically. Currently, five-day passes to all Disney parks in Orlando start at $286.50 for adults and $230.04 for children. In contrast, a seven-day pass to Yellowstone National Park is $20 per automobile or $10 for an individual hiker or bicyclist.

In some instances, new attractions might interfere with the goal of preserving the natural environment. Advertising, for example, would probably become ubiquitous.

What some consider an "inherent governmental function" would be in the hands of the highest bidders—the private companies who win the contracts to run the parks. It is often said that park employees are a special group, dedicated to serving the public. Vice President Dick Cheney stated, "People expect park rangers to know just about everything, and they usually do. The typical park ranger works as a historian, resource manager, law enforcement officer, curator, teacher—and sometimes paramedic and rescuer." Private enterprises might not want to pay the costs of finding and training employees who could fill all of these roles and display the commitment of current rangers.

PRESERVATION VERSUS ENJOYMENT

In 1872, President Ulysses Grant signed legislation establishing America's first national park, Yellowstone National Park. The 2.2 million acres of wilderness were "set apart as a public park or pleasuring ground for the benefit and enjoyment of the people." The goal of public access to the parks has sometimes come into conflict with the desire of Americans to preserve the natural environment. An example of this conflict is the controversy over whether the use of snowmobiles in Yellowstone National Park should be phased out.

If the parks were privatized, the goal of wilderness preservation might have to be sacrificed. To attract more visitors, some footpaths and animal trails would probably become paved roads, and some forested areas might be cleared to make way for new concessions. Additional electrical power lines might have to be run into the parks.

FOR CRITICAL ANALYSIS

1. *Some people claim that banning snowmobiles from national parks is "elitist" because snowmobiling is a working-class activity. How much weight should be given to this argument?*
2. *If the parks were not privatized, what could the Park Service do to obtain more income from its operations?*

Typically, whenever a policy decision is made, some groups will be better off and some groups will be hurt. All policymaking generally involves such a dilemma.

Part of the public-policy debate in our nation involves domestic problems. **Domestic policy** can be defined as all of the laws, government planning, and government actions that affect each individual's daily life in the United States. Consequently, the span of such policies is enormous. Domestic policies range from relatively simple issues, such as what the speed limit should be on interstate highways, to more complex ones, such as how best to protect our environment. Many of our domestic policies are formulated and implemented by the federal government, but a number of others are the result of the combined efforts of federal, state, and local governments.

In this chapter, we look at domestic policy issues involving health care, poverty and welfare, immigration, crime, and the environment. Before we start our analysis, though, we must look at how public policies are made.

Domestic Policy
Public plans or courses of action that concern internal issues of national importance, such as poverty, crime, and the environment.

★ The Policymaking Process

How does any issue get resolved? First, of course, the issue must be identified as a problem. Often, policymakers simply have to open their local newspapers—or letters from their constituents—to discover that a problem is brewing. On rare occasions, a crisis, such as that brought about by the terrorist attacks of September 11, 2001, creates the need to formulate policy. Like most Americans, however, policymakers receive much of their information from the national media. Finally, various lobbying groups provide information to members of Congress.

As an example of policymaking, consider the Medicare reform bill, which was the last major piece of legislation to pass through Congress before the onset of the 2004 election cycle. Medicare is a program that pays health-care expenses for Americans over the age of sixty-five. As initially created in the 1960s, Medicare did not cover the cost of prescription drugs. The new bill provides a direct drug benefit beginning in 2006. (Certain discounts were available immediately.)

No matter how simple or how complex the problem, those who make policy follow a number of steps. We can divide the process of policymaking into at least five steps: agenda building, policy formulation, policy adoption, policy implementation, and policy evaluation. (See Figure 15–1 on page 487.)

Agenda Building

First of all, the issue must get on the agenda. In other words, Congress must become aware that an issue requires congressional action. Agenda building may occur as the result of a crisis, technological change, or mass media campaigns, as well as through the efforts of strong political personalities and effective lobbying groups.

Advocates for the elderly, including AARP (formerly the American Association of Retired Persons), had demanded a Medicare drug benefit for years. Traditionally, liberals have advocated such benefits. Yet the benefit was created under President George W. Bush—a conservative Republican. Bush's advocacy of Medicare reform was essential to its success.

Bush had already backed measures, such as outlawing "partial-birth" abortions, to solidify his conservative support. He now needed to show moderates that they did not have to vote for a Democrat to get action on domestic issues. A Medicare drug benefit would "steal the clothes of the other party," a time-honored political maneuver. For example, Democratic president Bill Clinton (1993–2001) championed a welfare reform bill that limited the number of years in which any one person could receive benefits. Conservatives were much more pleased with this reform than liberals.

Policy Formulation

During the next step in the policymaking process, various policy proposals are discussed among government officials and the public. Such discussions may take place in the printed media, on television, and in the halls of Congress. Congress holds hearings, the president voices the administration's views, and the topic may even become a campaign issue.

Many Republicans in Congress were opposed to any major new social-spending program. Many also disliked Medicare because they saw it as a government insurance program. These members of Congress believed that insurance programs should be run by private businesses. To win their support, the Republican leadership advocated a degree of "privatization." Under this plan, private companies would administer the drug benefit. In a six-city demonstration project, plans administered by private companies would compete with traditional Medicare. The Democratic leadership opposed privatization, claiming that it threatened the very existence of Medicare.

The Republicans also proposed measures that would benefit the insurance and pharmaceutical industries. For example, the government would not use its immense bargaining power to obtain lower prices for Medicare drugs and would discourage the importation of lower-cost drugs from Canada. Finally, the Republicans proposed that to keep the cost of the bill down, not all drug expenses would be covered. To reduce costs, the Republican plan had a "doughnut hole" in which out-of-pocket drug expenses greater than $2,250 but under $3,600 were not covered. The Democrats wanted more coverage—they wanted the "hole" filled.

Policy Adoption

The third step in the policymaking process involves choosing a specific policy from among the proposals that have been discussed. In the end, the Republican proposals were adopted, and the bill passed by the narrowest of margins. The progress of the bill through Congress revealed some of the intense partisanship that has become common in recent years. For example, the Republicans refused to allow any Democrats from the House to participate in the conference committee that reconciled the House and Senate versions of the bill—a startling departure from tradition.

Almost at the last minute, AARP endorsed the bill, which may have guaranteed its success. A significant minority of the Democratic members of Congress broke with their party to support the bill, and that was enough to balance out the Republicans who refused to vote for it.

Policy Implementation

The fourth step in the policymaking process involves the implementation of the policy alternative chosen by Congress. Government action must be implemented by bureaucrats, the courts, police, and individual citizens. In the example of the Medicare reform bill, the main portion of the legislation was not to come into effect until 2006. For the most part, therefore, implementation did not begin immediately. Some sections of the bill did become effective in 2004, however. These included a series of drug discount cards, sponsored by the government in cooperation with various insurance companies, which would provide some savings on prescription drugs right away. Because the Bush administration hoped to elicit a positive political response to the Medicare reform, it organized a major advertising campaign for the new cards, paid for by taxpayers through the Department of Health and Human Services. In May 2004, the federal Government Accountability Office ruled that the advertisements were illegal.

AGENDA BUILDING

June 3, 1997 AARP members rally to show their strong support for Medicare benefits.

July 3, 1997 John Rother, chief lobbyist of AARP, with mail from retirees. "We got Congress to pay attention," he said.

July 12, 2001 President Bush with a copy of a proposed discount card for lower prices on prescription drugs for seniors.

POLICY FORMULATION

June 12, 2003 President Bush speaks to seniors during a round-table discussion about Medicare at a Connecticut hospital.

June 17, 2003 House minority leader Nancy Pelosi criticizes a Republican version of the Medicare drug bill in committee hearings.

June 18, 2003 Bush in a bipartisan meeting with senators on Medicare reform in the White House.

POLICY ADOPTION

July 15, 2003 Members of the House-Senate Conference Committee on Medicare begin their meeting at the Capitol.

November 24, 2003 Senate Majority Leader Bill Frist with Republican leaders after the Senate voted to end debate on the Medicare drug bill.

November 25, 2003 AARP executives speak about AARP's support of the Medicare bill during a news conference.

POLICY IMPLEMENTATION

December 8, 2003 President Bush signs the Medicare Prescription Drug, Improvement and Modernization Act of 2003 at Constitution Hall in Washington.

May 3, 2004 On the first day senior citizens can sign up for the Medicare prescription drug discount cards, seniors meet with House Speaker Dennis Hastert to raise questions and express confusion about the new program.

June 14, 2004 President Bush meets the employees at a Hy-Vee Pharmacy in Liberty, Missouri. Bush discussed health care, including Medicare and the new prescription drug card.

FIGURE 15–1

The Policymaking Process: The Medicare Reform Bill

Four of the five steps of the policymaking process, as exemplified by the Medicare reform bill of 2003. The fifth step—evaluation—cannot begin until 2006, when all provisions of the new act have gone into effect.

AARP protest (Gray Panther photo)
Lobbyist (AP Photo/Susan Walsh)
Bush with card (White House Photo)
Roundtable (White House photo by Eric Draper)
Pelosi (AP Photo/Dennis Cook)
Bipartisan (White House photo by Paul Morse)
Frist et al. (AP Photo/Terry Ashe)
AARP execs (AP Photo/Susan Walsh)
Bush signs bill (White House photo by Paul Morse)
Q&A on cards (AP Photo/Stephen J. Carrera)
Bush at pharmacy (AP Photo/Susan Walsh)

Policy Evaluation

After a policy has been implemented, it is evaluated. Groups inside and outside the government conduct studies to determine what actually happens after a policy has been in place for a given period of time. Based on this feedback and the perceived success or failure of the policy, a new round of policymaking initiatives will be undertaken to improve on the effort. How effective the Medicare reform act will be in providing cost-effective support for the medical expenses of the elderly remains to be seen. Within a few more years, though, Congress will have received significant feedback on the results of the act's implementation.

 # Health Care

Spending for health care is estimated to account for about 15 percent of the total U.S. economy. In 1965, about 6 percent of our income was spent on health care (as shown in Figure 15–2), but that percentage has been increasing ever since. Per capita spending on health care is greater in the United States than almost anywhere else in the world. Measured by the percentage of the *gross domestic product* devoted to health care, America spends more than twice as much as the citizens of Australia or Canada—see Figure 15–3. (The gross domestic product, or GDP, is the dollar value of all final goods and services produced in a one-year period.)

The Rising Cost of Health Care

There are numerous explanations for why health-care costs have risen so much. At least one has to do with changing demographics—as you learned in Chapter 1, the U.S. population is getting older. Life expectancy has gone up, as shown in Figure 15–4 on the facing page. The top 5 percent of those using health care incur over 50 percent of all health-care costs. The bottom 70 percent of health-care users account for only 10 percent of health-care expenditures. Not surprisingly, the elderly make up most of the top users of health-care services. Nursing home expenditures are generally made by people older than age seventy. The use of hospitals is also dominated by the aged.

Advanced Technology.   Another reason that health-care costs have risen so dramatically is advancing technology. A CT (computerized tomography) scanner

FIGURE 15–2

Percentage of Total National Income Spent on Health Care in the United States

The portion of total national income spent on health care has risen steadily since 1965.

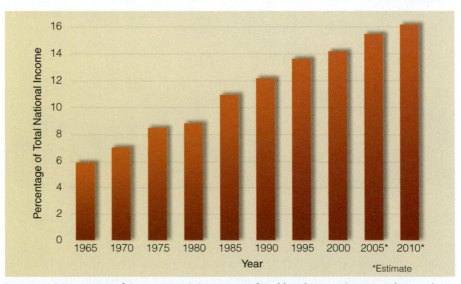

Sources: U.S. Department of Commerce; U.S. Department of Health and Human Services; Deloitte and Touche LLP; VHA, Inc.

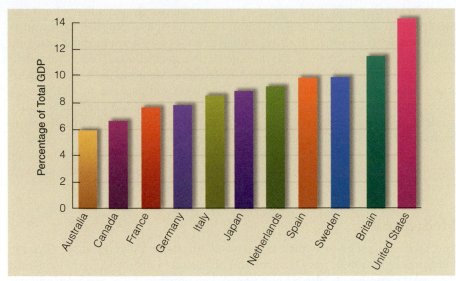

Cost of Health Care in Economically Advanced Nations

Cost is given as a percentage of total gross domestic product (GDP).

SOURCE: Organization for Economic Cooperation and Development, *OECD Health Data,* 3d ed., 2003.

costs around $1 million. An MRI (magnetic resonance imaging) scanner can cost over $2 million. A PET (positron emission tomography) scanner costs around $4 million. All of these machines became increasingly available in recent decades and are in demand around the country. Typical fees for procedures using them range from $300 to $500 for a CT scan to as high as $2,000 for a PET scan. The development of new technologies that help physicians and hospitals prolong human life is an ongoing process in an ever-advancing industry. New procedures that involve even greater costs can be expected in the future.

The Government's Role in Financing Health Care. Currently, government spending on health care constitutes about 45 percent of total health-care spending. Private insurance accounts for about 35 percent of payments for health care. The remainder—less than 20 percent—is paid directly by individuals or by philanthropy. Medicare and Medicaid are the main sources of hospital and other medical benefits for 35 million U.S. residents, most of whom are over the age of sixty-five.

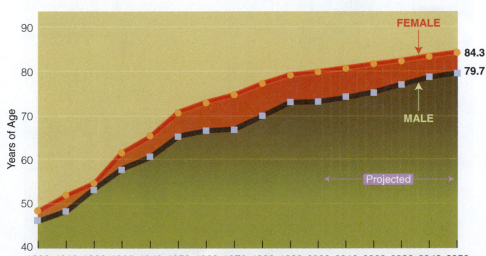

FIGURE 15–4

Life Expectancy in the United States

Along with health-care spending, life expectancy has gone up. Therefore, we are presumably getting some return for our spending.

SOURCE: Social Security Administration, Office of the Chief Actuary.

Medicare
A federal health-insurance program that covers U.S. residents over the age of sixty-five. The costs are met by a tax on wages and salaries.

Medicaid
A joint state-federal program that provides medical care to the poor (including indigent elderly persons in nursing homes). The program is funded out of general government revenues.

Medicare is specifically designed to support the elderly, regardless of income. **Medicaid**, a joint state-federal program, is in principle a program to subsidize health care for the poor. In practice, it often provides long-term health care to persons living in nursing homes. (To become eligible for Medicaid, these individuals must first exhaust their financial assets.) Medicare, Medicaid, and private insurance companies are called *third parties*. Caregivers and patients are the two primary parties. When third parties pay for medical care, the demand for such services increases; health-care recipients have no incentive to restrain their use of health care. One result is some degree of wasted resources.

The government also buys health insurance for its own employees, including members of Congress. How good is the deal that federal employees get? We examine that question in the *Politics and Health Care* feature.

Medicare

The Medicare program, which was created in 1965 under President Lyndon Johnson (1963–1969), pays hospital and physicians' bills for U.S. residents over the age of sixty-five. As already mentioned, beginning in 2006, Medicare will pay for at least part of the prescription drug expenses of the elderly. In return for paying a tax on their earnings (currently set at 2.9 percent of wages and salaries) while in the workforce, retirees are ensured that the majority of their hospital and physicians' bills will be paid for with public funds.

Over the past forty years, Medicare has become the second-largest domestic spending program, after Social Security. Government expenditures on Medicare have routinely turned out to be far in excess of the expenditures forecast at the time the program was put into place or expanded. In Chapter 16, you will learn what impact Medicare currently has on the federal budget and what impact it is likely to have in the future. For now, consider only that the total outlays on Medicare are high enough to create substantial demands to curtail its costs.

One response by the federal government to soaring Medicare costs has been to impose arbitrary reimbursement caps on specific procedures. To avoid going over Medicare's reimbursement caps, however, hospitals have sometimes discharged patients too soon or in an unstable condition. The government has also cut rates of reimbursement to individual physicians and physician groups, such as health

A physician examines a patient. Managed-care programs, which have become popular with employers in recent years, often reimburse only a limited number of health-care providers. How might we allow patients to visit physicians of their own choosing and simultaneously control health-care costs? © Corbis. All Rights Reserved.

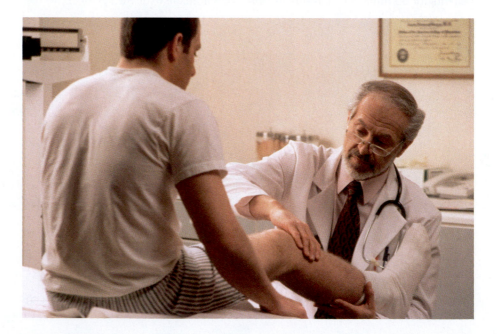

POLITICS AND HEALTH CARE
Health Care for Members of Congress

Members of Congress enjoy many perks, including a private gymnasium, free close-in parking at Ronald Reagan National Airport, subsidized lunches, and much more. They also enjoy a generous health-care plan. Why shouldn't everyone have the same good deal that Congress gets? John Kerry, for one, asked this question during his presidential campaign. George W. Bush has asked the same question. This raises another issue: Just how good is the congressional plan?

THE FEDERAL EMPLOYEES HEALTH BENEFITS (FEHB) PROGRAM

Members of Congress are eligible for coverage under the Federal Employees Health Benefits Program (FEHB) on the same basis as any other federal employee. The FEHB offers its participants an unusually wide range of health-care options. In Washington, D.C., for example, federal employees can choose from nineteen different plans, ranging from fee-for-service options to health maintenance organizations (HMOs). Those living elsewhere in the country are guaranteed access to at least a dozen plans.

The plans are provided by private insurance companies, and the federal Office of Personnel Management negotiates the terms of each plan with the companies. The rule for all federal employees, whether they deliver the mail or

serve in Congress, is that the government picks up 72 percent of the average premium. The employee pays the rest through payroll deductions.

FEHB ADVANTAGES

The FEHB is in many ways similar to what a generous private-sector employer might offer. It has a number of special advantages, however. There are no "preexisting condition" restrictions. In many private health-insurance plans, the insurance company refuses to cover any illness the employee already had when he or she was hired. If the illness is a serious one, such as heart disease or AIDS, having a policy that refuses to cover preexisting conditions is almost like having no insurance at all.

Federal employees can keep FEHB coverage after retirement. Family members of a federal employee can keep FEHB coverage if the covered family member dies. The FEHB will even cover persons who have obtained divorces from covered federal employees. In all, 8.3 million Americans are covered by the FEHB.

FOR CRITICAL ANALYSIS

What would the results be if the government provided subsidies that let everyone in the nation obtain insurance through private insurance companies?

maintenance organizations (HMOs). One consequence has been a nearly 15 percent reduction in the amount the government pays for Medicare services provided by physicians. As a result, physicians and HMOs have become reluctant to accept Medicare patients. Several of the nation's largest HMOs have withdrawn from certain Medicare programs. A growing number of physicians now refuse to treat Medicare patients.

The Uninsured

Over 40 million Americans—15 percent of the population—do not have health insurance. The proportion of the population that is uninsured varies from one part of the country to another. In Hawaii and Minnesota, only 7 percent of working adults lack coverage. In Texas, however, the figure is 27 percent. According to the Congressional Black Caucus Foundation, African Americans, Hispanics, and Asian/Pacific Islanders make up over half of the year-round uninsured, despite constituting 29 percent of the total U.S. population. Hispanic Americans are the most likely to be uninsured, with only 35 percent of working Hispanic adults under coverage.[1]

---

[1]"CBCF Denounces Rise in the Number of Uninsured: Census Figures Reveal Minorities Hardest Hit," CBCFHealth.org, part of the Congressional Black Caucus Foundation, Inc., February 10, 2004. This article is online at http://www.cbcfhealth.org/content/contentID/2404.

According to surveys, being uninsured has negative health consequences. People without coverage are less likely to get basic preventive care, such as mammograms; less likely to have a personal physician; and more likely to rate their own health as only poor or fair.

The Uninsured Employed.   The uninsured population is relatively young, in part due to Medicare, which covers almost everyone over the age of sixty-five. Also, younger workers are more likely to be employed in entry-level jobs that do not come with health-insurance benefits. The current system of health care in the United States assumes that employers will provide health insurance. Many small businesses, however, simply cannot afford to offer their workers health insurance. Insurance costs are now approaching an average of $9,000 a year for each employee, according to Kate Sullivan, director of health-care policy at the United States Chamber of Commerce.[2]

Shifting Costs to the Uninsured.   A further problem faced by the uninsured is that when they do seek medical care, they must usually pay much higher fees than would be paid on their behalf if they had insurance coverage. Large third-party insurers, private or public, normally strike hard bargains with hospitals and physicians over how much they will pay for procedures and services. The uninsured have less bargaining power. As a result, hospitals attempt to recover from the uninsured the revenues they lost in paying third-party insurers. A further result is that individual health-insurance policies (those not obtained through an employer) are extremely costly.

In any given year, most people do not require expensive health care. Young, healthy people in particular can be tempted to do without insurance. One benefit of insurance coverage, however, is that it protects the insured against catastrophic costs resulting from unusual events. Medical care for life-threatening accidents or diseases can run into thousands or even hundreds of thousands of dollars. An uninsured person who requires this kind of medical care may be forced into bankruptcy.

One Alternative: National Health Insurance

The United States is the only advanced industrial country with a large pool of citizens who lack health insurance. Western Europe, Japan, Canada, and Australia all provide systems of universal coverage. Such coverage is provided through **national health insurance.** In effect, the government takes over the economic function of providing basic health-care coverage. Private insurers are excluded from this market. The government collects premiums from employers and employees on the basis of their ability to pay and then provides basic services to the entire population.

Because the government provides all basic insurance coverage, national health-insurance systems are often called **single-payer plans.** Such plans can significantly reduce administrative overhead, because physicians need only deal with a single set of forms and requirements. The number of employees required to process claims is also lowered. In France, for example, which has national health insurance, administrative overhead is 5 percent of total costs, compared to 14 percent in the United States.[3] The French experience suggests that containing unnec-

National Health Insurance
A plan to provide universal health insurance under which the government provides basic health insurance to all citizens. In most such plans, the program is funded by taxes on wages or salaries.

Single-Payer Plan
A plan under which one entity has a monopoly on issuing a particular type of insurance. Typically the entity is the government, and the insurance is basic health coverage.

---

[2]Robin Toner, "Texas Leads the Nation in the Number of Uninsured Workers," *The New York Times,* May 5, 2004.

[3]Paul V. Dutton, "Health Care in France and the United States: Learning from Each Other," Washington, D.C.: The Brookings Institution, 2002. This article is online at **http://www.brookings.edu/fp/cusf/ analysis/dutton.htm**.

essary procedures may be more difficult with a single-payer plan, however. National health-insurance systems are also sometimes called *socialized medicine.* It should be noted, though, that only health insurance is socialized. The government does not employ most physicians, and in many countries the hospitals are largely private as well.[4]

The Canadian System.   Americans seeking an example of national health insurance often look to the Canadian system. Canada's program, however, is atypical in many respects. Canada is the only country with national health insurance that in effect outlaws private parallel health-care services for its wealthier citizens (funded in most countries by supplementary insurance). Canadian hospitals are also subject to an unusual degree of government control. Finally, the Canadian plan does not cover eyeglasses, most dental care, or prescription drugs.

If the United States ever established national health insurance, Americans would probably not accept such restrictions but instead would opt for a model with much greater participation by private enterprise. The health-care systems of France, Germany, and Japan are probably more relevant as models than the system in Canada, because the systems in these countries allow additional benefits for people who are willing to pay for them.

National Health Insurance in the United States?   Since the time of President Harry Truman (1945–1953), some liberals have sought to establish a national health-insurance system in this country. During his first two years in office, President Bill Clinton (1993–2001) attempted to steer such a proposal through Congress. Clinton's plan, developed by a panel chaired by his wife, Hilary Rodham Clinton, provided for a large degree of private-sector participation, though it imposed heavy regulation on the private sector. Clinton's plan was dauntingly complex, and he failed to build the political groundwork necessary for such a major change. Private insurance companies knew Clinton's program would deprive them of a major line of business and naturally did everything in their power to stop the bill.

---

[4]Britain is an exception. Under the British "National Health," most (but not all) physicians are employed by the government.

A nurse gives a woman a flu shot at a physician's office. Preventative medicine is usually very cost effective. How might our health-care system encourage people to take better care of themselves? (David Young-Wolff/PhotoEdit)

In the end, the proposal was defeated. Indeed, Clinton's proposal may have been an important reason why the Republicans gained control of Congress in the 1994 elections. Clinton's failure meant that national health insurance would not be seriously considered in the United States for many years. Should the Democrats ever gain control of both Congress and the presidency, however, it is possible that the issue will be revived.

Another Alternative: A Health Savings Account

Republicans in Congress have legislated a health savings account (HSA) program as an alternative to completely changing the U.S. health-care industry. Most taxpayers can set up a tax-free HSA, which must be combined with a high-deductible health-insurance policy. Eligible individuals or families can make an annual tax-deductible contribution to an HSA up to a maximum of $2,550 for an individual and $5,150 for a family. Funds in the HSA accumulate tax free, and distributions of HSA funds for medical expenses are also exempt. Any funds remaining in an HSA after an individual reaches age sixty-five can be withdrawn tax free. The benefits can be impressive—a single person depositing around $1,500 each year with no withdrawals will have hundreds of thousands of dollars in the account after forty years.

For those using an HSA, the physician-patient relationship remains intact because third-party payers do not intervene in paying or monitoring medical expenses. The patients, rather than third parties, have an incentive to discourage their physicians from ordering expensive tests for every minor ache and pain because they are allowed to keep any money saved in the HSA. Some critics argue that HSA participants might also forgo necessary medical attention and develop more serious medical problems as a consequence. Also, HSAs do not address the issue of universal access to health care. After all, even if HSAs became common, not everyone would be willing or able to participate.

★ Poverty and Welfare

Throughout the world, poverty has historically been accepted as inevitable. The United States and other industrialized nations, however, have sustained enough economic growth in the past several hundred years to eliminate mass poverty. In fact, considering the wealth and high standard of living in the United States, the persistence of poverty here appears bizarre and anomalous. How can there still be so much poverty in a nation of so much abundance? And what can be done about it?

Income Transfer
A transfer of income from some individuals in the economy to other individuals. This is generally done by government action.

A traditional solution has been **income transfers.** These are methods of transferring income from relatively well-to-do to relatively poor groups in society, and as a nation, we have been using such methods for a long time. Before we examine these efforts, let us look at the concept of poverty in more detail and at the characteristics of the poor.

The Low-Income Population

We can see in Figure 15–5 that the number of people classified as poor fell steadily from 1961 to 1968—that is, during the presidencies of John Kennedy and Lyndon Johnson. The number remained level until the recession of 1981–1982, under Ronald Reagan, when it increased substantially. The number fell during the "Internet boom" of 1994–2000, but then it started to rise again.

The threshold income level that is used to determine who falls into the poverty category was originally based on the cost of a nutritionally adequate food plan

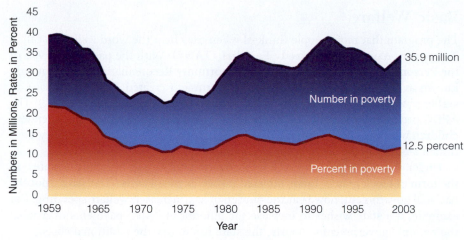

Note: The data points represent the midpoints of the respective years.
SOURCE: U.S. Census Bureau, Current Population Reports, *Income, Poverty, and Health Insurance Coverage in the United States: 2003*, U.S. Government Printing Office, 2004. Online at http://www.census.gov/prod/2004pubs/p60-226.pdf.

designed by the U.S. Department of Agriculture in 1963. The threshold was determined by multiplying the food-plan cost times three, on the assumption that food expenses constitute approximately one-third of a poor family's expenditures. Until 1969, annual revisions of the threshold level were based only on price changes in food. After 1969, the adjustments were made on the basis of changes in the consumer price index (CPI). The CPI is based on the average prices of a specified set of goods and services bought by wage earners in urban areas.

The low-income poverty threshold thus represents the income needed to maintain a specified standard of living as of 1963, with the purchasing-power value increased year by year to reflect the general increase in prices. For 2004, for example, the official poverty level for a family of four was about $18,850.

The official poverty level is based on pretax income, including cash but not **in-kind subsidies**—food stamps, housing vouchers, and the like. If we correct poverty levels for such benefits, the percentage of the population that is below the poverty line drops dramatically.

In-Kind Subsidy
A good or service—such as food stamps, housing, or medical care—provided by the government to low-income groups.

The Antipoverty Budget

It is not always easy to determine how much the government spends to combat poverty. In part, this is because it is not always easy to decide whether a particular program is an antipoverty program. Are grants to foster parents an antipoverty measure? What about job-training programs? Are college scholarships for low-income students an antipoverty measure? President George W. Bush's federal budget for 2005 allocated $16 billion for such scholarships.

Bush's 2005 budget allocated about $396 billion, or about one-sixth of all federal expenditures, to federal programs that support persons of limited income (scholarships included).[5] Of this amount, $188 billion was for Medicaid, which funds medical services to the poor. The states were expected to contribute an additional $142 billion to Medicaid. Medical care is by far the largest portion of the antipoverty budget. One reason medical spending is high is that there is a widespread belief that everyone should receive medical care that at least approximates the care received by an average person. No such belief supports spending for other purposes, such as shelter or transportation. Elderly people receive 70 percent of Medicaid spending.

[5]This sum does not include the Earned Income Tax Credit, which is not part of the federal budget.

**Temporary Assistance
to Needy Families (TANF)**
  A state-administered program in which
  grants from the national government are
  used to provide welfare benefits. The
  TANF program replaced the Aid to
  Families with Dependent Children
  (AFDC) program.

Supplemental Security Income (SSI)
  A federal program established to provide
  assistance to elderly persons and persons
  with disabilities.

Food Stamps
  Coupons issued by the federal government
  to low-income individuals to be used for
  the purchase of food.

An instructor (standing) with a welfare
recipient during a workshop at the
Philadelphia Workforce Development
Corporation (PWDC). The PWDC is a
nonprofit organization that helps people
on welfare to find employment. (Mike
Mergen/Bloomberg News/Landov)

Basic Welfare

The program that most people think of when they hear the word *welfare* is called
Temporary Assistance to Needy Families (TANF). With the passage in 1996 of
the Personal Responsibility and Work Opportunity Reconciliation Act, popularly
known as the Welfare Reform Act, the government created TANF to replace an
earlier program known as Aid to Families with Dependent Children (AFDC). The
AFDC program provided "cash support for low-income families with dependent
children who have been deprived of parental support due to death, disability, continued absence of a parent, or unemployment."

Under the TANF program, the U.S. government turned over to the states, in
the form of block grants, funds targeted for welfare assistance. The states, not the
national government, now bear the burden of any increased welfare spending. For
example, if a state wishes to increase the amount of TANF payments over what
the national government supports, the state has to pay the additional costs.

One of the aims of the Welfare Reform Act was to reduce welfare spending. To
do this, the act made two significant changes in the basic welfare program. One
change was to limit most welfare recipients to only two years of assistance at a
time. The second change was to impose a lifetime limit on welfare assistance of
five years. The Welfare Reform Act has largely met its objectives. During the first
five years after the act was passed, the number of families receiving welfare payments was cut in half. The 2005 federal budget allocated $18 billion to the TANF
block grants.

Welfare Controversies

Whether known as AFDC or TANF, the basic welfare program has always been
controversial. Conservative and libertarian voters often object to welfare spending
as a matter of principle, believing that it reduces the incentive to find paid employment. Because AFDC and TANF have largely supported single-parent households,
some also believe that such programs are antimarriage. Should "welfare mothers"
be required to obtain paid employment? We examine this question
in the *Which Side Are You On?* feature. (We also look at the effect of
day care on the employment of mothers in the *Global View* feature
on page 498.)

Finally, certain people object to welfare spending out of a belief
that welfare recipients are "not like us." In fact, non-Hispanic whites
made up only 31 percent of TANF recipients in the early 2000s. As a
result of all these factors, basic welfare payments in the United States
are relatively low when compared with similar payments in other
industrialized nations. In 2004, the average monthly TANF payment
nationwide was about four hundred dollars per family.

Other Forms of Government Assistance

The **Supplemental Security Income (SSI)** program was established
in 1974 to provide a nationwide minimum income for elderly persons
and persons with disabilities who do not qualify for Social Security
benefits. The 2005 budget allocated $43 billion to this program.

The government also issues **food stamps,** coupons that can be
used to purchase food. Food stamps are available to low-income
individuals and families. Recipients must prove that they qualify by
showing that they have a low income (or no income at all). Food
stamps go to a much larger group of people than TANF payments.
President Bush's 2005 budget allocated $31 billion to the food
stamp program. The food stamp program has become a major part

WHICH SIDE ARE YOU ON?
Should Welfare Mothers Work outside the Home?

A major objective of the Welfare Reform Act of 1996 was to encourage welfare recipients to take paid employment. The Temporary Assistance for Needy Families (TANF) program reduced the funds available for basic welfare payments but increased spending on "welfare to work" programs. The act also provided a day-care subsidy for the children of welfare recipients who were entering the work force. Taking care of small children, however, is hard work all by itself. Mothers who enter the work force have less time available for their children. Is it really a good idea to demand that poor women seek employment?

MOTHERS SHOULD STAY HOME TO RAISE THEIR CHILDREN

Some observers think that welfare mothers can often make a greater contribution to society by raising their children than by filling the kind of minimum-wage jobs that are typically available to them. Many conservatives believe that it is better for middle-class mothers of small children to stay home and rely on the husband's paycheck. If this is so, then staying home should also be a desirable arrangement for single mothers in poverty. Such mothers need government support. Also, a large number of welfare recipients not only supervise small children but also take care of family members with disabilities, such as severe retardation or degenerative diseases. Recipients themselves may suffer from these conditions.

MOTHERS SHOULD TAKE PAID WORK

Those who say that almost all welfare recipients should take paid work believe that many of them have succumbed to a culture of dependency, for which employment is the cure. Adults serve as role models for their children. When children see adults assuming responsibility for feeding the family—instead of relying on the government—the children will grow up to be responsible adults. It is more important for a parent to model responsible behavior than to be with the children on a full-time basis.

Polling data suggest that most welfare mothers do want employment, although some would rather stay home with

A working mother drops her son off at a day-care center before heading to her place of employment. What are the benefits and drawbacks of the widespread use of day care? (Lon C. Diehl/Photoedit)

infants under one year of age. This supports the belief that such women should seek employment.

WHAT'S YOUR POSITION?

Under what circumstances, if any, should poor women with children stay out of the work force?

GOING ONLINE

For the latest developments in welfare, check out the Web site of the Child Welfare League of America at **http://www.cwla.org/advocacy**. The Annie E. Casey Foundation Web site at **http://www.aecf.org** provides a wealth of information on this topic. The Welfare Information Network at **http://www.financeprojectinfo.org/win** offers commentary ranging from liberal to conservative.

of the welfare system in the United States, although it was started in 1964 mainly to benefit farmers by distributing surplus food through retail channels.

The **earned-income tax credit (EITC) program** was created in 1975 to help low-income workers by giving back part or all of their Social Security taxes. Currently, about 15 percent of all taxpayers claim an EITC, and an estimated $33 billion a year is rebated to taxpayers through the program.

Earned-Income Tax Credit (EITC) Program
A government program that helps low-income workers by giving back part or all of their Social Security taxes.

GLOBAL VIEW
Day Care in Western Europe

Encouraging poor mothers to work outside the home is established policy in the United States. One prerequisite to employment is finding a place for the children while the mother works. What effect does the availability of day care have on the employment behavior of mothers? For answers, consider the experience of various countries in Europe.

DIFFERENT COUNTRIES, DIFFERENT POLICIES

Some people believe that mothers of small children should not enter the work force. This, in fact, is the policy in several nations, including Germany, Italy, and Spain. In these countries, government programs provide financial support to nonworking mothers, regardless of income. Another factor discourages mothers from working in these nations—day care that matches work schedules is generally unobtainable.

In contrast, day care is widely available in the United States, even if in many instances it is expensive or of poor quality. Other nations also do not try to discourage the employment of mothers. France and the Scandinavian countries have subsidized day-care systems that support mothers who enter the labor force.

NO DAY CARE, NO BABIES

As a result of national policies, many mothers in Germany, Italy, and Spain do stay home. These policies have an unin-tended consequence, however. A large number of women remain in the work force and never become mothers, even though polling data suggest that women in these nations are no less willing to have children than women in other countries.

The demographic consequences are noticeable. In Chapter 1, you learned that the *fertility rate* measures the average number of children that a group of women are expected to have over a lifetime. As you can see in the accompanying table, the fertility rate in European countries that have day-care systems is higher than it is in countries that do not have such systems.

Day Care Available	Fertility Rate
France	1.85
Denmark	1.74
Norway	1.78
Sweden	1.66

Day Care Unavailable	Fertility Rate
Germany	1.38
Italy	1.27
Spain	1.27

SOURCE: Bureau of the Census.

FOR CRITICAL ANALYSIS

Why might mothers of small children be motivated to seek paid employment?

Homelessness—Still a Problem

The plight of the homeless remains a problem. Indeed, some observers argue that the Welfare Reform Act of 1996 has increased the number of homeless persons. There are no hard statistics on the homeless, but estimates of the number of people without a home on any given night in the United States range from a low of 230,000 to as many as 750,000 people.

It is difficult to estimate how many people are homeless because the number depends on how the homeless are defined. There are *street people*—those who sleep in bus stations, parks, and other areas. Many of these people are youthful runaways. There are the so-called *sheltered homeless*—those who sleep in government-supported or privately funded shelters. Many of these individuals used to live with their families or friends. While street people are almost always single, the sheltered homeless include many families with children. Homeless families are the fastest-growing subgroup of the homeless population.

The homeless problem pits liberals against conservatives. Conservatives argue that there are not really that many homeless people and that most of them are alcoholics, drug users, or the mentally ill. Conservatives contend that these individuals should be dealt with by either the mental-health system or the criminal justice system. In contrast, many liberals argue that homelessness is caused by a reduction in welfare benefits and by excessively priced housing. They want more shelters to be built for the homeless.

Some cities have "criminalized" homelessness. Many municipalities have outlawed sleeping on park benches and sidewalks, as well as panhandling and leaving personal property on public property. In some cities, police sweeps remove the homeless, who then become part of the criminal justice system.

Since 1993, the U.S. Department of Housing and Urban Development has spent billions of dollars on programs designed to combat homelessness. Yet because there is so much disagreement about the number of homeless persons, the reasons for homelessness, and the possible cures for the problem, there has been no consistent government policy. Whatever policies have been adopted usually have been attacked by one group or another.

★ Immigration

Time and again, this nation has been challenged and changed—and culturally enriched—by immigrant groups. All of these immigrants have faced the problems involved in living in a new and different political and cultural environment. Most of them have had to overcome language barriers, and many have had to deal with discrimination in one form or another because of their color, their inability to speak English fluently, or their customs. The civil rights legislation passed during and since the 1960s has done much to counter the effects of prejudice against immigrant groups by ensuring that they obtain equal rights under the law.

One of the questions facing Americans and their political leaders today is the effect of immigration on American politics and government. Another issue is the impact of immigration and interracial marriages on the traditional civil rights agenda. Still another issue is whether immigrants from countries where some citizens are known to support terrorism should be allowed to enter this country at all.

DID YOU KNOW . . .
That the Greenville County Department of Social Services in South Carolina wrote to a food stamp recipient, "Your food stamps will be stopped . . . because we received notice that you passed away. May God bless you. You may reapply if there is a change in your circumstances"**?**

A visitor to Ellis Island looks at an exhibit of some of the many immigrants who found a new life in America. Immigrants are usually younger than the population as a whole. What consequences follow from this fact? (W. L. Stryker)

The Continued Influx of Immigrants

Today, immigration rates are among the highest they have been since their peak in the early twentieth century. Currently, about one million people a year immigrate to this country, and people who were born on foreign soil now constitute over 10 percent of the U.S. population—twice the percentage of thirty years ago.

Since 1977, four out of five immigrants have come from Latin America or Asia. Hispanics have overtaken African Americans as the nation's largest minority. If current immigration rates continue, by the year 2075 minority groups collectively will constitute the "majority" of Americans. If Hispanics, African Americans, and perhaps Asians were to form coalitions, they could increase their political power dramatically and would have the numerical strength to make significant changes. According to Ben Wattenberg of the American Enterprise Institute, in the future the "old guard" white majority will no longer dominate American politics.

Some regard the high rate of immigration as a plus for America because it offsets the low birthrate and aging population. Immigrants expand the work force and help to support, through their taxes, government programs that benefit older Americans, such as Medicare and Social Security. If it were not for immigration, contend these observers, the United States would be facing even more serious problems than it already does with funding these programs (see Chapter 16). In contrast, nations that do not have high immigration rates, such as Japan, are experiencing serious fiscal challenges due to their aging populations.

Immigration and America's Security

Soon after the attacks on the World Trade Center and the Pentagon, many political leaders began looking at our immigration policies with security issues in mind. After all, the terrorists were from other countries (mainly Saudi Arabia). The most vocal critics of our immigration policy literally want to shut America's door to immigrants. That the terrorist attacks occurred while the American economy was suffering from a recession did not, of course, help matters. Anti-immigrant forces often have used high unemployment as a reason to restrict immigration. The 9/11 events simply provided these critics with an additional argument to support their views.

At John F. Kennedy airport in New York, a U.S. customs agent fingerprints a Korean student entering the United States on a student visa. Authorities now scan fingerprints and take photographs of arriving foreigners as part of a program that Homeland Security secretary Tom Ridge said will make borders "open to travelers but closed to terrorists." (AP Photo/Mary Altaffer)

Student Visas. Several of the 9/11 hijackers were in this country legally on student visas. Indeed, newly approved student visas for two of the hijackers arrived at their flight school in Florida two months after the attacks, emphasizing how inefficient, understaffed, and underfunded the U.S. agency handling immigration services has been for years. The State Department's inspector general pointed out that one consulate in a "suspect" country had an annual travel budget of only $300 to perform background checks on over 100,000 visa applicants.

According to those who support reducing immigration to further America's security, all visa applicants from suspect areas of the world should be subject to stricter scrutiny. This includes travelers from any nations in which anti-American groups such as al Qaeda have found supporters—for example, Somalia, Pakistan, Bosnia, the Philippines, Indonesia, and Saudi Arabia.

New Security Guidelines. U.S. immigration authorities give out over 500,000 student visas each year. Many of these visas go to individuals from countries where some residents are known to support terrorism. Under new security guidelines, U.S. immigration authorities conduct additional checks on these students. Universities must report to the government whether students who requested visas actually enroll in course work at their campuses. After all, many of the 9/11 hijackers never showed up for classes despite having received valid student visas.

★ Crime in the Twenty-First Century

The issue of crime has been on the national agenda for years now. Although crime rates have fallen in the last several years, virtually all polls taken in the United States in the last ten years have shown that crime remains one of the major concerns of the public. A related issue that has been on the domestic policy agenda for decades is controlling the use and sale of illegal drugs—activities that are often associated with crimes of violence. More recently, finding ways to deal with terrorism has become a priority for the nation's policymakers.

Crime in American History

In every period in the history of this nation, people have voiced their apprehension about crime. Some criminologists argue that crime was probably as frequent around the time of the American Revolution as it is currently. During the Civil War, mob violence and riots erupted in several cities. After the Civil War, people in San Francisco were told that "no decent man is in safety to walk the streets after dark; while at all hours, both night and day, his property is jeopardized by incendiarism [arson] and burglary."[6] In 1886, *Leslie's Weekly* reported, "Each day we see ghastly records of crime . . . murder seems to have run riot and each citizen asks . . . 'who is safe?'" From 1860 to 1890, the crime rate rose twice as fast as the population.[7] In 1910, one author stated that "crime, especially in its more violent forms and among the young, is increasing steadily and is threatening to bankrupt the Nation."[8]

From 1900 to the 1930s, social violence and crime increased dramatically. Labor union battles and race riots were common. Only during the three-decade period from the mid-1930s to the early 1960s did the United States experience, for the first time in its history, stable or slightly declining overall crime rates.

What most Americans are worried about is violent crime. From the mid-1980s to 1994, its rate rose relentlessly. The murder rate per 100,000 people in 1964 was 4.9, whereas in 1994 it was estimated at 9.3, an increase of almost 100 percent. Since 1995, however, violent crime rates have declined. Some argue that the cause of this decline has been

A police officer writes down a woman's report of a crime in her neighborhood. Research indicates that cooperation between the police and ordinary citizens is a highly effective method of combating crime. In what ways can police-community relations be improved? (Michael Newman/Photoedit)

[6]President's Commission on Law Enforcement and Administration of Justice, *Challenge of Crime in a Free Society* (Washington, D.C.: Government Printing Office, 1967), p. 19.
[7]Richard Shenkman, *Legends, Lies, and Cherished Myths of American History* (New York: HarperCollins, 1988), p. 158.
[8]President's Commission, *Challenge of Crime,* p. 19.

the growing economy the United States has generally enjoyed since about 1993. Others claim that the $3 billion of additional funds the federal government has spent to curb crime in the last few years has led to less crime. Still others claim that an increase in the number of persons who are jailed or imprisoned is responsible for the reduction in crime. Some have even argued that legalized abortion has reduced the population that is likely to commit crimes. You can see changes in the rates of violent crimes, homicides, and thefts in Figures 15–6, 15–7, and 15–8, respectively.

Many people have heard that the United States has the highest crime rates in the world. This is not actually true. Total crime rates are higher in some other countries, including Britain, Denmark, and Sweden, than in the United States. You are much more likely to be robbed in London than in New York City. What the United States has is not a high total crime rate, but a *murder* rate that is unusually high for an advanced industrialized nation. Explanations for this fact vary from easy access to firearms to a cultural predisposition to settling disputes with violence. It is worth noting, however, that many countries in Asia, Africa, and Latin America have much higher homicide rates than the United States.

Crimes Committed by Juveniles

A disturbing aspect of crime is the number of serious crimes committed by juveniles, although the number of such crimes is also dropping, as shown in Figure 15–9 on page 504. The political response to this rise in serious juvenile crimes has been varied. Some cities have established juvenile curfews. Several states have begun to try more juveniles as adults, particularly juveniles who have been charged with homicides. Still other states are operating "boot camps" to try to "shape up" less violent juvenile criminals. Additionally, victims of juvenile crime and victims' relatives are attempting to pry open the traditionally secret juvenile court system.[9]

Some worry that the decline in serious juvenile crimes is only temporary. The number of youths between the ages of fifteen and seventeen will rise from about nine million today to almost thirteen million in the year 2010. It is thus understandable that there is grave concern about preventing an even worse juvenile crime problem in the years to come.

---

[9]See Chapter 5 for details on the rights of juveniles in our legal system.

FIGURE 15–6

Violent Crime Rates

Violent crime rates have declined since 1994, reaching the lowest level ever recorded in 2002. The crimes included in this chart are rape, robbery, aggravated and simple assault, and homicide.

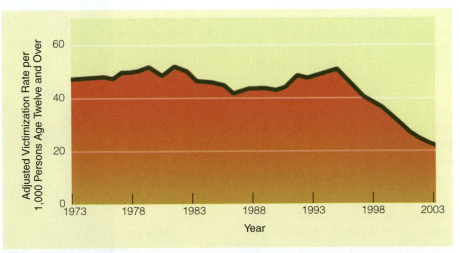

SOURCES: U.S. Department of Justice. Rape, robbery, and assault data are from the *National Crime Victimization Survey*. The homicide data are from the Federal Bureau of Investigation's *Uniform Crime Reports*.

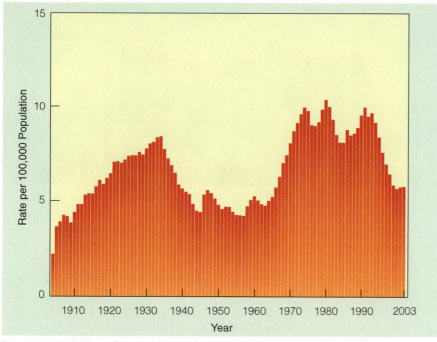

SOURCE: U.S. Department of Justice; National Center for Health Statistics, *Vital Statistics*.

FIGURE 15–7

Homicide Rate

Homicide rates recently declined to levels last seen in the late 1960s. The 2001 rate does *not* include deaths attributed to the 9/11 terrorism attacks.

The Cost of Crime to American Society

For the perpetrator, crime may pay in certain circumstances—a successful robbery or embezzlement, for example—but crime certainly costs the American public. One study suggests that when everything is added up, including the expenses of the legal system, the costs of private deterrence, losses by victims, and the value of time wasted by criminals and victims, the annual burden of crime in the United States exceeds a trillion dollars each year.[10]

The Office for Victims of Crime, a unit of the U.S. Department of Justice, has estimated that the direct tangible costs to crime victims, including the costs of

---

[10]David A. Anderson, "The Aggregate Burden of Crime," *Journal of Law and Economics,* Vol. 42, No. 2 (October 1999).

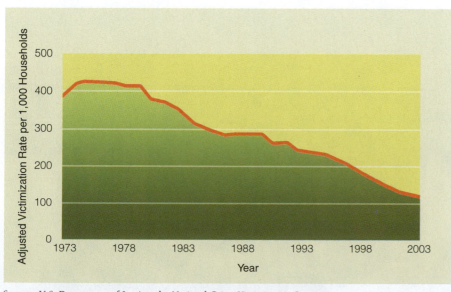

SOURCE: U.S. Department of Justice, the *National Crime Victimization Survey.*

FIGURE 15–8

Theft Rates

Theft rates continue to decline. *Theft* is defined as completed or attempted theft of property or cash without personal contact.

FIGURE 15–9

**Serious Violent Crime
by Perceived Age of Offender**

The number of serious violent crimes committed by juveniles has generally declined since 1993. The crimes included are rape, robbery, aggravated assault, and homicide.

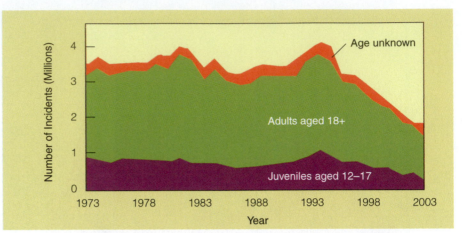

SOURCES: U.S. Department of Justice. Rape, robbery, and assault data are from the *National Crime Victimization Survey*. The homicide data are from the FBI's *Uniform Crime Reports*.

medical expenses, lost earnings, and victim assistance, are $105 billion annually. Pain, suffering, and reduced quality of life increase the cost to $450 billion annually. Check fraud costs an estimated $10 billion each year. Fraud involving stocks, bonds, and commodities costs about $40 billion a year. Telemarketing fraud costs another $40 billion (though the recently established "do not call" list may have curbed this expense somewhat). Insurance fraud costs about $80 billion a year.[11]

The Prison Population Bomb

Many Americans believe that the best solution to the nation's crime problem is to impose stiff prison sentences on offenders. Such sentences, in fact, have become national policy. In 2002, the number of persons held in U.S. jails and prisons exceeded two million for the first time. About two-thirds of the incarcerated population was held in state or federal prisons. The other third was held in local jails. About 60 percent of the persons held in local jails were awaiting court action. The other 40 percent were serving sentences.

---

[11]These estimates are online at http://www.ojp.usdoj.gov/ovc/ncvrw/2004/pg5b.html.

A group of young inmates begin "boot camp" by marching in line at the Sumter County Correctional Institution in Bushnell, Florida. What can be done to reach troubled youths before they commit crimes that lead to imprisonment? (© Bettmann/CORBIS)

The number of incarcerated persons has grown rapidly in recent years. In 1990, for example, the total number of persons held in U.S. jails or prisons was still only 1.1 million. From 1995 to 2002, the incarcerated population grew at an average of 3.8 percent annually. The rate of growth has slowed since 2002, however.

The Incarceration Rate. Some groups of people are much more likely to find themselves behind bars than others. Men are more than ten times more likely to be incarcerated than women. Prisoners are also disproportionately African American. To measure how frequently members of particular groups are imprisoned, the standard statistic is the **incarceration rate.** This rate is the number of people incarcerated for every 100,000 persons in a particular population group. To put it another way, an incarceration rate of 1,000 means that 1 percent of a particular group is in custody. Using this statistic, we can say that U.S. men have an incarceration rate of 1,309, compared to a rate of 113 for U.S. women. Table 15–1 shows selected incarceration rates by gender, race, and age. Note the very high incarceration rate for African Americans between the ages of twenty-five and twenty-nine—at any given time, almost 13 percent of this group are in jail or prison.

International Comparisons. The United States has more people in jail or prison than any other country in the world. That fact is not necessarily surprising, because the United States also has one of the world's largest total populations. More to the point, the United States has the highest reported incarceration rate of any country on earth.[12] Figure 15–10 on the following page compares U.S. incarceration rates, measured by the number of prisoners per 100,000 residents, with incarceration rates in other major countries.

Prison Construction. To house a growing number of inmates, prison construction and management have become sizable industries in the United States. Ten years ago, prison overcrowding was a major issue. In 1994, for example, state prisons had a rated capacity of about 500,000 inmates but actually held 900,000 people. The prisons were therefore operating 80 percent above capacity. Today, after a major prison construction program, state prisons are operating between 1 and 16 percent above capacity, although the federal prison system is still 31 percent above capacity. Since 1980, Texas has built 120 new prisons, Florida has built

Incarceration Rate
The number of persons held in jail or prison for every 100,000 persons in a particular population group.

[12]North Korea probably has a higher incarceration rate than the United States, but that nation does not report its incarceration statistics. The incarceration rate for political prisoners alone is estimated to be between 650 and 900 per 100,000 inhabitants. North Korea also holds an unknown number of prisoners as common criminals. See Pierre Rigoulot, "Comparative Analysis of Concentration Camps in Nazi Germany, the Former Soviet Union and North Korea," 2002. This article is online at the Web site of Human Rights without Frontiers. Go to **http://www.hrwf.net/html/north_korea___political_prison.html**.

TABLE 15–1

Incarceration Rates per 100,000 Persons for Selected U.S. Population Groups

	MEN	**WOMEN**
Non-Hispanic White, Total	649	68
Non-Hispanic White, Aged 25–29	1,615	170
Non-Hispanic Black, Total	4,810	349
Non-Hispanic Black, Aged 25–29	12,877	752
Hispanic, Total	1,740	137
Hispanic, Aged 25–29	4,339	314
All Groups	1,309	113

SOURCE: "Prison and Jail Inmates at Midyear 2002," *Bureau of Justice Statistics Bulletin*, U.S. Department of Justice (2003).

FIGURE 15–10

Incarceration Rates around the World

Incarceration rates of major nations measured by the number of prisoners per 100,000 residents. The statistics are for years from 2002 to 2004, depending on the nation. Some authorities believe that the estimate for China is too low.

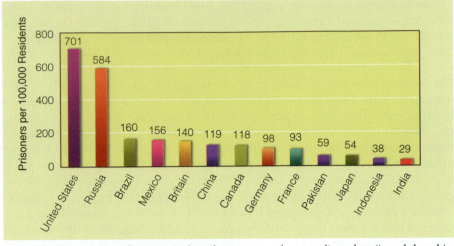

SOURCE: International Centre for Prison Studies. The most recent data are online at http://www.kcl.ac.uk/depsta/rel/icps/worldbrief/highest_to_lowest_rates.php.

84, and California has built 83. In 1923, there were only 61 prisons in the entire United States.

Nationwide, local jails are operating at 93 percent of capacity. That figure conceals major differences among jurisdictions, however. Seventeen of the fifty largest jail jurisdictions are operating at over 100 percent of their rated capacity. Clark County, Nevada (Las Vegas) is 66 percent above capacity and Maricopa County, Arizona (Phoenix) is 52 percent above capacity.

Effects of Incarceration. When imprisonment keeps truly violent felons behind bars longer, it prevents them from committing additional crimes. The average predatory street criminal commits fifteen or more crimes each year when not behind bars. But most prisoners are in for a relatively short time and are released on parole early, often because of prison overcrowding. Then many find themselves back in prison because they have violated parole, typically by using illegal drugs. Indeed, of the more than 1.5 million people who are arrested each year, the majority are arrested for drug offenses. Given that from twenty to forty million Americans violate one or more drug laws each year, the potential "supply" of prisoners seems virtually limitless. Consequently, it may not matter how many prisons are built; there will still be overcrowding as along as we maintain the same legislation on illegal drugs.

Federal Drug Policy

Illegal drugs are a major cause of crime in America. A rising percentage of arrests are for illegal drug use or drug trafficking. The violence that often accompanies the illegal drug trade occurs for several reasons. One is that drug dealers engage in "turf wars" over the territories in which drugs can be sold. Another is that when drug deals go bad, drug dealers cannot turn to the legal system for help, so they turn to violence. Finally, drug addicts who do not have the income to finance their habits often resort to a life of crime—assault, robbery, and sometimes murder.

The war on drugs and the increased spending on drug interdiction over the years have had virtually no effect on overall illegal drug consumption in the United States. Mandatory sentences, which have been imposed by the federal government since the late 1980s for all federal offenses, including the sale or possession of illegal drugs, are also not an ideal solution. Mandatory sentences lead to a further problem—overcrowded prisons. Furthermore, almost half of the 1.5

million people arrested each year in the United States on drug charges are arrested for marijuana offenses—and of these, almost 90 percent are charged with possession only.

While the federal government has done little to modify its drug policy, state and local governments have been experimenting with new approaches to the problem. Many states now have special "drug courts" for those arrested for illegal drug use. In these courts, offenders typically are "sentenced" to a rehabilitation program. Although efforts in some states to legalize marijuana have failed, eight states have adopted laws that allow marijuana to be used for certain medical purposes. Inevitably, though, state initiatives to legalize the use of marijuana for any reason run into problems because they conflict with federal drug policy.

Confronting Terrorism

Of all of the different types of crimes, terrorism can be the most devastating. The victims of terrorist attacks can number in the hundreds—or even in the thousands, as was the case when hijacked airplanes crashed into the Pentagon and the World Trade Center on September 11, 2001. Additionally, locating the perpetrators is often extremely difficult. In a suicide bombing, the perpetrators have themselves been killed, so the search is not for the perpetrators but for others who might have conspired with them in planning the attack.

Terrorism is certainly not a new phenomenon in the world, but it is a relatively new occurrence on U.S. soil. And certainly, the 9/11 attacks made many Americans aware for the first time of the hatred of America harbored by some foreigners—in this case, a network of religious fundamentalists in foreign countries. As you have read elsewhere in this text, immediately after 9/11 the U.S. government took many actions, including launching a war in Afghanistan, as part of a "war on terrorism." Congress quickly passed new legislation to fund these efforts, as well as a number of other acts, such as the Aviation Security Act discussed in Chapter 7.

Some of the actions taken in the wake of 9/11, such as the war in Afghanistan, were widely supported by the public. Others, such as the enactment of the USA

Ayman Gheith, right, and Omar Choudhary, left, were among three men detained by police on Interstate 75 in Florida in 2002. A woman reported to police that she had overheard them making terrorist threats while dining at a restaurant in Georgia. The men, medical students on their way to Miami to begin hospital internships, were later cleared of any wrongdoing. The incident led Muslim Americans to claim that they were victims of racial profiling. Police defended their actions, saying any threat of terrorism would be taken seriously. (AP Photo/J. Pat Carter)

AMERICA'S SECURITY
Those Colored Alert Levels

From time to time, you hear it on the radio—"Alert level elevated to orange." Weeks later, you may read in the newspaper that the alert level is back to yellow. You may ask yourself, "What was that all about?"

THE TERRORISM ALERT SYSTEM

The five levels of terrorism alerts issued by the Department of Homeland Security (DHS) are:

- Green: Low risk of terrorist attacks.
- Blue: Guarded condition. General risk of terrorist attacks.
- Yellow: Elevated condition. Significant risk of terrorist attacks.
- Orange: High risk of terrorist attacks.
- Red: Severe risk of terrorist attacks.

When the alert level rose to orange over the Christmas and New Year's holidays in 2003–2004, sharpshooters were deployed on Las Vegas Boulevard, extra patrols checked a North Dakota dam, and helicopters circled Times Square. Police collected overtime pay. The federal government promised to reimburse state and local governments for their costs, but the reimbursements rarely cover all such expenses.

How much does an orange alert cost in total? David Heyman of the Center for Strategic and International Studies estimates that the total cost of security during a week of orange alert is one billion dollars. This figure rep-resents the total security cost—it is not the difference between a yellow and an orange alert. Fixed homeland security costs amount to $880 million a week regardless of the alert level, so the true cost of an elevated level may be closer to $120 million a week.

IS IT WORTH IT?

Is the color-coded alert level system useful? Some doubt it. The DHS provides little or no specific information about likely targets or methods of terrorism. Some contend that the warning system, already an object of derision for late-night comedians, is inuring Americans to genuine threats. John D. Cohen, a former police officer with the Progressive Policy Institute, believes that the system should be scrapped. He maintains that terrorism prevention should be a "part of everyday business" instead of an occasional emergency responsibility for state and local authorities.*

FOR CRITICAL ANALYSIS

In what ways could the alert level system be beneficial? In what ways might it be counterproductive?

---

*The Democratic Leadership Council, "Idea of the Week: Real Preparation, Not Security Alerts," *New Democrat Daily,* June 6, 2003. This article is online at **http://www.pscommllc.com/news/ndol_real_preparation.html**.

Patriot Act and President Bush's executive order establishing military tribunals (see Chapter 4), have been criticized for infringing too greatly on Americans' civil liberties. (Is the system of colored terrorist alert codes a reasonable tool for combating terrorism? We examine that question in the *America's Security* feature above.) The extension of the war on terrorism to include a military attack against Iraq in 2003 was also criticized by many Americans as well as citizens of countries around the globe. Certainly, at this point there is no end in sight to the war on terrorism. As with all policies, the nation's policy with respect to terrorism will be evaluated—and perhaps modified—over time.

 ## Environmental Policy

Americans have paid increasing attention to environmental issues in the last three decades. A major source of concern for the general public has been the emission of pollutants into the air and water. Each year, the world atmosphere receives twenty million metric tons of sulfur dioxide, eighteen million metric tons of ozone pollutants, and sixty million metric tons of carbon monoxide.

Environmentalism

Environmental issues are not limited to concerns about pollution. A second major concern is the protection of the natural environment. The protection of endangered species is an example of this type of issue. The movement to protect the environment has been based on two major strands of thought since its beginnings in the early 1900s. One point of view calls for *conservation*—that is, a policy under which natural resources should be used, but not abused. A second view advocates *preservation*. Under this policy, natural preserves are established that are isolated from the effects of human activity.

The Environmentalist Movement. In the 1960s, an environmentalist movement arose that was much more focused on pollution issues than the previous conservation movement. A series of high-profile events served to awaken environmental interest. In 1962, Rachel Carson, of the U.S. Fish and Wildlife Service, published *Silent Spring*,[13] in which she detailed the injurious effects of pesticides on a variety of wild species. In 1969, an oil spill off the coast of Santa Barbara, California, drew national attention. That same year, the Cuyahoga River in Cleveland actually caught fire due to flammable chemicals floating on top of the water.

---

[13]Boston: Houghton Mifflin, 1962; repr., Boston: Mariner Books, 2002.

These three photos illustrate some of the environmental problems that persuaded Congress to pass the National Environmental Policy Act of 1969. Top: The Cuyahoga River in 1969—firefighters extinguish a fire that started on the river and spread to a wooden trestle bridge. Lower left: Workers clean a beach after a 1969 oil spill in Santa Barbara, California. Lower right: In 1945, municipal workers spray the pesticide DDT at Jones Beach, New York, while children frolic. (Cuyahoga River photo courtesy of the EPA; Santa Barbara photo courtesy of the California Environmental Protection Agency; Jones Beach photo, Library of Congress)

In 1970, the environmental movement organized the first Earth Day, which proved to be a very successful way of drawing attention to environmentalism and its concerns. Pollution control was a popular goal, and during the 1960s and 1970s Congress passed numerous bills aimed at cleaning up the nation's air and water. We will describe some of these efforts in greater detail shortly.

Ecology. In the 1970s, a number of environmental activists began to advocate policies that were more controversial than pollution control. These policies represented a radical elaboration of the older preservationist philosophy and a rejection of the conservationist principle of wise use. Not only did the new line of thought reject the conservation of natural resources for use by people, but some activists also argued that the human race itself was the problem. Along with the new thinking came a new label—the ecology movement. *Ecology* refers to the total pattern of relationships between organisms and their environment.

Cleaning Up the Air and Water

The government has been responding to pollution problems since before the American Revolution, when the Massachusetts Bay Colony issued regulations to try to stop the pollution of Boston Harbor. In the 1800s, states passed laws controlling water pollution after scientists and medical researchers convinced most policymakers that dumping sewage into drinking and bathing water caused disease. At the national level, the Federal Water Pollution Control Act of 1948 provided research and assistance to the states for pollution-control efforts, but little was done.

Environmental Impact Statement (EIS)

A report that must show the costs and benefits of major federal actions that could significantly affect the quality of the environment.

The National Environmental Policy Act. The year 1969 marked the start of the most concerted national government involvement in solving pollution problems. As mentioned, in that year, the conflict between oil-exploration interests and environmental interests literally erupted when an oil well six miles off the coast of Santa Barbara, California, exploded, releasing 235,000 gallons of crude oil. The result was an oil slick, covering an area of eight hundred square miles, that washed up on the city's beaches and killed plant life, birds, and fish. Hearings in Congress revealed that the Interior Department had no guidance in the energy-environment trade-off. Congress soon passed the National Environmental Policy Act of 1969. This landmark legislation established, among other things, the Council on Environmental Quality. It also mandated that an **environmental impact statement (EIS)** be prepared for all major federal actions that could significantly affect the quality of the environment. The act gave citizens and public-interest groups concerned with the environment a weapon against the unnecessary and inappropriate use of natural resources by the government.

A curtain of smog shrouds the Los Angeles skyline. Strict air-pollution standards for automobiles have been phased in over the past several years to curb such air pollution. How do policymakers measure the economic impact of clean-air policies? (AP Photo/Nick Ut)

Curbing Air Pollution. Beginning in 1975, the government began regulating tailpipe emissions from cars and light trucks in an attempt to curb air pollution. In 1990, after years of lobbying by environmentalists, Congress passed the Clean Air Act of 1990. The act established tighter standards for emissions of nitrogen dioxide (NO_2) and other pollutants by newly built cars and light trucks. California was allowed to establish its own, stricter standards. By 1994, the maximum allowable NO_2 emissions (averaged over each manufacturer's "fleet" of vehicles) were about a fifth of the 1975 standard. The "Tier 2" system, being phased in between 2004 and 2007, reduces maximum fleet emissions by cars and light trucks to just over 2 percent of the 1975 standard. In 2008–2009, the standards will be extended to trucks weighing between 6,000 and 8,500 pounds.

Stationary sources of air pollution were also made subject to more regulation under the 1990 act. The act required 110 of the oldest coal-burning power plants in the United States to cut their emissions 40 percent by 2001. Controls were placed on other factories and businesses in an attempt to reduce ground-level ozone pollution in ninety-six cities to healthful levels by 2005 (except in Los Angeles, which has until 2010 to meet the standards). The act also required that the production of chlorofluorocarbons (CFCs) be stopped completely by 2002. CFCs are thought to deplete the ozone layer in the upper atmosphere and increase the levels of harmful radiation reaching the earth's surface. CFCs were formerly used in air-conditioning and other refrigeration units.

In 1997, in light of evidence that very small particles (2.5 microns, or millionths of a meter) of soot might be dangerous to our health, the Environmental Protection Agency (EPA) issued new particulate standards for motor vehicle exhaust systems and other sources of pollution. The EPA also established a more rigorous standard for ground-level ozone, which is formed when sunlight combines with pollutants from cars and other sources. Ozone is a major component of smog.

Water Pollution. One of the most important acts regulating water pollution is the Clean Water Act of 1972, which amended the Federal Water Pollution Control Act of 1948. The Clean Water Act established the following goals: (1) make waters safe for swimming, (2) protect fish and wildlife, and (3) eliminate the discharge of pollutants into the water. The act set specific time schedules, which were subsequently extended by further legislation. Under these schedules, the EPA establishes limits on discharges of types of pollutants based on the technology available for controlling them. The 1972 act also required municipal and industrial polluters to apply for permits before discharging wastes into navigable waters.

The Clean Water Act also prohibits the filling or dredging of wetlands unless a permit is obtained from the Army Corps of Engineers. The EPA defines *wetlands* as "those areas that are inundated or saturated by surface or ground water at a frequency and duration sufficient to support, and that under normal circumstances do support, a prevalence of vegetation typically adapted for life in saturated soil conditions." In recent years, the broad interpretation of what constitutes a wetland subject to the regulatory authority of the federal government has generated substantial controversy.

Perhaps one of the most controversial regulations concerning wetlands was the "migratory-bird rule" issued by the Army Corps of Engineers. Under this rule, any bodies of water that could affect interstate commerce, including seasonal ponds or waters "used or suitable for use by migratory birds" that fly over state borders, were "navigable waters" subject to federal regulation under the Clean Water Act as wetlands. In 2001, after years of controversy, the United States Supreme Court struck down the rule. The Court stated that it was not prepared to hold that isolated and seasonal ponds, puddles, and "prairie potholes" become "navigable waters of the United States" simply because they serve as a habitat for migratory birds.[14]

Cost-Effective Solutions

Before the mid-1980s, environmental politics seemed to be couched in terms of "them against us." "Them" was everyone involved in businesses that cut down rain forests, poisoned rivers, and created oil spills. "Us" was the government, and

---

[14]*Solid Waste Agency of Northern Cook County v. U.S. Army Corps of Engineers,* 531 U.S. 159 (2001).

it was the government's job to stop "them." Today, particularly in the United States, more people are aware that the battle lines are blurred.

According to the EPA, we are spending about $210 billion annually to comply with federal environmental rules. There is a bright side, however. A report issued by the Office of Management and Budget in 2003 concluded that the health and social benefits of enforcing tough new clean-air regulations are five to seven times greater than the costs of compliance. The government has become interested in how to solve the nation's environmental problems at the lowest cost. Moreover, U.S. corporations are becoming increasingly engaged in producing recyclable and biodegradable products, as well as helping to solve some environmental problems.

The Costs of Clean Air.   Cost concerns clearly were in the minds of the drafters of the Clean Air Act of 1990 when they tackled the problem of sulfur emissions from electric power plants. Rather than tightening the existing standards, the law simply limited total sulfur emissions. Companies had a choice of either rebuilding old plants or buying rights to pollute. The result was that polluters had an incentive to not even attempt to deal with exceptionally dirty plants. When closing down such plants, they could sell their pollution rights to those who valued them more. The law is straightforward: An electric utility power plant is allowed to emit up to one ton of sulfur dioxide into the air in a given year. If the plant emits one ton of sulfur dioxide, the allowance disappears. If a plant switches to a fuel low in sulfur dioxide, for example, or installs "scrubbing equipment" that reduces sulfur dioxide, it may end up emitting less than one ton. In this circumstance, it can sell or otherwise trade its unused pollution allowance, or it can bank it for later use.

These rights to pollution allowances are being traded in the marketplace. Indeed, there is a well-established market in "smog futures" offered on the Chicago Board of Trade and the New York Mercantile Exchange.

There Have Been Improvements.   The United States is making fairly substantial strides in the war on toxic emissions. According to the Environmental Protection Agency, in the last thirty years U.S. air pollution has been cut in half. Airborne lead is 3 percent of what it was in 1975, and the lead content of the average American's blood is one-fifth of what it was in that year. Airborne sulfur dioxide concentrations are one-fifth of the levels found in the 1960s. Carbon monoxide concentrations are a quarter of what they were in 1970. Water pollution is also down. Levels of six persistent pollutants in U.S. freshwater fish are about one-fifth of their 1970 levels. One reason for these successes is the increased awareness of the American public of the need for environmental protection. To a large extent, this increased awareness has been brought about through the efforts of various environmental interest groups, which have also exerted pressure on Congress to take action.

Regulating Hazardous Waste: Superfund

In 1980, Congress passed the Comprehensive Environmental Response, Compensation, and Liability Act (CERCLA), commonly known as Superfund. The basic purpose of Superfund, which was amended in 1986 by the Superfund Amendments and Reauthorization Act, is to regulate the clean-up of leaking hazardous-waste disposal sites. A special federal fund was created for that purpose. Superfund provides that when a release or a threatened release from a site occurs, the EPA can clean up the site and recover the cost of the clean-up from (1) the person who generated the wastes disposed of at the site, (2) the person who transported the wastes to the site, (3) the person who owned or operated the site at the time of the disposal, or (4) the current owner or operator. Liability is usually assessed on anyone who might have been responsible—for example, a person who generated only a fraction of the hazardous waste disposed of at the site may nevertheless be liable for all of the clean-up costs.

By 2005, about half of the designated sites on Superfund's high-priority list had been cleaned up—at a cost of about $21 billion. Large-volume waste contributors have also incurred legal expenses that average over one-third of the actual cost of cleaning up a site. Legal fees have averaged $32,000 among small-volume waste contributors, which is almost equal to the amount that these parties spent on clean-ups. Critics of the program claim that the potential benefits of such expensive toxic waste clean-ups are not worth the cost.

The Endangered Species Act

Inspired by the plight of disappearing species, Congress passed the Endangered Species Preservation Act in 1966. In 1973, Congress passed a completely new Endangered Species Act (ESA). The ESA made it illegal to kill, harm, or otherwise "take" a species listed as endangered or threatened. The government could purchase habitat critical to the survival of a species or prevent landowners from engaging in development that would harm a listed species.

The ESA proved to be a powerful legal tool for the ecology movement. In a famous example, environmental groups sued to stop the Tennessee Valley Authority from completing the Tellico Dam on the ground that it threatened habitat critical to the survival of the snail darter, a tiny fish. In 1978, the United States Supreme Court ruled in favor of the endangered fish.[15] Further controversy erupted in 1990, when the Fish and Wildlife Service listed the spotted owl as a threatened species. The logging industry blamed the ESA for a precipitous decline in national forest timber sales in subsequent years.

---

[15]*Tennessee Valley Authority v. Hill,* 437 U.S. 153 (1978). In 1979, Congress exempted the snail darter from the ESA. In 1980, snail darters were discovered elsewhere, and the species turned out not to be in danger.

A logger prepares to cut a tree during a forest-thinning operation in the Stanislaus National Forest near Dorrington, California. How much consideration should we give to the needs of the timber industry when establishing national forestry policies? (AP Photo/Rich Pedroncelli, File)

The ESA continues to be a major subject of debate. There are signs, however, that the government and environmentalists may be seeking common ground. Both sides are shifting toward incentives for landowners who participate in protection programs. "Regulatory incentives really do result in landowners doing good things for their land," said William Irvin of the World Wildlife Fund.[16] Still, environmental groups accused the Bush administration of underfunding the act and undermining the species-listing process by shifting control from the Fish and Wildlife Service to the secretary of the interior.

Global Warming

In the 1990s, scientists working on climate change began to conclude that average world temperatures will rise significantly in the twenty-first century. Gases released by human activity, principally carbon dioxide, may produce a "greenhouse effect," trapping the sun's heat and slowing its release into outer space. In fact, many studies have shown that global warming has already begun, although the effects of the change are still modest. Christine Todd Whitman, who headed the Environmental Protection Agency from 2001 to 2003, called global warming "one of the greatest environmental challenges we face, if not the greatest."

The Kyoto Protocol. In 1997, delegates from around the world gathered in Kyoto, Japan, for a global climate conference sponsored by the United Nations. The conference issued a proposed treaty aimed at reducing emissions of greenhouse gases to 5.2 percent below 1990 levels by 2012. Only thirty-eight developed nations were mandated to reduce their emissions, however—developing nations faced only voluntary limits. The U.S. Senate voted unanimously in 1997 that it would not accept a treaty that exempted developing countries, and in 2001 President Bush announced that he would not submit the Kyoto protocol to the Senate for ratification. By 2004, 122 nations had ratified the protocol. Its rejection by the United States, however, raised the question of whether it could ever be effective.

The Global Warming Debate. While the majority of scientists who perform research on the world's climate believe that global warming will be significant, there is considerable disagreement as to how much warming will actually occur. It is generally accepted that world temperatures have already increased by at least 0.6 degrees Celsius over the last century. Scenarios by the United Nation's Intergovernmental Panel on Climate Change predict increases ranging from 2.0 to 4.5 degrees Celsius by the year 2100. More conservative estimates, such as those by climate experts James Hansen and Patrick Michaels, average around 0.75 degrees Celsius.[17]

Global warming has become a major political football to be kicked back and forth by conservatives and liberals. Some conservatives have seized on the work of scientists who believe that global warming does not exist at all. (Some of these researchers work for oil companies.) If this were true, there would be no reason to limit emissions of carbon dioxide and other greenhouse gases. A more sophisticated argument by conservatives is that major steps to limit emissions in the near future would not be cost effective. Bjorn Lomborg, a critic of the environmental movement, believes that it would be more practical to take action against

Bjorn Lomborg, director of Denmark's Environment Assessment Institute, speaks at the Copenhagen Consensus conference in May 2004 in Copenhagen. Eight world-renowned professors of economics, among them several Nobel laureates, made up an expert panel that discussed and prioritized solutions to serious global challenges. (EPA/Bjarke Orsted/Landov)

Bjørn Lomborg
Director, The Environmental Assessment Institute

[16]"Endangered Species Act Turns 30 as Environmental Strategy Shifts," *The Charleston Post and Courier,* Charleston, S.C., January 2, 2004.

[17]J. E. Hansen, "Defusing the Global Warming Time Bomb," *Scientific American,* March 2004, p. 69–77. This article is also online at http://www.sciam.com/media/pdf/hansen.pdf.

According to a study by the National Aeronautics and Space Administration, Arctic sea ice has been decreasing at a rate of 9 percent per decade since the 1970s. Researchers suspect the loss of Arctic sea ice may be caused by the buildup of greenhouse gases in the atmosphere. The first image shows the minimum sea ice concentration in 1979, and the second shows minimum sea ice in 2003. The red line highlights the change. The changes in Arctic ice may be a harbinger of global climate change. (NASA images)

global warming later in the century, when the world is (presumably) richer and when renewable energy sources have become more competitive in price.[18]

★ Domestic Policy: Why Is It Important Today?

Whether policy is made by the president or by Congress, policymaking affects you perhaps more than any other aspect of government. Certainly, if you fly, you saw how policymaking affected the ease, or lack thereof, of getting on a plane after new security measures were implemented following 9/11. Other results of policy changes may not be so obvious, even though they are important. For example, you may not realize how much cleaner the air is in New York, Minneapolis, and other cities than it was thirty-five or more years ago. Older people with long memories may be able to tell the difference, however.

The way we finance health care is a major political issue that has obvious implications for your pocketbook or wallet. The degree of success the government has in preventing crime may affect your peace of mind and perhaps even determine how willing you are to leave your home at night. Clean air and water are always major concerns. Serious climactic change could affect you directly as well. Global warming could lead to inadequate water supplies from precipitation in your region or make it unpleasant to remain outside in the summer. Domestic policy determines how we address these issues and other matters of national concern.

[18]Bjorn Lomborg, *The Skeptical Environmentalist* (Cambridge, England: The Cambridge University Press, 2001), pp. 258–324.

MAKING A DIFFERENCE ★ Environmental Trade-Offs

Environmental problems will undoubtedly be some of the most important domestic issues in the coming decades. For example, every energy policy involves environmental questions. To make things more complicated, the parallel struggles of coping with energy problems and preserving our environment tend to work at cross-purposes.

Land use is another topic that can require difficult political trade-offs. Landowners naturally want the freedom to do whatever they wish with their property. But what if a farm family at some distance from town wants to sell its property so that developers can put up tract housing? Should the state or local government be able to block such a development on the ground that it would foster "urban sprawl"?

Why Should You Care?

The trade-off between energy development and preserving the environment has a direct impact on your pocketbook and your quality of life. In 2004, gasoline prices rose dramatically. High gas prices affect your mobility. Yet increased oil drilling might despoil nature reserves, and no one wants to live next door to a refinery.

Land-use issues can have an even more direct effect on your life. On the one hand, a housing development might destroy a local scenic view. On the other hand, failure to build new housing will increase the value of existing housing. As a result, you might have to pay more to rent an apartment or, eventually, to buy a house.

What Can You Do?

Energy policy is a national issue, and you can have an impact on policy by getting involved with national organizations through their Web sites. The following environmental groups have taken a special interest in energy issues:

National Environmental Policy Institute
http://www.nepi.org

(This organization is particularly interested in telecommuting as a way of saving time and natural resources.)

Friends of the Earth
http://www.foe.org

Wilderness Society
http://www.wilderness.org

For a contrasting point of view, go to the home page of the Heritage Foundation at **http://www.heritage.org** and look for its list of research issues. Then click on "Energy & Environment."

Land-use policies are usually set at the state or local level. There are some national groups that organize around these issues, however. For a slow-growth perspective, visit the Smart Growth Network at **http://www.smartgrowth.org**.

For counterarguments, check the Web site of the Thoreau Institute at **http://ti.org**.

 **Key Terms**

domestic policy 485	food stamps 496	Medicaid 490	Supplemental Security Income (SSI) 496
earned-income tax credit (EITC) program 497	incarceration rate 505	Medicare 490	Temporary Assistance to Needy Families (TANF) 496
environmental impact statement (EIS) 510	income transfer 494	national health insurance 492	
	in-kind subsidy 495	single-payer plan 492	

Chapter Summary

1 Domestic policy consists of all of the laws, government planning, and government actions that affect the lives of American citizens. Policies are created in response to public problems or public demand for government action. Major policy problems discussed in this chapter include health care, poverty and welfare, crime, the environment, and immigration.

2 The policymaking process is initiated when policymakers become aware—through the media or from their constituents—of a problem that needs to be addressed by the legislature and the president. The process of policymaking includes five steps: agenda building, policy formulation, policy adoption, policy implementation, and policy evaluation. All policy actions necessarily result in both costs and benefits for society.

3 Health-care spending is about 15 percent of the U.S. economy and is growing. Reasons for this growth include the increasing number of elderly persons, advancing technology, and higher demand because costs are picked up by third-party insurers. A major third party is Medicare, the federal program that pays health-care expenses of U.S. residents over the age of sixty-five. The federal government has tried to restrain the growth in Medicare spending, but it has also expanded the program to cover prescription drugs.

4 About 15 percent of the population does not have health insurance—a major political issue. Most uninsured adults work for employers that cannot afford to offer health benefits. Hospitals tend to charge the uninsured higher rates than they charge insurance companies or the government. One proposal for addressing this problem is a national health-insurance system under which the government provides basic coverage to all citizens. Another proposal advocates health savings accounts (HSAs) that would allow people to save for their medical expenses tax free.

5 In spite of the wealth of the United States, a significant number of Americans live in poverty or are homeless. The low-income poverty threshold represents the income needed to maintain a specified standard of living as of 1963, with the purchasing-power value increased year by year based on the general increase in prices. The official poverty level is based on pretax income, including cash, and does not take into consideration in-kind subsidies (food stamps, housing vouchers, and so on).

6 The 1996 Welfare Reform Act transferred more control over welfare programs to the states, limited the number of years people can receive welfare assistance, and imposed work requirements on welfare recipients. The reform act succeeded in reducing the number of welfare recipients in the United States by at least 50 percent.

7 America has always been a land of immigrants and continues to be so. Today, more than 9 million immigrants from other nations enter the United States each year, and over 10 percent of the U.S. population consists of foreign-born persons. The civil rights legislation of the 1960s and later has helped immigrants to overcome some of the effects of prejudice and discrimination against them.

8 There is widespread concern in this country about violent crime, particularly the large number of crimes that are committed by juveniles. The overall rate of violent crime, including crimes committed by juveniles, has been declining since 1995, however. In response to crime concerns, the United States has incarcerated an unusually large number of persons. Crimes associated with illegal drug sales and use have also challenged policymakers. A controversial issue today is whether federal drug policy, as reflected in the Controlled Substances Act of 1970, should take priority over state laws that legalize the use of marijuana for certain medical purposes. A pressing issue facing Americans and their government today, of course, is terrorism—one of the most devastating forms of crime. Government attempts to curb terrorism will no doubt continue for some time to come.

9 Pollution problems continue to plague the United States and the world. Since the 1800s, a number of significant federal acts have been passed in an attempt to curb the pollution of our environment. The National Environmental Policy Act of 1969 established the Council on Environmental Quality. That act also mandated that environmental impact statements be prepared for all legislation or major federal actions that might significantly affect the quality of the environment. The Clean Water Act of 1972 and the Clean Air Act amendments of 1990 constituted the most significant government attempts at cleaning up our environment. Recent environmental controversies have centered on the Endangered Species Act and global warming.

Selected Print and Media Resources

SUGGESTED READINGS

Davis, Devra Lee. *When Smoke Ran Like Water: Tales of Environmental Deception and the Battle against Pollution.* New York: Basic Books, 2004. Davis, an epidemiologist, describes the health consequences of polluted air. She provides historical examples, such as the Donora Fog of 1948 that sickened a small town in Pennsylvania.

Easterbrook, Gregg. *The Progress Paradox: How Life Gets Better While People Feel Worse.* New York: Random House, 2003. Easterbrook points to real improvements in recent years in fighting crime, cleaning up the environment, and enhancing the material prosperity of most Americans. Nevertheless, pessimism remains popular.

Ehrenreich, Barbara. *Nickel and Dimed: On (Not) Getting By in America.* New York: Owl Books, 2002. Released on audio CD in 2004. What is life like for the working poor? Commentator and humorist Barbara Ehrenreich sought to live for a few months working at minimum-wage jobs. Here, she describes her experiences.

Hage, Dave. *Reforming Welfare by Rewarding Work: One State's Successful Experiment.* Minneapolis: University of Minnesota Press, 2004. Hage describes the Minnesota Family Investment Program, a pilot program in welfare reform. He illustrates the story with first-hand accounts of three families.

Herzlinger, Regina, and Nancy R. McPherson. *Market-Driven Healthcare: Who Wins, Who Loses in the Transformation of America's Largest Service Industry.* New York: Basic Books, 1999. The authors advocate moving away from our current third-party payment system and allowing consumer demand to lead the health-care market. The result, they contend, would be convenient, cost-effective services. Herzlinger and McPherson are professors at the Harvard Business School.

LeBow, Robert H. *Heath Care Meltdown: Confronting the Myths and Fixing Our Failing System.* Chambersburg, Penn.: Alan C. Hood and Company, 2003. LeBow, a physician and more recently a quadriplegic, details the limits of current health-care insurance plans. He advocates a universal single-payer system.

Miller, Roger LeRoy, *et al. The Economics of Public Issues,* 14th ed. Reading, Mass.: Addison-Wesley, 2003. Chapters 4, 8, 11, 13, 19, 20, 22, 24, and 27 are especially useful. The authors use short essays of three to seven pages to explain the purely economic aspects of numerous social problems, including health care, the environment, and poverty.

MEDIA RESOURCES

The Age of Terror: A Survey of Modern Terrorism—A four-part series, released in 2002, that contains unprecedented interviews with bombers, gunmen, hijackers, and kidnappers. The interviews are combined with photos from police and news archives. The four tapes are *In the Name of Liberation, In the Name of Revolution, In the Name of God,* and *In the Name of the State.*

America's Promise: Who's Entitled to What?—A four-part series that examines the current state of welfare reform and its impact on immigrant and other populations.

A Day's Work, A Day's Pay—This 2002 documentary by Jonathan Skurnik and Kathy Leichter follows three welfare recipients in New York City from 1997 to 2000. When forced to work at city jobs for well below the prevailing wage and not allowed to go to school, the three fight for programs that will help them get better jobs.

Drugs and Punishment: Are America's Drug Policies Fair?—In this 1996 BBC production, British journalist Charles Wheeler examines America's drug use and the hail of new drug laws instituted under the Reagan administration. Former drug czar William Bennett defends the government's position.

Traffic—A 2001 film, starring Michael Douglas and Benicio Del Toro, that offers compelling insights into the consequences of failed drug policies. (Authors' note: Be aware that this film contains material of a violent and sexual nature that may be offensive.)

Young Criminals, Adult Punishment—An ABC program that examines the issue of whether the harsh sentences given out to adult criminals, including capital punishment, should also be applied to young violent offenders.

e-mocracy ★ The Internet and Domestic Policy

Today, the World Wide Web offers opportunities for you to easily access information about any domestic policy issue. The *Logging On* section that follows lists a variety of Web sites where you can learn more about domestic policy issues and how they affect you. Many other sites are available as well. For example, would you like to learn more about prisons and imprisonment rates in different countries? The Web site of the International Center for Prison Studies (ICPS) can help. A URL for the ICPS is **http://www.kcl.ac.uk/depsta/rel/icps/worldbrief/world_brief.html**. Would you like to take a turn at proposing a federal budget, and allocate spending among different programs, domestic or otherwise? You can find a budget simulation game at **http://www.kowaldesign.com/budget**. Of course, most news media outlets have their own Web sites, which are useful to keep up to date on the latest domestic policy developments.

Logging On

To find more information on poverty in the United States and the latest research on this topic, go to the Web site of the Institute for Research on Poverty at

http://www.ssc.wisc.edu/irp

For current statistics on poverty in the United States, go to

http://www.census.gov/hhes/www/poverty.html

The National Governors Association offers information on the current status of welfare reform and other topics at

http://www.nga.org

The Federal Bureau of Investigation offers information about crime rates at its Web site:

http://www.fbi.gov/ucr/ucr.htm

You can also find statistics and other information on crime in the United States at the Web site of the Bureau of Justice Statistics. Go to

http://www.ojp.usdoj.gov/bjs

Using InfoTrac for Online Research

One of the most heavily disputed topics covered in this chapter is global warming. What temperature changes can we expect in the twenty-first century? Which scenarios are realistic? New articles on global warming are published constantly. As an exercise, try to obtain updated information on the severity of this effect. You can find relevant information by visiting InfoTrac. To access InfoTrac, go to

http://www.infotrac-college.com

Log on, go to InfoTrac College Edition, and then go to the Keyword search page. Type "global warming" into the text box and click on "Search." Read a dozen or so short articles that seem, from their titles, to be most helpful in providing information that is current and accurate.

ONLINE REVIEW

At **http://politicalscience.wadsworth.com/schmidt12**, you will find a free Study Guide to this book. For each chapter, there are two online quizzes to help you master the material.

• The **PoliPrep Self Study Assessment** provides a pre-test for each major section of the chapter. PoliPrep then generates a customized study plan. After you complete the study plan, a post-test evaluates your progress.

• The **Tutorial Quiz** for each chapter provides questions on the chapter contents, including the features. The questions are organized to match the major sections of the chapter.

CHAPTER 16

Economic Policy

- Good Times, Bad Times

- Fiscal Policy

- Monetary Policy

- World Trade

- The Politics of Taxes

- The Social Security Problem

521

WHAT IF . . .
Every Adult Were Guaranteed a Job?

BACKGROUND

Some psychologists say that unemployment is one of the most traumatizing events in a person's life. Certainly, unemployment imposes costs on the entire economy, not just on the unemployed individuals. Since the Great Depression of the 1930s, fighting unemployment has been a major goal of the federal government. Legislation passed under President Harry Truman (1945–1953) made full employment a national goal, and so did the Humphrey-Hawkins Act of 1978. Neither bill had any real enforcement mechanism, however.

The government cannot force private businesses to hire employees. Therefore, the only way to guarantee a job to every adult would be for the government to become the *employer of last resort.* If such a program were implemented, what would it look like, and how would it work?

WHAT IF EVERY ADULT WERE GUARANTEED A JOB?

To get a sense of what a guaranteed jobs program would be like, consider the last time the federal government attempted to implement a major jobs program. At the start of the Great Depression, the unemployment rate reached 25 percent. In response, the administration of President Franklin Roosevelt (1933–1945) adopted several emergency employment measures.

Members of the Civilian Conservation Corps received a dollar a day (about $13 in 2005 dollars) plus room and board for disaster relief, reforestation, and flood control. Beginning in 1935, the Works Progress Administration (WPA) employed 8.5 million people. If a guaranteed jobs program were created today, presumably millions of Americans would be hired to pick up litter, look in on the elderly, care for the children of working mothers, and perform dozens of other hard-to-fill jobs.

None of Roosevelt's programs eliminated unemployment altogether. The programs were also expensive, and any modern-day guaranteed jobs program would be even more costly. Taxes would have to go up to pay for the program.

THE MINIMUM-WAGE PROBLEM

On average, WPA workers received approximately the minimum wage. (When the minimum wage was first created in 1938, it was twenty-five cents an hour.) Because unemployment was so widespread, paying WPA workers that much did not mean they were pulled away from private-sector jobs. Today, however, major sectors of the economy, including the retail and restaurant industries, depend on minimum-wage workers. If the government offered minimum-wage jobs to everyone, these industries would probably not be able to hire enough workers. One solution would be to have the legislation establishing the jobs program set the pay for government jobs of last resort at less than the minimum wage.

Even if the guaranteed jobs program offered a "subminimum wage," minimum-wage jobs would probably become harder to fill. Many minimum-wage jobs involve hard work, and employees must always worry that they might be fired. Participants in a jobs program would not have to be so concerned about losing their jobs and would probably not work very hard. Some employees might prefer such an environment.

THE IMMIGRATION PROBLEM

Immigrants could perform any minimum-wage jobs that citizens did not want to take. For citizens of nations in Asia, Africa, and Latin America, migrating to America is economically attractive. Even the lowest wages in the United States are much higher than the prevailing wages in most of these countries. Of course, the government would not let illegal immigrants participate in a federal guaranteed jobs program and might bar legal immigrants who have not yet become citizens as well. If there were more minimum-wage jobs available in the private sector, however, the number of immigrants might increase. Even now, America has a problem with illegal immigration. A guaranteed jobs program could make the problem much worse.

FOR CRITICAL ANALYSIS

1. *How would the problems created by a federal guaranteed jobs program compare with the benefits of such a program?*
2. *If some participants in a federal guaranteed jobs program did not perform satisfactory work, what should the government do?*

Nowhere are the principles of public policymaking more obvious than in the economic decisions made by the federal government. The president and Congress (and to a growing extent, the judiciary) are constantly faced with questions of economic policy. A major economic policy issue is how to maintain stable economic growth without falling into either excessive unemployment or *inflation* (rising prices). **Inflation** is defined as a sustained upward movement in the average level of prices.

One possible method of dealing with unemployment is described in the *What If . . .* feature that opened this chapter. Other issues discussed in this chapter include world trade, taxes, and the impact that Social Security will have on the federal budget in future years.

Inflation
A sustained rise in the general price level of goods and services.

 Good Times, Bad Times

Other than the fundamental tasks of maintaining law, order, and national security, no governmental objective is more important than the maintenance of economic stability. Like any economy that is fundamentally capitalist, the U.S. economy experiences ups and downs. Good times—booms—are followed by lean years. If a slowdown is so severe that the economy actually shrinks for six or more months, it is called a **recession.** Recessions, in part because they bring increased unemployment, are political poison for a sitting president, even though a president's power to control the economy is actually not that great. The government tries to moderate the effects of such downturns. In contrast, booms are historically associated with another economic problem that the government must address—rising prices, or inflation. We will turn to the topic of inflation shortly. First, we consider the problem of excessive unemployment.

Recession
Two or more successive quarters in which the economy shrinks instead of grows.

Unemployment

One political goal of any administration is to keep the rate of unemployment down. **Unemployment** is the inability of those who are in the work force to find a job. There are several reasons why individuals become unemployed. Some people enter the labor force for the first time and have to look for a job. Some people are fired or laid off and have to look for a job. Others just want to change occupations. **Full employment** is defined as a level of unemployment that makes allowances for normal movement between jobs. Full employment is widely considered to be a desirable state of affairs, but the nation does not always have it. During recessions, unemployment rises well above the full-employment level. For example, during the last serious business slowdown in 2001–2003, the rate of unemployment increased from 4.0 to 6.5 percent.

Unemployment
The inability of those who are in the labor force to find a job; defined as the total number of those in the labor force actively looking for a job but unable to find one.

Full Employment
An arbitrary level of unemployment that corresponds to "normal" friction in the labor market. In 1986, a 6.5 percent rate of unemployment was considered full employment. Today, it is assumed to be around 5 percent.

Unemployment Becomes an Issue. For much of American history, unemployment was not a problem that the federal government was expected to address. In the early years of the republic, most people would have doubted that the national government could do much about unemployment. By the late 1800s, many people had come to believe that as a matter of principle, the government should not fight unemployment. This belief followed from an economic philosophy that was dominant in those years—*laissez-faire economics.* (You learned about the concept of *laissez-faire*—French for "let it be"—in Chapter 1.) Advocates of this philosophy believed then (and believe now) that government intervention in the economy is almost always misguided and likely to lead to negative results. A second barrier to any federal government action against unemployment was the doctrine of *dual federalism,* which was described in Chapter 3. Under this theory, *only* state governments had the right to address a problem such as unemployment.

The Great Depression of the 1930s ended popular support for dual federalism and *laissez-faire* economics. As the depression took hold, unemployment initially exceeded 25 percent. Relatively high rates of unemployment—over 15 percent—persisted for more than ten years. As described in the chapter-opening *What If . . .* feature, one of the methods that the Roosevelt administration adopted to combat the effects of the depression was direct government employment of those without jobs.

Since the passage of the Social Security Act of 1935, the federal government has also offered a program of unemployment insurance. The program is the government's single most important source of assistance to the jobless. Not all unemployed workers are eligible, however. In fact, only about one-third of the unemployed receive benefits. Benefits are not available to employees who quit their jobs voluntarily or are fired for cause (for example, constantly showing up late for work). They are also not paid to workers who are entering the labor force for the first time but cannot find a job. Unemployment insurance is a joint state-federal program and is paid for by a tax on employers.

Measuring Unemployment. Estimates of the number of unemployed are prepared by the U.S. Department of Labor. The Bureau of the Census also generates estimates using survey research data. Figure 16–1 shows how unemployment has gone up and down over the course of American history.

Critics of the published unemployment rate calculated by the federal government believe that it fails to reflect the true numbers of discouraged workers and "hidden unemployed." Though there is no exact definition of discouraged workers or way to measure them, the Department of Labor defines them as people who have dropped out of the labor force and are no longer looking for a job because they believe that the job market has little to offer them.

Inflation

Rising prices, or inflation, can also be a serious political problem for any sitting administration, especially if prices are rising fast. As previously stated, inflation is a sustained upward movement in the average level of prices. Another way of defining inflation is as a decline in the purchasing power of money over time. The government measures inflation using the **consumer price index,** or **CPI.** The Bureau of Labor Statistics (BLS) identifies a market basket of goods and services

Consumer Price Index (CPI)
A measure of the change in price over time of a specific group of goods and services used by the average household.

In 1933, young members of the Civilian Conservation Corps (CCC) clear rocks from a trail in the Snoqualmie National Forest in Washington state. Today, government employees' unions, fearing competition, often oppose programs under which the government hires former welfare recipients or other low-paid individuals. How should such concerns be addressed? (© Corbis. All Rights Reserved.)

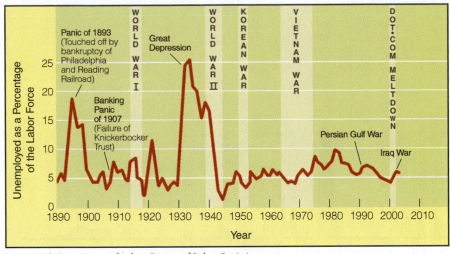

SOURCE: U.S. Department of Labor, Bureau of Labor Statistics.

FIGURE 16–1

More Than a Century of Unemployment

Unemployment reached lows during World Wars I and II of less than 2 percent and a high during the Great Depression of more than 25 percent.

purchased by the typical consumer and regularly checks the price of that basket. Over a period of many years, inflation can add up. For example, today's dollar is worth (very roughly) one-twentieth of what a dollar was worth a century ago. Figure 16–2 shows the changing rates of inflation in the United States since 1860.

The Business Cycle

As noted earlier in the chapter, the economy passes through boom times and recessions. Economists refer to the regular succession of economic expansions and contractions as the *business cycle*. This term may be less appropriate than it used to be because *cycle* implies regular recurrence, and in the years since World War II (1939–1945) contractions and expansions have varied greatly in length. Figure 16–3 on the following page shows business cycles since 1880. Note that the long-term upward trend line is shown as horizontal, so all changes in business activity focus around that trend line.

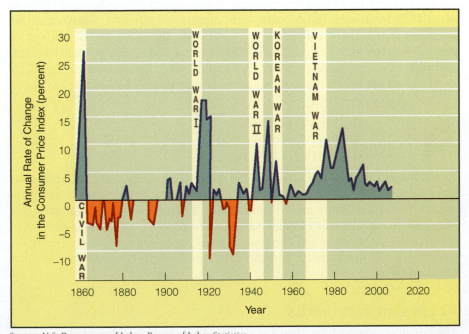

FIGURE 16–2

Changing Rates of Inflation, 1860 to the Present

From the Civil War until World War II, the United States experienced alternating inflation and deflation. (*Deflation* is a sustained decrease in the average price level.) Since World War II, deflation has not been a problem. The vertical yellow bars represent wartime.

SOURCE: U.S. Department of Labor, Bureau of Labor Statistics.

FIGURE 16-3

National Business Activity, 1880 to the Present

Variations around the trend of U.S. business activity have been frequent since 1880.

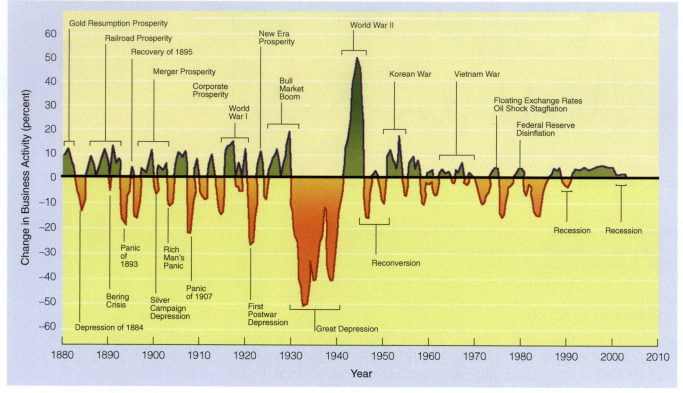

SOURCE: *American Business Activity from 1790 to Today,* 67th ed. (AmeriTrust Co., January 1996); plus authors' updates.

An extremely severe recession is called a *depression,* as in the example of the Great Depression. By 1933, actual output was 35 percent below the nation's productive capacity. By 1932, the net income of farm operators was barely 20 percent of its 1929 level, even though total farm output had risen by 3 percent in the interim. Between 1929 and 1932, more than five thousand banks, one out of every five, failed, and their customers' deposits vanished. Compared with this catastrophe, recessions since 1945 have been mild. Nevertheless, limiting the effects of recessions has been a major policy goal of every administration that has had to confront such a slowdown.

 Fiscal Policy

To smooth out the ups and downs of the national economy, the government has several policy options. One is to change the level of taxes or government spending. The other possibility involves influencing interest rates and the money side of the economy. We will examine taxing and spending, or **fiscal policy,** first. Fiscal policy is the domain of Congress. A fiscal policy approach to stabilizing the economy is often associated with a twentieth-century economist named John Maynard Keynes.

Keynesian Economics

The British economist John Maynard Keynes (1883–1946) originated the school of thought called **Keynesian economics,** which supports the use of government

Fiscal Policy
The federal government's use of taxation and spending policies to affect overall business activity.

Keynesian Economics
A school of economic thought that tends to favor active federal government policymaking to stabilize economy-wide fluctuations, usually by implementing discretionary fiscal policy.

spending and taxing to help stabilize the economy. (*Keynesian* is pronounced *kayn-zee-un*.) Keynes believed that there was a need for government intervention in the economy, in part because after falling into a recession or depression, a modern economy may become trapped in an ongoing state of less than full employment.

Government Spending. Keynes developed his fiscal policy theories during the Great Depression. He believed that the forces of supply and demand operated too slowly on their own in such a serious recession. Unemployment meant people had less to spend, and because they could not buy things, more businesses failed, creating additional unemployment. It was a vicious cycle. Keynes' idea was simple: in such circumstances, the *government* should step in and undertake the spending that is needed to return the economy to a more normal state.[1]

Government Borrowing. Government spending can be financed in a number of ways, including increasing taxes and borrowing. For government spending to have the effect Keynes wanted, however, it was essential that the spending be financed by borrowing, and not by taxes. In other words, the government should run a **budget deficit**—it should spend more than it receives. If government spending in a recession were financed by taxation, the government would be spending funds that would, for the most part, have otherwise been spent by the taxpayer.

Normally, businesses constantly borrow funds to expand future production. Consumers also borrow to finance items that cannot be paid for out of current income, such as a house or a car. In a recession, however, borrowing slows down. Businesses may not believe that they can sell the new goods or services that would allow them to repay the funds they might borrow. Consumers may be fearful of incurring long-term obligations at a time when their jobs might be threatened.

When the government borrows during a recession, this borrowing replaces the borrowing that businesses and consumers would normally undertake. By running a budget deficit, therefore, the government not only makes up for reduced spending by businesses and consumers, but reduced borrowing as well.

Discretionary Fiscal Policy. Keynes originally developed his fiscal theories as a way of lifting an economy out of a major disaster such as the Great Depression. Beginning with the presidency of John F. Kennedy (1961–1963), however, policymakers have attempted to use Keynesian methods to "fine-tune" the economy. This is discretionary fiscal policy—*discretionary* meaning left to the judgment or discretion of a policymaker. For example, President George W. Bush advertised his tax cuts of 2001 and 2003 as a method of stimulating the economy to halt the economic slowdown of those years.

Kennedy was the first American president to explicitly adopt Keynesian economics. In 1963, during a mild business slowdown, Kennedy proposed a tax cut. Congress did not actually pass the necessary legislation until early 1964, after Kennedy had been assassinated. The economy picked up—the tax cut was a success.

Discretionary Fiscal Policy Failures. Subsequent presidents did not have the same success as Kennedy with their fiscal policies. Lyndon Johnson, Kennedy's successor, presided over a boom that was partially fueled by spending on the Vietnam War (1964–1975). In principle, Johnson should have asked for a tax increase to pay for the war. He was afraid of the political consequences, however; the Vietnam War was unpopular enough already. Instead of raising taxes, Congress borrowed money and ran a budget deficit. This, of course, is the exact opposite of what Keynes would have recommended. One of the results seemed to be inflation.

Budget Deficit
Government expenditures that exceed receipts.

John Maynard Keynes, the famous British economist, at his home in London in 1929. (© Corbis. All Rights Reserved.)

---

[1]Robert Skidelsky, *John Maynard Keynes: The Economist as Savior 1920–1937: A Biography*. New York: Penguin USA, 1994.

Wage and Price Controls
Government-imposed controls on the maximum prices that may be charged for specific goods and services, plus controls on permissible wage increases.

Ending an inflationary spiral can be politically dangerous. It may result in a recession. Johnson's successors, presidents Richard Nixon, Gerald Ford, and Jimmy Carter, were reluctant to take that risk and, in any event, may have lacked the political support needed for serious anti-inflationary measures. Nixon, in particular, chose to fight inflation not with fiscal or monetary policies but by instituting a comprehensive system of **wage and price controls.** Eventually, Nixon had to lift the controls, and when he did, inflation came roaring back stronger than ever. In the end, inflation was halted through the use of monetary policy, which you will read about shortly.

The Thorny Problem of Timing

Attempts to fine-tune the economy face a timing problem. Have you ever taken a shower, turned on the hot water, and had the water come out cold? Then, in frustration, you gave the hot water faucet another turn and were scalded? What happened was that there was a lag between the time you turned on the faucet and the time the hot water actually reached the showerhead. Policymakers concerned with short-run stabilization face similar difficulties.

It takes a while to collect and assimilate economic data. Time may go by before an economic problem can be identified. After an economic problem is recognized, a solution must be formulated. There will be an action time lag between the recognition of a problem and the implementation of policy to solve it. Getting Congress to act can easily take a year or two. Finally, after fiscal policy is enacted, it takes time for it to act on the economy. Because the fiscal policy time lags are long and variable, a policy designed to combat a recession may not produce results until the economy is already out of the recession.

Automatic Stabilizers

Automatic, or Built-In, Stabilizers
Certain federal programs that cause changes in national income during economic fluctuations without the action of Congress and the president. Examples are the federal income tax system and unemployment compensation.

Not all changes in taxes or in government spending require new legislation by Congress. Certain automatic fiscal policies—called **automatic,** or **built-in, stabilizers**—include the tax system itself and government transfer payments such as unemployment insurance.

You know that if you work less, you are paid less, and therefore you pay lower taxes. The amount of taxes that our government collects falls automatically during a recession. Some economists consider this an automatic tax cut. Like other tax cuts, it may help reduce the extent of a recession.

Similar to the tax system, unemployment compensation payments may boost total economy-wide demand. When business activity drops, many laid-off workers automatically become eligible for unemployment compensation from their state governments. They continue to receive an income, although certainly it is less than they had when they were employed.

Deficit Spending and the Public Debt

U.S. Treasury Bond
Debt issued by the federal government.

The federal government typically borrows by selling **U.S. Treasury bonds.** The sale of these federal government bonds to corporations, private individuals, pension plans, foreign governments, foreign businesses, and foreign individuals adds to this nation's *public debt.* In the last few years, foreigners have come to own over 40 percent of the U.S. public debt. Twenty years ago, foreign ownership of the U.S. public debt was only 15 percent.

The Public Debt in Perspective.   Did you know that the federal government has accumulated trillions of dollars in debt? Does that scare you? It certainly would if you thought that we had to pay it back tomorrow. But we do not.

Gross Public Debt
The net public debt plus interagency borrowings within the government.

There are two types of public debt—gross and net. The **gross public debt** includes all federal government interagency borrowings, which really do not matter. This is similar to your taking an IOU ("I owe you") out of your left pocket and putting it into your right pocket. Currently, federal interagency borrowings account for close to $3 trillion of the gross public debt. What is important is the **net public debt**—the public debt that does not include interagency borrowing. Table 16–1 shows the net public debt of the federal government since 1940.

This table does not take into account two very important variables: inflation and increases in population. A better way to examine the relative importance of the public debt is to compare it to the **gross domestic product (GDP),** as is done in Figure 16–4. (The *gross domestic product* is the dollar value of all final goods and services produced in a one-year period.) There you see that the public debt reached its peak during World War II and fell thereafter. Since about 1960, the net public debt as a percentage of GDP has ranged between 30 and 50 percent.

Are We Always in Debt?   From 1960 until the last few years of the twentieth century, the federal government spent more than it received in all but two years. Some observers consider these ongoing budget deficits to be the negative result of Keynesian policies. Others argue that the deficits actually result from the abuse of Keynesianism. Politicians have been more than happy to run budget deficits in recessions, but they have often refused to implement the other side of Keynes's recommendations—to run a *budget surplus* during boom times.

In 1993, however, President Bill Clinton (1993–2001) obtained a tax increase as the nation emerged from a mild recession. For the first time, the federal government implemented the more painful side of Keynesianism. In any event, between the tax increase and the "dot-com boom," the United States had a budget surplus each year from 1998 to 2002. Some commentators predicted that we would be running federal government surpluses for years to come. All of those projections went by the wayside because of several events.

One event was the "dot-com bust" followed by the 2001–2002 recession, which lowered the rate of growth of not only the economy but also federal government tax receipts. Another event was a series of large tax cuts passed by Congress in 2001 and 2003 on the urging of President George W. Bush. These cuts, by themselves, were more than enough to erase the surplus.

The third event took place on September 11, 2001. Basically, as a result of the terrorist attacks, the federal government spent much more than it had planned to spend on security against terrorism. Finally, the government had to pay for the war in Iraq in 2003 and the occupation of that country thereafter. The federal budget deficit for 2004 was close to $400 billion. Few people now think there will be government budget surpluses in the near future.

TABLE 16–1

Net Public Debt of the Federal Government

YEAR	TOTAL (BILLIONS OF CURRENT DOLLARS)
1940	$ 42.7
1945	235.2
1950	219.0
1960	237.2
1970	284.9
1980	709.3
1990	2,410.1
1992	2,998.6
1993	3,247.5
1994	3,432.1
1995	3,603.4
1996	3,747.1
1997	3,900.0
1998	3,870.0
1999	3,632.9
2000	3,448.6
2001	3,200.3
2002	3,528.7
2003	3,878.4
2004	4,420.8*
2005	4,791.9*
2006	5,074.1*
2007	5,333.0*

*Estimate.

SOURCE: U.S. Office of Management and Budget.

Net Public Debt
The accumulation of all past federal government deficits; the total amount owed by the federal government to individuals, businesses, and foreigners.

Gross Domestic Product (GDP)
The dollar value of all final goods and services produced in a one-year period.

FIGURE 16–4

Net Public Debt as a Percentage of the Gross Domestic Product

During World War II, the net public debt grew dramatically. It fell thereafter but rose again from 1975 to 1995. The percentage fell after 1995, only to rise again after the events of 9/11.

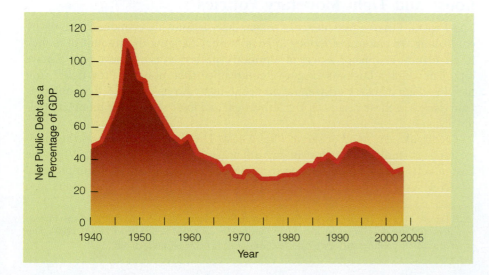

Federal Reserve System (the Fed)
The system created by Congress in 1913 to serve as the nation's central banking organization.

Federal Open Market Committee
The most important body within the Federal Reserve System. The Federal Open Market Committee decides how monetary policy should be carried out.

Monetary Policy

Controlling the rate of growth of the money supply is called *monetary policy*. This policy is the domain of the **Federal Reserve System,** also known simply as the **Fed**. The Fed is the most important regulatory agency in the U.S. monetary system.

The Fed performs a number of important functions. Perhaps the Fed's most important task is its ability to regulate the amount of money in circulation, which can be defined loosely as checking account balances and currency. The Fed also provides a system for transferring checks from one bank to another. In addition, it holds reserves deposited by most of the nation's banks, savings and loans, savings banks, and credit unions.

Organization of the Federal Reserve System

A board of governors manages the Fed. This board consists of seven full-time members appointed by the president with the approval of the Senate. The twelve Federal Reserve district banks have twenty-five branches. The most important unit within the Fed is the **Federal Open Market Committee.** This is the body that actually determines the future growth of the money supply and other important economy-wide financial variables. This committee is composed of the members of the Board of Governors, the president of the New York Federal Reserve Bank, and presidents of four other Federal Reserve banks, rotated periodically.

Alan Greenspan testifies during a Senate Banking Committee hearing on his fifth nomination for chairman of the Federal Reserve Board in 2004. (UPI Photo/ Greg Whitesell/Landov)

The Board of Governors of the Federal Reserve System is independent. The president can attempt to influence the board, and Congress can threaten to merge the Fed into the Treasury Department, but as long as the Fed retains its independence, its chairperson and governors can do what they please. Hence, any talk about "the president's monetary policy" or "Congress's monetary policy" is inaccurate. To be sure, the Fed has, on occasion, yielded to presidential pressure, and for a while the Fed's chairperson had to observe a congressional resolution requiring him to report monetary targets over each six-month period. But now, more than ever before, the Fed remains one of the truly independent sources of economic power in the government.[2]

Loose and Tight Monetary Policies

Monetary Policy
The utilization of changes in the amount of money in circulation to alter credit markets, employment, and the rate of inflation.

The Federal Reserve System seeks to stabilize nationwide economic activity by controlling the amount of money in circulation. Changing the amount of money in circulation is a major aspect of **monetary policy.** You may have read a news report in which a business executive complained that money is "too tight." You may have run across a story about an economist who has warned that money is "too loose." In these instances, the terms *tight* and *loose* refer to the monetary policy of the Fed.

Credit, like any good or service, has a cost. The cost of borrowing—the interest rate—is similar to the cost of any other aspect of doing business. When the cost of borrowing falls, businesspersons can undertake more investment projects. When it rises, businesspersons will undertake fewer projects. Consumers also

---

[2]Axel Krause, "The American Federal Reserve System: Functioning and Accountability" (Paris, France: Groupement d'etudes et de recherches, Notre Europe, Research and Policy Paper No. 7, 1999). This paper is available online at http://www.notre-europe.asso.fr/fichiers/Etud7-en.pdf.

react to interest rates when deciding whether to borrow funds to buy houses, cars, or other "large-ticket" items.

If the Fed implements a **loose monetary policy** (often called an "expansionary" policy), the supply of credit increases and its cost falls. If the Fed implements a **tight monetary policy** (often called a "contractionary" policy), the supply of credit falls and its cost increases. A loose money policy is often implemented as an attempt to encourage economic growth. You may be wondering why any nation would want a tight money policy. The answer is to control inflation. If money becomes too plentiful too quickly, prices (and ultimately the price level) increase and the purchasing power of the dollar decreases.

Loose Monetary Policy
Monetary policy that makes credit inexpensive and abundant, possibly leading to inflation.

Tight Monetary Policy
Monetary policy that makes credit expensive in an effort to slow the economy.

Time Lags for Monetary Policy

You learned earlier that policymakers who implement fiscal policy—the manipulation of budget deficits and the tax system—experience problems with time lags. Similar problems face the Fed when it implements monetary policy.

Sometimes accurate information about the economy is not available for months. Once the state of the economy is known, time may elapse before any policy can be put into effect. Still, the time lag when implementing monetary policy is usually much shorter than when implementing fiscal policy. The Federal Open Market Committee meets eight times a year and can put a policy into effect relatively quickly. However, a change in the money supply may not have an effect for several months.

The Way Federal Reserve Policy Is Announced

No matter what the Fed has on its mind, the way it signifies current monetary policy is by making announcements about an interest rate target. Nevertheless, when the chair of the Fed states that the Fed is lowering "the" interest rate from, say, 2.75 percent to 2.50 percent, something else is really meant. The interest rate referred to is the *federal funds rate,* or the rate at which banks can borrow excess reserves from other banks. The direct impact of this interest rate on the economy is modest. To have a significant effect on interest rates throughout the economy, the Fed must increase or restrain the growth in the money supply.

The Fed Tackles Inflation

For much of the twentieth century, the Fed's implementation of monetary policy had dismal results. Researchers point out that until the last two or so decades, the Fed's policies turned out to be procyclical rather than anticyclical—that is, by the time the Fed started pumping money into the economy, it was usually time to do the opposite. By the time the Fed started reducing the rate of growth of the money supply, it was usually time to start increasing it.

The Fed's greatest blunder occurred during the Great Depression. The Fed's policy actions at that time resulted in an almost one-third decrease in the amount of money in circulation. Some economists believe that the Fed was responsible for turning a severe recession into a full-blown depression.

Volckernomics. The Fed's finest hour came under chairperson Paul Volcker. Volcker, who was appointed by President Carter in 1979, was convinced that the Fed had to act against the inflation that had built up under Presidents Johnson, Nixon, and Carter. In 1979, the change in the CPI hit 13.3 percent per year. Volcker was prepared to tighten the

A federal employee performs quality control on new U.S. currency at the Bureau of Printing and Engraving in Washington, D.C. Some observers have called for the abolition of the hundred-dollar bill in an attempt to make criminal transactions more difficult. What problems might result from such a step? (UPI Photo/Roger L. Wollenberg/Landov)

On the left, in May 2004: In the Chicago suburbs, a service station employee changes the prices on the marquee to reflect rising gasoline prices. Rising costs of crude oil have a depressing effect on the economy. What would happen if the Fed, to counteract a slowdown in business caused by high oil prices, increased the rate of growth of the money supply?

On the right, in August 1938: In Santa Fe, New Mexico, a gasoline station owner has posted a sign to explain his prices. (Left: Frank Polich/Bloomberg News/Landov; right: Lange, Dorothea, Library of Congress)

money supply by enough to end inflation even if the result was to tip the nation into a recession. In 1980, Carter was defeated in his reelection bid by Ronald Reagan, a conservative Republican. Volcker interpreted this development as a green light to tighten the money supply further.

As the money supply tightened, interest rates soared. The prime rate, a key interest-rate benchmark, peaked at 21.5 in December 1980. It had been 11.5 as recently as 1979. The subsequent recession was by some measures the most severe contraction since the Great Depression. (You can check out the peak in unemployment in Figure 16–1 on page 525.)

A Policy Success.   There were political consequences. We now think of Ronald Reagan as a very popular president. In 1982, though, he was not popular at all. Ironically, the recession that caused this unpopularity was not Reagan's doing. Reagan had no authority to order Volcker to run a tight monetary policy. Reagan did, however, refrain from criticizing the chair of the Fed in public. The policies that Reagan was able to affect—taxes and spending, or fiscal policy—were loose. Reagan's tax cuts ran counter to Volcker's tight monetary policy. It was monetary policy, however, that proved to be more powerful.

By 1982, inflation was back down to 3.8 percent per year. Volcker eased away from the tight monetary policy. Slowly, people began to realize that the period of high inflation had come to an end. Reagan reappointed Volcker as chair in 1983. In 1987, however, he picked a new chair, Alan Greenspan, who has served ever since.[3]

---

[3]See Brian Trumbore, "Paul Volker—Part 1" and "Paul Volker—Part 2," at http://www.buyandhold.com/bh/en/education/history/2000/paul_volker1.html and paul_volker2.html. Also see the text of an interview with Volker shown in 2000 on the PBS program *Commanding Heights*. It is available at http://www.pbs.org/wgbh/commandingheights/shared/minitextlo/int_paulvolcker.html.

Monetary Policy versus Fiscal Policy

A tight monetary policy is effective as a way of taming inflation. (Some would argue that ultimately, a tight monetary policy is the only way that inflation can be fought.) If interest rates go high enough, people *will* stop borrowing. How effective, though, is a loose monetary policy at ending a recession?

Under normal conditions, a loose monetary policy will spur an expansion in economic activity. At any given time, there are businesses that are considering whether to borrow. If interest rates are low, businesses are more likely to do so. Low interest rates also reduce the cost of new houses or cars and encourage consumers to spend.

Recall from earlier in the chapter, however, that in a serious recession businesses may not want to borrow no matter how low the interest rate falls. Likewise, consumers may be reluctant to make major purchases even if the interest rate is zero. In these circumstances, monetary policy is ineffective. Using monetary policy is like "pushing on a string," because the government has no power to *make* people borrow money. Here is where fiscal policy becomes important. The borrowing *can* take place—if the government does it itself.

 World Trade

Most of the consumer electronic goods you purchase—flat-screen television sets, boom boxes, and digital cameras—are made in other countries. Many of the raw materials used in manufacturing in this country are also purchased abroad. For example, more than 90 percent of bauxite, from which aluminum is made, is brought in from other nations.

World trade, however, is a controversial topic. From 1999 through 2001, meetings of major trade bodies such as the World Trade Organization were marked by large and sometimes violent demonstrations against "globalization." Opponents of globalization often refer to "slave" wages in developing countries as a reason to restrict imports from those nations. Others argue that we should restrict imports from countries that do not follow the same environmental standards as the United States.

Although economists of all political persuasions are strong believers in the value of international trade, this is not true of the general public. In a public opinion poll taken in 2004, only 23 percent of Americans wanted the government to actively promote international trade, while 43 percent wanted the government either to slow down international trade or end it altogether. Of those surveyed, 63 percent believed that trade costs more jobs than it creates.[4]

Imports and Exports

Imports are those goods (and services) that we purchase from outside the United States. Today, imports make up about 14 percent of the goods and services that we buy. This is a significant share of the U.S. economy, but actually it is quite small in comparison with many other countries.

We not only import goods and services from abroad; we also sell goods and services abroad, called **exports.** Each year we export over $700 billion of goods. In addition, we export about $300 billion of services. The United States exports about 12 percent of GDP. As with imports, our exports are a relatively small part of our economy compared with those of many other countries.

Imports
Goods and services produced outside a country but sold within its borders.

Exports
Goods and services produced domestically for sale abroad.

---

[4]Steven Kull, *Americans on Globalization, Trade, and Farm Subsidies* (College Park, Md.: Program on International Policy Attitudes, 2004).

World Trade Keeps Growing
In this chart, the volume of world trade and world GDP are both represented by indexes. The base year is 1950, which means that the index is set to equal 100 for that year. While world output has increased by about eight times since 1950, world trade has increased by more than twenty-one times.

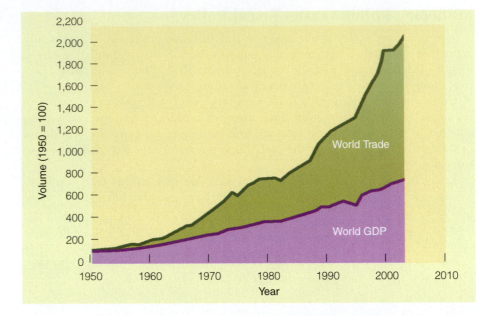

Back in the 1950s, imports and exports comprised only about 4 percent of the U.S. GDP. In other words, international trade has become more important for the United States. This is also true for the whole world. Consider Figure 16–5. There you see that since the 1950s, world trade has increased over twenty-one times.

The Impact of Import Restrictions on Exports

What we gain as a country from international trade is the ability to import the things we want. We must export other things to pay for those imports. A fundamental proposition for understanding international trade is the following:

In the long run, imports are paid for by exports.

Of course, in the short run, imports can also be paid for by the sale (or export) of U.S. assets, such as title to land, stocks, and bonds, or through an extension of credit from other countries. Other nations, however, will not continue to give us credit forever for the goods and services that we import from them.

Economists point out that if we restrict the ability of the rest of the world to sell goods and services to us, then the rest of the world will not be able to purchase all of the goods and services that we want to sell to them. This argument runs contrary to the beliefs of people who want to restrict foreign competition to protect domestic jobs. While it is certainly possible to preserve jobs in certain sectors of the economy by restricting foreign competition, there is evidence that import restrictions actually reduce the total number of jobs in the economy. Why? Because ultimately such restrictions lead to a reduction in employment in export industries.

Protecting American Jobs.   When imports are restricted to save jobs, one effect is to reduce the supply of a particular good or service and thus to raise its price to consumers. Economists calculate that restrictions on imports of clothing have cost U.S. consumers $45,000 *per year* for each job saved. In the steel industry, the cost of preserving a job has been estimated at approximately $750,000 per year. How much did it cost to save jobs in the automobile industry? We examine this question in the *Politics and Trade* feature.

Import Quota
A restriction imposed on the value or number of units of a particular good that can be brought into a country. Foreign suppliers are unable to sell more than the amount specified in the import quota.

Quotas and Tariffs.   The U.S. government uses two key tools to restrict foreign trade. They are import quotas and tariffs. An **import quota** is a restriction imposed

POLITICS AND TRADE
The High Cost of Saving U.S. Jobs

One of the best examples of how import restrictions raise prices to consumers has been in the automobile industry, where "voluntary" restrictions on Japanese car imports were in place for more than a decade. Due in part to the enhanced quality of imported cars, sales of domestically produced automobiles fell from nine million units per year in the late 1970s to an average of six million units annually between 1980 and 1982. As you can imagine, profits of U.S. automobile manufacturers fell as well. The U.S. automakers and the United Automobile Workers demanded protection from import competition.

POLITICIANS RESPONDED WITH TRADE RESTRICTIONS

Politicians from automobile-producing states were sympathetic to the "cause." The result was a "voluntary" agreement entered into by Japanese car companies. This agreement, which restricted U.S. sales of Japanese cars to 1.68 million units per year, began in April 1981 and continued into the 1990s in various forms.

THE COST PER JOB SAVED

Economist Robert W. Crandall estimated how much this "voluntary" trade restriction cost U.S. consumers. According to his estimates, the reduced supply of Japanese cars pushed their prices up by over $1,500 apiece. The higher price of Japanese imports, in turn, enabled domestic producers to hike their prices an average of over $600 per car. The total cost in the first full year of the program was more than $6.5 billion (expressed in today's dollars). Crandall also estimated that about 26,000 jobs were saved in automobile-related industries. Dividing $6.5 billion by 26,000 jobs yields a cost to consumers of more than $250,000 every year for each job saved in the automobile industry. U.S. consumers could have saved nearly $2 billion on their car purchases each year if, instead of implicitly agreeing to import restrictions, they had simply given $75,000 annually to every autoworker whose job was preserved by the "voluntary" import restraints.

FOR CRITICAL ANALYSIS

If it is so costly to save U.S. jobs through import restrictions, why do you think that politicians continue to pass import-restricting legislation?

---

on the value or the number of units of a particular good that can be brought into the United States. **Tariffs** are taxes specifically on imports. Tariffs can be set as a particular dollar amount per unit—say, 10 cents per pound—or as a percentage of the value of the imported commodity.

Tariffs have been a part of the import landscape for two centuries. One of the most famous examples of the use of tariffs was the Smoot-Hawley Tariff Act of 1930. It included tariff schedules for over 20,000 products, raising taxes on affected imports by an average of 52 percent. The Smoot-Hawley Tariff Act encouraged similar import-restricting policies by the rest of the world. Britain, France, the Netherlands, and Switzerland soon adopted high tariffs, too. The result was a massive reduction in international trade. According to many economists, this worsened the ongoing Great Depression.

Free Trade Areas and Common Markets.   To lower or even eliminate restrictions on free trade among nations, some nations and groups of nations have created free trade areas, sometimes called common markets. The oldest and best-known common market is today called the European Union (EU). As of 2004, the EU consisted of twenty-five member nations. These countries have eliminated almost all restrictions on trade in both goods and services among themselves.

On our side of the Atlantic, the best-known free trade zone consists of Canada, the United States, and Mexico. This free trade zone was created by the North American Free Trade Agreement (NAFTA), approved by Congress in 1993. There are additional regional free trade areas within Latin America and Asia.

Tariffs
Taxes on imports.

The World Trade Organization

Since 1997, the principal institution overseeing tariffs throughout the world has been the World Trade Organization (WTO). The goal of the nations that created the WTO was to lessen trade barriers throughout the world so that all nations can benefit from freer international trade.

What the WTO Does.   The WTO's many tasks include administering trade agreements, acting as a forum for trade negotiations, settling trade disputes, and reviewing national trade policies. Today, the WTO has more than 140 members, accounting for over 97 percent of world trade. Another 30 countries are negotiating to obtain membership. Since the WTO came into being, it has settled many trade disputes between countries, sometimes involving the United States.

For example, a few years ago, the United States, backed by five Latin American banana-exporting nations, argued before the WTO that the banana import rules of the European Union (EU) favored former European colonies in Africa and the Caribbean at the expense of Latin American growers and U.S. marketing companies. Specifically, Chiquita Banana claimed that its earnings had fallen because its competitors' bananas received preferential treatment from the EU. Because the EU would not back down, the United States imposed a 100 percent tariff on almost $200 million worth of EU items in nine categories. The right of the United States to impose the tariffs was backed by the WTO. Finally, the WTO brokered a deal between the United States and the EU. The EU agreed to dismantle its banana import policy that favored European multinationals and former European colonies. The United States agreed to drop the 100 percent tariff.

The WTO and Globalization.   Opponents of globalization have settled on the WTO as the embodiment of their fears. As noted earlier, WTO meetings in recent years have been the occasion for widespread and sometimes violent demonstrations. Indeed, the WTO raises serious political questions for many Americans. Although the WTO has arbitration boards to settle trade disputes, no country has veto power. Some people claim that a "vetoless" America will be repeatedly outvoted by the countries of Western Europe and East Asia. Some citizens' groups have warned that the unelected WTO bureaucrats based in Geneva, Switzerland, might be able to weaken environmental, health, and consumer safety laws if such laws affect international trade flows.

Bananas were the subject of a major trade dispute between the United States and Europe. Here, a worker in Honduras carries boxes in a banana-packing plant. If you buy apples, you have many choices, including Golden Delicious, Granny Smith, and McIntosh. Oranges may be mandarins, navels, or others. But in a world of more than five hundred banana varieties, U.S. and European consumers are loyal to just one, the Cavendish. The crop is huge and unvaried—a ready target for disease. Some scientists say it might be time to rethink our banana habits. (AP Photo/ Esteban Felix)

The United States is not the only country to have problems with the WTO. Beginning in 2001, the WTO sponsored a new round of trade talks called the Doha round, after the city in Qatar where the first talks were held. In 2003, however, the talks broke down completely at a meeting in Cancun, Mexico. At that meeting, economically advanced countries such as the United States and the nations of Western Europe pressed for new rules on cross-border investments, competition, government procurement, and trade facilitation. Developing countries opposed these priorities. A group of African nations demanded instead that wealthy nations open their markets to exports by poor farmers. When they were rebuffed, the Africans walked out.

The Balance of Trade and the Current Account Balance

You may have heard on the news that the U.S. **balance of trade** is "negative" by some large figure. What does this announcement mean? To begin with, a negative balance of trade exists when the value of goods imported into a country is greater than the value of its exports. This situation is called a trade deficit. The United States has consistently had a large trade deficit since the late 1970s.

The Current Account Balance. The balance of trade is limited to trade in goods. A broader concept is the **current account balance,** which includes the trade in services and a number of other items. The United States has enjoyed a positive balance of trade in *services* for a long time. (Does the recent practice of "outsourcing" service jobs abroad change this fact? We examine this question in the *Politics and Economics* feature on the next page.) Like the balance of trade, however, the current account balance is negative and has been growing more negative for years. Figure 16–6 shows the growth in the current account deficit.

Balance of Trade
The difference between the value of a nation's exports of goods and the value of its imports of goods.

Current Account Balance
A wider concept than the balance of trade. The current account balance includes the balance of trade in services, unilateral transfers, and other items.

FIGURE 16–6

The Current Account Deficit

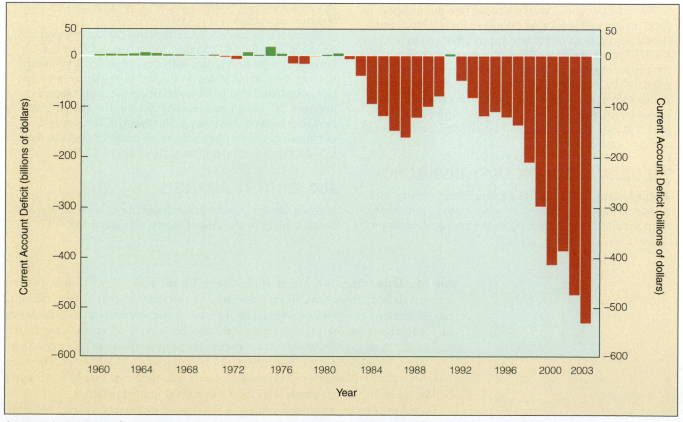

SOURCE: U.S. Department of Commerce, Bureau of Economic Analysis, U.S. International Transactions Accounts Data, Table 1, June

POLITICS AND ECONOMICS
Outsourcing: A Political Hot-Button Issue

Presidential candidate John Kerry had a name for heads of companies that outsourced telemarketing projects, customer services, and other white-collar jobs to foreign countries. He called them "Benedict Arnold CEOs." A well-known TV business analyst on CNN, Lou Dobbs, even started listing "unpatriotic" U.S.–based companies that were "sending this country's jobs overseas."

In 2004, Congress tried to pass a bill to prevent any type of outsourcing by the Department of State and the Department of Defense. Republican representative Don Manzullo of Illinois said, "You can't just continue to outsource overseas time after time after time, lose your strategic military base, and then expect this Congress to sit back and see the jobs lost and do nothing." When a Bush administration advisor publicly stated that the foreign outsourcing of services jobs was not such a bad idea, Kerry, as well as numerous other politicians, lambasted the Bush administration for even the suggestion that outsourcing could be viewed in a positive light.

THE JOBS LOST TO OUTSOURCING

According to Craig Barrett, chief executive of the chip maker Intel, American workers today face the prospect of "300 million well-educated people in India, China, and Russia who can do effectively any job that can be done in the U.S." Along the same lines of reasoning, Forrester Research predicts that 3.3 million services jobs will "move offshore" by the year 2015. According to *Business Week* editor Kathleen Madigan, "This is no longer about a few low-wage or manufacturing jobs. Now, one out of three jobs is at risk. These jobs could be shipped overseas in the name of cost cutting."

THE OTHER SIDE OF THE STORY: INSOURCING

A little-known fact is that numerous foreign nations outsource to the United States. In other words, we benefit from simultaneous insourcing as we engage in outsourcing.

Agents attend to customer calls at a "Smart Serve" call center in India. The call center employs over 1,000 young university graduates. College-educated Americans can often find better jobs than this. Does it always make sense to try to keep low-wage jobs in the United States? (Photograph: Sondeep Shankar/Bloomberg News/Landov)

Mexican companies that hire U.S. accountants outsource accounting services to the United States. E-mail and the Internet allow companies in Mexico to transfer financial data electronically. The services of U.S. accountants are in fact a less expensive substitute for those provided by Mexican accountants.

Therefore, to more fully understand the debate over outsourcing, you need to compare the outsourcing by U.S. firms to foreign companies with the outsourcing by foreign firms to the United States. In the last ten years, economists have estimated that labor outsourcing probably created between 20 and 25 million more jobs in the United States than it destroyed. For every dollar that U.S. firms spend on outsourcing, there appears to be an overall benefit to the U.S. economy from net insourcing of about $1.13.

FOR CRITICAL ANALYSIS

When a foreign automobile manufacturer, such as Toyota, builds a plant in the United States, who benefits?

Are We Borrowing Too Much from Other Countries? If we run a current account deficit, as we have in recent years, we can only finance it by increasing our obligations to other countries. The increasing current account deficit shown in Figure 16–6 on the previous page can also be viewed as an increase in the claims that foreigners have on our economy. These obligations to other countries can take a variety of forms. Foreigners can buy stocks on Wall Street. They can buy American businesses or real estate. Above all, they can buy U.S. Treasury bonds issued by the government to fund the federal budget deficit.

Have our obligations abroad, which by 2005 were increasing by over $500 billion per year, become too large? It is true that during the last fifteen years, the

United States has enjoyed a larger share of the world's economic growth than any country other than China. Many people in other nations therefore consider the United States an attractive place to invest. While foreign appetites for investment in America cannot be unlimited, the rise in the size of the current account deficit suggests that foreigners are still willing to invest in the United States.

The Politics of Taxes

Taxes are voted on by members of Congress. The Internal Revenue Code encompasses thousands of pages, thousands of sections, and thousands of subsections—our tax system is not very simple.

Americans pay a variety of different taxes. At the federal level, the income tax is levied on most sources of income. Social Security and Medicare taxes are placed on wages and salaries. There is an income tax for corporations, which has an indirect effect on many individuals. The estate tax is collected from property left behind by those who have died. State and local governments also assess taxes on income, sales, and land. Altogether, the value of all taxes collected by the federal government and by state and local governments is about 30 percent of the gross domestic product (GDP). This is a substantial sum but is less than what many other countries collect, as you can see in Figure 16–7.

Federal Income Tax Rates

Individuals and businesses pay taxes based on tax rates. Not all of your income is taxed at the same rate. The first few dollars you make are not taxed at all. The highest rate is imposed on the "last" dollar you make. This highest rate is the *marginal* tax rate. Table 16–2 on the following page shows the 2004 marginal tax rates for individuals and married couples. The higher the tax rate—the action on the part of the government—the greater the public's reaction to that tax rate. If the highest tax rate you pay on the income you make is 15 percent, then any method you can use to reduce your taxable income by one dollar saves you fifteen cents in tax liabilities that you owe the federal government. Individuals paying a 15 percent rate have a relatively small incentive to avoid paying taxes, but consider individuals who were faced with a tax rate of 94 percent in the 1940s.

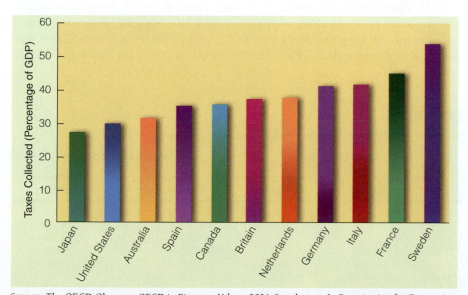

FIGURE 16–7

Total amount of taxes collected as a percentage of gross domestic product (GDP) in major industrialized nations.

SOURCE: The OECD Observer, *OECD in Figures—Volume 2004,* Supplement 1, Organization for Economic Cooperation and Development, 2004.

Loophole
A legal method by which individuals and businesses are allowed to reduce the tax liabilities owed to the government.

Progressive Tax
A tax that rises in percentage terms as incomes rise.

Regressive Tax
A tax that falls in percentage terms as incomes rise.

They had a tremendous incentive to find legal ways to reduce their taxable incomes. For every dollar of income that was somehow deemed nontaxable, these taxpayers would reduce tax liabilities by ninety-four cents.

Loopholes and Lowered Taxes

Individuals and corporations facing high tax rates will adjust their earning and spending behavior to reduce their taxes. They will also make concerted attempts to get Congress to add **loopholes** to the tax law that allow them to reduce their taxable incomes. When Congress imposed very high tax rates on high incomes, it also provided for more loopholes than it does today. For example, special provisions enabled investors in oil and gas wells to reduce their taxable incomes.

In 2001, President George W. Bush fulfilled a campaign pledge by persuading Congress to enact new legislation lowering tax rates. In 2003, rates were lowered again, retroactive to January 2003; these rates are reflected in Table 16–2. As a result of other changes contained in the new tax laws, the U.S. tax code became even more complicated than it was before.

Progressive and Regressive Taxation. As Table 16–2 shows, the greater your income, the higher the marginal tax rate. Persons with large incomes pay a larger share of their income in income tax. A tax system in which rates go up with income is called a **progressive tax** system. The federal income tax is clearly progressive.

The income tax is not the only tax you must pay. For example, the federal Social Security tax is levied on all wage and salary income at a flat rate of 6.2 percent. (Employers pay another 6.2 percent, making the total effective rate 12.4 percent.) In 2004, however, there was no Social Security tax on wages and salaries in excess of $87,900. (This threshold changes from year to year.) Persons with very high salaries therefore pay no Social Security tax on much of their wages. In addition, the tax is not levied on investment income (including capital gains, rents, royalties, interest, dividends, or profits from a business). The wealthy receive a much greater share of their income from these sources than the poor. As a result, the wealthy pay a much smaller portion of their income in Social Security taxes than do the working poor. The Social Security tax is therefore a **regressive tax.**

Who Pays? The question of whether the tax system should be progressive—and if so, to what degree—is subject to vigorous political debate. Democrats in general and liberals in particular favor a tax system that is significantly progressive. Republicans and conservatives are more likely to prefer a tax system that is proportional or even regressive. For example, President Bush's tax cuts made the fed-

TABLE 16–2

Marginal Tax Rates for Single Persons and Married Couples (2004)

SINGLE PERSONS		MARRIED FILING JOINTLY	
MARGINAL TAX BRACKET	**MARGINAL TAX RATE**	**MARGINAL TAX BRACKET**	**MARGINAL TAX RATE**
$ 0–$ 7,150	10%	$ 0–$ 14,300	10%
$ 7,151–$ 29,050	15%	$ 14,301–$ 58,100	15%
$ 29,051–$ 70,350	25%	$ 58,101–$117,250	25%
$ 70,351–$146,750	28%	$117,251–$178,650	28%
$146,751–$319,100	33%	$178,651–$319,100	33%
$319,101 and higher	35%	$319,101 and higher	35%

eral system somewhat less progressive, basically because they significantly reduced taxes on nonsalary income.

Overall, what kind of tax system do we have? The various taxes Americans pay pull in different directions. The Medicare tax, as applied to wages and salaries, is entirely flat—that is, neither progressive nor regressive. Because it is not levied on investment income, however, it is regressive overall. The federal estate tax is extremely progressive, because it is not imposed at all on smaller estates. (In 2004 and 2005, all estates below $1.5 million were exempt; for 2006 and 2007, the exemption will rise to $2 million.) Sales taxes are regressive because the wealthy spend a relatively smaller portion of their income on items subject to the sales tax. Table 16–3 lists the characteristics of major taxes. Add everything up, and the tax system as a whole is probably slightly progressive.[5]

The Social Security Problem

Closely related to the question of taxes in the United States is the viability of the Social Security system. Social Security taxes came into existence when the Federal Insurance Contribution Act (FICA) was passed in 1935. Social Security was established as a means of guaranteeing a minimum level of pension benefits to all persons. Today, many people regard Social Security as a kind of "social compact"—a national promise to successive generations that they will receive support in their old age.

To pay for Social Security, as of 2004, a 6.2 percent rate is imposed on each employee's wages up to a maximum of $87,900. Employers must pay in ("contribute") an equal percentage. In addition, a combined employer/employee 2.9 percent tax rate is assessed for Medicare on all wage income, with no upper limit. Medicare is a federal program, begun in 1965, that pays hospital and physicians' bills for persons over the age of sixty-five.

Social Security Is Not a Pension Fund

One of the problems with the Social Security system is that people who pay into Social Security think that they are actually paying into a fund, perhaps with their name on it. This is what you do when you pay into a private pension plan. It is not the case, however, with the federal Social Security system. That system is basically a pay-as-you-go transfer system in which those who are working are paying benefits to those who are retired.

Currently, the number of people who are working relative to the number of people who are retiring is declining. Therefore, those who continue to work will have to pay more in Social Security taxes to fund the benefits of those who retire. In 2025, when the retirement of the Baby Boomer generation is complete, benefits are projected to cost almost 25 percent of taxable payroll income in the economy, compared with the current rate of 16 percent. In today's dollars, that amounts to more than a trillion dollars of additional taxes annually.

Workers per Retiree

One way to think about the future bill that today's college students (and their successors) could face in the absence of fundamental changes in Social Security is to

TABLE 16–3
Progressive versus Regressive Taxes
PROGRESSIVE TAXES
Federal Income Tax
State Income Taxes
Federal Corporate Income Tax
Estate Tax
REGRESSIVE TAXES
Social Security Tax
Medicare Tax
State Sales Taxes
Local Real Estate Taxes

[5]Brian Roach, "GDAE Working Paper No. 03–10: Progressive and Regressive Taxation in the United States: Who's Really Paying (and Not Paying) Their Fair Share?" (Medford, Mass.: The Global Development and Environment Institute, Tufts University, 2003). This paper is online at http://www.ase.tufts.edu/gdae/Pubs/wp/03-10-Tax_Incidence.pdf.

FIGURE 16–8

Workers per Retiree

The average number of workers per Social Security retiree has declined dramatically since the program began.

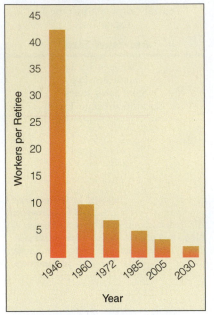

SOURCES: Social Security Administration and authors' estimates.

consider the number of workers available to support each retiree. As you can see in Figure 16–8, roughly three workers now provide for each retiree's Social Security, plus his or her Medicare benefits. Unless the current system is changed, by 2030 only two workers will be available to pay the Social Security and Medicare benefits due each recipient.

The growing number of people claiming the Social Security retirement benefit may pose less of a problem than the ballooning cost of Medicare. In the first place, an older population will require greater expenditures on medical care. In addition, however, medical expenditures *per person* are also increasing rapidly. Given continuing advances in medical science, Americans may logically wish to devote an ever-greater share of the national income to medical care. This choice puts serious pressure on federal and state budgets, however, because a large part of the nation's medical bill is funded by the government.

What Will It Take to Salvage Social Security?

The facts just discussed illustrate why efforts to reform Social Security and Medicare have begun to dominate the nation's public agenda. What remains to be seen is how the government ultimately will resolve the problem. What, if anything, might be done?

Raise Taxes.   One option is to raise the Social Security payroll tax rate. A 2.2 percentage point hike in the payroll tax rate, to an overall rate of 17.5 percent, would yield an $80 billion annual increase in contributions. Such a tax increase would keep current taxes above current benefits until 2020, after which the system would again technically be in "deficit." Another option is to eliminate the current cap on the level of wages to which the payroll tax is applied; this measure would also generate about $80 billion per year in additional tax revenues. Nevertheless, even a combined policy of eliminating the wage cap and implementing a 2.2 percentage point tax increase would not keep tax collections above benefit payments over the long run.

Other Options.   Proposals are also on the table to increase the age of full benefit eligibility, perhaps to as high as seventy. In addition, many experts believe that increases in immigration offer the best hope of dealing with the tax burdens and work force shrinkage of the future. Unless Congress changes the existing immigration system to permit the admission of a much larger number of working-age immigrants with useful skills, however, immigration is unlikely to relieve fully the pressure building due to our aging population. Still another proposal calls for partially privatizing the Social Security system in the hope of increasing the rate of return on individuals' retirement contributions. Would this be a workable solution? We examine this issue in the *Which Side Are You On?* feature.

★ Economic Policy: Why Is It Important Today?

Economic policy has a direct and obvious impact on your pocketbook or wallet. It can even be time-consuming. If you have attempted to fill out your own income tax forms recently, you discovered that due to complicated policy decisions by Congress and the Internal Revenue Service, it is harder and harder to understand how to fill out those forms, which are due on April 15 every year.

As we pointed out in Chapter 13, much domestic policymaking is carried out by nonelected appointees to government agencies. One of the most powerful appointees is the chair of the U.S. Federal Reserve System. That person can

WHICH SIDE ARE YOU ON?
Should Social Security Be Partially Privatized?

A major policy issue that has divided liberals and conservatives is whether Social Security should be privatized, at least partially. Privatization would allow workers to invest a specified portion of their Social Security payroll taxes in the stock market and possibly in other investment options, such as bonds or real estate. Although such a solution would have been unthinkable in past decades, today there is some support for the idea. Indeed, President George W. Bush's proposal that Social Security be partially privatized in this way drew significant support.

PARTIAL PRIVATIZATION COULD INCREASE THE RATE OF RETURN

Those who argue in favor of privatization point to the falling rate of return for Social Security contributions if the program is compared with a private investment plan.

FIGURE 16–9

Private Rates of Return on Social Security Contributions

Although those who paid in to Social Security in earlier years got a good deal, those who are paying in now and those who will contribute in the future are facing low or negative implicit returns.

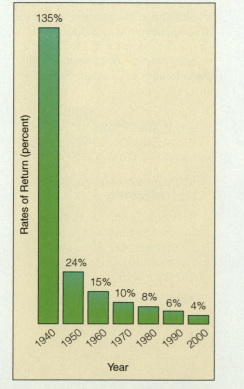

SOURCES: Social Security Trustees and authors' estimates.

Figure 16–9 shows that Social Security was a very good deal for those who paid into it in earlier generations. Today, the implicit rate of return is not so good. Looking into the future, the situation is worse. By 2020, the implicit rate of return may be negative, and it is likely to become increasingly negative in subsequent years. Advocates of privatization believe that investing Social Security contributions would yield greater returns for the average retired worker. In addition, the added investment in the nation's private sector could fuel economic growth, to everyone's benefit.

ANY PRIVATIZATION IS A THREAT TO SOCIAL SECURITY

A number of groups oppose the concept of partial privatization. These groups fear that the diversion of Social Security funds into individual investment portfolios could jeopardize the welfare of future retirees, who could be at the mercy of the volatile stock market. Opponents of partial privatization point out that such a plan might mean that workers would have to pay for two systems for many years—the benefits for today's retirees cannot simply be abolished.

For these people, the rate of return on Social Security contributions is also less of an issue than it might appear. Social Security was never meant to be an investment fund, and the program has always contained a certain "welfare" component that subsidizes the retirement of low-income individuals. This drives down the rate of return for the program as a whole. Finally, opponents worry that such a change could be the first step down a slippery slope toward the end of government-guaranteed retirement income.

WHAT'S YOUR POSITION?

Given the past performance of the stock market, just how risky would it be to invest a part of your Social Security contributions in the private sector?

GOING ONLINE

You can find arguments in favor of Social Security privatization at the Web site of the Cato Institute, a libertarian research organization. You can find Cato's home page at **http://www.cato.org** and the institute's arguments on Social Security at **http://socialsecurity.org**. The Social Security Network, a project of the Century Foundation, opposes privatization. Its Web site is at **http://www. socsec.org**.

determine how much you pay in interest when you decide to buy a car or a house. The Federal Reserve, through its monetary policies, ultimately determines the value, in terms of purchasing power, of the dollars you have in your wallet and checking account. Therefore, as long as we use money, monetary policy will directly affect you.

Economic policy mistakes by the president, Congress, or the Fed can have consequences that affect almost everyone in the country. High unemployment can place pressure on anyone who needs a job. The question of how we will handle the funding of Social Security and Medicare will probably continue to disturb both policymakers and the public throughout the lifespan of anyone who is now in college. Economic policy may seem abstract and irrelevant, but it is too important to ignore.

MAKING A DIFFERENCE

★ Learning about Social Security

The growing number of elderly people and increases in the cost of medical care will force changes in the Social Security and Medicare programs in years to come. The nature of these changes is still an open question.

Why Should You Care?

Unless you die before your time, you will grow old. Paying for your retirement will become an important issue. Even while you are still young, you may consider the cost of Social Security taxes on your wages or salary. What should the trade-off be between the interests of the elderly and the interests of younger persons who are members of the work force? Few questions will have a greater impact on your pocketbook, today and in the future.

What Can You Do?

Should Social Security and Medicare be changed as little as possible, to keep the system at least close to what currently exists? Or should we make more radical changes, such as replacing the existing programs with a sys-

tem of private pensions? You can develop your own opinions by learning more about the Social Security issue.

There are a variety of proposals for privatizing Social Security. Some call for a complete replacement of the existing system. Others call for combining a market-based plan with parts of the existing program. In general, advocates of privatization believe that the government should not be in the business of providing pensions and that pensions and health insurance are best left to the private sector. The following organizations advocate privatization:

National Center for Policy Analysis
12655 N. Central Expy.,
 Suite 720
Dallas, TX 75243–1739
972-386-6272

http://www.ncpa.org
http://www.teamncpa.org

Institute for Policy Innovation
250 S. Stemmons Freeway,
 Suite 215
Lewisville, TX 75067
972-874-5139

http://www.ipi.org

A variety of organizations oppose privatization in the belief that it will lead to reduced benefits for some or all older people. Opponents of privatization believe that privatization plans are motivated more by ideology than by practical considerations. Organizations opposing privatization include:

AARP
601 E. Street N.W.
Washington, DC 20049
800-424-3410

**http://www.aarp.org/
 socialsecurity**

National Committee to Preserve
 Social Security and Medicare
10 G Street N.E., Suite 600
Washington, DC 20002
202-216-0420

http://www.ncpssm.org

Key Terms

automatic, or built-in,
  stabilizers 528

balance of trade 537

budget deficit 527

consumer price index
  (CPI) 524

current account balance 537

exports 533

Federal Open Market
  Committee 530

Federal Reserve System
  (the Fed) 530

fiscal policy 526

full employment 523

gross domestic product
  (GDP) 529

gross public debt 528

import quota 534

imports 533

inflation 523

Keynesian economics 526

loophole 540

loose monetary policy 531

monetary policy 530

net public debt 529

progressive tax 540

recession 523

regressive tax 540

tariffs 535

tight monetary policy 531

unemployment 523

U.S. Treasury bond 528

wage and price controls 528

Chapter Summary

1 One of the most important policy goals of the federal government is to maintain economic growth without falling into either excessive unemployment or inflation (rising prices). Inflation is commonly measured using the Consumer Price Index (CPI) published by the U.S. Bureau of Labor Statistics. The regular fluctuations in the economy are called business cycles. If the economy fails to grow for six months or more, the nation is experiencing a recession.

2 Fiscal policy is the use of taxes and spending to affect the overall economy. Economist John Maynard Keynes is credited with developing a theory under which the government should run budget deficits during recessions to stimulate the economy. Keynes also advocated budget surpluses in boom times, but political leaders have been reluctant to implement this side of the policy. Time lags in implementing fiscal policy can create serious difficulties.

3 The federal government has run a deficit in most years since the 1930s. The deficit is met by U.S. Treasury borrowing. This adds to the public debt of the U.S. government. Although the budget was temporarily in surplus from 1998 to 2002, deficits now seem likely for many years to come.

4 Monetary policy is controlled by the Federal Reserve System, or the Fed. Monetary policy consists of changing the rate of growth of the money supply in an attempt to either stimulate or cool the economy. A loose monetary policy, in which more money is created, encourages economic growth. A tight monetary policy, in which less money is created, may be the only effective way of ending an inflationary spiral. Monetary policy may, however, be ineffectual in pulling the economy out of a severe recession—fiscal policy may be required.

5 World trade has grown rapidly since 1950. The United States imports and exports not only goods but services as well. While economists of all persuasions strongly support world trade, the public is less enthusiastic. Restrictions on imports to protect jobs are often popular. Ultimately, however, imports are paid for by exports. Restricting imports restricts exports as well, with resulting loss of employment in export industries. Trade restrictions also increase the cost of the affected goods to consumers.

6 Groups of nations have established free trade blocs to encourage trade among themselves. Examples include the European Union and the North American Free Trade Association (NAFTA). The World Trade Organization (WTO) is an international organization set up to oversee trade disputes and provide a forum for negotiations to reduce trade restrictions. The WTO has been a source of controversy in American politics.

7 The current account balance includes the balance of trade, which is limited to goods, and also the balance in the trade of services and other items. A possible problem for the future is the growing size of the U.S. current account deficit. This deficit is funded by foreign investments in the United States.

8 U.S. taxes amount to about 30 percent of the gross domestic product, which is not particularly high by international standards. Individuals and corporations that pay taxes at the highest rates will try to pressure Congress into creating exemptions and tax loopholes. Loopholes allow high-income earners to reduce their taxable incomes. The federal income tax is progressive; that is, tax rates increase as income increases. Some other taxes, such as the Social Security tax and state sales taxes, are regressive—they take a larger share of the income of poorer people. As a whole, the tax system is slightly progressive.

9 Closely related to the question of taxes is the viability of the Social Security and Medicare systems. As the number of people who are retired increases relative to the number of people who are working, those who are working may have to pay more for the benefits of those who retire. Proposed solutions to the problem include raising taxes, reducing benefits, allowing more immigration, and partially privatizing the Social Security system in hopes of obtaining higher rates of return on contributions.

Selected Print and Media Resources

SUGGESTED READINGS

Friedman, Milton, and Walter Heller. *Monetary versus Fiscal Policy.* New York: Norton, 1969. This is a classic presentation of the pros and cons of monetary and fiscal policy given by a noninterventionist (Friedman) and an advocate of federal government intervention in the economy (Heller).

Kotlikoff, Laurence J., and Scott Burns. *The Coming Generational Storm: What You Need to Know about America's Economic Future.* Cambridge, Mass.: MIT Press, 2004. The authors explain how an aging population will create a crisis in Social Security and Medicare funding. One possible flaw in the authors' argument

is their unquestioning use of very long-term demographic projections, which are inherently uncertain.

Slemrod, Joel, and Jon Bakija. *Taxing Ourselves: A Citizen's Guide to the Great Debate over Tax Reform,* second edition. Cambridge, Mass.: MIT Press, 2001. This volume is a clear, nonpartisan review of our tax system and the major proposals for revising it.

MEDIA RESOURCES

Alan Greenspan—This rather laudatory biography of the chairman of the Federal Reserve was released in 1999. Using Greenspan, the film looks at factors that influence the world and national economies.

e-mocracy ★ E-Commerce and Economic Policy

The age of e-commerce has brought with it several challenges for economic policymakers. One economic policy issue has to do with electronic money, or *e-money*. In one type of e-money, a balance of funds is recorded on a magnetic stripe on a card; each time the card is used, a computer terminal debits funds from the balance. Another type uses a microprocessor chip embedded in a so-called *smart card*. E-money is sometimes referred to as *e-cash* because it can be used like cash, meaning that no personally identifiable records are created. The problem for policymakers is that e-cash moves about outside the network of banks, checks, and paper currency. With the growth of e-cash, the traditional definition of money will no longer hold, giving the Federal Reserve less ability to control the money supply.

Logging On

You can keep up with actions taken by the Federal Reserve by checking the home page of the Federal Reserve Bank of San Francisco at

http://www.frbsf.org

For further information on Social Security, access the Social Security Administration's home page at

http://www.ssa.gov

For information on the 2005 budget of the U.S. government, go to

http://www.whitehouse.gov/omb/ budget/fy2005

Using InfoTrac for Political Research

The World Trade Organization continues to face trade disputes that are highly politicized. You can research a sample dispute by using InfoTrac. To use InfoTrac to research the WTO, go to

http://www.infotrac-college.com

Log in and go to InfoTrac College Edition, then go to the Keyword guide. Type "world trade organization cotton" in the search field. InfoTrac will present

you with a list of articles, with the most recent ones listed first. When choosing articles for your analysis, be sure to pick articles that represent the views both of the U.S. cotton industry and of cotton producers in developing countries.

ONLINE REVIEW

At **http://politicalscience.wadsworth. com/schmidt12**, you will find a free Study Guide to this book. For each chapter, there are two online quizzes to help you master the material.

• The **PoliPrep Self Study Assessment** provides a pre-test for each major section of the chapter. PoliPrep then generates a customized study plan. After you complete the study plan, a post-test evaluates your progress.

• The **Tutorial Quiz** for each chapter provides questions on the chapter contents, including the features. The questions are organized to match the major sections of the chapter.

Foreign Policy

WHAT IF . . .
North Korea Exploded a Nuclear Bomb?

BACKGROUND

It has long been American policy to try to limit the spread of nuclear weapons. A nuclear North Korea would be a particular problem for the United States, because North Korea is a potential military adversary. Indeed, as of 2004, the United States had 37,000 troops stationed in South Korea to help protect it from North Korea. In 1994, North Korea agreed to freeze a program for developing nuclear weapons in return for economic aid. In 2002, however, U.S. officials discovered a covert North Korean nuclear program that violated the 1994 agreement. In 2003, North Korea began testing long-distance rockets.

WHAT IF NORTH KOREA EXPLODED A NUCLEAR BOMB?

Almost every nation in the world (other than North Korea) believes that North Korea should not have nuclear weapons. That includes the five nations currently negotiating with North Korea: America, China, Japan, Russia, and South Korea. A North Korean nuclear test would mean that diplomatic efforts to persuade it to give up its nuclear weapons program had failed. The North Korean threat would quickly become one of the most important problems facing the United States and the world. We would be confronted with a series of unpalatable options.

One response could be a U.S. air strike to take out North Korea's nuclear development facilities at Yongbyon. Such a raid might be modeled on an Israeli attack in 1981, which destroyed a nuclear reactor in Iraq. The problem with such a strike in Korea is that, unlike Iraq, North Korea has an obvious way to hit back. It could attack South Korea. Even if North Korea were quickly defeated, the destruction and loss of life resulting from such a war could be extreme. For that reason, South Korea would probably mount a vigorous opposition to an air strike against Yongbyon. Such a strike might also cause serious problems in our relations with China.

Alternatively, if America proposed a response short of a military attack—such as economic sanctions—it would probably receive much support from around the world. Nations currently hostile to our policies in Iraq might rally to the United States as it confronted an unmistakable threat to world peace. Sanctions, however, might be ineffective.

NUCLEAR PROLIFERATION

If North Korea could not be disarmed by force, its neighbors, especially South Korea and Japan, might feel impelled to develop nuclear weapons as well. China's breakaway province of Taiwan might also aspire to nuclear capability, which would be a major issue for China. A further problem is that North Korea, perennially strapped for funds, could export nuclear technology to other countries. It might even sell weapons or know-how to terrorist organizations. North Korea has already provided missile technology to other nations—Pakistan, for example.

CAN DIPLOMACY RESOLVE THIS ISSUE?

A North Korean nuclear test could conceivably have taken place by the time you read this book. Still, two negotiating sessions between North Korea and the five nations mentioned above convened in 2004. A third session—in September—was put off as North Korea

sought to determine whether it would be negotiating with George W. Bush or John Kerry.

Both North Korea and the United States have made proposals. North Korea wants very substantial aid and security assurances in exchange for relatively limited moves to curtail its nuclear program. It also has not accepted verification procedures. The U.S. proposal calls for a complete and verifiable elimination of all aspects of the program in exchange for aid and assurances that are much more modest than those that North Korea has demanded. In principle, a settlement should be possible. American negotiators, however, are mindful of the fact that North Korea violated the last such agreement it made. Also, aiding North Korea, a totalitarian communist state with no aspirations to democracy, may undercut the Bush administration's efforts to encourage democracy throughout the world.

FOR CRITICAL ANALYSIS

1. *What motives might China have to dissuade North Korea from obtaining nuclear weapons?*
2. *If a settlement included a guarantee that the United States would not attack North Korea, what problems might that create?*

On September 11, 2001, Americans were forced to change their view of national security and of our relations with the rest of the world—literally overnight. No longer could citizens of the United States believe that national security issues involved only threats overseas or that the American homeland could not be attacked. No longer could Americans believe that regional conflicts in other parts of the world had no direct impact on the United States.

Within a few days, it became known that the attacks on the World Trade Center and on the Pentagon had been planned and carried out by a terrorist network named al Qaeda that was funded and directed by the radical Islamist leader Osama bin Laden. The network was closely linked to the Taliban government of Afghanistan, which had ruled that nation since 1996.

Americans were shocked by the complexity and the success of the attacks. They wondered how our airport security systems could have failed so drastically. How could the Pentagon, the heart of the nation's defense, have been successfully attacked? Shouldn't our intelligence community have known about and defended against this network? And, finally, how could our foreign policy have been so blind to the anger voiced by Islamist groups throughout the world?

In this chapter, we examine the tools of foreign policy and national security policy in the light of the many challenges facing the United States today. Nuclear proliferation is one of them, and we examined this question in the *What If . . .* feature that opened this chapter. One of the major challenges for U.S. foreign policymakers today is how best to respond to the threat of terrorism. We also review the history of American foreign policy.

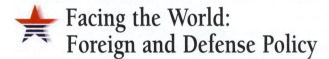

Facing the World: Foreign and Defense Policy

The United States is only one nation in a world with almost two hundred independent countries, many located in regions where armed conflict is ongoing. What tools does our nation have to deal with the many challenges to its peace and prosperity? One tool is **foreign policy.** By this term, we mean both the goals the government wants to achieve in the world and the techniques and strategies to achieve them. For example, if one national goal is to achieve stability in the Middle East and to encourage the formation of pro-American governments there, U.S. foreign policy in that area may be carried out through **diplomacy, economic aid, technical assistance,** or military intervention. Sometimes foreign policies are restricted to statements of goals or ideas, such as helping to end world poverty, whereas at other times foreign policies are comprehensive efforts to achieve particular objectives, such as changing the regime in Iraq.

As you will read later in this chapter, in the United States, the **foreign policy process** usually originates with the president and those agencies that provide advice on foreign policy matters. Congressional action and national public debate often affect foreign policy formulation.

National Security Policy

As one aspect of overall foreign policy, **national security policy** is designed primarily to protect the independence and the political integrity of the United States. It concerns itself with the defense of the United States against actual or potential (real or imagined) enemies, domestic or foreign.

U.S. national security policy is based on determinations made by the Department of Defense, the Department of State, and a number of other federal agencies, including the National Security Council (NSC). The NSC acts as an advisory body to the president, but it has increasingly become a rival to the State Department in influencing the foreign policy process.

Foreign Policy
A nation's external goals and the techniques and strategies used to achieve them.

Diplomacy
The process by which states carry on political relations with each other; settling conflicts among nations by peaceful means.

Economic Aid
Assistance to other nations in the form of grants, loans, or credits to buy the assisting nation's products.

Technical Assistance
The practice of sending experts in such areas as agriculture, engineering, or business to aid other nations.

Foreign Policy Process
The steps by which foreign policy goals are decided and acted on.

National Security Policy
Foreign and domestic policy designed to protect the nation's independence and political and economic integrity; policy that is concerned with the safety and defense of the nation.

Defense Policy
A subset of national security policies having to do with the U.S. armed forces.

Defense policy is a subset of national security policy. Generally, defense policy refers to the set of policies that direct the scale and size of the U.S. armed forces. Among the questions defense policymakers must consider is the number of major wars the United States should be prepared to fight simultaneously. Defense policy also considers the types of armed forces units we need to have, such as Rapid Defense Forces or Marine Expeditionary Forces, and the types of weaponry that should be developed and maintained for the nation's security. Defense policies are proposed by the leaders of the nation's military forces and the secretary of defense and are greatly influenced by congressional decision makers.

Diplomacy

Diplomacy is another aspect of foreign policy. Diplomacy includes all of a nation's external relationships, from routine diplomatic communications to summit meetings among heads of state. More specifically, diplomacy refers to the settling of disputes and conflicts among nations by peaceful methods. Diplomacy is the set of negotiating techniques by which a nation attempts to carry out its foreign policy.

Diplomacy may or may not be successful, depending on the willingness of the parties to negotiate. For example, in 1993, after years of refusing to negotiate or recognize each other's legitimacy, Israel and representatives of the Palestine Liberation Organization (the PLO) reached an agreement under which Israel returned control of Jericho and part of the West Bank to the Palestinians. As of 2004, however, relations between Israel and the Palestinians continued to erupt in conflict, and the United States, together with the leaders of the European Union, continued to use diplomatic tools to try to get the parties to resume peace negotiations. Another example of the failure of diplomacy is the second Gulf War in 2003. Negotiations were unsuccessful in resolving the global standoff caused by Iraqi president Saddam Hussein's refusal to comply with requirements imposed by the United Nations.

★ Morality versus Reality in Foreign Policy

From the earliest years of the republic, Americans have felt that their nation had a special destiny. The American experiment in democratic government and capitalism, it was thought, would provide the best possible life for men and women and be a model for other nations. As the United States assumed greater status as a power in world politics, Americans came to believe that the nation's actions on the world stage should be guided by American political and moral principles. As Harry Truman stated, "The United States should take the lead in running the world in the way that it ought to be run."

Moral Idealism
A philosophy that sees nations as normally willing to cooperate and to agree on moral standards for conduct.

Moral Idealism

This view of America's mission has led to the adoption of many foreign policy initiatives that are rooted in **moral idealism.** This philosophy sees the world as fundamentally benign and assumes that most nations can be persuaded to take moral considerations into account when setting their policies.[1] In this perspective, nations should come together and agree to keep the peace, as President Woodrow Wilson (1913–1921) proposed for the League of Nations. Many of the foreign policy initiatives taken by the United States have been based on this idealistic view of the world. The Peace Corps, which was created by President John Kennedy in 1961, is one example of an effort to spread American goodwill and technology that has achieved some of its goals.

Raquib Jamal is a business volunteer in Ghana helping farmers develop and run tourism businesses. Her work is an example of the moral idealism that is an important component of American foreign policy. (Peace Corps photo)

---

[1] Eugene R. Wittkopf, Charles W. Kegley, and James M. Scott, *American Foreign Policy,* 6th ed. (Belmont, Calif.: Wadsworth Publishing, 2002).

Political Realism

In opposition to the moral perspective is **political realism.** Realists see the world as a dangerous place in which each nation strives for its own survival and interests regardless of moral considerations. The United States must also base its foreign policy decisions on cold calculations without regard for morality. Realists believe that the United States must be prepared militarily to defend itself, because all other nations are, by definition, out to improve their own situations. A strong defense will show the world that the United States is willing to protect its interests. The practice of political realism in foreign policy allows the United States to sell weapons to military dictators who will support its policies, to support American business around the globe, and to repel terrorism through the use of force.

American Foreign Policy—A Mixture of Both

It is important to note that the United States never has been guided by only one of these principles. Instead, both moral idealism and political realism affect foreign policymaking. President George W. Bush drew on the tradition of morality in foreign policy when he declared that the al Qaeda network of Osama bin Laden was "evil" and that fighting terrorism was fighting evil. To actually wage war on the Taliban in Afghanistan, however, U.S. forces needed the right to use the airspace of India and Pakistan, neighbors of Afghanistan. The United States had previously criticized both of these South Asian nations because they had developed and tested nuclear weapons. In addition, the United States had taken the moral stand that it would not deliver certain fighter aircraft to Pakistan as long as it continued its weapons program. When it became absolutely necessary to work with India and Pakistan, the United States switched to a realist policy, promising aid and support to both regimes in return for their assistance in the war on terrorism.

The second Gulf War, in 2003, also revealed a mixture of idealism and realism. While the primary motive for invading Iraq was realistic (the interests of U.S. security), another goal of the war reflected idealism—the liberation of the Iraqi people from an oppressive regime and the establishment of a democratic model in the Middle East. Are idealist and realist values associated with the two major political parties? We examine this question in the *America's Security* feature on the next page.

★ Challenges in World Politics

The foreign policy of the United States, whether moralist, realist, or both, must be formulated to deal with world conditions. Early in its history, the United States was a weak, new nation facing older nations well equipped for world domination. In the twenty-first century, the United States faces different challenges. Now it must devise foreign and defense policies that will enhance its security in a world in which it is the global superpower and has no equal.

The Emergence of Terrorism

Dissident groups, rebels, and other revolutionaries have long engaged in terrorism to gain attention and to force their enemies to the bargaining table. Over the last two decades, however, terrorism has increasingly threatened world peace and the lives of ordinary citizens.

Terrorism and Regional Strife. Terrorism can be a weapon of choice in regional or domestic strife. The conflict in the Middle East between Israel and the Arab states is an example. Until recently, the conflict had been lessened by a series of painfully negotiated agreements between Israel and some of the Arab states. Those opposed to the peace process, however, have continued to disrupt the negotiations through

AMERICA'S SECURITY
Realism versus Idealism in Foreign Affairs

As you have learned in this chapter, two principles of American foreign policy are *moral idealism* and *political realism.* Realist foreign policy thinking often leads to the support of dictators. Realism has led to U.S. support of, for example, the royal family in Saudi Arabia and the less-than-democratic Egyptian President Hosni Mubarak. Realists have supported the status quo in the Middle East for decades because strong nondemocratic leaders in the Middle East have "kept things stable." Idealists, in contrast, have advocated the spread of democracy throughout the world. Democratic presidents Harry Truman (1945–1953) and John F. Kennedy (1961–1963) were promoters of idealism in foreign policy. In Kennedy's inauguration speech, he stated that we would "pay any price" and "bear any burden" in the cause of liberty. Of course, these presidents attempted to base their policies on political realism as well.

The question is whether each of these two viewpoints is specifically associated with a major political party. Clearly, America's security might be affected by which policy a given administration tends to favor.

POLITICAL ROLE REVERSALS

Beginning with Woodrow Wilson (1913–1921), idealism has been associated with Democratic presidents.

Realpolitik (a German word meaning "realistic politics") has traditionally been associated with Republicans. Indeed, the most famous advocate of *realpolitik* was Henry Kissinger, national security adviser to Republican president Richard Nixon (1969–1974).

Apparently, however, the George W. Bush administration adopted an idealist foreign policy. Bush argued that U.S. security requires the transformation of the Middle East into a zone of democracy to reduce terrorism in that area. His 2004 Democratic opponent, John Kerry, was not so sure. Kerry spoke more of a *stable* Iraq than of a democratic Iraq. Kerry's belief that the United States should make greater efforts to coordinate its actions with the world's other democratic nations also suggested realism instead of idealism.

A PARTISAN TURN

While it has been traditional for the two parties to present a united front on foreign policy issues, following the saying, "partisanship stops at the water's edge," the candidates certainly abandoned that practice in 2004. Bush and Kerry were eager to establish their policy differences in front of the voters as well as the rest of the world.

FOR CRITICAL ANALYSIS

Why might nations that are more democratic tend to be the home of fewer terrorists?

---

assassinations, mass murders, and bomb blasts in the streets of major cities within Israel. Other regions have also experienced terrorism. In September 2004, terrorists acting on behalf of Chechnya, a breakaway republic of Russia, seized a school at Besian in the nearby Russian republic of North Ossetia. In the end, at least 330 people—most of them children—were dead.

Terrorist Attacks against Foreign Civilians. In other cases, terrorist acts are planned against civilians of foreign nations traveling abroad to make an international statement. One of the most striking of these attacks was that launched by Palestinian terrorists against Israeli athletes at the Munich Olympics in 1972, during which eleven athletes were murdered. Other attacks have included ship and airplane hijackings, as well as bombings of embassies. For example, in 1998, terrorist bombings of two American embassies in Africa killed 257 people, including 12 Americans, and injured over 5,500 others.

September 11. In 2001, terrorism came home to the United States in ways that few Americans could have imagined. In a well-coordinated attack, nineteen terrorists hijacked four airplanes and crashed three of them into buildings—two into the World Trade Center towers in New York City and one into the Pentagon in Washington, D.C. The fourth airplane crashed in a field in Pennsylvania, after the passengers fought the hijackers. Why did the al Qaeda network plan and launch attacks on the United States? Apparently, the leaders of the network, including

Terrorist bombings have become increasingly destructive. Left: Rescue workers cover bodies following train explosions in Madrid, Spain, just three days before Spain's general elections in 2004. The bombs killed more than 170 and wounded more than 500. Upper right: The bombing of a nightclub on the island of Bali in Indonesia in 2002 killed over 180 tourists, most of them Australian. Al Qaeda was blamed for the bombing. Bottom right: Palestinians carry sacks of food through the remains of a market in Bethlehem, destroyed after a standoff between Israeli troops and Palestinians in 2002. (Left: AP Photo/Paul White; upper right: AP Photo/David Guttenfelder; bottom right: AP Photo/Achmad Ibrahim)

Osama bin Laden, were angered by the presence of U.S. troops on the soil of Saudi Arabia, which they regard as sacred. They also saw the United States as the primary defender of Israel against the Palestinians and as the defender of the royal family that governs Saudi Arabia. The attacks were intended to frighten and demoralize the American people, thus convincing their leaders to withdraw American troops from the Middle East.

The War on Terrorism

After 9/11, President George W. Bush implemented stronger security measures to protect homeland security and U.S. facilities and personnel abroad. The president sought and received congressional support for heightened airport security, new laws allowing greater domestic surveillance of potential terrorists, and new funding for the military.

Military Responses. The first military effort was directed against al Qaeda camps in Afghanistan and the Taliban regime, which had ruled that country since 1996. In late 2001, after building a coalition of international allies and

A satellite image of lower Manhattan shows the devastation after the collapse of the World Trade Center towers on September 11, 2001. Terrorists crashed two commercial airplanes into the twin towers. About three thousand people were killed in the terrorist attacks at the World Trade Center and the Pentagon. What might be the long-term effects of this horrible event on American foreign policy? (Department of Defense photo)

Army National Guard soldiers and Marines conduct foot patrols on the streets of Ghazni, Afghanistan, in 2004. How much political and security responsibility should the United States assume in Afghanistan following the defeat of the Taliban? (Department of Defense photo by Staff Sergeant Vernell Hall, U.S. Army)

anti-Taliban rebels within Afghanistan, the United States defeated the Taliban and supported the creation of an interim government that did not support terrorism.

During 2002 and early 2003, the U.S. government focused its attention on the threat posed by Saddam Hussein's government in Iraq. As you will read later in this chapter, after the first Gulf War, in 1991, Hussein was subject to various United Nations (UN) resolutions. These resolutions included mandates that Iraq allow UN weapons inspectors to search for and oversee the demolishing of weapons of mass destruction and related research facilities. Iraq's failure to comply with the UN requirements led to a standoff that lasted for over a decade.

Having tried and failed to convince the UN Security Council that the UN should take action to enforce its resolutions, President Bush decided to take unilateral action against Iraq. In March 2003, supported by a coalition of thirty-five other nations, including Britain, the United States invaded Iraq. Within three weeks, Hussein's government had toppled, and coalition forces were in control of Baghdad and most of the other major Iraqi cities. An insurgent resistance to the coalition forces followed, however. In December 2003, Hussein was finally located and arrested. The difficult task facing the victors continues to be establishing a new governing regime.

A New Kind of War. Terrorism has posed a unique challenge for U.S. foreign policymakers. The Bush administration's response has also been unique. In September 2002, President Bush enunciated what has since become known as the "Bush doctrine" or the doctrine of preemption:

> We will . . . [defend] the United States, the American people, and our interests at home and abroad by identifying and destroying the threat before it reaches our borders. While the United States will constantly strive to enlist the support of the international community, we will not hesitate to act alone, if necessary to exercise our right of self-defense by acting preemptively against such terrorists, to prevent them from doing harm against our people and our country.[2]

The concept of "preemptive war" as a defense strategy is a new element in U.S. foreign policy. The concept is based on the assumption that in the war on terrorism, self-defense must be *anticipatory*. As President Bush stated on March 17, 2003, just before launching the invasion of Iraq, "Responding to such enemies only after they have struck first is not self-defense, it is suicide."

The Bush doctrine has not been without its critics. Some point out that preemptive wars against other nations have traditionally been waged by dictators and rogue states—not democratic nations. By employing such tactics, the United States would seem to be contradicting its basic values. Others claim that launching preemptive wars will make it difficult for the United States to further world peace in the future. By endorsing such a policy itself, the United States could hardly argue against the decisions of other nations to do likewise when they feel potentially threatened.

Wars in Iraq

On August 2, 1990, the Persian Gulf became the setting for a major challenge to the international system set up after World War II (1939–1945). President Saddam Hussein of Iraq sent troops into the neighboring oil sheikdom of Kuwait,

---

[2]George W. Bush, September 17, 2002. The full text of the document from which this statement is taken can be accessed at **http://www.whitehouse.gov/nsc/nssall.html**. Other speeches and press releases made by President Bush prior to the attack on Iraq are available online at **http://www.whitehouse.gov/response/index.html**.

occupying that country. This was the most clear-cut case of aggression against an independent nation in half a century.

The Persian Gulf—The First Gulf War. At the formal request of the king of Saudi Arabia, American troops were dispatched to set up a defensive line at the Kuwaiti border. After the UN approved a resolution authorizing the use of force if Saddam Hussein did not respond to sanctions, the U.S. Congress reluctantly also approved such an authorization. On January 17, 1991, two days after a deadline for President Hussein to withdraw, U.S.–led coalition forces launched a massive air attack on Iraq. After several weeks, the ground offensive began. Iraqi troops retreated from Kuwait a few days later, and the first Gulf War ended, although many Americans criticized President George H. W. Bush for not sending troops to Baghdad to depose Saddam Hussein.

As part of the cease-fire that ended the Gulf War, Iraq agreed to abide by all UN resolutions and to allow UN weapons inspectors to oversee the destruction of its medium-range missiles and all chemical- and nuclear-weapons research facilities. Economic sanctions would continue to be imposed on Iraq until the weapons inspectors finished their jobs. In 1999, however, Iraq placed such obstacles in the path of the UN inspectors that the inspectors withdrew from the country.

The Persian Gulf—The Second Gulf War. After the terrorist attacks on the United States on September 11, 2001, President George W. Bush called Iraq and Saddam Hussein part of an "axis of evil" that threatened world peace. In 2002 and early 2003, Bush called for a "regime change" in Iraq and began assembling an international coalition that might support further military action in Iraq.

As already discussed, Bush was unable to convince the UN Security Council that military force was necessary in Iraq, so as pointed out before, the United States took the initiative. In March 2003, U.S. and British forces invaded Iraq and within a month had ended Hussein's decades-old dictatorship. The process of establishing order and creating a new government in Iraq turned out to be extraordinarily difficult. In the course of the fighting, the Iraqi army, rather than

A collage of images from the Second Gulf War in Iraq. Clockwise from the lower left, the photographs show the initial battles that began in March 2003, the fall of Baghdad, the capture of Saddam Hussein, and the protracted struggle with various insurgents that followed. (All photos courtesy of U.S. Military)

Crew members of the USS *Abraham Lincoln* salute President George W. Bush after he was given a ride on a fighter jet based on the aircraft carrier. President Bush declared to the crew, and later the nation, that major military operations in Iraq were a "mission accomplished." How can identification with the military be politically helpful to a president or a presidential candidate? (U.S. Navy photo by Photographer's Mate 3rd Class Tyler J. Clements)

surrendering, disbanded itself. Soldiers simply took off their uniforms and made their way home. As a result, the task of maintaining law and order fell on the shoulders of a remarkably small coalition expeditionary force. Coalition troops were unable to halt immediately the wave of looting and disorder that spread across Iraq in the wake of the invasion.

Occupied Iraq. The people of Iraq are divided into three principal ethnic groups. The Kurdish-speaking people of the North, who had in practice been functioning as an American-sponsored independent state since the First Gulf War, were overjoyed by the invasion. The Arabs adhering to the Shiite branch of Islam live principally in the South and constitute a majority of the population. The Shiites were glad that Saddam Hussein, who had murdered many thousands of Shiites, was gone. They were deeply skeptical of U.S. intentions, however. The Arabs belonging to the Sunni branch of Islam live in the center of the country, west of Baghdad. Although the Sunnis constituted only a minority of the population, they had controlled the government under Hussein. Many of them considered the occupation to be a disaster. Figure 17–1 shows the distribution of major ethnic groups in Iraq.

FIGURE 17–1

Ethnic/Religious Groups in Iraq

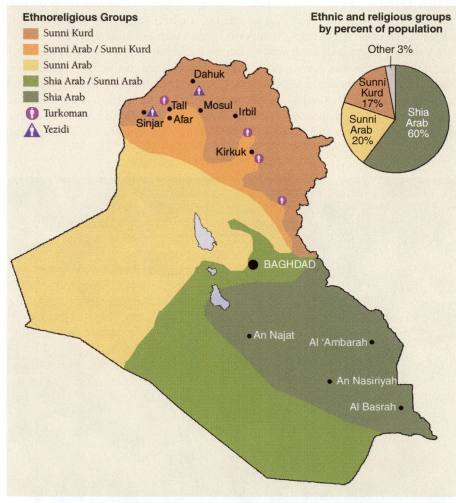

SOURCE: The Central Intelligence Agency, as adapted by Globalsecurity.org.

The preeminent Shiite leader was the Ayatollah Ali al-Sistani, the most senior Shia cleric in Iraq. Al-Sistani refused to meet with officials of the Coalition Provisional Authority (CPA) but was in constant contact with members of the Iraqi Governing Council. Beginning in late 2003, Al-Sistani made increasingly firm demands for elections to choose a new Iraqi government. The CPA, however, did not believe elections could be held before the end of 2004. Following a strategy established by President Bush, the CPA turned Iraqi sovereignty over to an interim government on June 30, 2004. Elections were scheduled for January 2005.

The Security Problem in Iraq. One reason the CPA did not believe that early elections were possible was the security situation in Iraq, which showed no signs of stabilizing in late 2003 and early 2004. Despite successes by coalition troops in locating and arresting armed rebels, the violence continued. It included suicide bombings and armed attacks on coalition forces, Iraqi police, and Shiite religious sites. Insurgents killed an average of fifty coalition troops per month between May 2003 and March 2004.

Uprisings in Spring 2004. In April 2004, four non-Iraqi civilian security personnel were murdered in the Sunni city of Fallujah, and their bodies were publicly defiled. U.S. Marines entered the city to locate and arrest the perpetrators. Almost at the same time, authorities in Baghdad closed a newspaper run by followers of the Shiite cleric Mutada al-Sadr. Al-Sadr, a radical, was the son of a famous Shiite martyr. The paper was closed on the ground that it had been fomenting violence. The result was simultaneous uprisings in the "Sunni triangle" west of Baghdad and in neighborhoods dominated by al-Sadr's militia in Baghdad and southern cities.

After several weeks, fighting was confined to Fallujah and the Shiite city of Najaf, where al-Sadr had established his headquarters. Public opinion polls in Iraq revealed that hostility toward the occupation forces had grown dramatically. To make matters worse, in May 2004 graphic photographs were published showing that U.S. guards at Abu Ghraib prison in Baghdad had subjected prisoners to physical and sexual abuse.

While coalition forces were able to maintain control of the country, they were now suffering monthly casualties comparable to those experienced during the initial invasion. Iraq had begun to be a serious political problem for President Bush. By May 2004, a majority of Americans no longer believed that going to war had been the right thing to do, and Bush's overall job-approval rating had fallen to 46 percent, his lowest mark since 9/11.

Nuclear Weapons

In 1945, the United States was the only nation to possess nuclear weapons. Several nations quickly joined the "nuclear club," however, including the Soviet Union in 1949, Great Britain in 1952, France in 1960, and China in 1964. Few nations have made public their nuclear weapons programs since China's successful test of nuclear weapons in 1964. India and Pakistan were the most recent nations to do so, detonating nuclear devices within a few weeks of each other in 1998. Several other nations are suspected of possessing nuclear weapons or the capability to produce them in a short time.

The United States and the Soviet Union. More than 32,000 nuclear warheads are known to be stocked worldwide, although the exact number is uncertain because some countries do not reveal the extent of their nuclear stockpiles. Although the United States and Russia have dismantled some of their nuclear weapons systems since the end of the **Cold War** and the dissolution of the

A member of a New York National Guard unit passes out candy to children in Alalaa, Iraq. The unit was engaged in an operation to locate explosives, identify targets, and gather intelligence. If, at some time in the future, the United States must fight another war similar to the one in Iraq, how might it ensure a more successful postwar occupation? (U.S. Army Photo by Sergeant April L. Johnson)

Cold War
The ideological, political, and economic confrontation between the United States and the Soviet Union following World War II.

This CIA photograph shows Yongbyon in North Korea. The area marked in red contains a nuclear research center and associated reprocessing facilities. What, if anything, can the United States legitimately offer to North Korea if that country abandons its nuclear weapons program? (Globalsecurity.org)

Soviet Union in 1991 (discussed later in this chapter), both still retain sizable nuclear arsenals. Even more troublesome is *nuclear proliferation*—that is, the development of nuclear weapons by additional nations.

Nuclear Proliferation.   The United States has attempted to influence late arrivals to the "nuclear club" through a combination of rewards and punishments. In some cases, the United States has promised aid to a nation to gain cooperation. In other cases, such as those of India and Pakistan, it has imposed economic sanctions as a punishment for carrying out nuclear tests.

In 1999, President Bill Clinton presented the Comprehensive Nuclear Test Ban Treaty to the Senate for ratification. The treaty, formed in 1996, prohibits all nuclear test explosions worldwide and provides for the establishment of a global network of monitoring stations. Ninety-three nations have ratified the treaty. Among those that have not are China, Israel, India, and Pakistan. In a defeat for the Clinton administration, the U.S. Senate rejected the treaty in 1999.

North Korea has admitted that it has a nuclear weapons development program, and there are reasons to believe that Iran has such a program as well. President George W. Bush described both nations as members of an "axis of evil," and the fear exists that one of them could supply nuclear materials to terrorists. In addition, Israel is known to possess more than one hundred nuclear warheads. South Africa developed six nuclear warheads in the 1980s but dismantled them in 1990. In 2003, Libya announced that it was abandoning a secret nuclear weapons program. Also, since the dissolution of the Soviet Union in 1991, the security of its nuclear arsenal has declined. There have been reported thefts, smugglings, and illicit sales of nuclear material from the former Soviet Union in the past decade.

With nuclear weapons, materials, and technology available worldwide, it is conceivable that terrorists could develop a nuclear device and use it in a terrorist act. In fact, a U.S. federal indictment filed in 1998, after the attack on the American embassies in Kenya and Tanzania, charged Osama bin Laden and his associates with trying to buy nuclear bomb-making components "at various times" since 1992.

The New Power: China

Since Richard Nixon's visit to China in 1972, American policy has been to gradually engage the Chinese in diplomatic and economic relationships in the hope of turning the nation in a more pro-Western direction. In 1989, however, when Chinese students engaged in extraordinary demonstrations against the government, the Chinese government crushed the demonstrations, killing a number of students and protesters and imprisoning others. The result was a distinct chill in Chinese-American relations.

Chinese-American Trade Ties.   After initially criticizing the administration of George H. W. Bush (1989–1993) for not being hard enough on China, President Bill Clinton came around to a policy of diplomatic outreach to the Chinese. An important reason for this change was the large and growing trade ties between the two countries. China was granted *most-favored-nation status* for tariffs and trade policy on a year-to-year basis. To prevent confusion, in 1998 the status was renamed **normal trade relations (NTR) status.** In 2000, over objections from organized labor and human rights groups, Congress approved a permanent grant of NTR status to China.

In 2001, Congress endorsed China's application to join the World Trade Organization (WTO), which effectively guaranteed China's admission to that body. For a country that is officially communist, China already permits a striking degree of free enterprise, and the rules China must follow as a WTO member will further increase the role of the private sector in China's economy.

Normal Trade Relations (NTR) Status
A status granted through an international treaty by which each member nation must treat other members at least as well as it treats the country that receives its most favorable treatment. This status was formerly known as *most-favored-nation status*.

GLOBAL VIEW
China—The Next Superpower?

China has experienced rapid economic growth for the last thirty years and today is one of the world's great economic powers. Adjusted for purchasing power, its gross domestic product (GDP) is now second only to that of the United States and is almost double that of Japan.

In 2001–2003, China's industrial output increased by almost 50 percent. Chinese demand for raw materials led to dramatic increases in the world prices of many commodities. China produces more steel than America and Japan combined. It consumes 40 percent of the world's output of cement. By 2004, many economists predicted a "correction"—a slowdown in the country's growth. No one expected, however, that a slowdown would be more than temporary.

CHINA'S ECONOMIC PROSPECTS

Goldman Sachs, an investment firm, has projected that China's GDP will surpass that of the United States by 2039, making China's economy the largest in the world. The Goldman Sachs projection may be an underestimate—it uses growth rates that are substantially less than the actual rates China has posted over the last thirty years.*

* Goldman Sachs, "Dreaming with BRICs: The Path to 2050," Global Economics Paper No. 99. This paper is online at **http://www. gs.com/insight/research/reports/99.pdf**.

WHAT ABOUT TAIWAN?

Inevitably, economic power translates into military potential. Is this a problem? It could be if China had territorial ambitions. Currently, China does not have an appetite for non-Chinese territory, and it does not seem likely to develop one. But China has always considered the island of Taiwan to be Chinese territory.

In principle, Taiwan agrees. Taiwan calls itself the "Republic of China" and officially considers its government to be the legitimate ruler of the entire country. This diplomatic fiction has remained in effect since 1949, when the Chinese Communist Party won a civil war and drove the anti-Communist forces off the mainland. China's position is that sooner or later, Taiwan must rejoin the rest of China. The position of the United States is that this must not come about by force.

Is peaceful reunification possible? China holds up Hong Kong as an example. Hong Kong came under Chinese sovereignty peacefully in 1997. The people of Taiwan, however, are far from considering Hong Kong to be an acceptable precedent.

FOR CRITICAL ANALYSIS

If China invaded Taiwan, should the United States go to war to protect it? Why or why not?

Chinese-American Tensions. China has one of the fastest-growing economies in the world. Given China's large population, projections suggest that the gross domestic product of China may match or exceed that of the United States during this century. This prospect has led to alarm in some quarters. Some U.S. observers and officials have argued that China is destined to become a great rival—or even an enemy—of the United States. What problems would be posed if China should become a superpower? We examine this question in the *Global View* feature.

In 1999, Wen Ho Lee, a Taiwanese-American nuclear scientist, was accused of spying for China and placed in solitary confinement for nine months. Asian American leaders contended that the Lee case was being used to stir up racial hostility toward Asian Americans. In 2000, a court found that while Lee had violated certain security guidelines, he was innocent of espionage. The judge apologized to Lee for the way in which the government had mishandled the case. Tensions between the Chinese and U.S. governments were also enhanced in 2001 by a dispute that followed a collision between a U.S. spy plane and a Chinese fighter jet. Still, after the September 11 attacks, China offered its full support to the United States in the war on terrorism and, for the first time ever, supplied intelligence to the United States about terrorist activities. The Chinese, however, did not support the American military action to overthrow Saddam Hussein.

Regional Conflicts

The United States played a role—sometimes alone, sometimes with other powers—in many regional conflicts during the 1990s and early 2000s.

Haiti.   The Caribbean nation of Haiti became a focal point of U.S. policy in the 1990s. The repressive military regime there ousted the democratically elected president Jean-Bertrand Aristide in 1992. In 1994, the Clinton administration sent troops to Haiti to assist in the reinstatement of President Aristide. Aristide's party won all subsequent elections, none of which was certified as fair by international observers. In February 2004, rebels seized control of several provincial cities. Aristide resigned and fled into exile aboard a U.S. airplane, and Haiti organized an interim government.

Cuba.   The United States has continued to face problems with Cuba. Tensions between the United States and Cuba increased significantly in late 1999 and 2000 after a little boy, Elian Gonzalez, survived a boat wreck in which his mother died. They had been crossing from Cuba to join relatives in Miami. With his mother dead, Elian became the prize in a political tug-of-war between Fidel Castro and the Cuban American population in Miami until the Clinton administration returned the young boy to his family in Cuba. Cuban American relations continue to be politically important because the Cuban American population can influence American election outcomes in Florida, a state that all presidential candidates try to win.

Israel and the Palestinians.   As a longtime supporter of Israel, the United States has undertaken to persuade the Israelis to negotiate with the Palestinian Arabs who live in the territories occupied by the state of Israel. The conflict, which began in 1948, has been extremely hard to resolve. The internationally recognized solution is for Israel to yield the West Bank and the Gaza Strip to the Palestinians in return for effective security commitments and abandonment by the Palestinians of any right of return to Israel proper. Unfortunately, the Palestinians have been unwilling to stop terrorist attacks on Israel, and Israel has been unwilling to dismantle its settlements in the occupied territories. Further, the two parties have been unable to come to an agreement on how much of the West Bank should go to the Palestinians and on what compensation (if any) the Palestinians should receive for abandoning all claims to settlement in Israel proper.

In December 1988, the United States began talking directly to the Palestine Liberation Organization (PLO), and in 1991, under great pressure from the United States, the Israelis opened talks with representatives of the Palestinians and other Arab states. In 1993, both parties agreed to set up Palestinian self-government in the West Bank and the Gaza Strip. The historic agreement, signed in Cairo on May 4, 1994, put in place a process by which the Palestinians would assume self-rule in the Gaza Strip and in the town of Jericho. In the months that followed, Israeli troops withdrew from much of the occupied territory, the new Palestinian Authority assumed police duties, and many Palestinian prisoners were freed by the Israelis.

The Collapse of the Israeli-Palestinian Peace Process.   Although negotiations between the Israelis and the Palestinians resulted in more agreements in Oslo, Norway, in 2000, the agreements were rejected by Palestinian radicals, who began a campaign of suicide bombings in Israeli cities. In 2002, the Israeli government responded by moving tanks and troops into Palestinian towns to kill or capture the terrorists. One result of the Israeli reoccupation was an almost complete collapse of the Palestinian Authority. Groups such as Hamas (the Islamic Resistance Movement), which did not accept the concept of peace with Israel even in principle, moved into the power vacuum.

This view shows a concrete wall that is part of Israel's new security barrier. This section separates the eastern neighborhoods of Jerusalem from the West Bank town of Abu Dis (to the rear). In choosing the route of the security barrier, how much consideration should Israel have given to its impact on the daily lives of the Palestinians? (REUTERS/Reinhard Krause/Landov)

In 2003, President Bush attempted to renew Israeli-Palestinian negotiations by sponsoring a "road map" for peace. First, the road map called for an end to terrorism by Palestinians. Later, it held out hopes for a Palestinian state alongside Israel. In its weakened condition, however, the Palestinian Authority was unable to make any commitments, and the "road map" process ground to a halt. In February 2004, Israeli Prime Minister Ariel Sharon announced a plan under which Israel would withdraw from the Gaza Strip regardless of whether a deal could be reached with the Palestinians. Sharon's plan met with strong opposition within his own political party, and by late 2004 it remained an open question whether the plan would actually be implemented.

Bosnia. After the end of the Cold War, Eastern Europe, a region that had been extremely stable while under Soviet domination, suddenly became an unknown quantity in U.S. policy. In Yugoslavia, a federation of six republics, the new leader—Slobodan Milosevic—attempted to replace communism with Serbian nationalism as the motivating ideology of government. As a result, four Yugoslav republics with non-Serb majorities seceded from the union in 1992. Two of these new nations—Croatia and Bosnia—contained sizable Serb-populated districts. Using the Yugoslav armed forces and, later, local Serb militias, the Serbs attempted to regain control of the Serb districts, plus additional territory. In Bosnia, the result was a four-year civil war among Serb, Croatian, and Bosnian Muslim forces.

As the front stabilized, the various parties engaged in "ethnic cleansing," or driving members of the opposing ethnic groups from their homes. Atrocities, including the murder of civilians and officially sponsored rapes, were common. Serb forces were responsible for the greater share of these, though Croatian forces also behaved badly. In July 1995, the Muslim-inhabited, UN–sponsored "safe area" of Srebrenica was overrun by Bosnian Serbs, who killed virtually the entire male population of the zone. This was the worst war crime committed in Europe since the end of World War II.

The fall of Srebrenica spurred the Western powers toward greater efforts to end the war. In August 1995, the army of Croatia, covertly equipped by Western interests, regained full control of that country's territory and began a sweep through Serb-controlled Bosnia. Together with a Western bombing campaign, this forced the Bosnian Serbs to accept a cease-fire. Under the North Atlantic Treaty Organization (NATO), forces from the United States and European nations maintained the resulting peace and oversaw the reconstruction of Bosnia.

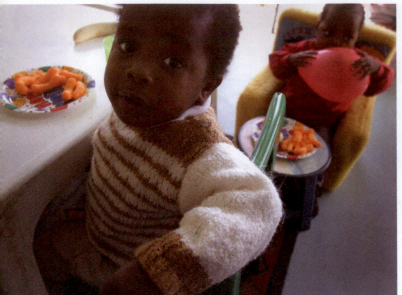

Children take their afternoon meal at the Cotlands Baby Sanctuary in Johannesburg, South Africa. Both of these children have AIDS and were abandoned at birth. They are receiving antiretroviral drugs and have managed to remain healthy. The South African government has discouraged the use of the drugs because of the high costs involved and because of controversial theories about AIDS held by top officials. (EPA/Kim Ludbrook/Landov)

Kosovo. In 1998, a second major crisis broke out in former Yugoslavia. For some years, the Albanian majority in the Serb province of Kosovo had agitated for independence from what remained of Yugoslavia. Yugoslav forces responded to the agitation in 1998 by attempting to drive the entire Albanian population out of the province. Through NATO, the United States mounted a bombing campaign in 1999 that forced Yugoslav forces to leave Kosovo. NATO and Russian forces then occupied the province.

AIDS in Southern Africa. During the early 2000s, the disease AIDS (acquired immune deficiency syndrome) spread throughout Southern Africa. This disease infects one-fourth of the populations of Botswana and Zimbabwe and is endemic in most other nations in the southernmost part of the continent. Millions of adults are dying from AIDS, leaving orphaned children. The epidemic is taking a huge economic toll on the affected countries because of the cost of caring for patients and the loss of skilled workers. The disease may be the greatest single threat to world stability emanating from Africa. The Bush administration put in place a special aid package directed at this problem amounting to $15 billion over five years.

African Civil Wars. The year 1994 brought disaster to the African nation of Rwanda. Following the death of that country's president, members of the Hutu tribe launched a campaign of genocide against the Tutsi tribe. More than half a million people were killed in a matter of weeks. The genocide campaign came to an abrupt end as a Tutsi guerrilla force, sponsored by neighboring Uganda, overthrew the Rwandan government. A large number of Hutus then fled from Rwanda. The United States played almost no part in this crisis until small military and civilian contingents were sent to assist the Hutu refugees.

In Angola, wars dating back as far as 1961 came to an end in 2002 with the death of rebel leader Jonas Savimbi, who had received U.S. support for several years in the 1970s. In 1996, civil war broke out in Zaire (now named Congo-Kinshasa). Rebels were aided by Rwandan and Ugandan forces, while Angolan and Zimbabwean forces entered the country to support the government. The civil war officially came to an end in 2002, and a coalition government was established in 2003. Several million deaths, primarily due to disease and malnutrition, were attributed to the war.

In 2004, the world woke up to a growing disaster in Darfur, a western province of Sudan. In the spring of 2004, Sudan had reached a tenuous agreement with rebels in the southern part of the country, but the agreement did not cover a separate rebellion in Darfur. Government-sponsored militias drove over a million inhabitants of Darfur from their homes and into refugee camps, where they faced starvation. In July 2004, the U.S. Congress labeled the situation as "genocide." At U.S. urging, the UN Security Council contemplated sanctions against Sudan.

 **Who Makes Foreign Policy?**

Given the vast array of challenges in the world, developing a comprehensive U.S. foreign policy is a demanding task. Does this responsibility fall to the president, to Congress, or to both acting jointly? There is no easy answer to this question, because, as constitutional authority Edwin S. Corwin once observed, the U.S. Constitution created an "invitation to struggle" between the president and

Congress for control over the foreign policy process. Let us look first at the powers given to the president by the Constitution.

Constitutional Powers of the President

The Constitution confers on the president broad powers that are either explicit or implied in key constitutional provisions. Article II vests the executive power of the government in the president. The presidential oath of office given in Article II, Section 1, requires that the president "solemnly swear" to "preserve, protect and defend the Constitution of the United States."

War Powers.   In addition, and perhaps more important, Article II, Section 2, designates the president as "Commander in Chief of the Army and Navy of the United States." Starting with Abraham Lincoln, all presidents have interpreted this authority dynamically and broadly. Indeed, since George Washington's administration, the United States has been involved in at least 125 undeclared wars that were conducted under presidential authority. For example, in 1950 Harry Truman ordered U.S. armed forces in the Pacific to counter North Korea's invasion of South Korea. Dwight Eisenhower threatened China and North Korea with nuclear weapons if the Korean peace talks were not successfully concluded. Bill Clinton sent troops to Haiti and Bosnia. In 2001, George W. Bush authorized an attack against the al Qaeda terrorist network and the Taliban government in Afghanistan. As described earlier, in 2003, Bush sent military forces to Iraq to destroy Saddam Hussein's government.

Treaties and Executive Agreements.   Article II, Section 2, of the Constitution also gives the president the power to make treaties, provided that two-thirds of the senators present concur. Presidents usually have been successful in getting treaties through the Senate. In addition to this formal treaty-making power, the president makes use of executive agreements (discussed in Chapter 12). Since World War II (1939–1945), executive agreements have accounted for almost 95 percent of the understandings reached between the United States and other nations.

Executive agreements have a long and important history. During World War II, Franklin Roosevelt reached several agreements with the Soviet Union and other countries. One agreement with long-term results was concluded at Yalta in the Soviet Crimea. In other important agreements, presidents Eisenhower, Kennedy, and Johnson all promised support to the government of South Vietnam. In all, since 1946 over eight thousand executive agreements with foreign countries have been made. There is no way to obtain an accurate count, because perhaps as many as several hundred of these agreements have been secret.

Other Constitutional Powers.   An additional power conferred on the president in Article II, Section 2, is the right to appoint ambassadors, other public ministers, and consuls. In Section 3 of that article, the president is given the power to recognize foreign governments through receiving their ambassadors.

Informal Techniques of Presidential Leadership

Other broad sources of presidential power in the U.S. foreign policy process are tradition, precedent, and the president's personality. The president can employ a host of informal techniques that give the White House overwhelming superiority within the government in foreign policy leadership.

First, the president has access to information. The Central Intelligence Agency (CIA), the State Department, and the Defense Department make more information available to the president than to any other governmental official. This information carries with it the ability to make quick decisions—and the president uses that ability often. Second, the president is a legislative leader who can influence the funds that are allocated for different programs. Third, the president can influence public opinion. President Theodore Roosevelt once made the following statement:

> People used to say to me that I was an astonishingly good politician and divined what the people are going to think. . . . I did not "divine" how the people were going to think; I simply made up my mind what they ought to think and then did my best to get them to think it.[3]

Presidents are without equal with respect to influencing public opinion, partly because of their ability to command the media. Depending on their skill in appealing to patriotic sentiment (and sometimes fear), they can make people believe that their course in foreign affairs is right and necessary. Public opinion often seems to be impressed by the president's decision to make a national commitment abroad. President George W. Bush's speech to Congress shortly after the September 11 attacks rallied the nation and brought new respect for his leadership. It is worth noting that presidents normally, although certainly not always, receive the immediate support of the American people in a foreign policy crisis.

Finally, the president can commit the nation morally to a course of action in foreign affairs. Because the president is the head of state and the leader of one of the most powerful nations on earth, once the president has made a commitment for the United States, it is difficult for Congress or anyone else to back down on that commitment.

Other Sources of Foreign Policymaking

There are at least four foreign policymaking sources within the executive branch, in addition to the president. These are (1) the Department of State, (2) the National Security Council, (3) the intelligence community, and (4) the Department of Defense.

The Department of State.   In principle, the State Department is the executive agency that has primary authority over foreign affairs. It supervises U.S. relations with the nearly two hundred independent nations around the world and with the United Nations and other multinational groups, such as the Organization of American States. It staffs embassies and consulates throughout the world. It has

---

[3]Sidney Warren, *The President as World Leader* (New York: McGraw-Hill, 1964), p. 23.

In October 2002, President George W. Bush signed a joint resolution from Congress authorizing the use of military force against Iraq to dismantle all of Iraq's weapons of mass destruction. Although the president is the commander in chief, the Constitution does not give him or her the authority to declare war. That authority rests solely with Congress. (AP Photo/Ron Edmonds)

about 32,000 employees. This number may sound impressive, but it is small compared with, say, the 67,000 employees of the Department of Health and Human Services. Also, the State Department had an annual budget of only $11.1 billion in fiscal year 2005, one of the smallest budgets of the cabinet departments.

Newly elected presidents usually tell the American public that the new secretary of state is the nation's chief foreign policy adviser. Nonetheless, the State Department's preeminence in foreign policy has declined since World War II. The State Department's image within the White House Executive Office and Congress (and even with foreign governments) is quite poor—a slow, plodding, bureaucratic maze of inefficient, indecisive individuals. There is a story about how Premier Nikita Khrushchev of the Soviet Union urged President John Kennedy to formulate his own views rather than to rely on State Department officials who, according to Khrushchev, "specialized in why something had not worked forty years ago."[4] In any event, since the days of Franklin Roosevelt, the State Department has often been bypassed or ignored when crucial decisions are made.

It is not surprising that the State Department has been overshadowed in foreign policy. It has no natural domestic constituency as does, for example, the Department of Defense, which can call on defense contractors for support. Instead, the State Department has what might be called **negative constituents**—U.S. citizens who openly oppose the government's policies. One of the State Department's major functions, administering foreign aid, often elicits criticisms. There is a widespread belief that the United States spends much more on foreign aid than it actually does. For 2005, President Bush's budget request allocated $21 billion to foreign economic aid, or about eighty-eight cents for every one hundred dollars of federal spending.

The National Security Council. The job of the National Security Council (NSC), created by the National Security Act of 1947, is to advise the president on the integration of "domestic, foreign, and military policies relating to the national security." Its larger purpose is to provide policy continuity from one administration to the next. As it has turned out, the NSC—consisting of the president, the vice president, the secretaries of state and defense, the director of emergency planning, and often the chairperson of the joint chiefs of staff and the director of the CIA—is used in just about any way the president wants to use it.

The role of national security adviser to the president seems to adjust to fit the player. Some advisers have come into conflict with heads of the State Department. Henry A. Kissinger, Nixon's flamboyant and aggressive national security adviser, rapidly gained ascendancy over William Rogers, the secretary of state. Although it is known that there were divisions over policy within George W. Bush's national security team, Secretary of State Colin Powell, National Security Adviser Condoleezza Rice, and Secretary of Defense Donald Rumsfeld all became important players and spokespersons for the administration.

The Intelligence Community. No discussion of foreign policy would be complete without some mention of the **intelligence community.** This consists of the forty or more government agencies or bureaus that are involved in intelligence activities. They are as follows:

1. Central Intelligence Agency (CIA).
2. National Security Agency (NSA).
3. Defense Intelligence Agency (DIA).
4. Offices within the Department of Defense.
5. Bureau of Intelligence and Research in the Department of State.
6. Federal Bureau of Investigation (FBI).

---

[4]Theodore C. Sorensen, *Kennedy* (New York: Harper & Row, 1965), pp. 554–555.

★★★★★★★★★★★★★★★★

DID YOU KNOW . . .

That it is estimated that the Central Intelligence Agency has more than 16,000 employees, with about 5,000 in the clandestine services**?**

Negative Constituents
Citizens who openly oppose the government's policies.

Intelligence Community
The government agencies that gather information about the capabilities and intentions of foreign governments or that engage in convert actions.

Henry Kissinger may have been the most influential national security advisor in U.S. history. Here, he is shown walking with President Nixon on the south lawn of the White House in 1971. Kissinger later became Nixon's secretary of state. (National Archives)

7. Army intelligence.
8. Air Force intelligence.
9. Drug Enforcement Administration (DEA).
10. Department of Energy.
11. Directorate of Information Analysis and Infrastructure Protection in the Department of Homeland Security.

The CIA, created as part of the National Security Act of 1947, is the key official member of the intelligence community.

Covert Actions. Intelligence activities consist mostly of overt information gathering, but covert actions also are undertaken. Covert actions, as the name implies, are carried out in secret, and the American public rarely finds out about them. The CIA covertly aided in the overthrow of the Mossadegh regime in Iran in 1953 and the Arbenz government of Guatemala in 1954. The agency was instrumental in destabilizing the Allende government in Chile from 1970 to 1973.

During the mid-1970s, the "dark side" of the CIA was partly uncovered when the Senate undertook an investigation of its activities. One of the major findings of the Senate Select Committee on Intelligence was that the CIA had routinely spied on American citizens domestically—supposedly, a prohibited activity. Consequently, the CIA came under the scrutiny of oversight committees within Congress, which restricted the scope of its operations. By 1980, however, the CIA had regained much of its lost power to engage in covert activities.

Criticisms of the Intelligence Community. By 2001, the CIA had come under fire for a number of lapses, including the discovery that one of its agents was spying on behalf of a foreign power, the failure to detect the nuclear arsenals of India and Pakistan, and, above all, the failure to obtain advance knowledge about the 9/11 terrorist attacks. With the rise of terrorism as a threat, the intelligence agencies have received more funding and enhanced surveillance powers, but these moves have also provoked fears of civil liberties violations. In 2004, the bipartisan 9/11 commission called for a new intelligence czar to oversee the entire intelligence community, with full control of all agency budgets. After initially balking at this recommendation, President Bush eventually joined his rival John Kerry in calling for at least a partial implementation of the commission's report.

The Department of Defense. The Department of Defense (DOD) was created in 1947 to bring all of the various activities of the American military establishment under the jurisdiction of a single department headed by a civilian secretary of defense. At the same time, the joint chiefs of staff, consisting of the commanders of the various military branches and a chairperson, was created to formulate a unified military strategy.

Although the Department of Defense is larger than any other federal department, it declined in size after the fall of the Soviet Union in 1991. In the subsequent ten years, the total number of civilian employees was reduced by about 400,000, to about 665,000. Military personnel were also reduced in number. The defense budget remained relatively flat for several years, but with the advent of the war on terrorism and the use of military forces in Afghanistan and Iraq, funding has again been increased.

★ Congress Balances the Presidency

A new interest in the balance of power between Congress and the president on foreign policy questions developed during the Vietnam War (1964–1975). Sensitive to public frustration over the long and costly war and angry at Richard

Nixon for some of his other actions as president, Congress attempted to establish limits on the power of the president in setting foreign and defense policy. In 1973, Congress passed the War Powers Resolution over President Nixon's veto. The act limited the president's use of troops in military action without congressional approval (see Chapter 12). Most presidents, however, have not interpreted the "consultation" provisions of the act as meaning that Congress should be consulted before military action is taken. Instead, presidents Ford, Carter, Reagan, George H. W. Bush, and Clinton ordered troop movements and then informed congressional leaders. Critics note that it is quite possible for a president to commit troops to a situation from which the nation could not withdraw without incurring heavy losses, whether or not Congress is consulted.

Congress has also exerted its authority by limiting or denying presidential requests for military assistance to various groups (such as Angolan rebels and to the government of El Salvador), and requests for new weapons (such as the B-1 bomber). In general, Congress has been far more cautious in supporting the president in situations in which military involvement of American troops is possible. Recently, however, Congress has shown a willingness to support the administration of George W. Bush in the use of military force to fight the war on terrorism.

At times, Congress can take the initiative in foreign policy. In 1986, Congress initiated and passed a bill instituting economic sanctions against South Africa to pressure that nation to end its policy of racial segregation (apartheid). President Ronald Reagan vetoed the bill, but the veto was overridden by large majorities in both the House and the Senate.

Domestic Sources of Foreign Policy

The making of foreign policy is often viewed as a presidential prerogative because of the president's constitutional power in that area and the resources of the executive branch that the president controls. Foreign policymaking is also influenced by a number of other sources, however, including elite and mass opinion and the *military-industrial complex*, described below.

Elite and Mass Opinion

Public opinion influences the making of U.S. foreign policy through a number of channels. Elites in American business, education, communications, labor, and religion try to influence presidential decision making through several strategies. A number of elite organizations, such as the Council on Foreign Relations and the Trilateral Commission, work to increase international cooperation and to influence foreign policy through conferences, publications, and research. The members of the American elite establishment also exert influence on foreign policy through the general public by encouraging debate over foreign policy positions, publicizing the issues, and using the media.

Generally, the efforts of the president and the elites are most successful with the segment of the population called the **attentive public.** This sector of the mass public, which probably constitutes 10 to 20 percent of all citizens, is more interested in foreign affairs than are most other Americans, and members of the attentive public are likely to transmit their opinions to the less interested members of the public through conversation and local leadership.

Attentive Public
That portion of the general public that pays attention to policy issues.

The Military-Industrial Complex

Civilian fear of the relationship between the defense establishment and arms manufacturers (the **military-industrial complex**) dates back many years. During President Eisenhower's eight years in office, the former five-star general of the

Military-Industrial Complex
The mutually beneficial relationship between the armed forces and defense contractors.

army experienced firsthand the kind of pressure that could be brought against him and other policymakers by arms manufacturers. Eisenhower decided to give the country a solemn and—as he saw it—necessary warning of the consequences of this influence. On January 17, 1961, in his last official speech, he said:

> In the councils of government, we must guard against the acquisition of unwarranted influence, whether sought or unsought, by the military-industrial complex. The potential for the disastrous rise of misplaced power exists and will persist. . . . Only an alert and knowledgeable citizenry can compel the proper meshing of the huge industrial and military machinery of defense with our peaceful methods and goals, so that security and liberty may prosper together.[5]

The Pentagon has supported a large sector of our economy through defense contracts. It also has supplied retired army officers as key executives to large defense-contracting firms. Perhaps the Pentagon's strongest allies have been members of Congress whose districts or states benefit from the economic power of military bases or contracts. After the Cold War ended in the late 1980s, the defense industry looked abroad for new customers. Sales of some military equipment to China raised serious issues for the Clinton administration. The war on terrorism provoked a new debate about what types of weaponry would be needed to safeguard the nation in the future. When President George W. Bush proposed legislation in 2002 to increase the Defense Department's budget substantially, weapons manufacturers looked forward to increased sales and profits.

★ The Major Foreign Policy Themes

Although some observers might suggest that U.S. foreign policy is inconsistent and changes with the current occupant of the White House, the long view of American diplomatic ventures reveals some major themes underlying foreign policy. In the early years of the nation, presidents and the people generally agreed that the United States should avoid foreign entanglements and concentrate instead on its own development. From the beginning of the twentieth century until today, however, a major theme has been increasing global involvement. The theme of the post–World War II years was the containment of communism. The theme for at least the first part of the twenty-first century may be the containment of terrorism.

The Formative Years: Avoiding Entanglements

Foreign policy was largely nonexistent during the formative years of the United States. Remember that the new nation was operating under the Articles of Confederation. The national government had no right to levy or collect taxes, no control over commerce, no right to make commercial treaties, and no power to raise an army (the Revolutionary army was disbanded in 1783). The government's lack of international power was made clear when Barbary pirates seized American hostages in the Mediterranean. The United States was unable to rescue the hostages and ignominiously had to purchase them in a treaty with Morocco.

The founders of this nation had a basic mistrust of European governments. George Washington said it was the U.S. policy "to steer clear of permanent alliances," and Thomas Jefferson echoed this sentiment when he said America wanted peace with all nations but "entangling alliances with none." This was also a logical position at a time when the United States was so weak militarily that it could not influence European development directly. Moreover, being protected by oceans that took weeks to traverse certainly allowed the nation to avoid entangling alliances.

[5]*Congressional Almanac* (Washington, D.C.: Congressional Quarterly Press, 1961), pp. 938–939.

During the 1800s, therefore, the United States generally stayed out of European conflicts and politics. In this hemisphere, however, the United States pursued an actively expansionist policy. The nation purchased Louisiana in 1803, annexed Texas in 1845, gained substantial territory from Mexico in 1848, purchased Alaska in 1867, and annexed Hawaii in 1898.

The Monroe Doctrine.   President James Monroe, in his message to Congress on December 2, 1823, stated that this country would not accept foreign intervention in the Western Hemisphere. In return, the United States would not meddle in European affairs. The **Monroe Doctrine** was the underpinning of the U.S. **isolationist foreign policy** toward Europe, which continued throughout the 1800s.

The Spanish-American War and World War I.   The end of the isolationist policy started with the Spanish-American War in 1898. Winning the war gave the United States possession of Guam, Puerto Rico, and the Philippines (which gained independence in 1946). On the heels of that war came World War I (1914–1918). In his reelection campaign of 1916, President Woodrow Wilson ran on the slogan "He kept us out of war." Nonetheless, the United States declared war on Germany on April 6, 1917, because that country refused to give up its campaign of sinking all ships headed for Britain, including passenger ships. (Large passenger ships of that time commonly held over a thousand people, so the sinking of such a ship was a disaster comparable to the attack on the World Trade Center.)

In the 1920s, the United States went "back to normalcy," as President Warren G. Harding urged it to do. U.S. military forces were largely disbanded, defense spending dropped to about 1 percent of total annual national income, and the nation returned to a period of isolationism.

The Era of Internationalism

Isolationism was permanently shattered by the bombing of the U.S. naval base at Pearl Harbor, Hawaii, on December 7, 1941. The surprise attack by the Japanese caused the deaths of 2,403 American servicemen and wounded 1,143 others. Eighteen warships were sunk or seriously damaged, and 188 planes were destroyed at the airfields. The American public was outraged. President Franklin Roosevelt asked Congress to declare war on Japan immediately, and the United States entered World War II. This unequivocal response was certainly due to the nature of the provocation. American soil had not been attacked by a foreign power since the occupation of Washington, D.C., by the British in 1814.

The United States was the only major participating country to emerge from World War II with its economy intact, and even strengthened. The Soviet Union, Japan, Italy, France, Germany, Britain, and a number of minor participants in the war were economically devastated. The United States was also the only country to have control over operational nuclear weapons. President Harry Truman had made the decision to use two atomic bombs, on August 6 and August 9, 1945, to end the war with Japan. (Historians still argue over the necessity of this action, which ultimately killed more than 100,000 Japanese and left an equal number permanently injured.) The United States truly had become the world's superpower.

The Cold War.   The United States had become an uncomfortable ally of the Soviet Union after Adolf Hitler's invasion of that country. Soon after World War II ended, relations between the Soviet Union and the West deteriorated. The Soviet Union wanted a weakened Germany, and to achieve this, it insisted that Germany be divided in two, with East Germany becoming a buffer against the West. Little by

This painting shows President James Monroe explaining the Monroe Doctrine to a group of government officials. Essentially, the Monroe Doctrine made the Western Hemisphere the concern of the United States. (Library of Congress photo)

Monroe Doctrine
A policy statement made by President James Monroe in 1823, which set out three principles: (1) European nations should not establish new colonies in the Western Hemisphere, (2) European nations should not intervene in the affairs of independent nations of the Western Hemisphere, and (3) the United States would not interfere in the affairs of European nations.

Isolationist Foreign Policy
A policy of abstaining from an active role in international affairs or alliances, which characterized U.S. foreign policy toward Europe during most of the 1800s.

British Prime Minister Winston Churchill, U.S. President Franklin Roosevelt, and Soviet leader Joseph Stalin met at Yalta from February 4 to 11, 1945, to resolve their differences over the shape that the international community would take after World War II. (Corbis/Bettmann)

Soviet Bloc

The Soviet Union and the Eastern European countries that installed Communist regimes after World War II and which were dominated by the Soviet Union.

Iron Curtain

The term used to describe the division of Europe between the Soviet Bloc and the West; coined by Winston Churchill.

Containment

A U.S. diplomatic policy adopted by the Truman administration to contain Communist power within its existing boundaries.

Truman Doctrine

The policy adopted by President Harry Truman in 1947 to halt Communist expansion in southeastern Europe.

little, the Soviet Union helped to install Communist governments in Eastern European countries, which began to be referred to collectively as the **Soviet bloc.** In response, the United States encouraged the rearming of Western Europe. The Cold War had begun.[6]

In Fulton, Missouri, on March 5, 1946, Winston Churchill, in a striking metaphor, declared that from the Baltic to the Adriatic Sea "an iron curtain has descended across the [European] continent." The term **iron curtain** became even more appropriate when Soviet-dominated East Germany built a wall separating East Berlin from West Berlin in August 1961.

Containment Policy.   In 1947, a remarkable article was published in *Foreign Affairs*. The article was signed by "X." The actual author was George F. Kennan, chief of the policy-planning staff for the State Department. The doctrine of **containment** set forth in the article became—according to many—the Bible of Western foreign policy. "X" argued that whenever and wherever the Soviet Union could successfully challenge the West, it would do so. He recommended that our policy toward the Soviet Union be "firm and vigilant containment of Russian expansive tendencies."[7]

The containment theory was expressed clearly in the **Truman Doctrine,** which was enunciated by President Harry Truman in his historic address to Congress on March 12, 1947. In that address, he announced that the United States must help countries in which a Communist takeover seemed likely. Later that year, he backed the Marshall Plan, an economic assistance plan for Europe that was intended to prevent the expansion of Communist influence there. By 1950, the United States had entered into a military alliance with the European nations commonly called the North Atlantic Treaty Organization, or NATO. The combined military power of the United States and the European nations worked to contain Soviet influence to Eastern Europe and to maintain a credible response to any Soviet military attack on Western Europe. Figure 17–2 on the next page shows the face-off between the U.S.–led NATO alliance and the Soviet-led Warsaw Pact.

Superpower Relations

During the Cold War, there was never any direct military conflict between the United States and the Soviet Union. Rather, confrontations among "client" nations were used to carry out the policies of the superpowers. Only on occasion did the United States directly enter a conflict in a significant way. Two such occasions were in Korea and in Vietnam.

After the end of World War II, northern Korea was occupied by the Soviet Union, and southern Korea was occupied by the United States. The result was two rival Korean governments. In 1950, North Korea invaded South Korea. Under UN authority, the United States entered the war, which prevented an almost certain South Korean defeat. When U.S. forces were on the brink of conquering North Korea, however, China joined the war on the side of the North, resulting in a stalemate. An armistice signed in 1953 led to the two Koreas that exist today. U.S. forces have remained in South Korea ever since.

The Vietnam War (1964–1975) also involved the United States in a civil war between a Communist North and pro-Western South. When the French army in Indochina was defeated by the Communist forces of Ho Chi Minh and the two

---

[6]See John Lewis Gaddis, *The United Nations and the Origins of the Cold War* (New York: Columbia University Press, 1972).
[7]X, "The Sources of Soviet Conduct," *Foreign Affairs,* July 1947, p. 575.

Vietnams were created in 1954, the United States assumed the role of supporting the South Vietnamese government against North Vietnam. President John Kennedy sent 16,000 "advisers" to help South Vietnam, and after Kennedy's death in 1963, President Lyndon Johnson greatly increased the scope of that support. American forces in Vietnam at the height of the U.S. involvement totaled more than 500,000 troops. More than 58,000 Americans were killed and 300,000 were wounded in the conflict. A peace agreement in 1973 allowed U.S. troops to leave the country, and in 1975 North Vietnam easily occupied Saigon (the South Vietnamese capital) and unified the nation. The debate over U.S. involvement in Vietnam became extremely heated and, as mentioned previously, spurred congressional efforts to limit the ability of the president to commit forces to armed combat. The military draft was also a major source of contention during the Vietnam War. Do events in Iraq justify bringing back the draft? We examine this question in the *Which Side Are You On?* feature on the following page.

The Cuban Missile Crisis.   Perhaps the closest the two superpowers came to a nuclear confrontation was the Cuban missile crisis in 1962. The Soviets placed missiles in Cuba, ninety miles off the U.S. coast, in response to Cuban fears of an American invasion and to try to balance an American nuclear advantage. President Kennedy and his advisers rejected the option of invading Cuba, setting up a naval blockade around the island instead. When Soviet vessels appeared near Cuban waters, the tension reached its height. After intense negotiations between Washington and Moscow, the Soviet ships turned around on October 25, and on October 28 the Soviet Union announced the withdrawal of its missile operations from Cuba. In exchange, the United States agreed not to invade Cuba in the future and to remove some of its own missiles that were located near the Soviet border in Turkey.

A Period of Détente.   The French word **détente** means a relaxation of tensions. By the end of the 1960s, it was clear that some efforts had to be made to reduce the threat of nuclear war between the United States and the Soviet Union. The Soviet Union gradually had begun to catch up in the building of strategic nuclear delivery vehicles in the form of bombers and missiles, thus balancing the nuclear

The atomic bomb explodes over Nagasaki, Japan, on August 9, 1945. (U.S. Air Force photo)

Détente

A French word meaning a relaxation of tensions. The term characterized U.S.–Soviet relations as they developed under President Richard Nixon and Secretary of State Henry Kissinger.

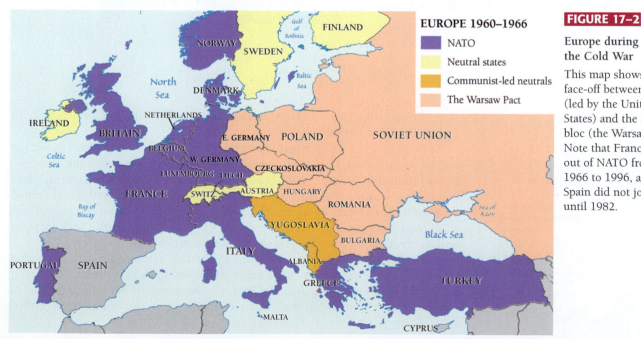

EUROPE 1960–1966

- NATO
- Neutral states
- Communist-led neutrals
- The Warsaw Pact

FIGURE 17–2

Europe during the Cold War

This map shows the face-off between NATO (led by the United States) and the Soviet bloc (the Warsaw Pact). Note that France was out of NATO from 1966 to 1996, and Spain did not join until 1982.

WHICH SIDE ARE YOU ON?
Should We Bring Back the Draft?

By law, male residents of the United States are required to register for the military draft after their eighteenth birthdays. From 1948 through 1973, all American men were subject to the draft, and draftees filled the ranks of the armed forces during war and peace. Since 1973, however, the armed forces have been composed entirely of volunteers.

In 2004, coalition troops in Iraq faced major uprisings. U.S. forces were stretched thin. The Department of Defense was compelled to extend the tours of duty for units that were about to be brought home. In particular, this meant extending the service of National Guard units. Most members of the National Guard had never anticipated that they would serve in a war zone.

In response, some members of Congress proposed enlarging the army. A few spoke up for bringing back the draft.

BRINGING BACK THE DRAFT WOULD PROMOTE FAIRNESS

Those who advocate bringing back the draft believe that universal service would be fairer than the current system. Now, almost no children of wealthy families enter the military. Only four members of the 107th Congress had children in one of the services. Draft advocates say that the military should not be limited to the lower classes—everyone should give something back to society. Alternative civilian service could be provided for those who do not wish to join the armed forces, but complete exemption should be unavailable.

A draft would prevent the kinds of troop shortages that the military is currently experiencing. In particular, it could eliminate the unfairness involved in stationing National Guard troops abroad for long periods of time. Finally, if there were a universal draft, Congress might be more cautious about endorsing wars.

THE DRAFT IS UNFAIR AND UNNECESSARY

Others fundamentally oppose forcing young people to give up one or more years of their lives to the government. The draft, they say, is a "tax" that falls most strongly on those who value their independence. If the government wants more soldiers, let it offer higher pay and better benefits. A draft would worsen already existing divisions in the country, as it did during the Vietnam War. Furthermore, the military really needs highly trained members who will reenlist, not large numbers of "warm bodies" who will leave as soon as they can.

WHAT'S YOUR POSITION?

If the draft were reinstated, should it include women? Why or why not?

GOING ONLINE

Draft registration is administered by the Selective Service System, which maintains a Web site at **http://www.sss.gov**. At this site, you can actually register online. For a pro-draft argument, check the Web site of Representative Charles Rangel at **http://www.house.gov/apps/list/press/ ny15_rangel/draftrelease.html**. An antidraft site that advocates civil disobedience is at **http://www. draftresistance.com**.

Strategic Arms Limitation Treaty (SALT I)

A treaty between the United States and the Soviet Union to stabilize the nuclear arms competition between the two countries. SALT I talks began in 1969, and agreements were signed on May 26, 1972.

scales between the two countries. Each nation acquired the military capacity to destroy the other with nuclear weapons.

As the result of lengthy negotiations under Secretary of State Henry Kissinger and President Nixon, the United States and the Soviet Union signed the **Strategic Arms Limitation Treaty (SALT I)** in May 1972. That treaty "permanently" limited the development and deployment of antiballistic missiles (ABMs) and limited the number of offensive missiles each country could deploy. To further reduce tensions, new scientific and cultural exchanges were arranged with the Soviets, as well as new opportunities for Jewish emigration out of the Soviet Union.

The policy of détente was not limited to the U.S. relationship with the Soviet Union. Seeing an opportunity to capitalize on increasing friction between the Soviet Union and the People's Republic of China, Kissinger secretly began negotiations to establish a new relationship with that nation. President Nixon eventually visited

China in 1972. The visit set the stage for the formal diplomatic recognition of that country, which occurred during the Carter administration (1977–1981).

The Reagan-Bush Years. President Ronald Reagan took a hard line against the Soviet Union during his first term, proposing the strategic defense initiative (SDI), or "Star Wars," in 1983. The SDI was designed to serve as a space-based defense against enemy missiles. Reagan and others in his administration argued that the program would deter nuclear war by shifting the emphasis of defense strategy from offensive to defensive weapons systems.

In November 1985, however, President Reagan and Mikhail Gorbachev, the Soviet leader, began to work on an arms reduction compact. The negotiations resulted in a historic agreement signed by Reagan and Gorbachev in Washington, D.C., on December 8, 1987. The terms of the Intermediate-Range Nuclear Force (INF) Treaty, which was ratified by the Senate, required the superpowers to dismantle a total of four thousand intermediate-range missiles within the first three years of the agreement.

Beginning in 1989, President George H. W. Bush continued the negotiations with the Soviet Union to reduce the number of nuclear weapons and the number of armed troops in Europe. Subsequent events, including developments in Eastern Europe, the unification of Germany, and the dissolution of the Soviet Union (in December 1991), made the process much more complex. American strategists worried as much about who now controlled the Soviet nuclear arsenal as about completing the treaty process. In 1992, the United States signed the Strategic Arms Reduction Treaty (START) with four former Soviet republics—Russia, Ukraine, Belarus, and Kazakhstan—to reduce the number of long-range nuclear weapons. President George W. Bush changed directions in 2001, announcing that the United States was withdrawing from the 1972 ABM treaty. Six months later, however, Bush and Russian President Vladimir Putin signed an agreement greatly reducing the number of nuclear weapons on each side over the next few years.

The Dissolution of the Soviet Union. After the fall of the Berlin Wall in 1989, it was clear that the Soviet Union had relinquished much of its political and military control over the states of Eastern Europe that formerly had been part of the Soviet bloc. No one expected the Soviet Union to dissolve into separate states as quickly as it did, however. Though Gorbachev tried to adjust the Soviet constitution and political system to allow greater autonomy for the republics within the union, demands for political, ethnic, and religious autonomy grew. In August 1991, anti-reformist conspirators launched an attempt to overthrow the Soviet government and to depose Gorbachev. These efforts were thwarted by the Russian people and parliament under the leadership of Boris Yeltsin, then president of Russia.

Instead of restoring the Soviet state, the attempted *coup d'état* hastened the process of creating an independent Russian state led by Yeltsin. On the day after Christmas in 1991, the Soviet Union was officially dissolved. Another uprising in Russia, this time led by anti-Yeltsin members of the new parliament who wanted to restore the Soviet Union immediately, failed in 1993. Figure 17–3 on the next page shows the new situation in Europe following the collapse of the Soviet Union.

In 2000, Yeltsin resigned due to poor health. He named Vladimir Putin, architect of the Russian military effort against the independence movement in the province of Chechnya, as acting president. A few months later, Putin won the presidency in a national election. As the United States launched its war on terrorism, Putin stood by President George W. Bush's side as an ally. Nonetheless, Russia opposed to the use of military forces in Iraq in early 2003, believing that a war against Iraq was unjustified.

DID YOU KNOW . . .
That Russia has suffered more battle deaths in putting down the rebellion in Chechnya than the Soviet Union experienced in its decades-long attempt to subdue Afghanistan?

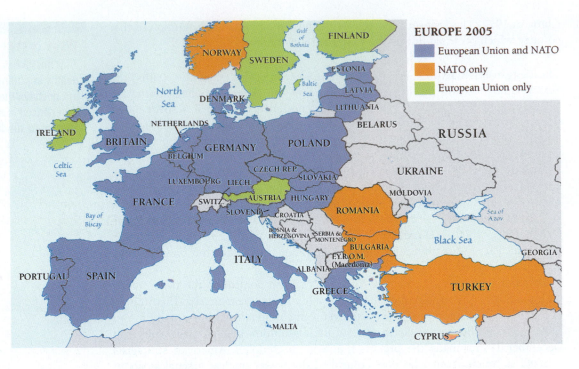

FIGURE 17-3

Europe after the Fall of the Soviet Union

This map shows the growth in European unity as marked by the participation in transnational organizations. The United States continues to lead NATO (and would be orange if it were on the map). Note the reunification of Germany and the creation of new states from former Yugoslavia and the former Soviet Union.

★ Foreign Policy: Why Is It Important Today?

The collapse of the Soviet Union in 1991 effectively left the United States as the only global superpower. It also brought to an end what had previously been a major shaping force in U.S. foreign policy—the containment of communism. For most of the second half of the twentieth century, the Cold War between the superpowers—the ideological battle between the "Communist evil" and the West—had provided a framework for U.S. foreign policy decision making.

Today, the United States has another ideological framework for its foreign policy—the war on terrorism. Nations that sponsor terrorism or that produce weapons of mass destruction that could fall into the hands of terrorists are the new "evil" that guides U.S. foreign policy. The Bush administration has implemented a policy of preemptive war and regime change, such as in Afghanistan and Iraq, in an attempt to eradicate, or at least curb, these "evil" forces in today's world.

Ultimately, every American is affected by this country's actions in the world arena. The stakes are high. Given the military and economic power of the United States, U.S. policy decisions will strongly affect the viability of multilateral organizations, including the United Nations, and the effectiveness of such organizations in handling worldwide challenges. U.S. decisions will also influence how the world copes with environmental degradation, the development and possible future deployment of nuclear and chemical weapons, and other problems that can have an impact not only on U.S. citizens but also on the global community. The United States is in a position to exert leadership in a world divided by different political, ethnic, and religious cultures. In the end, it is up to the American people to determine the form that such leadership will take.

MAKING A DIFFERENCE ★ Working for Human Rights

In many countries throughout the world, human rights are not protected. In some nations, people are imprisoned, tortured, or killed because they oppose the current regime. In other nations, certain ethnic or racial groups are oppressed by the majority population.

Why Should You Care?

The strongest reason for involving yourself with human rights issues in other countries is simple moral altruism—unselfish regard for the welfare of others. The defense of human rights is unlikely to put a single dollar in your pocket.

A broader consideration, however, is that human rights abuses are often associated with the kind of dictatorial regimes that are likely to provoke wars. To the extent that the people of the world can create a climate in which human rights abuses are unacceptable, they may also create an atmosphere in which national leaders believe that they must display peaceful conduct generally. This, in turn, might reduce the frequency of wars, some of

which could involve the United States. And wars always have costs—in the form of dollars, and in the form of American lives.

What Can You Do?

What can you do to work for the improvement of human rights in other nations? One way is to join an organization that attempts to keep watch over human rights violations. (Two such organizations are listed at the end of this feature.) By publicizing human rights violations, such organizations try to pressure nations into changing their practices. Sometimes, these organizations are able to apply enough pressure and cause enough embarrassment that victims may be freed from prison or allowed to emigrate.

Another way to work for human rights is to keep informed about the state of affairs in other nations and to write personally to governments that violate human rights or to their embassies, asking them to cease these violations.

If you want to receive general information about the position of the

United States on human rights violations, you can contact the State Department:

U.S. Department of State
   Bureau of Democracy,
   Human Rights, and Labor
2201 C St. N.W.
Washington, DC 20520
202-647-4000

http://www.state.gov/g/drl/hr

The following organizations are well known for their watchdog efforts in countries that violate human rights for political reasons:

Amnesty International U.S.A.
322 Eighth Ave., Fl. 10
New York, NY 10001
212-807-8400
http://www.amnestyusa.org

American Friends Service Committee
1501 Cherry St.
Philadelphia, PA 19102
215-241-7000
http://www.afsc.org

Key Terms

attentive public 567

Cold War 557

containment 570

defense policy 550

détente 571

diplomacy 549

economic aid 549

foreign policy 549

foreign policy process 549

intelligence community 565

iron curtain 570

isolationist foreign policy 569

military-industrial
   complex 567

Monroe Doctrine 569

moral idealism 550

national security policy 549

negative constituents 565

normal trade relations (NTR)
   status 558

political realism 551

Soviet bloc 570

Strategic Arms Limitation
   Treaty (SALT I) 572

technical assistance 549

Truman Doctrine 570

Chapter Summary

1 Foreign policy includes national goals and the techniques used to achieve them. National security policy, which is one aspect of foreign policy, is designed to protect the independence and the political and economic integrity of the United States. Diplomacy involves the nation's external relationships and is an attempt to resolve conflict without resort to arms. U.S. foreign policy is sometimes based on moral idealism and sometimes based on political realism.

2 Terrorism has become a major challenge facing the United States and other nations. The United States waged war on terrorism after the September 11 attacks. U.S. armed forces occupied Afghanistan in 2001 and Iraq in 2003.

3 Nuclear proliferation continues to be an issue due to the breakup of the Soviet Union and loss of control over its nuclear arsenal, along with the continued efforts of other nations to gain nuclear warheads. The number of warheads is known to be more than 32,000.

4 Ethnic tensions and political instability in many regions of the world provide challenges to the United States. The nations of Central America and the Caribbean, including Haiti, require American attention because of their proximity. Civil wars have torn apart Rwanda, Yugoslavia, and other countries. The Middle East continues to be a hotbed of conflict despite efforts to continue the peace process. In 1991 and again in 2003, the United States sent combat troops to Iraq. The second Gulf War, in 2003, succeeded in toppling the decades-long dictatorship in Iraq.

5 The formal power of the president to make foreign policy derives from the U.S. Constitution, which designates the president as commander in chief of the army and navy. Presidents have interpreted this authority broadly. They also have the power to make treaties and executive agreements. In principle, the State Department is the executive agency with primary authority over foreign affairs. The National Security Council also plays a major role. The intelligence community consists of government agencies engaged in activities varying from information gathering to covert operations. In response to presidential actions in the Vietnam War, Congress attempted to establish some limits on the power of the president to intervene abroad by passing the War Powers Resolution in 1973.

6 Three major themes have guided U.S. foreign policy. In the early years of the nation, isolationism was the primary strategy. With the start of the twentieth century, isolationism gave way to global involvement. From the end of World War II through the 1980s, the major goal was to contain communism and the influence of the Soviet Union.

7 During the 1800s, the United States had little international power and generally stayed out of European conflicts and politics, and so these years have been called the period of isolationism. The Monroe Doctrine of 1823 stated that the United States would not accept foreign intervention in the Western Hemisphere and would not meddle in European affairs. The United States pursued an actively expansionist policy in the Americas and the Pacific area, however.

8 The end of the policy of isolationism toward Europe started with the Spanish-American War of 1898. U.S. involvement in European politics became more extensive when the United States entered World War I on April 6, 1917. World War II marked a lasting change in American foreign policy. The United States was the only major country to emerge from the war with its economy intact and the only country with operating nuclear weapons.

9 Soon after the close of World War II, the uncomfortable alliance between the United States and the Soviet Union ended, and the Cold War began. A policy of containment, which assumed an expansionist Soviet Union, was enunciated in the Truman Doctrine. Following the frustrations of the Vietnam War and the apparent arms equality of the United States and the Soviet Union, the United States adopted a policy of détente. Although President Reagan took a tough stance toward the Soviet Union during his first term, his second term saw serious negotiations toward arms reduction, culminating in the signing of the Intermediate-Range Nuclear Force Treaty in 1987. After the fall of the Soviet Union, Russia emerged as a less threatening state and signed the Strategic Arms Reduction Treaty with the United States in 1992. The United States and Russia have agreed on some issues in recent years, such as the fight against terrorism, but have disagreed on other matters, such as the war against Iraq in 2003.

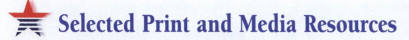

Selected Print and Media Resources

SUGGESTED READINGS

Lewis, Bernard. *What Went Wrong? Western Impact and Middle Eastern Response.* Oxford: Oxford University Press, 2002. Lewis, an outstanding scholar of the Middle East, provides a brief history of how the West and the Middle East have taken different paths in the last few centuries and how those choices have brought them into conflict.

Nye, Joseph S., Jr. *The Paradox of American Power: Why the World's Only Superpower Can't Go It Alone.* New York: Oxford University Press, 2002. Former assistant secretary of defense and now dean of Harvard's Kennedy School of Government, Joseph Nye stresses the importance of U.S. cooperation with the international community and indicates why the United States cannot "go it alone" in today's world arena.

O'Hanlon, Michael, and Mike M. Mochizuki. *Crisis in the Korean Peninsula: How to Deal with a Nuclear North Korea.* New York: McGraw-Hill, 2003. The authors provide a comprehensive introduction to the dangers posed by North Korea, which could become a greater threat to world peace than the current terrorist movements. They also offer a possible "grand bargain" to defuse the crisis.

Rashid, Ahmed. *Taliban: Militant Islam, Oil, and Fundamentalism in Central Asia.* New Haven, Conn.: Yale University Press, 2001. Written by a reporter who spent twenty-one years in Afghanistan, this book examines the causes of Islamic radicalism and of the anger against the United States expressed by the Taliban when that government was in power.

Woodward, Bob. *Plan of Attack.* New York: Simon and Schuster, 2004. This is the second of Woodward's masterful inside accounts of policymaking in George W. Bush's administration. *Bush at War* dealt with 9/11 and the war in Afghanistan. *Plan of Attack* covers the Second Gulf War in Iraq and its aftermath. Woodward reveals alarming problems in the way the war was conceived and planned, but he also shows the conviction and dedication of the people who carried out the policy.

MEDIA RESOURCES

The Aftermath: A Visit to Postwar Iraq—A 2003 program that features interviews with Iraqi clerics, businessmen, scholars, and street protestors, and also with U.S. soldiers and their commanders.

Black Hawk Down—This 2002 film recounts the events in Mogadishu, Somalia, in October 1993, during which two U.S. Black Hawk helicopters were shot down. The film, which is based on reporter Mark Bowden's best-selling book by the same name, contains graphic scenes of terrifying urban warfare.

The Fall of Milosevic—A highly acclaimed 2003 documentary by Norma Percy and Brian Lapping. This film covers the final years of the crisis in former Yugoslavia, including the war in Kosovo and the fall of Slobodan Milosevic, Serb nationalist leader and alleged war criminal. Except for Milosevic himself, almost all top Serb and Albanian leaders are interviewed, as are President Bill Clinton and British Prime Minister Tony Blair.

The 50 Years War—Israel and the Arabs—A two-volume PBS Home Video released in 2000. More balanced than some accounts, this film includes interviews with many leaders involved in the struggle, including: from Israel, Yitzhak Rabin, Shimon Peres, Benjamin Netanyahu, and Ariel Sharon; from the Arab world, Egypt's Anwar al-Sadat, Jordan's King Hussein, and Yasir Arafat; and from the United States, presidents Jimmy Carter, George H. W. Bush, and Bill Clinton.

Osama bin Laden: In the Name of Allah—A 2001 biography of the leader responsible for the terrorist attacks of September 11, 2001.

e-mocracy ★ Attacking Government Computer Systems

Attacks on the government's computer systems occur often and are sometimes successful. In 1996, hackers caused mischief at the computers of the Central Intelligence Agency and the Justice Department and destroyed the Air Force's home page. In early 1998, computer hackers accessed a series of nonclassified sites, caused major university and National Aeronautics and Space Administration computers to crash, and defaced military base home pages. It is clear from these episodes that the electronic network used by U.S. military and intelligence organizations is susceptible to access by amateurs, criminals, and spies.

Perhaps even more damage could be caused by interruptions to the global economic and banking system. During 1997, a survey of banks, universities, and companies showed that more than 60 percent had been accessed "illegitimately" during that year alone. In 2000, a series of computer viruses crippled businesses around the world. One of the most destructive viruses was eventually traced to a graduate student in the Philippines whose thesis had been rejected.

The potential consequences of successful attacks on government or business computer systems are great. Among the networks that, if impaired or destroyed, could interfere with the nation's activities are those that connect the military services; guide satellites for communications and defense; guide submarines; and control all air traffic, credit-card transactions, interbank transactions, and utility grids throughout the nation. The collapse of the World Trade Center towers in 2001 damaged telecommunications and Internet communications for all of lower Manhattan.

Logging On

Our government and the governments of other nations maintain hundreds of Web sites on foreign and defense policy. If you are interested in information about visas, passports, and individual countries, you can access the site maintained by the Department of State at

http://www.state.gov

For information about human rights, national security, and other issues from a European point of view, check a Web site maintained by the Swiss government, the International Relations and Security Network, at

http://www.css.ethz.ch

The Brookings Institution, a Washington, D.C., think tank, provides access to its research reports at the following Web site:

http://www.brook.edu

The Global Affairs Agenda, an interest group that promotes a progressive or liberal foreign policy, provides information about many topics at

http://www.fpif.org

For information about the intelligence community and about foreign countries, go to the Web site of the Central Intelligence Agency at

http://www.cia.gov

Freedom House, an organization that promotes its vision of democracy around the world, rates all nations on their democratic practices at

http://www.freedomhouse.org

Using InfoTrac for Political Research

You can use InfoTrac to research the latest developments in foreign affairs. To use InfoTrac to research foreign policy, go to

http://www.infotrac-college.com

Log in and go to InfoTrac College Edition, then go to the Keyword guide. Type one or more words in the search field—choose words that are likely to bring up articles on a particular foreign policy issue. One combination of words that yields a useful collection of articles is "israeli palestinian peace." InfoTrac will present you with a list of articles, sorted by date. Choose a number of recent ones, and use them to make your analysis.

ONLINE REVIEW

At **http://politicalscience.wadsworth.com/schmidt12**, you will find a free Study Guide to this book. For each chapter, there are two online quizzes to help you master the material.

• The **PoliPrep Self Study Assessment** provides a pre-test for each major section of the chapter. PoliPrep then generates a customized study plan. After you complete the study plan, a post-test evaluates your progress.

• The **Tutorial Quiz** for each chapter provides questions on the chapter contents, including the features. The questions are organized to match the major sections of the chapter.

State and Local Government

WHAT IF . . .
All States Offered School Vouchers?

BACKGROUND

There is a growing sense in this country that our educational system is in decline. Routinely, U.S. students test poorly in achievement, particularly in math and science, compared to students in such countries as Japan, Russia, and Germany.

Not surprisingly, many observers of the educational scene believe that the fault lies in our public school system. They argue that change is needed and that the easiest way to improve the system is to make schools compete with each other. Currently, parents normally are required to send their children to a public school in the particular district where the family's home is located. Generally, only families that are willing to spend from $3,000 to $10,000 a year for tuition at private schools (in addition to the property taxes they pay to support their local public school districts) have a choice as to which school their children will attend.

WHAT IF ALL STATES OFFERED SCHOOL VOUCHERS?

School choice sometimes involves open districts, meaning that parents can choose to send their children to public schools outside their districts. The aspect of school choice that generates substantial controversy, however, usually involves giving families vouchers, representing state funds, that can be used at any school, public or private.

In other words, a voucher would be worth some specified amount of money, such as $5,000, but only if it were redeemed by a bona fide public or private school. Any such plan would have to be set up by state or local government because that is where the responsibility for education currently lies.

Under such a system, parents would determine where their children went to school. The children could attend the same local public school, a public school in another district, or a private school anywhere. Private schools might accept the vouchers as full payment for tuition fees or request that additional fees be paid.

COMPETITION WOULD BECOME EVIDENT

Certainly, competition for students would develop. Public schools would have to compete not only among themselves (which they currently do in areas that have open districts) but also with private schools. Private schools would have to compete with all schools, including new competitors in the educational marketplace.

Some critics of school choice, particularly public school teachers and administrators, are uncomfortable with treating public education like a business. Because of the competitive environment that would be created by school choice, some public schools might not be able to keep and attract enough students to survive. These schools, unless further subsidized by state and local governments, would "go bankrupt" and disappear.

THE CONSTITUTIONAL ISSUE

Other critics of school vouchers claim that such programs are unconstitutional because they allow state funds to be used to pay for education at religious schools. For example, in a voucher program set up in Cleveland, Ohio, children from low-income families received state funds, in the form of vouchers, to attend the school of their choice. Most of the four thousand children in the program left public schools to attend Catholic educational institutions.

According to those who challenged the program, the use of tax dollars to support religious education violated the establishment clause of the First Amendment to the Constitution, which requires the separation of church and state (see Chapter 4). An Ohio court agreed and invalidated the program, but in 2002 the Supreme Court held that the voucher program was constitutional. The Court's majority reasoned that because families theoretically could use the vouchers to send their children not only to religious schools but also to secular private academies, suburban public schools, or charter schools, the program did not unconstitutionally entangle church and state.

FOR CRITICAL ANALYSIS

1. *Why are teachers' unions, such as the National Education Association, so adamantly against vouchers?*
2. *Given that the goal of our public school system is universal education, do you see school choice as hurting or helping students from low-income families? Explain.*

As you read in this chapter's opening *What If . . .* feature, it is up to the individual states to determine whether to allow school choice. There is no federal law that determines the issue, at least not yet. Within each state, even if a law allowing school choice were passed, local governments, particularly school boards, no doubt would have a large say in determining exactly how school choice would be made available in their particular areas.

This is true with respect to many state—and federal—policies. Typically, it is the local governing units in this country that give a human face to particular policies, such as welfare reform, and that deal directly with the persons affected by those policies. Indeed, many people, when they think of government, think of local agencies or sets of individuals—such as city councils, city or county commissioners, school boards, libraries, zoning boards, fire and police departments, and so on—and not their state governments or the federal government. Because they shape the environments in which all Americans live, the more than 87,000 local governmental units in the United States play a vital role in our federal system.

From a practical point of view, it is impossible to understand American politics and government today without a knowledge of how state and local governments operate—the topic of this chapter. We begin by examining the constitutional powers of the states as set forth by the founders in the U.S. Constitution. As you will see, local governments were not mentioned in the Constitution. The founders left their existence in the hands of state government.

Public education is a service that is largely controlled and funded by local (and to the lesser extent, state) governments, not by the federal government. This often creates conflict over specific education reforms, such as the use of school vouchers. Here, Reverend Timothy McDonald addresses a rally in Atlanta, Georgia, opposing school vouchers. What arguments do opponents of school vouchers use to defend their position? (AP Photo/Rick Bowmer)

★ The U.S. Constitution and the State Governments

We live in a federal system in which there are fifty separate state governments and one national government. The U.S. Constitution reserves a broad range of powers for state governments. It also prohibits state governments from engaging in certain activities. The U.S. Constitution does not say explicitly what the states actually may do. Rather, state powers are simply reserved, or residual: states may do anything that is not prohibited by the Constitution or anything that is not expressly within the realm of the national government.

The major reserved powers of the states are the powers to tax, spend, and regulate intrastate commerce, or commerce within a given state. The states also have general **police power,** meaning that they can impose their will on their citizens in the areas of safety (through, say, traffic laws), health (immunizations), welfare (child-abuse laws), and morals (regulation of pornographic materials).

Restrictions on state and local governmental activity are implied by the Constitution in Article VI, Clause 2:

> This Constitution, and the Laws of the United States which shall be made in Pursuance thereof; and all Treaties made, or which shall be made, under the Authority of the United States, shall be the supreme Law of the Land; and the Judges in every State shall be bound thereby, any Thing in the Constitution or Laws of any State to the Contrary notwithstanding.

In other words, it is the U.S. Constitution that is the supreme law of the land. No state or local law can be in conflict with the Constitution, with laws made by the national Congress, or with treaties entered into by the national government. Judicially, the United States Supreme Court has been the final arbiter of conflicts arising between the national government and state governments.

Police Power
Authority to promote and safeguard the health, morals, safety, and welfare of the people.

★ State Constitutions

The U.S. Constitution is a model of brevity, although at the cost of specificity. State constitutions, however, typically are excessively long and detailed. The U.S. Constitution has endured for two hundred years and has been amended only twenty-seven times. State constitutions are another matter. Louisiana has had eleven constitutions; Georgia, ten; South Carolina, seven; and Alabama, Florida, and Virginia, six. The number of amendments that have been submitted to voters borders on the absurd. For example, the citizens of Alabama have adopted 743 amendments to their state constitution.

Why Are State Constitutions So Long?

According to historians, the length and mass of detail of many state constitutions reflect the loss of popular confidence in state legislatures between the end of the Civil War and the early 1900s. During that period, forty-two states adopted or revised their constitutions. Those constitutions adopted before or after that period are shorter and contain fewer restrictions on the powers of state legislatures. Another equally important reason for the length and detail of state constitutions is that state constitution makers apparently have had a difficult time distinguishing between constitutional and statutory law. Does the Louisiana constitution need an amendment to declare Huey Long's birthday a legal holiday? Is it necessary for the constitution of South Dakota to authorize a cordage and twine plant at the state penitentiary? Does the California constitution need to discuss the tax-exempt status of the Huntington Library and Art Gallery? The U.S. Constitution contains no such details. It leaves to the legislature the nuts-and-bolts activity of making specific statutory laws.

In all fairness to the states, their courts do not interpret their constitutions as freely as the United States Supreme Court interprets the U.S. Constitution. Therefore, the states feel compelled to be more specific in their own constitutions. Additionally, the framers of state constitutions may feel obliged to fill in the gaps left by the very brief federal constitution.

The Constitutional Convention and the Constitutional Initiative

Constitutional Initiative
An electoral device whereby citizens can propose a constitutional amendment through petitions signed by the required number of registered voters.

Two of the several ways to effect constitutional changes are the state constitutional convention and the constitutional initiative. As of 2005, over 230 state constitutional conventions had been used to write an entirely new constitution or to attempt to amend an existing one. In eighteen states, the constitution can be amended by **constitutional initiatives.**[1] An initiative allows citizens to place a proposed amendment on the ballot without calling a constitutional convention. The number of signatures required to get a constitutional initiative on the ballot varies from state to state; it is usually between 5 and 10 percent of the total number of votes cast for governor in the last election. The initiative process has been used most frequently in California and Oregon. Relatively few initiative amendments are approved by the electorate.

★ The State Executive Branch

All state governments in the United States have executive, legislative, and judicial branches. Here the similarity with the federal government ends. State governments do not always have strong executive branches.

A Weak Executive

During the colonial period, governors were appointed by the Crown and had the power to call the colonial assembly (the colonial legislative body) into session, recommend legislation, exercise veto power, and dissolve the assembly. The colo-

---

[1]These states are Arizona, Arkansas, California, Colorado, Florida, Illinois, Massachusetts, Michigan, Mississippi, Missouri, Montana, Nebraska, Nevada, North Dakota, Ohio, Oklahoma, Oregon, and South Dakota.

nial governor acted as commander in chief of the colony's military forces and was also the head of the judiciary.

Not surprisingly, the colonies' revolt against British rule centered on the all-powerful colonial governors. When the first states were formed after the Declaration of Independence, hostility toward the governor's office ensured a weak executive branch and an extremely strong legislative branch. By the 1830s, however, the state executive office had become more important. Since Andrew Jackson's presidency, all governors (except in South Carolina) have been elected directly by the people. Simultaneously, there was an effort to democratize state government by popularly electing other state government officials as well.

Under the tenets of Jacksonian democracy, the more public officials who are elected (and not appointed), the more democratic (and better) the system will be. Even today, some states have numerous state offices with independently elected officials. The direct election of so many executive officials makes it likely that no one will have much power, because each official is working to secure his or her own political support. Only if the elected officials happen to be able to work together cohesively can they get much done.

A slight majority of the states require that the candidates for governor and lieutenant governor run for election as a team. In some states where this is not required, however, the voters have at times chosen a governor from one political party and a lieutenant governor from another. In a few states, this has actually created a circumstance in which the governor is unwilling to leave the state in order to prevent the lieutenant governor from exerting power during the governor's travels.

Reforming the System

Most states follow the practice of electing numerous executive officials. Nonetheless, governors have exercised the authority of their office with increasing frequency in recent years. Governors, for example, have become a significant force in legislative policymaking. In theory, the governor enjoys the same advantage that the president has over Congress in his or her ability to make policy decisions and to embody these in a program on which the state legislative body can act. How the governor exercises this ability often depends on her or his powers of persuasion. A strong personality can make for a strong executive office. Personal skill, the strength of political parties and special interest groups, and the governor's use of the media can affect how much actual power she or he has.

Reorganization of the state executive branch to achieve greater efficiency has been attempted numerous times and in many states. There are some obstacles to

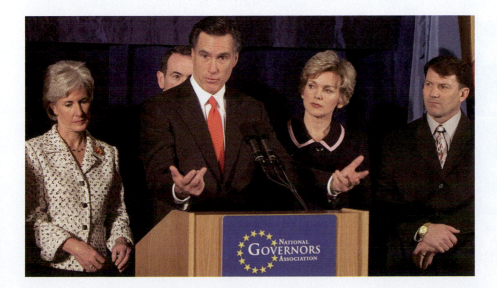

The National Governors Association is one of the most influential lobbying organizations in the country. It has also been an important source in providing governors with reports on a variety of innovative state programs. Governors from left to right are Kathleen Sebelius of Kansas, Mitt Romney of Massachusetts, Jennifer Granholm of Michigan, and Michael Rounds of South Dakota. (EPA/Mike Theiler/Landov)

reorganizing state executive branches, however. Voters do not want to lose their ability to influence politics directly. Both the voters and the legislators fear that reorganization will concentrate too much authority in the hands of the governor. Finally, many believe that numerous governmental functions, such as control of the highway program, should remain administrative rather than political.

Despite the fragmentation of executive power and doubts about the concentration of power in an executive's hands, the trend toward modernization has increased the powers of many of the states' highest executives. Based on a governor's ability to make major appointments, formulate a state budget, veto legislation, and exercise other powers, the National Governors Association ranks the governors of at least twenty-five states as powerful or very powerful executives. Only eleven states are assessed as giving their executives little or very little power.

Moreover, state governors—as well as legislators—are playing increasingly important roles as the states assume more authority over programs, such as welfare, that for decades have been controlled by the national government. The trend toward states' rights during the 1990s and early 2000s has allowed governors to become models of leadership on a number of issues affecting national politics, including crime, welfare, and education. A state governorship also may be a stepping-stone to the U.S. presidency. Seventeen of the nation's forty-three presidents (39 percent), including several recent presidents (Jimmy Carter, Ronald Reagan, Bill Clinton, and George W. Bush), served as state governors before assuming the presidential office. For these reasons, elections to state governorships tend to receive more national attention than in the past.

The Governor's Veto Power

The veto power gives the president of the United States immense leverage. Simply the threat of a presidential veto often means that legislation will not be passed by Congress. In some states, governors have strong veto power, but in other states, governors have no veto power at all. Some states give the governor veto power but allow only five days in which to exercise it. Thirteen states give the governor pocket veto power.

In forty-three states, the governor has some form of **item veto** power on appropriations. If the governor in such a state does not particularly like one item, or line,

Item Veto
The power exercised by the governors of most states to veto particular sections or items of an appropriations bill, while signing the remainder of the bill into law.

The seventeen presidents who served as state governors before assuming the presidential office.

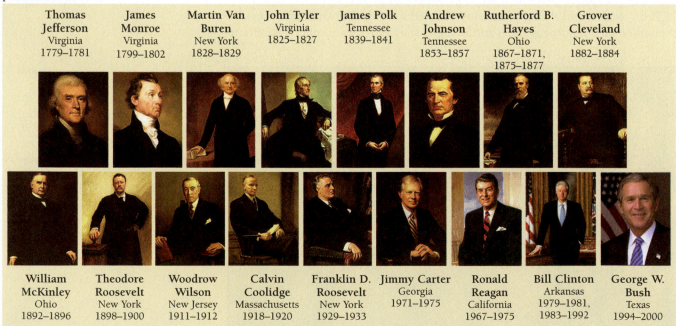

Thomas Jefferson	James Monroe	Martin Van Buren	John Tyler	James Polk	Andrew Johnson	Rutherford B. Hayes	Grover Cleveland
Virginia	Virginia	New York	Virginia	Tennessee	Tennessee	Ohio	New York
1779–1781	1799–1802	1828–1829	1825–1827	1839–1841	1853–1857	1867–1871, 1875–1877	1882–1884

William McKinley	Theodore Roosevelt	Woodrow Wilson	Calvin Coolidge	Franklin D. Roosevelt	Jimmy Carter	Ronald Reagan	Bill Clinton	George W. Bush
Ohio	New York	New Jersey	Massachusetts	New York	Georgia	California	Arkansas	Texas
1892–1896	1898–1900	1911–1912	1918–1920	1929–1933	1971–1975	1967–1975	1979–1981, 1983–1992	1994–2000

in an appropriations bill, he or she can veto that item. In twelve states, the governor can reduce the amount of the appropriation but cannot reduce it to zero. Nineteen states give governors the ability to use the item veto on more than just appropriations.

The State Legislature

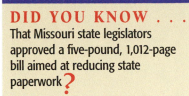

Although there has been a move in recent years to increase the power of governors, state legislatures are still an important force in state politics and state governmental decision making. The task of these assemblies is to legislate on such matters as taxes and the regulation of business and commerce, highways, school systems and the funding of education, and welfare payments. Allocation of funds and program priorities are vital issues to local residents and communities, and conflicts between regions within the state or between the cities and the rural areas are common.

State legislatures have been criticized for being unprofessional and less than effective. It is true that state legislatures sometimes spend their time considering trivial legislation (such as the official state pie in Florida), and lobbyists often have too much influence in state capitals. At the same time, state legislators are often given few resources with which to work. In many states, legislatures are limited to meeting only part of the year, and in some the pay is a disincentive to real service. In a number of states, state legislators are paid less than $10,000 per year. A complete list of state legislators' salaries, as well as other characteristics of state legislatures, is given in Table 18–1 on the following page.

We have seen earlier how a bill becomes a law in the U.S. Congress. A similar process occurs at the state level. Below, Figure 18–1 traces how an idea becomes a law in the Florida legislature. Similar steps are followed in other states (note that Nebraska has a unicameral legislature, however, so there is no second chamber process).

FIGURE 18–1

How an Idea Becomes a Law

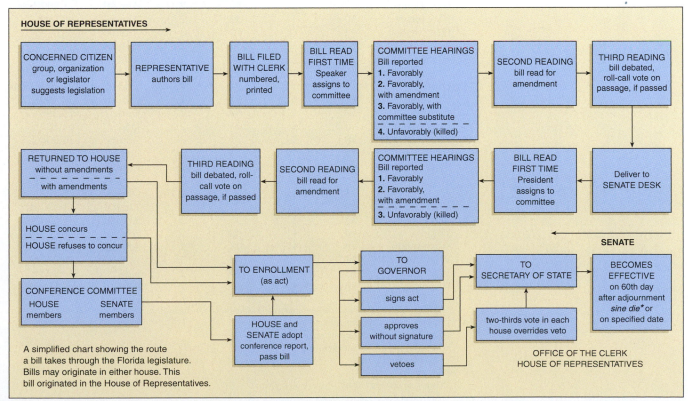

A simplified chart showing the route a bill takes through the Florida legislature. Bills may originate in either house. This bill originated in the House of Representatives.

Sine die means "without assigning a day for a further meeting."

SOURCE: Allen Morris and Joan Perry Morris, compilers, *The Florida Handbook, 2003–2004*, 29th ed. (Tallahassee, Fla.: Peninsular Books, 2003).

TABLE 18-1

Characteristics of State Legislatures

	Seats in Senate	Length of Term	Seats in House	Length of Term	Years Sessions Are Held	Salary*
Alabama	35	4	105	4	Annual	$10(d)†
Alaska	20	4	40	2	Annual	24,012†
Arizona	30	2	60	2	Annual	24,000†
Arkansas	35	4	100	2	Odd	12,796†
California	40	4	80	2	Even**	99,000†
Colorado	35	4	65	2	Annual	30,000†
Connecticut	36	2	151	2	Annual	28,000
Delaware	21	4	41	2	Annual	33,400
Florida	40	4	120	2	Annual	27,900†
Georgia	56	2	180	2	Annual	16,200†
Hawaii	25	4	51	2	Annual	32,000†
Idaho	35	2	70	2	Annual	15,646†
Illinois	59	‡	118	2	Annual	55,788†
Indiana	50	4	100	2	Annual	11,600†
Iowa	50	4	100	2	Annual	20,758†
Kansas	40	4	125	2	Annual	78.75(d)†
Kentucky	38	4	100	2	Annual	163.56(d)†
Louisiana	39	4	105	4	Annual	16,800†
Maine	35	2	151	2	Even	10,815§†
Maryland	47	4	141	4	Annual	31,509†
Massachusetts	40	2	160	2	Biennial**	50,123†
Michigan	38	4	110	2	Annual	77,400†
Minnesota	67	4	134	2	Odd††	31,140†
Mississippi	52	4	122	4	Annual	10,000†
Missouri	34	4	163	2	Annual	31,561†
Montana	50	4	100	2	Odd	71.83(d)†
Nebraska″	49	4	—	—	Annual	12,000†
Nevada	21	4	42	2	Odd	130(d)†
New Hampshire	24	2	400	2	Annual	200(b)
New Jersey	40	4	80	2	Annual	49,000
New Mexico	42	4	70	2	Annual	—†
New York	62	2	150	2	Annual	79,500†
North Carolina	50	2	120	2	Odd††	13,951†
North Dakota	47	4	94	4	Odd	125(d)†
Ohio	33	4	99	2	Odd**	51,674
Oklahoma	48	4	101	2	Annual	38,400†
Oregon	30	4	60	2	Odd	15,396†
Pennsylvania	50	4	203	2	Odd**	61,889†
Rhode Island	38	2	75	2	Annual	11,236
South Carolina	46	4	124	2	Biennial	10,400†
South Dakota	35	2	70	2	Annual	12,000†
Tennessee	33	4	99	2	Annual	16,500†
Texas	31	4	150	2	Odd	7,200†
Utah	29	4	75	2	Annual	120(d)†
Vermont	30	2	150	2	Annual	536(w)†
Virginia	40	4	100	2	Annual	18,000‡‡
Washington	49	4	98	2	Annual	32,064†
West Virginia	34	4	100	2	Annual	15,000†
Wisconsin	33	4	99	2	Odd**	44,333†
Wyoming	30	4	60	2	Annual	125(d)†

*Salaries annual unless otherwise noted as (d)—per day, (b)—biennium, or (w)—per week.
†Plus *per diem* living expenses.
‡Terms vary from two to four years.
§For odd year; $7,725 for even year.
″Unicameral legislature.
#For 2 years.
**Two-year session (that is, it meets every year).
††Annual at option of legislature.
‡‡Senate; House is 17,640.

SOURCE: Council of State Governments, *Book of the States* (Vol. 36, 2004 Edition).

Legislative Apportionment

Drawing up legislative districts—state as well as federal—has long been subject to gerrymandering—creative cartography designed to guarantee that one political party maintains control of a particular voting district. Malapportionment is the skewed distribution of voters in a state's legislative districts. The United States Supreme Court ruled in 1962 that malapportioned state legislatures violate the equal protection clause of the Fourteenth Amendment.[2] In a series of cases that followed, the Court held that legislative districts must be as nearly equal as possible in terms of population, and the grossest examples of state legislative malapportionment were eliminated.[3] The Supreme Court, however, allowed "benevolent, bipartisan gerrymandering" in certain states. Indeed, in 1977, the Supreme Court held that a state had an obligation under the 1965 Voting Rights Act to draw district boundaries to maximize minority legislative representation.[4] Thus, each decade, state and federal legislative districts must be redrawn to ensure that every person's vote is roughly equal and that minorities are represented adequately.

By the mid-1990s, however, the Supreme Court had reversed its position on what has been called "racial gerrymandering." In a series of cases, the Court held that voting districts that are redrawn with the goal of maximizing the electoral strength and representation of minority groups violate the equal protection clause.[5] (See Chapter 11 for a more detailed discussion of this issue.)

Term Limits for State Legislators

For more than a decade, a number of states have agreed that a legislator's tenure should be limited. Although the restrictions vary, seventeen states currently have laws restricting the number of terms a legislator can serve. In three other states— Oregon, Washington, and Massachusetts—term limits laws were thrown out by the respective state supreme courts, while Idaho's legislature repealed its voter-approved term limits law.

Advocates of term limits argue that lawmakers who have not spent years in public office will best represent the interests of voters. Special interest groups will have less chance to influence a politician who does not have a future campaign to finance. Opponents of term limits argue that the same inexperienced lawmakers who are less likely to be swayed by special interests are also more likely to lack the experience that is required to understand state policy. Such opponents, ironically, include current politicians who once voted for term limits but are now subject to its consequences.

Direct Democracy:
The Initiative, Referendum, and Recall

There is a major difference between the legislative process as outlined in the U.S. Constitution and the legislative process as outlined in the various state constitutions. Many states exercise a type of direct democracy through the *initiative*, the *referendum*, and the *recall*—procedures that allow voters to control the government directly.

The Initiative.   One technique lets citizens bypass legislatures by proposing new statutes or changes in government for citizen approval. Most states that permit the citizen legislative **initiative** require that the initiative's backers circulate a petition to place the issue on the ballot and that a certain percentage of the

DID YOU KNOW . . .
That the most expensive ballot initiative in history was California's Proposition 5 (the opposing sides of the 1998 proposition, which permitted video slot machines and card games on Indian reservations, spent a total of approximately $100 million)**?**

Initiative
A procedure by which voters can propose a change in state or local laws by gathering signatures on a petition and placing a proposed law on the ballot for the voters' approval.

---

[2]*Baker v. Carr,* 369 U.S. 186 (1962).

[3]*Reynolds v. Sims,* 377 U.S. 533 (1964); and other cases.

[4]*United Jewish Organizations of Williamsburg v. Cary,* 430 U.S. 144 (1977).

[5]*Miller v. Johnson,* 515 U.S. 900 (1995); *Shaw v. Hunt,* 517 U.S. 899 (1996); and *Bush v. Vera,* 517 U.S. 952 (1996).

Referendum
An electoral device whereby legislative or
constitutional measures are referred by the
legislature to the voters for approval or
disapproval.

Recall
A procedure enabling voters to remove an
elected official from office before his or her
term has expired.

A few years ago, the federal Drug
Enforcement Agency (DEA) confiscated
the marijuana supplies of an
organization in Santa Cruz, California,
that grows and distributes marijuana to
terminally ill patients. The distribution
of medical marijuana is legal under a
local ordinance. The Santa Cruz City
Council allowed the organization to
pass out marijuana to patients on the
steps of city hall after the DEA raid, as
seen here. Which side will normally
prevail when state or local ordinances
conflict with those of the federal
government? (AP Photo/Mike Fiala)

registered voters in the last gubernatorial election sign the petition. Twenty-four
states use the legislative initiative, typically those states in which political parties
are relatively weak and nonpartisan groups are strong. Legislative initiatives have
involved a range of issues, including crime victims' rights, campaign contributions, corporate spending on ballot questions, affirmative action, physician-
assisted suicide, and the medical use of marijuana. In some cases, voters have
passed state initiatives that are contrary to federal policy. For example, several
states have passed initiatives legalizing the use of marijuana for medical purposes,
a policy that conflicts with federal law.

The Referendum.   The **referendum** is similar to the initiative, except that the
issue (or constitutional change) is proposed first by the legislature and then
directed to the voters for their approval. The referendum is most often used for
approval of local school bond issues and for amendments to state constitutions. In
a number of states that provide for the referendum, a bill passed by the legislature
may be suspended by obtaining the required number of voters' signatures on petitions. A statewide referendum election is then held. If a majority of the voters disapprove of the bill, it is no longer valid.

The referendum was not initially intended for regular use, and indeed it was
employed infrequently in the past. Its opponents argue that it is an unnecessary
check on representative government and that it weakens legislative responsibility.
In recent years, the referendum has become increasingly popular as citizens have
attempted to control their state and local governments. Interest groups have been
active in sponsoring the petition drives necessary to force a referendum. Over
two-thirds of the states provide for the referendum.

The Recall.   The right of citizens to recall, or remove, elected officials is not
exercised frequently. **Recall** is a provision written into the constitutions of fifteen
states. It allows voters to remove elected state officials, including the governor,
before the expiration of their terms of office. In the case of judges, the recall can
terminate a lifetime appointment.

Citizens begin the recall process by circulating petitions demanding a
statewide vote to remove the offending officeholder. The number of signatures
required to bring about the election ranges from 10 to 40 percent of the last vote
for the office in question. If the required number of signatures is obtained, the
matter of whether to remove the incumbent is decided in a general election.

The recall and the initiative are examples of "pure democracy," in which the
people as a whole vote directly on important issues. Such measures are distinct in
theory and in practice from the norms of "representative democracy," in which
the people govern only indirectly, through their elected representatives. Should
recalls be harder to instigate—or easier? We examine this question in the *Which
Side Are You On?* feature.

★ The State Judiciary

In addition to the federal courts, each of the fifty states, as well as the District of
Columbia, has its own separate court system. Figure 18–2 on page 590 shows a
sample state court system. Like the federal court system, it has several tiers,
including trial courts, intermediate courts of appeal, and a supreme court.

Trial Courts

All states have major trial courts, commonly called circuit courts, district courts, or
superior courts. The number of judges and their terms in office vary widely. As in
the federal court system, the trial courts are of two types: those having limited juris-

WHICH SIDE ARE YOU ON?
Is the Recall Process Too Capricious?

In October 2003, the people of California voted to recall Democratic governor Gray Davis just eleven months after they had reelected him to the post. The margin was 55.4 percent to 44.6 percent. Californians then elected Republican Arnold Schwarzenegger, the famous actor and bodybuilder, as the new governor. Some claimed that it was unfair to recall an elected official so quickly after reelecting him, and that the recall process is capricious. Others thought that the election was a reaffirmation of democracy.

California Governor-elect Arnold Schwarzenegger and his wife, Maria Shriver, are showered with confetti following his acceptance speech in Los Angeles in 2003. Schwarzenegger was elected following the historic recall of Governor Gray Davis. (EPA/Francis Specker/Landov)

THE PROCESS IS TOO CAPRICIOUS—IT CAN BE UNDERTAKEN ON A WHIM

Those who believed that the recall process is too capricious claimed that the justification offered for recalling Davis—that he was incompetent, basically—was much too vague. According to these recall opponents, recalls should be reserved for politicians who commit crimes or other impeachable offenses. Admittedly, when he ran for reelection Davis was not altogether truthful about the probable size of the state's budget deficit. If that kind of behavior sufficed for a recall, however, politicians everywhere would be in trouble.

A further complaint about the California process was that it was much too easy for frivolous candidates to get on the recall ballot. (Candidates had to file only 65 signatures and pay a fee of $3,500.) There were 135 names on the ballot.

Finally, recall opponents pointed out that Davis needed over 50 percent of the vote to remain in office. Once Davis was out, any rival could win with a mere *plurality* (the largest number of votes, not necessarily more than 50 percent). With such rules, a sitting official is not given a fair chance.

THE PROCESS IS NOT TOO CAPRICIOUS—THE PEOPLE HAVE A RIGHT TO CHANGE THEIR MINDS

Recall advocates say that it is wrong to accuse the people of being capricious because they have changed their minds. The results of the recall demonstrate the value of the proce-dure. Recall advocates argue that Schwarzenegger has been a much more effective governor than Davis. The free-for-all nature of the race to replace Davis was actually one of the great advantages of the campaign. It allowed the people to choose a socially moderate Republican who probably could not have won his party's primary election. Nor did Californians have any trouble picking the top candidates out of the 135 names on the ballot—the top four contenders got 93.4 percent of the vote. The only problem with recalls, advocates say, is that only fifteen states permit them.

WHAT'S YOUR POSITION?

What failings in an incumbent should be sufficient to justify a recall election?

GOING ONLINE

For complete information on the California recall of 2003, visit **http://www.california-recall.com/archived-site**. A second site with links to recall information is located at **http://www.igs.berkeley.edu/library/htRecall2003.html**.

---

diction and those having general jurisdiction.[6] Cases heard before these courts can be appealed to the state appellate court and ultimately to the state supreme court.

Appellate Courts

About three-fourths of the states have intermediate appellate courts between the trial courts of original jurisdiction and the highest state appellate court, or the supreme court. These are usually called courts of appeals. Salaries of state judges vary widely, but higher pay is given to appellate and supreme court members.

---

[6]See Chapter 14 for a definition of these terms.

The highest state appellate courts are usually called simply supreme courts, although they are also labeled the supreme judicial court (Maine and Massachusetts), the court of appeals (Maryland and New York), the court of criminal appeals (Oklahoma and Texas, which also have separate supreme courts for appeals in noncriminal cases), or the supreme court of appeals (West Virginia). The decisions of each state's highest court on all questions of state law are final. Only when issues of federal law are involved can a decision made by a state's highest court be overruled by the United States Supreme Court.

Judicial Elections and Appointments

State court judges are either elected or appointed, depending on the state and (often) on the level of court involved—the procedures vary widely from state to state. In some states, including Delaware, the procedure is similar to the way federal judges are appointed—the judges are appointed by the governor and confirmed by the upper chamber of the legislature. In other states, all state court judges are elected, either on a partisan ballot (as in Arkansas) or on a nonpartisan ballot (as in Kentucky). In several states, judges in some of the lower courts are elected, while those in the appellate courts are appointed. Additionally, depending on the state, judges who are appointed may have to run for reelection if they wish to serve a second term.

FIGURE 18–2

A Sample State Court System

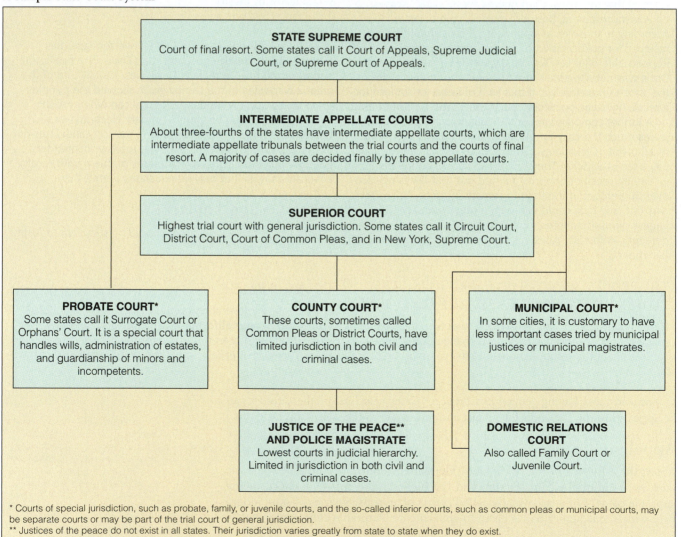

SOURCE: William P. Statsky, *Introduction to Paralegalism: Perspectives, Problems, and Skills*, 6th ed. (Clifton Park, N.Y.: Thompson Delmar Learning, 2002).

How Local Government Operates

Local governments are difficult to describe because of their great dissimilarities and because, if we include municipalities, counties, towns, townships, and special districts, there are so many of them. We limit the discussion here to the most important types and features of local governments.

The Legal Existence of Local Government

As mentioned earlier, the U.S. Constitution makes no mention of local governments. Article IV, Section 4, merely states that "[t]he United States shall guarantee to every State in this Union a Republican Form of Government." Actually, then, the states do not even have to have local governments. Consequently, every local government is a creature of the state. The state can create a local government, and the state can terminate the right of a local government to exist. Indeed, states often have abolished entire counties, school districts, cities, and special districts. Since World War II (1939–1945), almost twenty thousand school districts have gone out of existence as they were consolidated with other school districts.

Because the local government is the legal creation of the state, does that mean the state can dictate everything the local government does? For many years that seemed to be the case. The narrowest possible view of the legal status of local governments follows **Dillon's rule,** outlined by Judge John F. Dillon in his *Commentaries on the Law of Municipal Corporations* in 1872. He stated that municipal corporations may possess only powers "granted in express words . . . [that are] necessarily or fairly implied in or incident to the powers expressly granted."[7] Cities governed under Dillon's rule have sometimes been dominated by the state legislatures, depending on the extent of the authority granted to the cities by the legislatures. Those communities wishing to obtain the status of a municipal corporation have petitioned the state legislature for a **charter.**

In a revolt against state legislative power over municipalities, the home rule movement began. It was based on **Cooley's rule,** derived from an 1871 decision by Michigan judge Thomas Cooley stating that cities should be able to govern themselves.[8] Since 1900, about four-fifths of the states have allowed **municipal home rule,** but only with respect to local concerns for which no statewide interests are involved. A municipality must choose to become a **home rule city;** otherwise, it operates as a **general law city.** In the latter case, the state makes certain general laws relating to cities of different sizes, which are designated as first class cities, second class cities, or towns. Once a city, by virtue of its population, receives such a ranking, it follows the general law established by the state. Only if it chooses to be a home rule city can it avoid such state government restrictions. In many states, only cities with populations of 2,500 or more can choose home rule.

Local Governmental Units

There are four major types of local governmental units: municipalities, counties, towns and townships, and special districts.

Municipalities. A municipality is a political entity created by the people of a city or town to govern themselves locally. Currently, there are over nineteen thousand municipalities within the fifty states. Almost all municipalities are fairly small cities. Only about two hundred cities have populations over one hundred thousand, and

Dillon's Rule
The narrowest possible interpretation of the legal status of local governments, outlined by Judge John F. Dillon, who in 1872 stated that a municipal corporation can exercise only those powers expressly granted by state law.

Charter
A document issued by a government that grants to a person, a group of persons, or a corporation the right to carry on one or more specific activities. A state government can grant a charter to a municipality.

Cooley's Rule
The view that cities should be able to govern themselves, presented in an 1871 Michigan decision by Judge Thomas Cooley.

Municipal Home Rule
The power vested in a local unit of government to draft or change its own charter and to manage its own affairs.

Home Rule City
A city with a charter allowing local voters to frame, adopt, and amend their own charter.

General Law City
A city operating under general state laws that apply to all local governmental units of a similar type.

---

[7]John F. Dillon, *Commentaries on the Law of Municipal Corporations*, 5th ed. (Boston: Little, Brown, 1911), Vol. 1, Sec. 237.
[8]*People v. Hurlbut*, 24 Mich. 44 (1871).

County
The chief governmental unit set up by the state to administer state law and business at the local level. Counties are drawn up by area, rather than by rural or urban criteria.

New England Town
A governmental unit in the New England states that combines the roles of city and county in one unit.

Town Meeting
The governing authority of a New England town. Qualified voters may participate in the election of officers and in the passage of legislation.

Town Manager System
A form of town government in which voters elect three selectpersons, who then appoint a professional town manager, who in turn appoints other officials.

Selectperson
A member of the governing group of a town.

Township
A rural unit of government based on federal land surveys of the American frontier in the 1780s. Townships have declined significantly in importance.

only nine cities (Chicago, Dallas, Houston, Los Angeles, New York, Philadelphia, Phoenix, San Antonio, and San Diego) have populations over a million. City expenditures are primarily for water supply and other utilities, police and fire protection, and education. About three-fourths of municipal tax revenues come from property taxes. Municipalities often rely heavily on financial assistance from both the federal and state governments.

Counties.   The difference between a **county** and a municipality is that a county is usually not created at the behest of its inhabitants. The state sets up counties on its own initiative to serve as political extensions of the state government. Counties apply state law and administer state business at the local level.

There are over three thousand counties within the United States; they vary greatly in both size and population. San Bernardino County in California is the largest geographically, with 20,102 square miles. New York County in New York is possibly the smallest, with less than 22 square miles. County populations within California alone range from millions of residents, as in Los Angeles County, to barely a thousand, as in Alpine County.

County governments' responsibilities include zoning, building regulations, health, hospitals, parks, recreation, highways, public safety, justice, and record keeping. Typically, when a municipality is established within a county, the county withdraws most of its services from the municipality; for example, the municipal police force takes over from the county police force. County governments are extremely complex entities, a product of the era of Jacksonian democracy and its effort to bring government closer to the people. There is no easy way to describe their operation in summary form. Indeed, the county has been called by one scholar "the dark continent of American politics."[9]

Towns and Townships.   A unique governmental creation in the New England states is the **New England town**—not to be confused with the word *town* when used as just another name for a city. In Maine, Massachusetts, New Hampshire, Vermont, and Connecticut, the unit called the town combines the roles of city and county in one governing unit. A New England town typically consists of one or more urban settlements and the surrounding rural areas. Consequently, counties have little importance in New England. In Connecticut, for example, they are simply geographic units.

From the New England town is derived the tradition of the **town meeting,** an annual meeting at which direct democracy was—and continues to be—practiced. Each resident of a town is summoned to the annual meeting at the town hall. Those who attend levy taxes, pass laws, elect town officers, and appropriate money for different activities.

Normally, few residents show up for town meetings today unless an item of high interest is on the agenda or unless family members want to be elected to office. The town meeting takes a day or more, and few citizens are able to set aside such a large amount of time. Because of the declining interest in town meetings, many New England towns have adopted a **town manager system:** the voters simply elect three **selectpersons,** who then appoint a professional town manager. The town manager in turn appoints other officials.

Townships operate somewhat like counties. Where they exist, there may be several dozen within a county. They perform the same functions that the county would otherwise perform. Most midwestern states have townships, and they are also found in New York, New Jersey, and Pennsylvania. A township is not the same thing as a New England town, because it is meant to be a rural government rather than a city government. Moreover, it is never the principal unit of local

---

[9]Henry S. Gilbertson, *The County, the "Dark Continent of American Politics"* (New York: National Short Ballot Association, 1917).

government, as are New England towns. The boundaries of most townships are based on federal land surveys that began in the 1780s, mapping the land into six-square-mile blocks called townships. They were then subdivided into thirty-six blocks of one square mile each, called sections. Along the boundaries of each section, a road was built.

Although townships have few functions left to perform in many parts of the nation, they are still politically important in others. In some metropolitan areas, townships are the political unit that provides most public services to residents who live in suburban **unincorporated areas.**

Special Districts and School Districts.   The most numerous local government units are special districts. Currently, there are more than thirty-five thousand special districts (see Table 18–2). Special districts are one-function governments that usually are created by the state legislature and governed by a board of directors. Special districts may be called authorities, boards, corporations—or simply districts.

One important feature of special districts is that they cut across geographic and governmental boundaries. Sometimes special districts even cut across state lines. For example, the Port of New York Authority was established by an interstate compact between New Jersey and New York in 1921 to develop and operate the harbor facilities in the area. A mosquito control district may cut across both municipal and county lines. A metropolitan transit district may provide bus service to dozens of municipalities and to several counties.

School districts, although listed separately in Table 18–2, are essentially a type of special district. Except for school districts, the typical citizen is not very aware of most special districts. Indeed, most citizens do not know who furnishes their weed control, mosquito abatement, water, or sewage service. Part of the reason for the low profile of special districts is that most special district administrators are appointed, not elected, and therefore receive little public attention.

Consolidation of Governments

With over eighty thousand separate and often overlapping governmental units within the United States, the trend toward consolidation in recent years is understandable. **Consolidation** is the union of two or more governmental units to form a single unit. Typically, a state constitution or a state statute will designate consolidation procedures.

Consolidation is often recommended for metropolitan-area problems, but to date there have been few consolidations within metropolitan areas. The most successful consolidations have been **functional consolidations**—particularly of city and county police, health, and welfare departments. In some cases, functional consolidation is a satisfactory alternative to the complete consolidation of governmental units. One of the most successful examples of functional consolidation was started in 1957 in Dade County, Florida. The county government, now called Miami-Dade, is a union of twenty-six municipalities. Each municipality has its own governmental entity, but the county government has the authority to furnish water, planning, mass transit, and police services and to set minimum standards of performance. The governing body of Miami-Dade is an elected board of county commissioners, which appoints an executive mayor.

A special type of consolidation is the **council of governments (COG),** a voluntary organization of counties and municipalities that attempts to tackle area-wide problems. More than two hundred COGs have been established, mainly since 1966. The impetus for their establishment was, and continues to be, federal government grants. COGs are an alternative means of treating major regional problems that various communities are unwilling to tackle on a consolidated basis either by true consolidation of governmental units or by functional consolidation.

Unincorporated Area
An area not located within the boundary of a municipality.

TABLE 18–2

Local Governments in the United States

Counties	3,034
Municipalities	19,431
(mainly cities and towns)	
Townships	16,506
(less extensive powers)	
Special districts	35,356
(water supply, fire protection, hospitals, libraries, parks and recreation, highways, sewers, and so on)	
School districts	13,522
Total	**87,849**

SOURCE: U.S. Census Bureau, *Preliminary Report, 2002 Census of Governments.*

Consolidation
The union of two or more governmental units to form a single unit.

Functional Consolidation
Cooperation by two or more units of local government in providing services to their inhabitants. This is generally done by unifying a set of departments—for example, the police departments—into a single agency.

Council of Governments (COG)
A voluntary organization of counties and municipalities concerned with area-wide problems.

The power of COGs is advisory only. Each member unit simply selects its council representatives, who report back to the unit after COG meetings. Nonetheless, today several COGs have begun to have considerable influence on regional policy. These include the Metropolitan Washington Council of Governments, the Supervisors' Inter-County Commission in Detroit, and the Association of Bay Area Governments in the San Francisco Bay Area.

How Municipalities Are Governed

We can divide municipal representative governments into four general types of plans: (1) the commission plan, (2) the council-manager plan, (3) the mayor-administrator plan, and (4) the mayor-council plan.

The Commission Plan.   The commission form of municipal government consists of a commission of three to nine members who have both legislative and executive powers. The salient aspects of the commission plan are as follows:

1. Executive and legislative powers are concentrated in a small group of individuals, who are elected at large on a (normally) nonpartisan ballot.
2. Each commissioner is individually responsible for heading a particular municipal department, such as the department of public safety.
3. The commission is collectively responsible for passing ordinances and controlling spending.
4. The mayor (an office that is only ceremonial) is selected from the members of the commission.

The commission plan, originating in Galveston, Texas, in 1901, had its greatest popularity during the first twenty years of the twentieth century. It appealed to municipal government reformers. They looked on it as a type of business organization that would eliminate the problems they believed to be inherent in the long ballot and in partisan municipal politics. Unfortunately, vesting both legislative and executive power in the hands of a small group of individuals means that there are no checks and balances on administration and spending. Also, because the mayoral office is ceremonial, there is no provision for strong leadership. Not surprisingly, only about one hundred cities today use the commission plan—Tulsa, Salt Lake City, Mobile, Topeka, and Atlantic City are a few of them.

The Council-Manager Plan.   In the council-manager form of municipal government, a city council appoints a professional manager, who acts as the chief executive. He or she typically is called the city manager. In principle, the manager is there simply to see that the general directions of the city council are carried out. The important features of the council-manager plan are as follows:

1. A professional, trained manager can hire and fire subordinates and is responsible to the council.
2. The council or commission consists of five to seven members, elected at large on a nonpartisan ballot.
3. The mayor may be chosen from within the council or from outside, but he or she has no executive function. As with the commission plan, the mayor's job may be largely ceremonial, or it may be limited to chairing council meetings. The city manager works for the council, not the mayor (unless, of course, the mayor is part of the council).

Today, about two thousand cities use the council-manager plan. About one-third of the cities with populations of more than 5,000 and about one-half of the cities with populations of more than 25,000 operate with this type of plan. Only four large cities with populations of more than 500,000—Cincinnati, Dallas, San Antonio, and San Diego—have adopted this plan.

An elderly activist is led out of a Los Angeles City Council meeting by police officers. The council was hearing a resolution against the war in Iraq (which began the following month). The resolution was passed at the next meeting. Are local government resolutions on foreign policy a reasonable way to express popular opinion or are they a waste of time? Why? (AP Photo/Ann Johansson)

The major defect of the council-manager scheme, as with the commission plan, is that there is no single, strong political executive leader. It is therefore not surprising that large cities rarely use such a plan.

The Mayor-Administrator Plan. The mayor-administrator plan is often used in large cities where there is a strong mayor. It is similar to the council-manager plan except that the political leadership is vested in the mayor. The mayor is an elected chief executive. She or he appoints an administrative officer, whose function is to free the mayor from routine administrative tasks, such as personnel direction and budget supervision.

The Mayor-Council Plan. The mayor-council form of municipal government is the oldest and most widely used. The mayor is an elected chief executive, and the council is the legislative body. Virtually all councils are unicameral. The council typically has five to nine members, except in very large cities. For example, in Chicago, the council has fifty members. Council members are popularly elected for terms as long as six, but normally four, years.

The mayor-council plan can either be a strong-mayor type or a weak-mayor type. In the *strong mayor–council plan,* the mayor is the chief executive and has virtually complete control over hiring and firing employees, as well as preparing the budget. The mayor exercises strong and positive leadership in the formation of city policies. The *weak mayor–council plan* separates executive and legislative functions completely. The mayor is elected as chief executive officer; the council is elected as the legislative body. This traditional division of powers allows for checks and balances on spending and administration.

About 50 percent of American cities use some form of the mayor-council plan. Most recently, the mayor-council plan has lost ground to the council-manager plan in small and middle-sized cities.

Machine versus Reform in City Politics

For much of the late nineteenth and early twentieth centuries, many major cities were run by "the machine." The machine was an integrated political organization. Each city block within the municipality had an organizer, each neighborhood had a political club, each district had a leader, and all of these parts of the machine had a boss—such as William Tweed in New York, Richard Daley in Chicago, Edward Crump in Memphis, or Tom Pendergast in Kansas City. The machine became a popular form of city political organization in the 1840s, when the first waves of European immigrants came to the United States to work in urban factories. Those individuals, often lacking the ability to communicate in English, needed help; and the machine was created to help them.[10] The urban machine drew on the support of the dominant ethnic groups to forge a strong political institution that was able to keep the boss (usually the mayor) in office year after year. The machine was oiled by *patronage*—rewarding faithful party workers and followers with government employment and contracts. The party in power was often referred to as the patronage party.[11]

According to sociologist Robert Merton, the machine offered personalized assistance to the needy, helped to establish local businesses, opened avenues of upward social mobility for the underprivileged, and afforded a locus of strong political authority and responsibility.[12] Others, however, viewed party machines and the behind-the-scenes government that they often involved as contrary to our principles of government. In their classic work on city politics, Edward Banfield and James Q. Wilson also gave a critical appraisal of machine politics:

> [M]achine government is, essentially, a system of organized bribery. The destruction of machines . . . permit[s] government on the basis of appropriate motives, that is, public-regarding ones. In fact it has other highly desirable consequences—especially greater honesty, impartiality, and (in routine matters) efficiency.[13]

When the last of the big-city bosses, Mayor Richard Daley of Chicago, died in December 1976, an era died with him. The big-city machine began to be in serious trouble in the 1960s, when community activists organized to work for a more professional and efficient municipal government. Soon, governments of administrators rather than politicians began to appear. Fewer offices were elective; more were appointive.

Switching from a political to an administrative form of urban government was a way to break up the centralized urban political machine. In some cities, the results have been beneficial to most citizens. In others, decentralization has gone so far that there is no strong leader who can pull together discordant factions to create and follow a coherent policy. Consequently, in cities with a greatly decentralized government typified by numerous independent commissions and boards, much that should be done does not get done, particularly when an area-wide concern is involved. This is an especially severe problem for less economically privileged people, who used to be able to rely on machine-sponsored activities and on the machine's political clout to help them compete against wealthier citizens for a share of the city's services. Reform is in some ways a middle-class preoccupation, whereas the less advantaged may believe themselves better served by machine politics.

Governing Metropolitan Areas

Large cities are often faced with problems that develop in part from a shrinking employment base. When employers move out of a city, there is a smaller tax base, and more people are out of work. Less tax revenue means fewer funds to pay for schools and to meet other municipal obligations, including fighting crime and

---

[10] See Harvey W. Zorbaugh, *The Gold Coast and the Slum: A Sociological Study of Chicago's Near North Side* (Chicago: University of Chicago Press, 1929).

[11] See, for example, Harold F. Gosnell, *Machine Politics: Chicago Model* (Chicago: University of Chicago Press, 1937).

[12] Robert Merton, *Social Theory and Social Structure* (Glencoe, Ill.: Free Press, 1957), pp. 71–81.

[13] Edward C. Banfield and James Q. Wilson, *City Politics* (New York: Vintage Books, 1963), p. 12.

assisting those who are unemployed. These developments feed on themselves, leading to more crime, more poverty, an even smaller job base, and other problems.

But crime, as well as such problems as traffic congestion and pollution, is not contained within municipal political boundaries. For this reason, solutions are sometimes sought for a metropolitan area as a whole. Annexation by a city of the surrounding suburbs is one solution; consolidation of city and county governments into a single government is another. People who live in the suburbs often oppose such measures, however, particularly when they and the residents of a city are of different races or social classes, or have different political agendas.

A third possible solution to problems that spread beyond limited political boundaries is to set up a system of metropolitan government. With this method, a single entity, such as a county, concerns itself with the problems of an entire metropolitan area, and smaller entities, such as individual city governments, concern themselves with local matters. People who live in the suburbs often oppose this solution, however, for the same reasons that they oppose other measures: they want to preserve their communities and lifestyles as they are.

A fourth solution is the creation of special districts, each of which is concerned with a specific service—an area's water supply or public transportation system, for example. Special districts are more popular than the other solutions, in part because they can deal with a single matter relatively more efficiently without concern for social issues or class conflict.

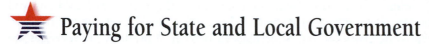 Paying for State and Local Government

Examining the spending habits of a household often gives relevant information about the personalities and priorities of the household members. Examination of the expenditure patterns of state and local governments likewise can be illuminating.

State and Local Government Expenditures

Table 18–3 shows state expenditures, by function, in percentages. Table 18–4 shows these data for local governments. Education and highways are major expenses at both the state and local level. (Most state spending on education is for colleges and universities; most local spending is for elementary and secondary schools.) Because of the growth of Medicaid—the health-care program for the poor—welfare is now the leading expense at the state level. Local governments, in contrast, spend heavily on utilities such as water, electricity, and public transit.

Compare state and local spending on education with spending by the federal government, which allocates only about 4 percent of its budget to education. Despite high expenditures, state and local governments are finding that their educational programs are not always producing well-educated students. As mentioned in the chapter-opening *What If . . .* feature, several states have been implementing various education reforms, such as school vouchers.

State and Local Government Revenues

State and local expenditures have to be paid for somehow. Until the twentieth century, almost all state and local expenditures were paid for by state and local revenues raised within state borders. Starting in the twentieth century, however, federal grants to state and local governmental units began to pay some of these costs.

Figure 18–3 on the next page shows the percentages of revenues in various categories received by state and local governments. The most important tax at the state level is the **general sales tax.** Whereas the federal government obtains about 45 percent of its total revenues from the personal income tax, states obtain only

General Sales Tax
A tax levied as a proportion of the retail price of a commodity at the point of sale.

TABLE 18–3

State Expenditures (in percentages)

EXPENDITURE	PERCENTAGE
Welfare including Medicaid	26.2
Education	19.5
Highways	13.2
Employee retirement	10.0
Unemployment compensation	4.6
Prisons and jails	4.2
Hospitals	4.2
Interest on general debt	3.4
Health	3.3
Utilities	2.8
Natural resources	2.1
Financial administration	2.1
Workers' compensation	1.1
Police	1.0
Other	2.3

SOURCE: U.S. Census Bureau, August 2004.

TABLE 18–4

Local Expenditures (in percentages)

EXPENDITURE	PERCENTAGE
Education	43.2
Utilities	12.6
Highways	5.4
Police	4.9
Hospitals	4.7
Interest on general debt	3.9
Sewerage	3.6
Welfare	3.5
Parks and recreation	2.9
Health	2.6
Housing and community development	2.5
Fire protection	2.3
Employee retirement	2.0
Prisons and jails	1.7
Other	4.1

SOURCE: U.S. Census Bureau, August 2004.

FIGURE 18–3

State and Local Government Revenues

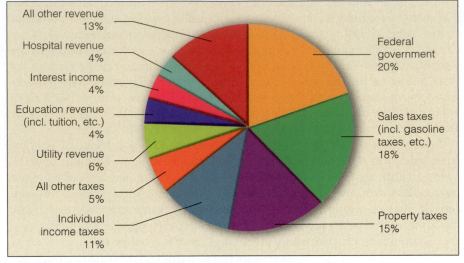

SOURCE: U.S. Census Bureau, August 2004.

about 11 percent in this way. By 2004, seven states still did not have a personal income tax. Other taxes assessed by states include corporate income taxes and fees, permits, and licenses at both the state and local governmental levels, as well as inheritance and gift taxes at the state level. At the local level, the most important tax is the **property tax.** More than 95 percent of property tax revenues are raised by local governments. Generally, the types of taxes that states levy vary widely from state to state.

There is considerable variation in the amounts of state and local taxes collected per capita. According to the most recently available statistics, state and local governments in Connecticut, New Jersey, and New York collect more than $4,000 per capita, while governments in Alabama, Mississippi, and Tennessee collect less than $2,500. There is also substantial variation in the degree to which taxes are collected at the state level, as opposed to locally. The state governments of Arkansas, Delaware, and Hawaii collect over four-fifths of the state and local taxes, while the state governments of Colorado, New York, and Texas collect less than half of the state and local total.

Nontax revenue includes federal grants to state and local governments. Today, federal grants to state and local governments total about $360 billion annually and provide about 20 percent of state government income. The grants are not always without "strings," however. Federal programs in such areas as education, highway construction, health care, and law enforcement may dispense cash subject to certain conditions (see Chapter 3).

Revenue from publicly operated services and businesses are additional sources of income for state and local governments. Publicly operated services include universities and hospitals, as well as municipal utilities such as water, electric power, and bus systems. More than a third of the states sell liquor at a profit through state-operated stores. Other state-run businesses include Washington's ferries and North Dakota's commercial banks. Further nontax revenue sources include court fines and interest on loans and investments. In the 1980s, state lotteries became an increasingly popular way to raise revenues.

Fiscal Policy Lessons

In the 1980s, when state budgets more than doubled, most states tried to close the gap between state income and spending by raising taxes. Many of these states con-

---

Property Tax

A tax on the value of real estate. This tax is a particularly important source of revenue for local governments.

tinued this policy into the early 1990s. By 1999, however, it became clear that states' attempts to reduce their budget deficits by increasing taxes were not especially successful at lowering those deficits. In fact, many states actually harmed, rather than helped, their economies. At the same time, other states attempted to balance their budgets by cutting spending instead of raising taxes. This policy proved more successful, resulting in balanced budgets and improved state economies. By the mid-1990s, many of these states were proposing state tax cuts to encourage the development of business and further improve their local economies.

The Fiscal Crisis of the States. The "dot-com bust" of 2001, however, hit most state governments hard. By 2003, Texas faced a budget deficit of $10 billion, and California's shortfall had reached $38 billion. The 2003 revenue shortfalls were 23 percent of the budget in Alaska and Arizona, and 24 percent in New York. Only Wyoming and New Mexico managed to avoid running a deficit. The National Governors Association announced that the states faced the "most dire fiscal situation since World War II." Governors and state legislators found themselves caught between two highly vocal groups—those who opposed cutting spending on education, health care, and other services, and those who opposed higher taxes.

The budgetary crisis had several causes. During the 1990s, most states expanded their spending on health care, education, and criminal justice. During the dot-com boom, tax revenues were more than sufficient to fund the increases. As noted, some states even cut their tax rates. The dot-com collapse, however, slashed projected revenue increases and in some states caused revenues to drop. Both the sales tax and the income tax are sensitive to changes in the economic environment, and many states continue to be dependent on revenues from these two taxes. Furthermore, most states are formally required to balance their budgets and cannot automatically fund a deficit by borrowing in the way that the federal government funds its deficit.

Poor Productivity. An additional problem for the states is that the tasks they perform are somewhat resistant to *productivity improvements*. America's farms and factories have posted dramatic improvements over the years in the volume of goods produced by the labor of each individual farmer or worker—in other words, these industries have improved their productivity. It is harder to attain such improvements in service industries. Some services, notably education and law enforcement, require face-to-face interaction with the public. It is difficult to cut the amount of such interaction without reducing the quality of the service. Still, from 1993 to 2000, productivity in a typical private-sector service industry rose by about 20 percent. The productivity of government services rose by much less than that.

Health-Care Costs. Increased health-care costs were a major part of the states' budget problems. Health-insurance premiums rose nationally at a rate of 13 percent in 2002 and 14 percent in 2003, and health-insurance costs for state employees grew as well. Furthermore, the states faced large increases in the cost of Medicaid, the program that provides health-care services to the poor. Do federal Medicaid subsidies lead the states to spend more on Medicaid? We look at this question in the *Politics and State Budgets* feature on the next page.

Recovery from the Crisis. In 2004, as the national economy began to recover from the slowdown, state budget difficulties also began to ease. State government finances, however, remain precarious, and the states need several good years to completely resolve their problems.

This 2004 photo shows an interview with incoming Louisiana Governor Kathleen Blanco. Blanco stated that her top priority was jobs. Especially given the fiscal crisis of the states, does it make sense to lower state business taxes in an attempt to lure new business into the state? Why or why not? (AP Photo/Bill Haber)

POLITICS AND STATE BUDGETS
Medicaid Grows by Leaps and Bounds

Medicaid is the joint state-federal program that funds health-care services for the poor. All states are expected to pick up at least 50 percent of the cost of the program. For low-income states, the federal share is higher. In Mississippi, the poorest state, the federal share exceeds 77 percent.

In 1984, 30 million U.S. residents were enrolled in Medicaid. By 2004, that number had climbed to 41 million. In 2005, state and federal Medicaid spending amounted to 16.6 percent of all health-care spending, up from 10.6 percent in 1980. As a share of the states' spending, Medicaid has doubled since 1987, and for many states it has become the number-one budget problem.

MEDICAID AND THE BUDGET CRUNCH

The business slowdown of 2001–2003 had a serious effect on many state budgets. By 2002, the states had begun to address Medicaid costs. By 2003, forty-nine states had established cost-containment plans, twenty-five had cut benefits, twenty-seven had restricted eligibility, and thirty-seven had frozen or cut payments to health-care providers.

How did the states get into this situation? Certainly, health-care costs have been rising across the board for many years. Medicaid is also one of the "automatic stabilizers" you learned about in Chapter 16—that is, more people become eligible for Medicaid when unemployment goes up. Some people argue, however, that there is a special

reason that Medicaid spending rose so much. They believe that the rise was due, in part, to the federal subsidy.

THE OPM (OTHER PEOPLE'S MONEY) SYNDROME

A typical state receives three dollars in federal funds for every two dollars it spends on Medicaid. This is an attractive proposition even for conservative lawmakers. Conservative state legislators may advocate low tax rates, but they rarely object when federal funds come into their state. Consider again a typical state. A reduction in the state's Medicaid spending of $1.00 leads to a $1.50 reduction in federal receipts.

The states are responsible for controlling costs, while the federal government pays most of the bill. According to some observers, the result is what the insurance industry calls a *moral hazard.* This term refers to the danger of people taking greater risks with a home or car because it is insured, and if something happens to it they will not lose financially. Similarly, during the boom years of the 1990s, the states may not have controlled the growth in Medicaid costs as much as they would have if they were paying the entire bill.

FOR CRITICAL ANALYSIS

How appropriate is the application of the concept of moral hazard to the problem of Medicaid financing?

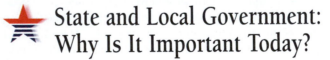

★ State and Local Government: Why Is It Important Today?

While the federal government often helps state and local governments with the costs of providing certain programs, many of the services you and your neighbors rely on most are implemented, maintained, and funded by state and local governments.

In recent years, the federal government has transferred many of the programs previously under its control to the states, with more likely to come. Currently, the states are responsible for making and monitoring welfare distributions to their poor residents. At the beginning of 2002, President George W. Bush signed a bill into law giving each state the responsibility to test its students yearly in reading and math—the "No Child Left Behind" act discussed in Chapter 3. States already have some responsibility, and will soon have more, for environmental control and clean-up within their borders. Although the federal government typically offers at least some financial support for such ventures, states often have to dip into their own tight budgets to pay some or all of the costs of providing government services.

Though we often think of "government" in terms of the federal government, your state and local governments affect much of your daily life. The state where you live can make a significant difference with respect to the amount of funds allocated for education and the curriculum being taught. As state budgets shrink, public schools often must be closed or suffer cutbacks in funding. Everything from school funding to the annoying pothole in your town square and the number of local police officers is under the jurisdiction of your state or local government. When you want that pothole fixed or the number of police officers increased, you do not call your representative in the U.S. Congress. Rather, you call your neighbor down the street who happens to be on the city council. State and local governments are as important, if not more so, as the federal government when it comes to providing for the everyday wants and needs of citizens.

MAKING A DIFFERENCE

★ Learning about Local Politics and Government in Your Community

Your local government bodies are usually close by. If you would like to learn how government operates, local government is a logical place to start.

Why Should You Care?

What government does or fails to do in the areas of education, health, employment, and crime affects you, your family, and your friends. Your sense of adventure, concern, curiosity, or injustice may urge you to take an active part in the government of a society with which you might not be particularly content. Yet getting involved on the national level may seem complicated, and national issues may not be of immediate concern. You may not even know exactly where you stand on many of those issues.

Every week, however, decisions are being made in your community that directly affect your local environment, transportation, education, health, employment, rents, schools, utility rates, freedom from crime, and overall quality of life. The local level is a good place to begin discovering who you are politically.

What Can You Do?

Many neighborhoods have formed neighborhood associations for the purposes of protecting their interests. One way to learn about issues that directly affect you (such as whether a street in your neighborhood should be widened or a park created) is to attend a local neighborhood association meeting. Another way to familiarize yourself with local political issues is to attend a city council meeting. Think about the issues being discussed. How do these issues and their outcomes concern you as an individual? What is your position on each issue?

If you are interested in education and educational reform, you can attend a school board meeting. Typically, the board will devote a substantial amount of time to budgetary decisions. Pay close attention to how the board believes school funds should be allocated. What are the board's primary concerns and priorities? Do you agree with the board's views? Find out if the school district is considering proposals to implement innovative educational programs.

Getting involved in a campaign for a local or state office is another way to learn about political issues that affect your community or your state. You also can participate at the local level in campaigns by candidates seeking national office, such as candidates running for Congress. Working at the "grassroots" level for a political candidate gives you firsthand knowledge of how the politics of democracy actually works.

Finally, to observe the judicial branch of government at work, you can watch the proceedings in your local courts. An important court at the local level is the small claims court. Small claims courts hear disputes involving claims under a certain amount, such as $2,500 or $5,000 (the amount varies from state to state). Lawyers are not required, and many small claims courts do not permit lawyers. Other local courts are described in Figure 18–2 on page 590. For information on your local courts and on when you can attend court proceedings, call the courthouse clerk.

★ Key Terms

★ Chapter Summary

1 The United States has more than 87,000 separate governmental units. State and local governments perform a wide variety of highly visible functions, such as education, police and fire protection, and so on.

2 Under the U.S. Constitution, powers not delegated expressly to the federal government are reserved to the states. The states may exercise taxing, spending, and general police powers. State constitutions are often very long, owing to the desire of their framers to include much of what we would consider statutory law because of a loss of popular confidence in state legislatures in the late 1800s. Other reasons include state courts' reluctance to interpret state constitutions as freely as the United States Supreme Court interprets the U.S. Constitution.

3 In colonial America, the governors of the colonies were vested with extensive powers. Following the Revolutionary War, most states established forms of government in which the governor received very limited powers. After Andrew Jackson's presidency, however, all governors (except in South Carolina) were elected directly by the people. Most governors have the right to exercise some sort of veto power; many enjoy item veto power.

4 State legislatures deal with matters such as taxes, schools, highways, and welfare. They also must redraw state and federal legislative districts each decade to ensure that every person's vote is roughly equal to that of others

and that minorities are adequately represented in both the state legislature and Congress. Voters may exercise some direct control over state government through the use of the initiative, referendum, and recall. Every state has its own court system. Most such systems have several levels of courts—including trial courts, intermediate courts of appeal, and a supreme court.

5 There are over 19,000 municipalities in the United States, most of which are small cities. The more than three thousand counties in this country are merely extensions of state authority and apply state laws at the local level. In New England, many of the functions of municipalities and counties are combined in towns. Municipalities may be governed by a commission consisting of members with executive and legislative powers, or they may be administered according to a council-manager, mayor-administrator, or mayor-council plan. Most major cities used to be run by political machines, which freely dispensed favors to supporters. In recent decades, however, machine politics have become almost completely extinct.

6 State spending is funded by sales and personal income taxes and is concentrated on higher education, welfare (including Medicaid), and highways. Local spending, which is mainly funded by property taxes, goes largely to the public schools and to utility services such as water, electricity, and transit.

★ Selected Print and Media Resources

SUGGESTED READINGS

Bartlett, Randall. *The Crisis of America's Cities.* New York: M. E. Sharpe, 1999. This book offers a colorful overview of America's urban history and the crises facing metropolitan areas today. The author predicts that cities will continue to lose jobs, population, and economic activity to suburbs and "edge cities" on their peripheries.

Cannon, Lou. *Governor Reagan: His Rise to Power.* New York: PublicAffairs, 2003. With two books on Reagan under his belt, Lou Cannon is the recognized expert on the late former president. Here, he assesses Reagan's years as governor of California. Despite Reagan's fame as a conservative standard-bearer, his policies for the state were pragmatic, and his term in office was a political success.

Coppa, Frank J. *County Government: A Guide to Efficient and Accountable Government*. Westport, Conn.: Praeger, 2000. The author gives an excellent review of the historical foundations of county government in the United States. In addition, he shows how charter reform can address the issues that face local governments.

Kane, Larry. *Larry Kane's Philadelphia*. Philadelphia: Temple University Press, 2000. Larry Kane is the best-known local television news anchor in Philadelphia. In almost four decades in journalism, he has accumulated a wealth of information about Philadelphia city government. This anecdote-filled volume not only provides an intimate look at big city government but also gives the reader an inside view of TV news.

Solamine, Michael E., and James L. Walker. *Respecting State Courts: The Inevitability of Judicial Federalism*. Westport, Conn.: Greenwood Press, 1999. The authors make a case for the value of judicial federalism—the division of judicial power between the federal and state court systems. They emphasize the important role played by state courts in implementing federal civil rights, interpreting their own state constitutions, and dealing with special problems, such as the death penalty.

MEDIA RESOURCES

Can the States Do It Better?—A program examining devolution—shifting federal powers back to the states—and what this means for the states with respect to, among other things, school reform.

City Hall—A 1996 drama about corruption at City Hall in New York and a mayor, played by Al Pacino, who is willing to break the law to fulfill his presidential aspirations.

The Last Hurrah—A film based, in part, on the career of James Curley (1874–1958) of Massachusetts, who played a leading role in creating and running Boston's political machine in the first half of the twentieth century. When Curley was convicted of mail fraud and sent to prison in 1947, he refused to resign as mayor and maintained his office while in jail.

Our Town—A 1980 film based on Thornton Wilder's play about day-to-day life and politics in a small, picturesque community—Peterborough ("Grover's Corners" in the play) in New Hampshire.

e-mocracy ★ Public Access to Information on the Internet Is Growing

Individuals conduct only a tiny fraction—less than 1 percent—of their fund transactions with federal, state, and local governments over the Internet each year. This percentage should increase sharply over the next decade as activities such as voting, paying fines, and registering automobiles become more accessible on the Internet.

The type of information one can access on the Internet is also growing and is certainly not limited to government resources. Now, the places where that information can be accessed are growing as well. Children are becoming more exposed to cyberspace as public schools add computers to their classroom tools. Community centers, public libraries, and other local organizations or entities often have computers that can be used by patrons who otherwise would not have the means to obtain such access or information. Shoppers at a mall in Medford, Oregon, can use computers in an office space run by the Oregon Department of Employment to look for available job opportunities. As a result of these innovations, standing in long lines at the post office to file taxes or at the employment office to apply for a job might one day become a thing of the past.

Logging On

If you are interested in state law codes (statutes) and state court cases, go to

http://www.findlaw.com/ casecode/state.html

Information on state governments, including their constitutional powers, education, and finances, can be accessed by clicking on "State Governments" at

http://www.vote-smart.org/ resource_govt101_01.php

Another excellent source for information on state governments is the following Web site:

http://www.statesnews.org

You can access the *Book of the States,* a biennial publication of the Council of State Governments, from the preceding site, or access it directly at

http://www.csg.org/CSG/Products/ book+of+the+states/default.htm

The National Governors Association offers a wide variety of information on issues and data relating to state governments at

http://www.nga.org

The National Conference of State Legislators is a good source for state information as well. Its URL is

http://www.ncsl.org

You can find a wealth of data on state and local governments at the "Map Stats" site of the U.S. Census Bureau by simply clicking on states and counties on the maps. Go to

http://quickfacts.census.gov/qfd

Piper Resources offers a Web site with numerous links to state and local government resources. You can access this site at

http://www.statelocalgov.net

Using InfoTrac for Political Research

In the election of 2004, as in any major election, numerous state initiatives and referenda were decided in addition to choosing the president, the House of

Representatives, and one-third of the Senate. How the voters reacted to the propositions put before them may tell you a great deal about political trends affecting the American people. You can research initiative and referenda results in 2004 by using InfoTrac. To use Info-Trac, go to

http://www.infotrac-college.com

Log in and go to InfoTrac College Edition, then go to the Keyword guide. Type "referendum 2004" in the search field. (Using "initiative" will not work well because that word has so many different meanings.) InfoTrac will present you with a list of articles that describe what the voters did in the 2004 election. Review several of the articles, and look for patterns.

ONLINE REVIEW

At **http://politicalscience.wadsworth. com/schmidt12**, you will find a free Study Guide to this book. For each chapter, there are two online quizzes to help you master the material.

• The **PoliPrep Self Study Assessment** provides a pre-test for each major section of the chapter. PoliPrep then generates a customized study plan. After you complete the study plan, a post-test evaluates your progress.

• The **Tutorial Quiz** for each chapter provides questions on the chapter contents, including the features. The questions are organized to match the major sections of the chapter.

In Congress, July 4, 1776

A Declaration by the Representatives of the United States of America, in General Congress assembled. When in the Course of human Events, it becomes necessary for one People to dissolve the Political Bands which have connected them with another, and to assume among the Powers of the Earth, the separate and equal Station to which the Laws of Nature and of Nature's God entitle them, a decent Respect to the Opinions of Mankind requires that they should declare the causes which impel them to the Separation.

We hold these Truths to be self-evident, that all Men are created equal, that they are endowed by their Creator with certain unalienable Rights, that among these are Life, Liberty, and the Pursuit of Happiness—That to secure these Rights, Governments are instituted among Men, deriving their just Powers from the Consent of the Governed, that whenever any Form of Government becomes destructive of these Ends, it is the Right of the People to alter or to abolish it, and to institute new Government, laying its Foundation on such Principles, and organizing its Powers in such Forms, as to them shall seem most likely to effect their Safety and Happiness. Prudence, indeed, will dictate that Governments long established should not be changed for light and transient Causes; and accordingly all Experience hath shewn, that Mankind are more disposed to suffer, while Evils are sufferable, than to right themselves by abolishing the Forms to which they are accustomed. But when a long Train of Abuses and Usurpations, pursuing invariably the same Object, evinces a Design to reduce them under absolute Despotism, it is their Right, it is their Duty, to throw off such Government, and to provide new Guards for their future Security. Such has been the patient Sufferance of these Colonies; and such is now the Necessity which constrains them to alter their former Systems of Government. The History of the present King of Great-Britain is a History of repeated Injuries and Usurpations, all having in direct Object the Establishment of an absolute Tyranny over these States. To prove this, let Facts be submitted to a candid World.

He has refused his Assent to Laws, the most wholesome and necessary for the public Good.

He has forbidden his Governors to pass Laws of immediate and pressing Importance, unless suspended in their Operation till his Assent should be obtained; and when so suspended, he has utterly neglected to attend to them.

He has refused to pass other Laws for the Accommodation of large Districts of People, unless those People would relinquish the Right of Representation in the Legislature, a Right inestimable to them, and formidable to Tyrants only.

He has called together Legislative Bodies at Places unusual, uncomfortable, and distant from the Depository of their Public Records, for the sole Purpose of fatiguing them into Compliance with his Measures.

He has dissolved Representative Houses repeatedly, for opposing with manly Firmness his Invasions on the Rights of the People.

He has refused for a long Time, after such Dissolutions, to cause others to be elected; whereby the Legislative Powers, incapable of Annihilation, have returned to the People at large for their exercise; the State remaining in the mean time exposed to all the Dangers of Invasion from without, and Convulsions within.

He has endeavoured to prevent the Population of these States; for that Purpose obstructing the Laws for Naturalization of Foreigners; refusing to pass others to encourage their Migrations hither, and raising the Conditions of new Appropriations of Lands.

He has obstructed the Administration of Justice, by refusing his Assent to Laws for establishing Judiciary Powers.

He has made Judges dependent on his Will alone, for the Tenure of their offices, and the Amount and payment of their Salaries.

He has erected a Multitude of new Offices, and sent hither Swarms of Officers to harrass our People, and eat out their Substance.

He has kept among us, in Times of Peace, Standing Armies, without the consent of our Legislatures.

He has affected to render the Military independent of, and superior to the Civil Power.

He has combined with others to subject us to a Jurisdiction foreign to our Constitution, and unacknowledged by our Laws; giving his Assent to their Acts of pretended Legislation:

For quartering large Bodies of Armed Troops among us:

For protecting them, by a mock Trial, from Punishment for any Murders which they should commit on the Inhabitants of these States:

For cutting off our Trade with all Parts of the World:

For imposing Taxes on us without our Consent:

For depriving us, in many cases, of the Benefits of Trial by Jury:

For transporting us beyond Seas to be tried for pretended Offences:

For abolishing the free System of English Laws in a neighbouring Province, establishing therein an arbitrary Government, and enlarging its Boundaries, so as to render it at once an Example and fit Instrument for introducing the same absolute Rule into these Colonies:

For taking away our Charters, abolishing our most valuable Laws, and altering fundamentally the Forms of our Governments:

For suspending our own Legislatures, and declaring themselves invested with Power to legislate for us in all Cases whatsoever.

He has abdicated Government here, by declaring us out of his Protection and waging War against us.

He has plundered our Seas, ravaged our Coasts, burnt our towns, and destroyed the Lives of our People.

He is, at this Time, transporting large Armies of foreign Mercenaries to compleat the works of Death, Desolation, and Tyranny, already begun with circumstances of Cruelty and Perfidy, scarcely paralleled in the most barbarous Ages, and totally unworthy the Head of a civilized Nation.

He has constrained our fellow Citizens taken Captive on the high Seas to bear Arms against their Country, to become the

Executioners of their Friends and Brethren, or to fall themselves by their Hands.

He has excited domestic Insurrections amongst us, and has endeavoured to bring on the Inhabitants of our Frontiers, the merciless Indian Savages, whose known Rule of Warfare, is an undistinguished Destruction, of all Ages, Sexes and Conditions.

In every state of these Oppressions we have Petitioned for Redress in the most humble Terms: Our repeated Petitions have been answered only by repeated Injury. A Prince, whose Character is thus marked by every act which may define a Tyrant, is unfit to be the Ruler of a free People.

Nor have we been wanting in Attentions to our British Brethren. We have warned them from Time to Time of Attempts by their Legislature to extend an unwarrantable Jurisdiction over us. We have reminded them of the Circumstances of our Emigration and Settlement here. We have appealed to their native Justice and Magnanimity, and we have conjured them by the Ties of our common Kindred to disavow these Usurpations, which, would inevitably interrupt our Connections and Correspondence. They too have been deaf to the Voice of Justice and of Consanguinity.

We must, therefore, acquiesce in the Necessity, which denounces our Separation, and hold them, as we hold the rest of Mankind, Enemies in War, in Peace, Friends.

We, therefore, the Representatives of the UNITED STATES OF AMERICA, in General Congress Assembled, appealing to the Supreme Judge of the World for the Rectitude of our Intentions, do, in the Name, and by the Authority of the good People of these Colonies, solemnly Publish and Declare, That these United Colonies are, and of Right ought to be, Free and Independent States; that they are absolved from all Allegiance to the British Crown, and that all political Connection between them and the State of Great-Britain, is and ought to be totally dissolved; and that as Free and Independent States, they have full Power to levy War, conclude Peace, contract Alliances, establish Commerce, and to do all other Acts and Things which Independent States may of right do. And for the support of this declaration, with a firm Reliance on the Protection of divine Providence, we mutually pledge to each other our lives, our Fortunes, and our sacred Honor.

How to Read Case Citations and Find Court Decisions

Many important court cases are discussed in references in footnotes throughout this book. Court decisions are recorded and published. When a court case is mentioned, the notation that is used to refer to, or to cite, the case denotes where the published decision can be found.

State courts of appeals decisions are usually published in two places, the state reports of that particular state and the more widely used *National Reporter System* published by West Publishing Company. Some states no longer publish their own reports. The *National Reporter System* divides the states into the following geographic areas: Atlantic (A. or A.2d, where *2d* refers to *Second Series*), South Eastern (S.E. or S.E.2d), South Western (S.W., S.W.2d, or S.W.3d), North Western (N.W. or N.W.2d), North Eastern (N.E. or N.E.2d), Southern (So. or So.2d), and Pacific (P., P.2d, or P.3d).

Federal trial court decisions are published unofficially in *West's Federal Supplement* (F.Supp.), and opinions from the circuit courts of appeals are reported unofficially in West's *Federal Reporter* (F., F.2d, or F.3d). Opinions from the United States Supreme Court are reported in the *United States Reports* (U.S.), the *Lawyers' Edition of the Supreme Court Reports* (L.Ed.), West's *Supreme Court Reporter* (S.Ct.), and other publications. The *United States Reports* is the official publication of United States Supreme Court decisions. It is published by the federal government. Many early decisions are missing from these volumes. The citations of the early volumes of the *U.S. Reports* include the names of the actual reporters, such as Dallas, Cranch, or Wheaton. *McCulloch v. Maryland*, for example,

is cited as 17 U.S. (4 Wheat.) 316. Only after 1874 did the present citation system, in which cases are cited based solely on their volume and page numbers in the *United States Reports*, come into being. The *Lawyers' Edition of the Supreme Court Reports* is an unofficial and more complete edition of Supreme Court decisions. West's *Supreme Court Reporter* is an unofficial edition of decisions dating from October 1882. These volumes contain headnotes and numerous brief editorial statements of the law involved in the case.

State courts of appeals decisions are cited by giving the name of the case; the volume, name, and page number of the state's official report (if the state publishes its own reports); the volume, unit, and page number of the *National Reporter;* and the volume, name, and page number of any other selected reporter. Federal court citations are also listed by giving the name of the case and the volume, name, and page number of the reports. In addition to the citation, this textbook lists the year of the decision in parentheses. Consider, for example, the case *United States v. Curtiss-Wright Export Co.,* 299 U.S. 304 (1936). The Supreme Court's decision of this case may be found in volume 299 of the *United States Reports* on page 304. The case was decided in 1936.

Today, many courts, including the United States Supreme Court, publish their opinions online. This makes it much easier for students to find and read cases, or summaries of cases, that have significant consequences for American government and politics. To access cases via the Internet, use the URLs given in the *Logging On* section at the end of Chapter 14.

In 1787, after the newly drafted U.S. Constitution was submitted to the thirteen states for ratification, a major political debate ensued between the Federalists (who favored ratification) and the Anti-Federalists (who opposed ratification). Anti-Federalists in New York were particularly critical of the Constitution, and in response to their objections, Federalists Alexander Hamilton, James Madison, and John Jay wrote a series of eighty-five essays in defense of the Constitution. The essays were published in New York newspapers and reprinted in other newspapers throughout the country.

For students of American government, the essays, collectively known as the Federalist Papers, are particularly important because they provide a glimpse of the founders' political philosophy and intentions in designing the Constitution—and, consequently, in shaping the American philosophy of government.

We have included in this appendix three of these essays: Federalist Papers No. 10, No. 51, and No. 78. Each essay has been annotated by the authors to indicate its importance in American political thought and to clarify the meaning of particular passages.

Federalist Paper No. 10

Federalist Paper No. 10, penned by James Madison, has often been singled out as a key document in American political thought. In this essay, Madison attacks the Anti-Federalists' fear that a republican form of government will inevitably give rise to "factions"—small political parties or groups united by a common interest—that will control the government. Factions will be harmful to the country because they will implement policies beneficial to their own interests but adverse to other people's rights and to the public good. In this essay, Madison attempts to lay to rest this fear by explaining how, in a large republic such as the United States, there will be so many different factions, held together by regional or local interests, that no single one of them will dominate national politics.

Madison opens his essay with a paragraph discussing how important it is to devise a plan of government that can control the "instability, injustice, and confusion" brought about by factions.

Among the numerous advantages promised by a well-constructed Union, none deserves to be more accurately developed than its tendency to break and control the violence of faction. The friend of popular governments never finds himself so much alarmed for their character and fate as when he contemplates their propensity to this dangerous vice. He will not fail, therefore, to set a due value on any plan which, without violating the principles to which he is attached, provides a proper cure for it. The instability, injustice, and confusion introduced into the public councils have, in truth, been the mortal diseases under which popular governments have everywhere perished, as they continue to be the favorite and fruitful topics from which the adversaries to liberty derive their most

specious declamations. The valuable improvements made by the American constitutions on the popular models, both ancient and modern, cannot certainly be too much admired; but it would be an unwarrantable partiality to contend that they have as effectually obviated the danger on this side, as was wished and expected. Complaints are everywhere heard from our most considerate and virtuous citizens, equally the friends of public and private faith and of public and personal liberty, that our governments are too unstable, that the public good is disregarded in the conflicts of rival parties, and that measures are too often decided, not according to the rules of justice and the rights of the minor party, but by the superior force of an interested and overbearing majority. However anxiously we may wish that these complaints had no foundation, the evidence of known facts will not permit us to deny that they are in some degree true. It will be found, indeed, on a candid review of our situation, that some of the distresses under which we labor have been erroneously charged on the operation of our governments; but it will be found, at the same time, that other causes will not alone account for many of our heaviest misfortunes; and, particularly, for that prevailing and increasing distrust of public engagements and alarm for private rights which are echoed from one end of the continent to the other. These must be chiefly, if not wholly, effects of the unsteadiness and injustice with which a factious spirit has tainted our public administration.

Madison now defines what he means by the term faction.

By a faction I understand a number of citizens, whether amounting to a majority or minority of the whole, who are united and actuated by some common impulse of passion, or of interest, adverse to the rights of other citizens, or the permanent and aggregate interests of the community.

Madison next contends that there are two methods by which the "mischiefs of faction" can be cured: by removing the causes of faction or by controlling their effects. In the following paragraphs, Madison explains how liberty itself nourishes factions. Therefore, to abolish factions would involve abolishing liberty—a cure "worse than the disease."

There are two methods of curing the mischiefs of faction: the one, by removing its causes; the other, by controlling its effects.

There are again two methods of removing the causes of faction: the one, by destroying the liberty which is essential to its existence; the other, by giving to every citizen the same opinions, the same passions, and the same interests.

It could never be more truly said than of the first remedy that it was worse than the disease. Liberty is to faction what air is to fire, an aliment without which it instantly expires. But it could not be a less folly to abolish liberty, which is essential to political life, because it nourishes faction than it would be to wish the annihilation of air, which is essential to animal life, because it imparts to fire its destructive agency.

The second expedient is as impracticable as the first would be unwise. As long as the reason of man continues fallible, and he is at liberty to exercise it, different opinions will be formed. As long as the connection subsists between his reason and his self-love, his opinions and his passions will have a reciprocal influence on each other; and the former will be objects to which the latter will attach themselves. The diversity in the faculties of men, from which the rights of property originate, is not less an insuperable obstacle to a uniformity of interests. The protection of these faculties is the first object of government. From the protection of different and unequal faculties of acquiring property, the possession of different degrees and kinds of property immediately results; and from the influence of these on the sentiments and views of the respective proprietors ensues a division of the society into different interests and parties.

The latent causes of faction are thus sown in the nature of man; and we see them everywhere brought into different degrees of activity, according to the different circumstances of civil society. A zeal for different opinions concerning religion, concerning government, and many other points, as well of speculation as of practice; an attachment to different leaders ambitiously contending for preeminence and power; or to persons of other descriptions whose fortunes have been interesting to the human passions, have, in turn, divided mankind into parties, inflamed them with mutual animosity, and rendered them much more disposed to vex and oppress each other than to co-operate for their common good. So strong is this propensity of mankind to fall into mutual animosities that where no substantial occasion presents itself the most frivolous and fanciful distinctions have been sufficient to kindle their unfriendly passions and excite their most violent conflicts. But the most common and durable source of factions has been the various and unequal distribution of property. Those who hold and those who are without property have ever formed distinct interests in society. Those who are creditors, and those who are debtors, fall under a like discrimination. A landed interest, a manufacturing interest, a mercantile interest, a moneyed interest, with many lesser interests, grow up of necessity in civilized nations, and divide them into different classes, actuated by different sentiments and views. The regulation of these various and interfering interests forms the principal task of modern legislation and involves the spirit of party and faction in the necessary and ordinary operations of government.

No man is allowed to be a judge in his own cause, because his interest would certainly bias his judgment, and, not improbably, corrupt his integrity. With equal, nay with greater reason, a body of men are unfit to be both judges and parties at the same time; yet what are many of the most important acts of legislation but so many judicial determinations, not indeed concerning the rights of single persons, but concerning the rights of large bodies of citizens? And what are the different classes of legislators but advocates and parties to the causes which they determine? Is a law proposed concerning private debts? It is a question to which the creditors are parties on one side and the debtors on the other. Justice ought to hold the balance between them. Yet the parties are, and must be, themselves the judges; and the most numerous party, or in other words, the most powerful faction must be expected to prevail. Shall domestic manufacturers be encouraged, and in what degree, by restrictions on foreign manufacturers? [These] are questions which

would be differently decided by the landed and the manufacturing classes, and probably by neither with a sole regard to justice and the public good. The apportionment of taxes on the various descriptions of property is an act which seems to require the most exact impartiality; yet there is, perhaps, no legislative act in which greater opportunity and temptation are given to a predominant party to trample on the rules of justice. Every shilling with which they overburden the inferior number is a shilling saved to their own pockets.

It is in vain to say that enlightened statesmen will be able to adjust these clashing interests and render them all subservient to the public good. Enlightened statesmen will not always be at the helm. Nor, in many cases, can such an adjustment be made at all without taking into view indirect and remote considerations, which will rarely prevail over the immediate interest which one party may find in disregarding the rights of another or the good of the whole.

The inference to which we are brought is that the *causes* of faction cannot be removed and that relief is only to be sought in the means of controlling its *effects*.

Having concluded that "the causes of faction cannot be removed," Madison now looks in some detail at the other method by which factions can be cured—by controlling their effects. This is the heart of his essay. He begins by positing a significant question: How can you have self-government without risking the possibility that a ruling faction, particularly a majority faction, might tyrannize over the rights of others?

If a faction consists of less than a majority, relief is supplied by the republican principle, which enables the majority to defeat its sinister views by regular vote. It may clog the administration, it may convulse the society; but it will be unable to execute and mask its violence under the forms of the Constitution. When a majority is included in a faction, the form of popular government, on the other hand, enables it to sacrifice to its ruling passion or interest both the public good and the rights of other citizens. To secure the public good and private rights against the danger of such a faction, and at the same time to preserve the spirit and the form of popular government, is then the great object to which our inquiries are directed. Let me add that it is the great desideratum by which alone this form of government can be rescued from the opprobrium under which it has so long labored and be recommended to the esteem and adoption of mankind.

Madison now sets forth the idea that one way to control the effects of factions is to ensure that the majority is rendered incapable of acting in concert in order to "carry into effect schemes of oppression." He goes on to state that in a democracy, in which all citizens participate personally in government decision making, there is no way to prevent the majority from communicating with each other and, as a result, acting in concert.

By what means is this object attainable? Evidently by one of two only. Either the existence of the same passion or interest in a majority at the same time must be prevented, or the majority, having such coexistent passion or interest, must be rendered, by their number and local situation, unable to concert and carry into effect schemes of oppression. If the impulse and the opportunity be suffered to coincide, we well know that neither moral nor religious motives can be relied on as an adequate control. They are not found to be such on the injustice and violence of individuals, and lose their efficacy in proportion to the number combined together, that is, in proportion as their efficacy becomes needful.

From this view of the subject it may be concluded that a pure democracy, by which I mean a society consisting of a small number of citizens, who assemble and administer the government in person, can admit of no cure for the mischiefs of faction. A common passion or interest will, in almost every case, be felt by a majority of the whole; a communication and concert results from the form of government itself; and there is nothing to check the inducements to sacrifice the weaker party or an obnoxious individual. Hence it is that such democracies have ever been spectacles of turbulence and contention; have ever been found incompatible with personal security or the rights of property; and have in general been as short in their lives as they have been violent in their deaths. Theoretic politicians, who have patronized this species of government, have erroneously supposed that by reducing mankind to a perfect equality in their political rights, they would at the same time be perfectly equalized and assimilated in their possessions, their opinions, and their passions.

Madison now moves on to discuss the benefits of a republic with respect to controlling the effects of factions. He begins by defining a republic and then pointing out the "two great points of difference" between a republic and a democracy: a republic is governed by a small body of elected representatives, not by the people directly; and a republic can extend over a much larger territory and embrace more citizens than a democracy can.

A republic, by which I mean a government in which the scheme of representation takes place, opens a different prospect and promises the cure for which we are seeking. Let us examine the points in which it varies from pure democracy, and we shall comprehend both the nature of the cure and the efficacy which it must derive from the Union.

The two great points of difference between a democracy and a republic are: first, the delegation of the government, in the latter, to a small number of citizens elected by the rest; secondly, the greater number of citizens and greater sphere of country over which the latter may be extended.

In the following four paragraphs, Madison explains how in a republic, particularly a large republic, the delegation of authority to elected representatives will increase the likelihood that those who govern will be "fit" for their positions and that a proper balance will be achieved between local (factional) interests and national interests. Note how he stresses that the new federal Constitution, by dividing powers between state governments and the national government, provides a "happy combination in this respect."

The effect of the first difference is, on the one hand, to refine and enlarge the public views by passing them through the medium of a chosen body of citizens, whose wisdom may best discern the true interest of their country and whose patriotism and love of justice will be least likely to sacrifice it to temporary or partial considerations. Under such a regulation it may well happen that the public voice, pronounced by the representatives of the people, will be more consonant to the public good than if pronounced by the people themselves, convened for the purpose. On the other hand, the effect may be inverted. Men of factious tempers, of local prej-

udices, or of sinister designs, may, by intrigue, by corruption, or by other means, first obtain the suffrages, and then betray the interests of the people. The question resulting is, whether small or extensive republics are most favorable to the election of proper guardians of the public weal; and it is clearly decided in favor of the latter by two obvious considerations.

In the first place it is to be remarked that however small the republic may be the representatives must be raised to a certain number in order to guard against the cabals of a few; and that however large it may be they must be limited to a certain number in order to guard against the confusion of a multitude. Hence, the number of representatives in the two cases not being in proportion to that of the constituents, and being proportionally greatest in the small republic, it follows that if the proportion of fit characters be not less in the large than in the small republic, the former will present a greater option, and consequently a greater probability of a fit choice.

In the next place, as each representative will be chosen by a greater number of citizens in the large than in the small republic, it will be more difficult for unworthy candidates to practice with success the vicious arts by which elections are too often carried; and the suffrages of the people being more free, will be more likely to center on men who possess the most attractive merit and the most diffusive and established characters.

It must be confessed that in this, as in most other cases, there is a mean, on both sides of which inconveniencies will be found to lie. By enlarging too much the number of electors, you render the representative too little acquainted with all their local circumstances and lesser interests; as by reducing it too much, you render him unduly attached to these, and too little fit to comprehend and pursue great and national objects. The federal Constitution forms a happy combination in this respect; the great and aggregate interests being referred to the national, the local and particular to the State legislatures.

Madison now looks more closely at the other difference between a republic and a democracy—namely, that a republic can encompass a larger territory and more citizens than a democracy can. In the remaining paragraphs of his essay, Madison concludes that in a large republic, it will be difficult for factions to act in concert. Although a factious group—religious, political, economic, or otherwise—may control a local or regional government, it will have little chance of gathering a national following. This is because in a large republic, there will be numerous factions whose work will offset the work of any one particular faction ("sect"). As Madison phrases it, these numerous factions will "secure the national councils against any danger from that source."

The other point of difference is the greater number of citizens and extent of territory which may be brought within the compass of republican than of democratic government; and it is this circumstance principally which renders factious combinations less to be dreaded in the former than in the latter. The smaller the society, the fewer probably will be the distinct parties and interests composing it; the fewer the distinct parties and interests, the more frequently will a majority be found of the same party; and the smaller the number of individuals composing a majority, and the smaller the compass within which they are placed, the more easily will they concert and execute their plans of oppression. Extend the sphere and you take in a greater variety of parties and interests; you make it less probable that a majority of the whole will have a common motive to invade the rights of other citizens; or if such a common motive exists, it will be more difficult for all who feel it to discover their own strength and to act in unison with each other. Besides other impediments, it may be remarked that, where there is a consciousness of unjust or dishonorable purposes, communication is always checked by distrust in proportion to the number whose concurrence is necessary.

Hence, it clearly appears that the same advantage which a republic has over a democracy in controlling the effects of faction is enjoyed by a large over a small republic—is enjoyed by the Union over the States composing it. Does this advantage consist in the substitution of representatives whose enlightened views and virtuous sentiments render them superior to local prejudices and to schemes of injustice? It will not be denied that the representation of the Union will be most likely to possess these requisite endowments. Does it consist in the greater security afforded by a greater variety of parties, against the event of any one party being able to outnumber and oppress the rest? In an equal degree does the increased variety of parties comprised within the Union increase this security. Does it, in fine, consist in the greater obstacles opposed to the concert and accomplishment of the secret wishes of an unjust and interested majority? Here again the extent of the Union gives it the most palpable advantage.

The influence of factious leaders may kindle a flame within their particular States but will be unable to spread a general conflagration through the other States. A religious sect may degenerate into a political faction in a part of the Confederacy; but the variety of sects dispersed over the entire face of it must secure the national councils against any danger from that source. A rage for paper money, for an abolition of debts, for an equal division of property, or for any other improper or wicked project, will be less apt to pervade the whole body of the Union than a particular member of it, in the same proportion as such a malady is more likely to taint a particular county or district than an entire State.

In the extent and proper structure of the Union, therefore, we behold a republican remedy for the diseases most incident to republican government. And according to the degree of pleasure and pride we feel in being republicans ought to be our zeal in cherishing the spirit and supporting the character of federalists.

Publius
(James Madison)

Federalist Paper No. 51

Federalist Paper No. 51, also authored by James Madison, is another classic in American political theory. Although the Federalists wanted a strong national government, they had not abandoned the traditional American view, particularly notable during the revolutionary era, that those holding powerful government positions could not be trusted to put national interests and the common good above their own personal interests. In this essay, Madison explains why the separation of the national government's powers into three branches—executive, legislative, and judicial—and a federal structure of government offer the best protection against tyranny.

To what expedient, then, shall we finally resort, for maintaining in practice the necessary partition of power among the several departments as laid down in the Constitution? The only answer that can be given is that as all these exterior provisions are found to be inadequate the defect must be supplied, by so contriving the interior structure of the government as that its several constituent parts may, by their mutual relations, be the means of keeping each other in their proper places. Without presuming to undertake a full development of this important idea I will hazard a few general observations which may perhaps place it in a clearer light, and enable us to form a more correct judgment of the principles and structure of the government planned by the convention.

In the next two paragraphs, Madison stresses that for the powers of the different branches (departments) of government to be truly separated, the personnel in one branch should not be dependent on another branch for their appointment or for the "emoluments" (compensation) attached to their offices.

In order to lay a due foundation for that separate and distinct exercise of the different powers of government, which to a certain extent is admitted on all hands to be essential to the preservation of liberty, it is evident that each department should have a will of its own; and consequently should be so constituted that the members of each should have as little agency as possible in the appointment of the members of the others. Were this principle rigorously adhered to, it would require that all the appointments for the supreme executive, legislative, and judiciary magistracies should be drawn from the same fountain of authority, the people, through channels having no communication whatever with one another. Perhaps such a plan of constructing the several departments would be less difficult in practice than it may in contemplation appear. Some difficulties, however, and some additional expense would attend the execution of it. Some deviations, therefore, from the principle must be admitted. In the constitution of the judiciary department in particular, it might be inexpedient to insist rigorously on the principle: first, because peculiar qualifications being essential in the members, the primary consideration ought to be to select that mode of choice which best secures these qualifications; second, because the permanent tenure by which the appointments are held in that department must soon destroy all sense of dependence on the authority conferring them.

It is equally evident that the members of each department should be as little dependent as possible on those of the others for the emoluments annexed to their offices. Were the executive magistrate, or the judges, not independent of the legislature in this particular, their independence in every other would be merely nominal.

In the following passages, which are among the most widely quoted of Madison's writings, he explains how the separation of the powers of government into three branches helps to counter the effects of personal ambition on government. The separation of powers allows personal motives to be linked to the constitutional rights of a branch of government. In effect, competing personal interests in each branch will help to keep the powers of the three government branches separate and, in so doing, will help to guard the public interest.

But the great security against a gradual concentration of the several powers in the same department consists in giving to those who administer each department the necessary constitutional means and personal motives to resist encroachments of the others. The provision for defense must in this, as in all other cases, be made commensurate to the danger of attack. Ambition must be made to counteract ambition. The interest of the man must be connected with the constitutional rights of the place. It may be a reflection on human nature that such devices should be necessary to control the abuses of government. But what is government itself but the greatest of all reflections on human nature? If men were angels, no government would be necessary. If angels were to govern men, neither external nor internal controls on government would be necessary. In framing a government which is to be administered by men over men, the great difficulty lies in this: you must first enable the government to control the governed; and in the next place oblige it to control itself. A dependence on the people is, no doubt, the primary control on the government; but experience has taught mankind the necessity of auxiliary precautions.

This policy of supplying, by opposite and rival interests, the defect of better motives, might be traced through the whole system of human affairs, private as well as public. We see it particularly displayed in all the subordinate distributions of power, where the constant aim is to divide and arrange the several offices in such a manner as that each may be a check on the other—that the private interest of every individual may be a sentinel over the public rights. These inventions of prudence cannot be less requisite in the distribution of the supreme powers of the State.

Madison now addresses the issue of equality between the branches of government. The legislature will necessarily predominate, but if the executive is given an "absolute negative" (absolute veto power) over legislative actions, this also could lead to an abuse of power. Madison concludes that the division of the legislature into two "branches" (parts, or chambers) will act as a check on the legislature's powers.

But it is not possible to give to each department an equal power of self-defense. In republican government, the legislative authority necessarily predominates. The remedy for this inconveniency is to divide the legislature into different branches; and to render them, by different modes of election and different principles of action, as little connected with each other as the nature of their common functions and their common dependence on the society will admit. It may even be necessary to guard against dangerous encroachments by still further precautions. As the weight of the legislative authority requires that it should be thus divided, the weakness of the executive may require, on the other hand, that it should be fortified. An absolute negative on the legislature appears, at first view, to be the natural defense with which the executive magistrate should be armed. But perhaps it would be neither altogether safe nor alone sufficient. On ordinary occasions it might not be exerted with the requisite firmness, and on extraordinary occasions it might be perfidiously abused. May not this defect of an absolute negative be supplied by some qualified connection between this weaker department and the weaker branch of the stronger department, by which the latter may be led to support the constitutional rights of the former, without being too much detached from the rights of its own department?

If the principles on which these observations are founded be just, as I persuade myself they are, and they be applied as a criterion to the several State constitutions, and to the federal Constitution, it will be found that if the latter does not perfectly correspond with them, the former are infinitely less able to bear such a test.

In the remainder of the essay, Madison discusses how a federal system of government, in which powers are divided between the states and the national government, offers "double security" against tyranny.

There are, moreover, two considerations particularly applicable to the federal system of America, which place that system in a very interesting point of view.

First. In a single republic, all the power surrendered by the people is submitted to the administration of a single government; and the usurpations are guarded against by a division of the government into distinct and separate departments. In the compound republic of America, the power surrendered by the people is first divided between two distinct governments, and then the portion allotted to each subdivided among distinct and separate departments. Hence a double security arises to the rights of the people. The different governments will control each other, at the same time that each will be controlled by itself.

Second. It is of great importance in a republic not only to guard the society against the oppression of its rulers, but to guard one part of the society against the injustice of the other part. Different interests necessarily exist in different classes of citizens. If a majority be united by a common interest, the rights of the minority will be insecure. There are but two methods of providing against this evil: the one by creating a will in the community independent of the majority—that is, of the society itself; the other, by comprehending in the society so many separate descriptions of citizens as will render an unjust combination of a majority of the whole very improbable, if not impracticable. The first method prevails in all governments possessing an hereditary or self-appointed authority. This, at best, is but a precarious security; because a power independent of the society may as well espouse the unjust views of the major as the rightful interests of the minor party, and may possibly be turned against both parties. The second method will be exemplified in the federal republic of the United States. Whilst all authority in it will be derived from and dependent on the society, the society itself will be broken into so many parts, interests and classes of citizens, that the rights of individuals, or of the minority, will be in little danger from interested combinations of the majority. In a free government the security for civil rights must be the same as that for religious rights. It consists in the one case in the multiplicity of interests, and in the other in the multiplicity of sects; and this may be presumed to depend on the number of interests and sects; and this may be presumed to depend on the extent of country and number of people comprehended under the same government. This view of the subject must particularly recommend a proper federal system to all the sincere and considerate friends of republican government, since it shows that in exact proportion as the territory of the Union may be formed into more circumscribed Confederacies, or States, oppressive combinations of a majority will be facilitated; the best security, under the republican forms, for the rights of every class of citizen, will be diminished; and consequently the stability and independence of some member of the government, the only other security, must be proportionally increased. Justice is the end of government. It is the end of civil society. It ever has been and ever will be pursued until it be obtained, or until liberty be lost in the pursuit. In a society under the forms of which the stronger faction can readily unite and oppress the weaker, anarchy may as truly be said to reign as in a state of nature, where the weaker individual is not secured against the violence of the stronger; and as, in the latter state, even the stronger individuals are prompted, by the uncertainty of their condition, to submit to a government which may protect the weak as well as themselves; so, in the former state, will the more powerful factions or parties be gradually induced, by a like motive, to wish for a government which will protect all parties, the weaker as well as the more powerful. It can be little doubted that if the State of Rhode Island was separated from the Confederacy and left to itself, the insecurity of rights under the popular form of government within such narrow limits would be displayed by such reiterated oppressions of factious majorities that some power altogether independent of the people would soon be called for by the voice of the very factions whose misrule had proved the necessity of it. In the extended republic of the United States, and among the great variety of interests, parties, and sects which it embraces, a coalition of a majority of the whole society could seldom take place on any other principles than those of justice and the general good; whilst there being thus less danger to a minor from the will of a major party, there must be less pretext, also, to provide for the security of the former, by introducing into the government a will not dependent on the latter, or, in other words, a will independent of the society itself. It is no less certain than it is important, notwithstanding the contrary opinions which have been entertained, that the larger the society, provided it lie within a practicable sphere, the more duly capable it will be of self-government. And happily for the republican cause, the practicable sphere may be carried to a very great extent by a judicious modification and mixture of the *federal principle*.

Publius
(James Madison)

Federalist Paper No. 78

In this essay, Alexander Hamilton looks at the role of the judicial branch (the courts) in the new government fashioned by the Constitution's framers. The essay is historically significant because, among other things, it provides a basis for the courts' power of judicial review, which was not explicitly set forth in the Constitution (see Chapters 3 and 14).

After some brief introductory remarks, Hamilton explains why the founders decided that federal judges should be appointed and given lifetime tenure. Note how he describes the judiciary as the "weakest" and "least dangerous" branch of government. Because of this, claims Hamilton, "all possible care" is required to enable the judiciary to defend itself against attacks by the other two branches of government. Above all, the independence of the judicial branch should be secured, because if judicial powers were combined with legislative or executive powers, there would be no liberty.

WE PROCEED now to an examination of the judiciary department of the proposed government.

In unfolding the defects of the existing Confederation, the utility and necessity of a federal judicature have been clearly pointed out. It is the less necessary to recapitulate the considerations there urged, as the propriety of the institution in the abstract is not disputed; the only questions which have been raised being relative to the manner of constituting it, and to its extent. To these points, therefore, our observations shall be confined.

The manner of constituting it seems to embrace these several objects: 1st. The mode of appointing the judges. 2d. The tenure by which they are to hold their places. 3d. The partition of the judiciary authority between different courts, and their relations to each other.

First. As to the mode of appointing the judges; this is the same with that of appointing the officers of the Union in general, and has been so fully discussed in the last two numbers, that nothing can be said here which would not be useless repetition.

Second. As to the tenure by which the judges are to hold their places; this chiefly concerns their duration in office; the provisions for their support; the precautions for their responsibility.

According to the plan of the convention, all judges who may be appointed by the United States are to hold their offices during good behavior; which is conformable to the most approved of the State constitutions and among the rest, to that of this State. Its propriety having been drawn into question by the adversaries of that plan, is no light symptom of the rage for objection, which disorders their imaginations and judgments. The standard of good behavior for the continuance in office of the judicial magistracy, is certainly one of the most valuable of the modern improvements in the practice of government. In a monarchy it is an excellent barrier to the despotism of the prince; in a republic it is a no less excellent barrier to the encroachments and oppressions of the representative body. And it is the best expedient which can be devised in any government, to secure a steady, upright, and impartial administration of the laws.

Whoever attentively considers the different departments of power must perceive, that, in a government in which they are separated from each other, the judiciary, from the nature of its functions, will always be the least dangerous to the political rights of the Constitution; because it will be least in a capacity to annoy or injure them. The Executive not only dispenses the honors, but holds the sword of the community. The legislature not only commands the purse, but prescribes the rules by which the duties and rights of every citizen are to be regulated. The judiciary, on the contrary, has no influence over either the sword or the purse; no direction either of the strength or of the wealth of the society; and can take no active resolution whatever. It may truly be said to have neither force nor will, but merely judgment; and must ultimately depend upon the aid of the executive arm even for the efficacy of its judgments.

This simple view of the matter suggests several important consequences. It proves incontestably, that the judiciary is beyond comparison the weakest of the three departments of power; that it can never attack with success either of the other two; and that all possible care is requisite to enable it to defend itself against their attacks. It equally proves, that though individual oppression may now and then proceed from the courts of justice, the general liberty of the people can never be endangered from that quarter; I mean so long as the judiciary remains truly distinct from both the legislature and the Executive. For I agree, that "there is no liberty, if the power of judging is not separated from the legislative and executive powers." And it proves, in the last place, that as liberty can have nothing to fear from the judiciary alone, but would have everything to fear from its union with either of the other departments; that as all the effects of such a union must ensue from a dependence of the former on the latter, notwithstanding a nominal and apparent separation; that as, from the natural feebleness of the judiciary, it is in continual jeopardy of being overpowered, awed, or influenced by its co-ordinate branches; and that as nothing can contribute so much to its firmness and independence as permanency in office, this quality may therefore be justly regarded as an indispensable ingredient in its constitution, and, in a great measure, as the citadel of the public justice and the public security.

Hamilton now stresses that the "complete independence of the courts" is essential in a limited government, because it is up to the courts to interpret the laws. Just as a federal court can decide which of two conflicting statutes should take priority, so can that court decide whether a statute conflicts with the Constitution. Essentially, Hamilton sets forth here the theory of judicial review—the power of the courts to decide whether actions of the other branches of government are (or are not) consistent with the Constitution. Hamilton points out that this "exercise of judicial discretion, in determining between two contradictory laws," does not mean that the judicial branch is superior to the legislative branch. Rather, it "supposes" that the power of the people (as declared in the Constitution) is superior to both the judiciary and the legislature.

The complete independence of the courts of justice is peculiarly essential in a limited Constitution. By a limited Constitution, I understand one which contains certain specified exceptions to the legislative authority; such, for instance, as that it shall pass no bills of attainder, no ex-post-facto laws, and the like. Limitations of this kind can be preserved in practice no other way than through the medium of courts of justice, whose duty it must be to declare all acts contrary to the manifest tenor of the Constitution void. Without this, all the reservations of particular rights or privileges would amount to nothing. Some perplexity respecting the rights of the courts to pronounce legislative acts void, because contrary to the Constitution, has arisen from an imagination that the doctrine would imply a superiority of the judiciary to the legislative power. It is urged that the authority which can declare the acts of another void, must necessarily be superior to the one whose acts may be declared void. As this doctrine is of great importance in all the American constitutions, a brief discussion of the ground on which it rests cannot be unacceptable.

There is no position which depends on clearer principles, than that every act of a delegated authority, contrary to the tenor of the commission under which it is exercised, is void. No legislative act, therefore, contrary to the Constitution, can be valid. To deny this, would be to affirm, that the deputy is greater than his principal; that the servant is above his master; that the representatives of the people are superior to the people themselves; that men acting by virtue of powers, may do not only what their powers do not authorize, but what they forbid.

If it be said that the legislative body are themselves the constitutional judges of their own powers, and that the construction they put upon them is conclusive upon the other departments, it may be answered, that this cannot be the natural presumption, where it is not to be collected from any particular provisions in the Constitution. It is not otherwise to be supposed, that the Constitution could intend to enable the representatives of the people to substitute their will to that of their constituents. It is far more rational to suppose, that the courts were designed to be an intermediate body between the people and the legislature, in order, among other things, to keep the latter within the limits assigned to their authority. The interpretation of the laws is the proper and peculiar province of the courts. A constitution is, in fact, and must be regarded by the judges, as a fundamental law. It therefore belongs to them to ascertain its meaning, as well as the meaning of any particular act proceeding from the legislative body. If there should happen to be an irreconcilable variance between the two, that which has the superior obligation and validity ought, of course, to be preferred; or, in other words, the Constitution ought to be preferred to the statute, the intention of the people to the intention of their agents.

Nor does this conclusion by any means suppose a superiority of the judicial to the legislative power. It only supposes that the power of the people is superior to both; and that where the will of the legislature, declared in its statutes, stands in opposition to that of the people, declared in the Constitution, the judges ought to be governed by the latter rather than the former. They ought to regulate their decisions by the fundamental laws, rather than by those which are not fundamental.

This exercise of judicial discretion, in determining between two contradictory laws, is exemplified in a familiar instance. It not uncommonly happens, that there are two statutes existing at one time, clashing in whole or in part with each other, and neither of them containing any repealing clause or expression. In such a case, it is the province of the courts to liquidate and fix their meaning and operation. So far as they can, by any fair construction, be reconciled to each other, reason and law conspire to dictate that this should be done; where this is impractable, it becomes a matter of necessity to give effect to one, in exclusion of the other. The rule which has obtained in the courts for determining their relative validity is, that the last in order of time shall be preferred to the first. But this is a mere rule of construction, not derived from any positive law, but from the nature and reason of the thing. It is a rule not enjoined upon the courts by legislative provision, but adopted by themselves, as consonant to truth the propriety, for the direction of their conduct as interpreters of the law. They thought it reasonable, that between the interfering acts of an equal authority, that which was the last indication of its will should have the preference.

But in regard to the interfering acts of a superior and subordinate authority, of an original and derivative power, the nature and reason of the thing indicate the converse of that rule as proper to be followed. They teach us that the prior act of a superior ought to be preferred to the subsequent act of an inferior and subordinate authority; and that accordingly, whenever a particular statute contravenes the Constitution, it will be the duty of the judicial tribunals to adhere to the latter and disregard the former.

It can be of no weight to say that the courts, on the pretense of a repugnancy, may substitute their own pleasure to the constitutional intentions of the legislature. This might as well happen in the case of two contradictory statutes; or it might as well happen in every adjudication upon any single statute. The courts must declare the sense of the law; and if they should be disposed to exercise will instead of judgment, the consequence would equally be the substitution of their pleasure to that of the legislative body. The observation, if it prove anything, would prove that there ought to be no judges distinct from that body.

If, then, the courts of justice are to be considered as the bulwarks of a limited Constitution against legislative encroachments, this consideration will afford a strong argument for the permanent tenure of judicial offices, since nothing will contribute so much as this to that independent spirit in the judges which must be essential to the faithful performance of so arduous a duty.

The independence of the judges is equally requisite to guard the Constitution and the rights of individuals from the effects of those ill humors, which the arts of designing men, or the influence of particular conjunctures, sometimes disseminate among the people themselves, and which, though they speedily give place to better information, and more deliberate reflection, have a tendency, in the meantime, to occasion dangerous innovations in the government, and serious oppressions of the minor party in the community. Though I trust the friends of the proposed Constitution will never concur with its enemies, in questioning that fundamental principle of republican government, which admits the right of the people to alter or abolish the established Constitution, whenever they find it inconsistent with their happiness, yet it is not to be inferred from this principle, that the representatives of the people, whenever a momentary inclination happens to lay hold of a majority of their constituents, incompatible with the provisions of the existing Constitution, would, on that account, be justifiable in a violation of those provisions; or that the courts would be under a greater obligation to connive at infractions in this shape, than when they had proceeded wholly from the cabals of the representative body. Until the people have, by some solemn and authoritative act, annulled or changed the established form, it is binding upon themselves collectively, as well as individually; and no presumption, or even knowledge, of their sentiments, can warrant their representatives in a departure from it, prior to such an act. But it is easy to see, that it would require an uncommon portion of fortitude in the judges to do their duty as faithful guardians of the Constitution, where legislative invasions of it had been instigated by the major voice of the community.

But it is not with a view to infractions of the Constitution only, that the independence of the judges may be an essential safeguard against the effects of occasional ill humors in the society. These sometimes extend no farther than to the injury of the private rights of particular classes of citizens, by unjust and partial laws. Here also the firmness of the judicial magistracy is of vast importance in mitigating the severity and confining the operation of such laws. It not only serves to moderate the immediate mischiefs of those which may have been passed, but it operates as a check upon the legislative body in passing them; who, perceiving that obstacles to the success of iniquitous intention are to be expected from the scruples of the courts, are in a manner compelled, by the very motives of the injustice they meditate, to qualify their attempts. This is a circumstance calculated to have more influence upon the character of our governments, than but few may be aware of. The benefits of the integrity and moderation of the judiciary have already been felt in more States than one; and though they may have displeased those whose sinister expectations they may have disappointed, they must have commanded the esteem and applause of all the virtuous and disinterested. Considerate men, of every description, ought to prize whatever will tend to beget or fortify that temper in the courts; as no man can be sure that he may not be to-morrow the victim of a spirit of injustice, by which he may be a gainer to-day. Any every man must now feel, that the inevitable tendency of such a spirit is to sap the foundations of public and private confidence, and to introduce in its stead universal distrust and distress.

That inflexible and uniform adherence to the rights of the Constitution, and of individuals, which we perceive to be indispensable in the courts of justice, can certainly not be expected from judges who hold their offices by a temporary commission. Periodical appointments, however regulated, or by whomsoever made, would, in some way or other, be fatal to their necessary independence. If the power of making them was committed either to the Executive or legislature, there would be danger of an improper complaisance to the branch which possessed it; if to

both, there would be an unwillingness to hazard the displeasure of either; if to the people, or to persons chosen by them for the special purpose, there would be too great a disposition to consult popularity, to justify a reliance that nothing would be consulted but the Constitution and the laws.

Hamilton points to yet another reason why lifetime tenure for federal judges will benefit the public: effective judgments rest on a knowledge of judicial precedents and the law, and such knowledge can only be obtained through experience on the bench. A "temporary duration of office," according to Hamilton, would "discourage individuals [of 'fit character'] from quitting a lucrative practice to serve on the bench" and ultimately would "throw the administration of justice into the hands of the less able, and less well qualified."

There is yet a further and a weightier reason for the permanency of the judicial offices, which is deducible from the nature of the qualifications they require. It has been frequently remarked, with great propriety, that a voluminous code of laws is one of the inconveniences necessarily connected with the advantages of a free government. To avoid an arbitrary discretion in the courts, it is indispensable that they should be bound down by strict rules and precedents, which serve to define and point out their duty in every particular case that comes before them; and it will readily be conceived from the variety of controversies which grow out of the folly and wickedness of mankind, that the records of those precedents must unavoidably swell to a very considerable bulk, and must demand long and laborious study to acquire a competent knowledge of them. Hence it is, that there can be but few men in the society who will have sufficient skill in the laws to qualify them for the stations of judges. And making the proper deductions for the ordinary depravity of human nature, the number must be still smaller of those who unite the requisite integrity with the requisite knowledge. These considerations apprise us, that the government can have no great option between fit character; and that a temporary duration in office, which would naturally discourage such characters from quitting a lucrative line of practice to accept a seat on the bench, would have a tendency to throw the administration of justice into hands less able, and less well qualified, to conduct it with utility and dignity. In the present circumstances of this country, and in those in which it is likely to be for a long time to come, the disadvantages on this score would be greater than they may at first sight appear; but it must be confessed, that they are far inferior to those which present themselves under other aspects of the subject.

Upon the whole, there can be no room to doubt that the convention acted wisely in copying from the models of those constitutions which have established good behavior as the tenure of their judicial offices, in point of duration; and that so far from being blamable on this account, their plan would have been inexcusably defective, if it had wanted this important feature of good government. The experience of Great Britain affords an illustrious comment on the excellence of the institution.

Publius
(Alexander Hamilton)

Justices of the U.S. Supreme Court since 1900

Chief Justices

NAME	YEARS OF SERVICE	STATE APP'T FROM	APPOINTING PRESIDENT	AGE AT APP'T	POLITICAL AFFILIATION	EDUCATIONAL BACKGROUND*
Fuller, Melville Weston	1888–1910	Illinois	Cleveland	55	Democrat	Bowdoin College; studied at Harvard Law School
White, Edward Douglass	1910–1921	Louisiana	Taft	65	Democrat	Mount St. Mary's College; Georgetown College (now University)
Taft, William Howard	1921–1930	Connecticut	Harding	64	Republican	Yale; Cincinnati Law School
Hughes, Charles Evans	1930–1941	New York	Hoover	68	Republican	Colgate University; Brown; Columbia Law School
Stone, Harlan Fiske	1941–1946	New York	Roosevelt, F.	69	Republican	Amherst College; Columbia
Vinson, Frederick Moore	1946–1953	Kentucky	Truman	56	Democrat	Centre College
Warren, Earl	1953–1969	California	Eisenhower	62	Republican	University of California, Berkeley
Burger, Warren Earl	1969–1986	Virginia	Nixon	62	Republican	University of Minnesota; St. Paul College of Law (Mitchell College)
Rehnquist, William Hubbs	1986–	Virginia	Reagan	62	Republican	Stanford; Harvard; Stanford University Law School

*SOURCE: Educational background information derived from Elder Witt, *Guide to the U.S. Supreme Court,* 2d ed. (Washington, D.C.: Congressional Quarterly Press, Inc., 1990). Reprinted with the permission of the publisher.

Associated Justices

NAME	YEARS OF SERVICE	STATE APP'T FROM	APPOINTING PRESIDENT	AGE AT APP'T	POLITICAL AFFILIATION	EDUCATIONAL BACKGROUND*
Harlan, John Marshall	1877–1911	Kentucky	Hayes	61	Republican	Centre College; studied law at Transylvania University
Gray, Horace	1882–1902	Massachusetts	Arthur	54	Republican	Harvard College; Harvard Law School
Brewer, David Josiah	1890–1910	Kansas	Harrison	53	Republican	Wesleyan University; Yale; Albany Law School
Brown, Henry Billings	1891–1906	Michigan	Harrison	55	Republican	Yale; studied at Yale Law School and Harvard Law School
Shiras, George, Jr.	1892–1903	Pennsylvania	Harrison	61	Republican	Ohio University; Yale; studied law at Yale and privately
White, Edward Douglass	1894–1910	Louisiana	Cleveland	49	Democrat	Mount St. Mary's College; Georgetown College (now University)
Peckham, Rufus Wheeler	1896–1909	New York	Cleveland	58	Democrat	Read law in father's firm
McKenna, Joseph	1898–1925	California	McKinley	55	Republican	Benicia Collegiate Institute, Law Department
Holmes, Oliver Wendell, Jr.	1902–1932	Massachusetts	Roosevelt, T.	61	Republican	Harvard College; studied law at Harvard Law School

Name	Years of Service	State App't from	Appointing President	Age at App't	Political Affiliation	Educational Background*
Day, William Rufus	1903–1922	Ohio	Roosevelt, T.	54	Republican	University of Michigan; University of Michigan Law School
Moody, William Henry	1906–1910	Massachusetts	Roosevelt, T.	53	Republican	Harvard; Harvard Law School
Lurton, Horace Harmon	1910–1914	Tennessee	Taft	66	Democrat	University of Chicago; Cumberland Law School
Hughes, Charles Evans	1910–1916	New York	Taft	48	Republican	Colgate University; Brown University; Columbia Law School
Van Devanter, Willis	1911–1937	Wyoming	Taft	52	Republican	Indiana Asbury University; University of Cincinnati Law School
Lamar, Joseph Rucker	1911–1916	Georgia	Taft	54	Democrat	University of Georgia; Bethany College; Washington and Lee University
Pitney, Mahlon	1912–1922	New Jersey	Taft	54	Republican	College of New Jersey (Princeton); read law under father
McReynolds, James Clark	1914–1941	Tennessee	Wilson	52	Democrat	Vanderbilt University; University of Virginia
Brandeis, Louis Dembitz	1916–1939	Massachusetts	Wilson	60	Democrat	Harvard Law School
Clarke, John Hessin	1916–1922	Ohio	Wilson	59	Democrat	Western Reserve University; read law under father
Sutherland, George	1922–1938	Utah	Harding	60	Republican	Brigham Young Academy; one year at University of Michigan Law School
Butler, Pierce	1923–1939	Minnesota	Harding	57	Democrat	Carleton College
Sanford, Edward Terry	1923–1930	Tennessee	Harding	58	Republican	University of Tennessee; Harvard; Harvard Law School
Stone, Harlan Fiske	1925–1941	New York	Coolidge	53	Republican	Amherst College; Columbia University Law School
Roberts, Owen Josephus	1930–1945	Pennsylvania	Hoover	55	Republican	University of Pennsylvania; University of Pennsylvania Law School
Cardozo, Benjamin Nathan	1932–1938	New York	Hoover	62	Democrat	Columbia University; two years at Columbia Law School
Black, Hugo Lafayette	1937–1971	Alabama	Roosevelt, F.	51	Democrat	Birmingham Medical College; University of Alabama Law School
Reed, Stanley Forman	1938–1957	Kentucky	Roosevelt, F.	54	Democrat	Kentucky Wesleyan University; Foreman Yale; studied law at University of Virginia and Columbia University; University of Paris
Frankfurter, Felix	1939–1962	Massachusetts	Roosevelt, F.	57	Independent	College of the City of New York; Harvard Law School
Douglas, William Orville	1939–1975	Connecticut	Roosevelt, F.	41	Democrat	Whitman College; Columbia University Law School
Murphy, Frank	1940–1949	Michigan	Roosevelt, F.	50	Democrat	University of Michigan; Lincoln's Inn, London; Trinity College
Byrnes, James Francis	1941–1942	South Carolina	Roosevelt, F.	62	Democrat	Read law privately

Associate Justices (continued)

Name	Years of Service	State App't From	Appointing President	Age at App't	Political Affiliation	Educational Background*
Jackson, Robert Houghwout	1941–1954	New York	Roosevelt, F.	49	Democrat	Albany Law School
Rutledge, Wiley Blount	1943–1949	Iowa	Roosevelt, F.	49	Democrat	University of Wisconsin; University of Colorado
Burton, Harold Hitz	1945–1958	Ohio	Truman	57	Republican	Bowdoin College; Harvard University Law School
Clark, Thomas Campbell	1949–1967	Texas	Truman	50	Democrat	University of Texas
Minton, Sherman	1949–1956	Indiana	Truman	59	Democrat	Indiana University College of Law; Yale Law School
Harlan, John Marshall	1955–1971	New York	Eisenhower	56	Republican	Princeton; Oxford University; New York Law School
Brennan, William J., Jr.	1956–1990	New Jersey	Eisenhower	50	Democrat	University of Pennsylvania; Harvard Law School
Whittaker, Charles Evans	1957–1962	Missouri	Eisenhower	56	Republican	University of Kansas City Law School
Stewart, Potter	1958–1981	Ohio	Eisenhower	43	Republican	Yale; Yale Law School
White, Byron Raymond	1962–1993	Colorado	Kennedy	45	Democrat	University of Colorado; Oxford University; Yale Law School
Goldberg, Arthur Joseph	1962–1965	Illinois	Kennedy	54	Democrat	Northwestern University
Fortas, Abe	1965–1969	Tennessee	Johnson, L.	55	Democrat	Southwestern College; Yale Law School
Marshall, Thurgood	1967–1991	New York	Johnson, L.	59	Democrat	Lincoln University; Howard University Law School
Blackmun, Harry A.	1970–1994	Minnesota	Nixon	62	Republican	Harvard; Harvard Law School
Powell, Lewis F., Jr.	1972–1987	Virginia	Nixon	65	Democrat	Washington and Lee University; Washington and Lee University Law School; Harvard Law School
Rehnquist, William H.	1972–1986	Arizona	Nixon	48	Republican	Stanford; Harvard; Stanford University Law School
Stevens, John Paul	1975–	Illinois	Ford	55	Republican	University of Colorado; Northwestern University Law School
O'Connor, Sandra Day	1981–	Arizona	Reagan	51	Republican	Stanford; Stanford University Law School
Scalia, Antonin	1986–	Virginia	Reagan	50	Republican	Georgetown University; Harvard Law School
Kennedy, Anthony M.	1988–	California	Reagan	52	Republican	Stanford; London School of Economics; Harvard Law School
Souter, David Hackett	1990–	New Hampshire	Bush	51	Republican	Harvard; Oxford University
Thomas, Clarence	1991–	District of Columbia	Bush	43	Republican	Holy Cross College; Yale Law School
Ginsburg, Ruth Bader	1993–	District of Columbia	Clinton	60	Democrat	Cornell University; Columbia Law School
Breyer, Stephen, G.	1994–	Massachusetts	Clinton	55	Democrat	Stanford University; Oxford University; Harvard Law School

Party Control of Congress since 1900

CONGRESS	YEARS	PRESIDENT	MAJORITY PARTY IN HOUSE	MAJORITY PARTY IN SENATE
57th	1901–1903	McKinley/T. Roosevelt	Republican	Republican
58th	1903–1905	T. Roosevelt	Republican	Republican
59th	1905–1907	T. Roosevelt	Republican	Republican
60th	1907–1909	T. Roosevelt	Republican	Republican
61st	1909–1911	Taft	Republican	Republican
62d	1911–1913	Taft	Democratic	Republican
63d	1913–1915	Wilson	Democratic	Democratic
64th	1915–1917	Wilson	Democratic	Democratic
65th	1917–1919	Wilson	Democratic	Democratic
66th	1919–1921	Wilson	Republican	Republican
67th	1921–1923	Harding	Republican	Republican
68th	1923–1925	Harding/Coolidge	Republican	Republican
69th	1925–1927	Coolidge	Republican	Republican
70th	1927–1929	Coolidge	Republican	Republican
71st	1929–1931	Hoover	Republican	Republican
72d	1931–1933	Hoover	Democratic	Republican
73d	1933–1935	F. Roosevelt	Democratic	Democratic
74th	1935–1937	F. Roosevelt	Democratic	Democratic
75th	1937–1939	F. Roosevelt	Democratic	Democratic
76th	1939–1941	F. Roosevelt	Democratic	Democratic
77th	1941–1943	F. Roosevelt	Democratic	Democratic
78th	1943–1945	F. Roosevelt	Democratic	Democratic
79th	1945–1947	F. Roosevelt/Truman	Democratic	Democratic
80th	1947–1949	Truman	Republican	Democratic
81st	1949–1951	Truman	Democratic	Democratic
82d	1951–1953	Truman	Democratic	Democratic
83d	1953–1955	Eisenhower	Republican	Republican
84th	1955–1957	Eisenhower	Democratic	Democratic
85th	1957–1959	Eisenhower	Democratic	Democratic
86th	1959–1961	Eisenhower	Democratic	Democratic
87th	1961–1963	Kennedy	Democratic	Democratic
88th	1963–1965	Kennedy/Johnson	Democratic	Democratic
89th	1965–1967	Johnson	Democratic	Democratic
90th	1967–1969	Johnson	Democratic	Democratic
91st	1969–1971	Nixon	Democratic	Democratic
92d	1971–1973	Nixon	Democratic	Democratic
93d	1973–1975	Nixon/Ford	Democratic	Democratic
94th	1975–1977	Ford	Democratic	Democratic
95th	1977–1979	Carter	Democratic	Democratic
96th	1979–1981	Carter	Democratic	Democratic
97th	1981–1983	Reagan	Democratic	Republican
98th	1983–1985	Reagan	Democratic	Republican
99th	1985–1987	Reagan	Democratic	Republican
100th	1987–1989	Reagan	Democratic	Democratic
101st	1989–1991	G. H. W. Bush	Democratic	Democratic
102d	1991–1993	G. H. W. Bush	Democratic	Democratic
103d	1993–1995	Clinton	Democratic	Democratic
104th	1995–1997	Clinton	Republican	Republican
105th	1997–1999	Clinton	Republican	Republican
106th	1999–2001	Clinton	Republican	Republican
107th	2001–2003	G. W. Bush	Republican	Democratic
108th	2003–2005	G. W. Bush	Republican	Republican
109th	2005–2007	G. W. Bush	Republican	Republican

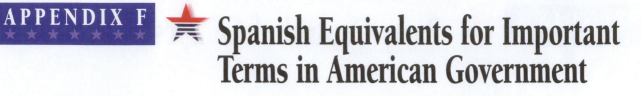
Acid Rain: Lluvia Acida
Acquisitive Model: Modelo Adquisitivo
Actionable: Procesable, Enjuiciable
Action-reaction Syndrome: Sídrome de Acción y Reacción
Actual Malice: Malicia Expresa
Administrative Agency: Agencia Administrativa
Advice and Consent: Consejo y Consentimiento
Affirmative Action: Acción Afirmativa
Affirm: Afirmar
Agenda Setting: Agenda Establecida
Aid to Families with Dependent Children (AFDC): Ayuda para Familias con Niños Dependientes
Amicus Curiae **Brief:** Tercer persona o grupo no involucrado en el caso, admitido en un juicio para hacer valer el intéres público o el de un grupo social importante.
Anarchy: Anarquía
Anti-Federalists: Anti-Federalistas
Appellate Court: Corte de Apelación
Appointment Power: Poder de Apuntamiento
Appropriation: Apropiación
Aristocracy: Aristocracia
Attentive Public: Público Atento
Australian Ballot: Voto Australiano
Authority: Autoridad
Authorization: Autorización

Bad-Tendency Rule: Regla de Tendencia-mala
"Beauty Contest": Concurso de Belleza
Bicameralism: Bicameralismo

Bicameral Legislature: Legislatura Bicameral
Bill of Rights: Declaración de Derechos
Blanket Primary: Primaria Comprensiva
Block Grants: Concesiones de Bloque
Bureaucracy: Burocracia
Busing: Transporte público

Cabinet: Gabinete, Consejo de Ministros
Cabinet Department: Departamento del Gabinete
Cadre: El núcleo de activistas de partidos políticos encargados de cumplir las funciones importantes de los partidos políticos americanos.
Canvassing Board: Consejo encargado con la encuesta de una violación.
Capture: Captura, toma
Casework: Trabajo de Caso
Categorical Grants-in-Aid: Concesiones Categóricas de Ayuda
Caucus: Reunión de Dirigentes
Challenge: Reto
Checks and Balances: Chequeos y Equilibrio
Chief Diplomat: Jefe Diplomático
Chief Executive: Jefe Ejecutivo
Chief Legislator: Jefe Legislador
Chief of Staff: Jefe de Personal
Chief of State: Jefe de Estado
Civil Law: Derecho Civil
Civil Liberties: Libertades Civiles
Civil Rights: Derechos Civiles
Civil Service: Servicio Civil
Civil Service Commission: Comisión de Servicio Civil
Class-Action Suit: Demanda en representación de un grupo o clase.

Class Politics: Política de Clase
Clear and Present Danger Test: Prueba de Peligro Claro y Presente
Climate Control: Control de Clima
Closed Primary: Primaria Cerrada
Cloture: Cierre al voto
Coattail Effect: Effecto de Cola de Chaqueta
Cold War: Guerra Fría
Commander in Chief: Comandante en Jefe
Commerce Clause: Clausula de Comercio
Commercial Speech: Discurso Comercial
Common Law: Ley Común, Derecho Consuetudinario
Comparable Worth: Valor Comparable
Compliance: De acuerdo
Concurrent Majority: Mayoría Concurrente
Concurring Opinion: Opinión Concurrente
Confederal System: Sistema Confederal
Confederation: Confederación
Conference Committee: Comité de Conferencia
Consensus: Concenso
Consent of the People: Consentimiento de la Gente
Conservatism: Calidad de Conservador
Conservative Coalition: Coalición Conservadora
Consolidation: Consolidación
Constant Dollars: Dólares Constantes
Constitutional Initiative: Iniciativa Constitucional
Constitutional Power: Poder Constitucional

Containment: Contenimiento
Continuing Resolution: Resolució Contínua
Cooley's Rule: Régla de Cooley
Cooperative Federalism: Federalismo Cooperativo
Corrupt Practices Acts: Leyes Contra Acciones Corruptas
Council of Economic Advisers (CEA): Consejo de Asesores Económicos
Council of Government (COG): Consejo de Gobierno
County: Condado
Credentials Committee: Comité de Credenciales
Criminal Law: Ley Criminal

De Facto **Segregation:** Segregación de Hecho
De Jure **Segregation:** Segregación Cotidiana
Defamation of Character: Defamación de Carácter
Democracy: Democracia
Democratic Party: Partido Democratico
Dillon's Rule: Régla de Dillon
Diplomacy: Diplomácia
Direct Democracy: Democracia Directa
Direct Primary: Primaria Directa
Direct Technique: Técnica Directa
Discharge Petition: Petición de Descargo
Dissenting Opinion: Opinión Disidente
Divisive Opinion: Opinión Divisiva
Domestic Policy: Principio Político Doméstico
Dual Citizenship: Ciudadanía Dual
Dual Federalism: Federalismo Dual
Détente: No Spanish equivalent

Economic Aid: Ayuda Económica
Economic Regulation: Regulación Económica
Elastic Clause, or Necessary and Proper Clause: Cláusula Flexible o Cláusula Propia Necesaria

Elector: Elector
Electoral College: Colegio Electoral
Electronic Media: Media Electronica
Elite: Elite (el selecto)
Elite Theory: Teoría Elitista (de lo selecto)
Emergency Power: Poder de Emergencia
Enumerated Power: Poder Enumerado
Environmental Impact Statement (EIS): Afirmación de Impacto Ambiental
Equality: Igualdad
Equalization: Igualación
Equal Employment Opportunity Commission (EEOC): Comisión de Igualdad de Oportunidad en el Empleo
Era of Good Feeling: Era de Buen Sentimiento
Era of Personal Politics: Era de Política Personal
Establishment Clause: Cláusula de Establecimiento
Euthanasia: Eutanasia
Exclusionary Rule: Regla de Exclusión
Executive Agreement: Acuerdo Ejecutivo
Executive Budget: Presupuesto Ejecutivo
Executive Office of the President (EOP): Oficina Ejecutiva del Presidente
Executive Order: Orden Ejecutivo
Executive Privilege: Privilegio Ejecutivo
Expressed Power: Poder Expresado
Extradite: Entregar por Extradición

Faction: Facción
Fairness Doctrine: Doctrina de Justicia
Fall Review: Revision de Otoño
Federalist: Federalista
Federal Mandate: Mandato Federal
Federal Open Market Committee (FOMC): Comité Federal de Libre Mercado

Federal Register: Registro Federal
Federal System: Sistema Federal
Federalists: Federalistas
Fighting Words: Palabras de Provocación
Filibuster: Obstrucción de iniciativas de ley
Fireside Chat: Charla de Hogar
First Budget Resolution: Resolució Primera Presupuesta
First Continental Congress: Primér Congreso Continental
Fiscal Policy: Politico Fiscal
Fiscal Year (FY): Año Fiscal
Fluidity: Fluidez
Food Stamps: Estampillas para Comida
Foreign Policy: Politica Extranjera
Foreign Policy Process: Proceso de Politica Extranjera
Franking: Franqueando
Fraternity: Fraternidad
Free Exercise Clause: Cláusula de Ejercicio Libre
Full Faith and Credit Clause: Cláusula de Completa Fé y Crédito
Functional Consolidation: Consolidación Funcional
Gag Order: Orden de Silencio
Garbage Can Model: Modelo Bote de Basura
Gender Gap: Brecha de Género
General Law City: Regla General Urbana
General Sales Tax: Impuesto General de Ventas
Generational Effect: Efecto Generacional
Gerrymandering: División arbitraria de los distritos electorales con fines políticos.
Government: Gobierno
Government Corporation: Corporación Gubernamental
Government in the Sunshine Act: Gobierno en la acta: Luz del Sol
Grandfather Clause: Clausula del Abuelo
Grand Jury: Gran Jurado
Great Compromise: Grán Acuerdo de Negociación

Hatch Act (Political Activities Act): Acta Hatch (acta de actividades politicas)
Hecklers' Veto: Veto de Abuchamiento
Home Rule City: Regla Urbana
Horizontal Federalism: Federalismo Horizontal
Hyperpluralism: Hiperpluralismo

Ideologue: Ideólogo
Ideology: Ideología
Image Building: Construcción de Imágen
Impeachment: Acción Penal Contra un Funcionario Público
Inalienable Rights: Derechos Inalienables
Income Transfer: Transferencia de Ingresos
Incorporation Theory: Teoría de Incorporación
Independent: Independiente
Independent Candidate: Candidato Independiente
Independent Executive Agency: Agencia Ejecutiva Independiente
Independent Regulatory Agency: Agencia Regulatoria Independiente
Indirect Technique: Técnica Indirecta
Inherent Power: Poder Inherente
Initiative: Iniciativa
Injunction: Injunción, Prohibición Judicial
Institution: Institución
Instructed Delegate: Delegado con Instrucciones
Intelligence Community: Comunidad de Inteligencia
Intensity: Intensidad
Interest Group: Grupo de Interés
Interposition: Interposición
Interstate Compact: Compacto Interestatal
In-Kind Subsidy: Subsidio de Clase
Iron Curtain: Cortina de Acero
Iron Triangle: Triágulo de Acero
Isolationist Foreign Policy: Politica Extranjera de Aislamiento
Issue Voting: Voto Temático
Item Veto: Artículo de Veto

Jim Crow Laws: No Spanish equivalent.
Joint Committee: Comité Mancomunado
Judicial Activism: Activismo Judicial
Judicial Implementation: Implementacion Judicial
Judicial Restraint: Restricción Judicial
Judicial Review: Revisión Judicial
Jurisdiction: Jurisdicción
Justiciable Dispute: Disputa Judiciaria
Justiciable Question: Pregunta Justiciable

Keynesian Economics: Economía Keynesiana
Kitchen Cabinet: Gabinete de Cocina

Labor Movement: Movimiento Laboral
Latent Public Opinion: Opinión Pública Latente
Lawmaking: Hacedores de Ley
Legislative History: Historia Legislativa
Legislative Initiative: Iniciativa de legislación
Legislative Veto: Veto Legislativo
Legislature: Legislatura
Legitimacy: Legitimidad
Libel: Libelo, Difamación Escrita
Liberalism: Liberalismo
Liberty: Libertad
Limited Government: Gobierno Limitado
Line Organization: Organización de Linea
Literacy Test: Exámen de alfabetización
Litigate: Litigar
Lobbying: Cabildeo
Logrolling: Práctica legislativa que consiste en incluir en un mismo proyecto de ley temas de diversa ídole.
Loophole: Hueco Legal, escapatoria

Madisonian Model: Modelo Madisónico

Majority: Mayoría
Majority Floor Leader: Líder Mayoritario de Piso
Majority Leader of the House: Líder Mayoritario de la Casa
Majority Opinion: Opinión Mayoritaria
Majority Rule: Regla de Mayoría
Managed News: Noticias Manipuladas
Mandatory Retirement: Retiro Mandatorio
Matching Funds: Fondos Combinados
Material Incentive: Incentivo Material
Media: Media
Media Access: Acceso de Media
Merit System: Sistema de Mérito
Military-Industrial Complex: Complejo Industriomilitar
Minority Floor Leader: Líder Minoritario de Piso
Minority Leader of the House: Líder Minorial del Cuerpo Legislativo
Monetary Policy: Politica Monetaria
Monopolistic Model: Modelo Monopólico
Monroe Doctrine: Doctrina Monroe
Moral Idealism: Idealismo Moral
Municipal Home Rule: Regla Municipal

Narrowcasting: Mensaje Dirigído
National Committee: Comité Nacional
National Convention: Convención Nacional
National Politics: Politica Nacional
National Security Council (NSC): Concilio de Seguridad Nacional
National Security Policy: Politica de Seguridad Nacional
Natural Aristocracy: Aristocracia Natural
Natural Rights: Derechos Naturales
Necessaries: Necesidades

Negative Constituents: Constituyentes Negativos

New England Town: Pueblo de Nueva Inglaterra

New Federalism: Federalismo Nuevo

Nullification: Nulidad, Anulación

Office-Block, or Massachusetts, Ballot: Cuadro-Oficina, o Massachusetts, Voto

Office of Management and Budget (OMB): Oficina de Administració y Presupuesto

Oligarchy: Oligarquía

Ombudsman: Funcionario que representa al ciudadano ante el gobierno.

Open Primary: Primaria Abierta

Opinion: Opinión

Opinion Leader: Líder de Opinión

Opinion Poll: Encuesta, Conjunto de Opinión

Oral Arguments: Argumentos Orales

Oversight: Inadvertencia, Omisión

Paid-for Political Announcement: Anuncios Politicos Pagados

Pardon: Perdón

Party-Column, or Indiana, Ballot: Partido-Columna, o Indiana, Voto

Party Identification: Identificación de Partido

Party Identifier: Identificador de Partido

Party-in-Electorate: Partido Electoral

Party-in-Government: Partido en Gobierno

Party Organization: Organización de Partido

Party Platform: Plataforma de Partido

Patronage: Patrocinio

Peer Group: Grupo de Contemporáneos

Pendleton Act (Civil Service Reform Act): Acta Pendleton (Acta de Reforma al Servicio Civil)

Personal Attack Rule: Regla de Ataque Personal

Petit Jury: Jurado Ordinario

Pluralism: Pluralismo

Plurality: Pluralidad

Pocket Veto: Veto de Bolsillo

Police Power: Poder Policiaco

Policy Trade-Offs: Intercambio de Politicas

Political Action Committee (PAC): Comité de Acción Política

Political Consultant: Consultante Político

Political Culture: Cultura Politica

Political Party: Partido Político

Political Question: Pregunta Politica

Political Realism: Realismo Político

Political Socialization: Socialización Politica

Political Tolerance: Tolerancia Política

Political Trust: Confianza Política

Politico: Político

Politics: Politica

Poll Tax: Impuesto sobre el sufragio

Poll Watcher: Observador de Encuesta

Popular Sovereignty: Soberanía Popular

Power: Poder

Precedent: Precedente

Preferred-Position Test: Prueba de Posición Preferida

Presidential Primary: Primaria Presidencial

President Pro Tempore: Presidente Provisoriamente

Press Secretary: Secretaría de Prensa

Prior Restraint: Restricción Anterior

Privileges and Immunities: Privilégios e Imunidades

Privitization, or Contracting Out: Privatización

Property: Propiedad

Property Tax: Impuesto de Propiedad

Public Agenda: Agenda Pública

Public Debt Financing: Financiamiento de Deuda Pública

Public Debt, or National Debt: Deuda Pública o Nacional

Public Interest: Interes Público

Public Opinion: Opinión Pública

Purposive Incentive: Incentivo de Propósito

Ratification: Ratificación

Rational Ignorance Effect: Effecto de Ignorancia Racional

Reapportionment: Redistribución

Recall: Suspender

Recognition Power: Poder de Reconocimiento

Recycling: Reciclaje

Redistricting: Redistrictificación

Referendum: Referédum

Registration: Registración

Regressive Tax: Impuestos Regresivos

Relevance: Pertinencia

Remand: Reenviar

Representation: Representación

Representative Assembly: Asamblea Representativa

Representative Democracy: Democracia Representativa

Reprieve: Trequa, Suspensión

Republic: República

Republican Party: Partido Republicano

Resulting Powers: Poderes Resultados

Reverse: Cambiarse a lo contrario

Reverse Discrimination: Discriminación Reversiva

Rules Committee: Comité Regulador

Rule of Four: Regla de Cuatro

Run-Off Primary: Primaria Residual

Safe Seat: Asiento Seguro

Sampling Error: Error de Encuesta

Secession: Secesión

Second Budget Resolution: Resolución Segunda Presupuestal

Second Continental Congress: Segundo Congreso Continental

Sectional Politics: Política Seccional

Segregation: Segregación

Selectperson: Persona Selecta

Select Committee: Comité Selecto

Senatorial Courtesy: Cortesia Senatorial

Seniority System: Sistema Señiorial

Separate-but-Equal Doctrine: Separados pero iguales

Separation of Powers: Separación de Poderes

Service Sector: Sector de Servicio

Sexual Harassment: Acosamiento Sexual

Sex Discrimination: Discriminacion Sexual

Slander: Difamación Oral, Calumnia

Sliding-Scale Test: Prueba Escalonada

Social Movement: Movimiento Social

Social Security: Seguridad Social

Socioeconomic Status: Estado Socioeconómico

Solidary Incentive: Incentivo de Solideridad

Solid South: Súr Sólido

Sound Bite: Mordida de Sonido

Soviet Bloc: Bloque Soviético

Speaker of the House: Vocero de la Casa

Spin: Girar/Giro

Spin Doctor: Doctor en Giro

Spin-Off Party: Partido Estático

Spoils System: Sistema de Despojos

Spring Review: Revisión de Primavera

Stare Decisis: El principio característico del ley comú por el cual los precedentes jurisprudenciales tienen fuerza obligatoria, no sólo entre las partes, sino tambien para casos sucesivos análogos.

Stability: Estabilidad

Standing Committee: Comité de Sostenimiento

State Central Committee: Comité Central del Estado

State: Estado

State of the Union Message:

Mensaje Sobre el Estado de la Unión

Statutory Power: Poder Estatorial

Strategic Arms Limitation Treaty (SALT I): Tratado de Limitación de Armas Estratégicas

Subpoena: Orden de Testificación

Subsidy: Subsidio

Suffrage: Sufrágio

Sunset Legislation: Legislación Sunset

Superdelegate: Líder de partido o oficial elegido quien tiene el derecho de votar.

Supplemental Security Income (SSI): Ingresos de Seguridad Suplementaria

Supremacy Clause: Cláusula de Supremacia

Supremacy Doctrine: Doctrina de Supremacia

Symbolic Speech: Discurso Simbólico

Technical Assistance: Asistencia Técnica

Third Party: Tercer Partido

Third-Party Candidate: Candidato de Tercer Partido

Ticket Splitting: División de Boletos

Totalitarian Regime: Régimen Totalitario

Town Manager System: Sistema de Administrador Municipal

Town Meeting: Junta Municipal

Township: Municipio

Tracking Poll: Seguimiento de Encuesta

Trial Court: Tribunal de Primera

Truman Doctrine: Doctrina Truman

Trustee: Depositario

Twelfth Amendment: Doceava Enmienda

Twenty-fifth Amendment: Veinticincoava Enmienda

Two-Party System: Sistema de Dos Partidos

Unanimous Opinion: Opinión Unánime

Underground Economy: Economía Subterráea

Unicameral Legislature: Legislatura Unicameral

Unincorporated Area: Area no Incorporada

Unit Rule: Regla de Unidad

Unitary System: Sistema Unitario

Universal Suffrage: Sufragio Universal

U.S. Treasury Bond: Bono de la Tesoreria de E.U.A.

Veto Message: Comunicado de Veto

Voter Turnout: Renaimiento de Votantes

War Powers Act: Acta de Poderes de Guerra

Washington Community: Comunidad de Washington

Weberian Model: Modelo Weberiano

Whip: Látigo

Whistleblower: Privatización o Contratista

White House Office: Oficina de la Casa Blanca

White House Press Corps: Cuerpo de Prensa de la Casa Blanca

White Primary: Sufragio en Elección Primaria/Blancos Solamente

Writ of *Certiorari*: Prueba de certeza; orden emitida por el tribunal de apelaciones para que el tribunal inferior dé lugar a la apelación.

Writ of *Habeas Corpus*: Prueba de Evidencia Concreta

Writ of *Mandamus*: Un mandato por la corte para que un acto se lleve a cabo.

Yellow Journalism: Amarillismo Periodístico

GLOSSARY

A

Acquisitive Model A model of bureaucracy that views top level bureaucrats as seeking constantly to expand the size of their budgets and the staffs of their departments or agencies so as to gain greater power and influence in the public sector.

Actual Malice In libel cases, either knowledge of a defamatory statement's falsity or a reckless disregard for the truth.

Administrative Agency A federal, state, or local government unit established to perform a specific function. Administrative agencies are created and authorized by legislative bodies to administer and enforce specific laws.

Advice and Consent The power vested in the U.S. Senate by the Constitution (Article II, Section 2) to give its advice and consent to the president on treaties and presidential appointments.

Affirm To declare that a court ruling is valid and must stand.

Affirmative Action A policy in educational admissions or job hiring that gives special consideration or compensatory treatment to traditionally disadvantaged groups in an effort to overcome present effects of past discrimination.

Agenda Setting Determining which public-policy questions will be debated or considered.

Amicus Curiae Brief A brief (a document containing a legal argument supporting a desired outcome in a particular case) filed by a third party, or *amicus curiae* (Latin for "friend of the court"), who is not directly involved in the litigation but who has an interest in the outcome of the case.

Anti-Federalist An individual who opposed the ratification of the new Constitution in 1787. The Anti-Federalists were opposed to a strong central government.

Appellate Court A court having jurisdiction to review cases and issues that were originally tried in lower courts.

Appointment Power The authority vested in the president to fill a government office or position. Positions filled by presidential appointment include those in the executive branch and the federal judiciary, commissioned officers in the armed forces, and members of the independent regulatory commissions.

Appropriation The passage, by Congress, of a spending bill, specifying the amount of authorized funds that actually will be allocated for an agency's use.

Aristocracy Rule by the "best"; in reality, rule by an upper class.

Arraignment The first act in a criminal proceeding, in which the defendant is brought before a court to hear the charges against him or her and to enter a plea of guilty or not guilty.

Attentive Public That portion of the general public that pays attention to policy issues.

Australian Ballot A secret ballot prepared, distributed, and tabulated by government officials at public expense. Since 1888, all states have used the Australian ballot rather than an open, public ballot.

Authoritarianism A type of regime in which only the government itself is fully controlled by the ruler. Social and economic institutions exist that are not under the government's control. Contrast *totalitarianism*.

Authority The right and power of a government or other entity to enforce its decisions and compel obedience.

Authorization A formal declaration by a legislative committee that a certain amount of funding may be available to an agency. Some authorizations terminate in a year; others are renewable automatically without further congressional action.

Automatic, or Built-In, Stabilizers Certain federal programs that cause changes in national income during economic fluctuations without the action of Congress and the president. Examples are the federal income tax system and unemployment compensation.

B

Balance of Trade The difference between the value of a nation's exports of goods and its imports of goods.

"Beauty Contest" A presidential primary in which contending candidates compete for popular votes but the results have little or no impact on the selection of delegates to the national convention.

Bias An inclination or a preference that interferes with impartial judgment.

Bicameral Legislature A legislature made up of two chambers, or parts. The U.S. Congress, composed of the House of Representatives and the Senate, is a bicameral legislature.

Bicameralism The division of a legislature into two separate assemblies.

Block Grants Federal programs that provide funds to state and local governments for general functional areas, such as criminal justice or mental-health programs.

Boycott A form of pressure or protest—an organized refusal to purchase a particular product or deal with a particular business.

Broad Construction A judicial philosophy that looks to the context and purpose of a law when making an interpretation.

Budget Deficit Government expenditures that exceed receipts.

Bureaucracy A large organization that is structured hierarchically to carry out specific functions.

Busing In the context of civil rights, the transportation of public school students from areas where they live to schools in other areas to eliminate school segregation based on residential patterns.

C

Cabinet An advisory group selected by the president to aid in decision making. The cabinet includes the heads of fifteen executive departments and others named by the president. Depending on the president, the cabinet may be highly influential or relatively insignificant in its advisory role.

Cabinet Department One of the fifteen departments of the executive branch (State, Treasury, Defense, Justice, Interior, Agriculture, Commerce, Labor, Health and Human Services, Homeland Security, Housing and Urban Development, Education, Energy, Transportation, and Veterans Affairs).

Capitalism An economic system characterized by the private ownership of wealth-creating assets and also by free markets and freedom of contract.

Capture   The act of gaining direct or indirect control over agency personnel and decision makers by the industry that is being regulated.

Case Law   The rules and principles announced in court decisions. Case law includes judicial interpretations of common law principles and doctrines as well as interpretations of constitutional law, statutory law, and administrative law.

Casework   Personal work for constituents by members of Congress.

Categorical Grants   Federal grants-in-aid to states or local governments that are for very specific programs or projects.

Caucus   A closed meeting of party leaders to select party candidates or to decide on policy; also, a meeting of party members designed to select candidates and propose policies.

Charter   A document issued by a government that grants to a person, a group of persons, or a corporation the right to carry on one or more specific activities. A state government can grant a charter to a municipality.

Checks and Balances   A major principle of the American government system whereby each branch of the government exercises a check on the actions of the others.

Chief Diplomat   The role of the president in recognizing foreign governments, making treaties, and making executive agreements.

Chief Executive   The role of the president as head of the executive branch of the government.

Chief Legislator   The role of the president in influencing the making of laws.

Chief of Staff   The person who is named to direct the White House Office and advise the president.

Civil Disobedience   A nonviolent, public refusal to obey allegedly unjust laws.

Civil Law   The law regulating conduct between private persons over noncriminal matters. Under civil law, the government provides the forum for the settlement of disputes between private parties in such matters as contracts, domestic relations, and business relations.

Civil Liberties   Those personal freedoms that are protected for all individuals and that generally deal with individual freedom. Civil liberties typically involve restraining the government's actions against individuals.

Civil Rights   Generally, all rights rooted in the Fourteenth Amendment's guarantee of equal protection under the law.

Civil Service   A collective term for the body of employees working for the government. Generally, the term is understood to apply to all those who gain government employment through a merit system.

Civil Service Commission   The initial central personnel agency of the national government; created in 1883.

Class-Action Suit   A lawsuit filed by an individual seeking damages for "all persons similarly situated."

Clear and Present Danger Test   The test proposed by Justice Oliver Wendell Holmes for determining when government may restrict free speech. Restrictions are permissible, he argued, only when speech presents a "clear and present danger" to the public order.

Climate Control   The use of public relations techniques to create favorable public opinion toward an interest group, industry, or corporation.

Closed Primary   A type of primary in which the voter is limited to choosing candidates of the party of which he or she is a member.

Coattail Effect   The influence of a popular candidate on the electoral success of other candidates on the same party ticket. The effect is increased by the party-column ballot, which encourages straight-ticket voting.

Cold War   The ideological, political, and economic impasse that existed between the United States and the Soviet Union following World War II.

Commander in Chief   The role of the president as supreme commander of the military forces of the United States and of the state National Guard units when they are called into federal service.

Commerce Clause   The section of the Constitution in which Congress is given the power to regulate trade among the states and with foreign countries.

Commercial Speech   Advertising statements, which increasingly have been given First Amendment protection.

Common Law   Judge-made law that originated in England from decisions shaped according to prevailing customs. Decisions were applied to similar situations and thus gradually became common to the nation.

Communism   A revolutionary variant of socialism that favors a partisan (and often totalitarian) dictatorship, government control of all enterprises, and the replacement of free markets by central planning.

Concurrent Powers   Powers held jointly by the national and state governments.

Concurring Opinion   A separate opinion prepared by a judge who supports the decision of the majority of the court but who wants to make or clarify a particular point or to voice disapproval of the grounds on which the decision was made.

Confederal System   A system of government consisting of a league of independent states, each having essentially sovereign powers. The central government created by such a league has only limited powers over the states.

Confederation   A political system in which states or regional governments retain ultimate authority except for those powers they expressly delegate to a central government. A voluntary association of independent states, in which the member states agree to limited restraints on their freedom of action.

Conference Committee   A special joint committee appointed to reconcile differences when bills pass the two chambers of Congress in different forms.

Consensus   General agreement among the citizenry on an issue.

Consent of the People   The idea that governments and laws derive their legitimacy from the consent of the governed.

Conservatism   A set of beliefs that includes a limited role for the national government in helping individuals, support for traditional values and lifestyles, and a cautious response to change.

Conservative Coalition   An alliance of Republicans and southern Democrats in the House or the Senate to oppose liberal legislation and support conservative legislation.

Consolidation   The union of two or more governmental units to form a single unit.

Constituent   One of the people represented by a legislator or other elected or appointed official.

Constitutional Initiative   An electoral device whereby citizens can propose a constitutional amendment through petitions signed by the required number of registered voters.

Constitutional Power   A power vested in the president by Article II of the Constitution.

Consumer Price Index (CPI)   A measure of the change in price over time of a specific group of goods and services used by the average household.

Containment   A U.S. diplomatic policy adopted by the Truman administration to "build situations of strength" around the globe to contain Communist power within its existing boundaries.

Continuing Resolution   A temporary law that Congress passes when an appropriations bill has not been decided by the beginning of the new fiscal year on October 1.

Cooley's Rule   The view that cities should be able to govern themselves, presented in an 1871 Michigan decision by Judge Thomas Cooley.

Cooperative Federalism   The theory that the states and the national government should cooperate in solving problems.

Corrupt Practices Acts   A series of acts passed by Congress in an attempt to limit and regulate the size and sources of contributions and expenditures in political campaigns.

Council of Governments (COG)   A voluntary organization of counties and municipalities concerned with area-wide problems.

County   The chief governmental unit set up by the state to administer state law and business at the local level. Counties are drawn up by area, rather than by rural or urban criteria.

Credentials Committee   A committee used by political parties at their national conventions to determine which delegates may participate. The committee inspects the claim of each prospective delegate to be seated as a legitimate representative of his or her state.

Criminal Law   The law that defines crimes and provides punishment for violations. In criminal cases, the government is the prosecutor because crimes are against the public order.

Current Account Balance A wider concept than the balance of trade. The current account balance includes the balance of trade in services, unilateral transfers, and other items.

D

***De Facto* Segregation** Racial segregation that occurs because of past social and economic conditions and residential patterns.

***De Jure* Segregation** Racial segregation that occurs because of laws or administrative decisions by public agencies.

Dealignment A decline in party loyalties that reduces long-term party commitment.

Defamation of Character Wrongfully hurting a person's good reputation. The law has imposed a general duty on all persons to refrain from making false, defamatory statements about others.

Defense Policy A subset of national security policy that generally refers to the set of policies that direct the scale and size of the U.S. armed forces.

Democracy A system of government in which ultimate political authority is vested in the people. Derived from the Greek words *demos* ("the people") and *kratos* ("authority").

Democratic Party One of the two major American political parties that evolved out of the Republican Party of Thomas Jefferson.

Democratic Republic A republic in which representatives elected by the people make and enforce laws and policies.

Détente A French word meaning a relaxation of tensions. The term characterizes U.S.–Soviet policy as it developed under President Richard Nixon and Secretary of State Henry Kissinger. Détente stressed direct cooperative dealings with Cold War rivals but avoided ideological accommodation.

Devolution The transfer of powers from a national or central government to a state or local government.

Dillon's Rule The narrowest possible interpretation of the legal status of local governments, outlined by Judge John F. Dillon, who in 1872 stated that a municipal corporation can exercise only those powers expressly granted by state law.

Diplomacy The total process by which states carry on political relations with each other; the settling of conflicts among nations by peaceful means.

Diplomatic Recognition The formal acknowledgment of a foreign government as legitimate.

Direct Democracy A system of government in which political decisions are made by the people directly, rather than by their elected representatives; probably possible only in small political communities.

Direct Primary An intraparty election in which the voters select the candidates who will run on a party's ticket in the subsequent general election.

Direct Technique An interest group activity that involves interaction with government officials to further the group's goals.

Discharge Petition A procedure by which a bill in the House of Representatives may be forced out of a committee (discharged) that has refused to report it for consideration by the House. The discharge petition must be signed by an absolute majority (218) of representatives and is used only on rare occasions.

Dissenting Opinion A separate opinion in which a judge dissents from (disagrees with) the conclusion reached by the majority on the court and expounds his or her own views about the case.

Diversity of Citizenship A basis for federal court jurisdiction over a lawsuit that involves citizens of different states or (more rarely) citizens of a U.S. state and citizens or subjects of a foreign country. The amount in controversy must be at least $75,000 before a federal court can take jurisdiction in such cases.

Divided Government A situation in which one major political party controls the presidency and the other controls the chambers of Congress or in which one party controls a state governorship and the other controls the state legislature.

Divisive Opinion Public opinion that is polarized between two quite different positions.

Domestic Policy Public plans or courses of action that concern internal issues of national importance, such as poverty, crime, and the environment.

Dominant Culture The values, customs, language, and ideals established by the group or groups in a society that traditionally have controlled politics and government institutions in that society.

Dual Federalism A system of government in which the states and the national government each remain supreme within their own spheres. The doctrine looks on nation and state as co-equal sovereign powers. It holds that acts of states within their reserved powers are legitimate limitations on the powers of the national government.

E

Earned-Income Tax Credit (EITC) Program A government program that helps low-income workers by giving back part or all of their Social Security taxes.

Economic Aid Assistance to other nations in the form of grants, loans, or credits to buy the assisting nation's products.

Elastic Clause, or Necessary and Proper Clause The clause in Article I, Section 8, that grants Congress the power to do whatever is necessary to execute its specifically delegated powers.

Elector A person on the partisan slate that is selected early in the presidential election year according to state laws and the applicable political party apparatus to cast ballots for president and vice president. The number of electors in each state is equal to that state's number of representatives in both chambers of Congress.

Electoral College A group of persons called electors selected by the voters in each state and Washington, D.C.; this group officially elects the president and vice president of the United States. The number of electors in each state is equal to the number of each state's representatives in both chambers of Congress. The Twenty-third Amendment to the Constitution permits Washington, D.C., to have as many electors as the smallest state.

Electronic Media Communication channels that involve electronic transmissions, such as radio, television, and, to an increasing extent, the Internet.

Elite Theory A perspective holding that society is ruled by a small number of people who exercise power in their self-interest.

Emergency Power An inherent power exercised by the president during a period of national crisis, particularly in foreign affairs.

Enabling Legislation A statute enacted by Congress that authorizes the creation of an administrative agency and specifies the name, purpose, composition, functions, and powers of the agency being created.

Enumerated Powers Powers specifically granted to the national government by the Constitution. The first seventeen clauses of Article I, Section 8, specify most of the enumerated powers of Congress.

Environmental Impact Statement (EIS) As a requirement mandated by the National Environmental Policy Act, a report that must show the costs and benefits of major federal actions that could significantly affect the quality of the environment.

Equality The idea that all people are of equal worth.

Era of Good Feelings The years from 1817 to 1825, when James Monroe was president and there was, in effect, no political opposition.

Establishment Clause The part of the First Amendment prohibiting the establishment of a church officially supported by the national government. It is applied to questions of state and local government aid to religious organizations and schools, questions of the legality of allowing or requiring school prayers, and questions of the teaching of evolution versus fundamentalist theories of creation.

Exclusionary Rule A policy forbidding the admission at trial of illegally seized evidence.

Executive Agreement An international agreement made by the president, without senatorial ratification, with the head of a foreign state.

Executive Budget The budget prepared and submitted by the president to Congress.

Executive Office of the President (EOP)   An organization established by President Franklin D. Roosevelt by executive order under the Reorganization Act of 1939 to assist the president in carrying out major duties.

Executive Order   A rule or regulation issued by the president that has the effect of law. Executive orders can implement and give administrative effect to provisions in the Constitution, to treaties, and to statutes.

Executive Privilege   The right of executive officials to withhold information from or to refuse to appear before a legislative committee. Executive privilege is enjoyed by the president and by those executive officials accorded that right by the president.

Exports   Goods and services produced domestically for sale abroad.

Expressed Power   A constitutional or statutory power of the president that is expressly written into the Constitution or into statutory law.

F

Faction   A group or bloc in a legislature or political party acting together in pursuit of some special interest or position.

Fall Review   The time every year when, after receiving formal federal agency requests for funding for the next fiscal year, the Office of Management and Budget reviews the requests, makes changes, and submits its recommendations to the president.

Fascism   A twentieth-century ideology—often totalitarian—that exalts the national collective united behind an absolute ruler. Fascism rejects liberal individualism, values action over rational deliberation, and glorifies war.

Fed   The Federal Reserve System created by Congress in 1913 as the nation's central banking organization.

Federal Mandate   A requirement in federal legislation that forces states and municipalities to comply with certain rules.

Federal Open Market Committee   The most important body within the Federal Reserve System. The Federal Open Market Committee decides how monetary policy should be carried out by the Federal Reserve System.

Federal Question   A question that pertains to the U.S. Constitution, acts of Congress, or treaties. A federal question provides a basis for federal jurisdiction.

Federal Register   A publication of the executive branch of the U.S. government that prints executive orders, rules, and regulations.

Federal System   A system of government in which power is divided between a central government and regional, or subdivisional, governments. Each level must have some domain in which its policies are dominant and some genuine political or constitutional guarantee of its authority.

Federalist   The name given to one who was in favor of the adoption of the U.S. Constitution and the creation of a federal union with a strong central government.

Feminism   The movement that supports political, economic, and social equality for women.

Filibuster   The use of the Senate's tradition of unlimited debate as a delaying tactic to block a bill.

First Budget Resolution   A resolution passed by Congress in May that sets overall revenue and spending goals for the following fiscal year.

Fiscal Policy   The federal government's use of taxation and spending policies to affect overall business activity.

Fiscal Year (FY)   A twelve-month period that is used for bookkeeping, or accounting, purposes. Usually, the fiscal year does not coincide with the calendar year. For example, the federal government's fiscal year runs from October 1 through September 30.

Focus Group   A small group of individuals who are led in discussion by a professional consultant to gather opinions on and responses to candidates and issues.

Food Stamps   Coupons issued by the federal government to low-income individuals to be used for the purchase of food.

Foreign Policy   A nation's external goals and the techniques and strategies used to achieve them.

Foreign Policy Process   The steps by which external goals are decided and acted on.

Franking   A policy that enables members of Congress to send material through the mail by substituting their facsimile signature (frank) for postage.

Free Exercise Clause   The provision of the First Amendment guaranteeing the free exercise of religion.

Free Rider Problem   The difficulty interest groups face in recruiting members when the benefits they achieve can be gained without joining the group.

Front-Loading   The practice of moving presidential primary elections to the early part of the campaign, to maximize the impact of certain states or regions on the nomination.

Front-Runner   The presidential candidate who appears to be ahead at a given time in the primary season.

Full Employment   An arbitrary level of unemployment that corresponds to "normal" friction in the labor market. In 1986, a 6.5 percent rate of unemployment was considered full employment. Today, it is assumed to be around 5 percent.

Functional Consolidation   The cooperation of two or more units of local government in providing services to their inhabitants.

G

Gag Order   An order issued by a judge restricting the publication of news about a trial in progress or a pretrial hearing in order to protect the accused's right to a fair trial.

Gender Discrimination   Any practice, policy, or procedure that denies equality of treatment to an individual or to a group because of gender.

Gender Gap   A term most often used to describe the difference between the percentage of women who vote for a particular candidate and the percentage of men who vote for the candidate. The term came into use after the 1980 presidential elections.

General Jurisdiction   Exists when a court's authority to hear cases is not significantly restricted. A court of general jurisdiction normally can hear a broad range of cases.

General Law City   A city operating under general state laws that apply to all local governmental units of a similar type.

General Sales Tax   A tax levied as a proportion of the retail price of a commodity at the point of sale.

Generational Effect   A long-lasting effect of events of a particular time on the political opinions or preferences of those who came of political age at that time.

Gerrymandering   The drawing of legislative district boundary lines for the purpose of obtaining partisan or factional advantage. A district is said to be gerrymandered when its shape is manipulated by the dominant party in the state legislature to maximize electoral strength at the expense of the minority party.

Government   The institution in which decisions are made that resolve conflicts or allocate benefits and privileges. It is unique because it has the ultimate authority within society.

Government Corporation   An agency of government that administers a quasi-business enterprise. These corporations are used when activities are primarily commercial. They produce revenue for their continued existence, and they require greater flexibility than is permitted for departments and agencies.

Government in the Sunshine Act   A law that requires all multiheaded federal agencies to conduct their business regularly in public session.

Grandfather Clause   A device used by southern states to exempt whites from state taxes and literacy laws originally intended to disenfranchise African American voters. It restricted the voting franchise to those who could prove that their grandfathers had voted before 1867.

Great Compromise   The compromise between the New Jersey and the Virginia plans that created one chamber of Congress based on population and one chamber representing each state equally; also called the Connecticut Compromise.

Gross Domestic Product (GDP)   The dollar value of all final goods and services produced in a one-year period.

Gross Public Debt The net public debt plus interagency borrowings within the government.

H

Hatch Act An act passed in 1939 that restricted the political activities of government employees. It also prohibited a political group from spending more than $3 million in any campaign and limited individual contributions to a committee to $5,000. The act was designed to control political influence buying.

Head of State In the United States, the role of the president as ceremonial head of the government.

Hispanic Someone who can claim a heritage from a Spanish-speaking country. The term is used only in the United States or other countries that receive immigrants—Spanish-speaking persons living in Spanish-speaking countries do not normally apply the term to themselves.

Home Rule City A city with a charter allowing local voters to frame, adopt, and amend their own charter.

I

Ideology A comprehensive set of beliefs about the nature of people and about the institutions and role of government.

Impeachment As authorized by Articles I and II of the Constitution, an action by the House of Representatives to accuse the president, vice president, or other civil officers of the United States of committing "Treason, Bribery, or other high Crimes and Misdemeanors."

Import Quota A restriction imposed on the value or number of units of a particular good that can be brought into a country. Foreign suppliers are unable to sell more than the amount specified in the import quota.

Imports Goods and services produced outside a country but sold within its borders.

Incarceration Rate The number of persons held in jail or prison for every 100,000 persons in a particular population group.

Income Transfer A transfer of income from some individuals in the economy to other individuals. This is generally done by way of the government. It is a transfer in the sense that no current services are rendered by the recipients.

Incorporation Theory The view that most of the protections of the Bill of Rights apply to state governments through the Fourteenth Amendment's due process clause.

Independent A voter or candidate who does not identify with a political party.

Independent Executive Agency A federal agency that is not part of a cabinet department but reports directly to the president.

Independent Expenditures Nonregulated contributions from PACs, ideological organizations, and individuals. The groups may spend funds on advertising or other campaign activities so long as those expenditures are not coordinated with those of a candidate.

Independent Regulatory Agency An agency outside the major executive departments charged with making and implementing rules and regulations to protect the public interest.

Indiana Ballot See *Party-Column Ballot.*

Indirect Technique A strategy employed by interest groups that uses third parties to influence government officials.

Inflation A sustained rise in the general price level of goods and services.

Inherent Power A power of the president derived from the loosely worded statements in the Constitution that "the executive Power shall be vested in a President" and that the president should "take Care that the Laws be faithfully executed"; defined through practice rather than through constitutional or statutory law.

Initiative A procedure by which voters can propose a law or a constitutional amendment.

In-Kind Subsidy A good or service—such as food stamps, housing, or medical care—provided by the government to low-income groups.

Institution An ongoing organization that performs certain functions for society.

Instructed Delegate A legislator who is an agent of the voters who elected him or her and who votes according to the views of constituents regardless of personal assessments.

Intelligence Community The government agencies that are involved in gathering information about the capabilities and intentions of foreign governments and that engage in covert activities to further U.S. foreign policy aims.

Interest Group An organized group of individuals sharing common objectives who actively attempt to influence policymakers.

Interstate Compact An agreement between two or more states. Agreements on minor matters are made without congressional consent, but any compact that tends to increase the power of the contracting states relative to other states or relative to the national government generally requires the consent of Congress. Such compacts serve as a means by which states can solve regional problems.

Iron Curtain The term used to describe the division of Europe between the Soviet Union and the West; popularized by Winston Churchill in a speech portraying Europe as being divided by an iron curtain, with the nations of Eastern Europe behind the curtain and increasingly under Soviet control.

Iron Triangle The three-way alliance among legislators, bureaucrats, and interest groups to make or preserve policies that benefit their respective interests.

Isolationist Foreign Policy Abstaining from an active role in international affairs or alliances, which characterized U.S. foreign policy toward Europe during most of the 1800s.

Issue Advocacy Advertising Advertising paid for by interest groups that supports or opposes a candidate or candidate's position on an issue without mentioning voting or elections.

Issue Network A group of individuals or organizations—which may consist of legislators or legislative staff members, interest group leaders, bureaucrats, the media, scholars, and other experts—that supports a particular policy position on a given issue, such as one on the environment, taxation, or consumer safety.

Item Veto The power to veto particular sections or items of an appropriations bill while signing the remainder of the bill into law. The governors of most states have this power.

J

Joint Committee A legislative committee composed of members from both chambers of Congress.

Judicial Activism A doctrine holding that the Supreme Court should take an active role in using its powers to check the activities of Congress, state legislatures, and administrative agencies when those government bodies exceed their authority.

Judicial Implementation The way in which court decisions are translated into action.

Judicial Restraint A doctrine holding that the Supreme Court should defer to the decisions made by the elected representatives of the people in the legislative and executive branches.

Judicial Review The power of the Supreme Court or any court to declare unconstitutional federal or state laws and other acts of government.

Jurisdiction The authority of a court to decide certain cases. Not all courts have the authority to decide all cases. Where a case arises and what its subject matter is are two jurisdictional factors.

Justiciable Question A question that may be raised and reviewed in court.

K

Keynesian Economics A school of economic thought, named after English economist John Maynard Keynes, that tends to favor active federal government policymaking to stabilize economy-wide fluctuations, usually by implementing discretionary fiscal policy.

Kitchen Cabinet   The informal advisers to the president.

L

Labor Movement   Generally, the full range of economic and political expression of working-class interests; politically, the organization of working-class interests.

Latent Interests   Public-policy interests that are not recognized or addressed by a group at a particular time.

Lawmaking   The process of deciding the legal rules that govern society. Such laws may regulate minor affairs or establish broad national policies.

Legislature   A governmental body primarily responsible for the making of laws.

Legitimacy   Popular acceptance of the right and power of a government or other entity to exercise authority.

Libel   A written defamation of a person's character, reputation, business, or property rights. To a limited degree, the First Amendment protects the press from libel actions.

Liberalism   A set of beliefs that includes the advocacy of positive government action to improve the welfare of individuals, support for civil rights, and tolerance for political and social change.

Libertarianism   A political ideology based on skepticism or opposition toward almost all government activities.

Liberty   The greatest freedom of individuals that is consistent with the freedom of other individuals in the society.

Limited Government   A form of government based on the principle that the powers of government should be clearly limited either through a written document or through wide public understanding; characterized by institutional checks to ensure that government serves the public rather than private interests.

Limited Jurisdiction   Exists when a court's authority to hear cases is restricted to certain types of claims, such as tax claims or bankruptcy petitions.

Line Organization   With respect to the federal government, an administrative unit that is directly accountable to the president.

Line-Item Veto   The power of an executive to veto individual lines or items within a piece of legislation without vetoing the entire bill.

Literacy Test   A test administered as a precondition for voting, often used to prevent African Americans from exercising their right to vote.

Litigate   To engage in a legal proceeding or seek relief in a court of law; to carry on a lawsuit.

Lobbyist   An organization or individual that attempts to influence the passage, defeat, or contents of legislation and the administrative decisions of government.

Loophole   A legal method by which individuals and businesses are allowed to reduce the tax liabilities owed to the government.

Loose Monetary Policy   Monetary policy that makes credit inexpensive and abundant, possibly leading to inflation.

M

Madisonian Model   A structure of government proposed by James Madison in which the powers of the government are separated into three branches: executive, legislative, and judicial.

Majoritarianism   A political theory holding that in a democracy, the government ought to do what the majority of the people want.

Majority   1) More than 50 percent; 2) Full age; the age at which a person is entitled by law to the right to manage her or his own affairs and to the full enjoyment of civil rights.

Majority Leader of the House   A legislative position held by an important party member in the House of Representatives. The majority leader is selected by the majority party in caucus or conference to foster cohesion among party members and to act as spokesperson for the majority party in the House.

Majority Opinion   A court opinion reflecting the views of the majority of the judges.

Majority Rule   A basic principle of democracy asserting that the greatest number of citizens in any political unit should select officials and determine policies.

Managed News   Information generated and distributed by the government in such a way as to give government interests priority over candor.

Mandatory Retirement   Forced retirement when a person reaches a certain age.

Massachusetts Ballot   See *Office-Block Ballot.*

Material Incentive   A reason or motive having to do with economic benefits or opportunities.

Media   The channels of mass communication.

Media Access   The public's right of access to the media. The Federal Communications Commission and the courts gradually have taken the stance that citizens do have a right to media access.

Medicaid   A joint state-federal program that provides medical care to the poor (including indigent elderly persons in nursing homes). The program is funded out of general government revenues.

Medicare   A federal health-insurance program that covers U.S. residents over the age of sixty-five. The costs are met by a tax on employment.

Merit System   The selection, retention, and promotion of government employees on the basis of competitive examinations.

Military-Industrial Complex   The mutually beneficial relationship between the armed forces and defense contractors.

Minority Leader of the House   The party leader elected by the minority party in the House.

Monetary Policy   The use of changes in the amount of money in circulation to alter credit markets, employment, and the rate of inflation.

Monopolistic Model   A model of bureaucracy that compares bureaucracies to monopolistic business firms. Lack of competition within a bureaucracy leads to inefficient and costly operations. Because bureaucracies are not penalized for inefficiency, there is no incentive to reduce costs or use resources more productively.

Monroe Doctrine   A policy statement included in President James Monroe's 1823 annual message to Congress, which set out three principles: (1) European nations should not establish new colonies in the Western Hemisphere, (2) European nations should not intervene in the affairs of independent nations of the Western Hemisphere, and (3) the United States would not interfere in the affairs of European nations.

Moral Idealism   A philosophy that sees all nations as willing to cooperate and agree on moral standards for conduct.

Municipal Home Rule   The power vested in a local unit of government to draft or change its own charter and to manage its own affairs.

N

Narrowcasting   Broadcasting that is targeted to one small sector of the population.

National Committee   A standing committee of a national political party established to direct and coordinate party activities during the four-year period between national party conventions.

National Convention   The meeting held every four years by each major party to select presidential and vice presidential candidates, to write a platform, to choose a national committee, and to conduct party business. In theory, the national convention is at the top of a hierarchy of party conventions (the local and state conventions are below it) that consider candidates and issues.

National Health Insurance   A plan to provide universal health insurance under which the government provides basic health insurance to all citizens. In most such plans, the program is funded by taxes on wages or salaries.

National Security Council (NSC)   A staff agency in the Executive Office of the President established by the National Security Act of 1947. The NSC advises the president on domestic and foreign matters involving national security.

National Security Policy   Foreign and domestic policy designed to protect the independence and political and economic integrity of a nation; policy that is concerned with the safety and defense of the nation.

Natural Rights   Rights held to be inherent in natural law, not dependent on governments. John Locke stated that natural law, being superior to human law, specifies certain rights of "life, liberty, and property." These rights, altered to become "life, liberty, and the pursuit of happiness," are asserted in the Declaration of Independence.

Necessaries   In contract law, necessaries include whatever is reasonably necessary for suitable subsistence as measured by age, state, condition in life, and so on.

Necessary and Proper Clause   See *Elastic Clause.*

Negative Constituents   Citizens who openly oppose government foreign policies.

Net Public Debt   The accumulation of all past federal government deficits; the total amount owed by the federal government to individuals, businesses, and foreigners.

New England Town   A governmental unit in the New England states that combines the roles of city and county in one unit.

Normal Trade Relations (NTR) Status   A status granted through an international treaty by which each member nation must treat other members at least as well as it treats the country that receives its most favorable treatment. This status was formerly known as *most-favored-nation* status.

O

Office of Management and Budget (OMB)   A division of the Executive Office of the President created by executive order in 1970 to replace the Bureau of the Budget. The OMB's main functions are to assist the president in preparing the annual budget, to clear and coordinate all departmental agency budgets, to help set fiscal policy, and to supervise the administration of the federal budget.

Office-Block, or Massachusetts, Ballot   A form of general election ballot in which candidates for elective office are grouped together under the title of each office. It emphasizes voting for the office and the individual candidate, rather than for the party.

Ombudsperson   A person who hears and investigates complaints by private individuals against public officials or agencies.

Open Primary   A primary in which any registered voter can vote (but must vote for candidates of only one party).

Opinion   The statement by a judge or a court of the decision reached in a case tried or argued before it. The opinion sets forth the law that applies to the case and details the legal reasoning on which the ruling was based.

Opinion Leader   One who is able to influence the opinions of others because of position, expertise, or personality. Such leaders help to shape public opinion.

Opinion Poll   A method of systematically questioning a small, selected sample of respondents who are deemed representative of the total population. Opinion polls are widely used by government, business, university scholars, political candidates, and voluntary groups to provide reasonably accurate data on public attitudes, beliefs, expectations, and behavior.

Oral Arguments   The verbal arguments presented in person by attorneys to an appellate court. Each attorney presents reasons to the court why the court should rule in her or his client's favor.

Order   A state of peace and security. Maintaining order by protecting members of society from violence and criminal activity is the oldest purpose of government.

Oversight   The responsibility Congress has for following up on laws it has enacted to ensure that they are being enforced and administered in the way Congress intended.

P

Pardon   The granting of a release from the punishment or legal consequences of a crime; a pardon can be granted by the president before or after a conviction.

Party Identification   Linking oneself to a particular political party.

Party Identifier   A person who identifies with a political party.

Party Organization   The formal structure and leadership of a political party, including election committees; local, state, and national executives; and paid professional staff.

Party Platform   A document drawn up by the platform committee at each national convention, outlining the policies, positions, and principles of the party; it is then submitted to the entire convention for approval.

Party-Column, or Indiana, Ballot   A form of general election ballot in which candidates for elective office are arranged in columns under their respective party labels and symbols. It emphasizes voting for the party, rather than for the office or individual.

Party-in-Government   All of the elected and appointed officials who identify with a political party.

Party-in-the-Electorate   Those members of the general public who identify with a political party or who express a preference for one party over another.

Patronage   Rewarding faithful party workers and followers with government employment and contracts.

Peer Group   A group consisting of members sharing common social characteristics. These groups play an important part in the socialization process, helping to shape attitudes and beliefs.

Pendleton Act (Civil Service Reform Act)   The law, as amended over the years, that remains the basic statute regulating federal employment personnel policies. It established the principle of employment on the basis of merit and created the Civil Service Commission to administer the personnel service.

Picket-Fence Federalism   A model of federalism in which specific programs and policies (depicted as vertical pickets in a picket fence) involve all levels of government—national, state, and local (depicted by the horizontal boards in a picket fence).

Pluralism   A theory that views politics as a conflict among interest groups. Political decision making is characterized by bargaining and compromise.

Plurality   The total votes cast for a candidate who receives more votes than any other candidate but not necessarily a majority. Most national, state, and local electoral laws provide for winning elections by a plurality vote.

Pocket Veto   A special veto power exercised by the chief executive after a legislative body has adjourned. Bills not signed by the chief executive die after a specified period of time. If Congress wishes to reconsider such a bill, it must be reintroduced in the following session of Congress.

Police Power   The authority to legislate for the protection of the health, morals, safety, and welfare of the people. In the United States, most police power is a reserved power of the states.

Political Action Committee (PAC)   A committee set up by and representing a corporation, labor union, or special interest group. PACs raise and give campaign donations on behalf of the organizations or groups they represent.

Political Consultant   A paid professional hired to devise a campaign strategy and manage a campaign. Image building is the crucial task of the political consultant.

Political Culture   The collection of beliefs and attitudes toward government and the political process held by a community or nation.

Political Party   A group of political activists who organize to win elections, operate the government, and determine public policy.

Political Question   An issue that a court believes should be decided by the executive or legislative branch.

Political Realism   A philosophy that sees each nation as acting principally in its own interest.

Political Socialization   The process through which individuals learn a set of political attitudes and form opinions about social issues. The family and the educational system are two of the most important forces in the political socialization process.

Political Trust   The degree to which individuals express trust in the government and political institutions, usually measured through a specific series of survey questions.

Politics   The struggle or process to decide which members of society get certain benefits or privileges and which members of society are excluded from benefits or privileges; more specifically, the struggle over power or influence within organizations or informal groups that can grant benefits or privileges.

Poll Tax A special tax that must be paid as a qualification for voting. The Twenty-fourth Amendment to the Constitution outlawed the poll tax in national elections, and in 1966 the Supreme Court declared it unconstitutional in all elections.

Popular Sovereignty The concept that ultimate political authority is based on the will of the people.

Precedent A court rule bearing on subsequent legal decisions in similar cases. Judges rely on precedents in deciding cases.

President Pro Tempore The temporary presiding officer of the Senate in the absence of the vice president.

Presidential Primary A statewide primary election of delegates to a political party's national convention to help a party determine its presidential nominee. Such delegates are either pledged to a particular candidate or unpledged.

Press Secretary The individual responsible for representing the White House before the media. The press secretary writes news releases, provides background information, sets up press conferences, and generally handles communication for the White House.

Prior Restraint Restraining an action before it has actually occurred. In relation to the press, prior restraint means censorship.

Privatization The replacement of government services with services provided by private firms.

Progressive Tax A tax that rises in percentage terms as incomes rise.

Property Anything that is or may be subject to ownership. As conceived by the political philosopher John Locke, the right to property is a natural right superior to human law (laws made by government).

Property Tax A tax on the value of real estate. This tax is limited to state and local governments and is a particularly important source of revenue for local governments.

Public Agenda Issues that commonly are perceived by members of the political community as meriting public attention and governmental action. The media play an important role in setting the public agenda by focusing attention on certain topics.

Public Figures Public officials, movie stars, and generally all persons who become known to the public because of their positions or activities.

Public Interest The best interests of the collective, overall community; the national good, rather than the narrow interests of a self-serving group.

Public Opinion The aggregate of individual attitudes or beliefs shared by some portion of the adult population. There is no one public opinion, because there are many different "publics."

Purposive Incentive A reason or motive having to do with ethical beliefs or ideological principles.

R

Ratification Formal approval.

Rational Ignorance Effect When people purposely and rationally decide not to become informed on an issue because they believe that their vote on the issue is not likely to be a deciding one; a lack of incentive to seek the necessary information to cast an intelligent vote.

Realignment A process in which a substantial group of voters switches party allegiance, producing a long-term change in the political landscape.

Reapportionment The allocation of seats in the House of Representatives to each state after each census.

Recall A procedure allowing the people to vote to dismiss an elected official from state office before his or her term has expired.

Recession Two or more successive quarters in which the economy shrinks instead of grows.

Redistricting The redrawing of the boundaries of the congressional districts within a state.

Referendum An electoral device whereby legislative or constitutional measures are referred by the legislature to the voters for approval or disapproval.

Registration The entry of a person's name onto the list of eligible voters for elections. To register, a person must meet certain legal requirements relating to age, citizenship, and residency.

Regressive Tax A tax that falls in percentage terms as incomes rise.

Remand To send a case back to the court that originally heard it.

Representation The function of members of Congress as elected officials in representing the views of their constituents.

Representative Assembly A legislature composed of individuals who represent the population.

Representative Democracy A form of government in which representatives elected by the people make and enforce laws and policies; may retain the monarchy in a ceremonial role.

Reprieve Postponing the execution of a sentence imposed by a court of law; usually done for humanitarian reasons or to await new evidence.

Republic A form of government in which sovereignty rests with the people, who elect agents to represent them in lawmaking and other decisions.

Republican Party One of the two major American political parties. It emerged in the 1850s as an antislavery party. It consisted of former northern Whigs and antislavery Democrats.

Reverse To annul or make void a court ruling on account of some error or irregularity.

Reverse Discrimination The charge that affirmative action programs requiring preferential treatment or quotas discriminate against those who do not have minority status.

Reverse-Income Effect A tendency for wealthier states or regions to favor the Democrats and for less wealthy states or regions to favor the Republicans. The effect appears paradoxical because it reverses traditional patterns of support.

Rule of Four A United States Supreme Court procedure according to which four justices must vote to hear a case in order for the case to come before the full Court.

Rules Committee A standing committee of the House of Representatives that provides special rules under which specific bills can be debated, amended, and considered by the House.

S

Safe Seat A district that returns the legislator with 55 percent of the vote or more.

Sampling Error The difference between sample results and the true result if the entire population had been interviewed.

Second Budget Resolution A resolution passed by Congress in September that sets "binding" limits on taxes and spending for the next fiscal year beginning October 1.

Select Committee A temporary legislative committee established for a limited time period and for a special purpose.

Selectperson A member of the governing group of a town.

Senate Majority Leader The chief spokesperson of the majority party in the Senate, who directs the legislative program and party strategy.

Senate Minority Leader The party officer in the Senate who commands the minority party's opposition to the policies of the majority party and directs the legislative program and strategy of his or her party.

Senatorial Courtesy In regard to federal district court judgeship nominations, a Senate tradition allowing a senator to veto a judicial appointment in his or her state by indicating that the appointment is personally not acceptable. At that point, the Senate may reject the nomination, or the president may withdraw consideration of the nominee.

Seniority System A custom followed in both chambers of Congress specifying that the member of the majority party with the longest term of continuous service will be given preference when a committee chairperson (or a holder of another significant post) is selected.

Separate-but-Equal Doctrine The doctrine holding that segregation in schools and public accommodations does not imply that one race is superior to another, and that separate-but-equal facilities do not violate the equal protection clause.

Separation of Powers The principle of dividing governmental powers among the executive, the legislative, and the judicial branches of government.

Sexual Harassment   Unwanted physical or verbal conduct or abuse of a sexual nature that interferes with a recipient's job performance, creates a hostile environment, or carries with it an implicit or explicit threat of adverse employment consequences.

Single-Payer Plan   A plan under which one entity has a monopoly on issuing a particular type of insurance. Typically the entity is the government, and the insurance is basic health coverage.

Slander   The public uttering of a false statement that harms the good reputation of another. The statement must be made to, or within the hearing of, persons other than the defamed party.

Social Contract   A voluntary agreement among individuals to secure their rights and welfare by creating a government and abiding by its rules.

Socialism   A political ideology based on strong support for economic and social equality. Socialists traditionally envisioned a society in which large privately owned businesses were taken over by the government or by employee cooperatives.

Social Movement   A movement that represents the demands of a large segment of the public for political, economic, or social change.

Socioeconomic Status   The value assigned to a person due to occupation or income. An upper-class person, for example, has high socioeconomic status.

Soft Money   Campaign contributions that evade contribution limits by being given to parties and party committees to help fund general party activities.

Solidary Incentive   A reason or motive having to do with the desire to associate with others and to share with others a particular interest or hobby.

Sound Bite   A brief, memorable comment that easily can be fit into news broadcasts.

Soviet Bloc   The Eastern European countries that installed Communist regimes after World War II and which were politically dominated by the Soviet Union.

Speaker of the House   The presiding officer in the House of Representatives. The Speaker is always a member of the majority party and is the most powerful and influential member of the House.

Spin   An interpretation of campaign events or election results that is most favorable to the candidate's campaign strategy.

Spin Doctor   A political campaign adviser who tries to convince journalists of the truth of a particular interpretation of events.

Splinter Party   A new party formed by a dissident faction within a major political party. Usually, splinter parties have emerged when a particular personality was at odds with the major party.

Spoils System   The awarding of government jobs to political supporters and friends; generally associated with President Andrew Jackson.

Spring Review   The time every year when the Office of Management and Budget requires federal agencies to review their programs, activities, and goals and submit their requests for funding for the next fiscal year.

Standing Committee   A permanent committee in the House or Senate that considers bills within a certain subject area.

Stare Decisis   To stand on decided cases; the judicial policy of following precedents established by past decisions.

State   A group of people occupying a specific area and organized under one government; may be either a nation or a subunit of a nation.

State Central Committee   The principal organized structure of each political party within each state. This committee is responsible for carrying out policy decisions of the party's state convention.

State of the Union Message   An annual message to Congress in which the president proposes a legislative program. The message is addressed not only to Congress but also to the American people and to the world. It offers the opportunity to dramatize policies and objectives and to gain public support.

Statutory Power   A power created through laws enacted by Congress.

Straight-Ticket Voting   Voting exclusively for the candidates of one party.

Strategic Arms Limitation Treaty (SALT I)   A treaty between the United States and the Soviet Union to stabilize the nuclear arms competition between the two countries. SALT I talks began in 1969, and agreements were signed on May 26, 1972.

Strict Construction   A judicial philosophy that looks to the "letter of the law" when interpreting the Constitution or a particular statute.

Subpoena   A legal writ requiring a person's appearance in court to give testimony.

Suffrage   The right to vote; the franchise.

Sunset Legislation   A law requiring that an existing program be reviewed regularly for its effectiveness and be terminated unless specifically extended as a result of this review.

Superdelegate   A party leader or elected official who is given the right to vote at the party's national convention. Superdelegates are not elected at the state level.

Supplemental Security Income (SSI)   A federal program established to provide assistance to elderly persons and disabled persons.

Supremacy Clause   The constitutional provision that makes the Constitution and federal laws superior to all conflicting state and local laws.

Supremacy Doctrine   A doctrine that asserts the superiority of national law over state or regional laws. This principle is rooted in Article VI of the Constitution, which provides that the Constitution, the laws passed by the national government under its constitutional powers, and all treaties constitute the supreme law of the land.

Swing Voters   Voters who frequently swing their support from one party to another.

Symbolic Speech   Nonverbal expression of beliefs, which is given substantial protection by the courts.

T

Tariffs   Taxes on imports.

Technical Assistance   The practice of sending experts with technical skills in such areas as agriculture, engineering, or business to aid other nations.

Temporary Assistance to Needy Families (TANF)   A state-administered program in which grants from the national government are given to the states, which use the funds to provide assistance to those eligible to receive welfare benefits. The TANF program was created by the Welfare Reform Act of 1996 and replaced the former AFDC program.

Third Party   A political party other than the two major political parties (Republican and Democratic). Sometimes, third parties are composed of dissatisfied groups that have split from the major parties. They act as indicators of political trends and as safety valves for dissident groups.

Ticket Splitting   Voting for candidates of two or more parties for different offices. For example, a voter splits her ticket if she votes for a Republican presidential candidate and for a Democratic congressional candidate.

Tight Monetary Policy   Monetary policy that makes credit expensive in an effort to slow the economy.

Tipping   A phenomenon that occurs when a group that is growing in population becomes large enough to change the political balance in a district, state, or country.

Totalitarian Regime   A form of government that controls all aspects of the political and social life of a nation. All power resides with the government. The citizens have no power to choose the leadership or policies of the country.

Town Manager System   A form of city government in which voters elect three selectpersons, who then appoint a professional town manager, who in turn appoints other officials.

Town Meeting   The governing authority of a New England town. Qualified voters may participate in the election of officers and in the passage of legislation.

Township   A rural unit of government based on federal land surveys of the American frontier in the 1780s. Townships have declined significantly in importance.

Tracking Poll   A poll taken for the candidate on a nearly daily basis as election day approaches.

Trial Court   The court in which most cases begin and in which questions of fact are examined.

Truman Doctrine   The policy adopted by President Harry Truman in 1947 to halt Communist expansion in southeastern Europe.

Trustee   In regard to a legislator, one who acts according to her or his conscience and the broad interests of the entire society.

Twelfth Amendment   An amendment to the Constitution adopted in 1804 that specifies the separate election of the president and vice president by the electoral college.

Twenty-fifth Amendment   An amendment to the Constitution adopted in 1967 that establishes procedures for filling vacancies in the two top executive offices and that makes provisions for situations involving presidential disability.

Two-Party System   A political system in which only two parties have a reasonable chance of winning.

U

U.S. Treasury Bond   Evidence of debt issued by the federal government; similar to corporate bonds but issued by the U.S. Treasury.

Unanimous Opinion   A court opinion or determination on which all judges agree.

Unemployment   The inability of those who are in the labor force to find a job; the total number of those in the labor force actively looking for a job, but unable to find one.

Unicameral Legislature   A legislature with only one legislative body, as compared with a bicameral (two-house) legislature, such as the U.S. Congress. Nebraska is the only state in the Union with a unicameral legislature.

Unincorporated Area   An area not located within the boundary of a municipality.

Unit Rule   A rule by which all of a state's electoral votes are cast for the presidential candidate receiving a plurality of the popular vote in that state.

Unitary System   A centralized governmental system in which local or subdivisional governments exercise only those powers given to them by the central government.

Universal Suffrage   The right of all adults to vote for their representatives.

V

Veto Message   The president's formal explanation of a veto when legislation is returned to Congress.

Voter Turnout   The percentage of citizens taking part in the election process; the number of eligible voters that actually "turn out" on election day to cast their ballots.

W

Wage and Price Controls   Government-imposed controls on the maximum prices that may be charged for specific goods and services, plus controls on permissible wage increases.

War Powers Resolution   A law passed in 1973 spelling out the conditions under which the president can commit troops without congressional approval.

Washington Community   Individuals regularly involved with politics in Washington, D.C.

Watergate Break-In   The 1972 illegal entry into the Democratic National Committee offices by participants in President Richard Nixon's reelection campaign.

Weberian Model   A model of bureaucracy developed by the German sociologist Max Weber, who viewed bureaucracies as rational, hierarchical organizations in which power flows from the top downward and decisions are based on logical reasoning and data analysis.

Whig Party   A major party in the United States during the first half of the 1800s, formally established in 1836. The Whig Party was dominated by anti-Jackson elements and represented a variety of regional interests. It fell apart as a national party in the early 1850s.

Whip   A member of Congress who aids the majority or minority leader of the House or the Senate.

Whistleblower   An insider who brings to public attention gross governmental inefficiency or an illegal action.

White House Office   The personal office of the president, which tends to presidential political needs and manages the media.

White House Press Corps   A group of reporters assigned full-time to cover the presidency.

White Primary   A state primary election that restricts voting to whites only; outlawed by the Supreme Court in 1944.

Writ of *Certiorari*   An order issued by a higher court to a lower court to send up the record of a case for review. It is the principal vehicle for United States Supreme Court review.

Writ of *Habeas Corpus*   *Habeas corpus* means, literally, "you have the body." A writ of *habeas corpus* is an order that requires jailers to bring a person before a court or judge and explain why the person is being held in prison.

Y

Yellow Journalism   A term for sensationalistic, irresponsible journalism. Reputedly, the term is an allusion to the cartoon "The Yellow Kid" in the old *New York World*, a newspaper especially noted for its sensationalism.

INDEX

A

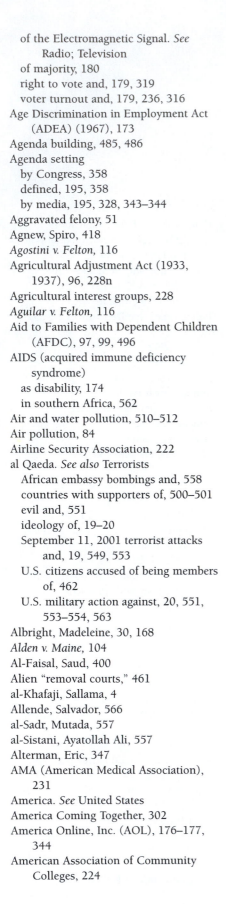

Chapter Opening Photo Credits

Chapter 1: REUTERS/Mannie Garcia /Landov; Chapter 2: AP Photo/Rusty Kennedy; Chapter 3: Ap Photo/Rich Pedroncelli; Chapter 4: AP Photo/Lee Marriner; Chapter 5: AP Photo/Starkville Daily News, Brian Loden; Chapter 6: AP Photo/Gregory Smith; Chapter 7: AP Photo/Bruce Brewer; Chapter 8: AP Photo/Rogelio Solis; Chapter 9: © Corbis. All Rights Reserved; Chapter 10: REUTERS/Jim Bourg /Landov; Chapter 11: UPI Photo/Michael Kleinfeld/Landov; Chapter 12: Greg Whitesell/UPI /Landov; Chapter 13: OSHA photo, U.S. Department of Labor; Chapter 14: REUTERS/Mickey Welsh/POOL /Landov; Chapter 15: REUTERS/Jeff Christensen /Landov; Chapter 16: Ken Cedeno/ Bloomberg News. /Landov; Chapter 17: AP Photo/Pool, Heidi Levine; Chapter 18: Bob Daemmrich/PhotoEdit.

Presidents of the United States

	Term of Service	Age at Inauguration	Political Party	College or University	Occupation or Profession
1. George Washington	1789–1797	57	None		Planter
2. John Adams	1797–1801	61	Federalist	Harvard	Lawyer
3. Thomas Jefferson	1801–1809	57	Jeffersonian Republican	William and Mary	Planter, Lawyer
4. James Madison	1809–1817	57	Jeffersonian Republican	Princeton	Lawyer
5. James Monroe	1817–1825	58	Jeffersonian Republican	William and Mary	Lawyer
6. John Quincy Adams	1825–1829	57	Jeffersonian Republican	Harvard	Lawyer
7. Andrew Jackson	1829–1837	61	Democrat		Lawyer
8. Martin Van Buren	1837–1841	54	Democrat		Lawyer
9. William H. Harrison	1841	68	Whig	Hampden-Sydney	Soldier
10. John Tyler	1841–1845	51	Whig	William and Mary	Lawyer
11. James K. Polk	1845–1849	49	Democrat	U. of N. Carolina	Lawyer
12. Zachary Taylor	1849–1850	64	Whig		Soldier
13. Millard Fillmore	1850–1853	50	Whig		Lawyer
14. Franklin Pierce	1853–1857	48	Democrat	Bowdoin	Lawyer
15. James Buchanan	1857–1861	65	Democrat	Dickinson	Lawyer
16. Abraham Lincoln	1861–1865	52	Republican		Lawyer
17. Andrew Johnson	1865–1869	56	National Union†		Tailor
18. Ulysses S. Grant	1869–1877	46	Republican	U.S. Mil. Academy	Soldier
19. Rutherford B. Hayes	1877–1881	54	Republican	Kenyon	Lawyer
20. James A. Garfield	1881	49	Republican	Williams	Lawyer
21. Chester A. Arthur	1881–1885	51	Republican	Union	Lawyer
22. Grover Cleveland	1885–1889	47	Democrat		Lawyer
23. Benjamin Harrison	1889–1893	55	Republican	Miami	Lawyer
24. Grover Cleveland	1893–1897	55	Democrat		Lawyer
25. William McKinley	1897–1901	54	Republican	Allegheny College	Lawyer
26. Theodore Roosevelt	1901–1909	42	Republican	Harvard	Author
27. William H. Taft	1909–1913	51	Republican	Yale	Lawyer
28. Woodrow Wilson	1913–1921	56	Democrat	Princeton	Educator
29. Warren G. Harding	1921–1923	55	Republican		Editor
30. Calvin Coolidge	1923–1929	51	Republican	Amherst	Lawyer
31. Herbert C. Hoover	1929–1933	54	Republican	Stanford	Engineer
32. Franklin D. Roosevelt	1933–1945	51	Democrat	Harvard	Lawyer
33. Harry S. Truman	1945–1953	60	Democrat		Businessman
34. Dwight D. Eisenhower	1953–1961	62	Republican	U.S. Mil. Academy	Soldier
35. John F. Kennedy	1961–1963	43	Democrat	Harvard	Author
36. Lyndon B. Johnson	1963–1969	55	Democrat	Southwest Texas State	Teacher
37. Richard M. Nixon	1969–1974	56	Republican	Whittier	Lawyer
38. Gerald R. Ford‡	1974–1977	61	Republican	Michigan	Lawyer
39. James E. Carter, Jr.	1977–1981	52	Democrat	U.S. Naval Academy	Businessman
40. Ronald W. Reagan	1981–1989	69	Republican	Eureka College	Actor
41. George H. W. Bush	1989–1993	64	Republican	Yale	Businessman
42. Bill Clinton	1993–2001	46	Democrat	Georgetown	Lawyer
43. George W. Bush	2001–	54	Republican	Yale	Businessman

*Church preference; never joined any church.
†The National Union Party consisted of Republicans and War Democrats. Johnson was a Democrat.

**Inaugurated Dec. 6, 1973, to replace Agnew, who resigned Oct. 10, 1973.
‡Inaugurated Aug. 9, 1974, to replace Nixon, who resigned that same day.
§Inaugurated Dec. 19, 1974, to replace Ford, who became president Aug. 9, 1974.